002332134

CQ PRESS **GUIDE TO**

U.S. HEALTH AND HEALTH CARE POLICY

CQ PRESS **GUIDE TO**

CQ PRESS GUIDE TO

U.S. HEALTH AND HEALTH CARE POLICY

EDITED BY

THOMAS R. OLIVER

University of Wisconsin School of
Medicine and Public Health

SAGE reference | CQPRESS

Los Angeles | London | New Delhi
Singapore | Washington DC

Los Angeles | London | New Delhi
Singapore | Washington DC

FOR INFORMATION:

CQ Press
An Imprint of SAGE Publications, Inc.
2455 Teller Road
Thousand Oaks, California 91320
E-mail: order@sagepub.com

SAGE Publications Ltd.
1 Oliver's Yard
55 City Road
London EC1Y 1SP
United Kingdom

SAGE Publications India Pvt. Ltd.
B 1/I 1 Mohan Cooperative Industrial Area
Mathura Road, New Delhi 110 044
India

SAGE Publications Asia-Pacific Pte. Ltd.
3 Church Street
#10-04 Samsung Hub
Singapore 049483

Acquisitions Editor: Jim Brace-Thompson
Editorial Assistant: Jordan Enobakhare
Production Editor: Tracy Buyan
Copy Editor: Sarah J. Duffy
Typesetter: C&M Digitals (P) Ltd.
Proofreader: Kristin Bergstad
Indexer: Joan Shapiro
Cover Designer: Michael Dubowe
Marketing Manager: Carmel Schrire

Printed in the United States of America.

Library of Congress Cataloging-in-Publication Data

Guide to U.S. health and health care policy / edited by Thomas R. Oliver.

p. ; cm.
Includes bibliographical references and index.

ISBN 978-1-4522-7073-9 (hardcover : alk. paper)

I. Oliver, Thomas R., editor.
[DNLM: 1. Health Policy—history—United States. 2. Health Planning—history—United States. 3. History, 20th Century—United States. 4. History, 21st Century—United States. 5. United States Government Agencies—history—United States. WA 11 AA1]

RA418.3.U6
362.10973—dc23   2014018781

14 15 16 17 18 10 9 8 7 6 5 4 3 2 1

★ SUMMARY TABLE OF CONTENTS

★ TABLE OF CONTENTS

★ LIST OF ILLUSTRATIONS

PART IV

CONTEMPORARY HEALTH POLICY ISSUES: PEOPLE AND POLICIES (1960s–TODAY)

PART V

U.S. RESPONSE TO GLOBAL
HEALTH CHALLENGES (1980s–TODAY)

★ ABOUT THE EDITOR

Thomas R. Oliver is professor of population health sciences in the School of Medicine and Public Health at the University of Wisconsin–Madison. There, he has served as director of the Master of Public Health program and of the Wisconsin Center for Public Health Education and Training and is a faculty affiliate of the Robert M. La Follette School of Public Affairs. Before coming to Wisconsin, he held faculty positions at the University of Maryland and Johns Hopkins University.

Trained in health administration and political science, Professor Oliver teaches courses in domestic and international health systems and policy and in the politics of health policy to a variety of professional and graduate students.

Over the course of his career, he has published a wide range of research examining major issues in health politics, policy, and system reform at all levels of government. He has focused much of his work on how ideas—whether specific concepts, evidence-based analysis, or paradigm shifts—are translated into action through leadership and institutional dynamics. Currently, he is studying the critical roles of inter-sectoral governance and leadership in strategies for population health improvement in the United States and other countries. Professor Oliver served as president of the Health Politics and Policy section of the American Political Science Association in 2010–2011 and is a member of the editorial board of the *Journal of Health Politics, Policy and Law*.

★ CONTRIBUTORS

Diana M. Bowman
University of Michigan

Claire D. Brindis
University of California, San Francisco

Jaclyn Bunch
Florida State University

Robert Cook-Deegan
Sanford School of Public Policy
Duke University

Cari Cuffney
University of Wisconsin–Madison

Rob A. DeLeo
Northeastern University

Michael W. Fahey
Independent Scholar

Thomas D. Fahey
California State University, Chico

Andrew Flescher
Stony Brook University

Daniel M. Fox
President Emeritus, Milbank Memorial Fund

Lance Gable
Wayne State University

Susan Giaimo
Marquette University

Scott L. Greer
University of Michigan

Michael K. Gusmano
The Hastings Center

Andrew S. Jessmore
University of Michigan

Christopher E. Johnson
University of Washington

Darrell J. Kozlowski
Independent Scholar

B. Rick Mayes
University of Richmond

Deborah R. McFarlane
University of New Mexico

Michael McGeary
Political Director and Senior Strategist at Engine

Evan M. Melhado
University of Illinois at Urbana-Champaign

Roy T. Meyers
University of Maryland, Baltimore County

Edward Alan Miller
University of Massachusetts, Boston

Pamela Nadash
University of Massachusetts, Boston

Kenrad E. Nelson
Johns Hopkins University

Ann M. Nguyen
Bastyr University

Rongal D. Nikora
University of New Mexico

Jonathan Oberlander
University of North Carolina at Chapel Hill

Thomas R. Oliver
University of Wisconsin–Madison

Mary K. Olson
Tulane University

Kant Patel
Professor Emeritus, Missouri State University

Beryl A. Radin
Georgetown University

Patrick Remington
University of Wisconsin–Madison

Thomas C. Ricketts
University of North Carolina at Chapel Hill

David A. Rochefort
Northeastern University

Samira Soleimanpour
University of California, San Francisco

David Barton Smith
Drexel University

Donald H. Taylor Jr.
Duke University

Carol S. Weissert
Florida State University

Beyond the Stable State—
New Challenges and Directions
for U.S. Health Policy

HE PHILOSOPHER AND SYSTEMS ANALYST Donald Schön argued that individuals, organizations, and societies bent on preserving the status quo were unlikely to prosper over the long run. In his 1971 book *Beyond the Stable State,* he acknowledged an innate human desire for stability and the certainty it brings. Schön concluded, however, that the pace and pervasiveness of technological change were so disruptive that efforts to maintain, or return to, a stable state were illusory and futile. Far better to proceed on the basis of these assumptions:

- The loss of the stable state means that our society and all of its institutions are in continuous processes of transformation. We cannot expect new stable states that will endure even for our own lifetimes.
- We must learn to understand, guide, influence and manage these transformations. We must make the capacity for undertaking them integral to ourselves and to our institutions.
- We must, in other words, become adept at learning. We must become able not only to transform our institutions, in response to changing situations and requirements; we must invent and develop institutions which are "learning systems," that is to say, systems capable of bringing about their own continuing transformation. (p. 30)

Schön warned that "dynamic conservatism"—a tendency to fight to remain the same—could provoke dysfunctional responses to technological change. Although his analysis was not focused on health systems per se, four decades later it can be seen as a prescient warning about the patchwork quilt of U.S. health and health care policy. Each time a health care program expanded its coverage or a new program extended coverage to a new segment of the population, it became harder to develop a system that might adequately serve all Americans.

Without an overarching framework to weigh potential tradeoffs of technological "advances," system change was driven by incentives to create new products and services that, most of the time, would increase individual patients' health status and producers' financial status but not necessarily improve systemwide effectiveness, efficiency, or equity. Startling progress in life expectancy and infant mortality for the country as a whole was offset by equally startling disparities in those same health outcomes across socioeconomic groups and geographic areas.

Progress was also offset by extravagant, seemingly inexorable growth in health care costs. On a per capita basis, they were two to three times higher in the United States than other advanced industrial countries and directly contributed to stagnant wage growth, personal bankruptcies, and fiscal stress in all levels of government. Without institutions capable of converting this feedback into more accountable and equitable uses of system resources, Americans were stuck in a perpetual state of "Doing Better and Feeling Worse," as John H. Knowles put it in his edited 1977 work by the same name.

Public policy can and must be part of strategies to achieve the triple aim of better health care, lower costs, and better health. As Schön noted, "If government is to learn to solve new public problems, it must also learn to create the systems for doing so and to discard the structure and mechanisms grown up around old problems" (p. 116).

Recent developments signal the possibility that leaders in the U.S. political and health systems have recognized the need for more constructive adaptation to, and exploitation of, technological change as it affects population health. The 2010 Patient Protection and Affordable Care Act (also known as the Affordable Care Act), with its wide array of interventions, is a major catalyst for change. In the wake of the Affordable Care Act, however, two 2013 reports by the Institute of Medicine (IOM)—*Best Care at Lower Cost: The Path to Continuously Learning Health Care in America* and *U.S. Health in International Perspective: Shorter Lives, Poorer Health*—assert there is even more to be done to improve the state of health and health care in the United States. The reports' sharp, unambiguous critiques should command the attention of U.S. citizens and policymakers alike.

BETTER GOVERNANCE OF HEALTH: AN INSIDE-OUT STRATEGY

The first IOM report, *Best Care at Lower Cost: The Path to Continuously Learning Health Care in America,* emphasizes an inside-out strategy for population health improvement through better methods of organizing, financing, and delivering personal health services. The basic problems to be addressed are poor stewardship of vast resources and ineffective translation of knowledge into improved practice:

> The past 50 years have seen an explosion of biomedical knowledge, dramatic innovation in therapies and surgical procedures, and management of conditions that previously were fatal, with ever more exciting clinical capabilities on the horizon. Yet, American health care is falling short on basic dimensions of quality, outcomes, costs, and equity. Available knowledge is too rarely applied to improve the care experience, and information generated by the care experience is too rarely gathered to improve the knowledge available. The traditional systems for transmitting new knowledge—the ways clinicians are educated, deployed, rewarded, and updated—can no longer keep pace with scientific advances. (p. 1)

BETTER GOVERNANCE FOR HEALTH: AN OUTSIDE-IN STRATEGY

The second IOM report, *U.S. Health in International Perspective,* documents and dissects the disappointing population health outcomes in the United States relative to international standards. Its overall assessment is succinctly captured in the report's subtitle: "Shorter Lives, Poorer Health." This report also recognizes the shortcomings of the U.S. health care system but attributes only part of Americans' comparatively poor health to the health sector.

The chief sources of lower life expectancy and quality of life in the United States are infant mortality and low birth weight, injuries and homicides, adolescent pregnancy and sexually transmitted diseases, HIV/AIDS, drug-related deaths, obesity and diabetes, heart disease, chronic lung disease, and disability. The IOM observes that those problems originate in or are compounded by physical environments, social and economic conditions, and behaviors as well as health systems and services. The inescapable conclusion is that the determinants of health are largely outside of the health care system, so disease prevention and health promotion must start where people live, work, and go to school.

In short, the IOM affirms the need for an *outside-in strategy* for population health improvement. This strategy rests on stronger governance *for* health, which must provide the authority and resources to pursue "health in all policies" across agencies of government and sectors of society.

SCOPE AND CONTENT OF THE *GUIDE TO U.S. HEALTH AND HEALTH CARE POLICY*

I believe that we need to pursue both strategies for population health improvement: inside-out *and* outside-in. With the vast resources it has been granted, our health care system must be more productive, and some of those resources need to be shifted outside the walls of our medical centers into the community to address the root causes of preventable death, disease, and disability whenever possible. When you read the chapters of this book, I think you will discover that most of them point in the same direction. We can address the needs of each population group, solve our most pressing problems, and draw nearer to our social and policy goals only by addressing the social determinants of health as well as smarter provision of health services.

The chapters of this *Guide* offer an opportunity to readers to contribute to more effective learning systems in health and public policy by enabling them to be better informed about

- the historical paths to our present health system and policies;
- some of the most important institutions in health policy development and administration;
- past and current efforts to address major health problems and the health needs of different population groups;
- and emerging threats to public health that will require careful analysis and creative policy responses.

Part I: Evolution of American Health Care Policy is a historical overview of health care policy in the United States. In Chapter 1, Kant Patel describes how government's responsibilities in the health sector emerged in the colonial era and grew to their present scope and significance. He notes the relatively limited role of government until well into the twentieth century, when a variety of major policy shifts laid the foundation for a substantial expansion of government-funded research, facilities, and health services. In Chapter 2, Jonathan Oberlander addresses the puzzle of why the United States is the only advanced industrial nation in the world without universal health care for its citizens and outlines nearly a century of failed efforts to achieve that goal. He then explains the circumstances that allowed passage of the Affordable Care Act in 2010, its significance as a major policy and political achievement, and the unfinished journey still ahead for advocates of universal health care.

Part II: Government Organizations that Develop, Fund, and Administer Health Policy offers insight into health policy development in the three branches of the U.S. federal government as well as the importance of intergovernmental support and coordination on key health issues. In Chapter 3, Beryl Radin provides an overview of the structure and functions of the Department of Health and Human Services. She describes the extraordinary range of the department's activities, the potential conflicts among policy, management, and political priorities, and the general limitations on the department's power in the context of the U.S. political system. In Chapter 4, Rob DeLeo explains the difficult role of the Centers for Disease Control and Prevention (CDC) as an agency charged with anticipating and heading off threats to public health both in the United States and abroad as a partner in global health protection. In most cases, the CDC must deal with unavoidable uncertainty, and its history illustrates the risks associated with underreaction or overreaction to potential health hazards. In Chapter 5, Mary Olson examines the responsibilities of one of the most well-known health agencies, the Food and Drug Administration (FDA). She demonstrates how the FDA must continually strike a balance between helping make new drugs and medical devices available to providers and patients and ensuring the safety of those products, all under intense scrutiny by industry, consumer advocates, and politicians. In Chapter 6, Thomas Oliver describes the history and continually expanding mission of the Centers for Medicare and Medicaid Services, which funnels nearly $1 trillion annually into the U.S. economy. He analyzes the agency's basic functions of financing, regulation, and innovation and how the Affordable Care Act adds critical responsibilities for ensuring access, improving quality, and containing the costs of both public and private health insurance. In Chapter 7, Christopher Johnson and Ann Nguyen portray the important role of health care in the Department of Defense and the Department of Veterans Affairs, which together serve more than eighteen million active duty service members and veterans of the nation's wars. The authors describe important changes in the departments' health care programs over time and highlight new strategies to address the challenges posed by mental health and substance abuse

disorders. In Chapter 8, Darrell Kozlowski outlines the constitutional role of the U.S. Supreme Court and the implications for adjudicating contested health policies, whether obscure policies or headline-makers such as the Affordable Care Act. He also identifies key responsibilities of the Department of Justice in prosecuting health care fraud and abuse, promoting fair competition in the health care industry, and upholding civil rights guaranteed under the Americans with Disabilities Act. In Chapter 9, Roy Meyers examines the key institutional actors and processes in government budgeting, a complex but extraordinarily influential element of health policy design, resource allocation, and evaluation. In Chapter 10, Carol Weissert and Jaclyn Bunch provide an overview of the major role of states in U.S. health policy and the changing patterns of intergovernmental relations in this area. They offer important examples of the interplay between federal and state action, including the Medicaid program, the Children's Health Insurance Program, the Employee Retirement and Income Security Act of 1974, the Health Insurance Portability and Accountability Act of 1996, and state-led efforts at comprehensive health care reform.

Part III: Contemporary Health Policy Issues: Goals and Initiatives reviews the central functions of the health care system and major policies related to those functions. In Chapters 11 and 12, Evan Melhado presents a rich history of health planning in the United States. His account captures the many sponsors, participants, purposes, and jurisdictions involved in health planning for the better part of a century and how efforts to establish planning as a scientific discipline failed in the face of the raw politics of resource allocation. In Chapter 13, Donald Taylor surveys many different sources of government support for health care: investment in research and facilities, public health insurance programs, direct provision of services, tax subsidies for private insurance, and health benefits for federal employees. In Chapter 14, Michael McGeary and Robert Cook-Deegan recount the emergence of the modern biomedical research complex in the United States. They highlight the critical juncture of World War II and how it led to a massive government-academic partnership, as well as the role of influential advocates in the postwar expansion of the National Institutes of Health They point out that, despite its tremendous success, the biomedical establishment still faces challenges in sustaining its historical growth, generating new biomedical innovation, and ensuring research conforms to ethical standards. In Chapter 15, Thomas Ricketts describes the often overlooked pluralism of the health care workforce: the many occupations, clinical roles, legal privileges and duties, and settings of their work. He reviews the history of numerous policy initiatives to build, redeploy, and reconfigure the workforce to align with national priorities, and he questions the ability of policy to solve seemingly universal problems of overspecialization, mismatches of supply and demand, geographic maldistribution, and lack of interdisciplinary teamwork. In Chapter 16, Michael Gusmano provides a close view of several generations of policies and programs to improve the equality of U.S. health care. He demonstrates that innovative strategies can emerge from government, from private purchasers, or through patient movements. There is little evidence, however, that there are easy policy solutions for drastically reducing poor-quality care or substantially increasing excellent "value-based" care. In Chapter 17, Rick Mayes directs our attention to the relative capacities in the public and private sectors to rein in health care costs. His analysis suggests that government—especially through Medicare—is a major source of innovation in cost containment and that many of its strategies have been adopted in the private sector. Conversely, numerous techniques honed in private managed care plans have subsequently been adopted in Medicare and Medicaid. In Chapter 18, Andrew Flescher offers an analysis of some ethical challenges that arise in the formulation or conduct of health policies. He poses the question of whether there is a right to health care and presents both philosophical arguments and empirical evidence to answer it. He also takes up two other contentious issues, asking if health care rationing is justified and what protection is required for human subjects in medical experiments.

Part IV: Contemporary Health Policy Issues: People and Policies focuses on health and health care policies aimed at special populations and problems. In Chapter 19, Samira Soleimanpour and Claire Brindis highlight the distinctive health needs of children and trends in children's health status. They identify significant disparities in child health and well-being related to race, ethnicity, and socioeconomic factors and a long history of policy initiatives to improve not only children's access to health care but also nutrition, education, family planning, product safety, and prevention of child abuse. In Chapter 20, Deborah McFarlane and Rongal Nikora explain why health policies focusing on women are appropriate and necessary and the pattern of policy development in particular areas such as reproductive health, access to health insurance, women's health research, and long-term care. In Chapter 21, David Barton Smith highlights the historical origins of our contemporary concern with racial and ethnic health disparities. A combination of mass migrations and new policies set in motion changes in the U.S. health care system that substantially reduced disparities in treatment. Far more needs to be done, however, to eliminate racial and ethnic disparities in health outcomes. In Chapter 22, Pamela Nadash and Edward Alan Miller raise a number of inconvenient truths about the current state of aging and health care policy in the United States. They remind us that the aging population is an inescapable driver of health care needs and spending, and describe the myriad forms of institutional and community-based services that have developed over time. They also probe the politics of aging and to what extent interests on behalf of the elderly are organized and influential. In Chapter 23, Cari Cuffney and Patrick Remington examine the leading causes of death in the United States and find dramatic improvement in population-wide trends since 1960. They also report significant disparities, however, in mortality rates for subpopulations based on age, gender, race, geographical location, and socioeconomic status. They focus on some specific issues—infant deaths, vaccine-preventable infections, HIV, smoking, and heart disease—and describe programs and policies that are effective means of reducing mortality from those causes. In Chapter 24, David Rochefort delivers an in-depth history of mental health policy, which features episodic bursts of activity followed by retreat or neglect. He shows how the recent adoption of mental health parity legislation and the Affordable Care Act offer hope to the mentally ill and their families, and he advocates that their needs might be met through better access to mainstream health care and better integration of care for mental and physical conditions. In Chapter 25, Thomas Fahey and Michael Fahey trace back to the 1960s the emergence of what is now universally recognized as an obesity epidemic and examine the diverse policy approaches to slowing or reversing the epidemic. While there are mixed opinions on the degree of personal responsibility for obesity, the authors conclude that governmental policies can be effective and are essential ingredients in a social response. Chapter 26, Susan Giaimo discusses the connections among money, election campaigns, and influence in the policy process and reflects on the relative influence of some key interest groups and think tanks. She revisits three major episodes in U.S. health policy—the adoption of Medicare and Medicaid in 1965, the defeat of President Clinton's health care reform plan in 1993 and 1994, and the enactment of the Affordable Care Act in 2010—to clarify how interest groups shaped the outcomes.

Part V: U.S. Response to Global Health Challenges considers strategies for meeting a mix of old and new threats to public health. It also acknowledges the reality that the health and well-being of Americans depends on policies and practices in other countries and multilateral governance. In Chapter 27, Kenrad Nelson reviews the many threats posed by infectious diseases. Each disease has its unique attributes, but there are common elements in successful strategies to contain or eliminate their threats. In Chapter 28, Lance Gable analyzes how many of the concepts and tactics used to plan for and prevent epidemics are being updated for a broader range of public health emergencies, namely, responses to natural or human-made disasters. He reviews the history of emergency preparedness and assesses the current capacity of the U.S. government to limit the damage from potentially catastrophic events. In Chapter 29, Diana Bowman, Andrew Jessmore, and Scott Greer reflect on the inability of the United States or any other nation to isolate itself from threats to modern public health. Increasingly, infectious or communicable diseases (such as HIV/AIDS, SARS, avian flu) do not respect borders, but the same can be said of many noncommunicable diseases and injuries. The authors discuss how international action can be mobilized to attack common health threats, such as tobacco, and some of the chief limitations to such strategies. In Chapter 30, Daniel Fox comments

on the strengths and weaknesses of different analytical approaches to health politics and policy. To best understand the governance of a sector—in this case, the connection between public policy and population health outcomes—he emphasizes the value of empirical, historically grounded analysis. That approach can best inform readers about what actors, in concert with whom, took particular actions in pursuit of particular goals. I would concur with Fox that this is important information for participants who hope to be effective in the next round of health policy development and implementation.

—*Thomas R. Oliver*

PART I ★ **EVOLUTION OF AMERICAN HEALTH CARE POLICY (BEGINNINGS TO TODAY)**

chapter 1

Origins and Development of Government's Role in Health Policy (Colonial Era to Present)[1]

Kant Patel

HE UNITED STATES REMAINS THE ONLY MAJOR industrialized country in the world without national health insurance. Today, a majority of Americans are covered through private health insurance, usually bought through their employers. Health care is largely financed, administered, and delivered through the private sector. However, it is important to note that if one uses internationally accepted standards for health accounting, public spending accounts for almost 60 percent of U.S. spending on health care. This discrepancy arises because, in the United States, tax expenditures of state and local government on health coverage for their employees and retirees are counted as private spending.

The federal government today performs a variety of important roles in the health care field. First, the federal government in collaboration with state and local governments performs public health functions through the Centers for Diseases Control, Department of Agriculture, and Department of Defense. Second, the federal government provides health services to veterans, American Indians, and Alaska Natives. Third, through public health insurance programs such as Medicare, Medicaid, and the Children's Health Insurance Program, the federal government covers the health care needs of individuals—such as the elderly, the poor, the permanently disabled, and poor children who cannot afford private health insurance for one reason or another. Yet almost forty-eight million Americans fall through the holes in this safety net and remain uninsured today. Although the United States spends far more on health care than any other country in the world, it does not rank near the top on many health care indicators and suffers from problems related to high costs, access, and inequality.

Perhaps it is not too surprising that scholarly and journalistic literature has described the U.S. health care system as broken, sick, a disgrace, wasteful and built for waste, scandalous, accidental, an oxymoron, fragmented, and unsystematic.[2] The patients in the U.S. health care system are often described as overdosed, overtreated, and overdiagnosed.[3] The present-day health care system has evolved over several centuries into a patchwork of public and private sector health programs and policies, often without any coordination.

HEALTH CARE IN COLONIAL TIMES, 1600s–1700s

In an effort to alleviate potential settlers' and investors' widespread anxieties about the dangers of migrating to North America and the potential hostility of Native Americans, early explorers at the beginning of the 1600s described the eastern sea coast (present-day New England) in idyllic terms as made up of bountiful gardens and a paradise that would be hospitable and healthy for their constitution as well as support European plantations with minimum efforts.[4] Instead, what the new settlers found was a world that was a melting pot of disease such as malaria, typhoid, and yellow fever.[5] Settlers also brought several diseases with them to the Americas. Colonies were often swept by deadly epidemics, such as smallpox, measles, scarlet fever, plagues, typhus, and diphtheria, against which doctors were helpless.

Out of necessity, the doctors relied on Old World medicine and practices such as purging, puking, sweating, and bleeding since modern medical procedures and pharmaceuticals were not yet developed. The drugs they used were primarily medicinal herbs, called "simples," which seldom relieved the patients' symptoms; beyond that, doctors could do little else but offer moral support.[6] In the early settlements, European trained doctors were very few, and they existed in short supply as the population grew. Consequently, colonists were forced to train their own doctors by a system of apprenticeship or send young men of promise to Europe for proper medical training.[7]

European medicine has a rich history and it began with the age of Pericles. It was Hippocrates (460–370 BCE) who is credited with giving Greek medicine its scientific foundation and its ethical ideals. He has been called the "Father of Medicine" and is known for, among other things, disassociating medicine from philosophy, organizing existing knowledge into systematic science, and giving physicians high moral aspirations.[8] The Greek medicine ultimately migrated to Rome and established a respectable footing. Romans made hygienic contributions to science, such as cremation, well-ventilated houses, sewers, drains, and public baths. The fall of the Roman Empire ushered in the Middle Ages (1096–1438) and the period of feudalism. The Christian virtue of compassion for the weak and suffering led to new directions in nursing the sick and building hospitals for their care. It also led to advancement in medical laws and chartering of medical universities. The period of the Renaissance (1400s–1600s) led to revival of learning and reformation. During this period the invention of printing, revival of learning, discovery of America, and advancement in travel and commerce laid the foundation of modern physics and chemistry. The seventeenth century was characterized by individual scientific endeavors. English medicine produced the first book on vital statistics. The condition of medicine was further improved by creation of scientific societies. By the seventeenth century, Europe had become the great center of medical education.[9] Thus, it is not surprising that colonists sent their young men of promise to Europe for medical training.

Epidemics and Little Treatment

A series of epidemics struck the eastern seaboard of New England between 1616 and 1619 and wiped out nearly 95 percent of the Native Americans living there. The Native Americans were described by early travelers and settlers as the enemies of God's chosen people, and the effect of the plague was described as having made the region much more fit for the English people to inhabit. Thus, the settlement of New England was seen as divinely ordained by the colonial ideology and as further evidence that Christ had endorsed the migration. The plagues were viewed as a divine force acting directly on the "Promised Land," opening the space for migration and cultivation.[10]

Of course, the English settlers were by no means immune to the same diseases. Many of them were also stricken by epidemics of smallpox, measles, and diphtheria. Because the colonists during that time had very little understanding of the transmission or nature of most diseases, sickness was generally attributed to an act of God. The smallpox epidemic in 1689 was considered an act of God.[11] Faith in divine protection against illness helped raise morale, but it also created a fear of divine wrath.[12] The 1721 smallpox epidemic that struck New England was believed to be God's punishment to colonists for breaking their covenant with him.[13] This link between medicine and theology in New England lasted throughout the seventeenth century and was fused into the religious life of the Puritan community.[14] It is not too surprising, then, that health guides and medical advice during that time consisted of urging individuals to avoid behaviors and emotions (anger, fear, grief, envy) that could lead to ill health and diseases. Health was seen as a private good and individual responsibility.[15]

Many of these diseases came from Europe, and vaccination to prevent disease such as smallpox was not available until 1800. Consequently, attempts were made to block importation of such diseases by the establishment of quarantine at the seaports as early as 1648. The quarantine function during the colonial times was left up to local governments. Because these quarantines were imposed by the government, one can argue that the principle of government responsibility for the safeguarding of the public's health was established.[16] In recognition that overcrowding on a ship can pose serious health problems, one of the first public health laws in Massachusetts limited the number of passengers on a ship based on the size of the ship. In addition, a vague sense of connection between sickness and purification led the town of Boston in 1634 to prohibit residents from depositing fish or garbage near common landings.[17] The end of the Civil War (1861–1865) helped usher in the sanitary revolution in the United States, and by the end of 1860s, most cities had established effective health boards.

Relief for the Poor

Provision for the sick poor in colonial America was essentially seen as a problem of relief for the poor; programs for relief varied considerably among colonies. The English settlements again adopted the principle of local responsibility as set down in the Elizabethan poor law of 1601 under which each parish or town was responsible for taking care of its own needy individuals. Responsibility for relief of the poor in the sparsely populated southern colonies was vested in the county rather than in a parish or a town. In 1642, in accordance with English customs, the Plymouth Colony passed a law making each town responsible for its own poor. However, it was not uncommon to see pregnant women, the sick, disabled, or homeless driven out of town to avoid the burden of taking care of them. Even in towns that provided help and care, the sick poor were granted minimal material and medical relief. Institutional provision for the sick was rare; instead, clergy generally undertook visitation of the sick. The main feature of the colonial provision for the care of the sick poor was its very unsystematic nature.[18]

By the early 1700s, most colonial assemblies had established the practice of quarantine at their ports to prevent spread of diseases. The first preventive medicine, a smallpox inoculation, was imported from Great Britain in 1720, which was followed by improved vaccination around 1800.

Key Developments in Health Care Policy

Several important developments occurred in the second half of the eighteenth century. Many of these developments were influenced and shaped by policies developed in Europe and were subsequently adopted in colonial America. Developments in American medicine regarding medical schools, medical training, hospitals, and medical treatment were significantly influenced and shaped by medical developments in Europe. For example, doctors in colonial America took eighteenth century England as their model in establishing the social structure of medicine in early America in an attempt to transform physicians from an "occupational profession" to a "status profession."[19]

One was the development of public health policies and sanitation laws passed by local governments: regulating butchers, requiring cleanliness in slaughterhouses, impounding stray cows and horses, and requiring the removal of dead animals from the streets. The increasing population and crowded conditions in growing cities also led local governments to pass laws regulating food and water supplies.

The second major development was the creation of university medical education with the establishment of the first medical school at the College of Philadelphia in 1765, followed by the medical school of King's College in New York in 1768. However, this development was disrupted by the American War of Independence (1775–1783).[20]

The third major development was the emergence of hospitals. Hospitals in the eighteenth century, however, were rare and generally found in urban areas such as New York and Philadelphia. One category of hospital that emerged frequently in the second half of the seventeenth century was the military hospital; they varied in the comprehensiveness of the services they provided, which ranged from mobile "lying hospitals" to permanent regimental hospitals to general hospitals.[21]

The origin of the federal government's role in health policy following independence can be traced to provision of medical and hospital care for merchant seamen and sailors when, in 1798, Congress passed an Act for the Relief of Sick and Disabled Seamen to finance the construction and operation of public hospitals at seaports. This was the first instance in which any level of government established a health program for a specific group of people (e.g., the Marine Hospital Service, renamed the Public Health Service in 1912).[22]

Thus, throughout the eighteenth century, government played a very minor role in health policy except for a limited role in the area of public health. Health care was essentially seen as a private good and individual responsibility, except for care of the sick poor by local towns.

HEALTH CARE IN THE NINETEENTH CENTURY

During the nineteenth century, public health activities were devoted to preventing the spread of communicable diseases and were confined primarily to major cities until the Civil War. Only after the Civil War did state boards of health become common. By the end of the nineteenth century, boards of health had been established in most large cities and at the state level. Their functions were limited to enforcement of sanitary regulations and control of certain communicable diseases. The scope of health departments and associations did not expand until the turn of the twentieth century. For example, the American Public Health Association, composed mainly of social workers, was founded in 1872, and the phrase *social work* emerged in the late 1890s as a way to describe professional activities in the first two decades of the twentieth century.

The engraving "United States Marine Hospital at Chelsea, Massachusetts" depicts an early hospital that was established for sick and disabled seamen. In July 1798, Congress passed and President John Adams (1797–1801) signed an Act for the Relief of Sick and Disabled Seamen. The law taxed mariners' wages at the rate of twenty cents per month to finance health care for ailing sailors in ports throughout the country.

SOURCE: Courtesy of the American Antiquarian Society, Worcester, Massachusetts.

General hospitals, as we know them today, did not exist, primarily due to the lack of advances in science and medicine at that point in time.[23] Poorhouses and almshouses provided care for destitute persons. Between 1830 and 1860, marine hospitals proliferated; during the Civil War, however, the Marine Hospital System was neglected, and the number of hospitals decreased. Then, in 1869, Congress reviewed the Marine Hospital System and passed the first Reorganization Act in 1870. Under this law, the system was federalized and formally organized as a national agency with a central headquarters.[24] Also, in 1878, Congress passed a National Quarantine Act to prevent persons with communicable diseases from entering the country.

In the early 1800s, all forms of medicine were practiced together. In 1806, New York became the first state to pass the first licensing laws in the United States when it passed the Medical Practice Act. The law allowed the state to license physicians, and unlicensed practitioners were fined for practicing without a license. Many states followed New York's example and passed similar licensing laws. However, many early Americans who remembered the sacrifice they had made for their freedom viewed such laws as too restrictive of their rights and freedom. During the 1820s and 1830s, opposition to such laws led many states to repeal their licensing laws. The definition of "irregular" physician was revised to allow just about every form of medicine to be practiced.

In 1847, the American Medical Association (AMA) was formed to upgrade medical education and promote professionalization of medical practice. One of the first actions the AMA took was to establish a Committee on Medical Education, which was replaced in 1904 by the Council on Medical Education, with considerably expanded powers to investigate and recommend improvement in medical training. The AMA invited an outside group, the Carnegie Foundation for Advancement of Teaching, to investigate medical schools. The group's representative, Abraham Flexner, visited each of the medical schools in the country and made his report in 1910. The Flexner Report recommended adoption of the German model of medicine with science-based training, strengthening of first-class medical schools, and elimination of inferior medical schools. The AMA implemented most of the recommendations of the Flexner Report, which paved the way ultimately for the professionalization of U.S. medical education and practice.

During the latter part of the nineteenth century, physicians and pharmacists were the sole dispensers of professionally recognized health services. Most physicians were trained through apprenticeships with practicing physicians. Later, private and public medical schools were established to train physicians. Physicians made their living treating patients for fees and received very little, if any, money from the government. The same was true of pharmacists, who later developed drugstores to supplement their income from prescriptions. Thus, private practice and fee-for-service was firmly established in the early U.S. health care system.

The last quarter of the nineteenth century saw a steady advance in medical science. Antiseptic surgery was highly developed by 1875; the science of microbiology was introduced; and techniques of vaccination were developed. The advent of anesthesia and antisepsis made general hospitals relatively safe places for surgery.[25]

Early general hospitals were established mostly by voluntary community boards and churches. The growing national economy made it possible for hospitals to obtain capital funds from philanthropists and operating funds from paying patients. Voluntary hospitals, because of their charitable and nonprofit charters, were obligated to provide care for the poor. Physicians began to admit patients to hospitals for surgeries. Patients paid for hospital charges and physicians' fees; in return, hospitals provided physicians with their facilities to provide free care for the poor. In 1875, there were very few general hospitals in the country. The tremendous growth in the number of U.S. hospitals occurred in the early twentieth century.

HEALTH CARE IN THE TWENTIETH CENTURY

During the first three decades of the twentieth century, American medicine and medical practice in particular were transformed from an unscientific and uncertain art lacking public support, respect, and prestige to a highly scientific discipline and organized profession enjoying prestige, status, and position of considerable political power and influence. This transformation, which was largely social in nature rather than political, emerged from three key developments.[26]

The Makeover of American Medicine, 1900–1930s

The first major development was the consolidation of medical schools and the standardization of medical education following the Flexner Report, published in 1910. In response to the Flexner Report, the process of consolidation of medical education proceeded at a rapid pace. By 1915, in eliminating inferior schools, the number of medical schools had decreased from 131 to 95. Similarly, the number of graduates from medical schools dropped from 5,440 to 3,536. The AMA became a national accrediting agency for medical schools, and many states came to accept its judgments regarding medical schools.[27] By the 1940s, the AMA had become a powerful political force and a major player in shaping U.S. health care policy.

The second major development was the separation of public health services from the private practice of medicine, whereby public health officers were not allowed to practice medicine. One catalyst for the development of an

POLITICS AND HEALTH CARE POLICY

American Ambivalence about the Role of Government in Health Care

Americans' reluctance to embrace universal health insurance is reflected in their ambivalence about the role of government, especially the federal government, in the health care field. This reluctance and ambivalence is rooted in their belief that health care is a private and not a public good and thus is an individual responsibility and not the government's collective responsibility to provide health care for everyone. Moral stigmas, however, are often constructed and employed in the debate about public health issues such as alcohol and drug use, abortion, and homosexual behavior.

Americans have often been torn between two political paradigms—individualism and individual responsibility (classical liberalism) on the one hand and yearning for a sense of community and desire for collective action (communitarianism) on the other. Classical liberalism insists on drawing a clear line between the public and private sphere and individuals' private sphere to be protected from government interference. However, early Americans often celebrated a notion of community and shared mutual assistance, shared public life, and civic duty.

During colonial times, English settlers and their descendants believed that diseases were an expression of Divine Providence and that there was a relationship among health, disease, and the natural order. Individuals should avoid behaviors and emotions that could lead to disease, and thus the means to perfect health was within everyone's grasp. This central idea that individuals were responsible for maintaining their own health has remained the core of Americans' belief. The vision of health care as a collective good requiring collective government action has emerged occasionally in U.S. history (e.g., the early sanitation reform movement), only to be quickly submerged by Americans' central belief in health care as a private good and an individual moral responsibility. In the early twentieth century, public health's focus on personal hygiene fit perfectly with the public's belief that health care was within individual control. In the United States, pursuit of wellness is linked with living a moral life. Exercise and eating healthy are seen as an individual's responsibility. For example, in 1990, the secretary of health and human services argued in *Healthy People 2000* that personal responsibility (i.e., responsible and enlightened behavior by each and every individual) is a key to good health. Even today, many chronic diseases, such as diabetes, cancer, and heart disease, are seen as individual responsibilities not requiring government action in prevention and treatment.

SOURCES: Mary Ann Jimenez, "Concepts of Health and National Health Care Policy: Views from American History," *Social Service Review* 71: 1 (1997): 34–50; James A. Morone, "Enemies of the People: The Moral Dimension to Public Health," *Journal of Health, Politics, Policy and Law* 224 (August 1997): 993–1020; see also James A. Morone, *Hellfire Nation: The Politics of Sin in American History* (New Haven, CT: Yale University Press, 2003).

institutional schism between public health and private medicine was the 1915 Welch-Rose Report, which focused more on medical research than on practical education. Another catalyst was the Rockefeller Foundation's decision in 1916 to advocate and support the establishment of separate schools of public health because the foundation believed that insufficient attention was being paid to the environmental and social causes of diseases. The establishment of separate schools of public health during the 1910s and 1920s created a dichotomous model of health care in U.S. medicine. One model is the preventive model of health care exemplified by public health functions focusing on the study of population health, prevention of diseases, and promotion of health and wellness. The second model of health care, the curative model, came to be associated with diagnosing, treating, caring for, and curing individuals after they suffer from an illness or disease.[28]

By the 1930s, physicians in private practice had come to view public health and government expansion in health care as antithetical to their economic self-interest and began to oppose government policies and programs expanding government's role in the field of health care. Federal government funding of biomedical research, particularly through the emerging National Institutes of Health, helped raise clinical medicine to a place of prominence in U.S. society. By

the 1950s, the curative model had become the dominant model of health care in the United States.

The third significant development during this period was the rise of the third-party insurance payment system. Before the 1930s, medical insurance programs were nonexistent. During the Great Depression of the 1930s, the incomes of hospitals and physicians declined; many people could not afford to pay hospitals or physicians for their medical services. Realizing that they could operate better with a steady income, hospitals began to sponsor prepayment plans, which came to be known as the Blue Cross plans. Similarly, prepayment plans for physicians' services in the hospital, especially surgery, began to appear. Sponsored by state medical societies, they became known as Blue Shield plans. Both the Blue Cross and the Blue Shield plans were very successful; in turn, this led to a proliferation of other private health insurance plans. The third-party payment system replaced the financing system based on direct one-on-one financial transactions between patient and physician.

Expanded Role for the Federal Government in Health Policy, 1900–1960

The role of the federal government in health policy changed dramatically in the twentieth century. As mentioned earlier, in the early part of the twentieth century, the government played a very limited role. The beginning of the federal government's role in health policy can be traced to the early 1920s, and it expanded significantly until the 1960s. Despite efforts to reduce the role of federal government in the second half of the twentieth century, the government today remains a major player in health policy.

Limited Federal Role, 1900s–1930s

The federal government's involvement in health policy began to evolve in the 1920s. While European nations were establishing compulsory sickness insurance programs during the late nineteenth and early twentieth centuries, the U.S. federal government took no action to subsidize voluntary sickness funds or to make sickness insurance mandatory nationwide. Mandatory national health insurance became a political issue briefly in the United States on the eve of World War I (1914–1918). The progressive reformers' hopes of adopting a national compulsory sickness insurance program, however, were soon dashed by robust opposition from physicians, pharmaceutical companies, and insurance companies. In addition, both labor unions and business, fearing competition from government in social welfare programs, failed to support the reformers. By 1920, the movement for compulsory sickness insurance had faded from the political agenda (which is further discussed in Chapter 2).

Under pressure from the labor movement and children's advocates, Congress passed the Sheppard-Towner Act in 1921. It established the first federal grant-in-aid program for local child health clinics. Many local health departments refused to accept these grants because the AMA and local medical societies strongly opposed the program. Congress allowed the program to terminate in 1928. Thus, the federal government's role in health care remained limited during the nineteenth and early twentieth centuries.

Liberal Mandate and the Expanded Federal Role, 1930s–1960s

The election of Franklin D. Roosevelt (1933–1945) and the beginning of the New Deal signified the start of a liberal mandate under which the role of the government in health care expanded significantly; it culminated in Lyndon B. Johnson's (1963–1969) War on Poverty and the creation of Medicare and Medicaid programs in 1965. During this period, many Democratic administrations proposed and initiated new federal health care programs.

Advances in medical technology and the discovery of antibiotics changed the focus of medical care from prevention of disease through inoculation and hygiene to curing of illnesses.[29] For the first time, sulfa drugs and penicillin gave physicians the true power to cure. In 1934, during the Great Depression, the Federal Emergency Relief Administration gave the first federal grants to local governments for public assistance to the poor, including financial support for medical care.

The Social Security Act of 1935 provided for unemployment compensation, old-age pensions, and other benefits. The early planning of the legislation had initially included a proposal for establishing health insurance as part of the package. However, the Roosevelt administration did not want to jeopardize the enactment of the entire law because of strong opposition to health insurance by the medical profession. Therefore, national health insurance was omitted from the final legislative proposal. The Social Security Act did extend the role of the federal government in health care by including provisions designed to strengthen public health services.

During 1935 and 1936, Senator Robert Wagner (D-NY; in office 1927–1949), a sponsor of the Social Security Act, introduced an amendment to the act that would have provided federal grants to the states for the organization of health insurance plans covering workers and their dependents. The onset of World War II (1939–1945) postponed any serious consideration of such a plan, and similar attempts to establish a health insurance program under the Harry S. Truman administration (1945–1953) were defeated during the 1940s. Thus, the medical profession succeeded in defeating proposals for any sort of national health insurance.

In 1937, the establishment of the National Cancer Institute (NCI), with a broad mandate for ascertaining the cause, prevention, and cure of the disease, reflected the increased role of the federal government in health care in general and in public health services in particular. The law authorized the NCI to conduct research in its own laboratories and to award grants to nongovernment scientists and institutions for training scientists and clinicians. It paved the way for public funding of biomedical research through the National Institutes of Health (NIH) and the National Science Foundation (NSF).

Health Care as an Employment Benefit

One of the most significant policy developments in shaping the present-day U.S. health care system was strengthening the link between employment and the private health insurance system that occurred during World War II. During the 1940s, the federal government encouraged the development of private, voluntary insurance plans. Congress gave voluntary insurance plans a financial boost by legislating that health insurance and pensions were fringe benefits and exempt from a wartime freeze on wages. Thus, employers could offer their workers health care fringe benefits by paying for part or all of the cost of their insurance premiums. In 1943, the War Labor Board ruled that controls over wages and prices imposed by the 1942 Stabilization Act did not apply to fringe benefits such as health insurance. This led many employers to use health insurance benefits to attract and retain workers. In 1948 and 1949, the National Labor Relations Board gave further impetus to workplace health coverage by ruling that health insurance and other employee welfare plans were subject to collective bargaining.[30]

A 1951 ruling by the Internal Revenue Service (IRS) that employers' costs for workers' premiums were a tax-deductible expense made large-scale development of private health insurance viable. In a 1954 landmark decision, the IRS ruled that employer-sponsored insurance benefits were exempt from income tax and added this provision to the tax code.[31] This determination extended the tax exemption of employee contributions, reduced the uncertainty surrounding the tax treatment of employer contribution, and provided the statutory basis for tax treatment of employer contributions, which previously were buried in individual administrative tax court cases. Under this ruling, health benefits are tax-exempt; that is, the value of the benefit is excluded in determining an employee's taxable income and the employer's health care contribution is treated as a deductible business expense just like wages and materials. Employer-sponsored health benefits can be excluded from personal income taxes also at the state level. This is considered the single largest tax subsidy in the federal budget. According to a report by the Urban Institute, this tax exemption reduced the federal tax revenue by $268 billion in 2011.[32]

The current U.S. health care system is built on this employment-based health insurance approach adopted during World War II. This development established and solidified the private health care insurance market and has been one of the major hurdles to creation of a national health insurance system in the United States.

After World War II, the Truman administration called for the expansion of hospitals, increased support for public health, maternal and child health services, and federal aid for medical research and education. In 1946, Congress passed the National Hospital Survey and Construction Act, also known as the Hill-Burton Act. This program provided federal funds to subsidize construction of hospitals in areas with bed shortages, mainly in rural counties. Physicians welcomed Hill-Burton funds and actively sought them for construction of new hospitals for reasons of prestige, convenience, and service.

In 1946, Congress also passed the National Mental Health Act. This law provided federal grants to states for research, prevention, diagnosis, and treatment of mental

KEY DECISIONS: HEALTH CARE CRISES AND SOLUTIONS

Tax Treatment of Employer-Sponsored Health Insurance and the Internal Revenue Code of 1954

By the early 1940s, Blue Cross and Blue Shield insurance plans had become very popular. At that time, however, the government's tax policy relating to the tax exempt status of employers' payment to insurance companies for group medical and hospitalization premiums on behalf of their employees was rather confusing. It applied only to direct employer contributions to group plans issued by commercial insurance companies and not to private programs of employee associations such as unions or other private plans. Previous IRS administrative rulings had created confusion about eligibility and about what constituted an insurance plan. The Revenue Act of 1951 allowed taxpayers age sixty-five and over to deduct medical expenses up to 5 percent of minimum income for themselves and their spouse. Thus, not all taxpayers were eligible for this tax exemption.

One of the most significant policy decisions in shaping today's U.S. health care system was the 1954 IRS ruling that dramatically strengthened the direct link between employment and private health insurance systems. The IRS ruled that all employer-sponsored insurance benefits were exempt from income tax and added this provision to the tax code. Internal Revenue Code of 1954, Sections 106 and 213, state:

SEC. 106. CONTRIBUTIONS BY EMPLOYER TO ACCIDENT AND HEALTH PLANS.

Gross income does not include contributions by the employer to accident or health plans for compensation (through insurance or otherwise) to his employees for personal injuries or sickness.

SEC 213. MEDICAL, DENTAL, ETC., EXPENSES.

(a) ALLOWANCE OF DEDUCTION.—There shall be allowed as a deduction expenses paid during the taxable year, not compensated by insurance or otherwise, for medical care of taxpayer, his spouse or a dependent (as defined in section 152).

SOURCE: Internal Revenue Code of 1954, pp. 32, 69, http://constitution.org/uslaw/sal/068A_itax.pdf. For more information on the 1954 tax code, see also, Selma Mushkin, "The Internal Revenue Code of 1954 and Health Programs," *Public Health Reports* 70: 8 (August 1955): 791–800.

disorders. During the 1950s, there was further expansion of public health services at the federal level. The NIH greatly expanded support of biomedical research.

From the 1920s to the 1950s, efforts to establish a system of national health care or insurance for the entire population had failed because of charges from the medical profession and others that such plans would constitute "socialized medicine." Faced with opposition to comprehensive change, advocates of a national health insurance system changed their strategy and objectives and turned to an incremental strategy. They began to push for a limited system of public health insurance programs for specific needy groups, such as the elderly. The elderly were a perfect target group for providing help because of their greater medical need, their often inadequate financial resources, and the loss of employment-based group medical insurance upon retirement. Thus, the elderly were deemed worthy and were not stigmatized as a failed group, as were welfare recipients.[33]

The result was passage of the Kerr-Mills Act (also known as the Medical Assistance Act) by Congress in 1960. The law provided federal matching payments to states for vendor (provider) payments and allowed states to include the medically needy (i.e., elderly, blind, and disabled persons with low income who were not on public assistance). The act also suggested the scope of services to be covered, such as hospital stays, nursing home care, physicians' services, and other health services. It required each state to plan for institutional and non-institutional care as a condition of federal cost-sharing. State participation in the program was optional, and states were left free to determine eligibility and the extent of services provided. Most important, the act established the concept of "medical indigency." However, the Kerr-Mills program proved to be neither effective nor adequate. It failed to provide significant relief for a substantial portion of the elderly population. This was largely due to limited participation by states, a unique feature of the U.S. federal system and a precursor to some states' opposition to the Patient Protection and Affordable Care Act of 2010. Clearly, the issue of financing health care for the elderly had not been resolved and remained on the political agenda.

On February 21, 1963, President John F. Kennedy (1961–1963) delivered his "Special Message on Aiding Our Senior Citizens." The key proposal included the creation of Medicare to meet the medical needs of the elderly. The assassination of Kennedy in November 1963 left the task of carrying on the battle for Medicare to his successor, Lyndon B. Johnson (1963–1969). Johnson adopted most of Kennedy's unfinished legislative proposals and incorporated them into the Great Society's War on Poverty program. After civil rights, Medicare was second in the administration's priorities. Johnson won a landslide victory in the 1964 presidential election, allowing him to claim a public mandate for his programs. Equally important, the Democrats won major

victories in the congressional elections. The administration now had enough votes in the House and Senate for the passage of its major health care proposals.

In 1965, Congress passed the Medicare program for the elderly and the Medicaid program for the poor as amendments to the Social Security Act of 1935. This final product was a classic compromise between three competing proposals. It included a compulsory health insurance program for the elderly, financed through payroll taxes (Medicare Part A, the Johnson administration proposal), a voluntary insurance program for physicians' services subsidized through general revenues (Medicare Part B, the Republican proposal), and an expanded means-tested program administered by the states (Medicaid, the AMA proposal).

In addition to Medicare and Medicaid, a number of other health programs, such as Maternal and Infant Care, the Special Food Service Program for Children, and community health centers, were created during the 1960s as part of Johnson's War on Poverty. Both Medicare and Medicaid dramatically increased access to health care.

However, increased access also resulted in increased health care expenditures leading to efforts at cost containment. In 1966, for example, Congress passed the Comprehensive Health Planning Act, an attempt at health care facilities planning through the states. Comprehensive health planning agencies were to be established in every state and in local areas. Their principal focus was hospital planning. The law attempted to synthesize the goal of cost containment with the goal of providing access and quality care to everyone. This law was replaced in 1974 by the National Health Planning and Resource Development Act. The law required each state to adopt certificate-of-need (CON) laws. The CON laws require hospitals to document community need in order to obtain approval for major capital expenditure for expansion of facilities and services. The act also established a network of health system agencies (HSAs) at state and local levels to administer CON laws. Overall, the attempt to contain health care costs through "planning" was not very successful because health care costs continued to rise. The explanations for lack of success include the fact that HSAs were captured by the hospital industry they were supposed to regulate. In addition, even though consumers were represented on HSA boards, representatives of the health care providers dominated the HSA meetings. Also, there was a general lack of public support for HSAs and CON laws.

REDUCING THE ROLE OF THE FEDERAL GOVERNMENT IN HEALTH POLICY, 1970s–2008

The election of Richard M. Nixon (1969–1974) to the presidency in 1968 signaled an end to the liberal mandate and an ascendency of a conservative political ideology. This period witnessed the initiation and implementation of several policy initiatives utilizing "managed competition," "managed care," and "consumer choice" strategies to devolve more authority and flexibility to state governments, reduce and/or contain health care costs (public and private sector), reduce the role of the federal government, expand the role of the private sector, induce competition in the marketplace, and increase consumer choices in health care. At the same time, the "managed" part recognized some role for the government in managing competition and care. Providing consumers with increased choice when they purchase insurance, reduction and elimination of many regulatory approaches to cost containment, and new forms of prepaid health care delivery organizations became the main focus.

Efforts at Health Care Cost Containment

By the 1970s, health care costs had risen dramatically. Total national health care expenditures increased from $27.1 billion in 1960 to $74.3 billion in 1970. During this same period, federal health care expenditures increased from $2.9 billion to $17.8 billion, while state and local governments' health care expenditures increased from $3.7 billion to $9.9 billion. Similar increases were evident in hospital care and physician services. From 1966 to 1970, Medicare expenditures increased from $1.6 billion to $7.1 billion, while Medicaid expenditures increased from $1.3 billion to $5.3 billion. Increases in medical care inflation outstripped overall inflation.[34] Consequently, policymakers' concerns began to shift from increasing access to containing rising health care costs. During the 1970s and 1980s, the federal government undertook a combination of regulatory and market-oriented policy initiatives in an effort to contain costs.

Beginning in 1971, the Nixon administration sought to curtail health care costs. In his message to Congress on February 18, 1971, Nixon argued that the United States was investing more of the nation's resources in the health of people but was not getting full return on that investment.[35] Despite Nixon's conflicts with the Democratic-controlled Congress, a number of cost-containment initiatives were begun during this time.

One of the factors often cited as responsible for increased health care costs is the overuse of health care resources. The rising costs of Medicare and Medicaid created concern in Congress about the cost of, as well as the quality of care provided by, these programs. Congress created the Professional Standards Review Organizations (PSROs) through the Social Security Amendments Act of 1972. This was a regulatory mechanism to encourage efficient and economical delivery of health care in the two large public sector programs, Medicare and Medicaid. More than two hundred local PSROs were created and staffed by local physicians to review and monitor care provided to Medicare

and Medicaid patients by hospitals, skilled nursing homes, and extended-care facilities.

In 1973, the Health Maintenance Organization Act was passed. It was a modest plan. Health Maintenance Organizations (HMOs) were a new form of health care delivery organizations, in which enrollees pay a fixed fee (capitation) in advance, and in return they receive a comprehensive set of health services. The idea behind HMOs was that they would operate more efficiently because they would have an incentive to reduce costs and increase their profits; they would help make traditional health delivery organizations such as hospitals economically more efficient by providing competition for health care services.

During the 1970s, the federal government also emphasized health planning to contain rising health care costs. The rationale for planning was based on the argument that there was an abundance of health care facilities and services: too many hospitals, too many hospital beds, and too much medical equipment. Unnecessary expansion and duplication led to overuse of health care resources. In 1974, Congress passed the National Health Planning and Resource Development Act. This law replaced the Comprehensive Health Planning Act and other health planning programs such as the regional medical programs and the Hill-Burton programs. The law required all states to adopt certificate-of-need (CON) laws by 1980. CON laws required hospitals to document community needs to obtain approval for major capital expenditures for expansion of facilities and services. The act also established a network of health systems agencies at state and local levels to administer the CON laws.

Many of the Ronald Reagan administration (1981–1989) of the policy initiatives resulted in reexamination of the role of federal government in financing and administering health services and a significant change in the health care sector. During the first three years of the Reagan administration, funding for health planning and health maintenance organizations was eliminated. The PSROs were renamed Peer Review Organizations (PROs) and their funding was reduced from $58 million in 1980 to $15 million in 1983, effectively ending the program. The Reagan administration also succeeded in replacing twenty-one categorical grant programs in the areas of prevention, mental health, maternal and child health care, and primary care with four block grants. Funding for Medicare and Medicaid was also reduced.[36]

The biggest innovation of the Reagan administration was the introduction in 1983 of the Prospective Payment System, mandated by the Deficit Reduction Act of 1982, for reimbursement to hospitals under the Medicare program in the hope of reducing costs and making hospitals more efficient. Under the new system, illnesses were classified into one of 468 diagnosis-related groups. Each category was assigned a treatment rate, and hospitals were reimbursed according to these rates. If hospitals spent more money on treatment, they absorbed the additional costs. If they spent less money than the established rates, they kept the overpayment as profit. The new system was phased in over a period of time and went into full effect in 1987.

Giving States More Authority and Flexibility: Medicaid Waivers

Two types of waivers are available under the Medicaid program. Demonstration waivers allow states to experiment with alternative approaches to program delivery. Program waivers, established under the Omnibus Budget Reconciliation Act of 1981,[37] give the federal executive branch authority to give states freedom in their Medicaid programs to (a) restrict the "freedom of choice" beneficiaries had to select from among Medicaid providers, (b) adopt payment approaches other than fee-for-service, and (c) allow states to offer Home Community-Based Health Services (HCBS) as an alternative to nursing home care. The administrations of George H.W. Bush (1989–1993), William J. Clinton (1993–2001), and George W. Bush (2001–2009) made frequent use of such waivers. During the Clinton years, the number of HCBS waivers increased by almost 50 percent, from 155 to 231, and the number of Medicaid enrollees covered by waivers increased by 225 percent from 236,000 to 768,000. The hallmark of the Clinton years with respect to Medicaid waivers was the approval of seventeen comprehensive waivers that moved large number of Medicaid enrollees into managed care. Of the eighty-nine proposals, including renewals, submitted during the Clinton years, 57 percent were approved. By August 2006, the Bush administration had approved 72 percent of all waiver proposals, and forty-four states and the District of Columbia had obtained approval for 149 waivers. Granting program waivers by the federal authority to states has become an important policy tool in the U.S. federal system.[38]

Health Care Reform

President Clinton presented his plan to overhaul and establish universal health insurance to the nation in a speech before a joint session of Congress in September 1993. The proposed reform plan was based on six general principles: security, simplicity, savings, choice, quality, and responsibility. The proposal, entitled the Health Security Act, would have provided universal coverage through an employer mandate and provided federal subsidies for poor persons and workers without insurance. The plan was very much based on the concept of managed competition. Several competing health care reform plans emerged in Congress from both Democrats and Republicans. As the debate over these competing plans intensified, however, none of the plans managed to attract majority support. There were many reasons that led to the failure of health

care reform at the time. The major reasons included an intense opposition to the Clinton plan from some powerful interest groups, such as the insurance industry and small business groups, and the fact that Republicans in Congress refused to support reform, concluding that opposing Clinton's health care reform was in their political best interest because they wanted to use the failed reform effort as a campaign issue in the Congressional elections of 1996.[39] By the late summer of 1994, President Clinton's Health Security Act was declared dead and buried. Another window of opportunity for establishing a universal health insurance system had opened and closed.

Welfare Reform

In 1996, Congress passed and President Clinton signed into law the bill known as the Personal Responsibility and Work Opportunity Act of 1996. The new law included changes in welfare, supplemental security income, child support enforcement, and food stamp and social services. The main feature of the law is the Temporary Assistance to Needy Families program, under which states are given a block grant to design their own welfare program. The Medicaid program was left virtually intact, but the linkage between the two was broken.

Health Insurance Reforms

The failure of the Health Security Act led Congress to pass some incremental reforms designed to address specific problems in the health care field. One of the crowning achievements of the 104th Congress was passage of the Health Insurance Portability and Accountability Act of 1996, which President Clinton signed into law in August. Two of the major provisions of the bill are placing limits on insurance companies' authority to deny coverage or to impose preexisting condition exclusions and guaranteeing portability of insurance coverage when a person leaves his or her job voluntarily or involuntarily.

Children's Health Insurance Program

President Clinton and the Republican-controlled Congress managed to address another issue that had become an area of concern: the increased number of children who lacked health insurance coverage. The Balanced Budget Act of 1997 provided funds to expand health insurance coverage for children by creating the State Children's Health Insurance Program as part of Title XXI of the Social Security Act. State governments have taken advantage of this program and have expanded health insurance coverage to uninsured children in their states. When the program was reauthorized in 2009 during the administration of Barack Obama (2009–), it was renamed the Children's Health Insurance Program (CHIP).

Stem Cell Policy and Politics

During the 1990s, embryonic stem cell research generated a significant amount of controversy and heated discussion among its supporters and opponents, especially concerning the question of whether the federal government should fund such research. In August 2001, President George W. Bush announced his policy decision. He argued that as a result of private research, more than sixty genetically diverse stem cell lines were already in existence that had been created from embryos that were already destroyed. Furthermore, he argued that these stem cell lines had the ability to regenerate themselves indefinitely, creating more opportunity for research. Thus, he would allow federal funds to be used for research only on these existing stem cell lines where the life-and-death decision had already been made. Several state governments, however, have embraced and funded such research. The federal government exercises control only over stem cell research that it funds. There are no restrictions on stem cell research carried on in the private sector.

Restrictions on Reproductive Health

The term *reproductive health* is generally used to describe policies concerning abstinence, contraception, abortion, and assisted reproductive technologies. Federal support for abstinence-only education flourished during the second Bush administration. The abstinence education movement was a key aspect of the Bush administration's attempt to promote a conservative moral framework and sexual ethic.[40]

The Bush administration also tried to restrict access to abortion; President Bush signed the Partial Birth Abortion Ban Act into law on November 5, 2003.[41] The law outlaws a specific abortion procedure medically called "intact dilation and extraction (D&X)." In April 2007, the Supreme Court upheld the law.[42]

The Bush administration also made two major changes in international abortion and family planning policy, reinstating the "Mexico City policy" from the Reagan and George H.W. Bush eras. Under this policy, the United States will not fund any foreign organization that provides abortion services.[43] President Bush also signed a directive reviving the Global Gag Rule. This rule precludes awarding of federal government money earmarked for international population assistance and funded by the United States Agency for International Development to nongovernmental organizations in other countries that perform, counsel, or advocate for abortion services even in cases involving rape or incest.[44]

Consumer Directed Health Care

In the post–managed care era, the George W. Bush administration encouraged the idea of consumer-directed health care. Under this vision, patients take on the role of consumers, who use information and the Internet to comparison shop and make informed choices about their own health care and tailor their own custom-made health benefit packages. The major instruments of consumer-driven health care are high-deductible health insurance plans (HDHP) and health savings accounts used to pay for routine health care expenditures until deductibles are met, at which point an HDHP's catastrophic coverage kicks in. The concept behind consumer-directed health care is that it would make consumers more cost conscious, work against over-insurance and overuse of health services, and lead to cost savings in health care.

Medicare Modernization Act of 2003 and the Prescription Drug Benefit

By the early 2000s, rapidly rising prescription drug costs and growing concern about the affordability of needed drugs helped elevate this issue to the national policy agenda. The problem of the high cost of prescription drugs is most acute for many seniors, especially those with low income, multiple health problems, or both. In 2003, President Bush signed into law the Medicare Modernization Act, which went fully into effect on January 1, 2006. The law added Part D to Medicare, under which individuals are eligible for prescription drug coverage if they are entitled to benefits under Medicare Part A and/or enrolled in Part B. Beneficiaries can obtain the Part D drug benefit by either joining a private Prescription Drug Plan for drug coverage only, or under Medicare Part C, joining a Medicare Advantage plan that covers both medical services and prescription drugs. This was the largest expansion of the Medicare program since its inception in 1965.

RETURN OF THE LIBERAL MANDATE? 2009–PRESENT

By 2008, a consensus was emerging that a solution for problems related to the U.S. health care system as a whole was overdue. The number of uninsured Americans had increased from 39.8 million in 2001 to 46.3 million in 2008.[45]

Health Care Reform: Patient Protection and Affordable Care Act

Senator Barack Obama's (D-IL) victory in the 2008 presidential election set the stage for yet another effort to reform the U.S. health care system and establish a universal health insurance system. President Obama made health care reform a top priority of his administration. The Obama administration outlined a few general principles to Congress and let Congress work out the specifics and details of the reform plan. The general principles outlined were insurance market reform, shared responsibility, Medicaid expansion and tax credits, public health and workforce investments, lowering health care costs, and improving quality.[46] However, the Republican Party, just as it had done with the Clinton reform attempt, mounted strong opposition to Obama's reform plan. After more than a year of very partisan and divisive national and congressional debate, Congress passed, and the president signed into law on March 23, 2010, the Patient Protection and Affordable Care Act (PPACA). The law aims to provide universal health insurance coverage through a combination of individual mandates, tax credits, insurance exchanges, expansion of Medicaid, and several insurance market reforms. President Obama had finally broken a century-long logjam on overhauling the U.S. health care system.

The Role of State and Local Governments in Health Care

The topic of health care politics and policy in the United States is indivisible from issues of U.S. federalism. The distribution of authority and responsibility between different levels of government within a federal system is a topic of continuous debate. Health care policy has not been immune from this debate. Initially, the role of the federal government and of state and local governments was very limited. During colonial times, local governments played a minimal role in health policy. During much of the nineteenth century, the role of state and local governments was confined to public health activities. The role of local governments in public health was stimulated by great epidemics of diseases such as smallpox and fever in the late eighteenth and early nineteenth centuries. Municipalities established health boards or health departments to deal with problems of sanitation, poor housing, and quarantine.

Similarly, the states' role in public health was initially limited to special committees or commissions to control communicable diseases. In 1855, the first state health department was established in Louisiana. State governments also played a significant role in personal health care through the establishment of state mental hospitals.

By the beginning of the twentieth century, state and local governments were active in the delivery of personal health services. During the first decade of the century, state governments also began the regulation and licensure of hospitals. At the end of World War II, detailed state regulations and licensure procedures for hospitals became more common. President Kennedy's New Frontier programs and President Johnson's Great Society and War on Poverty programs brought new resources, rules, and enforcement from the national government to state and local governments. This ushered in a period of cooperative federalism with national, state, and local governments working together as partners. In this new partnership, the national government took the lead and state governments became avenues for innovations.

During the 1960s and 1970s, state governments took on many new functions; some of them fundamentally changed the traditional public health activities of subnational governments. The federal health programs of the 1960s dramatically increased the role of state and local governments in health care. Enhanced federal support for the delivery of health care services by institutions that traditionally served the poor (e.g., public hospitals, local health departments) increased. The establishment of the joint federal-state Medicaid program also increased revenues available to public hospitals and local health departments. In the 1980s, state and local governments were not only heavily involved in traditional public health activities, such as health monitoring, sanitation, and disease control, but were also key participants in the financing and delivery of personal health care services, particularly to the poor through Medicaid and other programs. The traditional public health focus on sanitation and communicable diseases also expanded to cover a broad range of protection against human-made environmental and occupational hazards to personal health.

Today, state governments are heavily involved in the regulation and licensure of health care facilities, such as hospitals and nursing homes, and in licensing health care professionals, such as physicians and nurses. Furthermore, they have become important purchasers of health care services, especially for the poor through the Medicaid program. Thus, state and local governments play an important role, not only in public health activities but also in health care financing, delivery, and regulation of services.

During the 1990s, many state governments attempted innovative approaches to health care reform in general and Medicaid reform in particular in order to deal with problems of rising health care costs and access to health care.[47] Several state governments enacted market-based health insurance reforms in the 1990s. Significant increases in the use of Medicaid waivers under the Clinton and George W. Bush administrations allowed state governments to experiment with different approaches to deliver health services under Medicaid. State governments are also playing a major role providing health insurance coverage to children under the CHIP program.

The PPACA has significant implications for state governments, and they will play a crucial role in influencing the policy as well as its implementation.[48] The health care reform relies heavily on Medicaid expansion for achieving universal coverage. The law established a nationwide income floor at 133 percent of the federal poverty level, eliminating eligibility inequities across the states. However, reliance on Medicaid to achieve universal coverage was thrown into uncertainty when, in July 2012, the U.S. Supreme Court, by a vote of 7–2, ruled that the penalty imposed by the PPACA on states for not expanding their Medicaid programs to cover more uninsured poor people was too coercive and thus states had the option not to expand their Medicaid programs. The PPACA is unlikely to establish universal health insurance coverage for two reasons. First, undocumented immigrants are excluded from receiving any health benefits under this law. Second, several states governed by a Republican governor and/or a Republican-controlled state assembly have refused to expand their Medicaid program to expand coverage to more uninsured individuals in their states. It remains to be seen how many states will opt out of expansion of the Medicaid program.[49]

LOOKING TO THE FUTURE

Health care policy in the United States is a result of a combination of decisions made and initiatives undertaken by various levels of government and the private sector. Although the role of federal, state, and local governments in health care policy had expanded significantly in the twentieth century, the U.S. health care system remains a mostly private system. Policymakers have mainly followed a middle road between a totally private health care system and a completely publicly financed national health care system.

The federal government's health policy initiatives have focused primarily on concerns about access (equality), quality of care, and cost efficiency. The federal role in health care in the twenty-first century has gone through four distinct stages. The first stage was characterized by policies designed to increase access through expansion of health care facilities, services, and resources. The second stage was characterized by policies specifically designed to provide equal access and quality care to needy groups such as the elderly and the poor. The third stage was characterized by policies designed to contain rising health care costs. The fourth stage was characterized by political transformation of the U.S. health care system through managed care, managed competition, and consumer-driven health care.

In the past, the federal government always followed an incremental approach by creating specific policies such as Medicare, Medicaid, and numerous categorical grant programs targeted at narrowly defined groups or problems. This is consistent with the American public's belief that health care is a private good; likewise, the public has never wholeheartedly accepted the notion that health care is a public good and as such has never fully committed to the notion of health care as an individual right. How the PPACA changes the landscape of the U.S. health care system remains to be seen.

See also **Chapter 2: The Long Struggle for Universal Health Care (1900s–Present); Chapter 3: The Department of Health and Human Services: Responsibilities and Policies (1953–Present); Chapter 4: The Centers for Disease Control and Prevention: Anticipatory Action in the Face of Uncertainty (1946–Present); Chapter 5: The Food and Drug Administration (1962–Present); Chapter 6: The Centers for Medicare and Medicaid Services (1965–Present); Chapter 7: The Departments of Defense and Veterans Affairs: Responsibilities and Policies (1947–Present); Chapter 10: Federalism.**

NOTES

1. This chapter is an abridged and revised version by the author of Chapter 2 in the 4th edition of *Health Care Politics and Policy in America* (M.E. Sharpe). The book is authored by Kant Patel and Mark Rushefsky.

2. Anthony Lewis, "A Sick System," *New York Times,* June 3 1991, A17; Joanne Lynn, *Sick to Death and Not Going to Take It Anymore! Reforming Health Care for the Last Years of Life* (Berkeley: University of California Press, 2004); Jonathan Cohn, *Sick: The Untold Story of America's Health Care Crisis—and the People Who Pay the Price* (New York: HarperCollins, 2008); Barbara Ehrenreich, "Our Health-Care Disgrace," *Time,* December 10, 1990, 1–12; Milton Terris, "A Wasteful System That Doesn't Work," *Progressive* 54: 10 (1990): 14–16; Humphrey Taylor, "U.S. Health Care: Built for Waste," *New York Times,* April 17, 1990, A25; Susan Dentzer, "America's Scandalous Health Care," *U.S. News and World Report,* March 12, 1990, 24–28, 30; Michael D. Reagan, *The Accidental System: Health Care Policy in America* (Boulder, CO: Westview, 1999); J.D. Kleinke, *Oxymorons: The Myth of a U.S. Health Care System* (San Francisco: Jossey-Bass, 2001); Michael McCarthy, "Fragmented US Health-Care System Needs Major Reform," *Lancet* 357: 9258 (2001): 782; Einer Elhauge, ed., *The Fragmentation of U.S. Health Care: Causes and Solutions* (New York: Oxford University Press, 2010); Grace Budrys, *Our Unsystematic Health Care System,* 3rd ed. (Lanham, MD: Rowman & Littlefield, 2011).

3. John Abramson, *Overdosed America: The Broken Promise of American Medicine* (New York: HarperCollins, 2004); Shannon

Brownlee, *Overtreated: Why Too Much Medicine Is Making Us Sicker and Poorer* (New York: Bloomsbury, 2007); Gilbert H. Welch; Lisa Swartz; and Steve Woloshin, *Overdiagnosed: Making People Sick in the Pursuit of Health* (Boston: Beacon, 2011).

4. Cristobal Silva, "Miraculous Plagues: Epidemiology on New England's Colonial Landscape," *Early American Literature* 43: 2 (June 2008): 249–275.

5. Richard H. Shyrock, "The Health of the American People: An Historical Survey," *Proceedings of the American Philosophical Society* 90: 4 (September 1946): 251–258.

6. James H. Means, "Homo Medicus Americanus," *Daedalus* 92: 4 (Fall 1963): 701–723.

7. Ibid.

8. Fielding H. Garrison, *An Introduction to the History of Medicine* (Philadelphia: Saunders, 1960).

9. Ibid.

10. Silva, "Miraculous Plagues." See also, Elaine G. Breslaw, *Lotions, Potions, Pills, and Magic: Health Care in Early America* (New York: New York University Press, 2012).

11. Kant Patel and Mark Rushefsky, *The Politics of Public Health in the United States* (New York: M.E. Sharpe, 2005).

12. Shyrock, "The Health of the American People."

13. John D. Burton, "'The Awful Judgments of God Upon the Land': Smallpox in Colonial Cambridge," *New England Quarterly* 74: 3 (September 2001): 495–506.

14. Rosemary A. Stevens, *American Medicine and the Public Interest* (Berkeley: University of California Press, 1998).

15. Patel and Rushefsky, *The Politics of Public Health in the United States.*

16. Means, "Homo Medicus Americanus."

17. John Duffy, *The Sanitarians: The History of American Public Health* (Chicago: University of Illinois Press, 1990).

18. Albert Deutsch, "The Sick Poor in Colonial Times," *American Historical Review* 45: 3 (April 1941): 560–579.

19. Paul Starr, *The Social Transformation of American Medicine* (New York: Basic Books, 1982).

20. Stevens, *American Medicine and the Public Interest.*

21. David R. Starbuck, "Military Hospitals on the Frontier of Colonial America," *Expedition* 39: 1 (1997): 33–46.

22. Patel and Rushefsky, *The Politics of Public Health in the United States.*

23. Charles E. Rosenberg, *The Care of Strangers: The Rise of America's Hospital System* (New York: Basic Books). See also, Rosemary Stevens, *In Sickness and in Wealth: American Hospitals in the Twentieth Century* (New York: Basic Books, 1989).

24. U.S. Health Resources Administration, *Health in America: 1776–1976* (Rockville, MD: U.S. Department of Health, Education and Welfare, 1976).

25. Rosemary A. Stevens, Charles E. Rosenberg, and Lawton R. Burns, *History and Health Policy in the Unites States* (New Brunswick, NJ: Rutgers University Press, 2006). See also, Rosemary A. Stevens, *The Public-Private Health Care State: Essays on the History of American Health Care Policy* (New Brunswick, NJ: Transaction, 2007).

26. Paul Starr, *The Social Transformation of American Medicine* (New York: Basic Books, 1982).

27. Ibid.

28. Patel and Rushefsky, *The Politics of Public Health in the United States.*

29. Merton C. Bernstein and Joan B. Bernstein, *Social Security: The System That Works* (New York: Basic Books, 1988).

30. Thomas C. Buchmueller and Alan C. Monheit, "Employer-Sponsored Health Insurance and the Promise of Health Insurance Reform" (NBER Working Paper 14839, National Bureau of Economic Research, Cambridge, MA, 2009), http://www.nber.org/papers/w14839. See also Melissa A. Thomasson, "The Importance of Group Coverage: How Tax Policy Shaped U.S. Health Insurance" (NBER Working Paper 7543, National Bureau of Economic Research, Cambridge, MA, 2000), http://www.nber.org/papers/w7543.pdf.

31. Ibid. See also Selina Mushkin, "The Internal Revenue Code of 1954 and Health Programs," *Public Health Reports* 70: 8 (August 1955): 791–800.

32. Lisa Clemens-Cope, Stephen Zuckerman, and Dean Resnick, "Limiting the Tax Exclusion of Employer-Sponsored Health Insurance Premiums: Revenue Potential and Distributional Consequences" (Washington, DC: Urban Institute, 2013), http://www.rwjf.org/content/dam/farm/reports/issue_briefs/2013/rwjf405948.

33. Anne L. Schneider and Helen M. Ingram, *Deserving and Entitled: Social Constructions and Public Policy* (Albany: State University of New York Press, 2004).

34. Katharine R. Levit et al., "National Health Expenditures, 1993," *Health Care Financing Review* 16: 1 (Fall 1994): 247–294.

35. Richard M. Nixon, "Message to Congress," *Weekly Compilation of Presidential Documents* (Washington, DC: Office of the Federal Register, February 18, 1971).

36. David L. Ginsberg, "Health Care Policy in the Reagan Administration: Rhetoric and Reality," *Public Administration Quarterly* 11: 1 (Spring 1987): 59–70.

37. Frank J. Thompson and Courtney Burke, "Federalism by Waiver: Medicaid and the Transformation of Long-Term Care," *Publius* 39: 1 (2008): 22–48.

38. Frank J. Thompson and Courtney Burke, "Executive Federalism and Medicaid Demonstration Waivers: Implications for Policy and Democratic Process," *Journal of Health Politics, Policy and Law* 32: 6 (December 2007): 971–1004.

39. Theda Skocpol, *Boomerang: Health Care Reform and the Turn against Government* (New York: W.W. Norton, 1997); David Broder and Haynes Johnson, *The System: American Way of Politics at a Breaking Point* (Boston: Little, Brown, 1996); Jacob S. Hacker (*The Road to Nowhere: The Genesis of President Clinton's Plan for Health Security* (Princeton, NJ: Princeton University Press, 1997).

40. Andrzej Kulczyski, "Ethics, Ideology, and Reproductive Health Policy in the United States," *Studies in Family Planning* 38: 4 (December 2007): 333–351.

41. Deborah R. McFarlane, "Reproductive Health Policy in President Bush's Second Term: Old Battles and New Fronts in the United States and Internationally," *Journal of Public Health Policy* 27: 4 (2006): 405–426.

42. Kulczyski, "Ethics, Ideology, and Reproductive Health Policy."

43. McFarlane. "Reproductive Health Policy in President Bush's Second Term." See also Henry A. Waxman, "Politics and Science: Reproductive Health," *Health Matrix: Journal of Law-Medicine* 16: 1 (Winter 2006): 5–25.

44. Kulczyski, "Ethics, Ideology, and Reproductive Health Policy."

45. Khalid J. Quazi, "Health Care Reform in the United States: Fact, Fiction and Drama," *British Journal of Medical Practitioners* 2: 4 (2009): 5–7.

46. Katherine Hayes, "Overview of Policy, Procedure, and Legislative History of the Affordable Care Act," *National Academy of Elder Law Attorneys* 7: 1 (March 2011): 1–9.

47. Teresa A. Coughlin and Stephen Zuckerman, "State Responses to New Flexibility in Medicaid," *Milbank Quarterly* 86: 2 (2008): 209–240.

48. John Dinan, "Shaping Health Reform: State Government Influence in the Patient Protection and Affordable Care Act," *Publius* 41: 3 (June 2011): 395–420.

49. David Von Drehle et al., "Here's What We Know for Sure: Obama's Health Care Reform Is Constitutional, Congress May Not Hold States Hostage to Its Every Whim," *Time,* July 16, 2012, 30–41.

FURTHER READING

Duffy, John. *The Sanitarians: The History of American Public Health.* Chicago: University of Illinois Press, 1990.

Morone, Jim. *Hellfire Nation.* New Haven, CT: Yale University Press, 2004.

Patel, Kant, and Mark Rushefsky. *Health Care Politics and Policy in America,* 5th ed. New York: M.E. Sharpe, 2014.

Skocpol, Theda. *Boomerang: Health Care Reform and the Turn against Government.* New York: W.W. Norton, 1997.

Starr, Paul. *The Social Transformation of American Medicine.* New York: Basic Books, 1982.

Stevens, Rosemary A. *The Public-Private Health Care State: Essays on the History of American Health Care Policy.* Piscataway, NJ: Transaction, 2007.

Stevens, Rosemary A., Charles E. Rosenberg, and Lawton R. Burns. *History and Health Policy in the Unites States.* New Brunswick, NJ: Rutgers University Press, 2006.

Warner, John H., and Janet A. Tighe. *Major Problems in the History of American Medicine and Public Health: Documents and Essays.* Boston: Houghton Mifflin, 2001.

chapter 2

The Long Struggle for Universal Health Care (1900s–Present)

Jonathan Oberlander

THE UNITED STATES REMAINS AN INTERNATIONAL outlier, the only rich democratic country in the world with a large population lacking health insurance. Nearly one hundred years after the first proposal for national health insurance appeared in the United States, Americans are still debating the merits of health care reform, the perils of "socialized medicine," and the tensions between individual liberty and government aid. Why has universal health insurance proven so difficult to achieve in the United States? How did efforts to expand insurance coverage shape the development of the U.S. medical care system? Finally, after a century dominated by failure, how did reformers manage to secure passage of the 2010 Patient Protection and Affordable Care Act?

BEGINNINGS: HEALTH CARE REFORM IN THE PROGRESSIVE ERA

In 1912, Theodore Roosevelt, formerly president of the United States (1901–1909), ran unsuccessfully for another term as president as the nominee of the Progressive Bull Moose Party. His platform included support for compulsory health insurance for industrial workers.[1] Health insurance represented a key protection for workers against the risk of lost wages in industrializing economies, a protection that reformers in the United States wanted to add (sick pay was a core feature of early health insurance proposals), following the lead of nations such as Great Britain and Germany.

Roosevelt's defeat meant that pressure for health care reform initially came from outside the government.[2] In 1915, the American Association of Labor Legislation (AALL), a reform group comprising predominantly academic social scientists, labor leaders, and lawyers, introduced a model bill for compulsory health insurance. Given the limited role of the federal government in social policy at the time, the group intended to push for the bill in the states. Reformers believed that the case for government action in health care was compelling: providing health insurance and sick pay to workers would safeguard them against income losses from illness, give them access to medical services,

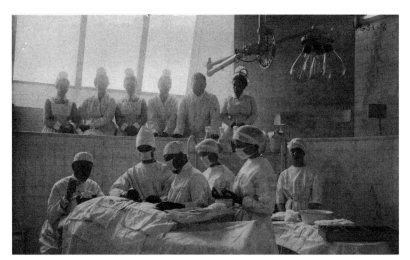

In this photograph from the early 1900s, the beginning of health insurance in the United States, a patient undergoes serious surgery. Back then, the major cost associated with illness was the loss of wages. Thus, some people purchased "sickness insurance," similar to today's disability insurance. Even though the need for universal health insurance has been debated since the 1900s, and after hundreds of health care proposals, the nation still lacks universal health care.

SOURCE: Library of Congress, Prints and Photographs Division.

help keep them healthy, and enhance productivity and companies' bottom lines.

The AMA: From Support to Opposition

Health insurance appeared to be an inevitable step in the progress of industrial societies. The labor association's health reform efforts initially drew support from the American Medical Association (AMA), the primary organization representing physicians. The AMA's Committee on Social Insurance reasoned that physicians' "blind opposition, indignant repudiation, bitter denunciation of these [compulsory health insurance] laws is less than useless; it leads nowhere and leaves the profession in a position of helplessness as the rising tide of social development sweeps over it."[3] In a 1916 editorial, the *Journal of the American Medical Association* praised national health insurance, gushing that "no other social movement in modern economic development is so pregnant with benefit to the public."[4]

Buoyed by its earlier achievement in pressing states to adopt industrial accident insurance, as well as the medical profession's cooperation, the AALL believed its campaign for health insurance legislation would quickly succeed. The group's model bill was introduced in fifteen states, and commissions to study health insurance were formed in ten states. Yet by 1920, the momentum for compulsory health insurance had stalled due to opposition from key groups, the overconfidence of reformers, bad timing, and defeats in key states such as New York.[5]

After its initially receptive stance, the American Medical Association reversed course. In 1920, the AMA, influenced by a revolt from conservative segments of its membership against the national leadership, formally declared its opposition "to the institution of any plan embodying the system of compulsory insurance . . . controlled or regulated by any state or the federal government."[6] The group's shift also reflected concerns that compulsory health insurance would threaten the growing incomes and social status of American physicians. In addition to the turnaround from organized medicine, national health insurance confronted a wide array of interests whose hostility the AALL had seriously underestimated, including the insurance industry, pharmaceutical companies, employers, and even the American Federation of Labor, whose leader Samuel Gompers feared that a government insurance program would strengthen workers' loyalties to the state at the expense of unions (later, however, the labor movement would become a prominent advocate of national health insurance). Commercial insurers, which at that time generally did not offer health care coverage, opposed reformers' inclusion of a death benefit to pay for funeral expenses in health insurance bills since it threatened their business.[7]

The U.S. entry into World War I (1914–1918) sealed the fate of health reform. Opponents exploited the association of health insurance with the enemy, declaring national health insurance a "German plot." The AALL did not effectively counter this opposition, "naively assuming that a reform which they thought should be deemed good by everyone would triumph on its own merits."[8] It did not, and the first campaign for national health insurance ended in defeat.

FDR AND THE NEW DEAL

Compulsory health insurance had no chance of adoption during the 1920s. Conservative Republicans consolidated their hold on national politics, while Progressivism gave way to a public philosophy critical of government activism and content with the prevailing social order. The identification of compulsory health insurance with Bolshevism following the 1917 Russian Revolution, which triggered fears of a socialist takeover in the United States, further hindered reformers. National commissions continued to study issues pertaining to the costs and distribution of medical care, but in the absence of favorable political circumstances, health insurance remained a topic for intellectual inquiry rather than government action.

However, Franklin Delano Roosevelt's (1933–1945) election as president and the coming of the New Deal created a new opportunity for health care reform. The Great Depression legitimized a greater role for the federal government in assuring economic security, and the Roosevelt administration pursued a variety of new programs designed to revive the economy and protect Americans against hardship. Roosevelt had huge congressional majorities to work with: after their victories in the 1934 midterm elections, Democrats held sixty-nine seats in the Senate and 322 in the House of Representatives. Roosevelt's own experiences also could have been expected to predispose the president to action on health care. Since 1921, FDR had battled polio, which paralyzed him from the waist down, and he founded a polio rehabilitation facility at Warm Springs, Georgia. Roosevelt thus came into office with extensive personal experiences with illness and medicine.[9]

The prospects for action on health care appeared promising. The mandate of the Committee on Economic Security, created by FDR in 1934 to draft a program of social insurance legislation, included health insurance. Yet the 1935 Social Security legislation, which encompassed unemployment insurance, old-age pensions, and aid for dependent children, omitted any program of national health insurance. The original Social Security bill had contained a single line authorizing study of health insurance, prompting a concerted campaign of opposition from the AMA. Fearing that the controversy would jeopardize enactment of the entire bill, the Roosevelt administration decided to defer pushing for government health insurance and ordered the line removed from the legislation.

That decision, though, did not mark the end of New Deal health insurance proposals. In 1939, Senator Robert Wagner (D-NY; in office 1927–1949) introduced a national health bill, and beginning in 1943, the introduction of national health insurance legislation in Congress—cosponsored by Wagner; Senator James Murray (D-MT; in office 1934–1961), and Representative John Dingell Sr. (D-MI; in office 1933–1955)—became an annual event. The Murray-Wagner-Dingell legislation was significantly broader than Progressive era plans, providing comprehensive coverage for all Americans, not just industrial workers. Reformers now explicitly advocated for universal health insurance.

However, Roosevelt remained reluctant to endorse the proposals. There were some indications that he intended to press anew for health insurance legislation following his reelection to a fourth term in 1944. Yet FDR never did push forthrightly for universal health insurance. His indifference to health care reform remains a puzzle.[10] Roosevelt certainly had no shortage of extraordinary, urgent issues to deal with, from the Great Depression to World War II (1939–1945). Reviving the economy and mobilizing the country for war were much more important priorities than overhauling the health care system. After Republicans made huge gains in the 1938 congressional elections, Roosevelt's influence with Congress waned. In addition, FDR was also reluctant to take on the American Medical Association. It would fall to his successor to wage that fight.

Truman versus the AMA

Following Roosevelt's death, Vice President Harry S. Truman (1945–1953) ascended to the presidency. Truman became the first president to formally endorse universal health insurance, arguing in a November 1945 message to Congress that the United States should ensure "health security for all" and "that financial barriers in the way of attaining health shall be removed . . . [as] the health of all its citizens deserves the help of the Nation."[11] Truman supported extending the Social Security system to cover the costs of medical care for all workers and their dependents, with the government picking up premium costs for low-income persons. National health insurance, three decades after it had first appeared as an idea in the United States, at last had gained support from a president.

Further Opposition to Truman's Plan

Still, Truman's proposal went nowhere.[12] A de facto majority of conservative Democrats and Republicans, known as the conservative coalition, held the balance of power in Congress. Even though Democrats had majorities in the House of Representatives and the Senate, key committees were ruled by conservative Democratic chairs who wanted no part of national health insurance. Additionally, the American Medical Association strongly opposed the

Truman health plan, as did congressional Republicans. Senator Robert Taft (R-OH; in office 1939–1953) declared it "the most socialistic measure that this Congress has ever had before it."[13] Truman himself did not exert much effort to push for the legislation. In the 1946 elections, Republicans gained majorities in the House and Senate, bottling up much of Truman's Fair Deal agenda and foreclosing any opportunity to enact universal insurance. Truman derided the Republican majorities as a "do-nothing Congress."

After unexpectedly winning the 1948 presidential election, and with Democrats having regained their congressional majorities, Truman again asked Congress to pass universal health insurance. The American Medical Association launched an intense campaign against the legislation, taking advantage of emerging Cold War fears to redefine the health debate as an issue of socialized medicine. The AMA declared that supporters of the Truman plan included "all who seriously believe in a socialistic State. Every left-wing organization in America . . . [and] the Communist party."[14] The AMA, though, went far beyond crude red-bashing in its offensive against the Truman administration. In 1949, it launched what was then the most expensive lobbying campaign in U.S. political history to raise public anxieties about national health insurance, warning that "socialized medicine," a term without specific meaning that opponents applied loosely to any effort to increase government involvement in the financing of medical care, would inevitably erode the quality of care. The AMA also forged alliances with groups, such as the Chamber of Commerce, that found common cause in distrust of big government, while pushing, in conjunction with the insurance company Blue Cross, private ("voluntary") insurance as the "American way."[15] Indeed, the rapid growth of employer-sponsored private insurance in the 1940s provided opponents with an alternative to national health insurance and created another political obstacle for the Truman administration.[16]

The Truman administration could not overcome the AMA's opposition, the stigma of socialized medicine, the power of the conservative coalition in Congress, the rise of private insurance, and Truman's puzzling reluctance to push more strongly for enactment of his plan. Moreover, efforts to pass universal health insurance again fell short. There were two major consequences for U.S. health policy. The defeat of national health insurance cleared the way for further growth of private health insurance coverage. During the 1940s and 1950s, employer-sponsored insurance spread widely as unions negotiated for health benefits. In turn, the share of Americans with private coverage rose from about 10 percent in 1940 to more than 60 percent by 1955.[17] Linking insurance to employment provided insurers with a convenient risk pool and a reliable source of premium payments. Private insurance also benefited from government largesse:

Truman's Message to Congress

On November 19, 1945, President Harry S. Truman sent a special message to Congress recommending a comprehensive health care program. Truman thus became the first U.S. president to endorse national health insurance. His message made the case for universal insurance and sought to deflect opponents' charges of socialized medicine, arguments that would echo in health reform debates for the next seven decades:

November 19, 1945

To the Congress of the United States:

. . . Our new Economic Bill of Rights should mean health security for all, regardless of residence, station, or race—everywhere in the United States. . . .

I recommend solving the basic problem by distributing the costs through expansion of our existing compulsory social insurance system. This is not socialized medicine.

Everyone who carries fire insurance knows how the law of averages is made to work so as to spread the risk, and to benefit the insured who actually suffers the loss. If instead of the costs of sickness being paid only by those who get sick, all the people—sick and well—were required to pay premiums into an insurance fund, the pool of funds thus created would enable all who do fall sick to be adequately served without overburdening anyone. That is the principle upon which all forms of insurance are based. . . .

People should remain free to choose their own physicians and hospitals. . . . Likewise physicians should remain free to accept or reject patients. They must be allowed to decide for themselves whether they wish to participate in the health insurance system full time, part time, or not at all. . . .

None of this is really new. The American people are the most insurance-minded people in the world. They will not be frightened off from health insurance because some people have misnamed it "socialized medicine." . . .

Socialized medicine means that all doctors work as employees of government. The American people want no such system. No such system is here proposed.

Under the plan I suggest, our people would continue to get medical and hospital services just as they do now—on the basis of their own voluntary decisions and choices. Our doctors and hospitals would continue to deal with disease with the same professional freedom as now. There would, however, be this all-important difference: whether or not patients get the services they need would not depend on how much they can afford to pay at the time.

I am in favor of the broadest possible coverage for this insurance system. I believe that all persons who work for a living and their dependents should be covered under such an insurance plan. This would include wage and salary earners, those in business for themselves, professional persons, farmers, agricultural labor, domestic employees, government employees and employees of non-profit institutions and their families.

In addition, needy persons and other groups should be covered through appropriate premiums paid for them by public agencies. . . .

We are a rich nation and can afford many things. But ill-health which can be prevented or cured is one thing we cannot afford. . . .

SOURCE: Harry Truman, "Special Message to the Congress Recommending a Comprehensive Health Program," November 19, 1945, http://www.trumanlibrary.org/publicpapers/index.php?pid=483.

the federal government subsidized employer-sponsored coverage by excluding from taxable income premium payments made by employers on behalf of workers. A second consequence was that reformers decided the time had come for a new strategy if they were to succeed in enacting federal health insurance. That strategy was Medicare.

The Medicare Strategy

By 1949, Truman administration officials were looking for a different, politically pragmatic approach to health care reform. Wilbur Cohen and I.S. Falk, advisers to Oscar Ewing, the head of the Federal Security Agency that administered Social Security, sought to reverse reformers' losing fortunes by "resurrect[ing] health insurance in a dramatically new and narrower form."[18] They developed a plan to provide federal health insurance to beneficiaries of Social Security payments for Old Age and Survivors Insurance. In June 1951, Ewing publicly announced a proposal for sixty days of hospitalization insurance a year for the seven million elderly retirees receiving Social Security, saying "it is difficult for me to see how anyone with a heart can oppose this."[19]

The substantive case for the government to cover the elderly was compelling. While seniors required more medical services than younger populations, their uninsurance rate was much higher and they had much lower incomes. Once retirees left employer-sponsored coverage, they had trouble obtaining coverage since insurers saw them as a bad (expensive) risk. Before Medicare's enactment, just about one-half of seniors had any health insurance and only 25 percent had meaningful coverage.

Still, politics were the primary rationale for focusing on the elderly. By limiting federal health insurance to seniors, reformers hoped to improve its legislative prospects. They wanted to draw on seniors' sympathetic image as a population deserving of government assistance to overcome Americans' cultural ambivalence about social welfare programs and to dampen fears of socialized medicine. By limiting benefits to sixty days of hospital coverage, Medicare's advocates hoped to moderate the opposition of their most formidable opponent, the American Medical Association. Furthermore, by tying federal health insurance to Social Security, they hoped to build on the program's familiarity and popularity. The Medicare strategy was, then, one of incrementalism, shaped by the Truman plan's defeat and the constraints of U.S. politics, including public ambivalence about government power and the barriers to passing health insurance legislation in Congress.

The strategy worked, but only after more than a decade of congressional debate and a major shift in the U.S. political landscape. The same sides that had earlier fought over national health insurance re-formed, with liberals and labor unions supporting Medicare (union-affiliated seniors' groups joined the fray) and conservatives, business groups, and organized medicine opposing it. AMA president David Allman declared in 1957 that the Medicare proposal "is at least nine parts evil to one part sincerity" and "the beginning of the end of the private practice of medicine."[20] Ronald Reagan, an actor and former president of the Screen Actors Guild who later would become governor of California and president of the United States, famously warned in a 1961 AMA recording that if Medicare passed, then a slippery slope of socialism would surely follow, as "behind it will come other federal programs that will invade every area of freedom as we have known it in this country."[21]

While Medicare attracted considerable support in Congress, it could not overcome the opposition of the conservative coalition and Representative Wilbur Mills (D-AR; in office 1939–1977), chair of the powerful House Ways and Means Committee. The 1964 elections, which produced a landslide victory for President Lyndon B. Johnson (1963–1969) and brought overwhelming Democratic Party majorities to both the House and Senate, transformed Medicare's political fortunes. Johnson pushed immediately for Medicare's enactment and Mills acquiesced. Indeed, Mills orchestrated, with Johnson's support, a major, unanticipated expansion of the program. Mills worried that Medicare's limited benefits package would disappoint seniors and, by adding coverage for physician services on his terms, he sought to preempt any future efforts to liberalize program benefits by raising Social Security payroll taxes.

The 1965 Social Security amendments that established Medicare also created Medicaid, a joint federal-state program to finance medical care for low-income Americans. Medicaid built on existing federal programs that gave states payments to fund medical care services for low-income seniors and other recipients of government aid. Yet Medicaid became part of the 1965 law largely because Wilbur Mills wanted to prevent Medicare from expanding in the future to cover all Americans. Mills believed that establishing a separate medical care program for the poor would defuse political pressures to expand Medicare into universal health insurance, while also helping to limit future increases in payroll taxes (Medicaid was funded through general revenues).[22]

The enactment of Medicare and Medicaid was an extraordinary development in U.S. health policy. In a nation where universal coverage had proven elusive, the coming of Medicare and Medicaid transformed the boundaries of health insurance in the United States. The federal government committed itself to financing medical care for the elderly and many low-income citizens, giving Washington a prominent and unprecedented role in the health care system. The programs' adoption also established a pattern of demographic incrementalism in U.S. health policy. Thereafter, policymakers would focus on expanding public insurance coverage to politically sympathetic, deserving populations such as pregnant women, children, and persons with disabilities.

Although Medicare advocates were pragmatists and believed in the political virtues of incrementalism, they also never abandoned their vision of universal coverage. As Robert Ball, one of the program's key architects later explained, "insurance for the elderly [was] a fallback position, which we advocated solely because it seemed to have the best chance politically."[23] Medicare advocates such as Ball envisioned the program as a first step, the cornerstone of national health insurance. The goal was to establish federal health insurance for the elderly, demonstrate that it could work, and then eventually expand federal insurance to cover the rest of the population, with children next in line.

That plan—creating a "Medicare for All" or a single-payer system—has never come close to fruition. In 1972, Medicare did expand to cover persons with permanent disabilities who were recipients of Social Security Disability Insurance and persons with end-stage kidney disease. Yet Medicare did not expand further or evolve into the universal system that its planners had hoped and anticipated that it would become. However, Medicare and Medicaid, in an unexpected way, did help to bring the issue of national health insurance back to the agenda.

Opportunity Lost: Nixon, Democrats, and Health Reform

During most of the twentieth century, health care costs were not a public policy issue in the United States. Spending more on medical care, policymakers believed, would ensure that Americans enjoyed the benefits of new therapies and produce a healthier population. When he proposed universal health insurance in 1945, Truman noted that the United States spent only 4 percent of national income on health services: "We can," he flatly stated, "afford to spend more."[24]

Even in 1965, concern over the level of national health spending simply did not exist. Medicare and Medicaid were enacted with scant attention to their impact on national health care spending and without meaningful limits on program expenditures (which private insurance plans at the time lacked as well). Reformers focused on expanding access to insurance, not restraining costs. The Medicare statute explicitly circumscribed the federal government's ability to control spending, and program administrators, in a quest to ensure the program's successful implementation, formulated generous payment policies aimed at conciliating the health care industry.

Nonetheless, the enactment of Medicare and Medicaid transformed the politics of health care. The government was now picking up a significant share of the tab, making health care spending a political issue. As Medicare and Medicaid's costs quickly rose and consumed a growing share of the federal budget, policymakers took notice: the federal government now had a powerful incentive to care about health care spending. Spending more on medical care was no longer seen as an unmitigated good; instead, it loomed as a threat to the budget and the economy. In 1971, President Richard M. Nixon (1969–1974) warned that "medical costs have gone up twice as fast as the cost of living. Hospital costs have risen five times as fast as other prices . . . costs have skyrocketed . . . but we are not getting a full return on our investment." Rising costs jeopardized not only public budgets, but also access to medical care. "For growing numbers of Americans," Nixon explained, "the cost of care is becoming prohibitive. And even those who can afford most care may find themselves impoverished by catastrophic medical expenditure."[25]

The spread of private employer-sponsored insurance—by 1980, nearly 80 percent of Americans had private insurance[26]—and enactment of Medicare and Medicaid had greatly broadened Americans' access to health care coverage. Yet not all Americans were covered, and concerns persisted about inequalities in access to medical care and gaps in the insurance system. Rising costs—fueled by the advent of Medicare, whose inflationary payment policies helped drive

up costs in the entire health care system—deepened those concerns. Nixon, a Republican, proposed a "comprehensive national health insurance program" to "ensure that no American family will be prevented from obtaining basic medical care."[27] Nixon's plan would have required employers to insure their workers and established a new program to cover the unemployed and low-income Americans (replacing Medicaid for families on welfare). By embracing the idea of moving toward universal coverage through an employer mandate and private insurance, the plan marked a major turning point in U.S. health policy. In 1974, Nixon would issue an even more ambitious proposal with the same core principles but more generous benefits and comprehensive coverage than his original plan.

Given that a Republican president had endorsed the goal of universal coverage and proposed his own plan, it appeared that national health insurance's time had finally come. Indeed, bipartisan interest in health care reform was strong. Congress considered twenty-two different health care reform bills in 1971.[28] One of those bills, a proposal to create a government-run national health insurance program, was introduced by Senator Edward "Ted" Kennedy (D-MA; in office 1962–2009), who had made health care a signature issue. Nixon's proposal was intended, in part, to provide an alternative to Kennedy's plan and neutralize Kennedy's threat to Nixon as a potential Democratic candidate for president in the 1972 elections. Other congressional Democratic leaders—Democrats held majorities in the House and Senate throughout Nixon's presidency—including Wilbur Mills, the chair of the House Ways and Means Committee, were also interested in passing health insurance legislation. Even the American Medical Association, the traditional bastion of opposition to universal coverage, offered its own plan to subsidize Americans' voluntary purchase of private insurance with tax credits. An air of inevitability surrounded health reform during the early 1970s.

What seemed inevitable, though, never happened. Despite all the momentum and favorable political conditions, proposals for universal health insurance again failed to clear Congress. Plenty of support existed for reform, but there was little consensus on what kind of reform to enact. Absent consensus on which plan to pass, Congress failed to enact any of them.[29]

Political, partisan, and ideological divisions fractured the health reform coalition. Nixon wanted reform that relied on private insurance. Liberal Democrats such as Ted Kennedy, as well as labor unions, alternatively favored a single-payer national health system where the federal government would operate one insurance program for all. Russell Long (D-LA; in office 1948–1987), chair of the Senate Finance Committee, preferred the less expensive option of assuring everyone catastrophic coverage for high-cost medical expenses. In 1974, Kennedy and Mills joined together to offer a compromise bill and then entered into secret negotiations with the Nixon administration to try to work out agreement on a plan that they all could support. That agreement never came. Labor leaders regarded Kennedy's compromises with Mills, accepting higher patient cost-sharing and an administrative role for private insurers, as a sellout and pressed him to wait instead for what they believed would be more favorable political circumstances that would enable passage of a single-payer system.[30] Their opposition made it difficult to forge a compromise plan, as did Nixon's wilting political power, sapped by the deepening Watergate scandal that would eventually force him out of the White House.[31]

From health reformers' perspective, waiting for a better plan proved to be a historic miscalculation. After Nixon was forced to resign the presidency in 1974, his successor, Gerald R. Ford (1974–1977), showed less interest in advancing health care reform, focusing instead on curbing inflation and government spending. Democrats did make sizable gains in the 1974 midterm elections, expanding their congressional majorities, but the chances for national health insurance were fading nonetheless. Amid the Watergate scandal, the Vietnam War (1945–1975), and an economy simultaneously stricken by high unemployment and galloping inflation (a double shot of economic trouble ominously termed *stagflation*), public faith in government eroded. Before Medicare passed in 1965, 76 percent of Americans, according to opinion polls, trusted the government to do the right thing all or most of the time; by 1974 that percentage had dropped to 36 percent and would continue to fall for the remainder of the decade.[32] In the mid-1970s, U.S. politics pivoted away from liberalism to a new conservative era, and as the country moved rightward, the fortunes of universal coverage dramatically dropped.

The shift in the political winds proved sufficiently powerful that Richard Nixon, a Republican, was arguably more liberal on health care than President Jimmy Carter (1977–1981). Carter, who like predecessor Gerald Ford had to battle budget deficits and inflation, did not push seriously for enactment of national health insurance, instead focusing on an ultimately unsuccessful effort to pass legislation aimed at slowing down hospital spending. That emphasis augured a new period in which universal health insurance was subordinated to health care cost containment, and especially to the goal of restraining federal expenditures on medical care, as a public policy priority. Thereafter, when proposals for universal coverage did reach the agenda, they would have to include measures that promised to control health care spending. The campaign for universal coverage was now linked to the perhaps even politically more difficult crusade of taming medical inflation.

Universal health insurance had no chance of enactment during Ronald Reagan's (1981–1989) presidency. Reagan, a conservative Republican committed to downsizing the welfare state, did not pursue universal health insurance. As the federal deficit increased sizably during the 1980s, the chances for national health insurance appeared even more remote, and the Reagan administration and Congress focused instead on Medicare reform. However, a confluence of rising medical care costs, an expanding uninsured population, and a faltering economy would soon bring health care reform back onto the agenda.

Medicaid Fills the Gap

For a half-century, from 1930 to 1980, the share of Americans covered by health insurance grew. To be sure, the United States never secured universal coverage. Millions of Americans fell through cracks in the safety net, because they were not old enough to qualify for Medicare, did not work for a business that offered coverage, or did not qualify for Medicaid because they were not sufficiently poor or did not fit one of the program's restricted demographic categories (e.g., children, pregnant women). Still, the combination of employer-sponsored private health insurance and government programs for the elderly and (some of the) poor helped expand access to health insurance. During the 1980s, though, that expansionary trend would reverse and the number and share of Americans without any health insurance would grow. Rising health care costs—insurance premiums rose much more rapidly than workers' wages—were beginning to erode the foundation of employer-sponsored insurance, increasing the uninsured population.[33]

Comprehensive health care reform nonetheless remained off the agenda in the 1980s, a poor match for the political, economic, and fiscal constraints of Reagan's America. Yet the rise of the uninsured prompted a turn to incremental health reform. Congress, led by the enterprising Representative Henry Waxman (D-CA; in office 1975–2014), chair of the subcommittee on health and environment of the House Energy and Commerce Committee, enacted a series of laws expanding Medicaid that liberalized coverage for pregnant women and children. The Medicaid expansions marked a return to the strategy of demographic incrementalism: find sympathetic, politically attractive populations and formulate proposals to improve their access to health insurance that would be difficult to oppose (and that might draw bipartisan support even from those who were opposed to broader health reform plans). Building up an existing program was politically easier than creating a new one, and because Medicaid was a joint federal-state program, some conservatives were more comfortable with this model of health insurance expansion than with a program run entirely by Washington. States additionally appreciated the fact that Medicaid costs were paid mostly by the federal government, while federal policymakers could find comfort that at least some of the tab would be picked up by the states, further enhancing the political appeal of Medicaid expansion.[34]

The expansions helped move Medicaid away from its historic ties to welfare as more working American families qualified under the new eligibility standards and broadened Medicaid's reach in the health care system. They also presaged a major effort a decade later to provide health insurance to children. Yet the incremental expansions did not help many uninsured adults who could not fit easily into a sympathetic demographic category, and they could not keep pace with the ongoing erosion of employer-sponsored health insurance. The number of uninsured continued to rise, exceeding thirty-four million by 1990. A de facto safety net—including emergency rooms, public hospitals, community health centers, other health clinics, and some community physician practices—emerged to provide medical services to the growing numbers of Americans without coverage. However, the size of the uninsured population and their medical care needs far exceeded the resources and reach of this loose safety net.

Universal Health Insurance Returns to Central Stage

During 1989–1991, the U.S. economy slipped into recession. Concerns about America's eroding economic competitiveness, faltering growth, diminishing job prospects, and rising federal budget deficits were accompanied by worries over soaring health care costs. Health insurance premiums for employer-sponsored plans rose by an astounding average of 19 percent during 1989–1990. Against that backdrop, in 1991, Pennsylvania held a special election for a U.S. Senate seat, pitting Republican Richard Thornburgh, formerly governor of the state and attorney general for the George H.W. Bush administration (1989–1993), against Democrat Harris Wofford, the state's secretary of labor and industry who previously had helped found the Peace Corps and been president of Bryn Mawr College. It appeared to be a mismatch, and opinion polls initially had the Republican Thornburgh leading by more than 40 percentage points.[35]

Harris Wofford, advised by up-and-coming political strategists James Carville and Paul Begala, decided to make health care a defining issue of the campaign. One memorable Wofford campaign ad made a powerful case for health reform:

> The Constitution says those accused of a crime have the right to a lawyer, yet millions of Americans aren't able to see a doctor. They either don't have health insurance or they are afraid medical costs will bankrupt them. If criminals have the right to a lawyer, I think working Americans should have the right to a doctor.[36]

Wofford managed to tap into Pennsylvanians' anxiety about the economy and dissatisfaction with President George H.W. Bush's perceived lack of engagement with domestic issues and connect it to the growing sense of health care insecurity that many voters felt.

Wofford's (in office 1991–1995) stunning upset victory catapulted health care reform back into the spotlight. During the 1991–1992 congressional session, Democrats introduced a variety of health reform bills, ranging from single-payer national health insurance to "play or pay" proposals for universal coverage that required employers to either finance their workers' coverage or pay a tax that would fund a new government program for the uninsured. Republicans, too, got in on the act, with President Bush proposing a plan to give tax credits to some of the uninsured and to regulate the insurance industry to make coverage more accessible.

The Rise and Demise of the Clinton Health Plan

When Democrat William J. Clinton (1993–2001) won the 1992 presidential election, the stars seemed aligned for enactment of health care reform. Health care had been a major issue in the 1992 campaign, and Clinton was intent on taking it on. Because of the recession and rising insurance premiums, health reform was now a middle-class issue as Americans worried about its affordability and losing coverage altogether if they lost their jobs. The uninsured population surpassed thirty-nine million in 1993, and more than 15 percent of U.S. residents lacked coverage. Underinsurance, the exposure of Americans with coverage to high costs, was also a significant problem. Businesses, too, wanted relief from rising costs, giving the reform coalition a powerful ally, and the American Medical Association appeared prepared to accept universal insurance. Even the insurance industry appeared amenable to reform. With the end of the Cold War and demise of the Soviet Union in 1991, there was talk of a coming "peace dividend" available to invest in social programs and a renewed focus on domestic policy issues. Democrats held sizable majorities in the House and Senate, and were eager to press ahead with their agenda after twelve years of Republican presidents. The Clinton administration believed it had a novel, politically compelling health plan that achieved liberal ends (universal coverage) through conservative means (competing private insurance plans). Clinton, an extraordinary politician, gifted speaker, and remarkable translator of arcane policy issues, seemed like the perfect messenger for overhauling the health care system.

The Clinton administration appointed a task force, chaired by the president's wife, Hillary Rodham Clinton, to work out the details of its plan. In September 1993, President Clinton implored a joint session of Congress: "after decades of false starts, we must make this our most urgent priority: giving every American health security, health care that can never be taken away, health care that is always there."[37] The speech received rave reviews, public opinion was favorable, and hopes for the passage of reform soared.[38]

The optimism was soon extinguished. A year after Clinton's speech, health care reform lay in ruins, the president's Health Security Act having failed, along with all other alternative proposals, to pass either house of Congress. There were many health reform failures during the twentieth century, but of those failures, this was perhaps the most profound, since no president had tried harder to enact universal coverage than Bill Clinton.

The favorable conditions that the Clinton administration saw for health reform during 1993–1994 proved to be a mirage. While Democrats had large majorities in Congress, they lacked the extraordinary majorities that Franklin D. Roosevelt and Lyndon B. Johnson had enjoyed when Congress enacted Social Security and Medicare. In 1993, Democrats held fifty-seven seats in the Senate, short of the sixty necessary to overcome a filibuster. Moreover, they lacked a congressional majority that supported the Clinton plan's mandate on employers to provide health insurance, without which the plan could not pass.[39] The Democratic Congressional Caucus included substantial numbers of Southern Democrats, many of whom were politically moderate and fiscally conservative, and skeptical about the president's plan. The Clinton administration, in short, had partisan Democratic majorities in the House and Senate but lacked the liberal programmatic majorities necessary to enact universal health insurance.

Moreover, Democrats were divided. While the president offered his plan, some congressional Democrats had their own ideas and resented that the administration had not solicited more congressional input. Key Democrats offered alternative proposals rather than get behind the president's plan, complicating efforts to assemble a majority behind any one bill. Foreign policy crises and domestic scandal distracted the administration, damaging its efforts to sell reform.

The Clinton administration seriously underestimated the strength of the opposition. Republicans in Congress initially appeared resigned to the passage of some type of health care legislation, with a group of GOP senators, including Bob Dole (R-KS; in office 1969–1996), then the Senate minority leader, signing on to cosponsor an alternative bill that included an individual mandate to obtain health insurance. Yet Republicans subsequently decided to fiercely resist reform. And while many stakeholder groups at first supported the goal for reform, as the debate dragged on and the details of the plan became clearer, their support evaporated. The insurance industry, worried about federal regulation and constraints on their profits, became a fervent opponent of the Clinton plan, as did the National Federation of Independent Businesses, which lobbied on behalf of small businesses and strongly opposed the employer mandate. Meanwhile, the anticipated allies—big business, the AMA, AARP did not rally to the administration's side.

The Clinton plan also failed because of the plan itself. The administration ambitiously sought to reorganize the delivery of U.S. health care, encouraging the spread of HMOs and establishing new insurance pools (known as Health Alliances) for most Americans to purchase insurance. Many insured Americans, however, were satisfied with their arrangements, confused by the plan, and anxious about changes that might jeopardize their health security and the quality of their medical care. Public support for health reform plummeted as well-insured, middle-class Americans lost confidence in a plan that promised health security but appeared to make their own health care circumstances less secure (an appearance exacerbated by opponents' scare tactics). Moreover, the plan lacked a strong constituency in Congress: it proved too liberal for moderate Republicans and conservative Democrats and too conservative for liberals to enthusiastically embrace.[40]

In short, everything that could go wrong for the Clinton administration did. In the aftermath of health reform's demise, Republicans won majorities in both the House and Senate in the 1994 congressional elections for the first time in forty years. The political perils of comprehensive health reform had been vividly demonstrated, and it would be fifteen years before another president and Congress would dare to tackle the issue.

A Return to Incrementalism

In a familiar pattern, following the Clinton plan's defeat, reformers took a more incremental tack. In 1996, Congress passed the Health Insurance Portability and Accountability Act, cosponsored by senators Ted Kennedy and Nancy Kassebaum (R-KS; in office 1978–1997), which aimed to make it easier for Americans with coverage who changed jobs to maintain insurance even if they had preexisting medical conditions. Then in 1997, Congress enacted, again with significant bipartisan support, the State Children's Health Insurance Program (SCHIP), cosponsored by Senators Ted Kennedy and Orrin Hatch (R-UT; in office 1977–). SCHIP was a joint state-federal program that built on Medicaid to provide coverage for the children of low-income, working families. SCHIP quickly made a difference, helping to reduce the uninsurance rate among children ages eighteen and younger from 12.6 percent in 1999 to 10 percent in 2002.[41]

Incremental policies to extend coverage were politically attractive because they were less costly, less controversial, less threatening to the status quo, and consequently more bipartisan, making them easier to run through the congressional gauntlet than more ambitious plans. Along with the virtues of incremental reforms came their inevitable vices, however, including avoiding serious efforts to contain health care spending and to secure universal coverage for all Americans, and adding to the complexity of U.S. health care arrangements. Indeed, while health insurance coverage for children improved, in 2007, a decade after

SCHIP's enactment, more than eight million children remained uninsured. Most of those children were eligible for but not enrolled in Medicaid or SCHIP, a testament to the byzantine insurance system. Medicaid alone had a staggering fifty different eligibility pathways. Meanwhile, employer-sponsored insurance continued to erode. In 2007, nearly forty-six million U.S. residents lacked insurance, up from thirty-nine million in 1999.

However, universal health insurance remained off the political radar. Republican President George W. Bush (2001–2009) pushed for an expansion of Medicare benefits to add prescription drug coverage and for a substantial increase in funding for community health centers that serve low-income and uninsured patients.[42] However, although Bush showed no interest in more comprehensive health reform, the political fortunes of national health insurance were about to take another, historic twist.

PRESIDENT BARACK OBAMA AND HEALTH CARE REFORM

In December 2007, the U.S. economy entered into a recession, and in the fall of 2008, a series of crises in the banking and financial system exacerbated the situation, making it the nation's worst economic downturn since the start of the Great Depression in 1929. All together, the U.S. economy lost a staggering 8.8 million jobs from December 2007 to February 2010.[43] The Great Recession helped Democrat Barack Obama (2009–) win the 2008 presidential election. It also helped propel health reform back onto the agenda as the health insurance system's acute vulnerability to economic troubles was again revealed. As the economy teetered, employer-sponsored insurance declined and the uninsured population rose precipitously from 45.7 million in 2007 to 50.7 million in 2009. A decade of incremental reforms had not redressed the gaping holes in the U.S. health insurance system.

Still, when Barack Obama took office in January 2009, it was unclear, even after campaigning on the issue, if he would take up the universal coverage cause. A host of formidable challenges—stabilizing the financial system, reviving the economy, a skyrocketing budget deficit, foreign policy challenges in Iraq, Afghanistan, and beyond—confronted the new president. Obama decided nonetheless to pursue an ambitious health care plan, telling aides, some of whom cautioned him to follow a more incremental course, that he felt "lucky."[44]

The Obama administration had much more than luck going for it.[45] While Democrats enjoyed House majorities almost the same as they had enjoyed during 1993–1994 when Bill Clinton was president, they held sixty seats in the Senate, giving Democrats an all-important filibuster-proof majority. Congressional Democrats, having seen how internal divisions had previously doomed health reform, were also more determined to coordinate their efforts and unify around a single plan this time around. The chairs of the three committees in the House with major jurisdiction jointly sponsored a "tricommittee" bill, a sign of the new cooperation. That task was made easier by an emerging consensus in the Democratic Party around a health reform plan modeled after what Massachusetts had adopted in 2006, with subsidies to help the uninsured purchase coverage, establishment of new purchasing pools for the uninsured and small businesses, regulation of insurers to stop them from excluding or charging higher premiums to persons with preexisting medical conditions, expansion of Medicaid, and mandates on individuals to obtain and larger employers to offer insurance or pay penalties. Those policies would become the foundation of the Patient Protection and Affordable Care Act's strategy for expanding health insurance coverage.

The Obama administration learned much from the Clinton misadventures. In virtually every strategic decision, it did the opposite of what the Clintons had tried. President Obama tried to move health care quickly, capitalizing on Democrats' large majorities. The Obama administration did not present a detailed plan of its own, instead deferring to and working with congressional Democrats to develop legislation. However, in what would become a crucial decision, Obama pushed Democratic leaders in Congress to create the option to pass a health care bill through budget reconciliation, which required only a simple majority to pass legislation through the Senate rather than the super-majority necessary to end a filibuster. The Obama administration took a more modest approach to health reform than had the Clinton administration, promising not to unsettle medical care arrangements for the already insured. It also sought to avoid a multi-front battle with stakeholder groups and managed to win support from the American Medical Association, the American Hospital Association, and PhRMA, a lobbying group for the pharmaceutical industry. The administration also benefited from the support of a new well-funded, pro-reform group: Health Care for America Now.

The Obama administration, though, faced plenty of formidable hurdles. Congressional Democrats were more unified than they had been fifteen years earlier, but divisions persisted. Liberals insisted on creating a new "public option" for the uninsured: a Medicare-like, government-operated plan, which would compete in the new insurance pools, an idea that was anathema to conservative Democrats (the public option would not make it into the final bill). Coverage of abortion services became another divisive intraparty issue that jeopardized passage of health reform in the House of Representatives. Further, it remained unclear whether the Obama administration could count on all sixty Senate Democrats to break a filibuster and vote for health reform, and if not, whether Democrats could find a handful of Senate Republicans to join the coalition. Partisan polarization in Congress was the highest it had been since after the Civil War (1861–1865), meaning the administration could count on strong Republican resistance. Barack Obama sought to enact a New Deal and Great Society–type health care program but in a bitter partisan environment and without the massive party majorities that Presidents Roosevelt and Johnson had enjoyed. Moreover, there were policy dilemmas aplenty, including how to finance a major expansion of health insurance and ensure that it did not add to, and preferably reduced, the federal budget deficit, a stipulation critical to securing support from fiscally conservative "Blue Dog" Democrats.

In addition, despite the Obama administration's carefully crafted strategies, lots went wrong during 2009–2010. It was seemingly unprepared for the intense opposition to and fury against "Obamacare," as the president's plan was nicknamed, which erupted during town-hall meetings in the summer of 2009 as the conservative Tea Party movement emerged. The Democrats' focus group–tested mantra of "quality, affordable health care" was drowned out by Republicans' false warnings of impending "death panels." Predictably, Congress was much slower in producing a bill than the Obama administration wanted. That delay nearly proved politically fatal when, in January 2010, Republican Scott Brown's (R-MA; in office 2010–2013) upset win in a special Senate election in Massachusetts to fill the seat left vacant by Senator Ted Kennedy's death deprived Senate Democrats of their sixty-vote majority, almost derailing reform after the House and Senate had already passed health care legislation but had yet to agree on a joint bill.

After a century filled with misfortune and missteps and dominated by failure, this time health reformers surmounted all of the obstacles. After Brown's victory, steeled by the determination of President Obama and Speaker of the House Nancy Pelosi (D-CA; in office 1993– , as Speaker 2007–2011) to press ahead, Democrats enacted the 2010 Patient Protection and Affordable Care Act (PPACA)—not a single Republican voted for the final bill—by having the House first pass the Senate version of the legislation and then pass a second "sidecar" bill to address problems with that version, which the Senate then passed using budget reconciliation.

The health reform fight, though, did not end with the law's passage. Republicans immediately pledged to "repeal and replace" Obamacare, and twenty-six states filed suit in federal courts to challenge the constitutionality of the law's individual mandate and Medicaid expansion. The U.S. Supreme Court eventually heard the case and in summer 2012 narrowly upheld the individual mandate and thereby the health reform law as constitutional, though the court also limited the federal government's ability to take Medicaid

funds away from states that refused to expand program eligibility. President Obama's victory in the 2012 presidential elections over Republican nominee Mitt Romney ensured that the major provisions of the PPACA designed to expand insurance coverage would move forward. Health care reform had survived, just barely, a dramatic series of legislative, legal, and electoral gauntlets.

UNFINISHED JOURNEY

The 2010 Patient Protection and Affordable Care Act marks a milestone in the American struggle for universal coverage. It is the most important health care law and coverage expansion since Medicare and Medicaid were enacted in 1965. It breaks the cycle of incrementalism and inaction that has governed U.S. health policy for four decades. The PPACA will make health insurance more accessible and affordable for the uninsured and more secure for Americans who already have coverage.

Yet the advent of Obamacare does not end the nation's long struggle for universal health insurance. The law will not produce universal coverage. In 2016, after the PPACA's coverage provisions are fully implemented, the nonpartisan Congressional Budget Office estimates that 25 million Americans will gain coverage but that 31 million persons will remain uninsured. Many Republican-governed states continue to resist the law and are refusing to expand their Medicaid programs, meaning that many low-income Americans will not gain access to coverage, at least in the short run. The PPACA does not create a new health insurance system as much as it attempts to fill in gaps in the existing system, and the resulting complexity and confusion mean that other Americans who are eligible for new benefits are still likely to fall through the cracks. Moreover, many of the health insurance policies available under the law do not offer comprehensive coverage and will require enrollees to pay substantial sums for medical care to cover deductibles and copayments.

Still, the Patient Protection and Affordable Care Act is arguably as much as and perhaps more than the Obama administration could reasonably have been expected to achieve given the powerful constraints on health reform. A century of struggles over universal health care has amply demonstrated the daunting barriers to health care reform in the United States. A fragmented political system makes the passage of legislation through Congress difficult and compels compromise even when presidents have legislative majorities from their own party. A host of interest groups are invested in the status quo and resistant to changes that threaten their role in the system and their bottom lines. Americans are ambivalent about government and often fearful of excessive public power, a fear that reform opponents can exploit. Debates over health reform

State Resistance to Obamacare

The 2010 Patient Protection and Affordable Care Act (commonly known as the Affordable Care Act or Obamacare) aims to increase access to health insurance in the United States. The Affordable Care Act greatly expands the role of the federal government in the health insurance system, providing the uninsured with subsidies to purchase coverage, creating new purchasing pools for the uninsured and small businesses, regulating insurers to prohibit practices that make coverage unaffordable or inaccessible for persons with preexisting conditions, and mandating individuals to obtain and larger businesses to offer health insurance or pay penalties.

States also have an important role to play in the Affordable Care Act's implementation. They are responsible for enforcing some of the law's insurance regulations, can establish new health insurance pools (called health insurance exchanges), and must decide whether to expand eligibility in their Medicaid program to meet standards envisioned by the law. Therein lies one of the dilemmas that Obamacare has encountered: its implementation depends in part on states whose leaders are intensely opposed to the law and want it overturned.

State resistance to Obamacare has been much stronger than the administration and other health reform advocates anticipated. Only sixteen states and the District of Columbia initially decided to establish their own health insurance exchanges, the largely online marketplaces where the uninsured and small businesses will shop for coverage. Seven states chose to partner with the federal government, and twenty-seven states decided to cede control over these exchanges to the federal government. The states that chose not to establish exchanges were largely governed by Republicans, this despite the fact that insurance purchasing pools were originally an idea promoted by the GOP.

Meanwhile, the Supreme Court's ruling making Obamacare's Medicaid expansion effectively optional for states (in response to a suit brought by twenty-six states challenging the law's constitutionality) created another, unexpected front in the health reform battle. As of October 1, 2013, twenty-six states had indicated they would not expand their Medicaid programs, meaning that many low-income residents of those states would remain uninsured. The widespread opposition to Medicaid expansion, again concentrated in politically conservative, Republican states, came despite the availability of generous federal funding and pressures from hospitals to accept the program to reduce the financial burden of uninsured patients. Washington would initially pay all of the costs of the expansion and 90 percent after 2020, a financial arrangement that many policy analysts mistakenly believed would persuade all but a few states to go along with the expansion.

State resistance to the Affordable Care Act could weaken over time if the law survives intact after the 2016 elections and is further entrenched into the health care system. The initial scope and intensity of resistance to health care reform was extraordinary; state opposition to Obamacare underscored how controversial the law remained even after its enactment. It also underscored the extent to which U.S. politics is currently polarized along ideological and partisan lines. Not a single Republican in Congress voted for the Affordable Care Act. While state Republican responses to the law have been more diverse (some GOP states have embraced insurance exchanges or the Medicaid expansion), the concentration of opposition to its implementation in Republican-led states indicates that polarization is not simply a congressional issue. While the federal government will run exchanges in states that do not create their own, it may be harder to inform residents about new health insurance options and the law's benefits in states that refuse to cooperate with the federal government. In addition, if more states do not reverse their decisions to reject the Medicaid expansion, the Affordable Care Act will leave more Americans uninsured than expected. The evolution of state attitudes toward Obamacare will be a major story in U.S. health politics going forward.

trigger ideological and partisan divisions over the role of government and markets and the values of individualism and community.

The patchwork health care system that the United States has built over the last century—employer-sponsored insurance, Medicare, Medicaid—complicates reform efforts because most Americans already have coverage and it is hard politically to move away from a system, however incoherent or irrational, that has been institutionalized over decades. During the past fifty years, universal insurance proposals have become more conservative, more reliant on private insurance, and less universal. If the PPACA is incomplete, inelegant, and complex, it is because this powerful array of barriers shapes and constrains the kind of health care reform that is possible in the United States, limiting how far reformers can budge the convoluted and irrational status quo.

The Patient Protection and Affordable Care Act builds on the nation's patchwork health insurance system, the only politically feasible path reform could have taken in 2010. Ongoing fights over repealing health care reform and the law's implementation at both the federal and state levels will reveal just how far down the path to universal coverage the United States travels. A century after Americans first debated government health insurance, we still have a long way to go.

See also **Chapter 1: Origins and Development of Government's Role in Health Policy (Colonial Era to Present); Chapter 17: Strategies for Health Care Cost Containment (1980s–Present); Chapter 18: Health and Health Care Policy: Ethical Perspectives (1970s–Present); Chapter 19: Children's Health and Health Care Policy (1960s–Present); Chapter 20: Women's Issues and**

American Health Care Policy (1960s–Present); Chapter 21: Minorities, Immigrants, and Health Care Policy: Disparities and Solutions (1960s–Present); Chapter 22:

Aging and Health Care Policy (1990s–Present); Chapter 26: Interest Groups, Think Tanks, and Health Care Policy (1960s–Present).

NOTES

1. This section draws on Jonathan Oberlander, *The Political Life of Medicare* (Chicago: University of Chicago Press, 2003).
2. Paul Starr, *The Social Transformation of American Medicine* (New York: Basic Books, 1982), 243.
3. Quoted in Robert J. Myers, *Medicare* (Bryn Mawr, PA: McCahan Foundation, 1970), 5.
4. Quoted in Ronald Numbers, *Almost Persuaded: American Physicians and Compulsory Health Insurance* (Baltimore: Johns Hopkins University Press, 1978).
5. Beatrix Hoffman, *The Wages of Sickness: The Politics of Health Insurance in Progressive America* (Chapel Hill: University of North Carolina Press, 2001).
6. Quoted in Daniel Hirshfield, *The Lost Reform: The Campaign for Compulsory Health Insurance in the United States from 1932 to 1943* (Cambridge, MA: Harvard University Press, 1970), 25.
7. Starr, *Social Transformation of American Medicine*, 252.
8. Quoted in Oberlander, *The Political Life of Medicare*, 20.
9. David Blumenthal and James A. Morone, *The Heart of Power: Health and Politics in the Oval Office* (Berkeley: University of California Press, 2009), 24–28.
10. Ibid., 53–56.
11. Harry Truman, "Special Message to the Congress Recommending a Comprehensive Health Program," November 19, 1945, http://www.trumanlibrary.org/publicpapers/index.php?pid=483.
12. See Monte M. Poen, *Harry S. Truman Versus the Medical Lobby: The Genesis of Medicare* (Columbia: University of Missouri Press, 1979).
13. Quoted in Blumenthal and Morone, *The Heart of Power*, 77.
14. Quoted in Eugene Feingold, *Medicare: Policy and Politics: A Case Study and Policy Analysis* (San Francisco: Chandler, 1966).
15. See Starr, *Social Transformation*, 280–285.
16. Jacob Hacker, *The Divided Welfare State: The Battle over Public and Private Social Benefits in the United States* (New York: Cambridge University Press, 2002), 221–237.
17. Ibid., 214.
18. Theodore Marmor, *The Politics of Medicare* (New York: Aldine, 1973), 23.
19. Ibid., 14–15.
20. See "Organization Section: Highlights of A.M.A. Clinical Session," *Journal of the American Medical Association* 165: 16 (1957), 2090–2092.
21. Quoted in Oberlander, *The Political Life of Medicare*, 27.
22. Marmor, *The Politics of Medicare*, 79.
23. Robert Ball, "What Medicare's Architects Had in Mind," *Health Affairs* 14: 4 (1995): 62–72.
24. Truman, "Special Message to the Congress."
25. Richard Nixon, "Special Message to the Congress Proposing a National Health Strategy," February 18, 1971, http://www.presidency.ucsb.edu/ws/?pid=3311.

26. Hacker, *The Divided Welfare State*, 214.
27. Nixon, "Special Message to the Congress."
28. Blumenthal and Morone, *The Heart of Power*, 231.
29. See Rick Mayes, *Universal Coverage: The Elusive Quest for National Health Insurance* (Ann Arbor: University of Michigan Press, 2004), 88–108.
30. Stuart Altman and David Shactman, *Power, Politics and Universal Health Care: The Inside Story of a Century-Long Battle* (Amherst, NY: Prometheus Books, 2011), 27–61.
31. Blumenthal and Morone, *The Heart of Power*, p. 244-245.
32. Gallup, "Trust in Government," http://www.gallup.com/poll/5392/trust-government.aspx.
33. Richard Kornick and Todd Gilmer, "Explaining the Decline in Health Insurance Coverage, 1979–1995," *Health Affairs* 18: 2 (1999): 30–47.
34. Lawrence Brown and Michael Sparer, "Poor Program's Progress: The Unanticipated Politics of Medicaid Policy," *Health affairs* 22: 1 (2003): 31–44.
35. Theda Skocpol, *Boomerang: Health Care Reform and the Turn against Government* (New York: W.W. Norton, 1997), 26–30.
36. John M. Baer, "Woffer Uses Soft Sell in His First TV Ads," *Philly.com*, September 10, 1991, http://articles.philly.com/1991-09-10/news/25801370_1_democrat-harris-wofford-dick-thornburgh-tv-ads.
37. "Clinton's Health Plan; Transcript of President's Address to Congress on Health Care," *New York Times*, September 23, 1993, http://www.nytimes.com/1993/09/23/us/clinton-s-health-plan-transcript-president-s-address-congress-health-care.html?pagewanted=all&src=pm
38. Paul Starr, "What Happened to Health Care Reform?" *The American Prospect* no. 20 (Winter 1995): 20–31.
39. Ibid.
40. Jonathan Oberlander, "Learning from Failure in Health Care Reform," *New England Journal of Medicine*, 357: 17 (2007): 1677–1679.
41. Genevieve Kenney, Jennifer Haley, and Alexandra Tabay, "Children's Insurance Coverage and Service Use Improve," in *Snapshots of American Families III* (Washington, DC: Urban Institute, July 2003).
42. Robert Mickey, "Dr. StrangeRove; or, How Conservatives Learned to Stop Worrying and Love Community Health Centers," in *The Health Care "Safety Net" in a Post-Reform World* (New Brunswick, NJ: Rutgers University Press, 2012), 21–66.
43. Christopher J. Goodman and Stephen M. Mance, "Employment Loss and the 2007–2009 Recession: An Overview," *Monthly Labor Review* (Washington, DC: Bureau of Labor Statistics, April 2011), 3–12.
44. Jonathan Cohn, "How They Did It," *The New Republic*, May 20, 2010.
45. Jonathan Oberlander, "Long Time Coming: Why Health Reform Finally Passed," *Health Affairs* 29: 6 (2010): 1112–1116.

FURTHER READING

Altman, Stuart, and David Shactman. *Power, Politics and Universal Health Care: The Inside Story of a Century-Long Battle.* Amherst, NY: Prometheus Books, 2011.

Blumenthal, David, and James A. Morone. *The Heart of Power: Health and Politics in the Oval Office.* Berkeley: University of California Press, 2009.

Gordon, Colin. *Dead on Arrival: The Politics of Health Care in Twentieth-Century America.* Princeton, NJ: Princeton University Press, 2003.

Hacker, Jacob. *The Divided Welfare State: The Battle over Public and Private Social Benefits in the United States.* New York: Cambridge University Press, 2002.

Hoffman, Beatrix. *Health Care for Some: Rights and Rationing in the United States Since 1930.* Chicago: University of Chicago Press, 2012.

Jacobs, Lawrence R., and Theda Skocpol. *Health Care Reform and American Politics: What Everyone Needs to Know.* New York: Oxford University Press, 2010.

Marmor, Theodore. *The Politics of Medicare.* New York: Aldine, 1973.

Mayes, Rick. *Universal Coverage: The Elusive Quest for National Health Insurance.* Ann Arbor: University of Michigan Press, 2001.

McDonough, John E. *Inside National Health Reform.* Berkeley: University of California Press, 2009.

Oberlander, Jonathan. *The Political Life of Medicare.* Chicago: University of Chicago Press, 2003.

Quadagno, Jill. *One Nation Uninsured: Why the U.S. Has No National Health Insurance.* New York: Oxford University Press, 2005.

Rothman, David J. *Beginnings Count: The Technological Imperative in American Health Care.* New York: Oxford University Press, 1997.

Starr, Paul. *Remedy and Reaction: The Peculiar American Struggle over Health Care Reform.* New Haven, CT: Yale University Press, 2011.

———. *The Social Transformation of American Medicine.* New York: Basic Books, 1982.

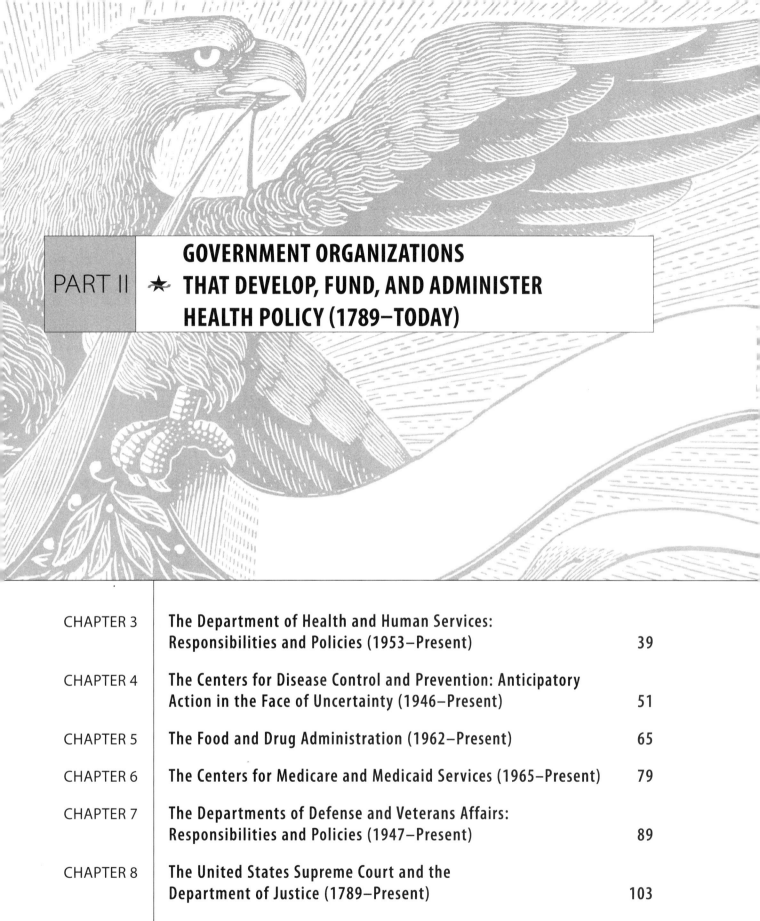

PART II ★ GOVERNMENT ORGANIZATIONS
THAT DEVELOP, FUND, AND ADMINISTER
HEALTH POLICY (1789–TODAY)

chapter 3

The Department of Health and Human Services

Responsibilities and Policies (1953–Present)

Beryl A. Radin

O NE COULD CHARACTERIZE THE CURRENT health system as an example of American exceptionalism: it highlights limited government, faith in markets, and individual rather than group responsibility.[1] While the uniqueness of U.S. history is often expressed as a rationale for American superiority and separation from international norms, critics argue that the concept of exceptionalism is a way to avoid dealing with problems in U.S. society. The changes that have occurred as a result of the recent health reform debate are examples of this conceptual conflict. Advocates for change are attempting to balance an acceptance of some historical patterns with the need to address problems faced by significant elements of the American public. These are issues that provide the context for an examination of the current and future structure of the U.S. health system. While one might have expected the debate about the federal role in health and health care to focus on the structure of government, that policy development process did not include serious attention to the mechanisms of implementing the system that emerges from the policy formulation process.

THE STRUCTURE OF HHS TODAY

In its current structure, the Department of Health and Human Services (HHS) is an organization that reflects two characteristics: first, that health programs and policies are located in the same agency as a number of human service activities, and second, that the health programs within the department are highly fragmented and operate under quite different assumptions and processes.

Both characteristics are not surprising to a student of the U.S. political system. The structure of shared power among the three branches of government (legislative, executive, and judicial) has led to a system that is accurately referred to as a crazy quilt, a patchwork of different approaches that are not always compatible or consistent with one another. The programs that are currently within the HHS portfolio have emerged over many eras as a result of the different decision-making environments of those times and through the pressure of separate constituencies.

This set of complex pressures has created a governmental system that is required to respond to three different types of expectations: policy expectations, political expectations, and management and internal process expectations. Policy expectations are defined within the contours of program design and different policy cultures.[2] The structure of a block grant program that provides funds to third parties to deliver the service is quite different from a program that provides services directly to the public. Historical relationships tied to some policy and program areas have high levels of agreement on program goals, objectives, and implementation technologies, while other areas are characterized by contentiousness and conflict.

Political expectations flow from the complex set of relationships that are attached to the U.S. decision-making system as well as other aspects of fragmented authority. Shared powers have created pressures for all administrative agencies. Those powers shared between the White House and the Congress are especially difficult, because both institutions are required to deal with top-level appointments, the budget, program authority, and relationships with a range of actors concerned about governance. These expectations emerge from the White House, from multiple committees and subcommittees of Congress, and from interest groups and others who may be involved in the implementation of programs. Expectations vary from program to program and often include conflicting demands.

Management and internal process expectations of the activity of a federal department involve classic management

FIGURE 3.1 **Current HHS Organizational Chart**

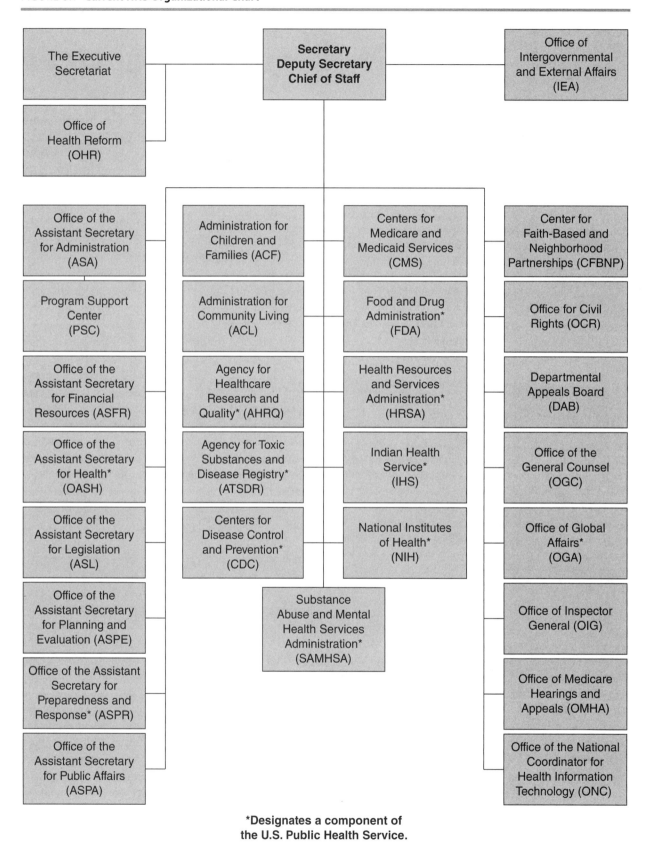

***Designates a component of
the U.S. Public Health Service.**

SOURCE: U.S. Department of Health and Human Services, "HHS Organization Chart," http://www.hhs.gov/about/orgchart.

issues. They include leadership approaches, questions of centralization and decentralization, development of the budget, legislation and regulations, relationships with other agencies, and interactions between career staff and political appointees.

Balancing these three types of expectations is incredibly demanding. In response to these three imperatives over the years, the structure of HHS has changed dramatically. Indeed, one can look at the more than sixty years of the department as a time of constant change, reflecting not only substantive policy changes but also the use of shifts in organizational structure to communicate other agendas.[3]

Beginnings of the Department of Health and Human Services

The Department of Health and Human Services began in 1953 as the Department of Health, Education and Welfare (HEW). It was a relatively small organization that reflected the minimal federal role in social policy. Rufus Miles, a former top official in the department, argued that it is "the foremost institutional expression of five social revolutions that have, within a single generation, completely altered the relationship between U.S. citizens and their national government."[4] The five social revolutions were the New Deal, the education revolution, the civil rights revolution, the health revolution, and the consumer rights revolution.

By 1973, HHS included two hundred programs administered through thirteen operating agencies and ten regional offices. At the same time that programs were created utilizing broad social welfare strategy rhetoric, they were also devised in a form that acknowledged the limited role of the federal government. In the late 1970s, the education programs within the department were separated and moved into a new cabinet department, the Department of Education.

During this period, many of the health programs were placed under an assistant secretary for health, who had responsibility for the Public Health Service, the entity that included the National Institutes of Health (NIH); the Food and Drug Administration (FDA); the Centers for Disease Control (CDC); the Health Resources Administration; the Health Services Administration; and the Alcohol, Drug Abuse and Mental Health Administration. Further shifts occurred in the early 1990s, when the Social Security Administration became a freestanding agency outside of HHS.[5] Despite the exit of these two program areas, at the turn of the twenty-first century, HHS contained approximately three hundred programs with an operating budget of nearly $880 billion.

As the current structure indicates, when the health programs within the department are aggregated both in size and in budget, they represent the majority of activities within HHS. Health programs and activities are spread throughout the structure, and it is difficult to clearly differentiate health efforts from human services activities. However, the program units within the department each report directly to the

MAP 3.1 **HHS Regional Offices**

To better serve the needs of the American public, the Department of Health and Human Services (HHS) is organized into ten regional offices spanning the nation. The president appoints the regional director for each region; the regional directors ensure that HHS maintains close contact with state, local, and tribal partners.

SOURCE: Adapted from Health and Human Services by DWJ BOOKS LLC.

cabinet secretary; the assistant secretary for health was moved from an operating program role to a staff function. Until 1995, the program units found within the Public Health Service reported to the Office of the Assistant Secretary for Health (OASH). Although some of the units traditionally bypassed this intervening level and in practice dealt directly with the secretary, OASH played the role of formal decision maker within the department, particularly as it involved the budget development process. The change in the structure removed this level and defined the role of the Office of the Assistant Secretary for Health as a staff unit.

In spite of the shifts that have taken place in the departmental structure (both as HEW and as HHS) over more than fifty years, few people have been satisfied with the management, mission, structure, and governance of the agency.[6] When the federal government's involvement in social programs increased dramatically in the 1960s, new attention was focused on the operations of the Department of Health, Education and Welfare.[7] To that point, the department operated much like a collection of separate entities. Some described the department as a feudal system where power and authority were found in separate components.

By the mid-1960s, however, the Office of the Secretary had emerged as a force within the department. The span of activity grew wider as the federal government became a more important force in the society. Building on two processes, controlling the budget process and the determination of departmental positions on legislation, the Office of the Secretary grew and played a role attempting to mold together the separate forces within the program components and reaching for a common set of department policy goals. Yet the specialized knowledge and expertise required to administer the programs were often missing from the staff at the centralized Office of the Secretary.

From that time on, most secretaries of the department have searched for management systems that provide policy leadership and offer a way for them to oversee departmental administrative matters and programs. In a few cases, efforts at management reform have accentuated attempts to identify interdependencies and shared issues across program elements. Most efforts, however, emphasized attempts to control the separate elements within the department. This agenda drew on several strategies. In some cases, the attempt to control the program components was handled through manipulation of the organizational structure, moving program components into new configurations in which they were required to work with previously separate and autonomous elements.

The 1990 GAO Report

A report issued by the General Accounting Office (GAO) in 1990 depicted the approach that was predominant until 1993.[8] According to the GAO, a management system should be able to identify issues, define goals and objectives, develop strategies, create monitoring systems, oversee operations, and receive feedback on performance. In its analysis, the GAO wrote that the efforts within the department did not go far enough and that HHS was not able to create a system that actually required the operating programs to respond to the will of the secretary. The GAO found that the lack of departmental strategic planning was a "key element missing" from the HHS system.

Although the GAO report did acknowledge some of the forces and constraints that made it difficult to encourage central management in HHS, it was clear that the GAO analysts sought ways to overcome these difficulties. As new cabinet secretaries have been appointed, they have searched for ways to organize a coordinated national response to the nation's health challenges. Two relatively recent reports represent this recurring effort to rationalize what is viewed as an extremely difficult and less-than-effective system. One of the reports was issued by a committee of the Institute of Medicine of the National Academies of Science, a study that was commissioned by two members of the U.S. House of Representatives. The chair and ranking member of the House Committee on Oversight and Government Reform asked the Institute of Medicine to "undertake a study of whether HHS is really organized to meet the public health and healthcare cost challenges that our nation faces."[9] The report did not call for a major reorganization, but it crafted a strategy that emphasized the importance of reaching both White House agreement and congressional support or action on health policy. It emphasized five goals:

1. Define a twenty-first-century vision.
2. Foster adaptability and alignment.
3. Increase effectiveness and efficiency of the U.S. health care system.
4. Strengthen the HHS and the U.S. public health and health care work forces.
5. Improve accountability and decision-making.[10]

There was little in this report that dealt with the non-health portions of the department or the institutionalized attributes of the U.S. political system that created the fragmentation found in the system. The report read as if HHS is a health department that emphasizes the direct provision of services. It clearly represented a set of policy perspectives that were not always found in the design of the programs themselves.

The Second Report

Issued by a study panel from the National Academy of Social Insurance and the National Academy of Public Administration, a second report focused on administrative issues in expanding access to health care. The report[11] issued in July 2009 was funded by the Robert Wood Johnson Foundation, the largest philanthropic organization devoted to health and health care. One of the chapters in the report focused specifically on designing administrative organizations and outlined proposals to create new organizations, considering issues related to organizational design, funding, operational flexibilities, levels of political independence and accountability, and the structure of its management. The findings and recommendations of the chapter emphasized three issues as it reviewed administrative perspectives:

1. Organizations that use governmental powers and funds and make public policy must be accountable as well as effective.

2. Many administrative problems do not have solutions that require new organizational designs.

3. The Federal Reserve System (FED) does not provide an appropriate model for an entity to manage a national health insurance system.[12]

Both of these reports indicate a high level of frustration with the U.S. political system about the ability to address problems that are entrenched in the health policy world. While structural and organizational issues are emphasized, the critics of the current system have not settled on a strategy that seems to shift the debate in a way that addresses these entrenched problems and combines policy, political, and administrative expectations. Both of these reports indicate that there has been very limited consideration of the appropriate details involved in organizing the federal health system. That which has been developed appears to be somewhat unrealistic or limited in scope.

DEVISING THE PATIENT PROTECTION AND AFFORDABLE CARE ACT (PPACA)

The election of Barack Obama (2009–) as president in November 2008 provided an opening for serious consideration of shifts in the health policy world. Often described as the most significant overhaul of the U.S. health care system since the passage of Medicare and Medicaid in 1965, Obama's administration began a process that highlighted two goals: decreasing the number of uninsured Americans and, at the same time, reducing the costs of health care.

The Political and Structural Context

The program that emerged in March 2010 after a difficult political process illustrated the continued reality of the six elements discussed earlier and below.

American Ambivalence about Creating a Public Health Sector

Critics of the U.S. health system have often noted that the United States is one of the very few developed countries that have neither a separate and freestanding department of health nor a serious governmental commitment to providing health services to its citizens. At the same time, the United States spends more money on health services than any other developed country and invests in expensive technologies that drive up the cost of health care. Efforts to address this situation have been made for more than sixty years, and presidents from Harry S. Truman (1945–1953) on have advanced proposals to remedy this situation. Thus, the drive by the Obama administration to enact a health reform policy traveled along a political path that had not produced much success beyond the enactment of the Medicare and Medicaid programs in 1965 under Lyndon B. Johnson (1963–1969). Also, comprehensive efforts at reform during the Clinton administration (1993–2001) encountered political obstacles that meant that progress toward broader insurance coverage or serious cost containment since 1965 had been limited to periodic, incremental initiatives such as expanding eligibility for Medicaid, prospective payment systems for Medicare services, establishment of the Children's Health Insurance Program, and prescription drug coverage for Medicare beneficiaries. Skepticism about the federal role in health is built around three areas: financing responsibilities, a regulatory role, and responsibility for delivering services. Disagreement about the appropriate path to take transcends and crosses the two major political parties.

The ambivalence about confronting this issue has resulted in two often conflicting policy strategies: one that focuses on the private sector and one that highlights the public role. First, the U.S. health system rests on dependence on the private sector to provide services, and second, the public role has been defined in a fragmented, suboptimizing way that operates at the margins of the system. Even Medicare, the most extensive of the national health programs, was constructed around the private sector where private third parties play an important role in administering the benefits.[13]

Rather than attempting to develop a universal system, the United States has emphasized programs and policies in areas that do not appear to be addressed by private activity. Thus, the federal programs work at the margins of the system. A sizeable sector of the current federal health portfolio is designed to compensate for limits of the private sector. For example, programs involving Indian health services, rural health services, and services for low-income citizens are now included in the repertoire of federal activities, because they have not been created by the private sector. In addition, a number of federal programs focus on a research and development role, ranging from funding for research itself to the development of health professionals in underserved areas. These separate programs have resulted from the fragmentation of the U.S. political system: the shared powers among the legislative, executive, and judiciary as well as the separate jurisdictional authority in Congress, where programs are the responsibility of different committees and subcommittees.

Early in the Obama health reform deliberations, it appeared clear that the policy design used in many parts of the globe, a single-payer system, would not be considered, because the effort was about not just what the federal government would provide in terms of health services but also what changes were required of the players from the private sector.

Actually, the ambivalence about creating a comprehensive health system is expressed in the structure of HHS itself. The current system emphasizes freestanding program units that operate as silos with distinct legislative supporters and interest groups. These interest groups include organizations that represent clients of programs but, more important, the providers of programs with large budgets. These separate programs have to compete inside of HHS with welfare programs, a range of programs for children, and activities focused on the elderly. In addition, health programs are also found in other departments and agencies such as the Department of Labor, the Environmental Protection Agency, the Department of Education, the Department of State, the Department of Veterans Affairs, the Department of Defense, and the Social Security Administration. Thus, the boundaries between various types of health programs are difficult to define.

It is logical to view fragmentation as a way of keeping the federal role in health to a minimum. Although one might have assumed that the departure of the education programs and the Social Security Administration would create some momentum to clarify the definition of organizational mission, that has not really occurred within HHS. Many health programs therefore stay beneath the radar only to surface when some major problem or crisis emerges.

The current debate over health reform also reinforces American ambivalence about the responsibility of the public sector in this policy area. None of the serious proposals were constructed as pure public interventions; none of the proposed congressional or presidential schemes focused on the government as the single payer or the sole deliverer of services. In fact, it is worth pointing out that the price paid for abandoning provisions in House proposals for a new federal health insurance program for those under age sixty-five (the "public option") was tepid support for, or even outright opposition to, the version of health care reform undertaken in the PPACA from the most liberal constituencies in the Democratic Party, the groups theoretically most in favor of action toward universal health insurance coverage. The controversy about a very limited public option is evidence of the continuation of this classic American approach.

Separation of Functions within HHS

The individual program units within the department are organized around three separate functions: service delivery, financing, and research.[14] Even when all of the programs seemed to report to a single assistant secretary for health, they operated in very independent ways. Service delivery functions are the major task of the Health Resources and Services Administration, the Indian Health Service, the Substance Abuse and Mental Health Services Administration, and some parts of the Centers for Disease Control and Prevention. Financing functions are mainly found in the Centers for Medicare and Medicaid Services, which emphasize the fiscal role. The research functions predominate in the National Institutes of Health and the Agency for Healthcare Research and Quality but are also found in the CDC and the FDA, which also plays a regulatory role. Most of the units also have some level of investment in training activities, but these are not at the core of their work.

The three functions are intertwined with the three sets of expectations: policy, political, and management expectations are found (and often differ) in the service,

President Barack Obama talks with HHS Secretary Kathleen Sebelius in the Oval Office. Secretary Sebelius (in office 2009–2014) played a major role in developing the specifics of the Patient Protection and Affordable Care Act of 2010. Sebelius is also a strong advocate of policies supporting people with mental health issues.

SOURCE: Pete Souza/White House/Handout/The White House/Corbis.

financing, and research functions. Thus, in addition to varied functions, the program units' accountability relationships are also fragmented. They report to different congressional committees and subcommittees. They also respond to the perspectives of different interest groups and employ staff members with different training and perspectives. Despite efforts to centralize responsibilities in the Office of the Secretary (or even in the Office of the Assistant Secretary for Health), the decentralized accountability relationships limit the ability of the top official in the department to pull programs and policies together. This fragmentation has led to situations that seem to be highly irrational. For example, it has been difficult to integrate research findings into fiscal reimbursement policies or to find ways to deliver services that include the practices that flow from the research. Similarly, drug developments that are financed through federal funds are often given to pharmaceutical companies and integrated into the private sector market.

This problem reaches beyond HHS itself because health-related programs reach into other departments and agencies. During the administration of President William J. Clinton, efforts by public health officials to develop a needle exchange program to limit the spread of HIV/AIDS were stopped by Justice Department officials who believed that such an exchange program seemed to be supporting illegal drug use.

Just a few months after President Obama took office, his administration created two offices charged with development of the health reform effort. While the White House Office of Health Reform was usually viewed as the pivotal player in the development process, as it required agreement between Congress and the White House, it had a counterpart inside HHS. An HHS Office of Health Reform was created in the Office of the Secretary, and it was composed of approximately ten high-level officials whose responsibilities were linked to the White House efforts. While these individuals had experience in the health sector, the policy adoption process demanded skill and understanding of the vagaries of the political environment, because the imperative was to get the legislation passed by Congress.

After passage of the PPACA, the office was divided and charged with two responsibilities. It was expected to oversee implementation of the law as well as to develop health care reform rules. The latter was named the Office of Consumer Information and Insurance Oversight. Nearly a year after passage of the new law, however, the office was renamed the Center for Consumer and Insurance Oversight and moved from the Office of the Secretary to the Centers for Medicare and Medicaid Services (CMS). Placing the unit inside CMS was viewed as a way of linking the new policy to some of the existing policies and programs in HHS and also of protecting administrative support for the PPACA. Approximately seven staff members remain in the Office of Health Reform in the Office of the Secretary, while the Center for Consumer Information and Insurance Oversight in CMS has a staff of more than two hundred people.

Thus, despite passage of the PPACA, there continues to be activity emerging from different parts of HHS. While political concerns are found in most of those locations, the specialized policy focus is likely to be stronger inside the program units than in the Office of the Secretary. Depending on the issue at hand, management issues can be found in a range of locations.

The Reality of Federalism and Separation of Powers

In addition to the constraints imposed by historical reliance on the private sector, the U.S. health system is also limited by the institutional structure of the U.S. political system. It is extremely difficult for the executive branch to clearly define a national or federal role in health policy because it does not have the authority to create policies and programs

The Clinton Administration's Consideration of Needle Exchange Programs

Although the Office of National Drug Control Policy (ONDCP) involved representatives from a range of affected federal programs in its operations, there were times when the perspective of this office did not mesh with the concerns of HHS. A rather dramatic clash in perspectives was found in the debate over the Clinton administration's policy on needle exchange programs for drug users to reduce the spread of HIV and AIDS (and other communicable diseases such as hepatitis). Research that was supported and analyzed by the public health agencies in HHS indicated that programs involving the exchange of used needles for new needles were able to reduce the incidence of HIV in that population. However, the staff in the ONDCP believed that providing needles for drug users would encourage drug use. That position prevailed in the Clinton administration until a compromise position was eventually crafted to give the secretary of HHS the authority to fund programs that can show that they are effective in reducing the transmission of HIV and do not increase drug abuse.

SOURCE: Beryl A. Radin, *The Accountable Juggler: The Art of Leadership in a Federal Agency* (Washington, DC: CQ Press, 2002).

on its own. Rather, it is limited by the system of shared powers with the legislative branch as well as the judiciary. As has been noted, the fragmentation that has been part of the U.S. system has largely emerged from the role of Congress and those who influence the legislative decision making.

The second major constraint that inhibits efforts to achieve national alignment in health policy stems from the structure of the U.S. federal system. The fifty states have significant differences in the way that they approach the health system, reflecting population, historical, and cultural experiences. In addition, a number of states have given authority and responsibility for health programs to counties and other local levels of government.

As a result, many health programs have been constructed around shared responsibility between the federal government and states and/or localities.[15] For example, the large Medicaid program historically required states to contribute approximately 50 percent of the cost of the program (the specific percentage of the federal matching funds—now between 50 and 74 percent—is determined by state attributes). Efforts to develop data systems were constructed on voluntary grounds; states were provided with funds to devise data systems if they agreed to particular requirements. A number of programs are structured as block grants that provide states with significant discretion to determine how the federal funds are used. Negotiated agreements (such as performance partnerships) have been advanced as a way to deal with collaborative and shared responsibilities. As a result, there is significant variation in the health policy and program landscape across the country.

Although earlier health reform efforts did not emphasize the role of states, the PPACA did draw on the experience of Medicaid and thus the important role of states in expanding coverage. For example, the highly publicized health care reform law in Massachusetts, the most immediate precursor to the 2010 federal legislation, relied heavily on an expansion of Medicaid coverage to approach near universal coverage. Expansion of Medicaid, however, gives states the opportunity to decline to participate in the process.[16] States can opt out of Medicaid expansion (including individuals and families with incomes of 133 percent of the poverty level). States also have the opportunity to create their own health insurance exchanges (American Health Benefits Exchanges) that can be used by individuals and small business to buy insurance. The discretion provided to states is expected to result in a continuation of variability across the country in terms of access to providers, consumer take-up, and eligibility.

Financing the System

The complexity of relationships and actors in the United States makes it very difficult to clearly define "the health system" in the country. If the parameters of that system are not agreed upon, it becomes almost impossible to find a way to determine its cost. Do we focus only on the costs directly assumed by the government (national, state, and local)? How do we monetize the indirect role played by government that supports the various elements of the private sector? How do we characterize the profit that is assumed to be a legitimate part of the private sector's role?

In its account of the enactment of the PPACA, reporters from the *Washington Post* characterized this system as a contradiction:

> American medicine remains the envy of the world. The United States has many of the best hospitals. It has well-trained, highly skilled and innovative doctors. It produces the lion's share of the most significant advances in biomedical research.
>
> Yet the same country has constructed a health-care system that is wasteful, inefficient, increasingly irrational—and unsustainably expensive. We spend a fortune on medical care, and yet we're lagging behind other nations in several major categories that define a healthy country.[17]

One could add other expressions of this set of contradictions to this list. Debates about health policy over the years have often focused on issues related to cost. The citizenry cannot seem to accept the arguments that begin with the assumption that health is a public good and thus we should try to find the least costly way to achieve that good. In addition, the citizenry cannot decide who should pay for these services—the individual, the workplace, or the government. Finally, there is a lack of consensus on the level of profit that is appropriate for the private sector and, in a related fashion, whether that profit margin should be regulated by the government.

The repertoire of health programs that now make up the HHS portfolio illustrate various ways to dance around these contradictions. Changes in program design are required to be budget neutral. Costs are calculated on a combination of long- and short-run bases. To make things even more complex, the contemporary concern about the budget deficit has made it more difficult to devise ways to find new revenues and to modernize the current system.[18] Programs that involve states face their own form of fiscal stress; efforts to encourage change through waivers are limited by budget neutrality requirements.[19]

Henry Aaron, a well-respected health economist at the Brookings Institution, has described the current situation as one in which health costs are blamed for the budget and entitlement crisis. He notes that the long-term problem is private and public health care spending, not a general budget shortfall or entitlements. Three broad strategies are available to deal with the fiscal problem: Increase taxes to finance general government; curtail public spending, including Medicare and Medicaid benefits; and reform the health system, private and public. The three strategies are not mutually exclusive. All may be used. The first two do not deal with the whole problem, the economic pressures generated by increases in both private and public health care spending. The third strategy does.[20]

Difficulties Focusing on Health Prevention Approaches

The U.S. public health community has long recognized that policies and programs that emphasize health prevention are effective in terms of both dealing with health problems and achieving cost savings. However, many of the programs in the federal government repertoire have a crisis orientation and do not lend themselves to approaches that require a longer term perspective.

A 1988 report from the Institute of Medicine reinforced these concerns. It asserted that "this nation has lost sight of its public health goals and allowed the system of public health activities to fall into disarray."[21] Health policy experts Rick Mayes and Thomas Oliver note that most public health professionals do not feel comfortable operating in the political arena and are particularly uncomfortable arguing for imposing immediate burdens in exchange for uncertain and often long-term benefits. They differentiate between the practice of medicine and that of public health. The practice of medicine is visible—indeed, often flashy—while public health succeeds when resources are used to keep something bad from happening. Yet these results are often abstract, dispersed, and delayed. For example, when public health is able to achieve safe drinking water that prevents the transmission of a gastrointestinal infection, these benefits are not immediately visible.

To some degree this reflects the ambivalence in the society about a public investment in health. However, it also is supported by the commitment in the U.S. system to an annual budget process; focusing on annual expenditures makes it difficult to assess outcomes that require a multi-year perspective.

There have been attempts in the federal government to try to compensate for this short-term orientation. *Healthy People*, the national health objectives that emphasize prevention, was first published by HHS in 1979 and subsequently revised in 2000, 2010, and will be again in 2020.[22] Although issued by the federal government, many of the recommendations in the documents have called for action by nongovernment players. *Healthy People* has been created by scientists both inside and outside of government and identifies a range of public health priorities and measureable objectives around two overarching goals: increasing quality and years of healthy life and eliminating health disparities.

Although the health sector has one of the most robust data sets in the federal government, there have been both budget and authority limitations placed on some attempts to

gather information that would provide the basis for a sophisticated assessment of policy and program outcomes.

Soon after the PPACA was signed into law, President Obama signed an executive order creating the National Prevention, Health Promotion and Public Health Council. The council brings together seventeen federal departments and agencies to plan and coordinate prevention efforts across the government and the nation. While the council does not have a direct role in the administration of programs, it is responsible for making recommendations to the president and Congress that help the nation shift from a focus on sickness and disease to one based on wellness and prevention programs in the federal government.

Conflict between Management Approaches and the Expertise of Health Professionals

One of the classic problems facing professionals in the government is the conflict between the perspective of managers and those of the professionals who work in the bureaucracy. This is not a problem that is unique to the United States nor is it limited to the health sector. The bureaucratic managers tend to emphasize issues related to efficiency and control while the professionals focus on the norms defined by their professions and also tend to highlight issues related to quality and personal autonomy.[23]

This conflict is similar to the tension that is found in hospitals where there are differences between doctors and administrators or in research settings where there is stress between scientists and managers. Although the current health reform debate has focused on the decisions by insurance companies that limit the discretion of both providers and consumers, the broader issue of conflict between managers and health professionals is likely to surface in the implementation of any new health policy design.

During the past decade or so, efforts to impose performance standards and measurement on health programs provided a snapshot of problems facing health professionals.[24] In 1998, three of the nation's preeminent health care accrediting organizations—the American Medical Association's Accreditation Program, the Joint Commission on Accreditation of Healthcare Organizations, and the National Committee for Quality Assurance—announced a collaborative effort designed to coordinate performance measurement activities across the entire health care system. Each of the three organizations involved in the collaborative effort defined performance measurement at different levels of the health care system. Others were also involved in the effort to assess and improve the nation's quality of care. The Institute of Medicine of the National Academy of Sciences began an effort in 1996 titled "Crossing the Quality Chasm," documenting the serious and pervasive nature of health quality through a series of reports and meetings. The Agency for Healthcare Research and Quality in the Department of

Health and Human Services was designed to support research that would help improve the quality, safety, efficiency, and effectiveness of health care.

Despite some skepticism, it was not surprising that the availability of this data created a set of dynamics that moved beyond the original concerns of those involved in creating a set of performance measures. Originally focused on behaviors in the private sector, the availability of the measures defined by the Healthcare Effectiveness Data and Information Set moved them to be used in the public sector both for performance requirements and for reimbursement policies. Some of the measures became the basis for the federal government in the Centers for Medicare and Medicaid Services to issue reporting requirements in Medicare. As the years have progressed, the quality focus of the measures seems to have been overpowered by a concern about cost savings. The effort to focus on quality seems to have collided with imperatives of cost savings and cost control.

LOOKING TO THE FUTURE

All of the preceding factors must be considered in the implementation of any structure that may emerge from the current health policy debate. Clearly, they will surface in different ways, depending on the construct of the policy change and the structural determination that might follow that decision.

As the PPACA moves through a decade of implementation, by 2020, it is possible that HHS will look quite different than it does today. At least five possibilities could emerge from this process:

1. Pull out all of the health programs and put them in a new cabinet-level department. It is not likely that a separate department will avoid any of the problems discussed in this chapter but would give symbolic status to a separate department.

2. Spin off the separate entities within the health portfolio but keep them inside HHS, organized by function. The research, financing, services, and regulatory functions could be given more autonomy. This would continue the fragmentation but organize the programs by function rather than historical organization.

3. Spin off the separate entities within the health portfolio as individual agencies organized either by function (e.g., a regulatory body) or by program type. Some might be independent or highly specialized, while others may have minimal change. This would give visibility to the priority areas defined by the policy change.

4. Keep all existing programs within HHS but consolidate them inside the department. This would

---

KEY DECISIONS: HEALTH CARE CRISES AND SOLUTIONS

HHS and the Organ Procurement and Transplantation Network

The development of organ transplantation settings in the 1970s created a need for an organization that represented all U.S. transplant centers and other medical settings that were involved in the transplant process. In 1977, the United Network for Organ Sharing (UNOS) was created as a service to the more than ninety transplant centers across the country. With the passage of the National Organ Transplant Act, the HHS secretary was authorized to establish a national Organ Procurement and Transplantation Network (OPTN) in the private sector. The OPTN is responsible for establishing membership criteria and medical criteria for organ allocation and operates a twenty-four-hour computer system for listing patients awaiting transplants and matching donated organs with those patients. It also provides twenty-four-hour organ placement assistance and works actively to increase the organ supply.

In 1986, UNOS was awarded the federal contract to establish and operate the OPTN. As a result, it serves to not only articulate the needs of the transplantation network but also determine the policies and criteria that govern the activity. The organization itself is structured to represent eleven regions, and its board includes transplant surgeons or physicians, patients, donors, and family members. The UNOS computer-matching system generates a priority ranking of patients in specific geographical areas. The federal law requires that organs be allocated to patients based on medical criteria, not social criteria or economic status.

Over the years, UNOS has worked closely with the Office of Special Programs in HRSA [Health Resources and Service Administration]. In effect, the federal agency is dependent on UNOS to implement the program. In 1998, HHS issued regulations that attempted to provide greater equity in the organ transplantation system, moving toward a more national rather than regional allocation of organs. UNOS did not agree with these proposed regulations and was able to use its close relationship with members of Congress to block their implementation. However, in 2000, HHS was able to separate some of the functions that it had contracted to UNOS, and, while retaining UNOS's administration of the network, HHS gave another nonprofit group responsibility for the scientific registry of transplant recipients.

SOURCE: Beryl A. Radin, *The Accountable Juggler: The Art of Leadership in a Federal Agency* (Washington, DC: CQ Press, 2002).

provide a way to address the problems discussed through internal decision making and might minimize external opposition to change.

5. Maintain the current structure. This would minimize internal disruption and allow the policy changes to be implemented incrementally.

None of these possible options avoids the attributes that provide the context for the structure and operation of a U.S. health bureaucracy. It will be impossible to avoid acknowledgment of the ambivalence in U.S. society about public health; it will not avoid the complex and diverse functions and activities within the health portfolio; it must operate in a government structure of shared powers and federalism and assumptions about decision-making processes; financing issues are likely to continue; and it has to assume tension between managers and health professionals.

Given all that, the federal department charged with implementation of the PPACA is likely to continue to look quite different than its international counterparts. Moving toward decreasing the number of uninsured Americans and slowing growth in the overall costs of health care are not likely to move along a direct or clear pathway.

See also **Chapter 4: The Centers for Disease Control and Prevention: Anticipatory Action in the Face of Uncertainty (1946–Present); Chapter 5: The Food and Drug Administration (1962–Present); Chapter 6: The Centers for Medicare and Medicaid Services (1965–Present); Chapter 7: The Departments of Defense and Veterans Affairs: Responsibilities and Policies (1947–Present); Chapter 8: The United States Supreme Court and the Department of Justice (1789–Present); Chapter 10: Federalism: Cooperation and Conflict between State and Federal Health Care Responsibilities (1960s–Present).**

NOTES

1. Seymour Martin Lipset, *American Exceptionalism: A Double-edged Sword* (New York: W.W. Norton, 1996). See also James Marone, *The Democratic Wish: Popular Participation and the Limits of American Government* (New York: Basic Books, 1990).

2. See Beryl A. Radin, *The Accountable Juggler* (Washington, DC: CQ Press, 2002), 22–23.

3. See Beryl A. Radin and Joshua M. Chanin, eds., *Federal Government Reorganization: A Policy and Management Perspective* (Sudbury, MA: Jones and Bartlett, 2009). Among the reasons for reorganization decisions are the following: surrogate for policy change, public demand for change, imprinting of new actors, subordinating to private sector values, diffused innovation, improving policy technology, and a drive for stability and conflict avoidance (p. 3).

4. Rufus E. Miles Jr., *The Department of H.E.W.* (New York: Praeger, 1974), Introduction.

5. See Radin, *The Accountable Juggler.*

6. See Beryl A. Radin, "When Is a Health Department Not a Health Department: The Case of the US Department of Health and Human Services," *Social Policy & Administration* 44: 2 (April 2012): 142–154.

7. This is described in Beryl A. Radin, *Managing in a Decentralized Department: The Case of the US Department of Health and Human Services* (Arlington, VA: PricewaterhouseCoopers Endowment for the Business of Government, October 1999).

8. U.S. General Accounting Office, *Management of HHS: Using the Office of the Secretary to Enhance Departmental Effectiveness* (GAO HRD-90-51, Washington, DC: U.S. General Accounting Office, February 1990), 3.

9. Letter from Representatives Waxman and Davis to Harvey V. Fineberg, President of the Institute of Medicine, June 20, 2007.

10. ISchaeffer, L.D., Schultz, J.A., Institute of Medicine, et al., *HHS in the 21st Century: Charting a New Course for a Healthier America* (Washington, DC: National Academies Press, 2009), 4–5.

11. National Academy of Social Insurance and National Academy of Public Administration, *Administrative Solutions in Health Reform* (Washington, DC: National Academy of Social Insurance, July 2009).

12. Ibid., 43–44.

13. See, for example, Jonathan Oberlander, *The Political Life of Medicare* (Chicago: University of Chicago Press, 2003).

14. Each of the program units may contain activities in all three functions, but their major goals tend to emphasize just one of the functions.

15. The Medicare program, by contrast, does not include a specific role for states.

16. See Frank J. Thompson, *Federalism, Policy Durability, and Health Reform* (Washington, DC: Georgetown University Press, 2012), ch. 6.

17. The Staff of The Washington Post, *Landmark: The Inside Story of America's New Health-Care Law and What It Means for Us All* (New York: Public Affairs, 2010), 65.

18. David M. Cutler and Judy Feder, *Financing Health Care Reform: A Plan to Ensure the Cost of Reform Is Budget-Neutral* (Washington, DC: Center for American Progress, June 2009).

19. Thompson, *Federalism, Policy Durability*, chs. 4 and 5.

20. Henry J. Aaron, "Budget Crisis, Entitlement Crisis, Health Care Financing Problem—Which Is It? *Health_Affairs* 26: 6 (2007): 1627.

21. Quoted in Rick Mayes and Thomas R Oliver, "Chronic Disease and the Shifting Focus on Public Health: Is Prevention Still a Political Lightweight?" *Journal of Health Politics, Policy and Law* 37: 2 (April 2012): 185.

22. See Healthy People Web site, http://www.healthypeople.gov.

23. See Eliot Freidson, *Professionalism, The Third Logic: On the Practice of Knowledge* (Chicago: University of Chicago Press, 2001).

24. These have taken two forms that require performance information and measures across the federal government: the Government Performance and Results Act of 1993 and the

Program Assessment Rating Tool used by the Bush administration. See discussion in Beryl A. Radin, *Challenging the Performance Movement: Accountability, Complexity and Democratic Values* (Washington, DC: Georgetown University Press, 2006), ch. 4.

FURTHER READING

Cutler, David M., and Judy Feder. *Financing Health Care Reform: A Plan to Ensure the Cost of Reform Is Budget-Neutral.* Washington, DC: Center for American Progress, 2009.

Institute of Medicine. *HHS in the 21st Century: Charting a New Course for a Healthier America.* Washington, DC: National Academies Press, 2009.

Mayes, Rick, and Thomas R. Oliver. "Chronic Disease and the Shifting Focus on Public Health: Is Prevention Still a Political Lightweight?" *Journal of Health Politics, Policy and Law* 37: 2 (2012): 181–200.

Miles, Rufus E., Jr. *The Department of H.E.W.* New York: Praeger, 1974.

National Academy of Social Insurance and National Academy of Public Administration. *Administrative Solutions in Health Reform.* Washington, DC: National Academy of Social Insurance, July 2009.

Radin, Beryl A. *The Accountable Juggler: The Art of Leadership in a Federal Agency.* Washington, DC: CQ Press, 2002.

———. "When Is a Health Department Not a Health Department: The Case of the US Department of Health and Human Services." *Social Policy & Administration* 44: 2 (2012): 142–154.

Thompson, Frank J. *Federalism, Policy Durability, and Health Reform.* Washington DC: Georgetown University Press, 2012.

chapter 4

The Centers for Disease Control and Prevention

Anticipatory Action in the Face of Uncertainty (1946–Present)

Rob A. DeLeo

THE U.S. SYSTEM OF GOVERNMENT IS OFTEN described as a reactive sequence wherein policymakers respond to existing and manifest social ills. Powerful incentive structures exist for fixing problems, as voters reward candidates and leaders for treating problems, not preventing them. However, in the public health arena, success is achieved not by purely reacting to current conditions and problems, but by anticipating, preparing for, and ideally preventing emerging and existing health threats. As the nation's premier public health agency, the Centers for Disease Control and Prevention (CDC) is acutely aware of the inherent difficulties associated with being a proactive agency in a reactive system. The CDC is simultaneously responsible for *preventing* the onset of noncommunicable diseases (e.g., obesity, smoking related cancers, heart disease), which are typically associated with lifestyle and environmental factors, while *preparing* the nation for potential outbreaks of communicable diseases (e.g., pandemic influenza, severe acute respiratory syndrome, other emerging diseases) that have the capacity to rapidly spread from person to person. In both instances, the CDC is called on to act with anticipation, staving off and mitigating dangers before they blossom into full-blown problems.

THE CDC'S ORGANIZATIONAL STRUCTURE

The largest federal agency outside of the Washington, D.C., area, the CDC is the nation's premier public health agency. The CDC is an action-oriented institution that provides substantive policy solutions to pressing public health problems. With responsibilities spanning both the international and domestic arenas, the CDC is subdivided into a number of freestanding centers, institutes, and offices (CIOs), thus accommodating greater specialization, resource sharing, and a more efficient division of labor.

The CDC's organizational structure in part reflects a distinction between noncommunicable and communicable diseases. Organization units are often differentiated by the extent to which they focus on one of these two topical areas, although many straddle both domains. Communicable diseases are infectious and contagious, meaning they can spread from human to human or from animal to human. Examples include influenza, malaria, and HIV/AIDS. Because these diseases are constantly evolving and adapting over time, public health practitioners struggle to address mutated versions of existing germs. Influenza viruses, for example, typically undergo genetic changes each year, necessitating entirely new vaccines. In addition, novel viruses once thought to infect only animals can mutate and develop traits allowing them to sicken humans as well. Because humans lack immunity to these animal diseases, novel viruses pose enormous threats to human health and well-being. Thus, the CDC must constantly change best practice approaches and organizational focus relative to these rapidly changing health threats.

Communicable Diseases, Disease Outbreaks, and Bioterrorism Attacks

Although various CIOs have jurisdiction over communicable diseases, none have a more explicit mandate than the Office of Infectious Diseases, which is broadly tasked with organizing scientific research and policy to reduce infectious diseases domestically and globally. A number of Office of Infectious Diseases branches focus on specific diseases, including the National Center for Immunization and Respiratory Diseases, the National Center for Emerging and Zoonotic Infectious Diseases, and the National Center for HIV/AIDS, Viral Hepatitis, STD, and TB Prevention.

A number of other CDC branches play an important role in preparing for communicable diseases, although they

FIGURE 4.1 **CDC Organizational Chart**

CENTERS FOR DISEASE CONTROL AND PREVENTION (CDC)

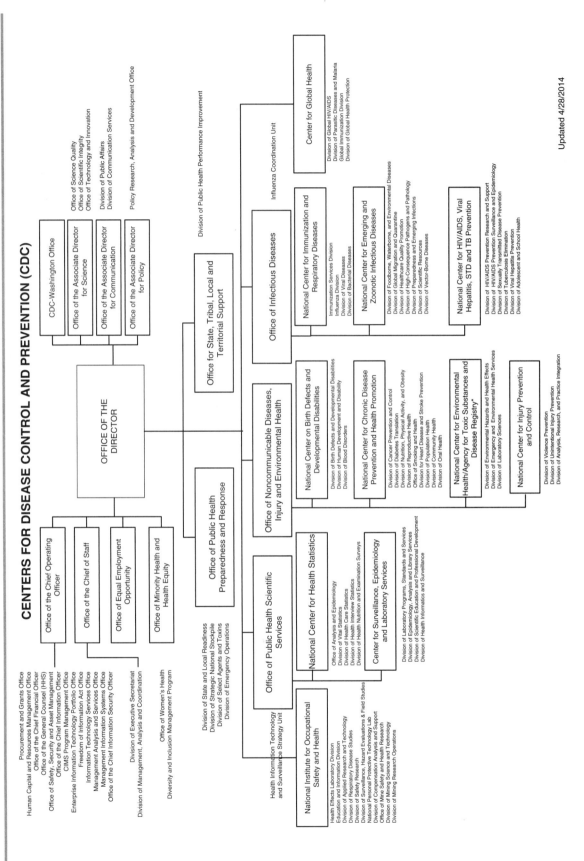

SOURCE: Centers for Disease Control and Prevention, "Department of Health and Human Services, Centers for Disease Control and Prevention," http://www.cdc.gov/maso/pdf/CDC_detailed.pdf.

Updated 4/28/2014

maintain jurisdiction over noncommunicable diseases as well. The Epidemic Intelligence Service deploys teams of trained epidemiologists, famously known as the "disease detectives," across the globe to investigate and survey potential disease outbreaks. The Epidemic Intelligence Service is housed within the Center for Surveillance, Epidemiology and Laboratory Services, which is a division of the Office of Public Health Scientific Services.[1]

The CDC also prepares the nation for disease outbreaks and bioterror attacks. This responsibility falls squarely on the Office of Public Health Preparedness and Response, which coordinates domestic and, on occasion, international public health preparedness activities. Vaccine acquisition and distribution is particularly important to public health preparedness. To this end, the Office of Public Health Preparedness and Response oversees the Strategic National Stockpile, a repository of critical vaccines and other medicines. The Strategic National Stockpile, the largest stockpile of vaccines in the United States, is intended to provide important medicines to states and localities in the event that their stockpiles are exhausted during a severe health event, be it a terrorist attack, natural disaster, or disease outbreak.

Noncommunicable Diseases

Noncommunicable diseases, by contrast, are not infectious and cannot be readily transferred from person to person. Instead, they are typically associated with lifestyle and environmental factors. Examples include various types of cancer, heart disease, diabetes, asthma, kidney disease, and certain autoimmune deficiency disorders.[2] Combating noncommunicable diseases demands addressing an array of social determinants of individual health, ranging from eating habits to sexual conduct, substance abuse to economic disparities. The World Health Organization (WHO) reports noncommunicable diseases are the leading cause of death in all regions except Africa, killing more than thirty-six million people each year.[3]

Organizationally, occupational and environmental hazards are often grouped with noncommunicable diseases, a testament to the fact that they too pose serious public health risk but lack the capacity to spread from human to human. The CDC's Office of Noncommunicable Diseases, Injury and Environmental Health coordinates most agency activities in this area. Similar to the Office of Infectious Diseases, the Office of Noncommunicable Diseases, Injury and Environmental Health houses a number of distinct centers, each specializing in different aspects of noncommunicable disease prevention. The National Center for Chronic Disease Prevention and Health Promotion is one of the largest centers and offers programs in a array of areas, including nutrition promotion, cancer prevention, smoking cessation, and heart

disease prevention, to name a few. The National Center on Birth Defects and Developmental Disabilities addresses a variety of health ailments unique to newborns and children. Its programs span the developmental spectrum from pregnancy (e.g., promoting health behavior among pregnant mothers) to early childhood development (e.g., screening for various developmental disabilities). This center also spearheads agency efforts to assist adult individuals with disabilities.

Similar to its approach to dealing with infectious diseases, the CDC employs surveillance strategies to monitor noncommunicable disease. The Office of Public Health Scientific Services and, more specifically, the National Center for Health Statistics coordinate most of these surveillance activities. The National Center for Health Statistics collects and disseminates statistics on an array of topic areas, including life expectancy, birth rates, nutrition status, and immunization rates.

As indicated above, noncommunicable diseases are also associated with environmental factors, such as living and workplace conditions. The Office of Noncommunicable Diseases, Injury and Environmental Health includes centers with jurisdiction over the environment and workplace, including the National Center for Environmental Health and the National Center for Injury Prevention and Control. Outside of the Office of Noncommunicable Diseases, Injury and Environmental Health, the National Institute for Occupational Safety and Health is responsible for promoting health in the workplace. Although the National Institute for Occupational Safety and Health cannot develop legally binding regulatory policy (as can its counterpart, the Occupational Health and Safety Administration in the Department of Labor), it conducts important research on occupational health risks and develops recommendations.

The CDC's organizational structure also partially reflects its distinctive position as both a domestic and global actor. Federalism, the division of power between the national government and the states, unquestionably shapes the CDC's domestic activities. This arrangement constitutes both a gift and a curse. On the one hand, devolving certain functions to the states allows for shared responsibilities and, ideally, a quicker response to local needs. What is more, states have represented important arenas for experimenting with innovative public health reforms. On the other hand, decentralization makes it difficult to coordinate national initiatives, as each state is marked by distinctive norms, rules, and cultures. What is more, marked economic disparities exist across the states, in turn resulting in considerable gulfs in public health capacity. The Office of State, Tribal, Local and Territorial Support coordinates CDC activities at the state level, providing technical and resource support.

Global Health Initiatives

Finally, global health initiatives are spearheaded by the CDC's Center for Global Health. With staff working all over the globe, the Center for Global Health is not merely a surveillance agency, but instead strives to improve public health in traditionally underprivileged countries. As described in greater detail below, these activities range from training local public health practitioners to improving access to clean drinking water.

HISTORICAL PERSPECTIVE

Much like the diseases and germs it seeks to identify, track, and eradicate, the CDC's history has been marked by a seemingly perpetual state of flux. Organizational changes have been driven by an array of internal and external factors, including emergence of new diseases, political realignments, social demands, and leadership changes. Of course, for students of public administration, this trajectory is by no means unique and virtually all organizations are sensitive to their environment—cultural, political, social, and otherwise—as well as the emergence of new demands.[4] Yet in the case of the CDC, these changes have been particularly pronounced, a testament to the inherent difficulties associated with governing—and anticipating—highly uncertain problems.

Although it currently represents one of the largest and most reputable public health agencies in the world, the CDC emerged from relatively humble beginnings. The CDC is descended from the U.S. Public Health Service's Malaria Control in War Areas program, a World War II era (1939–1945) agency responsible for preventing the spread of malaria among U.S. troops. Focusing its efforts on the southern United States, which was a haven for malaria's vector organism, the mosquito, the Malaria Control in War Areas nearly eradicated the disease in less than two years.[5]

In 1946, Congress renamed the Malaria Control in War Areas program the Communicable Disease Center (CDC) and expanded its mission to include a host of communicable diseases, including typhus, plague, sand-fly fever, and dysentery, to name a few. The CDC, which was technically a branch of the U.S. Public Health Service, opened in Atlanta, Georgia, after Emory University gifted the agency fifteen acres of land for the bargain-buster price of $10. Unlike the National Institutes of Health, which tended to focus on supporting basic research, the CDC would provide practical and applied service to the U.S. states.[6]

Growth and Importance

The CDC quickly established itself as an important player in the public health arena. The agency pioneered a "disease-centered" approach to surveillance, challenging the conventional wisdom that monitoring germs could take place only on a patient-by-patient basis. Conversely, the CDC set out to track the diseases themselves, dispatching teams of scientists across the United States to gather samples of scores of diseases and amassing information in a running database. This approach remains the CDC's modus operandi to this day.[7]

The CDC continued to expand throughout the late 1940s and obtained jurisdiction over a variety zoological diseases and eventually sexually transmitted diseases. The most significant expansions came during the Cold War, as policymakers looked to the CDC to protect the nation against a biological weapon attack. Similar to the Central Intelligence Agency, the CDC would provide intelligence or advanced warning of manufactured epidemics. Drawing from its disease-centered, surveillance-based approach, the CDC established the Epidemic Intelligence Service, which was responsible for protecting both civilians and military personnel.[8] Staffing the new Epidemic Intelligence Service (EIS) required an in-house training program, as very few colleges or universities offered degree programs in epidemiology at this time. Epidemic Intelligence Service officers, popularly known as "disease detectives," went through a two-year postgraduate training program in applied epidemiology. Over the course of its more than fifty-year history, the EIS has tracked some of the world's deadliest diseases, including tuberculosis, polio, West Nile Virus, and AIDS.[9]

The Asian Flu Pandemic

The Epidemic Intelligence Service quickly proved its worth, despite the fact that the Soviet Union never used biological weapons against U.S. citizens. The group led the response to a polio vaccine contamination incident in 1955. The contaminated vaccine, which was produced by Cutter Laboratories, sickened forty thousand children, five of whom died. The Epidemic Intelligence Service also led the charge against the Asian influenza pandemic of 1957–1960. While the United States suffered considerable—and tragic—losses of life and economy in both instances, policy recommendations generated by the Epidemic Intelligence Services were credited for having saved innumerable lives, especially in the pandemic. In the wake of these disasters, the CDC and its surveillance-based approach were seen as a viable solution for a variety of health threats. In turn, the CDC secured jurisdiction over all communicable diseases. The CDC capitalized on this newfound approval by expanding its Venereal Disease Branch, obtaining sole control over the Tuberculosis Program, codifying national influenza guidelines, and establishing a polio surveillance program.[10]

Improving Life for All

President Lyndon B. Johnson's (1963–1969) Great Society programs of the 1960s reimagined the capacity of government to improve the lives of everyday citizens. Just as Johnson and other reformers recognized the profound impact people's lifestyle and environment could have on their capacity to thrive in the United States, so too did public health practitioners recognize the profound implications these often-ignored variables could have on health outcomes. From combating sexually transmitted disease to convincing the general public to receive vaccinations, combating disease, it seemed, was an exercise in biology, economics, and sociology. The CDC launched important domestic programs to vaccinate school-age children, remove lead paint from homes, and even assist in family planning. The agency also took over publication of the *Morbidity and Mortality Weekly Report*, an important vehicle for disseminating public health information gathered by the U.S. states.[11]

This period also saw the CDC solidify its reputation as a global leader in public health. The CDC provided enormous financial and personnel support to the WHO's smallpox eradication campaign. By the 1960s, smallpox, a deadly disease causing painful skin ulcerations, was endemic in sub-Saharan Africa and parts of Asia. The CDC's concern with smallpox reflected the agency's belief that the eradication of disease threats abroad was essential to preventing their transmission to the United States. With the help of the United States and the Soviet Union, a long-time proponent of smallpox eradication, the WHO's Smallpox Eradication Unit significantly reduced incidences of the disease and by 1980 smallpox was eradicated, no longer occurring naturally.[12]

The late 1960s and 1970s were periods of turmoil at the CDC, as the organization underwent more than eight reorganizations and even a handful of name changes. Even worse, the agency's botched response to the 1976 swine influenza outbreak significantly undermined its legitimacy. By the early 1980s, conservative reformers, energized by the election of President Ronald Reagan (1981–1989), sought to dismantle the federal bureaucracy and devolve power back to the states. In turn, the CDC suffered significant budget cuts.[13]

A Primary Prevention Approach

Throughout the late 1970s and into the 1980s, many public health practitioners advocated for a *primary prevention* approach. The CDC was pegged to lead the charge against an array of noncommunicable diseases, like cardiovascular disease, dental disease, various cancers, and even alcoholism. Combating these diseases required changing individual behavior. The CDC used tried-and-true public health interventions, such as surveillance and extensive data collection, to fight noncommunicable diseases. To accommodate this new mandate, the CDC added host centers, including the now-defunct Center for Health Promotion and Education and the Center for Environmental Health. In addition, the National Institute for Occupational Safety and Health, which was already a branch of the CDC, was relocated to Atlanta, signifying the agency's commitment to prevention in the workplace. This massive organizational restructuring

POLITICS AND HEALTH CARE POLICY

The Swine Flu Affair (1976)

In January 1976, a number of U.S. Army recruits stationed at Fort Dix, New Jersey, reported suffering from respiratory distress. A number of these men were hospitalized. One of the infected individuals chose to forgo medical services and died. Further testing by the CDC revealed the man died from a rare strain of swine influenza. Early reports indicated the virus was similar to the 1918 Spanish flu virus, which had sickened more than 500 million people worldwide. One of deadliest pandemics in human history, the Spanish flu was estimated to have killed between 50 and 100 million people.

The outbreak of swine flu sent panic through the public health community, which feared the incident was a precursor to pandemic. CDC representatives and other officials urged President Gerald Ford to launch a nationwide immunization campaign. Weeks later, Ford initiated the National Immunization Program, which aimed to inoculate the entire country by December 1976. The proposed initiative was unprecedented in its size and scope. Congress appropriated $135 million to support the new program and adopted legislation relaxing liability standards for vaccine producers.

Inoculations began October 1, 1976, but were abruptly halted on December 16, 1976, in the face of mounting evidence that the vaccine caused serious and often life-threatening side effects. Specifically, more than fifty cases of Guillain-Barre Syndrome (GBS), a paralyzing nervous system disorder, were reported across the country. Further investigations revealed that the vaccine caused upwards of five hundred cases of GBS. Twenty-five of these individuals died.

The National Immunization Program proved a gross miscalculation, as the feared swine flu pandemic never came to be. The swine flu debacle dramatically undermined the CDC's legitimacy. The CDC was lambasted for its "alarmist" response to the Fort Dix outbreak and was subsequently tagged as the agency that "cried wolf." The fallout from this event still haunts the CDC, and critics continue use the swine flu affair to undermine agency calls for preventative action.

SOURCE: Richard E. Neustadt and Harvey V. Fineberg, *The Swine Flu Affair: Decision-Making on a Slippery Disease* (Washington, DC: U.S. Department of Health, Education and Welfare, 1978).

was capped by yet another name change. The term *prevention* was symbolically added to the agency's title, and it became the Centers for Disease Control and Prevention.[14]

AIDS and Its Impact

No sooner had the CDC reoriented itself to better address noncommunicable diseases than the world was introduced to one of the deadliest diseases of the twentieth century, Acquired Immune Deficiency Syndrome (AIDS). AIDS posed extraordinary challenges for the public health community and most notably the CDC. Scientific uncertainty fueled rampant stigmatization of AIDS's earliest victims, many of whom were gay males and intravenous drug uses, and outright denial of the outbreak. In many regards, the government's response to AIDS was the antithesis of its response to the swine flu of 1976. Whereas the "swine flu affair" was marked by a swift and decisive reaction or, in the eyes of many, overreaction, it took years before elected officials even acknowledged AIDS. Indeed, despite its enormous human toll, AIDS did not become a policy priority until the late 1980s, when it was redefined as a viable public health threat for all Americans, not just intravenous drug users and gay males, as had once been supposed.[15]

AIDS remained a priority throughout the 1990s. By 1993, more than 200,000 Americans had died from the epidemic. The disease once again highlighted the relationship between lifestyle and disease. The social climate of the 1990s, which was far more liberal and accommodating to discussions about intercourse and other personal matters, allowed the CDC to launch a series of campaigns educating the public as to the importance of practicing safe sex. The CDC continued its work in the area of noncommunicable diseases as well and even began investigating interventions to combat gun violence.[16] Thus, by the end of the twentieth century, the CDC had solidified its position as a leading public health agency, capable of governing a range of distinct problems and coordinating large-scale domestic and global initiatives.

THE TWENTY-FIRST-CENTURY BALANCING ACT: NEW CHALLENGES, OLD THEMES

The dawn of the twenty-first century ushered in a new era of U.S. public health. The tragic events of September 11, 2001, the 2001 anthrax attacks, and even Hurricane Katrina in 2005 refocused policymaker attention on the importance of domestic preparedness. At the same time, advances in information technology coupled with dramatic increases in international travel have seemingly globalized the practice of public health, allowing both knowledge and germs to disseminate at an unprecedented rate. On the domestic front, medical practitioners have called attention to the relationship between the American lifestyle and noncommunicable

diseases, such as obesity, heart disease, and cancer. Despite their distinctive features, all of these problems demand that the CDC maintain a proactive approach to public health.

Disease Prevention in a Changing Health Care Landscape

The medical community has long debated the value of curative versus preventative medicine. Whereas curative or treatment based medicine (e.g., emergency medical interventions, surgery) seeks to "fix" an existing medical condition, preventative medicine (e.g., programs encouraging a healthy diet and exercise, regular health care screenings) tries to prevent ailments from occurring at all. Historically, the pendulum has swung decidedly in favor of the curative paradigm. In 1988, for every 3 cents the United States spent on prevention, it spent 97 cents on treatment. Some observers estimate this distribution currently favors treatment over prevention by a 1 : 99 cents ratio.[17] Yet a wealth of literature shows preventative medicine saves not only lives, but money as well. The American Public Health Association found that

A graphic warning poster published by the CDC shows the extent of the wound after a cancerous lung is removed. In the United States, more than 443,000 smoking-related deaths occur each year; this huge number includes individuals affected indirectly, such as babies born prematurely to pregnant women who smoke and victims of second-hand smoke.

SOURCE: Centers for Disease Control and Prevention.

AIDS in the Early 1980s

As part of its stockpiling responsibilities, the CDC dispatches rare drugs to U.S. states and health practitioners. In winter 1981, the agency received an unusually high number of requests from New York and California for a drug called pentamidine, which is used to treat *Pneumocystis carinii* pneumonia. While an underlying immune-compromising disease, like kidney disease or leukemia, typically causes *Pneumocystis carinii* pneumonia, the 1981 requests were curiously used to treat otherwise healthy young men.

In summer 1981, CDC officers went to Los Angeles, hoping to learn more about the mysterious infections. The officers discovered the infected individuals shared a number of commonalities. All sought help for oral yeast infections. All had cytomegalovirus infections, a herpes virus often linked to cancer. All were gay men. The CDC published its findings in the *Morbidity and Mortality Weekly Report (MMWR)*.

A month later, Epidemic Intelligence Service officers gathered a second trough of information on the virus from New York and California. The officers reported that a number of the patients also had Kaposi's sarcoma, a very rare form of cancer that typically strikes only older men. Twenty-six cases of Kaposi's sarcoma were diagnosed between January 1980 and July 1981. Eight of these cases resulted in death. A second article was published in the *MMWR* describing these inexplicable cases of Kaposi's sarcoma in gay men. In turn, many in the field came to refer to the outbreak as Gay Related Immunodeficiency Disease (GRID).

The CDC convened an informal Kaposi's Sarcoma and Opportunistic Infection (KSOI) Task Force to study the outbreak, but was hamstrung by budget shortages. Despite these budgetary limitations, the task force quickly made a number of important discoveries. In winter 1982, it traced the virus to heterosexual intravenous (IV) drug users, which implied that the disease was blood-borne. Testing also revealed KSOI was sexually transmitted. By April 1982, the task force reported more than 300 cases of Kaposi's sarcoma or *Pneumocystis* pneumonia, 119 of which resulted in death.

Despite these alarming figures, the KSOI outbreak received virtually no media or policymaker attention. Some observers argued that by linking the disease to a socially marginalized population—gay men—the CDC actually contributed to this pervasive disinterest. The CDC's concerns were heightened after the disease was dis-covered among hemophiliacs who received blood transfusions from clinics in Florida, Colorado, and Ohio. This development confirmed that the disease was in fact blood-borne and that it was a virus, as viruses are one of the few contaminants that can survive the filtering process used by blood blanks. Shortly thereafter, the disease was discovered among Haitian immigrants.

In response to these findings, the CDC renamed the virus Acquired Immune Deficiency Syndrome (AIDS), a more inclusive and sexually neutral title than KSOI or GRID. In an attempt to prevent further contamination of the nation's blood supply, the CDC convened a series of meetings with representatives from the government, blood banks, the pharmaceutical industry, the Hemophilia Foundation, and the National Gay Task Force. The CDC asked that blood donations from high-risk populations, most notably gay men, be prohibited. Their request was met by denial and indignation. Blood banks and hemophiliac advocates were unwilling to compromise the nation's already limited blood supply, which relied heavily on donations from gay men. The gay community called the proposal discriminatory.

Despite a second rash of infections among the children of IV drug users, a more sympathetic population, stakeholders continued to ignore the CDC's plea for help. By 1983, the number of reported AIDS cases reached 1,200 incidences, with more than 450 deaths. By June, new cases were being reported at a rate of five to six per day. In the face of this dramatic uptick, the CDC gave the task force a permanent home in the Center for Infectious Disease.

New Information

In the months to come, a windfall of new information reshaped scientific and, eventually, social understanding of the virus. With the help of their colleagues from the Pasteur Institute in Paris, U.S. scientists isolated the source of the virus in April 1984. Additionally, CDC immunologists discovered that heating blood could effectively kill the virus, effectively preventing further contamination vis-à-vis blood banks. Perhaps most important, international disease surveillance efforts traced the disease to Zaire, Africa, which was in the midst of a significant AIDS outbreak. The Zaire discovery proved instrumental in changing public perceptions of the virus, as most of the victims there were heterosexual. By mid-1983, the public and government were finally ready to acknowledge the AIDS virus and recognize its significance. Denial turned to mass hysteria and almost overnight AIDS was declared a serious problem, worthy of immediate government attention.

Society's initial reaction, or lack thereof, to the AIDS outbreak reflects the enormous difficulties associated with anticipating and preventing new diseases. The pervasive denial of the early 1980s was the result of a number of factors. First, gay men and IV drug users were not seen as sympathetic populations, and many Americans believed the disease was the result of their own behavior. As a relatively new immigrant group, Haitians also constituted a relatively marginalized group. Although hemophiliacs were hardly isolated from the mainstream, they constituted a very small percentage (0.9 percent) of early AIDS patients and were thus unlikely to mobilize widespread concern. Second, the conservative movement of the 1980s ushered in a wave of budget cuts at the national level, and many reformers hoped to devolve public health responsibilities to the states. Financial shortfalls severely hindered the CDC's capacity to respond to the disease and disseminate viable information. Finally, the legacy of the swine flu debacle of 1976 undermined the CDC's calls for preventative action. The CDC was accused of "crying wolf," despite compelling evidence that AIDS constituted a significant threat.

SOURCE: Elizabeth W. Etheridge, *Sentinel for Health: A History of the Centers for Disease Control* (Berkeley: University of California Press, 1992).

every 10 percent increase in funding for community-based prevention programs reduces deaths due to preventable disease by 1 percent to 7 percent.[18] Further, a 2008 study by the Trust for America's Health argued prevention-based programs could save the country $16 billion over a period of five years.[19]

As the Barack Obama administration (2009–) geared up for its much-anticipated health care reform push in 2010, public health proponents advocated for increased investment in prevention. Their arguments cited significant increases in noncommunicable disease incidences over the course of the last twenty years.[20] From 1980 to 2011, diabetes rates more than tripled in the United States, from 5.5 million to 19.6 million.[21] Tobacco use is estimated to be responsible for roughly one in every five deaths per year, and more than 16 million Americans currently suffer from a disease caused by smoking.[22] More than one-third (34.9 percent) of all U.S. adults were obese in 2011–2012.[23] Rates of obesity among U.S. children aged 6 to 11 exploded from 7 percent in 1980 to 18 percent in 2012. Obesity among adolescents aged 12 to 19 increased from 5 percent to 21 percent over that same period.[24]

The Patient Protection and Affordable Care Act and the CDC

The Patient Protection and Affordable Care Act (PPACA) of 2010 established the National Prevention, Health Promotion, and Public Health Council (Prevention Council), elevating "prevention as a national priority, providing unprecedented opportunities for promoting health through all policies."[25]

Because public health prevention closely intersects with various social and economic factors, the Prevention Council consists of cabinet-level officials from seven federal agencies as well as representatives of other national agencies, offices, and councils. The PPACA also mandates a twenty-five-member, presidentially appointed advisory group, consisting of stakeholders not employed by the federal government.[26]

The Surgeon General heads the Prevention Council and CDC staff provide analytic and technical support through the Office of the National Prevention Strategy. Among the Prevention Council's most important early tasks was the development of a National Prevention Strategy, which would guide the national prevention efforts. The Prevention Strategy, which was released in 2011, identifies four strategic directions: (1) health and safe environments, (2) clinical and community preventative services, (3) empowered people, and (4) the elimination of health disparities. In addition, the Prevention Strategy specifically describes a number of priority areas, including tobacco-free living, preventing substance abuse, healthy eating, and sexual health. To achieve these broad ends, the Prevention Strategy suggests more than seventy-six specific federal actions.[27]

While the Prevention Council lacks the authority to fund its goals, the PPACA established a separate Prevention and Public Health Fund to support investment in prevention activities at the national and state levels. The PPACA authorized $18.75 billion in funding between FY 2010 to FY 2022 in support of preventative programs. It was widely assumed this money would support Prevention Council

FIGURE 4.2 **Adults Diagnosed with Diabetes**

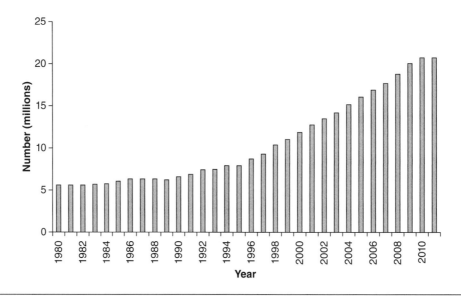

SOURCE: Centers for Disease Control and Prevention, "Number (in Millions) of Civilian, Noninstitutionalized Adults with Diagnosed Diabetes, United States, 1980–2011," http://www.cdc.gov/diabetes/statistics/prev/national/figadults.htm.

recommendations. With the help of the Prevention Fund, the Prevention Council is credited for having inspired a number of important initiatives, ranging from a $1.2 million medical information technology program in Virginia to a blood pressure and tobacco use screening initiative in Iowa.[28]

Many in the public health community applauded the Prevention Council's efforts. Dr. Kimberlydawn Wisdom, vice president of community health and equity and chief wellness officer at Henry Ford Health System, stated:

> In just one year, the National Prevention Strategy has served as a catalyst in leading multiple sectors across the nation away from focusing primarily on curing disease and sickness toward a culture of ensuring health and wellness and thereby preventing chronic conditions.[29]

Barbara Otto, chief executive officer at Health & Disability Advocates, seconded this praise:

> As a member of the Advisory Group on Prevention, Health Promotion, and Integrative and Public Health, I know the NPS has put the country on a path that will eliminate health disparities, empower people, and ensure anyone that wants to be healthy has access to the resources and support that can help them achieve this goal.[30]

Critics of the National Prevention Council and the Prevention Fund

Despite these achievements, the National Prevention Council and the Prevention Fund have come under significant political fire, and the CDC has been at the center of this debate. In 2012, Senator Susan Collins (R-ME; in office 1997–) and Representative Darrell Issa (R-CA; in office 2001–) charged that the agency used the Prevention Fund to support campaigns to change state laws, a violation of federal law. Others deemed the Prevention Fund a CDC "slush fund" and harshly criticized a number of efforts. Representative Cliff Stearns (R-FL; in office 1989–2013) called attention to one of the Prevention Fund's anti-obesity programs, which used remote school "drop-off sites" to encourage students and staff to walk farther distances to school. Stearns lambasted the proposal, arguing:

> Perhaps [the CDC] is telling Congress that we should eliminate mass transit as part of our war against obesity. Incredibly, this same program also funded free pet spaying and neutering. While a laudable goal, the Department of Health and Human Services should focus its limited resources on human health.[31]

Budget Cuts

In the wake of these controversies and in the face of widespread budgetary shortfalls, the Prevention Fund was significantly reduced. In February 2012, Republicans cut $6.5 billion from the $15 billion program as part of a deficit reduction package. This amounted to roughly 37 percent of the Prevention Fund's total budget. (This money was later used to keep Medicare payments stable.) Additionally, the Obama administration used $454 million of the $1 billion in 2013 Prevention Fund money to help pay for the PPACA's federal insurance exchange program.[32]

The Prevention Fund debate and the criticisms leveraged against the CDC reflect the difficulties associated with "selling" preparedness—or any other anticipatory public health program for that matter. According to health care scholars Rick Mayes and Thomas Oliver, prevention money is easy to cut because it is largely invisible: "If public health measures are effective, the problems they are aimed at are often solved or never even materialize, thereby making them virtually invisible."[33] For the time being, the Prevention Fund appears to be on solid footing.

A Renewed Focused on Preparedness

The Federal Emergency Management Agency broadly defines preparedness as "a continuous cycle of planning, organizing, training, equipping, exercising, evaluating, and taking corrective action in an effort to ensure effective coordination during incident response."[34] Preparedness is an exercise in proactive governance in that it seeks to ready the nation for emerging threats. While preparedness can rarely prevent disasters from occurring, it can greatly mitigate effects.

Studies show preparedness and planning can improve both households' and large organizations' capacity to act in the face of crisis. At the household level, families that took the time to plan performed, and fared, significantly better than those who did not. Planning measures include everything from stockpiling food and water to developing an evacuation plan. Studies are much more mixed as to the benefits of preparedness at the organizational level, but have generally concluded positive outcomes can result from a professional and well-constructed preparedness plan.[35] Preparedness is also cost-effective. One study estimates that every $1 spent on preparedness translates to roughly $15 in future damage mitigation savings.[36]

Yet, much like prevention, policymakers have historically overlooked disaster and emergency preparedness. Andrew Healy and Neil Malhotra found policymakers have few incentives to actually invest in preparedness policy because voters do not reward politicians for preparedness spending. Instead, significant electoral gains were reported for policymakers that supported disaster relief efforts. The authors conclude this creates a distorted incentive structure wherein policymakers have little reason to invest in preparedness.[37] Just as prevention's lack of tangibility stymies efforts to bolster funding and policymaker support, preparedness is plagued because most disasters are infrequent and often do not impose sustained negative impacts.[38] Thus, in a constrained budgetary environment, it is relatively easy to ignore preparedness.

The events of September 11, 2001, partially undermined this ambivalence by revealing gaping holes in the nation's preparedness infrastructure. The attacks ultimately resulted in a wholesale restructuring of the federal emergency management bureaucracy, culminating in the creation of the Office of Homeland Security. These deficiencies were again highlighted by the response to Hurricane Katrina in 2005, which was marred by systemic failures at all levels of government, In turn, further presidential directives mandated the establishment of national preparedness strategies and guidelines, drawing attention to the need to strengthen the country's resilience to emergencies.

The Pandemic and All-Hazards Preparedness Act

The importance of public health seemingly crystallized after the anthrax attacks of 2001. In 2006, Congress passed the Pandemic and All-Hazards Preparedness Act (PAHPA). PAHPA codified an "all-hazards" approach to preparedness, investing in readiness activities for both manufactured and naturally occurring threats. This broad umbrella encompassed natural disasters as well as public health threats, including biological and chemical attacks and emerging diseases (e.g., pandemic influenza). In the wake of PAHPA, the CDC profited from a sizable increase in preparedness funding, allowing it to strengthen existing programs while launching new efforts. The Strategic National Stockpile has increased its supplies of anthrax, plague, tularemia, and, most recently, smallpox vaccines (to be used in the event of a bioterror attack). The agency also improved its Global Disease Detection program, allowing for a more rapid detection of diseases abroad. At the same time, the CDC has worked diligently to empower state public health departments to respond quickly to crisis. The Laboratory Response Network, which was established in 1999, uses CDC experts to train state and local laboratories to both screen for and rule out the presence of biological agents. Before 1999, the CDC completed all detection testing. Today, more than 150 of these "sentinel" and "reference" laboratories exist in the United States.[39]

Much like preventative medicine, preparedness also necessitates individual cultural and lifestyle change. Empowering individuals to act in the face of crisis is a critical determinant of successful preparedness. The CDC uses a number of innovative public outreach campaigns, although none has generated as much discussion as "Preparedness 101: Zombie Apocalypse." Concerns about general public disinterest in planning and preparedness prompted the CDC to create a blog depicting a hypothetical zombie apocalypse. Using the apocalypse as context, the blog described the key elements of family preparedness, like stockpiling an emergency safety kit (e.g., water, food, medication, tools) and devising an emergency plan (e.g., identifying emergency contacts, selecting designated family meeting places, determining an evacuation route).[40]

"Preparedness 101: Zombie Apocalypse" quickly became an Internet sensation. Postings on the CDC's website typically generate one thousand to three thousand hits a week. Preparedness 101, in contrast, generated thirty thousand in a single day, crashing the agency's server. Within hours of the post, "Zombie Apocalypse" was trending on Twitter. "Preparedness 101: Zombie Apocalypse" was such a success that the agency launched a YouTube video contest challenging citizens to upload videos demonstrating how they would prepare for an apocalyptic situation. The campaign was considered an effective way to generate public interest in preparedness, although some observers jokingly contended the CDC's plan, which discouraged the stockpiling of weapons, would not serve citizens well in the face of an actual zombie outbreak.[41]

Realizations of Preparedness

The updated public health preparedness system has been tested on a number of occasions. Pandemic influenza has posed perhaps the most significant challenge and a number of novel strains of influenza have threatened the United States since 2000. The outbreak of H5N1 avian influenza in China in 2003 sparked worldwide concerns about the prospect of pandemic influenza. Some feared such an event could sicken millions of people worldwide and cripple the global economy. The CDC and other federal departments initiated a multimillion-dollar pandemic preparedness program, but the pandemic never came to fruition. Critics charged the CDC's concerns were grossly overblown, even drawing parallels between the avian influenza situation and the swine flu affair of 1976.[42]

However, the public health community's fears were confirmed in 2009, after a rare strain of H1N1 swine influenza sparked a global pandemic. The virus, which originated in Mexico, is estimated to have sickened nearly sixty million Americans, resulting in roughly twelve thousand deaths. The CDC's response received mixed grades. Observers commended the agency's surveillance and response efforts, which, per usual, were informed by sound epidemiological practice. However, widespread influenza vaccine shortages drew harsh criticisms from congressional Republicans, who charged that the Department of Health and Human Services, the CDC, and, ultimately, the Obama administration were ill prepared to deal with an event of this magnitude.[43]

Taken together, the swine and avian influenza outbreaks illustrate the enormous difficulties associated with public health preparedness. On the one hand, the CDC is expected to ensure that the nation is ready for potential and thus inherently uncertain events. On the other hand, the organization is chided for raising alarm about events that fail to manifest. While the tragic events of September 11, 2001, the 2001 anthrax attacks, and Hurricane Katrina have afforded the agency a little bit more leeway, the CDC is perpetually walking a fine line between vigilance and over-reaction, an unenviable task in today's polarized political environment.

PUBLIC HEALTH IN THE GLOBAL ERA

The term *globalization* denotes the international integration and exchange of ideas, products, and culture. Although these types of exchanges are hardly new, the level of global interconnectedness observed in the first two decades of the twenty-first century has been unprecedented. Rapid advances in information technology and travel have "flattened" the world, allowing exchanges of information, money, and the movement of people to occur at once unimaginable rates.[44] This latest round of globalization has proven a double-edged sword, simultaneously creating new markets and opportunities while increasing inequality and patterns of marginalization.[45]

This modern era of globalization has heightened interest in global public health, or the notion that health problems transcend national boundaries. Notions of global health are grounded in both altruism and self-interest. Many observers argue the presence of a global ethic that compels wealthier nation-states, organizations, and individuals to assist disadvantaged populations. Significant health disparities continue to exist. Recent surveys report a thirty-six-year gap in life expectancy across countries. Upwards of 21,000 children die before their fifth birthday as a result of malaria, diarrhea, pneumonia, and other diseases. More than 1 billion people live in hunger.[46] In 2010, there were an estimated 216 million cases of malaria and 655,000 deaths; 91 percent of all these deaths occurred in the African region.[47]

Global Health and National Security

At the same time, global health is believed to be essential to national security and domestic public health. Proponents of this view argue that the same interconnectedness linking economies and people also accommodates the rapid transmission of germs. Global travel patterns allow diseases originating in Asia to spread to the United States in less than twenty-four hours. The 2002–2003 severe acute respiratory syndrome (SARS) outbreak was instrumental in highlighting the nation's vulnerability to foreign-born germs. Originating in the Guangdong Province of China in February 2002, the disease rapidly spread across Asia. By March 2003, SARS had reached the shores of the United States and Canada. The novel virus proved incredibly lethal, sickening upwards of 8,000 people and killing 775.[48]

Commenting on the implications of the SARS outbreak, Secretary of State John Kerry (in office 2013–), then Secretary of Health and Human Services Kathleen Sebelius (in office 2009–2014), and Assistant to the President for Homeland Security and Counterterrorism Lisa Monaco (in office 2013–) wrote: "The emergence of SARS was a wake-up call for the World Health Organization and its members, including the United States. The world had to do more to prevent, detect, and respond to new biological threats."[49] Investment in foreign health systems, it is assumed, not only improves the lives of individuals living in those countries, but also reduces the likelihood of future disease outbreaks and, in turn, improves the nation's health security. In this regard, global public health, much like prevention and preparedness, promises highly intangible returns in that success is measured by the nonevent as opposed to the treatment of a problematic condition. Not surprisingly, mobilizing political support for global health is extraordinary difficult, especially in the current economic climate. Indeed, it is hard to justify investment in foreign nations' health care infrastructures given financial woes plaguing many Americans.

In many ways, the CDC's involvement in global health dates back to its original mandate to combat tropical diseases, or diseases associated with warm climates. Large-scale humanitarian efforts as well as the campaign to eradicate smallpox shifted the agency's focus away from tropical medicine, which largely centered on the Western Hemisphere, to a more encompassing international approach. Much of the contemporary work in the area of global public health can be traced to the 2000 United Nations Summit, which established a series of Millennium Development Goals (MDGs). The MDGs targeted certain priority areas for member nations. Three of these goals were specifically devoted to global health (MDG 4: child health; MDG 5: maternal health; and MDG 6: tuberculosis, HIV, and malaria). The three health MDGs help guide the actions of U.S. health actors.[50]

Presidential Health Initiatives

Much to the surprise of his critics, President George W. Bush (2001–2009) launched one of the most ambitious global health initiatives to date, expanding the budget and power of the CDC as well as other health agencies. President Bush made substantial investments in AIDS, malaria, and tuberculosis through the President's Emergency Plan for AIDS Relief, the President's Malaria Initiative, and the Global Fund to Fight AIDS, Tuberculosis and Malaria. Of these three programs, the President's Emergency Plan for AIDS Relief was widely considered the cornerstone of the Bush administration's global health agenda, allocating nearly $15 billion to combat global HIV/AIDS over a five-year period. The largest bilateral health assistance program in the history of the United States, the President's Emergency Plan for AIDS Relief funding has supported the CDC's Global AIDS Program. Working with host governments, nongovernmental organizations, private organizations, the WHO, and other groups, the Global AIDS Program assists countries with a range of AIDS-related activities, including surveillance, medical capacity building, and prevention and treatment services campaigns.[51]

Given the significant investments of his predecessor, President Barack Obama inherited a strong global public health infrastructure. Less than four months into his first term, President Obama proposed a $63 billion Global Health Initiative, to be funded over a six-year period. Drawing from the lessons of the President's Emergency Plan for AIDS Relief program, the Global Health Initiative proposed a more integrated approach to global public health that could address a range of diseases while addressing systemic flaws in international health systems. Although the Bush administration made substantial investments in global public health, some charged these efforts were overly focused on AIDS.[52] Through the Global Health Initiative, the Obama administration hoped to stimulate greater funding for other diseases, such as malaria, which also were being targeted by philanthropic agencies, such as the Bill & Melinda Gates Foundation.[53] At the same time, many observers argued that global public health necessitated empowering actors in impacted countries to become active participants in the production and procurement of health services. To this end, the Global Health Initiative explicitly sought to invest in the rebuilding of public health infrastructures in developing countries. Such activities range from funding hospital or health center maintenance projects to securing clean drinking water supplies. A Global Health Initiative office was established in the State Department, although the CDC and the U.S. Agency for International Development (USAID) were identified as "core" agencies.[54]

New Global Health Priorities

In 2009, CDC Director Dr. Thomas Frieden (in office 2009–) listed global health as one of the agency's top five priorities. He established the Center for Global Health, which manages more than $2.5 billion in U.S. global health investments annually. The bulk of the center's funding supports HIV/AIDS programs (roughly $1.772 billion), a testament to the legacy of the President's Emergency Plan for AIDS Relief program. Substantial investments are also made in the areas of disease detection ($108 million), malaria ($49 million), and public health capacity development ($24 million).[55] In only its first year, the Center for Global Health boasted a number of important achievements. In 2010, it provided millions of people with vaccinations, antiviral treatment, and other medicines while bolstering public health infrastructures worldwide and helping to organize a multinational disease surveillance network.[56]

Yet by most accounts the Global Health Initiative has not met its original, albeit lofty, goals. The $63 billion promised by the Obama administration has largely consisted of money cobbled together from existing health funding streams, as opposed to new allocations. Additional cuts were imposed during the 2012 sequestration. What is more, many critics charge the program's fragmented structure, which shares power and funding streams between the Department of State, the CDC, and USAID, has hindered efforts to promote a coordinated response. Finally, the overt focus on HIV/AIDS vis-à-vis the President's Emergency Plan for AIDS Relief makes it exceedingly difficult to achieve broader health goals, such as strengthening the capacity of local public health systems.[57]

CDC officials have recently implied a renewed concentration on global health security. In February 2014, Director Frieden announced a $40 million partnership with the Department of Defense to strengthen the CDC Quarantine Station program, which screens for contaminated individuals and goods at U.S. ports and entry points. He added that the president will request an additional $45 million for the CDC in the upcoming fiscal year to develop disease and health surveillance networks in other countries: "The vision is for host nations to establish their own laboratory networks, emergency operations centers, and prevention capabilities to create a new, globally interconnected line of defense."[58] Only time will tell whether the proposed program can overcome the institutional inertia militating against global health programs.

LOOKING TO THE FUTURE BY REFLECTING ON THE PAST

The CDC's structure, key functions, and resources are subject to significant fluctuation over time as it adapts to changes in both the threats to public health and its political environment. Diseases are incredibly unpredictable, constantly changing and evolving over time. As evidenced in the swine flu affair, accurately forecasting the next great outbreak is enormously difficult, if not impossible, as novel germs can dissipate just as quickly as they emerged. Complicating matters further, acting in haste, it seems, can be just as damaging to a public health agency's reputation as not acting at all. In essence, the CDC must strike the "perfect" balance between overreaction and inaction. Policymaker preferences have proven equally amorphous, imposing challenging and often contradictory demands. The early response to AIDS, for example, was hampered not by poor epidemiology or even scientific ineptitude but by a lack of political— better yet, social—motivation to even acknowledge the arrival of one of the deadliest viruses of the modern era. One thing that is certain, however, is that the CDC will be called on once again to act—to anticipate, prevent, and prepare—in the face of acute uncertainty. Ultimately, this inherently treacherous process will continue to shape the CDC's mission and legacy, just as it has done since 1946.

See also Chapter 1: Origins and Development of Government's Role in Health Policy (Colonial Era to Present); Chapter 2: The Long Struggle for Universal Health Care (1900s–Present); Chapter 3: The Department of Health and Human Services: Responsibilities and Policies (1953–Present); Chapter

27: Continuing Challenges of Infectious Disease (1980s–Present); Chapter 28: Emergency Preparedness: Bioterrorism, Armed Conflict, Natural Disasters, and Other Public Health Threats (2000s–Present); Chapter 29: Twenty-first-Century Challenges to Health and Health Care: Noncommunicable Diseases, Environmental Threats, and Human Rights (2000s–Present); Chapter 30: The Governance of Population Health: Reflections on the Analytical Approaches of Contributors to the *Guide.*

NOTES

1. For a more in-depth review of the work of the Epidemic Intelligence Service, see Maryn McKenna, *Beating Back the Devil: On the Front Lines with the Disease Detectives of the Epidemic Intelligence Service* (New York: Free Press, 2004).

2. Olusoji Adeyi, Owen Smith, and Sylvia Robles, *Public Policy and the Challenge of Chronic Noncommunicable Diseases* (Washington, DC: World Bank, 2007).

3. World Health Organization, "Noncommunicable Disease," March 2013, http://www.who.int/mediacentre/factsheets/fs355/en.

4. For a good description of this phenomenon, see W.D. Kay, *Defining NASA: The Historical Debate over the Agency's Mission* (Albany: State University of New York Press, 2005). Also see Karl E. Weick and Kathleen M. Sutcliffe, *Managing the Unexpected: Assuring High Performance in an Age of Complexity* (San Francisco: Jossey-Bass, 2007).

5. Elizabeth W. Etheridge, *Sentinel for Health: A History of the Centers for Disease Control* (Berkeley: University of California Press, 1992).

6. Ibid.

7. Ibid.

8. McKenna, *Beating Back the Devil.* See also Stephen B. Thacker, Andrew L. Dannenberg, and Douglas H. Hamilton, "Epidemic Intelligence Services of the Centers for Disease Control and Prevention: 50 Years of Training and Service in Applied Epidemiology," *American Journal of Epidemiology* 154: 11 (2001): 985–992.

9. Mark Pendergrast, *Inside the Outbreaks: The Elite Medical Detectives of the Epidemic Intelligence Service* (New York: Mariner Books, 2011).

10. Etheridge, *Sentinel for Health.*

11. Ibid.

12. Ibid.

13. Ibid.

14. Ibid.

15. Randy Shilts, *And the Band Played On: Politics, People, and the AIDS Epidemic* (New York: St. Martin's Press, 2007).

16. See Centers for Disease Control and Prevention, "CDC Timeline," 2014, http://www.cdc.gov/about/history/timeline.htm.

17. Halley S. Faust, "Prevention vs. Cure: Which Takes Precedence?" *Medscape Public Health & Prevention* 3 (May 2005).

18. American Public Health Association, "Prevention and Public Health Fund," 2014, http://www.apha.org/advocacy/Health+Reform/PH+Fund.

19. Joshua T. Cohen, Peter J. Neumann, and Milton C. Weinstein, "Does Preventative Care Save Money? Health Economics and the Presidential Candidates," *New England Journal of Medicine*, February 2008, 661–663.

20. Similar concerns have been raised in the international arena. In 2011, the UN General Assembly issued a formal declaration on noncommunicable diseases, calling them a direct threat to the health and economic well-being of low- to middle-income countries. The declaration was accompanied by a series of discussions regarding low-cost solutions to noncommunicable diseases, including diabetes education, cervical cancer screening, and the promotion of athletics. See Neil Canavan, "UN General Assembly Urges Action on Noncommunicable Diseases," *Medscape Medical News*, September 21, 2001; Thomas R. Oliver and Rick Mayes, "Chronic Disease and the Shifting Focus of Public Health: Is Prevention Still a Political Lightweight?" *Journal of Health Politics, Policy, and Law* 37: 2 (2012): 181–200.

21. Centers for Disease Control and Prevention, "Number (in Millions) of Civilian, Noninstitutionalized Adults with Diagnostic Diabetes, United States, 1980–2011," 2011, http://www.cdc.gov/diabetes/statistics/prev/national/figadults.htm.

22. Centers for Disease Control and Prevention, "Smoking & Tobacco Use," February 14, 2014, http://www.cdc.gov/tobacco/data_statistics/fact_sheets/fast_facts.

23. Centers for Disease Control and Prevention, "NCHS Data Brief: Prevalence of Obesity among Adults," October 2013, http://www.cdc.gov/nchs/data/databriefs/db131.htm.

24. Centers for Disease Control and Prevention, "Childhood Obesity Facts," February 27, 2014, http://www.cdc.gov/healthyyouth/obesity/facts.htm.

25. Howard K. Koh and Kathleen G. Sebelius, "Promoting Prevention through the Affordable Care Act," *New England Journal of Medicine* 363 (September 30, 2010): 1296–1299.

26. Elizabeth Rigby, "How the National Prevention Council Can Overcome Key Challenges and Improve Americans' Health," *Health Affairs* 30: 11 (2011): 2149–2156.

27. See U.S. Department of Health and Human Services, "National Prevention Strategy," June 16, 2011, http://www.surgeongeneral.gov/initiatives/prevention/strategy.

28. American Public Health Association, "Prevention and Public Health Fund," 2014, http://www.apha.org/advocacy/Health+Reform/PH+Fund.

29. Trust for America's Health, "Trust for America's Health Statement on the Anniversary of the National Prevention Strategy," June 13, 2012, http://healthyamericans.org/newsroom/releases/?releaseid=265.

30. Ibid.

31. Susan Crabtree. "Health Care Law's Prevention Money Called Slush Fund," *Washington Times*, May 9, 2012, http://www.washingtontimes.com/news/2012/may/9/health-care-laws-prevention-money-called-slush-fun.

32. Sarah Kliff, "The Incredible Shrinking Prevention Fund," *Washington Post*, April 19, 2013, http://www.washingtonpost.com/blogs/wonkblog/wp/2013/04/19/the-incredible-shrinking-prevention-fund.

33. Ibid.

34. Federal Emergency Management Agency, "National Preparedness," February 20, 2013, https://www.fema.gov/national-preparedness.

35. Kathleen J. Tierney, Michael K. Lindell, and Ronald W. Perry, *Facing the Unexpected: Disaster Preparedness and Response in the United States* (Washington, DC: Joseph Henry Press).

36. Andrew Healy and Neil Malhotra, "Myopic Voters and Natural Disaster Policy," *American Political Science Review* 103: 3 (August 2009): 387–406.

37. Ibid.

38. Tierney, Lindell, and Perry, *Facing the Unexpected*.

39. For more information on the Laboratory Response Network, see Centers for Disease Control and Prevention, "The Laboratory Response Network: Partners in Preparedness," May 2, 2013, http://www.bt.cdc.gov/lrn.

40. See Centers for Disease Control and Prevention, "Preparedness 101: Zombie Apocalypse," May 16, 2011, http://blogs.cdc.gov/publichealthmatters/2011/05/preparedness-101-zombie-apocalypse.

41. Mike Stobbe, "CDC's 'Zombie Apocalypse' Advice an Internet Hit," *Huffington Post*, May 20, 2011, http://www.huffingtonpost.com/2011/05/21/zombie-apocalypse-advice-cdc_n_865078.html.

42. See Lawrence K. Altman, "When a Novel Flu Is Involved, Health Officials Get Jumpy," *New York Times*, December 30, 1997, http://www.nytimes.com/1997/12/30/science/the-doctor-s-world-when-a-novel-flu-is-involved-health-officials-get-jumpy.html?pagewanted=all&src=pm. See also Marc Siegel, "A Pandemic of Fear," *Washington Post*, March 26, 2006. http://www.washingtonpost.com/wp-dyn/content/article/2006/03/24/AR2006032401716.html.

43. See Sheryl Gay Stolberg, "Shortage of Vaccine Poses Political Test for Obama," *New York Times*, October 28, 2009, http://www.nytimes.com/2009/10/29/us/politics/29shortage.html.

44. See Thomas L. Friedman, *The World Is Flat: A Brief History of the Twenty-first Century* (New York: Farrar, Straus and Giroux, 2005).

45. See Ida Susser, ed., *The Castells Reader on Cities and Social Theory* (Hoboken, NJ: Wiley-Blackwell, 2002).

46. World Health Organization, "Fact File on Health Inequities," 2014, http://www.who.int/sdhconference/background/news/facts/en.

47. Centers for Disease Control and Prevention, "Impact of Malaria," November 9, 2012, http://www.cdc.gov/malaria/malaria_worldwide/impact.html.

48. John Kerry, Kathleen Sebelius, and Lisa Monaco, "Why Global Health Security Is a National Priority," *CNN*, February 14, 2014, http://www.cnn.com/2014/02/12/opinion/kerry-sebelius-health-security.

49. Ibid.

50. Kevin M. De Cock, "Trends in Global Health and CDC's International Role, 1961–2011," *Morbidity and Mortality Weekly Report* 60: 4 (October 7, 2011): 104–111.

51. For further reading on the PEPFAR and other programs, see U.S. President's Emergency Plan for AIDS Relief, "PEPFAR's Role in the United States Global Health Initiative," 2014, http://www.pepfar.gov/documents/organization/149853.pdf. See also Centers for Disease Control and Prevention, "Global HIV/AIDS at CDC—Overview," November 14, 2013, http://www.cdc.gov/globalaids/global-hiv-aids-at-cdc/default.html.

52. Ted Alcorn, "What Has the US Global Health Initiative Achieved?" *Lancet* 380 (October 6, 2012): 1215–1216.

53. For example, in 1999 the Gates Foundation launched a multi-million-dollar "Malaria Vaccine Initiative," which sought to accelerate funding for RTS,S, a promising malaria vaccine, and ensure its distribution to the developing world. Since then, the Gates Foundation has invested more than $2 billion in malaria-related projects. See Bill & Melinda Gates Foundation, "What We Do: Malaria Strategy Overview," 2014, http://www.gatesfoundation.org/What-We-Do/Global-Health/Malaria; Malaria Vaccine Initiative, http://www.malariavaccine.org.

54. Alcorn, "What Has the US Global Health Initiative Achieved?"

55. Centers for Disease Control and Prevention, "Global Health Funding," July 15, 2013, http://www.cdc.gov/globalhealth/globalhealthfunding.htm.

56. For a much more detailed overview of the Center for Global Health's work, see Centers for Disease Control and Prevention, "What We're Doing: CDC Activities around the World," March 4, 2014, http://www.cdc.gov/globalhealth/what/default.htm.

57. Alcorn, "What Has the US Global Health Initiative Achieved?"; William C. Hsiao, "Why Is a Systemic View of Health Financing Necessary?" *Health Affairs* 26: 4 (2007): 950–961; Pablo Gottret, George J. Schieber, and Hugh R. Waters, eds., *Good Practices in Health Financing: Lessons from Reforms in Low- and Middle-Income Countries* (Washington, DC: World Bank, 2008).

58. Thomas R. Frieden, "Why Global Health Security Is Imperative," *The Atlantic*, February 13, 2014, http://www.theatlantic.com/health/archive/2014/02/why-global-health-security-is-imperative/283765.

FURTHER READING

Etheridge, Elizabeth W. *Sentinel for Health: A History of the Centers for Disease Control.* Berkeley: University of California Press, 1992.

Garrett, Laurie. *Betrayal of Trust: The Collapse of Global Public Health.* New York: Hyperion, 2000.

Neustadt, Richard E., and Harvey V. Fineberg. *The Swine Flu Affair: Decision-Making on a Slippery Disease.* Washington, DC: U.S. Department of Health, Education, and Welfare, 1978.

Osterholm, Michael. "Getting Prepared." *Foreign Affairs* 84: 4 (2005): 24–37.

Pendergrast, Mark. *Inside the Outbreaks: The Elite Medical Detectives of the Epidemic Intelligence Service.* New York: Mariner Books, 2011.

chapter 5

The Food and Drug Administration (1962–Present)

Mary K. Olson

THE U.S. FOOD AND DRUG ADMINISTRATION (FDA) is one of the most powerful and recognized regulatory agencies in the world. The agency has a mission to protect the public health through a broad range of responsibilities that include the regulation of food, drugs, cosmetics, dietary supplements, medical devices, vaccines, and other biological products. The agency also recently received new authority for regulating tobacco products.

The rationale for FDA regulation is one of asymmetric information. Because the attributes, purity, and quality of these products are difficult to observe, consumers and physicians may lack information needed to make informed choices among products and firms may lack sufficient incentives to invest in product quality. To address these problems, politicians have delegated substantial regulatory authority to the FDA, and consequently the agency has developed extensive expertise. This expertise has increased the legitimacy of the agency among medical professionals and the public and provided advantages for the agency in its relationship with Congress over time.

This chapter focuses on the most visible and probably the most contentious area of responsibility of the FDA: the regulation of prescription drugs. The FDA faces an important policy dilemma in the regulation of prescription drugs. On one hand, it has a mission to protect public health by keeping dangerous or ineffective drugs off the market. On the other hand, the agency also has a mission to advance public health by accelerating patient access to useful new medicines. Achieving both these objectives has proven to be challenging to the agency, because the regulations designed to protect consumers from unsafe or ineffective products may also delay the approval of other, useful medicines, and hence reduce drug access. Policymakers have struggled to find an appropriate balance between these two objectives in pharmaceutical regulation. Important changes in the external environment in which the agency operates also have affected the evolution of FDA policy. Public health crises, advances in technology and complexity of drugs, the emergence of the AIDS advocacy movement in the 1980s, concern over high drug prices, powerful stakeholders, and politics have all influenced pharmaceutical regulation. Following are an examination of the key episodes of policy development in the regulation of prescription drugs as well as an exploration of the role of various economic, social, and political factors in shaping FDA policy.

SAFETY CONCERNS AND POLICY REFORM: 1906–1962

The adulteration of food and drug products and the adverse effects of dangerous drugs on public health were motivating forces for developing early FDA regulations. Drug-related tragedies have served as an important catalyst for reforms that increased the stringency of pharmaceutical policy over time. In the early 1900s, concerns focused on adulterated food and dangerous drug products known as "patent medicines." Contrary to the name, these products were typically unpatented, heavily advertised, and promoted as cures, but they did not work as promoted. Some of these medicines included dangerous or habit-forming ingredients such as cocaine, opium, or heroin, which were undisclosed on the labels. The publication of Upton Sinclair's *The Jungle* (1906), which documented unsanitary conditions in Chicago's meatpacking plants, and a series of articles by journalist Samuel Hopkins Adams in *Collier's Weekly*, which exposed the dangers of the patent medicines, raised awareness of these problems and increased political pressure for reform.

The Pure Food and Drug Act of 1906

The Pure Food and Drug Act of 1906 prohibited the manufacture and interstate trade of adulterated or misbranded food and drug products. The act also required firms to give an accurate listing of ingredients on the labels of patent medicines, including habit-forming ingredients. Congress delegated enforcement authority for the act to the Bureau of Chemistry in the U.S. Department of Agriculture, which was renamed the Food and Drug Administration in 1931. Although the act made it possible for the government to prosecute firms that violated the law, it did not require firms to test products for safety prior to marketing. This shortcoming led to additional efforts to increase regulation of the patent medicine industry in the 1930s.

The Food, Drug, and Cosmetics Act (1938)

In 1937, a drug tragedy involving Elixir Sulfanilamide, a liquid sulfa drug, produced greater momentum for regulatory change. Unknown to consumers, the elixir contained a poisonous solvent and resulted in more than one hundred deaths. The languishing efforts to strengthen FDA regulation gained new momentum with the tragedy and Congress reacted by passing the 1938 Food, Drug, and Cosmetics Act, which required firms to test products for safety prior to marketing and to file that information with the FDA. The act also gave the FDA the power to regulate drug labels to ensure that there were adequate instructions for safe use and

An FDA food inspector visually examines packaged foods for signs of contamination, mold, or other health-related problems. In 2011, Congress passed the Food Safety Modernization Act, which gives the FDA authority to expand its food safety regulations by aiming to prevent contamination rather than focusing on responses to contaminated foods. The law enables the FDA to issue mandatory food recalls, require more complete inspections of food facilities, and implement more oversight over food importers.

SOURCE: Food and Drug Administration.

that therapeutic claims were accurate. While the new law represented an increase in regulatory authority for the agency, it provided the FDA with only limited screening power over new drugs. The burden of proof fell on the agency to reject a drug within a fixed period in order to prevent its sale to consumers. Although the FDA could examine the information provided by firms and look for safety problems at the time of filing, the time limit meant that new drugs could reach the market without approval after 60 days, and in some cases 180 days, unless the FDA could show them to be unsafe. Also, because the 1938 act did not require any scientific evidence about a drug's effects relating to its therapeutic claims, it was difficult for the agency to enforce the act's provisions. Consequently, consumers and physicians lacked any clinical information about whether drugs actually worked as claimed.

Growth of the FDA

In 1940, the FDA moved from the Department of Agriculture into the Department of Federal Security, the precursor to the Department of Health and Human Services. The move reaffirmed the agency's status as a public health agency with a mission to protect consumers from dangerous drugs. Change was also occurring in the pharmaceutical industry. The number, complexity, and toxicity of new drugs grew after the 1938 act due to the emergence of new technologies and advances in scientific knowledge, that facilitated drug discovery. These changes made it harder for the agency to ensure the safe use of the newer more toxic drugs. In response, the agency created the new category of "prescription drugs," whose use required physician supervision. Conflicts emerged between the FDA, pharmaceutical firms, and medical professionals about which drugs fell into this new category. To resolve these conflicts, Congress passed the Humphrey-Durham Amendment in 1951, which required drugs that were habit-forming or potentially harmful to be dispensed by prescription and used under physician supervision. Even with the new category of medicines, physicians still fundamentally lacked knowledge about the clinical effects of new drugs.

The biggest expansion in pharmaceutical regulatory authority occurred in response to a global drug tragedy involving the drug thalidomide. In 1961, researchers discovered that thalidomide, used as a sedative for pregnant women throughout Europe and Canada, was responsible for thousands of severe birth defects in which infants were born with missing or truncated limbs. The drug was not yet available in the United States, because an FDA reviewer, Frances Kelsey, questioned its safe use and held up its approval. U.S. physicians, however, had been distributed samples of the drug for premarket study. The FDA recalled those samples after Kelsey provided testimony to Congress about the adverse effects of thalidomide. Both the global scale of the tragedy and the powerful images of deformed babies spread fear about drug safety and concern about the adequacy of existing drug regulations. Senator Estes Kefauver (D-TN; in office 1949–1963) had been conducting hearings into high drug prices and exaggerated therapeutic claims for drugs before the scandal, but the near miss of a U.S. tragedy expanded the Senate's focus to include drug safety.

The 1962 Drug Amendments

As a result, Congress passed the 1962 Drug Amendments, which significantly increased the requirements for new drug approval and established the foundation for modern drug regulation. At the center of the 1962 Amendments was a new requirement for firms to demonstrate that drugs were safe and effective for their intended use prior to marketing. The law indicated that to obtain FDA approval, firms must provide "substantial clinical evidence" of a drug's safety and effectiveness. In addition, the law removed the time limit within which the FDA was supposed to act to reject a new drug, thereby eliminating the prospect of automatic approval. This effectively shifted the burden of proof from the FDA to firms to obtain explicit approval before entering the U.S. market. As a further expansion of regulatory authority, the law required firms to submit their premarket clinical testing plans to the FDA (prior to beginning any studies with human subjects) and inform the FDA of any serious adverse drug reactions experienced by patients during those tests. The 1962 Amendments also gave the FDA oversight of prescription drug advertising and promotion.

New Approval Procedures

In addition to the creation of new standards for approval, the 1962 Drug Amendments led to the creation of a complex, multistage set of procedures to govern the development, approval, and production of new drugs. Firms begin with preclinical studies and testing in animals to determine which drug compounds are reasonably safe for human testing. Before testing the drug on any human subjects, firms must submit an Investigational New Drug (IND) application to the FDA. The IND must contain results from toxicology studies, animal studies, and other preclinical tests; plans for clinical testing in humans; details of the manufacturing process; and results from any clinical studies conducted outside the United States. The IND allows for FDA input earlier in the development process than prior to the reform,

and it allows the FDA to place a hold on problematic applications until the firm addresses the agency's concerns. Without a clinical hold, however, most INDs become effective after thirty days.

Firms can then begin three phases of clinical testing to gather evidence of safety and effectiveness. In Phase I, firms test for drug safety in a small number of healthy human subjects (twenty to eighty subjects). In Phase II, firms conduct controlled clinical tests in a small number of human subjects with the target disease to develop preliminary data on effectiveness. In Phase III, firms conduct large-scale placebo-controlled randomized clinical studies to confirm a drug's effectiveness (six hundred to three thousand subjects on average). In cases where the use of a placebo is unethical, some Phase III studies may compare the target drug to the current treatment. Firms then submit all data and results from these tests to the FDA in the form of a New Drug Application (NDA).

Regulators review these NDAs to determine if there is sufficient evidence for approval, focusing on whether a drug's benefits exceed its known risks. While NDAs are being reviewed, the FDA may also negotiate with the manufacturer concerning a drug's labeling, review promotional materials, assess the need for post-marketing study requirements (i.e., Phase IV studies), and inspect the firm's manufacturing facilities. Phase IV studies take place after a drug's approval. These studies serve to expand the safety and efficacy profile of selected drugs in a large population following drug launch and can include formal therapeutic trials or comparisons with existing medicines. Phase IV studies are also sought where there are lingering questions about whether serious adverse events are associated with a drug.

Impact of New Procedures

The new procedures governing the development and approval of new drugs served several important roles. First, the IND application allowed the FDA to standardize the process of clinical drug development and the notion of what constituted clinical evidence. Second, the process enabled the agency to provide input into planned clinical tests or reject poorly formulated INDs at an earlier stage of a drug's development. Third, the complexity of this process helped insulate the agency from changing political tides or other outside pressures that might reduce regulatory stringency in drug approval over time. Even if policymakers or regulators wanted to reduce regulatory stringency in response to political pressure at some point in the future, it would be difficult for them to do so with the stringent regulatory procedures and evidentiary requirements that are in place.

For example, the FDA typically requires firms to conduct two Phase III large-scale controlled clinical studies to establish substantial evidence of effectiveness. This evidentiary standard, referred as the gold standard for drug approval, has been the subject of debate and controversy. It has greatly added to the cost and length of the FDA approval process since 1962. In addition, the FDA also requires companies to submit raw data from clinical trials so that the agency can ensure that clinical results reported by firms are accurate. These requirements have increased the size of NDAs as well as the time and effort required to review them.

Although there had been conflict among politicians about efforts to increase drug regulation prior to thalidomide, the tragedy resulting from this drug served to unite politicians across party lines. Receiving unanimous support in Congress, the 1962 Amendments made the FDA drug approval requirements the most stringent in the world. Although many countries also responded to the thalidomide tragedy with increased drug regulation, few at the time adopted a mandatory efficacy requirement for new drug approval and none adopted regulatory procedures as stringent as the FDA's. These procedures and the FDA's regulatory standard for "substantial clinical evidence" of safety and efficacy helped cement the FDA's role as a world leader in the regulation of pharmaceuticals. In recent years, there has been a convergence in pharmaceutical regulation relating to the clinical development and manufacturing processes of drugs in response to the international harmonization of drugs.

KEY DECISIONS: HEALTH CARE CRISES AND SOLUTIONS

The 1962 Drug Amendments

FDA Commissioner Margaret Hamburg commemorated the fiftieth anniversary of the passage of the 1962 Drug Amendments by tracing the path to reform and discussing how this seminal legislation transformed the FDA, advanced science and public health, and contributed to the growth and prosperity of the pharmaceutical industry:

> The story of how the Amendments became the law of the land goes back to 1956, when a German manufacturer introduced thalidomide, a sedative that rapidly became, throughout the world, a popular therapy for morning sickness in the first trimester in pregnancy. Within five years, the drug was used by thousands of future mothers in 46 countries—with disastrous consequences for their babies, who were either stillborn or, more frequently, born with deformed and truncated limbs.

> The U.S. was spared this heartbreaking tragedy by FDA's drug reviewer Dr. Frances Kelsey, a physician and former teacher of pharmacology at the University of South Dakota. In 1960, during her very first month as an FDA employee, Dr. Kelsey took the bold step of banning thalidomide from marketing while insisting on evidence of its safety.

> And when a growing torrent of reports about malformed babies bore out her position, FDA drafted legislation for keeping Americans safe from harmful drugs. These measures were adopted by Senator Kefauver, a crusader for truthful marketing, and formed the basis for most of the drug-testing requirements of the Kefauver-Harris Amendments.

> The key force behind this transformation was a requirement that new drugs had to be proven effective in the crucible of rigorous scientific investigation—and be approved by FDA—before they could be marketed in the United States. In the highly specific language of the Amendments, the claim of a drug's effectiveness has to be shown though "adequate and well-controlled investigations" conducted by "experts qualified by scientific training and experience."

> The resulting evidence has to be sufficient to convince these experts that, the law says, "the drug will have the effect it purports or is represented to have under the conditions of use prescribed, recommended, or suggested in the labeling."

> With the passage of the Amendments, FDA was no longer a helpless bystander while unproven medicines were streaming to pharmacies and patients' bedsides. FDA could now place a "clinical hold" on noncompliant drug trials; it could inspect drug facilities to enforce good manufacturing practices; it could insist on truthful advertising of prescription drugs.

> Most importantly, the new powers in the 1962 law bolstered an FDA capacity that makes our agency pivotal and highly engaged, while advancing progress for the pharmaceutical industry and the public health. That capacity was the talent of FDA's highly skilled scientists, policy makers and regulators to initiate—and adapt to—change.

> There can be no doubt that the Kefauver-Harris Amendments, with their rigorously science-based standards, triggered vast progress for FDA and for the public we serve. And notably, despite initial skepticism, Kefauver-Harris has had much the same effect on the pharmaceutical industry. To comply with the challenging drug requirements that Dr. Kelsey helped shape, firms greatly upgraded their scientific know-how, equipment, strategies and processes.

> Arguably, the 1962 law laid the foundation for today's modern pharmaceutical industry, which is one of the most advanced and prosperous sectors of our economy.

SOURCE: Margaret A. Hamburg, "The 1962 Kefauver-Harris Drug Amendments: An Appreciation," October 2, 2012, http://www.fda.gov/newsevents/speeches/ucm324201.htm.

Understanding the Influence of Drug Tragedies

The early history of FDA regulation shows that drug tragedies have motivated important policy changes. Because drug tragedies raise fears among the public about the safety of the nation's supply of drugs, it is not surprising that they have been associated with increases in policy stringency and the standards for product approval. Both politicians and the public tend to view drug-related tragedies as agency failures to protect consumers from unsafe drugs. When such harm occurs, it leads to heightened scrutiny of the FDA, which serves to draw attention to the shortcomings or weaknesses of existing regulations. For these reasons, drug tragedies have served as a catalyst for legislative change by increasing the pressure on politicians for timely action to avert future tragedies.

Political opportunities for policy change also increase because drug tragedies make politicians less responsive to industry arguments against stronger regulations. In 1962, some politicians favored weaker regulatory reforms, but changed their position to support stronger reforms after observing the effects of thalidomide and the public's reaction to the tragedy. For all these reasons, drug tragedies will continue to shape future FDA legislation.

Drug tragedies may also affect the decisions made by FDA regulators. In particular, the threat of future drug tragedies may lead regulators to be more cautious in the review of new drugs. Such caution may arise from the professional norms of the FDA's scientific and medical staff to protect public health over other agency or political goals. It may also arise from a desire to enhance the agency's reputation as a protector of the public health. Cautious reviewer behavior could also arise because of incentives created in the political environment. Failures to approve beneficial drugs have not produced the same kind of political consequences for the agency as drug tragedies. At the time, there were no political rewards for accelerating drug access and little punishment from politicians for taking too long to review new drugs. These divergent political consequences could help explain the FDA's historical emphasis on safety over access in reviewing new drugs prior to 1992.

In addition to drug tragedies, one cannot ignore the effects of two other factors that contributed to policy change. First, increases in the supply of new drugs that were more complex or toxic leads to greater informational asymmetries and greater uncertainty for physicians and patients about drug effects. These factors also increase the likelihood of observing a drug tragedy in the absence of reform. Second, policy entrepreneurs such as Senator Estes Kefauver, who was an advocate for expanded FDA regulation, or regulators such as Frances Kelsey, who possessed scientific expertise (that politicians lacked), played important roles in helping politicians navigate the path to reform and the content of reform after thalidomide.

EMERGING DRUG ACCESS PROBLEMS: 1969–1992

Since passage of the 1962 Drug Amendments, there have been important changes in the regulatory environment that have raised demands for improved drug access. First, the time required to develop and test new drugs increased substantially. In 1982, William Wardell and his coauthors showed that preclinical and clinical testing increased from 30 months in 1960, to 100 months in 1970, to 120 months in 1980.[1] Longer periods of drug development and testing limit drug access by delaying the entry of new drugs into the market. Second, the cost of developing new drugs also increased. In 2003, Joseph DiMasi and his coauthors estimated that the total capitalized cost (in 2000 dollars) per new drug approval increased from $138 million in the 1970s, to $318 million in the 1980s, to $802 million in the 1990s.[2] Higher costs of drug development make it more difficult for new drugs to enter the market. Third, a number of scholars noted that the number of new drug approvals declined after the 1962 Amendments.[3] Although some decline was expected given that the new law was designed to keep dangerous or ineffective drugs off the market, there was growing concern that the increased costs of drug development and length of the approval process may be discouraging the entry of useful drugs into the U.S. market.

Beginning in the late 1970s, research showed that the timing of U.S. approvals lagged behind other countries, presumably due to the tougher FDA regulations. In 1978, William Wardell found a lag of up to seven years in the United States compared to the United Kingdom for new drug approvals in 1972 to 1976.[4] In 1989, Kenneth Kaitin and colleagues found that the United States lagged behind the United Kingdom in the availability of new drugs in 1977 to 1987 in every therapeutic category with the greatest lags for respiratory (5.1 years), cardiovascular (3.2 years), central nervous system (3.2 years), and anticancer (2.9 years) drugs.[5] With growing evidence of a U.S. drug lag, pharmaceutical firms began to press politicians and regulators for changes to improve drug access.

The Rise and Importance of Generic Drugs

Confronted with high prescription drug prices, consumers were particularly concerned about the lack of access to cheaper generic drugs. Generic drugs are copies of already approved, innovative brand-name drugs whose patents have expired. While brand-name prescription drugs typically have high prices, which reflect their therapeutic advantages over existing remedies, the prices of the imitative generic drugs are often much lower. As the cost of drug approval increased, generic drug manufacturers became less willing to enter branded drug markets following patent expiration. The problem was that the 1962 regulatory standard for approval was the same for brand-name drugs and generic drugs. The FDA responded to consumer concerns about generic drug access by introducing an Abbreviated New Drug Application (ANDA) for generic drugs in 1969.

The ANDA did not require generic drug manufacturers to demonstrate clinical evidence of safety and efficacy as required for brand-name drug approval, thereby reducing the cost and time required to approve generic drugs. Instead, the manufacturer simply needed to show that a new generic drug was bioequivalent to the existing brand-name drug, a less stringent and less costly regulatory standard. The agency's rationale was that since branded drugs had been available in the market for several years prior to the entry of generics, additional evidence of a drug's effectiveness was unnecessary. As long as a firm could show that a new generic drug was bioequivalent to the branded drug, the FDA could safely approve it. The FDA used the rulemaking process to introduce the ANDA, so no new legislation was required. The ANDA provided an abbreviated pathway to generic drug approval and increased generic drug entry.

When ANDA was first introduced, the FDA could make it available only to pre-1962 patented drugs. Extending the ANDA to post-1962 patented drugs would require new legislation. As more drugs came off patent in the late 1970s and 1980s, generic drug producers were unable to use the simplified application. Consequently, consumers again faced high prescription drug prices and a lack of access to cheaper generic drugs by the early 1980s. This led to greater political pressure to increase the availability of generic drugs.

At the same time, branded drug manufacturers were concerned about the costs and length of the FDA's approval process and the effects of regulatory delay on their profits in the 1980s. Because branded drugs were typically patented prior to FDA approval, delays in the review process directly translated into less time for firms to earn monopoly profits on their branded drugs. Following patent expiration, branded drugs could face competition from generic drug producers. The patent life remaining on a drug after its FDA approval, referred to as a drug's effective patent life, had been falling since the late 1960s. A 1993 government study by the Office of Technology Assessment showed that the average effective patent life for new brand-name drugs declined from 13.2 years between 1968 and 1972, to 11.9 years between 1973 and 1977, to 9.2 years between 1978 and 1982.[6] Branded firms argued that smaller effective patent lives and reduced monopoly profits discouraged new branded drug research and innovation. These trends led to increased political pressure from branded drug firms to strengthen incentives for research.

The Hatch-Waxman Act (1984)

Congress responded to these dual interests in 1984 with the passage of the Drug Price Competition Act and the Patent Term Restoration Act, referred to as the Hatch-Waxman Act. This act represented a bipartisan political compromise negotiated between the two key committee leaders in the House and Senate, Henry Waxman (D-CA; in office 1975–) and Orrin Hatch (R-UT; in office 1977–), respectively, to address the competing concerns of consumers and pharmaceutical firms. To facilitate generic drug entry, the Drug Price Competition Act allowed generic drug manufacturers to use the ANDA process for generic versions of branded drugs patented after 1962. To strengthen incentives for innovative drug research, the Patent Term Restoration Act gave branded drugs additional patent life to offset time lost due to delays in the drug review process.

The Hatch-Waxman Act increased generic drug availability and intensified the amount of price competition in the market following the patent expiration of branded drugs. The act also provided some limited extensions in the effective patent lives of new drugs to compensate for delays in drug approval. However, upon the expiration of these patent extensions, the effects of generic drug competition on branded drug markets were substantial. In 1996, Henry Grabowski and John Vernon estimated that branded drug markets lost more than half of their market share to generic drugs within the first year after patent expiration under the Hatch-Waxman Act.[7]

It is interesting to note that the Hatch-Waxman Act did nothing to alter the stringency or complexity of the branded drug approval process to address firms' concerns about the costs and length of this process. Although consumer demands for more generic drugs and more price competition led to a less stringent standard for generic drug approval, the demands of firms to address the effects of regulatory delay for branded drug approval led to patent life extensions. Politicians were not willing to weaken the regulatory standard for branded drug approval set forth in the 1962 Amendments and potentially compromise drug safety. Because Hatch-Waxman did nothing to combat the forces producing delays in branded drug approval, these delays continued and increased over time.

The 1980s was a particularly challenging time for the FDA. The industries regulated by the FDA were growing and their demands for product approval were increasing.[8] The Hatch-Waxman Act increased the number of new generic drug applications. New legislation governing the regulation of medical devices in the late 1970s led to an increase in the number of medical device application submissions. Advances in biotechnology and the development of biopharmaceuticals also contributed to the increased demand for branded drug approvals. Even though the FDA's regulatory responsibilities were growing in the 1980s, its resources were shrinking. The FDA experienced significant cuts in its annual budget appropriations following the election of President Ronald Reagan (1981–1989).[9]

With few agency resources, the workloads of drug reviewers increased, the speed of new drug approval slowed down, and the pipeline of unapproved drugs grew. On average, the FDA took an additional 2.5 years to review and approve new drug applications between 1980 and 1992.[10] Together with the length of drug development and testing, delays in the review of new drugs further limited patient access to new medicines. In 2003, DiMasi and his coauthors estimated that it took twelve years on average to move a new drug from the laboratory to the market.[11]

Strengthening the FDA

By the late 1980s, politicians recognized the need for both stable leadership at the FDA and greater FDA funding, especially following a generic drug scandal in which some FDA employees took illegal payments from generic drug firms to speed the approval of their drugs. Congress passed legislation in 1989 that made the head of the FDA a presidential appointee subject to Senate confirmation, and legislation in 1990 that guaranteed a minimum budget of $500 million for the agency. The first presidential appointee to run the FDA was David Kessler in 1990.[12]

Responding to the AIDS Crisis

These changes at the FDA also coincided with the beginning of the AIDS crisis. In the late 1980s and early 1990s, AIDS activists who were frustrated with lack of treatments for the deadly disease and the slow pace of new drug approval, demanded that the agency accelerate the development and approval of AIDS drugs. The political pressure on the agency from AIDS activists was targeted and intense. Their efforts helped the agency better understand the costs of delay. The FDA responded to the political pressure from AIDS activists with new procedures to help improve AIDS patients' access to new drugs. The agency introduced treatment INDs and a parallel track program to give patients with life-threatening diseases early access to promising investigational therapies prior to approval. The agency also relaxed certain statutory requirements in the testing of AIDS drugs. Subpart E procedures allowed for the elimination of Phase III studies prior to approval, while accelerated approval procedures permitted sponsors to use surrogate endpoints other than survival or morbidity to demonstrate a drug's efficacy in clinical studies. The agency also introduced a special therapeutic classification just for AIDS drugs to help prioritize their approval.

The FDA achieved some success in accelerating both patient access to new AIDS drugs and the approval of new AIDS drugs. This success, however, led to increased political pressures on the agency and Congress from other patient advocates and firms to reduce regulatory delays for all drugs. The FDA argued that it required more resources to combat regulatory delays and Congress responded with new legislation, which introduced industry funding for new drug review.

IMPROVING DRUG ACCESS WITH INDUSTRY-FUNDED USER FEES

The passage of the 1992 Prescription Drug User Fee Act (PDUFA) gave the agency new resources and shifted the agency's emphasis toward speedy review. PDUFA required drug manufacturers seeking product approval to pay fees to the FDA to help finance the review of new drug applications. In return, firms received agency commitments to expedite the review of new drug applications. These commitments took the form of agency performance goals that were included in letters from the agency's commissioner, David Kessler, to congressional committee leaders.[13]

Two key goals specified new drug review targets for the approval of priority-rated drug applications, which offer a significant therapeutic advance over existing remedies, and for standard-rated drugs, which offer little to no therapeutic gain over existing remedies. The goals stated that the agency should review and act on 90 percent of priority drug applications in six months and 90 percent of standard drug applications in twelve months. Another PDUFA performance goal directed the FDA to eliminate its backlog of NDAs awaiting approval within twenty-four months of the establishment of the program.[14] The FDA was required to file annual reports to Congress on the status of meeting its performance goals. PDUFA had a fixed term of five years, after which new legislation was required to reauthorize the program.

PDUFA transformed the FDA and brought an influx of new revenues for the agency's drug review division. The program created new rewards for the timely approval of new drugs. The performance goals and reporting requirements increased FDA accountability and allowed industry and other stakeholders to assess the agency's performance prior to the program's renewal. Agency administrators recognized that program renewal depended on their ability to meet the drug review targets. A failure to reduce delays could result in both nonrenewal of PDUFA at the end of five years and the loss of future fee revenues. The threat of nonrenewal created substantial political pressure for the agency to meet its drug review targets. The renewal process also allowed stakeholders to adjust the program to ensure its effectiveness. PDUFA had the support of patients and disease activists, medical professionals, and the pharmaceutical industry at the time of its passage. The drug industry, which had opposed user fees in the past, now supported the program largely because of the new agency performance goals introduced by Commissioner Kessler.

Agency performance dramatically changed under PDUFA. From 1992 to 1998, the mean review time for new chemical entities fell from thirty months to twelve months.[15] In addition to faster drug reviews, there was also an increase in the number of new drugs receiving FDA approval and the probability of FDA approval during this time. These changes represented a substantial departure from the delays in drug approval in the 1980s and early 1990s and showed that the FDA was successfully responding to the demands for speeding new drug approval under PDUFA. These factors contributed to the program's renewal in the 1997 Food and Drug Administration Modernization Act (PDUFA II) for another five years.

PDUFA II increased user fees, raised agency revenue targets, and lowered the review deadline for standard rated drugs from twelve months to ten months. PDUFA II added new performance goals to ensure the timeliness of communications between the FDA and sponsors during the process of clinical development. It included timelines for the FDA to schedule sponsor-requested meetings prior to the submission of INDs or NDAs, to resolve disputes with sponsors that arise during clinical development, to respond to sponsor questions about study protocols, and to develop guidance for industry. These new performance goals were a response to the problem of regulatory delays in the clinical development period. PDUFA II also included a provision allowing the FDA to accept a single large-scale controlled clinical study (instead of two) as "substantial evidence" of effectiveness, when deemed appropriate by the agency.

Both the new resources and the stronger incentives to meet drug review deadlines under PDUFA help explain the reductions in FDA review times. By 2002, drug industry user fees accounted for more than 60 percent of the agency's human drug review resources and roughly 15 percent of its overall agency budget. FDA drug review times had fallen by almost 60 percent since enactment of PDUFA. There was some evidence in 2003, from Ken Kaitin and Catherine Cairns, that clinical development times had fallen from a high of 7.2 years in 1993–1995 to 5.5 years in 1999–2001 under PDUFA II.[16] These factors led to another program renewal in the 2002 Public Health Security and Bioterrorism Preparedness and Response Act (PDUFA III). PDUFA III raised fees and revenue targets for the FDA. The program also expanded the FDA's interactions and communication with firms during testing phases and the review cycle, with the goal of providing firms with better information during the process to avoid unnecessary delays later. However, there were some unanticipated effects of PDUFA. Increased turnover among agency staff and an environment of intense pressure on reviewers to meet drug review deadlines raised concern that PDUFA was skewing the agency's focus on speedy review and approval at the expense of other agency activities and objectives.

SAFETY CONCERNS CHALLENGE PDUFA

Between the late 1990s and early 2000s, public concerns were beginning to emerge about drug safety following a number of high-profile drug withdrawals. In 2002, Mary Olson noted that in a relatively short period, between 1997 and 2001, ten FDA-approved drugs were withdrawn from the market for safety reasons.[17] In contrast, in 1995, Olav Bakke and his coauthors found that only ten drugs had been withdrawn from the market for safety reasons between 1974 and 1993.[18] This jump in the number of safety-related drug withdrawals in the PDUFA era raised new questions about the possible effects of this reform on the safety of new drugs. There were also reports about growing internal agency conflicts over drug safety. Many reviewers in the agency expressed concern that the quality of the drug review process had worsened during their tenure because of the time pressures created by PDUFA as reported in a 2003 study of the FDA's drug approval process by the Inspector General's Office in the Department of Health and Human Services.[19]

In debates during PDUFA's renewal in 2001, stakeholders discussed the potential for conflicts of interest by having the regulated industry fund drug reviews. Some stakeholders were also concerned about the lack of FDA funds for monitoring drug safety problems following FDA approval. Both consumer advocates and drug industry representatives agreed that post-marketing drug safety activities at the agency had been underfunded by Congress since the start of the PDUFA program. However, it is interesting to note that PDUFA prohibited the FDA from using any user fee revenues for its post-marketing drug safety activities prior to 2002. PDUFA user fee revenues could only support efforts to accelerate drug reviews and could not support other agency activities, such as post-marketing drug safety surveillance. In response to these concerns, policymakers relaxed this restriction in PDUFA III in 2002 and permitted some fee revenues to support limited post-marketing drug safety monitoring. However, questions about the effects of PDUFA on drug safety and on the potential for conflicts of interest inside the agency remained largely unresolved.

The Withdrawal of Vioxx and the FDA

In 2004, Merck withdrew its blockbuster arthritis drug Vioxx from the market for safety reasons, after evidence linked its use with increased risk of heart attacks and stroke since its approval in 1999. An FDA study found that the use of Vioxx, a Cox-2 anti-inflammatory drug, led to more than 27,000 heart attacks between 1999 and 2003.[20] The release of this information led to substantial scrutiny and criticism of the agency among the public, medical professionals, and policymakers. Medical professionals took the agency to task for its slow response to the evidence of increased heart attack risk with the drug.[21] At the time of Vioxx's withdrawal, Congress was investigating the agency over its handling of evidence relating to pediatric antidepressants and suicidal thinking in children. Those investigations revealed evidence of bias in the firm's publication strategy (seeking to publish only positive studies and to hide those with unfavorable results), which also reduced public confidence in the safety of drugs. Although controversy over pediatric antidepressants had set the stage, the withdrawal of the blockbuster drug Vioxx brought the public's concerns to a new level and reduced public confidence in the FDA. As politicians and the public questioned the agency's priorities in drug regulation in the PDUFA era, the calls for reform increased. In the wake of mounting criticism, the FDA asked the Institute of Medicine to convene a committee of experts from outside government to assess the U.S. drug safety system and make recommendations to improve the system.[22]

The Institute of Medicine's Report

The Institute of Medicine's (IOM) 2007 report identified important shortcomings in the U.S. drug safety system from its fifteen-month study. These problems include insufficient FDA authority and tools for addressing drug safety problems that occur after approval, underfunding of post-marketing drug safety activities, problems with the agency's organizational culture and coordination problems among agency staff, limited post-approval drug safety data, insufficient monitoring of drug safety after approval, ineffective communication of new risk information, and insufficient transparency/public access to a drug's benefit and risk information. The report noted that these problems had become more pronounced because of the pressures created by PDUFA as well as increases in the number, complexity, and potency of prescription drugs marketed, increases in use of drugs for chronic conditions, and other changes that affected the way in which drugs were being promoted, used, and prescribed.

To address these problems, the IOM report recommended that the FDA be given new duties, authorities, and resources to ensure drug safety, especially in the post-marketing period, and that the agency develop a lifecycle approach for the assessment of a drug's risks and benefits. The IOM report also recommended that the agency take numerous steps to restore agency accountability and transparency to the public by communicating safety concerns in a timely and effective way.[23] These findings combined with the crisis of public confidence in the FDA following the withdrawal of Vioxx increased the political pressure for congressional action.

RESPONDING TO NEW SAFETY CONCERNS UNDER PDUFA

The approaching renewal of PDUFA in 2007 created an opportunity for politicians to address public and professional concerns about the FDA's oversight of drug safety. PDUFA IV became a vehicle for Congress to strengthen the U.S. drug safety system. The 2007 Food and Drug Administration Amendments Act (PDUFA IV) not only reauthorized the user fee program, but also gave the FDA new authority, tools, and resources to identify and address drug safety problems that occur after a drug's approval. The 2007 act increased user fee revenues and allowed the agency to use those revenues for hiring new agency personnel to monitor and analyze drug safety after approval. It also included several provisions to increase agency accountability for drug safety by requiring the agency to increase the availability of risk-benefit information for the public, to improve risk communications to the public, and to increase the transparency of its decision making.

Although Vioxx was the source of much negative attention and controversy for the FDA, the scrutiny of the agency's policies following the Vioxx removal led to an expansion of FDA authority under the 2007 act. Unlike past expansions of regulatory authority, which focused on the pre-market screening process for new drugs, the 2007 act expanded the agency's powers in the period after a drug's launch, known as the post-marketing period.

The agency received new authority to require and enforce Phase IV post-marketing studies, which included studies agreed to as a condition of approval to address unresolved questions about a drug's effects. Although the agency could request such studies prior to 2007, it had lacked the necessary enforcement tools for ensuring the completion of such studies. Without such enforcement tools, it is not surprising that many firms had failed to complete their Phase IV studies. In a 2005 report by the consumer group Public Citizen, Larry Sasich and coauthors showed that among the most innovative new drugs approved from 1990 to 1994, 87 percent had not completed their phase IV studies five to ten years after approval.[24] In September 2004, there were 1,191 open post-marketing study commitments reported in the 2005 *Federal Register*, of which only 18 percent were ongoing, while 68 percent were pending or not yet initiated.[25] Failure to complete Phase IV studies, especially those agreed to as a condition of approval, left patients and physicians without essential risk-benefit information to make informed prescribing decisions. The 2007 act gave the FDA power to levy new fines and civil penalties against firms that did not complete their Phase IV study commitments, which ranged from $250,000 for each violation and to $10 million for an ongoing violation. The law also made the FDA responsible for tracking and reporting on the status of these studies annually to consumers in the *Federal Register*.

The 2007 law also gave the agency new tools, including Risk Evaluation and Mitigation Strategies (REMS), to help manage risks among marketed drugs after FDA approval. If the agency had concerns that a drug's use might be associated with serious unintended risks when marketed, it could require firms to develop REMS to help limit the potential risks, misuse, or abuse of a drug. Typical REMS could include provisions to ensure appropriate risk communication to patients (Medication Guides), safe use conditions, adequate prescriber education or training, and in some cases patient monitoring or patient registries. In addition, the agency gained new authority to require changes to safety labeling after approval in response to new risk information.

To restore public confidence in the FDA, the 2007 act also sought to increase agency accountability and transparency to the public in its expanded set of drug safety activities. The act required the agency to improve the availability of new risk information and the timeliness of risk communications to the public by conducting regular, biweekly screening of the Adverse Event Reporting System (AERS) database and posting a quarterly report of any new safety information or potential signals of serious risks identified through AERS on its Web site. The 2007 act also required the agency to conduct systematic evaluations of the safety of new drugs eighteen months after approval or after a drug's use by ten thousand patients in order to analyze any new potential safety issues and report its summary findings on its website for physicians and patients.

The FDA was also required to develop a more proactive system of identifying and analyzing post-marketing drug safety problems through its Sentinel initiative, which is a national electronic system for tracking product safety after approval. Sentinel offers a broad data network drawn from automated health care data systems such as electronic health records, administrative claims databases, and registries to allow the FDA to investigate potential drug safety issues quickly and securely. The 2007 act set new goals for the expansion of Sentinel and required FDA to work with partners from public, academic, and private entities to develop the system.

To help restore public confidence in the supply of drugs and the regulated industry, the 2007 act included new requirements for firms to increase transparency by disclosing more data to the public about all the clinical studies conducted for drugs. Firms were required to register within twenty-one days of the enrollment of the first patient all Phase II, III, and IV drug trials in the publically available National Institutes of Health online database, www.clinicaltrials.gov. The act required the creation of a clinical trials results database for approved drugs that, when fully implemented, will include a set of Internet links to key FDA documents, summary tables of primary and secondary outcomes, expanded results, and information about serious adverse events. Firms were required to submit clinical trials results within one year of the trial completion or within thirty days of a drug's approval.

MOVING FORWARD: FINDING A NEW BALANCE

In the modern era of drug regulation, policymakers have come to recognize that even with stringent preapproval evaluation requirements, some drugs that reach the market may harm consumers. The approach to reform taken in the 2007 act shows that current policymakers are not willing to sacrifice the gains made in accelerating drug access under PDUFA or accelerated approval programs to try to prevent future drug tragedies. Instead, the reform targets the agency's ability to track and respond to drug safety problems that occur after approval. The 2007 act strikes a new balance among the agency's safety and access goals. By strengthening the FDA's ability to identify, manage, and act on new safety problems that emerge after approval, policymakers hope to limit or reduce patients' exposure to drug-related risks.

If successful, then the agency could continue its efforts to accelerate drug access in the future. The 2012 FDA Safety and Innovation Act (PDUFA V) takes a step in this direction with its provisions to accelerate the development and approval of new antibiotics and other drugs serving unmet medical needs for life-threatening or rare diseases. The 2012 act also builds on past efforts to improve communications between firms and regulators during the FDA review processes by adding two new sponsor-agency meetings to make sure that sponsors are aware of REMS requirements or advisory committee issues earlier in the process in order to prevent unnecessary delays that could slow a drug's approval. If the efforts to strengthen post-marketing surveillance do not reduce serious drug-related risks for consumers and drug tragedies continue, then expect heightened political pressure for regulatory change.

The Regulation of Follow-on Biologics: New Challenges

The regulation of follow-on biologics (the analog to generic drugs) presents new challenges for the agency moving forward. Biologics are medicinal products derived from living organisms through recombinant DNA synthesis or other biotech processes. They are structurally more complex and have more inherent heterogeneity than chemically synthesized drugs. They offer high value and have been used to treat serious conditions such as cancer, rheumatoid arthritis, and multiple sclerosis, but they are also much more expensive than other drugs. Biologics currently represent the fastest-growing segment of the pharmaceutical industry.

FDA Authority to Regulate Tobacco Products

There has always been some ambiguity over whether the FDA should have a role in the regulation of tobacco products. The quandary facing the FDA was that if the product was deemed to be a drug intended to affect the structure and function of the body, it would have to be banned because it could not meet the agency's safety and efficacy criteria for approval. The prospect of such a ban was considered to be politically infeasible. Prior to the 1990s, previous agency leaders assumed that the agency lacked the jurisdiction to regulate tobacco. Only when cigarette manufacturers tried to make therapeutic claims about cigarettes (e.g., as a weight loss aid) did the agency act to challenge those claims.

By the early 1990s, smoking was known to be a dangerous public health problem. The addictive effects of nicotine as a drug were formally recognized in a 1988 Surgeon General's report. More than 400,000 preventable deaths per year were attributed to smoking-related diseases according to the Centers for Disease Control and Prevention. In response to citizen petitions from anti-tobacco groups who wanted the FDA to regulate cigarettes as a drug, David Kessler, the first presidentially appointed commissioner of the FDA, approached the problem from a different perspective. He assembled a small group of officials inside the FDA to more closely examine the question of FDA jurisdiction, assess whether a cigarette could be considered a drug, and explore the possible options for the regulation of tobacco. They collected enough new evidence to convince the commissioner that the industry had known about the addictive effects of nicotine and that tobacco firms had acted to increase the addictiveness of their products. This led the commissioner to begin to build a case for regulation.

The agency faced political obstacles in building its case, especially given the strength of the tobacco lobby among politicians. In the early 1990s, efforts to introduce tobacco control legislation languished in the House of Representatives. In 1994, those efforts got a boost when Commissioner Kessler provided testimony about the evidence gathered by his group about nicotine addictiveness and tobacco industry practices to increase addictiveness. A turning point came in spring 1995 when Commissioner Kessler delivered a speech at Columbia University in which he framed the issue of youth smoking as a pediatric disease that was on the rise. He also characterized cigarettes as nicotine delivery mechanisms and provided evidence that tobacco companies were aware of the addictive properties of nicotine and that they had been targeting young smokers. This characterization of smoking as a pediatric disease created new momentum and opportunities for the FDA to act.

The FDA used its rulemaking process to introduce regulations to curb youth access to cigarettes and smokeless tobacco products, while leaving them on the market for adults. The agency's final rule, published in 1996, established a federal minimum age of eighteen to purchase tobacco products and strengthened enforcement by requiring age verification as a condition of sale and banning most cigarette vending machines, free samples, and self-service displays. In addition, the rule limited advertising practices designed to attract children, required a minimum package size of twenty cigarettes, and required companies to launch a public health education campaign to make children aware of the dangers of smoking. The final rule set a goal to reduce by one-half children's use of tobacco products.

Tobacco manufacturer Brown & Williamson sued the FDA to prevent the implementation of the new youth access regulations. In 2000, in a 5–4 decision, the Supreme Court struck down the FDA's final rule, concluding that Congress had not given the agency authority to regulate tobacco. In the Court's majority opinion, however, the justices acknowledged smoking as "one of the most troubling public health problems facing our nation today" and indicated that the agency had provided ample evidence of a problem. The ruling basically shifted the emphasis to Congress to address the issue.

In 2009, Congress passed legislation providing the FDA with the jurisdiction to regulate the tobacco industry. Under the Family Smoking Prevention and Tobacco Prevention and Control Act, the FDA was directed to issue a final rule on cigarettes and smokeless tobacco that is identical to the provisions of the agency's 1996 final rule. The act gave the FDA authority to regulate tobacco sales, advertising, and labeling. The agency could create standards for tobacco products, but it could not require the elimination of nicotine content. The FDA could require stronger health warnings and the disclosure of nicotine content on cigarette labels. Although the FDA's 1996 final rule was overturned by the Supreme Court in 2000, it eventually became law because of the actions of David Kessler and the agency's case for reform.

SOURCES: Department of Health and Human Services, FDA, 21 C.F.R. Part 1140, *Federal Register* 75: 53 (2010): 13225, http://www.gpo.gov/fdsys/pkg/FR-2010-03-19/pdf/2010-6087.pdf; David Kessler, "Taking on Big Tobacco: David Kessler and the FDA" (C120-96-1349.3) (Cambridge, MA: Harvard University, Kennedy School of Government Case Program, 1997); David Kessler, *A Question of Intent: A Great American Battle with a Deadly Industry* (New York: Public Affairs, 2001); "Remarks by David A. Kessler, M.D., Commissioner of Food and Drugs," Columbia University School of Law, New York, March 8, 1995.

High prices for these valuable drugs and their increasing use by patients have led to heightened political pressure for cheaper alternatives. Unfortunately, the Hatch-Waxman Act does not apply to most biological products. Furthermore, the complexity of these products makes it impossible for follow-on manufacturers to establish bioequivalence or create identical copies of these drugs. With no established abbreviated pathway for the approval of follow-on biologics, there has been little price competition in biologic markets.

The Biologic Price Competition and Innovation Act, which passed as part of the 2010 Patient Protection and Affordable Care Act, gave the FDA the authority to develop an abbreviated pathway for the approval of follow-on biologics or biosimilars. The goal is to create more price competition for biological products after their patents expire, much like the competition observed in generic drug markets. The act establishes two levels of biosimilarity: highly similar, which implies that there are no clinically meaningful differences in terms of safety, purity, and potency; and interchangeable, which offers a more stringent standard that would allow the substitution of a follow-on drug for an originator's drug at the pharmacy level. The FDA has developed guidelines to help firms understand the requirements to establish a drug's biosimilarity. However, the FDA retains discretion to determine the nature of the requirements for biosimilarity on a case-by-case basis. Unlike the process for generic drugs, the abbreviated process for follow-on biologics is likely to be more complex, costly due to requirements for clinical study, and subject to more delays. This could increase uncertainty for firms and slow down the approval of follow-on biologics.

FUTURE DIRECTIONS FOR FDA POLICY

Clearly, interests for food and drug safety and drug access have influenced the evolution of FDA policy. While early pharmaceutical reforms were a response to public concern about the safety of the supply of drugs, later reforms were a response to concerns about delays in drug access. This chapter also illustrates how important changes in the agency's external environment have contributed to policy change. In particular, public health crises have led to a strengthening of drug safety regulations, which raised the cost of and delayed branded drug entry, while high prescription drug prices and the absence of price competition in branded drug markets have led to greater availability and access to generic drugs. The rise of the AIDS advocacy movement led to reforms to accelerate patient access to and approval of new AIDS medicines. The introduction of industry-funded user fees has resulted in faster reviews for all drugs and important changes in the regulatory landscape, some of which may have undermined the public's confidence in the agency.

Advances in drug innovation, complexity, and technology will continue to create new challenges for the agency, such as those described in the regulation of follow-on biologics.

In terms of the future direction of FDA policy, recent reforms provide some insight. Policies adopted after the withdrawal of Vioxx, for example, addressed problems revealed in the FDA's oversight of drug safety, but those reforms also preserved the agency's programs for accelerating drug access. The PDUFA program, in particular, has helped institutionalize the agency's commitment to accelerating drug access even in the event of drug tragedies. This suggests that the FDA has struck a new balance between safety and access goals in the modern era of pharmaceutical regulation. Restoring public confidence in the agency has been challenging, but the reforms to increase agency accountability, transparency in decision making, and the availability of risk-benefit information about drugs may help alleviate public and professional fears about conflicts of interest and skewed agency priorities in the PDUFA era.

See also **Chapter 3: The Department of Health and Human Services: Responsibilities and Policies (1953–Present); Chapter 4: The Centers for Disease Control and Prevention: Anticipatory Action in the Face of Uncertainty (1946–Present); Chapter 6: The Centers for Medicare and Medicaid Services (1965–Present); Chapter 7: The Departments of Defense and Veterans Affairs: Responsibilities and Policies (1947–Present); Chapter 8: The United States Supreme Court and the Department of Justice: Responsibilities and Policies (1789–Present); Chapter 9: Budgeting and Health Care Policy (1970s–Present).**

NOTES

1. William M. Wardell, Maureen S. May, and A. Gene Trimble, "New Drug Development by United States Pharmaceutical Firms," *Clinical Pharmacology and Therapeutics* 32 (1982): 407–417.
2. Joseph A. DiMasi, Ronald W. Hansen, and Henry G. Grabowski, "The Price of Innovation: New Estimates of Drug Development Costs," *Journal of Health Economics* 22: 2 (2003): 151–185.
3. See Sam Peltzman, "An Evaluation of Consumer Protection Legislation: The 1962 Drug Amendments," *Journal of Political Economy* 81 (1973): 1049–1091; Henry Grabowski, John Vernon, and Lacy G. Thomas, "Estimating the Effects of Regulation on Innovation: An International Comparative Analysis of the Pharmaceutical Industry," *Journal of Law and Economics* 21 (1978): 133–163; Peter Temin, *Taking Your Medicine: Drug Regulation in the United States* (Cambridge, MA: Harvard University Press, 1980).

4. William M. Wardell, "The Drug Lag Revisited: Comparison by Therapeutic Area of Patterns of Drugs Marketed in the United States and Great Britain from 1972 through 1976," *Clinical Pharmacology &Therapeutics* 24 (1978): 499–524.
5. Kenneth I. Kaitin et al., "The Drug Lag: An Update of New Drug Introductions in the United States and in the United Kingdom, 1977 through 1987," *Clinical Pharmacology & Therapeutics* 46: 2 (1989), 121–138.
6. U.S. Congress, Office of Technology Assessment, *Pharmaceutical R&D: Costs, Risks and Rewards*, OTA-H-522 (Washington, DC: U.S. Government Printing Office, February 1993).
7. Henry Grabowski and John Vernon, "Longer Patents for Increased Generic Competition in the US," *PharmacoEconomics* 10: Suppl 2 (1996): 110–123.
8. Mary K. Olson, "Regulatory Agency Discretion among Competing Industries: Inside the FDA," *Journal of Law, Economics, & Organization* 11 (1995): 379–405.
9. Ibid.

10. Mary K. Olson, "Regulatory Reform and Bureaucratic Responsiveness to Firms: The Impact of User Fees in the FDA," *Journal of Economics & Management Strategy* 9: 3 (2000): 363–395.

11. DiMasi, Hansen, and Grabowski, "The Price of Innovation."

12. Mary K. Olson, "Explaining Regulator Behavior in the FDA: Political Control vs. Agency Discretion," In *Advances in the Study of Entrepreneurship, Innovation, and Economic Growth, Volume 7,* edited by Gary Libecap, 71–108 (Greenwich, CT: JAI Press, 1996).

13. See "Letter from David A. Kessler, M.D., Comm. of Food and Drugs, to Rep. John D. Dingell & Rep. Norman Lent," *Congressional Record* (September 22, 1992): H9099-9100.

14. For all PDUFA performance goals, see "PDUFA Reauthorization Performance Goals and Procedures Fiscal Years 2013 through 2017," http://www.fda.gov/downloads/forindustry/userfees/prescriptiondruguserfee/ucm270412.pdf.

15. Mary K. Olson, "How Have User Fees Affected the FDA?" *Regulation* 25: 1 (2002): 20–25.

16. Kenneth I. Kaitin and Catherine Cairns, "The New Drug Approvals of 1999, 2000, and 2001: Drug Development Trends after the Passage of the Prescription Drug User Fee Act of 1992," *Drug Information Journal* 37 (2003): 357–371.

17. Mary K. Olson, "Pharmaceutical Policy and the Safety of New Drugs," *Journal of Law and Economics* 45: 2 (2002): 615–642.

18. Olav M. Bakke, Michael Manocchia, Francisco de Abajo, Kenneth I. Kaitin, and Louis Lasagna, "Drug Safety Discontinuations in the United Kingdom, the United States, and Spain from 1974 through 1993: A Regulatory Perspective," *Clinical Pharmacology & Therapeutics* 58: 1 (1995), 108–117.

19. Office of the Inspector General, Department of Health and Human Services, *FDA's Review Process for New Drug Applications: A Management Review* (OEI-01-01-00590) (Washington, DC: Department of Health and Human Services, March 2003).

20. Anna W. Mathews, "FDA Study Estimates Vioxx Linked to 27,000 Heart Attacks," Dow Jones Newswires, October 6, 2004.

21. See Eric J. Topel, "Failing the Public Health—Rofecoxib, Merck, and the FDA," *New England Journal of Medicine* 351: 17 (October 2004): 1707–1709; Barbara Martinez and Scott Hensley, "Cardiologist Calls for Inquiry into FDA's Handling of Vioxx," *Wall Street Journal*, October 7, 2004, B8.

22. Sandra Kweder, Statement before the Senate Finance Committee, U.S. Senate, November 18, 2004, http://www.finance.senate.gov/imo/media/doc/111804sktest.pdf.

23. Institute of Medicine, Committee on the Assessment of the U.S. Drug Safety System, *The Future of Drug Safety: Promoting and Protecting the Health of the Public* (Washington, DC: National Academy Press, 2007).

24. Larry Sasich, Peter Lurie, and Sydney M. Wolfe, *The Drug Industry's Performance in Finishing Post-marketing Research (Phase IV) Studies*, http://www.citizen.org/hrg1520.

25. Report on the Performance of Drug and Biologics Firms in Conducting Postmarketing Commitment Studies (Docket no. 2005N-0049), *Federal Register* 70: 33 (February 18, 2005).

FURTHER READING

Carpenter, Daniel. *Reputation and Power: Organizational Image and Pharmaceutical Regulation at the FDA*. Princeton, NJ: Princeton University Press, 2010.

Grabowski, Henry, John Vernon, and Lacy Glenn Thomas. "Estimating the Effects of Regulation on Innovation: An International Comparative Analysis of the Pharmaceutical Industry." *Journal of Law and Economics* 21 (1978): 133–163.

Institute of Medicine, Committee on the Assessment of the U.S. Drug Safety System. *The Future of Drug Safety: Promoting and Protecting the Health of the Public*. Washington, DC: National Academy Press, 2007.

Olson, Mary K. "Explaining Regulatory Behavior in the FDA: Political Control vs. Agency Discretion." In *Advances in the Study of Entrepreneurship, Innovation, and Economic Growth,* Volume 7, edited by Gary Libecap, 71–108. Bingley, UK: Emerald, 1996.

———. "Pharmaceutical Policy Change and the Safety of New Drugs." *Journal of Law and Economics* 45: 2 (2002): 615–642.

———. "Regulation of Safety, Efficacy, and Quality." In *Elsevier Encyclopedia of Health Economics*, edited by Anthony Culyer. United Kingdom: Elsevier, 2014.

———. "Regulatory Agency Discretion among Competing Industries: Inside the FDA." *Journal of Law, Economics & Organization* 11: 2 (1995): 379–405.

Peltzman, Sam. "An Evaluation of Consumer Protection Legislation: The 1962 Drug Amendments." *Journal of Political Economy* 81 (1973): 1049–1091.

Quirk, Paul J. "The Food and Drug Administration." In *The Politics of Regulation*, edited by James Q. Wilson. New York: Basic Books, 1980, chap. 6.

Temin, Peter. *Taking Your Medicine: Drug Regulation in the United States*. Cambridge, MA: Harvard University Press, 1980.

The Centers for Medicare and Medicaid Services (1965–Present)

Thomas R. Oliver

THE CENTERS FOR MEDICARE AND MEDICAID Services (CMS) is one of several important agencies within the U.S. Department of Health and Human Services (HHS). It helps pay for health services provided to more than 110 million Americans each year and is increasingly involved in shaping the organization, delivery, quality, and costs of health services for all Americans.

This chapter traces the agency's evolution since the mid-1960s, when the Medicare and Medicaid programs were established as part of the Great Society initiatives under President Lyndon B. Johnson (1963–1969). It begins by describing key administrative changes in the agency's history and its diverse contemporary portfolio of policies and programs and then outlines the main functions CMS performs in the U.S. health care system and how each function has expanded over time. Finally, it examines the political environment in which CMS operates and how that affects the accountability of the agency and its capacity to improve health system performance.

A BRIEF ADMINISTRATIVE HISTORY OF CMS

The Medicare and Medicaid programs were created at the same time—as Titles 18 and 19 of the Social Security Act, enacted in 1965. Yet they had very different beneficiaries, program structures, and administrative homes.[1] Medicare (Title 18) was a nearly universal social insurance program supported in part by mandatory payroll tax contributions of current workers in the expectation of health care coverage when those workers reached retirement age. As such, it was designed as a companion program to Social Security's old age and survivors' pensions and therefore was assigned to the Social Security Administration (SSA). The vision, as articulated by President Johnson, was that Medicare "will

take its place beside Social Security, and together they will form the twin pillars of protection upon which all our people can safely build their lives and their hopes."[2] The administrative and programmatic link to Social Security helped ensure a rapid and successful implementation of Medicare; in fact, it began providing coverage to nineteen million beneficiaries less than a year after legislative enactment.[3]

In contrast, Medicaid (Title 19) was designed for a low-income population with means-tested eligibility and was jointly paid for and administered by the federal government and states. It was commonly linked to cash assistance welfare programs and administered at the federal level by the Social and Rehabilitative Services Administration.

Changes under the Carter Administration

In 1977, at the request of President Jimmy Carter (1977–1981), Secretary Joseph Califano (in office 1977–1979) moved the Medicare and Medicaid programs to a new agency, the Health Care Financing Administration (HCFA) within the Department of Health, Education and Welfare (HEW). Among many reasons for the move, it was thought that SSA did not have sufficient expertise or organizational commitment to develop means to contain the rapidly rising costs of health care; it made little sense to have separate agencies running major health insurance programs, with some overlap of beneficiaries and administrative functions.[4] Also, it was seen by some as a stepping stone for implementing national health insurance should President Carter successfully pursue such an initiative.[5]

The new agency was not fully functional until June 1979, when HCFA completed the transfer of Medicaid staff from Washington to Baltimore to join the Medicare staff from the nearby offices of SSA.[6] The SSA remained as a separate agency in HEW and later became an independent agency in 1995.[7] Although the intent of the Carter administration

FIGURE 6.1 **Centers for Medicare and Medicaid Services**

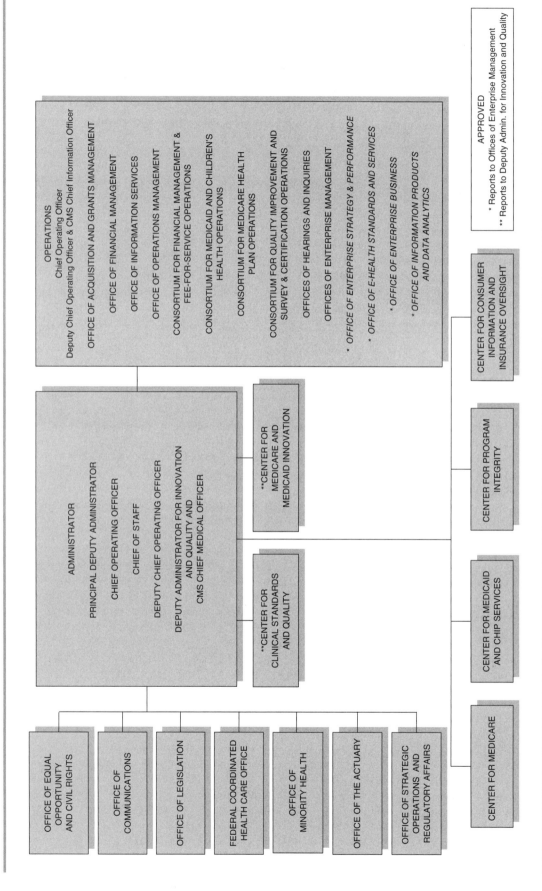

SOURCE: Centers for Medicare and Medicaid Services, "CMS Organizational Chart," http://www.cms.gov/About-CMS/Agency-Information/CMSLeadership/OrganizationalChartASP.html.

was to integrate the management of Medicare and Medicaid, full integration was and still is impossible due to the variation in eligibility, benefits, payment systems, and other program features along with the substantial role of states in the governance of Medicaid. The new agency was able to consolidate operations in the areas of quality assurance, program integrity (prosecuting fraud and abuse), and research and policy development.[8] In addition, it went from being simply a very large payer of health care bills to playing a leadership role in the nation's rapidly changing health care system.[9]

Further Reorganizations under Clinton, Bush, and Obama

A major reorganization of HCFA occurred under administrator Bruce Vladeck (in office 1993–1997) in 1997. The agency established new operations around its three main customers in the Center for Beneficiary Services, Center for Health Plans and Providers, and Center for Medicaid and State Operations (with states as partners for both Medicaid and the new State Children's Health Insurance Program [SCHIP]). The reorganization caused substantial disruption and confusion internally among staff transferred to new positions and externally among providers and other stakeholders in agency programs. However, it helped HCFA implement a major new set of responsibilities thrust upon it by the Balanced Budget Act of 1997, negotiated by President William J. Clinton (1993–2001) and congressional leaders.[10]

In 2001, the administration of President George W. Bush (2001–2009) undertook additional reorganization and gave the agency its current name, the Centers for Medicare and Medicaid Services. The name change was intended to better reflect the mission and commitment to be more responsive to health care consumers and providers.[11] It also would benefit the agency, presumably, to feature the names of its cornerstone programs with tens of millions of beneficiaries.

Under President Barack Obama (2009–), the agency was again assigned major new responsibilities in the wake of the American Recovery and Reinvestment Act of 2009 (ARRA) and the Patient Protection and Affordable Care Act of 2010 (PPACA). The most notable health provisions in ARRA were measures to expand adoption and meaningful use of electronic health records—an area in which the United States lags well behind most other advanced industrial countries.[12] The PPACA included hundreds of changes to CMS's existing programs and, importantly, added significant regulation of private health insurance and the development of new health insurance exchanges.

The current organization of CMS includes consolidated financial, information technology, and legal operations and several offices for specific administrative tasks. The main programmatic responsibilities of the agency are organized into six centers: Center for Medicare, Center for Medicaid and CHIP Services, Center for Program Integrity, Center for Consumer Information and Insurance Oversight, Center for Clinical Standards and Quality, and Center for Medicare and Medicaid Innovation (see Figure 6.1).

CURRENT ROLES OF CMS IN U.S. HEALTH POLICY

CMS is a relatively small agency as measured by its workforce. With 5,994 employees as of October 2013, CMS is considerably smaller than many of its sister agencies in the Department of Health and Human Services. The Centers for Disease Control and Prevention (CDC) with 12,825 employees, Food and Drug Administration (FDA) with 14,800 employees, Indian Health Service (IHS) with 15,541 employees, and National Institutes of Health (NIH) with 18,646 employees, are each two to three times as large as CMS.[13] The current number of employees at CMS is actually a substantial increase from its historical level of approximately 4,000 to 4,500, following a boost in staff to help implement provisions of ARRA and the PPACA.

By other measures, CMS is larger by far than any other federal government agency. It is projected to spend $901 billion in program benefits for an estimated 116 million Medicare, Medicaid, and CHIP beneficiaries in fiscal year 2014—more than one in three Americans.[14] The three public health insurance programs account for more than one-quarter of the entire federal budget, more than Social Security, defense spending, or all non-defense discretionary spending.[15]

The agency will spend an estimated $35 billion more on program administration, fraud and abuse enforcement, quality improvement organizations, and implementation of new insurance market reforms under the PPACA.[16] Although the administrative expenses are considerable, they constitute less than 4 percent of CMS spending on services for beneficiaries. Less than 1 percent of CMS's budget, in fact, is spent on the administration of Medicare, Medicaid, and CHIP themselves; that is an extraordinarily lean—some would argue too lean—amount of administrative resources given the scope and complexity of the agency's responsibilities and compared to private health insurance plans in the United States.[17]

Over time, the programs and policies assigned to CMS have expanded dramatically. While the agency's name highlights two very large, complicated programs—Medicare and Medicaid—it plays an even larger role in the health care system and U.S. social policy. Beryl Radin, in her study of HHS, noted the "highly diverse issue portfolio" of the department as a whole, with its many strategies to improve health, including the following:

- provision of resources for treatment or services
- support of research
- development of demonstration efforts
- requirements for or support of evaluations

- data collection, development of data systems, and information provision
- prevention programs
- public education
- regulation
- development of standards
- devising of partnerships
- support of or requirement for training
- provision or support of technical assistance
- support of outreach efforts to improve access to services
- improvement of state or local infrastructure
- improvement in the management of programs[18]

Today, CMS itself is involved in nearly all of these strategies. They help the agency fulfill four basic functions in the U.S. health care system: financing, regulation, innovation, and intergovernmental guidance and oversight. In addition, they fill a critical role in U.S. social policy in moderating the impact of economic and social inequalities.

Financing

The most visible function of CMS is financing of personal health services through Medicare, Medicaid, and CHIP. Although beneficiaries bear some financial responsibility for coverage under Medicare and CHIP, and states bear substantial responsibility for coverage under Medicaid and CHIP, the bulk of financing for all three programs is through federal revenues. The administrative challenges associated with each program have expanded over time through population growth, new eligibility standards, new benefits, and new payment systems. As of 2014, 38 million beneficiaries in the traditional fee-for-service program will generate more than 1.2 billion claims for payment by private claims administration contractors, and CMS will maintain more than 650 contracts with Medicare Advantage plans, covering 15.3 million beneficiaries.[19]

In 1972, Congress authorized Medicare coverage for individuals under age sixty-five with end-stage renal disease (requiring kidney dialysis) and those qualifying for permanent disability benefits from Social Security. Over time, Medicare also added coverage for hospice care, home health services, subacute hospital care, and outpatient prescription drugs. Beginning in 1983, a series of prospective payment systems was introduced to replace cost or charge-based reimbursement for inpatient hospital care, physician services, nursing home care, and home health care.[20] The new payment systems required considerable technical work within HCFA as well as its regional "fiscal intermediaries" and "carriers," private insurance companies that Medicare contracted with to review and pay claims from providers. In addition, legislation in 1982, 1997, and 2003 promoted membership in private health plans (now Medicare Advantage) as an alternative to the traditional coverage through Medicare Part A and Part B for almost all beneficiaries.[21]

Throughout the late 1980s and early 1990s, a series of federal laws expanded Medicaid eligibility for pregnant women, infants, and children up to age eighteen. Other legislative changes made more individuals, both under and over age sixty-five, eligible for long-term care.[22] By 2010, only 6 percent of Medicaid beneficiaries required long-term services and supports, either in institutional or community-based settings, but they accounted for 43 percent of all program spending.[23]

Through the PPACA, several million individuals who were previously uninsured will gain coverage through Medicaid. The expansion will not be as large as originally designed due to the Supreme Court decision in June 2012 that upheld the constitutionality of most elements of the PPACA but made expanded Medicaid eligibility, and federal funding for that purpose, an option rather than a requirement for state governments.

Regulation

CMS develops and administers regulations intended to protect not only the beneficiaries of its health insurance programs but also virtually all individuals receiving health care in the United States. The agency's regulatory function includes a wide range of activities dealing with issues from quality assurance to provider fraud to patient privacy. It fulfills its regulatory function directly and indirectly, often relying on key governmental and nongovernmental partners.

In the area of health care quality, CMS defers to the Joint Commission, the National Committee on Quality Assurance, and professional licensing bodies to certify the quality of health care facilities and health plans and to keep them eligible to receive Medicare and Medicaid payments. Other quality assurance is carried out through contracts with local Peer Review Organizations. Under the PPACA, a small proportion of hospitals' payments will be subject to satisfactory quality performance indicators. In addition, hospitals will be denied payments for "preventable readmissions," that is, care delivered to patients for conditions that could have been avoided through better in-hospital or follow-up care.[24]

Another aspect of health care quality is laboratory testing. Under the Clinical Laboratory Improvement Amendments of 1988, CMS shares responsibility with the FDA and the CDC for establishing and enforcing quality standards for all testing of specimens derived from humans in approximately 244,000 laboratory facilities. The goal is to ensure the accuracy, reliability, and timeliness of test results regardless of where the test was performed. The CMS Center for Clinical Standards and Quality also works hand in hand with state health departments, which are charged with conducting inspections required for state and federal certification.[25]

Over time, CMS has assumed a greater role in regulation of private insurance, traditionally an area reserved to state regulation. This role began with federal oversight and eventually standardization of "Medigap" policies sold to Medicare beneficiaries to cover the out-of-pocket costs for premiums, deductibles, and coinsurance in the traditional free-for-service program. It expanded when the Health Insurance Portability and Accountability Act of 1996 (HIPAA) established limited federal regulation of individual and small-group health insurance to protect access to health insurance for workers who change or lose jobs.[26] A second part of HIPAA has had far greater long-term impact; it requires HHS to establish and enforce national standards to both promote electronic health care transactions and protect individually identifiable patient records from being shared without the patient's permission.[27] This enormous task fell to CMS, which as of 2014 is implementing supplemental regulations to HIPAA security and privacy standards based on provisions in the PPACA.

The "My Healthcare, My Medicare" bus, sponsored by the Centers for Medicare and Medicaid Services, brings health care information to people across the country. Health care providers on the bus also make vaccines and inoculations available.

SOURCE: Mark Wilson/Getty Images.

CMS is actively engaged in efforts to prevent, detect, and prosecute fraud and abuse in Medicare, Medicaid, and CHIP. In general, fraud is the intentional billing for services or supplies not provided or altering claims to receive a higher payment. Abuse is billing for care that is not medically necessary, does not meet professional standards, or is not fairly priced. Providers and suppliers found guilty of such practices are subject to substantial civil and criminal penalties. The Center for Program Integrity at CMS has increasing data and analytic capacity, and works with the HHS Office of the Inspector General and the U.S. Department of Justice to investigate and prosecute potential fraud and abuse.[28] Major initiatives in the past have produced considerable savings, particularly after HIPAA and the Balanced Budget Act of 1997 added new incentives and resources for CMS in this area. The agency has been criticized, however, for information and analytical techniques that tend to catch unintentional billing errors and fail to detect systematic, intentional submission of fraudulent claims.[29]

Innovation

Leonard Schaeffer, the second administrator of HCFA (in office 1978–1980), asserted the agency's responsibility "to lead and leverage change in health care nationally" and attempted to instill a new organizational culture to do so.[30] This ambition revealed how much times had changed since 1965, when the legislation creating Medicare had enunciated the principle that governmental policy was not to interfere with the practice of medicine.[31] In fact, virtually from their inception, Medicare and Medicaid dramatically altered medical practice and the U.S. health care system. The challenge was to identify tools that could rein in the exploding costs of these programs and ensure that the positive effects they were making in people's lives would continue well into the future.

Over time, CMS has developed several tools for health care innovation. Dating back to 1972, the agency had authority to conduct research and demonstrations of new health care arrangements and policies. The results of such activities have been mixed. Perhaps the greatest success is the development of prospective payment systems for hospitals, physicians, nursing homes, and home health services.

Beginning in the 1980s, the agency negotiated with states over proposed waivers to expand Medicaid eligibility, covered services, and other program operations. Section 1915c waivers allowed states to develop home- and community-based services in lieu of care provided in hospitals and nursing homes, particularly for patients with long-term care needs. Section 1915b waivers allowed states to enroll Medicaid beneficiaries in managed care plans, trading their freedom of choice in providers for a more organized, comprehensive, and accessible system of care. This included the development of case management for beneficiaries with chronic health problems and special "carve outs" for the delivery of mental health and substance abuse services. Section 1115 waivers allowed states to conduct Medicaid demonstration projects, typically to expand eligibility to additional beneficiaries while implementing other reforms to maintain budget neutrality.[32] Among the most notable of the Section 1115 demonstrations was the Oregon Health Plan.[33] States were granted even more waiver options under the Health Insurance Flexibility and

Accountability demonstrations established by CMS in 2001 under President George W. Bush.

The PPACA has given new momentum to CMS efforts in the area of health system innovation. The Center for Medicare and Medicaid Innovation is heavily engaged in the demonstration of Accountable Care Organizations (ACOs), which are enthusiastically supported by former CMS administrators Mark McClellan (in office 2004–2006) and Donald Berwick (in office 2010–2011). The ACOs are groups of providers who voluntarily agree to take clinical and financial responsibility for the care of a defined population of patients. Through modified payments ("shared savings"), the ACOs are encouraged to provide more comprehensive, coordinated care than is typical under Medicare's regular payments and thereby improve the quality and efficiency of care. Thus far, 366 organizations across the United States caring for approximately 5.3 million Medicare beneficiaries have signed up to participate in the ACO program.[34]

In addition, CMS is running three major initiatives to accelerate adoption of patient-centered medical homes to improve the quality of primary care. The agency is working with eight states on the Multi-Payer Advanced Primary Care Practice demonstration. It is directly operating the Federally Qualified Health Center PCMH demonstration in five hundred sites and has mounted a new Comprehensive Primary Care Initiative, also involving five hundred practice sites. The last demonstration is run by the Center for Medicare and Medicaid Innovation, which has authority under the PPACA to scale up successful pilot projects without the need for congressional approval.[35]

Finally, CMS is responsible for developing new health insurance exchanges (marketplaces) authorized under the PPACA for individuals and small groups who do not have access to employer-sponsored health plans that meet standards of comprehensiveness and affordability. Many states elected to develop marketplaces on their own, with CMS guidance and approval. More than thirty states, however, relied on CMS to set up a federally facilitated marketplace (Healthcare.gov). Although the initial online enrollment suffered major problems and delays, in a remarkable turnaround, enrollment in the new health insurance marketplaces stood at more than eight million by March 2014, exceeding first-year projections by the Congressional Budget Office and the White House.[36,37]

SOCIAL POLICY

The programs administered by CMS are at once health care programs and instruments of broader social policy. They serve a number of purposes. Medicare, along with Social Security, is a critical source of income security in a society with widening economic disparities. The percentage of senior citizens in poverty is only about one-third of the level in the early 1960s, and Medicare is an important part of that improvement. Even

with retirement income from Social Security, half of all Medicare beneficiaries have an annual income below $22,502, twice the federal poverty level, and half have savings below $77,482, less than the cost of a single year of care in a skilled nursing home.[38] The financial protection of Medicare, therefore, keeps millions of beneficiaries from sliding into poverty during an already vulnerable period of life.

Medicare, CHIP, and an expanded Medicaid program have helped establish a far more egalitarian health care system. Each program dramatically improves access to health services, with utilization by beneficiaries generally approximating that of privately insured individuals and far above utilization by uninsured individuals. All participants, regardless of their social or economic status, in theory have access to the same facilities and quality of care as Americans with the best private insurance.

Medicare's most overt impact on social policy was the racial desegregation of hospitals in the South and Southwest and the desegregation of residency training programs throughout the country. Officials in the Johnson administration, from the president down, decided to apply the 1964 Civil Rights Act as they implemented Medicare in July 1966. They made clear that hospitals, in order to receive Medicare payments, would have to demonstrate that patients throughout inpatient wards were not segregated by race. In addition, all other aspects of hospital operations—staffing, food and water, and restrooms—were required to be desegregated. Volunteers from the district offices of Social Security, as well as public health officers directed by the Surgeon General, were recruited to carry out the inspections. In contrast to the federal government's role in school desegregation efforts, which began a decade earlier and continues in some communities to this day, the use of Medicare's economic power made an immediate and systematic impact on hospital desegregation, although various forms of discrimination continued under various guises even into the 1980s.[39] It should be noted that HEW officials did not attempt to desegregate ambulatory services, which would have posed a significantly more complex, decentralized, and costly enforcement problem.

Just as Medicaid has inadvertently become the largest payer for nursing home care, Medicare has inadvertently become the primary funder of graduate medical education, spending about $10 per year for the training and care provided by medical residents. Medicare and Medicaid serve another social purpose by making special payments to hospitals presumed to bear a large burden of uncompensated care. Hospitals with a disproportionate share of low-income patients, especially urban teaching hospitals, annually receive over $20 billion in payments from CMS.

Since the mid-1980s, Medicare has been the focal point of efforts to preserve rural health care systems, which are important to ensure reasonable equity in access to services for all beneficiaries and, in the eyes of Congress, as vital employers in rural economies. When the Medicare prospective payment

President Obama's Speech on Eight Million Enrolled

Enrollment in President Barack Obama's signature health care plan, the Patient Protection and Affordable Care Act of 2010, began with a rocky start, delaying the enrollment of many Americans. After resolving computer glitches and rebuilding the enrollment Web site, as well as extending the enrollment deadline, President Obama claimed victory in a speech on April 17, 2014, saying, "And this thing is working!" He went on to mention the extension of the Medicare Trust Fund:

I'd . . . like to say a few words about how the Affordable Care Act is now covering more people at less cost than most would have predicted just a few months ago.

The first open enrollment period under this law ended a little over two weeks ago. And as more data comes in, we now know that the number of Americans who've signed up for private insurance in the marketplaces has grown to 8 million people—8 million people. Thirty-five percent of people who enrolled through the federal marketplace are under the age of 35. All told, independent experts now estimate that millions of Americans who were uninsured have gained coverage this year—with millions more to come next year and the year after.

We've also seen signs that the Affordable Care Act is bringing economic security to more Americans. Before this law added new transparency and competition to the individual market, folks who bought insurance on their own regularly saw double-digit increases in their premiums. That was the norm. And while we suspect that premiums will keep rising, as they have for decades, we also know that since the law took effect health care spending has risen more slowly than at any time in the past 50 years.

In the decade before the Affordable Care Act, employer-based insurance rose almost 8 percent a year. Last year, it grew at half that rate. Under this law, real Medicare costs per person have nearly stopped growing. The life of the Medicare Trust Fund has been extended by 10 years. And the independent Congressional Budget Office now expects premiums for plans on the marketplace to be 15 percent lower than originally predicted.

So those savings add up to more money that families can spend at businesses, more money that businesses can spend hiring new workers. And the CBO now says that the Affordable Care Act will be cheaper than recently projected. Lower costs from coverage provisions will shrink our deficits by an extra $100 billion.

So the bottom line is, under the Affordable Care Act, the share of Americans with insurance is up, the growth of health care costs is down. Hundreds of millions of Americans who already have insurance now have new benefits and protections from free preventive care to freedom from lifetime caps on your care. No American with a preexisting condition like asthma or cancer can be denied coverage. No woman can be charged more just for being a woman. Those days are over. And this thing is working. . . .

SOURCE: "Press Conference by the President, 4/17/14," http://www.whitehouse.gov/the-press-office/2014/04/17/press-conference-president-41714.

system for inpatient hospital care was authorized in 1983, it threatened rural hospitals that relied on cost-based reimbursement to support a wide array of services despite relatively low volume of utilization. Congress directed that sole community hospitals in rural areas be paid the same DRG rate as urban hospitals—a rate higher than the costs of direct care of Medicare patients—to compensate for the limited census of patients and ensure the availability of acute care in many communities. Similarly, many rural hospitals qualify as "critical access hospitals" and receive payments set at 101% of reasonable costs for inpatient and outpatient services.[40]

THE POLITICAL ENVIRONMENT OF CMS AND ITS FUTURE

Scholars of bureaucracy have long observed that the capacity of a governmental agency depends on the relationships it has with important constituencies affected by its policies and programs.[41] Power flows not only down the organizational hierarchy from the president's priorities and support

but also from the bottom and sides via the attentive public (recipients of services, contractors, industry groups) and their ability to hold an agency accountable through direct pressure or through congressional oversight.

On the face of it, CMS should be widely appreciated for its stewardship of important entitlement programs, its tremendous financial support for beneficiaries and the health care industry, and its contributions to the significant gains in life expectancy in the United States since the 1960s. In reality, CMS operates in a difficult political environment that commonly features indifference or outright hostility.

When HCFA was established in the late 1970s, the Medicare program left the beneficiary-oriented culture and power base of SSA and entered a far more complicated political environment. The new agency's priorities shifted from the relatively simple task of ensuring access to services for beneficiaries through provider-friendly payment systems to the more challenging task of balancing the interests of patients and providers against the interests of taxpayers. In addition, Medicaid beneficiaries were viewed less favorably by policymakers and the general public, and as HCFA and then CMS assumed responsibilities for greater regulation of private insurance, the constellation of stakeholders shifted even further and placed greater demands on the agency.

James Q. Wilson examined how the interests at stake in an agency's policies and programs affect its ability to carry out its administrative responsibilities.[42] Today, the favorable "client politics" of Medicare, Medicaid, and CHIP—with their concentrated benefits for patients and diffuse costs to taxpayers—are often overshadowed by the contentious "entrepreneurial politics" of regulating health insurance practices and restraining payments—with their concentrated costs to health plans, suppliers, and providers and diffuse benefits for beneficiaries and taxpayers.[43] Even when concentrated benefits authorized by the PPACA are noticed—as they surely are by young adults who can remain on their parents' insurance coverage through age 25, by individuals with pre-existing conditions who can now obtain affordable coverage, or by seniors who get more of their prescription drug costs covered by Medicare—individuals do not connect those benefits to CMS, the agency responsible for ensuring compliance with legislation, because most of the changes come through private insurance plans.

When pressure for cost containment produces concessions from industry and professional groups, they look for opportunities to undo those deals. Since 1999, organized medicine has regularly sought and received from Congress reprieves from scheduled reductions in physician payments based on the Balanced Budget Act of 1997 and earlier reforms; the tactic is now so routine that it is referred to as the "doc fix," even though the likelihood that the implied threat by physicians to not accept Medicare patients will become a reality is highly unlikely.[44]

Entrepreneurial politics also are at play with industry efforts to repeal excise taxes on medical devices and private health plan premiums that were included in the PPACA; the quid pro quo was that the industry would gain millions of new paying customers, and the tax revenues would contribute toward the subsidies needed for low- and medium-income individuals and families signing up for coverage through the insurance marketplaces. The legislation also reduced payments to Medicare Advantage plans based on analysis that showed payments originally authorized under the Medicare Modernization Act of 2003 were substantially higher than the actual costs of care for enrolled beneficiaries.[45] The insurance industry is now mounting a campaign decrying the reduced payments, labeling them a "Medicare tax," in an effort to frighten beneficiaries into thinking their benefits will be reduced or quality of care will suffer, and encouraging them to join in the campaign to restore higher payments.

The political environment for CMS also includes the majoritarian politics associated with public health insurance and health care reform, with diffuse benefits and diffuse costs perceived by citizens and policymakers based on their broad

political values and ideology. As had occurred several decades earlier, with Social Security, the partisan conflict present during the creation of Medicare and Medicaid eventually subsided, and the general public and policymakers came to accept them as appropriate parts of a limited but growing American welfare state. The governance of health policy was largely bipartisan and progressed under both Republican and Democratic leadership in the White House and Congress.[46]

After the political furor and collapse of the health care reform proposals by President Clinton in 1994 and the subsequent election of new Republican majorities and leadership in both houses of Congress, the politics of consensus turned to a politics of dissensus.[47] What ensued is an extended battle, now two decades long, over the "modernization" of Medicare—a euphemism promoted primarily by conservatives who have continually set forth plans to shift all beneficiaries out of the traditional fee-for-service program into private health plans and shift more financial risk to both beneficiaries and health plans.[48]

Classical liberalism has always served as an ideological context for everything that CMS does.[49] Such a context gives primacy to individuals and markets, limiting collective responses even to near-universal problems such as the affordability of health insurance. The skepticism of government is evident even in periods of program expansion: while the Medicare Modernization Act and the PPACA both offered millions of Americans subsidies for health care coverage, the new coverage came primarily through private insurance companies rather than through "single payer" options. Still, the effort to placate private interests has not produced a settled, let alone supportive, environment for implementation of the PPACA. If anything, there is even greater animus toward government with the rise of the Tea Party wing of the Republican Party and its extreme hostility to what it calls "Obamacare."

Finally, the political environment for CMS includes constant interplay with state governments. States serve as partners in the Medicaid and CHIP programs, in licensing and certification of providers, and in insurance regulation. They also push CMS for greater autonomy in program design and management through waiver applications and other means. However, other state officials are not the only ones pressuring CMS to grant waivers and specific waiver provisions; the White House and many interest groups also get involved in intergovernmental bargaining on the highest profile requests.[50]

A political environment that is commonly hostile to CMS or the programs it administers has real consequences. The agency routinely has fewer administrative resources than it needs to perform progressively more complex and difficult responsibilities such as fraud and abuse enforcement, enforcing HIPAA's security and privacy rules, and building and regulating an online insurance marketplace under the PPACA. Administrators and close observers have for many years acknowledged the inability of the agency to adequately staff new initiatives.[51] In particular, CMS has had difficulty recruiting and retaining technical experts in the agency in areas such as information technology and clinical quality.

CMS GOING FORWARD

Few if any government agencies touch the lives of so many Americans in such important ways as CMS. Through its roles in health care financing, regulation, and innovation, CMS provides access to services for more than 100 million beneficiaries and is a critical leader in national health care reform. Over several decades, the agency has also served as an instrument of broader social policy, from enforcing civil rights to sustaining rural communities.

The effectiveness of CMS, now and in the future, depends on three things. First, it must secure adequate resources for an expanding set of responsibilities. Second, it must develop workable public-private partnerships to establish, refine, and sustain strategies for higher performing health systems. Third, it must adequately negotiate an uncertain and often unsupportive political environment so that, in the end, the agency succeeds in doing what is needed to help the beneficiaries who depend on it for health and financial security.

See also **Chapter 3: The Department of Health and Human Services: Responsibilities and Policies (1953–Present); Chapter 4: The Centers for Disease Control and Prevention: Anticipatory Action in the Face of Uncertainty (1946–Present); Chapter 5: The Food and Drug Administration (1962–Present); Chapter 8: The United States Supreme Court and the Department of Justice (1789–Present); Chapter 13: Government Financing of Health Care (1940s–Present); Chapter 18: Health and Health Care Policy: Ethical Perspectives (1970s–Present).**

NOTES

1. Theodore R. Marmor, *The Politics of Medicare,* 2nd ed. (New York: Transaction, 2000).
2. Nancy-Ann Min DeParle, "Celebrating 35 Years of Medicare and Medicaid," *Health Care Financing Review* 22 (Fall 2000): 1.
3. National Academy of Social Insurance, "Matching Problems with Solutions: Improving Medicare's Governance and Management" (Washington, DC: National Academy of Social Insurance, 2002), 24.
4. Ibid.
5. Robert A. Derzon, "The Genesis of HCFA," *Health Affairs* (July 26, 2005): W5-326.
6. Centers for Medicare and Medicaid Services, "Why Is CMS in Baltimore?" http://www.cms.gov/About-CMS/Agency-Information/History/Downloads/CMSInBaltimore.pdf.
7. In 1979, Congress split the Department of Health, Education and Welfare into two separate and reorganized entities: the Department of Education, which began operations in 1980, and the Department of Health and Human Services.
8. Derzon, "The Genesis of HCFA," W5-328.
9. Leonard D. Schaeffer, "Turning Medicare and Medicaid into Health Programs: The Role of Organizational Culture," *Health Affairs* (26 July 2005): W5-330.
10. National Academy of Social Insurance, "Matching Problems with Solutions," 25.
11. Ibid.
12. Bradford H. Gray, Thomas Bowden, Ib Johansen, and Sabine Koch, "Electronic Health Records: An International Perspective on 'Meaningful Use'" (New York: Commonwealth Fund, 2011).
13. Department of Health and Human Services, "Contingency Staffing Plan for Operations in the Absence of Enacted Annual Appropriations," http://www.hhs.gov/budget/fy2014/fy2014contingency_staffing_plan-rev2.pdf.
14. Centers for Medicare and Medicaid Services, "Justification of Estimates for Appropriations Committees, Fiscal Year 2014,"

http://www.cms.gov/About-CMS/Agency-Information/PerformanceBudget/Downloads/FY2014-CJ-Final.pdf, 2.
15. Congressional Budget Office, *The Budget and Economic Outlook: 2014 to 2024* (Washington, DC: Congressional Budget Office, February 2014), http://www.cbo.gov/publication/45010.
16. Centers for Medicare and Medicaid Services, "Justification."
17. John Iglehart, Doing More with Less: A Conversation with Kerry Weems. *Health Affairs* 28: 4 (2009): 688–696.
18. Beryl A. Radin, *The Accountable Juggler: The Art of Leadership in a Federal Agency* (Washington, DC: CQ Press, 2002), 49–50.
19. U.S. Government Accountability Office, *Medicare: Contractors and Private Plans Play a Major Role in Administering Benefits* (GAO-14-417T) (Washington, DC: U.S. Government Accountability Office, March 4, 2014), 1.
20. These are examined in more detail in Chapters 17 and 22 in this volume.
21. Thomas R. Oliver, "Medicare," in *Governing America,* edited by Paul J. Quirk and William Cunion, 651–661 (New York: Facts on File, 2011).
22. David G. Smith, *Entitlement Politics* (New York: Aldine de Gruyter, 2002), 24–30. See also Chapter 22 in this volume.
23. Kaiser Family Foundation, "Medicaid Long-Term Services and Supports (LTSS) Users Accounted for Nearly Half of Medicaid Spending, FY 2010," http://kff.org/medicaid/slide/medicaid-long-term-services-and-supports-ltss-users-accounted-for-nearly-half-of-medicaid-spending-fy-2010.
24. "Medicare Hospital Readmissions Reduction Program," *Health Affairs* (November 12, 2013), https://www.healthaffairs.org/healthpolicybriefs/brief.php?brief_id=102.
25. U.S. Food and Drug Administration, "Clinical Laboratory Improvement Amendments (CLIA)," http://www.fda.gov/medicaldevices/deviceregulationandguidance/ivdregulatoryassistance/ucm124105.htm.
26. Randall R. Bovbjerg, "Alternative Models of Federalism: Health Insurance Regulation and Patient Protection Laws," in *Federalism and Health Policy,* edited by John Holohan, Alan

Weil, and Joshua Wiener, 366–368 (Washington, DC: Urban Institute, 2003).

27. Centers for Medicare and Medicaid Services, "Health Insurance Portability and Accountability Act of 1996," http://www.cms.gov/Regulations-and-Guidance/HIPAA-Administrative-Simplification/HIPAAGenInfo/Downloads/HIPAALaw.pdf.

28. Centers for Medicare and Medicaid Services, "Medicare Fraud and Abuse: Prevention, Detection, and Reporting," November 2012, https://www.cms.gov/Outreach-and-Education/Medicare-Learning-Network-MLN/MLNProducts/downloads/Fraud_and_Abuse.pdf.

29. National Academy of Social Insurance, "Matching Problems with Solutions," 48–51.

30. Schaeffer, "Turning Medicare and Medicaid into Health Programs."

31. Thomas R. Oliver, "Analysis, Advice, and Congressional Leadership: The Physician Payment Review Commission and the Politics of Medicare," *Journal of Health Politics, Policy and Law* 18 (Spring 1993): 116.

32. On the rationale, prevalence, and impact of waiver programs, see Thomas Gais and James Fossett, "Federalism and the Executive Branch," in *The Executive Branch,* edited by Joel D. Aberbach and Mark A. Peterson (New York: Oxford University Press, 2005), 508–511; and Frank J. Thompson, *Medicaid Politics: Federalism, Policy Durability, and Health Reform* (Washington, DC: Georgetown University Press, 2012), 101–166.

33. Daniel M. Fox and Howard M. Leichter, "Rationing Care in Oregon: The New Accountability," *Health Affairs* 10: 2 (1991): 7–27; Daniel M. Fox and Howard M. Leichter, "The Ups and Downs of Oregon's Rationing Plan," *Health Affairs* 12: 3 (1993): 66–70; Lawrence D. Brown, "The National Politics of Oregon's Rationing Plan," *Health Affairs* 10: 2 (1991): 28–51; Jonathan Oberlander, "Health Reform Interrupted: The Unraveling of the Oregon Health Plan," *Health Affairs* 26: 1 (2007): 96–105.

34. David Muhlestein, "Accountable Care Growth in 2014: A Look Ahead," *Health Affairs* blog, January 29, 2014, http://healthaffairs.org/blog/2014/01/29/accountable-care-growth-in-2014-a-look-ahead.

35. David B. Klein, Miriam J. Laugesen, Nan Liu, "The Patient-Centered Medical Home: A Future Standard for American Health Care?" *Public Administration Review* 73: s1 (2013): S82–S92.

36. Amy Goldstein and Julie Eilperin, "HealthCare.gov: How Political Fear Was Pitted against Technical Needs," *Washington Post,* November 2, 2013.

37. Timothy Jost, "Implementing Health Reform: The Latest Affordable Care Act Coverage Numbers," *Health Affairs* blog, April 18, 2014, http://healthaffairs.org/blog/2014/04/18/implementing-health-reform-the-latest-affordable-care-act-coverage-numbers.

38. Kaiser Family Foundation, "Medicare at a Glance." Fact Sheet, November 2012.

39. Robert Ball, "What Medicare's Architects Had in Mind," *Health Affairs* 14 (Winter 1995): 62–72; David Barton Smith, *Health Care Divided: Race and Healing a Nation* (Ann Arbor: University of Michigan Press), pp. 115–66.

40. Centers for Medicare and Medicaid Services, "Critical Access Hospital: Rural Health Fact Sheet Series," December 2013. http://www.cms.gov/outreach-and-education/medicare-learning-network-MLN/MLNProducts/downloads/CritAcess Hospfctsht.pdf.

41. Norton Long, "Power and Administration," *Public Administration Review* 2 (1949): 257–264; James Q. Wilson, *Bureaucracy* (New York: Basic Books), 202–205.

42. Wilson, *Bureaucracy,* Ch. 5, 72–89; William T. Gormley and Steven J. Balla, *Bureaucracy and Democracy* (Washington, DC: CQ Press, 2004), 84–87.

43. Nancy-Ann DeParle, "What Does It Take to Run Medicare and Medicaid?" *Health Affairs* (July 26, 2005): W5-337.

44. Wesley Lowery, "For 17th Time in 11 Years, Congress Delays Medicare Reimbursement Cuts as Senate Passes 'Doc Fix,'" *Washington Post,* March 31, 2014, http://www.washingtonpost.com/blogs/post-politics/wp/2014/03/31/for-17th-time-in-11-years-congress-delays-medicare-reimbursement-cuts-as-senate-passes-doc-fix.

45. Brian Biles, Jonah Pozen, and Stuart Guterman, *The Continuing Cost of Privatization: Extra Payments to Medicare Advantage Plans Jump to $11.4 Billion in 2009* (New York: Commonwealth Fund, May 2009).

46. Jonathan Oberlander, *The Political Life of Medicare* (Chicago: University of Chicago Press, 2003), 106, 133; Thomas R. Oliver and Philip R. Lee, "The Medicare Modernization Act: Evolution or Revolution in Social Insurance?" in *Social Insurance and Social Justice,* edited by Leah Rogne, Carroll E. Estes, Brian R. Grossman, Brooke A. Hollister, and Erica Solway, 74–77 (New York: Springer, 2009).

47. Fay Lomax Cook and Meredith B. Czaplewski, "Public Opinion and Social Insurance: The American Experience," in *Social Insurance and Social Justice,* edited by Leah Rogne, Carroll E. Estes, Brian R. Grossman, Brooke A. Hollister, and Erica Solway, 253–237 (New York: Springer, 2009).

48. Oliver and Lee, "The Medicare Modernization Act," 66–67.

49. Robert Binstock and James Schulz, "Can Threats to Social Insurance in the United States Be Repelled?" in *Social Insurance and Social Justice,* edited by Leah Rogne, Carroll E. Estes, Brian R. Grossman, Brooke A. Hollister, and Erica Solway, 197–231 (New York: Springer, 2009).

50. Gormley and Balla, *Bureaucracy and Democracy.* Washington, DC: SAGE, 2013, 153–163.

51. Iglehart, "Changing with the Times: The Views of Bruce C. Vladeck," *Health Affairs* 16:3 (1997): 58–71; King, Burke, and Docteur, *Final Report of the Study Panel on Medicare's Governance and Management,* 36-39; Iglehart, "Doing More with Less: A Conversation with Kerry Weems."

FURTHER READING

King, Kathleen M., Sheila Burke, and Elizabeth Docteur, eds. *Final Report of the Study Panel on Medicare's Governance and Management.* Washington, DC: National Academy of Social Insurance, 2002.

Marmor, Theodore R. *The Politics of Medicare.* 2nd ed. New York: Transaction, 2000.

Radin, Beryl A. *The Accountable Juggler: The Art of Leadership in a Federal Agency.* Washington, DC: CQ Press, 2002.

Rogne, Leah, Carroll E. Estes, Brian R. Grossman, Brooke A. Hollister, and Erica Solway. *Social Insurance and Social Justice.* New York: Springer, 2009.

Smith, David G. *Entitlement Politics.* New York: Aldine de Gruyter, 2002.

Thompson, Frank J. *Medicaid Politics: Federalism, Policy Durability, and Health Reform.* Washington, DC: Georgetown University Press, 2012.

chapter 7

The Departments of Defense and Veterans Affairs

Responsibilities and Policies (1947–Present)

Christopher E. Johnson and Ann M. Nguyen

THE DEPARTMENTS OF DEFENSE (DoD) AND Veterans Affairs (VA) are the two largest governmental institutions in the United States. They are currently the nation's largest health care providers, with the DoD serving close to 9.6 million military members, retirees, and their families and the VA serving 8.7 million veterans who are enrolled in its health care system.[1,2] These seemingly integrated governmental functions of organizing the military and serving its veterans have existed since the birth of the country, evolving with wartime activity and continuously being reshaped by policy. Yet today, both are organized as independent parts of the federal government. The trend toward coordinated, patient-centered health care is encouraging new collaborations between the VA and DoD, and these integrations are bringing them closer together. One of the most poignant issues currently at hand is the growing concern about behavioral health disorders in both active duty service members and veterans. More and more men and women from these populations are being diagnosed with depression, anxiety, posttraumatic stress disorder, and substance abuse disorders.[3] In addition, there has been an alarming rise in suicide rates.[4] It is important to understand the evolution of the DoD's and VA's health care systems to better inform policies that can effectively unite these institutions and address these issues.

THE STRUCTURE OF THE DEPARTMENT OF DEFENSE TODAY

The DoD is the ultimate protector of the nation's survival. It is the largest governmental institution in the United States and is charged with coordinating and supervising all agencies and functions of the government concerned directly with national security and the U.S. armed forces. The activities of the DoD range from protecting U.S. interests in political and military crises to peacekeeping to humanitarian assistance.

Today, the secretary of defense, who serves as the principal defense policy adviser to the president, heads the Department of Defense. The secretary, who is appointed by the president with advice and consent from the Senate, has authority, direction, and control over the DoD. On February 26, 2013, Secretary of Defense Chuck Hagel (in office 2013–) was confirmed following a protracted confirmation process and replaced the retiring Leon Panetta (in office 2011–2013).[5] As his right hand, the deputy secretary of defense, the second-highest-ranking official in the DoD, is delegated full power and authority to act on behalf of the secretary. The department is headquartered at the Pentagon in Arlington, Virginia.[6]

The Department of Defense is a large entity comprising the Office of the Inspector General, the Office of the Secretary of Defense, the Joint Chiefs of Staff and the Joint Staff, and nine Unified Combatant Commands. It also has three military arms: the Department of the Army, the Department of the Navy, and the Department of the Air Force, which oversee the U.S. Army, Navy, Marine Corps, and Air Force, the joint forces of land, sea, and air. In addition, the department has seventeen Defense Agencies, which include the national intelligence services: the Defense Intelligence Agency, the National Security Agency, the National Geospatial-Intelligence Agency, and the National Reconnaissance Office. Also under the command of the secretary are DoD Field Activities, the National Guard Bureau, and other offices, agencies, activities, organizations, and commands established or designated by law, by the president, or by the secretary of defense. Collectively, the DoD maintains 555,000 facilities at five thousand sites on more than 28 million acres.[6,7] The military budget to support the DoD during fiscal year 2013 was an estimated $673 billion.[8]

FIGURE 7.1 Department of Defense Organizational Chart

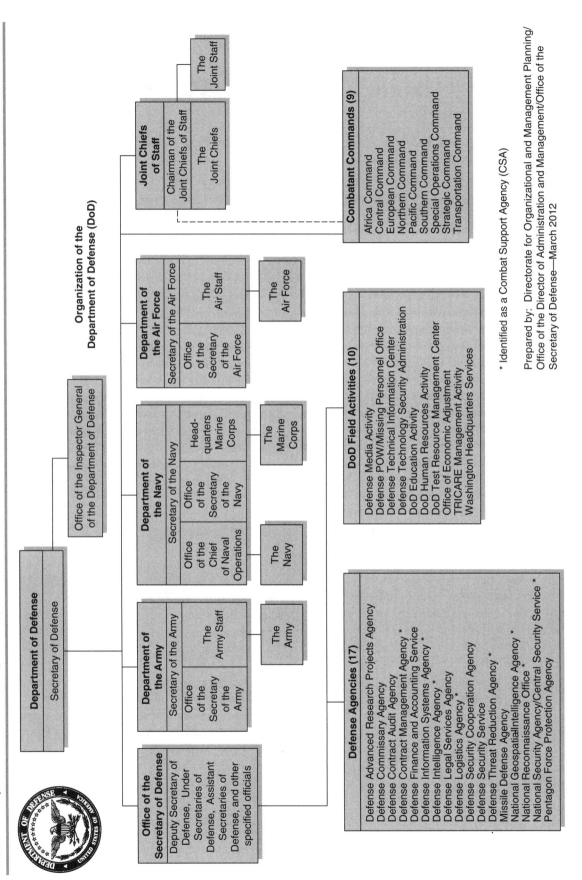

SOURCE: U.S. Department of Defense, "Organization of the Department of Defense," http://www.defense.gov/orgchart.

Due to its organizational magnitude, it is not surprising that the Department of Defense is the largest employer in the nation, with more than 1.4 million men and women on active duty and 718,000 civilian personnel. An additional 1.1 million serve in the National Guard and Reserve forces, and more than 2 million veterans and their family members receive benefits. As a result, as reported by the DoD, it is the nation's largest health care provider, serving 9.6 million military members (active, National Guard and Reserve, and retired) and their families.

Beginnings of the Department of Defense

The Department of Defense is the oldest government agency in the United States, and it has grown and evolved with the nation in response to changing domestic and international circumstances. Its military roots can be traced back to pre-Revolutionary times, but it was not until 1775, the beginning of the American War of Independence (1775–1783), that there was formal establishment of the U.S. Army, Navy, and Marine Corps. In 1789, Congress created the Department of War, the precursor to what is now the Department of Defense. One year later, the National Coast Guard was founded, followed by the Department of the Navy in 1798.[7]

As the different services grew, however, it steadily became apparent that centralization was key to reducing the growing numbers of deficits and inefficiencies reported during wartime. Between 1921 and 1945, at least fifty bills were offered to Congress to reshape the military; none were passed. Typical of most reforms, there was resistance with concerns on the role of the military in society and the threat of granting too much military power to the executive. World War II (1939–1945) proved to be the necessary impetus for change. The United States and its allies prevailed, but the war demonstrated that the organization of U.S. national security was seriously flawed. In 1945, President Harry S. Truman (1945–1953) proposed to Congress the unification of the different services under a single department. Months of long and arduous deliberations passed before President Truman was able to sign the National Security Act of 1947 into law on July 26, 1947. The National Security Act led to the creation of the "National Military Establishment," which enabled unified direction, authority, and control over the armed forces. The act created several new entities, including the U.S. Air Force, and placed the National Military Establishment under the control of a single secretary of defense. James V. Forrestal (in office 1947–1949) served as the nation's first secretary of defense. In 1949, the National Military Establishment was renamed the Department of Defense.[6]

Health Care in the DoD

For military personnel, health care was relatively unstructured until the Civil War (1861–1865). Around this time,

improvements in medical science, communication, and transportation were making centralized care more practical. Military health care continued to expand during World War I (1914–1918), as the U.S. Army Medical Department developed greater organization and structure in response to wartime necessities. Soldiers began to receive care right on the battlefield, and some access to care was being provided to dependents. Access to care, however, began to decline following World War II, as resources became sparse. In 1945, with the creation of a unified Department of Defense, the health care system faced another issue; the unification created conflict, as the Army, Navy, and Air Force each had its own medical service.

To address these issues, Congress passed the Dependents Medical Care Act of 1956 and the Military Medical Benefits Amendments of 1966. These acts created a single health care program for the U.S. Department of Defense Military Health System known as the Civilian Health and Medical Program of the Uniformed Services (CHAMPUS). Through CHAMPUS, the secretary of defense was able to contract with civilian health care providers.

In the late 1980s, costs escalated, claims processing became overwhelming, and beneficiaries were dissatisfied. In response, the DoD initiated a demonstration project, the CHAMPUS Reform Initiative (CRI), one of the first to introduce managed care features into CHAMPUS. Under the CRI, the Department of Defense intended to award three competitively bid contracts covering six states, but only one bid was received (made by Foundation Health Corporation, now Health Net, to cover California and Hawaii). Foundation covered the two states from August 1988 to January 1994.[9,10]

TRICARE

In 1993, President William J. Clinton (1993–2001) signed the Department of Defense Appropriations Act for Fiscal Year 1994, which set aside funds specifically for development of DoD medical and health care programs.[11] The DoD announced plans for a new program called TRICARE, a nationwide managed care program that would be completely implemented by May 1997. Under TRICARE, the United States was divided into twelve health care regions with an administrative organization at the core of each region to coordinate the health care needs of all military treatment facilities. The DoD subsequently awarded seven managed care contracts to cover the twelve regions.[12] Interestingly, TRICARE embodied many of the principles and organizational features of President Clinton's failed proposal for national health reform.

TRICARE has since undergone several restructuring initiatives, including realignment of contract regions and the addition of TRICARE for Life benefits in 2001 for those who are Medicare-eligible and TRICARE Reserve Select in

POLITICS AND HEALTH CARE POLICY

The Establishment of TRICARE

The Department of Defense (DoD) has been referred to as the nation's test bed for health care reform. The current military health benefit system reflects the evolving nature of health care in the United States over the past few decades. The Military Health System is one of the largest and most complex health organizations in the country, and it was certainly not immune to the challenges faced by the rest of the nation: rapidly increasing health care costs, uneven access to health care services, and separate benefit and cost-sharing packages for similarly situated categories of beneficiaries. In the 1960s, the federal government was under pressure to address these issues, hence it strategized to promote prepaid plans as a way to improve capacity and efficiency across the nation. During the presidency of Richard M. Nixon (1969–1974), Congress passed the Health Maintenance Organization (HMO) Act of 1973, which authorized federal funds to develop HMOs across the nation's health care system. The HMO Act also removed certain state restrictions for federally qualified HMOs and required employers with twenty-five or more employees (that offered health insurance) to include a federally certified HMO option.

The DoD recognized this emerging role of managed care. With congressional authorization, the DoD conducted a series of demonstration projects to test alternative approaches that included managed care. One of these projects was the revolutionary CHAMPUS Reform Initiative (CRI), which offered beneficiaries a triple-option benefit:

1. CHAMPUS Prime: an HMO-like option that required enrollment and offered enhanced benefits and low cost sharing

2. CHAMPUS Extra: a preferred provider organization–like option that required use of network providers in exchange for lower cost sharing

3. CHAMPUS Standard: an option that allowed freedom of choice in selecting providers but required higher cost-sharing and deductibles.

Congress mandated an external evaluation of CRI, in which the RAND Corporation reported that the average adult beneficiary with CRI benefit cost the government 9 percent more than the adult beneficiary with standard CHAMPUS. Despite of the CRI's failure to reduce costs, the U.S. General Accounting Office (now known as the Government Accountability Office) was impressed by the DoD's attempt to contain CHAMPUS costs for both the government and beneficiaries, increase access to health care, improve care coordination, ensure quality of care, and minimize administrative procedures. The DoD was likewise motivated by the beneficiaries' high level of satisfaction. The CRI demonstration project went through several iterations, with new initiatives that targeted major cost containment.

In 1993, the Department of Defense Appropriations Act of Fiscal Year 1994 required the DoD to develop, to the extent practical, health benefit options, including a uniform health benefit modeled after private sector HMOs. This act appropriated $9.6 billion toward expenses for the DoD's medical and health care programs. This provided the DoD with funding to design and establish TRICARE. The TRICARE program was inspired by the CRI and the subsequent demonstration projects, similarly featuring a triple-option benefit: TRICARE Standard, TRICARE Extra (a PPO option), and TRICARE Prime (an HMO option). With TRICARE, the DoD intended to control costs, improve beneficiary access to care, and provide high-quality care. The military health delivery system was reorganized into twelve regions, each headed by a lead agent who was responsible for monitoring and coordinating care in the region. This allowed for more effective cost control features, such as capitation budgeting and utilization management. Due to the size and complexity of the TRICARE program, the DoD phased its implementation over three years.

SOURCE: Philip M. Lurie, Richard R. Bannick, and Elder Granger, *The Department of Defense's TRICARE Health Benefits Program as a Critical Plank in the Federal Platform for Health Care Reform* (Arlington, VA: Institute for Defense Analysis, 2009).

2005 for service members in the National Guard and Reserve. Today, TRICARE provides civilian health benefits for military personnel, military retirees, and their dependents, including some members of the Reserve Component. TRICARE was initially managed by TRICARE Management Activity (TMA) under the authority of the assistant secretary of defense. On October 1, 2013, the DoD established the Defense Health Agency (DHA) to manage the activities of the Military Health System (MHS); the DHA is the centerpiece of the MHS governance reform. The intent behind the DHA is "to achieve greater integration of our direct and purchased health care delivery systems so that we accomplish the Department's Quadruple Aim: achieve medical readiness, improve the health of our people, enhance the experience of care, and lower our healthcare costs." TMA

has since been disestablished, and the DHA has assumed responsibility over TRICARE.[13]

In terms of quality and cost of care, over the past decade, there has been a dramatic increase in the overall share of the DoD budget that is allocated for TRICARE. The DoD spent $52 billion in 2012 to cover nearly 10 million TRICARE enrollees. This represents a growth from 6 percent of the budget in 2000 to 10 percent in 2012 and to a projected 11 percent of DoD's budget in 2028. The causes for this increase can be traced to new and expanded TRICARE benefits, increased utilization of TRICARE services, and the overall medical costs of recent wars. As potential solutions to the increase in costs associated with the plan, policymakers are looking to better management of chronic diseases, more effective administration of the military health care system, and increased cost-sharing for retirees who use TRICARE. Of the three potential solutions, increased cost-sharing for retirees is the most politically risky and difficult to implement. A bipartisan budget agreement was passed in December 2013 that found $6 billion in savings through the reduction of working-age military retirees' pensions. However, this provision was removed from the budget agreement via an omnibus spending agreement that was passed in January 2014. Given the requirements in the Budget Control Act of 2011, it is not clear how TRICARE and other parts of the military health care system will be able to maintain their current level of benefits without greater cost-sharing or other adjustments to financing of the DoD's health care programs.[14]

Contributions of Battlefield Medicine

Battlefield medicine has contributed in a number of ways to the advancement of new health delivery techniques in the civilian sector.[15] Tactical combat causality care, designed to aid first responders to life-threatening situations, is being used by civilian emergency medical systems. For example, early hemorrhage control and massive transfusion protocols are used in most Level 1 trauma centers in the United States. The battlefield medicine techniques for treating badly injured limbs were notably applied to victims of the 2013 Boston Marathon bombings. Also, advances in neurocritical care developed in the military are being examined as possible ways for civilians to respond to mass casualty events and crises.

THE STRUCTURE OF THE DEPARTMENT OF VETERANS AFFAIRS

The U.S. Department of Veterans Affairs (VA) is the most comprehensive veterans assistance system in the world. It is responsible for administering benefits and support to service members, veterans, their families, and survivors. The VA stands as the second largest government department in the United States and employs 280,000 people at more than seventeen hundred VA medical facilities, clinics, community living centers, domiciliaries, readjustment counseling centers, and benefits offices.[16] In 2012, the VA had a proposed budget of $132 billion.[17] In 2014, it requested a budget of $152.7 billion.[18] Despite the magnitude of the VA, its services and benefits are not used by all veterans. As of March 2013, there were about 22.3 million living veterans; about 8.76 million (39 percent) were enrolled in the VA health care system, 7 million (31 percent) were on life insurance policies supervised and administered by the VA, and only 3.6 million (16 percent) were receiving disability compensation. While the number of total veterans is on a downward trend, total expenditures are expected to increase over the next few years as a result of rising utilization.[1]

Today, the secretary of veterans affairs heads the Department of Veterans Affairs. The president, with the advice and consent of the Senate, appoints the secretary. Most recently serving in this role was Eric K. Shinseki (in office 2009–2014), a retired Army general who was nominated by President Barack Obama (2009–) and sworn in on January 21, 2009. The department itself has three main subdivisions, known as administrations, each headed by an undersecretary. The Veterans Benefits Administration is responsible for administering programs that provide financial and other forms of assistance, such as the Office of Disability Assistance (compensation, pension and fiduciary, insurance, and benefits assistance), the Office of Economic Opportunity (education, loan guaranty, and vocational rehabilitation and employment), and the Office of Field Operations. The Veterans Health Administration (VHA) is responsible for implementation of the medical assistance program. This is done through the administration and operation of VA medical centers, outpatient clinics, community-based outpatient clinics, and VA community living centers. It also conducts an array of biomedical research. The VHA is the largest entity within the VA, with more employees than all other elements of the VA combined. The National Cemetery Administration is responsible for providing burial and memorial benefits. It maintains operation of the National Cemetery System, which includes 131 of the 147 national cemeteries.[16]

Beginnings of the Department of Veterans Affairs

The Department of Veterans Affairs is a product of war. It is the nation's response to the question, "What can we do to support the men and women who have served our country in the time of war?" The origin of the VA dates back to 1636, when the Pilgrims of Plymouth Colony were at war with the Pequot Indians. The Pilgrims passed a law stating that the colony would support its disabled soldiers. During the American War of Independence, the Continental Congress of 1776 encouraged enlistment by expanding this support, providing pensions to disabled soldiers. Access to care also began to see improvement, as the very first domiciliary and medical facility for veterans was authorized in 1811, the assistance program was expanded to include widows and dependents, and state veteran homes were established following the Civil War.

World War I initiated a series of structural changes to veteran assistance. In 1917, as the United States entered the war, Congress established a new system of veterans' benefits that included programs for disability compensation, insurance for service persons and veterans, and vocational rehabilitation for the disabled. These programs, however, were administered by three different federal agencies: the Veterans Bureau, the Bureau of Pensions of the Interior Department, and the National Home for Disabled Volunteer

FIGURE 7.2 **Department of Veterans Affairs Organizational Chart**

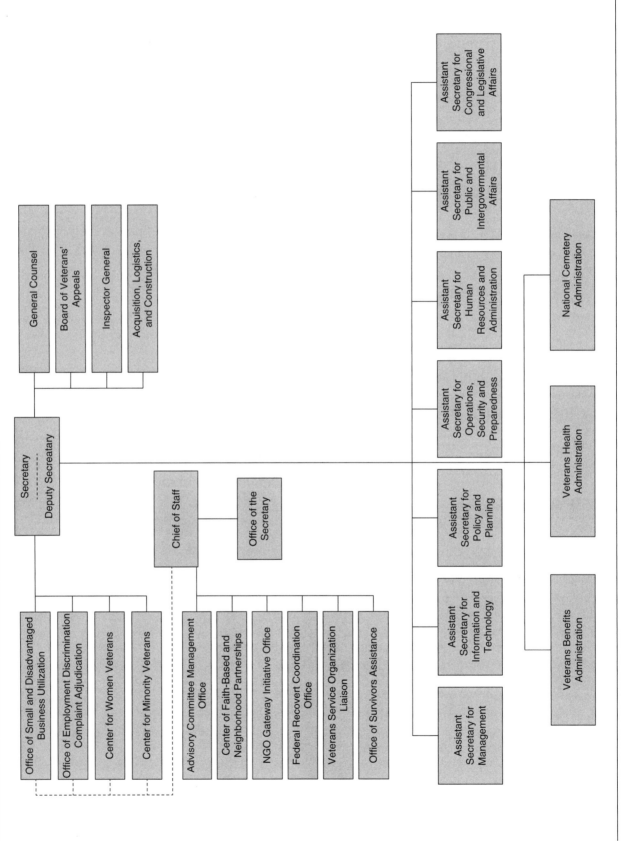

SOURCE: U.S. Department of Veterans Affairs, http://www.va.gov/ofcadmin/docs/vaorgchart.pdf.

Soldiers. In 1930, President Herbert Hoover (1929–1933) recognized the need to consolidate and coordinate government activities affecting war veterans; he established the Veterans Administration, bringing together the three bureaus.[16]

World War II ushered in another round of changes, this time to the quality of the benefits. The U.S. Department of Labor estimated that, after the war, fifteen million men and women from the armed services would be unemployed. They designed a series of education and training subsidization programs and introduced them into Congress as the Serviceman's Readjustment Act, informally known as the G.I. Bill. Met with unanimous support, the G.I. Bill was signed into law on June 22, 1944, by President Franklin D. Roosevelt (1933–1945). The law provided a range of benefits for returning World War II veterans, such as low-cost mortgages, low-interest loans to start a business, cash payments of tuition and living expenses to attend college, high school or vocational education, and one year of unemployment compensation. The G.I. Bill contributed more than any other program in history to the welfare of veterans and their families and to the growth of the nation's economy.[19]

Creating the Department of Veterans Affairs

The Veterans Administration continued its expansion and in 1973 assumed responsibility of the National Cemetery System. On March 15, 1989, the Department of Veterans Affairs was established as a cabinet-level position, signed into legislation by President Ronald Reagan (1981–1989) and taking effect under the presidency of George H.W. Bush (1989–1993). Under the administration of President Barack Obama, the VA is undergoing yet another transformation. Governed by three guiding principles—people-centric, results-driven, and forward-looking—the VA is focusing on sixteen major initiatives:

- eliminating veteran homelessness
- enabling twenty-first-century benefits delivery and services
- automating G.I. Bill benefits
- creating Virtual Lifetime Electronic Records
- improving veterans' mental health
- building Veterans Relationship Management capability to enable convenient, seamless interactions
- designing a veteran-centric health care model to help veterans navigate the health care delivery system and receive coordinated care
- enhancing the veteran experience and access to health care
- ensuring preparedness to meet emergent national needs
- developing capabilities and enabling systems to drive performance and outcomes

- establishing strong VA management infrastructure and an integrated operating model
- transforming human capital management
- performing research and development to enhance the long-term health and well-being of veterans
- optimizing the use of VA's Capital Portfolio by implementing and executing the Strategic Capital Investment Planning process
- improving the quality of health care while reducing cost
- transforming health care delivery through health informatics

Under the leadership of Secretary Shinseki, the VA undertook these initiatives with the expressed goal of becoming a high-performing, twenty-first-century organization to better serve its veterans.[16]

Health Care in the VA

Today, the Department of Veterans Affairs, through the Veterans Health Administration, provides primary care, specialized care, and related medical and social support services to enrolled veterans. The VHA is home to the largest integrated health system in the United States, a system that includes roughly 150 medical centers and nearly 1,400 community-based outpatient clinics, community living centers, Vet Centers, and domiciliaries. More than 53,000 independent licensed health care practitioners work in these facilities.[20]

Disabled soldiers, however, did not always have the luxury of a dedicated, wide-reaching health source. Before the nineteenth century, when care was needed it came from existing channels in the community and the state. The need for veterans' medical care became apparent with the Civil War. As casualties rose, Congress responded in 1865 by creating the National Home for Disabled Volunteer Soldiers. The homes initially served as room and board for disabled veterans, but by the late 1920s, they had evolved to provide a level of care comparable to a hospital.

The field changed dramatically in 1930 with the creation of the VA, which consolidated all veteran services. In 1945, Major General Paul Hawley (in office 1945–1947) was appointed as director of VA medicine. At the time, the VA had 5,600 beds and a lack of personnel. Staff shortages were projected to increase by a third or more. To address the problem of anticipated staff shortages, Hawley, who also served as the chairman of the Task Force on Federal Medical Services, gave recommendations for reorganization. Though only in the position for three years, Hawley is credited with starting the VA's hospital-based research program. He established a policy that affiliated new VA hospitals with medical schools, and he promoted resident and teaching fellowships at VA hospitals. As a result of the service integration and

Hawley's instrumental leadership, the VA's health care system grew from fifty-four hospitals in 1930 to ninety-seven hospitals in operation and twenty-nine newly built.

Quality measures became the next focus for veterans' health. In 1985, Congress passed Public Law 99-166, which mandated that the VA establish and conduct a comprehensive quality assurance program to monitor the quality of health care furnished by the VA. These outcome measures were then compared to national averages. In 1989, the Department of Veterans Affairs was established as a cabinet-level entity, when the quintessential role of the Veterans Health Administration was further affirmed. Quality measurement grew to a larger scale, and in 1991, the National VA Surgical Risk Study (NVASRS) was implemented in 44 VA medical centers. In 1994, NVASRS expanded to all 128 VHA hospitals that performed major surgery. The name of the study was thus changed to the National Surgical Quality Improvement Program.[21]

Beginning in 1995, the VHA underwent a major transformation to improve quality and efficiency of care for veterans, centered on the restructure of the VHA's field operations and its central office management. The new structure transformed its health care delivery system from a hospital-based system to one providing comprehensive services to an enrolled population. This included a reconfiguration of four delivery regions into twenty-two Veterans Integrated Service Networks. Underused inpatient beds and facilities were eliminated, and outpatient clinics were expanded. The Veterans' Health Care Eligibility Reform Act of 1996 set into motion a major restructure of eligibility rules, and in 1999, the VHA enrollment system was implemented.[22] The enrollment system, still in use today, tracks veterans who plan to use VHA services. Eligible veterans are assigned to one of eight priority groups based on their service-connected disabilities, service-related exposures, income, assets, and other factors. Nearly 80 percent of enrolled veterans, however, have access to other health care coverage. Most rely on the VHA only for outpatient care, mental health, and substance abuse counseling, services that are emphasized by the VHA and less likely covered by private insurance.[23] The 1990s were a remarkable period of innovation and quality improvement for the VHA. Quality of care improved substantially, and from 1997 to 2000, quality was significantly better than that in the Medicare fee-for-service program.[24–27]

KEY DECISIONS: HEALTH CARE CRISES AND SOLUTIONS

Vertically Integrated Service Networks

The Veterans Health Administration (VHA) underwent a major transformation in the 1990s, embracing the culture of "Patients First." A new structure was introduced based on the concept of coordinating and integrating the VHA's health care delivery assets and the creation of twenty-two Veterans Integrated Service Networks (VISNs). The VISN structure emphasizes quality patient care, customer satisfaction, innovation, personal initiative, and accountability. On March 17, 1995, the Department of Veterans Affairs Under Secretary for Health Kenneth W. Kizer (in office 1994–1999) presented the VHA's restructuring plan, titled "Vision for Change." In the excerpt below, Kizer shares his commitment to improving the quality of health care provided to veterans and describes the impetus and necessity for change:

The organizational model described in this document has been conceived with the intent of providing a structure that will facilitate the changes that need to occur, while at the same time retaining the many good things the system already does. The proposed structure optimizes VHA's ability to function as both an integrated and a virtual health care organization; it provides structural incentives for efficiency, quality and improved access; it builds in a formal means of ensuring a high degree of stakeholder involvement; and it provides for a level of accountability not typical of government agencies. Once operational, it should be apparent to our patients, Congress and the public that this is not only a better model than the present structure, but that it is also better than the various alternatives that call for doing away with VHA.

Important to note, however, is that in and of itself, the planned organizational structure merely provides a template upon which new attitudes and behavior will be encouraged and rewarded, and around which a new organizational culture can grow. This transformation will take time, and the difficulty of changing a decades-old culture in the second largest bureaucracy in the federal government should not be underestimated. The change will be neither easy nor painless. Nonetheless, if the veterans health care system is to remain viable it must fundamentally change its approach to providing care.

While the need for structural change is acute, it must be understood that this reorganization alone cannot heal all of the maladies of the veterans health care system. A number of other remedies are also needed. Among these are the development and use of system-wide clinical protocols and practice guidelines, a major Departmental commitment to providing more and better training for the VA workforce, and an overhaul of the veterans' health care eligibility criteria. Moreover, VA needs to explore opportunities to open up the system to additional users, within available resources, when that will enhance both the access to care and the quality of care provided to veterans.

SOURCE: U.S. Department of Veterans Affairs, "Vision for Change," http://www.va.gov/HEALTHPOLICYPLANNING/vision_for_change.asp.

In recent years, the VHA has pushed use of the Veterans Health Information System and Technology Architecture (VistA) as a means to document and coordinate care received by veterans in the system. The National Defense Authorization Act for Fiscal Year 2008 mandated that the DoD and VA secretaries "develop and implement electronic health record systems or capabilities that allow for full interoperability of personal health information between the Department of Defense and the Department of Veterans Affairs." There is huge value in an interoperable electronic health records system, particularly to streamline electronic medical, benefit, and administration information between the two departments. The act spearheaded multiple approaches, including the 2009 Virtual Lifetime Electronic Record and the 2011 Integrated Electronic Health Record. Despite joint efforts, unfortunately, the two departments faced incredible management challenges. Plans for integration were scrapped in 2013, resulting in a loss of more than $1 billion over the four-year attempt.[28] The failure to integrate electronic health records was a setback, but the VHA continues to use VistA, which has been identified as a key tool in the VHA's efforts to accurately measure performance and improve quality.

The VHA has also been working to transform the VA health care delivery system to one that provides more patient-centric care. In fiscal year 2010, the VHA began implementation of a patient-centered medical home model, now known as Patient Aligned Care Team (PACT), to its primary care sites. PACT strives to provide superb access to primary care (including alternatives to face-to-face care), seamless coordination of care between VA providers and with non-VA providers, and a patient-centered culture through the redesign of primary care practices and team roles. Veterans are assigned to a PACT, consisting of multidisciplinary clinical and support staff that deliver all primary care and coordinate the remainder of patients' needs, including specialty care.[29]

BEHAVIORAL HEALTH IN DOD AND VA

More than a decade has passed since the United States began engaging in armed conflict in Afghanistan and Iraq. Never before have U.S. military personnel been exposed to combat- and war-related stresses for such an extended period of time.[3] A staggering two million service members were deployed in support of overseas contingency operations (OCO). There was increased use of military reserve units and National Guard members to augment the regular armed forces, which exposed a wide swath of the U.S. population to combat-related stress in ways different than in previous wars. Active duty and recent veteran populations are increasingly likely to be temporary troops who reside in rural parts of the United States in disproportionate numbers. Since

September 11, 2001, troops have also regularly had their tours extended.[30] As of June 2008, more than 638,000 troops had been deployed more than once.[31] Given the increase in behavioral health issues in deployed units and veterans of armed conflict, both the DoD and the VA created organizational and policy responses to the increasing need for behavioral health services in this population.

Behavioral Health Services in the VA and DoD

In its medical centers, community-based outpatient clinics, and rehabilitation treatment programs, the VA provides behavioral health services that include treatment for post-traumatic stress disorder (PTSD), depression, and substance abuse disorders. These facilities may include specialty mental health care settings, mental health clinics, and primary care mental health services. Between 2006 and 2010, roughly 2.1 million veterans received mental health services through the VA. The numbers of veterans receiving these services increased from about 900,000 in 2006 to 1.2 million in 2010, with OCO veterans accounting for an increasing proportion.[32] In 2011, among OCO veterans who received health care services from the VA, mental health–related diagnoses were the second largest diagnostic category. A mental health diagnosis was given to 52 percent of this population.[3]

Overall Problem

A study about the prevalence of mental health disorders in service members deployed to Iraq found that 15.6 percent of marines and 17.1 percent of soldiers met the screening criteria for major depression, general anxiety, or PTSD.[33] Another study examined rates of mental illness among soldiers returning from Iraq between June 1, 2005, and December 31, 2006.[34] The participants completed self-reported questionnaires and clinician interviews four to ten months post-deployment. Among active duty personnel, 16.7 percent screened positive for PTSD, 0.6 percent reported suicide ideation, 14 percent reported interpersonal conflict, and 2.2 percent reported aggressive ideation. Reserve and National Guard soldiers reported significantly higher rates, with 24.5 percent screening positive for PTSD, 1.5 percent reporting suicide ideation, 13 percent reporting depressive symptoms, 15 percent screening positive for alcohol problems, 21.1 percent reporting interpersonal conflict, and 4 percent reporting aggressive ideation. Higher prevalence of mental health–related disorders were found in other studies, with one study reporting that in a sample of fifty female veterans returning from Iraq or Afghanistan, 78 percent reported needing some form of mental health treatment for one or more behavioral health problems.[35] Returning service personnel from the Iraq and Afghanistan theaters have documented problems with depression and PTSD, and studies indicate the need for early intervention and treatment.[36,37]

The shift in mental health care needs stems from an overall shift in demographics of the U.S. military and an increased reliance on the reserve and National Guard. During the current OCO, a greater proportion of U.S. military recruits tend to be from rural areas than from the general civilian population.[38] In the last decade, there also have been increasing numbers of men and women being deployed into combat. This has yielded an overall higher number of rural-dwelling veterans who have combat experience. The rural veteran population represents roughly 40 percent of the estimated 24 million veterans in the United States. A survey of 748,216 veterans found that rural-dwelling veterans in mental illness cohorts had worse physical and mental health component quality of life score summaries than their counterparts who live in urban areas. These differences were still significant after controlling for sociodemographic factors. Other empirical analyses support this finding, showing that rural residents in general have worse mental health services access and outcomes than the urban population.[39,40] Rural residents of all types face mental health care issues related to access, treatment stigmas, and poverty.[41–43] They have higher levels of depression, substance abuse, domestic violence, incest, and child abuse.[44,45] Rural residents also have more difficulty locating and maintaining health insurance coverage that provides for mental health conditions.[43]

For rural-dwelling veterans in particular, the added exposure to war- and combat-related stresses places them at an even higher risk for mental health–related issues than

President Barack Obama greets U.S. troops following his remarks at Bagram Air Field, Afghanistan, on May 1, 2012. President Obama has supported the expansion of mental health services for veterans and service members, and in August 2012, he signed an Executive Order to create an Interagency Task Force on Military and Veterans Mental Health.

SOURCE: Rex Features via AP Images.

nonveteran rural residents.[46] The implications of this from a mental health care utilization perspective are cause for serious concern. Gaps in mental health care are more likely for veterans who are younger, non-white, unmarried, homeless, and live in an area with limited access to VA facilities (e.g., rural areas).[47,48] Mental health services from the VA are thus targeting those populations.

Posttraumatic Stress Disorder

PTSD, a leading behavioral health issue in the veteran population, is an anxiety disorder induced by exposure to a traumatic event, such as witnessing injury or death. Symptoms include re-experiencing of the event, hyperarousal (irritability, anger, or hypervigilance), and diminished responsiveness to or avoidance of stimuli associated with the trauma.[3] Situations that can contribute to PTSD include armed conflict, the unexpected and sudden death of unit members, capture, terrorism, and accidents. These conditions are more present during current OCO than they were during the 1991 Gulf War, when most combat engagements were long-range tank battles and a massive Iraqi surrender. Current OCO, on the other hand, includes urban combat mixed with an unidentifiable enemy and prolonged deployment of combat forces.[49]

Between 2004 and 2009, 21 percent of the patients treated by the Veterans Health Administration were diagnosed with PTSD. Veterans with PTSD were found to be four to six times more costly for the VHA to treat during the first year as compared to the larger OCO population. PTSD is difficult to diagnose and identify in patients due to the stigma associated with admitting to mental health problems among veterans. For those OCO veterans being treated in VHA facilities, 26 percent have been diagnosed with PTSD; this number, however, does not include veterans that are being treated outside of the VHA. It is therefore estimated that an additional 5 percent to 25 percent of veterans in this population may have PTSD.[3] PTSD has been linked to increased suicide ideation,[50] increased aggression,[51] depressive symptoms,[52] and alcohol and drug abuse.[53]

Suicide

Suicides have increased at alarming rates for both veterans and active duty service members. There were 160 recorded suicides across all branches of the armed services in 2001, and this number steadily increased to 309 in 2009, representing a roughly 50 percent increase in suicides in the armed services.[4] Although this suicide rate is lower than the rate that exists per 100,000 in the U.S. civilian population,[54] the gap has begun to close, and with pronounced increases in the suicide rates among active duty service members in 2007 and 2008, there is concern that the gap may be even closer today. Active duty members at risk for suicide fall into a number of categories, such as prior suicide attempts, many mental disorders (including PTSD), substance abuse disorders, head trauma/traumatic brain injury, and those suffering from hopelessness, aggression and impulsivity, and problem-solving deficits. Additional risk factors include firearm access, life events, precipitating events, and triggers, as well as the suicides of others and the reporting of suicides.[54] In the 1990s, a program that influenced the decline of suicides and suicide attempts, however, was that of the U.S. Air Force, which worked to remove the stigma among pilots of reporting mental illness.

Alcoholism and Substance Abuse

Alcohol and illicit drug use declined in the U.S. military from 1980 to 1998. The large increases in the use of these substances, particularly alcohol abuse, occurred between 1998 and 2002.[55] Exposure to deployment-related stresses and comorbid behavioral health issues have caused a rise in alcohol and substance abuse in active duty and OCO veterans. Reserve and National Guard service members who were exposed to combat situations were found to be significantly more likely to experience new-onset, weekly heavy drinking, binge drinking, and alcohol-related problems.[56] Substance abuse is highly correlated with stressful and traumatic events and the mental health disorders that are associated with prolonged exposure to combat situations.[53] Depression, PTSD, and stressors related to deployment or return from deployment may increase alcohol and substance abuse as well as change the patterns in which these harmful behaviors are adopted as coping mechanisms.

The 2011 DoD Health Related Behaviors Survey of Active Duty Military Personnel[57] found alarming levels of alcohol and substance abuse among respondents. Among current drinkers, 39.6 percent reported binge drinking within the past month, and 84.5 percent identified themselves as "current drinkers." Of the heavy drinkers, 58.4 percent were considered "problem drinkers." Levels of illicit drug use were found to be low among active duty respondents. Only 1.4 percent reported drug-related substance abuse within the past twelve months. Roughly one-fourth of the active duty personnel reported using prescription drugs for any reason, with one-third identifying pain relief or sedatives as the reason for the prescription. Only 1.3 percent reported prescription drug abuse, with steroids and stimulants being the most common reasons for this misuse.

VA and DoD Responses to Increased Rates of Behavioral Health Issues

The VA provides care for veterans diagnosed with mental disorders at VHA hospitals, outpatient clinics, community-based outpatient clinics (CBOCs), and Vet Centers. Patients also can be sent to providers outside of the VA for treatment. The majority of patients with mental health–related issues are treated in CBOCs via mental health clinics or through specialty programs provided by PTSD Clinical Teams, Substance Abuse Teams, and Women's Stress Disorder Teams. The VA provides cognitive processing therapy and prolonged exposure therapy to patients in these settings. Evidence suggests that PTSD patients who undergo therapy require nine treatment sessions.[58] The VHA reported to the Congressional Budget Office that 40 percent of OCO veterans complete the full course of therapy. Additionally, 80 percent of OCO veterans who used VHA services and received new PTSD diagnoses had at least one follow-up visit. Less than one-half, however, completed their recommended number of treatment sessions within one year.[58] Barriers to completing recommended therapy include the distance between home and the location of care, difficulty scheduling appointments, negative perceptions of mental health care, and impaired judgment as a result of the condition itself or associated problems with substance abuse. Some veterans may also choose to receive mental health care from providers outside of the VHA.[3]

THE 2000s: RESPONDING TO THE MENTAL HEALTH CHALLENGE

In response to the growing mental health challenge, the federal government has focused on four major areas. The first policy initiative aimed to substantially increase the number of VA mental health providers serving veterans. Since 2005, the VA has hired more than 7,500 mental health professionals.[3] The goal for fiscal year 2013 was to hire an additional 1,600 mental health professionals and 800 peer specialists; as of January 29, 2013, the VA had hired 1,058 mental health clinic providers and 100 peer specialists.[59] The VA initiated an aggressive marketing and outreach campaign to recruit qualified trainees and residents to fill these positions. All Veterans Integrated Service Networks directors had to address improving mental health access in the fiscal year 2013 performance plans.

Second, the VA has initiated new efforts to enhance partnerships with community providers. A challenge facing the VA is providing services in areas that have a mental health professional shortage but are experiencing an increased demand for mental health services. The VA partnered with the U.S. Department of Health and Human Services to help identify local community partners that could help the VA meet this new demand.[59] The VA has established initial pilot projects and formal arrangements with eleven community-based mental health and substance abuse providers across seven states and four VISNs. Tele-mental health, staff sharing, and space utilization arrangements allow the VA to extend its service reach beyond its own facilities into areas that do not have a VA facility close to patients.

The third policy initiative involved strengthening suicide prevention efforts across the DoD and the VA. There are five suicide prevention initiatives sponsored by the DoD.[54] The DoD Suicide Prevention and Risk Reduction Committee consists of key stakeholders and each service's suicide prevention program manager. The Defense Centers of Excellence for Psychological Health and Traumatic Brain Injury is funding the Real Warriors Campaign, a public awareness campaign that promotes the processes of building resilience, facilitating recovery, and supporting reintegration of returning service members, veterans, and their families. Starting in 2008, the Department of Defense Suicide Event Report has been used by all service branches to conduct surveillance on suicide events. In 2009, the DoD Task Force on the Prevention of Suicide by Members of the Armed Forces was established. Last of all, the DoD and VA have cosponsored a joint suicide prevention conference since 2009.[54]

The VA also sponsors the Veterans Crisis Line (VCL), a tool that connects veterans in crisis and their families and friends with qualified responders through a confidential toll-free hotline, online chat, or text message. Any veteran presenting to a VA center in crisis must be evaluated within twenty-four hours. The Substance Abuse and Mental Health Services Administration's National Suicide Prevention Lifeline and community crisis centers back up the VCL. Since its launch in 2007, the VCL has answered more than 975,000 calls and made more than 32,500 life-saving rescues. The anonymous online chat service was added in 2009 and has since engaged in more than 127,000 chats. In November 2011, the VCL introduced a text messaging service, which has responded to more than 15,000 texts.[60] In September 2012, the VA and the DoD came together in a year-long joint effort to support the VCL, increasing its capacity by 50 percent.[59]

The fourth and final policy initiative promotes mental health research and the development of more effective treatment methodologies. When someone is identified as being an OCO patient, that person is given a screening test that includes a primary care PTSD screen. This test has health risk–related questions designed to detect PTSD, depression, alcohol abuse, and traumatic brain injury. Patients that screen positive for a mental health condition are referred to a psychiatrist, a psychologist, or a clinician trained in mental health treatment. Even with this screening test, however, it remains difficult to identify veterans with mental disorders. Many disorders cannot be measured objectively (such as via a laboratory test), and they can be hidden or occur within other conditions. PTSD is sometimes misdiagnosed as insomnia or masked as irritability.[3]

To coordinate these efforts, President Obama signed an Executive Order on August 31, 2012, directing the Departments of Veterans Affairs, Defense, and Health and Human Services to take steps to ensure that veterans and service personnel receive the mental health services and supports that they need.[59] An Interagency Task Force on Military and Veterans Mental Health was formed, and it is co-chaired by designees of the secretaries of defense, veterans affairs, and health and human services. The task force is charged with coordinating and reviewing agency efforts to enhance veteran and military mental health and substance abuse treatment. The task force will also integrate federal capabilities with academia, industry, and other organizations to ensure that the communities are working together to promote "good health, prevent illness, and provide ready access to mental health and substance abuse services."[59]

Acknowledging the rapid growth in the total number of veterans that will require services, President Obama's 2014 budget proposal included a 4 percent increase to $63.5 billion in non-entitlement spending. Since 2009, the VA's overall budget has increased 41 percent to $140 billion. The 2014 budget proposal included $7 billion to expand mental health services, with emphasis on PTSD and military sexual trauma. Also, there have been dramatic reports about the VA's inability to process the mounting number of disability claims filed by veterans, and this new funding is designed to address these issues. On the health care side, the VA seems capable of meeting challenges within the VHA to provide care to the growing number of veterans returning to civilian life following the expected draw-down of U.S. military forces in the upcoming years.

See also **Chapter 3: The Department of Health and Human Services: Responsibilities and Policies (1953–Present); Chapter 4: The Centers for Disease Control and Prevention: Anticipatory Action in the Face of Uncertainty (1946–Present); Chapter 5: The Food and Drug Administration (1962–Present); Chapter 6: The Centers for Medicare and Medicaid Services (1965–Present); Chapter 8: The United States Supreme Court and the Department of Justice (1789–Present).**

NOTES

1. National Center for Veterans Analysis and Statistics, http://www.va.gov/vetdata.

2. U.S. Department of Defense. *Strategic Management Plan: The Business of Defense FY2014–FY2015,* 2013, http://www.defense.gov/pubs/pdfs/FY14-15_SMP.pdf.

3. Congressional Budget Office, *The Veterans Health Administration's Treatment of PTSD and Traumatic Brain Injury among Recent Combat Veterans* (Washington, DC: Congressional Budget Office, 2012).

4. Department of Defense Task Force on the Prevention of Suicide by Members of the Armed Forces, *The Challenge and the Promise: Strengthening the Force, Preventing Suicide and Saving Lives* (Falls Church, VA: Defense Health Board, 2010).

5. Jim Garamone, "Senate Confirms Hagel as Defense Secretary" (Press Release), February 26, 2013, http://www.defense.gov/news/newsarticle.aspx?id=119383.

6. Roger R. Trask and Alfred Goldberg, *The Department of Defense, 1947–1997: Organization and Leaders* (Washington, DC: U.S. Government Printing Office, 1997).

7. U.S. Department of Defense, "About the Department of Defense," http://www.defense.gov/about.

8. Office of Management and Budget, *Fiscal Year 2013 Historical Tables: Budget of the U.S. Government,* http://www.whitehouse.gov/sites/default/files/omb/budget/fy2013/assets/hist.pdf.

9. U.S. Department of Defense, "About MHS," http://www.health.mil/About-MHS.

10. Philip M. Lurie, Richard R. Bannick, and Elder Granger, *The Department of Defense's TRICARE Health Benefits Program as a Critical Plank in the Federal Platform for Health Care Reform* (Arlington, VA: Institute for Defense Analysis, 2009).

11. "H.R. 3116 (103rd): Department of Defense Appropriations Act, 1994" (Washington, DC: U.S. Government Printing Office, 1993).

12. U.S. General Accounting Office, *Defense Health Care: Despite TRICARE Procurement Improvements, Problems Remain* (Washington, DC: U.S. General Accounting Office, 1995).

13. Defense Health Agency, "About DHA," http://www.tricare.mil/tma/aboutDHA.aspx.

14. Congressional Budget Office, *Approaches to Reducing Federal Spending on Military Health Care* (Washington, DC: Congressional Budget Office, 2014).

15. Eric Elster, Eric Schoomaker, and Charles Rice, "The Laboratory of War: How Military Trauma Care Advances Are Benefiting Soldiers and Civilians," *Health Affairs* Blog, December 18, 2013, http://healthaffairs.org/blog/2013/12/18/the-laboratory-of-war-how-military-trauma-care-advances-are-benefiting-soldiers-and-civilians.

16. U.S. Department of Veterans Affairs, "History—VA History," http://www.va.gov/about_va/vahistory.asp.

17. "VA Announces Budget Request for 2012" (Press Release), February 14, 2011, http://www.va.gov/opa/pressrel/pressrelease.cfm?id=2054.

18. U.S. Department of Veterans Affairs, "Annual Budget Submission," http://www.va.gov/budget/products.asp.

19. U.S. Department of Veterans Affairs, *VA History in Brief,* 2006, http://www.va.gov/opa/publications/archives/docs/history_in_brief.pdf.

20. Veterans Health Administration, "About VHA," http://www.va.gov/health/aboutVHA.asp.

21. Shukri F. Khuri, Jennifer Daley, and William G. Henderson, "The Comparative Assessment and Improvement of Quality of Surgical Care in the Department of Veterans Affairs," *Archives of Surgery* 137: 1 (2002): 20–27.

22. Kenneth W. Kizer, *Vision for Change: A Plan to Restructure the Veterans Health Administration* (Washington, DC: Department of Veterans Affairs, 1995).

23. Congressional Budget Office, *Quality Initiatives Undertaken by the Veterans Health Administration* (Washington, DC: Congressional Budget Office, 2009).

24. Ashish K. Jha et al., "Effect of the Transformation of the Veterans Affairs Health Care System on the Quality of Care," *New England Journal of Medicine* 348: 22 (2003): 2218–2227.

25. Barbara Skydell, "Restructuring the VA Health Care System: Safety Net, Training, and Other Considerations," *National Health Policy Forum* 716 (1998): 14.

26. Jonathan B. Perlin, Robert M. Kolodner, and Robert H. Roswell, "The Veterans Health Administration: Quality, Value, Accountability, and Information as Transforming Strategies for Patient-Centered Care," *American Journal of Managed Care* 10: 11, pt. 2 (2004): 828–836.

27. Kenneth W. Kizer, *Prescription for Change: The Guiding Principles and Strategic Objectives Underlying the Transformation of the Veterans Health Administration* (Washington, DC: Department of Veterans Affairs, 1996).

28. U.S. Government Accountability Office, *Electronic Health Records: Long History of Management Challenges Raises Concerns about VA's and DOD's New Approach to Sharing Health Information* (Washington, DC: U.S. Government Accountability Office, 2013).

29. U.S. Department of Veterans Affairs, "Patient Aligned Care Team (PACT)," http://www.va.gov/health/services/primarycare/pact/index.asp.

30. Lawrence J. Korb et al., *Beyond the Call of Duty* (Washington, DC: Center for American Progress, 2007).

31. Department of Defense Contingency Tracking System, "Deployment File for Operations Enduring Freedom and Iraqi Freedom," June 2008, https://www.dmdc.osd.mil.

32. U.S. Government Accountability Office, *VA Mental Health: Number of Veterans Receiving Care, Barriers Faced, and Efforts to Increase Access* (Washington, DC: U.S. Government Accountability Office, 2011).

33. Charles W. Hoge, Jennifer L. Auchterlonie, and Charles S. Millikcn, "Mental Health Problems, Use of Mental Health Services, and Attrition from Military Service after Returning from Deployment to Iraq or Afghanistan," *Journal of the American Medical Association* 295: 9 (2006): 1023–1032.

34. Charles S. Milliken, Jennifer L. Auchterlonie, and Charles W. Hoge, "Longitudinal Assessment of Mental Health Problems among Active and Reserve Component Soldiers Returning from the Iraq War," *Journal of the American Medical Association* 298: 18 (2007): 2141–2148.

35. Gina P. Owens, Catherine J. Herrera, and Allison A. Whitesell, "A Preliminary Investigation of Mental Health Needs and Barriers to Mental Health Care for Female Veterans of Iraq and Afghanistan," *Traumatology* 15: 2 (2009): 31–37.

36. Christine Eibner, "Invisible Wounds of War: Quantifying the Societal Costs of Psychological and Cognitive Injuries" (Santa Monica, CA: RAND, 2008).

37. Karen H. Seal et al., "Bringing the War Back Home: Mental Health Disorders Among 103,788 US Veterans Returning from Iraq and Afghanistan Seen at Department of Veterans Affairs Facilities," *Archives of Internal Medicine* 167: 5 (2007): 476–482.

38. Tim Kane, *Who Bears the Burden? Demographic Characteristics of U.S. Military Recruits Before and After 9/11* (Washington, DC: Heritage Foundation, Center for Data Analysis, 2005).

39. Amy E. Wallace et al., "Rural and Urban Disparities in Health-Related Quality of Life among Veterans with Psychiatric Disorders," *Psychiatric Services* 57: 6 (2006): 851–856.

40. Todd A. Mackenzie, Amy E. Wallace, and William B. Weeks, "Impact of Rural Residence on Survival of Male Veterans Affairs Patients after Age 65," *Journal of Rural Health* 26: 4 (2010): 318–324.

41. Brenda Happell et al., "Rural Physical Health Care Services for People with Serious Mental Illness: A Nursing Perspective," *Australian Journal of Rural Health* 20: 5 (2012): 248–253.

42. James D. Reschovsky and Andrea B. Staiti, "Access and Quality: Does Rural America Lag Behind?" *Health Affairs* 24: 4 (2005): 1128–1139.

43. Erica C. Ziller, Nathaniel J. Anderson, and Andrew F. Coburn, "Access to Rural Mental Health Services: Service Use and Out-of-Pocket Costs," *Journal of Rural Health* 26: 3 (2010): 214–224.

44. Angeline Bushy, "Health Issues of Women in Rural Environments: An Overview," *Journal of the American Medical Women's Association* 53: 2 (1998): 53–56.

45. K. Bryant Smalley et al., "Rural Mental Health and Psychological Treatment: A Review for Practitioners," *Journal of Clinical Psychology* 66: 5 (2010): 479–489.

46. Rural Assistance Center, "Returning Soldier and Veteran Health Frequently Asked Questions," http://www.raconline.org/topics/veterans/veteransfaq.php.

47. John F. McCarthy, Marcia Valenstein, and Frederic C. Blow, "Residential Mobility among Patients in the VA Health System: Associations with Psychiatric Morbidity, Geographic Accessibility, and Continuity of Care," *Administration and Policy in Mental Health and Mental Health Serviccess Research* 34: 5 (2007): 448–455.

48. Frederic C. Blow et al., "Ethnicity and Diagnostic Patterns in Veterans with Psychoses," *Social Psychiatry and Psychiatric Epidemiology* 39: 10 (2004): 841–851.

49. Steven L. Robinson, *Hidden Toll of the War in Iraq: Mental Health and the Military* (Washington, DC: Center for American Progress, 2004).

50. Jordan B. Bell and Ella C. Nye, "Specific Symptoms Predict Suicidal Ideation in Vietnam Combat Veterans with Chronic Post-traumatic Stress Disorder," *Military Medicine* 172: 11 (2007): 1144–1147.

51. Casey T. Taft et al., "Posttraumatic Stress Disorder Symptoms, Physiological Reactivity, Alcohol Problems, and Aggression among Military Veterans," *Journal of Abnormal Psychology* 116: 3 (2007): 498–507.

52. Coady B. Lapierre, Andria F. Schwegler, and Bill J. LaBauve, "Posttraumatic Stress and Depression Symptoms in Soldiers Returning from Combat Operations in Iraq and Afghanistan," *Journal of Traumatic Stress* 20: 6 (2007): 933–943.

53. Marc A. Schuckit, Tom L. Smith, and Yasmin Chacko, "Evaluation of a Depression-Related Model of Alcohol Problems in 430 Probands from the San Diego Prospective Study," *Drug and Alcohol Dependence* 82: 3 (2006): 194–203.

54. Rajeev Ramchand et al., *The War Within: Preventing Suicide in the US Military* (Santa Monica, CA: RAND, 2011).

55. Robert M. Bray and Laurel L. Hourani, "Substance Use Trends among Active Duty Military Personnel: Findings from the United States Department of Defense Health Related Behavior Surveys, 1980–2005," *Addiction* 102: 7 (2007): 1092–1101.

56. Isabelle G. Jacobson et al., "Alcohol Use and Alcohol-Related Problems before and after Military Combat Deployment," *Journal of the American Medical Association* 300: 6 (2008): 663–675.

57. Frances M. Barlas et al., *2011 Department of Defense Health Related Behaviors Survey of Active Duty Military Personnel* (Arlington, VA: U.S. Department of Defense, 2013).

58. Karen H. Seal et al., "VA Mental Health Services Utilization in Iraq and Afghanistan Veterans in the First Year of Receiving New Mental Health Diagnoses," *Journal of Traumatic Stress* 23: 1 (2010): 5–16.

59. U.S. Department of Defense, U.S. Department of Veterans Affairs, and U.S. Department of Health and Human Services, *Interagency Task Force on Military and Veterans Mental Health: 2013 Interim Report*, 2013, http://www.whitehouse.gov/sites/default/files/uploads/2013_interim_report_of_the_interagency_task_force_on_military_and_veterans_mental_health.pdf.

60. Veterans Crisis Line, "About the Veterans Crisis Line," http://veteranscrisisline.net/About/AboutVeteransCrisisLine.aspx.

FURTHER READING

Bossarte, Robert M. *Veteran Suicide: A Public Health Imperative.* Washington, DC: American Public Health Association, 2013.

Finley, Erin P. *Fields of Combat: Understanding PTSD among Veterans of Iraq and Afghanistan (The Culture and Politics of Health Care Work).* Ithaca, NY: Cornell University Press, 2011.

Greenwood, John T., F. Clifton Berry Jr. *Medics at War: Military Medicine from Colonial Times to the 21st Century.* Annapolis, MD: Naval Institute Press, 2005.

Jaycox, Lisa H., and Terri Tanielian. *Invisible Wounds of War: Psychological and Cognitive Injuries, Their Consequences, and Services to Assist Recovery.* Santa Monica, CA: RAND, 2008.

Kizer, Kenneth W. *Vision for Change: A Plan to Restructure the Veterans Health Administration.* Washington, DC: Department of Veterans Affairs, 1995.

Longman, Phillip. *Best Care Anywhere: Why VA Health Care Would Work Better for Everyone.* 3rd ed. San Francisco: Berrett-Koehler, 2012.

Lurie, Philip M., Richard R. Bannick, and Elder Granger. *The Department of Defense's TRICARE Health Benefits Program as a Critical Plank in the Federal Platform for Health Care Reform.* Arlington, VA: Institute for Defense Analysis, 2009.

Ramchand, Rajeev, Joie Acosta, Rachel M. Burns, Lisa H. Jaycox, and Christopher G. Pernin. *The War Within: Preventing Suicide In the U.S. Military.* Santa Monica, CA: RAND, 2011.

Schoenbaum, Michael. *Health Benefits for Medicare-Eligible Military Retirees: Rationalizing TRICARE for Life.* Santa Monica, CA: RAND, 2004.

Tick, Edward. *War and the Soul: Healing Our Nation's Veterans from Post-tramatic Stress Disorder.* Wheaton, IL: Quest Books, 2012.

Trask, Roger R. *The Department of Defense, 1947–1997: Organization and Leaders.* Washington, DC: U.S. Government Printing Office, 1997.

U.S. Congressional Budget Office. *The Veterans Health Administration's Treatment of PTSD and Traumatic Brain Injury among Recent Combat Veterans.* Washington, DC: CreateSpace, 2012.

U.S. Department of Veterans Affairs. *The Assessment and Treatment of Individuals with History of Traumatic Brain Injury and Post-Traumatic Stress Disorder: A Systematic Review of the Evidence.* Washington, DC: U.S. Department of Veterans Affairs, 2013.

U.S. Government Accountability Office. *Defense Health Care: Implementation Issues for New TRICARE Contracts and Regional Structure.* Washington, DC: Ulan Press, 2011.

———. *Defense Health Care Reform: Additional Implementation Details Would Increase Transparency of DOD's Plans and Enhance Accountability* (GAO-14-49). Washington, DC: U.S. Government Accountability Office, November 2013.

chapter 8

The United States Supreme Court and the Department of Justice (1789–Present)

Darrell J. Kozlowski

T IS COMMONLY ACCEPTED TODAY THAT THE SUPREME Court of the United States has the final word on all constitutional matters; this extraordinary power of the Court was established in the early years of the Republic and has been a central principle in the U.S. system of government for more than two hundred years. The Court's power of judicial review is grounded in Chief Justice John Marshall's (served 1801–1836) declaration in *Marbury v. Madison* (1803): "It is emphatically the province and duty of the judicial department to say what the law is."[1] Given the Court's considerable power in health care and social policy, the history and the scope of that power should be evaluated with care, sensitive to both the origins of judicial review and how the Court has acted since its beginnings.

The office of attorney general, which leads the Department of Justice (DOJ), was established by the Judiciary Act of 1789; the DOJ was elevated to cabinet-level status in 1870. Today, as it has since its beginnings, the DOJ works to ensure that all Americans are treated fairly and equally under the law; this is especially true in the realm of health care, where there are lists of cases in which unscrupulous providers and suppliers committed fraud, wasted taxpayer money, and discriminated against those in need. In the coming years, as more key provisions of the Patient Protection and Affordable Care Act (PPACA) are put into force, the mission statement of the DOJ will resonate throughout all health care fields:

> To enforce the law and defend the interests of the United States according to the law; to ensure public safety against threats foreign and domestic; to provide federal leadership in preventing and controlling crime; to seek just punishment for those guilty of unlawful behavior; and to ensure fair and impartial administration of justice for all Americans.[2]

THE THIRD BRANCH OF GOVERNMENT

Although Article III of the U.S. Constitution establishes the Supreme Court, it provides virtually no detail about the Court's structure or specific responsibilities:

> Section. 1.
> The judicial Power of the United States shall be vested in one supreme Court, and in such inferior Courts as the Congress may from time to time ordain and establish. The Judges, both of the supreme and inferior Courts, shall hold their Offices during good Behaviour, and shall, at stated Times, receive for their Services a Compensation, which shall not be diminished during their Continuance in Office.

> Section. 2.
> The judicial Power shall extend to all Cases, in Law and Equity, arising under this Constitution, the Laws of the United States, and Treaties made, or which shall be made, under their Authority;—to all Cases affecting Ambassadors, other public Ministers and Consuls;—to all Cases of admiralty and maritime Jurisdiction;—to Controversies to which the United States shall be a Party;—to Controversies between two or more States. . . .[3]

President Thomas Jefferson (1801–1809) complained that Marshall's assertion in *Marbury v. Madison* was a "gratuitous" exercise, given that "in the outset, [having] disclaimed all cognizance of the case [he] then went on to say what would have been their opinion."[4] Indeed, Marshall could have determined that the proper course of action in *Marbury* simply would have been to ask whether the Court had the power to hear this case, to state that it did not, and to dismiss it. Marshall, however, was keenly aware that the Supreme Court was seen as an afterthought in the U.S. governmental system. When Chief Justice Oliver Ellsworth (served 1796–1800) resigned in late 1800, President John Adams (1797–1801) renominated the first Chief Justice, John Jay (served 1789–1795), to replace Ellsworth. Jay was quickly confirmed by the Senate and Adams sent him a letter informing him of his appointment. Refusing the appointment, Jay tersely informed the president that he had better things to do than rejoin a Court that was "so defective" that it could not "acquire the public Confidence and Respect, which, as the last Resort of Justice of the nation, it should possess."[5] Adams considered others before appointing Marshall, who is now referred to as the Great Chief Justice.[6] Once confirmed, Marshall was determined to give the Court what he believed to be its rightful place. Thus, *Marbury* was the first in a series of judicial rulings asserting the authority of the Supreme Court.

Challenges to Judicial Review

The assertion of judicial authority was not always welcomed. For example, in his First Inaugural Address, Abraham Lincoln (1861–1865), referring to the infamous ruling in *Dred Scott v. Sandford* (1857), which held that blacks could not be U.S. citizens, contended that the Court's interpretation of the Constitution "must be binding . . . upon the parties" in the particular case before it, but otherwise are "entitled [only] to very high respect and consideration in all parallel cases."[7] Later, in 1937, President Franklin D. Roosevelt (1933–1945), provoked by ruling after ruling that invalidated key New Deal measures, offered his Court-packing plan in an ill-fated attempt to bypass a group of conservative justices, who appeared determined to undo the president's plans at every turn.

Each of these assaults on the tradition of judicial review was rebuffed. In 1957, when the governor of Arkansas attempted to defy the Court and preserve racial segregation in public schools, President Dwight D. Eisenhower (1953–1961) wanted to avoid the possibility of bloodshed in the highly charged situation. Yet as president and commander-in-chief, he recognized the importance of the rule of law, acting decisively to enforce the Court's ruling in *Brown v. Board of Education* (1954) that the concept of "separate but equal" had no place in the United States.

Evolution of the Court's Powers

What is the significance of these (and other) successful assertions of judicial review? Perhaps it is a reflection of what Associate Justice Robert Jackson (served 1941–1954) once famously observed about the Court: "We are not final because we are infallible, but we are infallible only because we are final."[8] Although it is reasonable to accept his view, there remain two significant issues.

The first issue to consider is that the vast majority of the Court's decisions are mundane. For example, a dispute about the proper labeling of generic drugs is of considerable importance for both the companies involved and the general public. Yet *Caraco Pharmaceutical Laboratories, LTD v. Novo Nordisk A/S* (2012) was far from headline news. Nonetheless, these types of cases are typical, occupying the vast majority of the Court's time. The second issue to remember is that views about the Court and how it rules are apt to be at least somewhat distorted when viewed as matters of high legal and political drama—the so-called landmark decisions.

Women and men march to the Supreme Court to demonstrate their support for the Patient Protection and Affordable Care Act of 2010 (PPACA). On June, 27, 2010, the Supreme Court upheld the constitutionality of the PPACA, including the provisions concerning women's reproductive rights and health.

SOURCE: Andrew Harrer/Bloomberg via Getty Images.

The National Federation of Independent Business v. Sebelius *(2012)*

The Patient Protection and Affordable Care Act of 2010, a sweeping piece of health care legislation, provoked deep debate from the moment it was introduced into Congress. Virtually everyone believed that the contested views would be resolved only when the measure reached the Supreme Court. In addition, many observers were convinced that how the Court ruled would turn not on the law, but on the philosophical predispositions of the individual justices. In *National Federation of Independent Business v. Sebelius* (2012), a decision that pleased virtually no one, a bare majority of the Court sustained one of the act's central provisions and perhaps the most controversial, the so-called individual mandate.

KEY DECISIONS: HEALTH CARE CRISES AND SOLUTIONS

The Medicare Modernization Act

The Medicare Prescription Drug, Improvement, and Modernization Act, also called the Medicare Modernization Act (MMA), was introduced into Congress in June 2003. It was signed into law by President George W. Bush (2001–2009) on December 8, 2003, after being passed by a close margin: 220 to 215 in the House of Representatives and 55 to 44 in the Senate. The MMA resulted in the largest overhaul of Medicare in the public health program's history. The most significant provision of the MMA is the introduction of an entitlement benefit for prescription drugs, known as Medicare Part D. Among other things, the MMA requires drug manufacturers to file documents with the DoJ, especially as concerns the entry of generic medications into the marketplace. Since Medicare's creation in 1965, the use of prescription drugs has grown significantly. As new and increasingly expensive drugs have become available, patients, particularly senior citizens for whom Medicare was designed, have found prescriptions more difficult to afford. The MMA was meant to address this problem.

Initially, the net cost of the program was projected at $400 billion for the ten-year period between 2004 and 2013. One month after the bill's passage, the administration estimated that the cost between 2006 (the first year the program started paying benefits) and 2015 would be $534 billion. As of February 2009, the estimated cost of the program for the period 2006 to 2015 was $549.2 billion.

SOURCES: Centers for Medicare and Medicaid Services, *Medicare Modernization Act Update—Overview,* http://www.cms.gov/Regulations-and-Guidance/Regulations-and-Policies/QuarterlyProviderUpdates/index.html; Vicki Kemper, "Medicare Drug Benefit Plan to Far Exceed Cost Estimate," *Los Angeles Times,* January 30, 2004.

The Court as Institution

It is important to recognize that the role the Court plays in health and health care policy is limited but, by definition, not truly final. Although the Court clearly has the last word about what particular terms in the Constitution actually mean, unless amended, that does not give the Court ultimate control. Most matters of social or health care policy that are contested involve very specific rulings or protocols enacted at all levels of government: federal, state, and local. Thus, the Court is setting law, not policy. At least since 1819, the basic rule is that judgments about policy are made by the political branches. The Supreme Court, Chief Justice John Marshall instructed in *McCulloch v. Maryland* (1819),

> must allow to the national legislature that discretion, with respect to the means by which the powers [the Constitution] confers are to be carried into execution, which will enable that body to perform the high duties assigned to it, in the manner most beneficial to the people.[9]

Thus, for example, the Court informs the nation exactly what it means when the Constitution states that Congress has the power to "regulate Commerce with Foreign Nations, and among the several States, and with the Indian Tribes."[10] That is, as a constitutional matter, the Court determines whether a given statute is a "proper" exercise of that judicially defined power.

Interpretation and Application of the Law

The difference between constitutional interpretation and the application of constitutional principles in legal construction is an important one. Congress, for example, cannot tell the Court what the term *commerce* means. Indeed, the rule that the Court has the final say in these matters is so ingrained

that individual justices have no misgivings in joining rulings affirming the Court's primacy, even when the underlying constitutional principle is one with which they disagree. For example, Chief Justice William H. Rehnquist (appointed as associate justice in 1972; served as chief justice 1986–2005) opposed the rule articulated in *Miranda v. Arizona* (1966), arguing in case after case that the "procedural safeguards" announced in *Miranda* "were not themselves rights protected by the Constitution."[11] Yet in a case describing a legislative provision that undermined *Miranda,* it was Rehnquist who wrote for the Court in *Dickerson v. United States* (2000), declaring that "*Miranda,* being a constitutional decision of this Court, may not be in effect overruled by an Act of Congress."[12]

That said, Congress can and frequently does step in after the fact to cure the constitutional defects the Court has identified in a particular statute, as in *National Federation of Independent Business v. Sebelius.* This means that the Supreme Court's decision is final in matters of statutory construction only in the sense that it resolves the particular constitutional question posed by the specific provision at issue in the case before it.

Constitutional Adjudication

One of the most important first principles in judicial review is that the Court understands the serious nature of constitutional adjudication. The Court knows that it and the "inferior" federal courts are overseen by individuals who are not elected and have life tenure. As a practical matter, the Court has responded to this "countermajoritarian difficulty" by adopting various rules of self-restraint that mean, at least in theory, that it will do everything it can to avoid deciding constitutional questions. One such rule suggests that if a given case poses both statutory and constitutional questions, and can be resolved on statutory grounds only, the Court will do so. Thus, the reality is that the Court decides very few cases, even as the requests that it do so have multiplied. As the Court notes on its Web site, its docket—the number of cases filed—has increased from about 1,460 in 1945 and 2,313 in 1960 to more than 10,000 per year. Yet the number of opinions issued has declined sharply since 1945, to the point where a Court that routinely decided hundreds of cases in the 1920s and 1930s now issues an average of seventy-five written opinions a year.[13]

There are two major reasons for this decline in Supreme Court decisions. One is statutory; the Court's appellate docket is controlled by Congress. Article III of the U.S. Constitution states that the Court's "original" jurisdiction, the power to file cases directly with the Court, is quite limited, extending only to "Cases affecting Ambassadors, other public Ministers and Consuls, and those in which a State shall be a party." In "all . . . other Cases," the Court has only "appellate Jurisdiction . . . under such Regulations as the Congress shall make."[14] Taken together, these provisions mean that the vast majority of the Court's cases come to it from lower courts, federal and state. Even then, however, the means by which the cases get to the Court need to be taken into account. One possibility is that the losing party exercises a right of appeal: in effect, it brings to the Court a case that it must hear. The other is that the losing party in a case

seeks discretionary review, filing a writ of certiorari, which asks the Court to take a case it has no obligation to accept.

The second reason for the contraction of the Court's docket is sagacious. The Court truly believes that the power of judicial review should be used cautiously. In particular, the Court has used its power to write the rules of constitutional interpretation to restrict the scope of its powers and the size of its docket.

Thus, the Court focuses on the standard of review: the degree of scrutiny the Court will employ when it considers constitutional questions. As a doctrinal matter, the standard of review now employed by the Court in most matters of health care policy is deferential. Consistent with the approach articulated in *McCulloch,* judgments about whether a given measure is good or bad policy are left to others. Therefore, as Justice Antonin Scalia (served 1986–) once observed, "a law can be both . . . folly and constitutional."[15]

The Spending Power

Article I, section 8 of the U.S. Constitution gives Congress the power to raise money and spend it for the "general Welfare of the United States." One of the major disputes resolved during the New Deal years focused on the extent to which spending measures could be used to effect policy. Consistent with earlier holdings, the Court initially rejected the idea that the federal funds could carry conditions that would allow the federal government to achieve certain national goals. Two specific concerns lay at the heart of these cases. The first was the extent to which a given federal spending measure was designed to achieve policy goals that the federal government could not accomplish directly. The second was the extent to which the conditions imposed intruded on traditional assumptions about the nature and scope of state sovereignty.

The judicial rules that emerged reflected a theme already discussed: the need for the federal courts to treat such matters with deference, entrusting to Congress judgments about both what constituted the general welfare and what the policies should be in such matters. As Chief Justice Burger (served 1969–1986) stressed in *Fullilove v. Klutznick* (1980):

> Congress has frequently employed the Spending Power to further broad policy objectives by conditioning receipt of federal moneys upon compliance by the recipient with federal statutory and administrative directives. This Court has repeatedly upheld against constitutional challenge the use of this technique to induce governments and private parties to cooperate voluntarily with federal policy.[16]

The increasing use of the spending power led to concerns that federal initiatives reached too far into the realm of issues traditionally determined by the states. The Court

FIGURE 8.1   **Select Health Care–Related Supreme Court Cases**

Health Care Reform

National Federation of Independent Business v. Sebelius (2012)

Birth Control and Abortion

Griswold v. Connecticut (1965)

Eisenstadt v. Baird (1972)

Roe v. Wade (1973)

Carey v. Population Services International (1977)

Planned Parenthood of Southeastern Pennsylvania v. Casey (1992)

Stenberg v. Carhart (2000)

Gonzales v. Carhart (2007)

End-of-Life Issues

Cruzan v. Director, Missouri Department of Health (1990)

Washington v. Glucksberg (1997)

Vacco v. Quill (1997)

Gonzales v. Oregon (2006)

SOURCE: http://www.supremecourt.gov.

Americans with Disabilities Act Barrier-Free Health Care Initiative

The Department of Justice (DOJ) regularly works with other government agencies to ensure that laws, especially those related to health care or discrimination, are actively enforced. In 2012, the DOJ announced a new initiative in which U.S. Attorneys' offices across the nation partnered with the DOJ's Civil Rights Division to target their enforcement efforts on a critical area for individuals with disabilities.

This new initiative will make sure that people with disabilities, especially those who are deaf or hard of hearing, have access to medical information provided to them in a manner that is understandable to them. The Barrier-Free Health Care Initiative is a multi-phase plan that will also involve other key issues for people with disabilities, including ensuring physical access to medical buildings.

"Access to health care remains an area of critical need for too many people with disabilities, especially those who are deaf or who have hearing loss," said Assistant Attorney General Perez. "The Barrier-Free Health Care Initiative will make sure people with disabilities are capable of physically accessing medical buildings and facilities and are not discriminated against when it comes to receiving potentially life-saving medical information. I look forward to continuing to work with U.S. Attorneys to advance ADA [Americans with Disabilities Act] compliance efforts nationwide."

The Civil Rights Division and U.S. Attorney's offices have long enforced the ADA in this area. This nationwide initiative seeks to focus and leverage the department's resources together and aggregate and echo the collective message that disability discrimination in health care is illegal and unacceptable. . . .

SOURCE: "Justice Department Announces Americans with Disabilities Act Barrier-Free Health Care Initiative by US Attorney's Offices Nationwide" (Press Release), July 26, 2012, http://www.justice.gov/opa/pr/2012/July/12-crt-931.html.

used two decisions to clarify the situation. In the first, *Pennhurst State School and Hospital v. Halderman* (1984), it stressed that the circumstances in question must be determined in advance so that compliance was truly voluntary. In the second, *South Dakota v. Dole* (1987), it sustained a congressional determination that states should raise their drinking ages to twenty-one or forfeit a portion of their federal highway funds. The Court ruled that such measures must meet four requirements: they must be "in pursuit of the 'general welfare,'" they must be "unambiguous," they must be "reasonable" and related to the national interest, and they must not be in violation of any other constitutional provision. In particular, the Court stressed that a "reasonable" measure was not one that was "so coercive as to pass the point at which 'pressure' turns into 'compulsion.'"[17]

New Restrictions and the PPACA

These specific restrictions on congressional power were not terribly burdensome, and the spending power was not deemed particularly controversial. However, in June 2012, a deeply divided Court handed down its decision on the Patient Protection and Affordable Care Act of 2010 in *National Federation of Independent Business v. Sebelius* (2012). In an opinion that many Court observers found deeply puzzling, Chief Justice John Roberts (served 2005–) declared that the "shared responsibility payment" required as part of the individual mandate could be sustained as a

"tax." Yet he also found that the means selected by Congress to induce the states to substantially increase their Medicaid programs crossed the line from simple alteration of the terms of the program into impermissible coercion.

The goal was to expand Medicaid to all non-Medicare-eligible individuals under age sixty-five (children, pregnant women, parents, and adults without dependent children) with incomes up to 133 percent of the federal poverty level based on modified adjusted gross income. The federal government would initially provide all of the new money required to do this, but it would decrease that payment gradually to 90 percent of the funding. It also conditioned continued payment of all Medicaid funds on participation in the expansion. The Court held that these conditions went too far and failed the Court's fourth requirement. The Court stressed the sheer size of the program, which in some states amounted to more than 10 percent of their respective budgets. Believing that the core agreement functioned as a contract between the federal government and the recipient state, Roberts stated that this "surprising, retroactive" provision was an impermissible attempt to "conscript" the states in ways that violated the Constitution. The Chief Justice expressly declined, however, to provide any particular guidance regarding how such lines should be drawn in the future, referring and resorting to a spending clause parallel to Justice Potter Stewart's (served 1958–1981) statement about obscenity, in effect declaring that "we will know it when we see it."

Establishing the Health Care Rights of Prisoners

In 1976, the U.S. Supreme Court established the standard of what a prisoner must plead in order to claim a violation of the Eighth Amendment protection against "cruel and unusual punishment." J.W. Gamble was a state prisoner who injured his back during prison labor, when a bale of cotton fell on him. He continued working, but later complained of back pain and stiffness. He was diagnosed with lower back strain and prescribed pain medication; however, he claimed that he failed to receive proper medical care, thus violating the Eighth Amendment.

In *Estelle v. Gamble* (1976), the Court found for the defendant, W.J. Estelle, director of the Texas Department of Corrections, because it viewed Gamble's failure to receive proper medical care as "inadvertent." Nevertheless, the case established the principle that the deliberate failure of prison authorities to address the medical needs of an inmate constitutes "cruel and unusual punishment." It held that "deliberate indifference to serious medical needs of prisoners constitutes the 'unnecessary and wanton infliction of pain' proscribed by the Eighth Amendment."

In 1993, the Supreme Court extended the requirement that inmates obtain medical care beyond what it established in *Estelle*. In *Helling v. McKinney* (1993), the Court heard the case of a Nevada prisoner, William McKinney, the cellmate of a five-pack-a-day smoker, who sought to be housed in a cell free of secondhand smoke. McKinney did not suffer from any illness, nor had he sought any medical treatment. Justice Byron White (served 1962–1993) wrote for a 7–2 majority that McKinney's claim that prison officials "have, with deliberate indifference, exposed him to levels of [secondhand smoke] that pose an unreasonable risk of serious damage to his future health" raised a valid claim under the Eighth Amendment. Justice White further noted that McKinney would have to prove both the scientific facts of the dangers of exposure to secondhand smoke and prove that community standards supported him, that "it violates contemporary standards of decency to expose *anyone* unwillingly to such a risk. In other words, the prisoner must show that the risk of which he complains is not one that today's society chooses to tolerate." He would also have to prove that prison officials acted with "deliberate indifference." Thus, if McKinney could prove that the secondhand smoke posed a serious threat to his future health and that the prison officials had deliberately ignored that threat, McKinney would be entitled to relief.

The DOJ and Health Care Fraud

In early 2014, Attorney General Eric Holder (in office 2009–) and Health and Human Services Secretary Kathleen Sebelius (in office 2009–2014) released the annual Health Care Fraud and Abuse Control (HCFAC) Program report. It showed that for every dollar spent on health care–related fraud and abuse investigations in the last three years, the government recovered $8.10. This was the highest three-year average return on investment in the seventeen-year history of the HCFAC Program.

The government's health care fraud prevention and enforcement efforts recovered a record-breaking $4.3 billion in taxpayer dollars in fiscal year 2013 from individuals and companies who attempted to defraud federal health programs. These recoveries, as noted in the HCFAC Program report, demonstrate President Barack Obama's (2009–) ongoing commitment to eliminate fraud, waste, and abuse, particularly in health care.

The success of the joint effort by the DOJ and HHS was made possible in part by the Health Care Fraud Prevention and Enforcement Action Team (HEAT), created in 2009 to prevent fraud, waste, and abuse in Medicare and Medicaid. Noted Attorney General Holder:

> With these extraordinary recoveries, and the record-high rate of return on investment we've achieved on our comprehensive health care fraud enforcement efforts, we're sending a strong message to those who would take advantage of their fellow citizens, target vulnerable populations, and commit fraud on federal health care programs. Thanks to initiatives like HEAT, our work to combat fraud has never been more cooperative or more effective. And our unprecedented commitment to holding criminals accountable, and securing remarkable results for American taxpayers, is paying dividends.[18]

The Patient Protection and Affordable Care Act and Health Care Fraud

New authority granted to HHS and the Centers for Medicare and Medicaid Services (CMS) under the PPACA was essential in reducing fraudulent activity in health care. Then Secretary Sebelius noted:

> We've cracked down on tens of thousands health [of] care providers suspected of Medicare fraud. New enrollment screening techniques are proving effective in preventing high risk providers from getting into the system, and the new computer analytics system that detects and stops fraudulent billing before money ever goes out the door is accomplishing positive results—all of which are adding to savings for the Medicare Trust Fund.[19]

The DOJ and HHS have improved their coordination through HEAT and are currently operating Medicare Fraud Strike Force teams. These teams use advanced data analysis techniques to identify high billing levels in health care fraud hot spots as well as fraud committed by criminals masquerading as health care providers or suppliers. The Justice Department's enforcement of the civil False Claims Act and the Federal Food, Drug and Cosmetic Act has produced similar record-breaking results. These combined efforts coordinated under HEAT have expanded local partnerships and helped educate Medicare beneficiaries about how to protect themselves against fraud.

Protecting Consumers and Taxpayers

In fiscal year 2013, the Justice Department opened 1,013 new criminal health care fraud investigations involving 1,910 defendants; a total of 718 defendants were convicted of health care fraud–related crimes during that year. The department also opened 1,083 new civil health care fraud investigations. In May 2013, for example, the strike force coordinated an operation that resulted in charges against eighty-nine individuals, including doctors, nurses, and other licensed medical professionals, for their alleged participation in Medicare fraud schemes involving about $223 million in false billings. The defendants who were found guilty and sentenced faced significant time in prison—an average of fifty-two months.

In March 2011, CMS began a new project to revalidate all 1.5 million Medicare providers and suppliers under the PPACA screening requirements. As of September 2013, more than 535,000 providers were subject to the new screening requirements, and more than 225,000 lost the ability to bill Medicare because of PPACA requirements. Since passage of the PPACA in 2010, CMS has revoked 14,663 providers' and suppliers' ability to bill the Medicare program.

Today, HHS and the Justice Department continue to work with the private sector to bring innovation to the fight against health care fraud. In addition to real-time data and information exchanges with the private sector, CMS and HHS offices worked with the Federal Bureau of Investigation to conduct ninety-three missions to detect, investigate, and reduce improper payments in fiscal year 2013.

Maintaining Competition in the Health Care Field

In addition to working to limit health care fraud and prevent discriminatory practices, the DOJ also strives to maintain competition among health care providers as well as among the many pharmaceutical companies. Competition in these areas provides incentive to keep costs low and to prevent monopolistic practices, such as the restraint of trade. Competition also leads to innovation, thus keeping the nation at the fore of the global health care industry. The DOJ has put forth a series of recommendations, including the following, to improve competition in health care markets:

1. Private payers, governments, and providers should continue experiments to improve incentives for providers to lower costs and enhance quality and for consumers to seek lower prices and better quality.

2. States should decrease barriers to entry into provider markets.

3. Governments should reexamine the role of subsidies in health care markets in light of their inefficiencies and potential to distort competition.

4. Governments should not enact legislation to permit independent physicians to bargain collectively.

5. States should consider the potential costs and benefits of regulating pharmacy benefit manager transparency.

6. Governments should reconsider whether current mandates best serve their citizens' health care needs. When deciding whether to mandate particular benefits, governments should consider that such mandates are likely to reduce competition, restrict consumer choice, raise the cost of health insurance, and increase the number of uninsured Americans.[20]

The DOJ concluded its recommendations by noting that consumer welfare is maximized by open competition and consumer sovereignty, even when complex products and services such as health care are involved. Thus, the department plays an important role in safeguarding the free market system from anticompetitive conduct by bringing enforcement actions against parties who violate antitrust and consumer protection laws.

LOOKING AHEAD

No doubt the DOJ and the U.S. Supreme Court will continue to play a major role in the nation's health care policy. As the various provisions of the PPACA go into effect, it is likely that the Court will be called upon to clarify the law. Certainly, it is equally likely that the Justice Department will develop new strategies to enforce the law and prevent health care fraud so that all Americans have access to the health care benefits as promised.

See also Chapter 3: The Department of Health and Human Services: Responsibilities and Policies (1953–Present); Chapter 4: The Centers for Disease Control and Prevention: Anticipatory Action in the Face of Uncertainty (1946–Present); Chapter 5: The Food and Drug Administration (1962–Present); Chapter 6: The Centers for Medicare and Medicaid Services (1965–Present); Chapter 7: The Departments of Defense and Veterans Affairs: Responsibilities and Policies (1947–Present).

NOTES

1. 5 U.S. (1 Cranch) 137, 177 (1803).

2. U.S. Department of Justice, "About DOJ," http://www.justice.gov/about/about.html.

3. "Constitution of the United States," http://www.archives.gov/exhibits/charters/constitution_transcript.html.

4. Letter from Thomas Jefferson to George Hay (June 2, 1807), in *The Writings of Thomas Jefferson,* Vol. 11, edited by Andrew A. Lipscomb and Albert Ellery Bergh (Washington, DC: Thomas Jefferson Memorial Association, 1903), 213–215.

5. Letter from John Jay to John Adams (January 2, 1801), in *The Documentary History of the Supreme Court of the United States, 1789–1800, Part 1: Appointments and Proceedings,* edited by Maeva Marcus, 146–147 (New York: Columbia University Press, 1985).

6. For the full, and not often told story, see Kathryn Turner, "The Appointment of Chief Justice Marshall," *William and Mary Quarterly* 17: 2 (1960): 143.

7. Abraham Lincoln, First Inaugural Address (March 4, 1861), in *A Compilation of the Messages and Papers of the Presidents,* Vol. 7, edited by James D. Richardson (Washington, DC: Bureau of National Literature, 1897), 5, 9.

8. *Brown v. Allen,* 344 U.S. 443, 540 (1953) (Jackson, J., concurring).

9. 17 U.S. (4 Wheat.) 316, 421 (1819).

10. "Constitution of the United States."

11. *Michigan v. Tucker,* 417 U.S. 433, 444 (1974).

12. 530 U.S. 428, 432 (2000).

13. The trend can be observed by comparing the data found in Felix Frankfurter and James M. Landis, "The Business of the Supreme Court at October Term, 1931," *Harvard Law Review* 46 (1931): 226–260, with that set forth in "The Supreme Court 2011 Term: The Statistics," *Harvard Law Review* 126 (2012): 388–403. Table VI in Frankfurter and Landis's article documents annual adjudication numbers for the years 1927–1931, ranging between a high of 327 and a low of 319. During its term starting in October 2011, the Court granted review and disposed of 66 cases out of the 7,685 considered.

14. "Constitution of the United States."

15. *CTS Corporation v. Dynamics Corporation of America,* 481 U.S. 69, 96–97 (1987) (Scalia, J., concurring).

16. *Fullilove v. Klutznick,* 448 U.S. at 474.

17. *South Dakota v. Dole,* 483 U.S. at 211.

18. U.S. Department of Health and Human Services, "Departments of Justice and Health and Human Services Announce Record-Breaking Recoveries Resulting from Joint Efforts to Combat Health Care Fraud" (press release), http://www.hhs.gov/news/press/2014pres/02/20140226a.html.

19. Ibid.

20. Federal Trade Commission and Department of Justice, "Improving Health Care: A Dose of Competition," July 2004, http://www.justice.gov/atr/public/health_care/204694/exec_sum.htm.

FURTHER READING

Belknap, Michal R. *The Supreme Court under Earl Warren, 1953–1969.* Columbia: University of South Carolina Press, 2005.

Kazmier, Janice L. *Health Care Law.* Independence, KY: Cengage Learning, 2008.

Leuchtenburg, William E. *The Supreme Court Reborn: The Constitutional Revolution in the Age of Roosevelt.* New York: Oxford University Press, 1995.

Maltz, Earl M. *The Chief Justiceship of Warren Burger 1969–1986.* Columbia: University of South Carolina Press, 2000.

Powe, Lucas A., Jr. *The Supreme Court and the American Elite 1789–2008.* Cambridge, MA: Harvard University Press, 2009.

Steiner, John E., Jr. *Problems in Health Care Law: Challenges for the 21st Century.* Burlington, MA: Jones & Bartlett, 2013.

Tushnet, Mark V. *A Court Divided: The Rehnquist Court and the Future of Constitutional Law.* New York: W.W. Norton, 2005.

U.S. Department of Health and Human Services. http://www.hhs.gov.

U.S. Department of Justice. http://www.justice.gov.

U.S. Supreme Court. http://www.supremecourt.gov.

chapter 9

Budgeting and Health Care Policy (1970s–Present)

Roy T. Meyers

THE CREATION OF MEDICARE AND MEDICAID in 1965 put health policy on the path to becoming the largest category in the federal budget. The federal government had long been involved in various activities to promote health; for example, spending on facilities for veterans' medical care began early in the nineteenth century. By 1953, when President Dwight D. Eisenhower (1953–1961) created the Department of Health, Education and Welfare (HEW), the federal government regularly conducted public health investigations, regulated food safety, financed hospital construction and medical education, and made grants for biomedical research.

Of course, periodically during the twentieth century, Congress and the president considered but rejected establishing a national health insurance system. The legislative breakthrough of 1965 created health insurance programs for the elderly and the poor, but it set an important precedent—health care was now an "entitlement" for these groups. If people met the program's eligibility requirements, then the federal government (with substantial assistance from state governments in the case of Medicaid) guaranteed payment for their medical care by participating providers. This guarantee had an open-ended impact on the budget—more money would be spent as both the number of beneficiaries and the costs of providing care increased.

Spending on Medicare and Medicaid quickly proved to be much higher than was expected at the time of enactment, primarily due to provider-friendly payment systems; the 1972 expansion of Medicare to cover those with end-stage renal disease, for example, was another notable contributor. By 1973, a rhetoric of "cost crisis" had become widespread, and President Richard M. Nixon (1969–1974) and Congress began to consider controls for these programs. Nixon also proposed a comprehensive plan for health insurance, a central component of which was an employer mandate, which for many reasons failed in Congress.[1]

One reason the plan failed was that by this time, Nixon had alienated Congress by threatening its "power of the purse." Article I of the U.S. Constitution prevents agencies from spending funds unless they receive appropriations from Congress. This implies that once funds are appropriated, agencies should spend them, except in extraordinary circumstances. Nixon disagreed, and shortly after his 1972 reelection, he refused to spend, or impounded, some appropriated funds, claiming that the programs were wasteful. Congress rightly believed that Nixon's action was unconstitutional, and it responded with the Congressional Budget and Impoundment Control Act of 1974. This law severely limited presidential authority on impoundments, but more important, it supplemented the long-standing congressional authorizations and appropriations processes with a new process by which Congress would establish its own budget.

NATIONAL HEALTH EXPENDITURES DATA AND FEDERAL BUDGET FUNCTIONS

According to the federal government's National Health Expenditures data, in calendar year 2012 (the most recent year available as of this writing), spending on health care in the United States was $2.79 trillion. This was 17.2 percent of the nation's gross domestic product (GDP). These data show the federal government spent $732 billion, and state and local governments spent $497 billion, but these figures exclude government health spending that was financed by employee payroll taxes and premiums paid to the Medicare trust funds.[2]

Turning to federal government budget data on health spending, one useful categorization is "budget functions," which breaks federal spending into about twenty major categories. For fiscal year 2013 (the most recent year for which data are available), which ran from October 1, 2012, to September 30, 2013, the Treasury Department reported that outlays for function 550 Health were $357 billion. Outlays are liquidations of obligations or, less formally, cash payments. The typical purposes of outlays in the health budget function are to reimburse medical providers for services they provide to patients, compensate civil servants in the Department of Health and Human Services (HHS), pay contractors for administering health insurance programs, grant funds to medical researchers housed at academic institutions and to states and localities for providing services, and pay for acquiring physical assets for the federal government, such as building a hospital on the campus of the National Institutes of Health (NIH).

The budget's "health" function is not intended to be a comprehensive measure of all government health spending. That function includes one of the federal government's most expensive health programs, Medicaid, along with many other programs in its "health care services" subfunction 551, and separate subfunctions for "health research training" and "consumer and occupational health and safety." However, there is an entirely separate budget function for Medicare, function 570, which had $498 billion in outlays in fiscal year 2013. Other budget subfunctions with substantial health spending were 703 Hospital and Medical Care for Veterans (where fiscal year 2013 outlays exceeded $50 billion) and 051 Defense, Military Personnel (where funding for health care in fiscal year 2012 was $52 billion, almost 10 percent of the regular defense budget).[3]

DISCRETIONARY SPENDING AND THE APPROPRIATIONS AND AUTHORIZATIONS COMMITTEES

While congressional budget resolutions group spending by budget functions, the authorizations and appropriations processes are much more important for the allocation of funds to departments and programs. Here, the critically important distinction is between discretionary and mandatory spending.

Discretionary Spending

By definition, a discretionary spending program is one that each year receives budget authority through the annual appropriations process. Budget authority is permission given to a department to obligate funds now or in the future. Liquidations of these obligations are outlays. In programs that pay personnel, the conversion speed of budget authority

to outlays, which is known as the "spend-out rate," is usually rapid, with the agency spending almost all of its budget authority in that year. In programs that purchase assets, spend-out rates can be much slower. Twelve annual appropriation bills are drafted by the appropriations committees of the House and Senate, after which they are considered by the whole House and Senate.

Almost all of the major operations by government, for the administration of health care services and the regulation of health, and almost all of the major grants and contracts for particular projects, are discretionary. If Congress were to follow routinely the schedule it has set out for itself, this would mean that by October 1 of each year, the major discretionary health programs would receive budget authority in four appropriations bills: the Labor, Health and Human Services, and Education bill (commonly called Labor-H); the Defense bill; the Military Construction and Veterans Affairs bill; and the Agriculture bill, which includes the Food and Drug Administration (FDA). Congress and the president have routinely failed to enact these bills on time, especially in recent years. Among the many reasons for the recent delays is the increased ideological polarization between the two major political parties. Delays for the Labor-H bill are more longstanding due to riders, provisions that affect spending but are more controversial because of their policy impact, such as bans on using government funds to finance abortions or family planning.

When regular appropriations bills are not enacted by the target date of October 1, Congress typically passes a continuing resolution, or CR, a law that gives departments budget authority for a limited period of time, usually from several weeks to several months. These bills typically require departments to spend at the current rate: the amount of spending authorized for the previous year, with no upward adjustments for inflation or for an increased demand for services. Departments also cannot use funds for purposes that were not in the previous year's budget, which is known as "no new starts."

In some years, numerous continuing resolutions have been required before Congress and the president finally agreed on the discretionary appropriations amounts and related policy disputes. The Library of Congress maintains a very helpful Web page on the "Status of Appropriations Legislation," which can be used to keep track of the progress, or lack of it, on these bills.[4] On several occasions Congress has failed to pass even a continuing resolution, which, under a strict interpretation of the U.S. Constitution, has meant that departments must cease their non-essential operations and send their unfunded employees home without pay. Perhaps as bad has been the regular threat of government shutdowns, which has forced departments to plan for shutdowns rather than carry out more productive activities.[5]

Authorizing Committees

While the provision of budget authority to discretionary programs is under the sole jurisdiction of appropriators, these programs typically must receive an authorization before being funded. The authorization committees have the responsibility to draft these bills before floor consideration. The Senate committee with the most jurisdiction in the discretionary health area is the cutely named Health, Education, Labor and Pensions Committee, or HELP. Armed Services and Veterans' Affairs oversee the aforementioned major health services programs for current and ex-military, and the same is the case in the House. The House, however, has no full committee that includes *health* in its title. There is a Health Subcommittee, which has jurisdiction over most nonmilitary discretionary health programs; it is part of the Energy and Commerce Committee, which is one of the House's most powerful committees.

Authorizing committees are responsible for creating departments and programs, and then overseeing their creations' behavior through hearings and investigations. These committees periodically try to pass revisions to their authorizations, subject to time being available on the legislative calendars. Authorization provisions are often tremendously important. For example, they have established the conditions of federal assistance for hospital construction, the rules for carrying out biomedical research, and the process for the regulation of food and drugs. Appropriators usually, but not always, defer to these committees' policy guidance.

For discretionary spending, authorizing committees also write into their bills permission for the appropriators to provide budget authority. That is, the process is intended to have two steps: first, the authorizers establish a program in great detail and provide a rough guide to how much funding could be provided; second, the appropriators decide how much funding will be provided. For the first step, the Congressional Budget Office (CBO), a nonpartisan group of budget experts, supplies a cost estimate that accompanies each bill when it is reported to the whole House or Senate. By convention, these projections assume that the appropriators will supply the full amounts of discretionary budget authority that are permitted in the authorizations and estimates the resulting outlays based on historical spend-out rates.

Despite that "full funding" assumption, *discretionary* means just that: the appropriators need not feel bound by what is often an authorizing committee's desire to expand funding for the program it has designed. It is rather common for appropriations to come in below authorized levels. However, the term *discretionary* is also in one sense a misnomer. Consider the Veterans Health Administration (VHA), the country's largest integrated health system, which is financed each year through the discretionary appropriations process. Practical and political realities require the appropriators to come close to the amount requested for this organization's budget, and it has often been the case that appropriations have exceeded presidential requests. In fact, given the practice of late appropriations bills, in 2009, Congress decided to provide the VHA with an advance appropriation, which means that the appropriation bill funds spending for the following fiscal year. That is, any delay in passing the appropriation bill by October 1 will not hurt the VHA, because its budget for the year starting on that date will already have been enacted in the previous year. Agencies within HHS are not so fortunate.

MANDATORY SPENDING, THE TAXATION COMMITTEES, AND HEALTH-RELATED TAXATION

The programs that are truly fortunate regarding the timing of budget approvals are so-called *mandatory* programs. This term is even more of a misnomer than *discretionary*, if the implication is that this spending cannot be reduced. That is incorrect in most cases, though there is no question that changing mandatory spending is not easy. For example, spending on Medicare, a mandatory program, has occasionally been reduced from its projected level, but this has required expenditure of substantial political capital, given the opposition by powerful interests that benefit from the program.

Mandatory Spending

The simplest start to understanding this type of spending has again to do with committee jurisdictions. In contrast to discretionary spending, which requires action by the appropriations committees, for mandatory spending, the appropriations committees have been written out of the process. The authorizing committees have taken over the appropriators' role by writing legislation that not only created a program but also provided that program with budget authority. Much like getting a beneficial card in the game Monopoly, a department with mandatory budget authority can go straight to the Treasury for its funding without having to get past the appropriators. So benefit payments for Medicare and Medicaid are mandatory, but the Centers for Medicare and Medicaid Services (CMS) must receive a discretionary appropriation to cover the costs of administering these programs.

Controlling Mandatory Health Care Spending

The authorization committees that control the most mandatory health spending are the Senate Finance Committee and the House Ways and Means Committee. These committees are especially powerful because they have exclusive jurisdiction over taxes and borrowing. This power can be politically precarious, given the tendency of Americans to rebel against taxes and to worry about government debt. On the other hand, jurisdiction over taxes has allowed these committees to greatly influence health policy, in two very different ways—the power to not collect taxes and the power to dedicate taxes.

The power to not collect taxes is used when Congress enacts tax preferences, which take many forms, including deductions, credits, exemptions, exclusions, and deferrals. The revenue losses from these preferences are called tax expenditures. The largest health tax preference by far, estimated to cost $203 billion in fiscal year 2013, is the exclusion from income taxation of employer-provided medical insurance premiums and medical care. It is also the costliest of all tax preferences, more than double the revenue loss from allowing the deduction of mortgage interest for owner-occupied homes.[6]

There is no doubt that this benefit is economic income to employees, but there is also no doubt that proposing to include this compensation in the income tax base is politically dangerous. The exception that proves this rule is the provision suggested early during consideration of the Patient Protection and Affordable Care Act (PPACA) to impose a tax on so-called Cadillac health insurance plans, those whose scope of benefits and low out-of-pocket costs for employees requires high annual premiums. By limiting the amount of private health insurance spending that can be excluded from taxation, government can limit its revenue losses and increase employee sensitivity to that spending. The near-term impact of this limit on the tax preference was greatly reduced in the adopted legislation after unions such as the United Mine Workers, who had negotiated strong health insurance coverage for those with very unhealthy occupations, lobbied against it. However, because the legislation did set a fixed dollar figure for the level at which the tax will apply, under the current law, as costs increase over time, more health insurance plans will become subject to the tax. Anticipation of this effect has already produced a lobbying campaign to amend the law.

Estimates of health tax expenditures, including eleven smaller health tax expenditures listed by the Office of Management and Budget, can be found in the Analytical Perspectives volume of the president's budget. This presentation is far less visible than the detailed descriptions of regular health spending programs in the rest of the budget. Like mandatory spending, health tax expenditures are not subject to annual review by appropriators. Apart from the occasional effort to carry out comprehensive reforms of the health care system or the tax code, health tax provisions receive very little scrutiny from the budget process.[7]

Medicare is a good example of the second benefit of having exclusive jurisdiction over taxation. The taxation committees may dedicate revenues to programs that they control, most notably through the Social Security Act of 1935.

Amendments to this act have created many programs, including Supplemental Security Income, child support enforcement, foster care and adoption assistance, "welfare" (now known as Temporary Assistance for Needy Families), and Medicare and Medicaid. (The House Energy and Commerce Committee now has primary jurisdiction over Medicaid.)

By statute, Medicare's Part A receives a share of payroll tax receipts to pay for the hospital insurance program. This dedication provides a source of budget authority separate from the general revenues of the Treasury, which are primarily from individual income taxes. As with Social Security, advocates of the program wanted to insulate Medicare's finances from general revenues and the appropriations process. The prior payment of dedicated taxes helped generate widespread perceptions of earned rights to program benefits, and Part A's finances were segregated in a so-called trust fund. Trust funds earn interest from the Treasury on the surplus of dedicated receipts that are not used to pay current benefits. The label *trust* also implies to some, mistakenly in fact, that the funds are sufficient to pay for all benefits and that they can never be used for other purposes.[8]

The trust fund structure is not the only approach for health mandatory spending. Most of Medicare's spending on outpatient services and prescription drugs is financed by general revenues and by premium payments from beneficiaries. Those premiums, along with co-insurance payments and substantial deductibles for inpatient hospital care, amount to several thousand dollars annually for an average beneficiary, who must either pay these costs directly or purchase supplemental "Medigap" insurance to cover them.

Medicare premiums are not counted as taxes, but as offsetting receipts, which are subtracted from outlays on the spending side of the budget. Medicaid is financed out of general revenues. The federal budget also includes taxes on tobacco and alcohol intended to reduce demand for these products, particularly among youth. These revenues are not dedicated to related programs, such as for substance abuse, though they have been used as offsets to allow increased spending on health programs in general. Offsets are increased revenues or reduced spending used to counteract the deficit-increasing effects of a spending increase or tax cut on the budget. A final financing source for health spending that deserves mention is government borrowing; because the federal government routinely runs a budget deficit (an excess of outlays over revenues), health spending contributes to the need to issue debt.

HEALTH BUDGETING IN THE EXECUTIVE BRANCH

Presidents and the executive branch at their command play a very significant role in health care budgeting. The Budget and Accounting Act of 1921 gave the president the responsibility to gather the spending estimates of agencies, modify them if desired, and present them as a comprehensive budget request to Congress. That act also created the General Accounting Office, now known as the Government Accountability Office (GAO), an agency of the legislative branch whose audits of health programs can be very influential.

The Budget and Accounting Act also led to the creation of a central budget office in the executive branch, which is now called the Office of Management and Budget (OMB). Its director is a political appointee, as are some subordinates; particularly important for health is the program associate director (PAD) for health. Health PADs typically have extensive political experience and have gone on to important health policy jobs, such as administrator of the CMS. Most of OMB's employees are civil servants, hired for their neutral competence: technical skills in policy analysis, management, and budgeting that are used in service of both Democratic and Republican administrations.

Importance of the OMB in Health Care Funding

OMB has many roles, including coordination of the administration's legislative program, but its most important responsibilities are to prepare the president's budget request and to oversee the execution of enacted budgets. It periodically issues specific guidelines to agencies about these activities, and these publications are available on OMB's Web page. Yet much of OMB's budget preparation work is not transparent to the public. In general, executive budget preparation is viewed as providing confidential advice to the president.

The budget preparation process begins with the budget "call," comprising broad guidance to departments about the president's priorities and the exceptionally detailed Circular A-11 that shows the format in which budget requests should be prepared. The process of budget preparation within domestic departments is designed to respond by early fall to OMB's requirements. Within HHS, for example, the various agencies, such as the NIH, Health Resources and Services Administration (HRSA), CMS, FDA, and Centers for Disease Control and Prevention (CDC), prepare requests that are reviewed by the department's budget office and the HHS secretary, with support units such as the assistant secretary for planning and evaluation weighing in. Each of these major agencies has its own budget office that runs a similar process within the department.

Once departments submit their budget requests, OMB's civil servant budget examiners (who are now formally called "resource management officers") review those requests in consultation with their bosses and make tentative decisions about which of the department's requests will be approved and which will be denied. The communication of these decisions to departments is called the "passback."

Passback day is usually not a happy day in departments, for it is rare for OMB to let a department's request through unscathed. A department proposal may be inconsistent with the president's program, or the examiner may believe that the department failed to show that a proposal would be cost-effective, or there simply may not be enough funding available even for a well-justified program.[9]

The next step in the process is potentially an appeal of the passback, which at its most serious stage can involve the HHS secretary petitioning directly the OMB director, senior White House staff, or the president. The word *potentially* is used because it is difficult to win appeals. Since in many years there has been substantial political concern about the size of the deficit and of the amount of government spending, the federal budget process has become a top-down process. This means that OMB has more influence than departments and that it takes a very strong argument to convince the White House to reverse its central budget office.

Performance versus Incrementalism

A distinctive element of executive budget preparation is its recent emphasis on what is broadly known as performance management. This approach seeks to replace a historically important method known as incrementalism, in which a proposed budget typically included only small changes to the previous year's budget. Over the past century, periodic attempts have been made to replace incrementalism with a more rational one in which the government takes a comprehensive view of its spending, estimates the projected benefits of alternative paths, and if necessary make substantial changes to the current budget. Some efforts to move toward rational budgeting have been particularly unrealistic, but the most recent approach has produced some improvements in the executive branch process. It started in 1993 when Congress passed the Government Performance and Results Act (GPRA), which required agencies to produce strategic plans, report periodically on their program results, and integrate their plans and results measurements with budget requests, management of operations, and personnel systems.

The Government Performance and Results Act

Implementation of GPRA has had mixed effects. A particular challenge has been that it placed the onus on the executive branch even though the legislative branch has substantial influence through the authorizations process on the statutory goals required of the agency and similar influence through the appropriations process on the resources available to address those goals. When Congress has been controlled by a different party than controls the presidency, legislators have complained, sometimes with cause, that departments failed to consult with Congress about their strategic plans.

On the other hand, many health agencies have made much progress generating and using performance data. GPRA called for a shift of focus toward outcomes, the intended results of programs, rather than looking solely at agency activities and their immediate outputs. This approach is consistent with existing efforts such as the decennial Healthy People goal-setting process and with the aspiration of the health field more generally to make decisions based on evidence.

In an analysis of how major HHS agencies had implemented GPRA through 2006, David and George Fredrickson found that despite the outcomes focus required by law (e.g., on healthier Americans), agencies in practice tended to focus on their operations and outputs (e.g., on the amount of services delivered). CMS reported quantitative figures on payment accuracy, while NIH reported qualitative findings about how the agency generated scientific knowledge. Outcome measurement happens to be quite challenging for many HHS-funded operations, particularly when this requires monitoring of the many contractors and grantees that provide health services funded by HHS (e.g., in substance abuse and mental health services). But even if outcomes could be determined with complete confidence, this information would rarely provide a definitive answer to the question: "Should we spend more or less on this program?" Evidence of a poorly performing program may indicate the need for reform and even more spending, rather than the termination of efforts to attain an important goal.[10]

The GPRA Modernization Act of 2010 made a modest extension of GPRA's aspirations, particularly to develop goals and strategies that cut across department jurisdictions. How far this approach can be pushed depends in part on how strongly the executive branch commits to it—but receptivity by Congress is also important. Though Congress mandated GPRA, the institution has often ignored department performance analyses. Many legislators are less interested in the cost-effectiveness of programs than they are in how much money will be spent, and especially where (in which states and districts) and on whom (beneficiaries, providers, grantees, and campaign donors).

While there is much truth to this characterization of congressional behavior, it can also be overstated. The appropriations committees require departments to supplement the president's budget with a justification book. Running in the many hundreds of pages, these documents provide committee staff with extensive detail on discretionary budgets: on personnel, building construction and maintenance, major contracts, the previous year's spending record and related accomplishments, and especially plans for new projects and programs. Agency leaders can expect many questions about these details, some about arcane matters, but also some about issues central to the agency's operations. In hearings and through personal communications, legislators and their staff also ask about special projects of interest to subcommittee members. Projects for specific beneficiaries that are inserted into the budget by legislators are known as earmarks; compared to other areas of the budget, most health budget accounts have few earmarks.

A particularly cynical view of legislative disinterest in effectively controlling spending observes that legislators are among the first to blame agencies for "fraud, waste, and abuse" (FWA) in health spending, even though they have not given agencies the full ability to control it. For years, after an offhand comment by a GAO official that "perhaps 10 percent" of Medicaid spending was fraudulent, this ratio was cited by legislators as an authoritative number when they would call attention to the problem and, in some cases, blame administrators for this supposed magnitude. But the real magnitude of FWA is by definition hard to estimate; if the government knew how all the misspending took place, it would be much easier to reduce that amount. CMS has recently stated that it believes a better estimate of improper payments is about one-third of the 10 percent imaginary figure.

Controlling Fraud and Waste

Over the past few decades, genuine progress has been made in fraud control; CMS and the Department of Justice have repeatedly succeeded in prosecuting providers who fraudulently billed Medicare and Medicaid. Yet many experts believe that additional investments are warranted. Health spending auditors and prosecutors can return many multiples of their salaries by preventing payments that providers do not deserve. Congressional practice is to not count increased funding for this purpose (known as program integrity appropriations) against some budget limits, but this has not been enough incentive to entice Congress to make much larger appropriations. Controlling fraudulent spending also requires effective regulation, which can be a political challenge when an influential provider group opposes such regulation, as has been the case with bidding procedures for durable medical equipment.[11]

State governments have also opposed stricter regulations, such as for Medicaid matching policies. Over the years, many states have imposed various taxes and fees on Medicaid providers, the proceeds of which have been recycled into the state medical systems, but which have increased the gross costs of the state programs. This increased the effective match rate to state spending that is provided by the federal government. At times, federal budget officials have labeled these practices as scams and the like, and periodically the federal government has limited its budget exposure by tightening its rules, though with very generous adjustment periods for the innovative states.[12]

While health FWA is often in the political spotlight, more generally the practice of budget execution—the implementation of enacted budgets—usually receives less attention than is deserved by its importance. Implementation of the PPACA is the clear exception. OMB plays a central role in controlling budget execution. Departments must report periodically to OMB on how they are spending their funds and must receive approval during each quarter of the fiscal year to spend portions of their enacted budgets (known as apportionments). OMB's Office of Information and Regulatory Affairs reviews proposed major health regulations that can have large impacts on budget costs. Finally, OMB is responsible for issuing sequestration orders, which require budget cuts that are triggered by the failure of Congress and the president to meet certain budget targets.[13]

To summarize, the executive budget preparation process is very hierarchical, with multiple deadlines and repeated adjustments from the point that a unit proposes its initial budget request. The process is very hard to observe from the outside. Although the process is oriented toward a rational approach, given the aforementioned delays in legislative budgeting, it's also fair to say that the executive process is often confused. How can it be possible to prepare a sensible budget request for next year when one does not know for months into the current year what the final approved budget is for that year? And that is not the only problem with how budget politics affects budget preparation and execution.

HEALTH IN THE CONGRESSIONAL BUDGET RESOLUTION AND IN BUDGET ENFORCEMENT

According to the Congressional Budget Act, Congress is supposed to pass its budget resolution by April 15. The process starts when separate resolutions are drafted by the budget committees of the House and Senate. The House Committee has a rotating membership and is a very partisan body; the Senate Committee retains its members as long as they would like to stay on the committee and is also now very partisan, much more so than it was in the past.

The budget resolution sets a floor for revenues and ceilings for budget authority, outlays, the deficit, and the debt. The resolution also divides the spending totals for budget authority and outlays between the various budget functions. However, since these budget functions do not match the jurisdictions of the appropriations and authorizations committees, the budget committees crosswalk, or transform, these allocations into those that match the various committee jurisdictions. Each appropriations committee receives its "302a" allocation, which constitutes all discretionary spending, and it then divides this amount between its twelve subcommittees, producing its "302b" ceilings. The appropriations subcommittees have the leeway to draft bills that reduce or increase health spending from the discretionary amounts assumed in the budget resolution.

The 302 ceilings are used during the rest of the appropriations process to make sure that subcommittees do not pass bills that provide more funding than the total allowed by the budget resolution. Legislators may raise a point of order against bills that violate the 302b ceilings. In addition, the Budget Control Act of 2011 created annual dollar limits on the two subtotals of defense and nondefense discretionary spending.

Budget Reconciliation

The budget resolution's total for mandatory spending is distributed to the authorization committees. Important enforcement procedures are based on these policy totals. A budget resolution may include reconciliation instructions to these committees to report changes in law that if enacted would reduce mandatory spending and/or increase revenues. Reconciliation bills are particularly important in the Senate because they cannot be filibustered, so they have served as vehicles for important changes to major entitlements. For example, the Balanced Budget Act of 1997 planned significant reductions in Medicare payments to providers, and created the State Children's Health Insurance Program. That is, reconciliation has been used not only to reduce spending, but also to increase spending on particular mandatory programs.[14]

The other enforcement control for mandatory spending is called "paygo." This rule requires that if Congress wants to create new mandatory spending or to provide new tax cuts, it must offset the resulting deficit increases with cuts in existing mandatory spending or with new tax increases. This rule, which was put in place in 1990, was a significant barrier, though not the most important one, to adoption of the Clinton health reform plan. In contrast, the temporary expiration of the paygo rule enabled passage of the Medicare Modernization Act of 2003, which created a prescription drug plan for outpatient Medicare beneficiaries. The projected cost of this expansion was limited by that year's budget resolution to $400 billion over a ten-year estimating period, but no offset was required. Passage of this bill was controversial in many respects; the House leadership used questionable methods to gain passage of the bill on the floor, and some actuarial estimates of the bill's cost were higher than the $400 billion ceiling, but those estimates were prevented from being released to the public.[15]

There are few defenders of the current congressional budget process, and for good reason. Over the past decade, Congress has frequently failed to pass a budget resolution. When this has happened, the cause has usually been policy disagreements between the parties over which they have been unwilling to compromise. Absent a budget resolution, the House and Senate set different ceilings for discretionary spending, making it more likely that there will be lengthy disputes over individual bills. Passage of the 2011 Budget

Control Act provided a substitute for budget resolution caps, but if the totals of this act are maintained over the next decade, the resulting nondefense discretionary spending will be less than 3 percent of GDP, which is below its percentage in 1962, when public expectations for government performance were much lower than they are today. For this reason, these projected cuts are widely believed to be politically unsustainable.

THE POLITICS OF HEALTH SPENDING CONTROL AND EXPANSION

The word *unsustainable* is more often used about mandatory spending for health care. For decades, the growth rate in federal health care spending has exceeded the growth rate of revenues. "Excess cost growth" can be also seen when comparing growth of the health sector of the economy to growth of the economy as a whole, and macroeconomic projections indicate that continuing this allocation of society's resources toward health care will eventually slow economic growth.[16] While health care cost growth has shrunk very recently, many projections assume significant excess cost growth over the coming decades. More spending on health benefits would crowd out spending in other parts of the budget and/or require large tax increases.[17]

Some advocates have argued that this projected growth of health spending is a crisis, one that threatens the financial viability of the country. Using the code word *entitlements*, by which they mean Medicare, Medicaid, and Social Security, these advocates have called for major reductions to spending on these programs. They have supported their claims by drawing from seventy-five-year actuarial projections that show Medicare's trust fund rapidly approaching insolvency. Other experts acknowledge that these projections show the need to shore up the program's finances, but reject the crisis imagery and the reliance on highly uncertain long-term estimates. They suggest that as the country's wealth increases, increased revenues can help close the financing gap, and they also note that the country still lacks an efficient and universal system for insuring for long-term care.[18]

Public Response to Health Care Spending and Growth

Most of the public has not responded to warnings of a health care funding problem by embracing proposed cuts in health care spending or increases in taxes. One of the most telling examples was the hand-lettered signs at Tea Party rallies that screamed: "Get the Government's Hands Off My Medicare!" However, that confusion about who runs Medicare is not shared by many elderly, or for that matter by many of their children; Medicare is one of the most successful and popular programs in U.S. history. In fact, the public is highly desirous of more spending on health in general. In public opinion polls, when asked whether government is spending "too little" or "too much" on health, the public typically chooses the former. For example, in 2012, Ellis and Stimson reported findings from the 2008 General Social Survey: when the public was asked about a range of public policies for which it was possible that "too little" was being spent, the option of "improving and protecting nation's health" was their top choice.[19] As is typical for such surveys, respondents were not simultaneously asked how reversing "too little" should be financed. A fundamental long-run question for health budgeting is thus: do we really want to increase spending for Medicare, Medicaid, and other health care payments if it will be financed by cuts to other spending and/or with higher taxes?

Many citizens and elected officials can be accused of ignoring that tradeoff, of respectively demanding and promising the proverbial free lunch. However, that criticism should not ignore the many plausible justifications for spending more on a broad range of health programs. Many rural and inner-city areas lack quality health care; HRSA budget increases might help. Substance abuse and mental health problems are quite serious; higher budgets for the Substance Abuse and Mental Health Services Administration and the VHA could assist those in need. Reductions in environmental pollution have saved many lives, including by reducing crime-stimulating exposures to lead; more research and enforcement funding for the Environmental Protection Agency could produce similar benefits. The CDC has an impressive record combating communicable diseases and other public health challenges. What are the chances that we won't need to spend more on these areas as the world becomes even more interconnected and as climate change creates more disease vectors? Also, regarding records of accomplishments, the massive government investment in biomedical research has clearly paid off in increased health outcomes, an argument used to support doubling the NIH budget over the period 1998 to 2003 (though funding in constant dollars has declined slightly since 2003). Is there much reason to doubt that more research spending, such as the proposed mapping of the fine details of the brain, would fail to produce findings that would benefit us?

That earlier NIH budget increase came about because Senator Arlen Specter (R-PA; in office 1981–2011) and a broad coalition of supporters mobilized to convince elected officials about the merits of a budget increase. More generally, health budgeting involves a multitude of affected interest groups as well as influential think tanks and for-profit consulting firms. These organizations interact in an "issue network" that on a daily basis exchanges research findings and rhetorical arguments about current health policy issues. The shifting coalitions of advocates for different types of health spending are often very influential, for they are well organized, geographically distributed, and politically skilled. There is not a legislator in the country who doesn't know successful doctors and hospital executives or is unaware of the influence exercised by the insurance companies represented by America's health insurance plans and by individual brokers.

Sometimes health provider interest groups have provided solutions to the financing challenges for expanded health spending. After the FDA was criticized for delays in its reviews of drug safety and efficacy in the mid-1990s, the pharmaceutical industry supported a proposal that they pay user fees to finance faster FDA reviews for generic drugs. Passage of the PPACA in 2010 was smoothed when major provider groups agreed that since expanded access would provide additional demand for their services, they would contribute new revenues, such as through excise taxes, to finance the law's early costs. That bargain has not completely held, however; interest groups, such as the providers of durable medical equipment, are now lobbying to repeal the taxes that affect them.

In other cases, the influence of provider groups has been a substantial barrier to desirable budget savings. This is because the government's health costs equal health providers' incomes, a truism of health budgeting that suggests why the process is often politically challenging for elected officials.[20] Nevertheless, many politicians prefer to claim that the policies they adopt to control health budgets will generate savings from providers' pockets and not from the patients. One justification for this approach is that the incomes and profits of U.S. health providers are substantially higher than the incomes and profits of comparable quality providers in other rich countries. However, with the PPACA's access expansion, the United States will need more providers in many important practice areas, limiting the potential for short-term savings. Over the longer run, the PPACA is projected to save substantial sums as it fosters new payment systems based on quality and as the government learns from numerous policy experiments authorized by the law.

Changing Health Funding Budgeting Procedures

U.S. budgeting has recently featured new procedures that some hoped would force difficult actions. One such approach for health budgets was the Sustainable Growth Rate Mechanism (SGR), which each year retroactively would reduce physicians' fees paid by the Medicare program to offset previous spending that exceeded a target related to inflation. Under the fee-for-service method used by Medicare, individual physicians are rewarded for providing more services. The SGR was intended to impose collective responsibility among physicians for controlling the

overall volume of services; all physicians were supposed to be punished for collectively exceeding the SGR target, whether they individually were contributing to the excess volume of services or not.

In practice, the SGR has been a failure. Repeatedly, Congress has voted to limit the adjustments; these actions have accumulated to schedule larger and larger cuts that will not be allowed to occur but that nevertheless are incorporated into budget projections.[21] A related approach was the establishment of the "excess general revenue funding trigger," which required the president to propose legislative changes for Medicare when it was funded with general revenues by more than an arbitrary 45 percent level. As with the SGR, this has not forced action.[22]

Another procedural approach for generating health budget savings is to form a group of health policy experts, insulated from day-to-day politics, to propose specific savings that are backed by evidence. The highly respected Medicare Payment Advisory Commission has generated many such proposals, but its influence has been more through an "enlightenment effect" of building support over the long run for good ideas rather than stimulating quick action by Congress and the president—who are not insulated from politics.[23] The PPACA creates a somewhat more powerful body, the Independent Payment Advisory Board (IPAB), which could force provider payment reductions in the future. Fifteen experts would recommend changes to Medicare's fee schedule if spending exceeded a specified amount, and their proposals would be implemented by HHS unless Congress disapproved them on a fast-track schedule. However, the IPAB may already be obsolete, for it seems likely that a replacement for the SGR will extend the PPACA's shift toward replacing fee-for-service payments with payments that reward the production of quality health outcomes.[24]

Each adoption of a major health policy change, such as Medicare's 1983 introduction of the prospective payment system for hospitals, has significantly changed health budgeting. In recent years there have been many proposals for large changes to the health sector, each accompanied by projections of budget savings. Among those that have not (yet) been adopted are a single-payer system, Medicare for All, replacing employer-based health insurance, block granting Medicaid, and a "premium support" to limit the government's portion of Medicare costs. The prospects of these approaches were all greatly diminished by passage of the PPACA, especially after the Supreme Court upheld most of the law and the 2012 reelection of President Obama effectively endorsed the law's continuation.

The PPACA's backers argued sensibly that access expansion was a prerequisite for cost control and quality improvement. The truth of this assertion will be tested as the law's benefits and mandates are phased in. Given its scope, full implementation of the law has been a tremendous challenge, and there will undoubtedly need to be significant changes made through both administrative and legislative actions. A particular challenge will be finding sufficient funds for administering the program. While the PPACA's authors used mandatory funding for administering parts of the law, opponents of the law have been fighting a rear-guard action against it by seeking to withhold the additional discretionary funding that is needed.

In sum, the PPACA has set in motion a dramatic transformation in how the country will budget for health; much uncertainty remains about how that transformation will proceed.

INTERGOVERNMENTAL ASPECTS OF HEALTH BUDGETING

In addition to federal budgeting for health, state and local governments also spend large amounts on health, often with matching assistance from the federal government. The largest state expenditures by far are for Medicaid. This program is typically the first or second largest component of state budgets, along with state spending on elementary and secondary education. States also spend large amounts on mental health and substance abuse services. Some local governments operate hospitals they own, many provide emergency medical services, and most provide public health services along with their states.

POLITICS AND HEALTH CARE POLICY

Debating and Projecting the Costs of the PPACA

Many authors have described the long and winding path to enactment of the PPACA, featuring ideological disputes about the extent to which government should guarantee health insurance, and political surprises such as the election of Scott Brown (R-MA; in office 2010–2013) to the Senate, which forced the Democrats to use budget reconciliation to pass critical elements of the reform.[25] Just as important as these factors was how the bill's budgetary costs and health insurance access expansions were projected by the Congressional Budget Office.

In 1994, in his testimony on the health proposal submitted by the Clinton administration before the House Ways and Means Committee, Robert D. Reischauer made an unusual plea:

> With your indulgence, I would like to close my remarks on a more personal note than is typical for the testimony of the Director of the Congressional Budget Office. I have appeared before committees and subcommittees of the Congress well over 100 times. On each of these occasions I have started with some customary remarks concerning how pleased I was to have the opportunity to testify.
>
> I did not start off that way today. I did not because I have considerable foreboding that the information contained in my statement and in the CBO report might be used largely in destructive rather than constructive ways—that is, it might be used to undercut a serious discussion of health reform alternatives or to gain some short-term partisan political advantage. I am not a babe in the woods who thinks that it is wrong to use CBO's objective analyses and estimates in the give-and-take of the political fray. But when this has happened in the past, it has quickly died down, and then CBO's input has been put to use in constructive ways to shape better policy.
>
> I fervently hope that will be the case once again. But I have not been encouraged by the recent debate, which at times has degenerated into semantic mud wrestling and name-calling. . . .

Reischauer continued by expressing a wish that the legislators would emulate their predecessors who passed the 1965 Medicare Act and write new legislation to make "America's health care system more equitable, more efficient, and less costly." His concerns were prescient; Congress passed no bill in 1994. This suggests a fascinating question: how did the Congressional Budget Office estimate the effects of the PPACA when the congressional practice of "semantic mud wrestling and name-calling" had greatly increased from its prior level? The short answer is that during consideration of both the Clinton health proposal and the PPACA, CBO's staff persevered despite an extraordinary workload and substantial political pressure to change its projections; the agency has a strong culture of independence and high-quality analysis.

There were many factors that produced the PPACA, but one was the increased capacity of the CBO to project the effects of major health policy changes. Besides the cost estimates mentioned above, CBO produces macroeconomic forecasts, policy analysis on major programs, and baseline projections and scorekeeping reports. The baseline is particularly important—it is a projection of spending and revenues under current law that is used to evaluate proposed changes to policy.

In 2007, CBO Director Peter Orszag, in anticipation of major health legislation, successfully requested from appropriators more funding to hire additional experts in health policy and budgets. These staff proceeded to build a sophisticated health insurance simulation model designed to estimate the effects on the budget and on insurance access from many possible changes to health policy. The model combined data from numerous sources—on business firms, federal programs, federal taxes,

With fifty state governments and almost forty thousand general purpose local governments in the United States, it is impossible to provide a succinct explanation of how these different governments budget for health. Powers vary substantially across governments; in some, the chief executives—governors, county executives, mayors—are relatively powerful; in others, legislative bodies have comparable powers. In most governments, however, the basics of state and local budgeting resemble the federal government's—the executive requests a comprehensive budget with the assistance of a central budget office, and then the legislature reviews, amends, and enacts a budget.

As with federal budgeting, there is widespread concern about how health spending may threaten fiscal sustainability.

Many state and local governments have promised health insurance benefits to their retirees, and accounting guidelines now require that more attention be paid to these "other post-employment benefits" (OPEB). Few governments have set aside funds to cover their OPEB liabilities, which are very costly, especially when added to the liabilities presented by the many underfunded pension plans. The new rules have led some governments to reduce their planned health benefits; many more will follow.

Long-term projections also show very large exposures over the next few decades from Medicaid spending. Most state leaders believe that controlling costs while maintaining and improving services for the growing population assisted by Medicaid will be a daunting challenge. Yet to many, that

and health providers—and used weights drawn from a voluminous review of empirical studies to estimate the effects of policy proposals. To build confidence in its approach, and to educate legislators about the policy tradeoffs, during 2007 and 2008, CBO released technical information about its modeling and two comprehensive reports: "Key Issues in Analyzing Major Health Insurance Proposals" and "Budget Options: Health Care." While CBO's analysis of the Clinton proposal discussed important administrative challenges of implementation, this topic received less attention during the PPACA's consideration.

Another difference from the Clinton approach was that President Obama largely deferred to Congress about the details of health reform, after he established major principles that he said should guide the reform. Obama also hired Orszag to be his OMB director. The five authorization committees with primary jurisdiction over health began to draft legislation, and they repeatedly requested informal estimates from CBO about the effects of their proposals. Those proposals that cost "too much" or that covered "too few" from the perspectives of their authors were modified or dropped. "Too much" was also guided by the Democrats' informal pledge to keep the total increase in spending for health care to no more than (an arbitrary target of) $900 billion over a ten-year period and by the president's pledge and the paygo requirement that the PPACA not increase the deficit over this span. The PPACA as enacted met those targets and was also projected to produce significant savings in the second decade of its implementation.

Though CBO's numbers were used to determine whether the legislation was affordable, these projections were also highly uncertain. It is impossible to predict with high confidence the behavior of providers, patients, and government administrators when legislation creates policies that are substantive changes from current practices. CBO exhibited the natural estimating caution of budget agencies by crediting the legislation with budget savings only when there was substantial evidence that those savings would likely occur, upsetting proponents of health reform.[26]

The uncertainty of projections increases the longer are the periods they cover. As required by statute, CBO provided point estimates of budgetary effects for individual provisions of the bill over the first ten-year period, but for the second decade, it estimated only how the total bill would affect government health care spending as a percentage of gross domestic product. CBO also repeatedly warned Congress that there were relatively large ranges around some of its point estimates.

One of the major financing sources for the PPACA came from reducing payments to Medicare Advantage comprehensive health plans, which many experts said were too generous. This both reduced the future expenditures of the Medicare hospital insurance trust fund and offset some of the costs of expanding access through Medicaid and exchange subsidies, leading to a dispute over whether this was "double-counting." The law also included a voluntary long-term care insurance program, the CLASS Act; premiums for the program would be collected in the first decade of PPACA implementation, helping to offset the projected effect of access expansion on the deficit. However, the CLASS Act also would lead to long-term outlays; the law would go into effect only if projected after passage of the PPACA to be actuarially sound. That it would not be was predictable given its voluntary participation, and HHS decided not to implement it. That was only one of many actions by HHS since passage of the law, actions that have led to revisions in CBO's original projections, though the law is still projected to reduce the deficit.

SOURCES: Congressional Budget Office, *Selected CBO Publications Related to Health Care Legislation, 2009–2010* (Washington, DC: Congressional Budget Office, December 2010); Richard S. Foster, "Estimated Effects of the 'Patient Protection and Affordable Care Act' on the Year of Exhaustion for the Part A Trust Fund, Part B Premiums and Part A and Part B Coinsurance Amounts" (Washington, DC: Office of the Actuary, Centers for Medicare and Medicaid Services, December 10, 2009); Paul N. Van de Water and James R. Horney, "Health Reform Will Reduce the Deficit: Charges of Budgetary Gimmickry Are Unfounded" (Washington, DC: Center for Budget and Policy Priorities, March 25, 2010); Jon R. Gabel, "Congress's Health Care Numbers Don't Add Up," *New York Times*, August 26, 2009; Philip G. Joyce, *The Congressional Budget Office: Honest Numbers, Power, and Policymaking* (Washington, DC: Georgetown University Press, 2011), Chs. 6 and 7; Bruce Vladeck, "Paralysis by Analysis," *Roll Call*, July 28, 2009; David M. Cutler, Karen Davis, and Kristof Stremikis, "Why Health Reform Will Bend the Cost Curve" (New York: Commonwealth Fund, December 2009).

problem is also an opportunity, for the states in effect run fifty different Medicaid programs. While important federal standards exist, the states have great flexibility in designing their programs, subject to approval from HHS through several waiver processes.

This diversity of Medicaid was increased by the Supreme Court's decision in *National Federation of Independent Business v. Sebelius* (2012), in which it determined by a 5–4 vote that the Patient Protection and Affordable Care Act was a constitutional exercise of the taxing power. The other important holding in this case, by a 7–2 vote, was that the PPACA's expansion of Medicaid could not be forced on the states. The PPACA provides very generous terms to the states for expanding the population covered by Medicaid, for those with incomes up to 138 percent of the federal poverty line: the full costs of expansion are covered by the federal government for the first three years and phased in to 90 percent thereafter. Yet partisan opposition to President Obama and ideological opposition to an expanded federal role in health insurance led twenty-one states, as of July 2013, to decide not to expand Medicaid, with six additional states undecided. Should all of these states decide not to participate, nearly two-thirds of those uninsured who would have been covered by the Medicaid expansion would still lack coverage. The loss of federal funds to these twenty-seven states has been estimated to total almost $600 billion over ten years. Nonparticipating states will also bear larger

costs for covering uncompensated care. That so much money would be left on the table suggests that many of the reluctant states will eventually join the expansion.[27]

REFORM THAT COULD IMPROVE HEALTH BUDGETING

Improvements to government budgeting will clearly be needed if the United States is to promote government financial sustainability and improve policymaking for health. While there are many good reasons for having an annual budget process, it is not well suited to planning and executing a major reform such as the PPACA.

In particular, there will need to be recognition that if governments are to budget sensibly for health, they must take an integrated view of the very complex health sector of society. One promising but politically controversial approach would be to reorganize what is now a very fragmented congressional committee system into one that empowers a Committee on Health in each body. That committee would respond to a periodic review of the health sector by the executive branch. The review would be a substantial expansion of the approach required by the GPRA Modernization Act, and it would use what can be learned from implementation of the PPACA. The review would assess health outcomes in the country and propose formal objectives for improving those outcomes. Based on the results of evidence-based studies, it would suggest how existing spending programs, tax preferences, and regulations could be modified, supplemented, and/or eliminated to foster attainment of health policy goals.[28] With this framework, the allocation of budgetary resources to health programs would have a stronger connection to national priorities and to science. Over the long run, it could evolve into a process covering both the public and private sectors, setting a global health sector budget, and using all-payer rate setting.[29]

See also **Chapter 3: The Department of Health and Human Services: Responsibilities and Policies (1953–Present); Chapter 4: The Centers for Disease Control and Prevention: Anticipatory Action in the Face of Uncertainty (1946–Present); Chapter 5: Food and Drug Administration (1962–Present); Chapter 6: The Centers for Medicare and Medicaid Services (1965–Present); Chapter 7: The**

A political carton expresses the view that U.S. health care costs continue to rise unabated. One goal of the Patient Protection and Affordable Care Act of 2010 was to control rising costs, but many observers doubt that stable health care costs will occur, in part because of people's expectations, which often demand the best and thus most expensive treatment.

SOURCE: Chris Madden/www.CartoonStock.com.

KEY DECISIONS: HEALTH CARE CRISES AND SOLUTIONS

Supreme Court Opinions in *National Federation of Independent Business v. Sebelius* (2012)

Chief Justice John Roberts (in office 2005–) wrote the majority opinion. Following are excerpts of the ruling that the Patient Protection and Affordable Care Act's Medicaid expansion could not be forced on the states:

The States also contend that the Medicaid expansion exceeds Congress's authority under the Spending Clause. They claim that Congress is coercing the States to adopt the changes it wants by threatening to withhold all of a State's Medicaid grants, unless the State accepts the new expanded funding and complies with the conditions that come with it. This, they argue, violates the basic principle that the "Federal Government may not compel the States to enact or administer a federal regulatory program. . . . "

In this case, the financial "inducement" Congress has chosen is much more than "relatively mild encouragement"—it is a gun to the head. Section 1396c of the Medicaid Act provides that if a State's Medicaid plan does not comply with the Act's requirements, the Secretary of Health and Human Services may declare that "further payments will not be made to the State." 42 U.S.C. §1396c. A State that opts out of the Affordable Care Act's expansion in health care coverage thus stands to lose not merely "a relatively small percentage" of its existing Medicaid funding, but *all* of it. . . . The States contend that the expansion is in reality a new program and that Congress is forcing them to accept it by threatening the funds for the existing Medicaid program. We cannot agree that existing Medicaid and the expansion dictated by the Affordable Care Act are all one program simply because "Congress styled" them as such. . . . If the expansion is not properly viewed as a modification of the existing Medicaid program, Congress' decision to so title it is irrelevant.

The Medicaid expansion, however, accomplishes a shift in kind, not merely degree. . . . It is no longer a program to care for the neediest among us, but rather an element of a comprehensive national plan to provide universal health insurance coverage. . . . As we have explained, "[t]hough Congress' power to legislate under the spending power is broad, it does not include surprising participating States with postacceptance or "retroactive" conditions. . . .

Nothing in our opinion precludes Congress from offering funds under the Affordable Care Act to expand the availability of health care, and requiring that States accepting such funds comply with the conditions on their use. What Congress is not free to do is to penalize States that choose not to participate in that new program by taking away their existing Medicaid funding.

Associate Justice Ruth Bader Ginsberg (in office 1993–), joined by Associate Justice Sonia Sotomayor (in office 2009–), dissented from the majority opinion about the Medicaid expansion. Following are excerpts from her opinion:

The Chief Justice . . . —*for the first time ever*—finds an exercise of Congress' spending power unconstitutionally coercive.

Medicaid, as amended by the ACA, however, is not two spending programs; it is a single program with a constant aim—to enable poor persons to receive basic health care when they need it. Given past expansions, plus express statutory warning that Congress may change the requirements participating States must meet, there can be no tenable claim that the ACA fails for lack of notice. Moreover, States have no entitlement to receive any Medicaid funds; they enjoy only the opportunity to accept funds on Congress' terms. Future Congresses are not bound by their predecessors' dispositions; they have authority to spend federal revenue as they see fit. The Federal Government, therefore, is not, as The Chief Justice charges, threatening States with the loss of "existing" funds from one spending program in order to induce them to opt into another program. Congress is simply requiring States to do what States have long been required to do to receive Medicaid funding: comply with the conditions Congress prescribes for participation.

Since 1965, Congress has amended the Medicaid program on more than 50 occasions, sometimes quite sizably. . . . Compared to past alterations, the ACA is notable for the extent to which the Federal Government will pick up the tab. . . . Nor will the expansion exorbitantly increase state Medicaid spending. . . . Finally, any fair appraisal of Medicaid would require acknowledgment of the considerable autonomy States enjoy under the Act.

The starting premise on which The Chief Justice's coercion analysis rests is that the ACA did not really "extend" Medicaid; instead, Congress created an entirely new program to co-exist with the old. The Chief Justice calls the ACA new, but in truth, it simply reaches more of America's poor than Congress originally covered. . . . Even if courts were inclined to second-guess Congress' conception of the character of its legislation, how would reviewing judges divine whether an Act of Congress, purporting to amend a law, is in reality not an amendment, but a new creation? At what point does an extension become so large that it "transforms" the basic law?

At bottom, my colleagues' position is that the States' reliance on federal funds limits Congress' authority to alter its spending programs. This gets things backwards: Congress, not the States, is tasked with spending federal money in service of the general welfare. And each successive Congress is empowered to appropriate funds as it sees fit. When the 110th Congress reached a conclusion about Medicaid funds that differed from its predecessors' view, it abridged no State's right to "existing," or "pre-existing," funds.

Departments of Defense and Veterans Affairs: Responsibilities and Policies (1947–Present); Chapter 8: The United States Supreme Court and the Department

of Justice (1789–Present); Chapter 10: Federalism: Cooperation and Conflict between State and Federal Healthcare Responsibilities (1960s–Present).

NOTES

1. Judith M. Feder, *The Politics of Federal Hospital Insurance* (Lexington, MA: Lexington Books, 1977); Paul Starr, *The Social Transformation of American Medicine* (New York: Basic Books, 1984).

2. Centers for Medicare and Medicaid Services, "National Health Expenditure Data: Historical," Tables 1 and 5, http://www.cms.gov/Research-Statistics-Data-and-Systems/Statistics-Trends-and-Reports/NationalHealthExpendData/NationalHealthAccountsHistorical.html.

3. Department of the Treasury, "Final Monthly Treasury Statement of Receipts and Outlays of the United States Government" (2013), https://www.fms.treas.gov/mts/mts0913.pdf; Congressional Budget Office, *Approaches to Reducing Federal Spending on Military Health Care* (January 2014), http://www.cbo.gov/publication/44993.

4. See Library of Congress, "Status of Appropriations Legislation for Fiscal Year 2014," http://thomas.loc.gov/home/approp/app14.html.

5. Philip G. Joyce, *The Costs of Budget Uncertainty: Analyzing the Impact of Late Appropriations* (Washington, DC: IBM Center for the Business of Government, 2012); Roy T. Meyers, "Late Appropriations and Government Shutdowns: Frequency, Causes, Consequences, and Remedies," *Public Budgeting and Finance* 17 (Fall 1997): 25–38.

6. Office of Management and Budget, "Analytical Perspectives, Budget of the United States Government, Fiscal Year 2014," 244–245, http://www.whitehouse.gov/omb/budget/Analytical_Perspectives.

7. See also Joseph R. Antos, "Is There a Right Way to Promote Health Insurance through the Tax System," *National Tax Journal* 54: 3 (2006): 477–490; Julie Kosterlitz, "Broad Coalition Prepares to Do Battle on Taxing Employee Fringe Benefits," *National Journal,* May 5, 1985, 956–960.

8. Theodore R. Marmor, *The Politics of Medicare,* 2nd ed. (New York: Aldine de Gruyter, 2000); Jonathan Oberlander, *The Political Life of Medicare* (Chicago: University of Chicago Press, 2003).

9. Barry White, "Examining Budgets for Chief Executives," in *Handbook of Government Budgeting,* edited by Roy T. Meyers, 462–484 (San Francisco: Jossey-Bass, 1999).

10. David G. Frederickson and H. George Frederickson, *Measuring the Performance of the Hollow State* (Washington, DC: Georgetown University Press, 2006); Alfred Ho, "The Governance Challenges of the Government Performance and Results Act: A Case Study of the Substance Abuse and Mental Health Administration," *Public Performance and Management Review* 30 (March 2007): 369–397.

11. Malcolm K. Sparrow, *License to Steal: How Fraud Bleeds America's Health Care System* (Boulder, CO: Westview Press, 2000); Alex Wayne, "Getting in Front of Health Fraud," *CQ Weekly,* February 16, 2009, 344–350.

12. See, for example, General Accounting Office, "Medicaid: States Use Illusory Approaches to Shift Program Costs to Federal Government" (Washington, DC: General Accounting Office, August 1994); Julie Rovner, "Congress, Administration Duel over State Medicaid Funds," *CQ Weekly,* October 26, 1991, 3130–3131.

13. C. Stephen Redhead, "Budget Control Act: Potential Impact of Sequestration on Health Reform Spending" (Washington, DC: Congressional Research Service, May 1, 2013).

14. James R. Horney and Paul N. Van de Water, "House-Passed and Senate Health Bills Reduce Deficit, Slow Health Care Costs, and Include Realistic Medicare Savings" (Washington, DC: Center for Budget and Policy Priorities, December 4, 2009).

15. Thomas R. Oliver, Philip R. Lee, and Helene L. Lipton, "A Political History of Medicare and Prescription Drug Coverage," *Milbank Quarterly* 82: 2 (2003): 283–354.

16. Glenn Follette and Louise Sheiner, "The Sustainability of Health Spending Growth," *National Tax Journal* 58: 3 (2005): 391–408.

17. See Congressional Budget Office, *The 2013 Long-Term Budget Outlook* (Washington, DC: Congressional Budget Office, September 2013), Chs. 2 and 7; Amitabh Chandra, Jonathan Holmes, and Jonathan Skinner, "Is This Time Different? The Slowdown in Healthcare Spending," Brookings Panel on Economic Activity (Fall 2013).

18. Joseph White, *False Alarm: Why the Greatest Threat to Social Security and Medicare Is the Campaign to "Save" Them* (Baltimore: Johns Hopkins University Press, 2003); Douglas Wolf and Nancy Folbre, *Universal Coverage of Long-Term Care in the United States: Can We Get There from Here?* (New York: Russell Sage Foundation, 2012).

19. Christopher Ellis and James A. Stimson, *Ideology in America* (New York: Cambridge University Press, 2012).

20. Robert G. Evans, "The TSX Gives a Short Course in Health Economics: It's the Prices, Stupid!" *Health Policy* 6: 2 (2010): 13–23.

21. Congressional Budget Office, *The Sustainable Growth Rate Formula for Setting Medicare's Physician Payment Rates* (Washington, DC: Congressional Budget Office, September 6, 2006); Drew Armstrong, "Medicare Patch Habit Too Painful to Break," *CQ Weekly,* June 16, 2008, 1595–1596.

22. U.S. Senate Committee on the Budget, Republican Staff, "Informed Budgeteer: The ABC&D's of the Trigger" (Washington, DC: U.S. Government Printing Office, April 3, 2008).

23. See also Bradford H. Gray, Michael K. Gusmano, and Sara R. Collins, "ACHPR and the Changing Politics of Health Services Research," *Health Affairs* (2003): W3-283–W3-307.

24. Ann Marie Marciarille and J. Bradford DeLong, "Bending the Health Cost Curve: The Promise and Peril of the Independent Payment Advisory Board," *Health Matrix* 75 (2012–2013): 75–121.

25. John E. McDonough, *Inside National Health Reform* (Berkeley: University of California Press, 2011); Paul Starr, *Remedy and*

Reaction (New Haven, CT: Yale University Press, 2011); Lawrence R. Jacobs and Theda Skocpol, *Health Care Reform and American Politics* (New York: Oxford University Press, 2012); Richard Kirsch, *Fighting for Our Health* (Albany, NY: Rockefeller Institute Press, 2011).

26. Jon R. Gabel, "Congress's Health Care Numbers Don't Add Up," *New York Times*, August 26, 2009; Bruce Vladeck, "Paralysis by Analysis," *Roll Call*, July 28, 2009; David M. Cutler, Karen Davis, and Kristof Stremikis, "Why Health Reform Will Bend the Cost Curve" (New York: Commonwealth Fund, December 2009).

27. John Holahona, Matthew Buettgens, and Stan Dorn. "The Cost of not Expanding Medicaid" (Menlo Park, CA: Kaiser Commission on Medicaid and the Uninsured, July 2013).

28. Roy T. Meyers, "The 'Ball of Confusion' in Federal Budgeting: A Shadow Agenda for Deliberative Budget Process Reform," *Public Administration Review* 69 (March/April 2009): 211–223; Paul Posner, Steve Redburn, Phil Joyce, and Roy T. Meyers, "Strengthening the Federal Budget Process" (Washington, DC: National Academy of Public Administration and American Society for Public Administration, July 12, 2012).

29. Joseph White, "Cost Control after the ACA," *Public Administration Review* 73: Special Issue (September 2013): S24–S33; Ezekiel Emanuel et al., "A Systemic Approach to Containing Health Care Spending," *New England Journal of Medicine* 367 (2012): 949–954; John Holahan et al., "Containing the Growth of Spending in the U.S. Health System" (Washington, DC: Urban Institute, October 2011); Bipartisan Policy Center, "A Bipartisan Rx for Patient-Centered Care and System-Wide Cost Containment" (Washington, DC: Bipartisan Policy Center, April 2013).

FURTHER READING

Feder, Judith M. *Medicare: The Politics of Federal Hospital Insurance.* New York: Harcourt, 1977.

Jacobs, Lawrence R., and Theda Skocpol. *Health Care Reform and American Politics: What Everyone Needs to Know.* New York: Oxford University Press, 2010.

Joyce, Philip G. *The Congressional Budget Office: Honest Numbers, Power, and Policymaking.* Washington, DC: Georgetown University Press, 2011. Chs. 6 and 7.

Marmor, Theodore. *The Politics of Medicare.* 2nd ed. Chicago: Transaction, 2000.

McDonough, John E. *Inside National Health Reform.* Berkeley: University of California Press, 2011.

Oberlander, Jonathan. *The Political Life of Medicare.* Chicago: University of Chicago Press, 2003.

Starr, Paul. *Remedy and Reaction.* New Haven, CT: Yale University Press, 2011.

———. *The Social Transformation of American Medicine.* New York: Basic Books, 1982.

chapter 10

Federalism

Cooperation and Conflict between State and Federal Health Care Responsibilities (1960s–Present)

Carol S. Weissert and Jaclyn Bunch

FEDERALISM AND HEALTH POLICY IN THE UNITED States are inextricably linked. Until fairly recently, states and localities provided most of the funding supporting health care for the poor and then, as now, directly provided public health services such as immunizations and provision of clean water. However, in 1965, the country enacted Medicare and Medicaid, providing a new federal role for health care coverage for the elderly and the poor. Since that time, federal and state spending in health has increased significantly and even in tough economic times continues to grow, at times squeezing out other state responsibilities like education. The federal role in regulating health has also stepped up since the mid-1960s, culminating in the Patient Protection and Affordable Care Act (PPACA), the most significant change in the delivery of health care in the United States since 1965. Over the past fifty years, states have led the way in innovative approaches to providing health care to the poor and in strategies for controlling costs. One state, Massachusetts, provided the blueprint for the individual mandate requirement in the PPACA (much to the dismay of its former Republican governor Mitt Romney [in office 2003–2007] when he was running for president in 2012).

It is essential in U.S. policy studies to understand the history of intergovernmental health policy over the past half century, especially the centralizing trends in adoption of policies (e.g., the increasing federal involvement in health policies formerly dominated by states), the cooperative efforts in the implementation of those policies, and the dynamic nature of federalism. Understanding the fundamentals of federal-state relationships as specified in the U.S. Constitution is also key. Finally, it is imperative to know that the next phase of intergovernmental health policy is beginning with the PPACA and the key role of the U.S. Supreme Court, whose 2012 ruling on the PPACA may play a defining role in the intergovernmental dynamics of health policy for years to come. While local governments play important roles in delivery of health care—particularly in public health—the federalism issues of the past fifty years are those at the level of Washington and the states.

FEDERALISM THEMES

The relationship between the federal government and the states was one of the most difficult issues for the Founders crafting the U.S. Constitution in 1787. They came up with the ingenious notion of federalism, or a sharing of responsibilities between two sovereign governments, a design that has served the country well and been adopted by around twenty-five other countries in the world. Yet defining federalism, especially delineating what functions are provided by the national or state government, has never been easy and conflicts over these responsibilities must be settled by the U.S. Supreme Court. Federalism has evolved over the more than two hundred years since its formation, sometimes favoring the powers of states, sometimes those of the national government.

Over the past fifty years, the trends have been toward centralizing, perhaps nowhere better illustrated than in health policy. Since 1965, the federal government has (1) taken on regulatory and financial support in health insurance that had long been a state responsibility; (2) shaped and participated in a massive shared health program for the poor that now makes up the largest category of state spending in most states; and (3) made states major, if often unwilling, partners in the most significant health policy program since 1965, the PPACA.

State Implementation

Throughout these centralizing developments, states have retained one ace in the hole: implementation. While the states may lose out on the front end of the policy development—its adoption—they retain their strong role in the implementation phase. In every intergovernmental health enactment, from Medicaid to the PPACA, it is the states that play a major role in putting those programs in place. In doing so, they can and do bargain with the federal government to make changes important to their states and their preferences. States sometimes play a role in designing policies, but often lose, even in areas such as insurance reform where their expertise exceeds that of Washington.

Finally, in the history of health care policy since 1965, the dynamic nature of federalism is a major theme. As the Founders expected, the relationships between federal and state governments change over time, with the federal level leading the way in some periods of history and the states taking on that role in other times. The Supreme Court plays a role in making these calls, but also important is the prevailing political context. In times when the national government is unable to make policy choices due to partisan disagreements that seemingly cannot be breached, states step up and act. When the states have difficulty treating all their citizens equally, as in the 1950s and 1960s, the federal government stepped in to take the dominant role. Woodrow Wilson (1913–1921), writing as a political scientist before he became president, noted that the relationship between the federal and state governments is the cardinal question of the constitutional system. Yet that question cannot be settled in one generation because every new issue in the nation's political and economic development defines it anew.

GETTING THE STATES TO ACT

Given the autonomy of states under the federal system, the national government cannot simply dictate to states what it would like them to do. So how can states be persuaded to act? The most effective way is by providing financial incentives through federal grants. In fiscal year 2012, some $600 billion went to states and localities in the form of federal aid. While federal grants can be traced to the Morrill Act of 1862, which made public lands available to states for support of agricultural and mechanical colleges, their use was quite modest until the 1930s. As part of President Franklin D. Roosevelt's (1933–1945) New Deal of the 1930s, federal grants were then provided to states for such economic programs as free school lunch, emergency relief work, and emergency highway funds. In the 1960s and early 1970s, federal grants proliferated and provided funds to states for social programs with goals of alleviating poverty, equalizing educational opportunities, cleaning the nation's air and water, and ensuring adequate health care for underserved populations. In 1965 alone, some 150 federal grants were passed. Between 1965 and 1970, the dollars provided through federal grants doubled, and then doubled again between 1970 and 1975.[1] In the years 2010 to 2011, federal grant funding increased thanks to the stimulus dollars designed to bolster state budgets through the worst of the Great Recession, marking the most dramatic increase in federal aid to state and local governments since the 1970s.[2]

However, with the carrots of grants, there are also sticks. One such stick is called a crossover sanction. This means that states can lose funds in a popular program if they fail to take some desired action in a separate program. Particularly popular is imposing penalties in the highway trust fund if states do not make desired federal changes. Early crossover sanctions dealt with transportation-related

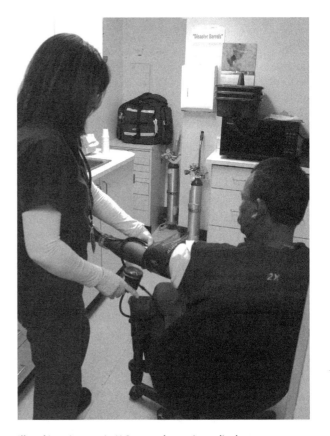

Illegal immigrants in U.S. custody await medical treatment at a U.S. Immigration and Customs Enforcement (ICE) Health Service Corps facility, part of the Department of Homeland Security (DHS). Formerly located in the Department of Justice, the ICE Health Service Corps became part of DHS in 2003; today, it provides direct care to about fifteen thousand detainees housed at twenty-one facilities across the nation. ICE also oversees medical care for more than seventeen thousand detainees housed at non-ICE facilities, which are located in all fifty states but are funded by the federal government, another example of federalism in action.

SOURCE: U.S. Immigration and Customs Enforcement Health Services.

issues such as lowering the speed limit and changing the minimum drinking age. A second generation of sanctions tied desired behavior to other funding programs. A good example is the 1992 Synar Amendment, which to this day punishes states that do not meet established targets for reducing tobacco sales to minors by reducing their substance abuse block grants by 40 percent.

Federal Mandates

Another way the federal government can persuade states to do what they may not otherwise want to is through partial preemption. This means that the federal government establishes rules and regulations calling for minimum national standards for a program. States can administer the program if they follow the standards; if not, the federal government will administer it. This approach was often used in laws pertaining to such issues as state occupational health and safety and group and individual insurance market standards.

Another type of stick is a direct order or mandate, in which the federal government orders lower governments to take certain types of action. Particularly troublesome for states is the tendency for Washington to mandate without federal financial assistance to pay for the newly required service. The 1990 Americans with Disabilities Act and the Drug-Free Workplace Act of 1988 mandated state action without providing adequate funding. However, the largest federal mandate is Medicaid. Congress has substantially broadened the scope and reach of the program over the past decade, arguing that the states could refuse the federal dollars for the entire program if they didn't want to make a particular change. The PPACA included a mandate to expand Medicaid eligibility to the near-poor population or states would lose all federal dollars contributed to their entire Medicaid program.

The PPACA also contained a partial preemption regarding the establishment and administration of insurance exchanges. If states acted by a given date, they could establish and run these exchanges; if states did not meet that deadline, the federal government would handle exchanges in those states. Politically, PPACA framers thought that states would not want the federal government to head these efforts but rather would prefer to use flexibility in the law to set up their own exchanges. They were wrong. Only sixteen states ended up setting up their own exchanges, and the federal government provided those cooperating with much more flexibility than it had initially intended.

Finally, sometimes Washington simply preempts state functions. During the eight years of the George W. Bush administration (2001–2009), there were fifty-seven preemption votes in Congress. In 2009, President Barack Obama (2009–) issued a memorandum to federal agencies asking them to proceed with caution before preempting states and

requiring agencies to revisit previous regulations of the past ten years. In his first term, President Obama said that new nationwide motor vehicle tailpipe standards for carbon would be decided with the strictest standards (from California) rather than preempting that state and others that wanted to exceed federal standards.

MEDICAID: THE SLEEPER PROGRAM WITH THE FINANCIAL WALLOP

Other federal health laws were passed in 1965—dealing with heart, cancer, and stroke programs; mental health; health professions; medical libraries; child health; and community health services—most involving state participation. Yet Medicare and Medicaid were the foremost health programs both then and now.

Medicare was the first major federal health program guaranteeing health care for a large civilian population in the country's history. Until Medicare, what public health coverage there was came largely from state and local governments. It took several decades, a determined Democratic president, and an extraordinary Democratic majority in both houses of Congress to get Medicare passed, but the result was monumental. During the discussion of the bill, the focus was on providing health care coverage for the elderly, but the final version included a separate program financing health care coverage for the poor. Medicaid built on a small federal program with voluntary state participation called Kerr-Mills and was a means-tested program available only to those who were poor or who met certain eligibility requirements (families with dependent children, the blind and disabled, the elderly). Importantly, Medicaid was funded by both the federal and state governments, while Medicare was funded totally by Washington and individual beneficiaries.

A Health Care Safety Net

Medicare and Medicaid had different target populations and different policy approaches. Medicare used a "social insurance" approach where health care would be available regardless of need, financed through the Social Security system. Medicaid was expected to be a small safety net program. Ironically, the inconsequential program for the poor did not live up to its second-tier billing and soon became a major spending endeavor for both Washington and the states. Expenditures increased from $0.9 billion in fiscal year 1966 to $5.1 billion by 1970 (a 54 percent average annual growth) and enrollment increased from four million to fourteen million over that time. Between 1971 and 2011, growth in Medicaid expenditures averaged 11.4 percent per year; average expenditures per enrollee grew at an average annual rate of 7.7 percent.[3]

Federal law requires that certain groups of persons be covered and certain services be provided to them. During times of fiscal stress, states often limit optional services such as dental care, eyeglasses, and prescription drugs. States can expand eligibility to include persons who are "medically needy," and states have flexibility in determining the reimbursement policies for most providers. Medicaid also pays safety-net hospitals for uncompensated care and helps fund health centers in underserved communities. All in all, Medicaid pays for 31 million children, 16 million non-elderly adults, 6 million seniors, and 9 million disabled persons. It also pays for Medicare premiums and copayments for 9 million very poor elderly people who quality for both Medicare and Medicaid, the most expensive group in both programs. The federal match varies from 50 percent in wealthier states such as Connecticut and Virginia to 74 percent in Mississippi.

Medicaid is the largest grant program to states, by far. Frank Thompson calls Medicaid the "Intergovernmental Colossus" due to its dominance of federal grants to states.[4] As indicated in Figure 10.1, health grants make up nearly half of all the total grants to state and local government, and most of this is Medicaid. The figure also shows the growth over time. The health grants share of total grants grew by 5 percentage points over the past dozen years. Medicaid accounts for more

than one-third of all federal outlays in health (including Medicare) and makes up nearly one-fourth of all state spending (including federal grants).

An Entitlement Program

Medicaid is an entitlement program, which means that federal and state governments must provide funding for services for those who meet the criteria specified in law. This is in contrast to federal (and state) programs that are appropriated a set amount of money and when the money runs out, the recipients will not get services. Entitlement programs grow when the number of recipients increases (as in difficult economic times) and are often politically viewed as "out of control" as a result. They are also politically very popular with recipients, particularly the other two major entitlement programs—Medicare and Social Security.

Perhaps the most troubling thing about Medicaid, especially for state officials, is not its size but its growth. Since program inception, the cost of Medicaid has generally increased faster than the U.S. economy and is expected to do so in the near future. As Figure 10.2 shows, there is considerable year-to-year variation in enrollment and spending for Medicaid. The trend is upward, and there is clearly an economic connection. When the economy was good, such as between 2002 and 2007, growth in Medicaid enrollment and

FIGURE 10.1 **Growth in Health Grants to State and Local Governments**

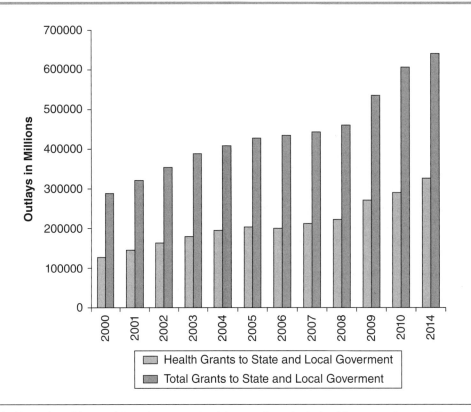

SOURCE: Historical Tables, Budget of the United States Government, Fiscal Year 2014, (2013, April 10). U.S Government Printing Office. Retrieved October 14, 2013.

spending fell. It rose again, only to fall again in 2012, and rose again in 2014. The trends depend largely on the economy, wage increases, price inflation, and state actions that reduce cost drivers such as provider payment rates and benefits.

State Innovations

Over the years, the states have made innovations and administrative improvements in Medicaid, including prior authorization requirements for expensive drugs or services, management information systems, and provider profiles that help control costs by identifying physicians whose practice patterns fall outside the normal range. They have moved Medicaid recipients to full-risk managed care arrangements, invoked competitive bidding strategies for choosing managed care vendors, and provided alternatives to nursing homes for elderly and disabled recipients. States have put in place these innovations through an important intergovernmental mechanism called grant waivers. With waivers, the federal government grants permission for states to fail to meet (that is, waive) certain federal requirements to operate a specific kind of program for a specific group. States have sought and received waivers for welfare, education, food stamps, and transportation, but one of the liveliest areas of waivers is Medicaid. Most interesting are Section 1115 waivers that allow states to set up experimental, pilot, or demonstration projects under Medicaid. The Massachusetts health program that served as a basic model for the PPACA was enabled by a Medicaid waiver. Oregon used the Section 1115

wavier to provide an innovative system whereby all of its poor citizens would be provided with a set of health care benefits. Florida received a waiver to put all its Medicaid recipients into managed care—even those in long-term care facilities.[5] Importantly, and not surprisingly, the PPACA also contains a number of opportunities for states to waive federal responsibilities.

Medicaid, overshadowed in the passage of Medicare in 1965, did not remain in the shadows for long. States quickly realized the value of a relatively generous federal match and began to draw down their state funding for programs benefiting children, the elderly, persons with disabilities, and hospitals. States also quickly learned some ways to maximize federal funding such as using "contributions" from hospitals and nursing homes to match federal dollars, thus increasing the total amount available to the program without using state general fund dollars. Medicaid was an intergovernmental game both then and now, especially as federal and state officials continue to bargain and compromise over what programs will be covered, how the funding is provided, and how much discretion states have.

THE HIDDEN PROVISION IN A PENSION BILL: ERISA 1974

One of the most important centralizing trends in health policy came in a largely ignored provision of a bill that did not deal primarily with health: the Employee Retirement

FIGURE 10.2 **Medicaid Spending and Enrollment Growth, 1998–2014**

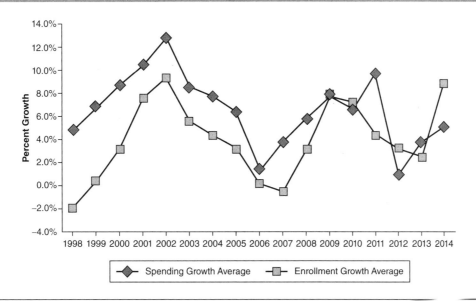

SOURCE: Kaiser Commission on Medicaid and the Uninsured, *Medicaid Enrollment June 2012 Data Snapshot,* August 2013. Spending Data from KCMU Analysis of CMS Form 64 Data for Historic Medicaid Growth Rates. FY 2012–2014 data based on KCMU survey of Medicaid officials in 50 states and DC conducted by Health Management Associates, October 2013.

NOTE: Enrollment percentage changes from June to June of each year. Spending growth percentages in state fiscal year.

Income Security Act (ERISA) of 1974. One of the ways in which Congress is not generally portrayed, in a typical "How a Bill Becomes a Law" graphic, is that the federalism provision of ERISA was not included in either the House or Senate bills; rather, it was put in *de novo* in the conference committee. A few House conferees inserted language that preempted state laws relating to "any employee benefit plan" to replace language that prevented states from legislating about subject matter regulated by the act. A second phrase was then added stating that no employee benefit plan shall be deemed an insurance company.

Together, the two provisions, added only ten days before final passage of the law, meant that companies that self-insured would be free of state regulation. This was a classic federal preemption of long-time state law. When the provision was enacted, there were relatively few such plans, but in the ensuing years more and more large employers decided to escape state insurance regulation through directly paying for their employees' health care costs and bearing the risk. Approximately 40 percent of Americans with private health coverage are in these self-insured programs. In the years since its passage, ERISA has hampered state health reforms, because any provision would apply to only 60 percent of insurance plans in the state, exempting from any employer mandate all self-insured firms. These ERISA-based limitations, and court cases supporting them, were especially troublesome in the 1980s and 1990s when states including Oregon, Massachusetts, and Washington wanted to provide universal coverage but found their efforts limited. The 2006 Maryland Fair Share Health Care Act was struck down by federal courts in 2006 and 2007, which may have helped steer designers of future state reforms toward the Massachusetts model with individual mandates.

GOVERNORS LEAD THE WAY IN THE 1980s

Governors led the way in protecting Medicaid from major cutbacks or significant program changes in the 1970s. In the 1980s governors, particularly southern governors, aggressively used Medicaid to reduce infant mortality and improve the health of their citizens. They lobbied Congress to allow states to enroll more babies and pregnant women and expanded programs in their own states. The Southern Governors Association was especially active in developing ways to provide health care for poor children.

Between 1984 and 1988, five federal laws mandated expansion of Medicaid to cover more children and pregnant woman and required twelve months of transitional Medicaid coverage for families leaving the nation's welfare program, Aid for Families with Dependent Children (AFDC), due to employment. These programs were supported by the governors who felt these needy populations should be covered, and the federal match inherent in the Medicaid program made coverage more appealing, sometimes to governors who could use the mandates as a tool for overcoming political resistance in their own states.

In 1986, the governors scored a victory from Congress when the first step was taken toward decoupling Medicaid from AFDC, the national welfare program. With the Omnibus Reconciliation Act of 1986, Congress amended the law to allow states to provide Medicaid to poor families with incomes above the state's AFDC standard without providing them with AFDC benefits. According to Shanna Rose, this decoupling of Medicaid eligibility from cash assistance was a major juncture in Medicaid history because, at the program level, it reduced the stigma of welfare that could be associated with Medicaid, what has been called "welfare medicine."[6]

Governors Work with Congress

The governors did not do it alone. They were aided by the chair of the House Commerce Committee's Subcommittee on Health and the Environment. Henry Waxman (D-CA; in office 1975–), who was on a mission to expand health care for the poor, and due to a heavily Democratic Congress, he was in a position to make it happen. He worked with the governors, especially the southern governors and the National Governors Association, to expand Medicaid incrementally, year by year. However, the partnership ran into difficulties in the later years of the 1980s, when tough fiscal times began to limit state revenues and governors and legislators had to choose between funding long-time state priorities such as education and the Medicaid expansion.

A rift in the warm relationship came from a 1988 law, the Medicare Catastrophic Coverage Act (MCCA). As the title suggests, the measure dealt primarily with Medicare, the federal-only program for the elderly, but there were two important components relating to Medicaid. First, the law required that the Medicaid program pay for premiums and deductibles for the elderly who were eligible for both Medicare (age and disability) and Medicaid (poor). These are known as "dual eligible." Some states were voluntarily providing this funding, but most were not as it was and would be costly. However, the law also provided this carrot or incentive for the states: Medicare would pay for prescription drug costs that most state Medicaid programs were then covering.

While many policy analysts thought the MCCA was an appropriate and needed law that protected senior citizens from health cost–related destitution, the intended recipients did not agree. Interest groups sprang up to fight the law, often barraging senior citizens with famously false information about how the law would affect them. In 1989, Congress repealed most of the provisions of the MCCA, with the exception of the mandate that states cover the dual eligible, a group that represented an increasingly heavy burden for state budgets in future years.[7]

In 1989, the governors at their national meeting adopted a measure calling on Congress and the White House to cease passage of any additional Medicaid mandate for two years. The relationship that had worked for both the states and Congress had ended. The measure passed unanimously and governors began to actively lobby against future mandates. There was one more mandate in the omnibus budget reconciliation act of 1990 that extended full Medicaid coverage to children and pregnant women once more and covered Early and Periodic Screening, Diagnosis and Treatment services to children under age twenty-one. However, it was the last Waxman mandate enacted. His incremental approach to expanding mandates, mostly with the support of the nation's governors, was over.

THE PAC-MAN OF STATE BUDGETS

As a result of these mandates and buy-in by the states, along with the increasing costs of medical services, total spending for Medicaid increased by more than 77 percent between 1980 and 1990. State spending for the program increased by 72 percent over the same time period. It is no wonder that Georgia Governor Zell Miller (in office 1991–1999) compared Medicaid spending to his state's native, rapidly growing kudzu plant. Others called it the Pac-Man of state budgets, likening it to the popular computer game of the time.

Democratic Governor Roy Romer (in office 1987–1999) of Colorado complained to President George H.W. Bush (1989–1993) at a 1992 National Governors Association meeting that he had to propose a tax increase to pay for Medicaid expenditures put upon his state by the federal government. Missouri Governor John Ashcroft (in office 1985–1993) asked all state agencies in 1991 to accept a 5 percent across-the-board cut to meet new federal Medicaid mandates in that state. Congressman Waxman claimed to be unmoved by the states pleas. However, his 1992 Medicaid proposal included two expansions, one fully funded by the federal government and one provided as a state option.

Implementation of the Waxman mandates also led to federal-state problems. For example, in early 1991, states were given only a few months to implement federally required changes in state methods of reimbursing services provided by federally qualified health centers. States were in the middle of a budget year in which there were no appropriations for the more expensive reimbursement system.

CLINTON HEALTH REFORM: FAILURE AND PERHAPS SUCCESS

In 1994, President William J. Clinton (1993–2001), a former governor, had an ambitious plan to reform health care. After a year of massive political coverage and public attention on what Clinton called the defining issue of his presidency, and without his 1,342-page draft ever passing a single committee in the House or Senate, the progress of health care reform ended. Clinton had chosen a major overhaul of health care, eschewing incremental approaches, but he did not have the support of key interests, Congress, or the public. While Clinton never again tried such comprehensive reform, the salience of the health issue and the education of the public about the need for reform contributed to the passage of several other important health measures during his tenure as president.

In 1996 and 1997, Congress passed two major health bills with large intergovernmental impacts. One, the Health Insurance Portability and Accountability Act (HIPAA), was important because it represented the federal government's entrance into an area formerly dominated by states, namely health insurance. Many thought it would be a "camel's nose under the tent" and indeed, the story of its implementation presages much of what happened with the implementation of the Patient Protection and Affordable Care Act. The second, the State Children's Health Insurance Plan (SCHIP), expanded health coverage for children, a group of deserving recipients whom members of both parties could support, at least initially.

HIPAA: THE CAMEL'S NOSE UNDER THE TENT

HIPAA is known popularly as the law addressing the disclosure of individuals' health status and diagnosis. For states, it is much more important for its combination of preemptions, mandates, and partial preemptions. The law is very complicated, but essentially provided federal minimum regulations over the individual insurance market and small business market (the same markets targeted in the PPACA fifteen years later). The law featured portability (allowing workers to change jobs without concern about losing insurance coverage), limited preexisting conditions, and regulated the individual and small group markets' underwriting techniques. The federal definition of preexisting conditions preempted state law, meaning that states with less protective policies had to strengthen their standards. In the area of portability from group to individual markets, states could adopt federal standards, adopt "fallback" or different standards, or do nothing and have federal officials enforce the federal fallback position. Mandates specified that states could not approve plans that excluded conditions such as pregnancy, diabetes, and hernias and set federal standards for administrative simplification of insurance forms. The law mandated that state health plans covering maternity care had to provide at least forty-eight hours of hospital stay after the delivery and that health plans had to provide equal lifetime and annual limitations for mental health and other coverage (called mental health parity).

One analyst called HIPAA "modest in scope, but far-ranging in implications."[8] HIPAA ended almost a century of federal deference to the states in health insurance regulation that began with a U.S. Supreme Court decision, *Paul v. Virginia* (1869), that declared insurance was *not* commerce, thus not an enumerated national responsibility. In 1945, after a later court reversed that finding, Congress passed a law providing that insurance was a state responsibility, but one that could be taken back by the federal government if the states failed to perform. ERISA chipped into this delineation of responsibility, and HIPAA widened the federal policy footprint.

Michael Doonan of the Brookings Institution argues that since the federal government was entering a new area, one in which federal agencies did not have experience, it relied heavily on states in the passage and implementation of the law.[9] Indeed, the National Association of Insurance Commissioners (NAIC) worked closely with Congress, particularly the Senate, in shaping the legislation. NAIC won on some issues but lost on others. However, it was during implementation of HIPAA that federal agencies worked most closely with the states and seemed to be most accommodating to their concerns.

HIPAA seemed to defy the common wisdom that Republicans support decentralization and Democrats support centralizing policies. In this law, conservatives supported federal regulations that preempted states at the request of business interests. Liberals wanted states to be able to enact consumer protections stronger than the federal government's standards.

STATE HEALTH INSURANCE FOR CHILDREN PROGRAM

SCHIP was enacted as part of the Balanced Budget Act of 1997 and funded at $20.3 billion for five years. It was a premier example of bipartisan support for a deserving group, poor children, namely those from working but low-income families. It was also strongly supported by state interest groups, the National Governors Association, and the National Conference of State Legislatures. SCHIP is a block grant. In a block grant, Congress specifies the policy area in which funds can be spent but the state or locality can decide, within the broad category, which programs best fit its needs. The first block grant was in health, in the Partnership for Health Act in 1966. Other health-related block grants are for maternal and child health, alcohol and drug abuse, mental health, and preventive health care.

The States and SCHIP

In SCHIP, states have considerable leeway in providing coverage for uninsured children in families with incomes below 200 percent of the federal poverty level. Any state that already covered children up to 200 percent could use the federal dollars to expand coverage to families with incomes of up to 250 percent of poverty. Federal dollars in SCHIP are matched with state dollars at rates that are more generous than the Medicaid matches. States can operate a separate program for children under this law or can expand Medicaid to service these children. If they choose to run their own program, they have some discretion concerning eligibility levels and benefits. The federal law built on state experiences in California, New York, and Florida in providing health care to children beyond Medicaid. In implementing SCHIP, nearly one-half of the states expanded Medicaid; fifteen states set up separate programs; the remainder chose to expand Medicaid and set up a new program. It was authorized for ten years; by the time of its renewal, however, the politics had changed. Republicans believed SCHIP was a back door to national health insurance. Republican President George W. Bush twice vetoed its reauthorization. When the Democrats had a unified Congress and a Democratic president in 2009, SCHIP became one of their first orders of business, and it was reauthorized and expanded. Also, it was renamed CHIP in that law.

DECOUPLING MEDICAID AND WELFARE

While the first step had been taken in 1986 in separating Medicaid and welfare, in 1996, a complete divorce was accorded between the two programs. The Welfare Reform Act of 1996, which replaced AFDC and changed from entitlement to a block grant called the Temporary Assistance for Needy Families (TANF), established a new Medicaid eligibility category for non-TANF adults. The divorce was important symbolically, because welfare has long been viewed as a stigma. Severing the "welfare medicine" moniker was important politically as well. Political scientists call this social construction of target populations. A negative social construction, such as that of "welfare queens" or "welfare medicine," can lead to punitive policies that can stymie the funding and flexibility of the program. Viewing Medicaid as "a health program" rather than "a welfare program" may improve its political acceptability, leading to growth and flexibility.

STATE INNOVATIONS IN HEALTH CARE

One of the great advantages of federalism, a sharing of power between national and state governments, is innovation. States can adopt policies that can be tried out in smaller venues and then adopted by other states or the federal government. Using states as "laboratories of democracy" has a long history in the United States. The 1921 Sheppard-Towner Act, providing social and medical assistance to pregnant women and babies, was copied from a

Connecticut law. States provided models for the 1935 Social Security Act, the 1973 Supplemental Security Income programs, Medicare's DRG-based payment system, SCHIP, and patients' bills of rights legislation. States adopted health savings accounts and managed care laws. They have adopted a number of antiabortion laws requiring women to view ultrasounds, impose additional waiting periods, cut funds for clinics, and ban abortions at the twentieth week after conception, the latter a provision that seemingly is in direct conflict with the threshold set by the U.S. Supreme Court.

Sometimes, states act when political difficulties prevent national action. States passed laws to reduce greenhouse gas emissions (California), allow assisted suicide (Oregon), and allow the use of marijuana for medical purposes (sixteen states). States also can act quickly when issues arise that engage or outrage constituencies. When a young Washington state high school student suffered a brain injury playing football, the state legislature crafted legislation mandating education for coaches and imposing new rules requiring removal from the game of head-injured players. Other states and Congress later passed similar laws, using the Washington law as a model.

MASSACHUSETTS PROVIDES THE MODEL FOR THE COUNTRY

The Massachusetts Health Insurance Reform law, passed in 2006, served as a basic model for the PPACA. Dubbed "Romneycare," it included individual mandates and exchanges or Web pages where individuals and small business can purchase insurance. Republican Governor Mitt Romney introduced his plan in 2005, in response to federal actions, yet another example of the importance of intergovernmental relationships in understanding health policy. It also was an example of how a Republican governor worked closely with key Democratic legislative leaders to achieve a major health reform.

Massachusetts, like many states, had been actively exploiting a loophole in the Medicaid law that allowed states to receive federal matching funds for supplemental payments for hospitals. In 2004, the George W. Bush administration balked at approving the waiver provisions with hundreds of millions of dollars going to safety-net providers. Governor Romney joined forces with Senator Edward "Ted" Kennedy (D-MA; in office 1962–2009) to work with federal staff to retain the federal matching funds by using them to cover the uninsured. The federal government wanted the state to extend coverage without expanding Medicaid and to provide sliding-scale premium support to recipients. The program that emerged required businesses with eleven or more full-time employees that did not provide a health insurance plan to pay an annual assessment for each uninsured employee. Individuals could purchase health insurance from the exchange-like entity, called Commonwealth Choice, with the help of subsidies, much like the PPACA. Medicaid was expanded to cover children whose family income was up to 300 percent of the federal poverty level. Penalties for individuals who do not have insurance were higher for those middle and higher income taxpayers over the age of twenty-six.

Ironically, given later political rhetoric surrounding the very similar PPACA, dubbed "Obamacare," Governor Romney characterized the individual mandate as "the ultimate conservative idea," where people take care of themselves without government interference.[10] At the time, he also pointed out that the idea for the exchange came from the conservative Heritage Foundation. While there is some disagreement about who originally conceived of exchanges, the Heritage Foundation did promote them for many years. There is probably more evidence that the Heritage Foundation did originate the individual mandate, a second major component of the PPACA, in 1989 as a health reform approach. Ironically, and showing that both parties can change their stances, when Barack Obama was running in the presidential primaries in 2008, he initially opposed the individual mandate, which his opponent Hillary Clinton supported.

PRESCRIPTION DRUGS, THE MMA, AND FEDERALISM

During President George W. Bush's first term, the signature health issue was prescription drugs. The Medicare Prescription Drug, Improvement, and Modernization Act (MMA) of 2004 expanded the Medicare program to cover prescription drugs for the elderly and persons with disabilities. Politically, the law was an important component of the president's campaign promises in 2000 and his planned reelection strategy for 2004. However, one key concern was cost. The president demanded that the new program cost no more than $400 billion over ten years, a relatively low number given the scope of the program. After passage of the measure (at 5:55 A.M., after voting time had been extended and major arm twisting occurred among Republicans, who held the House), it turned out that Medicare actuaries had predicted much higher estimated costs and had been ordered not to release their estimates.

While targeted to Medicare, the program directly affected some six million dual eligible (those eligible for both Medicare and Medicaid) and eight million who had prescription drug coverage through Medicaid and state drug programs. Unlike earlier health bills in the Clinton era (SCHIP and HIPAA), there was little recognition of the states' role of providing their own pharmacy programs and providing for prescription drugs for poor elderly in their Medicaid programs. In fact, as Martha Derthick notes, the

MMA is a centralizing program, giving the federal government additional responsibilities and sticking states with a supplemental role of providing additional or "wraparound" services with their own prescription drug programs.[11]

The low-ball cost numbers turned out to be important to states and involved something called a "clawback." Instead of having the federal government pay for all the state costs of the program, the law mandated state sharing of costs. Rather than federal grants going to states, state grants would go to the federal government. Over the first five years, estimates of state grants or clawbacks were about 13 percent of the cost of the program. Ironically, the states that had provided the most generous benefits to recipients paid the most in clawbacks. They were essentially penalized for being innovative or pioneering. Although states argued that this provision was a tax that infringed on state sovereignty and interfered with the functions of their sovereign governance, the Supreme Court declined to take the case. The implementation story was more typical. In implementing the MMA, the federal staff worked state by state to reach agreements on the transition of the program, a pattern that would be followed with the PPACA.

The MMA case remains unique today. There have been no other programs where states must contribute to federal programs based on the "savings" states would get from a national program. However, the clawback provisions are still in place, with states subsidizing the MMA. As part of the federal stimulus package in place from 2009 through 2011, the states were given $4.3 billion in financial relief by reducing their clawback payments. Yet this was temporary relief since the clawback payments resumed after the stimulus program ended.

THE PATIENT PROTECTION AND AFFORDABLE CARE ACT AND FEDERALISM

The Patient Protection and Affordable Care Act is all about federalism. To understand the PPACA, one must understand federalism. Three key aspects are reform of the insurance industry, establishment of state exchanges, and Medicaid expansion. State exchanges are a partial preemption; states have the opportunity to create their own exchanges, and if they do not, the federal government will do so. The Medicaid expansion as passed by Congress was a mandate. The insurance industry reform contained a number of full preemption provisions.

The PPACA builds on Medicaid, the federal-state health care program, not Medicare, the federal program for health care for the elderly and disabled. Also interesting, given the history of health policy discussed earlier, is that the PPACA did *not* pass on costs to the states as in the past. In fact, the Medicaid expansion was exceptionally generous, paying 100 percent of the costs for the first three years,

gliding down to a minimum of 90 percent of the costs by 2020. In an eerie replay of 1965, the Medicaid components of the PPACA were undervalued in the press coverage in 2009. Yet this expansion was essential to the widespread coverage of the PPACA, expected to add sixteen million uninsured persons to Medicaid and providing greater uniformity and federal direction.

The PPACA preempts state regulation of insurance in a variety of provisions constituting a major reform of the industry by abolishing a wide variety of practices that were permitted by state law while mandating coverage of certain services and populations. These provisions (with exceptions for grandfathered policies) include banning the exclusion of high-risk applications, the exclusion of preexisting condition, high premiums based on age and sex, and nonrenewal based on health experience, to name only a few.

Intergovernmental politics are also key to understanding the PPACA. Minutes after President Obama signed the law, Florida's attorney general filed a case in federal court claiming the PPACA was unconstitutional. The case was later joined by twenty-five other attorneys general. The issue was the requirement that every legal resident in the United States have health insurance, commonly known as the individual mandate. Also important was an argument over interstate commerce, a function of the federal government specified in the U.S. Constitution. The Obama administration argued that the provision requiring citizens to purchase health insurance fit the definition of interstate commerce.

Interstate commerce has long served as the constitutional rationale for federal takeover of state functions. It is important to remember that the Constitution sets forth a "compound republic" where both states and the national government are responsible to their citizens. The national government cannot direct, force, or commandeer states without a strong constitutional purpose. The interstate commerce clause (Article 1, section 8) has typically provided that rationale. Beginning in the mid-1800s, the Court has ruled liberally on the meaning of the constitutional phrase "regulate commerce among the several states," even arguing in 1942 in *Wickard v. Filburn* that a farmer who grows wheat only for his personal use still participates in interstate commerce and must abide by federal regulation.[12] While there were a few deviations in the string of decisions favoring the federal government's prerogative, the findings were fairly consistent. Most recently, a case similar to *Wickard* involved medical marijuana. In *Gonzales v. Raich* (2005), the Supreme Court upheld federal law on the commerce clause argument.[13] The court found that even though the plaintiff was growing marijuana for her own medicinal use, her action affects the interstate market and thus the federal law is constitutional, and it superseded state law allowing medical marijuana.

The Supreme Court and Interstate Commerce

At the core of the case brought by states against the Patient Protection and Affordable Care Act (PPACA), *National Federation of Independent Business v. Sebelius* (2012), was the interpretation of the constitution's interstate commerce provision. Challenged was the requirement that individuals must maintain "minimum essential" health insurance: either Americans purchase health insurance or they pay a penalty through the Internal Revenue Service (IRS). The administration argued that the economic effects of self-insurance by uninsured individuals affect interstate commerce. The court disagreed as described in the majority opinion by Chief Justice John Roberts:

The Constitution grants Congress the power to "regulate Commerce." . . . The power to regulate commerce presupposes the existence of commercial activity to be regulated. If the power to "regulate" something included the power to create it, many of the provisions in the Constitution would be superfluous.

Our precedent also reflects this understanding. As expansive as our cases construing the scope of the commerce power have been, they all have one thing in common: They uniformly describe the power as reaching "activity."

The individual mandate, however, does not regulate existing commercial activity. It instead compels individuals to become active in commerce by purchasing a product, on the ground that their failure to do so affects interstate commerce. Construing the Commerce Clause to permit Congress to regulate individuals precisely because they are doing nothing would open a new and potentially vast domain to congressional authority.

Further, the court found that the commerce clause was insufficient, citing precedent, such as the majority opinion of *United States v. Lopez* (1995):

Just as the separation and independence of the coordinate branches of the Federal Government serves to prevent the accumulation of excessive power in any one branch, a healthy balance of power between the States and the Federal Government will reduce the risk of tyranny and abuse from either front.

To uphold the Government's contentions here, we would have to pile inference upon inference in a manner that would bid fair to convert congressional authority under the Commerce Clause to a general police power of the sort retained by the States . . . To do so would require us to conclude that the Constitution's enumeration of powers does not presuppose something not enumerated . . . and that there never will be a distinction between what is truly national and what is truly local.

However, *National Federation of Independent Business v. Sebelius* did not strike this component of the PPACA completely; the component was upheld through the power of Congress to lay and collect taxes:

Under the mandate, if an individual does not maintain health insurance, the only consequence is that he must make an additional payment to the IRS. . . . That, according to the Government, means the mandate can be regarded as establishing a condition—not owning health insurance—that triggers a tax—the required payment to the IRS. Under that theory, the mandate is not a legal command to buy insurance. Rather, it makes going without insurance just another thing the Government taxes, like buying gasoline or earning income.

SOURCES: *United States v. Lopez* 18 U.S.C. 922 (1995); *National Federation of Independent Business v. Sebelius*, 183 L. Ed. 2d 450 (2012).

In 2012, in *National Federation of Independent Business v. Sebelius*,[14] the case involving more than half of the states, the court ruled in favor of the states on this point, saying that construing the commerce clause to permit Congress to penalize individuals precisely because they are doing nothing is not constitutional. However, the Court did not invalidate the PPACA. Even though the justices did not support the rationale as interstate commerce, they did conclude that the individual mandate was constitutional because the sanction for failing to comply with the mandate was a penalty remitted on the individual's income tax return. The Obama administration argued that this penalty is a tax on those who choose not to obtain insurance and thus is no different from a range of other federal taxes. The court agreed with this argument and upheld the law. (Ironically, throughout the debate on the bill during its congressional ordeal, the administration argued that the fee collected for not having insurance was *not* a tax.)

Another important issue, initially largely ignored by pundits, academics, and the press, was that the expansion of Medicaid, a mandate similar to those adopted in the 1990s, was an unconstitutional provision, essentially usurping state power. The provision required that states expand eligibility to those younger than age sixty-five earning up to 133 percent of the federal poverty level. If the states did not do this, they could lose all their Medicaid program dollars.

Previous Supreme Court decisions had ruled that Congress may not simply commandeer the legislative processes of the states by directly compelling them to act and enforce a federal regulation program.[15] However, the court had long upheld requirements and mandates on federal grants, asserting that states could reject the federal dollars if they did not want the additional requirements. In a verdict that surprised even the most sagacious court watcher, the justices ruled that the mandate to expand Medicaid in the Patient Protection and Affordable Care Act violated the Constitution by threatening existing Medicaid funding. In his opinion, Chief Justice Roberts argued that Congress has no authority to order the states to regulate according to its instructions. Congress may offer the states grants and require the states to comply with accompanying conditions, but the states must have a genuine choice whether to accept the offer. Losing all their Medicaid funds was not a realistic choice, he ruled.

The intergovernmental story of the PPACA was far from over, however. The implementation stage, where the states are major players, was just beginning. As in any partial preemption, states decided whether they wanted to implement exchanges or turn it over to the federal government. Map 10.1 illustrates the states that have implemented their own exchanges, the ones letting the federal government do it for them, and those that are doing something in between. While the PPACA envisioned only two types of exchanges,

federal and state, the Obama administration worked with states to develop a third category—a partnership that included some elements of federal control and some of state control. It was another example of how, in implementing federal law, states carry important sway.

The story, like that in earlier years, is of a dynamic federalism that is far from uniform. Citizens in some states will have Medicaid coverage very different from those in other states; the exchanges will also differ from state to state. In fact, one of the ironies of the Supreme Court decision, upholding exchanges but giving states more flexibility in Medicaid, is that the nation will experience more differences across the states in that program, with some citizens enjoying greater benefits than those in other states. Inequities across states has been dubbed "the price of federalism," which after *National Federation of Independent Business v. Sebelius* (2012) will be high indeed for those poorest of the poor living in states that have chosen not to expand Medicaid.[16]

FEDERALISM AND HEALTH CARE POLICY: IRONIES

There is no better example of the importance of federalism than health policy. One cannot understand health policy in the United States without factoring in the pivotal role played by states.

MAP 10.1 **State Implementation of PPACA Exchanges**

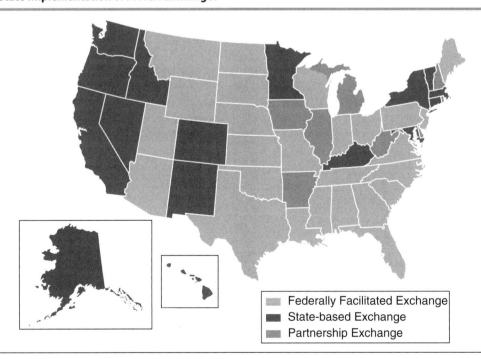

Legend:
- Federally Facilitated Exchange
- State-based Exchange
- Partnership Exchange

SOURCE: Kaiser Commission on Medicaid and the Uninsured, *Medicaid Enrollment June 2012 Data Snapshot,* August 2013. Spending Data from KCMU Analysis of CMS Form 64 Data for Historic Medicaid Growth Rates. FY 2012–2014 data based on KCMU survey of Medicaid officials in 50 states and DC conducted by Health Management Associates, October 2013.

Patient Protection and Affordable Care Act: Implementation of Insurance Exchanges and Medicaid Expansion

States play an important role in implementing the PPACA, signed into law by President Barack Obama in March 2010. Two components are key: (1) state exchanges that provide Internet-based information for comparing and purchasing health insurance with the assistance of federal subsidies where applicable and (2) a significant expansion of Medicaid. The provision in the PPACA relating to exchanges is what is called a "partial preemption." States have the choice to take on the services as defined by federal law or decline to do so and have the federal government perform the function in their states. The Medicaid expansion in the PPACA is an example of a mandate in which the federal government required states to provide services to new recipients (in this case, those at 133 percent of the federal poverty level).

Although the PPACA provided for only state or federal exchanges, a third type of exchange—a partnership—emerged as states began to implement the law. Sixteen states and the District of Columbia put in place their own state exchanges. Most of these states commissioned an independent public agency to run the marketplace. Four states have a state agency-run program, and Hawaii has delegated the responsibility to a nonprofit entity. Of the sixteen states to take part in this form of exchange, the majority have an executive office occupied by a Democrat. In fact, only about one in five of those states that elected for a state-based marketplace had a Republican governor.

Partnerships consist of a cooperative effort between the state and the federal government. Here, states may administer the functions of plan management, consumer assistance, or both. This choice commissions states with responsibilities such as verification of insurance plan qualification, management of qualified health plans, collection and transmission of data to the Department of Health and Human Services (HHS), support of consumers in the application process, and determination of eligibility and choices in plan selection. The remaining functions and responsibilities are handled by the secretary of health and human services at the federal level. Seven states have elected for a partnership-based exchange: Arkansas, Delaware, Illinois, Iowa, Michigan, New Hampshire, and West Virginia.

As of the 2013 federal deadline, the majority of U.S. states (twenty-seven) defaulted to the federally facilitated marketplace structure. In a federally facilitated marketplace, HHS performs all marketplace functions, but states may choose to run reinsurance or coordinate with the Center for Medicaid and CHIP Services regarding protocols of eligibility. However, this does not mean that the states that defaulted are not taking part in some active form of participation. Seven states with federally facilitated marketplaces (Kansas, Maine, Montana, Nebraska, Ohio, South Dakota, and Virginia) have received approval to participate with plan management activities, a role that usually occurs in either state-based or partnership exchanges. However, there is a distinctly Republican partisan skew in the states that defaulted to a federally facilitated program. Only two out of these twenty-seven states had a Democratic governor at the time of the deadline. Only Maine and New Jersey opted for federally facilitated exchanges with Democrats as the majority party in the upper chamber. (Although Nebraska has a federally facilitated exchange, it was not included in this assessment, because it does not have a bicameral system for its legislature.)

There have also been mixed responses in states regarding the option of expanding Medicaid coverage. The original expansion requirement would have mandated all states to provide Medicaid coverage for families with income up to 133 percent of the poverty level. The law called for 100 percent funding by the federal government for the first three years after expansion, followed by a gradual reduction in the subsidy to cover 90 percent of the funding by 2020. When the U.S. Supreme Court invalidated the Medicaid mandate, the program became voluntary.

SOURCES: Patient Protection and Affordable Care Act, Public Law 111-148 (March 23, 2010), as modified by the Health Care and Education Reconciliation Act of 2010, Public Law 111-152 (March 30, 2010), Title 1, Subtitle D, Section 1311; Claire McAndrew, "States and the Federal Government Working Together to Run Health Insurance Marketplaces," http://familiesusa2.org/assets/pdfs/health-reform/State-Exchange-Partnership-Responsibilities.pdf; Kaiser Family Foundation, "State Decisions for Creating Health Insurance Marketplaces, 2014," http://kff.org/health-reform/state-indicator/health-insurance-exchanges; Centers for Medicare and Medicaid Services, "Blueprint for Approval of Affordable State-Based and State Partnership Insurance Exchanges," http://www.cms.gov/CCIIO/Resources/Files/Downloads/hie-blueprint-11162012.pdf; Genevieve M. Kenney et al., "Opting in to the Medicaid Expansion under the ACA: Who Are the Uninsured Adults Who Could Gain Health Insurance Coverage?" http://www.urban.org/UploadedPDF/412630-opting-in-medicaid.pdf.

States serve as providers, financiers, administrators, initiators, and regulators of health care delivery in the United States. They help design and implement federal policies and implement their own policies and define and oversee local health-related activities. However, since 1965, the federal government has taken on more responsibilities formerly conducted by states, particularly in health insurance. Yet the implementation of health laws remains with the states.

The PPACA was expected to provide more uniformity for a Medicaid program with enormous variation from state to state. However, thanks to the U.S. Supreme Court's finding that the mandate was unconstitutional, the program will have more variation than ever, with some states expanding the program to the fullest, adding recipients and increasing the number of citizens with health insurance, and others providing a more restricted program and witnessing growing numbers of uninsured. Ironically, the inequities of federalism, where citizens of states have very different health care options depending on where they live, are growing from a program designed to do just the opposite.

See also Chapter 1: Origins and Development of Government's Role in Health Policy (Colonial Era to Present); Chapter 2: The Long Struggle for Universal Health Care (1900s–Present); Chapter 3: The Department of Health and Human Services: Responsibilities and Policies (1953–Present); Chapter 9: Budgeting and Health Care Policy (1970s–Present).

NOTES

1. David B. Walker, *The Rebirth of Federalism: Slouching toward Washington,* 2nd ed. (Chatham, NJ: Chatham House, 2000).
2. Timothy J. Conlan and Paul L. Posner, "Inflection Point? Federalism and the Obama Administration," *Publius* 41: 3 (2011): 421–446.
3. Centers for Medicare and Medicaid Services, *2012 Actuarial Report on the Financial Outlook for Medicaid* (Washington, DC: Centers for Medicare and Medicaid Services, 2012).
4. Frank J. Thompson, *Medicaid Politics: Federalism, Policy Durability and Health Reform* (Washington, DC: Georgetown University Press, 2012).
5. William G. Weissert and Carol S. Weissert, *Governing Health: The Politics of Health Policy,* 4th ed. (Baltimore: Johns Hopkins University Press, 2012).
6. Shanna Rose, *Financing Medicaid: Federalism and the Growth of America's Health Care Safety Net* (Ann Arbor: University of Michigan Press, 2013).
7. Richard Himelfarb, *Catastrophic Politics: The Rise and Fall of the Medicare Catastrophic Coverage Act of 1988* (University Park: Pennsylvania State University Press, 1995).
8. Kala Ladenheim, "Health Insurance in Transition: The Health Insurance Portability and Accountability Act of 1996," *Publius* 27: 2 (1997): 33–51.
9. Michael Doonan, *American Federalism in Practice: The Formulation and Implementation of Contemporary Health Policy* (Washington, DC: Brookings Institution, 2013).
10. Paul Starr, *Remedy and Reaction: The Peculiar American Struggle over Health Care Reform* (New Haven, CT: Yale University Press, 2011), 170.
11. Martha Derthick, "Going Federal: The Launch of Medicare Part D Compared to SSI," *Publius* 37: 3 (2007): 351–370.
12. *Wickard v. Filburn,* 317 U.S. 111 (1942).
13. *Gonzales v. Raich,* 545 U.S. 1 (2005).
14. *National Federation of Independent Business v. Sebelius,* 183 L.Ed 2d 450 (2012).
15. *New York v. United States,* 505 U.S. 144 (1992).
16. Paul Peterson, *The Price of Federalism* (Washington, DC: Brookings Institution, 1995).

FURTHER READING

Doonan, Michael. *American Federalism in Practice: The Formulation and Implementation of Contemporary Health Policy.* Washington, DC: Brookings Institution, 2013.

McDonough, John E. *Inside National Health Reform.* Berkeley: University of California Press, 2011.

Rose, Shanna. *Financing Medicaid: Federalism and the Growth of America's Health Care Safety Net.* Ann Arbor: University of Michigan Press, 2013.

Thompson, Frank J. *Medicaid Politics: Federalism, Policy Durability, and Health Reform.* Washington, DC: Georgetown University Press, 2012.

Weissert, William, and Carol Weissert. *Governing Health: The Politics of Health Policy,* 5th ed. Baltimore: Johns Hopkins University Press, 2014.

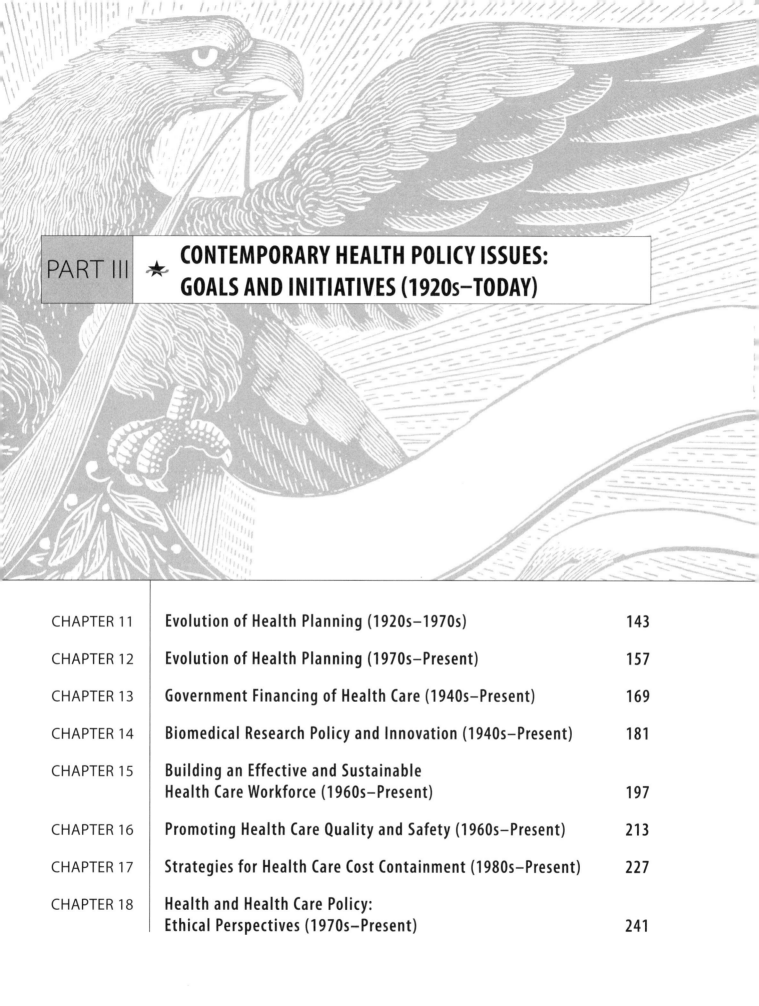

chapter 11

Evolution of Health Planning (1920s–1970s)

Evan M. Melhado

EXPLORING THE HISTORY OF HEALTH PLANNING in the United States serves at least three purposes: it exhibits features of policymaking that broadly characterized health care from the early twentieth century into the 1970s; it suggests how skepticism of government and commitment to markets ushered in new approaches; and, in the most recent period, it shows how altered policy contexts have created new settings for planning.[1] Planning ideas extend back into the 1920s; then gained influence in health care during the 1940s; took wing as a coalition-secured passage of the federal Hill-Burton Act (1946), which prepared the ground for a postwar expansion of the hospital sector; and flourished during the 1960s and 1970s as health care costs and expanded insurance coverage increased concurrently. Partisans saw planning as one means to further what they took to be the public interest in meeting the need for health care by rational expansion of the health system, distributing resources in accordance with need, and encouraging financing that would facilitate access to care.

During the 1960s and 1970s, when most observers of health care policy anticipated imminent passage of National Health Insurance (NHI), the planning and NHI agendas drew support from one another, because an efficient and rationally distributed health system would be required to keep NHI affordable. However, the failure of NHI proposals in 1974, the growth of skepticism about planning and governmental intervention, and the decline of regulatory regimes outside health care undermined support for planning. Moreover, experts and interest groups increasingly shifted the focus of policymaking in a variety of spheres away from the traditional public interest goals that planners had served and toward private markets responsive to a new conception of the public interest. Proponents saw markets as the sources of goods and services, including health care,

valued by citizens-cum-consumers and as the principal field for the autonomous exercise of consumer choice. The national push for planning ended in the early 1980s, but planning activity has emerged to support new health policy initiatives. The history of planning thus provides an avenue to portray premarket-era policymaking, its eclipse by market-oriented health care and health policy, and its succession by some recent novel forms, as discussed in Chapter 12.

BEGINNINGS OF HEALTH CARE PLANNING

The origins of health planning lay in the early twentieth century, as observers of health care from diverse fields, especially medicine, public health, the social sciences, social work, and endowed foundations, came to regard the then-emergent scientific medicine as offering novel, effective, and valuable health services, particularly in diagnosing and treating acute illnesses and accidents. The germ theory of disease, innovations in surgery, and new powers to measure physiological processes and diagnose diseases elicited from reformers a planning agenda that initially featured two major goals, but later included two more. One was to expand the supply and encourage the financing of scientifically based acute care. Another was to create institutions for economical deployment of the increasingly expensive resources—including hospitals, clinics, sterile operating rooms, diagnostic equipment, as well as the physicians and other skilled professionals who could exploit these novelties—that underlay scientific care and to facilitate linkages among medical generalists and specialists. Reformers emphasized two sorts of provider institutions: multispecialty group practice, for which modernizing urban dispensaries provided among the earliest models,[2] and hospitals, transformed from welfare institutions to modern workshops of scientific medicine for paying patients.[3] Such provider institutions would become community repositories of expensive capital, which could be deployed efficiently in regional hierarchies. Planning ideas emphasized the distribution of chiefly voluntary hospitals, and it was this concern that resulted in actual policy-making. Proposals to reorganize medical care, however, although of profound interest to some advocates of planning and other promoters of health care, elicited too much opposition, especially from the medical profession, to garner concrete results; this chapter leaves this story aside.[4]

Later on, additional perceptions fostered the third and fourth goals. Especially in the 1930s and 1940s, planners' awareness of the growing burden of chronic illnesses indicated the need to accommodate them into hierarchical arrangements, although financing mechanisms for chronic care remained controversial and therefore elusive; and awareness of urbanization, especially after World War II (1939–1945) and the subsequent suburbanization, shifted attention of hospital interests (especially in medical centers) and the corporate payers behind employees' health insurance plans toward urban hospitals. Planners hoped to create a hierarchical hospital system that constrained costs by limits on capital investment; subordinated both rural and urban community hospitals and small clinics as well as new, suburban institutions, to central-city teaching institutions; matched resources to the medical needs of the population; and provided high-quality care of the right kind (e.g., acute, chronic), in the right place (e.g., hospitals, less acutely oriented institutions), at the right time, to all who could pay for it.

Historical Framework

The story of U.S. health planning rests on discussions of policy and a series of federal and state legislative measures from the 1930s. Central to this history was a widespread, if also widely varied, approach to policy that Daniel M. Fox has characterized as "hierarchical regionalism."[5] Impressed by the progress of medical science, coalitions of reformers aimed for the efficient provision and broad dissemination of scientifically based care. Hierarchy was for them the best relationship to strive for among the diverse kinds of health care workers who possessed diverse levels of knowledge and skill. Regionalism for them was the means to supply each region (however defined) with services that were similar in kind and quality and distributed in relation to population. For health planning, the distribution of voluntary hospitals and the relationships among the diverse kinds of professionals who worked in them were central concerns.

The principal early source for this approach in the United States was the Committee on the Costs of Medical Care (CCMC), a group of physicians, public health professionals, economists, actuaries, and social scientists supported by several endowed foundations and active from 1927 to 1932.[6] The CCMC provided an early statement of

how the progress of medical science had rendered obsolete prevailing arrangements for care (solo practice that they deemed incapable of providing complex, scientific care and a supply and distribution of physicians and hospitals that did not correspond to distribution of population). Moreover, through its extensive studies of U.S. health care, the committee established the concept of need for care (defined by the existing state of science and technology), it documented the lack of human and material resources required to provide needed care, and it called attention to shortages of resources in both rural and urban areas. The recommendations of the committee included institutional arrangements for providing care on the community level in both hospitals and group practices, financing of care through prepayment, creation of a hierarchy of institutions for providing care and another for planning care, all to be coordinated to meet need efficiently. The committee aspired to bring advanced care from the urban centers, where its members understood medical resources to have been concentrated, out to the rural periphery, where rural health had been deemed a problem and resources to improve it seemed scarce. Because the CCMC ignited tremendous controversy, particularly around its call to impose group practice on doctors and force them into hierarchical arrangements, the coalition supporting it did not realize its ends in legislation.

THE HILL-BURTON ACT (1946)

However, during the 1930s, a new coalition arose that aimed to increase the supply of health services without antagonizing doctors and posing controversial proposals about financing care. A major early outcome of its efforts was the Hill-Burton program, created under the Hospital Survey and Construction Act (1946). Hill-Burton first introduced into federal legislation the idea of planned growth of health care resources; however, while it achieved its goal of growth in rural areas, it did little to foster a planned distribution of institutions or links between city and rural hinterland. Named for its initial Senate sponsors, J. Lister Hill (D-AL; in office 1938–1969) and Harold H. Burton (R-OH; in office 1941–1945), the act established a federal-state partnership to exploit federal subsidies for encouraging the planned growth in the number of especially nonprofit, acute-care hospitals, chiefly in poorer states and in areas with largely rural populations. The program eventually became moribund under the National Health Planning and Resources Development Act of 1974 (NHPRDA).

Urban Hospitals

Proliferation of urban hospitals after World War II also attracted attention. A variety of factors put these institutions under stress and led local coalitions to characterize their problems and create voluntary planning agencies, which arose chiefly in the 1950s and 1960s. Their goal was to organize urban hospitals into hierarchical systems that would provide care without needless duplication of services. Planners worked to gain federal support for their efforts, obtaining in 1966 a federal planning program, Comprehensive Health Planning (CHP).

Although the program had aroused high hopes for rationalizing the health system, it gradually attracted criticisms for its perceived failures, while cost inflation (i.e., the extent of inflation of health care costs above the rate of inflation in the overall economy), particularly under the impact of the new federal insurance programs of Medicare and Medicaid (enacted in 1965), led to calls for regulation of capital investment. As early as 1964 and especially in the 1970s, most states, following models of public utility regulation, tried to control costs by certificate of need (CON), which required sponsors of new or expansions of existing hospital facilities or services involving capital investments above a threshold to demonstrate the need for their projects. Finally, the NHPRDA ended Hill-Burton, mandated state-level CON, and reformed the planning structure created under CHP. The revamped planning program, however, had no greater success than CHP in reining in costs, and it, too, attracted diverse criticisms, leading to its demise through reduction in funding in 1981 and repeal in 1987.[7]

Regional Medical Programs

Two policy developments that were related to planning accompanied some of these developments, but they will not be treated here. One, the Regional Medical Programs (RMP; 1965–1974), also an expression of hierarchical regionalism, focused on scientific research in university medical centers and the dissemination of its innovations in patient care through hierarchies of care institutions,[8] while the health planning focused on the distribution of hospitals. Although CHP was supposed to coordinate RMP (among other diverse federal programs), it never did so, and RMP, too, was in effect ended under NHPRDA. Another set of programs, state hospital rate-setting, emerged from the late 1960s (at roughly the same time that state CON statutes were passed) in states that experienced rapid growth in hospital costs and Medicaid expenditures.[9] By the mid-1980s, some thirty states had developed mandatory prospective payment systems to limit the growth of hospital costs. After 1985, however, rate setting waned, to survive only in Maryland.[10]

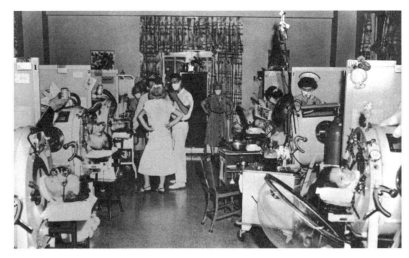

In a city hospital in 1953, patients with polio, one of the most dreaded infectious childhood diseases of the twentieth century, receive treatment with iron lungs and other respiratory devices. After World War II, a severe lack of accessible hospitals and a shortage of doctors and nurses hindered treatment and care. Fortunately, a polio vaccine was developed in the mid-1950s, and the disease was virtually eliminated in the United States and other industrialized nations.

SOURCE: © Bettman/Corbis.

ANTECEDENTS OF PLANNING

Early planning thought focused on local communities and their typically private, nonprofit hospitals. In the 1920s, professional organizations within medicine (medical societies, specialty organizations), governments, foundations, and the courts arrived at a consensus on the need to foster "small-town [acute-care] hospitals as ideal American institutions, institutions which simultaneously demonstrated community initiative, professional altruism, and diffusion of medical technology to consumers throughout the population."[11] From this period into the 1950s, and even beyond, observers lodged responsibility for meeting health care needs in local communities, expecting them to provide capital for plant and equipment, encourage patients' willingness to pay for services, and provide free care to the poor.[12] Despite this last aspiration, most community hospitals lay under private, voluntary ownership and served largely paying patients. Nevertheless, they were understood to serve as eleemosynary (that is, charitable or philanthropic) institutions, their services resembling what economists consider public goods (that is, as traditionally understood, goods or services deemed socially important but unlikely to be adequately supplied without collective action).

Although the major intellectual antecedents for planning lay in the work of the CCMC, after the controversies it set off, most proposals for regionalism emphasized that hierarchies could be made to rest on consensus, voluntary action, and subsidy from governments and foundations, without recourse to coercion.[13] In the 1940s and 1950s, a variety of regional hierarchies came to expression in the thinking of reformers and to realization in programs on the ground. Some programs for regionalizing hospital care lay in projects that relied on public or foundation funds to link peripheral rural with central urban hospitals through professional exchanges among staff and referrals of patients between institutions. Such cases included the efforts in 1931 of the Bingham Associates Fund at the Tufts New England Medical Center to support rural health services in New England by linking them to the academic medical center in Boston; the Rochester Regional Hospital Council, organized in 1946 to create cooperation between community hospitals and teaching hospitals; and the Hunterdon medical center in Flemington, New Jersey, which dated from the 1940s and featured links between the Hunterdon center and New York University-Bellevue Medical Center. These examples were diverse in structure and funding, but they served advocates of planning as models of coordinated planning and provision of urban-based health services in rural areas.[14]

RURAL VERSUS URBAN DEVELOPMENTS

The Hill-Burton program was an achievement of the coalition that took form during the war to expand the supply of health services. Under the legislation, each state designated a single agency, usually the state health department, to survey hospital resources in the state and write a state plan to guide the distribution of new hospitals and expansion of existing ones. After federal approval of the state plan, the state agency could approve funding for local projects that it judged consistent with the plan. The expectation of local engagement in creating health care resources emerged in the requirement that local sponsors of hospital projects had to provide one-third of the funding. Responding to traditional priorities, the formula for distributing federal funds to the states gave priority to poor states and rural areas. Reflecting the post-CCMC emphasis on voluntarism and seeking to avoid opposition in Congress and perhaps garner support there, advocates of the program downplayed hierarchy. Instead, they anticipated

FIGURE 11.1 **Coordinated Hospital Service Plan, 1944**

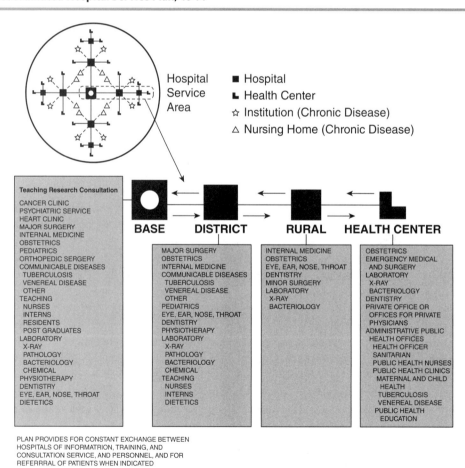

SOURCES: Thomas Parran Jr., "Statement of Dr. Thomas Parran, Surgeon General, United States Public Health Service," in *Wartime Health and Education: Hearings before a Subcommittee of the Committee on Education and Labor* (Washington, DC: U.S. Government Printing Office, 1944), testimony on 12 July; plate facing p. 1792.

that regional coalitions would emerge to build hospitals, and they hoped to create a setting for mutual bargaining and interaction representative of regional planning councils.[15] Congress amended the program frequently, supposedly to bring it more into conformity with planners' vision; however, the growth of voluntary hospitals that it fostered—of mostly small, freestanding, community hospitals, located mostly in less populated areas—scarcely conformed to plans.[16]

EXPANSION OF ETHNIC AND RELIGIOUSLY BASED HOSPITALS

Growth, equally unguided by planning goals, also characterized urban hospitals.[17] Ethnic and religious communities had created separate networks of health care institutions and professionals, but the cultural distinctions reflected in these institutions gradually diminished in importance. Advances in scientific standards of practice, the growth in professionalism among doctors and administrators, the reduced discrimination by hospital medical boards against Catholic and Jewish physicians, the eclipse of individual philanthropists by corporate donors, and the emergence in the suburbs during the 1950s and 1960s of a culturally less differentiated middle class that wanted scientific health care institutions in close proximity made culturally distinct institutions look to corporate donors and planners like inefficient duplication of resources. Growing needs for chronic care (shown by the tendency of chronic patients, after treatment for acute manifestations of their diseases, to remain in acute-care beds) reinforced concern for rationalizing the distribution of hospitals and beds in urban areas.[18] Planners, who formerly aimed to bring urban-based chronic-care services to

---

KEY DECISIONS: HEALTH CARE CRISES AND SOLUTIONS

The Hill-Burton Act

A reform coalition active during World War II aimed to prepare the country for the postwar expansion of its hospital system; the principal practical outcome of its efforts was the Hill-Burton or Hospital Construction and Survey Act, passed in 1946. The act provided federal subsidy in the form of grants-in-aid to the states to inventory existing hospitals and survey the need for new ones, and it provided additional grants to subsidize hospital construction. The act emphasized poorer states and rural areas, where health was deemed a problem and need for health care resources was deemed greater than in cities; it inaugurated planning in the U.S. hospital system, at least in principle; and it envisioned an integrated, efficient system for the equitable provision of advanced health services to the entire population. The U.S. Public Health Service, largely free from direction by an administration preoccupied with the war and its aftermath, allied itself with the coalition, and the head of the agency, Surgeon General Thomas Parran Jr. (in office 1936–1948), became the leading spokesman of the coalition before Congress. On February 27, 1945, appearing before the Senate Committee on Education and Labor, Parran summarized the features of the bill that formed the basis for the act:

> In summary, Mr. Chairman [Senator James E. Murray (D-MT; in office 1934–1961)], your committee is considering a bill which represents an important first step in the evolution of a national health program. The bill would give us the structural elements through which adequate health services can be made available to all our people.

> In order that these services may be fully integrated, and their maximum benefit realized, surveys of need for general and special hospitals would be made by competent experts in each State. These surveys would precede the drafting of master plans. New hospitals would be located and built in conformity with the master plan in each State, and would be architecturally sound, and functionally adequate.

> General hospitals, constituting service foci for the more equitable distribution of medical services, should be related administratively both to the large medical centers in the State and to the nearby small hospitals and health centers.

> Additional hospitals should be built for persons suffering from tuberculosis and mental diseases. Far better provision should be made for the care of chronic, convalescent, and cancer patients.

> Finally, obsolete hospital structures should be replaced by modern functional buildings.

> These services and facilities should be provided through the familiar pattern of grants-in-aid, varied in proportion to need.

> Hospitals of all types, diagnostic centers, health centers, and other health facilities should be planned, built, and operated solely for the purpose of insuring to every citizen the maximum benefit from all that medical science has to offer.

SOURCE: Thomas Parran Jr., "Statement of Dr. Thomas Parran, Surgeon General, United States Public Health Service," in *Hospital Construction Act: Hearing before the Committee on Education and Labor* (Washington, DC: U.S. Government Printing Office, 1945), 90–91.

outlying populations and had obtained some funds for this purpose under amendments to the Hill-Burton Act, passed in 1954, now applied their vision of hierarchy to urban settings.[19] Hoping to exploit additional funding for chronic care provided under the new major medical insurance that emerged after World War II, and eventually under Medicare and Medicaid, they sought to create a tightly coordinated cluster of facilities and services: a medical center. In this medical center, care, whether acute or chronic, could be organized to put "the right patient, in the right bed, with the right services, at the right time."[20] This was a grand vision for accommodation of chronic care, but it was never achieved.[21]

Moreover, pressure from corporations, in their roles as philanthropists who provided capital for hospitals and as purchasers of health insurance for employees paid for operating costs, eventually led to the creation of urban health planning agencies. Planners responded by analyzing the relations of capital investments and the resultant, much larger long-term operating expenses. To prevent duplication of facilities and services that would generate unneeded downstream costs, planners called for placing urban and suburban institutions, if not into a coordinated medical center, then at least into tight, rationalized hierarchies.[22]

Intensifying interest in this goal were substantial increases in rates for Blue Cross hospital insurance that in the late 1950s led state insurance commissioners to hold hearings and disallow premium increases. These circumstances encouraged the creation of local, voluntary planning agencies in a number of cities, beginning as early as 1938 in New York, and becoming commonplace in the late 1950s and 1960s. A particularly prominent and influential agency was the Hospital Planning Association of Allegheny County (Pittsburgh), and C. Rufus Rorem, who had been a staff economist for the CCMC, became the organization's first executive director (1960–1964).[23] Such institutions lacked roots in the earlier, rurally oriented programs that had inspired and reflected early thought about regionalization; instead, they responded to concerns of larger urban donors of capital, and they took up planning as their major activity.[24]

SUBURBANIZATION AND HEALTH PLANNING

Suburbanization proved a major concern of these bodies. Diverse ethnic populations, having migrated to new suburbs, created there a relatively uniform middle-class culture.[25] New suburban hospitals, emphasizing science over ethnicity and religion, drew support from voluntary health insurance and public investment in research, technological change, and training of skilled medical specialists. Suburban hospitals, including some new teaching hospitals, could now

supply many advanced services formerly offered only by urban teaching hospitals. The latter, suffering from loss of middle-class clienteles, declining physical plant, and reduced incomes, responded by rebuilding and modernizing, while many middle-sized urban hospitals, through expansion, merger, and affiliation with medical schools, imitated the major teaching hospitals. Engagement in undergraduate medical education and postgraduate specialty training, provision of advanced forms of care, and prosecution of research suggested the prestige and quality that could attract the middle class back to the central city.[26] Planners envisioned a regional, metropolitan system that would modernize central-city teaching institutions; encourage the merger of smaller urban institutions; and subordinate the rest, together with newer suburban hospitals, to the central-city teaching institutions. Such a hierarchy would protect the central hospitals from competition, limit capital investment by restraining the growth of suburban hospitals, match resources to the needs of the population, and provide high-quality care to all who could pay for it. In the hospital field planners called for "area-wide planning," a shorthand taken from the "metropolitan area-wide planning" that urban analysts had coined in the 1950s as a way to solve the "metropolitan problems" raised by the jurisdictional diversity of metropolitan areas.[27]

The need to modernize urban hospitals, felt even in the mid-1940s, became a theme that planners invoked in seeking congressional support and justifying outlays of capital. Congress responded modestly in 1964 with the Hill-Harris amendments to the Hill-Burton Act,[28] but modernizing hospital interests later found ways to borrow what they needed.

THE PLANNING MOVEMENT

Responding to these concerns from the mid-1950s, the American Hospital Association took an interest in the early planning bodies and, as the uproar over costs set in, worked with the U.S. Public Health Service to create consensus about planning. The chief intellectual outcome of these efforts was a 1961 report issued by the U.S. Public Health Service, *Areawide Planning for Hospitals and Related Facilities*,[29] which stated the case for planning, outlined its principles, and suggested means to institutionalize it. The report started "area-wide" on its career in health planning and served as a founding document of what advocates of planning palpably sensed as a movement. The chief practical outcome of support for area-wide planning was federal legislation in 1961 (An Act to Assist in Expanding and Improving Community Facilities and Services for the Health Care of the Aged and Other Persons and for Other Purposes) that beefed up earlier federal support for research on effective use of hospitals and, in the 1964 Hill-Harris amendments to Hill-Burton,[30] support for area-wide planning by private, voluntary organizations (known as "318 agencies" after the pertinent section of the Public Health Service Act).

In pursuing this agenda, the new agencies revealed a fault line that became a major reason for the delegitimization of planning by the early 1980s. Planners hoped to predicate planning on social science, not only because it promised rationalization in the distribution of resources, but also because they hoped the banner of science could compel cooperation of opposing interests and, generally, replace politics.[31] This "hard" approach to planning would discipline narrow interests to conform to the public interest, as stipulated by scientific study; it also would limit short-term capital investment and long-term operating expenditures and thus would occasion a reduction in the rate of cost inflation. In the late 1950s, when costs grew prominent and state insurance regulators rejected steep premium increases sought by Blue Cross (the nonprofit insurer created in the 1930s by hospital interests), planners, still lacking the hoped-for science, resorted to "putting out fires," that is, persuading sponsors of obvious cases of duplication to hold off.[32]

"ROEMER'S LAW" AND ITS IMPACT

Thereafter, however, the science remained elusive. The most nearly scientific result that seemed to support hard planning was the "Roemer effect" or "Roemer's law," named for its discoverer, Milton Roemer, a physician and professor who championed social medicine and applied the social sciences in its support.[33] In the late 1950s, he showed that, when insurance coverage was available, a bed built was a bed used.[34] Supply of resources, rather than reflecting medical need, created its own demand. The Roemer effect provided a rationale for the effort, initially on state level and later on the federal level, to impose hard planning through certificate of need (CON). However, such laws proved inadequate, and the deficiency of science led planners to resort to consultation among the interests, community organizing, and coalition building, the tools of soft planning. Despite the appeal of science, soft planning was what planners at the bottom preferred, what the Allegheny County agency had modeled, and what the American Hospital Association had consistently supported as preferable to science-based coercion and the ill will it elicited among representatives of interests. However, soft planning proved itself a political exercise. Eventually, aware that the track record of planning was thin, critics excoriated it also for its sub rosa practices and its lack of accountability to the public.

Proponents of planning believed they had set a movement in motion, and they now aimed to give it form and direction.[35] Contradictory developments emerged. On the federal level, Congress created in 1966 the first major federal mandate for planning, Comprehensive Health Planning (CHP), and amended and expanded the program the next

year.[36] The clamor over cost escalation having subsided, CHP would become a venue for soft planning, which advocates hoped would give them a long time horizon to create an orderly, hierarchical system. At roughly the same time, however, states struggling with large increases in hospital costs and with large and growing Medicaid budgets pressed for hard planning. The first CON law appeared in New York in 1964, and state CON legislation became widespread in the early 1970s.[37] Also, under the NHPRDA of 1974, the federal government mandated state-level CON as part of a broader national effort at cost containment. Along with Pittsburgh, Rochester, New York, was a prominent exemplar of area-wide health planning under the leadership of former Kodak executive and Health, Education and Welfare Secretary Marion Folsom (1955–1958). It was Folsom who started a CON review process in Rochester and then took it to the state level in New York. Ultimately, it was the local Blue Cross plan that underwrote and backed up the planning process there.[38] Planners in most communities, committed to the long-time horizons of soft planning, eventually proved unable to answer the growing number of voices calling for a short-term fix for cost inflation.

COMPREHENSIVE HEALTH PLANNING

Under CHP, planning received two kinds of support: grants for statewide comprehensive health planning under a single state agency, the "314(a)" or "a" agency (named for the section of the act), and project grants for local public or nonprofit agencies for comprehensive area-wide planning, "314(b)" or "b" agencies, which emerged from or replaced the former 318 agencies. Although one goal was to move planners from preoccupation with hospitals to comprehensive health care, in fact little other than hospital planning was attempted under CHP. Consistent with its political complexion, CHP never aspired to scientific planning. To reduce the fragmentation of public policy (i.e., the existence of assorted, partially overlapping, and partially conflicting programs), the administration of President Lyndon B. Johnson (1963–1969) pressed its theme of "creative federalism," featuring partnerships with lower level government and private groups. CHP, dubbed by the administration Partnership for Health, would exploit relations among governments at all levels; state and local planning agencies; and private, voluntary groups. Advocates hoped that the planning bodies would catalyze mutual engagement of the parties, lead them to consensus embodying the public interest, and unite them behind measures to meet it via local coalitions. In the spirit of the War on Poverty of the 1960s, which legitimized new, especially minority-group interests on the local level, the advisory councils of "a" agencies were to be broadly representative, and the councils and the boards of the "b" agencies were to contain majorities of consumers.

Such requirements were to persist under NHPRDA.[39] Funding of planning also reflected concerns about local participation. Just as Hill-Burton had required local groups to help fund hospital projects, CHP required a fourth of funding for "b" agencies to come from local sources.

The legislation thus created strong expectations about planning, but it denied a serviceable structure for its practice and stymied it at every turn. The "a" agencies, as entities of state government, could have been invested with enforcement powers but typically were not. Agencies could assemble interests, but not compel them to mobilize behind planners' notions of the public good. Although Congress wanted agencies to coordinate programs, the law gave them no authority or mechanism to do so; similar problems later marked the NHPRDA. Moreover, planners themselves encountered myriad problems: they expressed confusion about goals; lacked experience with comprehensive services; and worked without models, methods, and rational principles. While science remained elusive, politics dominated creation and staffing of agencies and pervaded their deliberations. Planning agencies thus scarcely could affect the development and distribution of hospitals or other health care resources. At most, planners succeeded in carrying out consultative practices, later dubbed the "forum function" of planning. In effect, however, the forum function was a means to subordinate the agencies and their planners to political maneuvering by the interests. As a means to rationalize health care, CHP was vacuous; as a political exercise, it privileged health care interests over reformers' notions of the public interest. It could hardly have been expected to engage in "promoting and assuring the highest level of health attainable for every person," as the declaration of purpose in the legislation had put it.[40] The act was far less a hard-headed program than a symbol of congressional aspiration to moderate cost escalation, improve access to care, and coordinate diverse programs, but it gave those jobs to the states, supposing that modest federal support would enable them to create the capacity to build coalitions to plan and organize health services.

CAPITAL FLOWS INVITE REGULATION

Efforts at hard planning emerged as voluntary hospitals gained improved access to capital. Philanthropy no longer met perceived needs for modernization, new technology, and new construction. The principal new route to capital for voluntary hospitals was borrowing, eventually through new tax-exempt instruments, secured by revenues from patients, created by the states beginning in the 1960s. Until then, however, the need for collateral proved an obstacle, since the only candidate for collateral, physical plant, had few alternative uses, and public opinion at the time would not tolerate foreclosure. Beginning in the 1950s, an alternative came

from third-party payers (commercial insurers and Blue Cross), which increasingly acknowledged the importance of capital costs and allowed reimbursement for them in the form of depreciation allowances; this critical change produced revenues that supported not only operations but also debt service. Anticipated revenues thus could replace collateral as security for loans. From about 1965, the Hill-Burton Act and philanthropy, formerly the major sources of capital, became ancillary to borrowing. Federal and state policy also fostered this change. A 1963 ruling by the Internal Revenue Service permitted tax-exempt borrowing but required a governmental agency to issue the bonds and in the end take over ownership of the facility. To avoid loss of ownership, beginning in the mid-1960s, the states created special finance authorities that granted access to a large supply of investors but left ownership in its original, voluntary hands. The advent of Medicare and Medicaid provided large revenues for much care that hospitals had previously provided as uncompensated charity, and Medicare reimbursement also included capital depreciation to help underwrite hospitals' plans for new construction and modernization.[41] Other federal policies, through amendments to Hill-Burton, supported borrowing through loan guarantees and interest subsidies, and additional federal supports appeared around 1970. By 1980, hospitals had acquired large volumes of capital from third-party reimbursement (public and private), tax-exempt borrowing, and federal loan guarantees.[42] Persistent cost escalation, however, elicited calls for change. Knowledge of the Roemer effect led analysts to blame cost increases on capital expenditures. State and federal policy thus had created a problem that demanded policy responses. Hard planning through capital controls became the favored solution.

From as early as the initial CHP legislation and in later measures, Congress had created some modest capital controls, giving local (or "b") agencies responsibility for "review and comment" on proposals for grants under various federal programs, and in 1972, under the Social Security amendments of that year, created section 1122 review, the first controls on capital investment and changes in service (later known jointly as CES controls) applied under federal mandate.[43] Through contracts between states and federal government, institutions that lacked state approval for certain capital expenditures and consequent changes in service would be denied reimbursement under Medicare, Medicaid, and the federal Maternal and Child Health program. Formal, if modest capital controls had become part of the federal health planning program. Their outcome was no better than that of CHP more broadly, however,[44] and Congress soon demanded reconstruction of planning.

The congressional response also reflected the poor outcomes of a bargain with hospital interests, which, because of cost escalation, faced delegitimization and feared governmental intervention. Hospitals promised that, while enjoying expanded access to capital, they would support discipline in its use. Beginning in 1968, hospital interests and planners backed or led state coalitions seeking CON laws, which many states introduced in the 1970s.[45] Under CON, creation or expansion of health facilities or significant changes of service would require a certificate of need from a state agency, an approach that hospitals and planners modeled on public utility regulation, which left intact ownership, management, and even self-regulation.[46] Most of the statutes gave local planning agencies only the power of review and comment, reserving decision making for a state agency (other than the "a" agency). However, under state CON, as under section 1122 review, planners persisted in formulating broad goals for rationalizing the health system, favored consultation, and exploited soft planning more than regulation. Congress decided to try again.

THE NATIONAL HEALTH PLANNING AND RESOURCES DEVELOPMENT ACT OF 1974

Reconstruction of the planning program took place under NHPRDA, the last major federal expression of planning as national policy. The act emerged after Congress temporarily renewed several antecedent programs (CHP, RMP, and Hill-Burton), which all expired in 1973. By 1974, the first two were moribund; NHPRDA was a reconstruction of CHP.[47] Just as contradictory pressures were at work in CHP (rationalizing the health system and constraining costs), so did the new program became enmeshed in opposing themes of national health policy (expanding entitlement to services under a resurgent movement for NHI and containing costs). A prevailing sense of crisis that had set in in the early 1970s had motivated widespread calls for NHI, both to expand entitlement and to provide leverage over the costs and structure of the health system.[48] Because proponents of NHI thought a national program would provide levers to rationalize health care, and proponents of planning had emphasized efficiency and distribution of resources in relation to need, the planning and NHI agendas grew linked. By 1974, when supporters of NHI in and out of government believed its passage imminent, reform of planning seemed urgent.[49]

The new legislation, however, was no better suited to its tasks than its predecessor.[50] The law called for local area-wide agencies (now called Health Systems Agencies) to cover the entire country and mandated state-level CON (i.e., power to review and approve). Like the CHP legislation, however, the new law, despite its ostensible focus on cost control, emphasized broad but vague goals; stipulated no clear, concrete subsidiary aims; delegated formulation of planning guidelines to the Department of Health, Education and Welfare (which failed to establish consensus on the matter); and tended to de-emphasize state functions in favor of direct relationships between federal and local agencies. Accordingly, local interests retained the power to interpret federal intentions. Although those interests included newer community constituencies, the new law, like its predecessor, did not allow them to balance the community and hospital interests that resisted subordination to planning. Dominant were the desire of hospitals to escape coercion and maintain and increase access to capital; the commitments of planners to their traditionally broad goals and soft planning; the desire of traditional community leaders to foster and showcase advanced health facilities and services; and the sanctity, in the minds of national legislators, of local coalitions and locally valued facilities.

THE FAILURE OF CONGRESSIONAL COST CONTROL

Congress had renewed its symbolic commitment to cost control and rationalization, but continued to hold back from imposing strict discipline on an industry that dealt, on a local level, with life and death. State CON laws that conformed to the act were slow to become operational; local agencies, lacking a specific charge, failed to focus on cost control; and local participants and the prevailing local incentives failed to encourage stringency. The legislation attempted to provide national focus to a program that had rested on federal encouragement of state and local initiatives, but it produced only marginal changes in planning practice and minor changes on the ground.

A prominent factor in the decline of planning under the act was the emergence of health services research, a multidisciplinary enterprise that in the 1970s had begun to show its mettle in fostering analysis and understanding of the health system.[51] In seeking variables to operationalize and measure, researchers seized on cost control, among other things. Studies revealed that planning and more particularly CON had little effect on capital investment or costs. The earliest and, in the event, most negative studies, published amid continued concern about cost escalation and a deregulatory movement outside health care that had gathered steam during the administration of President Jimmy Carter (1977–1981), tainted CON and the whole enterprise of planning.[52] Additional studies revealed previously unanticipated complexity in the decisions of hospitals to invest in capital projects and in the links between capital investment and operating costs, thereby suggesting that CON or other capital controls could not even in principle control costs.[53]

ONGOING COST ESCALATION

Other work suggested that the chief motors of cost escalation lay beyond the reach of planners, such as multiple sources of increased demand, retrospective reimbursement under fee-for-service, and public policies that encouraged technological advance.[54] In exploring agency operations, moreover, such studies suggested that regulators could not confine agency proceedings to principled practice, that planners shied away from hard planning, and that politics (and not fundamental principles) dictated the actions of agencies. Even where hard planning was attempted, it inevitably elicited opposition, which was often effective in courts, Congress and state legislatures, and national and state administrations. Moreover, research showed, logrolling by the interests in the deliberations of agency boards and sometimes even stonewalling in response to regulatory decisions undermined effectiveness. Resistance found support in local boosterism and in the broad and enduring conviction that more (and more advanced) care is better care. Health services researchers seemed to have demonstrated that the planning structure could never attain the goal of cost containment.[55]

Planners defended their programs, saying that critics' single-minded focus on cost control was inconsistent with the foundations of planning; that its benefits could not be captured by measurement; and that the forum function, if allowed to take its course, would gradually bring results.[56] Yet it was planners who had laid the groundwork for their own predicament. They had persistently focused on capital controls as the basis for moderating cost escalation, from "putting out fires" to CON. Although a minority of planners favored hard planning, most used concern about costs to sustain soft practice; even after the apparent lessons of the Roemer effect took hold, planners resisted stringency, upheld a broad agenda, and maintained a leisurely pace. Those interested in hard planning lacked any scientific principles beyond the Roemer effect (which research eventually showed insufficient), failed to resist the drift toward consultation, and courted criticism as unaccountable to the public. Between the indictments of researchers and a gathering policy stalemate in Washington that inhibited firm action on costs, the opportunity to use planning in the service of tight controls had passed. Planning was on the way out. Activities under NHPRDA sputtered along in the 1980s, until Congress finally repealed the act in 1987.[57]

HEALTH CARE PLANNING: WHAT THE NATION HAS LEARNED

The health planning movement that flourished in the United States during the 1960s and 1970s drew on the convictions of reformers, many of whom were social scientists and experts in health care, that the rise of scientific medicine had created valuable medical innovations that should be made available to the entire population. Ideas that had circulated in the late nineteenth century and gained prominence after World War I (1914–1918) about distributing health resources, as well as

the concept of need that the Committee on the Costs of Medical Care pressed on the nation from the early 1930s, suggested that a gap existed between what medical science could do in principle and the lack or maldistribution of the resources necessary to utilize new scientific knowledge in practice. Moreover, the traditional organization of medical care, which emphasized solo practice and freestanding hospitals, seemed ever less suitable, in the eyes of reformers, to the provision of scientifically based care. To encourage the creation of novel institutional arrangements for care and to efficiently create new health care resources that were increasingly expensive, advocates of modern medicine called for planning. However, interest in planning lay largely dormant until after World War II, when it emerged chiefly in connection with hospitals.

Preparing for the postwar expansion of hospitals, planners and hospital interests secured passage in 1946 of the Hill-Burton program, which subsidized the expansion of the hospital system and at least aspired to use planning in selecting and distributing projects. While planners continued to call for rational deployments of resources, construction took place through dispersed and local initiatives little guided by planning; and the importance of chronic care, while it found acknowledgment in amendments to the Hill-Burton Act, was scarcely realized on the ground. Instead the program resulted in unguided proliferation of chiefly acute-care hospitals in chiefly poor states and rural areas.

In the late 1950s, as cost inflation grew prominent, advocates pressed Congress to support planning, while they gradually reoriented themselves toward care in urban regions. Federal action fostered early urban-oriented planning agencies, and in 1966, Congress created the first major federal planning effort, Comprehensive Health Planning. Increased flow of capital into the health sector that resulted in part from the creation of Medicare and Medicaid and in part from the eclipse of philanthropy by borrowing, and the intensification of cost inflation in the late 1960s, heightened concern about duplication and maldistribution of resources and excess beds. Claims rising in the late 1960s that national health insurance, whatever its virtues as an expression of social justice, could also provide leverage over the health system that would constrain the rate of cost increases, supported planners' conviction that serious planning was needed. CHP, however, suffered from various disabilities, including planners' ambivalence about the virtues of hard-headed decision making and their predilection for leisurely, consultative practices; criticism that such soft planning elicited as unaccountable to the public; and congressional reticence to arouse the interests and create political discord in local communities.

Having concluded that CHP was ineffective while growing concerned about persistent cost escalation, Congress reconstructed the program in 1974. The new program mandated state-level regulation by certification of need, but in other respects bypassed state authority in favor of links with local communities. Many of the same difficulties that plagued CHP, however, also burdened the new program, while local politics surrounding planning agencies further inhibited substantive action. Studies by practitioners of an increasingly muscular health services research suggested that planning had few effects and many liabilities. The planning program fizzled out in the early 1980s. Many other, often underlying factors, such as the dissolution of community bonds and the immense flows of capital (and the business opportunities they afforded) into the health system, as well as the deregulatory movement outside health care, also contributed to the demise of health planning.

Meanwhile, newer voices calling for market-oriented health care suggested an alternative to traditional, top-down practices. Rather than plan and regulate the health sector, government should encourage the formation of markets in which market discipline would encourage the formation of the same kinds of large bureaucratic organizations that existed in other markets and that would require these organizations to plan as a matter of economic survival. Matching resources to need would become their task, and their success in achieving it would determine their profitability. The apparent exhaustion of planning and other, broadly similar forms of public policy encouraged more and more experts and political decision makers to think in terms of markets. Planning would be done, not under governmental sponsorship, but by private, typically profit-making organizations.

See also **Chapter 2: The Long Struggle for Universal Health Care (1900s–Present); Chapter 10: Federalism: Cooperation and Conflict between State and Federal Health Care Responsibilities (1960s–Present); Chapter 12: Evolution of Health Planning (1970s–Present); Chapter 13: Government Financing of Health Care (1940s–Present); Chapter 17: Strategies for Health Care Cost Containment (1980s–Present); Chapter 26: Interest Groups, Think Tanks, and Health Care Policy (1960s–Present).**

NOTES

1. This chapter relies heavily but not exclusively on the author's study, "Health Planning in the United States and the Decline of Public-Interest Policymaking," *Milbank Quarterly* 8: 2 (2006): 359–440.

2. Jonathan Engel, *Doctors and Reformers: Discussion and Debate over Health Policy, 1925–1950* (Columbia: University of South Carolina Press, 2002).

3. Proposals to provide especially public financing of care typically aroused intense opposition, and planners therefore emphasized the institutional arrangements supported by the growth of private insurance; David Rosner, *A Once Charitable Enterprise: Hospitals and Health Care in Brooklyn and New York, 1885–1915* (New York: Cambridge University Press, 1982); Rosemary A. Stevens, *In Sickness and in Wealth: American Hospitals in the Twentieth Century* (New York: Basic Books, 1989).

4. Daniel M. Fox, *Health Policies, Health Politics: The British and American Experience, 1911–1965* (Princeton, NJ: Princeton University Press, 1986), esp. chs. 5 and 7 and pp. 163–168; Jennifer Klein, *For All These Rights: Business, Labor, and the Shaping of America's Public-Private Welfare State* (Princeton, NJ: Princeton University Press, 2007).

5. Fox, *Health Policies, Health Politics.*

6. Engel, *Doctors and Reformers;* the final report of the committee was Committee on the Costs of Medical Care, *Medical Care for the American People* (Chicago: University of Chicago Press, 1932).

7. In 1981, the major federal planning program (begun in 1975, under Title XV of the Public Health Service Act, as created by PL 93-641), although not repealed, in effect lost its mandate with the passage of the Omnibus [Budget] Reconciliation Act; Bonnie Lefkowitz, with contributions by Eleanor D. Kinney and Cheryl Ulmer, *Health Planning: Lessons for the Future* (Rockville, MD: Aspen Systems, 1983), 26; the reconciliation act is PL 97-35; Congressional Quarterly Service, *Congress and the Nation: A Review of Government and Politics,* Vol. VI: 1981–1984 (Washington, DC: Congressional Quarterly Service, 1985), 531. Repeal of the federal planning program became effective only on January 1, 1987 (after passage in 1986 of an omnibus health bill, PL 99-660; Congressional Quarterly Service, *Congress and the Nation: A Review of Government and Politics,* Vol. VII: 1985–1988 (Washington, DC: Congressional Quarterly Service, 1990), 548, 550. Between these two events, the program limped along; see the two volumes by Congressional Quarterly Service just cited; Keith J. Mueller, "Federal Programs to Expire: The Case of Health Planning," *Public Administration Review* 48: 3 (1988): 719–725; William Shonick, *Government and Health Services: Government's Role in the Development of U.S. Health Services, 1930–1980* (New York: Oxford University Press, 1995), 465–470. However, in essence, the planning era ended with the budget act of 1981.

8. Created under PL 89-239, the Heart Disease, Cancer, and Stroke Amendments. See Daniel M. Fox, *Power and Illness: The Failure and Future of American Health Policy* (Berkeley: University of California Press, 1995), 68–69; Arthur D. Little and the Organization for Social and Technical Innovation, "Historical Background, Regionalization, Facilitation, Evaluation, Relationships," Vol. 2 of *A Study of the Regional Medical Program* (Cambridge, MA: Health Services and Mental Health Administration, 1970); Stevens, *In Sickness and in Wealth,* 277–279; Stephen P. Strickland, *The History of Regional Medical Programs: The Life and Death of a Small Initiative of the Great Society* (Lanham, MD: University Press of America, 2000).

9. John E. McDonough, *Interests, Ideas, and Deregulation: The Fate of Hospital Rate Setting* (Ann Arbor: University of Michigan Press, 1997).

10. Where it has been undergoing revision to comport with the major health care reform of the Obama administration, the

Patient Protection and Affordable Care Act (PL 111-148, as amended by the Health Care and Education Reconciliation Act, PL 111-152, passed in March 2010). See State of Maryland, Department of Health and Mental Hygiene, *Maryland's All-Payer Model* (2013), http://dhmh.maryland.gov/docs/Final%20Combined%20Waiver%20Package%20101113.pdf; I am indebted to Daniel M. Fox for calling my attention to this document. See also Rahul Rajkumar et al.. "Maryland's All-Payer Approach to Delivery-System Reform," *New England Journal of Medicine* 370: 6 (2014): 493–495.

11. Stevens, *In Sickness and in Wealth*, 125.

12. For example, Commission on Financing Hospital Care, *Financing Hospital Care in the United States,* 3 vols. (New York: Blakiston, vol. 1; New York: Blakiston Division, McGraw-Hill, vols. 2–3, 1954–1955); Commission on Hospital Care, *Hospital Care in the United States* (New York: Commonwealth Fund, 1947); C. Rufus Rorem, *The Public's Investment in Hospitals* (Chicago: University of Chicago Press, 1930).

13. Fox, *Health Policies, Health Politics*, 118, 163–168.

14. For example, Commission on Chronic Illness, *Care of the Long-term Patient*, Vol. 2 (Cambridge, MA: Harvard University Press, 1956), 292; New York State, Commission to Formulate a Long Range Health Program, *Planning for the Care of the Chronically Ill in New York State—Regional Aspects* (Albany, NY: Williams Press, 1945); Paul A. Lembcke, "Regional Organization of Hospitals," *Annals of the American Academy of Political and Social Science* 273 (1951): 53–61.

15. Fox, *Health Policies, Health Politics*, 118, 160, 166.

16. Alan Edward Treloar and Don Chill, *Patient Care Facilities: Construction Needs and Hill-Burton Accomplishments* (Chicago: American Hospital Association, 1961); Judith R. Lave and Lester B. Lave, *The Hospital Construction Act: An Evaluation of the Hill-Burton Program, 1948–1973* (Washington, DC: American Enterprise Institute, 1974); Gerard P. Walsh Jr., compiler, *Hospital Survey and Construction Act with Amendments, Contains Laws of the 79th through the 96th, 2d session, Congresses* (Washington, DC: U.S. Government Printing Office, 1981).

17. For example, Ray H. Elling, "The Hospital Support Game in Urban Center," in *The Hospital in Modern Society,* edited by Eliot Freidson, 73–111 (London: Free Press, 1963).

18. Paul Starr, *The Social Transformation of American Medicine: The Rise of a Sovereign Profession and the Making of a Vast Industry* (New York: Basic Books, 1982), 173–177; Kenneth Fox, *Metropolitan America: Urban Life and Urban Policy in the United States, 1940–1980* (Jackson: University Press of Mississippi, 1986); David J. Rothman, "The Hospital as Caretaker: The Almshouse Past and the Intensive Care Future," *Transactions and Studies of the College of Physicians of Philadelphia,* ser. 5, 12: 2 (1990): 151–174; Commission on Hospital Care, Hospital Care in the United States, 286–287, 376–377; Commission on Chronic Illness, Chronic Illness in the United States.

19. For example, New York State, *Planning for the Care of the Chronically Ill*; New York State, Commission to Formulate a Long Range Health Program, *A Program for the Care of the Chronically Ill in New York State* (Albany, NY: Williams Press, 1947); Treloar and Chill, *Patient Care Facilities*, 13, 14, 21, 29; United States Congress, House, Committee on Interstate and Foreign Commerce, *Public Health Service Act (Grant-in-Aid Amendments,* 83rd Congress, 2nd session (Washington, DC: U.S. Government Printing Office, 1954).

20. Evan M. Melhado, "Economists, Public Provision, and the Market: Changing Values in Policy Debate," *Journal of Health Politics, Policy, and Law* 23: 2 (1998): 215–263, esp. 231–233; Jack C. Haldeman, "The Ten Commandments of Progressive Patient Care," In *Proceedings of Workshop on Organization of Hospital Inpatient Services . . . January 25–28, 1961* (Chicago: American Hospital Association, 1961), 38–49 (39 for the quotation). Haldeman was then an assistant surgeon general of the Public Health Service and chief of its Division of Hospital and Medical Facilities.

21. Fox, *Power and Illness.*

22. John H. Hayes, ed., *Factors Affecting the Costs of Hospital Care,* Vol. 1 of *Financing Hospital Care in the United States* (New York: Blakiston, 1954–1955), 70; American Hospital Association, *Guides to Capital Financing of Hospitals: Proceedings of an Institute Conducted by American Hospital Association, Chicago, April 5–7, 1961* (Chicago: American Hospital Association, 1962), esp. chs. 6, 8, 19, and 20; Walter J. Rome, "The Time to Act Is Now for a Coordinated Hospital System," *Hospitals* 33: 23 (1959): 40–43, 110–112.

23. Samuel Levey and James Hill, "Rorem, C. Rufus," In *Encyclopedia of Health Services Research,* edited by Ross M. Mullner, 1050–1051 (Thousand Oaks, CA: Sage, 2009), doi:10.4135/9781412971942; Lewis E. Weeks and Howard J. Berman, *Shapers of American Health Care Policy: An Oral History* (Ann Arbor, MI: Health Administration Press, 1985), 132. For examples of how the new urban orientation of planning bodies influenced planning in Pittsburgh and elsewhere, see Evan M. Melhado, "Health Planning in the United States and the Decline of Public-Interest Policymaking," *Milbank Quarterly* 84: 2 (2006): 359–440, esp. 378–379.

24. "Activities in Hospital Councils around the U.S." [Part II], *Hospital Forum* 1: 15 (1958): 13; "Activities in Hospital Councils around the U.S." [Part III], *Hospital Forum* 1: 17 (1959): 17, 28–29; Clifford F. Hood, "Regional Hospital Planning in Allegheny County, Pennsylvania," *Chronic Illness Newsletter* 12: 66 (1961): 2–5; Robert M. Sigmond, "Hospital Planning in Allegheny County," *Group Practice* 13: 6 (1964): 370–374; United States Public Health Service, Division of Hospital and Medical Facilities, *Areawide Planning for Hospitals and Related Health Facilities* (Washington, DC: U.S. Government Printing Office, 1961), 11–13, 52–53.

25. David J. Rothman, *Strangers at the Bedside: A History of How Law and Bioethics Transformed Medical Decision Making* (New York: Basic Books, 1991), esp. 125–130; John C. Teaford, *City and Suburb: The Political Fragmentation of Metropolitan America, 1850–1970* (Baltimore: Johns Hopkins University Press, 1979).

26. Eli Ginzberg and the Conservation of Human Resources Staff, Columbia University, *Urban Health Services: The Case of New York* (New York: Columbia University Press, 1971); Alfred E. Miller, "The Changing Structure of the Medical Profession in Urban and Suburban Settings," *Social Science and Medicine* 11: 4 (1977): 233–243; Donald A. Faber, Austin S. Hall, and Michael L. Bobrow, "Downtown Hospitals Need not Go Downhill," *Modern Hospital* 109: 5 (1967): 107–108.

27. Lyle C. Fitch, "Fiscal and Political Problems of Increasing Urbanization," *Political Science Quarterly* 71: 1 (1956): 71–89. For "areawide," cf. for example, C. Rufus Rorem, "Appraisal and Priority Standards for Community Hospital Surveys," *American Journal of Public Health* 44: 9 (1954): 1134–1141; C. Rufus Rorem, "Voluntary Organizations in Medical Care Planning:

III. Community Hospital Planning Associations," *American Journal of Public Health* 54: 3 (1964): 455–457. The term *area-wide* thus did not derive from the efforts of planners in the 1940s to devise "hospital areas" to serve as the basis for organizing hierarchies that aimed to bring urban care to rural areas; see Joseph W. Mountin, Elliott H. Pennell, and Vane M. Hoge, *Health Service Areas: Requirements for General Hospitals and Health Centers* (Washington, DC: U.S. Government Printing Office, 1945).

28. Hospital and Medical Facilities Amendments of 1964, PL 88-443; Harald M. Graning and Anita H. Reichert, "The Hill-Harris Amendments of 1964 [PL 88-443] to the Hill-Burton Act for Construction and Modernization of Health Facilities," *Health, Education, and Welfare Indicators* 1964 (September): xxvi–xli.

29. United States Public Health Service, Areawide Planning for Hospitals and Related Health Facilities.

30. Hospital and Medical Facilities Amendments of 1964, PL 88-443; see Graning and Reichert, "The Hill-Harris Amendments of 1964."

31. To replace politics with science as wielded by professional experts was a prominent theme from the Progressive Era (roughly, 1900–1920) that long remained influential; see Evan M. Melhado, "American Health Reformers and the Social Sciences in the Twentieth Century," in *A Master of Science History: Essays in Honor of Charles Coulston Gillispie*, edited by Jed Z. Buchwald, 297–325 (Dordrecht, Netherlands: Springer, 2012).

32. Douglas R. Brown, "The Process of Area-wide Planning: Model for the Future?" *Medical Care* 11: 1 (1973): 1–11; Edward A. Lentz, "Changing Philosophy and Role of the Health Facilities Planning Agencies," in *Invitational Conference on Comprehensive Health Planning: Papers,* 47–56 (Chicago: American Hospital Association, 1969).

33. Emily K. Abel, Elizabeth Fee, and Theodore M. Brown, "Milton I. Roemer: Advocate of Social Medicine, International Health, and National Health Insurance," *American Journal of Public Health* 98: 9 (2008): 1596–1597.

34. Milton I. Roemer and Max Shain, *Hospital Utilization under Insurance* (Chicago: American Hospital Association, 1959); Max Shain and Milton I. Roemer, "Hospital Costs Relate to the Supply of Beds," *Modern Hospital* 92: 4 (1959): 71–73, 168.

35. George Bugbee, "The Areawide Health Facilities Planning Movement—Dimensions, Purposes, and Values," in *Papers from the Fourth Annual Institute for the Staffs of the Areawide Health Facility Planning Agencies,* 1–10 (Chicago: Center for Health Administration Studies, Graduate School of Business, University of Chicago, 1966); James H. Cavanaugh, "The Rise of the Areawide Planning Agency: A Survey Report," *Hospitals* 39, pt. 1: 15 (1965): 52–56; Jack C. Haldeman, "Area-wide Planning Gains Momentum," *Hospitals* 36: 19 (1962): 46–48; C. Rufus Rorem, "Areawide Planning Is Here to Stay," *Modern Hospital* 103: 2 (1964): 98–99, 168; Kenneth W. Wisowaty, Charles C. Edwards, and Raymond L. White, "Health Facilities Planning—A Review of the Movement," *Journal of the American Medical Association* 190: 8 (1964): 752–756.

36. James H. Cavanaugh and William McC. Hiscock, "Comprehensive Health Planning and Public Health Service Act of 1966 (PL-89-749)," *Health, Education, and Welfare Indicators* 1967 (January): 9–18.

37. Daniel M. Fox, "Sharing Governmental Authority: Blue Cross and Hospital Planning in New York City," *Journal of Health Politics, Policy, and Law* 16: 4 (1991): 719–746; William J.

Curran, "A National Survey and Analysis of State Certificate-of-Need Laws for Health Facilities," in *Regulating Health Facilities Construction: Proceedings of a Conference on Health Planning, Certificate of Need, and Market Entry,* edited by Clark C. Havighurst, 85–111 (Washington, DC: American Enterprise Institute, 1974).

38. Thomas R. Oliver, "Ideas, Entrepreneurship, and the Politics of Health Care Reform," *Stanford Law & Policy Review* 3 (Fall 1991): 160–80.

39. United States Congress, Senate, Committee on Labor and Public Welfare, *National Health Planning and Development and Health Facilities Assistance Act of 1974,* 93rd Congress, 2nd session (Washington, DC: U.S. Government Printing Office, 1974); United States Congress, House, Committee on Interstate and Foreign Commerce, *National Health Policy, Planning, and Resources Development Act of 1974,* 93rd Congress, 2nd session (Washington, DC: U.S. Government Printing Office, 1974); Steven Sieverts, *Health Planning Issues and Public Law 93-641* (Chicago: American Hospital Association, 1977), ch. 3.

40. United States Congress, House, Committee on Interstate and Foreign Commerce, *Comprehensive Health Planning and Public Health Services Amendments of 1966: October 11, 1966,* 89th Congress, 2nd session (Washington, DC: U.S. Government Printing Office, 1966), 9.

41. Judith Feder, *Medicare: The Politics of Federal Hospital Insurance* (Lexington, MA: Lexington Books, 1977).

42. American Hospital Association, *Capital Financing for Hospitals* (Chicago: American Hospital Association, 1974); Feder, *Medicare,* esp. ch. 5; John T. Ryan Jr., "Capital Needs of Hospitals: How Will They Be Met in the Next 20 Years?" *Hospitals* 32: 7 (1958): 32–35; Robert M. Sigmond, "Hospital Capital Funds: Changing Needs and Sources," *Hospitals* 39: 16 (1965): 52–55; Glenn Wilson, Cecil G. Sheps, and Thomas R. Oliver, "Effects of Hospital Revenue Bonds on Hospital Planning and Operations," *New England Journal of Medicine* 307: 23 (1982): 1426–1430.

43. Karen Davis et al., *Health Care Cost Containment* (Baltimore: Johns Hopkins University Press, 1990), 17–25; U.S. Department of Health, Education and Welfare, Health Services and Mental Health Administration, Comprehensive Health Planning Service, *The Review and Comment Responsibilities of State and Areawide Comprehensive Health Planning Agencies* (Washington, DC: U.S. Government Printing Office, 1973); U.S. Public Health Service, Health Resources Administration, *Evaluation of the Efficiency and Effectiveness of the Section 1122 Review Process* (Rockville, MD: Health Resources Administration, 1977).

44. Ibid.

45. For example, William J. Curran, "A National Survey and Analysis of State Certificate-of-Need Laws for Health Facilities," In *Regulating Health Facilities Construction: Proceedings of a Conference on Health Planning, Certificate of Need, and Market Entry,* edited by Clark C. Havighurst, 85–111 (Washington, DC: American Enterprise Institute, 1974); "State Regulation of Hospitals: Report of a New Modern Hospital Survey," *Modern Hospital* 115: 6 (1970): 62–75.

46. Clark C. Havighurst, ed., *Regulating Health Facilities Construction: Proceedings of a Conference on Health Planning, Certificates of Need, and Market Entry* (Washington, DC: American Enterprise Institute, 1974).

47. James F. Blumstein and Frank A. Sloan, "Health Planning and Regulation through Certificate of Need: An Overview," *Utah*

Law Review 1978 (1): 3–37; Bonnie Lefkowitz, with contributions by Eleanor D. Kinney and Cheryl Ulmer, *Health Planning: Lessons for the Future* (Rockville, MD: Aspen Systems, 1983); Sieverts, *Health Planning Issues*; John E. Wennberg and Alan W. Gittelsohn, *Health Planning and Regulation: The New England Experience* (Washington, DC: U.S. Government Printing Office, 1981).

48. Edward M. Kennedy, *In Critical Condition: The Crisis in America's Health Care* (New York: Simon & Schuster, 1972); Walter P. Reuther, "The Health Care Crisis: Where Do We Go from Here? The Eighth Annual Bronfman Lecture," *American Journal of Public Health and the Nation's Health* 59: 1 (1969): 12–20; Starr, *The Social Transformation of American Medicine*, 395–396, 404; U.S. Congress, Senate, Committee on Labor and Public Welfare, Subcommittee on Health, *Health Care Crisis in America, 1971*, 92nd Congress, 1st session (Washington, DC: U.S. Government Printing Office, 1971).

49. Edward M. Kennedy, "Excerpt from Comments on S. 2994 [forerunner of the National Health Planning and Resources Development Act of 1974, PL 93-641]," *Congressional Record*, 120, pt. 3 (February 8, 1974): 2822; Edward M. Kennedy, "Excerpt from Comments on S. 2994 [forerunner of the National Health Planning and Resources Development Act of 1974, PL 93-641]," *Congressional Record*, 120, pt. 28 (November 25, 1974): 37211–37213.

50. Pertinent items from the significant literature that can document this paragraph include those cited in supra n. 47 as well as Lawrence D. Brown, "Some Structural Issues in the Health Planning Program," in *Health Planning in the United States: Selected Policy Issues*, 2 vols., Vol. 2, 1–53 (Washington, DC: National Academy Press, 1981); Institute of Medicine, Committee on Health Planning Goals and Standards, *Health Planning in the United States: Selected Policy Issues*, 2 vols. (Washington, DC: National Academy Press, 1981); Basil J.F. Mott, "The New Health Planning System," in *Health Services: The Local Perspective*, edited by Arthur Levin, 238–254 (New York: Praeger, 1977); G. Gregory Raab, "Intergovernmental Issues Raised by the National Health Planning Program," *Journal of Health and Human Resources Administration* 1: 4 (1979): 570–595.

51. Daniel M. Fox, *Science and Convergence: Research, Health Policy, and the American States* (Berkeley: University of California Press, 2010), ch. 2.

52. Policy Analysis, *Evaluation of the Effects of Certificate of Need Programs*, 3 vols. (Springfield, VA: National Technical Information Service, 1981); David S. Salkever and Thomas W. Bice, "The Impact of Certificate of Need Controls on Hospital Investment," *Milbank Memorial Fund Quarterly/Health and Society* 54: 2 (1976): 185–214; Frank A. Sloan and Bruce Steinwald, *Insurance, Regulation, and Hospital Costs* (Lexington, MA: Lexington Books: 1980).

53. For example, Jerry Ginsburg et al., *Incentives and Decisions Underlying Hospitals' Adoption and Utilization of Major Capital Equipment* (Cambridge, MA: Abt Associates, 1975); Jonathan B. Brown and Harry M. Marks, "Buying the Future: The Relationship between the Purchase of Physical Capital and Total Expenditure Growth in U.S. Hospitals," in *Health Capital Issues: Papers Presented at the Health Capital Conference Sponsored by the Bureau of Health Facilities, February 19–20, 1980* (Washington, DC: U.S. Government Printing Office, 1981); ICF, *An Analysis of Programs to Limit Hospital Capital Expenditures: Final Report* (Springfield, VA: National Technical Information Service, 1980).

54. Drew E. Altman, "The Politics of Health Care Regulation: The Case of the National Health Planning and Resources Development Act," *Journal of Health Politics, Policy, and Law* 2: 4 (1978): 560–580; John K. Iglehart, "Washington Report: The Uncertain Future of Health Planning," *Journal of Health Politics, Policy, and Law* 5: 3 (1980): 579–582.

55. For example, Brown. "Some Structural Issues in the Health Planning Program"; Theodore R. Marmor and James A. Morone, "Representing Consumer Interests: Imbalanced Markets, Consumer Interests, and the HSAs," *Milbank Memorial Fund Quarterly/Health and Society* 58: 1 (1980): 125–165; Leonard Robins and Frank Thompson, "The National Government's Role in Health Planning: A Political Analysis," *Journal of Health and Human Resources Administration* 2: 4 (1980): 491–504; Bruce C. Vladeck, "Interest-Group Representation and the HSAs: Health Planning and Political Theory," *American Journal of Public Health* 67: 1 (1977): 23–28.

56. Harry P. Cain II, "Health Planning in the United States: The 1980s—A Protagonist's View," *Journal of Health Politics, Policy, and Law* 6: 1 (1981): 159–171; Institute of Medicine, Committee on Health Planning Goals and Standards, *Health Planning in the United States: Selected Policy Issues* 2 vols., Vol. 1 (Washington, DC: National Academy Press, 1981).

57. See supra, n. 7.

FURTHER READING

Altman, Drew E., Richard Greene, and Harvey M. Sapolsky. *Health Planning and Regulation: The Decision-making Process.* Washington, DC: AUPHA Press, 1981.

Fox, Daniel M. *Health Policies, Health Politics: The British and American Experience, 1911–1965.* Princeton, NJ: Princeton University Press, 1986.

Institute of Medicine, Committee on Health Planning Goals and Standards. *Health Planning in the United States: Selected Policy Issues.* 2 vols. Washington, DC: National Academy Press, 1981.

Lefkowitz, Bonnie, with contributions by Eleanor D. Kinney and Cheryl Ulmer. *Health Planning: Lessons for the Future.* Rockville, MD: Aspen Systems, 1983.

Melhado, Evan M., Walter Feinberg, and Harold M. Swartz, eds. *Money, Power, and Health Care.* Ann Arbor, MI: Health Administration Press, 1988.

Stevens, Rosemary A. *In Sickness and in Wealth: American Hospitals in the Twentieth Century.* New York: Basic Books, 1989.

chapter 12

Evolution of Health Planning (1970s–Present)

Evan M. Melhado

HEALTH CARE PROFESSIONALS AND SOME government officials began promulgating regional planning ideas as early as the 1920s. The general idea that health care planning would be in the public interest gained momentum, specifically after World War II (1939–1945). The movement flourished briefly during the 1960s and 1970s in response to expanded insurance coverage and rising health care costs in the wake of the creation of Medicare and Medicaid, as discussed in Chapter 11. By the 1980s, however, multiple factors coalesced to produce a new pro-competitive policy paradigm that was nearly the antithesis of traditional health planning. Remnants of the old planning regime are long gone, but new settings and approaches to health planning have emerged.

THE DECLINE AND FALL OF THE HEALTH PLANNING MOVEMENT

Beginning in the 1970s, various broad factors were at work to undermine the rationale and practice of health planning even as it reached its zenith in U.S. health policy. These factors—social, economic, and political—gave rise to a new market-oriented logic in health care and health policy that was incompatible with cooperative, consensus-based planning to meet community-wide needs.

Loosened Community Ties

Although health care, like politics, is fundamentally local, communities as such have ceased to be the focus of federal policymaking in health. In part, federal policies and their consequences encouraged hospital interests to behave less like eleemosynary institutions serving community goals than like business enterprises pursuing economic success. The capital flows that hospitals enjoyed required them to establish their accountability to lenders and investors by creating capital budgets and standardized accounting, practices that were formerly rare. Medicare reinforced these trends, as did the emergent investor-owned hospital industry, which compelled nonprofit hospitals, already strongly motivated by economic incentives,[1] to behave even more like businesses. Hospital administrators increasingly saw themselves as engaged in economic competition, not in providing community service.[2]

Also loosening community ties were the growing distance of planning agencies, Blue Cross plans, and philanthropists from local settings.[3] As metropolitan areas eclipsed rural hierarchies, metropolitan planning regions encompassed more than local communities (often defined by ethnicity, religion, culture, and race). Community groups, especially activists in the 1960s representing interests newly legitimized under President Lyndon B. Johnson's (1963–1969) War on Poverty, saw Health Systems Agencies as unsympathetic forces imposed from above. The nonprofit Blue Cross plans, the long-dominant payer created by local hospital interests, eventually felt competition from commercial firms to meet the needs of regional or national employers, abandoned community rating beginning even in the 1950s, and created structures that transcended local markets. Philanthropy, formerly derived from local elites, became the province of corporations, and they in turn operated in markets that grew beyond local communities. The management of multihospital systems, even if they began in local institutions, was often distant from them, and local hospitals themselves, under the impact of professionalism and the relative uniformity of suburban culture, grew less concerned about local practices and sensibilities. The economic forces that eroded community ties similarly eroded the extra-market culture, the social capital, of close community interactions. Local communities had ceased to be the chief context of heath care decision making and national policymaking for organizing and financing health services.

The Limits of Expertise

Another factor in the decline of planning was the impotence of experts, often in the employ of government, universities, and nonprofit institutions, who presumed to take the role of disinterested servants of the public interest.[4] However much planners rehearsed their ideas, and however much cost escalation seemed to create an opportunity for them to realize their goals with support on several governmental levels and among community groups, they routinely met powerful opposition that no legislative mandates and no consultation with supposedly enlightened interests could mitigate. Planners' preferences for soft planning, to which legislative mandates gave scope, may have blinded them to the full implications of their own agenda: it implied overturning the entire edifice of U.S. medical care, which, since the rise of scientific medicine, had given power to the medical profession, hospitals, and eventually insurers (especially Blue Cross)

to control the rate and distribution of capital investment. In its aspirations, therefore, soft planning was no less hard than direct regulation. The long time horizon of soft planning and the conviction of many planners that physicians and hospitals, themselves producers and beneficiaries of science, could be persuaded to support planners' goals, may have suggested to planners that rationalization of health care could be accomplished incrementally. Keeping the process going, however, in hopes that incrementalism would lead eventually to substantive change, succeeded only in preserving the ability of the interests to resist. Planners were no doubt correct that hard planning would only arouse intense opposition, but soft planning through consultation, when the ultimate stakes for the affected interests were very high and when those interests could wield powerful influence in their defense, was no viable avenue to reform. Moreover, a public and government impatient about cost escalation were unwilling to wait.

POLITICS AND HEALTH CARE POLICY

Certificate-of-Need Policies

Certificate-of-need (CON) policies established state-level regulation to rationalize the growth of the voluntary hospital sector and the distribution of hospitals. CON required sponsors of new capital investment in hospitals and their services to analyze the need, in a given service area, for the anticipated project and to obtain from a state regulatory agency permission to proceed in the form of a certificate of need. These policies emerged in the early 1960s, mostly in discussion but also in actual legislation in New York State, they arose in many states during the early 1970s at the behest chiefly of hospital interests, and they acquired federal mandate for state programs under the National Health Planning and Resources Development Act (NHPRDA) of 1974. By 1982, CON statutes existed in all states but Louisiana, which remained with the section 1122 capital controls created as part of the Social Security Amendments of 1972. After repeal of the federal planning program, some states abandoned CON, but up to at least 2011, thirty-six states, Puerto Rico, and the District of Columbia preserved them, despite the criticisms of CON that had helped sink the planning program and despite the disappearance of the planning institutions that had underlain CON regulation.

For about a decade before the spread of CON, statutory controls over hospital capital, variously labeled franchising, licensure, or CON, had been under discussion, as some planners held that only hard planning could compel urban and later also suburban hospitals to take into account broad community interest, as articulated by planners, in the rational and economical deployment and growth of hospital facilities and in avoidance of unnecessary duplication of facilities and services. Early research into the basis of planning led some planners to seek a "master plan," which, by virtue of its objective, scientific foundation, would garner support for planning goals. However, others, fearing that hard planning would elicit resistance, preferred a simple statement about the need for beds and their distribution. In the main, however, most planning agencies, recognizing that the scientific basis for planning was thin, worked chiefly by mobilizing local elites to avoid the most egregious examples of duplication. Soft planning remained dominant.

It was not planners' broad goals but capital flows into the hospital sector and intensifying cost escalation that elicited state CON statutes in the early 1970s. Facing a crisis of legitimacy, planners and hospital interests signaled willingness to discipline capital investment and, they hoped, thereby avoid additional governmental measures. Hospital interests therefore supported and often led state-based coalitions in support of CON policies. They covered more than the new construction and modernization of old facilities that CON had originally targeted. In response to technological change and market forces, they encompassed new equipment, services, and organizational settings (such as ambulatory surgery centers) that required capital investment, at least above a stipulated threshold, and in response to concerns about chronic care, CON laws encompassed additional kinds of institutions, such as nursing homes and dialysis centers. CON would constrain costs by limiting growth of a diverse group of institutions and services that generated costs under both public and private insurance programs.

However, once cost pressures set CON policies in motion, broader aspirations came to their support. Planners and reformers had long held that health services, because ever more effective, were of fundamental importance to citizens; that medical science possessed knowledge still unavailable in the form of novel services; that rational expansion of the health system was needed to create the resources to supply those services and assure their wide availability. These goals grew newly prominent in the late 1960s and early 1970s in the movement to enact a system of national health insurance (NHI). The Hill-Burton hospital construction program (1946–1974), the Regional Medical Programs (1965–1974), and Comprehensive Health Planning (CHP, 1966–1974) had all been motivated, at least in part, by these aspirations. The NHPRDA, which aimed to reform and coordinate these antecedents, gained support in part because it promised to lay the foundations for NHI. These diverse goals

The Limits of Science

Yet another theme was that in planning, as in other reform endeavors, experts' confidence in the power of science to serve the public interest proved to be misplaced. Reformers saw health services as the means to bring the fruits of scientific medicine to the population, and they held that planning could determine in the same scientific spirit that animated medical researchers the resources appropriate to meeting need, itself defined by the powers of science and technology. To determine the need for health facilities and services, to specify their rational geographic distribution, especially bed need, lay at the core of planners' interests.[5] Although much effort went into that kind of analysis, growing awareness of the diverse variables that could determine the distribution of beds, including of the elasticity of demand, implied that even in the application of science, value judgments were necessary about what things communities wanted and what they would pay for them.[6]

Additional factors inhibited a scientific approach. The complexities that researchers exhibited in decisions about capital investment, in the relation of investment to costs and in the effects of certificate-of-need (CON) regulation, also suggested that supposedly scientific planning could not control costs. Moreover, the rate of technological change demanded rapid responses in the supply and distribution of resources, but the factors that planners routinely invoked in trying to specify need—trends in population growth, in urban settlement, in economic development, and in medical technology—defied prediction in the short term and could not support concrete decisions about the character and location of facilities and personnel. Planners therefore called for flexible designs of new facilities to allow for future expansion and conversion of facilities to novel uses, activities that required not science but consultation, community organizing, and bargaining, all practices liable to the charge that planning, despite its claims to scientific foundations,

motivated Senator Edward M. Kennedy (D-MA; in office 1962–2009), a major sponsor of the NHPRDA. Reviewing the history of planning on the floor of the Senate, Kennedy argued for the legislation in light of these earlier programs:

> The important concept embodied in this legislation, that health financing should be closely related to health planning, has subsequently been reflected in almost all major proposal for national health insurance through a series of devices intended to assure that national health insurance does not pay for costly services which the planning process determines are unneeded.
>
> . . . [T]he ultimate objectives of the original [CHP] program were to promote the development of a healthful environment and a health care system in which quality health services would be available, accessible, and affordable for all persons. Despite the many changes made by S. 2994 [the Senate bill that, with few changes, became the NHPRDA], these objectives are continued in the proposed legislation. The means are changed, but the objectives are the same.

Contrary to expectation, NHI proposals failed in the 1970s, but the planning program lasted into the 1980s, and the CON policies in some form survived in a majority of states to the present. Why have CON policies persisted? Studies of CON offer conflicting accounts of its effectiveness but reveal that political considerations dominate regulatory proceedings. Persistence of CON thus likely reflects in part the alignment of contending forces and their skill in garnering broader support of the public, the courts, and legislatures. Hospital interests favor the programs, provided they are not too onerous, because they allow them to seize control over new or expanded services and keep out competitors, such as entrepreneurial physicians. The latter are opposed precisely because they experience CON as an unjustified barrier to market entry. Others, perhaps state officials and regulators, see an opportunity to impose requirements that providers serve poor and underserved populations, to uphold the centrality of major urban teaching hospitals, to limit the growth of cost-generating specialty and for-profit hospitals, to uphold quality standards, to constrain costs generally by limiting capital investment (one of the chief original rationales for CON now supported by studies of small area variations in costs), and to provide a forum for discussion of public policy (a longstanding feature of the soft planning that most planners had favored). Their rationales tenuous, their practices politicized, their outcomes of uncertain utility, CON policies nevertheless endure in the states as imperfect controls on a dynamic health system that generates enormous costs and often fails to meet what many take to be broad public goals.

SOURCES: U.S. Senate, 93rd Congress, 2nd session, *Congressional Record* 120: pt. 28 (November 25, 1974): 37211; William J. Curran, "A National Survey and Analysis of State Certificate-of-Need Laws for Health Facilities," in *Regulating Health Facilities Construction: Proceedings of a Conference on Health Planning, Certificate of Need, and Market Entry,* edited by Clark C. Havighurst, 85–111 (Washington, DC: American Enterprise Institute, 1974); Patrick Lenihan, "Certificate of Need (CON)," in *Encyclopedia of Health Services Research,* edited by Ross M. Mullner, 148–152 (Thousand Oaks, CA: Sage, 2009), doi:10.4135/9781412971942; Evan M. Melhado, "Health Planning in the United States and the Decline of Public-Interest Policymaking," *Milbank Quarterly* 84: 2 (2006): 359–440; National Conference of State Legislatures, "Certificate of Need: State Health Laws and Programs," http://www.ncsl.org/issues-research/health/con-certificate-of-need-state-laws.aspx; James B. Simpson, "State Certificate-of-Need Programs: The Current Status," *American Journal of Public Health* 75: 10 (1985): 1225–1229, United States Public Health Service, Health Resources Administration, *Evaluation of the Efficiency and Effectiveness of the Section 1122 Review Process* (Rockville, MD: Health Resources Administration, 1977); Tracy Yee, Lucy B. Stark, Amelia M. Bond, and Emily Carrier, "Health Care Certificate-of-Need Laws: Policy or Politics?" *National Institute for Health Care Reform Research Brief* 4 (2011): 1–8, http://www.nihcr.org/CON_Laws.

obscured unaccountable political activity.[7] Moreover, flexible designs risked imposing costs not compensated in the short term. The aspiration to replace politics with science lay in shambles.

In addition, the perceived failures of CON regulation caused health planning to be tainted with the antiregulatory animus that began in the 1970s in fields such as transportation and communications and grew apace thereafter.[8] Economists and other experts increasingly saw regulation as offering no scientific foundations to determine the levels of service and extent of competition, but instead as serving the regulated interests, depriving the public of efficient operations, and inhibiting innovation. Inside health care, was not CON the captive of the hospital industry? Why start a regulatory regime in health care when the public interest demanded its disestablishment elsewhere?

A Transformation of Policymaking

Also in ruins was the entire mode of public interest policymaking that planning had exemplified. Deriving from the Progressive Era at the turn of the twentieth century, it supposed that disinterested experts, especially in the employ of governments, foundations, and academic institutions (all nonprofit entities), exemplifying "social-trustee professionalism,"[9] could envision and advance a broad public interest. In the case of medical care, as planners saw it, glaring public needs were left unmet because the system of private, solo practice and freestanding hospitals, both oriented toward acute care, had not changed to meet the requirements of scientific practice and the growing awareness of chronic disease. Nonmarket arrangements had established themselves in medical care, experts believed, because society had deemed the provision of care too technical a matter and too valuable to be allowed to depend on market distribution. Experts replaced the market, but medical experts had not kept pace with change. Planners hoped to enlist medical and hospital experts in designing and fostering a system that could provide the most scientifically validated care in the most scientifically rational manner possible to serve the populations of local communities. Planners thus aimed to ally themselves in coalitions with governments, local elites, and heath care professionals in harmonious construction of modernized heath care arrangements. As planning foundered, however, new sensibilities emergent in diverse quarters suggested that the remedy for the widely acknowledged problems of health care lay precisely in the market arrangements that planners had long shunned.

Market arrangements in health care began in earnest during the 1980s and 1990s. Blue Cross plans, commercial insurers, Medicaid, and Medicare increasingly imposed standards on providers by regulating reimbursement, not by planning, however, but by contractual arrangements. It was not an overall vision of a reformed system that inspired these changes, but demands for efficiency and accountability to payers. Diminishing community ties, rising capital flows, and diversity of insurance programs made health care look ever more attractive as business activities rather than as public service. Gradually, as the legal barriers fell that had inhibited innovation in the organization of care, additional novel organizational and contractual arrangements continued to appear, managed-care organizations emerged to supply care to employees of firms on bases other than solo practice; independent hospitals often gave way to multihospital systems; new forms of out-of-hospital service appeared (in other kinds of institutions and in homes); and in general, market imperatives increasingly dominated health care on the ground.[10] The experts continued to play a role, but increasingly they embodied "expert professionalism," that is, working in the employ of the diverse interests active in health care markets or deeply interested in their workings. Not that they had abandoned public service, but notions of public service had changed into serving the interests, since a properly functioning market, in the view of experts, governments, and increasingly the public, is what served the public interest by providing goods and services, fostering efficient allocation of resources, and facilitating choice.[11]

Looking at the old regime, a sympathetic observer might see that the "social trustee professionalism" of the Progressive Era had brought valuable health services to a population that lacked them, even if professionals' grand visions often remained unrealized. A skeptical observer would point to structures of prestige and economic and legal advantage that privileged physicians, hospitals, and insurers over the public and patients. Advocates of the market claimed that by subjecting the interests to market discipline, the new heath care economy would serve the public better and that "expert professionalism" would help create and maintain a system that matched goods and services to demand; but critics hold that the new heath care economy privileges market values over extra-market values (interest in entitlement, distribution, affordability) and that it exposes care to the economic and moral hazards of business. Market-based care seems here to stay, but the extent to which it serves nonmarket goals remains a contested question. Passage of the Patient Protection and Affordable Care Act (PPACA) shows that extra-market values in health care, if much in dispute, are not dead; but under the act, as in the case of Medicare Part D (coverage for prescription drugs), traditional goals are to be attained by market mechanisms as much as possible.

NEW VENUES FOR HEALTH PLANNING

Planning has persisted in health care but no longer as a top-down national effort to control or even to guide the disposition of health care resources. Where can planning now be found? Outside of government, any participants in supplying health services must plan to create the institutions, assemble the personnel, engage in contracting with payers and providers, recruit patients, construct information systems, create mechanisms for accountability to patients and payers, and in general plan a complex organizational activity. Necessarily, therefore, planning exists throughout the health sector. Apart from these now typical activities, three settings for planning stand out as policy venues intended to advance something resembling traditional public-interest goals. One is the Accountable Care Organization (ACO), an idea that emerged midway through the first decade of this century. It is a clear successor to both the planning tradition and early advocacy of markets, both of which aimed to improve the quality, efficiency, and distribution of care. The second is community health improvement planning (CHIP) by local public health agencies and health care institutions.[12] The third, which emerged gradually after World War II and now commands much attention, rests on novel principles and practices in public health. All three have been promoted as serving goals that reflect extra-market values as traditionally conceived; all three lodge themselves in local communities and seek to create in diverse ways local commitments to improve population health; but all three face profound obstacles to their success.

Accountable Care Organizations

Early advocates of market-based health care argued that markets could solve the widely discussed problems of health care better than planning and regulation. Organized systems of care, like the health maintenance organizations (HMOs) that had been modeled on long-established prepaid group practices, would pursue population-oriented health provision, match resources to need, improve quality of care, and render its provision more efficient.[13] Newer HMOs, however, typically less tightly organized than the early models, largely failed to replicate their successes.[14] An explanation for this failure and a proposal for its remedy emerged from students of one form of irrationality in the structure of health care, geographically distinct patterns of health utilization and therefore spending that little affected the health of the populations served. Having observed and documented the power of supply to induce demand (i.e., characterized more broadly, the kind of phenomenon captured in Roemer's law about bed capacity), John Wennberg and colleagues at Dartmouth demonstrated that most of the variations in health care use among small areas involved primarily those chronic conditions for which physicians lacked consensus about the best course of treatment. Seeking to do their best for patients, physicians ordered more services in geographic areas having a larger supply of health resources, but in areas where supply was more limited, they practiced with more restraint and, interestingly, with higher quality.

To improve quality and constrain costs, these analysts concluded, payers should encourage more restrained practice by holding both physicians and hospitals accountable.[15] The ACO, proposed in the mid-2000s, fostered by Medicare and incorporated into the PPACA, has been held out as a promising means to that end.[16] Analysts could identify a local health system empirically by studying referral patterns in Medicare, they could attribute physicians to hospitals and patients to physicians, and they could identify the resultant rosters of physicians and hospitals as the providers accountable for the population they served. Planning would loom large as the ACO sought to match resources to need under "bundled payment" or "shared savings" mechanisms that encouraged more circumspect practice,[17] a corresponding reluctance of providers to expand the capacity of their local health system, and a commitment to invest in services—especially primary care—dedicated to long-term management and coordination of care for chronic disease patients. Thus, the ACO reflected the concerns of both traditional planners and early market advocates by seeking to improve the institutions of health care delivery and induce them to rationalize their functioning in accordance with public goals. The ACO also preserved the importance that traditional planners had accorded to limitations on capital investment, cost containment, and accommodating chronic disease.

Prospects for success of this approach are unclear. One novelty of the 1990s, which strongly resembles the recently envisioned ACO, also seemed to offer a path to coordinated and constrained practice. That was the physician-hospital organization, sometimes called an integrated delivery network. Some of these organizations styled themselves as fostering population health with improvements in quality and reductions in cost. Most proved ephemeral, however.[18] Proponents of the ACO acknowledge this precedent, and they also recognize that prevailing forms of reimbursement have acted since the 1990s to drive hospitals and physicians away from collaboration and into competition.[19] Moreover, the often novel planning tasks and practices that ACOs would need to undertake to control practice patterns and meet the stipulations of novel funding mechanisms entail high costs, offer still uncertain payoff, and risk incurring resistance from various quarters.[20] The promise of ACOs in lowering cost escalation of Medicare and therefore in relieving pressure on the federal budget thus defy safe prediction. Advocates of the ACO, however, may be correct that if accountable providers fail to curb cost escalation, Congress will do the job more directly through adjustments to future payments to providers of Medicare and Medicaid services.

Community Health Improvement Planning

This approach to planning derives from prominent reform efforts in U.S. public health that began in the 1980s and is now accelerating with new federal requirements under the

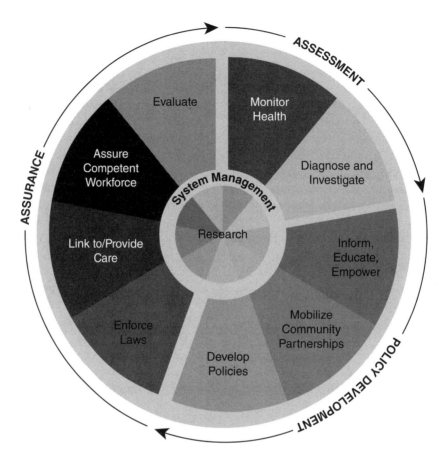

Three public health functions (identified in 1988 by the Institute of Medicine) are distributed over the Ten Essential Public Health Functions (as articulated in 1994 by a committee in the Department of Health and Human Services). Deployed together with the standards that the National Public Health Performance Standards Project first released in 2002, these ideas and practices have supported reforms of public health agencies in part to ensure their ability to carry out community public health improvement planning.

SOURCE: Centers for Disease Control and Prevention, "NPHPS: Strengthening Systems, Improving the Public's Health," http://www.cdc.gov/nphpsp/documents/nphpsp-factsheet.pdf.

PPACA that voluntary nonprofit hospitals must meet to secure exemption from federal taxes. Both fostered assessment of community health followed by planning and action to meet needs revealed by the assessment. Many of the reform efforts emerged from reactions to the state of disarray in public health characterized by a 1988 report from the Institute of Medicine (IOM), found elaboration in subsequent work by various public health organizations and additional IOM studies, and later drew strength from a second major IOM report in 2003. That study assessed the reforms already undertaken and argued for additional ones in the light of changed conditions.[21] The two reports, as well as several developments between them, helped provide intellectual foundations, standards, and tools to foster planning through community partnerships.

Reinforcing this interest in planning for public health through community partnerships were developments, motivated most recently by the PPACA, in the federal government to clarify the basis on which nonprofit hospitals could claim federal tax exemption; for CHIP, the pertinent issue is the extent and nature of the community benefits that hospitals must supply.[22] Under the reform law, nonprofit hospitals are to carry out "community health needs assessments" at least every three years and to devise an "implementation strategy" to meet needs revealed by the assessment. In fulfilling these requirements, hospitals are to take into account diverse representatives of the community. Organizations such as the National Association of City and County Health Officials, the Association of State and Territorial Health Officers, and the National Public Health Performance Standards Program have seized this development to bring hospitals together with local health departments and other community partners in carrying out assessments, building on them with community health improvement plans, and mobilizing the resources needed to carry them out.[23]

These and other efforts have created methods and models to encourage and guide improvement of the public health system; to make available exploitable data, models, and methods of performance evaluation; and to foster partnerships designed to investigate the health needs of communities, to build capacity to meet need, and to mobilize communities to bring improvements in population health. Although reformers in public health have aimed primarily to restore credibility to public health agencies that had grown isolated, ineffective, and under-resourced, as well as to encourage agencies to assume leadership in community partnerships,[24] the new capabilities, whatever the source of leadership in their deployment, can be targeted at recalcitrant public health issues that go beyond the capacities of medical treatment, particularly preventing and managing chronic conditions such as obesity, diabetes, asthma, and mental health.[25]

Whether these partnerships will succeed is uncertain.[26] Researchers thus far have been little able to demonstrate that partnerships can actually lead to improvements in population health, but they have been able to extract lessons from experience to characterize those partnerships that seem to be goal-oriented, stable, and capable of mounting programs and building capacity to carry out studies and launch initiatives.[27] Moreover, many settings, especially rural ones, lack resources, manpower, and technical ability to carry out community health assessments and planning.[28] Finally, the costs in energy, time, and effort to enroll, educate, and inspire, and diverse community stakeholders (i.e., to create community forms of social capital) can prove daunting, as can the need for constant efforts to maintain functional and committed relationships among them. CHIP seems to have promise, but its promise and its sustainability remain uncertain.

Public Health Transformed: The Social Determinants of Health

The third prominent context for health planning is actually a multiplicity of settings and approaches united largely by a concentration on the social determinants of health (SDH). A focus on SDH emerged from efforts after World War II to improve health globally, chiefly in developing countries; from the recognition in developed countries that the postwar effort to build up costly health care systems that focused high technology on acute conditions produced few improvements in population health and that chronic diseases increasingly required attention; from the perception that disparities in health in even developed countries mirrored those between wealthy and poor countries; from research documenting the influence of social and economic factors on health; and, in the United States, from unfavorable comparisons of its levels of population health with those in Great Britain.[29] Advocates of the SDH approach claimed that the roots of poor health lay in social and economic conditions ("the causes of the causes"), that public health policy needed to focus on social amelioration, and that heath care provision required reorientation from high-technology and often tertiary care to primary care and long-term disease management.

Intensifying these messages were novel concerns for the effects of gender discrimination, the claims of environmental justice, and more broadly social justice in the formation of social environments and the distribution of resources that affect health and well-being, broadly conceived. From this perspective, action on health requires efforts at diverse levels, participation of various public and private entities, development of community resources to create and empower local coalitions, and research and advocacy involving public and private agencies at all levels, as well as academic researchers.[30] This breadth of perspective has also fostered the conviction, especially in the World Health Organization and the European Union, that, because nearly all policy spheres outside health policy carry implications for population health, SDH mandated an "intersectoral" or "health in all policies" approach.[31] The health-in-all-policies perspective implies not only that planning from within the health sector should involve other sectors, but also that other forms of local and regional planning (such as transportation, zoning, and environmental protection) should explicitly accommodate health impacts in their own plans and policies. These ideas and practices have generated strong interest in the United States.[32]

A Global View to Health Planning?

One risk associated with SDH derives from its roots in studies of health on a global scale. Health services researchers abroad and in the United States have successfully demonstrated disparities in health among and within nations and linked them to differential social, environmental, and economic conditions. Their work has led advocates of SDH, such as the World Health Organization Commission on the Social Determinants of Health and the Commission to Build a Healthier America, to acknowledge the importance of national and local contexts, yet they suggest global adoption of a variety of generic policy measures that they assume are broadly applicable.[33] However, national and local contexts may well determine not only what is desirable, but whether globally defined goals can gain traction and, if so, whether programs can be mounted to attain them.[34]

Advocates of SDH who are mindful of particular contexts envisioned a transformation of public health from its narrowly professionalized, top-down practices to those that engage diverse constituencies, levels of action, and coalitions. This approach involved epistemological novelties, such as explicit inclusion of values in research (e.g., health or gender equity or environmental justice), belief in the codetermination of knowledge and social arrangements, and engagement of nonprofessional local activists and knowledgeable community members as analysts and researchers to work together with trained professionals.[35] In this kind of public health practice, planning would be needed at successive stages of activity, from the articulation of needs, to the analysis and investigation of causes, to the formulation of solutions, and to activism for achieving their realization. The perspective brings focus to local contexts, but recognizes that the scope of local activity is often dictated by policies articulated at diverse levels in diverse spheres. In this view, public health has vastly expanded its boundaries, its participants, its goals, and its methods.

Proponents of SDH and its implications for public health can point to many successes, but they also recognize the many obstacles in their way. Not least is that this expanded version of public health, despite its gradual emergence over several decades in several contexts, has yet to penetrate deeply into traditional realms of policymaking; that its costs in time, education, coalition building, research, analysis, activism, and funding of these activities and, should they succeed, of the programs they aim to create are hefty; that affected interests can mount effective opposition; and that policymakers and decision makers often have strong incentives to support opposing interests.[36] Much the same could be said of Community Health Improvement Planning, especially to the extent that it takes on themes of SDH. Recreating community capital, particularly in view of the forces that weakened traditional sensibilities of community cohesion and instead emphasized the imperatives of markets, business, individual autonomy, and choice, is a difficult proposition. Even the ACO, the fate of which depends more on managerial capacity and economic forces,

also relies on creating a sense of responsibility among providers for community health. Clearly, the particulars of the contexts for these novel forms of planning matter,[37] but whether, under market conditions, the localism that was long so prominent a feature of U.S. health policy can be reinvigorated is largely an unanswered question.

Although the old regime of health care planners is gone, the new approaches to health planning that have emerged since the rise of market-based policy reflect some of the themes at work in the history of traditional planning, especially the contrast between community solidarity and individualistic, economic incentives. All three of the newer venues for health planning aim to restore the emphasis of traditional planning on local communities. However, all three face significant obstacles in settings that, in comparison to the past, are less rich in social capital, more subject to centripetal influences deriving from both public policy and business imperatives, and more responsive to idealization of personal autonomy, individual choice, and market institutions.

See also **Chapter 2: The Long Struggle for Universal Health Care (1900s–Present); Chapter 10: Federalism: Cooperation and Conflict between State and Federal Health Care Responsibilities (1960s–Present); Chapter 11: Evolution of Health Planning (1920s–1970s); Chapter 13: Government Financing of Health Care (1940s–Present); Chapter 17: Strategies for Health Care Cost Containment (1980s–Present); Chapter 26: Interest Groups, Think Tanks, and Health Care Policy (1960s–Present); Chapter 29: Twenty-first-Century Challenges to Health and Health Care: Noncommunicable Diseases, Environmental Threats, and Human Rights (2000s–Present).**

NOTES

1. David Rosner, *A Once Charitable Enterprise: Hospitals and Health Care in Brooklyn and New York, 1885–1915* (New York: Cambridge University Press, 1982).

2. American Hospital Association, *Statement on the Financial Requirements of Health Care Institutions and Services: Approved by the House of Delegates February 12, 1969* (Chicago: American Hospital Association, 1969); American Hospital Association, *Capital Financing for Hospitals* (Chicago: American Hospital Association, 1974); David C. Clapp and Arthur B. Spector, "A Study of the American Capital Market and Its Relationship to the Capital Needs of the Health Care Field," in *Health Care Capital: Competition and Control*, edited by Gordon K. MacLeod and Mark Perlman, 275–303 (Cambridge, MA: Ballinger, 1978); Bradford H. Gray, *The Profit Motive and Patient Care: The Changing Accountability of Doctors and Hospitals* (Cambridge, MA: Harvard University Press, 1991).

3. For this paragraph, see Lawrence D. Brown, "Capture and Culture: Organizational Identity in New York Blue Cross," *Journal of Health Politics, Policy, and Law* 16: 4 (1991): 651–670; Robert Cunningham III and Robert M. Cunningham Jr., *The Blues: A History of the Blue Cross and Blue Shield System* (DeKalb: Northern Illinois University Press, 1997); Robert A. Dobbin, "Philanthropy Attracts Other Capital Sources," *Hospitals* 42: 20 (1968): 71–72, 76; Joyce C. Lashof and Mark H. Lepper, "Federal-State-Local Partnership in Health," in *Health in America: 1776–1996*, 122–137 (Washington, DC: U.S. Government Printing Office, 1976); Carl J. Schramm, "The Legal Identity of the Modern Hospital: A Story of Evolving Values," in *In Sickness and in Health: The Mission of Voluntary Health Care Institutions*, edited by J. David Seay and Bruce C. Vladeck, 65–86 (New York: McGraw-Hill, 1988); Bruce Spitz, "Community Control in a World of Regional Delivery Systems," *Journal of Health Politics, Policy, and Law* 22: 4 (1997): 1021–1050; United States Public Health Service,

An Evaluation of the Operation of Subarea Advisory Councils (Hyattsville, MD: Health Resources Administration, 1979).

4. Evan M. Melhado, "American Health Reformers and the Social Sciences in the Twentieth Century," in *A Master of Science History: Essays in Honor of Charles Coulston Gillispie,* edited by Jed Z. Buchwald, 297–325 (Dordrecht, Netherlands: Springer, 2012).

5. Odin W. Anderson, "Research in Hospital Use and Expenditures," *Journal of Chronic Diseases* 17: 9 (1964): 727–733; Daniel M. Fox, "The Consequences of Consensus: American Health Policy in the Twentieth Century," *Milbank Quarterly* 64: 1 (1986): 76–99; Herbert E. Klarman, "Health Planning: Progress, Prospects, and Issues," *Milbank Memorial Fund Quarterly/ Health and Society* 56: 1 (1978): 78–112.

6. Evan M. Melhado, "Economists, Public Provision, and the Market: Changing Values in Policy Debate," *Journal of Health Politics, Policy, and Law* 23: 2 (1998): 215–263.

7. J. Armand Burgun, "Flexibility—The Key to Holding Off Obsolescence," *Hospitals* 38: 19 (1964): 35–38; Jack C. Haldeman, "Here Are the Goals for Health Construction," *Modern Hospital* 93: 4 (1959): 70–74; Stuart E. Walker, "Hospital Obsolescence in a Metropolitan Area," *Hospital Progress* 44: 2 (1963): 66–68.

8. Evan M. Melhado, "Competition vs. Regulation in American Health Policy," in *Money, Power, and Health Care,* edited by Evan M. Melhado, Walter Feinberg, and Harold M. Swartz, 15–101 (Ann Arbor, MI: Health Administration Press, 1988).

9. Steven G. Brint, *In an Age of Experts: The Changing Role of Professionals in Politics and Public Life* (Princeton, NJ: Princeton University Press, 1994).

10. Carl F. Ameringer, *The Health Care Revolution: From Medical Monopoly to Market Competition* (Berkeley: University of California Press, 2008); Gray, *The Profit Motive and Patient Care*; M. Susan Marquis and Stephen H. Long, "Trends in Managed Care and Managed Competition, 1993–1997," *Health Affairs* 18: 6 (1999): 75–88; Robert H. Miller and Harold S. Luft, "Managed Care Plans: Characteristics, Growth, and Premium Performance," *Annual Review of Public Health* 15 (1994): 437–459; James C. Robinson, *The Corporate Practice of Medicine: Competition and Innovation in Health Care* (Berkeley: University of California Press, 1999).

11. Brint, *In an Age of Experts*; Daniel M. Fox, "Health Policy and the Politics of Research in the United States," *Journal of Health Politics, Policy, and Law* 15: 3 (1990): 481–499; Daniel T. Rodgers, *Age of Fracture* (Cambridge, MA: Belknap Press, 2011), ch. 2.

12. Not to be confused with the Children's Health Insurance Program, sometimes referred to by its acronym CHIP (or its former acronym, SCHIP, for State Children's Health Insurance Program), created under the Balanced Budget Act of 1997 and reauthorized under the PPACA. See National Conference of State Legislatures, "Children's Health Insurance Program (CHIP)," http://www.ncsl.org/research/health/childrens-health-insurance-program-overview.aspx; Centers for Medicaid and Medicare Services, "Children's Health Insurance Program (CHIP)," http://www.medicaid.gov/Medicaid-CHIP-Program-Information/By-Topics/Childrens-Health-Insurance-Program-CHIP/Childrens-Health-Insurance-Program-CHIP.html.

13. Ameringer, *The Health Care Revolution*; Melhado, "Competition vs. Regulation."

14. Alain C. Enthoven, *Health Plan: The Only Practical Solution to the Soaring Cost of Medical Care* (Reading, MA: Addison-Wesley, 1980); Bradford H. Gray, "The Rise and Decline of the HMO: A Chapter in U.S. Health-Policy History," in *History and Health Policy in the United States: Putting the Past Back In,* edited by Rosemary A. Stevens, Charles E. Rosenberg, and Lawton R. Burns, 309–339 (New Brunswick, NJ: Rutgers University Press, 2006); Melhado, "Competition vs. Regulation"; Robinson, *The Corporate Practice of Medicine.*

15. Elliott S. Fisher et al., "Creating Accountable Care Organizations: The Extended Hospital Medical Staff," *Health Affairs* 26: 1 (2007): w44–w57; Elliott S. Fisher et al., "Fostering Accountable Health Care: Moving forward in Medicare," *Health Affairs* 28: 2 (2009): w219–w231; Harold S. Luft, "From Small Area Variations to Accountable Care Organizations: How Health Services Research Can Inform Policy," *Annual Review of Public Health* 33 (2012): 377–392; John E. Wennberg, *Tracking Medicine: A Researcher's Quest to Understand Health Care* (New York: Oxford University Press, 2010).

16. Mark McClellan et al., "A National Strategy to Put Accountable Care into Practice," *Health Affairs* 29: 5 (2010): 982–990; Stephen M. Shortell, Lawrence P. Casalino, and Elliott S. Fisher, "How the Center for Medicare and Medicaid Innovation Should Test Accountable Care Organizations," *Health Affairs* 29: 7 (2010): 1293–1298;

17. Precedents for payment mechanisms emerged from discussions in the 1980s of physician payment under Medicare following that program's adoption of prospective payment of hospitals. See W. Pete Welch, "Prospective Payment to Medical Staffs: A Proposal," *Health Affairs* 8: 1 (1989): 34–49; W. Pete Welch and Mark E. Miller, "Proposals to Control High-Cost Hospital Medical Staffs," *Health Affairs* 13: 4 (1994): 42–57.

18. Lawton R. Burns and Mark V. Pauly, "Accountable Care Organizations: Back to the Future?" *LDI Issue Brief* 18: 2 (2012): 1–4; Robinson, *The Corporate Practice of Medicine,* ch. 8.

19. Robert A. Berenson, Paul B. Ginsburg, and Jessica H. May, "Hospital-Physician Relations: Cooperation, Competition, or Separation?" *Health Affairs* 26: 1 (2007): w31–w43.

20. Joy M. Grossman, Ha T. Tu, and Dori A. Cross, "Arranged Marriages: The Evolution of ACO Partnerships in California," *CHCF Regional Markets Issue Brief* 2013 (September): 1–17, http://www.chcf.org/~/media/MEDIA%20LIBRARY%20Files/PDF/A/PDF%20ArrangedMarriagesACOsCalifornia.pdf; Timothy K. Lake, Kate A. Stewart, and Paul B. Ginsburg, "Lessons from the Field: Making Accountable Care Organizations Real," *National Institute for Health Care Reform Research Brief* 2 (2011); Bridget K. Larson et al., "Insights from Transformations under Way at Four Brookings-Dartmouth Accountable Care Organization Pilot Sites," *Health Affairs* 31: 11 (2012): 2395–2406;

21. Institute of Medicine, Division of Health Care Services, Committee for the Study of the Future of Public Health, *The Future of Public Health* (Washington, DC: National Academy Press, 1988); Institute of Medicine, Board of Health Promotion and Disease Prevention, Committee on Assuring the Health of the Public in the Twenty-first Century, *The Future of the Public's Health in the Twenty-first Century* (Washington, DC: National Academy Press, 2003).

22. For historical context of the current situation, see Donna C. Folkemer et al., "Hospital Community Benefits after the ACA: The Emerging Federal Framework," *Hilltop Institute Issue Brief: Hospital Community Benefit Program* 2011 (January), http://www.hilltopinstitute.org/publications/HospitalCommunityBenefitsAfterTheACA-ScheduleHIssueBrief5-October2012.pdf; Erika K. Lunder and Edward C. Liu, "501(c)3 Hospitals: Proposed IRS Rules under § 9007 of the Affordable

Care Act" (Washington, DC: Congressional Research Service, July 27, 2012), http://www.naccho.org/topics/infrastructure/mapp/loader.cfm?csModule=security/getfile&pageID=237458; Mark Schlesinger, Bradford Gray, and Elizabeth Bradley, "Charity and Community: The Role of Nonprofit Ownership in a Managed Health Care System," *Journal of Health Politics, Policy, and Law* 21: 4 (1996): 697–750; Martha H. Somerville, "Community Benefit in Context: Origins and Evolution—ACA §9007," *Hilltop Institute Issue Brief: Hospital Community Benefit Program* 2012 (June), http://www.hilltopinstitute.org/publications/CommunityBenefitInContextOriginsAndEvolution-ACA9007-June2012.pdf; Centers for Disease Control and Prevention, Office for State, Tribal, Local, and Territorial Support, Public Health Law Program, "Summary of the Internal Revenue Service's April 5, 2013 Notice of Proposed Rulemaking on Community Health Needs Assessments for Charitable Hospitals," http://www.cdc.gov/phlp/docs/summary-irs-rule.pdf.

23. Association of State and Territorial Health Officials, "Community Health Needs Assessment," http://www.astho.org/Programs/Access/Community-Health-Needs-Assessments; Donna C. Folkemer et al., "Hospital Community Benefits after the ACA: Building on State Experience," *Hilltop Institute Issue Brief: Hospital Community Benefit Program* 2011 (April), http://www.hilltopinstitute.org/publications/HospitalCommunityBenefitsAfterTheACA-HCBPIssueBrief2-April2011.pdf; National Association of County and City Health Officials, "Community Benefit," http://www.naccho.org/topics/infrastructure/mapp/chahealthreform.cfm; National Association of County and City Health Officials, "Community Health Assessment and Improvement Planning," http://www.naccho.org/topics/infrastructure/CHAIP/; National Association of County and City Health Officials, "Statement of Policy: Role of Local Health Departments in Community Health Needs Assessments," http://www.naccho.org/advocacy/positions/upload/12-05-Role-of-LHDs-in-CHNA.pdf.

24. For example, Dennis Lenaway, Liza Corso, and Stephanie Bailey, "Accreditation as an Opportunity to Strengthen Public Health: CDC's Perspective," *Journal of Public Health Management and Practice* 13 4 (2007): 332–333.

25. For recent examples, see James Plumb et al., "Community-Based Partnerships for Improving Chronic Disease Management," *Primary Care Clinics in Office Practice* 39: 2 (2012): 433–447.

26. Julie Woulfe et al., "Multisector Partnerships in Population Health Improvement," *Preventing Chronic Disease* 7: 6 (2010): A119, http://www.cdc.gov/pcd/issues/2010/nov/pdf/10_0104.pdf.

27. Ibid.

28. Ruth E. Wetta et al., "Voices across Kansas: Community Health Assessment and Improvement Efforts among Local Health Departments," *Journal of Public Health Management and Practice* 20: 1 (2014): 39–42.

29. Mauricio Avendano et al., "Health Disadvantage in US Adults Aged 50 to 74 Years: A Comparison of the Health of Rich and Poor Americans with That of Europeans," *American Journal of Public Health* 99: 3 (2009): 540–548; James Banks et al., "Disease and Disadvantage in the United States and in England," *Journal of the American Medical Association* 295: 17 (2006): 2037–2045; Paula A. Braveman, Susan Egerter, and Robin E. Mockenhaupt, "Broadening the Focus: The Need to Address the Social Determinants of Health," *American Journal of Preventive Medicine* 40: 1, Suppl 1 (2011): S4–S18; Paula A. Braveman, Susan A. Egerter, and David R. Williams, "The Social Determinants of Health: Coming of Age," *Annual Review of Public Health* 32 (2011): 381–398; Linda Irvine et al., "A Review of Major Influences on Current Public Health Policy in Developed Countries in the Second Half of the 20th Century," *Journal of the Royal Society for the Promotion of Health* 126: 2 (2006): 73–78; Howard K. Koh et al., "Healthy People: A 2020 Vision for the Social Determinants Approach," *Health Education and Behavior* 38: 6 (2011): 551–557; Michael Marmot, "Achieving Health Equity: From Root Causes to Fair Outcomes," *Lancet* 370: 9593 (2007): 1153–1163; Michael G. Marmot and Ruth Bell, "Action on Health Disparities in the United States: Commission on Social Determinants of Health," *Journal of the American Medical Association* 301: 11 (2009): 1169–1171; World Health Organization, Secretariat of the Commission on Social Determinants of Health, *Action on the Social Determinants of Health: Learning from Previous Experiences* (Geneva: World Health Organization, 2005), http://www.who.int/social_determinants/resources/action_sd.pdf.

30. In addition to sources cited in the previous note, see Margaret Cargo and Shawna L. Mercer, "The Value and Challenges of Participatory Research: Strengthening Its Practice," *Annual Review of Public Health* 29 (2008): 325–350; Jason Corburn, *Toward the Health City: People, Places, and the Politics of Urban Planning* (Cambridge, MA: MIT Press, 2009); Meredith Minkler et al., "Sí Se Puede: Using Participatory Research to Promote Environmental Justice in a Latino Community in San Diego, California," *Journal of Urban Health* 87: 5 (2010): 796–812. Some of these themes have also animated the public health reforms discussed above under the heading CHIP; see, for example, Institute of Medicine, *The Future of the Public's Health*.

31. Institute of Medicine, Committee on Valuing Community-Based, Non-clinical Prevention Policies and Wellness Strategies, Board on Population Health and Public Health Practice, *An Integrated Framework for Assessing the Value of Community-Based Prevention* (Washington, DC: National Academy Press, 2012); Ilona Kickbusch, Warren McCann, and Tony Sherbon, "Adelaide Revisited: From Healthy Public Policy to Health in All Policies," *Health Promotion International* 23: 1 (2008): 1–4; Timo Ståhl et al., eds., *Health in All Policies: Prospects and Potentials,* http://www.euro.who.int/__data/assets/pdf_file/0003/109146/E89260.pdf.

32. As shown, for example, by the creation, under the Patient Protection and Affordable Care Act, of the National Prevention Council (see U.S. Department of Health and Human Services, "National Prevention Council," http://www.surgeongeneral.gov/initiatives/prevention/about/index.html) and the development by the council of the National Prevention Strategy (see U.S. Department of Health and Human Services, "National Prevention Strategy," http://www.surgeongeneral.gov/initiatives/prevention/strategy/index.html). The council sponsors an intersectoral approach to improve health and quality of life and to shift focus from treating disease to fostering health and wellness and improving quality of life. Another important indicator of U.S. interest, which provides a fulsome introduction to health in all policies and their reciprocal relation between health planning and other forms of local and regional planning, is Linda Rudolph et al., *Health in All Policies: A Guide for State and Local*

Governments (Washington, DC: American Public Health Association, 2013), http://www.apha.org/NR/rdonlyres/882690FE-8ADD-49E0-8270-94C0ACD14F91/0/HealthinAllPoliciesGuide169pages.PDF.

33. Braveman et al., "Broadening the Focus"; Koh et al., "Healthy People"; Michael Marmot et al., "Closing the Gap in a Generation: Health Equity through Action on the Social Determinants of Health," *Lancet* 372: 9650 (2008) 1661–1669.

34. Daniel M. Fox, "Health Inequality and Governance in Scotland since 2007," *Public Health* 127: 6 (2013): 503–513; Melhado, "American Health Reformers."

35. Supra, n. 29. Interest in engaging nonprofessional local activists and knowledgeable community members has also emerged in the reforms associated with CHIP. See, for example, Paul B. McGinnis et al., "Transitioning from CHIP to CHIRP: Blending Community Health Development with Community-based Participatory Research," *Family and Community Health* 33: 3 (2010): 228–237.

36. Cf. Daniel M. Fox, "The Politics of Achievable Mortality," *Public Health Reports* 125: 2 (2010): 168–170.

37. Jason Corburn, for example, points to the greater receptivity to for this approach in San Francisco over New York; see Corburn, *Toward the Health City: People, Places, and the Politics of Urban Planning* (Cambridge, MA: MIT Press, 2009). European advocates of SDH note that the greater commitments of EU countries than the United States to social solidarity, social equity, and social protection make for greater receptivity to public health based on SDH; see Marita Sihto, Eeva Ollila, and Meri Koivusalo, "Principles and Challenges of Health in All Policies," 1 in *Health in All Policies: Prospects and Potentials,* edited by Timo Ståhl, Matthias Wismar, Eeva Ollila, Eero Lahtinen, and Kimmo Leppo, http://www.euro.who.int/data/assets/pdf_file/0003/109146/E89260.pdf.

FURTHER READING

Altman, Drew E., Richard Greene, and Harvey M. Sapolsky. *Health Planning and Regulation: The Decision-making Process.* Washington, DC: AUPHA Press, 1981.

Ameringer, Carl F. *The Health Care Revolution: From Medical Monopoly to Market Competition.* California/Milbank Books on Health and the Public, Vol. 19. Berkeley: University of California Press, 2008.

Fox, Daniel M. *Health Policies, Health Politics: The British and American Experience, 1911–1965.* Princeton, NJ: Princeton University Press, 1986.

Gray, Bradford H. *The Profit Motive and Patient Care: The Changing Accountability of Doctors and Hospitals.* Cambridge, MA: Harvard University Press, 1991.

Institute of Medicine, Board of Health Promotion and Disease Prevention, Committee on Assuring the Health of the Public in the Twenty-first Century. *The Future of the Public's Health in the Twenty-first Century.* Washington, DC: National Academy Press, 2003.

Institute of Medicine, Board on Population Health and Public Health Practice, Committee on Valuing Community-Based, Non-clinical Prevention Policies and Wellness Strategies. *An Integrated Framework for Assessing the Value of Community-based Prevention.* Washington, DC: National Academy Press, 2012.

Institute of Medicine, Committee on Health Planning Goals and Standards. *Health Planning in the United States: Selected Policy Issues.* 2 vols. Washington, DC: National Academy Press, 1981.

Lefkowitz, Bonnie, with contributions by Eleanor D. Kinney and Cheryl Ulmer. *Health Planning: Lessons for the Future.* Rockville, MD: Aspen Systems, 1983.

Melhado, Evan M., Walter Feinberg, and Harold M. Swartz, eds. *Money, Power, and Health Care.* Ann Arbor, MI: Health Administration Press, 1988.

Rudolph, Linda, Julia Caplan, Karen Ben-Moshe, and Lianne Dillon. *Health in All Policies: A Guide for State and Local Governments.* Washington, DC: American Public Health Association, 2013. http://www.apha.org/NR/rdonlyres/882690FE-8ADD-49E0-8270-94C0ACD14F91/0/HealthinAllPoliciesGuide169pages.pdf.

Stevens, Rosemary A. *In Sickness and in Wealth: American Hospitals in the Twentieth Century.* New York: Basic Books, 1989.

Wennberg, John E. *Tracking Medicine: A Researcher's Quest to Understand Health Care.* New York: Oxford University Press, 2010.

chapter 13

Government Financing of Health Care (1940s–Present)

Donald H. Taylor Jr.

ABOUT EVERY OTHER DOLLAR FLOWING INTO the health care system is paid by governmental sources, particularly the federal, but also state governments, with the remainder being paid for via private means, both insurance and self-pay. However, governmental financing has played an even larger role in shaping the health care system, first in an era of initial and continued infrastructure building and later following the passage of the key insurance programs Medicare and Medicaid in 1965. Through Medicare, the federal government provided a predictable payer of broad-based health care services, and over time the inclusion of a service or therapy in Medicare's benefit package came to be viewed as a practical definition of what constituted "mainstream medical care." The federal government also plays a role as the largest employer in the United States, a nation in which most persons who are not elderly still get health insurance as a benefit of employment. Increasingly, the federal government has designed numerous policies to identify and respond to areas or groups with systematic problems accessing or benefiting from health care services. It was not always this way, however, in large part because for the first 150 years of the nation's history, medicine offered only a limited number of therapies or interventions that could improve the lives of the ill. For this reason, there was little pressure for government to become involved in medicine or health care delivery.

BEGINNINGS OF GOVERNMENTAL HEALTH CARE FINANCING

The Committee on the Costs of Medical Care report, published in 1933, heralded a change, and noted that for the first time medical science offered most patients treatments that actually increased their chances of survival and provided some hope of improving their lives.[1] Further, the report noted

that almost everyone in the United States could be considered underserved in the field of medical care—meaning they did not receive enough of it. The writers of the report made clear that they viewed increasing the receipt of health care services as a top public policy priority. The federal government has consistently responded to this reality since 1940 in ways that have greatly expanded the use and provision of health care. The primary federal means of this expansion has been federal financing of health care services, either directly or indirectly, and the development of increased infrastructure with which to carry out such a provision.

The Issues

The federal government has been involved in health care financing in myriad ways since 1940, both directly and indirectly. Six major areas of involvement are examined in this chapter:

1. Use of the tax code to finance health care, most importantly the tax exclusion of employer-paid benefits that arose during World War II (1939–1945), when wage and price controls were in place. This tax-free benefit remains in effect today. Other, more targeted efforts include federal tax credits for qualified long-term care insurance programs.

2. The federal government has played a huge role in expanding the health care delivery and research infrastructure that is also key to the training of physicians. Major examples are the Hill-Burton Hospital and Construction Act of 1946 and the National Institutes of Health (NIH) Act of 1950 that expanded research funding, furthering the development of academic medical centers where most physicians have been trained since 1940.[2,3]

3. The development of federal insurance programs such as Medicare, for persons age sixty-five and over and

select other groups, and Medicaid, a federal-state insurance program that provides both acute and long-term care services to persons who have low income and few assets (they are deemed to be "poor"). These programs filled major gaps in the employer-based private insurance system, beginning with their passage in 1965. The current financing mix in the U.S. health care system is roughly 50/50 government versus private payers. However, federal insurers—especially Medicare—have played a tremendous role in mainstreaming certain models of care (e.g., home health, hospice) as well as payment innovations such as Diagnostic Related Groups and Resource Based Relative Value Scale. Furthermore, Medicaid is the personification of federalism, with many variations in eligibility and benefits as states exercise their autonomy in running this program, a fact that is highlighted in the current Medicaid expansion (and lack of expansion) that is being undertaken by some states under the auspices of the Patient Protection and Affordable Care Act (PPACA).

4. The federal government is the largest employer in the United States and as such is a major provider and arranger of private health insurance for its employees. The Federal Employees Health Plan (FEHP) has a very large risk pool and provides many insurance choices to employees of the federal government, based on where they live. Notably, the optional long-term care insurance program that is arranged by the FEHP is the largest, most stable source of such insurance coverage in the United States. In addition, the federal government provides health insurance for both active duty military personnel and their dependents via a program called the Civilian Health and Medical Program of the Uniformed Services.

5. The federal government is also a direct provider of health care through its Department of Veterans Affairs (VA) health care system. The VA operates the largest hospital system in the United States and provides an example of joining the insurance provision (determined via service connected injury/disability) with direct provision of health care in government-owned facilities, overseen and delivered by government employees.[4] There are some smaller examples of direct provision of health care by the federal government, such as the Indian Health Service,[5] but the federal government is a much larger financier of health care than it is a direct provider.

6. The federal government plays an active role in responding to "special problems" in the health care sphere. Since the early 1970s, the federal government has maintained a system of identifying geographical areas and populations as being underserved and/or suffering from a shortage of medical providers. Designation of an area or population as being underserved makes it eligible for special programs such as the National Health Service Corps and Community Health Centers that are designed to respond to such special problem areas within the health care system.[6] Furthermore, the federal government maintains a system of data monitoring such as birth and death certificates, but also the real-time aggregation of reportable health events, notably infectious diseases such as influenza, syphilis, HIV, and emerging infections such as avian flu. The purpose of this effort is to identify such infectious disease problems so that a public health response can be launched. More recently, the federal government has expanded its attention to bioterrorism prevention, detection, and response.

USE OF THE TAX CODE TO FINANCE HEALTH CARE

During World War II, widespread wage and price controls were in place throughout the U.S. economy as the industrial output of the nation was refocused to a war economy. Such wage controls meant that employers could not compete for employees via higher wages. Several large employers asked Congress to create what we have come to call a "benefit" of employment, or a legal means for an employer to pay for something on behalf of an employee without this flow of money being taxable as income. The payment by employers of the majority of the health insurance premium for their employees is the most consequential example, in terms of both the revenue that it costs the federal government today as well as in understanding how the federal government finances health care today and since 1942 when Congress enabled such a benefit.

For example, a professor employed by a prestigious university receives health insurance for himself, his wife, and their three children. The university pays about 60 percent of the cost and the professor pays the remaining 40 percent of the premium for the particular insurance plan he has chosen. The law that Congress passed in 1942 allowed the health insurance premium paid by the university to not be counted as income, hence the creation of a form of compensation called a benefit. If this law had not been passed in 1942, then if an employer had provided health insurance to an employee, the amount of the premium would be taxable as income and hence would have run afoul of wage and price controls in force at that time.

During the 2008 presidential election, candidate Barack Obama made health care reform a primary issue. Soon after his inauguration in January 2009, his administration proposed a framework for legislation to vastly alter health care policies in the country. By fall 2009, the health care reform discussion was at full boil, filled with discussions about the appropriate role of the federal government in health care financing, with both the House and Senate proposing similar versions of reform. The rhetoric was often unhinged from the reality that around 160 million persons had private health insurance that was being subsidized by the federal government via the continued consideration of health insurance premiums paid by an employer on behalf of an employee as nontaxable compensation. As the cost of health insurance has rapidly increased along with the cost of care (these two are linked), wages have stagnated. Employers view wages plus benefits as overall compensation, and the rapid increase in health insurance premiums has brought about a shift from taxable compensation (wages) to nontaxable wages (health insurance premiums). In 2009, the cost to the U.S. Treasury was around $250 billion if one considers all the ways in which employers provided health insurance. This would make the tax-free nature of health insurance the third largest federal financing of health care provision after Medicare and Medicaid.[7] However, very few people who benefit from it understand how it works, because it is a passive subsidy, meaning no action must be taken for an individual to benefit from it. The hidden nature of this tax subsidy means that the 160 million persons receiving employer-provided health insurance are disconnected from the true cost of their health insurance. This subsidy of employer-provided health insurance underpins the federal government's role in financing health care in the United States. The subsidy provided to health insurance has helped to cement the role of employers as the providers of health insurance for persons who are not very poor or elderly, as well as setting the level of expected insurance coverage (benefits).

The Patient Protection and Affordable Care Act of 2010 includes a stipulation that in 2018 tax treatment of employer-paid insurance will be changed. The so-called Cadillac tax is implemented as a tax levied on insurance companies on the value of premiums that are above a given level. However, it is a tax that is designed to be avoided in that insurance companies will pass on this cost to employers, who in turn will do so with employees. The bottom line result should be slightly lower premiums for high-cost policies and slightly higher wages for such employees as well as compensation shifts from benefits that are not taxable to wages that are. Beyond the details of this tax, a key policy issue is that the tax subsidy that has been unlimited and little discussed for about seventy years is now being discussed openly in policy circles, with some preferring a more direct capping of the tax subsidy to the roundabout Cadillac tax. Moving away from the status quo would be a profound change that could, over time, curtail the degree to which a job is viewed as how most people obtain health insurance, especially given the move toward an exchange-based purchasing approach that not only is at the center of the Patient Protection and Affordable Care Act, but is typically a part of many reform efforts discussed either in opposition to, or agreement with, this new law.

THE FEDERAL GOVERNMENT'S ROLE IN EXPANDING HEALTH CARE INFRASTRUCTURE

At the close of World War II, a great deal of federal policy-making was turned toward health care services, just as in Great Britain. However, whereas Great Britain led with the implementation of the National Health Service to provide universal financing and provision of health care services, the United States focused early attention on infrastructure development. One of the more consequential efforts in this regard was passage of the Hill-Burton Hospital and Construction Act of 1946. This is one of the most important federal health-related laws that most people have never heard of, as it provided the planning and construction money for community hospitals throughout the nation, especially in the rural South, in areas that did not have a strong tradition of religious-oriented hospitals.

Around 6,800 health care facilities were built in four thousand communities under this program, injecting a large bolus of infrastructure spending into the health care system.[8] When viewed as coming on the heels of the Committee on the Costs of Medical Care report, Hill-Burton heeded the call to help produce the facilities and infrastructure necessary to deliver the health care innovations that scientific discoveries had made possible. Acceptance of Hill-Burton monies meant that hospitals had to have policies designed to accommodate persons who could not pay a full market rate for the care provided, a stipulation that had an initial thirty-year time horizon but that was extended in 1975 for a longer period of time, while also transferring the responsibility to ensure these policies were followed from the state to federal government. Hill-Burton's build-first, finance-later approach has generally continued throughout the decades since World War II. The implementation of that law provides a key part of the explanation of how, in 2013, the nation spent more than $8,000 per capita on health care services while at the same time around forty-five million persons live without any health insurance.

Further federal efforts to expand the health care infrastructure include passage of the Community Health Services and Facilities Act of 1961, which expanded building of health care infrastructure to health care facilities other than hospitals.[9] Through a series of extensions, the federal government has provided health care planning monies and stimulated the development of mental health facilities and other health care infrastructure.

One of the federal government's most profound health care infrastructure actions was passage of the National Institutes of Health Act of 1950. This commitment to basic and clinical research, supported by the federal government for the past sixty years, has meant that the United States has been a leader in such work globally but has also stimulated the infrastructure of universities and academic health care centers. NIH funds support both direct costs (the actual marginal or extra cost of undertaking a study) and indirect costs (a set percentage amount for the overhead of doing research). The NIH has poured vast amounts of money into universities and helped to support the training of physicians and other scientists in academic medical centers.

To provide a sense of the magnitudes involved, at Duke University's current NIH rate, for example, a $1 million grant (in direct costs) would provide not only that amount of money to complete the project proposed by university investigators and approved by the NIH-arranged team of researchers/experts, but an indirect cost amount equal to 54.1 percent, or $540,100. In other words, a $1 million grant from NIH actually results in flows of $1,540,100 to Duke University, with the indirect rate differing from university to university as negotiated between each university and the federal government. Such indirect cost recovery is not an accident of the system; it was an explicit investment in the infrastructure necessary to undertake basic science designed to yield medical advances as well as clinical and applied health care–related research.

DEVELOPMENT OF FEDERAL HEALTH INSURANCE PROGRAMS

Passage of the Social Security Act of 1935 provided the beginnings of a now near-universal pension program, which included disability insurance as well as child survivor and spouse coverage. Health insurance coverage was initially desired by President Franklin D. Roosevelt (1933–1945) as part of the Social Security Act, but that proved politically untenable and remained so for the next three decades.[10]

Medicare and Medicaid

Passage of Public Law 89-97 amended the Social Security Act and created the largest federal health insurance programs in the United States:

- Medicare, a federally run insurance plan that covers persons age sixty-five and older and who have standing in Social Security
- Medicaid, a federal-state run insurance plan for persons with very low incomes and few, if any, assets

In the 1960s, approximately half of the persons aged sixty-five and older had no health care insurance, a segment of the nation's population that had increased significantly in the twenty-five years since World War II, aided in part by the tax subsidy afforded to employer-sponsored health insurance. With the advent of health insurance, more persons had the financial means to avail themselves of the scientific discoveries that modern research and medicine increasingly

had to offer. Whereas in 1850, being uninsured was not a serious issue, because state-of-the-art medical science either had little to offer or was harmful (many doctors and nurses bled people with anemia), by 1960, there was an increasing desire to have access to mainstream health care services that were being made available in the health care facilities built by Hill-Burton and supported by the research base being driven by the NIH. Because health care needs generally increase with age, the health care system (physicians, hospitals) was eager to have a means of paying for the services that they were eagerly ready to provide.

The passage of Medicare and Medicaid may best be understood as an extension of the 1964 presidential election victory of Lyndon B. Johnson (1963–1969) as well as the subsequent civil rights victories and emerging Great Society programs that followed soon after. Amid this movement toward federal enforcement of equality and the right to vote was a drive to provide health insurance coverage to two groups: the elderly and the poor. Indeed, passage of Medicare and Medicaid are best understood as the cornerstones of the Great Society.

Medicare provided an immediate, predictable source of health care financing for the segment of the population that had the most health needs (those age sixty-five and older). Medicare does not and never did directly provide health care services to the elderly, but instead has provided to the elderly a means of financing mainstream health care services that persons with private, mostly employer-based insurance had during their working years. Passage of Medicare in part underlies a shift in the concept of insurance, which in the abstract is the trading of a fixed and known premium for protection against a potentially catastrophic cost in the form of health care. Such a cost could devastate a family by causing them to spend their money planned for rent, clothes, and education on health care. Medicare most certainly has prevented many elderly persons and their families from being devastated financially due to health issues; however, it has also financed a great number of health care services that otherwise would not have been obtained or received.

The post–World War II U.S. culture was eager to consume more high-tech, scientifically based health care services, and the health system was eager to provide those services while also getting paid to do so. Medicare stepped in and completed the transaction for the nation's elderly and the health care system. This predictable flow of payment for services provided to the nation's elderly has undoubtedly served to further expand the nation's health care infrastructure.

Medicare has also played an important role in being the de facto establisher of what is typically viewed as "mainstream health care." If a therapy or treatment is covered by the Medicare program, which typically happens if it has been shown to have some potential to benefit patients, then

The Unexpected Rise of Medicare Costs in the 1970s

Passage of Medicare in 1965 linked predictable insurance with the demographic of society most likely to need health care services. The deepening understanding of heart disease and stroke with the early publication of the Framingham study results led to increased attention paid to these leading causes of death among the elderly. In turn, a movement to encourage the elderly to have regular check-ups and to monitor blood pressure, moderate salt intake, and seek to stop smoking cigarettes was initiated, and a group of elderly persons—half of whom were uninsured in the early 1960s—had regular access to health care services financed by Medicare.

In addition to an understanding of prevention, the increase in biomedical research begun by the National Institutes of Health Act of 1950 started to pay off with the development of medical procedures to revascularize the heart, and thus provide a curative route to forestalling the leading cause of death in the United States. Coronary bypass surgery, which allows for blocked heart arteries to be repaired, was pioneered in the 1960s and mainstreamed in the 1970s with Medicare as the primary payer. Thus, the initial cost projections of Medicare proved to be too optimistic, foreshadowing a simple truth that makes cost control in Medicare difficult: it offers the promise of care payment for the sickest segment of the population and provides access to innovations tomorrow that are unknown today. The initial cost inflation problems of the 1970s simply foreshadowed the program's timeless problem of balancing the desire to finance more care with the understanding that the cost of that care has a huge impact on the federal budget.

that item of care tends to be covered by private health insurance plans as well. In this way, Medicare has played a consistent leadership role in the establishment of benefits.

A classic example of this type of leadership is exemplified by the hospice benefit, initially included in the Medicare program on a temporary basis via the Tax Equity and Economic Fairness Act of 1982 tax reform and later made a permanent part of the Medicare benefit package in 1985. Hospice is a holistic approach to the care of persons who are believed to be imminently dying (within six months) and typically offers an alternative choice to aggressive "do everything" care even if benefits are unknown (or nonexistent) and regardless of the cost. Hospice was initially a renegade movement of sorts, led by physicians, nurses, and other activists who were intent on restoring a more personal, dignified, and less technology-driven process of dying, reserving for patients the choice of how to face terminal illness. While hospice is today viewed as a mainstream option for someone facing a terminal illness (regardless of insurer), it was a fairly radical notion in the early 1980s. The decision by Medicare to cover hospice was a key part of mainstreaming this care option for patients and their families. If the Medicare program had not covered hospice initially in 1982 and permanently in 1985, there is a reasonable chance hospice would not be widely available today.

Medicaid was passed at the same time as Medicare, but the two insurance programs have many differences. Whereas Medicare is a federal government insurance program, Medicaid is a shared financial and administrative responsibility between the federal and state governments. Medicaid, like Medicare, finances physician and hospital services, the main sources of acute medical care provision. Both programs have provided other services as well, such as durable medical equipment, home health care services, and, in later years, hospice care and specialized services such as dialysis.

While Medicare has standardized eligibility for services nationally, Medicaid is a means-tested insurance program, with persons having to show they are poor, at least relative to the standards used in a given state. While Medicare has one set of eligibility standards, Medicaid provides flexibility to states to practically determine what constitutes being "poor" for purposes of eligibility for insurance. Further, while Medicare provides a common benefit package everywhere in the United States, Medicaid specifies a minimum benefit package but allows states to cover a more expansive set of services. Thus, Medicare is essentially a one-size-fits-all program, while Medicaid can be thought of as a slightly different program in each state, in terms of both how impoverished one must be to be eligible and what benefit package is covered.

The Medicaid program provides a practical example of the quintessential American notion of federalism—the concept that there are national standards and ideals, but that the states are often given broad discretion to interpret what these ideals mean in practice. The way the federal-state interaction plays out in practice in Medicaid is highly complex. First, there is a funding formula in which the federal government provides at least 50 percent of a state's Medicaid program (roughly; there are many details with different cost shares for different types of services) and up to nearly 80 percent for a state with a lower income, such as Mississippi. This means that the federal government pays at least half of the state's Medicaid program bill in a state such as New York, but pays for $8 in $10 dollars of Mississippi's Medicaid program—all based on the relative wealth of the state. In this way, Medicaid serves as a tremendous policy tool that redistributes money from relatively rich states to relatively poor ones.

This is done because the passage of Medicaid established an insurance program for poor persons, and did so with the knowledge that states had varying amounts of resources and interest in doing so. Thus, a federal standard is set, but the practical interpretation of what that standard means is granted to states, in consultation with the federal government.

Under Medicaid, states must cover a basic level of services and benefits for certain patients, which are requirements under federal law that must be followed. However, states have a great deal of discretion regarding both what is covered (benefits) and who is covered, in terms of both poverty level and the characteristics of individuals. This means that while every state has a Medicaid program that defines a set of benefits for persons who are judged to be eligible for them, exactly who they are and how poor they must be to qualify differs greatly across states.

Over time, the federal government has incentivized states to undertake more expansive Medicaid spending targeted at particular groups. The Children's Health Insurance Program (CHIP) is a classic example from the 1990s. The federal government provided expanded funding for the coverage of children via Medicaid and required states to cover all persons under age eighteen, up to 100 percent of the poverty level (age 0–1, 185 percent; 1–5, 133 percent; 6–17, 100 percent). Many states went far beyond this standard. Thus, there is a patchwork of eligibility levels by group, which differs by state. North Carolina, for example, covers children 0–5 up to 200 percent of the poverty level. Many other states have similar coverage for children but have not gone beyond minimums for other age groups. Using North Carolina as an example, an adult male who is not a part of a household with a pregnant woman or a child can never qualify for Medicaid on the basis of income alone. The decision to go beyond the federal minimum for children, but not for childless adults, is a policy choice that is reserved for the state of North Carolina alone.

The CHIP programs were particularly high-profile aspects of state Medicaid programs because they covered children, and the federal government provides a higher cost match rate than it does for a given state's Medicaid program. In many states, CHIP was a program set up to be administratively separate from the overall Medicaid program, signifying an attempt to reduce the stigma related to an insurance program that is viewed as "coverage for poor persons." The establishment of CHIP in 1997, in the aftermath of the demise of the Clinton health reform plan, was also the first signal that some movement toward expanding coverage would be taken, and the increased eligibility standards for children foreshadowed the use of the Medicaid expansion more generally in the PPACA.

The PPACA uses expanded Medicaid eligibility as a key part of its strategy to expand health insurance coverage in the United States, setting a standard of 133 percent of poverty for any person. In theory, this produces a route to universal insurance coverage for persons below this income level; however, such a standard will not be achieved, at least not in the short term, because of two issues. First, the Supreme Court ruling affirming the individual mandate also found that the Medicaid provisions of the law were coercive and therefore unconstitutional. Also, this made the Medicaid expansion the choice of the states, with some states saying they will not undertake the expansion, thus reducing the ability of the expansion to lead to universal coverage below a given income. This will maintain the quintessential Medicaid reality that the program will differ across states in terms of eligibility for services as well as by benefits, as some choose a more expansive package than do others.

Holes in Medicare Benefits

For the first forty years of Medicare's history, the benefit package covered by the program could be said to have two major "holes": coverage of prescription drugs and long-term care. Prescription drug coverage was not included in Medicare initially, and it took until 2003, when the Medicare Modernization Act was passed, to add a prescription drug coverage part to the program, which began in 2006 and which uses a model of subsidized private insurance coverage. The other major hole in coverage, long-term care, is still largely missing from Medicare's benefit package.

Long-term care (LTC) is help and support to enable a person to deal with a disability or the inability to complete activities of daily living (ADL), both instrumental ADLs like balancing a checkbook, shopping, cooking a meal, and successfully taking medicines and or basic ADLs such as eating, dressing, bathing, and going to the toilet. You must be able to successfully complete the first set of activities to live independently and be able to do the second set to live at all. The type of care that persons with such disabilities receive does not typically involve high-tech medical services, but custodial care. Medicare does not routinely pay for such LTC services except in limited circumstances, such as paying for up to one hundred days' cost to provide rehabilitation after an acute illness or injury. Recently, a court case expanded eligibility for such care, rescinding a policy that a patient had to show improvement from rehabilitation services or lose this coverage; now such care can be provided to patients who are said to have "plateaued" in order to maintain function.

Medicare's home-health benefit provides some care that could be understood to be LTC, but it has become more medicalized over time, essentially to stop the program from paying for custodial care (cooking, cleaning, running errands, facilitating physician appointments), which is not typically covered by the program. Similarly, hospice provides care, typically in patients' homes, typically for a period of days or weeks, just before death, so is not meant as an LTC benefit. The use of hospice has increased greatly in recent years, with about half of all Medicare decedents last year using at least one hospice care day prior to their death. Coterminous to the expansion of the benefit has been an increase in both the length and occurrence of very long periods of hospice use: the expected maximum period of the benefit is 180 days, though longer periods can and are provided. Because the vast majority of hospice care is provided in the home of a patient, there is potential for this to become a back door LTC benefit, and this is why there has been so much policy attention (from the Medicare Payment Advisory Commission and others) toward relatively long lengths of hospice use (short stays represent potential quality issues whereby patients suffer needlessly).

The exclusion of LTC coverage in Medicare is a nod to the cultural premise that while medical care is something to be covered by health insurance that finances access to high-tech medicine, LTC is believed to be the responsibility of families to care for one another during their frail years. While some LTC services are covered by Medicare, most notably a benefit of up to one hundred days for treatment in a skilled nursing facility (SNF), the care delivered in such settings must focus on rehabilitation and the return of a patient's functioning, and cannot simply be the provision of custodial care. A set of litigations against Medicare has forced a revision of the benefit determination for SNF (as well as in-home health) in that maintenance of function, and not more specifically the ability to improve function, is to be the standard for SNF eligibility in Medicare going forward.

Some families choose to provide LTC to one another on an informal basis, while those with the financial means may hire others to provide such care. Private LTC insurance is quite rare and expensive, but a private market for such insurance does exist and provides a product that allows families to hire others to either fully or partly provide this care.

Due to Medicare's not covering most LTC and very few persons having private LTC insurance, Medicaid has essentially become the default LTC insurance provider of last resort in the United States. Families tend to provide some care, but as disability increases and assets are used to finance either all or part of the increasing LTC burden that is present, individuals "spend down" to Medicaid or become eligible due to having low income from paying for LTC.

Children and pregnant women are among the largest groups of Medicaid beneficiaries because the federal government has mandated higher levels of coverage (one doesn't have to be as poor) for these groups, and many states have gone even further. For example, in North Carolina, pregnant women are covered up to 133 percent of the federal poverty level, while children are covered up to 185 percent; both policy choices are driven by the notion that such persons are worthy of coverage and that investment in their health care will pay dividends down the line.

POLITICS AND HEALTH CARE POLICY

Richard Nixon and the War on Cancer

On December 23, 1971, President Richard Nixon (1969–1974) said the following on National Public Radio:

> More people each year die of cancer in the United States than all the Americans who lost their lives in World War II. This shows us what is at stake. It tells us why I sent a message to the Congress the first of this year, which provided for a national commitment for the conquest of cancer, to attempt to find a cure.

So began the so-called War on Cancer, the use of a familiar image to focus the attention of the nation on a problem that was not military. In many ways, the campaign was the second act of the play that began with the National Institutes of Health Act of 1950, which answered the call of the Committee on the Costs of Medical Care to provide more biomedical research–based health care to the American people. "Cancer only" insurance policies, which made little sense from an actuarial sense, nevertheless were bought by many people because they especially feared death from cancer, a death that was driven by an individual's own cells gone awry, thereby defeating them from within.

What did this war look like? Large sums of money were devoted to research into cancer treatments and therapies. Prevention was a late arrival to the cause and has always been less well funded, not having the same romantic ring as does "curing cancer." Merged with the rise of the academic medical center and its research-driven existence, coverage of the War on Cancer via Medicare of the aged of society, ensuring predictable, stable payments for disease therapies, and the American cultural notion that with enough focused effort and persistence, we should be able to defeat anything, the campaign was waged on many fronts.

The success in the war is certainly uneven. Some diagnoses, such as pediatric leukemia, are now commonly treated with great results, and in many types of cancers survival after diagnosis has increased, although death rates have not shown as much consistent increase. Also, a decline in smoking, from around half of adults in 1950 to just over 20 percent today, has produced benefits in prevention of cancer, heart disease, and stroke, the three leading causes of death in the United States.

SOURCE: "The War on Cancer Turns 40," *NPR*, http://www.npr.org/2011/12/23/144190091/the-war-on-cancer-turns-40.

By comparison, to be eligible for Medicaid to pay for a nursing home in many states, an individual can have no more than $2,000 in assets and his or her income must be below a certain level, or the excess spent toward the cost of the nursing home. Thus, Medicaid serves as a default payer for nursing home care, the site of the most intensive 24/7 care available, and at a very high cost. The deductible could be thought of as one's wealth.

Many families do not desire to use Medicaid as the long-term payer for a loved one due to worries about quality of services as well as views that such care is not appropriate, at least as the first place to turn. However, the price of long-term care, both implicit in the case of informal care and the actual cost in the case of seeking market services to deliver such services, is very large.

For example, my family has recently priced assisted living facilities for a family member who now lives in such a facility. These facilities can provide most of the care that many disabled persons will need, other than care for full-blown dementia, and routinely care for patients who would have had to move to a nursing home just fifteen years ago. The monthly cost of assisted living care in the Durham/Chapel Hill area of North Carolina ranges from around $3,500 to $8,500 per month for assisted living, $5,000 to $7,500 per month for a skilled nursing facility, and as high as $11,000 per month for dementia care in a specialty facility. Very few people have amassed wealth or the insurance necessary to finance cost streams such as these for a long period of time, and Medicaid will step in and pay for individuals to live in a skilled nursing facility until death if there is no other option. Medicaid finances around 40 percent of the total nursing home bill for the United States today, showing it to be the de facto LTC insurer of last resort.

The ratios of coverage are similar nationally, with the costs differing from location to location, but again, few families have amassed the wealth necessary to afford such costly care. One tool offered comes from the National Long Term Care Clearinghouse, which provides detailed state-level information on the cost and availability of LTC nationwide.

THE FEDERAL GOVERNMENT AS EMPLOYER

The federal government is the largest employer in the United States, and as such provides health insurance to its employees. The subsidy that is availed by private

employers is also provided to employees of the federal government via the tax treatment of employer-provided health insurance. In that sense, it is no different from any other employer in the United States. A key difference is the scope of the employer, due to both the large number of employees and the fact that there is at least one federal employee in every county in the United States. This has led the FEHP to offer many insurance options, though the number of practical options varies greatly by locale. For example, a federal employee living in the Washington, D.C., metro area might have fifteen health insurance options, meaning plans with a means of using care (physicians and hospitals participating in a health insurance network). In other locales, such as Charlotte, North Carolina, there may be only three or four plans.

Most important, the structure of the FEHP shopping portal is somewhat similar to what an exchange in the PPACA is likely to resemble in terms of defined benefit packages with differences in options primarily being driven by premium/deductible tradeoffs along with the choice of providers afforded by a given plan. Federal employees now go to a Web-based interface each year during open enrollment and decide what plan to pick for the following year. The number of choices available to them depends on where they live. The PPACA exchanges through which private insurance is available, which began providing options in October 2013 for coverage that started on January 1, 2014,

CAT scans and other expensive tests have been an increasingly routine part of diagnoses in the U.S. health care system. A recent study by the Commonwealth Fund, a nonprofit health research organization, suggests the primary cause of the nation's skyrocketing costs is not poor overall health or too many hospital admissions but rather the costs that stem from greater access to technology, such as imaging and knee and hip replacements. When private and public health care spending is combined, the U.S. health care bill is bigger than that of any other industrialized nation.

SOURCE: Levent Konuk/Shutterstock.

are similar to the experiences of federal employees. The choices available differ by state, and most likely where an individual lives in a given state.

The federal government as an employer providing insurance is also notable due to the LTC insurance option provided to employees. This is an optional source of private LTC insurance coverage that is taken by only 5 percent of employees, but 5 percent of the federal government workforce is a relatively large risk pool. The premiums and benefits per premium available for the FEHP represent the most affordable private LTC insurance option in the United States, and the relatively low rate of uptake provides guidance that private LTC insurance is not going to ever represent a population-based answer to the financing and provision of LTC services.

A final way in which Medicare impacts the entire health care system is through its predominant funding role of graduate medical education (GME). Medicare not only pays direct subsidies to medical schools and residency programs to underwrite the cost of teaching and training physicians, but it also pays indirect GME payments, whereby care is reimbursed at a higher level for a teaching hospital, as compared to a non-teaching hospital, as a means of underwriting the teaching mission. This subsidy is not well understood and is a holdover from the original days of Medicare and the drive to expand the nation's health care infrastructure.

The logic of Medicare as financier was initially that more physicians were needed to provide medical care to the elderly. More recently, as the push to restrain Medicare cost inflation has become more acute, there have been suggestions of moving toward an all-payer approach to financing medical education, which would allow for reductions in Medicare's role in paying for graduate medical education.[11]

THE FEDERAL GOVERNMENT AS DIRECT PROVIDER OF HEALTH CARE

The federal government directly provides medical care to active duty service members and to veterans who are eligible for care via the VA health care system. The federal government is far more consequential as an insurance company or purchaser of health care via Medicare and Medicaid, as well as via the tax preference provided to employer-sponsored health insurance, but the VA hospital system is the largest integrated hospital system in the United States, and the VA also provides a full range of health care services to veterans who are eligible for care in this system.

The system of eligibility for services in the VA is complex and depends on the era in which military service was rendered. In short, different wars and different periods of military service have been afforded different standards of eligibility for care from the VA, typically with a fractional "service contingent" proportion. This simply means that veterans can be eligible for some services from the VA but not other services.

There are other ways in which the federal government directly provides some health care services, such as through the Indian Health Service. This is a section of the Health Resources and Services Administration that directly provides health care services to members of federally recognized American Indian tribes and Alaska Natives. The U.S. Public Health Service provides care and surveillance services for reportable infectious diseases.

IDENTIFYING AND RESPONDING TO SPECIAL PROBLEMS

An overarching theme of the 1933 Committee on the Costs of Medical Care report was the entire nation as underserved and in need of more health care provision. In response to the items noted above (infrastructure, federal insurance programs, and others), a fairly broad array of financing for health care was in place in the United States by the mid-1960s. However, the safety net was not seamless, as those persons with incomes above Medicaid eligibility, yet without employer-provided health insurance, found themselves uninsured. This reduced their ability to access health care services, left them vulnerable to financial ruin if they got sick, and also lessened the ability of health care provision to be found in some areas with inadequately insured populations.

Further, there are some regions that faced particularly burdensome challenges in terms of developing a stable health care infrastructure, notably rural areas. The reality is that the effective demand or ability to pay for services in large (geographically speaking) portions of the United States may never be able to maintain an independent health care delivery infrastructure. Such geographical problem areas are often characterized by the lack of medical providers and reduced access due to long travel times. Other types of underserved areas are often found in urban areas, where certain neighborhoods or particular ethnic groups have systematic difficulties accessing health care services,

Health Professional Shortage Areas and Medically Underserved Areas

In the 1970s, the federal government developed two designation methods—the Health Professional Shortage Area (HPSA) and Medically Underserved Area (MUA) methodologies—which were used to identify such areas for the purpose of making them eligible to receive special, targeted resources designed to improve availability of, access to, and use of health care services for such areas and populations or groups. The designation of an area as being either an HPSA or MUA, or a group or population as the same, does not typically guarantee the receipt of resources designed to ameliorate the access problems being faced, but instead makes them eligible. For example, there are many more communities and locations designated as eligible to receive a National Health Service Corps physician placement than there are actual physicians (and other health professionals) who are eligible to be placed in an underserved community, typically as a means of repaying federal support of the cost of the medical education.

These measures (HPSA and MUA) have been essentially unchanged since the mid-1970s, and attempts by both the William J. Clinton (1993–2001) and George W. Bush (2001–2009) administrations to update these designation methods via the federal rulemaking process failed. The PPACA provided for a Negotiated Rulemaking Committee to recommend a revised set of designation methods that would then be put forth via the federal rulemaking process. This group produced a report to the secretary of health and human services in October 2011, but new rules based on these recommendations have not yet been developed.

A SUSTAINABLE FEDERAL HEALTH CARE BUDGET

Government plays an expansive role in providing health care services in the United States, far beyond even the scope and reach implied by the fact that every other dollar paid into the system is paid for by government. The federal government in particular has long played an agenda-setting role and led in the mainstreaming of new benefits (hospice, home health) as well as in the development of insurance/payment of care innovations (Diagnostic Related Groups) and how physicians (Resource Based Relative Value Scale) and hospitals (Prospective Payment) are paid. Similarly, rules established by payers such as Medicare when rehabilitation services are legitimately reimbursed are commonly followed and copied by private insurers. Perhaps the most profound and least understood ways in which government policy impacts private insurance is via the federal tax code: the fact that employer-paid health insurance premiums are classified as a benefit and are therefore essentially tax-free income. This has expanded the amount of insurance that persons have had and has also disconnected individuals from the cost of their employer-based private health insurance, because they typically had no reason to know how much it cost.

As we move to the reality of the baby boom generation switching en masse from paying taxes into receiving Medicare and/or Medicaid (and Social Security), the long-time federal budget pressures are primarily driven by federal health care expenditures. This is not the case of only the federal government having a health care cost problem; the rate of cost inflation in health care is similar for government and private insurance payers. The reality is that these costs hit the federal budget at the same time the demographic reality of the baby boomers takes full effect (fewer people paying taxes per person receiving benefits). This makes the quintessential policy question of the next thirty years the need to achieve a sustainable federal health care budget, which can be done only by achieving a sustainable federal budget. This in turn can be achieved only with sustainable Medicare and Medicaid, which means collecting the money to finance the spending in the programs Americans want.

See also **Chapter 11: Evolution of Health Planning (1920s–1970s); Chapter 12: Evolution of Health Planning (1970s–Present); Chapter 14: Biomedical Research Policy and Innovation (1940s–Present); Chapter 15: Building an Effective and Sustainable Health Care Workforce (1960s–Present); Chapter 16: Promoting Health Care Quality and Safety (1960s–Present); Chapter 17: Strategies for Health Care Cost Containment (1980s–Present); Chapter 18: Health and Health Care Policy: Ethical Perspectives (1970s–Present); Chapter 24: Mental Health and Social Policy (1960s–Present).**

NOTES

1. Committee on the Costs of Medical Care, *Health Care for the American People*, 1933, http://www.ncbi.nlm.nih.gov/pmc/articles/PMC1658442/?page=1.
2. House of Representatives, Subcommittee of the Committee on Interstate and Foreign Commerce on S. 191, 79th Congress, 2nd session. Hospital Survey and Construction Act/Hill–Burton Act of March, 1946.
3. National Institute of Health, NIH Act of 1950.
4. U.S. Department of Veterans Affairs, "About VA," http://www.va.gov/health/aboutVHA.asp.
5. U.S. Department of Health Human Services, "Indian Health Service," http://www.ihs.gov.
6. U.S. Department of Health and Human Services, Indian Health Service, *Negotiated Rulemaking Committee on the Designation of Medically Underserved Populations and Health Professional Shortage Areas: Final Report to the Secretary*, http://www.hrsa.gov/advisorycommittees/shortage/nrmcfinalreport.pdf.

7. Kaiser Family Foundation, "Health Reform," http://kff.org/health-reform.

8. Northern Virginia Community College, "Hill Burton Act of 1946," http://www.nvcc.edu/home/bhays/dogwood/hillburtonact.htm.

9. Northern Virginia Community College, "Community Health Services and Facilities Act—1961 and beyond," http://www.nvcc.edu/home/bhays/dogwood/facilitiesact.htm.

10. Paul Starr, *Social Transformation of American Medicine* (New York: Basic Books, 1982);

11. Robert Wood Johnson Foundation, "Can Medicare Be Preserved while Reducing the Deficit?" *Timely Analysis of Immediate Health Policy Issues,* http://www.rwjf.org/content/dam/farm/reports/issue_briefs/2013/rwjf404766/subassets/rwjf404766_1.

FURTHER READING

Mayes, Rick, and Robert Berenson. *Medicare Prospective Payment and the Shaping of U.S. Health Care.* Baltimore: Johns Hopkins University Press, 2008.

Starr, Paul. *Remedy and Reaction: The Peculiar American Struggle over Health Care Reform.* New Haven, CT: Yale University Press, 2013.

———. *The Social Transformation of American Medicine.* New York: Basic Books, 1982.

Zelman, Walter A., and Robert A. Berenson. *The Managed Care Blues and How to Cure Them.* Washington, DC: Georgetown University Press, 1998.

chapter 14

Biomedical Research Policy and Innovation (1940s–Present)

Michael McGeary and Robert Cook-Deegan

SINCE THE END OF WORLD WAR II (1939–1945), national biomedical research policy in the United States has emphasized public support of a large and broad program of primarily basic research aimed at advancing knowledge of biological processes, on the premise that such knowledge would lead to better ways to cure or prevent diseases that afflict the American people. Public funding, primarily National Institutes of Health (NIH) research grants to biomedical scientists in academia, has always included some clinical research, drug development, and support for clinical trials, but the main responsibility for innovation, defined as turning new knowledge into practical uses, has been left to the private sector. There have been exceptions, usually driven by emergencies. In World War II, federal funding paid for the development of penicillin from inventing mass production methods to building the production plants for private industry to run. The War on Cancer Act of 1971 mandated extensive clinical research and drug development by the National Cancer Institute (NCI) because at that time the pharmaceutical industry was not developing cancer treatments. The NCI conducted the early developmental research on AZT, the first effective drug for treating infection by the AIDS virus, before turning it over to Burroughs-Wellcome to produce for sale, and the National Institute of Allergies and Infectious Diseases paid for numerous clinical trials of AZT and other AIDS drugs.

In the 1940s and 1950s, the March of Dimes raised most of the funding leading to the Salk and Sabin vaccines, which eliminated the scourge of polio in the United States. By that time, however, it was apparent that the federal government had much deeper pockets for sustained research and development (R&D), and the nonprofit foundations and disease-oriented charities turned to more targeted strategies of funding higher-risk research than NIH generally funds. Since federal R&D funding went flat ten years ago (except for a one-time injection of American Recovery and Reinvestment Act funds in 2009) and the private pharmaceutical industry cut back on R&D in response to the Great Recession that began in late 2008, foundations funded by multibillionaires have been able to play a larger role in deciding which research opportunities to pursue and what diseases to focus on (see Figure 14.1).

Until recently, national policy on health R&D has been to fund steady growth year after year, resulting in the establishment of a large biomedical research capacity in the nation's universities and their academic health centers, a large workforce of doctoral and other scientific researchers, and a large volume of research results reported in peer-reviewed journals. The prolonged steady state in federal biomedical research funding of recent years is unprecedented, but whether it is the new normal state or another blip in the steady expansion of funding of NIH and other federal health research agencies is anyone's guess.

The story of the 1980s was the strong expansion of the private for-profit biomedical research sector. The biotechnology industry emerged, comprising companies dedicated to exploiting commercial opportunities arising from molecular and cellular biology, mainly applied to medicine and agriculture. At the same time, research-intensive pharmaceutical firms undertook a remarkable increase in R&D funding that went from 12 percent of sales in the mid-1970s to 21 percent in 2012 and that surpassed federal funding in 1993. The biotech and research-based pharmaceutical industries developed and marketed many new biologicals and pharmaceuticals with great economic success. Recently, however, sales have diminished because of high-revenue drugs going off patent, competition from generics, increased costs of R&D, and lack of new "blockbuster" drugs in the R&D pipeline. The number of novel drugs approved by the Food and Drug Administration

FIGURE 14.1   **NIH Appropriations, 1953–2015 (in billions of constant 2009 dollars)**

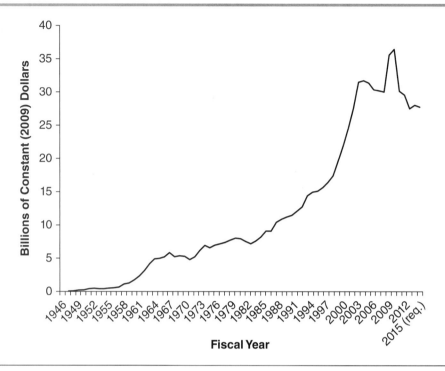

SOURCES: For 1946–2012: National Institutes of Health, "NIH Almanac," http://www.nih.gov/about/almanac/appropriations/part2.htm; for 2013–2015: National Institutes of Health, "NIH Congressional Justification Budget for FY 2015," http://officeofbudget.od.nih.gov/pdfs/FY15/FY2015_Overall_Appropriations.pdf.

NOTE: The totals for FY 2009 and FY 2010 each include approximately half of the $10.4 billion appropriated to NIH under the American Recovery and Reinvestment Act (ARRA) of 2009; the total for FY 2013 includes the $1.55 billion reduction in that year's appropriation because of sequestration.

(FDA) was flat starting in 2005 at about twenty-three a year until it jumped to thirty in 2011 and thirty-nine in 2012 before reverting to twenty-seven in 2013. It is not clear, however, if the new drugs will make up for the sales lost from drugs coming off patent.

Biomedical research has been buffeted by other forces in recent years. The closer relationships of researchers in academia and government with industry in the interests of enhancing medical innovation have also exposed the enterprise to charges of conflict of interest and greed. Promising research using fetal tissue drew the ire of antiabortion activists and involved successive U.S. presidents in decisions about how much and what kind of such research to allow. Research has created the capacity to clone living organisms, potentially including humans, and to alter germ lines for beneficial purposes with unknown side effects. These issues require extensive public debate to resolve.

HISTORICAL BACKGROUND OF BIOMEDICAL RESEARCH IN THE UNITED STATES

Before World War II, biomedical research in the United States was a small, almost entirely private endeavor. It was largely funded by philanthropic foundations such as the Rockefeller, Markle, Macy, and Kellogg Foundations and the Commonwealth and Milbank Memorial Funds as well as endowments from private donors. It was conducted in universities and privately funded research institutions such as the Rockefeller Institute for Medical Research (1901) and the Carnegie Institution of Washington (1902).[1] A burgeoning pharmaceutical industry, given a boost by the abrogation of German patents on chemicals and pharmaceuticals during World War I (1914–1918), conducted a certain amount of applied research and development. The private sector approach perhaps reached its zenith in 1938, with the founding of the National Foundation for Infantile Paralysis, known as the March of Dimes, which funded the development of the Salk and Sabin vaccines that essentially ended polio in the United States in the 1950s.[2] Then president Franklin D. Roosevelt (1933–1945), himself a victim of polio, strongly encouraged the March of Dimes efforts; the idea of mounting a "war" on polio through the National Institutes of Health was not politically feasible (although the establishment of the National Cancer Institute the year before was an early sign of the future substantial role of federal funding in attacking deadly diseases).

Before 1940, the federal government supported little biomedical research (indeed, little scientific research of any kind except agricultural research). Most federal involvement

Health and Human Services Secretary Kathleen Sebelius: Discovering New Therapeutic Uses for Existing Compounds

From time to time, the National Institutes of Health (NIH) has attempted to close the gap between scientific discovery and industrial development, for example, during the War on Cancer when thousands of compounds were synthesized and tested for anticancer activity with federal funds. In 2012, Health and Human Services Secretary Kathleen Sebelius announced that NIH would try a variation of this approach to help industry find promising new drugs to develop, seeking grants to retest compounds that were tested in the past for particular diseases against other diseases. The model for this program is AZT, which was synthesized and tested in the 1960s against cancer through a federal contract, but not pursued, although it demonstrated antiviral activity. When the AIDS epidemic hit, Burroughs-Wellcome (B-W), the pharmaceutical company that had licensed AZT, asked NIH to retest AZT against HIV, because the company did not have the containment facilities to handle such a dangerous virus. Samuel Broder, a physician and National Cancer Institute scientist, determined that AZT is very effective against HIV, after which he and other NIH researchers worked with B-W to develop AZT and conduct the clinical trials needed for FDA approval and to understand how to use the drug most effectively. An excerpt from Secretary Sebelius's May 3, 2012, announcement follows:

> When we look back over recent history, we see that biomedical research is responsible for some of our greatest progress, from the discovery of penicillin to the development of effective therapies for cancer. Diseases that had once been a death sentence have been eradicated or cured. Conditions that had once been disabling are now manageable.
>
> These achievements have not only saved the lives and improved the health of millions. They have also sparked enormous economic growth and created countless new jobs.
>
> At the beginning of a new century, we can see even bigger opportunities ahead. Last week, at the White House, I helped introduce our nation's first-ever Bio-economy Blueprint—this administration's commitment to strengthening bioscience research as a major driver of American innovation and economic growth.
>
> And keeping America on the forefront of the search for new cures and treatments is fundamental to achieving that vision.
>
> Yet the road from the research lab to an approved and marketable drug is a long one. And today there are many detours and obstacles along the way. It can take many years and hundreds of millions of dollars to bring one new drug from discovery to the marketplace, and most new projects fail in the early stages.
>
> If we want to find the cures of the 21st Century, we need to chart a clear path forward. And that is why this administration has undertaken a major effort to identify and remove roadblocks at every stage of the development process. . . .
>
> The drug AZT, for example, was originally tested against cancer and failed. Only later was it discovered to be an effective treatment for HIV—the first medicine we found to work against the virus. . . . In the search for new cures and treatments, these compounds offer a big advantage over those still being developed in the lab. They have already cleared many of the early clinical and regulatory hurdles, allowing researchers to identify new therapies more quickly—and allowing companies to bring them to market more efficiently.
>
> And yet, many of these compounds have not been re-evaluated. Or, if they are re-evaluated, that research is typically conducted through traditional partnerships of very limited size and scope.
>
> But today that is changing.
>
> I am proud to announce a new collaborative program that will allow far more researchers to study pharmaceutical-industry compounds and pursue vital new treatments for patients.
>
> Our goal is simple: to see whether we can teach old drugs new tricks. And to get there, we are taking an innovative approach: crowd-sourcing these compounds to our brightest minds and most inventive companies.
>
> Under the initiative we are launching today, any researcher with a promising scientific idea can apply for a new grant to test compounds from our partners against a variety of diseases and conditions.
>
> Through the program, the National Institutes of Health intend to provide at least $20 million in Fiscal Year 2013 to support the grants. And for their part, the companies will provide researchers with access to the compounds and all related data.
>
> This new kind of partnership is an investment—not only in our researchers, but in our nation.
>
> Because, when America's scientists have the tools and the resources to pursue the next great discoveries, we all benefit. It makes our nation stronger, healthier, and more competitive.

SOURCE: Kathleen Sebelius, "Discovering New Therapeutic Uses for Existing Compounds," May 3, 2012, http://www.hhs.gov/secretary/about/speeches/sp20120503.html.

in biomedical research was through the Public Health Service's (PHS) National Institute of Health, then a set of in-house laboratories that focused on communicable diseases, nutritional deficiencies, and other public health problems. The army and navy did not have formal research programs in their medical departments. The Veterans Administration (VA) did not yet conduct medical research either. The Food and Drug Administration, then in the U.S. Department of Agriculture (USDA), had only a small research effort.[3]

In 1938, for example, the PHS budget for research was not quite $3 million, about 3.6 percent of federal research expenditures that year, which totaled only $78.5 million. The FDA's research budget was $125,000. That year, the USDA, at $28.3 million, had the largest federal scientific research effort, followed by the navy at $9.1 million and army at $6.9 million.[4]

The federal government's main involvement in bio-medical research and innovation before World War II was through regulation of pharmaceuticals by the FDA and biologics (vaccines and antitoxins) by the NIH and through the patent system.

IMPACT OF WORLD WAR II

World War II transformed the role of the federal government in all areas of scientific research, including biomedical. The wartime R&D effort resulting from the funding of scientists and engineers in academic and industrial laboratories was so successful it fostered a growing appetite for federally funded R&D in the postwar period.

Even before the United States entered the war in December 1941, U.S. scientific leaders convinced President Roosevelt to harness the talents of U.S. scientific researchers in the war effort through the establishment of a civilian war agency, the National Defense Research Committee (NDRC). A year later, the NDRC was expanded to include medical research and renamed the Office of Scientific Research and Development (OSRD). The newly formed OSRD Committee on Medical Research (CMR) included leading academic and industrial scientists and engineers and representatives of the army and navy surgeons general and the PHS. The CMR worked closely with advisory committees of the National Academy of Sciences to identify and fund researchers to address the needs of the military services. The results included better methods of treating shock and trauma from burns and wounds, better whole blood storage and delivery methods, blood substitutes such as plasma, effective quinine substitutes for treating malaria, powerful insecticides (such as DDT) for improved sanitation, expanded knowledge of nutrition, aviation medicine, and, most salient to the general public, the mass production of penicillin.

Although penicillin was discovered by British researchers, most notably Alexander Fleming in 1928, its commercial development languished until World War II. The war made development difficult in Great Britain, so the discoverers of penicillin brought it to the United States, where the U.S. war effort developed mass production methods, conducted clinical evaluations, and made the "miracle drug" in such quantities that it was available without restrictions to the general public beginning in March 1945.[5]

When Japan surrendered in September 1945 after two cities—Hiroshima and Nagasaki—were destroyed by a new super weapon, the atomic bomb, which had been developed by U.S. scientists and engineers on a crash basis, science was widely seen as having played a critical part in winning the war. The public expected science to continue to address national needs. According to an analysis of newspaper editorials and stories from 1945:

> Americans expected science to give them great economic, medical, and strategic benefits. Science would facilitate the return to a peacetime economy by promoting new industries that would in turn create new markets and more jobs. It was believed that science should not only ensure the country's prosperity, but would also, through scientific research in medicine, enable Americans to live healthier, longer lives. Finally, Americans expected to provide the means to protect the healthy, prosperous nation from foreign aggressors.[6]

POSTWAR BIOMEDICAL RESEARCH SYSTEM

The postwar biomedical research system was shaped by many influences. A major influence was the success of OSRD in engaging academic scientists—who constituted the vast majority of America's scientific talent—in federally funded research through arrangements that respected the autonomy of the researchers and their universities. Another influence was the decentralized structure of the federal government around mission agencies, which strongly discouraged efforts to create a central science agency. The postwar period also witnessed the rise of influential citizen lobbyists advocating for ever-increasing federal funding of biomedical research. More indirect influences on the postwar biomedical research system included the advent of the Cold War in the late 1940s, which kept the federal government highly involved in the support of the national research enterprise generally (not just applied defense research), and the high rate of growth of the U.S. economy from 1945 through the 1960s, which facilitated large annual increases in federal R&D funding during those years.

Organization of Postwar Research

In 1945, as the war was ending, Vannevar Bush, who headed the NDRC and its successor, OSRD, wrote a report on the organization and funding of postwar science at the request of President Roosevelt. Bush duly wrote the report, but Roosevelt had died by the time he delivered it to President Harry S. Truman (1945–1953) in July 1945. In the report, which he called *Science—The Endless Frontier,* Bush proposed the establishment of a National Research Foundation (NRF) that would not conduct research itself. Rather, Bush's NRF, following the OSRD model, would support meritorious peer-reviewed research projects through grants to qualified nonfederal scientists in universities and industrial laboratories.[7] The NRF, organized around divisions for basic research, medical research, and defense research, would have been the central home of federal civilian R&D support.

Bush's vision of a national research foundation was not realized. His proposal that the NRF be governed by a board of mostly nonfederal scientists that would hire the head of the agency was vetoed by President Truman, who was ever mindful of presidential prerogatives. By the time the bill creating the National Science Foundation (NSF) was passed in 1950 with a director appointed by the president, the NIH and the armed services had established robust extramural research programs that were too entrenched to be transferred to the new agency.[8]

Bush had not realized that the armed services would be able to fund academic research under arrangements that preserved the autonomy and initiative of researchers. Before World War II, the services took a narrow contracting approach to the procurement of weapons, but by 1945, they were convinced that academic scientists and engineers were important assets and were willing to rely on scientific advisory groups, peer review, and open-ended research contracts to keep them engaged. The Office of Naval Research was only a step behind NIH in launching a large extramural research program at the end of the war.[9]

Bush also did not understand the intense desire of the medical research community to have its own agency, which was also strongly preferred by health research advocates for funding of disease-specific research. By the time the NSF was established in 1950, NIH's budget for health research was already larger than the $50 million for health research that Bush forecast for the entire NRF when it was up and running.[10] NSF's first full-year budget for research in all fields was $3.5 million, a fraction of NIH's budget of $57.7 million that year (fiscal year 1952), and NIH's research budget has continued to be considerably larger than NSF's to the present.

Development of the Competitive Research Grant Mechanism

One of OSRD's proudest achievements, the subject of an entire chapter in the official administrative history of the office, was the research contract:

A check of Army and Navy contract forms failed to disclose any which promised to be satisfactory. For the most

part they were aimed at procurement or production rather than research.... What was needed was a contract that would combine a maximum freedom for the exercise of scientific imagination on NDRC problems with those safeguards necessary for the expenditure of public funds.[11]

The key to the success of the OSRD contract was a simple performance clause developed in 1940:

The contractor agreed to conduct studies and experimental investigations in connection with a given problem and to make a final report of his findings and conclusions to the [NDRC] by a specified date. This clause was deliberately made flexible in order that the contractor would not be hampered in the details of the work which he was to perform. The objective was stated in general terms; no attempt was made to dictate the method of handling the problem.[12]

The need to develop such a flexible relationship between the government and researchers reflected a major potential obstacle to an enlarged national biomedical research system in the postwar period. Before the experience of World War II, leading scientists and engineers were very leery of, if not opposed to federal funding, fearing government dictation of their work. Their employers, the universities, were even more wary of federal funding and the strings that came with it. The first step was the creation of a science-friendly agency—the NDRC (succeeded by OSRD); the second was the development of funding and oversight procedures that preserved the institutional autonomy of the universities and the ability of researchers to decide what to investigate and how to investigate it. In addition to the research contract with a flexible performance clause, OSRD adopted a number of other science-friendly practices that have continued to this day. Those included using panels of nonfederal research experts to evaluate and recommend scientifically sound proposals for funding, which was the origin of the peer review systems now used by NIH, NSF, and other funding agencies, and paying for the overhead costs incurred by the university or other research institution.

The next step was to use grants rather than contracts to support research.

As a rule, individual investigators prefer the grant-in-aid to the contract. Grants allow the investigator to follow promising paths wherever they may lead. He need not be concerned with deviating from the terms of contract. He has fewer authorities with whom to deal and there are fewer inspectors and less supervision. Moreover, the entire initiative lies with him. He selects the field, the problem, and the specific subject and, having complete freedom in the conduct of the work, is under no obligation to "find something," or to meet a fixed time schedule. His proposal and his results are judged by his peers.[13]

Before World War II, research grants were often used by foundations, but only two small federal agencies had authority to use grants instead of contracts, the National Cancer Institute and the National Advisory Committee on Aeronautics. NCI had been imposed on the PHS in 1937 by Congress, which was responding to a new force that came into full bloom after World War II: citizen advocates lobbying for federal funding for research on specific diseases. In its first year, NCI awarded ten extramural grants totaling $91,000. During the war, PHS leaders worked with Congress to revise and codify the statutes governing the PHS. The PHS Act of 1944 cleverly made NCI a part of NIH rather than a separate PHS agency and broadened NCI's grant authority to all of the PHS. That development positioned NIH to convert the OSRD contracts that were transferred to the PHS after the war into grants and to form the nucleus of an NIH extramural research grant program.[14]

The Office of Scientific Research and Development was disbanded shortly after the end of the war. Because Bush's proposed National Research Foundation was stalled, active OSRD contracts were transferred to the army, navy, and, in the case of medical research, the PHS in September 1945. As early as August 1944, NIH Director Rolla Dyer was discussing such a transfer with A.N. Richards, head of the Committee on Medical Research.[15] Dyer explained in some detail how the PHS could administer the projects through an organization that would have the flexibility of the CMR organization and that would draw on most of the same personnel. His plan was to transfer members of the CMR and its National Academy of Sciences reviewing bodies to the Public Health Services, which would then take over OSRD's responsibilities using the PHS grants system that had been developed by NCI.[16]

About fifty to sixty contracts, totaling nearly $1 million, were transferred. Most of them were converted into grants and continued. Some large contracts for clinical testing of penicillin in the treatment of venereal disease were terminated, freeing up funds NIH could use to launch its new extramural grants program. The new system was organized at the beginning of 1946 under a separate office of research grants (renamed the Division of Research Grants in 1950 and the Center for Scientific Review in 1997 with no change in functions). The grants office was organized around panels of expert nonfederal scientists who reviewed research proposals in their research area for technical merit. Those disciplinary panels of scientific peers were and are key in legitimizing federal funding of basic research in the eyes of nonfederal scientists. The peer review system assures the science community that funding will go to the best science and individual scientists that their research proposals will be considered without regard to personal, political, or other nonscientific considerations.

Rise of Citizen Advocates for Federal Health Research Funding

The creation of the NCI before the war was a harbinger of postwar biomedical research politics, in which federal funds would be mobilized to address a series of specific diseases by coalitions of citizen activists and congressional patrons.[17] Cancer, then the most dreaded of all diseases, seemed to be increasing at an alarming rate during the 1920s and 1930s, which justified an unprecedented federal role in addressing chronic diseases, not just communicable diseases and other public health problems that traditionally defined the scope of federal health responsibilities.[18]

The effort to conquer polio through private voluntary action was successful, but financially exhausting for the March of Dimes. The March of Dimes raised more than $600 million dollars between 1938 and 1962, of which about 11 percent went to research, but even these sums were tiny compared with the need for further R&D and for clinical care.[19] Within a few years after World War II, federal funding of biomedical research exceeded philanthropic funding.

The career of Mary Lasker illustrates the political advocacy approach.[20] Her husband, Albert Lasker, made a fortune pioneering the modern advertising and public relations industry. The Laskers started a foundation in 1942 with $50,000, which began awarding the prestigious Lasker Awards in 1946. In 1945, Mary Lasker joined the board of the American Association for the Control of Cancer and offered to help it raise more money if it would devote 25 percent to research. The organization, later renamed the American Cancer Society, raised $4 million, compared with less than $1 million in 1944.[21] In 1946, the American Cancer Society raised $10 million. Soon, however, Lasker decided that the federal government had much deeper pockets. She teamed with Florence Mahoney, whose husband owned the Cox newspaper chain, to use modern public relations techniques and the power of the press to advocate for more federal medical research funding. Lasker and Mahoney also cultivated close relationships with key members of Congress who supported their vision of federal funding of health research, beginning with donations to Claude Pepper's Senate campaigns (in the Senate 1936–1951; in the House of Representatives 1963–1989). In 1946, Lasker and Mahoney were involved in the establishment of the National Institute of Mental Health, NIH's second categorical institute (after NCI); Lasker had provided the funds for the National Committee for Mental Hygiene to hire a lobbyist in 1945. In recognition for her support of the National Heart Act of 1948, which established the National Heart Institute, Lasker was the first layperson appointed as a member of an NIH institute's national advisory council. Her crowning achievement was passage of the War on Cancer Act in 1971, rallying supporters in response to cuts in the NCI's budget in the late 1960s. Mahoney was a leader in the establishment of the National Institute on Aging in 1974.

Although Lasker and Mahoney have passed from the scene, their legacy lives on. Currently, hundreds of diseases have one or more voluntary groups pressing Congress, the administration, and NIH for more funding of biomedical research, along with umbrella groups such as Research!America coordinating efforts to present a united front to decision makers.

A scientist examines a culture through a microscope. In the future, innovations in research and technology will likely improve many aspects of health care. Indeed, the American public can expect scientific research to improve their lives, especially in the areas related to health.

SOURCE: B. Boissonnet/BSIP/SuperStock.

The Categorical Approach to Biomedical Research Funding

Before World War II, the NIH was organized around scientific disciplines and medical fields, such as divisions of biologic standards, chemistry, industrial hygiene, infectious diseases, pathology, pharmacology, public health methods, and zoology. The disease-focused NCI was a new kind of animal to PHS leaders, who feared that they would be forced to spend more scarce research dollars on cancer than there was good science to support. After the war, however, they began to realize that categorical institutes were an excellent way to gain larger appropriations than disciplinary units did. By the end of 1950, the NIH, pluralized to become the National Institutes of Health, had added six institutes: the National Institute of Mental Health (1946), National Heart Institute (1948), National Institute of Dental Research (1948), National Microbiological Institute (NMI) (1948), National Institute of Arthritis and Metabolic Diseases (NIAMD; 1950), and National Institute of Neurological Diseases and Blindness (1950). NIAMD replaced the Experimental Biology and Medicine Institute established in 1948. Not surprisingly, the NMI was renamed the National Institute of Allergy and Infectious Diseases in 1955.

Over time, the number of institutes has proliferated. Currently, there are twenty institutes and seven centers (gaining center status is often the first step in becoming an institute). Initially, NIH leaders accepted the disease-oriented categorical structure as a workable focus for research, which also had the advantage of "being socially understandable and still amenable to balancing scientific opportunity with perceived social needs."[22] Subsequently, NIH leaders and the scientific community began to oppose further proliferation, beginning with the establishment of the National Eye Institute, carved out of the National Institute of Neurological Diseases and Blindness in 1968, with partial success. In 2001, former NIH director Harold

Varmus (in office 1993–1999) proposed reorganizing NIH into five broadly based categorical institutes (for cancer, brain disorders, internal medicine, human development, and microbial and environmental medicine), arguing their broader scope would give them more adequate resources and flexibility to respond to public needs and promising research opportunities.[23] Fewer institutes would not only be more administratively manageable, they would better match the current emphasis in scientific research on multidisciplinary approaches to understanding fundamental cellular and molecular processes underlying multiple diseases and organ systems.

Reconciling Health Needs and Scientific Opportunity

The system of peer review of competitive research grant proposals helps NIH reconcile two sometimes conflicting imperatives: to assure the public that it is meeting the most important health needs and to assure the scientific community that it is funding the best science. A review of NIH structure in 1984 put it this way:

> The genius of the institution in shaping scientific excellence to health needs is found in the interplay of categorical research institutes and disciplinary study sections. The primarily disease-based institutes enable Congress to understand, appreciate, and support the research accomplishments and goals of the institutes, and also to express concerns and priorities about the need for further research. The study sections, on the other hand, cut across institute lines and ensure that appropriate scientific talent and ideas are brought to bear on the problems.[24]

In recent years, as research has become more multidisciplinary, the organization of NIH's Center for Scientific Review around more than one hundred disciplinary peer review groups (called study sections) and many ad hoc and special emphasis panels has been called into question. In 2000, an advisory panel recommended that as much science as possible be reviewed on an organ-system or disease basis, rather than by discipline-related study sections. A smaller number of "integrated review groups" (IRGs; the panel suggested twenty-four of these) would each address basic, translational, and clinical research in the context of the particular disease or physiological function being addressed.[25]

> This recommendation acknowledges the advent of molecular medicine, where biochemistry, genetics, molecular and cellular biology have become tools applied to virtually all fields of health-related research. Molecular medicine applications will be reviewed in the context of the biological questions addressed rather than lumped in discipline-related study sections where they will compete against each other.[26]

Currently, there are twenty-five IRGs, some disciplinary (e.g., cell biology, biological chemistry and macromolecular biophysics, immunology) but mostly disease- or organ-system based (e.g., AIDS, oncology, brain disorders, cardiovascular and respiratory). The study sections within each IRG are a mix of disciplinary and integrative bases. It remains to be seen if the shift toward disease-based study sections blurs the differences between the two approaches, the categorical and the disciplinary, thus affecting the creative tension between two demands—meeting public needs and supporting the most promising scientific opportunities.

SUPPORT OF BIOMEDICAL RESEARCH IN THE UNITED STATES

The positive experience of federally funded academic research and development during and after World War II provided the impetus for what quickly became the largest biomedical research and development enterprise in the world. Today, the United States is still the dominant force in biomedical research; it accounted for half the estimated $160.3 billion spent on health R&D in the world in 2005 (Japan, the next largest investor in health R&D, accounted for 10 percent).[27] The federal government was the largest funder in the early decades; the private for-profit sector became the largest funder beginning in the early 1990s. This investment has built an enormous infrastructure of biomedical researchers and research institutions conducting thousands of research projects at any given time. U.S. biomedical researchers publish almost 400,000 research reports in peer-reviewed journals annually.[28]

Periods of Growth

The growth of the biomedical research and development enterprise since 1946 can be divided into five periods:

1. *Rise of NIH, 1946–1967.* Transition from private funding to public funding by rapid growth of NIH appropriations.

2. *Federal dominance, 1968–1980.* Rebuilding a coalition with new players and resumed growth through the War on Cancer and the rise of molecular biology.

3. *Surge of pharmaceutical R&D and emergence of biotechnology, 1980–1998.* Mixed growth and stagnation of NIH funding, consistently faster growth of pharmaceutical research and development, birth and growth of the "new biotechnology," and emergence of the Human Genome Project.

4. *A final doubling, 1998–2003.* NIH's budget doubled through a concerted public advocacy campaign, alignment of interests, and bipartisan support, and the Human Genome Project produced a reference sequence.

5. *Volatility and turbulence, 2004–present.* Flat NIH budgets, stem cell research becomes a divisive issue in presidential politics, pressure for translating research into health goods and services mounts, financial collapse and federal deficit spending put pressure on NIH's budget, which is now large enough that it cannot grow without substantial compensating cuts elsewhere, and pharmaceutical firms begin to cut research budgets.

In the first period, public financing supplanted private funding. Before World War II, pharmaceutical companies, private philanthropy, and individual hospitals or local medical facilities (e.g., cancer centers) supported most health research; after the war the most powerful force became federal funding through NIH. Federal health research appropriations increased rapidly after the war, especially during the second half of the 1950s and the early 1960s.

The second period began with a decline in 1967-1969, caused by the dismantling of a political coalition that had to be rebuilt. NIH Director James A. Shannon (in office 1955–1968) and the chairs of the House and Senate appropriations subcommittees left (or died) in that period. Once the coalition was reconstituted, and the War on Cancer Act was passed in 1971, annual increases in federal health research budgets resumed.

Molecular biology became a dominant research paradigm. In this era of recombinant DNA, NIH policy—along with support from other federal research funders such as the

National Science Foundation, Department of Defense, and Veterans Administration—was the dominant force in biomedical research. Academic health centers expanded dramatically over those two decades and they became dependent on federal grants and contracts. Scientific careers also became dependent on NIH funding. Those features became fixtures in the national research enterprise, and remain so today.

The third period began in the 1980s, when the private for-profit R&D in pharmaceuticals, biotechnology, and devices began to grow even faster than federal funding. The biotechnology industry based on recombinant DNA and cell fusion technologies was tiny and fragile at the beginning of this period, but by the mid-1990s, several biotechnology firms had joined the ranks of pharmaceutical manufacturers, based primarily on high-value therapeutic proteins. Both pharma and biotech pursued research-intensive pathways to growth. By the late 1990s, industry was funding the

majority of biomedical R&D as it had before World War II, but at a thousand-fold greater magnitude. Although the federal government dwarfed private philanthropies in the amount of health R&D, large private philanthropic funding agencies were able to fill important gaps and became important in their chosen fields.

At the same time that industrial R&D was growing, the nature of science within NIH shifted gradually away from heavy dominance by investigator-initiated "cottage science" to larger-scale, instrument- and data-intensive efforts exemplified by the Human Genome Project, which emerged in 1985, was established in administrative units at NIH and the U.S. Department of Energy by 1990, and spawned a new NIH institute in 1997. The publicly funded Human Genome Project depended heavily on instruments that grew out of federally funded research but were then developed in private firms that then sold instruments and analytical tools to both publicly and privately funded

FIGURE 14.2 **Federal Health R&D and PhRMA Member Domestic R&D Expenditures, 1970–2012**

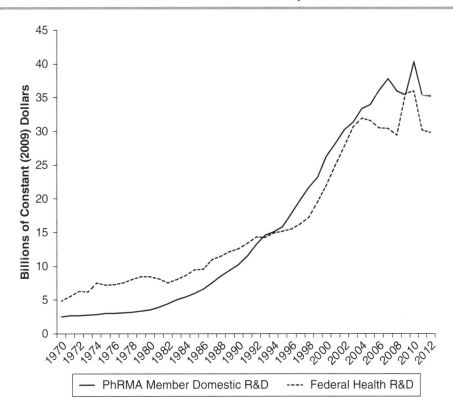

SOURCES: For PhRMA R&D: PhRMA, "2013 Profile: Biopharmaceutical Research Industry," Table 1, http://www.phrma.org/sites/default/files/pdf/PhRMA%20 Profile%202013.pdf; for federal health R&D: National Science Foundation, "Federal R&D Funding by Budget Function, Fiscal Years 2012–14," Table 24, http://nsf .gov/statistics/nsf14301.

NOTES: NIH accounts for most of federal health R&D; other federal agencies with health R&D expenditures include the Food and Drug Administration, Consumer Product Safety Commission, and Agency for Health Research and Quality. Federal health R&D totals for FY 2009 and FY 2010 each include approximately half of the $9.6 billion appropriated to NIH for R&D under the American Recovery and Reinvestment Act (ARRA) of 2009; they do not include the $1.5 billion in ARRA funding for R&D plant.

research institutions. One indication of the complex public-private research ecosystem in this era was Celera Genomics, created in 1998 to sequence the human genome in competition with the publicly funded international Human Genome Project.

By the late 1990s, federal funding of biomedical R&D became so large it could pose a threat to other publicly funded programs. In 1995, NIH Director Harold Varmus warned that NIH might have to accommodate "steady state" budgets, after five decades of nearly continual growth.[29] Instead, the NIH's budget doubled during the five years beginning in 1998. The doubling, which began in the last year of Varmus's tenure as NIH director, resulted from a concerted effort among countless health research advocates who orchestrated bipartisan support. Research!America and many disease advocacy groups rallied to the cause. The doubling survived a change in the party holding the White House, from Democratic President William J. Clinton (1993–2001) to Republican President George W. Bush (2001–2009), and to a new NIH director, Elias Zerhouni (in office 2002–2008).

Even as the doubling ended, however, the nation's priorities shifted sharply toward rebuilding military might in response to international terrorism. Biomedical research encountered unaccustomed political turbulence. One indicator that the size and scale of NIH's budget was changing the political economy of biomedical research politics was a remarkably explicit criticism from Senator Pete Domenici (R-NM; in office 1973–2008) in March 2004:

"I hate to say it, but the NIH is one of the best agencies in the world," an angry Domenici said as he spoke in opposition to an amendment by Sen. Arlen Specter (R-Pa.) to boost NIH funding by $1.5 billion. "But they've turned into pigs. You know, pigs! They can't keep their oinks closed. They send a Senator down there [to] argue as if they're broke.[30]

Domenici went on to point out that the research in the physical sciences funded by the National Science Foundation was slated to receive $3.6 billion in the FY 2005 budget, the same as in 2004. Domenici's outburst was all the more remarkable because he and his wife Nancy were long-standing stalwart supporters of health research, especially research on serious mental disorders. It signaled that NIH had become large enough that its continual growth encroached on other national priorities and other research institutions such as the Department of Energy–funded national laboratories, Los Alamos and Sandia, in Domenici's home state of New Mexico. NIH was getting more than $30 billion a year in today's dollars, so it could still be seen as the "jewel in the crown" of federally funded research with steady-state funding and should not have to squeeze funding for other R&D agencies or other worthy public programs.

Scale was not the only new element in the politics of biomedical research. The cloning of Dolly the sheep in 1996 and the discovery of human embryonic stem cells in 1998 injected controversy into biomedical research. Cloning rekindled anxieties about how biological research could refashion life on Earth. Concerns that had lain relatively dormant for a decade or more resurfaced, although they had never been far below the surface. Then the discovery of methods for identifying and creating human embryonic stem cell lines ignited a highly divisive debate about the moral legitimacy of science and applications that depended on the destruction of human embryos.

Human embryonic stem cell research added a new element to a long-standing controversy surrounding embryonic and fetal research. Special Olympics founder Eunice Kennedy Shriver's outrage at research done on fetuses in Sweden was one of the reasons for creating the nation's first bioethics commission, the National Commission for the Protection of Human Subjects of Biomedical and Behavioral Research in 1974, and fetal research was the topic of its first report. Congress included restrictions on fetal research in 1985's NIH authorization statute (PL 99-158), although research on embryos up to two weeks old was not covered by the definition. Those restrictions were removed by Congress during the first two years of the Clinton administration, and NIH was poised to begin funding some human embryonic research, although not research that would produce embryonic lines for research purposes, when the 1994 midterm elections gave Republicans a majority in both the House and Senate. Starting in 1995, language prohibiting research that entailed the destruction of human embryos was included in NIH funding bills. In his first formal public address as president, in August 2001, George W. Bush announced that federal agencies would not fund research involving human embryonic stem cell lines that had not already been created.

Those restrictions became a major issue in the 2004 presidential elections, an unusual case of a divisive biomedical research issue breaking along partisan lines in U.S. presidential politics. In contrast, the War on Cancer became part of a presidential election campaign, but in that case, candidates were vying for leadership of expansion; whereas for stem cell research, the parties broke in opposite directions, supporting or opposing human embryonic stem cell research.

The Bush administration restrictions were reversed by the first bill passed by a Democratic House and Senate during the administration of President Barack Obama (2009–). A federal district court then ruled some lines of research violated the statutory restrictions in funding bills, but a federal appeals court then reversed the lower court ruling. This back-and-forth meant NIH simply could not adopt its usual stance of placating all constituencies through a mutual war on disease, but instead was forced to pursue or not pursue lines of research that offended constituencies, tended to break along party lines, and separated most liberals from most conservatives as defined by U.S. political conventions of the decade.

NIH thus now finds itself with a relatively large budget in the Department of Health and Human Services. It has strong disease group advocates and academic health centers as major constituencies. It remains a highly regarded funding arm of government with bipartisan support in most areas. Yet there is intense pressure to reduce federal deficit spending, particularly in nondefense discretionary accounts. Moreover, funding decisions are being made amid more political turbulence than during most of NIH's seven decades of post–World War II growth. It is probably not a coincidence that NIH's budget peaked in real terms in 2004, when Domenici, a hitherto faithful supporter of NIH, voiced his complaint about more funding for NIH.

Yet predictions about long-term decline—or even leveling—of health research budgets have a way of being proven wrong. When Stephen Strickland wrote his book on health research in 1972, he clearly believed the era of continual growth was over and the politics of health research would change fundamentally. It turned out his book ended at the beginning of another surge built on the War on Cancer. After Harold Varmus warned about the inevitability of a steady-state budget, NIH's budget began to double. The future, of course, is uncertain and predictions fraught with peril. However, seven decades of growth suggest that health research is truly a national priority. In fact, continued NIH budget growth has been driven to an important degree by a series of advocacy movements, beginning with the War on Cancer in the 1970s. In the 1990s, the AIDS epidemic saw the emergence of a very strong and successful advocacy movement. Advocates for breast cancer and other women's health research learned how to be effective from the HIV/AIDS advocates. Subsequently, many other disease advocacy groups adopted the same tactics, with some success. The Alzheimer's Association, for example, has been very effective in increasing Alzheimer's research at the National Institute on Aging. Currently, however, there does not seem to be enough public concern about a particular health problem to launch a new crusade for increasing federal health research. Perhaps it will be Alzheimer's as the full impact of the disease becomes apparent with the aging of the baby boom generation.

Just as NIH faced questions over the propriety of its management after the budget expansion of the 1960s, NIH's budget doubling that ended in 2003 has been followed by

POLITICS AND HEALTH CARE POLICY

The Impact of the PPACA on Biomedical Research

The main purpose of the Patient Protection and Affordable Care Act (PPACA) is to ensure affordable health care insurance for Americans who do not qualify for Medicaid and do not have health care insurance, either because they have an existing condition that health insurers will not accept or because they cannot afford health insurance through their employers or on the individual policy market. However, the PPACA also includes specific provisions regarding biomedical research. One of these establishes a quick approval process at the Food and Drug Administration for "biosimilar" biologics (generic versions of large protein-based drugs).

The PPACA also established a new research initiative at the National Institutes of Health (NIH) called the Cures Acceleration Network, part of NIH's new National Center for Advancing Translational Sciences. The PPACA authorized $500 million a year for the network to support nonfederal researchers developing treatments for diseases or conditions that are rare, and for which market incentives are inadequate. However, appropriations were only $10 million in FY 2012 and $9 million in FY 2013.

The PPACA could be considered a giant experiment itself in how to expand access to quality health care at reasonable cost. This is because the law mandates evaluation of new approaches to pay for delivering health care that is high quality and efficient. These include demonstration projects on bundled payments, value-based purchasing, accountable care organizations, and patient-centered medical homes.

Some of the health care delivery research is being supported by a new Innovation Center at the Centers for Medicare and Medicaid Services. Other research is being conducted by the Patient-Centered Outcomes Research Institute created by the PPACA, a public-private organization that is comparing treatments and care strategies in terms of quality, effectiveness, and value.

Not everyone believes that the PPACA will benefit from research. The head of the Cleveland Clinic has warned that the PPACA provision that ties payments to the effectiveness of a new drug or medical device would reduce innovation or at least drive it out of the United States.

SOURCES: C. Stephen Redhead, Sarah A. Lister, Kirsten J. Colello, Amanda K. Sarata, and Elayne J. Heisler, "Discretionary Spending in the Patient Protection and Affordable Care Act (ACA), July 1, 2013. http://www.fas.org/sgp/crs/misc/R41390.pdf; Sabrina Eaton, "Cleveland Clinic's Toby Cosgrove: Affordable Care Act May Hurt Medical Research" Cleveland Plain Dealer, July 20, 2012, http://www.cleveland.com/healthfit/index.ssf/2012/07/cleveland_clinics_toby_cosgrov.html. Harry P. Selker and June S. Wasser, eds., The Affordable Care Act as a National Experiment: Health Policy Innovations and Lessons (New York: Springer, 2014).

concerns about accountability—conflict of interest and management of funds. Is the run of consistent growth since 1946 an indicator of a powerful long-term current in U.S. politics? Or is the nation's deep and abiding faith in health research and strong bipartisan support for federal funding bumping up against other policy priorities in a way that will constrain future growth? Has NIH become so large, and new biomedical research directions so controversial, that consistent growth will no longer be the pattern? Growth cannot continue at the pace of the surges in the past. The safest prediction may be that health R&D as a fraction of the national economy will continue to grow. Yet the safest prediction may not be very safe.

RESULTS OF BIOMEDICAL RESEARCH AND DEVELOPMENT

Federal funding, with increasing contributions from industry and philanthropy, has built and maintains a large biomedical research enterprise that provides inputs for innovation. Because of the nature of scientific research and long time lags between discovery and innovation, however, it is difficult to trace a straight line from a specific federally funded research advance to a particular drug, preventive intervention, or medical device. The need for innovation as measured by the burden of disease in the population is not necessarily congruent with the most promising opportunities for research advances. Much of basic research is not related to a specific disease. In the U.S. system of biomedical research, publicly funded research focuses largely on producing new knowledge, and private enterprise focuses on using extant knowledge to develop new products. There is overlap, to be sure. About 20 percent of the Pharmaceutical Research and Manufacturers of America (PhRMA) members' R&D expenditures go to basic and preclinical research, while NIH and other federal R&D agencies fund some clinical trials and other applied research and development activities. Generally, however, government and nonprofit funds support the R, more "basic" biological research, while commercial R&D focuses more on the D, developing products and services. Many steps have been taken to more closely couple research and invention. On the research side, for example, the Bayh-Dole Act of 1980 has encouraged movement of academic and federal research into products, although many other factors contribute to the process of converting academic science into socially valuable goods and services, most notably a very long history of academic-industrial relations in U.S. universities and the very practical value of "open science" research results as inputs to industrial R&D.[31] On the invention side, biopharmaceutical companies have moved more and

more into molecular and cellular biology, overlapping with academic science, to augment the industry's "absorptive capacity" for new product ideas and new methods of drug discovery.[32]

Whatever the impact of publicly funded open science and the increasing collaboration between industry and academic researchers, the U.S.-based biopharmaceutical sector of biotechnology companies and research-intensive pharmaceutical companies has been the most productive in the world. About 1,600 companies in the United State develop, manufacture, and market pharmaceuticals and biologicals, with annual sales of about $171 billion in 2011, roughly 12 percent less than the $195 billion in sales in 2008.[33] In 2010, about 138,000 persons worked for biotechnology firms, and 278,000 worked for pharmaceutical companies, although the latter number was 5.8 percent smaller than the peak of 295,000 in 2007 due to industry restructuring and consolidation, a trend that is expected to continue. PhRMA reports that in 2011, more than 5,400 drugs were in development worldwide. Approximately 3,400 of the drugs in development are being studied in the United States.[34] U.S. dominance of the world biopharmaceutical market could be eroding, however, as other nations increase their investment in biomedical R&D while U.S. investment stagnates. A recent study found that the U.S. share of R&D expenditures globally declined from 50.1 percent in 2007 to 44.4 percent in 2012.[35]

CURRENT ISSUES

The biomedical R&D enterprise is facing challenges. Nearly constant growth in federal funding support has ended, or at least been suspended, for a decade, disrupting a system that relied on growth. Despite the enormous past public and private investment in biomedical R&D, the rate of innovation, as measured by new medicines, has slowed. Efforts to bring academia, government, and industry closer together to foster a smoother transition from research to development has thrust a host of ethical issues into political prominence. Finally, biomedical research opportunities touch on socially sensitive beliefs and attitudes regarding cloning, use of fetal tissue, gene alteration, and other matters.

Federal Funding

It remains to be seen whether NIH funding will stay flat or begin growing again. Public support for health research is high, and reports of the end of NIH growth in the past were not borne out. On the other hand, the NIH budget of $30 billion is large enough to force it to compete with other public priorities. If NIH funding does not grow significantly faster than inflation, as it did most years since 1945, it will force painful changes in the way NIH conducts business.

NIH's practice is to approve research grants for three to five years but fund them year by year. Normally, this means about a quarter of NIH's extramural research funding (which constitutes 80 percent of its budget) is available for new grants as old grants end. However, many of the grants are renewed because they are productive, which reduces opportunities for young new researchers to get their first grants. In the past, this was resolved when NIH usually received significantly more funding than the president requested, and then that increase was programmed in the NIH budgets. This provided flexible funding that could be used to fund more new investigator grants and new research opportunities or needs that emerged. With flat funding, however, new projects can be launched only if existing grants end; it throws a terrible wrench into the gears of a system premised on monotonic growth. If newly minted PhDs and MDs are unable to launch independent research careers, the flow of fresh talent will be interrupted, and different approaches will be needed to ensure balance in the system.

Maintaining Innovation

Sales of medicines have slowed for several reasons, one of which is the lack of new blockbuster drugs to replace those coming off patent protection. They provide the resources that have allowed the pharmaceutical and biotechnology industries to invest heavily in R&D (more than 20 percent of sales revenues in recent years). Recent upticks in the number of new entities approved by the FDA in 2011 and 2012, and the promising sales potential of some of them, provide some hope that this situation is improving.

Ethical Concerns

Ironically, efforts to promote innovation through closer interactions between academia and industry are creating potential conflicts, perhaps more quickly than the affected institutions can revise their policies to handle such situations. In the first years of the twenty-first century, some fissures in the academic-industrial complex began to widen into public controversies. Long-time science and technology analyst Daniel Greenberg wrote that science had become dominated by the self-interest of academic scientists and their institutions and pointed to "ethical erosion."[36] Bioethicist Daniel Callahan called for priorities beyond profit and life extension to guide biomedical research.[37]

Muckraking has already forced changes in NIH policies and tightened the guidelines of medical societies on accepting fees from private industry. A series of congressional hearings, reacting to stories in the *Los Angeles Times*,[38] focused on senior administrators at NIH receiving substantial payments from industry partners, and a spate of books argued that the relationships between industry, academic medicine, and government had become too cozy. Two former editors of *The New England Journal of Medicine* and several academics wrote books about how the pharmaceutical industry systematically biased science in its favor, causing conflicts of interest and encouraging exploitation, greed, deceit, and corruption.[39] In September 2004, NIH seriously constrained intramural scientists' partnerships with industry, and new rules were codified in February 2005, while extramural academic research institutions began to evaluate their own policies.

Difficult Social Issues Raised by Biomedical Research

Biomedical research has created, and will no doubt continue to create, conflicts with powerful religious, political, and philosophical values and beliefs. New medicines and medical procedures call for careful patient protection procedures so that patients are not harmed by unexpected effects. The ability to make research advances by using fetal tissue, for example, has been stymied by antiabortion activists who fear that the use of tissues from aborted fetuses will encourage abortion. What about cloning? Should it be it banned because improved techniques might make it possible to clone human beings some day? Should genes be altered to prevent or cure disease in ways that can be inherited? These are issues that could create a backlash that affects the future of the biomedical research if not well handled.

LOOKING AHEAD

The explosive growth of biomedical research during and after World War II changed health research from a relatively small effort fueled by philanthropy to a complex system of government and nonprofit research strongly connected to large and diverse private R&D efforts in drugs, devices, and biologics. Relatively consistent growth for six decades has been followed by plateaus in research budgets for the past decade, punctuated by a two-year blip from the 2009 and 2010 economic "stimulus." With growth of scale has come complexity of politics.

See also **Chapter 11: Evolution of Health Planning (1920s–1970s); Chapter 12: Evolution of Health Planning (1970s–Present); Chapter 13: Government Financing of Health Care (1940s–Present); Chapter 15: Building an Effective and Sustainable Health Care Workforce (1960s–Present); Chapter 16: Promoting Health Care Quality and Safety (1960s–Present); Chapter 17: Strategies for Health Care Cost Containment (1980s–Present); Chapter 18: Health and Health Care Policy: Ethical Perspectives (1970s–Present).**

NOTES

1. Robert E. Kohler, *Partners in Science: Foundations and Natural Scientists, 1900-1945* (Chicago: University of Chicago Press, 1991); Eli Ginzberg and Anna B. Dutka, *The Financing of Biomedical Research* (Baltimore: Johns Hopkins University Press, 1989).

2. Jane S. Smith, *Patenting the Sun: Polio and the Salk Vaccine* (New York: William Morrow, 1990); John Rowan Wilson, *Margin of Safety* (Garden City, NJ: Doubleday, 1963).

3. John R. Steelman, *The Nation's Medical Research* (Washington, DC: U.S. Government Printing Office, 1947).

4. National Resources Committee, *Research—A National Resource,* 76th Congress, 1st session, House Document No. 122 (Washington, DC: U.S. Government Printing Office, 1939), 73–74.

5. James Phinney Baxter, *Scientists against Time* (Boston: Little, Brown, 1968).

6. Kenneth Macdonald Jones, "The Endless Frontier," *Prologue* 8 (1976): 35–46.

7. Vannevar Bush, *Science—The Endless Frontier* (Washington, DC: Office of Scientific Research and Development, 1945).

8. Robert Cook-Deegan and Michael McGeary, "The Jewel in the Federal Crown? History, Politics, and the National Institutes of Health," in *History and Health Policy in the United States: Putting the Past Back In,* edited by Rosemary A. Stevens, Charles E. Rosenberg, and Lawton R. Burns, 176-201 (New Brunswick, NJ: Rutgers University Press, 2006).

9. Harvey Sapolsky, *Science and the Navy: The History of the Office of Naval Research* (Princeton, NJ: Princeton University Press, 1990).

10. Bush, *Science*; Rufus Miles Jr., *The Department of Health, Education, and Welfare* (New York: Praeger, 1974).

11. Irvin Stewart, *Organizing Scientific Research for War: The Administrative History of the Office of Scientific Research and Development* (Boston: Little, Brown, 1948).

12. Ibid.

13. Steelman, *The Nation's Medical Research.*

14. Lynn Page Snyder, "Passage and Significance of the 1944 Public Health Service Act," *Public Health Reports* 109 (November–December 1994): 721-724.

15. Stephen P. Strickland, *Politics, Science, and Dread Disease: A Short History of United States Medical Research Policy* (Cambridge, MA: Harvard University Press, 1972).

16. Stewart, *Organizing Scientific Research for War*; Richard Mandel, *A Half Century of Peer Review, 1946-1996* (Bethesda, MD: National Institutes of Health, Division of Research Grants, 1996).

17. Daniel M. Fox, "The Politics of the NIH Extramural Program, 1937-1950," *Journal of the History of Medicine and Allied Sciences* 42 (1987): 447-466.

18. James T. Patterson, *The Dread Disease: Cancer and Modern American Culture* (Cambridge, MA: Harvard University Press, 1987); Strickland, *Politics, Science, and Dread Disease*; Nancy Carol Erdey, "The Armor of Patience: The National Cancer Institute and the Development of Medical Research Policy in the United States, 1937-1971," Doctoral dissertation, Case Western University, 1995.

19. Wilson, *Margin of Safety.*

20. Strickland, *Politics, Science, and Dread Disease*; Elizabeth Drew, "The Health Syndicate: Washington's Noble Conspirators," *Atlantic Monthly* (December 1967): 75-82; Judith Robinson, *Noble Conspirator: Florence S. Mahoney and the Rise of the National Institutes of Health* (Washington, DC: Francis Press, 2001).

21. Strickland, *Politics, Science, and Dread Disease.*

22. James Shannon, "The Background of Some Contemporary Problems," paper presented at Conference No. 3 on the Biomedical Sciences, Macy Foundation, 1975; available from NIH History Office. Shannon was director of the NIH from 1955 to 1968, the period of its greatest growth.

23. Harold Varmus, "Proliferation of the National Institutes of Health," *Science* 291 (2001): 1903, 1905.

24. Institute of Medicine, *Responding to Health Needs and Scientific Opportunity: The Organizational Structure of the National Institutes of Health* (Washington, DC: National Academy Press, 1984).

25. Panel on Scientific Boundaries for Review, "Phase 1 Report," (Bethesda, MD: Center for Scientific Review, National Institutes of Health, 2000), http://www.csr.nih.gov/archives/summary012000.htm.

26. Ellie Ehrenfeld, "From the CSR Director's Desk," *Peer Review Notes* (Bethesda, MD: Center for Scientific Review, National Institutes of Health, May 2000).

27. Mary Anne Burke and Stephen A Matlin, eds., *Monitoring Financial Flows for Health Research 2008,* Global Forum for Health Research, 2008.

28. Benjamin G. Druss and Steven C. Marcus, "Growth and Decentralization of the Medical Literature: Implications for Evidence-Based Medicine," *Journal of the Medical Library Association* 93 (October 2005): 499–501.

29. Harold Varmus, "Shattuck Lecture: Biomedical Research Enters the Steady State," *New England Journal of Medicine* 333 (1995): 811–815.

30. Jeff Earle, "Domenici Slams Specter and NIH 'Pigs.'" *The Hill,* March 17, 2004, http://psychrights.org/education/Congress/NIHPigs.htm.

31. Wesley M. Cohen and John P. Walsh, "Public Research, Patents and Implications for Industrial R&D in the Drug, Biotechnology, Semiconductor and Computer Industries," in *Capitalizing on New Needs and New Opportunities: Government-Industry Partnerships in Biotechnology and Information Technologies,* edited by Charles W. Wessner, 223–243 (Washington, DC: National Academy Press, 2002); David C. Mowery et al., *Ivory Tower and Industrial Innovation: University-Industry Technology Transfer before and after the Bayh-Dole Act* (Stanford, CA: Stanford Business Books, 2004).

32. Kira R. Fabrizio, "Absorptive Capacity and Innovation: Evidence from Pharmaceutical and Biotechnology Firms," *Research Policy* 38 (2009): 255–267; Iain Cockburn and Rebecca M. Henderson, "Absorptive Capacity, Coauthoring Behavior, and the Organization of Research in Drug Discovery," *Journal of Industrial Economics* 46 (1998): 157–182.

33. U.S. Bureau of the Census, "Number of Firms, Number of Establishments, Employment, and Annual Payroll by Enterprise Employment Size for the United States, All Industries: 2011. Statistics of U.S. Businesses," December 2013; International Trade Commission, "Pharmaceutical Industry Profile, 2010."

34. Pharmaceutical Research and Manufacturers of America, *2013 Biopharmaceutical Research Industry Profile* (Washington, DC: PhRMA, 2013), http://www.phrma.org/sites/default/files/pdf/PhRMA%20Profile%202013.pdf.

35. Justin Chakma et al., "Asia's Ascent—Global Trends in Biomedical R&D Expenditures," *New England Journal of Medicine* 370 (2014): 3–6.

36. Daniel S. Greenberg, *Science, Money, and Politics: Political Triumph and Ethical Erosion* (Chicago: University of Chicago Press, 2001).

37. Daniel Callahan, *What Price Better Health? Hazards of the Research Imperative* (Berkeley: University of California Press, 2003).

38. David Willman, "Stealth Merger: Drug Companies and Government Medical Research," *Los Angeles Times,* December 7, 2003, A1ff; David Willman, "National Institutes of Health: Public Servant or Private Marketeer?" *Los Angeles Times,* December 22, 2004, A1ff.

39. John Abramson, *Overdo$ed America: The Broken Promise of American Medicine* (New York: HarperCollins, 2004); Marcia Angell, *The Truth about Drug Companies: How They Deceive Us and What to Do about It* (New York: Random House, 2004); Jerome Kassirer, *On the Take: How Big Business Is Corrupting American Medicine* (New York: Oxford University Press, 2004); Jerry Avorn, *Powerful Medicines: Benefits, Risks, and Costs of Prescription Drugs* (New York: Alfred Knopf, 2004); Merrill Goozner, *The $800 Million Pill: The Truth behind the Cost of New Drugs* (Berkeley: University of California Press, 2004).

FURTHER READING

Chakma, Justin, Gordon H. Sun, Jeffrey D. Steinberg, Stephen M. Sammut, and Reshma Jagsi. "Asia's Ascent—Global Trends in Biomedical R&D Expenditures." *New England Journal of Medicine* 370: 3 (2014): 3–6.

Cook-Deegan, Robert, and Michael McGeary. "The Jewel in the Federal Crown? History, Politics, and the National Institutes of Health." In *History & Health Policy in the United States: Putting the Past Back In,* edited by Rosemary A. Stevens, Charles E. Rosenberg, and Lawton R. Burns, 176–201. New Brunswick, NJ: Rutgers University Press, 2006.

Moses, Hamilton, E. Ray Dorsey, David H. M. Matheson, and Samuel O. Thier. "Financial Anatomy of Biomedical Research." *Journal of the American Medical Association* 294 (2005): 1333–1342.

National Research Council and Institute of Medicine. *Enhancing the Vitality of the National Institutes of Health: Organizational Change to Meet New Challenges.* Washington, DC: National Academies Press, 2003.

Strickland, Stephen P. *Politics, Science, and Dread Disease: A Short History of United States Medical Research Policy.* Cambridge, MA: Harvard University Press, 1972.

chapter 15

Building an Effective and Sustainable Health Care Workforce (1960s–Present)

Thomas C. Ricketts

HEALTH CARE IS PRIMARILY A FUNCTION OF people, professionals, and supporting occupations providing care and support to patients. The workforce component of health care is simultaneously its identifying feature as well as a separate component of policymaking that affects the health of the population. We can separate a workforce sector from, say, financing, organization, or research, but all parts of health care delivery, preventive services, policymaking, and research require a trained and willing set of people to make the system work. Who are these people, how are they trained and classified, how are they paid, and how are they distributed according to the needs of the population? The focus here is on the policies that affect the health care workforce and how those policies evolved.

WHAT IS THE HEALTH CARE WORKFORCE?

The composition of the health care workforce is not well understood, as there are two ways to enumerate health care workers. One is by employment, counting people who earn salaries. The other is by profession, where the workers may or may not be salaried; they may be paid as owners or professionals in partnerships or some other income-sharing arrangement. The U.S. Bureau of Labor Statistics (BLS) also counts employed people in health care according to a set of broad categories that describe their workplace. These include the setting of their work:

Hospitals	34%
Nursing and residential care facilities	22%
Offices of physicians	17%
Home health care services	8%
Outpatient care services	4%
Other ambulatory settings	15%

The health care workforce is much more than doctors and nurses. The BLS classifies workers according to a long list of titles, the Standard Occupational Classifications, of which there are almost 850 in total, and 78 of those are classified under health care. The listing, though extensive, is of interest in how it provides a glimpse into the complexity of health care, and it is remarkable because it leaves out many types of health care workers who are integral to health and health care, including public health professionals, counselors, social workers, and behavioral health workers. The U.S. health care workforce is very large, complex, and crosses into many activities of the economy that might not be considered when thinking about health care services.

How Is Workforce Policy Determined, and How Do We Understand It?

Perhaps the best approach to understanding any policy, whether health workforce policy or policy in general, is as a "journalistic" task, that is, one must understand the who, what, where, when, why, and how of an issue to analyze it effectively.[1] John Kingdon described *how* one must focus on the people involved, in this case the special group of health professionals, and the *when*, meaning the time constraints on policymaking.[2] He illustrates the importance of the when by emphasizing the electoral cycle and the coming and going of "windows of opportunity." These are important in health workforce policy in many ways, and it is useful to ask whether we can understand when a window of opportunity opens in health workforce policy.

TABLE 15.1 **Bureau of Labor Statistics Standard Occupational Classifications in Category 29: Health Care Classifications**

Chiropractors	Occupational therapists	Nuclear medicine technologists	Genetic counselors
Dentists, general	Physical therapists	Radiologic technologists	Practitioners and technical workers, other
Oral and maxillofacial surgeons	Radiation therapists	Magnetic resonance imaging technologists	Home health aides
Orthodontists	Recreational therapists	Emergency medical techs and paramedics	Psychiatric aides
Prosthodontists	Respiratory therapists	Dietetic technicians	Nursing assistants
Dentists, all other specialists	Speech-language pathologists	Pharmacy technicians	Orderlies
Dietitians and nutritionists	Exercise physiologists	Psychiatric technicians	Occupational therapy assistants
Optometrists	Therapists, all other	Respiratory therapy technicians	Occupational therapy aides
Pharmacists	Veterinarians	Surgical technologists	Physical therapist assistants
Anesthesiologists	Registered nurses	Veterinary technicians	Physical therapist aides
Family and general practitioners	Nurse anesthetists	Ophthalmic medical technicians	Massage therapists
Internists, general	Nurse midwives	Licensed practical vocational nurses	Dental assistants
Obstetricians and gynecologists	Nurse practitioners	Medical records and HI technicians	Medical assistants
Pediatricians, general	Audiologists	Opticians, dispensing	Medical equipment preparers
Psychiatrists	Diagnosing and treating practitioners, other	Orthotists and prosthetists	Medical transcriptionists
Surgeons	Medical and clinical laboratory technologists	Hearing aid specialists	Pharmacy aides
Physicians and surgeons, all other	Medical and clinical laboratory technicians	Health technicians, all other	Veterinary assistants and lab animal caretakers
Physician assistants	Dental hygienists	Occupational health and safety specialists	Phlebotomists
Podiatrists	Cardiovascular technologists and technicians	Occupational health and safety technicians	Health care support workers, all other
	Diagnostic medical sonographers	Athletic trainers	

Key Groups

Important groups of the *who* in the workforce enjoy a special place in the overall policy world. These people are physicians who are given extraordinary power by the state to diagnose, treat, and control the lives of people. To a lesser extent, dentists, psychologists, and nurses also are allowed to do things to and for people that would otherwise be considered illegal interferences with personal liberties and daily living. Physicians can invade our bodies, determine whether we are sane or fit for work, and change how our bodies are configured. This power is delegated to the professions in return for their promise to act professionally for the benefit of the patient. These special people have a unique place in health policymaking because they are viewed both as experts in what constitutes the best way for them to work as well as dominating the knowledge and skills that make people healthier or that delay or forestall their demise.

Kingdon's *who* that are involved in general policymaking are also relevant to heath workforce policy. He identified elected officials, bureaucrats, the media, and various economic and policy stakeholders along with professionals. Other classes of actors not identified by Kingdon include "policy entrepreneurs," those people who push policy solutions as a career activity. In workforce policy, the dominant stakeholders include those who protect the franchises of medicine, dentistry, nursing, and pharmacy via their control of licensing laws as well as those who control the teaching and training systems that produce the professionals: the deans and leaders of academic health centers and medical, nursing, dental, and pharmacy schools. Another important group that is key to policymaking is Congress. The process that resulted in the Health Professions Educational Assistance Act of 1976 was carefully documented in a book edited by two of the key participants in the process, Lauren

LeRoy and Phil Lee.[3] *Deliberations and Compromise* tracked the legislative process that was dominated by two figures, Representative Paul G. Rogers (D-FL; in office 1955–1979) and Senator Edward M. Kennedy (D-MA; in office 1962–2009). They were viewed as the champions of health workforce policy, and their efforts kept the issue at the forefront of the congressional agenda for many years, including during the debates over the Patient Protection and Affordable Care Act (PPACA) on the part of Kennedy. There have not been obvious replacements for these two, and this represents a real barrier to the future of comprehensive health workforce policymaking.

Multiple Jurisdictions

The *where* of health workforce policy works in several dimensions. The United States has more than fifty separate jurisdictions that effectively control the legal aspects of workforce policy via their control of the licensing or "scope of practice" laws. These fifty-plus jurisdictions, with some additional federal systems like the Department of Veterans Affairs (VA) and the Department of Defense medical offices, offer the opportunity for wide variation. In one sense, that variation is only potential as there is a fairly uniform set of rules and laws that structure workforce policy: doctors are generally regulated in much the same way in Alaska as they are in New York, but important differences exist. In terms of the *where* of health workforce policy, some geographic variations exist, such as the regional concentration of osteopaths. Important national boundary issues, such as the importation or immigration of professionals trained outside the borders of the United States, are geographic elements of policy. One also can ask where workforce policy is made and refer to institutions such as Congress and state legislatures, advisory groups such as the Council on Graduate Medical Education (COGME), various commissions and committees such as the Pew Commission on Higher Education in Health, or professional associations and lobbies of various sorts. Congress has shown interest in shaping the health care workforce by supporting nursing education, adding a graduate medical education payment in Medicare payments, and creating a National Health Service Corps to provide primary care practitioners in underserved areas. State legislatures appropriate funds to build medical, nursing, pharmacy, dental, and other health-related schools in universities and colleges as well as to oversee the scope of practice of health professions. Congress also has given strong advisory powers to councils and committees that suggest changes to policy, as COGME does, and delegates decision-making power that gives external committees strong control over the payments made to professionals. The so-called Relative Value Update Committee, for example, essentially controls Medicare physician payment levels.[4] Because this mix of policy players

overlaps the *who* and *how* part of the analytical structure, it might be useful to divide the role of institutions and those of individuals or groups of individuals. It may be best to put the institutions under the category of *how*, because they are generally studied in terms of how they work. For example, how is workforce policymaking allocated among the various committees of Congress?

The *what* of workforce policy is a central and somewhat awkward question. What exactly is health workforce policy? Is it the skein of laws and regulations that are outlined in Table 15.2, or can we understand it more in the context of society and think more about the traditions of healing and gender, or power and hierarchy? That overlaps with the *why* realm. Why do we have health professionals in the first place, and why do we regulate them the way we do? What is the political economy of health professions? Is the way we treat health professionals under pressure to change? How must we structure our national policies in order to have a supply of effective and efficient health professionals?

The time element of policymaking for health care professionals, the *when*, especially for decisions affecting physicians, has a special quality that makes it different from other policy realms. This is the pipeline for training health care professionals, and it covers a relatively long time span. Because workforce policy is focused on people who have to complete training and

TABLE 15.2 **Physician Specialty Boards in 1960 and Their Founding Year**

Anesthesiology	1941
Colon and Rectal Surgery	1949
Dermatology	1932
Internal Medicine	1936
Neurological Surgery	1940
Obstetrics and Gynecology	1930
Ophthalmology	1917
Orthopedic Surgery	1935
Otolaryngology	1924
Pathology	1936
Pediatrics	1935
Physical Medicine and Rehab	1947
Plastic Surgery	1941
Preventive Medicine	1949
Psychiatry and Neurology	1935
Surgery	1935
Urology	1935

education processes that take substantial time—up to a decade from entry into training until independent practice—a real problem related to the lagging effects of policy decisions exists.

How is the process, and that is linked closely to the institutions that control society, politics, and policy. While there are special considerations in health workforce policymaking, including the need to defer to the professions, most of this policymaking still rests in the hands of the executive and legislative branches of the state and the national governments.

HISTORICAL DEVELOPMENT OF WORKFORCE POLITICS

In the period between 1960 and 1980, the United States was roughly equal to most developed nations in the proportion of economic activity devoted to health care. In 1980, the United States spent approximately $1,000 per capita on health care services, comparable to Switzerland, German, and Canada. By 2010, the nation was spending more than twice the Organisation for Economic Co-operation and Development average. This rapid growth rate was accompanied by an equally rapid expansion of the employed, wage-earning labor force in health care. Interestingly, the increase in the number of physicians, dentists, and other independent health care professionals was roughly equal to the rest of the developed nations. The United States remains squarely in the middle of the developed world distribution when it comes to physicians.

The U.S. health care structure has grown to be the largest in the world, taking up 17 percent of the nation's gross domestic product, consuming $3 trillion per year. The largest portion of that, perhaps 60 percent, goes to the wages for a workforce that "produces" health care: the doctors, nurses, dentists, assistants, therapists, administrators, and hundreds of other workers and health professionals who care for patients, prevent disease, organize that care and prevention, and handle the substantial amounts of data and money that go with this task.[5] That wage-based health care workforce is made up of approximately sixteen million people, 8.5 percent of the total number of employed persons in the United States. This number does not count professionals who are self-employed physicians, dentists, independent nurses, and psychologists. The U.S. health care workforce has grown very rapidly in the recent past, 2.2 percent per year—not as fast as the growth of health care expenditures, but much faster than overall employment growth, which, after the economic slowdown of 2007–2010, is just less than 1 percent per year.[6]

This economic place for health care has not necessarily meant that those who work in the system run the system. Before 1960, that may have been true. Paul Starr has carefully described the growth of the "professional dominance" of medicine, where doctors essentially controlled health care

with the support of legislation and favorable court rulings that strengthened their authority.[7] Organizationally, physicians were able to structure institutions and processes to their advantage as management remained weak and payers did not have the tools to control physician decision making or autonomy. Physicians lived in a "benign environment" where their "turf" was well protected.[8] That was to change starting in the 1960s with the inception of Medicare and Medicaid, programs that opened the federal purse to health care.[9] The rapid expansion of the market for health care attracted many new stakeholders into the system, and the practitioners were to see their influence decline as the overall cost of care rose.

How Did We Get Here? Federal Policies

Until the 1960s, the federal government had not been very involved in the training of practitioners nor their licensing and control—the exceptions being the medical corps in the military, the VA, and the Public Health Service hospitals. These amounted to a relatively small part of the overall volume of health care delivery but were very important in the development of new roles for personnel during wartime. The elevation of nurses to officer rank came soon after World War I (1914–1918), when it became apparent that they were crucial to the organization and performance of military medical care. That role was strengthened in World War II (1939–1945) and in the Korean War (1950–1953) and was anticipated in the 1941 Nurse Training Act, which gave schools of nursing support to increase their enrollments and strengthen their facilities. This was the first real involvement of the federal government in general health workforce policy, but it was not followed up with additional legislation for another twenty years and was viewed more as "emergency" planning for defense than it was as setting new policy.

At the same time, the performance of military medics expanded as they were the front-line users of new clinical and surgical approaches. Their skills and capacities became better appreciated in the Vietnam War (1945–1975) and prompted the development of a new, mid-level profession, the physician assistant. These transitions were more or less organic and reflected the pressure of the need for clinical skills to take care of patients as much as a desire to reform the professions.

In the 1960s, Congress felt it had the opportunity and the power to begin to weigh in on shaping the health care workforce in the United States as it debated the first of several "health professional" or "health manpower" acts. Various stakeholders had forewarned of a potential shortage of physicians, nurses, dentists, and other clinical professions that were emerging as existing schools could not keep up with the rapid postwar growth and the first signs of an aging population. The federal government had begun to invest heavily in higher education with the G.I. Bill and additional support for colleges and universities through loan repayment plans as well as direct support for science and engineering training programs.

Major Legislation

The first of the health workforce legislative packages, the Health Professional Educational Assistance Act of 1963, provided construction money for health professions schools. These funds were tied to increased enrollment requirements and were intended to assist with schools' operating expenses. The law also authorized and appropriated funds for loans and scholarship programs. For the first time, there was direct support to medical schools in general and this established the presence of the federal government in health-related education institutions. The pattern was established for the federal government to take an active role in shaping the workforce, but surprisingly, not overall health workforce policy or planning.

The 1963 legislation was followed by the Nursing Training Act, which provided loan guarantees, faculty development funds, construction funds, and support for additional costs of expansion.[10] This law set the template for future support for training: a shortage was determined to exist, the specific profession(s) was considered a national resource, and the best way to expand numbers was to stimulate the training system by expanding existing and building new schools and lowering the costs of entry into the profession by subsidizing the costs through loans and scholarships. Nearly every subsequent piece of federal health workforce legislation followed this pattern.

However, perhaps the greatest influence for the expansion of the workforce came via the choice to create a social health insurance program for the elderly in the form of Medicare and to set the table for a rapid expansion of subsidies for the care of certain population groups in Medicaid. In 1965, Congress amended the Social Security Act to provide for medical care for the elderly (Medicare) and developed a system to give grants to the states for medical assistance to certain categories of the poor (Medicaid). The legislation passed on a vote of 307–116 in the House and 70–24 in Senate, and President Lyndon B. Johnson (1963–1969) signed it into law on July 30, despite vigorous opposition from the American Medical Association. The linkage between the workforce and the Medicare program was first discussed at a White House Conference on Aging held in 1961.

Following the pattern set by the nursing bill, the 1965 Health Professions Educational Assistance Amendments provided scholarships, loans, and construction aid to schools of medicine, osteopathy, and dentistry. This new law also set the stage for the concept of designated shortage areas that would be targeted for support through loan forgiveness or some other direct aid. The law included a provision that would allow doctors and dentists to have 50 percent of their loans forgiven if they practiced in personnel shortage areas. These shortage areas were not defined a priori; states were allowed to designate them, usually by county, based on provider-to-population guidelines issued by the Department of Health, Education and Welfare (HEW). This set the precedent of designation as a contingency for support, a process that continues to the present.

Following Precedent

In the 1960s, the idea that health care systems could be planned and coordinated caught hold and Congress responded with the Comprehensive Health Planning Act. This was a first step toward planning for health services, personnel, and facilities in federal-state-local partnerships. The planning agencies that emerged in the states that took up the program began to develop targets and goals for practitioner-to-population ratios and to assess local systems for how well they met these targets. In New York, the health planning agency worked within a set of strong state regulations that gave it decision-making power over the establishment of new facilities and some degree of control over staffing targets in those institutions and regions in New York State. Health workforce planning became a part of an overall planning mindset, something that built on more intentional planning that was occurring in other countries and based on notions of regionalization to optimize access. Early contributors to this planning movement were Isidore Falk, Joseph Mountin, Milton Roemer, Leonard Rosenfeld, and Conrad Seipp, all of whom saw the value in using formal policies and law to allocate health care resources based on population need. The idea that physicians, dentists, and nurses could be either assigned or induced to practice in places where they were needed based on regional standards of access to care appropriate to the population became a central tenet of workforce planning.[11]

The federal government recognized the need for an agency to coordinate the various grant and loan programs and in 1967 created the Bureau of Health Manpower within HEW. By this time, the number of professions that were included in federal support and assistance programs grew to include allied health as well as optometry, dentistry, veterinary medicine, osteopathic medicine, pharmacy, and podiatry, creating the awkward acronym of MODVOPP to refer to the professions.

The idea that there were areas in the nation with critical shortages of doctors took hold, and a plan was developed by Senator Warren Magnuson (D-WA; in office 1944–1981) to create some form of organization or structure that would recruit doctors from medical schools and then induce them to go into those underserved places in return for payment of the costs of their medical school. Thus, the National Health Service Corps was created by the Emergency Health

Personnel Act. Enactment of this law had to overcome a thorny legal question of whether the federal government could actually employ practitioners who would be located in communities and treat patients who were not linked to the federal government.[12]

The Comprehensive Health Manpower Training Act of 1971 included all of the so-called MODVOPP professions and their schools but replaced institutional formula grants with capitation grants, thus tying federal support to individuals with the goal of expanding production of health care professionals. Each school would receive a fixed sum of money for each student in return for agreeing to increase its enrollment by a specified percentage. There were no strategic objectives for the increases, that is, there was no central planning entity that set a national goal for the workforce; the schools were asked to respond to the incentives and largely did so. This new legislation, however, included oversight and monitoring authority and there was a sense that this signaled a shift in federal policy from support of independent schools to control of programs.

It was possible at this time, in the mid-1960s, for some key congressional staff to observe that health care workforce policy had settled into a basic framework: federal support is provided to the nation's health professions schools, which agree, as a quid pro quo, to serve national need identified by Congress.[13] This remains the framework, but it is a bit frayed by ideological arguments that push toward private sector solutions for a health care workforce market.

PERSISTENT ISSUES IN HEALTH CARE WORKFORCE POLICY

Growth of the U.S. health care workforce lagged behind employment sectors in the rest of the economy in the 1960s. Professionals were in short supply at the end of that decade, and health care needed to quickly modernize. In the 1960s, the states were the primary policy players in health professions politics. They licensed a range of professionals and controlled the scope of practice of pharmacists, dentists, nurses, and physicians. Some states did not recognize osteopathic medicine as a distinct profession; chiropractic was not universally recognized by the states until 1974, and it was not until 1987 that a court found the American Medical Association (AMA), American College of Surgeons, and American College of Radiologists guilty of antitrust and conspiracy in their efforts to restrain the practice of chiropractic medicine. That kind of struggle over the scope of practice remains to this day. The process of specialization is not unique to medicine; in an economic sense, it is simply the process of progressive division of labor to accomplish tasks more efficiently and can be applied to complex medical work as well as less complex occupational tasks in health care. All of the health professions have undergone significant specialization, but the trend began in medicine and soon spilled over to nursing, dentistry, pharmacy, and the supporting technologies and technical fields that emerged as innovations were adopted in health care.

Progressive Specialization: A Core Feature of the U.S. Health Care Workforce

Before the late 1970s, no one had heard of a *nurse practitioner* or a *physician assistant*. The term *family doctor* was just a general term, and the term *primary care* was hardly to be found in the literature. Many professions and labor categories related to now-familiar technology were yet to be imagined. There existed recognized medical and surgical specialties, and one—general practice—was considered "moribund."[14] In 1960, as seen in Table 15.2, there were seventeen specialty boards that awarded certification in their focused field of medicine but with very few subspecialty classifications.

In the 1960s, a movement began to create even more focused medical specialty qualifications. Only a few more full-specialty boards were created after the 1960s (allergy and immunology, 1971; nuclear medicine, 1971; thoracic surgery, 1971; emergency medicine, 1979; family medicine, 1969; and medical genetics, 1991). Yet these twenty-four boards began to recognize subspecialties at an ever-increasing rate; there now exist 145 American Board of Medical Specialties classifications. The American Board of Osteopathic Medicine also recognizes specialties and subspecialties, and there are a range of other certifications for specific procedures or practice focus such as laparoscopic surgery and what might be termed *alternative medical work,* including certifications by the American Board of Integrative and Holistic Medicine. There is an alternative to the American Board of Medical Specialties (ABMS) and the Osteopathic board in the American Board of Physician Specialties which offers certification in sixteen specialties that mirror the core specialties under the ABMS.

The splitting of medicine into so many discrete specialties has shifted the balance of power in the house of medicine. In the 1950s and 1960s, the AMA could count on a strong membership base to bring the voice of medicine to national policy debates, and strong individual state medical associations could do the same in the states; by the 1990s, that single voice was losing its focus as the politics of medical care payment began to recognize differences between groups of doctors. The specialty groups began to find their interests were best served by separate representation. During the national debate over President William J. Clinton's (1993–2001) health reform from 1990 to 1993, the splintering effect became obvious, as there was strong disagreement with the AMA, and the new specialty groups, such the American Academy of Family Physicians, began to take a more progressive stance toward reform while groups representing orthopedic surgery and radiology resisted change. More important, for the profession of medicine, other stakeholders, primarily insurance companies, were more powerful in the debate as organized medicine was losing its power.[15,16]

This pattern of progressive specialization[17] represented a tendency to make medical care more efficient in a production sense as practitioners who focus their work improve the quality of care they provide and become more proficient, able to do more in less time. However, there is an alternative explanation for this tendency that has to do with the way doctors are paid and the degree to which they can control that process. Characteristics that promote the dominance of the professions are their control over the intellectual content of their work, their special knowledge, and their ability to determine what is a legitimate, and therefore reimbursable, activity. This knowledge is a protected realm that allows doctors to demarcate their professional roles and supports their need for autonomous control over other professions as well as patients.

Dentistry

While individual dentists may have focused their work on selected procedures and patients, dentistry did not formally develop specialty designations until 1976, when dental public health was recognized. This was followed by endodontics in 1983 and seven other specialty boards afterward. Each of these specialties has its own professional association and these, in turn, liaise with the American Dental Association. The dental profession has maintained its professional dominance in the field of oral health care by controlling the application of innovations and technology. Dentists have resisted the expansion of the scope of practice of dental hygienists and dental assistants, allowing them to do only a limited range of tasks although they are often capable of providing a much larger range of services than permitted.[18]

Nursing

Nursing did not follow a path toward formal specialization but began to splinter in its own way along more occupational lines. In 1960, like today, nursing represented the largest single group of health care workers, with about 500,000 registered nurses and half as many vocational or practical nurses. Nursing had emerged as a gender-linked profession that saw its role as separate from a curing activity, and instead more of a caring activity with a service and occupational principle. Nurses were professional in that they had a special code of ethics, but their work was seen as supportive and separate, a job. The ideas of Florence Nightingale, that nurses should be engaged in a broadly applicable reparative process, did not underpin a strong professional role: rather nurses were given a *vocation,* a term rejected by Nightingale.[19] The role of nurses was largely shaped by their position in hospitals where their work was organized along an industrial model that viewed them as production-linked employees paid on a wage basis.[20]

Nursing began its search for a special professional identity late in the twentieth century when the construction of a theory of nursing became an important task in schools of nursing, which began to view nursing as an academic health profession rather than an occupational role. By 2010, there were almost two million nurses, and new graduate nurses were being trained by faculty more often with PhDs than by physicians or senior experienced nurses who shared duty on hospital wards and who saw their work as practical rather than theory-based.

The search for a more professional place in the field of health care was given a very strong push with the release of the "Future of Nursing" report in 2011 from the Institute of Medicine.[21] This document called for a general upgrading of the scope of practice for nurses, allowing to them to work to the full extent of their training—a form of practice that was not subservient or inferior to the work of physicians.[21] The process of professionalization was one of acceptance of the complexity of nursing that deserved equal status with other healing professions. A strong symbol of that improvement of status and power was the emergence of the Doctor of Nursing Practice degree (DNP) that was foreseen as the future standard for preparation of nurses, beyond the Bachelor of Science in Nursing or the various master's specializations and clearly separate from the two-year or vocationally trained nurse, the Associate of Arts in Nursing or the Licensed Practical Nurse. That splitting of the profession according to training was accompanied by conflicts and concerns that "up-skilling" and "degree creep" were antithetical to the need to reduce costs and make care more efficient. One report found:

> Professionals and the academy have yet to state clearly the problems for which the new professional doctorates are the solution. . . . Leaders of graduate education need to find effective ways to include industry in the discussion about the role and nature of these new degree.[22]

Nevertheless, the clinical doctorate is viewed by the individual professions, including physical therapy, pharmacy (which achieved this in the PharmD), and nursing, as the new norm and the most appropriate level of training for clinical practice.

Primary Care: Symbol or Solution?

Primary care has emerged as a key element in health care delivery. As such, it is not necessarily a profession or a discipline, but something a bit more. The special position of primary care was described in 1978 by an international conference organized by the World Health Organization in the form of the "Declaration of Alma-Ata":

> Primary health care is essential health care based on practical, scientifically sound and socially acceptable

methods and technology made universally accessible to individuals and families in the community through their full participation and at a cost that the community and country can afford to maintain at every stage of their development in the spirit of self-reliance and self-determination. It forms an integral part both of the country's health system, of which it is the central function and main focus, and of the overall social and economic development of the community. It is the first level of contact of individuals, the family and community with the national health system bringing health care as close as possible to where people live and work, and constitutes the first element of a continuing health care process.[23]

Thirty years later, a follow-up conference attempted to revive the spirit of that original declaration. Primary care is as much a symbol to promote social justice, as the Alma-Ata declaration states, as it is a sector of the health care workforce. In the United States, the debate over primary care became one not of how to best allocate the benefits of society justly, but of how to structure and support health care workforce policymaking. In the United States, primary care is a contested concept and several disciplines and professions struggle to control the symbolic meaning of it.

Primary care is a term anyone involved in the medical or health care fields would presently recognize and likely understand in a general sense or have a clear opinion about its meaning. Since the mid-1960s, the term has gained worldwide usage in technical, scientific, and lay publications variously to describe practitioners, symptoms, diagnoses, organizations, and an array of services. From that time, the term *primary care* has been at the center of controversy over the best way to organize the delivery of medical care in the United States. Its definition has held important political and practical consequences for the training of physicians and mid-level practitioners. Yet primary care has meant mainly a pathway to reforming medicine, making it more rational and more equitable. However, once the concept of primary care came to refer to every category of medical specialty practice where first contact care was provided, it began to lose its distinctive meaning. Despite this erosion of the impact of the concept, primary care remains an important organizing model for practitioners and scholars attempting to change and rationalize the U.S. health care system from a pluralistic collection of potentially competing interests and individuals to a more coordinated, more equitable national system.

Primary care was used in the Report of the National Advisory Commission on Health Manpower as a signifier for basic medical care, and the concept was rapidly expanded to reform the U.S. health care system at the local level. The funding of the first Office of Economic Opportunity Neighborhood Health Centers in 1964 and the approval of the new specialty of family medicine in 1969 predate general use of the term itself by a few years and

organized attempts at a definition of primary care by a decade. The relationship of these two developments to what is now considered primary care is taken for granted; indeed, the ideals embodied in those reforms (accessibility of services, comprehensiveness of care, coordination of care, accountability to the patient) have become parts of subsequent definitions of primary care. Those same two realignments in the system also contain the seeds of a conceptual struggle within primary care itself: whether the responsibility for coordination and accountability for primary care should be based on a professional model, such as family practice, or on content similar to the medical training model embodied in general pediatrics or general medicine, or on an organizational model such as the neighborhood or community health center. Many policymakers thought that the family practice model was implicit in the legislation creating the new programs, while others looked to reform through other organizations.

The interpretation of primary care as a professional versus an organizational phenomenon continues as physicians, primarily family physicians, compete with other professions and disciplines for primacy and ownership of the term. Primary care became an issue to the medical profession because it represented, on the conceptual level, a central organizing paradigm for family medicine. At the same time, other specialties and professions made claim to a shared responsibility for delivering primary care. In the 1970s, the emergence of family medicine as a viable new specialty with strong political support that translated into appropriations and grants threatened the older specialties; they responded by presenting themselves as the preferred providers of primary care. Claims were made that the primary care needs of the nation were being met by a hidden system of primary care being provided by specialists.[24] A debate emerged over the role of specialists in primary care and the degree to which the traditional specialties should be supported for their contribution to primary care. A major national study of the content of care of specialties, including primary care, was launched with the implicit goal of documenting that hidden system; this was the so-called Mendenhall Studies by RAND. The conflict over ownership of primary care between family practice and the more traditional medical specialties and the new professions of nurse practitioner (NP) and physician assistant (PA) has not been resolved, especially in academic medical centers; however, a political compromise was reached with regard to federal support of residency training programs in primary care, with pediatrics and general internal medicine departments receiving some direct support for primary care residency training and NP and PA programs fitting in under a general rubric of support to primary care. This persists into the present, as primary care is the binding element in most federal workforce policy.

The "New Health Practitioners"

The origins of the NP can be traced back to efforts to solve the problem of access to primary care services in remote, rural, and otherwise underserved areas. PAs were originally conceived as a way to make use of the skills acquired by military corps and to provide a mechanism for handling the less demanding chores that fell on medical residents. Loretta Ford and Henry Silver are credited with generating the idea of nurse practitioners at the University of Colorado in 1966, but similar ideas sprung up in other places at around the same time.[25]

The idea caught on quickly, and by 1973, there were 65 NP training programs; by 2009, that number had risen to 323. The number of nurse practitioners in the United States is difficult to determine as there are multiple descriptors, classifications, and licensing requirements. The total ranges from 180,233 (2011), according to the *American Journal of Nurse Practitioners* Pearson Report and based on license and training data, to 105,780 (2010), according to the Bureau of Labor Statistics, and 106,073 according to the Agency for Health Care Research and Quality.[26] The last estimate breaks down the number by primary and non-primary care practice and estimates that 52 percent of NPs are in primary care. In contrast, of 70,383 PAs, 43 percent are considered in primary care. The inventories of PAs are much more reliable as there is a common qualification and an annual inventory is compiled by the PA Association. Nurse practitioners, on the other hand, are represented by a number of professional associations and have not generated a common taxonomy for the development of an inventory.

Nurse practitioners actually represent a variety of advanced practice nursing (APN) roles and designations, including clinical nurse specialist, specialist practitioner, nurse therapist, and nurse consultant. Their appearance was preceded by the nurse midwife, the nurse anesthetist, and the psychiatric nurse, but those professional roles were seen as a focused practice of nursing and they took on specific roles that had historical acceptance (nurse midwives) or were necessary in rural areas (nurse anesthetists). The new APNs were prepared for a much broader field of practice; at least that was the intention. In general, they were nurses with additional training in direct patient care provided either in certificate programs but more often in a curriculum that awarded a master's degree. PAs, on the other hand, developed a fairly consistent curriculum, not tied to a degree, but a certification that usually involved two years of mostly clinical training.

State laws vary widely in the degree to which NPs and PAs are allowed to practice.[27] Practice acts are controlled by state legislatures, and all states recognize NPs, nurse midwives, and PAs in some form or another; they are allowed to practice very similarly to physicians or they are restricted in their scope of work. States may limit the ability of practitioners to prescribe drugs, require them to adhere to a specific set of protocols, or require them to work under direct supervision of a physician.

The initial challenge for NPs and PAs was to prove they were able to provide care equal in quality and efficacy to that of physicians. This was done relatively early in their existence with a study supported by the U.S. Office of Technology Assessment and reinforced by multiple, subsequent well-designed studies.[28,29,30] In 1977, the Rural Health Clinic Act extended Medicare and Medicaid coverage to NPs in rural clinics, and later amendments added PAs. They were first paid at rates lower than physicians, but this was modified to become equal reimbursement for certain office visits. Nevertheless, they were not immediately accepted in many communities when they were offered as substitutes for primary care physicians who did not choose to practice there.[31] Despite the strong evidence of their efficacy and strong demand for their services, some physicians continue to resist accepting NPs as equals. Nevertheless, NPs and PAs are now an integral, almost indispensable professional classification in health care delivery.[32,33]

Tort Reform and the Supply of Physicians

In the 1970s, another important element in the workforce policy field emerged with vigor: the issue of malpractice law and its effects on the workforce; although almost all of the controversy has to do with physicians. In 1975, in the face of what were seen as soaring medical malpractice insurance premiums and the flight of commercial insurers from California, which threatened to leave its health care providers bereft of coverage, the state legislature passed the landmark Medical Injury Claims Reduction Act calling for a variety of tort reforms and limitations on the malpractice awards a plaintiff can receive. This law set the tone for a recurring policy debate over whether the U.S. tort system was the best way to punish erring physicians and serve as a guarantor of high-quality medical care; it also raised the issue of whether misguided malpractice laws affected the supply of physicians.[34] From the 1970s until today, there has been constant pressure on Congress and state legislatures to enact tort reform, which usually meant capping punitive damages, changing the rules of evidence, and sometimes, removing the issue from the courts.

By 2010, the debates began to mature, with a much broader choice of policy options being offered as states, selected institutions, and professional groups sought to break the impasse. Although no national legislation has reformed the system, many states have implemented changes, but those can hardly be considered reform.[35,36,37] The list of currently discussed alternatives includes caps on noneconomic damages, pretrial screening panels, certificate of merit requirements, attorney-fee limits, joint-and-several liability rule reform, collateral source rule reform, periodic payment, and statutes of limitation/repose, as well as six more innovative, less tested reforms: schedules of noneconomic damages, health courts, disclosure-and-offer programs, safe harbors for adherence to evidence-based clinical practice guidelines, subsidized reinsurance that is made conditional upon meeting particular patient safety goals, and enterprise medical liability.[38] These live alongside the earlier proposals that focus on reducing the amount of liability.

STRATEGIES FOR SHAPING THE HEALTH CARE WORKFORCE

The 1976 Health Professions Educational Assistance Act required medical schools to have 50 percent of their graduates entering primary residencies by 1980. This was the first explicit limiting criterion set on health professions schools and it was met by a storm of controversy as the definitions of primary care became muddied—the notion that the target was for overall production, with some schools specializing in primary care and others ignoring it altogether.

The same law continued capitation payments but no longer required enrollment increases as a condition for funding; it also added mandates, as a condition for receiving federal financial support, that recipient schools reserve positions in their classes for U.S. students studying at foreign medical schools. The latter provision was heatedly opposed by U.S. medical schools as an unwarranted infringement on their right to determine admissions. Northwestern, Indiana, and Yale universities announced that they would not comply, even if it meant loss of federal funding. The provision was subsequently dropped.

Foreign medical graduates became an important point of controversy as their number began to grow rapidly in the 1970s and rose in importance after the implementation in 1984 of the Graduate Medical Exam support via the Medicare program. U.S. medical schools were given incentives to expand in the 1970s, and there was a slight uptick in the number of schools that opened in the 1970s and 1980s; the overall proportion of International Medical Graduates (IMGs) in the United States was headed toward 25 percent, as the number of postgraduate residencies exceeded the number of graduating medical students by one-fourth. The role and place of IMGs in the U.S. health care system was now firmly established and subject not only to workforce policy but also to immigration policy. The entry into practice of IMGs was controlled by quotas and targets, and the medical establishment became a part of the debate over who and how many people should be allowed to enter the United States.

In 1976, over the strenuous opposition of the hospital industry, Congress tightened immigration rules by amending the Immigration and Nationality Act to restrict the entry of alien physicians into the United States. The hospitals viewed residents as a form of "cheap labor," and there was growing concern that the Medicare GME funds were not accounted for.[39] The legislation imposed stringent constraints on the licensure of international medical graduates, including the requirement of passage of the VISA and/or FLEX exam, declaring that "there is no longer an insufficient number of physicians and surgeons in the United States" and that "there is no further need for affording preference to alien physicians and surgeons in admission to the United States."[39] This discovery of a balance in the supply of practitioners was not apparent to all.

Grasping at the Future: The Uncertain Science of Projections

Much of the policy discussion around the health workforce has been stimulated by some form of prediction that there will be too many or too few of any given health professional group. The future of nursing in the twenty-first century was seen to be threatened by a severe shortage of nurses and the people who can teach nurses.[40] The fear of shortages and surpluses has cycled through the history of projections of the physician supply. The first truly large-scale effort to estimate the need for physicians and match that to supply was completed by the Graduate Medical Education National Advisory Committee (GMENAC), which in 1981 issued a prediction of an impending serious oversupply of physicians.[41] The work done by the GMENAC, over the course of four years, included an attempt to consider the productivity of NPs and PAs and other health professionals and how that might change when they considered overall supply; that inclusion has rarely appeared in subsequent efforts to determine how many physicians the nation needs.[42]

The GMENAC modeling attempted to unpack the need and demand for health care services, then relate them to the productivity of physicians, NPs, and PAs. This mix of demand, and the need the committee termed "requirements," was based on extrapolations of population clinical needs and the capacity of practitioners to meet those needs. The projections for the GMENAC were performed under the auspices of its Modeling Panel and were reported as part of the multiple volumes issued by the GMENAC.[43,44] Much of this work was accomplished by federal staff in the Division of Manpower Analysis in the Bureau of Health Manpower, assisted by staff from the National Center for Health Services Research. Multiple external contracts were let to support the work, including one to "computerize the physician requirements model" to permit GMENAC to examine manpower implications under various assumptions."[45] The work of the GMENAC can still be viewed as a template for the conduct of any projection work as subsequent efforts have not been able to match the detailed and comprehensive approach of that effort. A very important characteristic of the GMENAC work was the careful documentation of the assumptions that went into the projections and modeling, as well as a comprehensive summary of the process. This documentation of assumptions should be the hallmark of any projections and modeling work undertaken by the federal government.

Graduate Medical Education: An Issue for the Future?

Doctors are acutely aware of the long training process that allows them to practice, but much of the public is unaware that the pathway includes postgraduate residencies that often last longer than the four years spent in medical school. By the 1970s, the proliferation of specialties and the emphasis on advanced training to master new technologies and knowledge made graduate medical education (GME) a requisite rather than an option for practice. By 2012, there had been a rapid expansion in medical school enrollment without a concurrent plan to expand graduate medical education positions. However, policy toward GME is very mixed given the apparent gap between the number of graduates coming out of medical schools and the places available for them in approved residencies. Policy proposals range from those that cut GME funding (e.g., Deficit Reduction Commission recommendations) or increase GME funding (e.g., the Resident Physician Shortage Reduction Act of 2013, also known as the Nelson, Shumer, Reid bill). Debates over how best to support GME have become contentious; numerous organizations, including the Macy Foundation, the American College of Physicians, the American Academy of Family Physicians, the American Medical Association, and the Association of American Medical Colleges, have been assembling data and publishing evidence to support their positions on how the nation should change GME and who should pay for it. Numerous papers have recently been issued calling for increased accountability of GME dollars with better alignment between funding of GME positions and the nation's health workforce needs.[46,47,48]

GME has become a very complicated problem as federal support for residency training is tied to the Medicare program and, in turn, linked to the per patient payments for hospital care. This mixes patient care and training, and it bases support on the intensity of care, with more complex, specialty-based care getting proportionately more linked GME funds. In addition, the payments go only to hospitals that host the care. The original idea was that there was a cost to training doctors that reduced the productivity of a hospital. This was originally considered an indirect and relatively difficult-to-calculate amount. The Tax Equity and Fiscal Responsibility Act of 1982 (TEFRA) budget reconciliation legislation established indirect payments to make up for the reduction in productivity. The TEFRA was followed in 1987 with support to hospitals for the "direct" costs of training

residents—essentially, the costs of their stipends. Later amendments created caps on the numbers of residents who could be included in the calculation of the Indirect Medical Education and Direct Medical Education formulae—these are the two streams of payment that go to teaching hospitals, the first to pay for the salaries of residents in training and the latter to pay for the forgone productivity of the hospitals due to the need to supervise and train residents. This cap has become contentious as it essentially throttles the pipeline of physician supply in the United States and accounts for more than $12 billion in costs to Medicare. In 1986, COGME was authorized by Congress as a policy-recommending body to help iron out conflicts the in the prioritization of funding for GME in selected specialties. COGME gradually shifted its emphasis to promoting primary care and has become more of a stakeholder on that side of disputes than an objective deliberative group.

Relying on less rigorous projections of an oversupply, in 1995, the Pew Health Professions Commission called for the closing of 20 percent of the nation's medical schools by the year 2005 and a cutback of 25 percent in training slots for physicians, registered nurses, and pharmacists to reduce a projected surplus of such personnel and reducing Medicare GME allowances to hospitals to 110 percent of U.S. graduates. The AMA, the American Nurses Association, and the Association of American Medical Colleges (AAMC) described the projections as flawed and the recommendations overblown. A 1996 Institute of Medicine report, "The Nation's Physician Workforce: Options for Balancing Supply and Requirements," called for a freeze in the number of U.S. medical schools as well as their class size, and a reduction in the number of residency slots by limiting access to graduate medical education for international medical graduates and to more closely match the number of residency positions to the level of graduates of U.S. medical schools.

Over the next decade, the surplus disappeared, and the Association of American Medical Colleges issued a warning in 2006 that seeing a doctor in the future would be very difficult if the nation did not expand medical enrollments by 30 percent, because there would be a gap between the number of doctors needed and the number in practice.[49] None of these predictions came true, as there was a very rapid expansion of nursing education and more trained nurses went back into practice. For the doctor supply, the number of medical and osteopathic graduates will exceed the 30 percent the AAMC called for, as there was an explosion of new medical schools and most existing schools expanded their class size; the next big challenge will be where to train them after they graduate from medical school.

That projections of the future supply of physicians and the need or demand for them are controversial should come as no surprise; any projection will inevitably be ambushed by what was unknown when it was constructed.

The PPACA Health Workforce Commission and Its Abandonment

The modern history of the struggle to create a "sustainable health care workforce" can be traced back to the "Report of the National Advisory Commission on Health Manpower," issued in November 1967. This was the first such national commission created by the federal government (in this case by presidential appointment) to provide policy direction for the entire U.S. health care workforce. The report saw very rapid increases in medical care costs, "rising at twice the rate of overall prices," and a coming severe shortage of doctors, nurses, dentists, and other health professionals that amounted to a "crisis":

> There *is* a crisis in American health care . . . the contradiction of increasing employment of health manpower and decreasing personal attention of patients. *The crisis, however, is not simply one of numbers.* It is true that substantially increased numbers of health manpower will be needed over time. But if additional personnel are employed in the present manner and within the present patterns and systems of care, they will not avert, or even perhaps alleviate the crisis. *Unless we improve the system* through which health care is provided, care will continue to become less satisfactory, even though there are massive increases in cost and in numbers of health personnel.

Several characteristics of that commission were and remain unique. It was a national group that included a very broad spectrum of stakeholders. It was chaired by the head of the Cummins Engine Company but included experts in health care delivery and training, as well as employers and labor representatives. It also was charged with anticipating the nation's needs for the entire health care workforce, not just one profession, and it was structured to include panels focusing on consumers, education, supply, federal use of health manpower, foreign medical graduates, hospital care, new technologies, and the organization of health services.

The National Advisory Commission on Health Manpower was the last time such a group was given national prominence until the Patient Protection and Affordable Care Act (PPACA) created a National Health Care Workforce Commission. The commission was given a broad charge to "serve(s) as a national resource for Congress, the President, States and localities" and to coordinate the work of federal agencies, develop and commission evaluations of programs and policies, and "encourage innovations to address population needs, changes in technology, and other environmental factors." Unfortunately, that commission was never able to meet because it was caught up in the partisan fight over President Barack Obama's (2009–) health care plan, dubbed "Obamacare." Republicans, who had gained control of the House of Representatives after the midterm elections of 2012, set an agenda that was based on resistance to full implementation of the PPACA, vowing to, if not repeal the law, not support any element that required further funding. This specific strategy of resistance was largely symbolic and tied to an attempt to negate the signature legislative achievement of the administration—health reform. The $3 million appropriation that the commission required, a very small amount in the context of the federal budget, was denied by the House, even as a special "anomaly" to Continuing Resolutions passed to keep the federal government at work. Without an appropriation, the commission was, under law, unable to meet.

SOURCES: James W. Begun and Ronald C. Lippincott, *Strategic Adaptation in the Health Professions* (San Francisco: Jossey-Bass, 1993); Uwe E. Reinhardt, "U.S. Health Care Stands Adam Smith on His Head," *BMJ* 335: 7628 (2007): 1020.

The surprising thing is that they would be criticized for not being accurate, because their purpose has almost always been to change anticipated trends. For example, the GMENAC projection of a surplus was used to change policy, thus changing the trends that would then lead to a shortage. The more recent AAMC forecasts have similarly prompted the expansion and opening of medical schools and put strong pressure on the debate over how to support graduate medical education.[50]

Economists came early to the task of determining need and supply of nurses, dentists, and doctors.[51,52] Labor economics importantly contributed to the discussion of the emergence of new health professionals, and the measures of efficiency and productivity in reference to their contributions helped make the case for their acceptance and supported the notion that we could calculate accurate descriptions of the costs and benefits of medical professions.

The process of examining supply compared to need for practitioners, especially physicians, became a central task for analysis, and a series of projections intended to influence policy were developed. Theses were variously based on benchmarks,[53] HMO staffing patterns,[54] stock and flow and existing utilization,[55] or combinations of these methods in the GMENAC model that had predicted oversupply; federal consensus models that had hedged toward shortages[56]; and macro-trend analysis[57] combined with demand assumptions of the AAMC estimates of severe future shortages. This kind of work has been described as less than useful, because the projections turned out to be wrong, either because we do not really know how many physicians there are[58] or because we do not really understand the relationship between physician supply and health outcomes.[59] Projections or models have to be adaptable to change and sensitive to policy questions that arise in the short term.[60]

HEALTH CARE WORKFORCE POLICY AFTER THE PPACA

By the late 1980s, the policy structures and patterns of policymaking for the health workforce had settled into a distinct policy field. The federal government had focused its workforce activities in the Health Resources and Services Administration and given some limited coordinating powers to that agency. That work was formally coordinated by the 1998 Health Professions Education Partnerships Act, which reauthorized and consolidated forty-four federal health professions programs, such as AHECs, the National Health Service Corps, primary care training support and others, into a Primary Care Cluster. The law established an Advisory Committee on Training in Primary Care and Dentistry that was supposed to provide policy guidance for this coordination and do so across professions. Nursing, however, continued to have a separate identity in the HRSA, and projects and activities within HRSA and other parts of the Department of Health and Human Services, such as the National Institute for Nursing Research, tended to identify as nursing rather than primary care.

The PPACA, passed in 2010, included what was essentially an updated reauthorization of the existing health professions programs but added some new wrinkles, including the Teaching Health Centers provision that supported GME in Federally Qualified Health Centers, a new center for health workforce data analysis capacity, and a National Health Care Workforce Commission. That last provision represented an effort, long in gestation, to generate some form of policy advisory group that might take on the challenges that a rapidly specializing workforce might create when the system needs much more coordination and cooperation.

The current trend is toward comprehensive consolidation in the health care delivery system. Today, health care is not delivered by independent community-based hospitals but through horizontally and vertically integrated systems of care that attempt to generate efficiencies as well as quality improvements through coordination. The effects on the workforce are being felt as new roles and work classifications emerge. The Accountable Care Organizations and Patient Centered Medical Homes emerging as a result of the PPACA or as fulfillment of long trends toward consolidation are asking for patient navigators, transition nurses, and extensivists who coordinate care across settings and among specialties, not to mention the institutional role of hospitalists and

How the training and educational support of the health care workforce is executed is a key and continuous concern of policymakers. In this laboratory, a group of medical students undergo a series of tests as part of their education.

SOURCE: Fotokosticc/iStockphoto.

nocturnalists who are specializing their work to meet the demands of the workflow. Part of this effort is generating new pressure to combine a public health or population approach with curative care, a long-standing goal that has resisted resolution.[61]

One anticipated effect of the passage of the PPACA is an increase in demand for services as more people gain insurance coverage. This is expected by some to generate a growing gap between the ability of the system to provide care and the supply of professionals who can see patients when they ask for care.[62] Even the existence of this gap is hotly debated and drags to the forefront conflicts among "new health professionals," primary care physicians, and specialists.[63,64]

Despite the central role of the workforce in the overall effectiveness of health care delivery, the topic still finds itself relegated to the second tier of policy concerns. Costs and financing clearly occupy the attention and actions of policymakers and institutional leaders, while quality, safety, and outcomes are front and center in the minds of professionals and practitioners and the policy networks that support them. There are important and salient discussions taking place over who is to be trained, and how, in order to make health care more efficient and effective, but these discussions continue to be uncoordinated and without a real set of policy structures to which they can be directed.

See also **Chapter 11: Evolution of Health Planning (1920s–1970s); Chapter 12: Evolution of Health Planning (1970s–Present); Chapter 13: Government Financing of Health Care (1940s–Present); Chapter 14:**

AHECs as Common Ground for Health Professions and the Planning Impulse

An innovative program that combined ideas of regionalization by connecting health professions schools to more distant communities came in the form of the Area Health Education Centers (AHEC) program, also a product of the Comprehensive Health Manpower Training Act (1971). The AHEC program, which is still authorized and funded, but under threat of complete defunding from recent administrations, is a unique example of both the desire to plan for the health workforce and recognition that market forces are more likely to affect the supply of practitioners at the local level. AHECs conceptually emerged from a report of the Carnegie Commission on Higher Education, issued in fall 1970, titled "Higher Education and the Nation's Health." The report called for closer cooperation between medical schools and communities and suggested the creation of Area Health Education Centers. President Richard M. Nixon (1969–1974) included a description of these proposed centers in a message to Congress in 1971, and following the passage of the Comprehensive Health Manpower Training Act of 1971, the AHEC program was established in 1972 in the Bureau of Health Manpower Education. AHECs were not mentioned by name in the act but were clearly part of the considerations leading up to its passage. The bureau, acting on the authorization in the act to support projects for training programs to improve the distribution of health personnel by area of specialty, issued a call for interest and subsequently a request for proposals, which was addressed to twenty-seven potential program sponsors. By fall 1972, eleven university health science centers were selected, and contracts were developed for five years with the universities. This group became known as the first generation of AHECs.

The Generations of AHEC

The first-generation AHECs set up regional centers to link the more centralized health professions schools with rural communities. They were to act as locations for continuing education and outreach programs to recruit students into the various schools. The second generation of AHECs was authorized by the Health Professions Educational Assistance Act of 1976, which formally named and defined an AHEC as "a cooperative program of one or more medical or osteopathic schools and one or more nonprofit private or public health education centers." The law also allowed the extension of funding for the original eleven AHECs for two years. Four additional AHECs were funded in 1977 under substantially modified criteria for eligibility. In 1979, three planning contracts were awarded to the University of California, San Francisco for a statewide program in collaboration with seven other medical schools; the University of Kansas School of Medicine; and Eastern Virginia Medical Authority. Between 1978 and 1981, the national program continued, but some states reported difficulty in meeting the requirements of their contracts. In 1978, federal funding for the Texas program was withdrawn.

In 1981, the Omnibus Reconciliation Act reauthorized the AHEC program. Policy changes in the newly created Health Resources and Services Administration (HRSA), which called for greater HRSA involvement in the program operation, shaped the third generation of AHECs. Additional special initiative projects available to AHECs were included in the Public Health Service Act and the Health Professions Training Assistance Act of 1985. The AHEC program was reauthorized by the 1988 Health Professions Reauthorization Act, which established Health Education Training Centers that focused on specific populations. The 1992 Health Professions Educations Extension Amendments created model or state-supported AHECs. Through these generations of AHECs and multiple reauthorizations, the legislation has been consistent in its emphasis on linking academic centers with communities, focusing on primary and preventive care, improving access, and reducing disparities.

The Health Professions Education Partnerships Act of 1998 reauthorized the AHEC program; it was renewed by Congress through 2010 when it was again authorized as part of the Patient Protection and Affordable Care Act (PPACA), this time for a finite five-year period. Although the Obama administration, as earlier administrations had done, recommended elimination of the appropriations for AHEC and related "pipeline" programs, it has managed to live on by being reinstated in continuing resolutions that have marked the "new normal" for funding the federal government in recent years.

Coordination of the Health Care Workforce

The AHEC program is worth emphasizing because it is the single national program that is charged with coordinating the various health professions into programs and projects, and it is charged with doing so on a regional basis. The original legislation called for the AHECs to engage in health planning activities and data gathering to support planning, but that has not been the case. The program's 1998 goals ("To enhance access to quality health care, particularly primary and preventive care, by improving the supply and distribution of health care professionals through community/academic partnerships") were modified and appended by the PPACA to include "develop and implement strategies to foster and provide community-based training and education to individuals seeking careers in health professions within underserved areas . . . in collaboration with other Federal and State health care workforce development programs, the State workforce agency, and local workforce investment boards, and in health care safety net sites" and "conduct and participate in interdisciplinary training that involves physicians, physician assistants, nurse practitioners, nurse midwives, dentists, psychologists, pharmacists, optometrists, community health workers, public and allied health professionals, or other health professionals, as practicable." These goals are the sole federal guidance for any real coordination of the health care workforce across professions.

Unfortunately, the AHECs themselves, with a few exceptions, are not prepared to influence the health professions schools, and in most states they function as "special projects" offices that support and conduct so-called pipeline programs that recruit minorities to health professions and support some programs that recruit and retain professionals in rural and underserved areas. The latter activity in itself overlaps with other workforce support programs that are, in turn, implemented at the state level by federally funded technical assistance programs via another branch of the Health Resources and Services Administration that oversees almost all workforce-related activities in the national government.

Biomedical Research Policy and Innovation (1940s–Present); Chapter 16: Promoting Health Care Quality and Safety (1960s–Present); Chapter 17: Strategies for

Health Care Cost Containment (1980s–Present); Chapter 18: Health and Health Care Policy: Ethical Perspectives (1970s–Present).

NOTES

1. Ricketts T.C. "Public Health Policy and the Policy Making Process", in *Principles of Public Health Practice*, 3rd ed., edited by F. Douglas Scutchfield and C. William Keck, 86–115 (Stamford, CT: Cengage Learning, 2011).

2. John W. Kingdon, *Agendas, Alternatives and Public Policies*, 2nd ed. (New York: HarperCollins, 1995).

3. Lauren LeRoy and Philip Randolph Lee, eds., *Deliberations and Compromise: The Health Professions Educational Assistance Act of 1976* (Cambridge, MA: Ballinger, 1977).

4. Andis Robeznieks, "RUC Panel Makes Limited Changes to Improve Transparency and Surveys," *Modern Healthcare* 43: 45 (2013): 12.

5. Robert Kocher and Nikhil R. Sahni, "Rethinking Health Care Labor," *New England Journal of Medicine* 365: 15 (2011): 1370–1372.

6. Altarum Institute, *Health Market Insights from the Bureau of Labor Statistics (BLS) December 2011 Employment Data* (Washington, DC: Altarum Institute, 2012).

7. Paul Starr, *The Social Transformation of American Medicine* (New York: Basic Books, 1982).

8. James W. Begun and Ronald C. Lippincott, *Strategic Adaptation in the Health Professions* (San Francisco: Jossey-Bass, 1993).

9. Uwe E. Reinhardt, "US Health Care Stands Adam Smith on His Head," *BMJ* 335: 7628 (2007): 1020.

10. Donald E. Yett, "The Nursing Shortage and the Nurse Training Act of 1964," *Industrial and Labor Relations Review* 19: 2 (1966): 190–200.

11. Ernest W. Saward, ed., *The Regionalization of Personal Health Services*, rev. ed. (New York: Prodist, 1976).

12. Eric Redman, *The Dance of Legislation: An Insider's Account of the Workings of the United States Senate* (New York: Simon & Schuster, 1973).

13. Stephan Lawton and JoAnne Glisson, "Congressional Deliberations: A Commentary," in *Deliberations and Compromise: The Health Professions Educational Assistance Act of 1976*, edited by Lauren LeRoy and Philip Randolph Lee, 1–19 (Cambridge, MA: Ballinger, 1977).

14. Nicholas J. Pisacano, "History of the Specialty," https://www.theabfm.org/about/history.aspx.

15. Haynes Johnson and David S. Broder, *The System: The American Way of Politics at the Breaking Point* (Boston: Little, Brown, 1996).

16. Mark A. Peterson, "From Trust to Political Power: Interest Groups, Public Choice, and Health Care Markets," *Journal of Health Politics, Poilicy and Law* 26 (October 2001): 1145–1163.

17. Karyn B. Stitzenberg and George F. Sheldon, "Progressive Specialization within General Surgery: Adding to the Complexity of Workforce Planning," *Journal of the American College of Surgeons* 201: 6 (2005):925–932.

18. Burton Edelstein, "The Dental Safety Net, Its Workforce, and Policy Recommendations for Its Enhancement," *Journal of Public Health Dentistry* 70: Suppl 1 (2010): S32–S39.

19. Florence Nightingale, *Notes on Nursing: What It Is and What It Is Not* (New York: D. Appleton, 1912).

20. Rosemary Stevens, *In Sickness and in Wealth: American Hospitals in the Twentieth Century* (New York: Basic Books, 1989).

21. Institute of Medicine, *The Future of Nursing: Leading Change, Advancing Health* (Washington, DC: National Academies Press, 2011).

22. Task Force on the Professional Doctorate, *A Report to the Board of Trustees from the Task Force on the Professional Doctorate* (Urbana, IL: Higher Learning Commission, North Central Association of Colleges and Schools, 2006).

23. International Conference on Primary Health Care, Declaration of Alma-Ata. Alma-Ata, Uzbek SSR, World Health Organization (1978).

24. Linda Aiken et al., "The Contribution of Specialists to the Delivery of Primary Care: A New Perspective," *New England Journal of Medicine* 300 (1979): 1363–1370.

25. Silver, H. K., L. C. Ford, and L. R. Day, "The Pediatric Nurse Practitioner Program: Expanding the Role of the Nurse to Provide Increased Health Care to Children," *JAMA* 204: 4 (1968): 298–302.

26. Agency for Healthcare Research and Quality, *Primary Care Workforce Facts and Stats: Overview* (Rockville, MD: AHRQ, 2012).

27. Yong-Fang Kuo et al., "States with the Least Restrictive Regulations Experienced the Largest Increase in Patients Seen by Nurse Practitioners," *Health Affairs* 32: 7 (2013): 1236–1243.

28. U.S. Congress, Office of Technology Assessment, *Nurse Practitioners, Physician Assistants, and Certified Nurse Midwives: A Policy Analysis* (Washington, DC: U.S. Government Printing Office, 1986).

29. Kathleen A. Baldwin et al., "Acceptance of Nurse Practitioners and Physician Assistants in Meeting the Perceived Needs of Rural Communities," *Public Health Nursing* 15: 6 (1998): 389–397.

30. Mary O. Mundinger et al., "Primary Care Outcomes in Patients Treated by Nurse Practitioners or Physicians: A Randomized Trial," *Journal of the American Medical Association* 283: 1 (2000): 59–68.

31. Miranda Laurant et al., "The Impact of Nonphysician Clinicians: Do They Improve the Quality and Cost-effectiveness of Health Care Services?" *Medical Care Research and Review* 66: 6 Suppl (2009): 36S–89S.

32. Michael J. Dill et al., "Survey Shows Consumers Open to a Greater Role for Physician Assistants and Nurse Practitioners," *Health Affairs* 32: 6 (2013): 1135–1142.

33. Lars E. Peterson et al., "Most Family Physicians Work Routinely with Nurse Practitioners, Physician Assistants, or Certified Nurse Midwives," *Journal of the American Board of Family Medicine* 26: 3 (2013): 244–245.

34. Daniel P. Kessler, William M. Sage, and David J. Becker, "Impact of Malpractice Reforms on the Supply of Physician

Services," *Journal of the American Medical Association* 293: 21 (2005): 2618–2625.

35. David M. Studdert et al., "Claims, Errors, and Compensation Payments in Medical Malpractice Litigation," *New England Journal of Medicine* 354: 19 (2006): 2024–2033.

36. Ash Samanta et al., "The Role of Clinical Guidelines in Medical Negligence Litigation: A Shift from the Bolam Standard?" *Medical Law Review* 14: 3 (2006): 321–366.

37. Michelle M. Mello et al., "'Health Courts' and Accountability for Patient Safety," *Milbank Quarterly* 84: 3 (2006): 459–492.

38. Michelle M. Mello and Allen Kachalia, *Evaluation of Options for Medical Malpractice System Reform* (Washington, DC: Medicare Payment Advisory Commission, 2010).

39. Eugene C. Rich et al., "Medicare Financing of Graduate Medical Education," *Journal of General Internal Medicine* 17: 4 (2002): 283–292.

40. Peter I. Buerhaus, "Is a Nursing Shortage on the Way?" *Nursing Management* 30: 2 (1999): 54–55.

41. Donald M. Steinwachs, "GMENAC's Projection of a Future Physician Surplus: Implications for HMOs," *Group Health Journal* 4: 1 (1983): 7–11.

42. Jonathan P. Weiner et al., "Assessing a Methodology for Physician Requirement Forecasting: Replication of GMENAC's Need-Based Model for the Pediatric Specialty," *Medical Care* 25: 5 (1987): 426–436.

43. Graduate Medical Education National Advisory Committee, *Report to the Secretary, Department of Health and Human Services, Volume III Geographic Distribution Technical Panel* (Washington, DC: Office of Graduate Medical Education, Health Resources Administration, Department of Health and Human Services, 1981).

44. Graduate Medical Education National Advisory Committee, *Report of the Graduate Medical Education National Advisory Committee to the Secretary, Department of Health and Human Services, Volume 1* (Washington, DC: Office of Graduate Medical Education, 1980).

45. Graduate Medical Education National Advisory Committee, *Interim Report of the Graduate Medical Education National Advisory Committee to the Secretary, Department of Health Education and Welfare* (Washington, DC: Department of Health, Education and Welfare, Health Resources Administration, 1979).

46. Stoney Abercrombie et al., "GME Reform," *Annals of Family Medicine* 11: 1 (2013): 90.

47. John K. Iglehart, "Financing Graduate Medical Education—Mounting Pressure for Reform," *New England Journal of Medicine* 366 (2012): 1562–1563.

48. Medicare Payment Advisory Commission, *Report to the Congress: Improving Medicare's Payments for Inpatient Care and for Teaching Hospitals* (Washington, DC: Medicare Payment Advisory Commission, 2000).

49. Association of American Medical Colleges, *AAMC Statement on the Physician Workforce* (Washington, DC: Association of American Medical Colleges, 2006).

50. Darrell G. Kirch, Mackenzie K. Henderson, and Michael J. Dill, "Physician Workforce Projections in an Era of Health Care Reform," *Annual Review of Medicine*, 63 (2012): 435–445.

51. Uwe E. Reinhardt, *Physician Productivity and the Demand for Health Manpower: An Economic Analysis* (Cambridge, MA: Ballinger, 1975).

52. Frank A. Sloan, "Access to Medical Care and the Local Supply of Physicians," *Medical Care* 15: 4 (1977): 338–346.

53. David C. Goodman et al., "Benchmarking the US Physician Workforce: An Alternative to Needs-Based or Demand-Based Planning," *Journal of the American Medical Association* 276: 22 (1996): 1811–1817.

54. Donald M. Steinwachs et al., "A Comparison of the Requirements for Primary Care Physicians in HMOs with Projections Made by the GMENAC," *New England Journal of Medicine* 314: 4 (1986): 217–222.

55. William D. Marder et al., *Physician Supply and Utilization by Specialty: Trends and Projections* (Chicago: American Medical Association, 1988).

56. Bureau of Health Professions, *Physician Supply and Demand* (Rockville, MD: Health Resources and Services Administration, Department of Health and Human Services, 2006).

57. Richard A. Cooper and Thomas E. Getzen, "The Coming Physician Shortage," *Health Affairs* 21: 2 (2002): 296–299.

58. Douglas O. Staiger, David I. Auerbach, and Peter I. Buerhaus, "Comparison of Physician Workforce Estimates and Supply Projections," *Journal of the American Medical Association* 302: 15 (2009): 1674–1680.

59. David C. Goodman and Elliott S. Fisher, "Physician Workforce Crisis? Wrong Diagnosis, Wrong Prescription," *New England Journal of Medicine* 358: 16 (2008): 1658–1661.

60. Erin P. Fraher et al., "Projecting Surgeon Supply Using a Dynamic Model," *Annals of Surgery* 257: 5 (2013): 867–872.

61. Barbara Starfield, "Public Health and Primary Care: A Framework for Proposed Linkages," *American Journal of Public Health* 86: 10 (1996): 1365–1369.

62. Atul Grover and Lidia M. Niecko-Najjum, "Physician Workforce Planning in an Era of Health Care Reform," *Academic Medicine* 88: 12 (2013): 1822–1826.

63. Arthur L. Kellermann et al., "Primary Care Technicians: A Solution to the Primary Care Workforce Gap," *Health Affairs* 32: 11 (2013): 1893–1898.

64. Linda V. Green, Sergei Savin, and Yina Lu, "Primary Care Physician Shortages Could Be Eliminated through Use of Teams, Nonphysicians, and Electronic Communication," *Health Affairs* 32: 1 (2013): 11–19.

FURTHER READING

Iglehart, John K. "A New Day Dawns for Workforce Redesign." *Health Affairs* 32: 11 (2013): 1870.

Institute of Medicine. *The Future of Nursing.* Washington, DC: National Academies Press, 2010. http://iom.edu/Reports/2010/The-Future-of-Nursing-Leading-Change-Advancing-Health.aspx.

Sklar, David P. "How Many Doctors Will We Need? A Special Issue on the Physician Workforce." *Academic Medicine* 88: 12 (2003): 1785–1787.

chapter 16

Promoting Health Care Quality and Safety (1960s–Present)

Michael K. Gusmano

THE PATIENT PROTECTION AND AFFORDABLE Care Act of 2010 (PPACA) is known, primarily, for expanding access to health insurance through an individual mandate, the creation of state health insurance exchanges, and enlarging the Medicaid program. Along with the provisions designed to expand access, the PPACA places significant emphasis on improving the quality of medical care by funding research, collecting and disseminating quality data, and reorganizing the health care system to create greater incentives for high-quality, patient-centered care.

The focus on quality is a relatively recent phenomenon. When the federal government created the Medicare and Medicaid programs in 1965, most policymakers assumed that the United States had the best health care system in the world and its primary concern was overcoming financial barriers to that system. By the early 1970s, researchers began publishing data that raised serious questions about the safety and quality of medical care in the United States. By the start of the twenty-first century, the issue of health care quality had grown in prominence.

PAYERS, PROVIDERS, AND QUALITY: FROM NONINTERFERENCE TO VALUE-BASED PURCHASERS

Enhancing access to mainstream health care was the principal concern of the architects of the Medicare program.[1] Following the program's enactment in 1965, Congress mandated quality assurance programs for Medicare beneficiaries,[2] but very little emphasis was placed on improving the quality or efficiency of health care delivery in the United States. To the contrary, the noninterference clause of Title 18 explicitly sought to limit the ability of the government to regulate providers:

Nothing in this title shall be construed to authorize any Federal officer or employee to exercise any supervision or control over the practice of medicine or the manner in which medical services are provided . . . or to exercise any supervision or control over the administration or operation of any . . . institution, agency, or person [providing health care services].[3]

The Medicare law did establish minimal quality standards for hospitals that wanted to participate in the program. Any hospital that wanted to participate had to be certified by the Joint Commission on the Accreditation of Hospitals, now called the Joint Commission on the Accreditation of Healthcare Organizations (JCAHO).[4] JCAHO's accreditation process draws on structure (who provides care and where), process (how care is provided), and outcomes approaches to the measurement of quality advocated for by Avedis Donabedian in his seminal 1966 article "Evaluating the Quality of Medicare Care."[5] Since the early 1990s, JCAHO has also drawn on theories of continuous quality improvement developed by W. Edwards Deming, Walter A. Shewart, and Joseph M. Juran.[6] The only quality standard for physicians was the requirement that services had to be "medically necessary."

There were two reasons for the initial lack of emphasis on quality. First, legislators were concerned about the willingness of physicians to participate in the Medicare program. They feared that if they attempted to place more stringent requirements on providers, the act might not pass Congress at all. Second, most people assumed that expanding access to the mainstream health care system would be enough to improve the quality of care received by Medicare beneficiaries. "If access to mainstream health care were assured, it was reasoned, Medicare enrollees would enjoy the best in health care that the nation could offer, and quality would be a 'nonissue.'"[7] Even after decades of evidence that the U.S. health care system suffers from significant quality problems, the idea that the United States has the "best health care system in the world" still resonates with members of Congress.[8]

Concerns about Quality Care

In the half-century since the enactment of Medicare, the federal government has become much more aggressive with providers. Interest in developing quality of care grew with the increase in medical cost inflation in the early 1970s,[9] but the role of the government as a relatively passive bill payer did not change significantly until much later. When the Health Care Financing Administration (HCFA) was created in 1977, it was endowed with an institutional legacy from the Social Security Administration (SSA), which had previously administered the Medicare program. Reflecting the standard operating principles at SSA, the principal goals were seen as efficiently and fairly processing the paperwork associated with billing and reimbursement for services. This emphasis on efficient claims processing was reinforced by legislative prohibitions against government influencing the "practice of medicine." Along with SSA's focus on beneficiaries' enrollment and access to entitled benefits, in deference to hospitals and physicians, the main administrative elements of the Medicare program were carried out by regional insurance companies (Part A fiscal intermediaries and Part B carriers). Policymakers may have assumed that in the process of paying claims under the rubric of "medically necessary" and "usual, customary, and reasonable" services, these administrative agents were in effect screening for quality as well.

Although Medicare had incorporated an early form of utilization review into its Professional Standards Review Organization program in the mid-1970s, this function was seen to be explicitly delegated to regional groups of medical professionals and did little to change the core mission of the agency administering the program nationally.[10] To the extent that the agency had involvement with Medicare beneficiaries, it was primarily to ensure that they understood their benefits under the program. This orientation was reflected in portrayals of HCFA's core mission, typically characterized as a bill payer.

Not long after HCFA was established, the Medicare program began to shift away from the passive orientation toward clinical practice. The most prominent of the federal quality assurance programs were Experimental Medical Care Review Organizations (EMCROs), Professional Standards Review Organizations (PSROs), and Utilization and Quality Control Peer Review Organizations (PROs).[11] In these programs, quality assurance was closely linked to utilization review and the attempt to control overuse of services, and therefore excessive costs that might occur under cost-based reimbursement. Between 1970 and 1975, the National Center for Health Services Research and Development administered

the EMCROs, which were voluntary physician organizations established to review inpatient and outpatient services reimbursed by Medicare and Medicaid. The organizations were largely focused on research and development and evidence regarding their effectiveness is mixed.[12] In a four-year case study of the New Mexico EMCRO, Robert H. Brook and colleagues found that while the program had succeeded in reducing the inappropriate use of injectable drugs, it had no impact on hospital inpatient services and failed to produce cost savings in the state's Medicaid program.[13]

The EMCROs were prototypes for the PSROs, established under the 1972 Social Security Amendments. The law gave decision-making power to local physicians and prohibited the federal government from owning the data generated by the local PSRO agencies. It also forbade the development of national practice norms. Despite these limitations, one American Medical Association leader called it "the most dangerous government intrusion into medical practice in American history."[14] Overheated rhetoric notwithstanding, the PSROs produced little net cost savings or evidence of quality improvement, and the program ended in 1981.[15] Almost immediately after the demise of the PSRO program, Congress created Peer Review Organizations in the Tax Equity and Fiscal Responsibility Act of 1982, to ensure quality care for beneficiaries. PROs, unlike PSROs, were given performance-based contracts and both for-profit and non-profit organizations were eligible for such contracts. PROs were also given greater ability to sanction providers and enjoyed greater independence from HCFA than PSROs.[16]

The adoption of the prospective payment system for inpatient care in 1983 was explicitly aimed at changing the ways in which hospital treatment was provided as well as the extent to which facilities specialized in the delivery of particular services.[17] Later in the decade, comparable changes were made in the payment for outpatient services through the adoption of the Resource-Based Relative Value System, explicitly designed to encourage greater use of more efficient outpatient services.[18] The adoption of prospective payment was a significant moment in the quality story, because from the perspective of the Physician Payment Review Commission (PPRC), the volume targets represented the stick to be accompanied by the carrot of new investment in outcomes research to help physicians use evidence to guide their clinical decision making (i.e., reduce inappropriate services).[19]

Another important development in the 1980s was the decision by HCFA to publish hospital mortality rates. William Roper, as HCFA administrator (and President Ronald Reagan's [1981–1989], also a leading health adviser), not only supported administrative pricing but was also the one who approved publication of hospital mortality rates.[20] This was a bold, transformational moment in alerting hospitals (and health professionals in general) that times had changed. If President Reagan was willing to set price controls, promote health maintenance organizations (HMOs), and go public with mortality rates, it was a signal that more aggressive efforts by the government to monitor and encourage quality may be on the way.

Although these changes gave the program as a whole greater influence over the delivery of services to Medicare beneficiaries, they had a smaller impact on HCFA's ability to actively oversee this influence. Quality oversight over clinical practices was largely delegated to regional PROs. The primary oversight for the new inpatient and outpatient payment systems was given to new special-purpose commissions, ProPAC and PPRC, respectively. The Balanced Budget Act of 1997 consolidated the two commissions into a single agency, labeled MEDPAC. The unwillingness of Congress to authorize greater authority within HCFA can be attributed in part to a government divided along partisan lines. For all but five years of HCFA's existence, the party of the president differed from the party with majority control of at least one house of Congress. Perhaps more important, this reflected the ongoing power struggle between Congress and the president. The legacy of the Watergate scandal and other struggles in the 1970s had not vanished, and there was a new budget process that demanded more technical expertise in the legislative branch. In addition, the commissions had substantial representation from the industry and professions it was overseeing. Congress preferred both the concessions to industry and the creation of a forum in which interests could negotiate with each other, instead of engaging in direct, individual lobbying of members and staff.

HCFA's Shift in Orientation

These delegations of authority outside HCFA delayed the transformation of that agency's core mission. Nevertheless, some competing strands of health services research helped sow the seeds for changes that were adopted in the late 1980s and early 1990s. Robert Brook and colleagues at the RAND Corporation laid out the evidence on inappropriate care, which raised significant questions about the quality of physician care in the United States.[21] Pioneering researcher John Wennberg, meanwhile, established the key theme of practice variations without making claims as to what was the right volume or rate.[22] These studies led to the creation, in 1989, of the Agency for Health Care Policy and Research. In addition, significant change was evident by the early 1990s, reflected in two different agency initiatives. The first, begun in 1991, involved a shift in the ways in which HCFA pursued quality assurance, moving away from a model based on policing inappropriate practices toward one that favored active collaboration with health care providers to encourage quality improvement.[23] Although largely implemented outside the agency under the auspices of the PROs, this change in policy nonetheless signaled an effort to exert greater direction over the ways in which

medical care quality was defined and services improved over time. In 1992, the agency started its Health Care Quality Improvement Initiative, which involved the use of uniform outcome measures to assess quality of care.

A more dramatic and potentially pervasive change occurred in 1994, with the announcement that HCFA would henceforth understand its core mission to be a "patient-centered value-based purchaser" of medical care.[24] The agency underwent a significant structural reorganization intended to support this change in mission. At least in principle, this transformation represented a radical shift from the passive orientation to the health care system that had dominated HCFA's raison d'etre for almost two decades. The accompanying rationale suggested that the agency would increasingly seek to emulate the role that employers and other large purchasers were playing in selectively contracting and encouraging more efficient and effective medical care, which was a central feature of President William J. Clinton's (1993–2001) proposal for combining universal insurance coverage with "managed competition." Since the mid-1990s, HCFA (and now the Centers for Medicare and Medicaid Services) has adopted exactly such an approach. In 2005, Judith Eichner and former HCFA administrator Bruce Vladeck argued that the Centers for Medicare and Medicaid Services (CMS) had "imposed a set of quality improvement standards in its requirements for the [Medicare Advantage] program, which is at least as rigorous as the most well-developed private accreditation standards (such as JCAHO and URAC)."[25]

This more aggressive approach has accelerated in recent years. In 2008, for example, CMS decided to use a financial incentive to improve safety and quality. Medicare and Medicaid stopped reimbursing participating hospitals for so-called never events, derived from a list developed by the National Quality Forum,[26] which was created in 1998 based on a recommendation of the President's Advisory Commission on Consumer Protection and Quality in the Health Care Industry.[27] CMS also eliminated enhanced reimbursement for preventable hospital-acquired infections.[28] In its press release, CMS described the new reimbursement rules as part of its "transformation of its public payer role into that of an active purchaser."[29] More recently, the PPACA has empowered CMS to extend its efforts to influence quality through payment reforms and experiments designed to reorganize the health care delivery system for the purpose of encouraging value rather than volume. The evidence for pay-for-performance is mixed,[30] but federal and state policymakers, as well as corporate leaders, have embraced this approach.[31] For example, the PPACA authorized a Hospital Value-Based Purchasing program in Medicare, under which payments to hospitals will be based on measures of quality of care rather than quantity of service.

Business Efforts in the 1980s

The efforts by HCFA and CMS to become value-based purchasers were, in many respects, preceded by the private sector. HCFA's approach to quality improvement was rather timid until the mid-1980s, but corporate leaders began pursuing mechanisms for improving the quality of medical care they were purchasing for their employees in the 1980s. By the mid-1980s, many large employers had turned to managed care to help control health care costs. Several Fortune 500 companies, including Bank of America, Ford, General Motors, and Xerox, wanted better information about the quality of care offered by the health plans they offered to their employees. In response, the National Committee for Quality Assurance (NCQA) worked with corporate leaders to develop standards for health plans.

NCQA was established in 1979 at the request of the federal Office for Health Maintenance Organizations, by the Group Health Association of America and the American Association of Foundations for Medical Care. In 1988, NCQA reorganized itself and created a board that included representatives of corporations, consumers, and quality experts. Health plans are still on the NCQA board, but they are a minority.[32] NCQA developed accreditation standards for health plans in 1991. In 1993, it started publishing report cards based on the Healthcare Effectiveness Data and Information Set. Today, NCQA publishes health plan report cards in *Consumer Reports*.

In theory, health plan report cards allow corporations, public purchasers, and individuals to compare plans on the basis of comparable quality measures. There is little evidence, however, that people "vote with their feet" and select health plans on the basis of health plan report cards.[33] Elbel and Schlesinger found that, even when patients experience significant problems with their plans, most people "do not formally voice their complaints or exit health plans."[34] These findings are consistent with a number of studies that evaluate the use of safety and quality information by the public. In 1988, for example, Bruce Vladeck found that the publication of hospital mortality data did not influence the selection of hospitals by consumers, "be they patients or physicians who admit patients."[35] More recent assessments of the response to quality information have reached similar conclusions.[36] Nevertheless, policymakers hope to disseminate NCQA and other quality data to people who will select plans in the state health plan "exchanges" created by the PPACA.[37]

Despite their limitations, there are some positive assessments of report cards. Judith Hibbard's research, for example, indicates that report cards can be useful if they provide information that is salient and does not involve a heavy cognitive burden.[38] Gwyn Bevan and Christopher Hood argue that it is not consumers or patients, but rather health care administrators (and boards), who are influenced by quality ratings.[39] Bevan and Hood's work in the United Kingdom suggests that poor report card marks may generate "reputational damage," which executives want to avoid. Similarly, the other important hook for voluntary quality monitoring such as by NCQA is the fact that health plans must submit to NCQA assessment and ratings in order to participate in the Part C Medicare Advantage program and most state Medicaid managed care programs

PATIENT MOVEMENTS AND QUALITY

Concerns about the cost of health care encouraged the federal government and private corporations to influence the practice of medicine and improve the quality of health care. Cost pressures faced by major payers were not the only factor that led to a growing focus on health care quality. In the 1970s, a broad range of consumer advocacy groups, inspired by the success of the civil rights movement, challenged organized medicine to improve its responsiveness to patients and the quality of its care.[40,41]

Women's Issues

For decades, the medical profession ignored health care problems faced exclusively by women. In some cases, physicians engaged in practices that put their female patients at risk.[42] Diethylstilbestrol was prescribed to women to prevent miscarriages even though the daughters of women who took it frequently developed vaginal cancer, doctors performed unnecessary hysterectomies and Cesarean-sections without discussing alternatives with their patients, and women were kept out of medical school and denied the ability to challenge the male domination of the medical profession. The women's health movement called on the medical profession to end the sexist practices.[43] The National Women's Health Network, the National Abortion and Reproductive Rights Action League, and the Women's Defense Fund work to keep women's health issues on the policy agenda. Women have also lobbied for better funding to address their concerns, and in 1990, the National Institutes of Health established the Office of Research on Women's Health.[44]

The spread of managed care in the 1990s raised new concerns about the quality of care for women. The push to reduce health care expenses led to so-called drive-through mastectomies and drive-through deliveries in which women were forced to leave the hospital following surgery and/or childbirth before they were healed and without adequate community-based care. These concerns and others led to a backlash against managed care and a call for a new "patients' bill of rights," but the advocacy of patients against the abuses of managed care was different in character. The backlash against managed care practice was not marked primarily by an organized campaign by patients or patient groups. Rather, it was a collection of individual protests, later joined by organized medicine, which hoped that it could "recoup legitimacy with patients . . . as a defender of consumer rights vis-à-vis the managed care industry."[45]

Mental Health Issues

Advocates for persons with mental illness, including patients themselves, have also lobbied for changes in policy and practice for more than a century. The National Institute of Mental Health, a professional association, worked with the Joint Commission on Mental Health on the background report that led to the establishment of the Community Mental Health Centers Act of 1963. This program provided a community-based alternative for the thousands of people who were being released from state mental hospitals. Although the community support required to handle rapid deinstitutionalization, particularly during the 1970s and 1980s, was inadequate, the existence of community mental health centers (CMHCs) improved the situation.

The first modern mental health patient rights group organized by former patients, the Oregon Insane Liberation Front, was established in late 1969; there are now dozens of patient organizations focused on mental illness. Like organizations to promote the rights of women and people with disabilities, many of these groups were inspired by the civil rights movement. In 1979, two mothers of children with schizophrenia helped to form another patient advocacy organization, the National Alliance for the Mentally Ill (NAMI). Thousands of families from across the country joined NAMI affiliates to provide mutual support, challenge psychiatric practices that blamed families for the disease, and advocate for change.[46] Such mobilization is often dual-purpose: it is designed to improve the quality of care and typically also to expand the quality of insurance coverage (by being instrumental in working with key members of Congress, insurers, employers, and others in mental health parity).

By 1999, the surgeon general's report on mental health recognized the important role of mental health patients/survivors and family groups in shaping mental health policy. Yet some argue that the professional mental health community and policymakers have only a "shallow acceptance of community empowerment."[47] Patients who do not follow the advice of mental health professionals are usually labeled "manipulative noncompliant, or lacking in insight" and "coercive tactics still enable providers to deal with consumers expediently, rather than therapeutically."[48] As Edward Foulks asserts, "after 150 years of advocacy and reform to improve the care of people with mental illness in the United States, there still remains much work to be done."[49]

Breast Cancer Concerns

The past thirty years have also witnessed the growth of patient advocacy efforts associated with particular diseases and conditions. Before the 1970s, breast cancer was rarely discussed in public and largely ignored by media, policymakers, and the general public. The 1970 book *Our Bodies, Ourselves,* published by the Boston Women's Health Book Collective, raised awareness, and the willingness of First Lady Betty Ford and Governor Nelson A. Rockefeller's wife Happy to go public with their fights against the disease inspired other women to share their experiences.

This set in motion several campaigns to raise money for research and advocacy. The Susan G. Komen Foundation was founded in 1982, and the National Alliance for Breast Cancer Organization, a large umbrella organization with hundreds of members, was established in 1986.[50] During the 1990s, the National Breast Cancer Coalition, Breast Cancer Action, and several local breast cancer support organizations were established. In addition to providing support to women with breast cancer, these organizations encouraged political activism to find a cure and improve treatment. These efforts resulted in a quadrupling of federal dollars for breast cancer research, and the National Breast Cancer Coalition convinced Congress to channel "more than one billion dollars for breast cancer research through the Department of Defense."[51,52,53, 54] In all of these cases, the effectiveness of the advocacy was helped by and may have depended to a considerable extent on, the leaders' ability to work on a bipartisan, if not nonpartisan, basis. Nearly all of the significant achievements described above were facilitated by both Democrats and Republicans.

Consumer Representation in Government Programs

The involvement of patients in the health policy process is usually the result of demands by people and organizations outside of government, but this is not always the case. At the same time that patient organizations were becoming a more important voice in health policy, reformers within government were trying to institutionalize the voice of patients in health policy. The Neighborhood Health Center Program, established in the 1960s, and Health Systems Agencies, established in the 1970s, both tried to guarantee a voice for nonprofessionals in these programs. More recently, state governments have tried to facilitate the role of patient organizations by supporting networks of such organizations. The results of these efforts have been mixed, but they reflect the continued enthusiasm among most policymakers for establishing a role for patients in the health policy process.

The Neighborhood Health Center Program was part of the Economic Opportunity Act (EOA) of 1964, which was the centerpiece of President Lyndon B. Johnson's (1963–1969) War on Poverty. The EOA provided funding to new community agencies in which the poor would participate to provide education, job training, health care, and other services to low-income individuals.[55] The neighborhood health center models that were funded by the Office of Economic Opportunity combined the delivery of health services with community organization by providing comprehensive health care, training and employing community residents, and involving them in community development.[56]

Community participation has always been a central feature in the federal government's funding of Community Health Centers (CHCs). When Congress created Neighborhood Health Centers in 1964 and then CHCs (and Community Mental Health Centers) in 1975, the legislation stated clearly that consumer participation in the running of the centers was paramount.[57] Because the location of CHCs and CMHCs was restricted to impoverished, underserved areas, the users of the centers have always been the poor, primarily Medicaid recipients and the uninsured.[58] In addition to consumer membership on the center boards, many of the staff as well as project directors at the centers are members of minority groups that match the racial and ethnic composition of the community. The National Association of Community Health Centers (NACHC) also had strong consumer representation. Fifty percent of the votes in the House of Delegates—the ultimate decision-making body of the NACHC, which establishes policy and programs, creates and reviews budgets, and elects association officers—are cast by consumers.[59] This community participation provision embodied in legislation and put into practice at each of the centers and in their national policy organization endowed CHCs (as well as CMHCs) with authority, and political clout, to represent the interests of the poor.

As CHCs grew in number, they established a formal political voice. The NACHC was established in 1973, and in 1976, it created a Department of Policy Analysis to have a more concerted impact on legislation pertaining to health care for the poor. The NACHC has been successful in affecting public policy in several areas. Despite this success, there have always been problems with regard to board control. Community participation was often limited, and effective control even more so, although success varied tremendously from one community to the next. According to Alice Sardell, CHCs were more effective at providing conventional clinical services than in providing the outreach or innovation needed to reach groups that had atypical needs or especially pronounced barriers to access.

Efforts to institutionalize patient voice into health policy and practice have continued in recent years. The Food and Drug Administration (FDA), for example, created an advisory committee system in the 1960s that is still used as a mechanism for allowing patients and other consumers to help evaluate the benefits and risks of new drugs.[60] The law that reauthorized the Prescription Drug User Fee Act (PDUFA) in 2012 called for increasing the role of the public in the FDA decision-making process.[61]

In 1995, the Agency for Healthcare Research and Quality (AHRQ) developed the Consumer Assessment of Healthcare Providers and Systems (CAHPS) to assess consumer experiences with health care in a variety of settings. Although there is little evidence that the public uses information from CAHPS to make decisions about health plans or providers, there is some evidence that it is used by plans themselves in their quality improvement efforts.[62]

After decades of advocacy by patients and consumers to improve the quality of health care and fight for greater patient voice in health care decisions, Rachel Grob argues that the status of patient-centered care "remains deeply contested." She points out that a 2012 meta-analysis of patient-centered care interventions did not identify any that involved patients in the implementation of an intervention, and only one included patients in the design.[63] The Patient-Centered Outcomes Research Institute (PCORI), created in 2010 by the PPACA, is designed to overcome this limitation and produce "evidence-based information that comes from research guided by patients, caregivers and the broader health care community." In its first cycle of funding, PCORI provided $40.7 million for "patient-centered comparative clinical effectiveness research projects."[64]

Focusing Events: IOM Publications on Safety and Quality

Political scientists who study agenda change often point to "focusing events" that alter the political landscape and lead directly to changes in the policy agenda. Nothing had a more dramatic effect on the health policy agenda with regard to quality than two reports by the Institute of Medicine (IOM). *To Err Is Human: Building a Safer Health Care System,* published in 1999, reported that preventable medical errors in U.S. hospitals resulted in an estimated 44,000 to 98,000 deaths each year.

Crossing the Quality Chasm, published two years later in 2001, generated a bit less media attention than *To Err Is Human,* but it offered a comprehensive agenda for reform. The report called for improvements in health care safety, effectiveness, patient-centeredness, timeliness, efficiency, and equity. Its recommendations were consistent with many of the efforts by patient advocates described above, because it tied quality issues "more closely to patients' experiences, cost, and social justice."[65]

Since these reports were issued, there has been considerable disagreement about the extent to which they have resulted in change. Many observers express frustration over the lack of substantial improvements in safety or quality in the wake of these reports.[66] Others argue that, although more change is needed, quality has improved measurably since these reports were issued. Despite disagreements about the extent to which the U.S. health care system has addressed the problems and achieved the goals articulated by these reports, there is a little disagreement that they fundamentally altered the policy debate and, as Vladeck and

KEY DECISIONS: HEALTH CARE CRISES AND SOLUTIONS

98,000 Deaths!

In 1999, the Institute of Medicine published a report titled *To Err Is Human: Building a Safer Health Care System,* in which it documented the magnitude of medical error in U.S. hospitals. One of the major headlines from the report—that as many as 98,000 people die in hospitals each year as a result of medical error—garnered considerable news coverage and had a clear impact on the health policy agenda. The report delivered a blistering attack on the entire health care system, arguing that a host of factors— from the attitudes of clinicians to the liability system, the incentives from third-party payers, and the fragmented nature of the delivery system—contributed to what it categorized as an "epidemic of medical error."

An excerpt from the introduction to the report points out the key issues:

Health care in the United States is not as safe as it should be—and can be. At least 44,000 people, and perhaps as many as 98,000 people, die in hospitals each year as a result of medical errors that could have been prevented, according to estimates from two major studies. Even using the lower estimate, preventable medical errors in hospitals exceed attributable deaths to such feared threats as motor-vehicle wrecks, breast cancer, and AIDS.

Medical errors can be defined as the failure of a planned action to be completed as intended or the use of a wrong plan to achieve an aim. Among the problems that commonly occur during the course of providing health care are adverse drug events and improper transfusions, surgical injuries and wrong-site surgery, suicides, restraint-related injuries or death, falls, burns, pressure ulcers, and mistaken patient identities. High error rates with serious consequences are most likely to occur in intensive care units, operating rooms, and emergency departments.

Beyond their cost in human lives, preventable medical errors exact other significant tolls. They have been estimated to result in total costs (including the expense of additional care necessitated by the errors, lost income and household productivity, and disability) of between $17 billion and $29 billion per year in hospitals nationwide. Errors also are costly in terms of loss of trust in the health care system by patients and diminished satisfaction by both patients and health professionals. Patients who experience a long hospital stay or disability as a result of errors pay with physical and psychological discomfort. Health professionals pay with loss of morale and frustration at not being able to provide the best care possible. Society bears the cost of errors as well, in terms of lost worker productivity, reduced school attendance by children, and lower levels of population health status.

Rice put it, "leaders throughout the system are now paying appropriate attention" to the issues of safety and quality.[67]

From Practice Variation to Comparative Effectiveness Research

The Medicare utilization review programs described above were unsuccessful in containing costs and produced little evidence of quality improvement. They did, however, generate some of the first evidence that use of physician and hospital services was marked by wide, unexplained variations.[68] Interest in this issue among health services researchers began in the 1970s and has grown to a point that some analysts suggest that it has become an "obsession."[69] John Wennberg and his colleagues found that the types and numbers of procedures ordered by physicians varied greatly by geographic region in various New England states and Iowa. The researchers concluded that such variation was primarily the result of individual practice styles on the part of physicians.[70] Similarly, research begun by Robert Brook and his colleagues at the RAND Corporation in the early 1980s suggested that physicians were providing therapies to patients when scientific evidence did not support their use.[71]

The National Center for Health Care Technology (NCHCT) was established in 1978 to conduct comprehensive assessments of health technologies and to advise the Health Care Financing Administration on Medicare coverage issues. Only four years later, the Reagan administration eliminated the NCHCT. Some of its work was taken up by the National Center for Health Services Research, but the demise of the NCHCT was driven, in part, by objections from industry and medical professionals. Opponents argued that the agency's work represented inappropriate regulation of industry.[72]

After the NCHCT was eliminated, the Institute of Medicine created the Council on Health Care Technology (CHCT) in 1986 in response to congressional concerns about the continued need for health technology assessment. CHCT conducted only two formal evaluations and the IOM did not seek additional funding for the program after 1989. The council's demise coincided, however, with the establishment of the Agency for Health Care and Policy Research (AHCPR). William Roper, who became administrator for the Health Care Financing Administration in 1986, promoted the use of Medicare databases to address some of these concerns by monitoring quality of care. Influenced by

Wennberg, Roper, and others, several congressional leaders, including Senate Majority Leader George Mitchell (D-ME, in office 1980–1995), Senator David Durenberger (R-MN, in office 1978–1995)—the ranking Republican on the Senate Finance Committee—and Representative Bill Gradison (R-OH, in office 1975–1983)—the ranking Republican on the Health Subcommittee of Ways and Means—heralded the idea that evidence-based approaches could save Medicare billions of dollars by identifying unnecessary health care services in high-cost areas without harming patients.[73]

In response to these concerns, AHCPR was created in 1989 with bipartisan congressional and professional support to carry out outcomes studies, develop practice guidelines, and conduct and coordinate health services research. In the first few years of its operation, the agency established a new program for developing practice guidelines as well as fourteen new Patient Outcomes Research Teams (PORTs), multidisciplinary centers focused on particular medical problems (e.g., back pain, myocardial infarction), to determine "what worked."[74] AHCPR frequently assisted the White House, under both the George H.W. Bush (1989–1993) and William J. Clinton (1993–2001) administrations, in assessing the implications of different health reform policy options. Although the leaders of the agency hoped that these efforts would demonstrate the value of AHCPR to policymakers, its association with the Clinton health reforms was later seen as a liability.

Despite some initial success, a broad government reduction agenda (the so-called Contract with America) was introduced in 1995, when the Republicans gained control of both the House and Senate, and the AHCPR's performance fell under significant scrutiny, to such an extent that it risked being eliminated during the 1996 budget appropriations. AHCPR's vulnerability to termination was attributable to many factors, several of which related to the strategies underlying its creation,[75] but the opposition of influential lobby groups also had a substantial effect. In particular, the North American Spine Society (NASS), an association of back surgeons who, in collaboration with the Center for Patient Advocacy, mounted a serious attack on the agency in 1995 after its PORT on low-back pain concluded that "there was no evidence to support spinal-fusion surgery and that such surgery commonly had complications." A letter-writing campaign to gain congressional support was organized, and the NASS used personal contacts to obtain the backing of a number of Republican politicians.

During this same time period, the Office of Technology Assessment, a congressional support agency established in 1972, which also focused on cost-effectiveness, was eliminated.[76] Unlike with the Office of Technology Assessment, a series of behind-the-scenes negotiations that involved lobbying by the former members of Congress who had helped to create the AHCPR and the fact that many of the problems that underpinned its establishment remained (e.g., practice variations, cost concerns), allowed the agency to survive, albeit with a new name, the Agency for Healthcare Research and Quality. The agency deliberately eliminated the word *policy*, abandoned its practice guideline program, and took a 21 percent budget cut. As John Wennberg put it:

[T]the unfortunate political history of ... AHCPR ... illustrate[s] the risks inherent in efforts to evaluate the common practices ... stable funding; strong peer review to assure good science and freedom from conflicts of interest that affect judgments; policies that sustain the careers of leading scientists over a professional lifetime (keeping them free of dependency on funding from the drug and device companies whose products they evaluate); and deep commitment on the part of the scientific establishment sufficient to withstand the wrath of practitioners and others with vested interests who find their favorite theories slain by evidence or demand for their services reduced because informed patients want less.[77]

Members of the National Women's Health Network demonstrate their support of the Institute of Medicine (IOM) guidelines. In 2008, Congress, through the Medicare Improvements for Patients and Providers Act, requested that the IOM study the best methods for developing clinical practice guidelines. Ultimately, the IOM developed eight standards for developing rigorous, trustworthy guidelines.

SOURCE: National Women's Health Network/Raising Women's Voices 2011.

Even after the agency's near-death experience, health experts continued to push for evidence-based medicine (EBM) and comparative effectiveness research (CER), with support from several members of Congress. These calls increased in volume and intensity as the debate for health care reform picked up steam prior to the 2008 presidential campaign.

POLITICS AND HEALTH CARE POLICY

From AHCPR to AHRQ

In 1989, the Agency for Health Care Policy and Research (AHCPR), later the Agency for Healthcare Research and Quality (AHRQ), was created with bipartisan support to carry out outcomes research, develop practice guidelines, and conduct and coordinate health services research. In the years that followed, federal spending on such research increased substantially.

In the first few years of its operation, the new agency was, by several measures, successful. It implemented its legislative mandate, saw an increase in its budget during the early 1990s, and was involved in the health system reform efforts of both the George H.W. Bush and William J. Clinton administrations. However, a broad government-reduction agenda, the so-called Contract with America, was introduced following Republican victories in the 1994 midterm elections; the agency's performance fell under significant scrutiny, and it was nearly eliminated.

AHCPR's vulnerability to a government shutdown was attributable to many factors, many (if not all) of which relate to the strategies underlying its creation. A review of the agency focused on its ability to meet the original expectations of Congress, with several governmental reports pointing to the ineffectiveness of its practice guideline program in improving practice and the unlikelihood that its comparative effectiveness work would ever lead to cost savings. In particular, the guidelines were not seen as user-friendly and were considered to be in potential conflict with other federal agencies and private sector groups issuing clinical practice guidelines. Its comparative effectiveness work was deemed ineffectual and disappointing.

Beyond concerns that the agency had failed to meet congressional expectations, several members of the new Republican majority in the House of Representatives were hostile toward the agency because they associated it with the despised Clinton Health Security Act, which had never come up for a vote in Congress. Because the agency would have assumed some monitoring responsibilities under the Clinton health reform proposal, some members argued that the defeat of health care reform meant that the agency was no longer necessary. Others, including members of the House Budget Committee, argued that the agency had engaged in advocacy on behalf of the administration. This accusation is the primary reason the word *policy* was eliminated from its name when it was rechristened the Agency for Healthcare Research and Quality.

In 1995, the North American Spine Society (NASS), an association of back surgeons, in collaboration with the Center for Patient Advocacy, mounted a serious attack on AHCPR after the agency's Patient Outcomes Research Team on low-back pain concluded that "there was no evidence to support spinal-fusion surgery and that such surgery commonly had complications" and issued practice guidelines based on this research. A letter-writing campaign to gain congressional support was organized and the groups used personal contacts to obtain the backing of a number of Republican politicians who led the congressional attack on the agency. One of the agency's chief detractors was Representative Sam Johnson (R-TX, in office 1991–), who distributed a "Dear Colleague" letter in which he called it the "Agency for High Cost Publications and Research." Later, he offered amendments on the House floor to eliminate the agency.

Although NASS is often given full credit for AHCPR's "near-death experience," the relative success of its lobbying efforts was due to unique historical circumstances, primarily the rise of Newt Gingrich (R-GA, in office 1979–1999, as Speaker 1995–1999) as Speaker of the House and the Republican victories during the 1994 midterm elections. Indeed, several other agencies, including the highly respected Office of Technology Assessment, which was established in 1972, were eliminated as part of this broader political effort. In many ways, it is remarkable that the agency survived at all. Thanks to behind-the-scenes lobbying by a bipartisan group of former members of Congress who helped to create the AHCPR, along with Gail Wilensky, the administrator of HCFA during the George H.W. Bush administration, and the fact that many of the problems (e.g., practice variations, the cost issue) that underpinned its establishment remained, the agency survived—with a new name and a 21 percent budget cut.

Using CER for Medicare Coverage Decisions

Medicare pays for medically needed and necessary services provided to elderly and disabled individuals. In 1989, amid growing complaints that its coverage process was unpredictable, unclear, and lengthy, HCFA (now CMS) pushed regulation stating that for purposes of coverage, a technology would need to be safe, effective, non-investigational, appropriate, and accepted by the medical community. Including cost-effectiveness as an explicit criterion for selected cases was also proposed, the first time that HCFA had supported cost-effectiveness as a factor in coverage decisions. The proposal met substantial opposition from professional and industry groups, especially regarding its cost-effectiveness provision, who feared rationing of important technologies would follow, leaving seniors to pay for or forgo necessary care, and was eventually withdrawn.[78]

CER and the Health Care Reform of 2009–2010

In late 2006 and early 2007, a shift from a Republican to a Democratic congressional majority renewed focus on health care and the need for comprehensive reform.[79] Democratic members of Congress began to advocate for CER as a mechanism to address quality by encouraging the use of evidence-based practice. A 2007 House proposal called for a new CER program within the AHRQ. Senators Max Baucus (D-MT, in office 1978–2014) and Kent Conrad (D-ND, in office 1992–2013) introduced legislation (S 3408) that would establish a nongovernmental, public-private entity, based on the idea that a nongovernmental body would offer a more efficient, transparent, and accepted mechanism to integrate CER into U.S. health care. Neither proposal was adopted, but these ideas were incorporated into the PPACA.

Interest in CER continued to grow during the 2008 presidential campaign. Although CER garnered bipartisan support in the campaign, once Barack Obama (2009–) was elected in November 2008 and the Democrats took control of Congress, Republican support waned, with many party leaders distancing themselves from or opposing the issue.[80] Opponents of CER argued that it would lead to rationing of care and "cookbook medicine." To address fears that CER would be used to ration care, the final law prohibits the use of quality-adjusted life years (QALYs) to reinforce the fact that consideration of costs would not be prescribed in the research and that findings published by the IOM would not dictate coverage, reimbursement, or other policy recommendations.

In the end, the language for a public-private research institute, PCORI, prevailed. In particular, the law charges PCORI with identifying research priorities, establishing an agenda, and carrying out CER. To realize these aims, the institute draws on a dedicated trust fund of dollars from the Medicare program and contributions from private insurers. Under the PPACA, PCORI will distribute approximately $3 billion to finance CER during its first decade.[81] Previously, the American Recovery and Reinvestment Act (ARRA) of 2009 included $1.1 billion for establishing comparative effectiveness research. The ARRA established the Federal Coordinating Council for Comparative Effectiveness Research to coordinate CER efforts by the federal government.[82] The PPACA also provides substantial funding to AHRQ to disseminate CER findings and link databases and disease registries to improve evidence.

From HMOs to ACOs: Reorganizing the Health Care System to Improve Quality

Along with the generation of quality information, policymakers have repeatedly tried to reorganize the delivery of care to improve the quality of care. Since the 1970s, policymakers have turned to managed care and, more recently, accountable care organizations to improve the quality and efficiency of health care services in the United States. Theodore Marmor and Jonathan Oberlander argue that there is little evidence to support the faith that policymakers place in these organizational innovations and that they reflect a search for a "holy grail" that will reduce costs while improving quality.[83]

Paul Ellwood first suggested changing the name of prepaid group practice organizations to "health maintenance organizations" in order emphasize the potential of HMOs for improving quality of care.[84] The administration of Richard M. Nixon (1969–1974) embraced this linguistic shift, because they thought it would provide an effective counter to Senator Edward Kennedy's (D-MA, in office 1962–2009) proposals for more comprehensive health reform. Ellwood argued that the incentives in these organizations would lead them to "do everything possible to keep or make their members healthy."[85]

Capitated payments provide HMOs and other managed care organizations (MCOs) with the incentive to avoid inappropriate use of inpatient services associated with the fee-for-service system. MCOs also have an incentive to encourage less expensive outpatient treatments and home care alternatives.[86] MCOs may also encourage preventative care.[87] While this aspect of MCO care is often seen as an advantage for younger enrollees, it may also benefit older patients "whose decreased reserves and likelihood of compromising illnesses often result in less than optimal outcomes from late, heavily intrusive intervention."

In addition to its expansion in the private sector, managed care has been used on a voluntary basis by the Medicare program and, often, on a mandatory basis by state Medicaid programs for acute health care services. A major concern about managed care provision is that strong incentives to control costs most often limit necessary medical services, particularly for vulnerable groups whose care may be costly, difficult to deliver, and difficult to evaluate.[88] Vulnerable groups including children, adults, and the elderly who suffer from chronic medical, mental, and emotional conditions. Concerns about obtaining appropriate services and paying for those services are paramount for most families with chronically ill relatives. MCOs sometimes try to minimize costs by limiting hospitalization referrals and expensive therapeutic services. As a result of these concerns and the belief that managed care was being used primarily to reduce costs, not to improve efficiency, there was a backlash against managed care in the 1990s.[89]

Despite this backlash, managed care has become the dominant form of health insurance in the United States.[90] Furthermore, the idea of developing an organizational strategy that can address the problems of cost and quality still enjoys support from policymakers and corporate leaders. The PPACA, for example, encourages CMS to proliferate "accountable care organizations" (ACOs). ACOs are, in many ways, an extension of the work started by John Wennberg and developed further in the *Dartmouth Atlas of Health*. They respond to the question raised by evidence on variations: how do we get to the right rate (mix) of services? The answer is to do what is needed to achieve the best outcomes, and the Dartmouth data suggest that more is not always better. ACOs are supposed to let clinicians and their own managers, not government regulators, decide how to attain better health outcomes for their population of patients by ensuring that their patients get appropriate care (reducing undertreatment) while avoiding unnecessary care. Politically, the idea of ACOs has been championed by former CMS administrator Mark McClellan, a Republican appointee, and Don Berwick, former CMS administrator under President Obama and an architect and advocate of many quality improvement initiatives in the PPACA as well as in the private health care sector. Like the original HMOs, ACOs are an organizational mechanism designed to provide health care providers with an incentive to offer high-quality care at the lowest possible price. ACOs are affiliations of health care providers that accept risk for a population of patients. In addition to private sector efforts to create ACOs, the PPACA created the Medicare Shared Savings Program. To participate, ACOs must provide care to at least five thousand Medicare fee-for-service patients and agree to participate for three years. If ACOs achieve quality standards (using thirty-three quality measures) while providing care for less than it would have cost Medicare otherwise, they will be eligible to receive a share of these savings.[91]

Continuing the Quest for High-Quality, Cost-Effective Health Care

The issues of access, cost, and quality are often called the "three-legged stool" of health policy, but until recently, quality did not received a great deal of attention. In the decades since the adoption of Medicare and Medicaid, this situation has changed. In the 1970s, patient groups began to organize and make demands for health care that was more responsive to their needs. In the 1980s, major institutional payers began to ask questions about, and demand accountability for, the product they were purchasing.

Disturbing evidence of problems with safety and quality has pushed the issue of quality into the national spotlight. Finding solutions to these problems, however, has not been easy. Stakeholders have resisted challenges to existing practices and technologies, and the fears of rationing, coupled with ideological opposition to government, have made it difficult to develop an evidence base for improving quality and even more difficult to use this evidence for making decisions about coverage and payment.

Along with these political barriers, there are fundamental disagreements about the meaning of quality and how to measure "value for money" in health care.[92] Furthermore, the evidence supporting a number of important efforts to improve quality, from the use of managed care to the dissemination of information to payers and consumers, is mixed. Despite these challenges, public and private payers are experimenting with innovations in the payment and the delivery of care designed to focus the attention of providers and patients on quality, and the implementation of the PPACA has pushed the issue of quality even higher on the policy agenda.

See also **Chapter 11: Evolution of Health Planning (1920s–1970s); Chapter 12: Evolution of Health Planning (1970s–Present); Chapter 13: Government Financing of Health Care (1940s–Present); Chapter 15: Building an Effective and Sustainable Health Care Workforce (1960s–Present); Chapter 17: Strategies for Health Care Cost Containment (1980s–Present); Chapter 18: Health and Health Care Policy: Ethical Perspectives (1970s–Present); Chapter 24: Mental Health and Social Policy (1960s–Present).**

NOTES

1. Robert M. Ball, "What Medicare's Architects Had in Mind," *Health Affairs* 14:4 (1995): 62–72; Theodore Marmor, *The Politics of Medicare* (Chicago: Aldine, 1973).
2. Kathleen N. Lohr, ed., *Medicare: A Strategy for Quality Assurance, Volume I* (Washington, DC: National Academy Press, 1990).
3. Marilyn Moon, *Medicare Now and in the Future* (Washington, DC: Urban Institute Press, 1993).
4. Ball, "What Medicare's Architects Had in Mind."
5. Avedis Donabedian, "Evaluating the Quality of Medical Care," *Milbank Memorial Fund Quarterly* 44: 3, pt. 2 (1966): 166–203.
6. David Blumenthal and Charles M. Kilo, "A Report Card on Continuous Quality Improvement," *Milbank Quarterly* 76: 4 (2001): 625–648; W. Edwards Deming, *Out of the Crisis* (Cambridge: Massachusetts Institute of Technology, Center for the Advanced Engineering Science, 1986); Joseph M. Juran, *A History of Managing for Quality* (Milwaukee, WI: ASQC Quality Press, 1995); Walter A. Shewhart, *Statistical Method from the Viewpoint of Quality Control* (Mineola, NY: Dover, 1986).
7. Moon, *Medicare Now and in the Future,* 97.
8. Michael K. Gusmano, "Health Systems Performance and the Politics of Cancer Survival," *World Medical & Health Policy* 5: 1 (2013): 76–84.
9. Bradford H. Gray, "The Legislative Battle over Health Services Research." *Health Affairs* 11: 4 (1992): 38–66; Paul Starr, *The Social Transformation of American Medicine* (New York: Basic Books, 1982), 398–400.
10. Bradford Gray and Marilyn Fields, eds., *Controlling Costs and Changing Patient Care? The Role of Utilization Management* (Washington, DC: National Academy Press, 1989).
11. Lohr, *Medicare,* 138.
12. Robert H. Brook, Kathleen N. Williams, and John E. Rolph, "Controlling the Use and Cost of Medical Services: The New Mexico Experimental Medical Care Review Organization—A Four Year Case Study," *Medical Care* 16: 9, Suppl (1978): 1–76.
13. Ibid.

14. Starr, *The Social Transformation*, 400.

15. Lohr, *Medicare*.

16. Kathleen Lohr, *Peer Review Organizations: Quality Assurance in Medicare* (Santa Monica, CA: Rand, 1985).

17. Judith Bentkover et al., "Medicare's Payment of Hospitals," in *Renewing the Promise: Medicare and Its Reform,* edited by David Blumenthal, Mark Schlesinger, and Pamela B. Drumheller, 90–114 (New York: Oxford University Press, 1988).

18. David G. Smith, *Paying for Medicare: The Politics of Reform* (New York: De Gruyter, 1992); William C. Hsiao, Daniel L. Dunn, and Diana K. Verrilli, "Assessing the Implementation of Physician-Payment Reform," *New England Journal of Medicine* 328: 13 (1993): 928–933; Thomas R. Oliver, "Analysis, Advice, and Congressional Leadership: The Physician Payment Review Commission and the Politics of Medicare," *Journal of Health Politics, Policy and Law* 18: 1 (1993): 113–174.

19. Oliver, "Analysis, Advice."

20. David J. Rothman and David Blumenthal, *Medical Professionalism in the New Information Age* (New Brunswick, NJ: Rutgers University Press, 2010).

21. Mark R. Chassin et al., "Does Inappropriate Use Explain Geographic Variations in the Use of Health Care Services? A Study of Three Procedures," *Journal of the American Medical Association* 258: 18 (1987): 2533–2537.

22. John Wennberg and Alan Gittelsohn, "Variations in Medical Care among Small Areas," *Scientific American* 246 (1982): 120–135; John E. Wennberg, Benjamin A. Barnes, and Michael Zubkoff, "Professional Uncertainty and the Problem of Supplier Induced Demand," *Social Science & Medicine* 16 (1982): 811–824.

23. Stephen F. Jenks and Gail R. Wilensky, "The Health Care Quality Improvement Initiative," *Journal of the American Medical Association* 268: 7 (1992): 900–903.

24. John K. Iglehart, "Changing with the Times: The Views of Bruce C. Vladeck," *Health Affairs* 16: 3 (1997): 58–71.

25. Judith Eichner and Bruce Vladeck, "Medicare as a Catalyst for Reducing Health Disparities," *Health Affairs* 24: 2 (2005): 365–375.

26. "CMS Improves Patient Safety for Medicare and Medicaid by Addressing Never Events" (Press Release, August 4, 2008), http://www.cms.gov/Newsroom/MediaReleaseDatabase/Fact-Sheets/2008-Fact-Sheets-Items/2008-08-042.html.

27. Christina Bielaszka-DuVernay, "Improving Quality and Safety" (Health Policy Brief), *Health Affairs,* April 15, 2011.

28. "CMS Improves Patient Safety,"

29. Ibid.

30. Sandra J. Tannenbaum, "Pay for Performance in Medicare: Evidentiary Irony and the Politics of Value," *Journal of Health Politics, Policy and Law* 34: 5 (2009): 717–746.

31. Jill Bernstein, Deborah Chollet, and Stephanie Peterson, "Financial Incentives for Health Care Providers and Consumers" (Princeton, NJ: Mathematica Policy Research, May 2010).

32. Mark R. Chassin and Margaret E. O'Kane, "History of the Quality Improvement Movement," in *Toward Improving the Outcome of Pregnancy III,* edited by Scott D. Berns, 1–8 (White Plains, NY: March of Dimes, 2010).

33. Margaret O'Kane, "Increasing Transparency on Health Care Costs, Coverage and Quality," Testimony before the Senate Commerce, Science and Transportation Committee, February 27, 2013, http://pharmacychoice.com/News/article.cfm?ARTICLE_ID=1031043.

34. Brian Elbel and Mark Schlesinger, "Responsive Consumerism: Empowerment in Markets for Health Plans," *Milbank Quarterly* 87: 3 (2009): 633–682.

35. Bruce C. Vladeck et al., "Consumers and Hospital Use: The HCFA 'Death List,'" *Health Affairs* 7: 1 (1988): 122–125.

36. Andrew J. Epstein, "Do Cardiac Surgery Report Cards Reduce Mortality? Assessing the Evidence," *Medical Care Research and Review* 63 (2006): 403–426; David H. Howard, "Quality and Consumer Choice in Healthcare: Evidence from Kidney Transplantation," *Topics in Economic Analysis and Policy* 5: 1 (2005): 1–20.

37. O'Kane, "Increasing Transparency."

38. Judith H. Hibbard and Ellen Peters, "Supporting Informed Consumer Health Care Decisions: Data Presentation Approaches that Facilitate the use of Information in Choice," *Annual Review of Public Health* 24 (2003): 413–433.

39. Gwyn Bevan and Christopher Hood, "Have Targets Improved Performance in the English NHS? *BMJ* 332 (2006): 419.

40. Sydney A. Halpern, "Medical Authority and the Culture of Rights," *Journal of Health Politics, Policy and Law* 29: 4–5 (2004): 835–852.

41. Beatrix Hoffman et al., eds., *Patients as Policy Actors* (New Brunswick, NJ: Rutgers University Press, 2011).

42. Marc A. Rodwin, "Patient Accountability and Quality of Care: Lessons from Medical Consumerism, Patients' Rights, Women's Health and Disability Rights Movements," *American Journal of Law & Medicine* 20: 1&2 (1994): 147–167.

43. Beatrice Hoffman, "Health Care Reform and Social Movements in the United States," *American Journal of Public Health* 93 (2003): 75–85.

44. Rodwin, "Patient Accountability and Quality of Care."

45. Halpern, "Medical Authority," 836.

46. Edward Foulks, "Advocating for Persons Who Are Mentally Ill: A History of Mutual Empowerment of Patients and Profession," *Administration and Policy in Mental Health* 27: 5 (2000): 353–367.

47. Robert Bernstein, "A Seat at the Table: Trend or an Illusion?" *Health Affairs* 25: 3 (2006): 730–733.

48. Ibid.

49. Foulks, "Advocating for Persons."

50. Vicki Brower, "The Squeaky Wheel Gets the Grease," *EMBO Reports* 6: 11 (2005): 1014–1017.

51. Bob Riter, "A Very Brief History of the Breast Cancer Advocacy Movement," http://www.cancerlynx.com/breastadvocacy.html.

52. Susan Braun, "The History of Breast Cancer Advocacy," *Breast Journal* 9: s2 (2003): S101–S103.

53. Karen L. Baird, "The New NIH and FDA Medical Research Policies: Targeting Gender, Promoting Justice," *Journal of Health Politics, Policy and Law* 24: 3 (1999): 531–565.

54. Maureen Hogan Casamayo, *The Politics of Breast Cancer* (Washington, DC: Georgetown University Press, 2001).

55. James A. Morone, *The Democratic Wish: Popular Participation and the Limits of American Government* (New York: Basic Books, 1990).

56. Alice Sardell, *The U.S. Experiment in Social Medicine: The Community Health Center Program, 1965–1986* (Pittsburgh, PA: University of Pittsburgh Press, 1988).

57. Ibid., 101.

58. Michael K. Gusmano, Gerry Fairbrother, and Heidi Park, "Exploring the Limits of the Safety Net: Community Health Centers and Care for the Uninsured," *Health Affairs* 21: 6 (2002): 188–194.

59. Colleen M. Grogan and Michael K. Gusmano, *Healthy Voices/ Unhealthy Silence: Advocacy and Health Policy for the Poor* (Washington, DC: Georgetown University Press, 2007).

60. Food and Drug Administration, "Patient Representatives to FDA Advisory Committees," http://www.fda.gov/ForConsumers/ByAudience/ForPatientAdvocates/PatientInvolvement/ucm123861.htm.

61. Jill Wechsler, "FDA User Fee Renewal Addresses Drug Shortages, New Drug Development," *Formulary* 47 (2011): 125–126.

62. Tim Lake, Chris Kvam, and Marsha Gold, "Literature Review: Using Quality Information for Health Care Decisions and Quality Improvement, Final Report" (Princeton, NJ: Mathematica Policy Research, May 2005).

63. Rachel Grob, "Behind the Jargon: The Heart of Patient-Centered Care," *Journal of Health Politics, Policy and Law* 38: 2 (2013): 457–465.

64. Patient-Centered Outcomes Research Institute, "Governance and Leadership," http://www.pcori.org/about/governance-and-leadership.

65. Donald Berwick, "A User's Manual for the IOM's 'Quality Chasm' Report," *Health Affairs* 21: 3 (2002): 80–90.

66. Peter Pronovost, Bryan Sexton, and David Thompson, "Five Years after to Err Is Human," *Journal of Critical Care* 20: 1 (2005), 76–78; Robert M. Wachter, "The End of the Beginning: Patient Safety Five Years after 'To Err Is Human,'" *Health Affairs* 23 (2004): W4-534–W4-545.

67. Bruce C. Vladeck and Thomas Rice, "Market Failure and the Failure of Discourse: Facing up the to Power of Sellers," *Health Affairs* 28: 5 (2009): 1305–1315.

68. Gray, "The Legislative Battle," 247.

69. Sandra J. Tanenbaum, "Reducing Variation in Health Care: The Rhetorical Politics of a Policy Idea," *Journal of Health Politics, Policy and Law* 38: 1 (2013): 5–26; Joseph White, "Prices, Volume, and the Perverse Effects of the Variations Crusade," *Journal of Health Politics, Policy and Law* 36: 4 (2011): 775–790.

70. John E. Wennberg, Jean L. Freeman, and William J. Culp, "Are Hospital Services Rationed in New Haven or Over-Utilised in Boston?" *Lancet* 329: 8543 (1987): 1185–1189; John E. Wennberg, "Dealing with Medical Practice Variations: A Proposal for Action," *Health Affairs* 3: 2 (1984): 6–32; John E. Wennberg and Alan Gittelsohn, "Small Area Variations in Health Care Delivery," *Science* 182 (1973): 1102–1108.

71. Brook et al., "Controlling the Use and Cost"; Robert H. Brook et al., "A Method for Detailed Assessment of the Appropriateness of Medical Technologies," *International Journal of Technology Assessment in Health Care* 2 (1986): 53–63; Robert H. Brook et al., "Geographic Variations in the Use of Services: Do They Have Any Clinical Significance?" *Health Affairs* 3: 2 (1984): 63–73; Robert H. Brook, "Practice Guidelines and Practicing Medicine: Are They Compatible?" *Journal of the American Medical Association* 262 (1989): 3027–3030.

72. Dennis Cotter, "The National Center for Health Technology: Lessons Learned," *Health Affairs* Blog, January 22, 2009, http://healthaffairs.org/blog/2009/01/22/the-national-center-for-health-care-technology-lessons-learned.

73. Bradford H. Gray, Michael K. Gusmano, and Sara Collins, "AHCPR and the Politics of Health Services Research," *Health Affairs Web Exclusive*, June 25, 2003, http://content.healthaffairs.org/content/early/2003/06/25/hlthaff.w3.283.full.pdf+html.

74. Bryan Luce and Rebecca Singer Cohen, "Health Technology Assessment in the United States," *International Journey of Technology Assessment in Health Care* 25: Suppl 1 (2009): 33–41.

75. Gray et al., 2093.

76. Corinna Sorenson, Michael K. Gusmano, and Adam Oliver, "The Politics of Comparative Effectiveness Research: Lessons from Recent History," *Journal of Health Politics, Policy and Law* 39: 1 (2014): 139–170.

77. John E. Wennberg, "The More Things Change . . . : The Federal Government's Role In the Evaluative Sciences," *Health Affairs* Suppl (2003): W3-308–W3-310.

78. Susan Bartlett Foote, "Why Medicare Cannot Promulgate a National Coverage Rule: A Case of Regula Mortis," *Journal of Health Politics, Policy and Law* 2: 5 (2002): 707–730.

79. Kavita Patel, "Health Reform's Tortuous Route to the Patient-Centered Outcomes Research Institute," *Health Affairs* 29: 10 (2010): 1777–1782.

80. John K. Iglehart, "The Political Fight over Comparative Effectiveness Research," *Health Affairs* 29: 10 (2010): 1757–1760.

81. Thomas Sullivan, "PCORI," http://www.policymed.com/pcori.

82. Sorenson et al., "The Politics of Comparative Effectiveness Research."

83. Theodore Marmor and Jon Oberlander. 2012. "From HMOs to ACOs: The Quest for the Holy Grail in U.S. Health Policy." *Journal of General Internal Medicine*, doi:10.1007/s11606-012-2024-6.

84. Starr, *The Social Transformation*.

85. Lawrence D. Brown, *Politics and Health Care Organizations: HMOs as Federal Policy* (Washington, DC: Brookings Institution, 1982).

86. Mark Schlesinger and Pamela Brown Drumheller, "Medicare and Innovative Insurance Plans," in *Renewing the Promise: Medicare and Its Reform*, edited by David Blumenthal, Mark Schlesinger, and Pamela Brown Drumheller, 133–159 (New York: Oxford University Press, 1988).

87. Harold S. Luft, "How Do Health Maintenance Organizations Achieve Their Savings?" *New England Journal of Medicine* 298: 24 (1978): 1336–1343.

88. Mark Schlesinger and David Mechanic, "Challenges for Managed Competition from Chronic Illness," *Health Affairs* Suppl (1993): 123–137.

89. Robert E. Hurley, "The Puzzling Popularity of the PPO," *Health Affairs* 23 (2004): 56–68.

90. Thomas R. Oliver, "Policy Entrepreneurship in the Social Transformation of American Medicine: The Rise of Managed Care and Managed Competition," *Journal of Health Politics, Policy and Law* 29: 4–5 (2004): 701–734.

91. Thomas L. Greaney, "Accountable Care Organizations—The Fork in the Road," *New England Journal of Medicine* 364: 1 (2011): e1.

92. Michael K. Gusmano and Daniel Callahan, "Value for Money: Use with Care," *Annals of Internal Medicine* 154: 3 (2011): 207–208.

FURTHER READING

Elbel, Brian, and Mark Schlesinger. "Responsive Consumerism: Empowerment in Markets for Health Plans." *Milbank Quarterly* 87: 3 (2009): 633–682.

Hoffman, Beatrix. "Health Care Reform and Social Movements in the United States." *American Journal of Public Health* 93 (2003): 75–85.

Tannenbaum, Sandra J. "Pay for Performance in Medicare: Evidentiary Irony and the Politics of Value." *Journal of Health Politics, Policy and Law* 34: 5 (2009): 717–746.

Strategies for Health Care Cost Containment (1980s–Present)

B. Rick Mayes

THE BIGGEST AND MOST INTENSE BATTLE IN the U.S. health care system during the past three decades has been over two interrelated questions: first, who will control the manner in which medical care is paid for, and, second, how much will it cost? Many health care experts believe that Medicare's efforts at cost control, primarily in the form of the program's seminal transition to and continual modification of prospective payment of health care providers, has both triggered and repeatedly intensified the economic restructuring of the U.S. health care system. Medicare is an almost $600 billion public health insurance program for individuals sixty-five years of age and older; individuals under sixty-five with certain disabilities (with eligibility dependent on the severity of the disability and the resultant consequences for a person's ability to work), and those with end-stage renal disease). With regard to how the program reimburses for care, "Medicare sets prospectively the payment amount (rates) providers will receive for most covered products and services, and providers agree to accept them as payment in full," according to the Medicare Payment Advisory Commission. "Thus, in most instances, providers' payments are based on predetermined rates and are unaffected by their costs or posted charges."[1]

MEDICARE'S VAST INFLUENCE

Medicare payment reforms have empowered the federal government's effort at cost control in ways that are similar to health care systems in other industrialized countries.[2] They have (1) given the U.S. government de facto control over the price of most medical care and (2) ended the era, dating back to the 1920s, in which doctors' and hospitals' authority over medical prices and decision making went virtually unquestioned.[3] The key to Medicare's role as the leading catalyst for change in the U.S. health care system is the program's immense size and influence.[4] As the single largest individual buyer of health care and the "first mover" in the annual payment game between those who provide medical care and those who pay for it, Medicare invariably drives the behavior of both medical providers and private payers.

Medicare's revolutionary transition from traditional cost reimbursement (generally paying hospitals and physicians what they submitted in the way of costs) to a prospective payment model began in 1983. In that year, Congress changed the program's method of paying hospitals to a system of predetermined payment amounts for individual diagnosis-related groups (DRGs). In 1989, following the success of DRGs in restraining the rate of growth in Medicare's hospital expenditures, Congress enacted a similar program—a resource-based relative-value scale with a standardized fee schedule—for Medicare's reimbursement of physicians. The program went into effect in 1992. With the Balanced Budget Act of 1997, Congress reformed the reimbursement processes of the remaining cost-based components of Medicare, including outpatient ambulatory services and post-acute care (such as skilled nursing facilities and home health agencies). By 2003, twenty years after Medicare started the payment revolution in America's health care system, the program had become fully "prospectivized" in its reimbursement of all medical providers. Medicare also plays a significant role in supporting the education of health professionals, particularly medical school graduates training as residents in the nation's more than one thousand teaching hospitals. The program's direct and indirect financial support of medical training (direct in the form of paying the salaries of the residents and the supervising physicians' time, around $3 billion, and indirect in the form of subsidizing other hospital expenses associated with running training programs, around $6–$7 billion) amounted to upwards of $10 billion in 2012.

Each time Congress changed one part of Medicare from cost reimbursement to prospective rate-setting, the overall growth of the program's expenditures slowed. A significant, albeit temporary, measure of cost control was achieved. Yet these spending reductions have often come at the expense of health care providers compensating by increasing their revenues from private payers. "When Medicare slows its rate of expenditure growth," explains David Abernethy, former senior Medicare specialist and Staff Director of the House Ways and Means Health Subcommittee, "hospitals' overall rate of revenue growth slows and that, in the end, puts the final pressure on private payers."[5] This increased use of cost shifting (or cross-subsidization or differential pricing) by medical providers, in which changes in administered prices of one payer lead to compensating changes in prices charged to other payers for care, propelled the growth of private sector efforts (namely, managed care in the 1990s) to achieve similar cost control.

Ultimately, the change in Medicare's reimbursement policy altered the balance of power between the federal government and medical providers. By increasing the scope and extent of Medicare's regulation through prospective payment, Congress for the first time gained the upper hand in its financial relationship with hospitals and then with physicians in terms of setting medical prices. Yet the federal government has done little to extend Medicare's success in controlling prices to controlling the volume of services provided.[6] Therefore, although Medicare's Prospective Payment System (PPS) has been more influential than anything else in rationalizing health care prices in the United States, the program has never gained major and lasting control over utilization or total costs. Thus, Medicare's rate of expenditure growth and relatively meager results at cost containment in recent years remain issues of enormous political concern.[7]

Moreover, Medicare does not cover all health care costs for its beneficiaries. The program's Part A benefits cover inpatient hospital stays, skilled nursing facility stays, home health visits, and hospice care, but there is a deductible ($1,156 in 2012) and coinsurance requirements. The program's Part B benefits cover physician visits, outpatient services, preventive services, and home health visits, but there is also a monthly premium that beneficiaries must pay ($140 in 2012). Also, Part D, the voluntary, subsidized outpatient prescription drug benefit that George W. Bush (2001–2009) signed into law in 2003 and that went into effect in 2006, also includes deductibles and monthly premiums that vary by drug plan and beneficiary income.

Passage of Medicare's Prospective Payment System Driven by the Need for Cost Containment

In the late 1970s and early 1980s, rampant medical inflation forced policymakers to search for ways to control Medicare's rapidly escalating costs. With doctors and hospital executives in control of the U.S. health care system for decades, virtually unrestricted cost reimbursement had become the dominant model for financing public and private medical care. Independent not-for-profit hospitals and physicians practicing alone or in small groups dominated the medical landscape. Notes Bradford Gray,

> Third-party payers (both private and public) played their financing role passively, reluctant to interfere with medical decision-making and the doctor-patient relationship. They paid for medical care by reimbursing for costs incurred or charges billed by health care providers and did little to control which services were provided or how much they cost.[8]

The medical inflation that grew directly out of these delivery structures and payment systems became unsustainable. In 1980, hospital spending grew 16.4 percent, as the nation's total health care expenditures reached $230 billion, a threefold increase from $69 billion in 1970.[9] In Ronald Reagan's (1981–1989) first full year in office, hospital spending increased 17.5 percent.[10] The following year the country slipped into the worst recession in half a century, with the unemployment rate reaching almost 11 percent.

Out of financial necessity, therefore, Congress and a handful of state governments commissioned experiments in alternative reimbursement systems. The most promising conceptual innovation, prospective payment with predetermined reimbursement rates, was the product of pioneering research at the University of Michigan and Yale University. Using data from Connecticut's hospitals, Yale professors John Thompson and Robert Fetter demonstrated that medical care could be standardized and measured. As a result, policymakers and administrators were able, for the first time, to compare prices across different hospitals for the same services. They found an enormous amount of unjustifiable variation, which called into question medical providers' authority to regulate their own affairs.

Rising Medical Costs

The deadly combination of inexorably rising medical inflation and deep economic deterioration forced elected leaders to pursue the radical reform of Medicare to keep the program from insolvency. Federal policymakers—led primarily by President Reagan's health and human services secretary, Richard Schweiker (in office 1981–1983)—eventually turned to the one alternative reimbursement system that analysts and academics had studied more than any other and even tested with apparent success in New Jersey: prospective payment with DRGs. Rather than simply reimbursing hospitals whatever costs they incurred in treating Medicare patients, the new model would pay hospitals a predetermined, set rate based on a patient's diagnosis. The payment would be unrelated to any specific hospital's costs. Instead, it would be a national payment based on the costs of a general hospital. Thus, if a hospital could treat a patient for less than the standard DRG payment, it could keep the savings as a profit. If it cost the hospital more, it had to absorb the difference as a financial loss. Once Republican leaders became convinced that PPS could be used to reduce federal budget deficits, as well as create new profit and efficiency incentives for hospitals based on an increase in volume, the political obstacles to radically transforming Medicare finally dissolved.

Realigning Financial Incentives

Ironically, the most significant change in health policy since the passage of Medicare and Medicaid (the publicly financed, federal-state health insurance program for low-income Americans) in 1965 went virtually unnoticed by the general public. Nevertheless, the change was significant. For the first time in U.S. history, the federal government acquired a sizeable measure of power in its financial relationship with the hospital industry. Together with Congress's development and use of the budget reconciliation process, Medicare's new prospective payment system with DRGs infringed on the hospital industry's sovereignty and autonomy. Also, the new and vastly increased amount of government regulation that Medicare's PPS represented was paradoxical in that it purported to mimic the dynamic forces of the free market. By realigning financial incentives, policymakers designed the new system to bring Medicare's rate of cost growth under control.

Developing a new hospital reimbursement model was one thing; enacting it was another. A financial crisis affecting Social Security between 1982 and 1983 provided the Reagan administration and leading members of Congress with the necessary legislative opportunity to pass Medicare's prospective payment system as part of a larger and even more urgent package of welfare state reforms. Mushrooming budget deficits (stemming from President Reagan's major tax cuts passed in 1981), together with the highest unemployment rate and the worst recession in decades, created a sense of fiscal and economic crisis. When the Social Security boards of trustees released their annual reports on April 1, 1982, they noted that the Social Security system would be unable to pay cash benefits beginning in July 1983. Medicare's trust funds were in somewhat better shape, they reported, but the program still faced serious financial problems, including bankruptcy, by the late 1980s or early 1990s, unless changes were made.[11]

Following a decade of development, experimentation, and analysis, the passage of Medicare's new prospective payment system with DRGs represented something of an administrative revolution. Key to policymakers' success was the strange political attraction of prospective payment.

Hospital industry representatives were already desperate for any alternative to the Tax Equity and Fiscal Responsibility Act (TEFRA), budget legislation that was primarily aimed at quickly increasing tax revenue to reduce deficits. However, congressional leaders of both parties and Reagan administration officials wanted increased control of Medicare to restrain the program's rate of growth, despite the fact that prospective payment required significantly increased government regulation and control of health care. Also, with Social Security literally on the verge of bankruptcy in 1983, policymakers finally had a legislative vehicle for comprehensive Medicare reform that was unstoppable.

CHALLENGES POSED BY CHANGES IN MEDICARE

Following the rapid passage of Medicare's reimbursement system, a new set of concerns arose: Would the system actually work? Would Medicare's rate of expenditure growth subside? How would hospitals respond to the new incentives? Would any particular set of hospitals be wiped out financially by the new system? How would patients be affected, if at all? The only thing policymakers did know for sure was that, with a program as immense as Medicare, it was impossible to change just one thing.[12] The ripple effects of moving to a prospective payment system were bound to be extensive.

Phase-In Years of Medicare's New Hospital Cost Containment System

As it turned out, Medicare's new payment model had a major impact on hospital administration during its four-year phase-in period. During this time, the hospital industry's financial view of Medicare patients changed significantly. Instead of providing as much care as could be medically justified, hospitals shifted their focus to increasing efficiency and shortening Medicare patients' length of stay. In so doing, the PPS operated as a huge shock to the nation's hospital industry, because it completely reengineered the billing structure accounting for approximately 40 percent of every hospital's total revenue. The rate of growth in Medicare's hospital expenditures slowed considerably. Substantial cost control was accomplished with regard to Medicare hospital payment. No change in the private sector could ever have effected so much change in the U.S. health care system in so short a period of time. The Medicare payment reforms "were the most drastic and far-reaching changes in federal health policy since the passage of Medicare itself," notes David Smith. They were "remarkable for the comprehensiveness and sophistication of their design—indeed, the sheer technical achievement was astonishing."[13]

Medicare's transition to its new prospective payment system changed the focus of care. In fact, never had so much change in hospital management transpired in so short a period of time. Previously, because Medicare paid hospitals whatever costs they incurred, hospitals had no incentive to control their operating expenses. Higher costs translated into increased payments from Medicare, which administrators could, and often did, use to expand their hospitals' programs and services.[14] The PPS completely upended this status quo. By categorizing all hospital services and procedures, the new system allowed policymakers to know what medical care would cost *before* Medicare beneficiaries received it; the PPS established predetermined payment amounts for 467 different diagnosis-related groups. (In fact, the number of DRGs has increased over the years to approximately 536 to account for new procedures and services.) If the hospital managed to treat a Medicare patient for less than the DRG allotted, it kept the "savings" as profit. Conversely, if the hospital incurred more costs than the DRG allotted, it had to absorb the difference as a loss.[15] As a result, the structure of Medicare's financial incentives flipped. By separating an individual hospital's level of reimbursement from its production costs, the PPS triggered a radical change in hospital administration. The focus shifted from providing as much care as possible to maximizing the overall profit from each Medicare patient.[16]

The initial success of Medicare's new reimbursement model encouraged a number of key congressional leaders and the staff of the Health Care Finance Administration (HCFA; the predecessor to the Centers for Medicare and Medicaid Services) to make a series of changes that, ironically, resulted in the PPS becoming *more* complex and political rather than less (as originally intended). The process began in the mid-1980s when senior congressional leaders turned to the PPS as a new and hugely effective deficit reduction device. By simply restraining the annual increases in Medicare's hospital payment rates, Congress was able to divert tremendous amounts of government revenue for reducing annual deficits and increasing spending in other areas of the federal budget. Congress repeatedly adjusted Medicare's payment rates at levels below annual increases in medical inflation, which would not have been enormously consequential had the hospital industry as a whole restrained its cost growth. However, it did not. In the late 1980s and early 1990s, hospitals' costs continued to increase at their pre-PPS levels.

Yet "squeezing" Medicare payments to all hospitals for larger fiscal objectives struck many policymakers as unfair, because some hospitals were in a much better position than others to absorb a decline in Medicare reimbursement. Therefore, Congress began selectively targeting increased payment rates to specific hospital groups (teaching, rural, inner-city). Along the way, the original goal of the PPS—to establish one set of national, wage-adjusted payment rates—became eclipsed by the new goal of using the PPS to address major federal budget imbalances. In essence, as Medicare payment policy became increasingly subordinated to fiscal policy, Congress sought ways to try to ensure that the inevitable "rough justice" of moving to a national, standardized payment system would remain as financially fair as possible to the nation's hospital industry.

Medicare's PPS Triggers Private Sector Cost Containment with Managed Care

As Congress tightened Medicare's reimbursement policies, hospitals responded by increasing their charges to private payers. "Why it took private payers until the early 1990s before they began to marshal even a modicum of countervailing market power" is perplexing, notes Uwe Reinhardt.[17] However, employers eventually found their paradigmatic response: managed care. Prepaid group practice, a form of managed care, did precede Medicare's PPS, but organized medicine's traditional opposition to any form of reimbursement other than the fee-for-service model associated with indemnity insurance kept managed care marginalized for decades. What ultimately made market incentives sufficient to induce a paradigm shift in the private sector away from indemnity insurance and toward managed care was the success of Medicare's PPS in controlling health care costs in the public sector. What is ironic about the rapid shift in the U.S. health care system from a predominantly not-for-profit ethos to a more corporate orientation is that it was largely the incidental byproduct of federal policy initiatives designed to control Medicare's costs.[18] In other words, before business behavior triggered the managed care revolution, and the increased commercialization of health care that followed in its wake, it was largely a response to and an unintended consequence of government policymaking—in this instance, Medicare payment reforms.

By examining the connections between Medicare's subordination to budget policy and the rise of managed care, one finds that government policymakers in the late 1980s increasingly used the PPS as a powerful tool to address federal budget imbalances and increase spending on other government programs at the expense of health care providers (particularly hospitals but also physicians). Instead of increasing the payroll tax for Medicare (1.45 percent paid by workers and 1.45 percent by employers and deposited into Medicare's Part A Hospital Insurance Trust Fund) or making the program's beneficiaries pay more for their medical care, government leaders unintentionally increased less visible tax expenditures—tax revenue forgone—by precipitating a significant increase in health insurance costs for businesses.[19] In short, Congress and the George H.W. Bush administration (1989–1993) made it clear that the government was only going to control Medicare's hospital costs; employers were on their own.[20] The hospital industry responded to Congress's systematic reduction in Medicare's generosity by increasing the charges billed to their privately insured patients.[21] By its very definition, this billing behavior (most commonly referred to as "cost shifting") was simply passed along the payment chain and contributed significantly to large annual increases in private health insurance premiums.

Ironically, federal tax revenue was forgone in this budgetary process, because private businesses simply absorbed the increased costs charged by hospitals. Over time, therefore, an increasing number of employers responded to the growing imperative for cost control by ditching more expensive indemnity insurance for their workers in favor of cheaper managed care alternatives. This linkage illustrates that nothing can transform an industry more quickly and profoundly than when the government—if it is an industry's single largest customer—dramatically alters how it pays for goods and services.

Managed Care

Managed care as a term hardly existed until the early 1990s. Yet employers' shifting of their workers away from fee-for-service health insurance was facilitated by the managed care industry's ability to quickly construct networks of participating providers.[22] Between 1988 and 1993, managed care organizations responded to employers' demands for more cost control by consolidating and applying extensive utilization review and guideline development to their more traditional fee-for-service insurance offerings.[23] The traditional managed care organizations, such as staff- or group-model health maintenance organizations (HMOs)—for example, Kaiser Permanente—required significant expenditures in "bricks and mortar" when entering new markets. This served as a major barrier to entry because they were vertically integrated organizations that operated their own physical facilities in different geographic locations and whose physicians worked solely for the managed care organization.[24]

Beginning in the late 1980s and early 1990s, however, many new for-profit HMOs experienced rapid growth because they were "virtual organizations" or "organizations without walls," built largely on contractual (paper) relationships with community providers.[25] These new HMOs began competing with the traditional prepaid group practices by contracting with networks of private physicians called independent practice associations (IPAs). In this newer type of HMO, physicians would provide care for HMO patients in their own offices, but not at a shared clinic. This model kept health plans from having to invest in "bricks and mortar" or hire their own personnel. The IPA approach also enabled HMOs to enter new markets more quickly and with much lower capital expenses than the traditional prepaid group practices.

The initial shift to managed care had a self-reinforcing quality to it that fed back into the momentum away from fee-for-service insurance. Managed care organizations initially attracted and enrolled low-risk individuals who were least likely to object to restrictions on utilization of services and physician choice.[26] Because these low-risk individuals also tended to be healthier than the general population, they did not increase operating costs; on the contrary, they increased the profitability of managed care organizations.[27] Meanwhile, by expanding their provider base and involving in their systems more physicians whose predominant practice was fee-for-service, managed care organizations developed to the point that employers took them more seriously and found them significantly more attractive.[28] Why? Because by increasing their number of affiliated medical providers, managed care organizations essentially became more effective "managed cost" plans, which could negotiate lower prices on behalf of larger numbers of patients and then pass the savings on to employers.[29] Before this balance of power shifted to payers in the early 1990s, providers had set prices and determined fees in most markets.[30] The advent of Medicare's PPS provided private payers with a critical benchmark for categorizing and comparing medical providers' prices.[31]

Cost Control or a Temporary Success?

During the mid-1990s, employers experienced minimal to no growth in their health insurance costs, largely because managed care clamped down on medical spending and decreased hospitals' ability to charge privately insured patients more. The United States spent almost $120 billion less on health care in 1996 than the Congressional Budget Office had predicted in its 1993 forecast.[32] With declining private payments from managed care, the hospital industry finally achieved significant cost control.

Ultimately, therefore, much of the (temporary) success in containing Medicare's cost growth came at the expense of hospitals increasing their revenue from privately insured patients. Exactly how much hospital cost shifting was specifically caused by Medicare's PPS is difficult, if not impossible, to determine. Nevertheless, employers simply bought into the cost shifting argument made by ProPAC, health policy journalists, and others, regardless of how much empirical support there was for it. This confounds the causation question, because if employers believed that cost shifting was driving the inflation in their health care costs (and then acted on this belief), then that belief was a powerful influence in its own right.

Moreover, causality comes in different forms.[33] With respect to prospective payment, explains David Smith, the image of a river and flooding rains is helpful. The rain comes down (cost drivers are continually raising the cost of medicine), and there are many tributaries—new medical technology, rising prices, more elderly patients—filling the river. The PPS functioned, in part, as a diverting dam that helped to keep the flood away from Medicare. Yet the water was simply diverted back into the river. In other words, only Medicare was (temporarily) sheltered from ever-increasing medical inflation, and, after the PPS went into effect, the flooding problem became even worse because more water (cost drivers) was now moving down a smaller channel. In short, a huge part of the medical economy, Medicare, was no longer doing its part to absorb a significant portion of ever-increasing medical inflation because it was containing health care cost growth. This left employers in the private sector to make up the difference.[34]

This cost-shifting phenomenon became a major motivation for businesses to begin moving their workers into various forms of cheaper managed care. The responsibility for either paying more for medical care or accepting increased rationing—which the government chose not to do—now fell squarely on employers and other purchasers in charge of health care spending.[35] They quickly moved many of their employees out of traditional indemnity insurance and into various forms of managed care.

HMOs, however, sowed the seeds for future trouble by not fundamentally altering or improving the delivery of health care (as staff- and group-model HMOs such as Harvard Community Health, Kaiser Permanente, and Group Health had done for years in specific areas of the country, such as Boston, California, and Seattle, respectively). Instead, insurers simply employed the term HMO and focused on using contracting leverage to both negotiate discounts from medical providers and impose distant controls on them. The health care that resulted from these new arrangements was hardly more "managed" than it had been under traditional indemnity insurance. For these reasons, and others, managed care's cost containment efforts in the private sector eventually proved enormously unpopular and acrimonious in the latter half of the 1990s.

Medicare's Subsequent Cost Containment Success with Physician Expenditures

The cost-control success associated with Medicare's DRGs for hospitals led policymakers to rationalize the program's reimbursement of physicians. They adopted a resource-based relative-value scale (RBRVS) with a standardized fee schedule. One goal was to reduce payments to surgeons and specialists and increase them to internists and general practitioners. The main goal of the RBRVS and fee schedule, however, was to slow the rate of cost growth of Medicare Part B (which covers physician visits, outpatient services, preventive services, and home health visits and accounted for 20 percent of benefit spending in 2012); Part B benefits are subject to a deductible ($140 in 2012), and cost-sharing generally applies for most Part B benefits. When the new

payment system went into effect in 1992, the growth in volume and intensity of Medicare's spending on physician services slowed dramatically. Thus, the federal government succeeded in shifting another balance-of-power arrangement, in this instance, from physicians to Medicare.

Through most of the 1990s, Medicare's RBRVS-based fee schedule was viewed as a significant success by most observers. A sign of its acceptance is the fact that, much more than is the case with DRGs, the RBRVS system that was adopted and maintained by Medicare became adopted by most private payers.[36] Before the RBRVS system, the private insurers that abandoned the inflationary "usual, customary, and reasonable" payment approach often used relative value scales that had been based on historic charges, thereby perpetuating the alleged distortions among the various categories of services.[37] Private payers now typically rely on the RBRVS relativities, even if they often use different conversion factors to reflect local market factors that dictate their ability to negotiate fees with physicians.[38] Perhaps because organized medicine was given a major role in maintaining and updating the RBRVS system through the Relative-Value Scale Update Committee, physicians generally accepted the resultant shift in relativities of different services, even if they continued to strenuously object to expenditure limits (cost containment).

An added benefit of the expenditure limitation mechanism was that it was formula-driven. Congress merely needed to tinker with some parts of the formula, based on recommendations from the Physician Payment Review Commission (PPRC) and HCFA could meet its obligations to make the necessary changes in the payment systems that the contractors administered without any disruption in the flow of dollars to physicians for services rendered.[39] With control over budgetary expenditures for Part B (physician services), Congress did not concern itself much with "winners and losers" among the medical profession. Congress and the HCFA were more than happy to let the American Medical Association preside over inevitable "food fights" within the profession when cutting the pie of physician expenditures. Already having control over physician expenditures, Congress subsequently did not need to include physician payment as a target of savings in the Balanced Budget Act of 1997.

Paying on the basis of input costs, however, ignores whether the services provide value for patients. The assumption had been that what professionals decide to do with their professional time is the best determinant of value. Yet even in the mid-1980s, some had argued that Medicare should set the relative values not just on how physicians combine inputs to produce services but also on what it gets as outputs of a fee schedule in terms of benefit to beneficiaries and the program.[40] That is, relative values should reflect relative value, not merely resource costs. Now, with more

President Clinton's and President Obama's Addresses to Congress

President William J. Clinton's (1993–2001) nationally televised address to a joint session of Congress on September 22, 1993, marked one of the high points of public support for health care reform during the effort that began during his campaign in 1991 and ended in failure in September 1994. It was the first presidential address ever to Congress solely devoted to health care reform (Lyndon Johnson [1963–1969] urged Congress to pass Medicare in honor of his martyred predecessor, John F. Kennedy [1961–1963], who had pushed for the program's enactment).

Early polls showed overwhelming margins of public support for President Clinton's plan. Four months later, in January 1994, Clinton reiterated his pledge to veto any health care reform legislation that emerged from Congress but fell short of universal coverage. However, support for the president's plan eroded over the course of spring 1994 and disintegrated entirely by the end of that summer. Democratic allies in Congress splintered into supporting different alternatives to Clinton's plan, Republicans united in total opposition, and the general public grew less supportive and more concerned about government efforts at reform in general.

Unless we do this [pass health care reform], . . . health care costs will devour more and more and more of our budget. Pretty soon all of you or the people who succeed you will be showing up here and writing out checks for health care and interest on the debt and worrying about whether we've got enough defense, and that will be it, unless we have the courage to achieve the savings that are plainly there before us.

President Barack Obama's (2009–) nationally televised health care reform address to a joint session of Congress on September 29, 2009, sixteen years after president Clinton's address, was delivered to a more partisan, divided audience. In contrast to Clinton's speech, Obama did not have a detailed presidential reform plan that he was promoting or trying to explain to the public. Instead, he listed a number of principles he argued were essential for any legislative proposal to receive his signature. In this way, he delegated far more power to congressional leaders in determining the details of the eventual Patient Protection and Affordable Care Act that he signed into law on March 23, 2010. Another key difference between the two presidents' efforts is that Democrats were the majority in both the House and the Senate for Obama, while Clinton had only a Democrat majority in the House during his effort.

Then there's the problem of rising cost. We spend one and a half times more per person on health care than any other country, but we aren't any healthier for it. This is one of the reasons that insurance premiums have gone up three times faster than wages. It's why so many employers—especially small businesses—are forcing their employees to pay more for insurance, or are dropping their coverage entirely. It's why so many aspiring entrepreneurs cannot afford to open a business in the first place, and why American businesses that compete internationally are at a huge disadvantage. . . .

Finally, our health care system is placing an unsustainable burden on taxpayers. When health care costs grow at the rate they have, it puts greater pressure on programs like Medicare and Medicaid. If we do nothing to slow these skyrocketing costs, we will eventually be spending more on Medicare and Medicaid than every other government program combined. Put simply, our health care problem is our deficit problem. Nothing else even comes close. Nothing else. Now, these are the facts. Nobody disputes them. We know we must reform this system. The question is how.

than two decades of evidence that physician practice patterns and costs vary significantly without important differences in quality or patient satisfaction, there is increasing recognition that purchasers, including Medicare, may not be getting their money's worth for their major investment in physician services. More specifically, while the volume and intensity of physician services vary across the country, the variations seem to make no difference in either quality or patient satisfaction.[41]

The introduction of Medicare's new physician payment reform also further complicated the doctor-hospital relationship. Many specialist surgeons petitioned their hospitals to help them make up their income losses from Medicare, while hospital administrators increasingly pursued joint ventures with physicians for outpatient services in order to enhance their institutions' revenues, which they increasingly needed to offset the declining generosity of Medicare's hospital payments.[42]

Ultimately, though, the main problem with the Medicare physician fee schedule lies in the coupling of fixed budgets with fee-for-service reimbursements. First, the appropriate amount to be budgeted for physician services may be difficult to determine.[43] Using historic costs ignores the reality that technology changes, the population's burden of illness changes, and other factors may significantly alter how much should be allocated to any particular provider sector, such as physician services. The 1997 Balanced Budget Act (BBA) altered the calculation of the volume performance standard by tying spending-per-beneficiary on physician services to the rate of growth in the national economy, as reflected in growth in the real gross domestic product; the new expenditure limitation was called the Sustainable Growth Rate (SGR).[44] Whatever the theoretical merits of tying Medicare beneficiary needs for physician services to how the national economy is doing, the new SGR approach has proved unworkable and is currently subject to intense attention by Congress and its advisory bodies.

Second, in a fixed, national budget arrangement, all physicians have an incentive to overprovide, because gains from overprovision would typically exceed the losses from the pro rata reductions that the application of the expenditure limitation produces.[45] Under this system, prudent physicians are penalized financially, while profligate ones are rewarded. The PPRC had hoped that organized medicine would step up to the challenge of national expenditure limits by taking responsibility for rationalizing the volume of services through the establishment of clinical practice guidelines, enhanced peer review, and other professionally grounded approaches to reducing excessive volume and intensity of services.[46] It never happened, nor has Medicare ever achieved significant and sustained cost containment with regard to the program's physician expenditures.

Maintaining Health Care Cost Containment Proves Impossible

Following President Clinton's landslide reelection in fall 1996, representatives from both parties returned to using Medicare as a huge cost-containment mechanism in passing the Balanced Budget Act of 1997. The BBA constituted the ultimate subordination of Medicare to larger fiscal policy goals; it achieved approximately 73 percent of its total budgetary savings ($224 billion) from reductions in Medicare spending.[47] The BBA also attempted to capitalize on the cost containment potential of managed care by encouraging millions of Medicare beneficiaries to enroll in private health plans as part of a new Medicare+Choice program.

Temporary cost control by both Medicare and managed care in the private sector ultimately led to an economic reckoning that the U.S. health care system experienced in the late 1990s and the early 2000s. Health care reform by way of "managed competition" in the free market offered only a temporary solution to the nation's ongoing struggle with medical inflation.[48] Both the BBA's major Medicare cuts and the final death throes of restrictive managed care left medical providers in 1998 and 1999

MAP 17.1 **Medicare Spending during the Last Two Years of Life for Chronically Ill Patients**

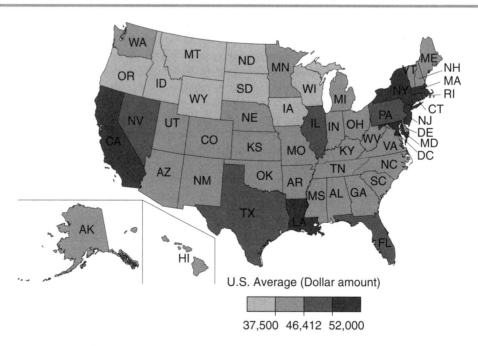

U.S. Average (Dollar amount)

37,500   46,412   52,000

The amount of Medicare spending on chronically ill patients varies by state, with New Jersey spending an average of almost $60,000 per patient and North Dakota spending less than $33,000 per patient. The spending associated with chronically ill and end-of-life patients continues to be a major factor in the government's and the health care community's work to control costs.

SOURCE: Adapted from the *Dartmouth Atlas of Health Care* by DWJ BOOKS LLC.

with declining payments from both public and private payers. Hospitals and home health agencies were particularly hard hit. When increasing cost pressures returned in the late 1990s, growing numbers of medical providers and managed care organizations found profitability difficult to achieve and bankruptcy a growing threat.

Eventually, renewed cost pressures, the BBA's significant Medicare cuts, and years of minimal (or nonexistent) payment increases from private payers left (1) the hospital industry with its lowest overall margins in a decade; (2) most physicians with increased workloads, less autonomy, and often reduced incomes; and (3) a slew of bankruptcies and near-bankruptcies among a wide variety of health care management and delivery organizations.[49] Yet medical providers were not alone. Even as managed care organizations experienced their own severe "profitability crisis," the consumer and physician backlash against them led to an aggressive legislative and legal assault on the industry. The general public came to view commercial managed care as responsible for turning doctors "into entrepreneurs who maximize profits by minimizing care."[50]

The Managed Care Revolution Stalls

Medical providers hastened the demise of traditional, restrictive managed care by consolidating into larger networks and practice groups, which vastly improved their bargaining leverage. A roaring economy in the late 1990s aided their efforts, because it led employers to request more generous and less restrictive health plans. By the early 2000s, most hospitals and physicians were receiving sizeable payment increases. Private health plans followed suit and pursued their own consolidation strategy. Many managed care organizations and traditional health insurance companies either merged or exited the market altogether. The surviving plans, facing less competition and more employer willingness to pay higher costs, quickly restored their profitability by dropping money-losing patient populations and increasing premiums. Employers also shifted more and more of their employees out of low-cost HMOs into less restrictive preferred provider organizations, which allowed them to increase their employees' level of cost-sharing.[51]

The result is that the managed care revolution—which was principally about the private sector forcing medical providers (primarily hospitals and physicians) to provide discounts to health plans and

employers—stalled and surrendered. Managed care organizations dropped most of the business practices that had restrained (at least temporarily) health care inflation in the United States. Many of them also dropped their participation in Medicare+Choice, after years of overreaching for "easy" Medicare profits, which left millions of the program's beneficiaries scurrying to reestablish their coverage under the program's traditional fee-for-service arrangements.

This increased consolidation and the declining effectiveness of market forces triggered a return to rampant medical inflation in the 2000s. Health plans and hospitals successfully negotiated significant payment increases after years of minimal or no revenue growth, which restored the majority of them to solid financial health. However, skyrocketing health insurance costs and a sluggish economy left an additional five million Americans without health insurance coverage by 2003.[52] Medical-related bankruptcies increased substantially, as did the costs of and enrollment in Medicaid.

In the midst of these and other deteriorating health care trends, President George W. Bush and Congress passed the largest expansion of Medicare since the program's enactment in 1965. The 2003 Medicare Prescription Drug, Improvement, and Modernization Act differed from the pattern established between the 1983 Social Security reforms and the 1997 BBA. It added a hugely expensive (almost $550 billion between 2006 and 2015) drug benefit with major

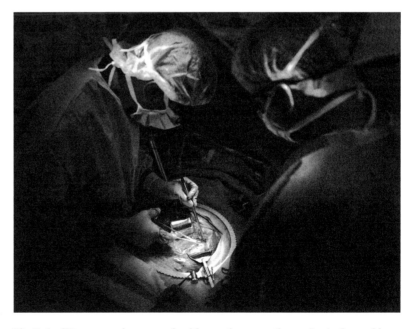

The United States spends more on health care than any other nation in the world, about $8,200 per person per year as of 2012. That figure is more than two-and-a-half times higher than most developed nations in the world, including relatively wealthy European countries such as Sweden, France, and the United Kingdom. U.S. health care now accounts for 18 percent of gross domestic product.

SOURCE: Brendan Smialowski/AFP/Getty Images.

coverage gaps for millions of people who spend moderate to high amounts on prescription drugs.[53] It injected the first elements of means-testing into Medicare, by which wealthier beneficiaries will pay more than poor beneficiaries for both their Part B (physician and outpatient) services and Part D drug benefits. It also pushed the program toward increased privatization with a financial overcommitment to private health plans that enroll Medicare beneficiaries. These measures have not resulted in any noteworthy health care expenditure restraint.

Currently, while about thirty-three million Medicare beneficiaries voluntarily enroll in the program's Part D

Section 3403 of the Patient Protection and Affordable Care Act: The Independent Medicare Advisory Board (also known as the Independent Payment Advisory Board)

This section of the Patient Protection and Affordable Care Act establishes specific target growth rates for Medicare and charges the Independent Payment Advisory Board (IPAB) with ensuring that Medicare expenditures stay within these limits. The IPAB must also make recommendations to Congress as to how to control health care costs more generally. As noted by Bruce Vladeck in 1999 in *Health Affairs*, the IPAB

will have significant authority to curb rising Medicare spending if per beneficiary growth in that spending exceeds target growth rates. In a process that began in 2013, recommendations made by the 15-member board will go to Congress for rapid consideration; Congress must adopt these or enact savings of similar size in Medicare. If Congress doesn't act within a specified timetable, the secretary of health and human services (HHS) must implement the board's recommendations. The board is not allowed by law to recommend changes in premiums, benefits, eligibility, or taxes, or other changes that would result in "rationing" of care to Medicare beneficiaries.

SEC. 3403. INDEPENDENT MEDICARE ADVISORY BOARD.

(a) BOARD.—(1) IN GENERAL.—Title XVIII of the Social Security Act (42 U.S.C. 1395 et seq.), as amended by section 3022, is amended by adding at the end the following new section:

INDEPENDENT MEDICARE ADVISORY BOARD

SEC. 1899A. (a) ESTABLISHMENT.—There is established an independent board to be known as the "Independent Medicare Advisory Board."

(b) PURPOSE.—It is the purpose of this section to, in accordance with the following provisions of this section, reduce the per capita rate of growth in Medicare spending—

(1) by requiring the Chief Actuary of the Centers for Medicare & Medicaid Services to determine in each year to which this section applies (in this section referred to as "a determination year") the projected per capita growth rate under Medicare for the second year following the determination year (in this section referred to as "an implementation year");

(2) if the projection for the implementation year exceeds the target growth rate for that year, by requiring the Board to develop and submit during the first year following the determination year (in this section referred to as "a proposal year") a proposal containing recommendations to reduce the Medicare per capita growth rate to the extent required by this section; and

(3) by requiring the Secretary to implement such proposals unless Congress enacts legislation pursuant to this section.

(c) BOARD PROPOSALS.—

(1) DEVELOPMENT.—

(A) IN GENERAL.—The Board shall develop detailed and specific proposals related to the Medicare program in accordance with the succeeding provisions of this section.

(B) ADVISORY REPORTS.—Beginning January 15, 2014, the Board may develop and submit to Congress advisory reports on matters related to the Medicare program, regardless of whether or not the Board submitted a proposal for such year. Such a report may, for years prior to 2020, include recommendations regarding improvements to payment systems for providers of services and suppliers who are not otherwise subject to the scope of the Board's recommendations in a proposal under this section. Any advisory report submitted under this subparagraph shall not be subject to the rules for congressional consideration under subsection (d).

pharmaceutical program, it was designed (and continues to operate) largely on financing from general revenues, which are 80 percent of the program's total cost. Many leading Republicans in Congress were hopeful that forcing the new benefit to be financed from general revenues would make its total cost more transparent and, thus, of greater concern in annual budget negotiations. On the individual level, policymakers also tried to restrain the new benefit's cost growth by including a "donut hole," whereby once a Medicare beneficiary reaches $2,930 of Part D spending on pharmaceuticals in a calendar year, he or she becomes responsible for any additional drug costs accrued up to $4,800, at which point Part D coverage reengages. Part of the 2010 Patient Protection and Affordable Care Act includes a gradual phasing out of the donut hole until its closure by 2020. Part D has been less costly than originally predicted, largely due to the fact that only about 77 percent of Medicare beneficiaries have enrolled in the benefit (rather than the original estimate of 93 percent). Yet monthly premiums have increased each year of operation by approximately 10 percent and are predicted to continue increasing by the same annual rate. Additionally, total Part D expenditures will increase from roughly $85 billion in 2013 to around $150 billion by 2020.

THE IMPACT OF THE PATIENT PROTECTION AND AFFORDABLE CARE ACT ON HEALTH CARE COSTS

The need for health care cost containment has only become more urgent in recent years. The landmark passage of the Patient Protection and Affordable Care Act (PPACA) in March 2010, along with its constitutional upholding by a slim 5–4 Supreme Court vote and President Obama's reelection in November 2012, will dramatically increase the number of insured people with access to more health care. Roughly thirty million currently uninsured individuals were expected to gain insurance coverage starting in 2014, which will cost hundreds of billions of dollars by the end of the decade. Also, as a demographic tidal wave (the baby boom generation) began retiring in 2010, the government's longtime use of Medicare as a fiscal "cash cow" for other budgetary purposes has become much more problematic despite the fact that the PPACA depends on hundreds of billions of dollars in reduced future Medicare payments to health care providers—mostly hospitals and physicians—to finance expansions in health insurance coverage. Furthermore, with health care expenditures constituting 18 percent of gross domestic product and on course to reach expenditures of 20 percent by 2020, employers and government leaders are hoping that alternative reimbursement models such as bundled episode payments and capitation to medical homes and Accountable Care Organizations will engender better quality and slow cost growth.[54] To date,

TABLE 17.1 **Federal Government Spending on and Financial Support of Health Care in the United States**

Program	Approximate Amount of Federal Spending (2011)
Tax expenditure on employer-provided health insurance	$260 billion
Medicare	$550 billion
Medicaid (federal portion)	$275 billion
Children's Health Insurance Program (federal portion)	$8 billion
Department of Veterans Affairs	$90 billion
Indian Health Service	$4 billion
National Institutes of Health	$31 billion
TOTAL	$1.3 trillion

SOURCES: Department of Health and Human Services, Office of Management and Budget, Congressional Budget Office.

unfortunately, preliminary pilot studies have given little reason for observers to be overly optimistic about any major health care cost containment in the near future.

Ultimately, as health economist Victor Fuchs observes,

It is difficult to see how the health sector can continue to expand rapidly at the expense of the rest of the economy, but every past prediction of a sustained slowing of the growth of health expenditures has been proved wrong. Rapid growth may continue as a result of political gridlock regarding the form that curbs on expenditures should take. There is no public consensus about how much care should be provided for the poor and sick or how it should be done. Similarly, there's no public consensus regarding efforts to increase the efficiency of care. A rational approach to the financing, organization, and delivery of care seems politically impossible. However, the observation by [Alexis] de Tocqueville [the French political thinker who toured the United States in the 1830s] that in the United States "events can move from the impossible to the inevitable without ever stopping at the probable" may prove to be prescient.[55]

See also **Chapter 13: Government Financing of Health Care (1940s–Present); Chapter 14: Biomedical Research Policy and Innovation (1940s–Present); Chapter 16: Promoting Health Care Quality and Safety (1960s–Present); Chapter 18: Health and Health Care Policy: Ethical Perspectives (1970s–Present); Chapter 20: Women's Issues and American Health Care Policy (1960s–Present); Chapter 21: Minorities, Immigrants, and Health Care Policy: Disparities and Solutions (1960s–Present); Chapter 26: Interest Groups, Think Tanks, and Health Care Policy (1960s–Present).**

NOTES

1. See Medicare Payment Advisory Commission, *Report to the Congress: Medicare Payment Policy* (Washington, DC: March 2002), 4.

2. Jill S. Quadagno and Debra Street, "Ideology and Public Policy: Antistatism in American Welfare State Transformation," *Journal of Policy History* 17 (Spring 2005): 64.

3. See Paul Starr, *The Social Transformation of American Medicine* (New York: Basic Books, 1982).

4. See Bruce C. Vladeck, "The Political Economy of Medicare," *Health Affairs* 18: 1 (1999): 27.

5. Interview with the author.

6. See Gail R. Wilensky and Joseph P. Newhouse, "Medicare: What's Right? What's Wrong? What's Next?" *Health Affairs* 18: 1 (1999): 92–106.

7. Medicare Boards of Trustees, Federal Hospital Insurance and Federal Supplementary Medical Insurance Trust Funds, *2005 Annual Report*.

8. Bradford H. Gray, *The Profit Motive and Patient Care: The Changing Accountability of Doctors and Hospitals* (Cambridge, MA: Harvard University Press, 1991), 3.

9. Starr, *The Social Transformation of American Medicine*, 380.

10. Congressional Budget Office, *Hospital Cost Containment Model: A Technical Analysis* (Washington, DC: Congressional Budget Office, 1981).

11. John K. Iglehart, "Health Policy Report: Medicare's Uncertain Future," *New England Journal of Medicine* 306 (1982): 1308–1312.

12. James A. Morone and Andre B. Dunham, "The Waning of Professional Dominance," *Journal of Health Politics, Policy & Law* 3 (1984): 73-87.

13. David G. Smith, *Paying for Medicare: The Politics of Reform* (New York: Aldine de Gruyter, 1992), 3–4.

14. U.S. Department of Health and Human Resources, *Report to the Congress: Impact of the Medicare Hospital Prospective Payment System* (Washington, DC: U.S. Department of Health and Human Resources, 1984), I-2.

15. Office of Technology Assessment "Medicare's Prospective Payment System: Strategies for Evaluating Cost, Quality, and Medical Technology" (Washington, DC: U.S. Government Printing Office, 1985), 3.

16. U.S. Department of Health and Human Resources, *Report to the Congress*, I-4.

17. See Uwe E. Reinhardt, "Columbia/HCA: Villain or Victim?" *Health Affairs* 17: 2 (1998): 32.

18. Gray, *The Profit Motive and Patient Care*, 6.

19. For more on this common government approach to fiscal policy, see Christopher Howard, *The Hidden Welfare State: Tax Expenditures and Social Policy in the United States* (Princeton, NJ: Princeton University Press, 1997).

20. See Walter A. Zelman and Robert A. Berenson, *The Managed Care Blues and How to Cure Them* (Washington, DC: Georgetown University Press, 1998), 33–34.

21. See Stuart Guterman, Jack Ashby, and Timothy Greene, "Hospital Cost Growth Down," *Health Affairs* 15: 3 (1996): 134–139.

22. Douglas R. Wholey et al., "HMO Market Structure and Performance: 1985–1995," *Health Affairs* 16: 6 (1997): 75–84.

23. Marsha R. Gold, "DataWatch: HMOs and Managed Care," *Health Affairs* 10: 4 (1991): 189–206.

24. Jon Gabel, "Ten Ways HMOs Have Changed during the 1990s," *Health Affairs* 16: 3 (1997): 136.

25. Ibid., 134–145.

26. Mark V. Pauly and Sean Nicholson, "Adverse Consequences of Adverse Selection," *Journal of Health Politics, Policy and Law* 24 (1999): 925.

27. Ibid.

28. See Gold, "DataWatch," 192–193.

29. See Elizabeth W. Hoy, Richard E. Curtis, and Thomas Rice, "Change and Growth in Managed Care," *Health Affairs* 10: 4 (1991): 18–36.

30. George C. Halvorson, "Health Plans' Strategic Responses to a Changing Marketplace," *Health Affairs* 18: 2 (1999): 28–29.

31. See Grace M. Carter et al., "Use of Diagnosis-Related Groups by Non-Medicare Payers," *Health Care Financing Review* 16: 2 (1994): 127–158.

32. Uwe Reinhardt, "Calm before the Storm: Will There Be a Second Revolution in American Health Care?" 1997 Duke University Private Sector Conference, Session 1: The Status of Managed Care and Evolutionary Trends.

33. Chain causation: your car hit mine and knocked it into the car in front of me. Causal network: affecting one part of a related network, such as an intrusion into an environment or habitat. Contributing causes, which are common in tort cases, such as environmental pollution.

34. Email exchange with the author, August 13, 2005.

35. See Kenneth E. Thorpe, "Managed Care as Victim or Villain?" *Journal of Health Politics, Policy and Law* 24: 5 (1999): 950.

36. Zachary Dyckman and Peggy Hess, "Survey of Health Plans Concerning Physician Fees and Payment Methodology" (Washington, DC: Medicare Payment Advisory Committee, June 2003), 13–15.

37. See Jack Hadley et al., "Alternative Approaches to Constructing a Relative Value Schedule," in *Medicare Physician Payment Reform—Issues and Options*, edited by John F. Holahan and Lynn M. Etheredge, 29–46 (Washington, DC: Urban Institute Press, 1986).

38. Dyckman and Hess, "Survey of Health Plans," 15.

39. Smith, *Paying for Medicare*, 270.

40. See Jack Hadley and Robert A. Berenson, "Seeking the Just Price: Constructing Relative Value Scales and Fee Schedules," *Annals of Internal Medicine* 106: 3 (1987): 461–466.

41. See Elliott S. Fisher et al., "The Implications of Regional Variations in Medicare Spending," Parts 1 and 2, *Annals of Internal Medicine* 138 (2003): 273–298; John E. Wennberg, Elliott S. Fisher, and Jonathan S. Skinner, "Geography and the Debate over Medicare Reform," *Health Affairs* (2003): W3-586–W3-602.

42. See Michael Hagland, "The RBRVS and Hospitals: The Physician Payment Revolution on Our Doorstep," *Hospitals* 65: 4 (1991): 24–27.

43. John Holahan, "Physician Reimbursement," in *National Health Insurance: Conflicting Goals and Policy Choices,* edited by Judy Feder, Theodore R. Marmor, and John Holahan, (Washington, DC: Urban Institute Press, 1980), 107.

44. Government Accountability Office, *Medicare Physician Payments: Concerns about Spending Target System Prompt Interest in Considering Reforms* (Washington, DC: U.S. Government Printing Office, October 2004), 4.

45. Holahan, "Physician Reimbursement," 107.

46. See Physician Payment Review Commission, *Annual Report to Congress: 1989* (Washington, DC: Physician Payment Review Commission, April 1989), 207–217.

47. Stuart Guterman, "Putting Medicare in Context: How Does the Balanced Budget Act Affect Hospitals?" (Washington, DC: Urban Institute, July 2000), 2; Brian Biles et al., "The Cost of Privatization" (Washington, DC: Commonwealth Fund, December 2004).

48. Stephen Heffler et al., "Health Spending Growth up in 1999; Faster Growth Expected in the Future," *Health Affairs* 20: 2 (2001): 193–203.

49. "Trends and Indicators in the Changing Health Care Marketplace" (Washington, DC: Kaiser Family Foundation, 2005).

50. See Deborah A. Stone, "Bedside Manna: Medicine Turned Upside Down," *The American Prospect*, (March-April 1997): 42–48.

51. See Robert E. Hurley, Bradley C. Strunk, and Justin S. White, "The Puzzling Popularity of the PPO," *Health Affairs* 23: 2 (2004): 56–68.

52. U.S. Census Bureau, *Income, Poverty and Health Insurance Coverage in the United States: 2003* (Washington, DC: U.S. Government Printing Office, August 2004).

53. See Bruce Stuart, Linda Simoni-Wastila, and Danielle Chauncey, "Assessing the Impact of Coverage Gaps in the Medicare Part D Drug Benefit," *Health Affairs* (2005):W5-167–W5-179.

54. Austin B. Frakt and Rick Mayes, "Beyond Capitation: How New Payment Experiments Seek to Find the 'Sweet Spot' in Amount of Risk Providers and Payers Bear," *Health Affairs* 31: 9 (2012): 1951–1958.

55. Victor R. Fuchs, "Major Trends in the U.S. Health Economy since 1950," *New England Journal of Medicine* 366 (2012): 977.

FURTHER READING

Altman, Stuart, and David Shactman. *Power, Politics, and Universal Health Care: The Inside Story of a Century-Long Battle.* Amherst, NY: Prometheus Books, 2011.

Fuchs, Victor. "Major Trends in the U.S. Health Economy since 1950." *New England Journal of Medicine* 366 (2012): 973–977.

Mayes, Rick, and Robert Berenson. *Medicare Prospective Payment and the Shaping of U.S. Health Care.* Baltimore: Johns Hopkins University Press, 2008.

Starr, Paul. *Remedy and Reaction: The Peculiar American Struggle over Health Care Reform.* New Haven, CT: Yale University Press, 2013.

Health and Health Care Policy

Ethical Perspectives (1970s–Present)

Andrew Flescher

MERICANS HAVE ENTERED AN ERA THAT warrants renewed ethical attention to the way in which we undertake health care delivery and conduct biomedical experiments in this country. In light of technology's advancing frontiers, new questions about health care provision and research abound. What sorts of policies should the nation responsibly adopt in light of the reality that health care is more expensive than ever before despite persistent disparities in health care access?[1] What is the fairest, most humane way to attend to our growing elderly population? Do we need to do a better job of restructuring shared resources through rationing and, if so, how should we go about it? How should experiments in the health sciences be conducted so as to preserve the autonomy and respect of those whose voluntary participation makes such experimentation possible? What is the attitude that society ought to adopt toward innovations such as stem cell research, human cloning, and pre-genetic testing? These issues provoke a reexamination of some traditional suppositions in public health and health care policy.

SOCIAL JUSTICE AND THE ETHICAL IMPETUS FOR HEALTH CARE REFORM

Americans are pressed to account for two unfortunate points of comparison with other developed nations: (1) the nation provides coverage for a smaller percentage of its citizenry than other countries that are similarly circumstanced while (2) spending more money than any other country in the world on health care. Not only is the United States inefficient in terms of the delivery of health care compared to other nations, but that care is also inequitable, for there is a significant correlation between the set of Americans who lack coverage and those who are either racial minorities, are less educated, or live below the poverty line. Specifically, one

in two uninsured Americans has an income below 138 percent of the poverty level, one in five has not finished high school, one in two identifies as a racial or ethnic minority, one in five has limited English proficiency, one in two does not have a usual source of health care, two in five did not visit any health care provider in the last year, and one in two has not been insured for the past year.[2] How could the United States be getting so little for its investment, which disproportionately shortchanges already disadvantaged populations? A large part of the answer has to do with the idiosyncratic features of the U.S. health care system, as well as American values, which make health care in the United States more expensive and less equitable than anywhere else.

The figures pertaining to the cost of health care are staggering. The nation's expenditures on health care are growing faster than any other part of the economy. In 2011, the United States spent almost 18 percent of gross domestic product (GDP) on health care, or $2.7 trillion. By 2019, expenditures are projected to be an even larger percentage of GDP, reaching about $4.7 trillion.[3] For decades, health care costs have significantly exceeded the rate of general inflation. Health care is too expensive for many Americans to afford. Just before the passage of the Patient Protection and Affordable Care Act (PPACA) in 2010, nearly one in four Americans reported having problems paying medical bills; by 2005, nearly one million people had experienced medical bankruptcy.[4] What makes health care so expensive in the United States, and what might be done to stem the tide of its rising costs?

Multiple Health Care Factors

A number of factors play into what drives up the costs of health care in the United States. First of all, in societies such as ours, where health care is a booming industry and private providers profit from its delivery, there is typically little administrative simplicity. This makes that portion of health care delivery not related to equipment, medication, or personnel very expensive. According to some estimates, up to one third of all health care costs in private industry are administrative, in comparison to the much lower figure of just more than 3 percent in the case of Medicare.[5] In most other developed countries, where health care is not quite so privatized, the costs associated with administration, and thus the overall costs, are significantly lower.

Second, in contrast to countries such as Great Britain and Switzerland, where the government is empowered to regulate most of the costs associated with health care delivery, in the United States, outside of public insurance programs, there are seldom negotiated prices up front for things such as medical supplies, procedures, or medications.[6] Negotiation does occur but only after the fact at the level of reimbursement, in the form of discounted payments on billed charges. This leads to two sorts of problems: (1) in the context of a fee-for-service system, the overall lack of governmental regulation drives up the cost of goods as they would be driven up in the case of goods in any other market, and (2) negotiations for reimbursements on a case-by-case basis leads to a situation in which different payers are willing to accept different charges and pay different amounts of those charges, leading to cost-shifting (as well as outrageous charges for the uninsured), rather than cost containment.[7] Thus, the lack of price regulation is both unsustainable and lacking in transparency.

Furthermore, as a result of the nation's dominant model of "individualized care," there is little incentive for consumers who have managed to secure ample coverage to avail themselves of their health care benefits conservatively and responsibly. This leads to a situation of both waste and disparity, where some individuals lack any coverage while others overuse health care. In the United States, where top-of-the-line equipment and medicines exist, we must also deal with the enormous costs to support these technologies and resources to a greater degree than anywhere else. Therefore, in valuing "the best and the latest," we also make the decision not to restrict the availability of medical equipment that is both costly and often most in need of consistent maintenance.[8]

However compassionate and well-intended our health care system's commitment to acquiring and widely disseminating the newest and most cutting-edge equipment is, following this policy is potentially fiscally unsustainable. This consideration leads to a fifth reason health care is so expensive in the United States: Americans do not relish discussions about rationing care. Indeed, the general public is reluctant even to acknowledge that rationing is already occurring in the health care system (as it inevitably will in any situation that involves the allocation of finite resources), just not necessarily in a manner that is supported by a transparent discussion about the nation's values and wishes to have health care support in U.S. society. While in the overall picture rationing is not as big a driver of health care costs as is the failure to successfully regulate prices, the nation's resistance to participating in debates about what to ration contributes to a situation in which people harbor unrealistic expectations of what health care should be provided, despite the large amounts of taxes and tax subsidies used to pay for it.

Cultural Issues

Thus, it appears that there are some culturally specific reasons that account for why health care is so expensive in the United States, while at the same time its delivery is not as efficient as it is elsewhere. These realities have led to some undesirable trends. The large population of uninsured or underinsured Americans—at the time of the 2008 presidential election, close to eighty million individuals—causes about forty-five thousand premature deaths a year.[9] If one believes that in a developed nation such as the United States, no one ought to die of a treatable disease, then these figures represent a lapse incommensurate with the ambition reflected in other similarly circumstanced nations to attend to the health care needs of their least well off.

Contributing to the problem of ineffective distribution of existing resources are the emergence of several other potentially unsustainable features of the nation's health care system, including unfunded mandates that are expensive to secure, such as the Health Insurance Portability and Accountability Act of 1996; long-term health planning goals that are not sufficiently outcomes-based; a lack of incentive in our fee-for-service system for physicians and other health care providers to prescribe only what is medically necessary; and a culture of "defensive medicine" governed by the ever-present threat of malpractice accusations. The upshot of these factors on the eve of the PPACA was a health care delivery system containing little distributive justice. Despite the fact that in 2010, at the time of the passage of the PPACA, close to 150 million Americans received health care through Medicare, Medicaid, the Children's Health Insurance Program, community health centers, and other programs that combined to serve as a safety net for the least well off, only a privileged minority had the fewest roadblocks to accessing health care or stood to benefit from the highest quality resources.

SHOULD HEALTH CARE BE CONSIDERED A RIGHT?

The reality that the United States has a health care system that imposes substantial economic burdens and effectively denies needed care to many leads to a fundamental philosophical question: should health care be considered a right? Life is not fair, and we are not all born in the same bed. What arguments can be made for redistributing resources so as to bring closer together the plight of the privileged and that of the disadvantaged? Alternatively, what arguments can be brought forth to refute the notion of health care as a right? The extent to which a nation's laws ought to compel its citizens to do more than merely not interfere in the affairs of others is a subject of significant debate in any civilized society. That individuals should abide a principle of non-violation where they are prohibited from harming others does not necessarily require them to contribute to the provision of health care for everybody. Is government supposed to do more than secure and enforce laws that fulfill the principle of non-violation, and if so, does this "more" extend to providing health care coverage for everyone?

Throughout the nation's history, the government has enacted laws that entail at least moderate proactive governmental intervention beyond the principle of non-violation, for example, tax impositions deemed necessary to prevent society from lapsing into a chaotic or uncivil state. On occasion, legislation has favored proactive redistribution of resources, but with the exception of the elderly and permanently disabled (who have Medicare) and the very poor (who have access to Medicaid), redistributive programs have targeted very specific geographic areas, population groups, and services. If access to affordable health care is to be considered a *right,* then society will have to furnish new arguments to suggest that civility is centrally about more than one's avoidance of wrongdoing, that it is also about securing the conditions of justice and flourishing of all people, the fulfillment of which may require a (presumably justifiable) impingement on the liberty of some. Even if the government establishes universal provision of basic health care, members of society who are well off are going to have to subsidize others who are struggling. What are the available ethical arguments to sustain the view that the rich ought to subsidize the poor? What are the arguments that refute this view?

Moral Arguments for a Right to Health Care

One of the most enduring and powerful arguments in the arsenal of someone who believes health care is a right is made manifest in Immanuel Kant's "categorical imperative," according to which, in deciding how to act, we are to bracket our own station in life and do what we would wish someone else in our shoes do.[10] On this analysis, we do not make of our own case an exception, ever, and realize that were we to look at ourselves as one among others, objectively, we would want ourselves and everyone to have health care. The political theorist John Rawls concretized Kant's categorical imperative with his notion of a "veil of ignorance" and insisted that when we morally deliberate we not consider class, gender, religion, or any other tangible detail about ourselves when making policy decisions in society.[11]

With such a procedural constraint in place, we would on the basis of rational persuasion likely want everyone to be eligible for basic health care. Utilitarians, who argue that we ought always to act on behalf of "the greatest good for the greatest number" of people, also would be in favor of a health care system with massive redistribution of resources to cover as many people as possible. In its insistence on maximizing available resources, utilitarianism enjoins the robust redistribution of wealth so as to meet this end. An "ethics of virtue," in kind, dictates that it is unbecoming of citizens of a flourishing society to allow their neighbors to die of a treatable disease.

Civility itself, according to this argument, requires us to provide certain basic goods for everyone, such as shelter, food, freedom from violence, the ability to pursue and choose a form of life, education up to a certain age, and basic health care for everyone.[12] In this virtue-based approach, we cannot fully be human if we are not communally oriented enough to worry about the welfare and well-being of those around us. Another argument in favor of universal health care can find support in some interpretations of the "natural law" tradition, according to which we ought to live in a nation in which those with excess ought to give what they can spare to the impoverished. John Locke spoke of a "surplusage" among the wealthy to which the needy in society had an inalienable right.[13]

Pragmatic Arguments for a Right to Health Care

Thus, there is no shortage of moral arguments of which we can avail ourselves to find justification for the idea that those who have resources ought to provide for those who do not. Supplementing the above arguments are a few pragmatic ones designed to appeal to the rational egoist on his or her own terms. The first is based on reciprocal self-regard: who gets sick is a lottery, which means that because anyone could be sick some day, it is mutually beneficial to support a system in which all would be covered. The second pragmatic argument appeals more directly to self-interest. We are all better off if as many people as possible in society are healthy. Conversely, we suffer social ills when we live in a society without adequate child care, preventive medicine measures, strategies for addressing communicable infectious diseases, and so forth. According to this reasoning, even if we are guaranteed that we ourselves are to be healthy in the immediate or near future, we will have better quality of life on a number of levels the healthier others around us remain.

Compelling arguments also abound to suggest that health care, while clearly something that would be nice to be able to provide for everyone, is not, strictly speaking, a right. A right is an entitlement, something one possesses from the outset of one's existence, which confers on the providers of that right a duty to provide it, whether they like it or not. Those who object to the notion of health care as a right believe that morality, in essence, is about the avoidance of wrongdoing, not about the proactive duty to enhance or even save other lives. On the basis of what authority, they ask, can I be *persuasive* (and not just assertive) that health care is a universal right? The one who argues against conceiving of health care as a right grants that some believe that we owe the stranger what we owe the near and dear and that we ought to treat the neighbor as we would ourselves, but points out that these beliefs are based on religious ideals about the world and our connection to one another. They are not universalizable recommendations on the basis of which to formulate societal rules. Life is not perfect or perfectly fair. Those in favor of universal health care, they argue, do not have the legitimacy to impose their metaphysical assumptions about the universe on everyone else.

Arguments against a Right to Health Care

Both moral and pragmatic arguments arise in defense of the view that health care is not a right. First, there is an interpretation of the "natural rights" tradition, somewhat different from John Locke's understanding, according to which one ought never to be compelled, through the arm of the state, to care for another. This libertarian understanding of the natural law tradition maintains that all forms of helping others, including attending to the health needs of others, while always good and noble activities in which to participate, ought not to be regarded as compulsory and therefore enforceable. On governmental involvement in health care, a recent Libertarian Party platform stated:

> The proper and most effective source of help for the poor is the voluntary efforts of private groups and individuals. We believe members of society will become more charitable and civil society will be strengthened as government reduces its activity in this realm.[14]

Consistent with this in-principle objection to governmental intervention into health care is the touchstone notion heralded by most libertarians that health care, like other goods one wishes to secure for oneself, is a matter of personal responsibility. Thus, many worry that in a system of universal care the onus for dealing with individual decisions to smoke, ride motorcycles, or even eat certain unhealthy foods on a regular basis will transfer from the one deciding to take part in those activities to the society in which they occur. When queried about the occasions on which individuals become sick due to what is evidently no culpable activity on their part, libertarians tend to reply that even in these instances it behooves us to acknowledge that life is an assumed risk from the moment of birth. That life comes with no guarantees, however, does not imply that health care should be considered an entitlement, the financial means for which should be provided by the state.

Aside from the question of what individuals do or do not owe their neighbor, there is, not surprisingly, additional libertarian resistance to campaigns by governmental agencies to protect the public against communicable diseases through immunization programs. Herein exists another fault line between the libertarian versus communitarian approach to medicine. The former, which prizes the individual over the collective, believes that laws that require vaccines overreach, violating the rights of individuals who are penalized for refusing government-mandated immunization programs. The most famous legal case pertaining to this issue is *Jacobson v. Massachusetts* (1905), which occurred in response to a smallpox outbreak in 1902 and was decided by the Supreme Court. It involved a Lutheran minister who harbored a number of unspecific fears about the smallpox vaccine, leading him to reject the Board of Health's mandate that he inoculate himself against the disease. The decision, which upheld the community's right to protect its citizens by enforcing compulsory vaccination laws, reflects society's belief that there are occasions on which individual liberty over one's body is not to be regarded as a trump card. Today, the libertarian lobby stands at the forefront of arguing against governmental mandates to vaccinate children and other susceptible populations, even following the outbreak of a contagious disease.

Supplementing this libertarian argument against universal health care is a utilitarian one of a different sort than the pro–universal coverage utilitarian argument mentioned above. While providing everyone with health care may be a worthy objective, in reality it is just too complex and costly to implement. There are so many hidden costs entailed in providing universal coverage that any sort of reform in a direction away from the current market-driven model is likely to bankrupt the entire system. For example, there are hidden costs in the technologies of health care, which any extra utilization is bound to exacerbate. MRI machines need to be maintained; when a person receives plasma transfusions, he or she needs to be put on immunosuppressant drugs. These things are all expensive and will become too costly if everyone in society becomes eligible to use them, or so libertarians claim. Universal health care, argue opponents of reform, will inevitably lead to an unsustainable overutilization on the part of the individuals who are suddenly covered. Moreover, they argue, the mere assumption that health care is free will lead to overutilization. If human beings *perceive* health care is a right, they will avail themselves of it with undue frequency if there are not countervailing methods of matching services and needs.

Interference with Clinical Judgment

Critics of governmentally supported universal coverage worry that the minute control over health care is ceded to third parties. Even if that control pertains merely to the financing of health care, the country invites circumstances under which physicians are forced to abdicate control over the welfare and well-being of their patients. Hence, there is the fear of "death panels," in which the state will supposedly determine who will live and who will die.[15] Universal coverage necessitates rationing to prevent overutilization, but, ask critics, who decides what ought to be covered? Finally, there are other practical considerations that speak in favor of a capitalistic system of health care delivery. While capitalism leads to disparity, it is also necessary for innovation. Price-fixing, for example, as in the case of pharmaceutical companies, is likely to disincentivize those researching the best new medications.

Thus, there is apparently no shortage of views one could espouse in defending or attacking the idea of health care as a right to which all citizens of a country should have affordable access. If health care is a right that society has to safeguard, then how might the nation administer this right to its citizens? It will be helpful to look at the Patient Protection and Affordable Care Act in some depth and examine the respects in which it both manages and fails to address some of the issues addressed above.

THE PATIENT PROTECTION AND AFFORDABLE CARE ACT AND COST CONTAINMENT

While the Patient Protection and Affordable Care Act (PPACA), signed into law in 2010, does not attend to all of the potential elements of reform enumerated above, it does address at least some of the important ethical matters that surface when determining how best to care for the worst off in society. First, in providing strong incentives for health care providers to deliver health care more efficiently and less redundantly, it is expected to reduce long-term health care costs over the long haul.[16] The Congressional Budget Office (CBO) predicted the PPACA is going to cost $940 billion over ten years, but reduce the deficit by $143 billion in the first ten years and $1.2 trillion in the second ten years.[17] Even if the CBO projections of savings are accurate, the new cost-saving incentives in the law will ensure that it at least does not cost money over the long haul. This said, the rate of growth in national health care spending has in fact fallen to historical lows in the past four years. The CBO projections are much higher than actual spending trends, at least for now.[18] How much this can be attributed to the PPACA, directly or indirectly, versus the general economy and other factors is subject to considerable debate, but it is certainly the case that by conscripting into participation paying healthy customers, costs incurred by sicker participants will much better be able to be absorbed, thereby addressing the issue of health care access, if not rising health care costs.

ETHICAL PRINCIPLES FOR POTENTIAL RATIONING OF HEALTH CARE

The Patient Protection and Affordable Care Act identifies no basic medical services that are to be precluded from coverage by insurance plans, as a result of which almost no part of Medicare is pared down to contain costs. In other words, the PPACA goes no distance toward tackling the tricky but essential question of rationing. If society wishes to consider basic health care a universal right, then society had better think carefully about what sorts of health care ought to be included. What principles might the nation adopt to determine what constitutes basic health care? Answering this question requires making some value judgments as well as adopting rules that provide for being as fair as possible in determining what should be covered and what should not. The default rule of thumb, "services shall be provided according to whoever is best in a position to pay," arbitrarily advantages the rich and privileged. What guidelines might be less discriminatory?

Ezekiel Emanuel, the medical ethicist and one-time adviser on health care for the Obama administration, introduces four rules by which we might form utilitarian principles for allocating scarce resources.[19] The first, "treat all people equally," insists on assigning no disadvantage based on who one is, where one comes from, and what the handicaps are under which one labors. One way to implement the maxim is to have a lottery to determine who receives services when there is not enough to go around; another is to enforce a policy of "first come, first served." A second rule would be to decide as a society to favor a specific disadvantaged demographic, for example, the worst off, the youngest among us, or those individuals with the most life years ahead of them. A third rule to follow is that of straightforward utility: act to maximize total benefit in terms of saving the most lives or, alternatively, the most life years. In this case, pay for those medical goods and services that affect the most people and make some hard choices with regard to people suffering from rare or costly diseases. Finally, perhaps adopt policies that promote and reward social usefulness by virtue of attending first to those members of societies deemed especially valuable. We do this to a certain extent already, for example, by making sure health care professionals are the first to receive critical vaccinations that enable them to work safely in health care settings.

Each of these four rules has its advantages but is also rife with problems from the perspective of social justice. In the first rule, "treat all people equally," lotteries are resistant to corruption but seem blind to socially relevant factors that would seem to bear on what is just (such as race, class, gender, sexual orientation, and so forth). Likewise, "First come, first served" protects the doctor-patient relationship but by unduly favoring well-connected or wealthy patients, thereby violating fairness. The second rule, "favor the worst off," appeals to customary rules of rescue that go out of their way to protect the most vulnerable, but fails to prioritize the practical consideration of looking at which resources will in the long run bear most fruit. (Society might consider whether it is economically efficient or ethically sagacious to keep alive babies born prematurely at the twenty-fifth week of pregnancy.) Favoring the youngest, likewise, protects longevity but unduly prioritizes one demographic over others. Third, while a straightforward "greatest good for the greatest number" sort of logic arguably benefits the most, it too ignores other trumping considerations, not the least of which is the view that all of life is valuable, not just the lives judged to have the most qualitative potential. Finally, deriving principles by heavily weighing the roles certain important people or groups fulfill in society is, while perhaps socially efficient, also discriminatory in its own right and laden with its own set of value judgments.

It appears that when we think as a society about how best to go about rationing (as opposed to letting those in power or who have an economic interest decide how best to ration), there is no easy solution. While Ezekiel Emanuel blames the overuse of medical care on the insistence in the Hippocratic Oath that physicians take any and every step to avoid harm to the patient,[20] he is not quite as decisive about exactly which services should be cut or what principles ought to be favored when actually going about rationing.

POLITICS AND HEALTH CARE POLICY

The Individual Mandate

Originally proposed by the Heritage Foundation in 1989 as the alternative to a single-payer national health insurance plan, and subsequently adopted by Congress as a key provision of the Patient Protection and Affordable Care Act (PPACA), the individual mandate confers on each citizen the responsibility of making sure he or she has health insurance. The individual mandate was first adopted as a key element in the Massachusetts package of health care reforms in 2006, which was negotiated by Democratic legislators and Republican governor Mitt Romney (in office 2003–2010) along with George W. Bush's (2001–2009) administration. By virtue of this historical precedent, it was included in congressional proposals in 2009 not only as a functional way to ensure buy-in from the health insurance industry but also as an attempt to secure at least some Republican support (which was not forthcoming, as legislative sponsors hoped it would be). The idea behind the individual mandate is that since who gets sick and who remains healthy is ultimately a cosmic lottery, it behooves all of us to support each other as a society by assuming the collective responsibility of providing health coverage for all. Because it is inappropriate for a civilized society to leave its poorest citizens to languish, proponents of the individual mandate maintain that individuals who are in the financial position to provide some protection against others getting sick ought to do so. According to an actuarial analysis, the individual mandate is necessary to make insurance premiums both affordable and economically feasible among large groups of enrollees. If only sick individuals buy into a health care system, then the risk pool will be narrow, and the system will quickly go bankrupt due to adverse selection. Through the individual mandate, the PPACA requires individuals not covered by their employers or other sources of insurance to cover themselves. Those who cannot demonstrate that they are below 133 percent of the poverty line will owe penalties to the Internal Revenue Service when they file their taxes for that year.[21]

The individual mandate is a controversial topic. Once embraced by the political right as an alternative to a single-payer system, critics of the Obama (2009–) administration, particularly libertarians, today claim that it coercively forces individuals into participating in an activity of which they want no part.[22] Defenders of the PPACA claim that because everybody gets sick at some point, and for the most part cannot control getting sick, the individual mandate requires us to pay only for a good we are already using and for which others are paying.

Moreover, symbolically it signals an attitude that "we are all in it together," so to speak. It is true that the premiums of those who are healthy defray the costs that are incurred by individuals who are ill on an ongoing basis, but in the future it could be the healthy person who gets sick later. A similar argument is used to justify payroll and income taxes on younger workers to support current Medicare beneficiaries. Critics of the individual mandate note that legislation that compels participation in a form of commerce flies in the face of a historically American preference for voluntary association, bucking the long-standing legacy of Alexis de Tocqueville, who once wrote: "democracy extends the sphere of individual freedom, socialism restricts it."[23] Lawyers on behalf of states that embraced this sentiment argued before the Supreme Court that just as no one can be compelled to eat broccoli, so is it the case that no one can be forced into an activity of commerce of which they want no part. In summer 2012, the Supreme Court considered constitutional objections to the PPACA, with Chief Justice Roberts, a conservative, casting the deciding vote in favor of upholding the individual mandate's constitutionality.[24]

OTHER PPACA PROVISIONS ON COVERAGE AND INSURANCE REGULATION

As crucial as the individual mandate is to the overall Patient Protection and Affordable Care Act, certain other features of the law bear elucidation.[25] Significantly, the PPACA does not de-privatize the process of acquiring coverage. Individuals, through a process of enrolling in state-administered health care exchanges, retain choices as to what kind of insurance plans they would like to purchase for themselves and their families (with premiums corresponding to appropriate level of coverage and deductibles). The enrollment process began October 1, 2013, in time for the individual mandate to go into effect January 1, 2014. The PPACA specifies that insurance companies cannot discriminate against prospective enrollees on the basis of their preexisting conditions, nor can they repeal coverage based on technicalities, as they were legally

However, Emanuel and his colleagues do consider a number of ways of combining the aforementioned principles into systems, for example, the United Network for Sharing, which allocates points based on principles such as "sickest first" and "gravity of prognosis"; the quality-adjusted life year (QALY) allocation; the disability-adjusted life year (DALY) allocation, which combines a QALY system with additionally calculated years based on certain health coefficients, such as freedom from chronically debilitating conditions; and the Complete Lives Systems, which combine DALY with the "bell-curve of life," or ages between the very young and old.[26] Thus, according to the approach recommended by the Complete Lives Systems, we would favor the population that is least vulnerable to disease (e.g., those between the ages of seven and eighty) in deference to the strategic assessment that this group has the best chance of surviving medical hardship and going on to flourish.

These combined systems, however, raise new questions about arbitrariness. For example, what exactly is "social usefulness," and how would one know? Should a child afflicted with an infectious disease get preference over an end-stage elderly cancer patient? Why or why not? Are there occasions on which social justice dictates that care is futile, or, if not completely futile, a squandering of the public's resources based on other existing priorities? Should we ever discriminate based on age and follow, for example, the recommendation of Daniel Callahan, who argues that the elderly (which he loosely defines as people in their mid-70s

allowed to do in the past. Moreover, by law, insurance companies can no longer set lifetime benefit caps and must offer their premiums at regulated rates. Young adults are now able to stay on their parents' insurance plans until the age of twenty-six, and the law makes anyone who subsists at 133 percent of the poverty line or below eligible for Medicaid. Still more measures in the law serve to alleviate some of the previously bankrupting features of health care in the United States. Up to four million Medicare recipients now have drug coverage to fill the so-called donut hole, which previously specified that once a certain cap had been reached for seniors, they would have to pay for their medications until they reached a threshold beyond which catastrophic coverage kicked in. The new law additionally earmarks $15 billion in a Prevention and Public Health Fund for programs including smoking cessation and introduces incentives to induce physicians to join together to form Accountable Care Organizations that help them coordinate and improve patient care, prevent illness, and reduce unnecessary hospital admissions. In keeping with this provision, the PPACA requires that health care providers move toward standardization of billing and medical records while adopting and implementing rules for the secure, confidential, electronic exchange of health information.

Thus, there are several provisions in the new law that constrain insurance companies not to avail themselves of an actuarial advantage by discriminating against potential enrollees or by cutting costs at the expense of the individuals such companies cover. Why, then, did the insurance companies strongly support the passage of the PPACA? The answer, in short, is that the individual mandate, if successfully implemented (which still remains to be seen), ensures that insurance companies will get enough additional healthy, paying customers to more than offset what all the rest of these provisions combined will cost them. This calculation alone underscores the significance of the PPACA being a national plan. Ensuring universal coverage is not merely left up to a particular state, in which case that state runs the risk of becoming a magnet for the sick. Indeed, the act is written to be comprehensive enough to be able to create conditions for universal access and affordability without inviting adverse selection. By law, it eliminates prior barriers to coverage such as preexisting conditions, stems the tide of Medicare fraud and waste, improves safety and quality of health care by investing in prevention and wellness, and, through the exchanges, does so in such a way that is consistent with our underlying identity as a country whose citizens prize choice and the retention of individualized care between physicians and their patients. Just so long as everyone is enrolled in some fashion, health care is more accessible and affordable for everyone.

PROPOSALS NOT ADOPTED IN THE PPACA

Several potential reforms were *not* included in the final version of the Patient Protection and Affordable Care Act, the absence of which unfortunately makes the lowering of the overall cost of health care unlikely. Most generally, the nation still does not have a single-payer plan in which revenue for universal health insurance coverage is collected through taxation, thus leaving many of the administratively complicated features of the current health care system intact or, worse, susceptible to becoming even more complicated. More pointedly, provisions for incentivizing hospitals to employ discharge specialists, present in the original draft of the act, got removed during congressional reconciliation. This is unfortunate, because such provisions would have made it easier to have professionals, such as social workers, consult with the families of terminally sick patients about when it made most sense for their loved ones to transition from hospital to hospice. Research has shown that this transition to hospice not only gives end-of-life patients far more comfort than when they are left to die in a hospital but also leads to better health outcomes and saves significant amounts of money. Sadly, critics of the PPACA successfully used the language of "death panels" to scare politicians out of supporting these provisions in the final version of the bill. Finally, nowhere in the PPACA is the crucial issue of rationing addressed. Should the nation enact provisions to preclude reimbursement for unnecessary duplication of medical tests? How shall the nation go about implementing such regulations? What shall be society's stance on care deemed futile? These sorts of issues seem especially politically difficult for us as a nation to discuss.

SOURCES: Gawande Atul, "Letting Go," *The New Yorker,* August 2, 2010, http://www.newyorker.com/reporting/2010/08/02/100802fa_fact_gawande; Kaiser Family Foundation, "Summary of the Affordable Care Act," April 25, 2013, http://kff.org/health-reform/fact-sheet/summary-of-new-health-reform-law.

or older) ought to be deprived of extraordinary means in intensive care settings in deference to sparing resources for the rest of the population?[27] "The trustees of Medicare projected its insolvency in eight years, and in a decade our overall national health care costs will double," wrote Callahan in 2012. "Not one of the most dominant diseases of aging has been cured, but more ways have been found to keep patients alive with them."[28] As Callahan points out, 65 percent of the nation's health care costs are incurred by 20 percent of the population, principally the elderly.[29] Yet as Callahan's critics are wont to point out, the economically obvious solution to the problem of an overburdened Medicare system would be less generous payments for all services, not denial of payments for services to certain beneficiaries. Such an approach would be not only more effective but also more humane. Clearly, the prospect of rationing, which Callahan thinks is necessary if the nation's health care system is to avoid bankruptcy in coming years, is fraught with the danger of making critical and consequential value judgments.

End-of-Life Care and Physician-Assisted Suicide

While the United States is slowly catching up to the rest of the developed world with respect to coming to terms with the idea that death is an important part of the life cycle, the fact of the matter is that, relative to citizens in other nations, the U.S. population, generally, still has a great deal of difficulty acknowledging death and establishing guidelines for how best to exhibit compassion in end-of-life cases. One of the trickiest ethical issues in the realm of medicine and public health policy is what to do with patients who do not have long to live and who are either suffering or no longer competent while facing scenarios that they may have regarded as degrading if they still had capacity. Although most Americans believe in the right to die, only 29 percent have a living will, perhaps not wishing to imagine themselves in a situation in which an advance directive would become relevant.[30]

In the absence of legally binding advance directives, what is the professional and moral obligation to patients who require extraordinary measures to be kept alive? What is the compassionate thing to do for such patients? Does it entail respecting the wishes of family members or friends? Finally, how do we resolve the tension between the principles of autonomy and well-being, especially when we must weigh them in lieu of any legal document unambiguously expressing what patients would have wanted? Complicating matters is a lack of uniformity among state laws in cases in which there is no advance directive and no formal proxy has been given.

The dilemma is no less pressing when family members, on behalf of a loved one, do want treatment withdrawn. Particularly in states that have restrictive end-of-life laws, patients are intubated or have feeding tubes installed even when the family provides evidence that this is not what their loved one would have wanted. To avoid such an occurrence, New York State passed the Family Health Care Decisions Act in June 2010, which establishes the authority of a patient's family member or close friend to "make health care decisions for the patient in cases where the patient lacks decisional capacity and did not leave prior instructions or appoint a health care agent." Under the law, this "surrogate" is eligible to speak on behalf of the patient and also has the authority to direct the withdrawal or withholding of life-sustaining treatment "when standards set forth in the statute are satisfied."[31]

The question of when it is appropriate to deprive patients of potentially lifesaving technologies is related to the issue of physician-assisted suicide, in which a physician, out of compassion, proactively helps a patient administer drugs that will end his or her life. The practice is legal in only four states: Oregon, Vermont, Washington, and Montana (the latter by court decree rather than legislation). With physician-assisted suicide, it is the patient who still autonomously "acts last." Oregon was the first state to legalize physician-assisted suicide; its Death with Dignity Act permits residents who are suffering from end-stage diseases and found to be sane to voluntarily self-administer life-ending medications under the supervision of a physician.[32] Perhaps surprisingly, Oregonians avail themselves of this legal right much less frequently than some predicted they would when the law was enacted.[33] This suggests that, even where physician assisted suicide is legal, those suffering from terrible diseases still by and large maintain a healthy regard for life and understand the significant step of ending their life. Importantly, physician-assisted suicide ensures that autonomy is preserved, as it is still the patient who makes the decisive move to end his or her life.

In Michigan, in one case, Jack Kevorkian, a practicing physician, publicly claimed to have helped more than one hundred people end their lives, many of whom had suffered from ALS (Lou Gehrig's Disease). Kevorkian was convicted of second-degree murder and sentenced to ten to twenty five years in prison when he moved beyond physician-assisted suicide (which in the state of Michigan was illegal) and himself administered the drugs that killed Thomas Youk, whose ALS symptoms had progressed to the point that he could not administer the drugs himself. Kevorkian maintained that he did not merely assist in this patient's death; he performed euthanasia by killing a man who did not have the ability to take his own life. At present, there is no state in which euthanasia is considered legal.

Should we permit patients to "die with dignity"? Moreover, is there any relevant difference between killing and letting die, that is, between euthanasia and physician-assisted suicide, if in both cases the intent is the same?[34] Again, much of the ethical analysis hinges on the extent to which we place emphasis on a patient's right to self-determination over the sanctity of life itself (which may or may not be based on religious beliefs). Other factors, such as how to interpret the injunction against harming that is entailed in the Hippocratic Oath, become relevant in considering any moral or legal distinction between physician-assisted suicide and euthanasia. As the average age of the U.S. population continues to rise in coming years, these ethical issues will become increasingly important to address within the health care system and through clear public policies.

MEDICAL ADVANCEMENT, EXPERIMENTS, AND HUMAN SUBJECTS

One response to the health care cost crisis offered by medical ethicists who are resistant to rationing pertains to medical advancement and the smarter use of technology. If health care providers are able to do more with what is available—and do a better job distinguishing the patients who present as sick from the ones who are actually sick—then this will place less of a burden on cutting medical goods and services deemed essential to vulnerable populations. In a recent study conducted at Stony Brook University in New York, involving two sets of 894 matched Emergency Department patients complaining of chest pain, researchers showed that the use of a new scanning device, a Coronary Computed Tomographic Angiography, in one of the groups was able to reduce the number of patients admitted to the hospital for further testing by 5.5 times the level of patients undergoing standard diagnostic procedure.[35] The upshot of such a finding is that as technology gets better, society in some cases can save significant amounts of money by using new diagnostic resources and being smarter about who is treated and under what circumstances. This, of course, needs to be weighed against the rising costs of technology in general, which is arguably the biggest factor in rising health care costs overall. How can we be smarter and more efficient with new technology? One way to make health care more economically viable is to use volunteers—patients who give their permission to serve as human subjects in tests of the efficacy of new technological resources, medications, and so forth—so that the medical community can accurately test outcomes. As we will see, the nation's history of respecting the autonomy of patients as subjects has not always been above reproach.

A senior citizen expresses her desire to make her own decision about her right to die. The issue of physician-assisted suicide, which is legal in Washington, Oregon, Vermont, and Montana, raises a variety of ethical issues. In the ruling Baxter v. Montana (2009), the Montana Supreme Court found no public policy against assisting suicide. In 2014, a judge in New Mexico ruled, "This court cannot envision a right more fundamental, more private or more integral to the liberty, safety and happiness of a New Mexican than the right of a competent, terminally ill patient to choose aid in dying."

SOURCE: AP Photo/Charles Dharapak.

The Tuskegee Syphilis and Willowbrook State School Experiments

In 1932, scientists and U.S. Public Health Service workers from the Tuskegee Institute began experiments on close to four hundred men in Macon County, Alabama, where 40 percent of the population suffered from syphilis. The goal of the experiment was to follow but not treat the men who had contracted the disease. The subjects—in general, impoverished, black, and undereducated—were not informed that they were being observed, much less not treated, for the potentially fatal disease they had contracted.[36] It was only forty years later, in 1972, when the story of Tuskegee broke, that some of the subjects received penicillin despite the fact that the antibiotic had become the main medication used for treating the disease as far back as the 1940s.[37] In a similarly disturbing case, children with intellectual disabilities at the Willowbrook State School in Staten Island, New York, were intentionally given hepatitis in an attempt to track the development of the viral infection. The study began in 1956 and lasted fourteen years.[38] Researchers explained away their deliberate infections and exposures through spurious utilitarian reasoning: given the high rate of infection in the institution it was practically inevitable that the children would catch the disease anyway, and we might as well scientifically benefit from that inevitability.[39]

The Cancer Cells of Henrietta Lacks

In a yet another case lacking informed consent, if not explicit deceit, Henrietta Lacks, a victim of cervical cancer, had her cells extracted and used without her permission by physician George Otto Gey. Cultured and eventually immortalized, these cells, now known as the HeLa cell line, were the first to be successfully cloned. Scientists have since grown about twenty tons of her cells, with which, to date, roughly eleven thousand patents are associated. Henrietta Lacks died in 1951, but her family did not learn of their mother's gift to science until the 1970s, much less receive any form of compensation for it.[40]

KEY DECISIONS: HEALTH CARE CRISES AND SOLUTIONS

The National Research Act of 1974

The National Research Act, signed into law July 12, 1974, called for the creation of a National Commission for the Protection of Human Subjects of Biomedical and Behavioral Research whose purpose was to identify the ethical guidelines for informing prospective participants about the nature of and the risks entailed in the experiments.[41] In 1979, this commission, under the auspices of the Department of Health, Education and Welfare, released the Belmont Report, which specified the boundaries between practice and research, enumerated the basic ethical principles by which human subjects would be recruited for experiments in this country (e.g., "respect for persons," "beneficence," "justice"), and outlined in careful detail what "informed consent" was to mean, including furnishing subjects with every available means to be given the opportunity to choose what should and should not happen to them. "Respect for persons" pertains to informing subjects of how they will be used in experiments and making sure that their consent is procured freely. "Beneficence" ensures that all subjects be treated ethically and in a way that keeps them free from harm. Finally, "justice" calls attention to the delicate balancing act of who bears the burdens and who reaps the benefits of research, making sure that in this calculation, the volunteering human subjects do not lose in the equation. The Belmont Report today still serves as the foundational precedent on which regulations in the United States on the use of human subjects in experimental research are based.

Nevertheless, debate persists about just how restrictive the recruitment of subjects in research ought to be. Are there special considerations along the lines of race, gender, culture, religion, and disability that the protocol of research ought to take into account? Does the Belmont Report go far enough to ensure that certain populations will not be discriminated against in the name of scientific advance? On the other hand, in using Tuskegee as one of its main cases in point, does the Belmont Report lay the ground for unrealistic guidelines for recruitment, unfairly constraining scientists' ability to conduct research by curtailing the potential participation of human subjects? Here, the criticism is that autonomy (i.e., ensuring that the subject has full control over any decisions that affect him or her) is never fully possible, and therefore, as written, the Belmont Report overregulates and is thus counterproductive. Also, what is "respect for persons" in the first place, and why should society assume that it is a trumping value, particularly when other goods lay in the balance? Is the Belmont Report philosophically sophisticated enough to deal with this thorny and nuanced distinction?

The question of recruiting human subjects is not the only one surrounding biomedical experimentation. There is also the question of "clinical equipoise," or what evidentiary standard should be adopted to determine when a new, better trial should be given preference over an existing one. The standard view is to err on the side of caution and not depart from customary practices before becoming convinced that a new method is superior. This is a difficult standard to maintain, however, as there is always so much financially at stake in determining how experimentally to proceed. Naturally, the situation becomes even more complicated if there is a debate about to whom researchers have their primary obligation. Are they most bound to protect their subjects? The scientific community? Prospective beneficiaries of their discoveries? Their funders? Furthermore, what should the standard of approval be for existing versus future treatment options? Is it ethical to assume by default that, all other things being equal, doing something is better than doing nothing? Under what circumstances should we follow a different, comparatively effective treatment option with the default option? How much should cost weigh into this discussion? Are we justified, for example, in prescribing a medication that is 95 percent as effective as the gold standard of treatment if the medication costs significantly less money? Where are the thresholds that serve as guides by which we answer these tough questions? The engine that powers scientific advance also invites new, contemporary quandaries for responsible scientists to consider.

Biomedical research becomes further complicated when one tackles the difficulties of ensuring that many populations whom researchers would ideally want represented are nevertheless excluded as subjects of clinical trials. In looking at the risks associated with teen births, for example, it is important to stratify age ranges; babies born to mothers between the ages of twelve and fifteen incur greater risks than mothers between the ages of fifteen and seventeen. However, for practical reasons, it is extremely difficult to involve enough of the younger group of teenagers in an experiment to get an adequately reliable sample size. (The risk of upsetting such individuals by including them in the experiment may outweigh the benefit of increasing the sample size.) There are countless such examples where clinicians and researchers must think about how responsibly to secure a legitimate sample size (and comparison or control group) while never failing to take into account the psychological, emotional, and in some cases physical needs of their prospective subjects.

SOURCES: Richard B. Miller, "How the Belmont Report Fails," *Medical Research Ethics* 4: 2 (2003), http://commons.pacificu.edu/cgi/viewcontent.cgi?article=1089&context=eip; National Commission for the Protection of Human Subjects of Biomedical and Behavioral Research, "The Belmont Report," April 18, 1979, http://www.hhs.gov/ohrp/humansubjects/guidance/belmont.html; Nancy Shore, "Re-conceptualizing the Belmont Report: A Community-Based Participatory Research Perspective," *Journal of Community Practice* 14: 4 (2006): 5–26; Peter Ubel and Robert Silbergleit, "Behavioral Equipoise: A Way to Resolve Ethical Stalemates in Clinical Research," *American Journal of Bioethics* 11: 2 (2011): 1–8.

STEM CELL RESEARCH, HUMAN CLONING, AND PRENATAL GENETIC TESTING

Just because we can do it, does this mean we should do it? More often than not, technological innovation arrives before society has taken the time to think through the full range of consequences of its implementation. At the same time, advances such as stem cell research, human cloning, and pre-genetic or prenatal testing potentially stand to improve the plight of victims suffering from currently incurable disease and otherwise increase the chances of human betterment in the long run. How long do we need to identify and weigh the benefits and costs of our utilization of new technologies, and what, if any, changes to our understanding of what it is in the first place to be a human being will such technologies precipitate? While it is too soon to address the answers to these questions in any thorough manner, it does behoove the biomedical ethicist to acknowledge that with our changing world come new contemporary issues for ethical reflection.

Stem Cell Issues

In 1998, John Gearhart of Johns Hopkins University, James Thomson of the University of Wisconsin, and colleagues figured out how to develop stem cell lines from human embryos, a significant advance beyond the previous technology in which stem cells could be produced only ad hoc, in tiny amounts, out of tissue from embryos or fetuses. Since that time, stem cell research, particularly research utilizing embryos, has come to represent a significant opportunity for scientists to help the body, when it is injured, grow new cells, make new blood, and, most important (and in distinction to adult stem cells), develop into differentiated cellular tissue.[42] In 2001, in one of his first acts in office, President George W. Bush (2001–2009), guided by conservative bioethicist Leon Kass, restricted federal funding for research on human embryos, permitting the money to be used only in connection with the sixty stem lines remaining after in vitro fertilization, that is, not on embryos that were specifically created for research. Citing ethical and religious concerns about humans being used as a means only, Bush's historic live press conference indicated not only a precedent for what was legitimate ethical use of stem cell technology, but also more broadly that the nation had entered an era in which biomedical ethics had become a primary concern for political reflection and policymaking.[43] In response to complaints that these stem lines, which actually numbered fifteen and not sixty, were inadequate, there was pushback in the U.S. Senate to fund research on all embryonic cells. Congress remained deadlocked, but Proposition 71 in California, passed in 2002, designated $3 billion in state revenues for stem cell research from human embryos. On March 9, 2009, President Barack Obama issued Executive Order 13505, removing the Bush restrictions on National Institutes of Health funding research on embryonic stem cells.

The principal objection to research on embryonic stem cells, and certainly Kass's main concern, pertains to the assertion that human embryos are considered a form of life and therefore of intrinsic value, not to be destroyed for any superseding purpose. In addition, some ethicists share the concern that if embryos can be used for research then this might represent its own inducement for abortion, even infanticide, or, equally chilling, a spur to procreate for reasons that neglect to consider the welfare and well-being of the human entity being created.[44] What such critics need to address, apart from establishing the moral status of the embryos they wish respected, is whether such respect ought legitimately to be considered a trump card that potentially stands in the way of curing dreadful diseases previously thought to be untreatable. This, in essence, amounts to a debate about the merits of engaging in utilitarian calculations. Are the stakes ever so high that the prospect of bringing about a great good will be considered enough to allow the formation of policies that permit the thing about which we once had grave reservations? In the case of stem cell research, we are still at the stage where we need to learn more about what fruits the use of embryos can yield.

Human Cloning

Human cloning is a different case than stem cell research in at least two respects: (1) unlike developing stem cell lines from embryonic stem cells, we are not yet able to clone human beings, and (2) it is less clear what good lies in the balance in the case of cloning. Here, the impetus for scientific research seems at least to be as much a matter of seeing what we can scientifically discover for its own sake as it is about helping other people. This makes the ethical case for cloning human beings weaker than the case for allowing public funds to be used for embryonic stem cell research. This said, there remain important potential reasons for considering human cloning, for example, to ease the production of stem cells or new medications or to solve human fertility problems. There is a vast literature on the extent to which human cloning will speed up the process of innovative medical breakthroughs. Thus, it would be shortsighted to think that cloning is only a matter of scientific hubris, curiosity, or a feature of some imperative to break new technological ground.

The specter of reproductive human cloning, not merely the creation of identical twins but the reproduction of a genetically identical copy of the same human being, came to widespread speculation when in the late 1990s the Roslin Institute near Edinburgh, Scotland, announced the birth of a lamb named Dolly, which had been cloned. The Institute waited until it received a patent for the technology before making the announcement.[45] Those in favor of cloning Dolly emphasized that, as in the case of stem cells, cloning humans could have many applications, among them regenerating seriously damaged or dead cells, as well as implications for retarding the aging process.[46] Additionally, some stress that cloning, like stem cell research, could have a positive overall effect on the quality of human life over time.[47] Opponents from religious perspectives stress the sacredness of all human life and worry about the prospect of human beings "playing God." They also harbor concerns about unwise ambitions to perfect a human race, as the Nazis infamously tried with their program of eugenics in the 1930s and 1940s.[48]

There are additionally some safety concerns with regard to cloning. The late novelist Michael Crichton made a career warning us about the consequences of this type of hubris. In his book *Jurassic Park*, the mathematician Ian Malcolm is surely speaking in Crichton's own voice when he says in response to the use of cloning technology used to bring the dinosaurs back to life:

> Broadly speaking, the ability of the park is to control the spread of life forms. Because the history of evolution is that life escapes all barriers. Life breaks free. Life expands to new territories. Painfully, perhaps even dangerously. But life finds a way.[49]

Here the concern is with regard to when the experiment *does* go right. As Francis Fukuyama observes, successful human cloning would alter who the human being fundamentally is.[50] It might even lead to a world of rampant discrimination, where human beings born of parents who did not avail themselves of the means to avoid genetic susceptibility to disease and deformity would be at a perennial disadvantage, as depicted in the riveting 1997 film *Gattaca*.

Prenatal Genetic Testing

This latter concern leads to the importance of ethically reflecting about a related scientific advance, prenatal genetic testing, for which, unlike human cloning, we do currently have the technology. Currently, the American College of Obstetricians and Gynecologists recommends that all women be screened to determine if their unborn fetuses will suffer from a disease or debilitating condition, such as Down syndrome.[51] As of 1999 in this country, 90 percent of women who tested positive for a fetus with Down syndrome elected to have an abortion.[52] Is Down syndrome, which is among the more mild conditions with which a newborn baby may be afflicted, a legitimate reason in itself to have an abortion? On the other hand, is it appropriate for anyone besides the potential mother, and perhaps the potential father, to weigh in on the answer to this question? Just who are the legitimate arbiters of what constitutes the quality of a future human life?

With the advent of prenatal genetic testing—a practice that is not only legal, but recommended in U.S. culture—all of these questions take center stage. Indeed, the very existence of prenatal genetic testing invites society to ponder the distinction between the legitimate goal of avoiding disease and disability on the one hand, and the questionable ambition of creating a society of individuals who possess desirable qualities and traits on the other. When the Human Genome Project has been fully completed, society might know more than it wishes to know. What are the psychological burdens when individuals learn about their propensity to pass on "defective" genes to the next generation? How will the information that is gathered in the process of completing the project be used? These questions and similar ones will accumulate the more gene-centric molecular science and the field of medicine becomes.

LOOKING AHEAD

The issues raised here signal that the nation has entered an era that warrants unprecedented attention to furnishing the next generation of students with a literacy of the basic concepts of health care reform and with an understanding of policy questions related to the attitude society ought to adopt toward the advancing frontiers of technology. Striking the right balance between technological optimism and ethical reservation is an art. New technological advances in the delivery of health care, the changing landscape of scientific research, and scientific innovation not even conceivable just a generation ago all represent contemporary realities that beckon us to consider what policies we might fashion in light of the new concerns that such realities precipitate.

More than ever before, ethical reflection, certainly in the area of biomedical technology, cannot be conducted from an armchair. As the nation and society strive for human betterment, hopefully they will not only create new technologies designed to alleviate suffering and promote fulfillment but also arrive at and implement compassionate policies commensurate with these new technologies. This ambition is and remains a human enterprise.

See also **Chapter 11: Evolution of Health Planning (1920s–1970s); Chapter 12: Evolution of Health Planning (1970s–Present); Chapter 13: Government Financing of Health Care (1940s–Present); Chapter 14: Biomedical Research Policy and Innovation (1940s–Present); Chapter 15: Building an Effective and Sustainable Health Care Workforce (1960s–Present); Chapter 16: Promoting Health Care Quality and Safety (1960s–Present); Chapter 17: Strategies for Health Care Cost Containment (1980s–Present).**

NOTES

1. There are many measures of disparities in access to health care. Although there are historically high numbers of uninsured individuals, expansions of the Community Health Centers program during the Bush and Obama administrations, along with Emergency Medical Treatment and Active Labor Act mandates for providing emergency care, might mean access to some type of health care is easier now than a couple of decades ago. The years before Medicare and Medicaid existed certainly had greater disparities in access for certain population groups, especially African Americans (who benefited from those programs not only directly but also indirectly since Medicare was used as an instrument to desegregate U.S. hospitals in many parts of the country). This said, it remains the case that not only do insured individuals in our country pay the least amount for the health care services they use, with the uninsured paying the highest prices, but an unprecedented more than a million Americans have now experienced medical bankruptcy while more than one-fourth of Americans have gone into debt over medical bills. Moreover, because of the historical accident that health insurance in this country is tied to one's employment status, we have a health care system that discriminates against the worst off (e.g., the unemployed). Finally, specialists are geographically located in disproportionate measure in the most well-off communities in the nation, ensuring that even if one did have the means to afford specialized health care in a geographically unfavorable area, one would have trouble accessing it.

2. As presented by Cara V. James, director of the Office of Minority Health, Centers for Medicare and Medicaid Services, at a talk she gave at the 2013 annual conference for the American Public Health Association ("Affordable Care Act: An Overview of CMS's Consumer Outreach and Education Efforts").

3. Centers for Medicare & Medicaid Services, "National Health Expenditures Projections, 2011–2021," http://www.cms.gov/ Research-Statistics-Data-and-Systems/Statistics-Trends-and-Reports/NationalHealthExpendData/Downloads/Proj2011 PDF.pdf. See also Richard Elmore, "National Health Expenditures Top 17% of GDP," *Health Care Technology News,* February 10, 2010, http://news.avancehealth.com/2010/02/growth-in-health-care-expenditure.html.

4. David U. Himmelstein, et al., "Illness and Injury as Contributors to Bankruptcy," *Health Affairs* (February, 2005), http://content. healthaffairs.org/content/suppl/2005/01/28/hlthaff.w5.63 .DC1. The Commonwealth Fund has data showing four in ten Americans reported going without care due to cost, and a similar percentage had trouble paying their medical bills: http://www.commonwealthfund.org/~/media/Files/News/ News%20Releases/2013/Nov/IHP%202013%20Survey%20 release%20FINAL%20111213_v2.pdf.

5. See Mark E. Litow, "Medicare versus Private Health Insurance: The Cost of Administration," January 6, 2006, http://www.cahi .org/cahi_contents/resources/pdf/CAHIMedicare TechnicalPaper.pdf; Steffie Woolhandler, Terry Campbell, and David U. Himmelstein, "Costs of Health Care Administration in the United States and Canada," *New England Journal of Medicine* 349 (2003): 768–775, http://www.pnhp.org/news/ Admin%20Cost%20study.pdf

6. See Walid F. Gellad et al., "What If the Federal Government Negotiated Pharmaceutical Prices for Seniors? An Estimate of National Savings," *Journal of Internal Medicine* 23: 9 (2008): 1435–1440. See also Center for Economic and Policy Research, "States Could Save $73 Billion by Negotiating Medicare Drug Prices," March 19, 2013, http://www.cepr.net/index.php/press-releases/press-releases/states-save-billions-negotiating-prescription-drug-prices.

7. Joseph White, "Cost Control after the ACA," *Public Administration Review* 73: 1 (2013): 24–33.

8. By contrast, in the Canadian health care system, technology is intentionally rationed, thereby saving both the cost of expensive equipment as well as the cost of maintaining it. Of course, there are consequences to this cost-saving measure. A case in point arguably pertains to the actress Natasha Richardson, who died of an epidural hematoma. Some physicians have insinuated that had she been better and sooner diagnosed than she was capable of being at the community health center near the Quebec ski resort where she had her accident, then she could have been treated and probably saved. Shortly after her accident, *The New York Post* published a controversial article explicitly attributing her avoidable death to rationing. While many physicians think that the alleged causal link is in this case a stretch, the issue of whether rationing of the sort that will cost a life here or there is ever justified given the enormous amount of savings at stake remains relevant. Cory Franklin, "Canadacare May Have Killed Natasha Richardson," *New York Post*, March 26, 2009, http://nypost.com/2009/03/26/canadacare-may-have-killed-natasha. To read a physician who demurs to Franklin's conclusions, see "Did the Canadian Health System Fail Natasha Richardson?" http://www.kevinmd.com/blog/ 2009/03/did-canadian-health-system-fail-natasha.html.

9. Andrew P. Wilper et al., "Health Insurance and Mortality in US Adults," *American Journal of Public Health* 99: 12 (2009): 1–7, http://www.ncpa.org/pdfs/2009_harvard_health_study.pdf.

10. Immanual Kant, *The Groundwork of the Metaphysics of Morals,* Translated by H. J. Paton (New York: Harper and Row, 1964), 72, ff.

11. John Rawls, *A Theory of Justice* (Cambridge, MA: Harvard University Press, 1971), 136–142.

12. For example, see Martha Nussbaum, "Non-Relative Virtues: An Aristotelian Approach," in *Midwest Studies in Philosophy* 13 (1998): 32–53.

13. John Locke, *Two Treatises of Government* (Cambridge, UK: Cambridge University Press, 1970), 41–42.

14. Ronald Pies, "The Libertarian Mind," December 3, 2010, http://thehealthcareblog.com/blog/2010/12/03/the-libertarian mind.

15. The misleading term *death panel* has been around for some time but was officially coined by Sarah Palin in August 2009 as a way of drumming up criticism of the Obama administration's efforts on behalf of health care reform. For an excellent article on the myths to which Palin's rhetoric led, see Brenda Nyhan, "Why the 'Death Panel' Myth Wouldn't Die: Misinformation in the Health Care Reform Debate," *The Forum* 8: 1 (2010), http:// www.dartmouth.edu/~nyhan/health-care-misinformation .pdf.

16. Atul Gawande, "Testing, Testing," *The New Yorker,* December 14, 2009, http://www.newyorker.com/reporting/2009/12/14/ 091214fa_fact_gawande.

17. Kaiser Health News Daily Report, "CBO Finds Health Overhaul Will Cost $940 Billion over 10 Years but Trim Deficit," March 18, 2010, http://www.kaiserhealthnews.org/Daily-Reports/2010/March/18/New-CBO-Numbers.aspx.

18. See Alexander J. Ryu et al., "The Slowdown in Health Care Spending in 2009–11 Reflected Factors Other Than the Weak Economy and Thus May Persist," *Health Affairs* 32: 5 (2013): 835–840; Anne B. Martin et al., "National Health Spending in 2012: Rate of Health Spending Growth Remained Low for the Fourth Consecutive Year," *Health Affairs* 33: 1 (2014): 67–77.

19. See especially Govind Persad, Alan Wertheimer, and Ezekiel J. Emanuel, "Principles for Allocation of Scarce Medical Interventions," *Lancet* 373: 9661 (2009): 423–431; Ezekiel J. Emanuel, *Healthcare, Guaranteed: A Simple, Secure Solution for America* (New York: Public Affairs, 2008).

20. Emanuel, *Healthcare, Guaranteed*, 66–67. See also Betsy McCaughey, "Obama's Health Rationer-in-Chief," *Wall Street Journal*, August 27, 2009, http://online.wsj.com/news/articles/SB10001424052970203706604574374463280098676.

21. See Kaiser Family Foundation, "Summary of the Affordable Care Act," April 25, 2013, http://kff.org/health-reform/fact-sheet/summary-of-new-health-reform-law. A summary even more concise is Jill Schlesinger, "Health Care Ruling: What It Means for You," *Money Watch*, June 28, 2012, http://www.cbsnews.com/8301-505123_162-57459511/health-care-ruling-what-it-means-for-you; this site also contains critical links to other sources, such as the full text to the Supreme Court hearing on the Patient Protection and Affordable Care Act.

22. Michael Cannon, "Perspectives on an Individual Mandate," October 17, 2008, http://www.cato.org/publications/commentary/perspectives-individual-mandate.

23. Alexis de Tocqueville, *Democracy in America*, translated by Harvey Mansfield and Delba Winthrop (Chicago: University of Chicago Press, 2000).

24. While siding with the four liberals on the bench who deemed the Patient Protection and Affordable Care Act constitutional, Roberts's majority decision also set a precedent for limiting government intrusion into commerce. This is to say, he specified that he rejected the Obama administration's main argument for constitutionality, claiming that the federal government had no authority under existing interstate commerce laws to enforce a mandate that individuals buy insurance for the health care they had not yet consumed. Thus, Roberts agreed with conservatives that inactivity with regard to any prospective purchase of a good or service, including health insurance, could not be regulated by the government. Nevertheless, he ultimately concluded that the PPACA, as well as the individual mandate (its main feature), was constitutional because it was within the federal government's purview to "lay and collect" taxes. (Since the individual mandate was never characterized as a tax when voted on in Congress, the Obama administration did not emphasize this justification in oral arguments before the Supreme Court). Roberts granted that there is ample precedent for such a tax, including George Washington's Militia Act of 1792, which required every "free able-bodied white male citizen" between the ages of eighteen and forty-five to "provide himself" ammunition, as well as the Act for the Relief of Sick and Disabled Seamen of 1798, signed into law by President John Adams, which compelled employers of seamen to pay to the Federal Treasury 20 cents per seaman per month to pay for "the temporary relief and maintenance of sick or disabled seamen."

25. For an elaboration of the principal features of the PPACA, see Kaiser Family Foundation, "Summary of the Affordable Care Act."

26. Persad, Wertheimer, and Emanuel, "Principles for Allocation."

27. Daniel Callahan, "Must We Ration Health Care for the Elderly?" *Journal of Law, Medicine & Ethics* 40 (2012): 1, 10.

28. Ibid., 11.

29. Ibid., 13.

30. Pew Research, "Strong Public Support for Right to Die," January 2005, http://www.people-press.org/2006/01/05/strong-public-support-for-right-to-die. For a discussion of why Americans avoid advance directives despite their support of the right over one's body in end-of-life cases, see Paula Span, "Why Do We Avoid Advance Directives?" *New York Times*, April 20, 2009, http://newoldage.blogs.nytimes.com/2009/04/20/why-do-we-avoid-advance-directives/?_php=true&_type=blogs&_r=0.

31. See the New York Bar Association's legal commentary on the law, https://www.nysba.org/FHCDA. This website contains detailed summaries of all the key provisions of the act.

32. See Oregon's website explaining this legislation, http://public.health.oregon.gov/ProviderPartnerResources/EvaluationResearch/DeathwithDignityAct/Pages/index.aspx.

33. Susan Hedlund, "Death with Dignity: The Oregon Experience," *The Forum* (2005), https://www.adec.org/AM/Template.cfm?Section=Resources_and_Links&Template=/CM/ContentDisplay.cfm&ContentID=1417.

34. For an argument that there is no moral difference, see, for example, James Rachels, "Killing and Letting Die," in *Encyclopedia of Ethics*, vol. 2, 2nd ed., edited by Lawrence Becker and Charlotte Becker, 947–950 (New York: Routledge, 2001), http://jamesrachels.org/killing.pdf.

35. Michael Poon et. al., "Associations between Routine Coronary Computed Tomographic Angiography and Reduced Unnecessary Hospital Admissions, Length of Stay, Recidivism Rates, and Invasive Coronary Angiography in the Emergency Department Triage of Chest Pain," *Journal of the American College of Cardiology* 62: 6 (2013): 543–552.

36. Gregory Pence, *Classic Cases in Medical Ethics: Accounts of the Cases that Shaped and Define Medical Ethics*, 5th ed. (Boston: McGraw-Hill, 2008), 220–230.

37. Ibid., 225.

38. Stephen Goldby et al., "The Willowbrook Letters: Criticisms and Defense" *The Lancet*, April 10, May 8, June 5, and July 10, 1971. This source is discussed in Philip A. Pecorino, "Human Experimentation," in *Medical Ethics* (2002), http://www.qcc.cuny.edu/socialsciences/ppecorino/MEDICAL_ETHICS_TEXT/Chapter_7_Human_Experimentation/Case_Study_Willowbrook_Experiments.htm.

39. Ibid.

40. Rebecca Skloot, *The Immortal Life of Henrietta Lacks* (New York: Broadway Books, 2010).

41. National Commission for the Protection of Human Subjects of Biomedical and Behavioral Research, "The Belmont Report," April 18, 1979, http://www.hhs.gov/ohrp/humansubjects/guidance/belmont.html.

42. Pence, *Classic Cases in Medical Ethics*, 125.

43. Ibid., 127.

44. Richard McCormick is a good example of one such ethicist. See, for example, "Experimentation on the Fetus: Policy Proposals," in *Appendix to Report and Recommendations: Research on the Fetus* (Washington, DC: National Commission for the Protection of Human Subjects of Biomedical and Behavioral Research, 1976).

45. Pence, *Classic Cases in Medical Ethics*, 141.

46. Frank Miele, "The Man Who Would Be Cloned," *Skeptic*, March 22, 1999, http://www.highbeam.com/doc/1G1-56222095.html.

47. See the Human Cloning Foundation's website: http://www.humancloning.com.
48. Leon Kass, *Human Cloning and Human Dignity: The Report of the President's Council on Bioethics* (New York: Public Affairs Press, 2002).
49. Michael Crichton, *Jurassic Park* (New York: Ballantine Books, 2012), 284.
50. Francis Fukuyama, *Our Post Human Future* (New York: Farrar, Straus & Giroux, 2002).
51. American College of Obstetricians and Gynecologists, "New Recommendations for Down Syndrome Call for Offering Screening to All Pregnant Women," December 31, 2006, http://www.acog.org/About_ACOG/News_Room/News_Releases/2006/New_Recommendations_for_Down_Syndrome.
52. Caroline Mansfield, Suellen Hopfer, and Theresa M. Marteau, "Termination Rates after Prenatal Diagnosis of Down Syndrome, Spina Bifida, Anencephaly, and Turner and Klinefelter Syndromes: A Systemic Literature Review," *Prenatal Diagnosis* 19 (1999): 808–812.

FURTHER READING

Amadeo, Kimberly. "Why Reform Health Care." *About.com*. July 2013. http://useconomy.about.com/od/fiscalpolicy/a/healthcare_reform.htm.

Berenson, Robert A., and Eugene C. Rich. "US Approaches to Physician Payment: The Deconstruction of Primary Care." *Journal of General Internal Medicine* 25: 6 (2010): 613–618. http://www.ncbi.nlm.nih.gov/pmc/articles/PMC2869428.

Caplinger, Dan. "Medicare Explained: Understanding the Basics from Part A to Part D." *Daily Finance*, May 14, 2013. http://www.dailyfinance.com/2013/05/14/medicare-explained-part-a-b-c-d/#!slide=976885.

Collins, Sara, Jennifer L. Kriss, Michelle M. Doty, and Sheila D. Rustgi. *Losing Ground: How the Loss of Adequate Health Insurance Is Burdening Working Families—Findings from the Commonwealth Fund Biennial Health Insurance Surveys, 2001–2007*. New York: Commonwealth Fund (August 2008). http://www.commonwealthfund.org/Publications/Fund-Reports/2008/Aug/Losing-Ground—How-the-Loss-of-Adequate-Health-Insurance-Is-Burdening-Working-Families—8212-Finding.aspx.

Emanuel, Ezekiel. *Health Care Guaranteed: A Simple, Secure Solution for America*. New York: Public Affairs, 2008.

Gabel, John R., Ryan Lore, Roland D. McDevitt, Jeremy D. Pickreign, Heidi Whitmore, Michael Slover, and Ethan Levy-Forsythe. "More Than Half of Individual Health Plans Offer Coverage That Falls Short of What Can Be Sold through Exchanges as of 2014." *Health Affairs* 31: 6 (2012): 1–8.

Harris, Dean M. *Ethics in Health Services and Policy: A Global Approach*. San Francisco: Jossey-Bass, 2011. Esp. chs. 7–9, 11–12.

Kaiser Family Foundation. "Five Key Questions about Medicaid and Its Role in State/Federal Budgets and Health Reform." May 1, 2012. http://www.kff.org/medicaid/upload/8139-02.pdf.

———. "Medicare: A Primer." http://kaiserfamilyfoundation.files.wordpress.com/2013/01/7615-03.pdf.

———. "The Uninsured and the Difference Health Insurance Makes." September 1, 2012. http://www.kff.org/uninsured/upload/1420-14.pdf.

Mitchell, C. Ben, Edmund D. Pellegrino, Jean Bethke Elshtain, John F. Kilner, and Scott Rae. *Biotechnology and the Human Good*. Washington, DC: Georgetown University Press, 2007.

More, Max, and Natasha Vita-More. *The Transhumanist Reader: Classical and Contemporary Essays on the Science, Technology, and Philosophy of the Human Future*. Chichester, UK: Wiley-Blackwell.

Physicians for a National Health Program. "What Is Single Payer?" 2014. http://www.pnhp.org/facts/what-is-single-payer.

Skloot, Rebecca. *The Immortal Life of Henrietta Lacks*. New York: Crown, 2010.

Sommers, Anna, and Peter J. Cunningham. "Medical Bill Problems Steady for U.S. Families, 2007–2010." *Tracking Report* 28. http://www.hschange.com/CONTENT/1268/1268.pdf. 2011.

Squires, David A. "The US Health Care System in Perspective: A Comparison of 12 Industrialized Nations." *Issues in International Health Policy* (July, 2011). http://www.commonwealthfund.org/~/media/Files/Publications/Issue%20Brief/2011/Jul/1532_Squires_US_hlt_sys_comparison_12_nations_intl_brief_v2.pdf.

Stone, Deborah. "AIDS and the Moral Economy of Insurance." *The American Prospect*, December 4, 2000. http://prospect.org/article/aids-and-moral-economy-insurance.

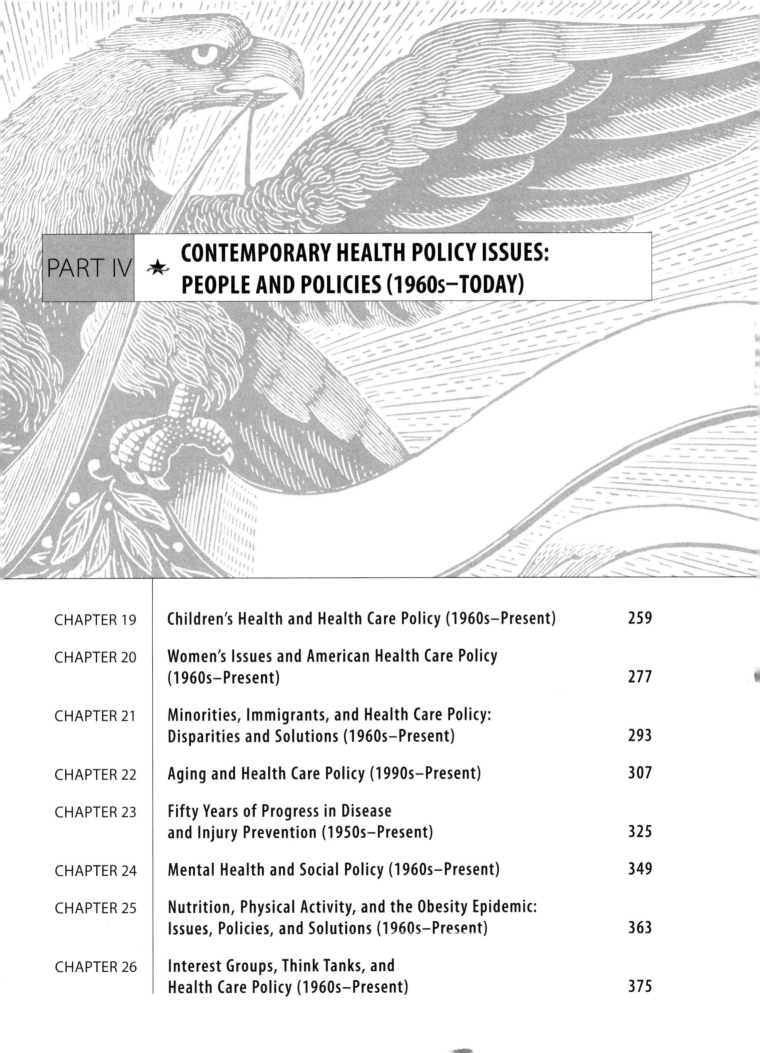

PART IV ★ **CONTEMPORARY HEALTH POLICY ISSUES:
PEOPLE AND POLICIES (1960s–TODAY)**

chapter 19

Children's Health and Health Care Policy (1960s–Present)

Samira Soleimanpour and Claire D. Brindis

WITH ITS ROOTS IN THE LATE 1800S and early 1900s, children's health policy in the United States has continued to flourish in the last fifty years. Several themes underlie the mosaic of changes in children's health policy. First, the publicly funded government sector has shifted from programs designed primarily to protect very poor children to increasing access to health care for all children. Second, many of these policies and programs were created in direct response to research demonstrating specific gaps in children's health needs. Finally, while the nation has made improvements in many child health indicators as a result of policy development, there have been growing social and economic disparities in nearly all of these indicators over time, requiring new strategies to bridge these gaps.

While policy development in the last fifty years has led to improvements in health care coverage and systems of care for children, the nation's poorest children continue to face significant challenges. It is essential to understand how the policies addressing children's health have evolved over the last five decades as well as to think about future directions.

TRANSITIONS IN CHILD HEALTH CONCERNS

With each decade from 1960 to 2010, the United States made significant strides in reducing mortality rates for children of all ages. In 1960, infant mortality rates were 26.0 per 1,000 live births, as compared to 6.1 per 1,000 in 2010.[1] Similarly, death rates for children ages one to four decreased from 109.1 to 26.5 per 100,000 and for children ages five to fourteen decreased from 46.6 to 12.9 per 100,000 in that same time period. Deaths in older youth ages fifteen to twenty-four decreased less dramatically, from 106.3 in 1960 to 67.7 in 2010.[2]

The causes of death in this time period have also shifted. Deaths due to infectious diseases, which were the leading cause in the earlier part of the century, have been replaced by injury as the greatest cause of morbidity and mortality in children, accounting for 37 percent of child deaths in 2010, as shown in Table 19.1.[3]

There has also been a dramatic increase in childhood chronic illnesses. Nationally, 43 percent of children currently have at least one of twenty chronic health conditions, including learning disabilities, asthma, environmental allergies, or conduct problems; this figure increases to 54 percent when overweight, obesity, or being at risk for developmental delays are included.[4] Furthermore, nearly one out of five children had conditions resulting in a special health care

TABLE 19.1 **Leading Causes of Death among Youth Ages 1–19, United States, 2010**

Cause of Death	Percentage (number)
Unintentional injuries (motor vehicle accidents, drowning, suffocation, poisoning, etc.)	37 (7,574)
Homicide	12 (2,478)
Suicide	9 (1,933)
Malignant neoplasms (cancer)	9 (1,863)
Congenital anomalies	5 (1,007)
Heart disease	3 (686)
Other	25 (4,941)
Total	100 (20,482)

SOURCE: Centers for Disease Control and Prevention. "Leading Causes of Death Reports, 1999–2010," http://webappa.cdc.gov/sasweb/ncipc/leadcaus10_us.html.

need (i.e., a condition requiring a higher level of care than normal children receive).[5] The causes for this rise are largely unclear and have been attributed to improved diagnosis, assessment, and awareness as well as to clear rises in these conditions, such as asthma, obesity, and mental health disorders.[6] Although some of these increases also can be attributed to greater childhood survival due to improved access to care and medical technology, children who survive early childhood can suffer from other, less lethal conditions as they age.

The disparities in these indicators between children of different ethnic and socioeconomic backgrounds are also of growing concern. Prevalence rates of asthma are higher for African American children (15 percent) and Hispanic or Puerto Rican children (18 percent) compared to white children (8 percent).[7] Nationwide, while an estimated one out of three children and adolescents is overweight or obese, Hispanic (38 percent) and African American (36 percent) children are more likely to be overweight or obese than white children (29 percent).[8] Finally, in terms of mental health, national data suggest that Hispanic and African American youth have higher rates of suicidal thoughts, depression, and school dropout than whites.[9,10]

Poverty compounds all of these issues and children are the poorest age group among Americans, with 22 percent of children under the age of eighteen living in poverty in 2012.[11] Children of color are disproportionately affected, with 38 percent of African American and 34 percent of Hispanic children living in poverty compared to 12 percent of white children.[12] Children living in poverty have significantly worse health outcomes than their peers, including higher infant mortality rates, lower academic achievement, and higher social, behavioral, and emotional problems, such as aggression or depression.[13,14,15]

In order to address their health needs, children require access to the health care system, yet a large percentage of children nationwide still face significant barriers, primarily lack of insurance coverage to pay for health services. Despite significant efforts to expand health care coverage to children of all ages, in 2012, there were 6.6 million children under eighteen years of age who were uninsured.[16] Minority children are increasingly more likely to be uninsured than their white peers. In 2012, 7 percent of white children were uninsured, compared to 9 percent of African American, 8 percent of Asian, and 14 percent of Hispanic children.[17]

Moreover, the health of U.S. children trails behind many other developed countries.[18] There has been a long history of having to advocate for maternal and child health (MCH) issues in the United States, in contrast to the international environment, where MCH issues have long been recognized as being prime in improving a nation's health. Yet unwavering child health advocates have helped to continuously bring children's issues to the forefront of advocacy and policy.

While a more comprehensive historical overview would examine all policy matters related to children's health, including women's and maternal health, education, child care, child welfare, housing, and juvenile justice, this review focuses on efforts aimed directly at supporting the health of children between the ages of zero and eighteen. In addition, the focus here is primarily on federal initiatives rather than those at the state or local level, though federal-state partnerships, which have always been a key component of child health policy activities, are discussed as well.

CHILD HEALTH POLICY IN HISTORY

The early part of the twentieth century marked the start of several national programs and policies that set the foundation for later child health policy development. The Children's Bureau, established in 1912, was a first step in establishing a federal infrastructure to support children's health. The bureau was charged with investigating and reporting on issues pertaining to the welfare of children. The bill arguing for this federal initiative was met with opposition from states that felt the federal government was taking too large a role in their responsibilities to protect children, but it also received support from social workers, public health advocates, and women's organizations.[19] This type of mixed reception has been a recurring theme in the U.S. child health policy arena.

The bureau's investigative work identified significant unmet health needs, most notably related to infant mortality, and subsequently led to enactment of the Sheppard-Towner Act in 1921 (also known as the Maternity and Infancy Act) to help address these needs. This act provided federal grants matched with state funds to implement MCH services and resulted in forty-seven states creating child health programs.[20] This act faced similar opposition as the bureau had and, as a result, was allowed to expire in 1929, which coincided with the start of the Great Depression. Many states subsequently struggled to meet the health needs of their growing populations of impoverished mothers and children.[21,22]

President Franklin D. Roosevelt's (1933–1945) New Deal economic programs were designed to combat the devastations caused by the Great Depression and included the passage of the landmark Social Security Act of 1935 (SSA). Based on input from the Children's Bureau, two components of the SSA directly supported children.[23] Title IV was an entitlement program that provided cash assistance through state welfare agencies to children who had lost their parents, and subsequently led to the Aid to Families with Dependent Children program. Title V provided discretionary grant funding to states from the federal government for the provision of MCH services, similar to the earlier Sheppard-Towner Act, and services for disabled children.[24] Title V has remained a significant legislative force in the child health policy landscape.

MAJOR HEALTH POLICY EXPANSIONS IN THE 1960s

The 1960s were a time of significant civil rights movements and a rising awareness of income inequality. This decade also marked a time of unparalleled expansions in child health policy development, as shown in Table 19.2.

In 1960, President Dwight D. Eisenhower (1953–1961) held the sixth White House Conference on Children and Youth—almost fifty years after the first in 1909. Poverty rates were at a record high, with one out of five families with children living in poverty. Although the conference did not focus specifically on health issues, concerns about improving health services for mothers and children were evident.[25]

TABLE 19.2 **Key U.S. Child Health Legislation, 1960–2010**

Decade	Legislation	Description
1960–1969	Social Security Act of 1935 Title V amendments, 1963 and 1965 Title XIX, 1965 and amendments in 1967	The Social Security Act (SSA) of 1935 included establishment of the Title V Maternal and Child Health Program, a federal-state partnership program to provide maternal and child services and services for "crippled children."
		In 1963, the Maternal and Child Health and Mental Retardation Planning Amendments amended Title V and added Title XVII, aimed at preventing mental retardation.
		In 1965, Title XIX amended the SSA to establish the Medicaid entitlement program to provide government health insurance to low-income children and families and other vulnerable populations.
		1n 1967, the Early Periodic Screening, Diagnostic and Treatment Program was added to Medicaid to cover a set of compulsory services for children, including preventive, dental, mental health, developmental, and specialty services.
	Economic Opportunity Act, 1964 Head Start	Head Start was designed to provide education, medical, nutrition, social, and parental support to level the playing field for low-income preschool children entering public schools.
	Community Health Centers	Community Health Centers were established to provide comprehensive, accessible, and affordable care in medically underserved neighborhoods, particularly in rural areas.
1970–1979	Highway Safety Act, 1970	Established the National Highway Traffic Safety Administration to reduce injuries and losses from motor vehicle accidents.
	Consumer Product Safety Act, 1970	Established the Consumer Product Safety Commission, an independent regulatory agency charged with identifying and addressing children's product hazards.
	Title X of the Public Health Service Act, 1970	Established Population Research and Voluntary Family Planning Programs to provide comprehensive family planning and related preventive health services for all eligible individuals, including adolescents.
	Child Nutrition Act of 1966, 1972 amendment	Established the Special Supplemental Food Program for Women, Infants, and Children to support low-income women and children up to age five at nutritional risk by providing foods to supplement diets, information on healthy eating, and referrals to health care.
	Child Maltreatment Act, 1974	Authorized federal funds to improve state response to physical abuse, neglect, and sexual abuse of children.
	Title VI of the Public Health Service Act, 1978; replaced by Title XX, 1981	Title VI established the Office of Adolescent Pregnancy Prevention to administer adolescent pregnancy and parenting programs, including health, education, and social services.
		Title XX, also known as the Adolescent Family Life legislation, legislated discretionary funds for research, care, and prevention demonstration projects and provided specific funding for abstinence-only programs.
1980–1989	Omnibus Budget Reconciliation Acts (OBRA) of 1981 and 1989—Title V amendments	OBRA 1981 formally changed the MCH Program to a block grant, combining seven categorical programs into one with decreased federal oversight.
		OBRA 1989 changed Title V to its current structure with increased accountability and reporting, and increased guidance on service design. It required Medicaid coverage of pregnant women and children age five and under in families with income below 134 percent of the federal poverty level.

(Continued)

TABLE 19.2 **(Continued)**

Decade	Legislation	Description
	National Minimum Drinking Age Act, 1984	Required states to raise the age at which individuals could legally purchase or publicly possess alcoholic beverages to 21 as a condition of receiving highway funds.
1990–1999	Personal Responsibility Work and Opportunity Reconciliation Act, 1996	Repealed the Aid to Families with Dependent Children welfare program and replaced it with the Temporary Assistance to Needy Families program (TANF), designed to encourage self-sufficiency by providing assistance to families with a five-year lifetime limit and promoting marriage and work.
	Balanced Budget Act, 1997	Amended the SSA to add Title XXI, establishing the State Children's Health Insurance Program (SCHIP) to provide coverage to children living in low-income families who were not eligible for Medicaid but lacked private insurance.
2000–2010	Children's Health Insurance Program (CHIP) Reauthorization Act, 2009	Reauthorized SCHIP to extend and expand the program, including providing additional funding to states to enroll more low-income children.
	American Recovery and Reinvestment Act, 2009	Also called the "stimulus bill," it was designed to promote economic growth by creating jobs and providing expanded funding to programs like Head Start, TANF, and Medicaid that were supporting low-income families affected by the Great Recession.
	Patient Protection and Affordable Care Act, 2010	Landmark legislation implementing health care reform with significant impacts on children, including barring preexisting condition exclusions and lifetime insurance spending limits and establishing health insurance exchanges to provide more affordable options to low-income families not eligible for Medicaid or CHIP.

SOURCES: Kaiser Family Foundation, "Kaiser Commission on Medicaid and the Uninsured," http://kff.org/about-kaiser-commission-on-medicaid-and-the-uninsured; Kaiser Family Foundation, Commission on Medicaid and the Uninsured, "Medicaid Legislative History: 1965–2000," http://kaiserfamilyfoundation.files.wordpress.com/2013/05/mrbleghistory.pdf; Georgetown University, "Maternal & Child Health Library," http://www.mchlibrary.info; U.S. Department of Health and Human Services, Health Resources and Services Administration, "MCH Timeline," http://mchb.hrsa.gov/timeline; Social Security Administration, "Social Security History," http://www.ssa.gov/history/index.html.

Child Development

President John F. Kennedy (1961–1963) was committed to building federal support for children's health policies and programs. He made intellectual and developmental disabilities a priority for his administration, largely due to his own family's personal experiences. The president's younger sister, Rosemary, was born with intellectual disabilities, and, later, the loss of his own infant son contributed to his personal interests in the field. In 1962, President Kennedy, with the support of Congress, established the National Institute of Child Health and Human Development, within the National Institutes of Health, with the directive to study developmental processes from conception and beyond.

To further expand efforts in this area, President Kennedy worked with Congress to pass the Maternal and Child Health and Mental Retardation Planning Amendment to Title V of the SSA (1963), the first major legislation to combat mental illness and retardation.[26] The Title V amendment provided states with funding to update their intellectual disabilities programs, increase maternity and infant care prevention efforts, and build facilities to support the prevention, care, and treatment of people with intellectual disabilities.[27]

Child Abuse

Largely due to "Battered Child Syndrome," a publication by Dr. Henry Kempe and colleagues, child abuse was receiving

considerable national attention. This article revealed the growing number of physically abused children being seen in hospitals, the extent of the injuries they suffered often at the hands of their parents or guardians, and medical professionals' hesitance to intervene in family dynamics. This public attention led to additional SSA amendments in 1962 to further expand states' child protection and welfare services. It also led to recommendations from the Children's Bureau for state legislation requiring doctors to report suspected abuse; all states instituted these laws by 1967.[28] Due to heightened recognition of the lack of federal efforts focused on this issue and support from numerous child advocacy groups, Congress passed the Child Abuse Prevention and Treatment Act in 1974. This act authorized federal funds to improve state response to physical abuse, neglect, and sexual abuse.[29]

War on Poverty

In late 1963, after Kennedy's assassination, President Lyndon B. Johnson (1963–1969) took office and declared an "unconditional war on poverty" in his first State of the Union address. His administration was successful in passing several policy initiatives aimed at improving the lives of children, specifically addressing disparities in health and educational outcomes between low-income children and their peers. The Food Stamp Act (1964) made the food stamp pilot programs initiated during Kennedy's time permanent and increased low-income households' access to improved levels of nutrition. The Elementary and Secondary Education Act (1965) and the Higher Education Act (1965) were significant initiatives reinforcing federal support for education policy. In 1966, President Johnson also signed the Child Nutrition Act, which built on the successes of the National School Lunch Act, to establish the School Breakfast and the Special Milk Programs designed to increase consumption of nutritious foods by low-income children.

Through Johnson's Great Society initiatives, several of the most significant programs and policies designed to support child health and development were also launched as part of the Economic Opportunity Act of 1964 (EOA). Many of these efforts were crafted during Kennedy's administration, while others stemmed from recommendations of Johnson's task forces who were appointed to examine specific health and social issues. The initiatives that more directly impacted children's health included Community Health Centers, Head Start, and Medicaid.

Community Health Centers

Community Health Centers (CHCs), known initially as Neighborhood Health Centers, began as a two-site demonstration project to provide comprehensive, accessible, and affordable care to the growing number of Americans living in poverty, particularly in rural areas. They were developed under the EOA as a strategy to boost employment, given the potential of creating jobs for community members to operate the centers. CHCs' initial successes led to federal expansion of the model nationwide.[30]

CHCs provide "comprehensive, culturally competent, quality primary health care services to medically underserved communities and vulnerable populations."[31] CHCs are a primary safety net provider for the underinsured and uninsured and incorporate several fundamental requirements, including (1) being located in a medically underserved community; (2) being governed by a community board, most of whose members are from the patient population; (3) providing comprehensive primary health care services as well as supportive services, including education, translation services, and transportation care; and (4) providing services on a sliding-scale fee based on patients' ability to pay. Unlike with other federal programs that passed funding through state governments, the federal government provides funding directly to the community organizations that operate the centers.

Congress permanently authorized the CHC program in 1975, ensuring its continued funding. After experiencing cutbacks in the 1980s, CHCs regained favor in large measure due to staunch advocacy by community supporters, as evidenced by significant funding expansions after the turn of the twenty-first century.[32] In 2012, more than twenty-one million people received services from nearly 1,200 CHCs operating some 8,900 sites nationwide; one-third of the patients were under the age of eighteen.[33]

Head Start

Launched in 1965, Head Start was a comprehensive child development program based on research that showed the impacts that poverty had on children's development and education. Head Start offered educational, medical, social, nutritional, and parent involvement components to low-income children and their families. Under the auspices of the EOA, it was conceptualized as a means of leveling the playing field for disadvantaged preschool children entering public schools and improving their long-term potential. It was also designed to generate employment opportunities in target communities.

Similar to funding for CHCs, Head Start agencies receive grant funds directly from the federal government, bypassing state governments. Despite research showing somewhat mixed findings on its impacts, Head Start experienced significant expansions since its inception, including increased funding in each decade. The program was expanded to include bilingual and bicultural services in the 1970s under President Jimmy Carter's administration (1977–1981). In 1994, under President William J. Clinton's administration (1993–2001), the program's reauthorization established Early Head Start to fund services to infants and toddlers, as well as referral services to help pregnant women access comprehensive prenatal and postpartum care. In 1998, the program was reauthorized to expand to full-day and full-year services. Head Start was reauthorized in 2007, with several provisions to strengthen program quality, including setting quality standards, increasing teacher qualifications, and increasing program monitoring and accountability; it was expanded again in 2009 to serve even more children and families. Federal funding supported 80 percent of program costs, while local public and private agencies were required to provide 20 percent. A portion of program enrollment must also be allocated to children with special health care needs. In 2012, Head Start received nearly $8 billion in funding and served more than 1.1 million children ages birth to five years and pregnant women.[34]

Medicaid

Perhaps the most significant contribution to improving children's access to health care was the enactment of Title XIX of the SSA, which established the Medicaid program in 1965. Medicaid was a means-tested entitlement program for low-income families and children, meaning anyone meeting eligibility criteria would be entitled to the services covered by the program. It was originally designed to provide medical assistance to all children of families receiving cash welfare assistance as well as other vulnerable populations. It has since evolved into the largest safety net provider of health

Project Head Start

As part of his War on Poverty, President Lyndon B. Johnson enacted an unprecedented number of federal programs focused on children, primarily sparked by research demonstrating the detrimental impacts of poverty on children's health and development. The following is an excerpt from Johnson's speech introducing Project Head Start, which began as a summer pilot program and continues to serve millions of U.S. children year-round.

> [I]t was less than 3 months ago that we opened a new war front on poverty. We set out to make certain that poverty's children would not be forevermore poverty's captives. We called our program Project Head Start.
>
> The program was conceived not so much as a Federal effort, but really as a neighborhood effort, and the response we have received from the neighborhoods and the communities has been most stirring and the most enthusiastic of any peacetime program that I can remember.
>
> Today, we are able to announce that we will have open, and we believe operating this summer, coast-to-coast, some 2,000 child development centers serving as many as possibly a half million children.
>
> This means that nearly half the preschool children of poverty will get a head start on their future.
>
> These children will receive preschool training to prepare them for regular school in September. They will get medical and dental attention that they badly need, and parents will receive counseling on improving the home environment.
>
> This is a most remarkable accomplishment and it has been done in a very short time. It would not be possible except for the willing and the enthusiastic cooperation of Americans throughout the country.
>
> I believe this response reflects a realistic and a wholesome awakening in America. It shows that we are recognizing that poverty perpetuates itself.
>
> Five and six year old children are inheritors of poverty's curse and not its creators. Unless we act these children will pass it on to the next generation, like a family birthmark.
>
> This program this year means that 30 million man-years—the combined life span of these youngsters—will be spent productively and rewardingly, rather than wasted in tax-supported institutions or in welfare-supported lethargy.
>
> I believe that this is one of the most constructive, and one of the most sensible, and also one of the most exciting programs that this Nation has ever undertaken. I don't say that just because the most ardent and most active and most enthusiastic supporter of this program happens to be the honorary national chairman, Mrs. Johnson.
>
> We have taken up the age-old challenge of poverty and we don't intend to lose generations of our children to this enemy of the human race.

SOURCE: Lyndon B. Johnson, "Remarks on Project Head Start," May 18, 1965, http://www.presidency.ucsb.edu/ws/?pid=26973.

care coverage for these children.[35] Medicaid was enacted as a companion program to Medicare; the latter was designed to provide government health coverage to the elderly and disabled. While Medicare was vetted more publicly and criticized for being a socialist health program, Medicaid was passed with less controversy.[36] Unlike Medicare, Medicaid had a legislative history through the public welfare system. Moreover, it was viewed as a response to serve the growing health needs of the poor, rather than a federal hospital insurance program like Medicare.[37]

Medicaid is a federal-state partnership program, with federal funding going to states, which, in turn, design their own program eligibility and service structures. Participation by states was voluntary and those that opted in received federal funding based on a predetermined formula that

accounted for their per capita income. States that participated were required to contribute matching funds to pay for a share of the costs. By 1972, all states except Arizona were participating in the program; Arizona joined in 1982.[38]

Early and Periodic Screening, Diagnostic and Treatment Program

The Great Society programs increasingly revealed the poor health status of the nation's children, the impacts of their life circumstances, and, thus, the high need for services. Additionally, findings from a government study documenting the poor health status of young military recruits also heightened recognition of the need for further health benefit expansions. The 1964 report, "One-Third of a Nation: A Report on Young Men Found Unqualified for Military

Service," found that many young men failed recruitment exams due to physical and mental health ailments that could have been addressed in childhood. Most of these young men came from severely disadvantaged and impoverished homes.[39] As a result, Congress amended Medicaid in 1967 to add the Early and Periodic Screening, Diagnostic and Treatment (EPSDT) program.[40] The program's purpose was "to discover, as early as possible, the ills that handicap our children" and to provide "continuing follow up and treatment so that handicaps do not go neglected."[41] EPSDT covered a set of compulsory services for all youth under the age of twenty-one who were enrolled in Medicaid, including preventive, dental, mental health, developmental, and specialty services. It ensured that children received preventive services and screenings at scheduled intervals. The EPSDT legislation was amended many times since its inception to broaden covered services, including additional vision, dental, hearing, and mental health care benefits.

To date, the federal government has not passed bicycle helmet laws; instead, most states have passed legislation requiring the use of bicycle helmets. To prevent head injuries, the mandatory wearing of helmets is strongly supported by both medical organizations and government agencies responsible for child and road safety.

SOURCE: RBFried/iStockphoto.

Expansions to Medicaid Eligibility

When Medicaid was enacted, federal law required that the states cover mandatory populations, including people receiving Aid to Families with Dependent Children (AFDC) and other cash assistance or welfare.[42] Medicaid's, and thus EPSDT's, eligibility ties to AFDC enrollment resulted in many children being ineligible for these programs in the late 1970s through the 1980s;[43] AFDC required children and parents to be below 42 percent of the federal poverty level (FPL) to be eligible. This led to amendments in the 1980s and 1990s to change eligibility for children, taking them from 42 percent of FPL to 100 percent for children ages six to eighteen and 133 percent for children five and under, and finally severing the programmatic ties between AFDC and Medicaid. Amendments to the program also expanded coverage to pregnant women.

CHILD HEALTH POLICY IN THE 1970s

The 1970s brought increased recognition of additional health issues affecting children, which were not necessarily new but garnered a new level of policy attention. Several concerns were addressed during this time period.

Injury Prevention

In 1966, the National Academy of Sciences released a report calling accidental injuries the "neglected epidemic of modern society."[44] Thus, President Richard M. Nixon (1969–1974) signed the Highway Safety Act (1970), establishing the National Highway Traffic Safety Administration, replacing similar predecessor agencies, to reduce injuries and losses from motor vehicle accidents through strategies like car safety regulations and child safety seat promotion. In response to research showing a lack of federal consumer safety protections, Congress enacted the Consumer Product Safety Act (1972) to establish the Consumer Product Safety Commission.[45] This commission was an independent regulatory agency charged with identifying and addressing children's product hazards, including cribs and car seats. Over time, these programs had major impacts on mortality and morbidity associated with child injury and motor vehicle safety.

Family Planning

The 1960s and 1970s also saw a rise in feminism, the women's rights movement, and the sexual revolution. In 1970, the Title X Family Planning program was enacted under the Public Health Service Act. Title X is the only federal grant program dedicated solely to providing individuals with comprehensive family planning and related preventive health services.[46] Title X increases access to family planning services for eligible individuals, including adolescents. In addition to clinical services, Title X also funds training for family planning clinic providers, research and evaluation to improve service delivery, and community-based education and outreach.

Federal funding for family planning has been the focus of much debate over the last forty years, particularly with respect to abortion. However, by statute, Title X funds cannot be used to pay for abortion services.[47] Three years after the Supreme Court upheld the legality of abortion with *Roe v. Wade* (1973), Congress passed the Hyde Amendment (1976), barring federal funding for abortion. This amendment has been reauthorized annually since, including in the 2010 Patient Care and Affordable Care Act (PPACA) signed by President Barack Obama (2009–).

Teenage Pregnancy

One of Congress's specific goals in creating the Title X program was to address the reproductive health needs of adolescents and to prevent unplanned teenage pregnancies.[48] Teen pregnancy had been a prominent health issue in the United States since the late 1950s, when it was at its highest rate (96 births per 1,000 women ages fifteen to nineteen). The subsequent years marked a steep decline in these rates, except for a temporary increase in the late 1980s.[49] By 2012, teen birth rates had decreased to a record low of 29 births per 1,000 women aged fifteen to nineteen.[50] Many factors contributed to these declines, including widespread pregnancy prevention education efforts directed to teenagers[51] and increased access to family planning services and contraception, particularly more effective long-acting methods. Despite these declines, for decades the United States consistently has had the highest rates of teenage pregnancy compared to any other industrialized nation.[52]

In response to these high rates, the Office of Adolescent Pregnancy Programs was created in 1978 to administer adolescent pregnancy and parenting programs, including health, education, and social services, under Title VI of the Public Health Service Act. In 1981, under President Ronald Reagan (1981–1989), Title XX, also known as the Adolescent Family Life Act, replaced Title VI and legislated discretionary funds for research, care, and prevention demonstration projects.[53] It also provided specific funding for abstinence-only programs, reflecting the administration's views on this issue.

Abstinence-only program funding was significantly expanded again in 1996 as part of welfare reform efforts through an amendment to the SSA's Title V MCH legislation. This amendment outlined eight specific requirements that programs had to meet to obtain funding, including teaching teens that sexual activity and bearing children outside the context of marriage was likely to have harmful consequences for the child, his or her family, and society.[54]

Several states declined this funding due to their own and others' research showing the ineffectiveness of these programs. Despite this research, federal support continued; however, in 2010, the Obama administration and Congress eliminated two discretionary funding streams, the Community-Based Abstinence Education grant program and the abstinence-only portion of the Adolescent Family Life Act. Federal funding still remained through Title V, when the program was revived as part of the 2010 Patient Protection and Affordable Care Act.

Nutrition

Malnutrition among low-income mothers and children was another pressing issue in the early 1970s. In addition to the existing food assistance programs, the Department of Agriculture established the Commodity Supplemental Food Program in 1969 to provide commodities to feed low-income pregnant women, infants, and children up to age six.[55] Yet physicians continued to testify to Congress that low-income pregnant mothers and their infants were presenting in their practices with ailments related to malnutrition at alarming rates. As a result, the Child Nutrition Act of 1966 was amended to establish the Special Supplemental Food Program for Women, Infants, and Children (WIC) as a two-year pilot program.[56] Due to its success and increasing demand, WIC was converted to a permanent program in 1974. In the same year, the Food Stamp Program became a nationwide program and was later amended in 1977 to expand eligibility and eliminate the need for individuals to purchase stamps.

NEW FEDERALISM IN THE 1980s

President Reagan's administration marked an era of New Federalism, which was characterized by efforts to decrease the role of the federal government and return authority back to the states. The government implemented a strategy of combining federal funding of multiple categorical programs and designating them to an overarching state block grant, accompanied by reduced funding and federal oversight.

Changes to Title V Program

The Title V MCH funding was formally changed to a block grant with the passage of the Omnibus Budget Reconciliation Act (OBRA) of 1981. This legislation combined several of MCH's categorical programs into one block grant: Title V's MCH and Crippled Children Services, Supplemental Security Income benefits for children with disabilities, and other programs, including hemophilia, sudden infant death syndrome, lead-based paint poisoning prevention, genetic diseases, and adolescent pregnancy prevention.[57] The belief was that having all of these programs combined into one program, administered by one state entity, would save significant federal spending and allow states the flexibility to establish and address their own local priorities.[58] States received very little guidance from the federal government on how services should be delivered and little expectation for accountability. Simultaneously, Medicaid faced significant changes, primarily due to the enforcement of stricter AFDC eligibility requirements, resulting in many mothers and children becoming ineligible and losing their health care coverage.[59]

During the 1980s, the changes to Title V and Medicaid reflected the tensions and competing priorities of the

Republican presidential administration and Congress.[60] The struggling economy early in the decade reduced funding for MCH programs and led to a plateau in MCH indicators, including infant mortality and pregnancy outcomes. The federal MCH Bureau and state MCH program leaders recognized the need for stronger federal-state partnerships in order to refortify their efforts. In partnership with MCH providers and administrators, as well as a strong community advocacy base comprising families receiving Title V services, they were able to successfully advocate for significant legislative changes in 1989 to address the constraints on resources and programming that resulted from the block grant shift. As a result, OBRA 1989 created the current structure of the Title V program. The most significant changes, as outlined in OBRA 1989, were stricter application rules for states, including conducting a needs assessment to identify priority areas and developing plans to address proposed goals in these areas; increased reporting and accountability requirements; and increased guidance on service design, including designating approximately one-third of funds to children's preventive and primary care and another one-third to serving children with special health care needs (previously referred to as "crippled children").[61] OBRA 1989 held state programs more accountable for their spending. Interestingly, this accountability was instituted at the urging of the MCH program directors who recognized the value of data and who themselves wanted a greater degree of accountability to demonstrate the impacts of their efforts,[62] as well as an interest from Congress in this information.

Substance Use Prevention

Growing national concerns about substance use led President Reagan and his wife, Nancy Reagan, to support widespread drug prevention and education programs for youth, including the "Just Say No" campaign. To help reduce alcohol-related accidents, the National Minimum Drinking Age Act (1984) was passed, which raised the age that individuals could legally purchase or publicly possess alcoholic beverages to twenty-one.[63] The impacts of increased drinking age laws are documented in the literature, particularly in relation to decreased consumption and traffic accidents.[64] According to data from the National Highway Traffic Safety Administration, alcohol-related traffic deaths in youth fell from 22 per 100,000 in 1982 to 10 per 100,000 in 1997, and more than 17,000 lives were saved as a result of these laws during that time period.[65]

CHILD HEALTH POLICY IN THE 1990s

The 1990s brought a change in presidential administrations from Republican George H.W. Bush (1989–1993) to Democrat Bill Clinton, and thus another wave of changes in policy efforts targeting children. During the 1990s, several programs connected to children's health care and well-being were expanded.

Expansion of Title V Programs

For Title V programs, the 1990s brought continued focus on assessing unmet service needs, increasing accountability and reporting, developing national standards of care, and continued strengthening of federal-state partnerships.[66] This translated into programming that targeted continuing national concerns about connecting children to health care coverage, supporting children with special health care needs, and decreasing rates of infant mortality.[67] In the early 1990s, the MCH Bureau launched the Bright Futures program, which provided guidelines for health supervision of infants, children, and adolescents. It also launched the Healthy Start Initiative, with support from President George H.W. Bush's administration, to fund community-driven approaches to reduce infant mortality. Several large-scale data collection efforts were also developed and implemented, including the Title V Information System, Discretionary Grant Information System, National Survey of Children's Health, and National Survey of Children with Special Health Needs.

Clinton Era Health Care Reform Efforts

Despite a failed attempt at a large-scale overhaul of the health care system during President Clinton's first year in office, several very significant pieces of legislation affecting children's health were enacted during Clinton's tenure. Among them were the Family Leave Act (1993), which expanded employment leave for new parents; establishment of the Vaccines for Children entitlement program to give federally purchased vaccines to states for use with low-income children; expansion of the Earned Income Tax Credit to lower taxes owed by working families; expansions of Head Start; the Child Health Act (2000), which authorized research on children's health issues; the Personal Responsibility and Work Opportunity Act (1996), which reformed welfare; and the Balanced Budget Act (1997), which established the State Children's Health Insurance Program.

Welfare Reform

Due partly to concern about the growing AFDC caseloads, the 1996 Personal Responsibility and Work Opportunity Act reformed the federal welfare system by repealing the AFDC program and replacing it with block grants to states through the new Temporary Assistance for Needy Families (TANF) program.[68] TANF's goals included providing assistance to needy families; promoting job preparation, work, and marriage; and preventing unplanned, out-of-wedlock pregnancies.[69] While some criticized AFDC for encouraging dependency on government assistance, TANF was designed to promote transitions from welfare to work. To this end, TANF had a five-year lifetime limit of participation, though some state limits were shorter, and a five-year wait period for new immigrants.[70] In 2012, an average of three million children received TANF benefits; nearly one-half were children whose parents were ineligible due to citizenship or non-income-related ineligibility.[71]

Children's Health Insurance Program

In 1997, the State Children's Health Insurance Program (SCHIP) was enacted with bipartisan support under the Balanced Budget Act, in part a response to the failure of the passage of health care reform.[72,73] SCHIP was designed to insure children up to age nineteen living in low-income working families (less than 200 percent of the FPL) who were ineligible for Medicaid. Eligibility is based on both federal and state requirements, reflecting both entitlement and block grant functions.

States had three options to insure eligible children through SCHIP: expanding their Medicaid programs, including beyond the 200 percent FPL ceiling; creating a separate insurance program; or implementing a combination of both strategies.[74] Several states created new, separate health insurance programs to counter the stigma that was associated with government assistance. Similar to Medicaid, the federal government provided a match to state funds, though SCHIP's match rate is higher to encourage state participation. Unlike Medicaid, federal funding was capped and each state received an annual allotment based on a formula that primarily accounted for the portion of the nation's uninsured and low-income children in that state.[75] States were also allowed to use a small portion of funds for outreach and enrollment activities. States were given flexibility in designing their programs, but they had to meet a standard of coverage that was equivalent to most comprehensive health insurance plans in their state or the basic plans offered to government workers.[76] Similar to Medicaid, SCHIP programs generally cover essential health services, including EPSDT services. SCHIP was renamed the Children's Health Insurance Program (CHIP) in 2009 when the program was reauthorized and expanded. In 2012, CHIP served 5.5 million children,[77] in addition to the nearly 31 million children served by Medicaid. Furthermore, between 1998 and 2011, the uninsured rate among low-income children decreased from 28 percent to approximately 10 percent, partly due to CHIP and Medicaid.[78,79]

CURRENT POLICY LANDSCAPE: 2000–2012

The election of George W. Bush (2001–2009) brought with it an era of "compassionate conservatism." Increasing attention to the failing educational system led his administration to focus many of its child-directed efforts on education,

most notably the No Child Left Behind Act of 2001, which focused on having all children reach academic proficiency by 2014. While President Bush did not pursue more comprehensive approaches to health care reform, his administration did engage in several important, if more incremental, health policy initiatives, including adding prescription drug benefits to Medicare and supporting the expansion of Community Health Centers.[80,81]

CHIP Reauthorization

The CHIP program came up for reauthorization during President Bush's second term. In 2007, several reauthorization bills were passed by Congress and vetoed by Bush, resulting in a debate about government involvement in health care. Conservatives felt there was too much involvement and income eligibility levels were too high. Another concern was "crowd out" of private insurance, specifically that those covered by private sources might drop their plans to obtain public coverage, thus crowding out the private industry. Studies have shown that a small portion of CHIP enrollees drop employer-sponsored coverage to enroll in public programs.[82,83]

To prevent CHIP from expiring, Congress passed a temporary extension, assuming a new president would reauthorize it, which President Obama did. As one of his first acts in office, he signed the CHIP Reauthorization Act (CHIPRA) in 2009. CHIPRA further enhanced children's coverage by expanding state funding and programmatic options and providing incentives to states for streamlining processes to identify, enroll, and retain coverage for eligible children who previously had not been enrolled, and subsequently increasing Medicaid and CHIP enrollment.

Health Care Reform: Patient Protection and Affordable Care Act

In 2010, President Barack Obama and his fellow Democrats in Congress succeeded in passing a historic health care reform effort through the enactment of the Patient Protection and Affordable Care Act. The PPACA had many provisions that impacted children's health coverage, services, and programs.[84] First, it created a minimum Medicaid income eligibility level to include all individuals with income below 134 percent of the FPL, though states had the option to opt out of this expansion as a result of the Supreme Court ruling in *National Federation of Independent Business v. Sebelius* (2012).

From January 2014, when this change in eligibility level went into effect, through 2016, the federal government pays the entire cost of covering newly eligible individuals, and then states will be expected to cover 10 percent of these costs. Federal support for CHIP was also expanded through the PPACA, primarily through an increase in the federal match rate. Additionally, children who are eligible for

POLITICS AND HEALTH CARE POLICY

The Reauthorization of the Children's Health Insurance Program

The Children's Health Insurance Program (CHIP) was initially passed in 1997 to expand coverage to uninsured children living in families who were ineligible for Medicaid, the nation's primary source of government health insurance for low-income children. As the program was reaching expiration in 2007, President George W. Bush and Congress could not agree on how CHIP should be reauthorized, leading Congress to pass a temporary extension. In 2009, President Barack Obama signed the reauthorization bill as one of his first acts in office, affirming his commitment to protecting the health and welfare of children and to overall health care reform. The following is an excerpt from his speech on February 4, 2009:

Today, with one of the first bills I sign—reauthorizing the Children's Health Insurance Program—we fulfill one of the highest responsibilities we have: to ensure the health and well-being of our nation's children.

It is a responsibility that has only grown more urgent as our economic crisis has deepened, health care costs have exploded, and millions of working families are unable to afford health insurance. Today in America, eight million children are still uninsured—more than 45 million Americans altogether.

It's hard to overstate the toll this takes on our families: the sleepless nights worrying that someone's going to get hurt, or praying that a sick child gets better on her own. The decisions that no parent should ever have to make—how long to put off that doctor's appointment, whether to fill that prescription, whether to let a child play outside, knowing that all it takes is one accident, one injury, to send your family into financial ruin. . . .

. . . This is not who we are. We are not a nation that leaves struggling families to fend for themselves. No child in America should be receiving her primary care in the emergency room in the middle of the night. No child should be falling behind at school because he can't hear the teacher or see the blackboard. I refuse to accept that millions of our kids fail to reach their full potential because we fail to meet their basic needs. In a decent society, there are certain obligations that are not subject to tradeoffs or negotiation—health care for our children is one of those obligations.

That is why we have passed this legislation to continue coverage for seven million children, cover an additional four million children in need, and finally lift the ban on states providing insurance to legal immigrant children if they choose to do so. Since it was created more than ten years ago, the Children's Health Insurance Program has been a lifeline for millions of kids whose parents work full time, and don't qualify for Medicaid, but through no fault of their own don't have—and can't afford—private insurance. For millions of kids who fall into that gap, CHIP has provided care when they're sick and preventative services to help them stay well. This legislation will allow us to continue and build on these successes.

But this bill is only a first step. The way I see it, providing coverage to 11 million children through CHIP is a down payment on my commitment to cover every single American. . . .

SOURCE: "Remarks by President Barack Obama on Children's Health Insurance Program Bill Signing," February 4, 2009, http://www.whitehouse.gov/the_press_office/RemarksbyPresidentBarackObamaOnChildrensHealthInsuranceProgramBillSigning

CHIP, but who cannot enroll due to federal allotment caps, would be eligible for tax credits in the state health insurance exchanges that were established in October 2013. These marketplaces, which can be state or federally sponsored, offer health insurance options for consumers who do not have employer-based coverage. Medicaid and CHIP eligibility determination and enrollment would also be coordinated with the exchanges' application process, making these processes more seamless.

The PPACA also included several insurance market reforms that impact children, including barring exclusions based on preexisting conditions; barring lifetime limits on spending; expanding mandatory coverage of essential health benefits, including mental health and prescription coverage; and increasing the age that dependent children can stay on their family's qualified health plans to twenty-six. Furthermore, the PPACA eliminates co-pays for services

recommended by the U.S. Preventive Services Task Force, immunizations recommended by the Centers for Disease Control and Prevention (CDC), and evidence-based preventive care and screenings based on the MCH Bureau's Bright Futures, the Institute of Medicine's recommendations regarding women's preventive health services, and other health supervision guidelines.[85]

Additional PPACA provisions affecting children included (1) amending Title V to provide state funding for evidence-based home visitation programs to improve MCH outcomes through parental support and education; (2) appropriating funding for Childhood Obesity Demonstration Projects authorized under CHIPRA; (3) establishing a national public health education campaign focused on oral health care prevention and education; (4) authorizing the CDC to award competitive Community Transformation Grants to state and local agencies for implementation of evidence-based community preventive health activities targeting chronic diseases and health disparities; (5) authorizing grants to states for abstinence and comprehensive pregnancy and sexually transmitted infections prevention education; (6) restoring Title V abstinence education funding; (7) expanding funding for the Community Health Center program; and (8) providing funding for School-Based Health Centers, a model of care that provides comprehensive health services to children and their families on school campuses.[86]

Despite the extensive provisions expanding coverage and access to services for low-income children and their families, there is still some uncertainty around the PPACA's long-term impacts, including the effects of exclusion of children who are not legal immigrants and maintenance of increased state responsibility for Medicaid expansions after the initial full federal coverage ends.

OVERARCHING THEMES FROM THE LAST FIVE DECADES

Since the 1960s, several prominent themes have emerged in the child health policy landscape. Today, a greater number of children and young adults are eligible for federally sponsored or funded health care than ever before.

Major Improvements in Child Health Indices

There has been consistent improvement in many measures of child health over time, though many health indices continue to document a burden of disease that requires policymakers' attention and continued monitoring. Overall mortality rates for children have declined, including mortality due to infectious diseases and infant mortality. Infectious diseases declined due to the widespread availability of vaccines and antibiotics as well as better hygiene and sanitation. However, in recent years, some parents have chosen to forgo immunizations, leading to new outbreaks of some preventable diseases that require intervention. The infant mortality rate has declined due to the nation's focus on advanced health care for pregnant woman, as well as for sick newborns, through neo-intensive care units and federally supported, regionalized perinatal care. Yet the declines have mainly been in birth weight–specific mortality and the same impact has yet to be seen in preterm birth and low birth weight.[87] Thus, the nation's rates have reached a plateau and remain above those of other industrialized countries, requiring innovative strategies to make further improvements.[88]

Furthermore, public health campaigns have helped to deter the impacts of many health risks, such as lead poisoning, sudden infant death syndrome, malnutrition, injuries, and teenage pregnancy. As a result of significant legislative efforts that have led to improvements in medical care, research, and health care coverage, children with developmental disabilities and other special health care needs are also living longer and healthier lives. Yet with these improvements there is an increasing need to support these children as they transition into adolescence and young adulthood.

There has also been a rise in chronic conditions with roots in prenatal and early childhood years, including mental health conditions and obesity. In the 1960s, the rates of overweight were somewhat negligible but, in 2010, one out of three children was overweight. Children who are overweight in preschool years are at higher risk of obesity in later childhood years, and children and adolescents who are obese are likely to be obese as adults, putting them at higher risk for adult health problems, such as heart disease, diabetes, and cancer.[89] Chronic conditions have become the focus of many large-scale federal, state, and local initiatives in the past decade and will likely continue to require attention until they are fully addressed.

Oral health is another area that has received minimal attention in the past, but is increasingly prioritized due to its significant effects on children's health and academic outcomes. Historically, there has been limited availability of coverage and access to affordable care, but the PPACA includes several provisions for the improvement of pediatric oral health as well as prevention and management of obesity and other chronic conditions that are causing considerable strains on health care spending, both during childhood years and throughout the life course.

Most important, the antecedents that contribute to these health issues have changed with the rapid changes in technology that have occurred in this time period. For example, the rise in fast food and processed foods has dramatically contributed to the obesity epidemic, and increased access to social media and the Internet has given rise to diverse issues, including bullying, violence, suicide, and less physical activity. Thus, as we look forward, we see that the changing trends in child health indicators also call for changing our strategies to ensure that policies and programming are proactively addressing both the needs of children and the underlying antecedents to health conditions, such as the built and surrounding environment, socioeconomic factors, community violence, distribution of health services, and access to healthy food and exercise.

Changing Demography and the Evolution of Health Disparities

In 1960, there were 64.5 million children in the United States, and after a drop from 1970 to 1990, the number increased to 74.1 million in 2010 and is projected to continue to increase.[90] Despite this growth, children have represented a smaller proportion of the population over time, decreasing consistently from 36 percent of the population in 1960 to 24 percent in 2010.[91] This trend is largely due to declining birth rates and an increase in the elderly population. As the proportion of children decreases, their visibility and ability to compete for resources to address their health needs also lessen.

There has also been a growing trend in health, social, and economic disparities among children, particularly youth of color. The U.S. population has become increasingly diverse in recent decades and the demographic of children reflects this diversity. From 1980 to 2010, the percentage of white children decreased from 74 to 54 percent, and it is projected to continue to decline. The proportion of Hispanic children increased consistently, from 9 percent in 1980 to 23 percent in 2010, and is projected to steadily increase in the future.[92] Furthermore, children from immigrant families are the fastest growing group of children.[93] Immigrant children are more likely to live in families with incomes below the FPL, who lack health insurance, and who are less likely to use public benefits.[94] Exclusion of these children from public programs, including Medicaid and CHIP, and, thus, lack of access to preventive care in childhood will likely lead to higher burdens of need as these children age, for example, as reflected in Hispanic rates of obesity and diabetes.

There are also increasing ethnic and socioeconomic disparities in children's health outcomes. Rates of asthma, infant mortality, obesity, sexually transmitted diseases, and poor mental health are higher for children of non-white backgrounds. These gaps are due to challenges in accessing care, including cultural and financial barriers, as well as disparities in the quality and level of care received. The child health field needs new strategies to reach these children and address inequalities as these health concerns have long-term and potentially costly impacts not only to the individual but also to society in general.

Changing Trends in Funding and Organization of Health Care

There have been changing trends in the organization and financing of health care and health care coverage available to children and their families. These trends have been responsive to filling gaps in coverage that have persisted, but there are still many children who do not have full access. Federal funding shifted from categorical funding to states to address specific health issues, to block grants with limited federal oversight, and back to a combination of both federal and state funding and administrative strategies. Funding for Medicaid and CHIP has continued to expand since these programs' inception, and ongoing amendments, including those in the PPACA, have brought much-needed revisions to streamline eligibility, expand coverage, and ensure that the programs cover essential health services that are recommended for children's healthy development.

Expansion of health care coverage and services remains highly dependent on federal-state partnerships, with federal decision making and state-level implementation. There is also tremendous variability in terms of how states operationalize federal programs, which greatly affects the ability and state-level variability in addressing children's health needs. For example, with half of the states refusing to expand the Medicaid program under the PPACA, many eligible families and children will continue to lack access to health insurance and, in turn, will have limited access to health care services.

Furthermore, despite expansions to many federal programs since the 1960s, federal spending on children's programs overall has received a smaller portion of the federal budget than programs for adults and the elderly. One study documented that, while spending on children's programs, including health, nutrition, housing, and social services, increased from $58 billion in 1960 to $445 billion in 2011 in real dollars, expenditures on children as a portion of the federal budget decreased overall. Since 1960, the portion of the domestic budget spent on children dropped 23 percent, while spending on older age groups in Social Security, Medicare, and Medicaid more than doubled.[95]

With growing research showing that the roots of many adulthood health conditions lie in early child development, we need to continue to reevaluate how our programs are structured and funded, including continuing to strengthen federal-state partnerships and setting minimum standards nationally that must be met with regard to insuring and serving low-income children and families. The PPACA has taken a step in this direction with the increased eligibility limits to 133 percent FPL for all individuals; careful monitoring and assessment of the uptake of the program will be necessary to ensure full compliance with these new policies.

LOOKING AHEAD

Retrospectively, it is apparent that progress, though sometimes uneven, has been made in children's health issues. Recognition of their special vulnerabilities, such as growing up in disadvantaged homes and susceptibility to the effects of their environments, has often highlighted the importance of systems thinking on the part of government, including providing stable health insurance, nutrition, and developmentally appropriate programs such as Medicaid, WIC, and Head Start. However, this support has also led to somewhat fragmented services, spread throughout many government offices that may not frequently communicate with each other, as shown in Table 19.3. Increased coordination between these systems can only benefit their constituents. With increasing availability of technology to connect health, social service, and education records with appropriate checks and balances, there is a potential window for helping coordinate care across a variety of systems.

Furthermore, children often get caught in the political winds of which entities—federal, state, local, or individual families—should be responsible for their welfare and to

TABLE 19.3 **Select Federal Agencies and Offices That Oversee Children's Health Policies and Programs, 2012**

Federal Agencies/Offices with Children's Health Initiatives/Programs	Related Federal Legislation
Department of Health and Human Services	
Substance and Mental Health Services Administration	Social Security Act, 1935
Center for Mental Health Services	Title V Maternal and Child Health Block Grant, 1935
Center for Substance Abuse Prevention	Title XIX Grants to States to for Medical Assistance Programs (Medicaid and Children's Health Insurance Program), 1965
Centers for Medicare and Medicaid Services	
Health Resources and Services Administration	Title XX, Adolescent Family Life Act, 1981
Maternal and Child Health Bureau	Title IV Grants to States for Aid and Services to Needy Families with Children and for Child-Welfare Service (Temporary Assistance to Needy Families Program)
HIV/AIDS Bureau	
Bureau of Primary Health Care	Title XXI State Children's Health Insurance Program, 1997
National Institutes of Health	Section 1928, Vaccines for Children Program
National Institute of Child Health and Human Development	Section 418, Funding for Child Care
National Institute of Mental Health	Public Health Service Act, 1944
National Institute on Drug Abuse	Title X, Family Planning Program, 1970
Centers for Disease Control and Prevention	Section 330, authorizing Health Center Program
Office of Infectious Diseases	Ryan White CARE Act, 1990
National Center for HIV/AIDS, Viral Hepatitis, STD, and TB Prevention	Patient Protection and Affordable Care Act, 2010
Office of Noncommunicable Diseases, Injury and Environmental Health	
National Center for Chronic Disease Prevention and Health Promotion	
National Center for Injury Prevention and Control	
National Center on Birth Defects and Developmental Disabilities	
Office of Public Health and Science	
Office of Population Affairs	
Adolescent Family Life Program	
Office of Women's Health	
Agency for Healthcare Research and Quality	
Administration for Children and Families	
Administration on Children, Youth and Families	
Children's Bureau	
Family and Youth Services Bureau	
Office of Head Start	
Office of Child Care	
Office of Early Childhood Development	
Department of Agriculture, Food and Nutrition Services	
Commodity Supplemental Food Program	Food Stamp Act, 1964, 1977
Child and Adult Food Program	National School Lunch Act, 1946
Fresh Fruit and Vegetable Program	Child Nutrition Act, 1966
National School Lunch Program	Agriculture and Consumer Protection Act, 1973
School Breakfast Program	Child Nutrition and WIC Reauthorization Act, 2004
Special Milk Program	Agriculture, Rural Development, Food and Drug Administration, and Related Agencies Appropriations Act, 2006
Summer Food Service Program	
Women, Infants and Children (WIC)	Healthy, Hunger-Free Kids Act, 2010
Supplemental Nutrition Assistance Program (formerly Food Stamps Program)	
Department of Education, Office of the Deputy Secretary	
Office of Elementary and Secondary Education	Elementary and Secondary Education Act, 1965
Office of Special Education and Rehabilitation Services	

Federal Agencies/Offices with Children's Health Initiatives/Programs	Related Federal Legislation
Office of English Language Acquisition, Language Enhancement, and Academic Achievement for Limited English Proficient Students	Individuals with Disabilities Education Act, 1990, 1997, 2004 (formerly Education for All Handicapped Children Act, 1975)
Environmental Protection Agency, Office of Children's Health Protection	Executive Order 13045: Protection of Children from Environmental Health Risks and Safety Risks, 1997
Department of Transportation, National Highway Traffic Safety Administration	Highway Safety Act, 1970

SOURCE: Adapted from Mary Kay Kenney, Michael D. Kogan, Stephanie Toomer, and Peter C. van Dyck, "Federal Expenditures on Maternal and Child Health in the United States," *Maternal and Child Health Journal* 16: 2 (2012): 271–287.

NOTE: As this chapter focuses on health legislation, not all legislation included in this table is discussed. This table is meant to provide an overview of the various federal agencies that oversee programs and initiatives that impact the lives of children in the United States.

what degree. With changing political administrations and congressional majorities often come changes in program funding and structure. Policy efforts have been most successful when passed with bipartisan support and with transparency of how the legislation is crafted and how benefits will be distributed—factors that will need to be sustained for legislation to demonstrate long-term impacts.

There is an increasingly concentrated poor underclass in the United States and their children contribute disproportionately to all poor children's health indicators. This is due to numerous factors, including racism, prejudice, and structural barriers. Fifty years of policy has not led to significant improvements for these children; they continue to have worse outcomes than their peers. Access to care is another important concern, with more than six million children still uninsured despite significant expansion in public insurance options. Most of these uninsured children are Hispanic, and with a growing minority population in the United States, strategies are needed to increase access to care for this population.

In terms of provision of care, there have been shifts from individualized health care from direct providers to encouraging a coordinated systems approach that aims to link health care and population health. The concepts of medical homes and coordinated systems of care that were popularized to address the needs of children with special health care needs are now being expanded to the general population. The PPACA incentivizes the use of electronic health records to encourage coordinated care management across systems as well as medical homes to manage children's overall health care across a network of providers. Reductions in children's chronic conditions will also rely on policies, like EPSDT and the PPACA, that continue to support long-term, preventive interventions that address the antecedents of these issues, rather than providing treatment after they develop. Moreover, a more holistic approach that incorporates the context in which children's health issues develop, including community and family settings, would be more beneficial than previous approaches of focusing on the health care sector only. The remaining challenge is how to craft legislation that addresses these contextual factors without seemingly infringing on individual families' liberties.

The quality of care that children receive also requires attention as future policies are developed, particularly in regard to youth of disadvantaged backgrounds. The PPACA's requirements that essential preventive services must be provided and that care must meet health supervision guidelines are encouraging. Further policy efforts in this vain are needed to address health disparities, as is careful evaluation of whether the intent of these policies is fully actualized.

It is important to keep in mind that, overall, children are healthier today than ever before. The policies that have supported their health have been effective in improving access to care. As we look ahead to the next fifty years and beyond, the challenge will be how to diminish the causes and impact of mortality and morbidity, such as chronic illness, injury, and obesity, and how to ensure that all children have equitable access to health care and resources regardless of their social or economic backgrounds. With increasing awareness of intergenerational, social, and environmental impacts of inequity on health status, and the importance of quality improvement in health care and population health, investments in children's health, prenatally and throughout adolescence and young adulthood, are key if individuals and society at large are to fully benefit.

See also **Chapter 3: The Department of Health and Human Services: Responsibilities and Policies (1953–Present); Chapter 4: The Centers for Disease Control and Prevention: Anticipatory Action in the Face of Uncertainty (1946–Present); Chapter 6: The Centers for Medicare and Medicaid Services (1965–Present); Chapter 13: Government Financing of Health Care (1940s–Present); Chapter 20: Women's Issues and American Health Care Policy (1960s–Present); Chapter 21: Minorities, Immigrants, and Health Care Policy:**

Disparities and Solutions (1960s–Present); Chapter 23: Fifty Years of Progress in Disease and Injury Prevention (1950s–Present); Chapter 24: Mental Health and Social

Policy (1960s–Present); Chapter 25: Nutrition, Physical Activity, and the Obesity Epidemic: Issues, Policies, and Solutions (1960s–Present).

NOTES

We are grateful to Bernard Guyer, MD, MPH; Zanvyl Krieger, professor of children's health, Emeritus, John Hopkins University, Bloomberg School of Public Health; and Peter van Dyke, MD, MPH, senior associate, Department of Population, Family and Reproductive Health, Johns Hopkins University, Bloomberg School of Public Health, and former associate administrator, Maternal and Child Health Bureau, Health Resources and Services Administration, U.S Department of Health and Human Services, for sharing their thoughtful insights and careful review. We also greatly acknowledge additional funding for this chapter from the Maternal and Child Health Bureau (primary grant number: U45 MC000023-14-00).

1. National Center for Health Statistics. Health, United States, 2012: With Special Feature on Emergency Care (Hyattsville, MD: National Center for Health Statistics, 2013), table 25, http://www.cdc.gov/nchs/data/hus/hus12.pdf.

2. Ibid.

3. Ibid.

4. Christina D. Bethell et al., "A National and State Profile of Leading Health Problems and Health Care Quality for U.S. Children: Key Insurance Disparities and Across-State Variations," *Academic Pediatrics* 11: 3, Suppl (2011): S22–S33.

5. Ibid.

6. Paul H. Wise, "The Transformation of Child Health in the United States," *Health Affairs* 23: 5 (2004): 9–25.

7. Moorman et al., "Current Asthma Prevalence—United States, 2006–2008," *Morbidity and Mortality Weekly Report* 60: 1, Suppl (2011): 84–86.

8. Cynthia L. Ogden et al., "Prevalence of High Body Mass Index in U.S. Children and Adolescents, 2007–2008," *Journal of the American Medical Association* 303: 3 (2010): 242–249.

9. Sheryl H. Kataoka, Lily Zhang, and Kenneth B. Wells, "Unmet Need for Mental Health Care among U.S. Children: Variation by Ethnicity and Insurance Status," *American Journal of Psychiatry* 159: 9 (2002): 1548–1555.

10. Margarita Alegria, Melissa Vallas, and Andres J. Pumariega, "Racial and Ethnic Disparities in Pediatric Mental Health," *Child and Adolescent Psychiatry Clinics of North America* 19: 4 (2010): 759–774.

11. Carmen DeNavas-Walt, Bernadette D. Proctor, and Jessica C. Smith, *Income, Poverty, and Health Insurance Coverage in the United States: 2012* (Current Population Reports, P60–245) (Washington, DC: U.S. Government Printing Office, 2013).

12. DeNavas-Walt et al., *Income, Poverty, and Health Insurance Coverage.*

13. Kristin Anderson Moore and Zakia Redd, *Children in Poverty: Trends, Consequences, and Policy Options* (Research Brief 2002-54) (Washington, DC: Child Trends, 2002).

14. Hirokazu Yoshikawa, J. Lawrence Aber, and William R. Beardslee, "The Effects of Poverty on the Mental, Emotional, and Behavioral Health of Children and Youth: Implications for Prevention," *American Psychologist* 67: 4 (2012): 272–284.

15. Patrice L. Engle and Maureen M. Black, "The Effect of Poverty on Child Development and Educational Outcomes," *Annals of the New York Academy of Sciences* 1136: 1 (2008): 243–256.

16. Moore & Redd, *Children in Poverty.*

17. Ibid.

18. National Research Council and Institute of Medicine, *Children's Health, the Nation's Wealth: Assessing and Improving Child Health* (Washington, DC: National Academies Press, 2004).

19. Vince L. Hutchins, "Maternal and Child Health Bureau: Roots," *Pediatrics* 94: 5 (1994): 695–699.

20. Lewis Margolis and Jonathan B. Kotch, "Tracing the Historical Foundations of Maternal and Child Health to Contemporary Times," in *Maternal Child Health: Programs, Problems and Policies in Public Health*, 3rd ed., edited by Jonathan B. Kotch, 11–34 (Burlington, MA: Jones & Bartlett Learning, 2013).

21. Ibid.

22. Theda Skocpol, *Protecting Soldiers and Mothers: The Political Origins of Social Policy in United States* (Cambridge, MA: Harvard University Press, 1995).

23. Margolis & Kotch, "Tracing the Historical Foundations."

24. Bernard Guyer, "The Evolution and Future Role of Title V," in *Children in a Changing Health System: Assessments and Proposals for Reform*, edited by Mark J. Schlesinger and Leon Eisenberg, 297–324 (Baltimore: Johns Hopkins University Press, 1990).

25. Health Resources and Services Administration, "MCH Timeline," http://mchb.hrsa.gov/timeline/

26. John F. Kennedy Presidential Library and Museum, "JFK and People with Intellectual Disabilities," http://www.jfklibrary .org/JFK/JFK-in-History/JFK-and-People-with-Intellectual-Disabilities.aspx.

27. Ibid.

28. Health Resources and Services Administration, "MCH Timeline."

29. John E.B. Myers, "A Short History of Child Protection in America," *Family Law Quarterly* 42: 3 (2008): 449–464.

30. Alice Sardell, *The U.S. Experiment in Social Medicine: The Community Health Center Program, 1965–1986* (Pittsburgh, PA: University of Pittsburgh Press, 1988).

31. Health Resources and Services Administration, "What Is a Health Center?" http://bphc.hrsa.gov/about/index.html.

32. Bonnie Lefkowitz, *Community Health Centers: A Movement and the People Who Made It Happen* (New Brunswick, NJ: Rutgers University Press, 2007).

33. Health Resources and Services Administration, "Health Center Data," http://bphc.hrsa.gov/healthcenterdatastatistics/index .html.

34. U.S. Department of Health and Human Services, Office of Head Start, "Head Start Program Facts: Fiscal Year 2012," http://eclkc.ohs.acf.hhs.gov/hslc/mr/factsheets/2012-hs-program-factsheet.html.

35. Kaiser Family Foundation, *Medicaid: A Primer* (Washington, DC: Kaiser Family Foundation, 2013).

36. Theodore R. Marmor, *The Politics of Medicare*, 2nd ed. (Piscataway, NJ: Transaction, 2000).

37. Judith D. Moore and David G. Smith, "Legislating Medicaid: Considering Medicaid and its Origins," *Health Care Financing Review* 27: 2 (2005/2006): 45–52.

38. Arizona Health Care Cost Containment System, "A Brief History of AHCCCS," http://www.azahcccs.gov/Careers/History.aspx.

39. Sara Rosenbaum et al., *National Security and U.S. Child Health Policy: The Origins of Continuing the Role of Medicaid and EPSDT* (Policy Brief) (Washington, DC: George Washington University, School of Public Health and Health Services, Department of Health Policy, 2005).

40. Sara Rosenbaum, Michelle Proser, and Colleen Sonosky, "Health Policy and Early Child Development: An Overview," http://www.commonwealthfund.org/~/media/Files/Publications/Fund%20Report/2001/Jun/Health%20Policy%20and%20Early%20Child%20Development%20%20An%20Overview/rosenbaum_early_450%20pdf.pdf.

41. Health Resources and Services Administration, "EPSDT Overview," http://mchb.hrsa.gov/epsdt/overview.html.

42. Kaiser Family Foundation, *Medicaid: A Primer*.

43. Cindy Mann, Diane Rowland, and Rachel Garfield, "Historical Overview of Children's Health Care Coverage," *The Future of Children* 13:1 (2003): 31–53.

44. Committee on Trauma and Committee on Shock, *Accidental Death and Disability: The Neglected Disease of Modern Society* (Washington, DC: National Academy of Sciences, 1996), http://www.ems.gov/pdf/1997-Reproduction-AccidentalDeathDissability.pdf.

45. "2011–2016 U.S. Consumer Product Safety Commission Strategic Plan" (Washington, DC: U.S. Consumer Safety Product Commission), http://www.cpsc.gov//PageFiles/123374/2011strategic.pdf.

46. U.S. Department of Health and Human Services, Office of Population Affairs, "Title X Family Planning," http://www.hhs.gov/opa/title-x-family-planning/index.html.

47. Ibid.

48. Rebecca Gudeman and Sara Madge, "The Federal Title X Family Planning Program: Privacy and Access Rules for Adolescents," *Youth Law News* 3: 1 (2011), http://www.youthlaw.org/publications/yln/2011/jan_mar_2011/the_federal_title_x_family_planning_program_privacy_and_access_rules_for_adolescents.

49. Heather Boonstra, "Teen Pregnancy: Trends and Lessons Learned," *Guttmacher Report on Public Policy* 5: 1 (2002), http://www.guttmacher.org/pubs/tgr/05/1/gr050107.html.

50. Brady E. Hamilton, Joyce A. Martin, and Stephanie J. Ventura, "Births: Preliminary Data for 2012," *National Vital Statistics Reports* 62: 3 (2013), http://www.cdc.gov/nchs/data/nvsr/nvsr62/nvsr62_03.pdf.

51. Brady E. Hamilton and Stephanie J. Ventura, "Birth Rates for U.S. Teenagers Reach Historic Lows for All Age and Ethnic Groups" *NCHS Data Brief* 89 (2012), http://www.cdc.gov/nchs/data/databriefs/db89.htm.

52. Ibid.

53. U.S. Department of Health and Human Services, Office of Population Affairs, "Title XX Adolescent Family Life," http://www.hhs.gov/opa/about-opa-and-initiatives/title-xx-afl/index.html.

54. U.S. Social Security Administration, "Separate Programs for Abstinence Education," http://www.ssa.gov/OP_Home/ssact/title05/0510.htm.

55. Oliveira et al., "History of the WIC program," in *The WIC Program: Background, Trends, and Issues* (October 2002), http://www.ers.usda.gov/publications/fanrr-food-assistance-nutrition-research-program/fanrr27.aspx#.UhzxlbyE5_N.

56. Ibid.

57. Peter van Dyck, "Maternal and Child Health: History to Remember" (2012), http://services.choruscall.com/links/hrsa110713.html.

58. Ibid.

59. Margolis & Kotch, "Tracing the Historical Foundations."

60. Ibid.

61. Hutchins, "Maternal and Child Health Bureau."

62. van Dyck, "Maternal and Child Health."

63. National Institutes of Health, National Institute on Alcohol Abuse and Alcoholism, "The 1984 National Minimum Drinking Age Act," http://alcoholpolicy.niaaa.nih.gov/the_1984_national_minimum_drinking_age_act_2.html.

64. Alexander C. Wagenaar and Traci L. Toomey, "Effects of Minimum Drinking Age Laws: A Review and Analyses of the Literature from 1960 to 2000," *Journal of Studies on Alcohol* Supplement 14 (March 2002): 206–225.

65. Robert B. Voas, A. Scott Tippetts, and James C. Fell, "Assessing the Effectiveness of Minimum Legal Drinking Age and Zero Tolerance Laws in the United States," *Accident Analysis and Prevention* 35: 4 (2003): 579–587.

66. Peter van Dyck, "A History of Child Health Equity Legislation in the United States," *Pediatrics* 112 (2003):727–730.

67. Ibid.

68. Pamela Loprest, Stefanie Schmidt, and Anne Dryden Witte, "Welfare Reform under PRWORA: Aid to Children with Working Families?" in *Tax Policy and the Economy*, Volume 14, edited by James M. Poterba, 157–203 (Cambridge, MA: MIT Press, 2000).

69. U.S. Department of Health and Human Services, Office of Family Assistance, "About TANF," http://www.acf.hhs.gov/programs/ofa/programs/tanf/about.

70. Karen C. Tumlin and Wendy Zimmerman, "Immigrants and TANF: A Look at Immigrant Welfare Recipients in Three Cities" (Occasional Paper Number 69) (Washington, DC: Urban Institute, 2003), http://www.urban.org/UploadedPDF/310874_OP69.pdf.

71. Olivia Golden and Amelia Hawkins, "TANF Child-Only Cases" (Washington, DC: Urban Institute, 2012), http://www.acf.hhs.gov/sites/default/files/opre/child_only.pdf.

72. *The Medicaid Resource Book, Appendix 1: Medicaid Legislative History: 1965–2000* (Washington, DC: Kaiser Family Foundation, 2007).

73. Alice Sardell and Kay Johnson, "The Politics of EPSDT Policy in the 1990s: Policy Entrepreneurs, Political Streams, and Children's Health Benefits," *Milbank Quarterly* 76 (1998): 175–205.

74. Jeanne M. Lambrew, "The State Children's Health Insurance Program: Past, Present and Future" (New York: Commonwealth Fund, 2007), http://www.commonwealthfund.org/usr_doc/991_Lambrew_SCHIP_past_present_future.pdf.

75. Kaiser Family Foundation, Commission on Medicaid and the Uninsured, "CHIP Financing Structure" (Washington, DC: Kaiser Family Foundation, 2009), http://kaiserfamilyfoundation.files.wordpress.com/2013/01/7910.pdf.

76. Centers for Medicare and Medicaid Services, "CHIP Benefits," http://www.medicaid.gov/Medicaid-CHIP-Program-Information/By-Topics/Childrens-Health-Insurance-Program-CHIP/CHIP-Benefits.html.

77. Kaiser Family Foundation, Commission on Medicaid and the Uninsured, "CHIP Enrollment: June 2012 Data Snapshot" (Washington, DC: Kaiser Family Foundation, 2013), http://kaiserfamilyfoundation.files.wordpress.com/2013/08/7642-08-chip-enrollment.pdf.

78. Kaiser Family Foundation, Commission on Medicaid and the Uninsured, "The Impact of Medicaid and SCHIP on Low-Income Children's Health" (Washington, DC: Kaiser Family Foundation, 2009), http://kaiserfamilyfoundation.files.word press.com/2013/01/7645-02.pdf.

79. Kaiser Family Foundation, Commission on Medicaid and the Uninsured, "The Uninsured: A Primer" (Washington, DC: Kaiser Family Foundation, 2012), http://kaiserfamilyfounda tion.files.wordpress.com/2013/01/7451-08.pdf.

80. Thomas R. Oliver, Philip R. Lee, and Helene L. Lipton, "A Political History of Medicare and Prescription Drug Coverage," *Milbank Quarterly* 82: 2 (2004): 283–354.

81. Robert W. Mickey, "Dr. StrangeRove, or: How Republicans Learned to Stop Worrying and Love Community Health Centers," in *The Health Care Safety Net in a Post-Reform World*, edited by Mark A. Hall and Sara Rosenbaum, 21–66 (New Brunswick, NJ: Rutgers University Press, 2012).

82. Lisa Dubay and Genevieve Kenney, "The Impact of CHIP on Children's Insurance Coverage: An Analysis Using the National Survey of America's Families," *Health Services Research* 44: 6 (2009): 2040–2059.

83. David B. Muhlestein and Eric E. Seiber, "State Variability in Children's Medicaid/CHIP Crowd-Out Estimates," *Medicare & Medicaid Research Review* 3: 3 (2013): E1–E22.

84. Association of Maternal Child Health Programs, "The Patient Protection and Affordable Care Act: Summary of Key Maternal and Child Health Related Highlights with Updates on Status of Implementation" (Washington, DC: Association of Maternal Child Health Programs, 2012), http://www.amchp.org/Policy-Advocacy/health-reform/resources/Documents/The%20 Patient%20Protection%20and%20Affordable%20Care%20 1-20-12.pdf.

85. Ibid.

86. Ibid.

87. Wise, "The Transformation of Child Health."

88. Steven H. Woolf and Laudan Aron, eds., *U.S. Health in International Perspective: Shorter Lives, Poorer Health* (Washington, DC: National Academies Press, 2013), http://www.iom.edu/ Reports/2013/US-Health-in-International-Perspective-Shorter-Lives-Poorer-Health.aspx.

89. CDC, National Center for Chronic Disease Prevention and Health Promotion, Division of Nutrition, Physical Activity and Obesity, "Basics about Childhood Obesity," http://www.cdc .gov/obesity/childhood/basics.html.

90. Child Trends, "Number of Children: Indicators on Children and Youth" (Bethesda, MD: Child Trends, 2012), http://www .childtrends.org/?indicators=number-of-children.

91. Ibid.

92. Child Trends, "Racial and Ethnic Composition of the Child Population: Indicators on Children and Youth" (Bethesda, MD: Child Trends, 2012), http://www.childtrends.org/? indicators=racial-and-ethnic-composition-of-the-child-population.

93. Child Trends, "Immigrant Children: Indicators on Children and Youth" (Bethesda, MD: Child Trends, 2013), http://www .childtrends.org/?indicators=immigrant-children#sthash .kbAd1rea.dpuf.

94. Ibid.

95. Julia Isaacs et al., *Kids' Share 2012: Report on Federal Expenditures on Children through 2011* (Washington, DC: Urban Institute, 2012).

FURTHER READING

Kotch, Jonathan B., ed. *Maternal and Child Health: Programs, Problems and Policies in Public Health,* 3rd ed. Burlington, MA: Jones & Bartlett Learning, 2013.

National Research Council and Institute of Medicine. *Children's Health, the Nation's Wealth: Assessing and Improving Child Health.* Washington, DC: National Academies Press, 2004.

Schlesinger, Mark J., and Leon Eisenburg, eds. *Children in a Changing Health System: Assessments and Proposals for Reform.* Baltimore, MD: Johns Hopkins University Press, 1990.

chapter 20

Women's Issues and American Health Care Policy (1960s–Present)

Deborah R. McFarlane and Rongal D. Nikora

AT FIRST GLANCE, AMERICAN WOMEN MAY appear to be advantaged relative to American men regarding their health. American women live five years longer than their male counterparts.[1] Table 20.1 shows that women visit their doctors more frequently than American men do. Women also practice more preventive health measures, including being less likely than men to smoke or engage in many other risky behaviors.

TABLE 20.1 **Life Expectancy, Doctor Visits, Smoking, by Gender**

	Life Expectancy (Years)	Annual Doctor Visits per Person	Smoking (%)
Women	81.4	3.8	18.1
Men	76.4	2.6	23.2

SOURCE: U.S. Census Bureau, "The 2012 Statistical Abstract," http://www.census.gov/compendia/statab.

These trends persist across racial lines. Table 20.2 shows that while white women live an average of almost two and a half years longer than white men, African American women live more than six years longer than black men. Repeating the same pattern, Hispanic women live nearly five years longer than Hispanic men.[2] In each of these groups, men are more likely than women to report that they have no personal doctor or health care provider.

The gender gap here is greater for minority groups than for whites. Hispanics are most likely to report having no regular health care provider. Table 20.2 also shows that black women, white women, and Hispanic women are each less likely to smoke than their male counterparts.[1,3] Indeed, Hispanic women are less than half as likely as Hispanic men to smoke.

TABLE 20.2 **Life Expectancy, Doctor Visits, Smoking, by Gender and Race**

Gender by Race	Life Expectancy (Years)	No Personal Doctor or Health Care Provider (%)	Smoking (%)
Black	74.3	NA	20.1
Women	77.4	16.9	18.7
Men	70.9	30.3	20.6
White	78.4	NA	20.8
Women	80.8	13.2	18.5
Men	75.9	22.6	20.1
Hispanic	81.0	NA	NA
Women	83.3	35.6	10.7
Men	78.4	49.1	20.7

SOURCES: U.S. Census Bureau, "The 2011 Statistical Abstract," http://www.census.gov/compendia/statab/2011/2011edition.html; American Lung Association, "Key Facts about Smoking among Hispanics," http://www.lung.org/stop-smoking/about-smoking/facts-figures/hispanics-and-tobacco-use.html; Elizabeth Arias, "United States Life Tables," *National Vital Statistics Reports* 61: 3 (2012): 1–64.

SEPARATE TREATMENT OF WOMEN'S HEALTH ISSUES: WHY?

Given the data above, the reasons for discussing women's health care separately from health care for everyone may not be apparent, but they are compelling. First, women have unique conditions and health risks related to reproduction. Second, women are less likely than men to have consistent health insurance, especially in the form of health insurance benefits provided by their employers. Third, a sparser research base exists for women's health care than for men's health care. Fourth, women experience more unnecessary treatments than men do, including surgery. Finally, because of their increased longevity, women outnumber men in many conditions related to aging. Women are more likely to spend the end of life widowed, experiencing declining health by themselves or in nursing homes. Each of these factors is echoed in minority populations, where circumstances are often exacerbated by actual or perceived racial bias.[4]

The Women's Health Movement (1960s and 1970s) and Beyond

During the 1960s and 1970s, the women's health movement jolted the health care establishment by successfully pushing for increased access to contraception and abortion, heightening public awareness of medical biases toward women, and providing the means for women to educate themselves about their health and health care. The movement formed alternative service organizations, the most famous of which was the Boston Women's Health Collective, which published the seminal *Our Bodies, Ourselves,* the self-health book still being published and updated. Eventually, mainstream providers followed the movement's lead by offering such services as hospital-sponsored birthing centers and other birthing alternatives, patient support groups, and considerably more patient education and information.[5]

Awareness of the women's health movement and the issues it championed encouraged more women to pursue medical education. Fortuitously, the 1972 enactment of Title IX of the Civil Rights Act coincided with the motivation of more women to enter medicine. Title IX precluded medical schools receiving federal financial assistance from maintaining quotas to limit the matriculation of women. The synergy of these factors led to many more female physicians. In 1970, only 9 percent of medical students were women; by 1980, that statistic was 25 percent.[5] By 2012, that number exceeded 47 percent.[6]

The women's health movement of this period had a major impact on contraception and abortion. Nevertheless, U.S. reproductive health politics remain contentious. Other difficult issues related to women's health endure, including long-term care, parity in clinical trials, and screening for domestic violence. In recent years, political struggles have ensued over funding breast cancer research and treatment, access to emergency contraception, and eliminating gender disparities in health insurance coverage.

Minority Women and Health Care Organizations

Minority women of color have also organized around health issues affecting their communities. These problems often reflected low incomes and lack of access to health care. "To the extent that women's income, especially in families headed by women, is low, then all the health problems associated with low income show up here."[7] In the early 1980s, when programs aimed at low-income people were cut, these cuts affected women disproportionate to men, particularly women of color. Two important organizations formed in

this decade to address these concerns: the National Black Women's Health Project (1981) and the National Latina Health Organization (1986).

Other groups have also emerged; two newer groups for and comprising minority women are highlighted in this chapter. The first, SisterSong, is devoted to reproductive justice for women of color. The second, the International Center for Traditional Childbearing, aims to promote better maternal and infant outcomes.

REPRODUCTIVE HEALTH

Reproductive health services focus on a woman's unique ability to become pregnant and bear children. They include contraceptive services, maternity services, induced abortion, and sexuality education. Given these topics and the nation's Puritan heritage,[8] it is hardly surprising that policymaking in this arena has been fraught with discord.

Suppressing Contraception: The Comstock Laws

In 1873, the federal government passed the Act for the Suppression of Trade in, and Circulation of, Obscene Literature and Articles of Immoral Use, prohibiting interstate trading in obscene literature and materials, including any contraceptives, abortifacients, or birth control information. Known as the Comstock law, this legislation spawned twenty-two state laws, called the "little Comstock laws," some of which went much further than the federal law. Fourteen states prohibited the verbal transmission of information about contraception or abortion. Eleven states made possession of instructions for the prevention of pregnancy a criminal offense. Four states authorized the search and seizure of contraceptive instructions. Connecticut alone flatly outlawed the act of controlling conception.[9]

Legacy from 1960s and 1970s

For nearly one hundred years, federal and state Comstock laws effectively made contraceptive practice illegal. Over time, these laws were gradually weakened, largely through the persistent efforts of Margaret Sanger, a nurse and a family planning pioneer, and the American Birth Control League. Abortion was also outlawed and codified in state criminal laws, but it was widely practiced. The convergence of technological innovations and legal decisions in the 1960s and 1970s created dramatic changes in reproductive health policy.

In 1960, the U.S. Food and Drug Administration approved the sale of oral contraceptive pills. Intrauterine devices (IUDs) also became available about this time. Both methods required access to physician care, and middle-class women rapidly embraced them. As a result, there was an increased disparity in the percentage of unwanted births between middle-class and poor women who were less likely to have access to regular medical care.

With President Lyndon B. Johnson's (1963–1969) War on Poverty and the civil rights movement in full swing, great interest arose in providing poor women with the same contraceptive opportunities that middle-class women enjoyed. Between 1965 and 1970, Congress mandated no fewer than four federal statutes to fund family planning services (Title V of the Public Health Service Act, the Maternal and Child Health block grant; Title IV-A of the Social Security Act, the Social Services Program for Mothers and Children, which was later converted to Title XX; Title XIX of the Social Services Program, the Medicaid program; and Title X of the Public Health Service Act, the categorical family planning program). In less than one hundred years, Congress had moved from prohibiting birth control to actively promoting it.[10]

The last vestiges of the Comstock laws were coming to an end. In 1965, in *Griswold* v. *Connecticut,* the U.S. Supreme Court overturned Connecticut's law prohibiting the use of birth control by anyone, married or single. In 1972, in *Eisenstadt v. Baird,* the U.S. Supreme Court overturned a Massachusetts Comstock law prohibiting unmarried women from obtaining contraception.

Abortion policy changed as well. The medical profession, which had successfully lobbied for making abortion a crime a century earlier, became a principal advocate for liberalizing abortion laws. By this time, abortion had become a safe procedure when performed by a competent medical practitioner. Between 1967 and 1972, most states considered changing their abortion laws, and nineteen states did. As a result, women living in states with restrictive laws flocked to less restrictive states to obtain abortions.[11,12]

A persistent question in U.S. federalism has been whether, in the absence of *Roe v. Wade* (1973), most states would have liberalized their abortion laws. While there can be no definite answer to this question, the liberalization of state abortion laws had stalled in the early 1970s. No state repealed any criminal abortion law between 1971 and 1973.[12]

The U.S. Supreme Court addressed abortion in 1973. In handing down a 7–2 decision in *Roe v. Wade*, the Court struck down every abortion law in the land, liberal and restrictive. The Court found that a woman's right to decide whether to terminate her pregnancy was a "fundamental right." Although *Roe* legalized abortion throughout the nation, it did not unify public opinion. Activity by interest groups supporting and denouncing the decision intensified, and abortion became arguably one of the most contentious issues of the twentieth century, a debate that shows no sign of abating in the first part of the twenty-first century.

Ongoing Issues in Women's Health Care

Reproductive health has become increasingly politicized since the 1970s. Its politics are partisan and polarized, often overwhelmed by the abortion debate. For example, since 1985, Congress has not managed to reauthorize the specialized or categorical family planning legislation, Title X of the Public Health Service Act, in spite of the fact that Title X expressly forbids funding or providing abortion services. Nevertheless, Title X continues to fund family planning services because Congress still appropriates funds for this program. Gender politics are ever present in reproductive health debates because contraceptive technology remains women-centered, and only women have abortions.

Reproductive health politics are set against a backdrop of contradictions. Although the vast majority of Americans are sexually active by their late teens, the average age of marriage is twenty-six.[13] Nevertheless, the federal government and many school districts continue to fund and stress abstinence-until-marriage curricula, which exclude birth control information and denigrate contraception, particularly male condoms.

With a preference for only two children, the average American woman is fertile for more than thirty years and trying not to become pregnant for most of that time. However, American women practice contraception less successfully than do most of their Western European counterparts, reporting that nearly half of their pregnancies are unintended. Fully half of Americans self-identify as pro-life or antiabortion, yet one in three American women is likely to have at least one induced abortion by age forty-five.[14]

The historical unfolding of reproductive health policy in the United States largely segregated reproductive health services from other health services. More than one-fourth of the twenty million American women who obtain contraceptive services from a medical provider receive care from a publicly funded family planning clinic, not from a general medical practice. When women do become pregnant, the same settings are unlikely to offer prenatal care. Similarly, specialized clinics that deliver abortion services find it difficult to be reimbursed for offering contraceptive services. Because it engenders controversy, sexuality education, especially with birth control information, is seldom integrated with other kinds of health education, although most American parents support it.

Clearly, sexuality education, maternity services, contraceptive practice, and the demand for abortion are integrally related. Each, however, is addressed by separate public policies, thus promoting fragmentation at the service level. There is still no unified national policy to reduce unintended pregnancy or promote birth planning. Even recent Institute of Medicine recommendations for women's preventive health, calling for full funding of contraceptive services under the Patient Protection and Affordable Care Act (PPACA), neglected to mention linkages to sex education and abortion.[15]

Roe v. Wade

In handing down its decision in *Roe v. Wade* on January 22, 1973, the U.S. Supreme Court held that a woman's right to choose abortion was constitutionally protected as part of her right to privacy, thus the Court overturned Texas law and abortion became legal throughout the country. For the majority, Justice Harry Blackmun wrote:

1. A state criminal abortion statute of the current Texas type, that excepts from criminality only a lifesaving procedure on behalf of the mother, without regard to pregnancy stage and without recognition of the other interests involved, is violative of the Due Process Clause of the Fourteenth Amendment.

a. For the stage prior to approximately the end of the first trimester, the abortion decision and its effectuation must be left to the medical judgment of the pregnant woman's attending physician.

b. For the stage subsequent to approximately the end of the first trimester, the State, in promoting its interest in the health of the mother, may, if it chooses, regulate the abortion procedure in ways that are reasonably related to maternal health.

c. For the stage subsequent to viability, the State in promoting its interest in the potentiality of human life may, if it chooses, regulate, and even proscribe, abortion except where it is necessary, in appropriate medical judgment, for the preservation of the life or health of the mother.

2. The State may define the term "physician," as it has been employed in the preceding paragraphs of this Part XI of this opinion, to mean only a physician currently licensed by the State, and may proscribe any abortion by a person who is not a physician as so defined.

The Court recognized that there were differences in how the beginning of life was defined but said that one view should not prevail (i.e., the Texas criminal code's being challenged). The Court also reviewed the three major reasons why states had criminalized abortion during the nineteenth century. The first was "that these laws were the product of a Victorian social concern to discourage illicit sexual conduct . . . it appears that no court or commentator has taken the argument seriously." The second concerned the danger of the procedure itself: "When most criminal abortion laws were first enacted, the procedure was a hazardous one for the woman. . . . Modern medical techniques have altered this situation. . . . Consequently, any interest of the State in protecting the woman from an inherently hazardous procedure, except when it would be equally dangerous for her to forgo it, has largely disappeared." The third reason was "the State's interest . . . in protecting prenatal life. In assessing the State's interest, . . . as long as at least potential life is involved, the State may assert interests beyond the protection of the pregnant woman alone." The last reason formed the basis of *Roe's* trimester framework.

Since 1973, there have been more than thirty-five U.S. Supreme Court decisions about different aspects of abortion. The most recent cases are *Lambert v. Wicklund* (1997), *Mazurek v. Armstrong* (1997), *Stenberg v. Carhart* (2000), *Ayotte v. Planned Parenthood of Northern New England* (2006), *Gonzales v. Carhart* (2007), and *Gonzalez v. Planned Parenthood Federation of America* (2007).

SOURCE: Cornell University Law School, "Roe v. Wade," http://www.law.cornell.edu/supremecourt/text/410/113.

Low-Income Women and Reproductive Health

The policies that emanate from reproductive health politics disproportionately affect low-income women, who are disproportionately African American and Hispanic. Poor women are much more likely than more affluent women to rely on publicly financed family planning clinics. Therefore, low-income women are vulnerable to policy restrictions and funding cutbacks. Public funding for family planning lags far behind the unmet need for contraceptive services, a fact reflected in the much higher rates of unintended pregnancy for low-income and minority women.[16]

Given these facts, it is not surprising that low-income and minority women have far higher abortion rates than do more affluent women. Women living at or below the federal poverty level are four times as likely to experience abortion as women living at or above three times the poverty rate. The abortion rate for Hispanic women is twice as high as

that for non-Hispanic white women, and the rate for African American women is three times higher than that for white women. Over time, overall abortion rates have been dropping, while racial and income disparities in abortion rates have been increasing.[17] Nevertheless, due to the federal Hyde amendment (which Congress passed in 1977 and which banned Medicaid coverage of abortion) and other state restrictions affecting state Medicaid programs, the vast majority of abortions to low-income women are paid out of pocket. Under the PPACA, this situation will continue unabated because of the restrictions shown in Table 20.3.

The Patient Protection and Affordable Health Care Act and Reproductive Health

The 2010 passage of the PPACA means that more women than ever will be affected by public policy either through Medicaid or through mandated state health insurance

TABLE 20.3 **Abortion Provisions in 2010 Patient Protection and Affordable Care Act**

Provision	Year Implemented
Abortion is not covered in temporary high risk pools.	2010
Abortion is prohibited from being considered an essential medical service.	2014
Federal funding cannot be used to purchase coverage for abortion beyond conditions specified by the Hyde amendment.	2010
With state health insurance exchanges, payments for abortion coverage must be segregated from other funds.	2014
For insurance plans offering abortion coverage, actuarial value must be calculated without including the savings.	2014
Insurance plans that offer abortion coverage cannot discriminate against providers who do not provide abortions.	2014

SOURCE: Adapted from Alina Salganicoff, Adara Beamesderfer, and Nisha Kurani, "Coverage for Abortion Services and the ACA," 2014, http://kff.org/womens-health-policy/issue-brief/coverage-for-abortion-services-and-the-aca.

exchanges when most of PPACA's provisions are implemented. Given the stringent abortion requirements for insurance companies, it is unlikely that abortion coverage will even be offered for women whose employers participate in the state health insurance exchanges. Moreover, pre-PPACA Medicaid abortion restrictions continue unabated.

On the contraceptive front, women should have gained better access to family planning services, including often costly birth control supplies and devices. Contraceptive care is among the essential benefits that health insurance is now required to cover, "without any premium, deductible, co-payment, or other fees."[18] However, some employers (e.g., Hobby Lobby) and religiously affiliated health providers (e.g., Catholic Health Services) object to paying for contraceptive coverage because of their moral objections to birth control. Because this issue is in litigation, questions remain about the future accessibility of contraceptive services for American women. More certainty exists for millions of undocumented immigrant women, who are specifically excluded from all PPACA benefits, including reproductive health services, except for maternity care.[19]

Advocacy by Women of Color

Until recently, much of the highly visible advocacy work for women's reproductive health care issues emanated from groups comprising mostly middle-class white women. That situation has changed, as more women of color have organized around reproductive health issues. Their organizations and mission statements reveal differences in the circumstances of women's lives as well as cultural traditions. For example, some minority women's health groups have articulated a broader reproductive rights agenda than the narrower pro-choice stance that they believe has been represented by mainstream reproductive health advocacy groups. Two examples of this trend are SisterSong and the International Center for Traditional Childbearing.

SisterSong

Formed in 1997, the SisterSong Women of Color Reproductive Justice Collective is dedicated to addressing the reproductive health needs of women of color. Acknowledging the importance of social justice, SisterSong includes "reproductive justice" in its mission statement. This term signifies a broad advocacy strategy, to confront racial, economic, cultural, and structural constraints on the reproductive health status of women of color.[20]

Organizationally, SisterSong is made up of eighty local, regional, and national grassroots organizations in the United States representing five primary ethnic populations/indigenous nations in the United States—Native American/Indigenous, Black/African American, Latina/Puerto Rican, Arab American/Middle Eastern, and Asian/Pacific Islander—"as well as white allies and men." SisterSong strives to fulfill its mission through work in public policy as well as health education and service delivery to its target communities, mostly in the United States but also abroad.[21]

International Center for Traditional Childbearing

Founded in Portland, Oregon, in 1991, the International Center for Traditional Childbearing (ICTC) is a nonprofit organization dedicated to addressing a critical issue related to reproductive health: high black infant mortality. In the United States, African American infant mortality is more than twice as high as non-Hispanic white infant mortality, a situation that has been linked in part to the compromised health status of many African American women, who face many stressors in daily living.[22] Actions taken by ICTC to combat this longstanding public health problem include promoting breastfeeding and training African American women to serve as certified midwives and doulas. The latter are professionals trained to provide physical and emotional support prior to, during, and after delivery, but unlike midwives, doulas do not provide clinical care.

ICTC's culturally sensitive approach emphasizes the role of spirituality and religiosity, along with cultural history and tradition, as a part of a holistic view of the individual and community health. Midwives embody roles as healers, spiritualists, public health activists, and community organizers. They stand with doulas in empowering a model of improved public health in African American communities.

WOMEN AND HEALTH INSURANCE

In the United States, health insurance is vital for accessing health care. Women with health coverage are more likely to obtain needed preventive, primary, and specialty care services, and they have better access to new advances in women's health. Figure 20.1 shows a patchwork of different private sector and publicly funded programs in the United States, which leaves one in six American women uninsured. Among the estimated ninety-six million women ages eighteen to sixty-four, most have some form of coverage. According to the Kaiser Family Foundation, among women in this age group, one in five is uninsured, which represents an estimated nineteen million women.

Women without health insurance are more likely to delay care, especially for preventive health services such as Pap smears and mammograms; much less likely to have a usual source of care; more likely to receive lower quality care when they are in the health system; more likely to forgo filling prescriptions; and more likely to have poorer health outcomes than women who are insured.[23,24] These facts are especially sobering when one considers that only 67 percent of American Indian females and 69 percent of Hispanic females have health insurance.[25] Six in ten uninsured women live in a family where at least one adult is working full-time. There is considerable variation among the states in insurance rates, ranging from 70 percent of women in Texas to 95 percent in Massachusetts.[24]

Women and Employer Health Insurance

Compared to their male counterparts, working women are much less likely to be covered by their employer's health insurance benefits. Two major reasons account for this gap.

First, women's employment careers are more likely to be intermittent because of interruptions for family reasons such as childbirth and childrearing or leaving jobs when their husbands are transferred. Second, women are disproportionately represented in part-time and temporary jobs, which have rarely offered health insurance benefits.[26]

Women are more likely than men to be covered as dependents on health insurance policies, so they can lose health insurance coverage if they become widowed or divorced. Here again, minority women face disadvantages in the private health insurance market. While census data from 1990 to 2010 show no disparity in the percentage of white and black women who are widowed, the percentage of African American women who never marry (41.4 percent in 2010) is more than double that for white women. Health insurance and other financial, social, and psychological benefits ascribed to marriage elude many African American women throughout their lives.

Delaying Care

Not having any or inconsistent health insurance coverage affects women's health care utilization. One common effect is delaying screening or needed care. Table 20.4 shows that white, black, and Hispanic women are more likely than their male counterparts to delay a doctor's visit due to costs.

Women and Medicaid

While women are less likely than men to benefit from employer-based health insurance, they are much more likely to be covered by Medicaid, the federal-state health insurance program for low-income individuals. Indeed, prior to the full implementation of the PPACA, 12 percent of all non-elderly women were covered by this program, and 58

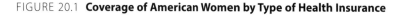

FIGURE 20.1 **Coverage of American Women by Type of Health Insurance**

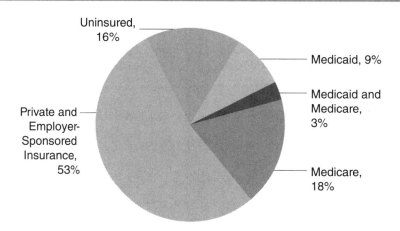

SOURCE: Kaiser Family Foundation, *Medicare and Medicaid Provide Health Coverage for Three in Ten Women* (Menlo Park, CA: Kaiser Family Foundation, May 15, 2013). http://kff.org/slideshow/the-role-of-medicaid-and-medicare-in-womens-health-care-jama-may-15-2013.

TABLE 20.4 **Percentage of No Doctor Visits in the Past Year Due to Cost (2006–2008)**

Race by Gender	No Doctor Visits (%)
Black	
Women	20.7
Men	18.2
White	
Women	14.7
Men	10.3
Hispanic	
Women	28.1
Men	21.8

SOURCES: Kaiser Family Foundation, "No Doctor Visit in Past Year Due to Cost for Men, by State and Race/Ethnicity, 2006–2008," http://kff.org/disparities-policy/state-indicator/no-doctor-visit-in-past-year-due-to-cost-2; Kaiser Family Foundation, "No Doctor Visit in Past Year Due to Cost for Women, by State and Race/Ethnicity, 2006–2008," http://kff.org/disparities-policy/state-indicator/no-doctor-visit-in-past-year-due-to-cost.

percent of Medicaid enrollees were female.[27] Traditionally, only poor women who were pregnant, had children living at home, or were disabled were eligible for Medicaid coverage, but there have always been many state differences.[24]

Nationally, Medicaid is an important program for women's health care. All states and the District of Columbia offer Medicaid benefits to low-income pregnant women. Indeed, 48 percent of all U.S. births are financed by Medicaid. Moreover, Medicaid funds 75 percent of all publicly supported family planning services. It also provides nearly half (43 percent) of all financial support for long-term care. Since 2002, thirty-one states expanded Medicaid eligibility to cover the costs of family planning services for low-income women, and every state has established Medicaid programs to pay for breast and cervical cancer treatment for certain low-income uninsured women.[24]

Despite its contribution to women's health care, Medicaid is fraught with challenges. Eligibility for pregnant women, meaning how poor they have to be to receive this health insurance, varies greatly from state to state. Coverage for non-pregnant adults is even less consistent. Only nine states and the District of Columbia even offer such Medicaid coverage to adults unless they have dependent children. Another barrier for women relying on Medicaid coverage is accessibility to health care providers. Physicians and other health professionals are not required to accept Medicaid patients. Many choose not to deal with Medicaid, due to low reimbursement rates and other problems.[28]

The original intent of the PPACA was to expand Medicaid in every state so that all individuals with very low incomes would qualify for coverage through the program. However, the U.S. Supreme Court decision in *National Federation of Independent Business v. Sebelius* (2012) made the Medicaid expansion optional in the states. This decision

impacts poor women more than men, particularly in states with ungenerous programs. Not surprisingly, it has a disproportionately negative effect on women of color, who are much more likely to be poor and uninsured.

Private Health Insurance and the Patient Protection and Affordable Care Act

The PPACA has changed private health insurance coverage for women. Dependents can now be covered up to age twenty-six; this measure was so popular that more than three million young adults were insured within the first two years of the PPACA's implementation. Insurers are prohibited from denying coverage based on preexisting conditions, and they are not allowed to vary premiums based on gender or health status. Insurers are required to cover essential benefits, including maternity care as well as preventive services and vaccines without copayments or patient cost-sharing. These services include Pap tests, mammograms, bone density tests, human papillomavirus (HPV) vaccines, contraceptives as prescribed by a provider, breastfeeding supplies, screening for domestic violence, and well-women visits.[24]

RESEARCH AND WOMEN'S HEALTH

Historically, medical research gave short shrift to women's health. The scant studies that were done focused on women's reproductive issues, but little else. This situation changed in the early 1990s, in no small part because of the work of women's health advocacy groups. Since that time, government support of women's health research has increased dramatically in terms of policies, regulations, and the organization of research efforts.

In 2008, to assess the impact of these changes, Congress directed the Institute of Medicine (IOM) to examine what had been learned from that research and how well it had been put into practice.

The findings of the IOM were mixed. Figure 20.2 shows that for some conditions, such as breast cancer, cardiovascular disease, and cervical cancer, women's health research had contributed to significant progress. For example, the IOM reported that studies targeting women, as well as improved detection and treatment, have led to reductions in incidence and mortality from both breast cancer and cervical cancer. Research findings also contributed to the 50 percent drop in cardiovascular mortality over the twenty-year time period examined (1980–2000). For other conditions, including depression, unintended pregnancy, and lung cancer, there had been little or no progress.

To explain the lack of progress in certain areas, the IOM identified some very broad contributing factors and noted the need for greater support of social and behavioral determinants of morbidity and mortality, including how to modify these determinants to improve health. The IOM also

Breast Cancer Advocacy in the 1990s

Perhaps the first example of women's organized activity related to breast cancer was the American Cancer Society's Reach to Recovery Program, which began in 1952. Organized by local affiliates, this program trained volunteer breast cancer survivors to provide support, including prostheses, to post-mastectomy patients. Volunteers visited patients in the hospital when their services were "ordered" by attending physicians. While it was innovative for its time, this program did not attempt to reform women's health services or affect public policy.

Breast cancer treatment captured far more attention during the 1970s due to a combination of factors. The women's health movement garnered publicity for women's health issues in general, and several prominent women (e.g., First Lady Betty Ford; Happy Rockefeller, wife of New York's then governor; actress and Ambassador Shirley Temple Black) shared their experiences with national media. Moreover, several studies and exposés critiqued radical mastectomy as standard treatment for this condition that affected so many women.

During the 1980s, the emergence of several regional organizations continued to raise the profile of breast cancer as a critical health issue. Among these were the Susan G. Komen Foundation, established in Texas in 1982, with awareness-raising efforts that include a now nationally recognized Race for the Cure 5K run/walk; Kendall Lakes Women Against Cancer, founded in Florida in 1985 to address possible environmental contaminants in a local cluster of breast cancer cases; and Baltimore-based patient and family support organization Arm-in-Arm in 1987. In that same year, First Lady Nancy Reagan revealed that she had also undergone breast cancer surgery. In a context of growing awareness of the widespread incidence of this condition, it was clear that the public was listening. The months immediately following the First Lady's announcement saw a substantial year-on-year increase in the proportion of women that reported having a mammogram performed in the past twelve months, from 26 percent to 38 percent. This momentum set the stage for the flurry of activism and advocacy that would emerge around breast cancer in the 1990s.

AIDS activism provided a strategic template for action for many of the organizations that gained prominence in breast cancer advocacy during the decade, a point revealed in interviews with the leaders of the National Alliance of Breast Cancer Organizations (NABCO), CAN ACT, Save Ourselves, and Breast Cancer Action. Similar to the gay community's approach to AIDS, breast cancer advocates sought to take ownership of living with the condition, with survivor-activists choosing to become "poster people" for the disease. The success of ACT UP and other vocal AIDS advocacy groups in winning gains in areas such as AIDS education and research is also credited with motivating the leadership of some breast cancer advocacy groups to bring a more aggressive, confrontational tone to their own efforts. Examples of this newfound assertiveness included mailings to members of Congress with no-nonsense messages of the realities of breast cancer as well as organized protests. A running theme throughout was equity in the use of public funds and in private insurance to address women's health issues on equal standing with issues primarily affecting men. Part of their demands included mandating that physicians receive informed consent from women before performing radical mastectomies and that physicians offer other treatment alternatives (e.g., lumpectomies) when viable. Others were that insurers provide equal coverage of procedures such as baseline mammograms and breast reconstruction; insurers frequently denied the latter as a "cosmetic" procedure, despite it being analogous to penile and testicular implants for men.

noted that future research needs to consider women's overall health and well-being and not just measure progress by each health condition.

While investments in women's health research have led to decreased rates of female mortality from some diseases, these achievements have not been enjoyed equally by women from all population groups in the United States. Large disparities in disease burden remain among different groups of women. Women who are socially disadvantaged because of their race or ethnicity, income level, or educational attainment have been underrepresented in many studies and have not benefited as much from the progress in women's health research.[29] In addition to its findings about extant studies, the IOM made recommendations for future research on women's health.

The first recommendation was that "U.S. government agencies and other relevant organizations should sustain and strengthen their focus on women's health, including the spectrum of research that includes genetic, behavioral, and social determinants of health and how they change during one's life." In addition to supporting women-only research, the IOM advised that women's health research should be integrated so that differences between men and women are routinely assessed.

The second recommendation addressed race and social class. Noting that women who experience social disadvantage also experience adverse health outcomes as well as barriers to care, but have not been well represented in studies of behavior and health, the IOM directed specific federal agencies to "develop targeted initiatives to increase research on the populations of women that have the highest risks and burdens of disease."[29]

The third recommendation dealt with the health conditions that had not improved after nearly two decades of women's health research (see Figure 20.1). Noting the propensity of research to focus on reductions in mortality, the

Another hallmark of the 1990s was the shift away from grassroots organizations concerned generally with women's health, which proliferated throughout the 1970s and early 1980s, toward a new wave of disease-specific organizations with national reach. In breast cancer advocacy, along with the earlier formation of NABCO in the late 1980s, this trend saw several grassroots organizations combine to form the National Breast Cancer Coalition (NBCC) in 1991. By 1993, NBCC was garnering vital financial support from a variety of corporate sponsors and philanthropic foundations, including Revlon Corporation, Lifetime Television, and the Streisand Foundation. NBCC efforts to lobby Congress for additional funding to combat breast cancer proved highly successful, leading to a massive increase in funding for research, from a planned $133 million to $211.5 million actually spent in fiscal year 1993. That same year, NBCC and other breast cancer advocacy groups led a signature drive to push for a national action plan on breast cancer, garnering 2.6 million signatures nationwide.

Another major step forward in breast cancer advocacy occurred in 1995, with official recognition of the month of October as National Breast Cancer Awareness Month (NBCAM). There is strong evidence that NBCAM (both prior to and after official recognition) was especially effective in driving increased use of mammograms in the mid-1990s, with November 1 diagnoses of breast cancer significantly higher from 1993 to 1995. However, equally impressive is the association of NBCAM with overall popular awareness of the issue of breast cancer. News articles on the disease rose dramatically, from fewer than fifty over the entire period from 1973 to 1985, to more than six hundred in 1993 and nearly two thousand in 1998.

Breast cancer advocacy and activism in the 1990s successfully reframed the issue from a focus on the victims of a disease to one of equity, particularly in the allocation of public funding for women's health research. In bringing national attention to a disease that carried a social stigma despite its near epidemic incidence in women, advocates established a greater role for patients and breast cancer survivors in setting the research agenda for the disease. Along the way, they developed mechanisms for working with government, thereby transforming the policymaking process with respect to women's health issues. In examining the political landscape that enabled breast cancer advocacy to achieve such popularity and prominence, three key factors stand out. The first is the enormous groundswell of support for action on breast cancer, evident from the runaway success of letter-writing and signature campaigns by advocacy groups. Second, the emergence of breast cancer on the national agenda was likely viewed by many politicians as low-hanging fruit, allowing them to gain favor with female voters over a highly salient, non-ideological women's health issue, while avoiding controversies associated with reproductive health issues like abortion. Third, and perhaps most important, may be the crosscutting impact of the disease itself. President William J. Clinton (1993–2001) had lost his own mother to the disease, while earlier high-profile revelations of breast cancer by First Ladies Betty Ford and Nancy Reagan likely did much to decouple the illness from associations with the moral politics that have often dominated women's health issues in the United States. The convergence of these factors may have facilitated the three key behaviors—advertising, credit claiming, and position taking—that members of Congress are thought to pursue in the quest for reelection, leading to big gains for advocacy groups in the fight against breast cancer.

SOURCES: Dennis Altman, "Rupture or Continuity? The Internationalization of Gay Identities," *Social Text 48* (1996): 77–94; Maureen Hogan Casamayou, *The Politics of Breast Cancer* (Washington, DC: Georgetown University Press, 2001); Grant D. Jacobsen and Kathryn H. Jacobsen, "Health Awareness Campaigns and Diagnosis Rates: Evidence from National Breast Cancer Awareness Month," *Journal of Health Economics* 30: 1 (2011): 55–61; David Mayhew, *Congress: The Electoral Connection* (New Haven, CT: Yale University Press, 1974); Sheryl Burt Ruzek and Julie Becker, "The Women's Health Movement in the United States: From Grass-Roots Activism to Professional Agendas," *Journal of the American Medical Women's Association* 54 (1999): 4–8; Carol S. Weisman, *Women's Health Care* (Baltimore: Johns Hopkins University Press, 1998).

directive here was to study the promotion of wellness and the quality of life in women. This recommendation alluded to the elderly female population by stating that "the end points examined in studies should include quality-of-life outcomes (for example, functional status or functionality, mobility, and pain) in addition to mortality."[29]

In developing the fourth recommendation, the IOM noted that "social factors and health-related behaviors and their interactions with genetic and cellular factors contribute to the onset and progression of multiple diseases; they act as pathways that are common to multiple outcomes."[29] The committee recommended that the National Institutes of Health (NIH) fund "research on common determinants and risk factors that underlie multiple diseases and on interventions on those determinants that will decrease the occurrence or progression of diseases in women."[29] Interestingly, NIH is mainly organized by disease-related institutes, so the IOM was saying that

women's health research demanded a different and more interdisciplinary approach.

The IOM noted the lack of enforcement of recruiting women for studies as well as reporting findings by gender. Consequently, the fifth recommendation addresses enforcement mechanisms and methodological issues.

Recognizing the difficulty of converting research findings into action, the sixth IOM recommendation was to fund studies that would translate research findings on women's health into clinical practice and public health policies.[29] This recommendation did not, however, mention the need to do so in ways that would benefit diverse groups of women.

Noting the confusion that ensues when conflicting research findings are made public, the IOM recommended that the U.S. Department of Health and Human Services appoint a task force to develop communication strategies to market research-based health messages to women. This

In 1913, fifteen physicians and business leaders in New York City formed the American Society for the Control of Cancer, now known as the American Cancer Society. In October 1983, in Dallas, Texas, about eight hundred people participated in the first Race for the Cure. Today, races and walks against breast cancer are held throughout the nation, with participants numbering in the millions.

SOURCE: © Joshua Roberts/Reuters/Corbis.

FIGURE 20.2   **Conditions Discussed by Institute of Medicine Committee on Women's Health Research, by Extent of Progress**

Conditions on Which Research Has Contributed to Major Progress

Breast cancer

Cardiovascular disease

Cervical cancer

Conditions on Which Research Has Contributed to Some Progress

Depression

HIV/AIDS

Osteoporosis

Conditions on Which There Has Been Little Progress

Unintended pregnancy

Maternal morbidity and mortality

Autoimmune diseases

Alcohol and drug addiction

Lung cancer

Gynecological cancers other than cervical cancer

Non-malignant gynecological disorders

Alzheimer's disease

SOURCE: Institute of Medicine, *Women's Health Research: Progress, Pitfalls, and Promise* (Washington, DC: National Academies Press, 2010), 276, http://www.iom.edu/reports/2010/womens-health-research-progress-pitfalls-and-promise.aspx.

recommendation did acknowledge differences in the circumstances of women's lives.[29]

Other groups have proposed future women's health research agendas. One such effort that coincided with the 2010 IOM report emanated from the NIH Office of Research on Women's Health.[30]

The impact of the abortion debate extends to the women's health research agenda. For example, over the years, pro-life advocates have claimed that induced abortion is associated with breast cancer. Concerned about that charge, the National Cancer Institute held a conference in 2003 to examine findings from various studies as well as the viewpoints of experts. Although recent studies have demonstrated no relationship between abortion and breast cancer, the issue is unlikely to disappear.[31] A related issue is embryonic stem cell research, which has the potential to help both women and men.[32]

WOMEN'S HEALTH CARE AND UNNECESSARY TREATMENTS

Relative to men, women on average also experience more surgical procedures over their lifetime,[33] many of them related to their reproductive systems. Data from the Organisation for Economic Co-operation and Development (OECD) confirm that American women have an age-standardized rate of hysterectomy of 366 per 100,000 females, more than triple the rate in Spain and the highest in the OECD. Similarly, the U.S. rate of Cesarean section births is 313 per 1,000 live births, compared to an OECD average of 242.[34]

Furthermore, there is ongoing controversy surrounding the necessity of a substantial portion of these and other surgical procedures (such as pacemaker implantation and bypass surgery), with evidence mounting that drugs and other surgical alternatives may be at least as efficacious in many instances.[35]

As much as one-third of the health expenditures in the United States may be unnecessary; women's health care is no exception in this regard and may be more pronounced. Childbirth offers a sobering example of unnecessary and expensive care. A recent study of 2,400 women in the United States who had recently given birth found that 41 percent of them had undergone labor induction, because of concerns that the fetus was too large or the due date had passed. In fact, research suggests that neither of these reasons alone merits an induction. Moreover, women who had labor induced for no medically significant reason were 67 percent more likely to require Cesarean section deliveries. Their infants were 64 percent more likely to require costly care in newborn intensive care units.[29]

According to the Institute of Medicine in 2010, nearly half of women who had previously delivered by Cesarean section wanted to deliver their next child vaginally, but were denied the possibility either by their doctor (24 percent) or by the hospital (15 percent). This practice occurred despite guidelines from the American College of Obstetricians and Gynecologists (ACOG) encouraging women to attempt vaginal deliveries after Cesarean sections.

Cesarean section deliveries have increased in recent decades, rising from 21 percent of births in the mid-1990s to about 32 percent in 2007. Much of this growth is due to greater emphasis on induced labor because of the convenience it affords both physicians and patients. However, this convenience comes at a cost, raising both expenditures and health risks. The Institute of Medicine suggested that financial incentives may play a role in sustaining the number of unnecessary procedures and treatments related to pregnancy and childbirth.[29] Indeed, efforts to curb such procedure actually mean substantial lost revenue.

Outside of pregnancy and childbirth, there are other unnecessary treatments. The United States has the highest rate of hysterectomies in the developed world.[34] Along similar lines, about more than one-half of women who have had full hysterectomies (typically removing the cervix) still report receiving Pap tests for cervical cancer. Fortunately, this figure has declined from nearly three-fourths in 2000. A similar decline has been reported for women less than twenty-one years of age (a low-risk group for whom testing is not recommended) receiving Pap tests, although more than half of this age group still reports have been screened.[36]

Racial and ethnic disparities also exist in unnecessary treatments and procedures. According to the National Center for Health Statistics, in 2013, African American women were more likely to receive unnecessary Pap tests than their white counterparts; the inverse relationship exists for Asian American women. Consistent with a long-standing trend, black women are more likely than white women to undergo hysterectomies.[37] African American women also experience higher rates of Cesarean section deliveries than white women, but black women have lower rates of induced labor.[38]

Responding to widespread concern about the overuse of various procedures and treatments in medical practice, twenty-six physician societies formulated lists that contained the top five to ten procedures that patients should question. Germane to women's health are the lists provided by the ACOG and the American Academy of Family Physicians (AAFP).[39] For one, the ACOG warns against scheduling the induction of labor prior to full-term (thirty-nine weeks) or up to two weeks after that date, performing annual cervical cancer screenings for women ages thirty to sixty-five, treating mild dysplasia (slightly abnormal cell growth) observed over fewer than two years, and screening for ovarian cancer in women at average risk for the disease.

The list compiled by the AAFP overlaps with some of the ACOG recommendations, but it directs patients and doctors to avoid Pap tests for women under age twenty-one and those older than sixty-five when there is an adequate history of prior screening and a low risk of cervical cancer. The AAFP also directs providers not to screen women younger than thirty years of age for cervical cancer with HPV testing, alone or in combination with cytology. If successful, these efforts to reduce unnecessary treatments will improve women's health while saving health care dollars.

AGING WOMEN AND HEALTH POLICY

The distribution of the population by gender is fairly even across younger age groups; however, because women have longer life expectancies, they represent a greater proportion of those aged sixty-five years and older. Women account for nearly 57 percent of all individuals aged sixty-five years and older, 60.8 percent of individuals aged seventy-five years and older, and more than two-thirds of individuals aged eighty-five years and older.[33]

Accounting for 59 percent of all Medicare beneficiaries, women covered by Medicare have significant health needs. They experience higher rates of many chronic health conditions than men do. However, the relatively high cost-sharing requirements for Medicare can be prohibitive for many seniors, especially women, who, on average, have far fewer financial resources than their male counterparts. Elderly women have lower average Social Security and pension benefits than men. In 2007, the median annual household income for women ages sixty-five and older was $20,400, substantially lower than $38,222 for older men.[40]

The Medicare program has had some notable gaps in coverage for long-term care, prescription drugs, and essential services such as vision and dental care. In addition, some preventive benefits important to older women's health, such as mammography, clinical breast exams, bone density tests, and visits for Pap test and pelvic exams, have required 20 percent coinsurance, which certainly can serve as a barrier to getting these services.

The PPACA has lowered some, but not all, of these barriers to care. Mammograms, colonoscopies, bone density tests, and certain other preventive services are covered by Medicare without a copayment; beneficiaries also receive free annual wellness checkups. However, vision and dental care are unchanged; annual eye exams still require a copayment, and routine dental work is simply not covered. The PPACA will eventually bring dramatic changes to prescription drug coverage. Beneficiaries facing the donut-hole gap in drug coverage under Medicare Part D now receive an automatic discount of 50 percent on covered prescription drugs. The donut hole is supposed to be completely eliminated by 2020.

The PPACA also affects Medicaid, another public insurance program vital to older women's health. In 2008, Medicaid covered nine million dual-eligible elderly and disabled people who qualified for both Medicare and Medicaid; 61 percent of these dual-eligible were women.[41] Here, with low-income elderly recipients, Medicaid pays premiums, deductibles, and coinsurance, which higher income Medicare beneficiaries have to pay themselves. The PPACA established a Medicare-Medicaid coordination office that has the responsibility to help the dual-eligible population access services, improve continuity of care, and reduce costs.[41]

This coordination is vital to the millions of women who rely on home health and nursing home care. Figure 20.3 shows that long-term care is predominantly a women's issue. Women comprise nearly three-fourths of the U.S. nursing home population. They represent more than two-thirds of home health users. With longer lives and lower incomes, women necessarily must rely on Medicaid for these services, because Medicare funds very minimal long-term care.

THE NEED FOR BETTER CARE AT LOWER COSTS

Again, it is not readily apparent why women's health care issues are discussed apart from men's issues. As shown, women live longer, smoke less, and generally engage in fewer risk-taking behaviors than men do. Moreover, women visit doctors more frequently and they use more medical services than do their male counterparts. Closer examination of the issues related to women's interaction with the U.S. health care system shows that women are less likely to have consistent health coverage, or any coverage for that matter, and they are more likely to delay medical care if they cannot afford it.

Race and class exacerbate these trends, because so many minority women, with the notable exception of Asian women, in all age groups have low incomes. Unfortunately, much remains unknown about health status and health services utilization in these groups. The paucity of data, especially from government sources, suggests that greater efforts are needed to gather and assess health data for Asian/Pacific Islander and American Indian/Alaska Native women, in particular, as well as various subsets of the Hispanic population. These data would provide more complete health profiles for these distinct pan-ethnic groupings and the subgroups of women that each represents.

These are changing times for U.S. health care. The implementation process of the Patient Protection and Affordable Care Act will continue over the course of several years, and it is impossible to know many of its future contours. For now, the PPACA is a mostly positive development for women's health. More women, particularly young women, have health coverage, and it should not be as precarious to retain coverage as it was in the past. More women can financially access preventive care for themselves and their families, and they should be able to afford birth control

FIGURE 20.3   **Gender of Long-Term Care Population**

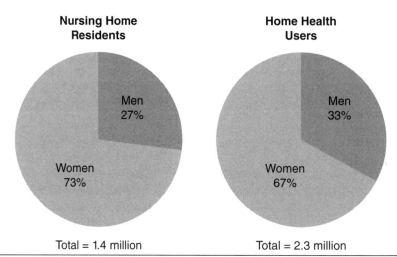

Distribution of Nursing Home Residents and
Home Health Users with Medicare, by Gender, 2008

Nursing Home Residents

Men 27%

Women 73%

Total = 1.4 million

Home Health Users

Men 33%

Women 67%

Total = 2.3 million

SOURCE: Kaiser Family Foundation, "Medicaid's Role for Women across the Lifespan: Current Issues and the Impact of the Affordable Care Act," *Women's Issue Brief*, December 2012.

NOTE: Nursing home residents refer to those ages 65 and older.

supplies. For the one in three to four American women who has an abortion, however, PPACA will not assist, which is a big gap in care. In addition, there are undocumented immigrant women who remain uncovered.

PPACA also benefits older women, who comprise the majority of elderly Americans. By closing the donut hole in Medicare prescription drug coverage, more prescriptions should be filled and fewer trade-offs made in how or whether to pay for them. The coordination of Medicare and Medicaid will also benefit the millions of women eligible for both programs; the coordination for both programs should benefit more women (and elderly men) than just the dual-eligibles.[42]

Because aging is feminized (i.e., disproportionately female), the development of comprehensive women's health policy must consider the quality of life. The greater longevity enjoyed by women is of dubious value if much of that extended lifespan is spent in poor health or in substandard housing or nursing homes.

The state of research into women's health, while much improved since the early 1990s, has much more ground to cover before parity with men—traditionally, the default subjects of most clinical studies—is achieved. The inclusion of women in clinical studies needs to be enforced by the funding agencies, journals, and research communities. Greater support for social and behavioral determinants is important for improving women's health status. While advocacy groups have been vital for pushing women's health into mainstream research, an epidemiologic base is needed to prioritize research endeavors, not just advocacy pressure. For example, lung cancer now kills more women than breast cancer, yet breast cancer receives six times the funding.[26]

Here again, race, ethnicity, and class present challenges for researchers and funders. The Institute of Medicine found that "women who experience social disadvantage as a result of race or ethnicity, low income, or low educational level suffer disproportionate disease burdens, adverse health outcomes, and barriers to care but have not been well represented in studies."[29] To improve health interventions, social and cultural factors must be understood. Moreover, research findings need to be disseminated more widely so that all women can benefit.

It is vital to keep in mind that the relationship between poverty and health is far more insidious than just health care insurance coverage. Women are more likely than men to live with a low income and its consequences. Women (and their children) who face food insecurity are likely to develop more physical and mental health problems than those who do not. For example, women on public assistance are more than twice as likely to report being physically abused by an intimate partner than women with higher incomes.[43] The convergence of these and other factors can undermine both health and quality of life.[44]

***See also* Chapter 19: Children's Health and Health Care Policy (1960s–Present); Chapter 21: Minorities, Immigrants, and Health Care Policy: Disparities and Solutions (1960s–Present); Chapter 22: Aging and Health Care Policy (1990s–Present); Chapter 23: Fifty Years of Progress in Disease and Injury Prevention (1950s–Present); Chapter 24: Mental Health and Social Policy (1960s–Present); Chapter 25: Nutrition, Physical Activity, and the Obesity Epidemic: Issues, Policies, and Solutions (1960s–Present); Chapter 26: Interest Groups, Think Tanks, and Health Care Policy (1960s–Present).**

NOTES

1. Census Bureau, "The 2012 Statistical Abstract," tables 104, 168, 204, http://www.census.gov/compendia/statab.

2. American Lung Association, "Key Facts about Smoking among Hispanics," http://www.lung.org/stop-smoking/about-smoking/facts-figures/hispanics-and-tobacco-use.html.

3. Elizabeth Arias, "United States Life Tables," *National Vital Statistics Reports* 61: 3 (2012): 1–64.

4. Brian D. Smedley, Adrienne Y. Stith, and Alan R. Nelson, *Unequal Treatment: Confronting Racial and Ethnic Disparities in Health Care* (Washington, DC: National Academies Press, 2009).

5. Carol S. Weisman, *Women's Health Care* (Baltimore: Johns Hopkins University Press, 1998).

6. Association of American Medical Colleges, "Women in Academic Medicine Statistics and Medical School Benchmarking, 2011–2012," https://www.aamc.org/members/gwims/statistics.

7. Kant Patel and Mark Rushefsky, *Health Care Politics and Policy in America,* 3rd ed. (Armonk, NY: M.E. Sharpe, 2006), 209.

8. For more discussion about how classical American liberal impulses to promote individual rights and property often conflict with moralistic impulses to shame or regulate others' behavior, see James A. Morone, *Hellfire Nation* (New Haven, CT: Yale University Press, 2003).

9. Janet F. Brodie, *Contraception and Abortion in Nineteenth Century America* (Ithaca, NY: Cornell University Press, 1994).

10. Deborah R. McFarlane and Kenneth J. Meier, *The Politics of Fertility Control: Family Planning and Abortion Policies in the American States* (Washington, DC: Congressional Quarterly Press, 2001).

11. Patrick J. Sheeran, *Women, Society, the State, and Abortion: A Structuralist Analysis* (Westport, CT: Praeger, 1987).

12. Laurence H. Tribe, *Abortion: The Clash of Absolutes* (New York: W.W. Norton, 1992).

13. Cheryl D. Fryar et al., "Drug Use and Sexual Behaviors Reported by Adults: United States, 1999–2002," *Advance Data from Vital Health Statistics* 384 (June 2007).

14. Guttmacher Institute, "Facts on Induced Abortion in the United States," February 2014, http://www.guttmacher.org/pubs/fb_induced_abortion.html.

15. Institute of Medicine, *Clinical Preventive Services for Women: Closing the Gaps* (Washington, DC: National Academies Press, 2011).

16. Guttmacher Institute, "Facts on Unintended Pregnancy in the United States," December 2013, http://www.guttmacher.org/pubs/FB-Unintended-Pregnancy-US.html.

17. Guttmacher Institute, "An Overview of Abortion in the United States," February 2014, http://www.guttmacher.org/presentations/ab_slides.html.

18. Robert Pear, "Contraceptives Stay Covered in Health Law," *New York Times*, June 29, 2013, A1.

19. Kinsey Hasstedt, "Toward Equity and Access: Removing Legal Barriers to Health Insurance Coverage for Immigrants," *Guttmacher Policy Review* 16: 1 (2013): 3–8, http://www.guttmacher.org/pubs/gpr/16/1/gpr160102.html.

20. SisterSong Women of Color Reproductive Justice Collective, "Mission Statement," http://www.sistersong.net./index.php?option=com_content&view=article&id=25&Itemid=66.

21. Ibid.

22. Donna Hoyert and Jiaquan Xu, "Deaths: Preliminary Data for 2011," *National Vital Statistics Reports* 61: 6.

23. Rongal D. Nikora, *The Political Determinants of Health: The Impact of Political Factors on Black and White Infant Mortality Rates in the United States* (PhD dissertation, Albuquerque, NM: University of New Mexico).

24. Kaiser Family Foundation, "Impact of Health Reform on Women's Access to Coverage and Care (Menlo Park, CA: Kaiser Family Foundation, April 2012), http://kaiserfamilyfoundation.files.wordpress.com/2013/01/7987-02.pdf.

25. Kaiser Family Foundation, "Women's Health Insurance Coverage" (Menlo Park, CA: Kaiser Family Foundation, October 2012), http://kaiserfamilyfoundation.files.wordpress.com/2013/01/6000-10.pdf.

26. Department of Health and Human Services, *Healthy People 2010: Women's and Men's Health: A Comparison of Select Indicators* (Washington, DC: U.S. Government Printing Office, July 2009), 6, http://www.womenshealth.gov/publications/federal-report/healthy-people/healthypeople2010-report-070109.pdf.

27. Patel and Rushefsky, *Health Care Politics*.

28. Kaiser Family Foundation, "State Health Facts, Medicaid Enrollment by Gender," http://kff.org/medicaid/state-indicator/medicaid-enrollment-by-gender.

29. Stephen Zuckerman and Dana Goin, *How Much Will Medicaid Physician Fees for Primary Care Rise in 2013? Evidence from a 2012 Survey of Medicaid Physician Fees* (Menlo Park, CA: Kaiser Family Foundation, December 2012), http://kaiserfamilyfoundation.files.wordpress.com/2013/01/8398.pdf.

30. Institute of Medicine, *Women's Health Research: Progress, Pitfalls, and Promise* (Washington, DC: Institute of Medicine, 2010), http://www.iom.edu/reports/2010/womens-health-research-progress-pitfalls-and-promise.aspx; Vivian W. Pinn et al., "Public Partnerships for a Vision for Women's Health Research in 2020," *Journal of Women's Health* 19: 9 (2010): 1603–1607.

31. Kant Patel and Mark Rushefsky, *The Politics of Public Health in the United States* (Armonk, NY: M.E. Sharpe, 2005).

32. Deborah R. McFarlane, "Reproductive Health Policies in President Bush's Second Term: Old Battles and New Fronts in the United States and Internationally," *Journal of Public Health Policy* 27: 4 (2006): 405–426.

33. Department of Health and Human Services, Health Resources and Services Administration, *Women's Health USA 2013* (Rockville, MD: U.S. Department of Health and Human Services, 2013).

34. Klim McPherson, Giorgia Gon, and Maggie Scott, *International Variations in a Selected Number of Surgical Procedures* (Paris: Organisation for Economic Co-operation and Development, 2013).

35. James Barron, "Unnecessary Surgery," *New York Times*, April 16, 1989, http://www.nytimes.com/1989/04/16/magazine/unnecessary-surgery.html?pagewanted=all&src=pm.

36. Centers for Disease Control and Prevention, "More Women Getting Pap Tests as Recommended" (press release), January 3, 2013, http://www.cdc.gov/media/releases/2013/p0103_pap_test.html.

37. Julia Bower et al., "Black-White Differences in Hysterectomy Prevalence: The CARDIA Study," *American Journal of Public Health* 99: 2 (2009): 300–307.

38. Joyce A. Martin et al. "Births: Final Data for 2010," *National Vital Statistics Reports* 61: 1 (2012): 1–72.

39. Kaiser Family Foundation, "Unnecessary Interventions Common in Maternity Care, Survey Finds" *Women's Daily Health Policy Report* (May 9, 2013).

40. Kaiser Family Foundation, *Medicare's Role for Women*. Menlo Park, CA: Kaiser Family Foundation, 2009. http://kaiserfamilyfoundation.files.wordpress.com/2013/01/7913.pdf

41. Grant D. Jacobsen and Kathryn H. Jacobsen, "Health Awareness Campaigns and Diagnosis Rates: Evidence from National Breast Cancer Awareness Month," *Journal of Health Economics* 30: 1 (2011): 55–61.

42. Centers for Medicare and Medicaid Services, "About the Medicare-Medicaid Coordination Office," http://www.cms.gov/Medicare-Medicaid-Coordination/Medicare-and-Medicaid-Coordination/Medicare-Medicaid-Coordination-Office/index.html.

43. American Bar Association Commission on Domestic and Sexual Violence, "Domestic Violence Statistics," http://www.americanbar.org/groups/domestic_violence/resources/statistics.html.

44. Kristen Shook Slack and Joan Yoo, "Food Hardship and Child Behavior Problems among Low-Income Children," *Social Service Review* 75 (2005): 511–536.

FURTHER READING

Alan Guttmacher Institute. "Facts on Publicly Funded Contraceptive Services in the United States." May 2013. http://www.guttmacher.org/pubs/fb_contraceptive_serv.html.

American Bar Association Commission on Domestic and Sexual Violence. "Domestic Violence Statistics." http://www.americanbar.org/groups/domestic_violence/resources/statistics.html.

Appleby, Julie. "Physicians Wade into Efforts to Curb Unnecessary Treatments." *Kaiser Health News,* April 4, 2012. http://www.kaiserhealthnews.org/Stories/2012/April/04/physicians-unnecessary-treatments.aspx.

Brodie, Janet Farrell. *Contraception and Abortion in Nineteenth Century America.* Ithaca, NY: Cornell University Press, 1994.

Casamayou, Maureen Hogan. *The Politics of Breast Cancer.* Washington, DC: Georgetown University Press, 2001.

Fryar, Cheryl D., Rosemarie Hirsch, Kathryn S. Porter, Benny Kottiri, Debra J. Brody, and Tatiana Louis. "Drug Use and Sexual Behaviors Reported by Adults: United States, 1999–2002." *Advance Data from Vital and Health Statistics* 384 (2007).

Jacobsen, Grant D., and Kathryn H. Jacobsen. "Health Awareness Campaigns and Diagnosis Rates: Evidence from National Breast Cancer Awareness Month." *Journal of Health Economics* 30: 1 (2011): 55–61.

McFarlane, Deborah R., and Kenneth J. Meier. *The Politics of Fertility Control: Family Planning and Abortion Policies in the American States.* Washington, DC: CQ Press, 2001.

Morgen, Sandra. *Into Our Own Hands: The Women's Health Movement in the United States, 1969–1990.* New Brunswick, NJ: Rutgers University Press, 2002.

Patel, Kant, and Mark Rushefsky. *Health Care Politics and Policy in America,* 3rd ed.. Armonk, NY: M.E. Sharpe, 2006.

Weisman, Carol S. *Women's Health Care.* Baltimore: Johns Hopkins University Press, 1998.

chapter 21

Minorities, Immigrants, and Health Care Policy

Disparities and Solutions (1960s–Present)

David Barton Smith

THE SECULAR, POLITICAL VERSION OF THE Golden Rule, as most pundits note, is "Those with the gold rule." That "gold" in the U.S. political system is a combination of money and votes. The magical tale beneath the presidential election victories of 1960 and 2012 was that both were the consequence of the actions of people who half a century prior had neither. Indeed, they faced difficulties that left but one choice: to vote with their feet. Two massive migrations, the second a direct consequence of the first, produced these victories and, in the process, transformed health policy in the United States.

POLITICS AND HEALTH CARE POLICY

A Tale of Two Elections: The 1960 Phone Call

Jailed for participating in a student-organized demonstration against segregated stores in Atlanta, Dr. Martin Luther King Jr. faced retaliation. While the local and state legal system released the student demonstrators, they sentenced King on a trumped-up traffic misdemeanor charge to four months hard labor on a prison road gang, transferred him to a rural state prison, and denied bail. Concerned about a brutal sentence that could cost him his life, Coretta King and civil rights leaders pressed the John F. Kennedy and Richard M. Nixon campaigns in the last week of a tightly contested election to intervene. Although African American voters generally viewed Nixon and the Republican Party more favorably than Kennedy and the Democrats, the Nixon campaign chose to ignore these appeals. At the same time, Kennedy's campaign strategists were desperate to avoid appearing to side with the civil rights activists, certain that would result in the loss of the southern states, the so-called solid south, and the election. Responding to the pleas of Harris Wofford, the campaign's liaison with the civil rights movement, Sargent Shriver, went behind the backs of the campaign's chief strategists and approached Kennedy while he was resting, exhausted from nonstop campaigning in the Chicago area. Shriver urged Kennedy to make a personal courtesy call to Mrs. King, and Kennedy agreed. He spoke briefly on the phone to her: "I know this must be very hard for you. I understand you are expecting a baby, and I just wanted you to know that I was thinking about you and Dr. King. If there is anything I can do to help, please feel free to call me." Enraged, Robert Kennedy, his brother's campaign manager, lashed out: "You bomb throwers have lost the whole campaign!" While the call and the subsequent change of heart and intervention by Robert Kennedy that got King out on bail were downplayed and caused only a brief ripple in the mainstream media, it changed the outcome of the election. Wofford and Shriver made arrangements for the distribution of "The Blue Bomb," two million leaflets to African American churches on the Sunday before the election. It described the call to Coretta King and touched a chord in the African American community long fragmented by party loyalties. Kennedy went on to win the election by a popular margin of 49.7 percent to Nixon's 49.5 percent. Without the African American vote, Nixon would have won 52 percent of the popular vote, carried Illinois and Michigan, and won the election. In the 1956 election, African Americans had voted 60 percent for the Republican Eisenhower. In 1960, however, 70 percent of African Americans voted for the Democrat Kennedy.

SOURCE: Taylor Branch, *Parting the Waters: America in the King Years 1954–63* (New York: Simon & Schuster, 1988), 352–378.

THE FIRST GREAT MIGRATION AND HEALTH CARE DISPARITIES

Between 1915 and 1960, in a period known as the Great Migration, almost six million African American citizens fled the south for northern cities to escape the caste system enforced by Jim Crow laws that denied equal opportunities for education, employment, health care, and the vote. Individuals who refused to accept these restrictions often faced violent reprisals.[1] Northern manufacturers seeking a supply of cheap unskilled labor, but cut off from the recruitment of European immigrants by World War I (1914–1918) and World War II (1939–1945), encouraged it. By 1960, that migration, as illustrated by the victory of John F. Kennedy (1960–1963), had begun to enter into the calculations of presidential candidates. Indeed, one could make the case that the entire civil rights and health care legislative agendas of the 1960s were in large part products of that migration.

The migrants, however, were only partially successful in escaping Jim Crow. America's health care system in the twentieth century had evolved in its shadow. Health care, segregated along racial lines by Jim Crow laws in the south and by informal understandings and residential segregation in the north, was separate and unequal. Even the training of physicians and their medical associations was separated by this racial divide. Minorities and the poor had both poorer health and less access to care. No one, however, labeled these differences as "disparities." Differences become disparities only when they are defined as a disturbing injustice in need of correction. Large racial differences (not disparities) in morbidity and mortality had been documented from the beginning of the twentieth century but used by many as evidence of racial inferiority and justification for segregated, inadequate care.[2] The life insurance industry and the emerging commercial health insurance industry used the racial differences in mortality rates for underwriting purposes. African Americans were either excluded from coverage as uninsurable or offered separate policies based on race-specific actuarial tables that raised the cost and limited the benefits of that coverage. Many African Americans were also excluded from health insurance coverage simply by where they lived and the nature of their employment (just as many new immigrants are today).

Differences in Health Care

Until the 1960s, differences in access to health care were not a major source of concern in the U.S. political system. Most providers of services accepted the racial and economic divisions as just the way things were. What limited access to care African Americans did have was justified by health officials representing the white majority as either evidence of their beneficence or self-interested public health protection from infectious diseases. The more limited access to mainstream medicine also served to supply teaching and research material for medical centers.

The Tuskegee Syphilis Study

The now infamous Tuskegee syphilis study was the poster child of the pre–civil rights era national mindset about health care. It was not, as some assume today, a secret rogue experiment. The study had been widely reported in the professional literature, and many in the medical, academic, and public health communities, both African American and white, not only were familiar with but also served in an advisory capacity overseeing the project and lending their support to the study. Lasting from 1932 to 1972, the study was the nation's longest experiment on the effect of withholding treatment. Three hundred ninety-nine African American males participated in a study that followed the natural course of the disease.[3] The central ethical justification for the study was the assumption that these individuals would have no access to adequate medical care anyway. Thus, whatever care was provided by the study was better than what they would receive without it. The project was shut down finally in 1972, long after the implementation of the Medicare and Medicaid programs and only after an exposé by an investigative reporter.

Health Care and the Civil Rights Movement

The shift to redefining health and health care differences as disparities began with John F. Kennedy's (1961–1963) election in 1960 and coincided with the growth in the influence of the civil rights movement. While statistics on racial differences in mortality and morbidity had been available for half a century, national statistics on the "smoking gun," the relationship between race and access to medical care, did not begin to be reported until around 1960, with the initiation of the National Health Interview Survey. An earlier effort to set a national policy agenda, conducted by a broad spectrum of national health professional groups and private foundations, the Committee on the Cost of Medical Care, looked at the relationship between income and access to care in selected geographic areas. However, the study chose to exclude African Americans from its surveys, concluding that "the procedure adopted could not procure satisfactory information from Negro families."[4] Did the National Health Interview Surveys that began to discover the national racial and income differences in access to care at the beginning of the 1960s help create the political will to do something about it, or did the political will to do something help create the surveys? Perhaps it was a little of both.

Coinciding with the release of statistics on the racial and economic differences in access to care and the growing influence of the civil rights movement, the life insurance industry voluntarily discontinued race-based practices for newly issued policies.[5] The standard industry race-based actuarial tables used in developing policies were desegregated. This was a key watershed for both life insurance and health care insurance. If policies now covered a racially integrated group with no distinctions by race, all policy holders and their underwriters, whether private or public, had a stake in reducing racial differences.

Nevertheless, the common use of the word *disparities* in describing racial and economic differences in health and health care did not come until well after the civil rights era. It appears to have been derived from the regulations promulgated to enforce Title VI of the 1964 Civil Rights Act. Those regulations spell out two types of discrimination prohibited by a recipient of federal funds: "disparate" treatment (overt discrimination) and "disparate" impact (discrimination resulting from facially neutral policies). For example, while disparate treatment would involve the refusal to treat a patient because of his or her race, disparate impact would involve relocating a hospital or medical practice to make it more difficult for persons of a particular race to access care. Concern about discrimination as a result of disparate treatment or impact underlies the labeling of health and health care differences as disparities. Addressing or eliminating such health and health care disparities did not become a central part of health policy reports and discussions until the 1990s. For the last three decades, the ten-year national health planning consensus documents have had as a major goal reducing or eliminating health and health care disparities.[6] For the last decade, following a legislative mandate, the Agency for Health Care Quality and Research has produced an annual report card on health care disparities in the United States.[7] All of these developments were a direct consequence of the transformation that began with Kennedy's election in 1960.

The Growing Storm

Nothing, however, could have prepared the pundits or the Kennedy administration for the events that would follow. Most assumed that only very cautious steps would be taken in addressing civil rights and the health care disparity problem. It was not in the interest of the Kennedy administration, setting its sights on reelection, to push hard. Yet they were caught up with everyone else in a groundswell over which they had little control. They were swept along by the sons and daughters of the Great Migration, by tragic events, and by the reaction of ordinary citizens to them.

Title VI of the Civil Rights Act of 1964

During the 1960 presidential campaign, Kennedy had glibly promised to end discrimination with "the stroke of a pen." That proved a difficult promise to keep. Harris Wofford, in his brief tenure at the Kennedy White House, became the unhappy custodian of thousands of pens sent to the White House to humorously prod the president into

action. One of the lessons of Harry S. Truman's (1945–1953) effort to integrate the military and federal agencies by executive order was that even in bastions of segregation, "those with the gold," in this case those controlling federal dollars, ruled. Even in Jackson, Mississippi, the crucible of later civil rights struggles, the Veteran's Administration (VA) hospital had been quietly integrated without protest in the early 1950s.[8] However, it was an entirely different matter for the executive branch to deny the distribution of federal funds that Congress had provided for segregated nonfederal institutions. The Kennedy administration began to quietly pressure medical schools and teaching hospitals receiving federal funding for research and training. In the early 1960s, the University of Mississippi Medical School Hospital in Jackson, just as other southern medical school facilities were quietly integrating, faced the threat of the loss of federal research and training dollars critical to their viability.

The Hill-Burton Act, however, had established the precedent clearly permitting the distribution of federal funds to segregated nonfederal organizations. Passed in 1946, the act provided matching federal funding for the construction and renovation of hospitals. States were given the authority to develop plans for the use of these matching funds in a manner that ensured that care in hospitals receiving funding

> did not discriminate on the basis of race, creed or color, but an exception will be made in cases where separate hospital facilities are provided for separate population groups, if the plan makes equitable provision on the basis of need for facilities and services of like quality for each such group. (Sec. 291e)[9]

This represented the only explicit authorization of the use of federal dollars for "separate but equal" Jim Crow purposes in federal legislation in the twentieth century. Southern states proceeded to distribute this funding for the construction of hospitals that excluded individuals because of race. Without a clear ruling by the courts that such a provision was unconstitutional, the executive branch, if challenged, could deny funding for racially segregated service and programs only in the nonexistent case where the authorizing act specifically prohibited racial segregation or discrimination in those services or programs.

This impasse was not overcome until March 1964, four months after Kennedy's assassination and in the midst of Lyndon B. Johnson's (1963–1969) effort to engineer the passage of a civil rights bill. A controversial section of that bill, Title VI, prohibited discrimination on the basis of race, color, and national origin in programs and activities receiving federal financial assistance. "Simple justice," Kennedy had argued in submitting the bill to Congress in June 1963, "requires that public funds, to which all taxpayers of all races contribute, not be spent in any fashion which encourages, entrenches, subsidizes or results in racial discrimination."[10] Passage of the bill and particularly this section did not prove that simple. In an effort to seek a remedy in the courts, the Kennedy Justice Department had intervened in a federal court case, arguing that the clause sanctioning segregation in the Hill-Burton Act was unconstitutional. The plaintiffs in the suit, African American physicians and dentists denied access to two Hill-Burton facilities restricted to white patients and physicians in Greensboro, North Carolina, won in the Fourth Circuit Court of Appeals in *Simkins v. Moses Cone Hospital* (1963). The Supreme Court, aware of its relationship to the pending legislation with unusual punctuality, declined review and let the Fourth Circuit decision stand. In so doing, it ruled on the unconstitutionality of a last-ditch effort to insert a similar Hill-Burton type of exemption in Title VI of the civil rights bill before it was even debated in the Senate. That debate, when it came, involved one of the longest filibusters in Senate history. At its end, more Republicans than Democrats voted for its passage. It was the high water mark of Republican support of civil rights and a profound watershed in national life. A geographic and racial realignment of the nation's two major political parties followed, with the Republicans replacing the Democrats as the dominant party in the south and the Democrats replacing the Republicans as the dominant party among African Americans.

The Enactment of Medicare

President Johnson, aided by a landslide victory in November 1964, produced a deluge of legislation that offered many opportunities to test the will of the federal government to enforce the two basic principles embodied in Title VI of the Civil Rights Act: (1) that all persons are entitled to nondiscriminatory, equal treatment from all organizations receiving federal funding and (2) that federal funds would be denied to any organization that failed to meet this requirement. The first real test came with passage of the Social Security amendments in July 1965. With the implementation of the Medicare and Medicaid programs, the federal share of funding for health care would triple from 9 percent to almost 30 percent. For most hospitals, the proportion of their revenue coming from state and federal government would jump to more than 50 percent. Many urged delay in any attempt to enforce Title VI. The implementation of the Medicare program faced resistance by many physicians and concerted opposition by some state and local medical societies. They feared that the same massive resistance in the south that had stalemated federal efforts to integrate public schools after the 1954 *Brown v. Board of Education* decision and passage of the Civil Rights Act would cripple the implementation of Medicare.

The Acid Test

For more than six months, it was uncertain what if anything would be done. Implementing the new program for a vulnerable population of almost twenty million beneficiaries required the active cooperation of almost all physicians and hospitals in the country. The Office of Equal Health Opportunity (OEHO), responsible for Title VI compliance, consisted of a skeleton staff of fewer than ten persons. They were responsible for certifying approximately eight thousand facilities by the July 1, 1966, deadline. Only in March 1966, however, did President Johnson's intentions become clear: Title VI compliance would be real, not a pro forma paper one, and Medicare would begin on schedule.

What happened then mystified both Johnson's segregationist and civil rights critics. OEHO sent out a form to every hospital on March 4, 1966, to complete in anticipation of on-site inspections. Earlier, in an effort to circumvent legislative budgetary restrictions on staffing, the Department of Health, Education and Welfare's (DHEW) secretary John W. Gardner (in office 1965–1968) had sent a memo to the head of his operating agencies. DHEW was now a civil rights organization. There was no legislative or court-ordered mandate to reorient the mission of DHEW; Gardner just did it. Each operational division would supply a quota of "volunteers" to staff the Title VI enforcement effort and cover their salaries and travel expenses.

A total of almost one thousand people volunteered. Gardner had stipulated that if there were not enough volunteers, staff would be drafted; but the growing civil rights commitment among federal civil servants, as in the general public, eliminated any need for draftees. About half of the volunteers came from the Public Health Service, and the other half came from local and regional offices of the Social Security Administration. The volunteers included bench scientists, an Alaska Native public health service nurse, a venereal disease inspector from New York City, and several medical students who had taken temporary positions in DHEW during a break from their schooling. Few had any experience relevant to the task they were about to embark upon.

The newly deputized volunteer compliance officers received little or no formal training. On April 6, 1966, OEHO scheduled a two-day training session for 119 compliance officer trainees.[11] Also in attendance as guests or consultants were representatives from the NAACP, the Urban League, the Southern Christian Leadership Conference, the Student Nonviolent Coordinating Committee, the American Jewish Committee, and the United Mine Workers. A similar two-day workshop was held a month later in Dallas, Texas, for another 120 trainees. Most of the volunteers, however, were just thrown into the job without even this degree of preparation. Nothing could have prepared them for what they would experience, and time was running out.

What worked in favor of this hastily cobbled together effort was the same Golden Rule that had worked so well earlier in integrating the VA hospitals and local Social Security Offices in the 1950s, even in the deep south. Medicare would ensure the financial viability of a hospital only if the Title VI requirements were met. If a hospital failed to comply, not only would local residents eligible for Medicare be unable to use their local hospital but also that hospital would face almost certain financial ruin. Hospital boards and administrators as well as the volunteer compliance officers all understood this. Most hospital administrators and boards were willing to integrate, assured that the federal government would take the blame and all the other hospitals would have to do so as well. It required no great act of courage, and most hospital officials were anxious to complete the traumatic transition as quickly and quietly as possible. For example, to paraphrase, a hospital official in a moderate-sized city telegrammed the regional office, "We have both a white and an African American hospital in our town, what should we do?" "Merge" was the one-word telegram sent in reply. It was done. In Alabama, a hospital had taken down the "White" and "Colored" waiting room signs for its clinic, but people still waited in the same places. The hospital was told to rope off one of the waiting rooms and place a sign in front of it: "Overflow waiting room, to be used only when the main waiting room is full." It was done. A compliance officer discovered that the Louisiana Red Cross blood bank used by all of the state's hospitals labeled blood "White" and "Colored." Not bothering to check with legal counsel about whether OEHO had the authority to do it, he sent a telegram to the Louisiana Hospital Association informing it that unless the blood supply in Louisiana was integrated, all the hospitals in the state would be out of compliance. The blood supply was integrated in a matter of hours. Not all hospitals were as cooperative and some attempted subterfuges, such as integrating the floors for the inspections and then resegregating them after the inspectors left. Local civil rights organizations and African American hospital employees were quick to bring this to the attention of the inspectors. In the midst of all of this, African American physicians who had long been frustrated by their inability to get privileges at local hospitals began to be actively recruited by hospital medical staffs, and African American nurses were hired for newly integrated nursing staffs.

On July 1, 1966, 6,593 acute care hospitals had their Title VI certifications and were accepting Medicare patients. Only 327 hospitals, many of them smaller facilities, were still awaiting Title VI clearance. While some of those granted clearance were still implementing integration plans, the transformation happened so quickly, completely, and quietly that, as one African American physician observed, "It was almost as if it had always been this way."[12] For hospital board members and executives, it was an easy decision to make. More than half their patients could now be generously reimbursed by the federal Medicare and Medicaid programs.

Refusal to comply with Title VI would mean the loss of more than half their potential revenues, a financial death spiral and almost certain closure. Even for the most entrenched Jim Crow zealots, there was something more important than race, namely getting the federal dollars to ensure solvency and avoid placing their institutions at a competitive disadvantage with other hospitals.

THE SECOND GREAT MIGRATION AND AN EXPANDED DEFINITION OF HEALTH CARE DISPARITIES

In October 1965, President Johnson signed the Immigration and Naturalization Act while next to the Statue of Liberty, which, because of previous immigration laws, had welcomed only white European immigrants. For those who had embraced the civil rights cause, it seemed just a final bit of embarrassing, overdue house cleaning. Johnson sought in his remarks to both reassure those who might fear its potential impact and embrace the principles enacted in the Civil Rights Act of the year before:

> [This Act] is not a revolutionary bill; it does not affect the lives of millions. It will not restructure our daily lives or add to our wealth and power. . . . Yet it is still one of the most important acts of this Congress and of this administration. For it does repair a very deep and painful flaw in the fabric of American justice. It corrects a cruel and enduring wrong in the conduct of the American Nation. This bill says simply that from this day forth those wishing to immigrate to America shall be admitted on the basis of their skills and their close relationship to those already here. This is a simple test, and it is a fair test. Those who can contribute most to this country—to its growth, to its strength, to its spirit—will be the first to be admitted to this land.[13]

Impact of the Immigration and Nationality Act of 1965

No one anticipated how revolutionary the effect of applying the nondiscrimination principles embedded in Title VI of the Civil Rights Act to immigration policies would be. Over the next fifty years, the foreign-born population of the United States would increase fourfold, but the number of European foreign born would decline by one-third. In contrast, the number of Asian foreign born would increase twenty-two-fold to more than 11 million, and the number of Latin American foreign born would increase twenty-three-fold to 22 million. In addition, the number of individuals born in Africa residing in the United States increased forty-five-fold to more than 1.6 million.[14,15] The United States had reinvented itself as a nation and, in the process, expanded the definition of health disparities and the challenges it posed for health policy and health care providers.

Title VI of the 1964 Civil Rights Act states, "No person in the United States shall, on the ground of race, color, or *national origin* [italics added], be excluded from participation in, be denied the benefits of, or be subjected to discrimination under any program or activity receiving Federal financial assistance."[16] The Supreme Court concluded in *Lau v. Nichols* (1973) that "national origin" was a proxy for language and that recipients of federal funding could be found liable for discrimination for failing to provide access to language services. In 2000, President William J. Clinton's (1993–2001) Executive Order 13166 facilitated the development of clarifying guidance to recipients of funding about how to meet this requirement and ensure meaningful access to limited-English-proficient (LEP) applicants and beneficiaries. For the earlier waves of European immigrants, whatever their degree of English proficiency, one could assume that they were still to a large extent embedded in the culture of Western medicine. For the newer waves of immigrants,

this could no longer be assumed, which led to a general recognition by both federal health agencies and recipients of funding that simply providing language services for the LEP population was not sufficient to achieve the intent. Eliminating national origin discrimination now required a degree of cultural competence, whatever that might entail, rather than just providing translation services. Foundations, service providers, and academic and federal health agencies continue to debate how this can be best achieved. In 2001, the Office of Minority Health released guidance for recipients of federal funding, or the "CLAS standards" (standards for Culturally and Linguistically Appropriate Services), which have helped further guide these discussions and program implementation.

Among these fourteen standards, only four related to making accommodations for those with limited English proficiency (Standards 4–7), which are mandated for all providers receiving federal support (e.g., a Title VI requirement). Three (Standards 1–3) that deal with the training and recruitment of staff and six (Standard 8–13) that deal with the organization and management are defined as

MAP 21.1   **Minority Populations in the United States**

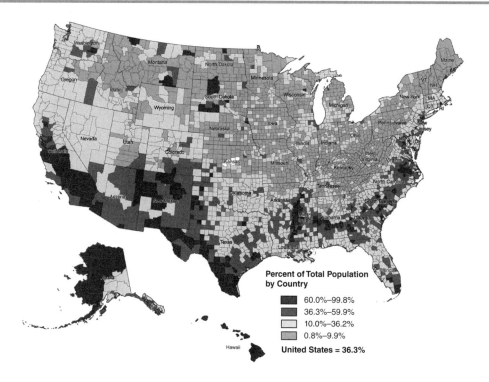

Percent of Total Population by Country

- 60.0%–99.8%
- 36.3%–59.9%
- 10.0%–36.2%
- 0.8%–9.9%

United States = 36.3%

In the contiguous forty-eight states, in general, non-white minorities are concentrated in the south as well as in urban areas in the north. Alaska and Hawaii, however, are populated by non-white majorities. Equal access to health care for all Americans, as well as new immigrants from regions other than Europe, remains a concern for the nation in the twenty-first century.

SOURCE: Rural Assistance Center.

NOTE: Alaska and Hawaii are not to scale.

CLAS "guidelines" and are recommended for federal, state, and national accrediting bodies. One (Standard 14) is "voluntary," with no penalties for noncompliance. The cost of meeting the "mandated" LEP standards are now reimbursable under Medicare, Medicaid, and the Children's Health Insurance Program (CHIP). The dynamics surrounding the implementation of the CLAS standards contrasted strikingly with those surrounding the enforcement off Title VI requirements with the implementation of Medicare. There has been more give-and-take and little resistance to the underlying intent. At least for those immigrants who are publicly or privately insured or who can afford to pay out of pocket, the "business case" for providing culturally competent services is straightforward. Culturally competent services attract more business, improve profitability, reduce malpractice risks, and improve the overall quality of care. The CLAS standards encourage providers to assess how well they are doing in addressing the LEP and cultural competence needs of their patients. Patient satisfaction surveys, conducted by many health plans and providers, now include standardized items to measure the effectiveness of their cultural competence and health literacy practices.[17] While the CLAS standards are in theory universal ones for the nation's health system, they are in practice more systematically developed in public and larger organizational settings than in private medical practices. Because these settings are the same locations that low-income and immigrant groups depend on for most of their medical care, this is perhaps one of the few instances in which these groups face a somewhat less fragmented and more user-friendly system of care than their more affluent and non-immigrant counterparts.

None of these standards or the evaluation of how well providers are meeting them, however, address the major problem producing foreign-born disparities in health insurance coverage. Low-income noncitizens are more than three times as likely to be uninsured as low-income citizens (60 percent as opposed to 28 percent).[18] Low-income noncitizens also are less likely to gain coverage through employment and, for the most part, are ineligible for Medicaid or CHIP. Not surprisingly, low-income noncitizens are twice as likely as native-born adult citizens to have no regular source of care and use health care providers at less than half the rate of citizens. Adding to the access problems related to coverage are the complex, ambivalent restrictions on Medicaid and other benefits for noncitizens, an often punitive governmental approach to undocumented migrants and the source of fear and distrust that all of this engenders in new immigrant communities.

The Patient Protection and Affordable Care Act, as argued by former Secretary of Health and Human Services Kathleen Sebelius (in office 2009–2014) in her speech to the National Hispanic Medical Association, may well make an important contribution to reducing health care access disparities in the immigrant population. If fully implemented, it will greatly expand health insurance coverage for the immigrant population. The expansion of Community Health Centers will also help increase access for those denied Medicare and Medicaid and those who are unable to afford private coverage. Pending immigration reform will also play a role in either reducing or increasing disparities in access for the nation's foreign-born population.

Disparities and Their Elimination

A new word, *disparities*, and the goal of eliminating them, entered the vocabulary and agenda of health policy in the aftermath of the civil rights era. What has happened and what has not? Improving the quality of health care involves improving structures, processes, and outcomes.[19] The structural aspects of quality refer to the settings in which care is organized, the process aspects of quality, what is done to whom and the outcomes aspects of quality, and what is accomplished in improving the health of the population served.

Structure

Acute care became less segregated but overall care more fragmented. A quiet revolution desegregated almost all hospital care in a matter of months in 1966. Reflecting this major structural shift, about seventy historically African American hospitals closed in the next two decades, casualties of that integration. Indeed, then presidential candidate Barack Obama (2009–) was slotted to give his nomination acceptance speech in the Bank of America North Carolina Panther Stadium that had been built over the demolished Good Samaritan Hospital, one of the oldest and best regarded of these facilities. By the end of the twentieth century, almost all the relics of that previous era, the separate wards and wings for indigent patients in the nation's hospitals, had disappeared as well.

That greater degree of hospital racial integration, however, was not achieved without costs. In racially mixed service areas, much of the bed supply was converted to private rooms, largely underwritten by Medicare and Medicaid. Length of stay in acute hospitals has dropped, and more of the care is provided in more segregated ambulatory and long-term care settings. Physician practices were exempted from compliance with Title VI, and for a variety of reasons nursing homes were never subjected to the same level of scrutiny as hospitals were.[20] The United States has the shortest length of stay and the fewest general hospital beds per one thousand population of any developed nation, yet it has the highest per capita cost for hospital care of any nation in the world. The structural changes following the implementation of Medicare and Medicaid, in part a response to Title VI compliance, have produced more fragmentation in the

The Culturally and Linguistically Appropriate Services (CLAS) Standards

Standard 1

Health care organizations should ensure that patients/consumers receive from all staff member's effective, understandable, and respectful care that is provided in a manner compatible with their cultural health beliefs and practices and preferred language.

Standard 2

Health care organizations should implement strategies to recruit, retain, and promote at all levels of the organization a diverse staff and leadership that are representative of the demographic characteristics of the service area.

Standard 3

Health care organizations should ensure that staff at all levels and across all disciplines receive ongoing education and training in culturally and linguistically appropriate service delivery.

Standard 4

Health care organizations must offer and provide language assistance services, including bilingual staff and interpreter services, at no cost to each patient/consumer with limited English proficiency at all points of contact, in a timely manner during all hours of operation.

Standard 5

Health care organizations must provide to patients/consumers in their preferred language both verbal offers and written notices informing them of their right to receive language assistance services.

Standard 6

Health care organizations must assure the competence of language assistance provided to limited English proficient patients/consumers by interpreters and bilingual staff. Family and friends should not be used to provide interpretation services (except on request by the patient/consumer).

Standard 7

Health care organizations must make available easily understood patient-related materials and post signage in the languages of the commonly encountered groups and/or groups represented in the service area.

provision of care. That fragmentation most adversely affects more vulnerable minority and low-income populations that lack the resources (e.g., transportation, out-of-pocket support of home care) of middle- and upper-income families in more medically resource-rich communities. The persistence of geographic and residential segregation contributes to most of the segregation and unequal distribution of resources that persist in health care.

Process

Although disparities in the overall volume of care received have been eliminated, the nation lacks any credible way to correct or even monitor disparate impact. Medicare and Medicaid produced a remarkable watershed that is often ignored in current health care reform debates. Between 1910

and 1966, during the development of the nation's health system, use of physicians and hospitals was significantly lower for lower income groups and for African Americans despite substantially poorer health. The volume of care received was directly related to income and inversely related to need. This "iron law" remained unbroken for a half-century. All statistics on health care use, no matter what kind of care, reflected this law. Medicare, Medicaid, and the civil rights movement that shaped both programs turned this around. The National Health Interview Surveys showed that African American age-adjusted admissions to hospitals that were only 75 percent of white use in 1964 climbed to 120 percent of white use in 2009. Similarly, age-adjusted physician contacts per year for African Americans climbed from 77 percent of white contacts in 1964 to 109 percent of white contacts in 2009. Among Medicare

Standard 8

Health care organizations should develop, implement, and promote a written strategic plan that outlines clear goals, policies, operational plans, and management accountability/oversight mechanisms to provide culturally and linguistically appropriate services.

Standard 9

Health care organizations should conduct initial and ongoing organizational self-assessments of CLAS-related activities and are encouraged to integrate cultural and linguistic competence-related measures into their internal audits, performance improvement programs, patient satisfaction assessments, and outcomes-based evaluations.

Standard 10

Health care organizations should ensure that data on the individual patient's/consumer's race, ethnicity, and spoken and written language are collected in health records, integrated into the organization's management information systems, and periodically updated.

Standard 11

Health care organizations should maintain a current demographic, cultural, and epidemiological profile of the community as well as a needs assessment to accurately plan for and implement services that respond to the cultural and linguistic characteristics of the service area.

Standard 12

Health care organizations should develop participatory, collaborative partnerships with communities and utilize a variety of formal and informal mechanisms to facilitate community and patient/consumer involvement in designing and implementing CLAS-related activities.

Standard 13

Health care organizations should ensure that conflict and grievance resolution processes are culturally and linguistically sensitive and capable of identifying, preventing, and resolving cross-cultural conflicts or complaints by patients/consumers.

Standard 14

Health care organizations are encouraged to regularly make available to the public information about their progress and successful innovations in implementing the CLAS standards and to provide public notice in their communities about the availability of this information.

SOURCE: Office of Minority Health, "National Standards for Culturally and Linguistically Appropriate Services," http://minorityhealth.hhs.gov/assets/pdf/checked/finalreport.pdf.

beneficiaries, the gap between African American and white use of services closed even more rapidly.[21] Comparably dramatic shifts took place between low- and high-income populations in the United States, with the low-income group of all races now having substantially higher rates of physician contacts and hospital admissions per year than high-income groups. Certainly, disparities have not been eliminated, and these gross differences may not even now fairly reflect the real differences in need. It is still a profound transformation in patterns of use and the culture of health care. Hospital parking lots are no longer mockingly referred to as delivery rooms for the indigent and minorities, and hospitals turn away uninsured emergency care at their peril. Disparities are now a focus of concern by both public and private health plans and health care providers.

However, are processes in place to ensure that more subtle disparities are corrected? The answer is not reassuring. Overall, disparities in treatment, whatever their cause, certainly persist, and these are now documented annually in the *National Health Care Disparities Report*. According to the most recent report, while overall quality of care is improving, disparities in quality and access are not. Yet efforts to enforce Title VI among health care providers now receiving more than $1 trillion in public funds has been ineffectual at best.

The magnitude of the struggle that remains is reflected by what the implementation of the Patient Protection and Affordable Care Act (PPACA) has left unresolved in addressing disparities. Section 1557 the nondiscrimination section of the PPACA invokes Title VI of the Civil Rights Act and

Secretary Sebelius's 2010 Speech to the National Hispanic Medical Association

In 2010, Secretary of Health and Human Services Kathleen Sebelius spoke to the National Hispanic Medical Association, pointing out the recent progress in health care access in minority communities. Her remarks struck a responsive chord. Indeed, few in the minority or immigrant community wanted to go back. In November 2012, Barack Obama won reelection with 91 percent of the African American vote, 73 percent of the Asian American vote, and 71 percent of the Latino vote, accounting for more than the 2.5 percent margin of victory in the popular vote. Sebelius reported:

The biggest single step we have taken to overcome disparities in years was the passing of the historic health care law, the Affordable Care Act. . . .

- Today there are 736,000 Latino young adults across the country that would have been uninsured but now have coverage under their parent's health plan.

- There are an estimated six million Latino Americans on Medicare who have access to new benefits like free preventive care and savings on prescription drugs when they hit the coverage gap known as the donut hole.

- There are new common sense rules of the road for insurance companies. For example, they can no longer deny coverage to children because of their preexisting conditions like asthma or diabetes.

- And we estimate that up to 9 million Latino Americans who are uninsured today will be eligible for coverage beginning in less than 2 years.

. . . [W]e're investing billions in more than 1,000 community health centers nationwide allowing them to construct and renovate buildings, add dental and mental health services, stay open longer, and serve millions of additional patients in the future—but those of you here today have gone one step further. As part of an organization like the National Hispanic Medical Association you've dedicated yourself to improving the health of Hispanic populations and you've dedicated yourself to putting an end to health disparities. . . . Health care disparities have been a constant source of injustice and inequality in our country and now that we have a renewed effort to combat such disparities, we cannot go back.

SOURCE: Kathleen Sebelius, National Hispanic Medical Association Conference, April 27, 2010, http://www.hhs.gov/secretary/about/speeches/sp20120427 .html.

---

subsequent acts prohibiting sex, disability, and age discrimination, stating, "an individual shall not on any of these grounds be excluded from participation in, be denied the benefits of, or be subjected to discrimination in any health program or activity, any part of which is receiving federal financial assistance." The prospects for ensuring the elimination of disparate treatment and impact through the implementation of the act, however, face many hurdles.

Two major problems that have dogged Title VI enforcement efforts since the elimination of the Public Health Services Office of Equal Health Opportunity and the creation of a centralized Office for Civil Rights (OCR) in the Department of Health, Education and Welfare in 1968 remain unresolved. First, OCR has lacked an adequate budget and staff. The flexibility that Secretary Gardner used to budget and staff the initial hospital Medicare Title VI compliance was lost in the reorganization. OCR has never had sufficient staff or budgets to effectively initiate its own compliance investigations or respond effectively to complaints. Second, it has been further handicapped by the failure to require collection of adequate data on race and ethnicity from providers and health plans. In the absence of such

information, it is not known what kind of discriminatory patterns exist or how pervasive they are among health care providers receiving federal funding. OCR is stuck in the embarrassing position of certifying compliance that no one is certain exists. While legislation intended to correct this periodically failed enactment by Congress, it was successfully included in the PPACA. Section 4302 of that act requires that any "federally conducted or supported health care or public health programs or survey . . . collects and reports data by race, ethnicity, sex, primary language and disability status for applicants, recipients or participants." Such data, standardized across providers, must be used to monitor disparities and made available for additional research and analysis by other agencies and the public. This new mandate, however, requires that separate specific funding be appropriated.

When all else fails, one of the critical safeguards built into the nation's system of government has been the right of private action to enforce the law in the courts. Until 2001, private actions could be brought on behalf of minorities or immigrant groups in the federal courts in cases involving disparate impact. It is relatively easy to present evidence of disparate impact: simply present the statistics that show a disparate pattern of use. It is rare and exceedingly difficult to present evidence of disparate treatment. One has to prove intent. That is possible only in the implausible case where there is evidence of admission of the intent to discriminate. The Supreme Court ruling in *Alexander v. Sandoval* (2001) blocks the right of private action in cases involving disparate impact. The PPACA failed to correct this impediment. As a result, while the federal office responsible for enforcing the nondiscrimination provisions in the PPACA lacks the resources in staff or data, private parties are blocked from attempting to address these shortcomings in court.

Of course, many might like to just assume that in the twenty-first century all of this is unnecessary. Given the nation's history, however, it would seem best to have a way to test this assumption and not just accept it as a matter of blind faith. Indeed, in both the housing and labor markets, the persistence of racial discrimination continues to be documented through federally funded testing programs that pair identical "testers" who differ only by race.[22,23] The Civil Rights Division of the Department of Justice continues to investigate and prosecute cases related to discrimination in both housing and employment. I was confidentially assured by a top Health and Human Services official in the mid-1990s that a similar testing program was in the process of development for health care, but no such program was ever implemented. The only thing close was a privately initiated research study simulating a testing program. Borrowing directly from the methodology used to test labor and housing discrimination, 720 physicians were given identical video scenarios at two national meetings of organizations of primary care physicians, which differed only in the race and sex of the actor portraying the patient. Physicians were less likely to recommend African Americans and females in these videos for cardiac catheterization.[24] The study was criticized methodologically for overstating its results, and the ethics of the study were questioned by some because the purpose of the study was not explained to the subjects. (Perhaps ironically, guidelines for the conduct of research involving human subjects, largely as a result of the Tuskegee scandal, now require a much greater degree of transparency.) No similar health care studies or federal testing programs have been conducted since then (1999). If one does not test for discrimination in health care, of course, one cannot prove it really exists or develop strategies for correcting the discrimination if it does. Lacking a grassroots groundswell similar to the one that forced the passage of the Civil Rights Act and Medicare in the 1960s, that is unlikely to happen.

Outcomes

Racial and economic health disparities in mortality rates declined between 1960 and 1980 but have since remained unchanged or widened despite overall health improvements.

Racial and economic disparities in rates of premature death (deaths before age sixty-five) and infant mortality rates (deaths before one year of age) shrank between 1966 and 1980.[25] Racial disparities in death rates more directly related to improvement in access to hospitals (infant mortality and deaths due to motor vehicle accidents) in southern states related to their desegregation declined markedly.[26,27] While there have been significant overall improvements in both premature death rates and infant mortality rates in all racial and income groups, disparities between African Americans and whites have remained unchanged since 1980. Black infant mortality rates were 2.23 times the rate of whites in 2010, and rates of African American years life lost (YLL) before age sixty-five remain substantially higher than the rate of white (1.6 times the rate of whites in 2010).

Adding complexity to the outcome disparity reduction puzzle, both Hispanic and Asian infant mortality and YLL before age sixty-five, as well as other measures of mortality risks, have long been consistently lower than non-Hispanic

A poster points out the increased emphasis on providing equal access to health care to minorities in the United States. Before the 1960s, whites and African Americans went to segregated health care facilities. Today, the federal government continues to reach out to African Americans and other minorities as well as to new immigrants from Latin America, Asia, and Africa.

SOURCE: Courtesy of Michigan Department of Community Health.

whites, despite indications of more limited access to care.[28] One possible explanation of this paradox would be the selective nature of immigration. Individuals do not choose to migrate if they are in poor health, and many, when they become sick, choose to return to more familiar cultural surroundings. Some researchers have suggested that healthier diets and lifestyle of recent immigrants may also contribute to these differences. However, most demographers and actuaries regard the effect of selective migration and reverse migration as a simpler and more plausible explanation for most of this pervasive statistical paradox.[29] A similar migration pattern has been observed among the nation's late-age migration to Florida, whose over-sixty-five population is markedly healthier than that of any other state.[30] Whatever the reason for this paradox, it has made the African American outcome disparities a more central concern of policymakers periodically since the 1960s. These efforts have focused on (1) addressing the social-economic, residential, and environmental differences that contribute to these health disparities and (2) redesigning health care to do a better job of compensating for these broader, underlying disparities. The second focus, not surprisingly, has proved a politically easier path to pursue than the first. The War on Poverty programs of the 1960s included extensive investment in developing community health centers. Their mission, then and now, has been to bridge the disparity gap through increased access and redesign of primary care. The PPACA makes a substantial investment in expanding and improving community health centers. The act also offers the opportunity to restructure the health system around primary care as opposed to specialty care that, following the model of other developed nations, many have advocated as a way of reducing health disparities.[31]

Why did African American disparities that had been declining hit an impasse after 1980? Disparities in outcomes, of course, are only partially related to disparities in access to appropriate care. Reductions in economic disparities accompanied the War on Poverty programs of the civil rights era. The post-1980 civil rights era backlash produced a rollback of these programs, a shift to rapidly growing economic disparities, and a fourfold increase in incarceration rates, all disproportionately affecting minority and immigrant communities. Neither overall economic trends (the per capita gross domestic product continued to rise at about the same rate), selective disease-specific trends (e.g., AIDS), nor selective changes in risk behavior (e.g., smoking) offer plausible alternative explanations to the shift toward increasing health disparities. Disparities in wealth, income, education, and environment all contribute to disparities in health. There is a limit to what can be accomplished in reducing health disparities without venturing beyond the conventional boundaries of health policy. Just as the earlier reductions in health disparities did, it will involve politics on a larger scale.

THE TWENTY-FIRST CENTURY

In the last fifty years or so, much as been accomplished in the struggle to eliminate minority and immigrant health disparities. What lessons does this review offer for health policy for the next half century? There would seem to be four:

Demographics are destiny. All of the changes in health policy described in this chapter were in large part a consequence of two demographic shifts in the United States. The first reflected the Great Migration of African Americans from the south to northern cities between 1910 and 1960. The second reflected the shift in immigration from Europe to Latin America and Asia from 1965 to the present. Both of these demographic shifts were unplanned products of the individual decisions of seemingly powerless disenfranchised people seeking a better life. Collectively, they produced a powerful force that transformed the nation's cultural, social, and political life and, with it, health policy.

Golden rules. These two demographic shifts were translated into votes and votes into federal funding priorities. The Title VI restriction on the flow of federal Medicare funding transformed health care. Copying from that success, the same language was included in Title IX of the 1972 Education Amendments prohibiting the use of federal funds in any educational institution that discriminates on the basis of sex and transformed the composition of medical schools and other programs. Most recently, this "Golden Rule" has worked wonders in converting governors who have been intractable opponents of the PPACA into reluctant participants in the federal funding providing expanded coverage under state Medicaid programs. Similarly, it may soon transform the way the nation cares for those with mental health care issues and drug dependency problems, providing services that can steer people away from the prison system and reduce the huge financial toll both on state and local budgets and on minority communities.

Eliminating disparate impact requires systemwide reform. Disparate treatment, the white and colored entrances and patient floors, were easy to eliminate quickly. Eliminating disparate impact has been a much harder and longer struggle. Title VI of the Civil Rights Act and its subsequent regulations avoided the politically contentious issue of defining what constituted disparate impact in terms of Title VI. For example, Title VI legal challenges of the relocation of hospitals from predominantly minority communities to more affluent white suburbs in the 1970s all failed. The disparate impact was obvious, but the business necessity arguments of the hospitals held sway in the courts. The corresponding migration of medical practices and other health-related services was never challenged, nor were the refusal of medical practices to accept Medicaid patients. Thus, in a largely privatized, market-driven system where the financial incentives encourage disparate access to care, further exacerbated by racial and economic residential segregation, the persistence of disparities is not surprising. In part, as the history of the implementation of the Medicare program illustrates, eliminating health care disparities is a matter of aligning the financial incentives of providers with that goal.

"The past is never dead. It's not even past."[32] The packaging may change, but not the underlying political issues. A week after the enactment of the Medicare and Medicaid legislation, President Johnson signed into law the Voting Rights Act of 1965. The unexpectedly high turnout of African Americans and other minorities in the 2012 election was pushback for perceived efforts to suppress the African American vote through enactment of voter ID laws and other measures. Much of the passion underlying efforts to cut the federal budget and restrict the role of the federal government are a similar reaction to the effectiveness of Title VI and subsequent federal legislation using similar language to alter the national social landscape. The many iterations of competitive market reform in health care have much in common with the efforts by some southern states to argue unsuccessfully for "freedom of choice" for patients in the implementation racial integration requirements for hospitals in the Medicare program. Southern political leaders wanted to let African Americans be "free" to choose whether they wanted to go to integrated hospital rooms and facilities. The answer of the federal civil rights compliance officers was "No, this is a federal program and we are all in this together." That answer also challenges the pervasive transformation of health care driven by private free market ideology. It asks the question: Who really owns the health care system? The conclusion of the 1963 *Simkins* decision that became Title VI of the Civil Rights Act was that not-for-profit hospitals were an "arm of the state," not private entities, and should respond to the collective needs of its citizens. Perhaps similar arguments will win the day

in the implementation of the PPACA, and health care can be insulated from the inevitable disparities and fragmentation of the free market.

What will happen to health policy about disparities over the next fifty years? We know that the non-Hispanic, white majority will become a minority. Will the new majority unite in policies that address health disparities? The divisions of race, ethnicity, and class have long contributed to the failure to ensure universal coverage that exists in every other developed country in the world. Yet the heirs of the two great migrations have much in common. They are the products of those motivated by the same desperation, courage, and belief in the possibility of a better world. They have much in common with the freed slaves and European immigrant groups a century and a half ago that created mutual-aid societies for protection. These associations gave birth to health insurance and other arrangements for caring for their members who became ill or incapacitated. The logic of solidarity, the purpose of joining such associations in the first place, dictated that the costs be spread equally among the members. The extent that the heirs of the two great migrations see themselves united by their common experience will determine the answer. Perhaps, according to Dr. Martin Luther King Jr., whose incarceration in a Georgia state prison demonstrated, "the arc of the moral universe is long, but it bends toward justice."[33]

***See also* Chapter 19: Children's Health and Health Care Policy (1960s–Present); Chapter 20: Women's Issues and American Health Care Policy (1960s–Present); Chapter 22: Aging and Health Care Policy (1990s–Present); Chapter 23: Fifty Years of Progress in Disease and Injury Prevention (1950s–Present); Chapter 24: Mental Health and Social Policy (1960s–Present); Chapter 25: Nutrition, Physical Activity, and the Obesity Epidemic: Issues, Policies, and Solutions (1960s–Present); Chapter 26: Interest Groups, Think Tanks, and Health Care Policy (1960s–Present).**

NOTES

1. Isabel Wilkerson, *The Warmth of Other Suns: The Epic Story of America's Great Migration* (New York: Random House, 2010).
2. Megan J. Wolff, "The Myth of the Actuary: Life Insurance and Fredrick L. Hoffman's *Race Traits and Tendencies of the American Negro*," *Public Health Reports* 121 (January–February 2006): 84–91.
3. James H. Jones, *Bad Blood: The Tuskegee Syphilis Experiment* (New York: Free Press, 1981).
4. Isadore S. Faulk, Margaret C. Kem, and Nathan Sinai, *The Incidence of Illness and the Receipt and Costs of Medical Care*

among Representative Families: Committee on the Cost of Medical Care Report No. 27 (Chicago: University of Chicago Press, 1933).
5. Mary L. Heen, "Ending Jim Crow Life Insurance Rates," *Northwestern Journal of Law & Social* Policy 4: 2 (2009): 360–399.
6. U.S. Department of Health and Human Services, "Healthy People 2020," http://www.healthypeople.gov/2020/default.aspx.
7. Agency for Health Care Research and Quality, *National Health Care Disparities Report 2011* (Rockville, MD: Agency for Health Care Research and Quality, 2012), http://www.ahrq.gov/research/findings/nhqrdr/nhdr11/nhdr11.pdf.

8. David Barton Smith, "Desegregating the Hospitals in Jackson, Mississippi," *Milbank Quarterly* 83: 5 (2005): 247–269.

9. Hospital Survey and Construction Act of 1964, U.S. Code, vol. 42, sec. 291e.

10. John F. Kennedy, "Special Message to Congress on Civil Rights and Job Opportunities, June 19, 1963," in *Public Papers of the Prsidents of the United States: John F. Kennedy* (Washington, DC: U.S. Government Printing Office, 1964), 492.

11. Office of Equal Health Opportunity, *Roster of Speakers, Program Staff, Consultants and Compliance Officer Trainees, Training Sessions April 4 & 5, 1966 and April 6 & 7* (Atlanta, GA: Office of Equal Health Opportunity, 1966).

12. E. H. Beardsley, "Goodbye to Jim Crow: The Desegregation of Southern Hospitals, 1945–70," *Bulletin of the History of Medicine* 60 (1986): 367–386.

13. *Public Papers of the Presidents of the United States: Lyndon Baines Johnson, 1965, Entry 546* (Washington, DC: U.S. Government Printing Office, 1966), 1037–1040.

14. *American Community Survey, 2010* (Washington, DC: U.S. Bureau of the Census, 2010).

15. *Dicennial Census, 1960* (Washington, DC: U.S. Bureau of the Census, 1960).

16. Civil Rights Act, Title VI, 1964.

17. Robert Weech-Maldanado et al., "The Consumer Assessment of Health Care Providers and Systems (CAHPS) Cultural Competence (CC) Item Set," *Medical Care* 50: 5 (2012): S22–S31.

18. Kaiser Commision on Medicaid and the Uninsured, "Immigrants' Health Care Coverage and Access," in *Key Facts* (Washington, DC: Kaiser Family Foundation, 2003).

19. Avedis Donabedian, *Exploring Quality Assessment and Monitoring: The Definition of Quality and Approaches to Its Assessment,* Vol. 1 (Ann Arbor, MI: Health Administration Press, 1980).

20. David Barton Smith, *Health Care Divided: Race and Healing a Nation* (Ann Arbor: University of Michigan Press, 1999), 225–235.

21. Martin M. Ruther and Allen Dobson, "Unequal Treatment and Unequal Benefits: A Re-examination of the Use of Medicare Services by Race: 1967–1976," *Health Care Financing Review* 2: 3 (1981): 55–83.

22. Michael E. Fix and Margery Austin Turner, eds., *A National Report Card on Discrimination in America: The Role of Testing* (Washington, DC: Urban Institute, 1998).

23. U.S. Department of Housing and Urban Development, "Racial and Ethnic Minorities Face More Subtle Housing Discrimination" (press release), June 11, 2013, http://portal.hud.gov/hudportal/HUD?src=/press/press_releases_media_advisories/2013/HUDNo.13-091.

24. Kevin A. Schulman et al., "The Effect of Race and Sex on Physicians' Recommendations for Cardiac Catheterization," *New England Journal of Medicine* 340 (1999): 618–626.

25. Nancy Krieger et al., "The Fall and Rise of US Inequalities in Premature Mortality 1960–2002," *PLOS Medicine* 5: 2 (2008): e46.

26. Douglas V. Almond, Kenneth Y. Chay, and Michael Greenstone, *The Civil Rights Act of 1964: Hospital Desegregation and Black Infant Mortality in Mississippi* (New York: Columbia University Press, 2008).

27. Haochi Zheng and Chao Zhou, *The Impact of Civil Rights Acts and Hospital Integration on Black-White Differences in Mortality: A Case Study of Motor Vehicle Accident Death Rates* (Minneapolis: University of Minnesota Press, 2009).

28. John M. Ruiz, Patrick Steffen, and Timothy B. Smith, "Hispanic Mortality Paradox: A Systematic Review and Meta-analysis of the Longitudinal Literature," *American Jounal of Public Health* 103: 3 (2012): e52–e60.

29. Alberto Palloni and Elizabeth Arias, "Paradox Lost: Explaining the Adult Hispanic Mortality Advantage," *Demography* 41: 3 (2004): 385–415.

30. David Barton Smith, *Reinventing Care: Assisted Living in New York City* (Nashville, TN: Vanderbilt University Press, 2003).

31. Barbara Starfield, "Refocusing the System," *New England Journal of Medicine* 359 (2008): 2087–2091.

32. William Faulkner, *Requiem for a Nun* (New York: Random House, 1950).

33. Theodore Parker, "Of Justice and Conscience," in *Ten Sermons on Religion* (Boston: Crosby, Nichols, 1853), 84–85.

FURTHER READING

Agency for Health Care Research and Quality. *National Health Care Disparities Report 2011.* Rockville, MD: Agency for Health Care Research and Quality, 2012. http://www.ahrq.gov/research/findings/nhqrdr/nhdr11/nhdr11.pdf.

Branch, Taylor. *Parting the Waters: America in the King Years 1954–63.* New York: Simon & Schuster, 1988.

Hoffman, Beatrix. *Health Care for Some: Rights and Rationing in the United States since 1930.* Chicago: University of Chicago Press, 2012.

Smedley, Brian, Adrienne Y. Stiths, and Alan R. Nelson, eds. *Unequal Treatment: Confronting Racial and Ethnic Disparities in Health Care.* Washington, DC: National Academies Press, 2002.

Smith, David B. *Health Care Divided: Race and Healing a Nation.* Ann Arbor: University of Michigan Press, 1999.

Wilkerson, Isabel. *The Warmth of Other Suns: The Epic Story of America's Great Migration.* New York: Random House, 2010.

chapter 22

Aging and Health Care Policy (1990s–Present)

Pamela Nadash and Edward Alan Miller

THINK ABOUT YOUR MOST RECENT VISIT TO the doctor's office. Who was in the waiting room? Chances are, it was packed with people age sixty-five and older. This imbalance, reflected in most other health care settings, shows the overwhelming influence of older people on the system. The cost of serving this population has an enormous impact on American politics and public policy, and the specific health care delivery challenges they pose also drive changes in the way services are provided.

Indeed, this trend is only just beginning. The population of people age sixty-five and older in the United States will grow rapidly over the next few decades, according to the U.S. Census. Between 2010 and 2050, it is projected to double, from 40.2 million people in 2010 to 88.5 million in 2050, increasing from 13 percent to 20 percent of the total population. Moreover, the population with the most significant health care needs—the "oldest old," eighty-five and older—will also grow rapidly, from 1.9 percent of the population in 2010 to 4.3 percent in 2050, putting ever more pressure on the nation's health care system.

THE IMPACT OF AGING ON U.S. HEALTH CARE POLICY

The aging of the population weighs most heavily on the Medicare program, which, according to the federal Centers for Medicare and Medicaid Services (CMS), constitutes 17 percent of the federal budget and exerts influence far beyond the 20 percent of national health care spending that it consumes. For example, its regulatory regime extends to any health care provider that serves Medicare beneficiaries, requiring hospitals and nursing homes, for example, to conform to Medicare requirements even if only some of their patients are covered by the program. A prominent example

is how the introduction of Medicare forced racial integration of hospitals across the south[1,2] Similarly, Medicare reimbursement policies shape reimbursement policy more generally and, for certain types of providers (e.g., home health, hospice), constitute their lifeblood, driving the industry as a whole. Although Medicare is the most obvious example, the need to serve older people has a huge impact on the policy and politics surrounding other public health programs; these include the Veterans Health Administration and publicly funded insurance for retired government employees at the local, state, and federal levels. Thus, the aging population has a critical impact on the country's public health care programs and the policies that shape them.

For most elderly Americans, the most important public health care program next to Medicare is Medicaid. Medicaid currently constitutes 7 percent of the federal budget and 23.7 percent and 16.7 percent of total and general fund expenditures, respectively, at the state level.[3] Although the majority of program recipients are women and children, a disproportionate amount of Medicaid spending is on older people, who, according to CMS, make up 10 percent of enrollees but use up about one-fourth of Medicaid dollars. As in the case of Medicare, the impact of Medicaid regulations and reimbursement strategies has an enormous effect on health care sectors that disproportionately serve older people, such as nursing homes, which consume 17 percent of Medicaid budgets. The aging population has an important impact, therefore, on Medicaid policies and politics at both the federal and state levels.

Aging also exposes critical vulnerabilities in the nation's health care system. On the one hand, public health has traditionally focused on eradicating and minimizing the impact of infectious disease and other systemic threats to health. On the other hand, medicine has focused on preventing and curing disease. Both of these approaches are inadequate to cope with the challenges of managing chronic conditions—often multiple, in older people—and maintaining or slowing declines in cognitive and functional status (an inherent part of many conditions associated with aging).

In particular, the health care system has failed to integrate the need for long-term services and supports; there is no comprehensive approach to financing such services, nor are they systematically incorporated into the health care continuum. Yet it is the challenges posed by these needs that are driving increasing costs in health care and for which the nation is so ill prepared. The history of health care policy from the 1990s onward is a story of growing recognition of these new challenges and developing mechanisms for adapting to them.

THE EVOLUTION OF THE MEDICARE PROGRAM

The classic treatment of Medicare's evolution can be found in Theodore Marmor's book *The Politics of Medicare*. Politically, there has been an ongoing battle regarding benefits expansions as well as the role the program plays in ensuring economic security among the elderly, all set against a background of intergenerational mistrust, whereby gains for one group are seen as losses for others. The pace of change in the program thus continues to reinforce one of Marmor's key themes: its incremental nature and the way in which expansions have been politically driven, rather than built on an informed response to programmatic needs. Also, as a reminder, although we automatically, and quite logically, think of Medicare when we think of aging and health care, it should be remembered that Medicare also serves a significant population of people age sixty-four and under who qualify on the basis of disability and comprise roughly 16 percent of beneficiaries. (A third, much smaller group of beneficiaries [0.7 percent] qualifies on the basis of an end stage renal disease diagnosis.)

FIGURE 22.1 **Key Legislation Discussed in This Chapter**

1989—PL 101-234 Medicare Catastrophic Coverage Repeal Act

1990—PL 101-508 Omnibus Budget Reconciliation Act (OBRA)

1997—PL 105-33 Balanced Budget Act (BBA)

2003—PL 108-173 Medicare Prescription Drug, Improvement, and Modernization Act (MMA)

2005—PL 109-171 Deficit Reduction Act (DRA)

2010—PL 111-148 Patient Protection and Affordable Care Act (PPACA) and Health Care and Education Reconciliation Act

Of course, the more recent history of the Medicare program (since the 1980s) has been dominated by the debate over the federal budget and the extent to which older people are responsible for the nation's budget deficit. It is certainly true that older people are responsible for 53 percent of entitlement spending overall,[4] with Medicare constituting a large piece of that; its costs are projected to increase substantially from roughly 3.7 percent of gross domestic product (GDP) in 2011 to 5.7 percent of GDP by 2035 and up to about 6.7 percent of GDP by 2086, according to the program's trustees. Because federal revenues are projected to increase more slowly, the gap between revenues and Medicare outlays may result in a large federal deficit. This increase in projected Medicare costs can be attributed not only to the increasing numbers of older people, but also to projected increases in per capita health care costs, which are partly attributable to the high cost of health care in old age—higher because the volume, intensity, and complexity of care increases—but are also attributable to the general upward trend in health care costs, even among younger populations. Indeed, Medicare has been more successful than commercial insurers in moderating increases in health care costs, no doubt due to the significant public policy tools available to the program.[5]

Shift to Prospective Payment

A major change to the Medicare program during the 1990s was the shift to prospective payment, where reimbursement is based on the appropriate costs of services, determined beforehand, rather than on the charges providers submit after care has been delivered. This shift aimed to rein in spending by establishing roughly uniform payment levels for defined services and by eliminating the incentive for providers to deliver more, but not better, care. In contrast to traditional fee-for-service reimbursement, providers reap financial rewards when they provide services more efficiently. This change in reimbursement policy had a substantial impact on hospitals, nursing homes, and home health agencies in particular, but also affected inpatient and outpatient rehabilitation centers. Moreover, another form of prospective payment, capitation, became more prominent as managed care came to play a larger role *in* the program.

The changes for hospitals were in fact a continuation of policies begun in the 1980s with the shift to diagnosis-related groups (DRGs) to reimburse Medicare-funded inpatient care, a shift that was extended to outpatient services in 2000 under provisions included in the 1997 Balanced Budget Act. DRGs are case-mix-adjusted rates, identifying clinically and financially similar patients, that are designed to cover all costs associated with a patient during his or her hospital stay. The shift to DRGs, along with other changes, resulted in significant reductions in hospital utilization, including reductions in the average length of stay (from 6.4 days in 1990 to 4.8 days in 2010, according to data from the Organisation for Economic Co-operation and Development). The financial incentives created by DRGs meant that it was no longer profitable for hospitals to treat certain patients and conditions, creating a need for alternative settings to handle these cases. Thus, more and more "post-acute" and specialty options became available, along with increasing pressure on nursing homes to function as short-term rehabilitation centers rather than long-term residences for people with high needs for support.

Similarly, the shift to prospective payment among nursing homes (skilled nursing facilities, or SNFs) had a significant impact. SNFs had traditionally been paid under a reasonable cost-based, retrospective system. However, between 1990 and 1997 Medicare payments for SNFs increased from $2.5 to $12 billion, according to CMS, as publicly held companies pursued profitable ancillary services, which led to rapid increases in physical, occupational, and speech therapy costs. In response, the 1997 Balanced Budget Act adopted case-mix methods under Medicare's new prospective payment system (PPS) for SNFs, beginning in 1999. Under this new system, reimbursement took the form of a fixed payment for a day of SNF resident care, adjusted for patient acuity and other factors.

As intended, prospective payment led to a sudden, dramatic decline in Medicare outlays for SNFs, by 16.2 percent in 1999. This also affected the profitability of ancillary services, resulting in financial losses among many operators, including bankruptcy of five of the nation's largest nursing home chains (representing nearly 1,800 facilities) during the late 1990s and early 2000s.[6] Due in part to perceived hardships on the part of the industry, the federal government enacted a series of Medicare "give-backs" with the Balanced Budget Refinement Act of 1999 and Benefits Improvement and Patient Protection Act of 2000, which temporarily added some of the per diem reimbursement lost by SNFs under the Balanced Budget Act. Thus, increases in SNF outlays remained in the double digits throughout the early 2000s, according to CMS.

Prospective payment was also introduced for the Medicare home health benefit, which had grown considerably during the 1990s, accounting for 10 percent of Medicare's benefit spending by 1996, according to federal data. To limit the use of the benefit as a form of long-term beneficiary support, Congress narrowed eligibility and created set payment rates for each sixty-day episode of care, regardless of the specific services delivered. This rate was adjusted for a variety of factors, most important, expected care needs and geographic location. This strategy appears to have been successful in controlling service utilization; prior to PPS, in 1996, the average number of visits per home health user was 72.6, according to CMS data. Post-PPS, it declined to 36.8 visits per user (in 2000) and has remained relatively constant, averaging 36.2 visits per home health user in 2010.

However, PPS was not necessarily effective in controlling total home health expenditures (in the Medicare fee-for-service program), which grew at an average annual rate of 8 percent between 2001 and 2011, in contrast to the program's overall average annual growth rate of 5.9 percent. This discrepancy is attributed, in part, to a shift toward more acute (and better compensated) case-mix classifications. A Congressional Research Service study of these trends also noted the increasing profit margins among home health agencies; the average margin in 2010 was 19.4 percent, up from 13.6 percent in 2003. Thus, PPS appears to have been only partly successful in moderating the cost of the home health benefit, and Congress continues to seek mechanisms for holding down its cost. This effort will likely become even more difficult following the federal court decision in *Jimmo v. Sebelius* (2012), which found Medicare's "improvement standard" illegal. This required beneficiaries to show a likelihood of medical or functional improvement before reimbursing skilled nursing and therapy services. Elimination of this standard expands eligibility to people needing services to maintain their existing health or functional status or to prevent decline, a potentially large group.

Medicare Managed Care

Of course, the most important way that prospective payment has transformed the Medicare program has been through its use of capitation payments to private managed care plans. By 2012, roughly 27 percent of all Medicare beneficiaries were enrolled. Managed care has been a part of Medicare since its inception—the original legislation allowed for "prepaid health plans"—and subsequent legislation, the Tax Equity and Fiscal Responsibility Act (TEFRA) of 1982, introduced health maintenance organizations (HMOs). It was TEFRA that enabled the true rise of managed care, resulting in the enrollment of roughly 1.6 million beneficiaries by 1992. In 1997, the Balanced Budget Act created Part C of the Medicare program, dubbed Medicare+Choice, and expanded the program to include private-fee-for-service plans and preferred provider organizations. By 1998, 6.9 million, 17.0 percent, of all Medicare beneficiaries were enrolled in 346 plans, according to CMS data. Part C was renamed Medicare Advantage with the Medicare Prescription Drug, Improvement, and Modernization Act of 2003, which created additional categories of private plans, including fee-for-service plans and managed care plans aimed at serving difficult-to-serve populations.

What accounted for the growth in managed care enrollment? From the consumer perspective, managed care had several advantages over traditional Medicare. Most important among these were the plans' lower costs and their administrative simplicity; typically, managed care plan enrollees have far less paperwork to manage. Moreover, they were comparatively inexpensive; many plans initially set premiums very low, some charging nothing on top of the Medicare Part B premium (which members pay directly to Medicare) as well as limiting cost-sharing. Under managed care, members pay a fixed amount (a copayment of $20, for example) toward doctor visits, rather than meeting a deductible and paying a coinsurance (typically 20 percent), as under traditional Medicare. Another benefit to such plans is enhanced benefits (made possible, in part, by the plans' more generous reimbursement from the government); some plans offer routine vision coverage, dental care, audiology services, and even fitness classes. Moreover, many plans included prescription drug coverage, providing beneficiaries with a much-desired benefit before the creation of Medicare Part D with the 2003 Medicare Modernization Act and saving beneficiaries from the headache of purchasing a stand-alone prescription drug plan post–Part D.

From the public policy perspective, the increasing role of managed care in Medicare has benefits that vary according to one's political point of view. Policymakers with a more market-oriented bent are attracted to managed care because of its potential to introduce market forces into Medicare, expanding choice for beneficiaries and shifting responsibility for managing the program away from government and toward the private sector. Policymakers with a more technocratic approach see an opportunity for systems improvement and are optimistic regarding managed care's potential to coordinate care, create systems change, and implement quality improvements. In addition, nearly all policymakers appreciate managed care's cost-cutting potential, although the question of whether it has in fact achieved this potential is still unresolved.

Central to the question of managed care's cost-effectiveness is the issue of how reimbursement levels are set. Reimbursement methodologies have undergone a number of shifts, reflecting differing views on the goal of managed care in the Medicare program. Under the original TEFRA legislation, payments were pegged at 95 percent of the fee-for-service equivalent, reflecting the original goal of introducing managed care: to save the program money through managing care more effectively. Subsequently, that rationale changed. The emphasis was now on expanding choice for beneficiaries by improving access to private health plans. Thus, to incentivize entry into the market, reimbursement was improved, most notably under the 2003 Medicare Modernization Act. These latter changes were a reaction to the revised payment methodologies introduced under the 1997 Balanced Budget Act, which had resulted in a wholesale withdrawal of plans from the program (from 346 in 1998 to 148 in 2003) and declining enrollment (from 6.9 million in 1998 to 5.3 million in 2003). Since the implementation of the Medicare Modernization

Act, however, enrollment has recovered, rising to 13.1 million in 2012, 27 percent of the total Medicare population.

The reimbursement changes that were put into place, however, have resulted in far higher payments to private plans. Indeed, one study found that payments to managed care organizations exceeded those for similar individuals enrolled in traditional Medicare by 14.2 percent in 2009,[7] and another calculated the total costs of these "overpayments" at $282.6 billion.[8] Provisions included in the Patient Protection and Affordable Care Act (PPACA) of 2010 sought to correct this discrepancy by introducing yet another shift in payment policy. The aim was to reduce federal payments to Medicare Advantage plans over time, bringing them in line with the average costs of care under traditional Medicare, thus saving the government an estimated $11 billion annually. Naturally, beneficiaries accustomed to the comparatively generous benefits available under Advantage plans see such reductions as benefit cuts.

The Adequacy of Medicare Coverage

If a key goal of the Medicare program is to protect beneficiaries from the financial risk that ill health imposes, rather than merely to provide basic health care coverage, then it is important to consider how much older adults actually spend on health care. From this perspective, the burden is ever increasing, with a Kaiser Family Foundation analysis of CMS's Medicare Current Beneficiary survey indicating median out-of-pocket health spending as a share of income increasing over time: from 12 percent in 1997 to 16 percent in 2006. Legislative changes under the PPACA only moderate this expanding burden, which is projected to exceed 25 percent by 2020.

This increase in out-of-pocket spending has occurred despite significant coverage expansions, several of which focused on increasing eligibility for low-income elders, often shifting costs to state Medicaid programs. Another eligibility expansion affected mostly younger people with disabilities, under the Ticket to Work and Work Incentives Improvements Act of 1999, which allowed certain working disabled people to retain eligibility.

Benefit coverage was also expanded. Most expansions were fairly minor. The Omnibus Budget Reconciliation Act of 1990 introduced coverage for screening mammography and partial hospitalization in community mental health centers. A major expansion, however, was created under the 2003 Medicare Modernization Act, which provided a new outpatient prescription drug benefit beginning in 2006. This benefit recognized the increasingly important role of medication in health care and the significant financial burden that it had come to place on older people. The legislation was also revolutionary in that it relied solely on private stand-alone prescription drug insurance plans, in accordance with the George W. Bush (2001–2009) administration's commitment to private sector solutions, a first in the Medicare program, where beneficiaries' right to "freedom of choice" has always meant the right to choose traditional Medicare. The PPACA built on these changes by making the cost-sharing built into Part D less onerous and by covering certain preventive services at no charge, including a yearly wellness visit, tobacco use cessation counseling, and screening for cancer, diabetes, and other chronic diseases.

Given these expansions, particularly the new drug benefit, which had contributed substantially to lowering beneficiaries' out-of-pocket burden, it can be unclear how out-of-pocket spending (calculated as a proportion of income) has remained so high. One important reason is the program's premium and cost-sharing arrangements. The bulk of out-of-pocket payments, 40 percent, are toward premiums; the Medicare Modernization Act increased Part B premiums for higher income individuals and imposed a new premium when it introduced Part D plans.[9] Deductibles, copayments, and coinsurance requirements also constitute significant obligations. These are seen as playing an important role in restraining utilization; indeed, policymakers are currently trying to overhaul Medigap supplemental insurance plans that people buy to protect themselves from these obligations (that is, deductibles and other cost-sharing), which have been associated with higher Medicare costs.[10] However, it is important to note that long-term services and supports constitute the next largest component of out-of-pocket spending, making up 19 percent of the median cost, a proportion that increases with age.

Coordinating Care for High-Cost Populations

Policy attention has focused on high-cost populations in the hope that marginal changes among these groups will cut costs considerably. Thus, there has been a focus on dual-eligible Medicare beneficiaries who also qualify for Medicaid on the basis of their low incomes and disability levels. Although their Medicare insurance is primary, state Medicaid programs supplement it, covering premiums and other cost-sharing obligations and providing services not covered by Medicare (such as long-term care). According to the Kaiser Family Foundation analysis of CMS data, this group comprised only 20 percent of the Medicare population in 2008 but consumed 31 percent of program expenditures; they also comprised 15 percent of the Medicaid population while using up 39 percent of its funding, with most (69 percent) going toward long-term services and supports. Average spending for duals is nearly twice as high as for other Medicare beneficiaries, with federal and state spending totaling $320 billion in 2011. This population is frail—55 percent have multiple chronic conditions as well as physical (44 percent) and cognitive (54 percent) impairment—and deficiencies in their care are widely acknowledged. Thus, there appears to

be considerable potential for providing more cost-effective, high-quality care by better coordinating Medicare and Medicaid services.

The primary mechanism for increasing coordination has been through specialized Medicare Advantage plans, known as Special Needs Plans (SNPs), authorized under the 2003 Medicare Modernization Act. Although SNPs enroll three Medicare subgroups—the dual-eligible, institutionalized beneficiaries, and those with severe or disabling chronic conditions—83 percent of enrollees (1.4 million) are in dual-eligible plans, known as D-SNPs, according to CMS data. Some D-SNPs genuinely improve service delivery, often by working with Medicaid managed care organizations to deliver a coordinated package of care, including long-term services and supports. However, most do not, resulting in legislation in the 2008 Medicare Improvements for Patients and Providers Act that required new or expanding D-SNPs to contract with state Medicaid agencies to develop such relationships. Despite this change, only about one-third of D-SNP contracts reviewed by the U.S. Government Accountability Office in 2012 contained any provisions for benefit integration, and only about one-fifth provided for active care coordination between D-SNPs and Medicaid agencies, indicating poor D-SNP performance on care integration.

The SNP program notwithstanding, several examples of good practice in care coordination do exist, the most notable of which is the Program for All-Inclusive Care for the Elderly (PACE), which combines capitation payments from both Medicare and Medicaid to deliver health and long-term care services to individuals needing a nursing home level of care. These bundled payments allow PACE to provide a broad range of services using multidisciplinary care teams. Although PACE began as a demonstration project, the 1997 Balanced Budget Act established the model as a permanent entity under the Medicare program. Unfortunately, while the PACE model has been found to deliver high-quality care, it has not been shown to save money.[11] Programs that attempt to improve care coordination under traditional fee-for-service arrangements have had similar results: the Medicare Coordinated Care Demonstration, for example, found that financial gains resulting from reduced rates of hospitalization were insufficient to offset intervention costs.[12]

Despite this history, the federal government is investing heavily in care coordination. The PPACA created a Federal Coordinated Health Care Office within CMS to identify how Medicare and Medicaid might work jointly to improve care. It also created the Center for Medicare and Medicaid Innovation to test payment and service delivery models that reduce costs while preserving quality. Together, the two centers have committed $1 billion to assess various care coordination strategies and incentives. While this focus on integrating care is impressive, there is concern that managed care organizations lack the expertise and capacity to care for this frail, difficult population. Their inexperience, coupled with CMS's requirement to demonstrate cost savings, suggests that managed care organizations might resort to more reliable methods of cost-cutting (such as service denials and favorable selection) rather than risk the uncertain benefits of innovation. Thus, the PPACA's emphasis on rigorous evaluation (as well as on related data collection efforts) is welcome. Other PPACA provisions promote experimentation with other forms of bundled payments to encourage providers to better handle transitions across service settings and reduce rehospitalizations.

Improving Care at the End of Life

Just as improvements in care coordination are driven by twin motivations, to save money and improve quality of care, so too are improvements to end-of-life care. Pragmatists will point to the savings potential represented by the estimated 32 percent of Medicare dollars spent in the last two years of life. However, most emphasize quality of life issues: patients and family members repeatedly report insufficient treatment of pain, inadequate emotional support, and poor physician communication. Most important, care at the end of life routinely fails to respect patient and family preferences, often by subjecting patients to unwanted costly, futile, and invasive treatments. Too often, older people die alone in hospitals, receiving medical treatments that they neither understood nor wanted.

From a health policy perspective, there are two primary dimensions of end-of-life care: palliative care and hospice care. Palliative care is an approach that focuses on reducing suffering; it may supplement, rather than replace, traditional curative treatment, and it is not solely provided at the end of life. Models vary but typically involve hospital-based multidisciplinary teams, which work with patients to provide symptom relief, identify patient goals, help patients make complex medical decisions, and provide practical, spiritual, and psychosocial support. Since the National Hospice Study established in the early 1980s that palliative care was effective in reducing costs and relieving suffering, it has become increasingly integrated into health care, but it still has a long way to go. The National Palliative Care Research Center, for example, estimates that half of all hospitals lack a palliative care program and that $6 billion in savings annually could be realized if penetration of palliative care increased to 90 percent of hospitals. In addition, too few doctors receive training in palliation.

In contrast, hospice is a Medicare benefit, added to the program in 1982. To qualify, patients must be expected to live for six months or less and abjure curative treatment for their terminal condition (but not for other conditions). The benefit's goal is to provide comfort care at the end of life, using a range of medical and other professionals. Although the hospice benefit has become increasingly well used (with an estimated 44 percent of all deaths occurring in hospice), it has several problems. First, patients often enter it too late and fail to get the maximum benefit; nearly two-thirds are enrolled for fewer than thirty days. Second, hospice seems to be particularly vulnerable to fraud.

To ensure that patient preferences are honored, advocates have experimented with a variety of legal tools, most of which are subject to state law. Most well known are advance directives. These include do-not-resuscitate orders, which specify the circumstances under which resuscitation should not be delivered; living wills, which provide guidance on general preferences about end-of-life care; and health care proxies and durable powers of attorney, which delegate medical decision making to specified individuals. However, studies routinely show that even where such instruments are utilized, they are ineffective, often because health care providers are unaware that they exist or decision makers fail to observe them. More recently, states have experimented with a different mechanism, known as MOLST or POLST (medical or physician order for life-sustaining treatment). Its distinguishing characteristic is that it is a standing medical order designed to follow the patient from treatment setting to treatment setting; in Oregon, the state that has implemented them most widely, these mechanisms have been found to be effective and reduce costs.

EVOLUTION OF THE MEDICAID PROGRAM

The story of aging and health care policy in the Medicaid program largely concerns the story of long-term services and supports. As noted previously, nearly a quarter of Medicaid spending goes toward older people. Of this, most goes toward long-term care; the remainder wraps around Medicare benefits, including covering premium and other cost-sharing requirements. (Prior to the Medicare Modernization Act, Medicaid also picked up the cost of prescription drug benefits.) State-level policymakers have little leverage over this latter category of expense, but do have a great deal of authority over long-term care. Consequently, there has been significant policy activity related to long-term care since the early 1990s, concentrated in two main areas: (1) a move toward reducing the role of nursing homes in long-term care, primarily by creating Medicaid-funded alternatives (often known as "rebalancing"), and (2) a continuing effort to ensure the quality of care provided to vulnerable populations receiving long-term services and supports.

To a certain degree, these two efforts are intertwined: home- and community-based services (HCBS) are considered by many to be of better quality almost by definition, because they are consistent with the majority preference to "age in place." Surveys regularly find that people in need of long-term services and supports prefer to remain in the least restrictive settings possible, as long as possible, typically by living at home, in a family member's home, or in an assisted living facility—rarely in a nursing home (typically less than 5 percent of those surveyed). Yet the primary objection to nursing homes is their high cost, which, according to the 2012 MetLife Market Survey, averaged $81,030 a year for a semi-private room and $90,520 for a private room. This compares to the $42,600 average yearly cost for assisted living, $18,200 for five days of adult day services and $29,120 to $30,576 for twenty-eight hours per week of homemaker, companion, and/or home health services. Policymakers have therefore taken several approaches to limit nursing home use.

The Shift away from Nursing Homes

By 1996, nursing homes accounted for 20 percent of Medicaid expenditures.[13] Thus, one of the first targets of policy attention in the 1990s was the 1980 Boren Amendment, the basis of much successful litigation by nursing homes,[14] due to its requirement that states set Medicaid payments for nursing facilities at rates that were reasonable and adequate to cover the costs of "efficiently and economically" operated facilities. The 1997 Balanced Budget Act repealed the Boren Amendment, aiming to increase state discretion over reimbursement. The repeal allowed states to exert downward pressure on reimbursement in the years following repeal,[15] although perhaps not as much as the nursing home industry had feared, due both to state concerns about quality and to the booming economy and budgetary surpluses of the late 1990s, which in fact led to some program expansions.

The financial troubles of the 2000s hit nursing homes hard. Both the recession of 2003 and the Great Recession of 2008 led to rising unemployment and higher Medicaid enrollment, just as state revenues dropped, placing extreme pressure on state Medicaid budgets. The Deficit Reduction Act of 2005 increased this pressure by reducing federal Medicaid spending by $26.5 billion over ten years. However, by 2009, the situation became so dire that Congress passed the American Recovery and Reinvestment Act of 2009, which enhanced federal Medicaid funding (by $87 billion) and provided a more limited extension of such support through June 2011. Meanwhile, states used a variety of strategies to cut nursing home costs. Although payment formulae limited nursing home reimbursement reductions to some extent, many states froze or reduced them. States also lowered bed hold payments, tightened eligibility requirements, and instituted certificate-of-need programs. The latter require state regulatory approval for the establishment or expansion of nursing homes, and/or moratoriums on new nursing home beds, on the assumption that empty beds tend to filled, regardless of genuine need. Such supply-side restrictions have fallen out of favor, although they remain on the books, as policymakers are shifting toward other methods of restraining utilization.

The Shift toward Home- and Community-based Services

The most popular strategy for restraining the cost of long-term care services and supports was to shift service delivery away from nursing homes; policymakers generally believed that, compared to nursing homes, HCBS are cost-effective. Clearly, per capita costs are substantially lower for those receiving HCBS than for institutional care. However, total costs are reduced only if the expense of expanding HCBS is less than the money saved through reduced nursing home expenditures. The question of the fiscal impact of expanding HCBS is a hotly debated one. Some studies show that such programs increase expenditures by serving people who are not at risk of nursing home care.[16] Others find that HCBS are in fact preventive of nursing home admission and save money,[17] while yet others find such services budget-neutral.[18] On balance, evidence supports the existence of a "woodwork effect" (whereby people claim services they might not otherwise have claimed) although its impact on budgets is unclear. Regardless, HCBS may be justified on grounds other than cost-saving potential, based on other perceived benefits, such as improved quality of life.[19]

Discussing the woodwork effect inevitably forces consideration of how public spending for long-term services and supports is justified. If people could get by without such support, why spend public money on it? This issue becomes even more complicated when we consider the role of family caregivers, known as "informal care" (in contrast to paid, "formal" care) because, it is assumed, formal care substitutes for informal, though little evidence supports this assumption. Such substitution is viewed as a bad thing if it makes family members less likely to take care of their own but a good thing if it enables caregivers to engage in paid employment (thus contributing to the tax base). In either case, informal care remains by far the most common source of support; at $450 billion in 2009, its estimated cost dwarfs the costs of all formal long-term care combined.[20]

The design of the Medicaid program has historically meant that nursing homes were the primary, if not the only, source of long-term services and supports. The original legislation made access to nursing home care, but not HCBS, an entitlement. States can use two primary mechanisms to provide Medicaid HCBS: using the optional personal care benefit or waiving sections of the Social Security Act (1915[c], which provides federal authority for HCBS for aged, disabled, and developmentally disabled populations, or 1115, which provides federal authority for broad-based research and demonstration projects, including, potentially,

HCBS). Many states went the waiver route, due to the wider range of services that could be provided (not just personal care) as well as the greater program control allowed (populations could be closely defined and services could be limited to certain areas of the state). Whichever route was chosen, the shift has been considerable: In 1990, 13 percent of the $32 billion Medicaid long-term care budget went toward HCBS, according to CMS data, while in 2009, 43 percent of the $122 billion directed toward long-term care did so. However, there is significant interstate variation: in 2009, some states spent as little as 10 percent of their Medicaid long-term care spending on HCBS waiver services, while others spent as much as 65 percent. Some states also operate state-only funded programs, comprising 5 percent of total spending on HCBS.

A particularly important moment in the shift toward HCBS was the Supreme Court decision in *Olmstead v. L.C.* (1999). The Court ruled that using public funds to care for disabled individuals in institutional settings violates the Americans with Disabilities Act of 1990, if these individuals could appropriately be treated in a "less restrictive environment," such as a home or community-based care setting.[21] Subsequently, the Bush administration launched its 2001 New Freedom Initiative, which outlined the federal government's approach to helping state and local governments meet the *Olmstead* requirements. These trends were taken even further in the 2005 Deficit Reduction Act, which contained several provisions promoting the expansion of Medicaid HCBS (see Table 22.1).

Broadening access to HCBS meant not only finding mechanisms to finance services, but also developing an infrastructure of providers and programs to deliver services. On the one hand, this has meant experimenting with ways to increase access to community-based options such as adult foster care, adult day services, and assisted living. On the other, it has meant other kinds of experimentation. Among

TABLE 22.1 **Key Home- and Community-Based Services Initiatives**

Medicaid Program	Authorizing Legislation	Enables States to
HCBS Waiver, §1915(c)	OBRA 1981	Provide HCBS to state-specified target group(s) of Medicaid beneficiaries meeting an institutional level-of-care requirement
Personal Care Benefit	Title XIX SSA	Opt to cover personal care as a state plan service
Managed Care Waiver, §1915(b)	OBRA 1981	Waive freedom of choice in Medicaid and require individuals to receive services through managed care plans
Medicaid HCBS, §1915(i)	DRA 2005	Opt to cover HCBS as a state plan service
Program of All-Inclusive Care for the Elderly, 1934(a)(3)(B)	BBA 1997	Pay PACE programs as a permanently recognized provider type under Medicaid (§1894(a)(3)(B) does this under Medicare)
Research and Demonstration Waiver, §1115	PWA 1962	Design experimental pilot projects aimed at better administering and promoting the goals of Medicaid
Self-Directed Personal Assistance Services, §1915(j)	DRA 2005	Offer self-directed personal assistance services as part of their state plan personal care benefit or HCBS waiver
Grants Program		**Funds States to**
Cash and Counseling	Line-item appropriation	Test the use of individualized budgets to deliver HCBS rather than services in kind
Money Follows the Person	DRA 2005	Transition Medicaid enrolled nursing home residents to the community (using $1.75 billion in federal funding)
Real Choice Systems Change Grants	Line-item appropriation	Develop the necessary regulatory, administrative, program, and funding infrastructure to rebalance their LTSS systems
Independence Plus	Line-item appropriation	Establish waiver or demonstration projects that give beneficiaries greater control over LTSS
State Balancing Incentive Payments	PPACA 2010	Accept extra money if their current Medicaid spending for community-based LTSS is less than that for LTSS in facilities
Community First	PPACA 2010	Expand HCBS offerings by providing an enhanced federal matching rate

NOTES: OBRA = Omnibus Budget Reconciliation Act; BBA = Balanced Budget Act; DRA = Deficit Reduction Act; PPACA = Patient Protection and Affordable Care Act; PWA = Public Welfare Amendments; LTSS = long-term services and supports.

the most notable was the Cash & Counseling Demonstration and Evaluation, which was conducted from 1998 to 2001.[22,23] Under consumer-directed care (also known as participant- or self-directed care), recipients are given an individualized budget over which they have control, rather than receiving services through agencies only. This budget can be used to pay for services, including personal care attendants (who can be relatives or neighbors), care supplies, assistive devices, and home modifications. Results from the demonstration were generally positive and the model has subsequently been expanded to fifteen states, with yet more states operating modified versions of the consumer-directed approach. Other innovations include the integrated care experiments mentioned previously in the section on dual-eligibles.

INDIVIDUAL OPTIONS FOR FINANCIAL PROTECTION

Few retirees report being very confident in having enough money to pay for either medical (24 percent) or long-term care expenses (18 percent) in retirement, figures that decline to 13 percent and 9 percent, respectively, among current workers.[24] Indeed, only about two-thirds of either retirees or workers report that they or their spouse has saved for retirement. Moreover, even among savers, the levels are low, in terms of both the proportion of workers and retirees that reports less than $1,000 in savings and investments (30 percent and 28 percent, respectively) and the proportion that reports less than $25,000 (60 percent and 55 percent). Thus, not only does the current population of elders lack sufficient resources to cover the catastrophic costs associated with long-term illness or disability, but so too does the population of future retirees.

Medigap Supplemental Insurance

Medicare has substantial coinsurance and deductible requirements and, until recently, lacked coverage for prescription drugs and preventive care. All but 12 percent of beneficiaries have therefore obtained supplemental coverage to help pay for Medicare cost-sharing, according to the Kaiser Family Foundation analysis of the Medicare Current Beneficiary Survey, including deductibles for Parts A and B ($1,184 and $147, respectively, in 2013) and 20 percent coinsurance for Part B. Sources of supplemental coverage include employer-sponsored benefits (25 percent), Medicaid (14 percent), Medicare Advantage (14 percent), or some combination thereof (10 percent). Sources of supplemental coverage also include private supplemental insurance, known widely as Medigap (24 percent); some Medigap policyholders (9 percent) combine Medigap coverage with other supplements such as an employer plan, Medicare Advantage, and/or Medicaid.

As employers have become increasingly less likely to offer retiree health benefits (coverage dropped from 66

percent to 25 percent between 1988 and 2012, according to the Kaiser Family Foundation/HRET Employer Health Benefits Survey), the private Medigap market has become more important. Initially, these plans were regulated by states, in most cases rather laxly, resulting in widespread consumer dissatisfaction and serious scandals. A national set of voluntary minimum standards was introduced under the 1980 federal "Baucus Amendments," but ongoing problems prompted further legislation in 1990 and 1994 to standardize the market (by requiring plans to conform to ten standard designs with precisely defined benefits) and to shift regulation from the states to the federal level. The goal was to simplify consumer choice, promote competition, and provide consumer protections. Subsequent legislation introduced plans with high deductibles, cost-sharing, and limits on annual out-of-pocket payments. However, Medicare program expansions mean that Medigap plans no longer need to provide coverage for prescription drugs and basic preventive services.

Private Long-Term Care Financing

In contrast to the robust Medigap market, the private long-term care insurance market is struggling. Although long-term care is precisely the kind of high-cost, low-probability risk that should spur people to buy insurance coverage, few Americans have taken steps to protect themselves against its potentially catastrophic costs. Just 5.7 percent to 7.4 percent of people age forty-five years or older had private long-term care insurance in 2010, despite the fact that an estimated 49 percent of those eighteen years or older could qualify and afford such coverage.[25] Thus, Medicaid and other public programs remained the primary payers for the nation's $207.9 billion long-term care bill in 2010 (paying 62.2 percent and 4.4 percent, respectively),[26] while 21.9 percent was paid out of pocket and 11.6 percent through long-term care insurance and other private sources.

Several explanations for the lethargic market are proposed. First, people are in denial; they avoid thinking about frailty and disability in old age and do little to prepare for it.[27] Second, many mistakenly believe that Medicare or private health insurance covers long-term services and supports.[28] Third, the policies themselves are off-putting; they must be kept in force for many years before any benefits are drawn, and they offer a myriad of choices regarding the daily benefit amount, waiting period, length of coverage, inflation protection, and other dimensions. They are also expensive. Although the average annual premium was $2,268 in 2010, that increases as purchasers age, up to $3,294 for people who buy at ages 70–74. Moreover, premiums are rising rapidly; for people aged 55–64, the average premium rose from $1,877 in 2005 to $2,255 in 2010.[29] Medical underwriting also eliminates as many as 15 percent to 20 percent of applicants, because they already have support needs or a preexisting condition that puts them at high risk for needing such supports.[30]

Insurers themselves have been under a great deal of stress. Some major carriers—Metlife, CUNA Mutual, CNA, Berkshire, Prudential Financial, Unum—have pulled out of the private long-term care insurance market altogether. Others—Genworth, John Hancock, Transamerica—have increased premiums, tightened underwriting, and/or emphasized more limited product lines, driving away potential customers. By 2010, there were just eleven companies selling meaningful numbers of long-term care insurance policies, down from more than one hundred in 2002.[31] This stress stems from a lower-than-expected number of lapsed policies and from near zero interest rates, which have lowered investment returns. The decline in the long-term care insurance market is worrying due to the lack of alternative public solutions to the long-term care financing problem. Instead, policymakers have focused on promoting private insurance as well as modest initiatives to spur personal planning, such as the "Own Your Future" long-term care awareness campaign launched in 2005 by CMS in collaboration with several states. Private insurance also became an employment benefit for federal employees and retirees. Additionally, the Health Insurance Portability and Accountability Act of 1996 provided tax clarification and minimum standards for private long-term care insurance policies, and the 2005 Deficit Reduction Act expansion of the Long-Term Care Partnership Program allowed individuals in participating states to protect substantially more assets when qualifying for Medicaid if they had previously purchased a private policy.

Policymakers also sought to ensure that potential Medicaid recipients had exhausted all their assets before qualifying for coverage. Currently, Medicaid rules prevent anyone found transferring assets for less than full market value for purposes of meeting Medicaid eligibility requirements from qualifying for coverage for a period of time. One of the 2005 Deficit Reduction Act's more controversial provisions tightened Medicaid eligibility rules regarding asset transfers, including extending the look-back period from three to five years and excluding individuals with more than $500,000 in home equity from qualifying for Medicaid coverage (up to $750,000 if a state chose), unless a spouse or child with a disability lived there. Previously, Medicaid disregarded the full value of an applicant's primary residence. The pertinence of such provisions is questionable, since few Medicaid applicants have significant assets.

The Community Living Assistance Services and Supports Act

The first broad-based, national proposal to address the financial risks posed by long-term care was the Community Living Assistance Services and Supports (CLASS) Act, a federally administered, voluntary, long-term care insurance. First introduced in Congress in November 2005 by the late Senator Edward M. Kennedy (D-MA, in office 1962–2009), CLASS was passed as part of the PPACA but was eventually abandoned. Unlike private plans, the program would not screen out those most at risk for using the program's modest lifetime benefit; premiums would have varied solely on the basis of age, with highly subsidized coverage being provided to the working poor and full-time students. To receive benefits, enrollees would have had to contribute five years of premiums, during three of which they would have been required to earn enough income to be credited for one quarter of Social Security benefits ($1,120 in 2011). At least two or three activities of daily living impairments, cognitive impairment, or their equivalent would have been required to receive benefits.

Despite its promise, CLASS had several major weaknesses, not the least of which was the voluntary nature of the program. Without a mandate, program actuaries could not find a way to make the program financially self-sustaining (as required by law). Because high-risk individuals are more likely to purchase insurance, the cost of premiums needed to cover program benefits would have been so high that lower risk individuals would have been deterred from purchasing, which would have led to even higher premiums, fewer lower risk subscribers, and so on. In addition, CLASS administration costs were limited to no more than 3 percent of premiums paid, an additional challenge.

For these reasons, implementation of the CLASS Act was suspended indefinitely by the Obama (2009–) administration on October 14, 2011, and repealed on January 2, 2013. In its place new legislation established a long-term care commission charged with developing and submitting a comprehensive plan for "the establishment, implementation, and financing of a comprehensive, coordinated, and high quality system that ensures the availability of long-term services and supports" to all those who need it.

IMPROVING THE QUALITY OF LONG-TERM SERVICES AND SUPPORTS

Quality is a perennial issue in long-term care. Persistent problems include a small but unacceptable proportion of residents that continue to experience actual harm due to poor care, government surveys designed to monitor care that routinely understate problems resulting in resident harm, government sanctions aimed at poor-quality homes that seldom go into effect, homes that cycle in and out of compliance, and federal oversight that is often inconsistent and limited in scope and effectiveness. Quality assurance in home-based settings poses even more significant challenges given the decentralized nature of service delivery. Thus, government has attempted a variety of methods for ensuring

The Demise of the CLASS Act

On October 14, 2012, U.S. Department of Health and Human Services (HHS) Secretary Kathleen Sebelius forwarded *A Report on the Actuarial, Marketing, and Legal Analyses of the CLASS Program* to Congress. In her transmittal letter, Secretary Sebelius reported that the Obama administration would not move forward with the CLASS program because it could not certify its financial viability as required by law.

> For 19 months, experts inside and outside of government have examined how HHS might implement a financially sustainable, voluntary, and self-financed long-term care insurance program under the law. . . . But despite our best analytical efforts, I do not see a viable path forward for CLASS implementation at this time.
>
> Because of [concerns about CLASS's viability] Congress required me to design a plan that would be actuarially sound and financially solvent for at least 75 years. The provision protected both taxpayers and beneficiaries. After all, if CLASS failed, no one would be hurt more than those who would pay into it and would be counting on it the most.
>
> With this in mind, experts across HHS . . . have worked steadily to find a path forward on CLASS. We have undertaken a methodical and comprehensive analysis of the statute and plan design options. We have broadly considered how to design potential benefit structures and reviewed those designs carefully to determine if they meet the twin tests of solvency and consistency with the law. We hired a chief actuary for the CLASS Office, engaged with other government actuaries, and worked with two outside actuarial firms in order to maximize the reliability of solvency estimates. I am proud of the careful and thorough approach that we have taken, engaging talented professionals across the Department and in the private sector.
>
> In [the attached report], you will find the results of our actuarial and policy analyses of the CLASS Act along with our legal analysis of multiple plan design options. While the report does not identify a benefit plan that I can certify as both actuarially sound for the next 75 years and consistent with the statutory requirements, it reflects the development of information that will ultimately advance the cause of finding affordable and sustainable long-term care options.
>
> The challenge that CLASS was created to address is not going away. By 2020, we know that an estimated 15 million Americans will need some kind of long-term care and fewer than three percent have a long-term care policy. These Americans are our family, our friends and our neighbors. If they are to live productive and independent lives, we need to make sure that they have access to the long-term care supports that make that possible.
>
> We also know that left unaddressed, long-term care costs to taxpayers will only increase. Without insurance coverage or the personal wealth to pay large sums in their later years, more Americans with disabilities will rely on Medicaid services once their assets are depleted, putting further strain on State and Federal budgets.
>
> The CLASS program seeks to address the critical need that Americans have for affordable long-term care services. The current market does not offer viable options for those unable to access private long-term care insurance. We look forward to continuing our work with you and your colleagues in Congress, consumer advocates, health care providers, insurers and other stakeholders to find solutions that ensure all Americans have the choices that best meet their needs.

SOURCE: "Secretary Sebelius' Letter to Congress about CLASS," October 14, 2011, http://www.ltcconsultants.com/articles/2011/class-dismissed/Sebelius-CLASS-Letter.pdf.

the quality of long-term services and supports, beginning with a fairly heavy-handed regulatory approach (most apparent in the plethora of regulations surrounding nursing homes) and shifting toward a more outcomes-based approach that integrates financial incentives with increased transparency regarding performance.

OBRA-Era Monitoring and Standards

In the late-1980s, the Institute of Medicine and the U.S. General Accounting Office produced strongly worded reports on nursing home quality, finding it "shockingly deficient."[32,33] In response, Congress passed the Nursing Home Reform Act, contained within the Omnibus Budget Reconciliation Act of 1987. Building on the previous infrastructure of standards and certification, the law continued the existing system—in which quality was periodically monitored through a survey process, resulting in deficiency citations where appropriate—but mandated new, higher standards of care, including minimum staffing regulations and quality-of-care monitoring with greater emphasis on resident outcomes and quality of life.[34] The Nursing Home Reform Act also established a new, more stringent enforcement system that better linked sanctions to the severity of the deficiency actions. Development of a Resident Assessment Instrument (RAI) was mandated as well. These changes went into effect in 1995, though they continued to evolve as the certification process changed and measurement techniques and data availability improved.

However, the impact of these provisions depends on enforcement, which has varied over time and across states. State inspectors are responsible for periodically surveying all nursing homes participating in Medicare or Medicaid, using a federally stipulated survey protocol. During the late 1990s, all states were more likely to cite their facilities for deficiencies contributing to actual harm or immediate jeopardy,[35] possibly due to the increased emphasis placed on regulatory enforcement under the Clinton administration.[36] This period also witnessed a proliferation of studies and reports identifying problems with the quality of nursing home care and the strategies necessary to improve it.[37,38] Subsequently, the rate of deficiency citations declined under the Bush administration, apparently due to a shift in the intensity of regulatory oversight as state inspectors downgraded the severity of deficiencies identified.[39] Other reports found considerable interstate inconsistencies in how surveys are conducted as well as understatement of serious quality problems.[40] Thus, the integrity of the survey process is an ongoing issue.

The Increased Role of Data

Other quality improvement efforts depend on having reliable data about patient status and outcomes. In nursing homes, the RAI system was implemented in 1998, aiming to improve quality by requiring nursing homes to develop individualized care plans, protocols for follow-up care, and algorithms to trigger residents' potential care needs. A key component is the Minimum Data Set (MDS), which, at defined intervals, describes the clinical conditions and needs of residents. This information is used to develop case-mix reimbursement, which adjusts nursing home payments on the basis of resident acuity, incentivizes providers to serve more resource intensive individuals, and monitors patients and report provider performance. Similarly, in the home health sector, the Outcome and Assessment Information Set is a standardized assessment instrument mandated by CMS for home health recipients, which is used in much the same way. In addition, state Medicaid agencies often administer their own assessment instruments to monitor patient and program performance in state-funded programs. Thus, the role of data, and techniques for collecting and using it, has expanded dramatically since the beginning of the 1990s.

An important way these data are being used is to increase public reporting of performance. For example, CMS launched the Nursing Home Compare website in 2002, which provides public information about the quality of care provided by nursing homes certified to treat Medicare and Medicaid patients.[41] Information posted on the site is based on the MDS, annual inspections, and staffing levels, and is updated on a quarterly basis. The site has evolved, adding separate scores for health inspections, staffing, and quality as well as a five-star rating system. Several states have established their own report cards as well. Similarly, the Home Health Compare website publishes information on home health agencies. Both of these efforts have occurred within the context of CMS-sponsored quality improvement initiatives addressing the industries as a whole.[42,43]

Data are also critical to experiments with pay-for-performance (P4P) in nursing homes, which seek to motivate quality improvement by tying reimbursement, in part, to performance on quality and efficiency measures. By 2010, there were fourteen states with planned or existing P4P programs.[44] On the Medicare side, CMS launched the Nursing Home Value-Based Purchasing Demonstration in 2009. Certain PPACA provisions promote P4P as well, and the law also includes provisions aiming to improve transparency in the nursing home sector, especially regarding disclosure of more detailed information about ownership, staffing, and expenditures.

Meanwhile, in the HCBS sector, the science of quality assurance is still under development. Traditionally, states receiving waivers have needed to provide CMS with several quality assurances, but how these assurances are met is up to each state (although subject to federal approval). Thus, there is no mandated reporting tool and states have considerable discretion in the data items they report and the methods used for monitoring. The need for far more work in this area is evidenced by a 2010 HHS Office of the Inspector General report, which found that seven out of twenty-five states studied did not have adequate quality assurance systems in place.

Nursing Home Litigation

One reason for the PPACA emphasis on transparency in the nursing home sector is the growing adoption of opaque ownership structures, which is in part a response to the rise in nursing home industry lawsuits. Traditionally the rate of litigation against nursing homes for negligence was quite low, compared to other providers. This began to change in the mid- to late 1990s, particularly in states such as Texas and Florida, which constituted more than half of the litigation identified in 2001.[45] During that time 88 percent of cases were settled and average recovery amounts reached $406,000 nationally. Indeed, the number of lawsuits in Florida increased rapidly, rising from 404 in 1997 to 752 in 2001 (in one sample of 2,378 nursing homes in forty-five states).[46]

Although certain types of nursing homes are more likely to be sued than others, it is unclear whether litigation effectively targets poor-quality facilities. Thus, while Johnson et al.[47] found that certain nursing homes—that is, larger for-profit homes with lower staffing levels and higher numbers of deficiencies located in states with residents' rights statutes—were more likely to experience a lawsuit, others found that the effect of quality on a home's risk of being sued was small.[48] More recently, litigation appears less frequent, possibly due to state statutes discouraging it and the formation of nursing home ownership structures aimed in part at limiting liability risk.[49] This is reflected in the average number of claims filed against the nation's five largest nursing home chains, which declined to 0.3 per 1,000 residents annually in 2006 from 1.5 annually in 1998.

The Culture Change Movement

A particularly important quality improvement innovation has been the "culture change" movement, which evolved in response to the perception that nursing homes are cold, clinical places where residents' needs come second to facility operators and staff. Culture change requires providers to adopt leadership processes, organizational redesigns, and environmental enhancements that allow facilities to respond to the values and preferences of care recipients. Two major components of this shift include elevating the role of direct care workers (who know their clients best) and transforming the physical plant into a more homelike environment.[50] The culture change movement officially began in 1997, after the first meeting of what is now known as the Pioneer Network,[51] and has evolved to include models such as the Eden Alternative, the Wellspring, and the Green House models. The movement was bolstered by support from CMS. First, it developed Quality Improvement Organizations in 2002, which worked with nursing homes to design and implement quality improvement projects. These increasingly adopted the tenets of the culture change movement, leading to increased media coverage and financial support from funders and a greater focus on both organization and clinical processes. CMS also launched a voluntary effort for quality improvement (the Advancing Excellence in America's Nursing Homes campaign), with nursing home participation growing from more than 3,000 facilities initially to 7,600 by 2009, supported by forty-nine Local Area Networks for Excellence in nearly every state, which were established to provide peer support, information, best practices, and technical systems.

INFLUENCE OF THE ELDERLY ON HEALTH POLITICS AND POLICY

A perennial question is the extent to which older people constitute a coherent political force. Certainly, there is a widely held perception, promoted in the media, that the

Senior citizens enjoy lunch in an assisted living facility, which serves adults who need help with everyday tasks—such as dressing, bathing, eating, or using the bathroom—but who do not need full-time nursing care. Often, assisted living facilities are part of a retirement community; others are near nursing homes so that a person can move easily if health care needs advance.

SOURCE: Stockbyte/Thinkstock.

"senior voting bloc" must be captured in any successful election campaign. However, over a series of elections, Robert Binstock has repeatedly disproved this theory. His findings show that older people, by and large, retain the political heterogeneity they demonstrated prior to turning sixty-five.[52,53] Age does not trump one's identity as a Mississippi conservative, for example, or a New York liberal.

On the other hand, voting may not be the primary means through which older people express political power. There is significant evidence that older people do respond to threats to programs that benefit them via other routes. Andrea Campbell, for example, shows how the creation of Social Security has in turn created a constituency that sustains it. Her book *How Policies Make Citizens: Senior Political Activism and the American Welfare State* systematically links specific policy changes to citizen actions, such as lobbying representatives and other political activities. This logic applies equally to the Medicare program. Her analysis of the repeal of the Medicare Catastrophic Coverage Act of 1988 connects the proportion of seniors in a district to the likelihood of Republican representatives to support repeal, after having initially voted for the legislation. This finding is consistent with research demonstrating the impact of constituent pressure (via letters, emails, or Capitol Hill visits) on individual representatives.[54]

Clearly, the politics surrounding aging have an enormous influence on policy, whether it be the negative images associated with neglected elderly people or with "greedy geezers" living it up on public monies.[55,56] Also, the meme of older people bankrupting our children's future appears to have political legs. However, apart from the research cited previously, there has been little serious attention to the impact of aging on the political landscape more generally and on health care policy more specifically. Although the impact of organized lobbying groups has received more attention, few rigorous studies exist. Nonetheless, it is apparent that seniors exert influence less as a voting bloc and

more through lobbying activities, including by sixty-six groups joined together under the banner of the Leadership Council of Aging Organizations. The largest and most influential of the Leadership Council's affiliates is the nearly forty-million-strong AARP (formerly the American Association of Retired Persons).

POLITICS AND HEALTH CARE POLICY

The American Association of Retired Persons (Now Known as AARP)

AARP was founded in 1958 by retired high school principal Dr. Ethel Percy Andrus. It evolved from the National Retired Teachers Association, which Dr. Andrus had formed in 1947 to provide retired teachers with the opportunity to purchase health insurance and to further her vision for productive aging, including promoting independence, dignity, and purpose; enhancing quality of life; and encouraging older people "to serve, not to be served." Currently, AARP describes itself as

> a nonprofit, nonpartisan organization . . . that helps people turn their goals and dreams into real possibilities, strengthens communities and fights for the issues that matter most to families such as healthcare, employment security and retirement planning [and] advocate[s] for consumers in the marketplace by selecting products and services of high quality and value to carry the AARP name as well as help our members obtain discounts on a wide range of products, travel, and services.

In 2011, AARP took in $1.36 billion in revenue from a variety of sources, primarily royalties from health, financial, and other products ($484 million, $203 million, and $18 million, respectively); membership dues ($266 million); and advertising revenues ($129 million). This is as opposed to $1.327 billion in expenses, including research and advocacy at the federal and state levels ($112 million), member service activities ($316 million), community benefits ($323 million), human resources, financial management, operations ($215 million), and publications ($174 million).

AARP is widely considered to be one of the more powerful interest groups in the country. Indeed, a 2006 study of health policy elites by Michael T. Heaney in the *Journal of Health Politics, Policy & Law* had AARP ranked first in influence by K Street lobbyists and fourth by congressional staff. Campaign donations are a minor part of the story. As an organization, AARP contributed just under $30,000 to political campaigns in 2011–2012, a major election year. It has spent far more lobbying federal officials, averaging $19.25 million annually, from 2007 to 2012 (although it spent much more [$36.3 million] in 2005, a year when Medicare was a particular focus of debate). Overall, the number of lobbyists representing AARP has grown steadily, rising from twenty-eight in 1998 to seventy-one in 2010.

How AARP policy is shaped, and the extent to which its positions correspond to the preferences of older people more generally, is difficult to determine. Certainly, AARP consistently faces allegations (typically from the right of the political spectrum) regarding conflicts posed by its money-making arm, the insurance products it sells. For example, conservatives most recently claimed that AARP supported the PPACA because it stood to gain more than $1 billion over ten years from increased Medigap sales. Consequently, Republican members of Congress asked the Internal Revenue Service to investigate the organization's tax-exempt status and called a joint Hearing on AARP's Organizational Structure, Management, and Finances before the House of Representatives Committee on Ways and Means Subcommittees on Health and Oversight in April 2011.

Perhaps AARP's influence was most pronounced during the debate over the 2003 Medicare Modernization Act, of which AARP played a critical role in ensuring passage. As Morgan and Campbell relate in *The Delegated Welfare State,* the bill was stalled in conference committee when Republicans reached out to the organization for support, which broke the stalemate and allowed the bill to proceed to the floor. They were able to do so with confidence because AARP had previously been quietly engaged in negotiations with the Republican leadership. Although the prescription drug benefit was seen as consistent with organizational and constituent goals, a huge win, these negotiations were controversial on two grounds: first, they had taken place without the knowledge of the Democratic leadership, and second, the deal included a toothless AARP requirement for a public sector demonstration project that would compete with the private plans favored by Republicans, a component that was clearly not honored. Thus, although the organization achieved its goal of an expanded drug benefit, it expended considerable political capital and incurred significant backlash. While Democrats by and large supported the concept of a new benefit, they were suspicious of the law's exclusive dependence on private plans to deliver the benefit and of its ban on allowing government to negotiate with drug manufacturers. Consequently, most Democrats voted against the bill; only sixteen supported it in the House, eleven in the Senate.

SOURCES: AARP, "AARP History," http://www.aarp.org/about-aarp/info-2009/History.html; AARP, "A Snapshot of AARP's 2011 Consolidated Expenses and Revenue," http://www.aarp.org/content/dam/aarp/about_aarp/leadership/2012-11/aarp-financial-snapshot-2011-final.pdf; AARP, "Who We Are," http://www.aarp.org/about-aarp; Michael T. Heaney, "Brokering Health Policy: Coalitions, Parties, and Interest Group Influence," *Journal of Health Politics, Policy and Law* 31: 5 (2006): 887–944; Center for Responsive Politics, "AARP," http://www.opensecrets.org/orgs/summary.php?id=D000023726; AARP, "AARP Responds to Congressional Inquiries," http://www.aarp.org/about-aarp/info-03-2011/website_overview.html; Kimberly J. Morgan and Andrea Louise Campbell, *The Delegated Welfare State: Medicare, Markets, and the Governance of Social Policy* (New York: Oxford University Press, 2011).

True Representation of Seniors' Interests

Although AARP is the behemoth among lobbying organizations, many other groups influence health policy toward older people. Single-issue organizations, such as the Alzheimer's Association, can have significant impact on research funding and family support issues. Another large category includes health care providers that cater largely to the older population. Clearly, physicians, hospitals, and nursing homes are all politically well organized and have a significant impact on policy. Increasingly influential, however, are the unions representing direct care workers, which include home health workers, certified nursing assistants, personal care attendants, and so forth. Direct care is an important area of employment opportunity for low-skilled workers; it is the largest occupational grouping in the country, and home health aides, followed by personal and home care aides, are projected to be the first and second fastest-growing occupations in the country between 2010 and 2020.[57] Factors surrounding the employment of this group, such as wage negotiations and licensing requirements, therefore, have a large impact on elder care programs and state finances, employment, and immigration policy more generally. The Service Employees International Union (SEIU) is ranked a "heavy hitter" by the Center for Responsive Politics,[58] and other unions are seeking to represent this group as well. In New York State, for example, the SEIU has become increasingly effective in negotiating better wages and conditions for these workers, which has a direct impact on the state's Medicaid budget.

The role of SEIU and other unions is particularly important given that there are not enough workers to serve an increasingly elderly population. This undersupply of geriatric expertise extends to every level. The direct care workforce presents particularly difficult challenges, because turnover is high and job satisfaction and pay are low, and although quality is a problem, instituting stricter licensing or training requirements is likely to further reduce supply. However, the problems are equally intractable in other health care professions. The supply of geriatricians is limited: only 7,500 exist where an estimated 17,000 are needed,[59] and they are among the lowest paid medical specialists. Nor is geriatrics integrated into general medical education, with only 23 percent of medical schools requiring a course.[60] The same story applies in the fields of nursing, pharmacy, dentistry, and social work. Thus, the health care workforce is ill prepared for the population it will be increasingly serving. Although the Institute of Medicine and other groups have issued various sobering reports, little action has been taken. Indeed, PPACA provisions regarding the health care workforce seem to have been put on hold indefinitely.

Despite the influence of AARP and other elder advocacy organizations, those in the field often bemoan the state of aging advocacy. Noted one knowledgeable observer, "It seems manifestly true that the energy and commitment of advocates has waned at the national level and in most states and communities. We need to find out why and what we can do about it."[61] The rise of neoconservatism and its emphasis on individualism, personal responsibility, and market forces has placed elder advocacy organizations on the defensive; so too has the portrayal of older Americans as a powerful and flourishing population cohort that consumes a disproportionate share of tax dollars. At the federal level, this dynamic has been exacerbated by ongoing debate over deficit reduction and entitlement reform. At the state and local level, it has been exacerbated by the Great Recession and its adverse implications for state and municipal coffers since 2008. John Rother,[62] formerly executive vice president of policy, strategy, and international affairs for AARP, observed that "we haven't built leadership support resources for the state or grassroots levels, where increasingly the action has moved. Many state advocates have been extraordinarily successful in recent years. . . . But we still lack the mechanisms to train and support such state-based advocacy across the country."

Certainly, the escalation of rhetoric regarding the role of programs serving older people in bankrupting the federal government seems to warrant an organized response from those who benefit from such programs. Yet the type of response generated in reaction to the Medicare Catastrophic Coverage Act (against which some seniors rose up to successfully achieve its repeal)[63] has not materialized. Indeed, many observers have noted the apparent contradiction that the Tea Party attracts considerable support from older people.[64] A variety of explanations for this lack of activity have been proposed: that seniors do not, in fact, constitute a coherent group likely to promote positive political change, except to the extent that they will oppose changes in programs benefiting them; that no obvious system exists for creating leaders or for building the political and intellectual capital needed to create a movement; that the current environment of scarcity makes it a bad time to push for change; and that ageism persists, along with the public perception that seniors have it comparatively good relative to the general population, based on the existence of public programs explicitly benefitting them.

It does not help that some of the issues that affect most older people receive little attention, both by the mass media and by the general public. Although most Americans interact with the long-term care system at some point in their lives, they do not rank the issue among the nation's most pressing problems and priorities.[65] When asked what should be the top priority for health reform in 2000, for example, only 8 percent of respondents identified "lack of long-term care options," far behind HMOs, costs, and Medicare prescription drugs (16 percent to 26 percent). When asked what should be the top priority for health reform in 2009, just 3 percent identified "providing stronger, affordable long-term care options," far below coverage, cost, fraud/waste, and insurance (13 percent to 19 percent).[66] There also has been comparatively little media attention devoted to long-term services and supports, again, despite the large number of Americans impacted.[67,68]

Of course, the federal government is a big playing field, with many players, making it a particular (and often expensive) challenge to lobby effectively. Many policies, particularly those related to long-term care services and supports, are set at the state level, requiring another type of political organization, potentially one where less well-organized and well-funded groups could have more influence. However, lobbying in the area of health care, at both the state and federal levels, requires considerable sophistication, given the intricacies of the health care system and its financing as well as the many powerful players affected by health care policy—making it even more challenging for seniors to have an impact. Those most affected by these policies—sick, frail, older people (and their families, who

are often exhausted by their caregiving responsibilities)—often have limited energy and ability to organize and lobby. Thus, true representation of aging interests in health care presents an ongoing conundrum.

See also **Chapter 6: The Centers for Medicare and Medicaid Services (1965–Present); Chapter 18: Health and Health Care Policy: Ethical Perspectives (1970s–Present); Chapter 20: Women's Issues and American Health Care Policy (1960s–Present); Chapter 21: Minorities, Immigrants, and Health Care Policy: Disparities and Solutions (1960s–Present); Chapter 23: Fifty Years of Progress in Disease and Injury Prevention (1950s–Present); Chapter 24: Mental Health and Social Policy (1960s–Present); Chapter 25: Nutrition, Physical Activity, and the Obesity Epidemic: Issues, Policies, and Solutions (1960s–Present); Chapter 26: Interest Groups, Think Tanks, and Health Care Policy (1960s–Present).**

NOTES

1. David Barton Smith, *Health Care Divided: Race and Healing a Nation* (Ann Arbor: University of Michigan Press, 1999).

2. Theodore Marmor, *The Politics of Medicare* (Hawthorne, NY: Aldine de Gruyter, 2000).

3. Kaiser Commission on Medicaid and the Uninsured, *Medicaid and Its Role in State/Federal Budgets and Health Reform* (Washington, DC: Kaiser Family Foundation, 2013), http://kaiserfamilyfoundation.files.wordpress.com/2012/05/8162-03.pdf.

4. Arloc Sherman, Robert Greenstein, and Kathy Ruffling, *Contrary to "Entitlement Society" Rhetoric, over Nine-Tenths of Entitlement Benefits Go to Elderly, Disabled, or Working Households* (Washington, DC: Center on Budget and Policy Priorities, 2012).

5. Cristina Boccuti and Marilyn Moon, "Comparing Medicare and Private Insurers: Growth Rates in Spending over Three Decades," *Health Affairs* 22: 2 (2003): 230–237.

6. Laura A. Dummit, *Nursing Homes: Aggregate Medicare Payments Are Adequate Despite Bankruptcies* (Washington, DC: U.S. General Accounting Office, September 5, 2000).

7. Brian Biles et al., *Realizing Health Reform's Potential: The Impact of Health Reform on the Medicare Advantage Program: Realigning Payment with Performance* (New York: Commonwealth Fund), http://www.commonwealthfund.org/~/media/Files/Publications/Issue%20Brief/2012/Oct/1637_Biles_impact_hlt_reform_Medicare_Advantage_rb.pdf.

8. Ida Hellander, David U. Himmelstein, and Steffie Woolhandler, "Medicare Overpayments to Private Plans, 1985–2012: Shifting Seniors to Private Plans Has Already Cost Medicare US $282.6 Billion," *International Journal of Health Services* 43: 2 (2013).

9. Kaiser Family Foundation, *How Much Skin in the Game Is Enough? The Financial Burden of Health Spending for People on Medicare* (Washington, DC: Kaiser Family Foundation, 2011), http://kff.org/medicare/report/how-much-skin-in-the-game-is-enough-the-financial-burden-of-health-spending-for-people-on-medicare.

10. Adam Atherly, "Supplemental Insurance: Medicare's Accidental Stepchild," *Medical Care Research and Review* 58 (2001): 133–134.

11. Patricia Neuman et al., "Dx for a Careful Approach to Moving Dual-Eligible Beneficiaries into Managed Care Plans," *Health Affairs* 31: 6 (2012): 1186–1194.

12. Randall S. Brown et al., "Six Features of Medicare Coordinated Care Demonstration Programs that Cut Hospital Admissions of High-Risk Patients," *Health Affairs* 31: 6 (2012): 1156–1166.

13. Joshua M. Wiener and David G. Stevenson, *Repeal of the "Boren Amendment": Implications for Quality of Care in Nursing Homes* (Washington, DC: Urban Institute, 1998), http://www.urban.org/UploadedPDF/anf30.pdf.

14. Edward Alan Miller, "Repealing Federal Regulation of State Health Policy: Lessons from the Boren Amendment," *Review of Policy Research* 28: 1 (2011): 5–23.

15. Christine E. Bishop, Michelle Visconti, and Linda Long, "Impact of Boren Amendment Repeal on Nursing Facility Services for Medicaid Eligibles," in *Report to Congress: Impact of Repeal of the Boren Amendment: Prepared in Response to Section 4711(b) of Public Law No. 105-33* (Washington, DC: U.S. Department of Health and Human Services, 2004).

16. Robert L. Kane et al., "Does Home- and Community-Based Care Affect Nursing Home Use?" *Journal of Aging and Social Policy* 25: 1 (2013): 146–160.

17. H. Stephen Kaye, Mitchell P. LaPlante, and Charlene Harrington, "Do Noninstitutional Long-Term Care Services Reduce Medicaid Spending?" *Health Affairs,* 28: 1 (2009): 262–272.

18. Steve Eiken, Brian Burwell, and Kate Sredl, "An Examination of the Woodwork Effect Using National Medicaid Long-Term Services and Supports Data," *Journal of Aging & Social Policy* 25: 2 (2013): 134–145.

19. Mitchell P. LaPlante, "The Woodwork Effect in Medicaid Long-Term Services and Supports," *Journal of Aging & Social Policy*, 25: 2 (2013): 161–180.

20. Lynn Feinberg et al., *Valuing the Invaluable: 2011 Update: The Growing Contributions and Costs of Family Caregiving* (Washington, DC: AARP Public Policy Institute, 2011), http://assets.aarp.org/rgcenter/ppi/ltc/i51-caregiving.pdf.

21. Sara Rosenbaum and Joel Teitelbaum, Olmstead *at Five: Assessing the Impact* (Washington, DC: Kaiser Family Foundation, 2004), http://kaiserfamilyfoundation.files.word press.com/2013/01/olmstead-at-five-assessing-the-impact .pdf.

22. Stacy B. Dale and Randall S. Brown, "How Does Cash and Counseling Affect Costs?" *Health Services Research Journal* 42: 1, Pt. 2 (2007): 488–509.

23. Pamela Doty, Kevin J. Mahoney, and Mark Sciegaj, "New State Strategies to Meet Long-Term Care Needs," *Health Affairs* 29: 1 (2010): 49–56.

24. Ruth Helman et al., *The 2012 Retirement Confidence Survey: Job Insecurity, Debt Weigh on Retirement Confidence* (Washington, DC: Employee Benefit Research Institute, 2012), http://www .ebri.org/pdf/surveys/rcs/2012/EBRI_IB_03-2012_No369_ RCS.pdf.

25. Barbara Lyons, Andy Schneider, and Katherine A. Desmond, "The Distributions of Assets in the Elderly Population Living in the Community" (Washington, DC: Kaiser Family Foundation, 2005), http://www.kff.org/medicaid/7335.cfm.

26. "Who Pays for Long-Term Care in the U.S.?" (Long Beach, CA: SCAN Foundation, 2013), http://www.thescanfoundation.org/ sites/thescanfoundation.org/files/who_pays_for_ltc_us_ jan_2013_fs.pdf.

27. Tompson et al., *Long-Term Care: Perceptions, Experiences, and Attitudes among Americans 40 or Older* (Chicago: Associated Press–NORC Center for Public Affairs Research, 2013). http:// www.apnorc.org/projects/Pages/long-term-care-perceptions- experiences-and-attitudes-among-americans-40-or-older.aspx.

28. Sheila P. Burke, Judith Feder, and Paul N. Van De Water, *Developing a Better Long-Term Care Policy: A Vision and Strategy for America's Future* (Washington, DC: National Academy of Social Insurance, 2005), http://www.nasi.org/usr_ doc/Developing_a_Better_Long-Term_Care_Policy.pdf.

29. "Who Pays for Long-Term Care in the U.S.?"

30. Anne Tumlinson, Christine Aguiar, and Molly O'Malley Watts, *Closing the Long-Term Care Funding Gap: The Challenge of Private Long-Term Care Insurance* (Washington, DC: Kaiser Commission on Medicaid and the Uninsured, 2009), http:// kaiserfamilyfoundation.files.wordpress.com/2013/01/closing- the-long-term-care-funding-gap-the-challenge-of-private- long-term-care-insurance-report.pdf.

31. Marc A. Cohen, "Long-Term Care Insurance: A Product and Industry in Transition," http://www.naic.org/documents/ committees_b_senior_issues_2012_fall_nm_ltc_hearing_ presentations_cohen_revised.pdf.

32. Institute of Medicine, *Improving the Quality of Care in Nursing Homes* (Washington, DC: National Academy Press, 1986).

33. U.S. General Accounting Office, *Medicare and Medicaid: Stronger Enforcement of Nursing Home Requirements Needed* (GAO-87-113) (Washington, DC: U.S. General Accounting Office, 1987).

34. Nicholas G. Castle and Jamie C. Ferguson, "What Is Nursing Home Quality and How Is It Measured?" *The Gerontologist* 50: 4 (2010): 426–442.

35. Edward Alan Miller, "Federal Administrative and Judicial Oversight of Medicaid: Policy Legacies and Tandem- Institutions under the Boren Amendment," *Publius* 38: 2 (2008): 315–342.

36. Centers for Medicare and Medicaid Services, "Assuring Quality Care for Nursing Home Residents" (press release), September 29, 2000, http://www.cms.hhs.gov/apps/media/press/release .asp?Counter=384.

37. Office of the Inspector General, *Quality of Care in Nursing Homes: An Overview* (Washington, DC: U.S. Department of Health and Human Services, 1999).

38. U.S. General Accounting Office, *Nursing Homes: Additional Steps Needed to Strengthen Enforcement of Federal Quality Standards* (GAO/HEHS-99-46) (Washington, DC: U.S. General Accounting Office, 1999).

39. U.S. General Accounting Office, *Nursing Home Quality: Prevalence of Serious Problems, While Declining, Reinforces Importance of Enhanced Oversight* (GAO-03-561) (Washington, DC: U.S. General Accounting Office, 2003).

40. U.S. Government Accountability Office, *Nursing Homes: Despite Increased Oversight, Challenges Remain in Ensuring High-Quality Care and Resident Safety* (GAO-06-117) (Washington, DC: U.S. Government Accountability Office, 2006).

41. Vincent Mor, "Improving the Quality of Long-Term Care with Better Information," *Milbank Quarterly* 83: 3 (2005): 333–364.

42. Centers for Medicare and Medicaid Services, "Nursing Home Quality Initiative," http://www.cms.gov/Medicare/Quality- Initiatives-Patient-Assessment-Instruments/Nursing HomeQualityInits/index.html .

43. Carol Hall Ellenbecker et al., "Patient Safety and Quality in Home Health Care," in *Patient Safety and Quality: An Evidence- Based Handbook for Nurses,* edited by Ronda G. Hughes (Rockville, MD: Agency for Healthcare Research and Quality, 2008).

44. Rachel M. Werner, R. Tamara Konetzka, and Kevin Liang, "State Adoption of Nursing Home Pay-for-Performance," *Medical Care Research and Review* 67: 3 (2010): 364–377.

45. David G. Stevenson and David M. Studdert, "The Rise of Nursing Home Litigation: Findings from a National Survey of Attorneys," *Health Affairs* 22: 2 (2003): 219–229.

46. Christopher E. Johnson et al., "Predicting Lawsuits against Nursing Homes in the United States, 1997–2001," *Health Services Research* 39: 6, Part I (2004): 1713–1731.

47. Ibid.

48. David M. Studdert et al., "Relationship between Quality of Care and Negligence Litigation in Nursing Homes," *New England Journal of Medicine* 364: 13 (2011): 1243–1250.

49. David M. Studdert and David G. Stevenson, "Nursing Home Litigation and Tort Reform: A Case for Exceptionalism," *The Gerontologist* 44: 5 (2004): 588–595.

50. Mary Jane Koren, "Improving Quality in Long-Term Care," *Medical Care Research & Review* 67: 4 (2010): 141S–150S.

51. Anna N. Rahman and John F. Schnelle, "The Nursing Home Culture-Change Movement: Recent Past, Present, and Future Directions for Research," *The Gerontologist* 48: 2 (2008): 142–148.

52. Robert H. Binstock, "Older Voters and the 2010 U.S. Election: Implications for 2012 and Beyond?" *The Gerontologist* 52: 3 (2012): 408–417.

53. Robert H. Binstock, "Older Voters and the 1992 Presidential Election," *The Gerontologist* 32: 5 (1992): 601–606.

54. Congressional Management Foundation, "Communicating with Congress: Perceptions of Citizen Advocacy on Capitol Hill" (Washington, DC: Congressional Management Foundation, 2011), http://www.congressfoundation.org/storage/documents/CMF_Pubs/cwc-perceptions-of-citizen-advocacy.pdf.

55. Robert H. Hudson, *The New Politics of Old Age Policy* (Baltimore: Johns Hopkins University Press, 2010).

56. James H. Schulz and Robert H. Binstock, *Aging Nation: The Economics and Politics of Growing Older in America* (Baltimore: Johns Hopkins University Press, 2006).

57. Paraprofessional Healthcare Institute, "Occupational Projections for Direct-Care Workers 2010–2020" (Bronx, NY: Paraprofessional Healthcare Institute, 2013), http://phinational.org/sites/phinational.org/files/phi_factsheet1update_singles_2.pdf.

58. Center for Responsive Politics, "Service Employees International Union," http://www.opensecrets.org/orgs/summary.php?id=d000000077.

59. American Geriatrics Society, "The Demand for Geriatric Care and the Evident Shortage of the Geriatric Workforce" (New York, NY: American Geriatrics Society, 2013), http://www.americangeriatrics.org/files/documents/Adv_Resources/demand_for_geriatric_care.pdf.

60. Chad Boult et al., "The Urgency of Preparing Primary Care Physicians to Care for Older People with Chronic Illnesses," *Health Affairs* 29: 5 (2010): 811–818.

61. Richard Browdie, "Introduction: Advocacy and Aging," *Generations* 28: 1 (2004): 5–7.

62. John Rother, "Why Haven't We Been More Successful Advocates for Elders? *Generations* 28: 1 (2004): 55–58.

63. Richard Himelfarb, *Catastrophic Politics: The Rise and Fall of the Medicare Catastrophic Coverage Act of 1988* (University Park: Pennsylvania State University Press, 1995).

64. Kate Zernike and Megan Thee-Brenan, "Poll Finds Tea Party Backers Wealthier and More Educated," *New York Times*, April 14, 2010, http://www.nytimes.com/2010/04/15/us/politics/15poll.html?hp&_r=2&.

65. Kaiser Family Foundation, "Kaiser Health News Index Survey/Health Poll Report Survey," http://www.kff.org/kaiserpolls/index2.cfm.

66. AARP, "AARP Bulletin Survey of Expectations for the President and Congress in 2010" (Washington, DC: AARP, 2009), http://assets.aarp.org/rgcenter/general/bulletin_expect10.pdf.

67. Felicia Mebane, "Want to Understand How Americans Viewed Long-Term Care in 1998? Start with Media Coverage," *The Gerontologist* 41: 1 (2001): 24–33.

68. Pew Research Center, "Previous State of the News Media Reports," http://www.journalism.org/2014/03/26/previous-state-of-the-news-media-reports.

FURTHER READING

Campbell, Andrea Louise. *How Policies Make Citizens: Senior Political Activism and the American Welfare State.* Princeton, NJ: Princeton University Press, 2003.

Marmor, Theodore. *The Politics of Medicare.* Hawthorne, NY: Aldine de Gruyter, 2000.

Schulz, James H., and Robert H. Binstock. *Aging Nation: The Economics and Politics of Growing Older in America.* Baltimore: Johns Hopkins University Press, 2006.

chapter 23

Fifty Years of Progress in Disease and Injury Prevention (1950s–Present)

Cari Cuffney and Patrick Remington

SINCE 1960, THE AGE-ADJUSTED DEATH RATE from all causes in the United States has decreased by nearly 50 percent (see Table 23.1). Although a full exploration of the reasons for this decline is beyond the scope of a single chapter, it is essential to understand the progress made in four of the leading causes of premature death: infant deaths, infectious diseases, chronic diseases, and injuries. We discuss these key issues, using examples of specific health problems and the potential impact of policies and programs that were developed to respond to each health problem. More broadly, we discuss recent trends in health policies in disease and injury prevention, including the impact of research into the causes of disease and incremental policymaking, as well as the future challenges to public health, most importantly achieving health equity—trends that have laid the foundation for more sound health care polices in the twenty-first century.

SCIENTIFIC RESEARCH AND POLICYMAKING

Changes in death rates due to disease and injury, as well as our understanding of the causes and development of health problems, have a profound influence on policy responses and the institutions responsible for public health. In order to take effective action, policymakers must have a clear understanding of the causes of the conditions policy is meant to change. Shifts in the leading causes of death in the 1960s, from infectious disease to chronic disease and injury, along with the development of social epidemiology, have changed our understanding of the causes of disease and injury. The social determinants of health include "the circumstances in which people are born, grow up, live, work, and age,"[1] as shaped by political, economic, and cultural forces. Rather than a single cause, single treatment approach, we now understand that disease and injury are multifactorial, having many causes. Social epidemiologists have demonstrated that health is not determined solely by health care and health behaviors, but rather by the multiple determinants of health, including education, socioeconomic status, the built environment, and the neighborhoods in which people live. This new understanding of the causes of disease and injury has broadened the range of intervention points by which policy can influence health outcomes. Future improvements in health outcomes will not be achieved by maintaining the traditional silos of health research, programs, and policies within the Centers for Disease Control and Prevention (CDC), National Institutes of Health (NIH), and local public health departments. Instead, a "health in all policies" approach, which considers all factors that influence health,[2] will be necessary to both continue to improve health outcomes and also address health inequities.

HEALTH EQUITY

While the United States has made significant progress in the control and prevention of disease and injury in the last half century (see Figure 23.1), improvement has not occurred at the same rate for all causes of death, nor have the benefits of progress been evenly distributed to all citizens. For example, all-cause mortality from cancer has decreased 11 percent since 1960 while lung cancer death rates have doubled, reflecting the lag between exposure, smoking, and health effect (see Table 23.1). Suicide and homicide rates remain largely unchanged, while the accidental poisoning death rate increased 600 percent in the last decade. Lack of progress in some areas may reflect the social construction of causes and populations. Drug use and mental health conditions are often labeled as deviant behaviors, resulting in the provision of fewer services with higher barriers to entry and reliance

TABLE 23.1 **Changes in Mortality Rates for the Leading Causes of Death, 1960–2010**

Cause of Death	1960	2010	Absolute Difference	Relative Risk, 2010 vs. 1960	Lives Saved
All causes	1,339.2	747	−592.2	0.56	1,828,391
Diseases of the heart	559	113.6	−445.4	0.20	1,375,153
Cerebrovascular disease	177.9	39.1	−138.8	0.22	428,539
Cancer	193.9	172.8	−21.1	0.89	65,145
(of trachea, bronchus, lung)	24.1	47.6	23.5	1.98	−72,555
(of colon, rectum, anus)	30.3	15.8	−14.5	0.52	44,768
Influenza and pneumonia	53.7	15.1	−38.6	0.28	119,176
HIV	10.2*	2.6	−7.6	0.26	23,465
Unintentional injury	62.3	38	−24.3	0.61	75,025
Motor vehicle–related injury	23.1	11.3	−11.8	0.49	36,432
Poisoning	1.7	10.6	8.9	6.24	−27,478
Suicide	12.5	12.1	−0.4	0.97	1,235
Homicide	5	5.3	0.3	1.06	−926

SOURCE: Data from National Center for Health Statistics, *Health, United States, 2012: With Special Feature on Emergency Care* (Hyattsville, MD: National Center for Health Statistics, 2013).

*1990 rate. All rates are per 100,000 population.

on the criminal justice system, rather than public health institutions, to address the problem.[3] In other cases, lack of understanding of the causes of disease has hampered policy efforts at prevention. For example, the causes of sudden infant death syndrome and some cancers are not well understood and require more basic research to inform decision making.

The use of national averages obscures underlying variations in health outcomes by subpopulations based on age, gender, race/ethnicity, geographic location, and socioeconomic status. Health disparities, differences in health outcomes between subpopulations, remain and in some cases have increased. These differences are not necessarily problematic in themselves; rather, they become inequities when the differences are "unnecessary and avoidable, but, in addition, are also considered unfair and unjust."[4] The classification of certain health disparities as health inequities implies a moral dimension and a demand for societal redress through policy.

Health inequities have become increasingly important in health policy. The Institute of Medicine (IOM) has clearly adopted health equity as a national goal through the definition of progress as "long, healthy lives for all."[5] The reduction of health inequities is key to achieving the goal of health equity. The Healthy People objectives, a set of national health goals published by the U.S. Department of Health

and Human Services each decade since 1990, first included "reducing disparities" by 2000, then progressed to "eliminating disparities" by 2010, and finally achievement of "health equity" by 2020. These changes reflect an increasing emphasis on the social determinants of health[6] and follow the capabilities approach outlined by Amartya Sen, which requires attention not only to reduction in inequities but also to improvements beyond the health care sphere in the capabilities of all individuals to enjoy long and healthy lives.[7] A review of the Healthy People 2010 objectives shows that 80 percent of health disparities have remained unchanged while an additional 13 percent have increased over the last twenty years.[8] Infant mortality is an excellent example of an area where enormous progress has been made in the last fifty years, yet stark inequities by race and ethnicity have persisted and even worsened over time.

INFANT DEATHS

The infant death rate, the risk of dying during the first year of life expressed per 1,000 live births, is "the most sensitive indicator of overall societal health"[9] according to both the CDC and the World Health Organization (WHO). The decline in infant death rates over the last century exceeds the reduction in the other leading causes of death in the United States.[10] In the United States in 1900, approximately

FIGURE 23.1 **Time Trends for the Leading Causes of Death, 1960–2010**

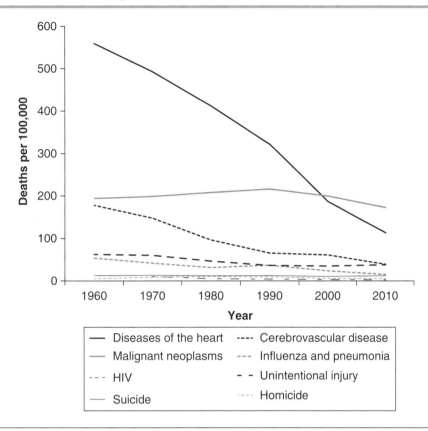

SOURCE: Data from National Center for Health Statistics, *Health, United States, 2012: With Special Feature on Emergency Care* (Hyattsville, MD: National Center for Health Statistics, 2013).

one of ten infants died before its first birthday. By 1960, the rate had declined by more than three-quarters, to 26 deaths per 1,000 live births, and in the past fifty years has declined another 75 percent to the current rate of 6.1 per 1,000 live births. Improvements in nutrition, advances in clinical medicine, improvements in access to health care, improvements in surveillance and monitoring of disease, increases in education levels, and improvements in standards of living contributed to this remarkable decline.[11] Research using a lifecourse approach, which evaluates the impact of health across the lifespan and between generations, continues to reveal a strong relationship between maternal preconception health and later birth outcomes with effects persisting across generations, from mother to child and even to grandchild.[12,13]

It is important to note that in the midst of this progress, the United States continues to perform poorly compared to other high-income nations on measures of infant mortality. The United States dropped from twelfth in the international rankings in 1960[14] to thirty-fourth in 2010.[15] In essence, the United States has made improvements, but those improvements have not been as large or as quick as the progress seen in other countries. In addition, geographic variations exist within the United States such that the worst-performing states have infant mortality rates twice that of the best-performing states.[16]

Healthy People 2020 seeks to reduce the overall infant mortality by 10 percent, to 6 per 1,000,[17] still far above the current average of 4.3 deaths per 1,000 live births observed in other high-income countries.[18] Three important contributors to infant deaths in the United States are maternal health, sudden infant death syndrome, and neural tube defects. These health problems, and the contributions of health policies to each, are described below.

Maternal Health

Maternal health is the health of the mother before, during, and between pregnancies and is an important predictor of the health of infants. Prenatal care, including blood tests, ultrasounds, and physician visits during pregnancy to discuss healthy behaviors such as diet (often eliminating smoking and alcohol use) and folic acid supplementation, has been the gold standard for improving maternal and infant health. The use of prenatal care is dependent on access, insurance status, and care-seeking behavior (such as timely knowledge of the pregnancy).

Prevention Programs and Policies: Expanding Health Insurance for the Poor

Medicaid, which pays for 41 percent of all births in the United States,[19] grew incrementally throughout the 1980s after a 1985 report by the Institute of Medicine, *Preventing Low Birthweight,* which identified access to prenatal care as an important policy option to improve birth outcomes.[20] The Deficit Reduction Act (1984) required Medicaid to cover all women with first-time pregnancies who were eligible under the Aid for Families with Dependent Children program.[21] States were then given the option in 1986 to expand Medicaid coverage to all pregnant women below 100 percent of the federal poverty level (FPL).[22] This option became a required mandate in 1988 and the income threshold was increased to 133 percent of FPL in 1989.[23] Many states choose to offer coverage at higher income thresholds, with thirty-one providing coverage to 200 percent of FPL or more and three planning to reduce coverage thresholds as of January 1, 2014, in favor of providing coverage through the state health insurance exchanges established in 2010 by the Patient Protection and Affordable Care Act (PPACA).[24]

North Carolina provides an example of the dramatic impact of increased access to prenatal care in reduction of the infant mortality rate. This state had the highest infant mortality rate in the country in 1988.[25] Since the introduction of the Baby Love campaign in 1987,[26] infant mortality has declined from 14.9 deaths per 1,000 live births in 1987 to 8.2 in 2008.[27] The abysmal 1988 ranking also prompted Governor James Martin (in office 1985–1993) to create the Commission on Reduction of Infant Mortality in 1989 to advise the state on the issue.[28] Progress in North Carolina mirrors that of the nation as a whole, as the state continues to have one of the highest infant mortality rates in the country, ranking forty-seventh out of fifty states based on 2007–2009 data, despite these large improvements.[29]

Sudden Infant Death Syndrome

Sudden infant death syndrome (SIDS) is the death of an infant that is sudden, unexpected, and without immediately obvious cause occurring in the first year of life.[30] It is the leading cause of death in infants between one month and twelve months of age.[31] The exact cause of SIDS is unknown and diagnosis is reliant on the exclusion of other identifiable causes of death. Risk factors are many and include co-sleeping of adults with infants, soft bedding, maternal smoking or exposure to secondhand smoke during pregnancy, prone and side sleeping of the infant, sex of the infant (higher rates in males), low birth weight, hyperthermia from over-swaddling, African American or Native American heritage, and possibly genetic factors.[32] The best form of prevention is parental education; however, disparities exist in who receives and has access to prenatal classes where this information is taught.[33] Since 1980, the SIDS rate has declined by two-thirds (see Figure 23.2).

Prevention Programs and Policies

SIDS was first defined as a cause of death in 1969 at the Second International Conference on Causes of Sudden Death in Infants.[34] The conference was held under growing parental demand for investigation into the causes of infant

FIGURE 23.2 **Rate of Sudden Infant Death Syndrome, 1980–2010**

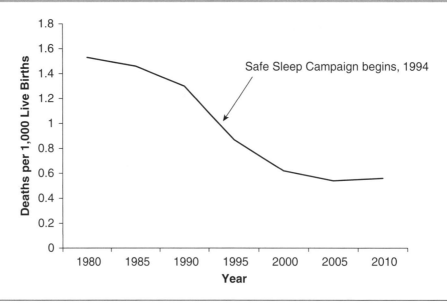

SOURCE: Data from the CDC and National Center for Health Statistics.

death. From 1964 to 1972, several organizations were established by parents who had lost infants, including the Mark Addison Roe Foundation (established in 1963), the Guild for Infant Survival (established in 1964), and the Washington Association for Sudden Infant Death Study (established in 1965). These were created to promote the study of SIDS and to lobby Congress for hearings and additional funding for SIDS research by the National Institute of Child Health and Human Development,[35] established in 1962 by President John F. Kennedy (1961–1963). Successful lobbying resulted in passage of the Sudden Infant Death Syndrome Act of 1974 and increased research on the causes of SIDS.[36]

There has been a steady decline in the rate of SIDS since the introduction in 1994 of the Safe Sleep campaign, formerly Back to Sleep, to educate parents on safe sleeping habits and provide cribs to families who cannot afford them. As of January 2014, a pilot case registry system is gathering additional information on SIDS deaths in nine states.[37] Some local educational campaigns have been highly controversial, such as the co-sleeping ads run in 2011 in Milwaukee, Wisconsin, which depicted babies asleep next to a large butcher's knife to illustrate the dangers of co-sleeping. Grassroots campaigns to provide cribs to low-income mothers have also emerged in response to the realization that disparities in infant mortality rates can, in part, be linked to socioeconomic status and the ability to purchase appropriate supplies, such as cribs, for safe sleep.[38]

Neural Tube Defects

Another leading cause of infant death is neural tube defects, which occur when elements of the central nervous system, the brain or spinal cord, fail to develop properly, causing neurological damage and disability. The most common neural tube defect is spina bifida, a birth defect of the spine in which a portion of the spinal column fails to close during development and may be exposed at birth. Another common neural tube defect is anencephaly, in which a portion of the brain or skull is not fully formed at birth.

The link between folic acid (a B vitamin) supplementation and decreased risk of neural tube defects has been well established and is an example of a classic progression of epidemiologic evidence from animal studies to the completion of randomized clinical trials.[39] Studies estimate a decrease between 19 percent[40] and 26 percent[41] in neural tube defects attributable to mandatory supplementation of all enriched grain products beginning in 1998 (see Figure 23.3). Researchers continue to investigate the genetic mechanisms and developmental timeline of the fetus in order to better understand additional risk factors for neural tube defects that can explain the remaining cases.[42,43]

Prevention Programs and Policies: Folate Supplementation

The first policy attempts to increase folate intake were directed at voluntary, individual behavior change. In September 1992, the U.S. Public Health Service recommended that all women of child-bearing age consume 0.4 mg of folic acid daily to prevent neural tube defects.[44] Voluntary recommendations failed to lower the incidence of neural tube defects due to low awareness of the recommendations, high rates of unplanned pregnancy (49 percent of all pregnancies in the United States[45]), and disparities between groups in uptake and action on the recommendations.[46] In March 1996, the FDA announced a requirement for all enriched grain products, including bread, flour, and cereals, to include folic acid supplementation beginning January 1, 1998.[47] This mandate has largely been a success, although there may be additional unintended effects of supplementation, such as protective

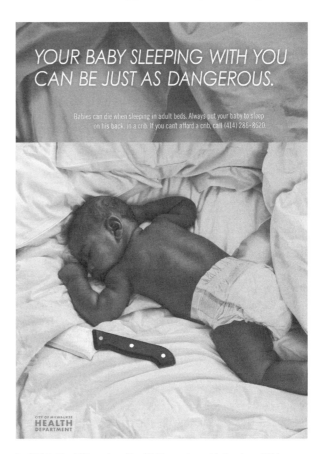

In 2011, the Milwaukee Health Department introduced this poster to publicize the city's Safe Sleep Campaign and to warn parents and other caregivers of the dangers of sleeping in the same bed as an infant. Unfortunately, the overall rate of infant deaths caused by an adult sleeping in the same bed has remained high in some areas, reaching an estimated 51 percent in Milwaukee alone.

SOURCE: City of Milwaukee Health Department Serve Marketing.

FIGURE 23.3 **Neural Tube Defect Rates and Folate Supplementation Policy, 1991–2006**

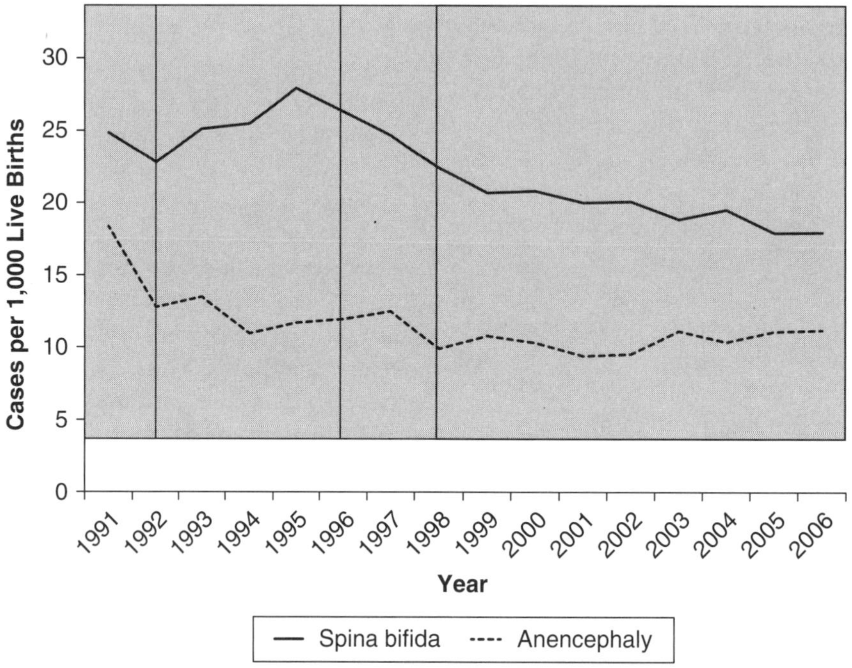

SOURCE: Data collected from the CDC and the National Vital Statistics System, excluding Maryland, New Mexico, and New York, which did not require reporting of spina bifida in all years.

NOTE: Prior to 1992 no recommendations for folate supplementation were in place. In the period 1992 to 1996, the FDA recommended folate intake for all women of child-bearing age. In 1996 the FDA mandated folate supplementation of all grain products, allowing producers until 1998 to comply. As of 1998, all producers were in compliance with the new regulation.

effects against cardiovascular disease[48] or possible increases in risk of colorectal cancer[49] and masking of vitamin B12 deficiencies.[50]

Summary of Progress in Reducing Infant Death Rates

Over the past fifty years, infant death rates have declined by almost 90 percent, a result of improvements in prenatal care, maternal nutrition, and reducing the risk of SIDS. Despite this progress, significant disparities in infant death rates by race and ethnicity have actually increased (see Figure 23.4).

In every decade from 1950 to 2000, the disparity between whites and blacks in infant mortality rates has increased, with the relative risk for blacks compared to whites rising from 1.6 in 1950 to 2.5 in 2000 (see Figure 23.5). Furthermore, the Healthy People 2020 goal for infant mortality was already achieved in white mothers when the infant mortality rate dropped to 5.7 per 1,000 live births in 2000.[51] This gap has only recently begun to shrink on a national scale,[52] while local variation remains high. For instance, the disparity between the white and black infant mortality rates in Milwaukee, Wisconsin, ranks among the nation's highest, with a rate of 6.4 for whites and 15.7 for blacks, with striking, highly localized variation within the city by census tract.[53] Targeted policy efforts at local, regional, and national levels

to eliminate disparities are needed if we are to achieve equity in infant birth outcomes and long, healthy lives for all.

INFECTIOUS DISEASES

Along with improvements in maternal and infant health, control of infectious diseases has been identified as one of the top ten great public health achievements in the twentieth century.[54] Infectious diseases are characterized by a single cause of illness, either a viral, bacterial, or parasitic agent, which is both necessary and sufficient for disease to occur; without the agent, disease is not possible. Declines in infectious disease deaths contributed to a sharp drop in infant and child mortality and to a nearly thirty-year increase in life expectancy. In 1900, the three leading causes of death were infectious diseases—pneumonia, tuberculosis, and diarrhea/enteritis. By 1960, heart disease and cancers had become the leading causes of death. These trends have continued over the past fifty years so that now infectious diseases of pneumonia, influenza, and human immunodeficiency virus (HIV) infection cause fewer than one in twenty deaths.[55]

The progress in reducing infectious disease deaths was based on the discovery that germs caused disease, resulting in a focus on improvements in sanitation and hygiene, discovery of antibiotics, and the implementation

FIGURE 23.4 **Infant Mortality Trends, by Race, 1950–2010**

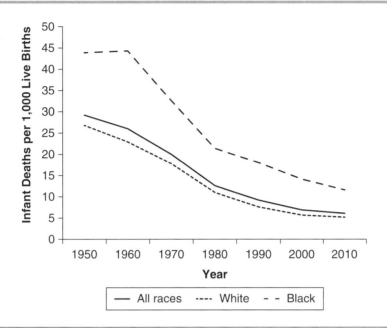

SOURCE: Data from National Center for Health Statistics, *Health, United States, 2012: With Special Feature on Emergency Care* (Hyattsville, MD: National Center for Health Statistics, 2013).

of universal childhood vaccination programs. A 2013 study estimates that 103.1 million infections have been avoided since 1924 through intensive vaccination efforts for eight of the major infectious diseases (smallpox, polio, measles, rubella, mumps, hepatitis A, diphtheria, and pertussis), with one-quarter of those (26 million) prevented in the last decade.[56] Vaccination eliminated smallpox in the United States in 1949, polio in 1979, and measles in 2000.

FIGURE 23.5 **Risk Ratios Comparing Infant Mortality Rates, Blacks : Whites**

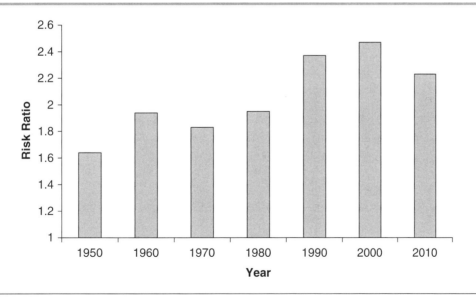

SOURCE: Data from National Center for Health Statistics, *Health, United States, 2012: With Special Feature on Emergency Care* (Hyattsville, MD: National Center for Health Statistics, 2013).

NOTE: Risk ratios are calculated as the infant mortality rates for blacks divided by the infant mortality rate for whites.

Despite this overall progress, many challenges remain. HIV infection, first recognized in 1981, is a pandemic still in progress. Vaccine hesitancy, concerns about the safety and efficacy of vaccinations that lead individuals to selectively vaccinate or not at all, threatens to erode progress already made in vaccine-preventable diseases. Only a small decrease in vaccine coverage is sufficient to reduce immunity in the population and open the door to epidemic infection. For instance, measles was eliminated in the United States in 2000 but continues to be imported in small numbers each year through immigration and international travel and can be catastrophic when introduced to unvaccinated populations.[57]

Vaccine-Preventable Infections

Many infections can now be avoided or their spread limited through vaccination. However, vaccines are only effective for those who have access to them. Limited implementation of recommended vaccine schedules in the elderly is a concern, and one study found that "only 64 percent had received or been offered a pneumococcal vaccine [and] nearly 10,000 deaths from pneumonia could be prevented annually by appropriate vaccinations."[58] Children are another vulnerable population for which access to vaccines must be guaranteed.

Prevention Programs and Policies: Expanding Access to Vaccines

Mass vaccination campaigns highlight an essential ethical dilemma in the field of public health: the tension between individual rights and the promotion of the common good and population health. Individual health choices are not always compatible with the health of the general public; for instance, unvaccinated individuals can be carriers of disease, and secondhand smoke infringes on the health of those who choose not to smoke. As part of their "police powers," states can pass legislation to regulate health behaviors to prevent the spread of disease.[59] Mass vaccination campaigns have highlighted this tension for more than a century. The Supreme Court ruled in *Jacobson v. Massachusetts* (1905) that states can require compulsory vaccinations, reasoning that individual freedoms can be subordinated to the promotion of the common good in certain cases.[60] This precedent has been used to defend school vaccination requirements and the rights of public schools to refuse admission to unvaccinated children.

Public schools have played an essential role in the provision and enforcement of vaccine requirements because they provide access to society's most vulnerable population, children, due to compulsory primary education laws, which require all children to attend school from the age of six through fifteen. State requirements are moderated by vaccine waivers, which allow parents to opt out of vaccination due to religious or personal objections. Studies have found that communities with higher rates of opt-out also have higher rates of infection and greater incidence of epidemic spread of disease.[61] Vaccine hesitancy was fueled by a 1998 study published in the *Lancet*, a highly respected journal, linking autism to thimerosal, a preservative containing trace amounts of mercury and used to prevent contamination of vaccine. Thimerosal was removed from all vaccines except seasonal flu by 2001 and numerous CDC studies since have been unable to detect a relationship between exposure and autism.[62] The 1998 study was retracted in 2010 when it was discovered that the investigator had used fraudulent data and had not revealed financial conflicts of interest regarding money received from lawyers seeking to sue vaccine manufacturers.

State requirements for vaccination also require increased access to vaccines for parents and children if they are to be successful. Section 317 of the Public Health Service Act of 1962 authorizes the Vaccine Assistance Act, the first national program to provide federal funding to states to purchase vaccines. In addition, the 1993 Vaccines for Children Program provides access to vaccines for children who are uninsured or underinsured.

Gardasil, the first vaccine licensed for human papillomavirus (HPV), provides an interesting case study. It was licensed in 2006 for four strains of HPV, a cause of both genital warts and cervical cancer. Immediately after approval, twenty-four states introduced legislation to mandate vaccination, yet only two states passed legislation.[63] Stumbling blocks for an HPV vaccine mandate include newness of the vaccine; sexual transmission and lack of transmission through casual contact; resistance to the promotion of the product through lobbying by the manufacturer, Merck; price; aversion to government coercion and vaccines generally; as well as the policymaking process.[64] Barriers to individual uptake of the HPV vaccine in the United States include lack of knowledge and information support from health care professionals, cost, the need for three visits over six months to complete the series, and perceived low risk, especially for younger ages and males.[65]

Australia provides an interesting case comparison to the United States. The vaccine is paid for by the state and provided to girls ages eleven through thirteen through the public school system in Australia, potentially eliminating barriers to care.[66] Early results show a high uptake rate in that country (70 percent) and a decrease in the incidence of genital warts of more than 90 percent.[67] Due to the long latency period from infection to clinical symptoms, it is too early to see potential effects on cervical cancer rates.

HIV Infection

HIV is a blood-borne disease transmitted through sexual contact, shared needles, contaminated blood supplies, or mother-to-child transmission during childbirth. Increasing viral load and subsequent symptoms result in Acquired Immunodeficiency Syndrome (AIDS). HIV emerged in the early 1980s as a completely unknown disease in populations of men who have sex with men and injection drug users in the cities of New York and San Francisco. Researchers quickly discovered cases in the general population, and an unprecedented research effort led to the discovery of the virus and antiretroviral therapies within a decade. Advances in antiretroviral therapies (ART) have converted a disease that was once a death sentence to a manageable chronic illness for those with access to appropriate treatments.

Prevention Programs and Policies: Screen and Treat

Lacking a cure or preventive vaccine, "screen and treat" has been the approach to controlling the HIV epidemic. In 2006, the CDC recommended universal, voluntary HIV screening using an opt-out methodology, which requires physicians to inform patients that an HIV test will be included with basic lab work unless the patient declines, for all adult patients in all health care settings, including pregnant women.[68] In 2013, the CDC reaffirmed this recommendation, specifying all patients between the ages of fifteen and sixty-five and pregnant women should be screened, regardless of risk status, with more regular screenings for those at high risk.[69] Implementation of the CDC's recommendation has been low, in part due to patient perceptions of social stigma or their own status as low-risk, as well as limitations on providers

who must navigate potentially awkward conversations with patients and competing priorities during limited appointment time with patients who may have multiple conditions to address at a single visit.[70] Screening is vital, as it is estimated that 20 percent of the 1.1 million infected individuals in the United States are unaware of their status[71] and contribute disproportionately to new HIV infections (50 percent of the 56,000 annual cases)[72], as seen in Figure 23.6.

President Barack Obama (2009–) renewed the federal commitment to HIV prevention when he established the HIV Care Continuum Initiative by executive order in July 2013.[73] He pledged an additional $100 million in funding to the NIH, in honor of World AIDS Day 2013, to identify new therapies.[74]

Hepatitis C

Another virus to emerge in the 1980s was Hepatitis C, which was first discovered in 1989.[75] Similar to HIV, the early symptoms of infection are not immediately life-threatening, but the disease follows a long temporal course and individuals may remain asymptomatic for years. There were only 849 confirmed cases of Hepatitis C in 2011 but estimates place the number of newly infected individuals that year at 17,000.[76] Increasing viral load in the later stages of infection leads to cirrhosis, liver cancer, and premature death. The population most at risk is the baby boomers, born between 1946 and 1964, and those exposed to infected blood through blood transfusions prior to 1992 or through shared needles.

FIGURE 23.6 **The HIV Care Continuum in the United States**

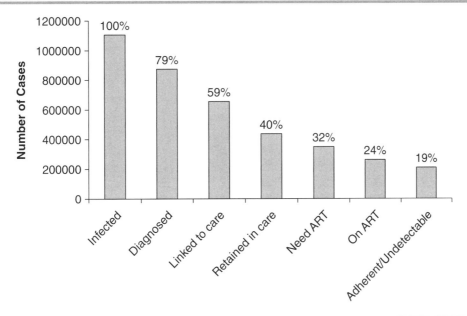

SOURCE: Adapted from Edward M. Gardner et al., "The Spectrum of Engagement in HIV Care and Its Relevance to Test-and-Treat Strategies for Prevention of HIV Infection," *Clinical Infectious Diseases* 52 (2011): 793–800, Figure 2.

The reasons for higher rates of infection in the baby boomer generation are unknown. Fortunately, the cure rate has risen from 6 percent in the 1980s to between 80 percent and 90 percent with the latest available drug treatments.[77]

Prevention Programs and Policies: A Hepatitis C–Free Future?

Mandatory screening of the blood supply for Hepatitis C began in 1992. In October 2012, the CDC recommended screening of all baby boomers for Hepatitis C infection.[78] Advances in antiretroviral therapy research driven by the HIV epidemic have also contributed to the discovery of a cure for Hepatitis C.[79] In November 2013, the Food and Drug Administration (FDA) approved a new line of drugs for Hepatitis C, with several similar drugs pending approval in 2014 and 2015. These new treatments have fewer side effects, a higher cure rate, and are of shorter duration than current available treatments. Questions remain regarding equitable access to these drugs, which could cost $90,000 for a single course of treatment.

Summary of Progress in Reducing Infectious Diseases

The progress in reducing death rates from infectious diseases over the past fifty years has largely been achieved through sanitation and maintained through mass vaccination. Despite this progress, challenges remain, such as concerns about vaccine safety that have led to lower rates of vaccine coverage and increased risk of future epidemics. Other infectious diseases have emerged as problems as well. For example, septicemia is a severe blood infection that killed 10.4 people per 100,000 in 2010 and is now the leading cause of infectious disease death.[80] Among hospitalizations, principal diagnosis rates of sepsis increased 153 percent from 2000 to 2009, and secondary diagnosis rates increased 66 percent in the same period.[81] Hospital-acquired infections have certainly contributed to the rise in sepsis rates, but how much they have contributed is unclear. Risk factors for hospital acquired infections include an aging population, more complex medical procedures, more individuals with chronic disease, and antibiotic-resistant strains of bacteria.[82] Finally, infection control has also been linked to prevention of chronic disease, such as cancer. An estimated 15 percent of all cancers are linked to viral agents, including liver cancer (Hepatitis C) and cervical cancer (HPV).[83] A cure for HIV remains elusive, but it has in many ways become a manageable chronic illness for those with access to treatment.

CHRONIC DISEASES

Chronic diseases are characterized by uncertain etiology, multiple risk factors, a long latency period, a prolonged course of illness, noncontagious origin, functional impairment or disability, and incurability.[84] In more general terms, a chronic disease can be defined as a disease that has a prolonged temporal course that does not resolve spontaneously, and for which a complete cure is rarely achieved. The course of a chronic disease can be viewed as a continuum from the "upstream" social and environmental determinants of health, which may take many years for symptoms of exposure to develop, to behavioral risk factors, chronic conditions, chronic diseases, and finally impairment, disability, and ultimately premature death.

For successful intervention, chronic disease requires a "persistent, long-term perspective" and many years to see results of upstream interventions.[85] This timeline is not always consistent with the U.S. policymaking system and the demands on policymakers for quick results within the timeline of election cycles. Finally, many chronic diseases have complex etiologies and are multifactorial in nature. For instance, smoking is a risk factor for both lung cancer and cardiovascular disease, the two leading causes of death from chronic disease in the United States. There is no silver bullet when it comes to chronic disease prevention, but rather a comprehensive, multipronged strategy is necessary for success.[86]

Many improvements in chronic disease mortality have resulted from increased screenings and federal investment in research. The long latency period between exposure and development of disease symptoms, as well as the multifactorial etiology of many chronic diseases, makes it difficult to develop a single, effective prevention policy. However, the "prolonged temporal course" of chronic disease means that screening and early detection is an effective secondary prevention measure.

Cancer

It is important to keep in mind that cancer is not a single disease, but rather a group of many cancers with diverse causes and clinical courses. Overall cancer death rates increased by 11 percent from 1960 to 1990, and have decreased 20 percent since that time. The decrease in cancer deaths is due to declines in lung, cancer, and prostate cancer deaths in men and breast and colon cancer deaths in women.[87] The trends by specific cancer are quite diverse, with some cancers decreasing (e.g., stomach cancer) and some increasing (e.g., lung cancer) during the past fifty years. In general, improvements in early detection and treatment through routine screening have led to significantly lowered mortality rates (see Figure 23.7 and Figure 23.8).

Risk factors for cancer are many and include exposure to tobacco, dietary factors, carcinogens (cancer-causing agents, such as asbestos), and genetic mutations (such as the BRCA1 and BRCA2 genes and breast cancer). Lung cancer is one exception to this rule, since it is known that a single agent, smoking, accounts for more than 80 percent of all lung cancers in the population.[88] The link between tobacco

FIGURE 23.7 **Site-Specific Cancer Trends, Males, 1930–2009**

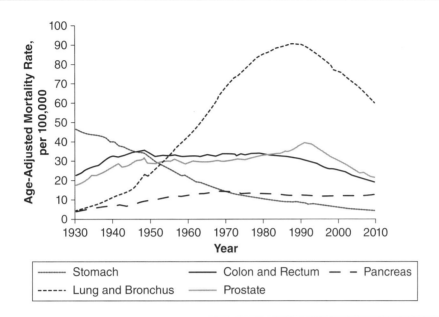

SOURCE: Adapted from the American Cancer Society. Rates are age-adjusted to the 2000 U.S. standard population. Note that rates cross three ICD thresholds, ICD-8 (1968–1978), ICD-9 (1979–1998), and ICD-10 (1999–2010), resulting in some change in the classification of death counts.

and adverse health outcomes was first identified in the 1950s, and in 1964 the U.S. Surgeon General released a landmark report on smoking and health that advised smokers to quit as soon as possible. Smoking rates peaked in 1965 at 42 percent of all adults and have since dropped 50 percent, to 19 percent in 2010.[89] Due to the long latency period between exposure (smoking) and disease, lung cancer rates have continued to rise during the same time period.

FIGURE 23.8 **Site-Specific Cancer Trends, Females, 1930–2009**

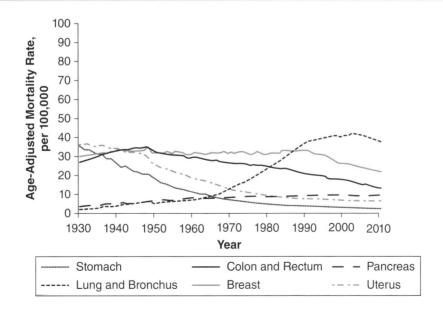

SOURCE: Adapted from the American Cancer Society. Rates are age-adjusted to the 2000 U.S. standard population. Note that rates cross three ICD thresholds, ICD-8 (1968–1978), ICD-9 (1979–1998), and ICD-10 (1999–2010), resulting in some change in the classification of death counts.

Tobacco Use among Youth and Young Adults

In March 2012, Secretary of Health and Human Services Kathleen Sebelius (in office 2009–2014) unveiled the *Surgeon General's Report on Tobacco Use among Youth and Young Adults.* It was the first report from the Surgeon General to specifically analyze tobacco use among youth ages twelve to seventeen and young adults ages eighteen to twenty-five in the United States. Teens and young adults represent a vulnerable population and deserve special attention in the prevention of tobacco-related disease and premature death if the United States is to achieve a tobacco-free generation.

Tobacco-related disease remains the leading cause of preventable death in the United States and one of the most well-documented linkages between exposure and adverse health outcomes. Adult smoking rates declined by 50 percent from 1965 to 2005, from 42 percent to 21 percent of all adults age eighteen years and older. Rates have dropped little in the last decade, remaining stable at 19 percent. It is known that smoking kills, yet one in five Americans continues to smoke, with two new smokers replacing every tobacco-related death each year.

Targeting youth and young adults to prevent use of tobacco products is essential to prevent future tobacco-related deaths. The teenage and young adult years are a critical period in human development in which individuals are more susceptible to outside influences and lifelong habits are formed. Tobacco use habits are formed early in life, with 90 percent of current smokers taking up smoking before the age of eighteen, and 99 percent starting before age twenty-six. Exposure to advertising in films, flavored products, and peer pressure all contribute to youth and young adult smoking rates.

The Obama administration has strengthened access to smoking cessation services through designation of tobacco use screening and cessation counseling as preventive services and essential health benefits under the Patient Protection and Affordable Care Act. The administration has also signed into law new legislation to limit the advertising of tobacco products to youth, including limits on "light" and "mild" labeling and candy- and fruit-flavored products.

Unfortunately, states are failing to meet the Centers for Disease Control and Prevention recommended funding levels for youth smoking prevention and cessation activities. According to a 2013 report by the nonprofit coalition Campaign for Tobacco-Free Kids, states will receive $25 billion in funding from the Master Tobacco Settlement of 1998 and taxation of tobacco products in fiscal year 2014. However, only 1.9 percent of that revenue is earmarked for youth smoking prevention and cessation activities.

SOURCES: U.S. Department of Health and Human Services, "Preventing Tobacco Use among Youth and Young Adults: A Report of the Surgeon General" (Rockville, MD: U.S. Department of Health and Human Services, 2012); Campaign for Tobacco-Free Kids, "Broken Promises to Our Children: The 1998 State Tobacco Settlement 15 Years Later," http://www.tobaccofreekids.org/what_we_do/state_local/tobacco_settlement.

Prevention Programs and Policies: Tobacco Prevention and Early Detection

President Richard M. Nixon (1969–1974) began the War on Cancer in 1971 with authorization of the National Cancer Act to improve funding for cancer research.[90] Despite the importance of cancer research, many critics argued that these investments did not lead to progress in reducing cancer death rates.[91] As a result, federal and state public health agencies began to focus on reducing smoking rates as a way to reduce overall cancer death rates. Research suggested that making progress in tobacco control required comprehensive, multilevel programs and policies. The WHO coined the term *MPOWER* to describe six evidence-based tobacco control measures: *monitoring* tobacco use and prevention policies; *protecting* people from tobacco smoke; *offering* help to quit tobacco use; *warning* people about the dangers of tobacco; *enforcing* bans on tobacco advertising, promotion, and sponsorship; and *raising* taxes on tobacco.[92]

An emerging policy challenge in the prevention of lung cancer is the regulation of e-cigarettes, or electronic nicotine delivery systems (ENDS). FDA classification of ENDS products as either a tobacco product or a pharmaceutical will affect the advertising and sales of the product. Lacking federal response, many states have already passed laws to classify ENDS products themselves, resulting in a patchwork of state-level laws and regulations. Concerns regarding ENDS products include lack of knowledge as to their efficacy as smoking cessation tools, potential unintended consequences of reduced stigma of smoking, and unknown effects of chemicals used in the fuel cartridge to create the vapor. Further basic research into the efficacy and safety of e-cigarettes is needed before they can be appropriately regulated.

As research demonstrated the effectiveness of mammography, public health efforts began to focus on strategies to increase breast cancer screening in the entire population. In 1990, the Breast and Cervical Cancer Mortality Prevention Act was passed to provide access to screening for low-income and underserved populations through the National Breast and Cervical Cancer Early Detection Program.

Despite overall progress in increasing cancer screening rates, the costs of screening must be weighed. False positives and the costs of more frequent screening and biopsies represent an opportunity cost of money not spent in other investments. In 2009, the United States Preventive Services Task Force, a panel of experts who evaluate the latest scientific

Big Tobacco

The Master Tobacco Settlement of 1998 ended litigation by forty-six states (excluding Florida, Minnesota, Mississippi, and Texas, who had already settled) against four of the major tobacco companies (Brown & Williamson, Lorillard, Philip Morris, and R.J. Reynolds) for damages suffered by the public health system, particularly Medicaid, for the high costs of treatment of smoking-related disease and smoking cessation programs. The states argued in their case that the tobacco companies had both deliberately failed to divulge information and presented misleading information regarding the negative health effects of smoking. Section III of the agreement outlines new regulations on the advertising and promotion of tobacco products, including limitations regarding youth advertising, lobbying, and health claims:

(q) Prohibition on Agreements to Suppress Research. No Participating Manufacturer may enter into any contract, combination or conspiracy with any other Tobacco Product Manufacturer that has the purpose or effect of: (1) limiting competition in the production or distribution of information about health hazards or other consequences of the use of their products; (2) limiting or suppressing research into smoking and health; or (3) limiting or suppressing research into the marketing or development of new products. Provided, however, that nothing in this subsection shall be deemed to (1) require any Participating Manufacturer to produce, distribute or otherwise disclose any information that is subject to any privilege or protection; (2) preclude any Participating Manufacturer from entering into any joint defense or joint legal interest agreement or arrangement (whether or not in writing), or from asserting any privilege pursuant thereto; or (3) impose any affirmative obligation on any Participating Manufacturer to conduct any research.

(r) Prohibition on Material Misrepresentations. No Participating Manufacturer may make any material misrepresentation of fact regarding the health consequences of using any Tobacco Product, including any tobacco additives, filters, paper or other ingredients. Nothing in this subsection shall limit the exercise of any First Amendment right or the assertion of any defense or position in any judicial, legislative or regulatory forum.

SOURCE: "Master Settlement Agreement," http://publichealthlawcenter.org/topics/tobacco-control/tobacco-control-litigation/master-settlement-agreement.

---

evidence and make recommendations for clinical practice, updated the recommended screening guidelines for breast cancer in women by increasing the age at first screening from forty to fifty years of age and lengthening the time between screenings from one year to two years, among great outrage from organizations dedicated to cancer elimination.[93] The updated recommendation reflected evidence that the cost of false positives, as well as more frequent screenings, did not justify the very small number of additional lives saved compared to biannual screening at a later age. Results published in February 2014 from the Canadian National Breast Screening Study, a randomized trial comparing mammography to clinical exam in women ages forty to fifty-nine, also showed no reduction in twenty-five-year mortality between groups and significant overdiagnosis in the mammography group.[94] Finally, access to and utilization of screening is not universal, limiting the effectiveness of early detection. In 2010, the cancer screening rates in eligible populations were as follows: 72.4 percent (breast), 83 percent (cervical), 58.6 percent (colorectal).[95]

In conclusion, changes in tobacco control policies and increases in cancer screening have led to reductions in cancer death rates since 1990. However, as with most progress in public health, disparities remain an area of concern in cancer treatment and prevention. Changes in tobacco use have created disparities in lung cancer based on both gender and ethnicity. Barriers to access to

screening and costly treatments mean that many more low-income and minority women are diagnosed with late-stage breast and cervical cancer each year than other groups.

Cardiovascular Disease

Cardiovascular disease (CVD), or heart disease, encompasses all diseases of the heart and blood vessels, including heart attack, heart failure, stroke, atherosclerosis (plaque build-up in the arteries), and arrhythmias. The Framingham Heart Study is the longest-running longitudinal cohort study of the risk factors for CVD in the United States. Begun in 1948, the study enrolled its third generation of participants in 2002. More than 2,473 articles have been published utilizing Framingham data.[96] Smoking, poor diet, lack of exercise, elevated alcohol consumption, and air pollution have all been identified as risk factors for cardiovascular disease. Improvements in these areas, as well as increased screening and treatment, have cut the risk of heart disease by 80 percent since 1960 (see Table 23.1 and Figure 23.1).

Prevention Programs and Policies: High Blood Pressure Detection and Control

The U.S. National High Blood Pressure Campaign is a collaboration between professional agencies, state health departments, and community organizations to educate the public and raise awareness and control of hypertension.[97]

Screening for hypertension and high blood cholesterol, followed by treatment with lifestyle changes (diet and exercise) and statins have dramatically lowered the death rate due to heart disease and stroke. However, only 64.7 percent of patients with hypertension receive recommended care, and poorly controlled hypertension still results in 68,000 deaths annually[98] and only 10.5 percent of participants received appropriate alcohol intervention.[99] The FDA has also tightened regulations on trans fats and voted to remove them from the national food supply entirely in 2013.[100]

Progress in the Reducing Chronic Diseases

Chronic disease is difficult to address via the policymaking process as prevention and treatment require long-term, committed programs that rarely show evidence of effectiveness in a single election cycle. The PPACA seeks to improve the management of chronic illness by incentivizing the use of preventive services through elimination of cost-sharing, co-pays, coinsurance, and deductibles to individuals for preventive services. It is possible that the effects of increased access to preventive services may not be seen for a generation. Unfortunately, increasing financial access does not always translate directly to implementation of evidence-based practices. Only 60 percent of patients receive recommended care,[101] meaning 40 percent of patients do not receive care that is known to be effective. Changes in physician reimbursement under the PPACA are designed to promote screening by tying payments to quality of care, including delivery of recommended preventive services.

Finally, the expanding understanding of the multiple determinants of health is breaking down silos of care and revealing new links between chronic disease and environmental risk factors. For example, evidence shows that dental health and periodontal disease are linked to increased risk of cardiovascular disease,[102,103] yet mandatory coverage of adult dental services was conspicuously absent from recent health care reforms (dental coverage is only an essential health benefit for children under the PPACA). Air pollution, in particular fine particulate matter less than 2.5 micrometers in diameter, is associated with increased risk of cardiovascular disease[104] as well as the development of asthma and the onset of asthmatic episodes.[105] The 1996 Atlanta Olympics and 2008 Beijing Olympics provide natural experiments showing a reduction in emergency room visits for asthma concurrent with reductions in traffic congestion to improve air quality for the games.[106,107] A 2013 study modeled the effects of reduced air pollution and increased active transport on health and found that 1,295 lives could be saved in the Midwest each year by replacing 50 percent of all car trips of less than three miles with bicycle transport, during the summer months only, through the combined reduction in air pollution (608 fewer deaths) and the physical benefits of active transport (687 fewer deaths).[108]

INJURIES AND VIOLENCE

Injuries and violence constitute a major public health problem in the United States, killing more than 180,000[109] and generating an additional 66 million[110] emergency room visits in 2010 alone. Mortality from injuries is the leading cause of death among ages of one to forty-four years in the United States, disproportionately affecting the young and those in their most productive working years.[111] The majority (60 percent) of the 180,811 injury deaths in the United States in 2010[112] were due to three causes: motor vehicle crashes (33,687 deaths), firearms (31,672 deaths), and accidental poisoning (42,917 deaths).

Dr. John Gordon was the first to apply the infectious disease triad (agent-host-environment) to injury, reframing the understanding of the causes of injury as well as where and when it is possible to intervene to prevent injury deaths. In Deborah Stone's typology of causal theories, accidental causes receive the least attention in the policymaking process, because their actions are unguided and the consequences are unintended, making responsibility for redress difficult to locate.[113] Early understandings of the causes of injury told a story of an individual behavior problem, rather than an environmental or systems approach, as well as that of an uncontrollable "accident," leaving little room for policy intervention since one cannot effectively control for unpredictable, random events.

The classification of injury by mechanism has strongly influenced the institutional location of injury surveillance and prevention activities. Worker safety is overseen by the Occupational Safety and Health Administration (OSHA) within the U.S. Department of Labor. Motor vehicle safety is monitored by the National Highway and Traffic Safety Administration (NHTSA) within the U.S. Department of Transportation. Firearms, homicide, and drug abuse prevention activities have been closely tied to the Drug Enforcement Agency and the Bureau of Alcohol, Tobacco, Firearms and Explosives, both housed in the U.S. Department of Justice, in addition to local law enforcement agencies. Between 1996 and 2013, the CDC and NIH were prohibited from gun control research and largely absent from conversations about this injury type.

Since OSHA's inception in 1971, worker fatalities have declined 65 percent while injury and illness rates are down 67 percent.[114] Shifts in the U.S. economy away from manufacturing and toward the service sector have significantly altered the conditions in which individuals work, further contributing to a decrease in on-the-job injuries.[115] Since 1970, when the NHTSA was established, deaths from motor vehicle crashes have fallen 60 percent, driving much of the decline in the all-cause injury mortality rate.

Motor Vehicle Crashes

Since 1960, the rate of death from motor vehicle crash has been reduced by one-half, from 23.1 per 100,000 population to 11.3 per 100,000. This progress is a result of efforts to address several of the risk factors for motor vehicle crash deaths, including vehicle safety (seatbelts, airbags, bumpers), driver characteristics (intoxication, age, seatbelt use, excessive speed), infrastructure, and the availability of prompt and effective medical care (trauma systems) in the event of a crash.

Prevention Programs and Policies: Motor Vehicle Safety

The application of policy to the problem of motor vehicle safety is a public health success story. In response to the rising death toll due to motor vehicle accidents, the Highway Safety Act was passed in 1966 under President Lyndon B. Johnson (1963–1969). This legislation established the National Highway Safety Bureau (renamed the National Highway and Traffic Safety Administration in 1970) within the Department of Transportation. Dr. William Haddon Jr., the father of injury epidemiology, was its first director. Section 402 of the act provides federal funding to state-level highway safety activities.[116] Motor vehicle safety is one of the best understood and well-studied areas of injury prevention.

Seatbelt installation was required of manufacturers in all new vehicles beginning in 1968[117]; however, availability of the new safety devices was not sufficient to change individual behavior. Low seatbelt usage rates among drivers and passengers prompted states to legally require seatbelt use beginning in 1988.[118] Since 1993, many states have moved from secondary enforcement of seatbelt laws to primary enforcement, allowing police to ticket drivers solely for lack of seatbelt use.[119] States have also been instrumental in establishing speed limits, the use of sobriety checkpoints to deter and enforce bans on drunk driving,[120] and graduated driver's licensing programs to reduce crashes among youth.[121] The right of state governments to screen for drunk drivers using sobriety checkpoints, temporary and unannounced locations where all vehicles are stopped and drivers screened for intoxication, was upheld by the Supreme Court in *Michigan Department of State Police v. Sitz* (1990), in which the Court reasoned that the searches were reasonable given the small inconvenience to innocent drivers who are stopped and the large government interest in preventing drunk driving.[122] However, not all states use this tactic and some have ruled that sobriety checkpoints are not legal under that state's constitution.

Personal stories of injury have galvanized individuals, communities, and consumer groups to act at local and national levels for change. Mothers Against Drunk Driving (MADD) was founded by Candy Lightner, whose daughter Cari was killed by a drunk driver in 1980. The organization has worked hard to change cultural norms and policy to reduce drunk driving. In 1990, MADD adopted a per se blood alcohol content (BAC) of 0.08 as part of its policy platform, and in 1993, the organization issued a report card rating each state's efforts to reduce drunk driving.[123] In 2000, President Bill Clinton (1993–2001) passed a crossover sanction, or unfunded mandate, requiring states to adopt a per se BAC of 0.08 or lose federal highway funds.[124]

When states have failed to implement policies, local municipalities have taken charge. The town of Carrboro, North Carolina, banned cell phone use while driving after a University of North Carolina–Chapel Hill student was hit by a distracted driver in 2010. The ban has been challenged by tow truck drivers who use their cell phones to call in from a job and the case is now pending in the North Carolina Supreme Court.

Homicide

While significant improvements have been made in the area of motor vehicle safety, the rates of homicide remained largely unchanged from 1960 to 2010. Two-thirds of all homicides are firearm-related.[125] Deaths from homicide are overwhelmingly among young African American males, representing an enormous loss to society in productivity and potential (see Figure 23.9 and Figure 23.10). A cross-sectional study of 2003 WHO data showed that firearm homicide rates are 19.5 times higher in the United States than in other Organisation of Economic Co-operation and Development nations,[126] yet studies suggest that the United States does not have a higher rate of violent crime.[127] Rather, high rates of poverty, inequality, and access to lethal weapons are risk factors for homicide. Social cohesion through the development of neighborhood associations has been identified as a protective factor in communities seeking to reduce homicide rates.[128]

Prevention Programs and Policies: Gun Control

A spate of mass shootings in 2012 prompted renewed interest in violence and gun control. In response, President Obama issued twenty-three executive orders regarding gun control in January 2013, including an order authorizing the CDC to conduct firearms research. The CDC previously funded firearms research in the 1980s and early 1990s, but was explicitly banned from doing so (along with the NIH) by Congress in 1996 under pressure from the National Rifle Association.[129] At least one study has identified an association between increased gun control laws and lower mortality from firearms at the state level, but results in the literature are mixed.[130]

Surveillance and lack of data regarding firearms remain barriers to research. The National Violent Death Reporting System was launched in 2002 by the CDC and modeled from an existing, privately funded surveillance

FIGURE 23.9 **Time Trends in Homicide Rates, by Gender and Race/Ethnicity, 1950–2010**

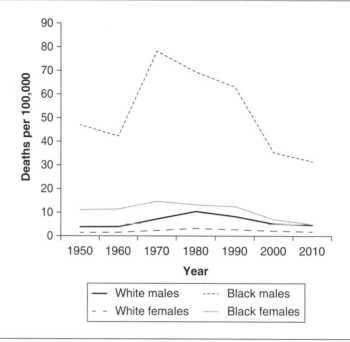

SOURCE: Data from National Center for Health Statistics, *Health, United States, 2012: With Special Feature on Emergency Care* (Hyattsville, MD: National Center for Health Statistics, 2013).

system.[131] This reporting system seeks to centralize data and improve identification of violent deaths of all types in the United States. It is currently funded by the CDC in eighteen states, with plans to expand to a fully national system.

FIGURE 23.10 **Homicide Rates, by Age, Gender, and Race/Ethnicity, 2010**

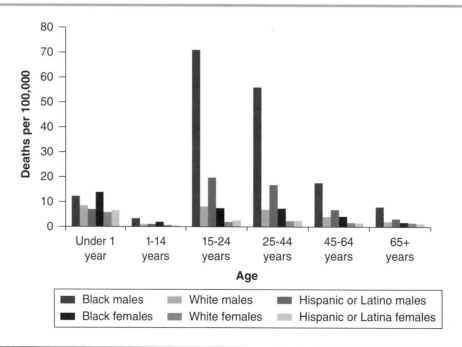

SOURCE: Data from National Center for Health Statistics, *Health, United States, 2012: With Special Feature on Emergency Care* (Hyattsville, MD: National Center for Health Statistics, 2013).

Suicide

The rates of suicide remained largely unchanged from 1960 to 2010. As of 2009, the United States lost more lives each year to suicide than to motor vehicle crashes.[132] Half of all suicides are firearm-related.[133] Firearms are a contributing, but not a necessary nor sufficient cause of violent death.[134] However, several studies have found significantly increased odds of both homicide and suicide when a gun is present in the home.[135,136]

Suicide rates have remained static in all groups since 1960 (see Figure 23.11). Given that suicide is a rare event and the known risk factors, including depression, drug use, presence of a firearm in the home, and military service, are common, it is very difficult to identify the individuals most at risk of suicide.[137] Death rates from suicide show an inverse pattern compared to homicide and are highest among older white males (see Figure 23.12). However, homicide and suicide do show similar trends in a common risk factor: exposure to firearms. Firearm-related suicide rates are 5.8 times higher in the United States than in other high-income nations, despite the country having a lower suicide rate overall.[138]

Prevention Programs and Policies: Mental Health Care

A strategic approach to suicide would include identification of high-risk subpopulations, identification and matching of effective interventions to these groups, identification of effective intervention settings, and establishment of timelines for research and intervention.[139] The Patient Protection and Affordable Care Act of 2010 and the Mental Health Parity and Addiction Equity Act of 2008 expand access to treatment services for those suffering from mental illness, a risk factor for suicide. Social stigma surrounding mental illness remains a barrier to accessing and receiving treatment, particularly for men, who are less likely than women to seek help.[140] Cyber-bullying among youth is a growing concern and another potential risk factor.

Accidental Poisoning

Accidental poisoning, largely due to prescription drug overdose, has exploded as a public health crisis in the last decade, increasing more than 600 percent since 2000 (see Figure 23.13). In 2012, accidental poisoning surpassed motor vehicle crashes in number of lives lost. This increase is largely due to opioid (painkillers) overdose, which caused more deaths in 2007 than cocaine and heroin combined.[141] A movement in the 1990s to treat chronic pain has resulted in increased opioid prescription, to the point that today the nation consumes 80 percent of the global supply, more per capita than any other country.[142]

Prevention Policies and Programs: Shifting from Legal to Public Health Approaches

The interaction between law enforcement, drug control policy, and drug abuse is complex. The Obama administration's

FIGURE 23.11 **Time Trends in Suicide Rates, by Gender and Race/Ethnicity, 1950–2010**

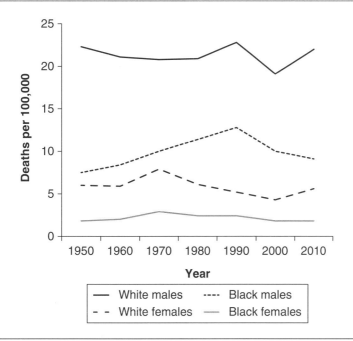

SOURCE: Data from National Center for Health Statistics, *Health, United States, 2012: With Special Feature on Emergency Care* (Hyattsville, MD: National Center for Health Statistics, 2013).

FIGURE 23.12 **Suicide Rates, by Age, Gender, and Race/Ethnicity, 2010**

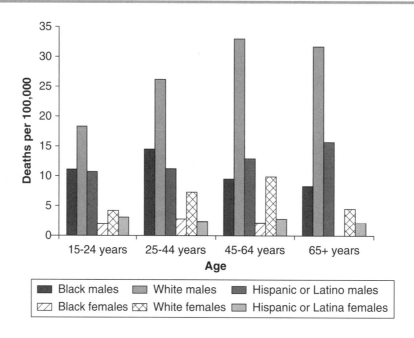

SOURCE: Data from National Center for Health Statistics, *Health, United States, 2012: With Special Feature on Emergency Care* (Hyattsville, MD: National Center for Health Statistics, 2013).

National Drug Control Strategy, published yearly since 2010, explicitly seeks to move drug abuse from the law enforcement sphere into the public health sector.[143] Current increases in drug overdose are not due to illegal drug use, but rather abuse of prescription drugs that were obtained legally, often by friends and family members. As such, the epidemic may

FIGURE 23.13 **Risk Ratios for the Leading Causes of Death, 1960 : 2010**

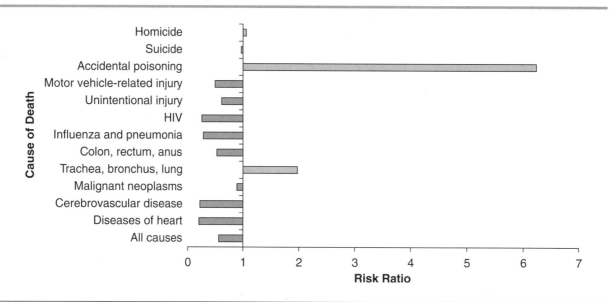

SOURCE: Data from National Center for Health Statistics, *Health, United States, 2012: With Special Feature on Emergency Care* (Hyattsville, MD: National Center for Health Statistics, 2013).

NOTE: Risk ratios (RRs) are calculated by dividing the cause-specific death rate in 1960 by the death rate in 2010. An RR of 1 indicates no change in the death rate. RRs less than 1 indicate a decrease in the death rate from 1960 to 2010, while RRs greater than 1 indicate an increase in the death rate.

require a different approach to drug control than has previously been used in the War on Drugs.

Primary prevention can be achieved through formulating drugs to prevent abuse, restricting access to prescriptions, and using prescription-tracking systems to prevent patients from filling multiple prescriptions at various locations. The PPACA and mental health parity laws also expand access to substance abuse and mental health treatment services. For increased access to be effective, individuals must also be aware of the dangers of drug abuse, particularly prescriptions. Secondary prevention can be achieved through access to opiate overdose reversal drugs, such as naloxone, to prevent death in the event of an overdose, as well as implementation of Good Samaritan laws to protect from legal prosecution individuals who call 911.

Progress in Injury Prevention

It is likely that there will be continued success in the prevention of motor vehicle crashes through innovations such as vehicle-to-vehicle (V2V) communications, which equip motor vehicles with sensors indicating location, speed, and warning signals to drivers. The NHTSA estimates that 80 percent of today's motor vehicle crashes could be avoided through the use of V2V technologies.[144] On February 3, 2014, the NHTSA announced that it will be paving the way for V2V technology based on results from the Safety Pilot program run jointly by the NHTSA and the Research and Innovative Technology Administration from 2011 through 2013 to evaluate the feasibility of these next-generation technologies.

In contrast, recent increases in suicide, homicide, and overdose rates threaten to erase gains made in other areas, such as motor vehicle safety. Experiences of interpersonal and self-directed violence are complex, often deeply personal events. The field of injury prevention currently lacks sufficient data and understanding of the underlying causes of these events, stymieing the development and evaluation of primary intervention programs as well as effective policy for prevention. Increased surveillance of violent death through the National Violent Death Reporting System (NVDRS) will fill a gap in the data needed for basic research and the identification of risk factors to inform effective policies in the future.

THE FUTURE OF DISEASE AND INJURY PREVENTION

Progress made in the prevention and control of disease and injury since 1960 has been monumental. Basic research into the causes of disease and injury informs policymaking, with clear causes resulting in more definitive policymaking, as is the case for vaccine-preventable diseases, smoking, and motor vehicle crashes. As understanding of the causes of disease and injury increase, the moral and ethical imperative for policy action increases. Progress thus far has been uneven between both health conditions and subpopulations. To achieve the next level of health for the nation—health equity—progress must accelerate in areas where inequities exist.

The extent of health-promoting policies highlights the tension between individual decision making and the promotion of population health. Effective public health interventions must balance individual rights with the common good, as seen in the recommended frequency of cancer screenings, mandates for folate supplementation, antismoking laws, mass vaccination campaigns, sobriety checkpoints, and even the individual mandate of the PPACA. Each of these policies infringes in some way on individual liberty in an effort to promote public health. The epidemiologic evidence can point us in the direction of interventions; however, political will and public perception will moderate the implementation of evidence-based policies.

In this chapter, we have also seen examples of incrementalism in policy development, for example, the slow expansion of Medicaid coverage of pregnant women in the 1980s and the link between evidence and decision making. Folate supplementation and seatbelt laws are further examples of evidence-based policies that had to be taken a step further (from recommendations to mandates) when additional evidence showed the limitations of voluntary behavior change. It is difficult to develop effective policy without data. A basic principle of quality improvement is that one cannot manage what is not measured. Development of data systems, such as the NVDRS, is essential to building evidence to establish the causal relationships surrounding SIDS, homicide, and suicide.

The Patient Protection and Affordable Care Act provides an important expansion of access to health care through increased rates of health insurance coverage. It is expected to continue the trend begun in the 1980s of expanding access to care for pregnant women through designation of maternity care as an essential health benefit and expansion of the Medicaid program (in many states). Designation of preventive services as an essential health benefit and the elimination of cost-sharing for these services have the potential to decrease rates of chronic illness and are a long-term investment in the health of the nation. Mental health parity and increased access to mental health services under the PPACA has the potential to lower rates of homicide and suicide. However, health care is not the only determinant of health, and future progress will require health promotion across sectors as well as intersectoral partnerships.

See also **Chapter 19: Children's Health and Health Care Policy (1960s–Present); Chapter 20: Women's Issues and American Health Care Policy (1960s–Present); Chapter 21:**

Minorities, Immigrants, and Health Care Policy: Disparities and Solutions (1960s–Present); Chapter 22: Aging and Health Care Policy (1990s–Present); Chapter 24: Mental Health and Social Policy (1960s–Present);

Chapter 25: Nutrition, Physical Activity, and the Obesity Epidemic: Issues, Policies, and Solutions (1960s–Present); Chapter 26: Interest Groups, Think Tanks, and Health Care Policy (1960s–Present).

NOTES

1. Commission on Social Determinants of Health, *Closing the Gap in a Generation: Health Equity through Action on the Social Determinants of Health* (Geneva, Switzerland: World Health Organization, 2008).

2. Lauren N. Gase, Radha Pennotti, and Kenneth D. Smith, "'Health in All Policies': Taking Stock of Emerging Practices to Incorporate Health in Decision Making in the United States," *Journal of Public Health Management and Practice* 19: 6 (2013): 529–540.

3. Anne Schneider and Helen Ingram, "Social Construction of Target Populations: Implications for Politics and Policy," *American Political Science Review* 87: 2 (1993): 334–347.

4. Margaret Whitehead, *The Concepts and Principles of Equity and Health* (Copenhagen, Denmark: World Health Organization, Regional Office for Europe, 1990).

5. Institute of Medicine, *Toward Quality Measures for Population Health and the Leading Health Indicators* (Washington, DC: National Academies Press, 2012).

6. Howard K. Koh, "A 2020 Vision for Healthy People," *New England Journal of Medicine* 362 (2010): 1653–1656.

7. Amartya Sen, "Why Health Equity?" *Health Economics* 11 (2002): 659–666.

8. U.S. Department of Health and Human Services, *Healthy People 2010 Final Review* (Washington, DC: U.S. Government Printing Office, 2011).

9. Centers for Disease Control and Prevention, "CDC Grand Rounds: Public Health Approaches to Reducing U.S. Infant Mortality," *Morbidity and Mortality Weekly Report* 62: 31 (2013): 625–628.

10. Ibid.

11. Centers for Disease Control and Prevention, "Ten Great Public Health Achievements—United States, 1900–1999," *Morbidity and Mortality Weekly Report* 48: 12 (1999): 241–243.

12. Michael C. Lu and Neal Halfon, "Racial and Ethnic Disparities in Birth Outcomes: A Life-Course Perspective," *Maternal and Child Health Journal* 7: 1 (2003): 13–30.

13. William C. Livingwood et al., "Impact of Pre-conception Health Care: Evaluation of a Social Determinants Focused Intervention," *Maternal and Child Health Journal* 14: 3 (2010): 382–391.

14. National Center for Health Statistics, *Health, United States, 2012: With Special Feature on Emergency Care* (Hyattsville, MD; National Center for Health Statistics, 2013).

15. Organisation for Economic Co-operation and Development, "OECD Family Database," http://www.oecd.org/social/family/database.

16. Commonwealth Fund, "Why Not the Best? Results from the National Scorecard on U.S. Health System Performance, 2011" (New York: Commonwealth Fund, October 2011), 26.

17. U.S. Department of Health and Human Services, Office of Disease Prevention and Health Promotion, "Maternal, Infant, and Child Health," http://www.healthypeople.gov/2020/topics objectives2020/objectiveslist.aspx?topicId=26.

18. Organisation for Economic Co-operation and Development, "OECD Family Database."

19. Centers for Medicare and Medicaid Services, "Pregnant Women," http://www.medicaid.gov/Medicaid-CHIP-Program-Information/By-Population/Pregnant-Women/Pregnant-Women.html.

20. Greg R. Alexander and Milton Kotelchuck, "Assessing the Role and Effectiveness of Prenatal Care: History, Challenges, and Directions for Future Research," *Public Health Reports* 116: 4 (2001): 306–316.

21. Kaiser Family Foundation, "Medicaid: A Timeline of Key Developments," http://kff.org/medicaid/timeline/medicaid-a-timeline-of-key-developments.

22. Ibid.

23. Ibid.

24. Kaiser Family Foundation, "Where Are States Today? Medicaid and CHIP Eligibility Levels for Children and Non-disabled Adults as of January 1, 2014," http://kff.org/medicaid/fact-sheet/where-are-states-today-medicaid-and-chip.

25. Julia L. DeClerque et al., "North Carolina's Infant Mortality Problems Persist: Time for a Paradigm Shift," *North Carolina Medical Journal* 65: 3 (2004): 138–146.

26. Patti Forest, "The Role of North Carolina Medicaid in Women's Health and Wellness," *North Carolina Medical Journal* 70: 5 (2009): 441–442.

27. Ibid.

28. "North Carolina Program Helps Keep More Babies Alive," *New York Times*, September 2, 1991, http://www.nytimes.com/1991/09/02/us/north-carolina-program-helps-keep-more-babies-alive.html.

29. Kaiser Family Foundation, "Infant Mortality Rate (Deaths per 1,000 Live Births), Linked Files, 2007–2009," http://kff.org/other/state-indicator/infant-death-rate.

30. Centers for Disease Control and Prevention, "Sudden Unexpected Infant Death and Sudden Infant Death Syndrome," http://www.cdc.gov/sids.

31. Ibid.

32. Rachel Y. Moon and Linda Fu, "Sudden Infant Death Syndrome: An Update," *Pediatrics in Review,* 33 (2012): 314–319.

33. Erin E. Tracy, Susan Haas, and Michele R. Lauria, "Newborn Care and Safety: The Black Box of Obstetric Practices and Residency Training," *Obstetrics and Gynecology* 120: 3 (2012): 643–464.

34. J. Bruce Beckwith, "Defining the Sudden Infant Death Syndrome," *Archives of Pediatric and Adolescent Medicine* 157 (2003): 286–290.

35. Michael P. Johnson and Karl Hufbauer, "Sudden Infant Death Syndrome as a Medical Research Problem since 1945," *Social Problems* 30: 1 (1982): 65–81.

36. Ibid.

37. Centers for Disease Control and Prevention, "CDC's Sudden Unexpected Infant Death Initiative," http://www.cdc.gov/sids/SUIDAbout.htm.

38. Cribs for Kids, "History," http://www.cribsforkids.org/history.

39. Andrew E. Czeizel and István Dudás, "Prevention of the First Occurrence of Neural-Tube Defects by Periconceptional Vitamin Supplementation," *New England Journal of Medicine* 327: 6 (1992): 1832–1835.

40. Margaret A. Honein et al., "Impact of Folic Acid Fortification of the US Food Supply on the Occurrence of Neural Tube Defects," *Journal of the American Medical Association* 285: 23 (2001): 2981–2986.

41. Centers for Disease Control and Prevention, "Spina Bifida and Anencephaly before and after Folic Acid Mandate— United States, 1995–1996 and 1999–2000," *Morbidity and Mortality Weekly Report* 53: 17 (2004): 362–365.

42. Andrew J. Copp and Nicholas D.E. Green, "Neural Tube Defects—Disorders of Neurulation and Related Embryonic Processes," *Wiley Interdisciplinary Reviews: Developmental Biology* 2: 2 (2013): 213–227.

43. Andrew J. Copp, Philip Sanier, and Nicholas D.E. Green, "Neural Tube Defects: Recent Advances, Unsolved Questions, and Controversies," *Lancet Neurology* 12: 8 (2013): 799–810.

44. Centers for Disease Control and Prevention, "Recommendations for the Use of Folic Acid to Reduce the Number of Cases of Spina Bifida and Other Neural Tube Defects," *Morbidity and Mortality Weekly Report* 41 (1991): RR–14.

45. Lawrence B. Finer and Mia R.S. Zolna, "Unintended Pregnancy in the United States: Incidence and Disparities, 2006." *Contraception* 84 (2011): 478–485.

46. Dale P. Lewis et al., "Drug and Environmental Factors Associated with Adverse Pregnancy Outcomes Part III: Folic Acid: Pharmacology, Therapeutic Recommendations, and Economics," *Annals of Pharmacotherapy* 32 (1998): 1087–1095.

47. U.S. Food and Drug Administration, "Food Standards: Amendments of Standards of Identity for Enriched Grain Products to Require Addition of Folic Acid," *Federal Register* 61 (1996): 8781–8797.

48. Carol J. Boushey et al., "A Quantitative Assessment of Plasma Homocysteine as a Risk Factor for Vascular Disease: Probable Benefits of Increasing Folic Acid Intakes," *Journal of the American Medical Association* 274 (1995): 1049–1057.

49. Joel B. Mason et al., "A Temporal Association between Folic Acid Fortification and an Increase in Colorectal Cancer Rates May Be Illuminating Important Biological Principles: A Hypothesis," *Cancer Epidemiology, Biomarkers & Prevention* 16: 7 (2007): 1325–1329.

50. Sarah G. Običan et al., "Folic Acid in Early Pregnancy: A Public Health Success Story," *FASEB Journal* 24 (2010): 4167–4174.

51. National Center for Health Statistics, *Health, United States, 2012.*

52. Abby Goodnough, "U.S. Infant Mortality Rate Fell Steadily from '05 to '11," *New York Times*, April 17, 2013, http://www.nytimes.com/2013/04/18/health/infant-mortality-rate-in-us-declines.html?_r=0.

53. "Mapping Milwaukee's Infant Mortality Crisis," *Journal Sentinel*, http://www.jsonline.com/news/130456803.html.

54. Centers for Disease Control and Prevention, "Ten Great Public Health Achievements—United States, 1900–1999," *Morbidity and Mortality Weekly Report* 48: 12 (1999): 241–243.

55. Ibid.

56. Willem G. van Panhuis et al., "Contagious Diseases in the United States from 1888 to the Present," *New England Journal of Medicine* 369: 22 (2013): 2152–2158.

57. Centers for Disease Control and Prevention, "Measles— United States, January 1–August 24, 2013," *Morbidity and Mortality Weekly Report* 62: 36 (2013): 741–743.

58. Elizabeth A. McGlynn et al., "The Quality of Health Care Delivered to Adults in the United States," *New England Journal of Medicine* 348: 26 (2003): 2635–2645.

59. Jorge E. Galva, Christopher Atchison, and Samuel Levey, "Public Health Strategy and the Police Powers of the State," *Public Health Reports* 120: Suppl 1 (2005): 20–27.

60. James Colgrove and Ronald Bayer, "Manifold Restraints: Liberty, Public Health, and the Legacy of *Jacobson v Massachusetts*," *Government, Politics, and Law* 95: 4 (2005): 571–576.

61. Jessica E. Atwell et. al., "Nonmedical Vaccine Exemptions and Pertussis in California, 2010," *Pediatrics* 132: 4 (2013): 624–630.

62. Centers for Disease Control and Prevention, "Timeline: Thimerosal in Vaccines (1999–2010)," http://www.cdc.gov/vaccinesafety/concerns/thimerosal/thimerosal_timeline.html.

63. James Colgrove, Sara Abiola, and Michelle M. Mello, "HPV Vaccination Mandates—Lawmaking amid Political and Scientific Controversy," *New England Journal of Medicine* 363: 8 (2010): 785–791.

64. Ibid.

65. Dawn M. Holman et al., "Barriers to Human Papillomavirus Vaccination among US Adolescents: A Systematic Review of the Literature," *Clinical Review and Education* 168: 1 (2014): 76–82.

66. Suzanne M. Garland, "The Australian Experience with the Human Papillomavirus Vaccine," *Clinical Therapeutics* 36: 1 (2014): 17–23.

67. Ibid.

68. Centers for Disease Control and Prevention, "Revised Recommendations for HIV Testing of Adults, Adolescents, and Pregnant Women in Health-Care Settings," *Morbidity and Mortality Weekly Report* 55: RR14 (2006): 1–17.

69. U.S. Preventive Services Task Force, *Screening for HIV: Final Recommendation Statement* (AHRQ Publication No. 12-05173-EF-3), http://www.uspreventiveservicestaskforce.org/uspstf13/hiv/hivfinalrs.htm.

70. Meghan B. Brennan et al., "Barriers and Facilitators of Universal HIV Screening among Internal Medicine Residents," *Wisconsin Medical Journal* 112: 5 (2013): 199–205.

71. Michael L. Campsmith et al., "Undiagnosed HIV Prevalence among Adults and Adolescents in the United States at the End of 2006," *Journal of Acquired Immune Deficiency Syndrome* 53 (2010): 619–624.

72. Centers for Disease Control and Prevention, "Estimates of New HIV Infections in the United States," http://www.cdc.gov/nchhstp/newsroom/docs/Fact-Sheet-on-HIV-Estimates.pdf.

73. Executive Order No. 13649, 78 F.R. 43057 (2013).

74. Barack Obama, "Remarks by the President on World AIDS Day," December 2, 2013, http://www.whitehouse.gov/the-press-office/2013/12/02/remarks-president-world-aids-day.

75. University of Chicago Medicine, "From a No-Name Virus to a Cure: Treatment Options Blossom for Hepatitis C," http://www.uchospitals.edu/news/features/hepatitisc-cure.html.

76. Centers for Disease Control and Prevention, "Hepatitis C FAQs for Health Professionals," http://www.cdc.gov/hepatitis/HCV/HCVfaq.htm.

77. Rui Tato Marinho and David Pires Barreira, "Hepatitis C, Stigma and Cure," *World Journal of Gastroenterology* 19, 40 (2013): 6703–6709.

78. Centers for Disease Control and Prevention, "Hepatitis C Testing for Anyone Born during 1945–1965: New CDC Recommendations," http://www.cdc.gov/features/hepatitisctesting.

79. Eddy Littler and Bo Oberg, "Achievements and Challenges in Antiviral Drug Discovery," *Antiviral Chemistry & Chemotherapy* 16 (2005): 155–168.

80. Centers for Disease Control and Prevention, National Center for Health Statistics, "About Underlying Cause of Death 1999–2010," http://wonder.cdc.gov/ucd-icd10.html.

81. Anne Elizhauser, Bernard Friedman, and Elizabeth Stranges, *Septicemia in U.S. Hospitals, 2009* (HCUP Statistical Brief #122) (Rockville, MD: Agency for Healthcare Research and Quality, October 2011), http://www.hcup-us.ahrq.gov/reports/statbriefs/sb122.pdf.

82. National Institute of General Medical Sciences, "Sepsis Fact Sheet," http://www.nigms.nih.gov/Education/factsheet_sepsis.html.

83. Harald zur Hausen, "Viruses in Human Cancers," *Science* 254: 5035 (1991):,1167–1173.

84. Matthew McKenna and Janet L. Collins, "Current Issues and Challenges in Chronic Disease Control," in *Chronic Disease Epidemiology and Control*, 3rd ed., edited by Patrick L. Remington, Ross C. Brownson, and Mark V. Wegner, 1–16 (Washington, DC: American Public Health Association, 2010).

85. Ibid.

86. Patrick L. Remington and Ross C. Brownson, "Fifty Years of Progress in Chronic Disease Epidemiology and Control," *Morbidity and Mortality Weekly Report* 60: Suppl. (2011): 70–77.

87. LeAnn D. Andersen et al., "Assessing a Decade of Progress in Cancer Control," *The Oncologist* 7 (2002): 200–204.

88. U.S. Department of Health and Human Services, *The Health Consequences of Smoking: A Report of the Surgeon General* (Atlanta, GA: U.S. Department of Health and Human Services, 2004).

89. National Center for Health Statistics, *Health, United States, 2012.*

90. Gina Kolata, "Hopeful Glimmers in Long War on Cancer," *New York Times*, November 4, 2013, http://www.nytimes.com/2013/11/04/booming/hopeful-glimmers-in-long-war-on-cancer.html?ref=health.

91. John C. Bailar and Elaine M. Smith, "Progress against Cancer?" *New England Journal of Medicine* 314 (1986): 1226–12232.

92. World Health Organization, "Tobacco Free Initiative," http://www.who.int/tobacco/mpower/en.

93. U.S. Preventive Services Task Force, "Screening for Cervical Cancer," http://www.uspreventiveservicestaskforce.org/uspstf/uspscerv.htm.

94. Anthony B. Miller et al., "Twenty Five Year Follow-up for Breast Cancer Incidence and Mortality of the Canadian National Breast Screening Study: Randomised Screening Trial," *BMJ* 348 (2014): g366.

95. Centers for Disease Control and Prevention, "Cancer Screening—United States, 2010," *Morbidity and Mortality Weekly Report* 61: 3 (2012): 41–45.

96. Framingham Heart Study, "Framingham Heart Study Bibliography," http://www.framinghamheartstudy.org/fhs-bibliography/index.php.

97. National Heart, Lung, and Blood Institute, "National High Blood Pressure Education Program Description," http://www.nhlbi.nih.gov/about/nhbpep/nhbp_pd.htm.

98. McGlynn et al., "The Quality of Health Care Delivered."

99. Ibid.

100. Tavernise, Sabrina. (November 7, 2013). "F.D.A. Ruling Would All but Eliminate Trans Fats." *New York Times.* http://www.nytimes.com/2013/11/08/health/fda-trans-fats.html.

101. Mark A. Schuster, Elizabeth A. McGlynn, and Robert H. Brook, "How Good Is the Quality of Health Care in the United States?" *Millbank Quarterly* 76 (1998): 517–563.

102. Jeffrey J. VanWormer et al., "Oral Hygiene and Cardiometabolic Disease Risk in the Survey of the Health of Wisconsin," *Community Dentistry and Oral Epidemiology* 41 (2013): 374–384.

103. Francesco D'Aiuto, Marco Orlandi, and John C. Gunsolley, "Evidence That Periodontal Treatment Improves Biomarkers and CVD Outcomes," *Journal of Periodontology* 84: 4 Suppl. (2013): S85–S105.

104. Gerard Hoek et al., "Long-Term Air Pollution Exposure and Cardio-Respiratory Mortality: A Review," *Environmental Health* 12: 43 (2013): 1–15.

105. Nina Annika Clark et al., "Effect of Early Life Exposure to Air Pollution on Development of Childhood Asthma," *Environmental Health Perspectives* 118: 2 (2010): 284–290.

106. Yi Li et al., "Impact of Air Pollution Control Measures and Weather Conditions on Asthma during the 2008 Summer Olympic Games in Beijing," *International Journal of Biometeorology* 55 (2011): 547–554.

107. Michael S. Friedman et al., "Impact of Changes in Transportation and Commuting Behaviors during the 1996 Summer Olympic Games in Atlanta on Air Quality and Childhood Asthma," *Journal of the American Medical Association* 285: 7 (2001): 897–905.

108. Maggie L. Grabow et al., "Air Quality and Exercise-Related Health Benefits of Reduced Car Travel in the Midwestern United States," *Environmental Health Perspective* 120: 1 (2012): 68–76.

109. Sherry L. Murphy, Jiaquan Xu, and Kenneth D. Kochanek, "Deaths: Final Data for 2010," *National Vital Statistics Reports* 61: 4 (2013): L1–118.

110. Centers for Disease Control and Prevention, "National Ambulatory Medical Care Survey: 2010 Summary Tables," http://www.cdc.gov/nchs/data/ahcd/namcs_summary/2010_namcs_web_tables.pdf.

111. National Center for Health Statistics, *Health, United States, 2012.*

112. Ibid.

113. Deborah Stone, *Policy Paradox: The Art of Political Decision Making,* 3rd ed. (New York: W.W. Norton, 2012).

114. Occupational Health and Safety Administration, "Commonly Used Statistics," https://www.osha.gov/oshstats/commonstats.html.

115. Tim F. Morse et al., "Are Employment Shifts into Non-Manufacturing Industries Partially Responsible for the Decline in Occupational Injury Rates?" *American Journal of Industrial Medicine* 52 (2009): 735–741.

116. Federal Highway Administration Safety Program, "Section 402 Highway Safety Funds," http://safety.fhwa.dot.gov/policy/section402.

117. U.S. Department of Transportation, National Highway Traffic Safety Administration. *Strategies to Increase Seat Belt Use: An Analysis of Levels of Fines and the Type of Law* (Washington, DC: U.S. National Highway Traffic Safety Administration, 2010).

118. James L. Nichols and Katherine A. Ledingham, "The Impact of Legislation, Enforcement, and Sanctions on Safety Belt Use" (NCHRP Report 601) (Washington, DC: National Cooperative Highway Research Program, 2008).

119. Ibid.

120. James C. Fell, John H. Lacey, and Robert B. Voas, "Sobriety Checkpoints: Evidence of Effectiveness Is Strong, but Use Is Limited," *Traffic Injury Prevention* 5: 3 (2004): 220–227.

121. Kelly F. Russell, Ben Vandermeer, and Lisa Hartling, "Graduated Driver Licensing for Reducing Motor Vehicle Crashes among Young Drivers," *Cochrane Database of Systematic Reviews* 10, CD003300.

122. *Michigan Department of State Police v. Sitz.* 496 U.S. 444 (1990).

123. Anne Russell et al., "MADD Rates the States: A Media Advocacy Event to Advance the Agenda against Alcohol-Impaired Driving," *Public Health Reports* 110: 3 (1995): 240–245.

124. David A. Sleet et al., "Scientific Evidence and Policy Change: Lowering the Legal Blood Alcohol Limit for Drivers to 0.08% in the USA," *Global Health Promotion* 18: 1 (2011): 23–26.

125. National Center for Health Statistics, *Health, United States, 2012.*

126. Erin G. Richardson and David Hemenway, "Homicide, Suicide, and Unintentional Firearm Fatality: Comparing the United States with Other High-Income Countries, 2003," *Journal of Trauma: Injury, Infection, & Critical Care* 70: 1 (2011): 238–243.

127. Lisa M. Hepburn and David Hemenway, "Firearm Availability and Homicide: A Review of the Literature," *Aggressive & Violent Behavior* 9 (2004): 417–440.

128. Bruce P. Kennedy et al., "Social Capital, Income Inequality, and Firearm Violent Crime," *Social Science & Medicine* 47 (1998): 7–17.

129. Richard F. Corlin, "The Secrets of Gun Violence in America: What We Don't Know Is Killing Us," *International Journal of Trauma Nursing* 8: 2 (2002): 42–47.

130. Eric W. Fleegler et al., "Firearm Legislation and Firearm-Related Fatalities in the United States," *Journal of the American Medical Association Internal Medicine* 173: 9 (2013): 732–740.

131. Malinda Steenkamp et al., "The National Violent Death Reporting System: An Exciting New Tool for Public Health Surveillance," *Injury Prevention* 12: Suppl II (2006): ii3–ii5.

132. National Center for Health Statistics, *Health, United States, 2012.*

133. Ibid.

134. Franklin E. Zimring, "Firearms, Violence, and the Potential Impact of Firearms Control," *Journal of Law, Medicine & Ethics* 32 (2004): 34–37.

135. Matthew Miller et al., "Household Firearm Ownership and Rates of Suicide across the 50 United States," *Journal of Trauma, Injury, Infection, and Critical Care* 62: 4 (2007): 1029–1035.

136. Linda L. Dahlberg, Robin M. Ikeda, and Marcie-jo Kresno, "Guns in the Home and Risk of a Violent Death in the Home: Findings from a National Study," *American Journal of Epidemiology* 160: 10 (2004): 929–936.

137. Elizabeth O'Conner et al., "Screening for and Treatment of Suicide Rise Relevant to Primary Care: A Systematic Review for the U.S. Preventive Services Task Force," *Annals of Internal Medicine* 158 (2013): 741–754.

138. Richardson and Hemenway, "Homicide, Suicide, and Unintentional Firearm Fatality."

139. Beverly Pringle et al., "A Strategic Approach for Prioritizing Research and Action to Prevent Suicide," *Psychiatric Services* 64: 1 (2013): 71–75.

140. National Center for Health Statistics, *Health, United States, 1995* (Hyattsville, MD: National Center for Health Statistics, 1996).

141. Centers for Disease Control and Prevention, "Unintentional Drug Poisoning in the United States," http://www.cdc.gov/homeandrecreationalsafety/pdf/poison-issue-brief.pdf.

142. Laxmaiah Manchikanti et al., "Therapeutic Use, Abuse, and Nonmedical Use of opioids: A Ten-Year Perspective," *Pain Physician* 13: 5 (2010): 401–435.

143. Office of National Drug Control Policy, "National Drug Control Strategy," 2010, http://www.whitehouse.gov/sites/default/files/ondcp/policy-and-research/ndcs2010.pdf.

144. Strickland, "How Autonomous Vehicles Will Shape the Future of Surface Transportation," Statement to the U.S. House, Committee on Transportation and Infrastructure, Subcommittee on Highways and Transit, November 19, 2013.

FURTHER READING

Bergman, Abraham. *The "Discovery" of Sudden Infant Death Syndrome.* Seattle: University of Washington Press, 1988.

Marmot, Michael. *The Status Syndrome: How Social Standing Affects Our Health and Longevity.* New York: Holt Paperbacks, 2005.

National Prevention Council. *National Prevention Strategy.* Washington, DC: U.S. Department of Health and Human Services, Office of the Surgeon General, 2011.

Rabinoff, Michael. *Ending the Tobacco Holocaust: How Big Tobacco Affects Our Health, Pocketbook and Political Freedom—And What We Can Do about It.* Santa Rosa, CA: Elite Books, 2010.

Russell, Louise B. *Educated Guesses: Making Policy about Medical Screening Tests.* Berkeley: University of California Press, 1994.

chapter 24

Mental Health and
Social Policy (1960s–Present)

David A. Rochefort

THE TRAGIC SCHOOL SHOOTING IN NEWTOWN, Connecticut, in December 2012, sharply heightened interest in the state of the nation's mental health system. Four days after the horrific event, a reporter for the *West Hartford News* wrote: "The magnitude of the slaughter of children in Newtown and the teachers who tried to help them may be the turning point in a national discussion on access to mental health treatment."[1] One mother of a troubled thirteen-year-old boy in Idaho wrote a blog entry titled "I am Adam Lanza's Mother," in which she drew an analogy between her distraught situation and that of the Newtown shooter's mother.[2] The posting went viral. Meanwhile, in the realm of public policy, state and federal lawmakers began exploring changes in mental health legislation and regulations, running the gamut from expanded services and training to simplified procedures for involuntary commitment. Amid all this activity, however, uncertainty remained as to the actual extent of psychological illness of the young man who took twenty-six lives at Sandy Hook Elementary School as well as the connection between any such disturbance and his appalling action.

Although greater prominence for mental health issues on the political agenda is a goal for mental health advocates, the kind of widespread concern brought about by Newtown qualifies as a mixed blessing at best. In his public comments, President Barack Obama (2009–) duly noted the fallacy of equating mental illness with the risk of violence: in fact, as the president stated, individuals who are mentally ill are more likely to be victims than perpetrators of violence, but such a point can easily become lost in an all-out media frenzy. Furthermore, for some who favor an absolutist position on the Second Amendment, the call for "fixing the mental health system" may be seen as a tactical ploy for resisting tough gun control measures rather than any real

commitment to the plight of those with mental illness.[3] Nor has past history demonstrated clear benefits when a spasmodic burst of interest in mental health care resulted from calamity and crisis. Instead, the outcome often proves to be a poorly planned and reactive investment of new resources that fails to be sustained over time.[4]

The truth is that the U.S. mental health system is a complex set of services, organizations, personnel, and funding mechanisms whose collective purpose has far more to do with promoting well-being, enhancing quality of life, and facilitating personal adaptation and functioning than with social control. Although the history of mental health care has often been marked by a tendency to distinguish persons with mental illness from other patient populations through stigmatization and separate treatment facilities, today the major impetus is for integration with general medicine and an end to exclusionary and discriminatory practices. From a mental health perspective, the importance of the Patient Protection and Affordable Care Act (PPACA) lies in the fact that it seeks not only to expand health insurance coverage for millions of Americans with psychiatric disorders but also to transform the delivery and financing of mental health services to improve the quality of care while implementing a positive philosophy of recovery. It would be naïve to look for quick or easy changes in mental health policy that could end the problem of school shootings. Yet to the extent that Newtown and other such tragedies can help build support for mental health reform as a vital work-in-progress, the interests of diverse stakeholders will coincide, both those who depend on access to care and those who desire a society in which fewer people suffer the anguish of untreated mental illness. This chapter reviews the long-term development of the U.S. mental health system, focusing on community-based care and the decisive role played by political advocacy and public policy in this movement.

HISTORICAL BACKGROUND OF MENTAL HEALTH CARE

The community-care revolution that took shape in the mental health field during the 1960s was driven by a vehement idealism as well as new treatment concepts. Yet it was as much a reaction against the established organization of care as it was an attempt to invent a different combination of philosophies and techniques. Prior to this time, the mental health system centered on institutions and the assumption that people with serious mental illness required residence in isolated, controlled environments. Public and private institutions alike existed, and it is important not to blur major distinctions between the two in regard to their provision of custodial supervision versus active treatment. Both kinds of facilities were similar, however, to the extent that they were guided by an overriding belief in long-term hospitalization as a tool for restoring psychological balance, separating patients from the pressures of community life, and relieving society of the burden of dealing with mental illness in its midst.

The first hospital in the United States to make specific arrangement for the segregated treatment of patients with psychological problems was the Pennsylvania Hospital in Philadelphia during the 1750s.[5] Not until establishment of the Virginia Eastern Lunatic Asylum in Williamsburg in 1770 was there a facility devoted solely to care of mentally ill patients. One of the most influential institutions of this early period in the history of psychiatry was Worcester State Hospital in Massachusetts, whose first patients arrived in 1833. Like other such facilities, Worcester State Hospital was a solution for the growing problem of the seriously mentally ill in the community, many of whom were either destitute and homeless or neglected in jails, poorhouses, and other local social welfare settings. Towns and municipalities generally were thankful for the relief provided by such hospitals and contributed toward the cost when their residents were admitted to state asylums.

Reforming Mental Health Care

As a result of the work of ardent reformers like Dorothea Dix, who began her career to expand the availability of mental hospitals across the United States and abroad with a crusade to augment facilities at Worcester State Hospital in the early 1840s, the institutional movement, likened by historian David Rothman to "a cult," spread rapidly.[6] According to one count, as many as four dozen mental institutions were operating in the United States by 1861. The majority were state facilities, with ten private institutions and the remainder a farrago of city, county, and family-managed institutions.[7]

While the federal government resisted calls to become involved as a major funder of mental health services in the states, it did agree in 1855 to establish a hospital for the insane, subsequently named Saint Elizabeth's, in Washington, D.C. The growth of this hospital over the following years was remarkable, as documented by Sarah Mondale in her 1989 award-winning film *Asylum*. By 1880, the patient census was 897; by 1900, it had risen to 2,076; and by 1963, the year in which the nation's first community mental health legislation was adopted, Saint Elizabeth's housed 6,577 residents.

Great confidence and optimism surrounded the mental hospital movement in its initial years. As noted, the hospitals were, at least in part, a humanitarian strategy for relocating patients from inappropriate local situations marked by harshness and negligence. Furthermore, the hospitals provided a vehicle for implementing the contemporary philosophy of "moral treatment" of mental illness through individualized patient care, kindness and emotional support, and medical attention. "The ideal hospital," writes historian Gerald N. Grob, "was modeled along the lines of a closely knit and cohesive family."[8] High rates of cure were anticipated and, for a while, the data seemed to bear out this hope.

By the late 1800s, however, claims of frequent cure among the state hospital population came to be recognized as unsubstantiated. The facilities themselves increasingly morphed into environments whose unhealthful features were painfully obvious, whether viewed from a psychiatric or general medical perspective. Staff psychiatrists shifted from giving patients individual psychological attention to experimenting with somatic interventions of various types. Many facilities became terribly overcrowded and decrepit as state legislatures refused to expand funding to keep up with growing numbers of patients. More and more, the gap widened between the quality of care in public and private institutions. Even in public facilities, glaring treatment disparities correlated with patients' class, ethnicity, and race.[9]

Attempts at Improvements during the Progressive Era

This degradation of mental health care in the United States did not go unnoticed. Indeed, reformers during the Progressive era at the start of the twentieth century strove to improve conditions in state mental hospitals and to create a range of alternative services. The latter, which may be considered an early impulse for a greater community orientation in the nation's mental health system, included such programs as psychopathic hospitals to provide short-term hospitalization for milder cases of mental illness, ambulatory care in outpatient clinics, and child guidance centers. Some hospitals, like Massachusetts General, took the lead in fashioning after-care services for discharged psychiatric patients. The Mental Hygiene Movement identified prevention of mental illness as a goal, preaching the importance of community education about good mental health and the value of early intervention. Yet despite such innovations, institutions remained generally custodial in nature, coming to resemble human warehouses rather than active treatment facilities, and they often failed to meet basic health and safety standards. Reflecting the dominance of the existing system, in many instances the alternative mental health services devised by Progressives merely ended up funneling more patients into the state hospitals.[10]

The essential problem was that the mental health system in this period lacked effective new treatments, new sources of funding, or a compelling new vision of the psychological self in society sufficient to catalyze a revolution in practice. By 1955, the residential census in state and county mental hospitals reached a peak of 559,000 patients across the nation. However, a collection of unexpected stimuli, from inside and outside the psychiatric world, would emerge on the scene during and after World War II (1939–1945) to finally set the stage for a different approach.

THE COMMUNITY MENTAL HEALTH REVOLUTION

Most students of public policy stress the powerful forces of inertia that support the status quo. Breakthroughs do occur, but they tend to be few and far between and dependent on the fortuitous opening of a window of opportunity.[11] Mental health policy is no exception to this pattern. When the community mental health revolution arrived in the 1960s, it reflected a professional and societal redefinition of the problem of mental illness, and it benefited from a general ethos of social reform absent during preceding decades.

An Increasing Awareness of Mental Health Issues

Before World War II, there was limited knowledge concerning the scope of mental illness in U.S. society.[12] The experience of war began to shed light on this question. Between 1942 and 1945, more than one in eight inductees was turned away from service for failing to pass the military's neurological and psychiatric screening exams. Approximately 37 percent of soldiers discharged because of disability had neuropsychiatric illnesses. Although such information was far from systematic or comprehensive, it went far in dispelling the notion of mental illness as a rare form of social deviance.

When pioneering studies in the field of psychiatric epidemiology appeared during the 1950s and early 1960s, many were shocked by estimates that perhaps as much as one-half of the population possessed mild or moderate symptoms of mental illness, while another one-fourth could be described as psychiatrically impaired.[13] Braced by such statistics, it was only a matter of time before mental health experts and other concerned observers started to refer to mental illness as the nation's "number-one public health problem."

During this period, the nation's system of mental hospitals fell further into disrepute. While mental health professionals and patients and their families had long known the deficiencies of public facilities, increasingly this disgraceful situation caught the attention of the mass media and mainstream America. Conscientious objectors who served as attendants in mental hospitals during World War II spurred on this development when they publicized the dire circumstances they had encountered. Journalists wrote scandalous exposés of the state hospital system in popular publications such as *Life* magazine and *Reader's Digest*. Among these observers, journalist Albert Deutsch went so far as to compare the horrific conditions he viewed in state hospitals to Nazi concentration camps. Social scientists added to the barrage of criticism in documenting the harmful effects of long-term institutional life, including seminal work on "total institutions" by sociologist Erving Goffman, who did his field work at St. Elizabeth's hospital. Together, these diverse streams of research and commentary converged to document the failure of public mental hospitals as the linchpin of the U.S. mental health system while underscoring the need for a bold alternative.

Due to wartime exigencies, military doctors experimented with new methods of treatment for psychiatric cases, including hypnosis and group therapy. The results they reported were promising. Most influential of all on the mental health treatment scene in the 1950s was the appearance of powerful new tranquilizing drugs that could help blunt patients' symptoms without strong sedative effects. In a field marked by pessimism and limited therapeutic options for the most severely ill, these medications brought hope and new service possibilities in the form of early discharge plans and day treatment programs. Indeed, as residential census data clearly exhibit, the administrative changes adopted by many public hospitals galvanized the process of deinstitutionalization years before any community mental health legislation on the national level. From a problem-definition perspective, the new drugs also bolstered the analogy between mental illness and other kinds of chronic medical conditions requiring long-term medical management.

In 1989, political scientist James Cameron emphasized the ideological underpinnings of community mental health care.[14] Of special significance was the emergence of an "environmental" conception of mental illness that evolved from psychoanalytic psychology and the behavioral sciences. Along with this framework came optimism about the feasibility of preventing mental illness, the goal of combating stress as a social problem, the focus on early intervention, and the ideal of serving the underprivileged through expanded access to care and social activism. Cameron stated:

> The community mental health movement included a strong claim to moral righteousness. Traditional state mental hospitals, where patients received little more

than custodial care, were considered anachronistic vestiges of an unenlightened past. This was contrasted to community-based care where patients could be treated in a normal setting, thereby facilitating adaptation to their social environment, and where far greater numbers of patients could be served.[15]

Changes in Mental Health Care Policy

The window of change in mental health care did not open all at once. It involved a series of legislative accomplishments over a span of years.[16] First came the National Mental Health Act of 1946, which provided new funding for professional training, created grants for basic research on mental illness and its treatment, and supported the development of community clinics as a pilot and demonstration effort. To supervise this new system of federal grants, the law also established the National Institute of Mental Health, which would become a major institutional stakeholder on behalf of a community-based system of care.[17] In 1955, Congress passed the Mental Health Study Act, which funded a comprehensive examination of the nation's mental health system by a Joint Commission on Mental Illness and Health. When the commission issued its final report in 1961, it strongly endorsed community care while recommending the downsizing of public mental hospitals. At a time of growing affluence in the U.S. economy, it also called for a major injection of federal funding for research, manpower, and service expansion in the mental health field.

The crowning jewel of postwar mental health policy, however, was the Community Mental Health Centers Act of 1963. To build momentum behind his legislative proposal, President John F. Kennedy (1961–1963) had convened Congress for a special message earlier in this same year, on February 5. In his speech, Kennedy borrowed many themes from the Joint Commission about the need for new directions in mental health treatment, the hopeful promise of new psychiatric drugs, and the objective of community integration of people with mental illness. Particularly harsh was his attack on public mental hospitals for their "cold mercy of custodial isolation." He set a goal of reducing the population housed inside these facilities by 50 percent or more over the next two decades. Less than a month before his assassination, Congress acted to give the president most of what he requested. This included funding to develop a network of community mental health centers (CMHCs) in some 1,500 local "catchment areas" around the country. Support would come on a matching basis, with the federal government playing the lead role in the first few years of a CMHC's existence. The only major item denied the administration was staffing for the centers due to complaints about "socialized medicine" by the American Medical Association (AMA). However, the administration of Lyndon B. Johnson (1963–1969) was able to add staffing money to the program

in 1965 owing to the president's landslide electoral victory in 1964 and the AMA's increasing absorption on another political front by the battle over Medicare.

IMPLEMENTATION CHALLENGES

By 1981, the last year before federal policymakers combined the program with alcohol and drug abuse services to form a block grant to the states, approximately eight hundred local mental health facilities had come into existence with support from the Community Mental Health Centers Act.[18] This number met only about one-half the original goal. Still, it meant the provision of services to more than three million clients yearly who benefited from short-term inpatient care, outpatient counseling, emergency intervention, partial hospitalization, and other modalities of active care. In a nod to the public health model, centers also were required to serve as resources for information and advice for other community agencies and to help improve the community's understanding of mental health and illness. Particularly for those with limited resources, the CMHCs represented a vital new arm of the treatment system and a resource that differed fundamentally in setting, philosophy, and organizational functioning from the traditional state hospitals.

Also quickly surpassed was President Kennedy's target for reducing the population in state and county mental hospitals.[19] By 1980, the year-end patient census inside these facilities fell to 132,000, a decline of 76 percent from the peak year of 1955. The actual number of hospitals did not decline very much, but facility size, gauged by inpatient beds, plummeted. On the other hand, admissions more than doubled over these same years, a telling sign that many discharged patients made repeated returns to the institution, a phenomenon termed the "revolving door syndrome." Overall, the precise role played by CMHCs in deinstitutionalization is debatable. It was the passage of Supplemental Security Income (SSI) in 1972 that added a critical impetus for moving patients into the community by helping to pay for housing. Moreover, research found a stronger correlation on the state level between inpatient declines in public mental hospitals and Medicaid payments to nursing homes than with the availability of community mental health centers. Indeed, in 1991 the U.S. Inspector General's Office issued a scathing report criticizing CMHCs for having failed to focus sufficiently on patients with serious mental illness.

Prisons and Mental Health Policy

Along with the movement of massive numbers of patients from state hospitals to nursing homes, another kind of "transinstitutionalization" accompanied the implementation of community mental health care. Increasingly, the population of local jails and state prisons included inmates with serious mental illnesses. By the late 1980s, a variety of studies had documented this trend.[20] Summarizing the latest, if still spotty, research on the scope of mental illness in the nation's correctional facilities, a 1990 editorial in the *American Journal of Public Health* declared "a prison crisis in mental health." Explained the authors:

> [T]he disappearance of community mental health services has accelerated the movement of individuals from the street to the penitentiary. Without sufficient funding for intermediate level mental health facilities, jails have become way-stations for the marginalized: places to confine individuals who cannot make bail or who are unable or unwilling to plea-bargain. Not surprisingly this group includes many who are mentally ill.[21]

Ironically, then, just as an idealistic generation of civil liberties lawyers fought to raise barriers to involuntary hospitalization of the mentally ill, those with mental health problems increasingly were being detained in the criminal justice system without benefit of clinical services. Many were innocent of having broken any major laws.

Homelessness and Mental Health

Another problem contributing to the criminalization of the mentally ill was homelessness. Homelessness is not a clear-cut issue either to define or to measure. Determining the association between mental illness and homelessness is complicated by a host of entangled variables like poverty, employment rates, changing population demographics, and housing availability.[22] The evidence is clear, however, that substantial numbers of homeless, perhaps as many as one-third, have symptoms of severe mental illness. Many have a history of contact with the mental health system, including time spent hospitalized. As persons with mental illness came to constitute an increasingly visible segment of the nation's homeless population throughout the 1980s, it drew biting criticism of the inadequacy of public mental health services, particularly in the nation's largest cities. The mentally ill homeless revealed a major gap in the shift from institutional to community care, which was the lack of careful planning and adequate funding for a spectrum of supervised and unsupervised housing arrangements. The emergency shelter system was, and continues to be, a poor response to the needs of this population group.

Programs of the National Institute of Mental Health

Architects of the community mental health movement understood better what they were reacting against than what they wanted to replace it with. Consequently, although the mental health system expanded dramatically in the volume of services delivered and in the number of people who received treatment as deinstitutionalization progressed, those with serious and chronic mental health problems often were

neglected. One of the first policy initiatives to respond to this reality was the Community Support Program (CSP) developed by the National Institute of Mental Health (NIMH) in the late 1970s.[23] CSP was a program of grants to the states to address the gaps and fragmentation of services for those with severe mental illness by focusing on coordination of resources and a comprehensive understanding of the psychological, medical, social, and daily living needs of this group. The fiscal footprint of CSP was small, however, and new service development modest. Thus, the plight of people with severe mental illness in the community continued to be of primary concern in a series of presidential-level task forces and commissions, from Jimmy Carter's (1977–1981) Presidential Commission on Mental Health, to the Surgeon General's Report on Mental Health during Bill Clinton's administration (1993–2001), to George W. Bush's (2001–2009) New Freedom Commission in the first decade of the twenty-first century.

While the political contexts and recommendations of these bodies differed in important ways, all identified those with severe and persistent mental disorders as an underserved population in need of wide-ranging improvements in the conceptualization, organization, and financing of the service system.[24] One consistent model of best practices recognized over the years has been the Program for Assertive Community Treatment, an intervention pioneered in Wisconsin during the 1970s featuring a process of multidisciplinary case management and an assortment of daily supports, in addition to clinical services, designed to help patients in the community avoid hospitalization. The program is at once practical and quite comprehensive, encompassing matters of housing, psychological and substance abuse treatment and rehabilitation, medication monitoring, crisis response, and help with such needs as finding employment, transportation, shopping, and household budgeting, all of which involve intensive staffing. Given the fact that many clients remain enrolled over long periods of time, it is an expensive package of services.

The community mental health revolution may have been symbolized by state hospital deinstitutionalization and passage of the CMHC Act, but the movement was actually much more far-reaching than these activities alone would indicate, and it was driven by activities in domains whose mental health policy significance often goes unrecognized. During the 1960s and 1970s, as the number of residents in state hospitals dropped, tremendous growth occurred in the number of inpatient psychiatric episodes in general hospitals, primarily hospitals without specialized psychiatric units.[25] Utilization of private mental hospitals also expanded. Taking into account all types of inpatient facilities, the number of episodes of mental hospitalization actually increased during the heyday of deinstitutionalization.

Private facilities were responding to the new financial opportunities that coincided with the arrival of community

The Rise of NAMI and the Politics of Mental Health Care

When community mental health care surfaced on the national agenda in the postwar era, there was, if not a total power vacuum, a state of disorganization and consequent weakness regarding interest group formation on this issue. A variety of organizations were active in calling for system reform and the new community approach, including the National Governors' Conference, the American Psychiatric Association, the American Psychological Association, and the National Committee Against Mental Illness, a foundation-supported lobby group. Another noteworthy source of advocacy at this time, the National Mental Health Association, was a direct descendant of the National Committee for Mental Hygiene founded during the Progressive era. However, it is unlikely that Congress would have moved so purposefully in establishing a community mental health program without steady pressure from within the government itself, primarily the National Institute of Mental Health (NIMH), which worked with and through external lobby groups to advance this policy preference. It also mattered a great deal that John F. Kennedy chose to make this cause a priority for his presidency.

Once adopted, the Community Mental Health Centers (CMHC) Act injected new resources into the mental health system, it fostered the turn away from public mental hospitals, and it stimulated development of a much more active and diverse set of organized interests for mental health care. At first, these stakeholders mounted concerted political pressure behind expansion of the CMHC program, constituting a highly effective "iron triangle" of bureaucratic, legislative, and interest group supporters. By the late 1970s, however, when President Jimmy Carter proposed the Mental Health Systems Act to update the CMHC program, open conflict erupted between state and local, community and hospital, and advocacy and provider interests over financial, service, and program commitments. Intense debate surrounded such issues as the importance of mental illness prevention versus treatment, comprehensive versus targeted service delivery, and future control of the CMHC network. The Mental Health Systems Act survived, without clearly resolving many of these tensions, only to be rescinded by the Ronald Reagan administration (1981–1989).

The founding of the National Alliance for the Mentally Ill (NAMI; now called the National Alliance on Mental Illness) in 1979 marked a critical step in the maturation of interest group formation inside the mental health policy arena. This organization emerged from a scattered collection of local family self-help groups in different parts of the country, its core tenet being that "mental illness is a disease of the brain," rather than a result of the environment. By the late 1980s, NAMI already could claim six hundred local and state affiliates across all fifty states and a membership of sixty thousand. Currently, the number of local affiliates and state organizations approximates twelve hundred. Although the two groups would end up cooperating on many issues, there were significant distinctions between NAMI and a traditional mental health advocacy organization like the National Mental Health Association (now called Mental Health America), whose concerns spanned a broad spectrum of psychological disorders and difficulties with a core mission of public information and education. NAMI's principal contribution, by contrast, was to demand increased resources in the public mental health system for those with severe and chronic mental illnesses by promoting the utility of community support services, diffusion of Wisconsin's Assertive Community Treatment model, affordable access to psychiatric medications, programs to combat homelessness and mental illness, and other initiatives. When a presidential proclamation launched the "Decade of the Brain" in July 1990, NAMI was a key actor behind the scenes pressuring for more work in neuroscience and neurochemistry as the route to improved understanding of mental disorder and its treatment. In 1992, NAMI fought for relocating NIMH research programs inside the National Institutes of Health to emphasize this link between medical science and mental health research.

mental health care. Medicare and Medicaid, enacted in 1965, provided coverage for patients in private psychiatric facilities and general hospitals. According to calculations by researchers, the Medicare program spent just less than $1 billion on mental health care in 1981, and four-fifths of this sum went for inpatient treatment. Medicaid expenditures cannot be so neatly tabulated, but this program also spent upward of $500 million on inpatient psychiatric care by the late 1970s.[26] Private hospitals found it in their interest to build capacity for delivering psychiatric services in line with new funding streams for these patients, just as it was in the interest of state officials to direct more patients to private facilities because of the cost savings realized by participation in the federal Medicaid program.

Medicaid's importance for the evolving mental health system has proven to be even greater than suggested by this assessment. In addition to its funding of inpatient mental health treatment, the program has subsidized a growing array of community mental health services. By choosing from a number of options—including case management, screening and diagnosis, rehabilitation, medication, occupational therapy, and more—states may leverage federal Medicaid dollars in building comprehensive systems of care for low-income and disabled residents who need attention for mental health conditions on a long-term basis. Resources on this scale dwarf the amounts directly invested by the federal government in community mental centers, even at the program's height. In short, it is not too much to say that

> Medicaid has evolved into one of the most important components of the health care safety net for people with mental disorders. The creation of the Medicaid program in 1965 began a process that fundamentally changed the rules governing the U.S. public mental health care system.[27]

NAMI took form primarily as a representative of family members of people with mental illnesses. In time, it was joined on the advocacy scene by a growing number of consumer/survivor organizations devoted to presenting the perspectives of those who had undergone treatment in the mental health system. As summarized by historian Nancy Tomes, the role of consumer/survivor groups went from "no part in the Mental Health Study Act of 1955, to a small but significant presence in the 1978 Carter Commission [on Mental Health], to a highly visible role in the 1999 surgeon general's report on mental health." While specific organizations differ in focus, the hallmark of the consumer movement includes an emphasis on self-help, self-determination, and an integrated program of health and social services aimed at recovery and rehabilitation. The voice of consumer/survivor groups has been particularly influential in the refinement and acceptance of this "recovery" model in the mental health system and its goal of facilitating the highest quality of life and independence of people who experience severe mental illness.

On many issues today, one can recognize the collective influence of a wide range of mental health interests. The coalition behind insurance parity for mental health conditions was a broad one, encompassing professional associations, institutional providers, mental health advocacy organizations, consumer/survivor groups, and researchers. Similarly, when a backlash against managed care occurred during the 1990s, mental health treatment abuses received substantial attention, and patients, their families, and mental health advocacy groups joined forces with provider interests to help force new regulatory controls on the managed care industry.

Yet other issues important to the mental health community have proved deeply divisive. Areas of disagreement between NAMI and consumer/survivor family groups, for example, concern the role of involuntary hospitalization and the use of medications in treatment. Further, although NAMI champions Assertive Community Treatment, consumer/survivor groups have balked sometimes at the dominance of professional decision making in this type of program. It would be wrong, however, to think of consumer/survivor interests as monolithic, for political differences also splinter this community. Pharmaceutical companies have sometimes cooperated with, sometimes opposed the demands of patients and advocacy groups. With respect to interprofessional conflict, one current flash point between psychiatrists and psychologists concerns the latter's attempt to gain prescribing privileges in a number of states. (Interestingly, NAMI has withheld its support from psychologists in this battle.) During the economic recession of the past several years, mental health budgets have sustained large cuts in different parts of the country. The threat posed by shrinking resources has induced open competition among rival programs, patient populations, and providers.

There is always a myriad of policy issues challenging mental health interest groups for a response. Alignments shift depending on the potential distribution of benefits for any specific matter. To a great extent, then, these political formations are ad hoc and arise out of calculations of self-interest and gain. On the other hand, there is also an evident tendency in the mental health policy domain for past political battles to result in lingering mistrust and cognitive distortions with a potential for interfering with the rational process of constituency building and pursuit of a coalition strategy.

SOURCES: Henry A. Foley, *Community Mental Health Legislation: The Formative Process* (Lexington, MA: D.C. Heath, 1975); David Mechanic, "Seizing Opportunities under the Affordable Care Act for Transforming the Mental and Behavioral Health System," *Health Affairs* 31: 2 (2012): 376–382; David A. Rochefort, *From Poorhouses to Homelessness: Policy Analysis and Mental Health Care*, 2nd ed. (Westport, CT: Auburn House, 1997); Agnes B. Hatfield, "The National Alliance for the Mentally Ill: The Meaning of a Movement," *International Journal of Health* 15: 4 (1987): 79–93; Nancy Tomes, "The Patient as a Policy Factor: A Historical Case Study of the Consumer/Survivor Movement in Mental Health," *Health Affairs* 25: 3 (2006): 720–729; Robert E. Drake and Patricia E. Deegan, "Are Assertive Treatment and Recovery Compatible?" *Community Mental Health Journal* 44: 1 (2008):75–77; Ron Honberg et al., *State Mental Health Cuts: The Continuing Crisis* (Arlington, VA: National Alliance on Mental Illness, 2011); Peter Margulies, "The Cognitive Politics of Professional Conflict: Law Reform, Mental Health Treatment Technology, and Citizen Self-Governance," *Harvard Journal of Law and Technology* 5 (Spring 1992): 24–63.

THE FIGHT FOR PARITY INSURANCE COVERAGE

Health insurance constitutes a principal battleground for those seeking to improve access to comprehensive and high-quality mental health care in our society.[28] Historically, private insurers were loath to begin paying for mental health treatment. They justified their position by noting this role had long been the province of state governments. They also feared an inability to exercise control over diagnosis and utilization of services for a category of disorders so ill defined at times and lacking in effective clinical interventions. It was not until the 1960s that commercial insurers routinely included benefits for inpatient and outpatient mental health care in their plans as they endeavored to compete for market share against the likes of Blue Cross and Blue Shield.

Even as insurance coverage for mental disorders spread, however, it was marked by various limitations not applied to other forms of medical care. Included were such features as higher deductibles and copays, caps on days of care or number of outpatient visits, and annual and lifetime spending ceilings. When Medicare was enacted in 1965, it followed the private insurance model in the area of outpatient mental health services by instituting heavy cost-sharing and an annual spending limit, although the program did not set any special limits regarding hospitalization for mental disorders beyond those in place for other conditions.

In general, mental health advocates viewed the imposition of all such insurance limitations on people seeking access to mental health care as a familiar denial of the reality of mental illnesses, unwarranted suspicion regarding the value of mental health treatments, stigmatization of mental illness as "different from" other health care problems, and an arbitrary exclusion of one group of subscribers from the full collective utility of the commodity of insurance. It was, in other words, the worst form of "mental health exceptionalism." What commenced was a decades-long struggle to eliminate these practices, a struggle for parity between coverage of health and mental health conditions that swung back and forth between the states and the federal government and did not reach culmination until passage of national health reform in 2010.

The campaign for reform began in the states during the 1970s and 1980s as a number of state legislatures adopted mandates for coverage of mental health services by private insurers. Such laws, which were far from universal and sometimes took the form of optional rather than compulsory benefits, fell far short of full parity coverage.[29] Nor did mandates apply to large "self-insuring" businesses or to public insurance programs. Yet they marked an important first step in expanding mental health benefits.

The parity push surfaced on the federal political agenda by the mid-1990s, at a time when insurance coverage was being transformed nationally due to the spread of managed care. Managed care relied on a host of new controls and payment strategies by insurers to restrict the amount and types of care delivered to subscribers. Ironically, although businesses and the private insurance industry had focused on the problems of managed care as a main line of attack against the Clinton health reform plan in 1993–1994, once that plan was defeated the two groups collaborated in quickly moving the bulk of the workforce under a managed care framework. This same period saw the majority of state governments secure federal waivers to move Medicaid enrollees into managed care. Mental health was a primary target of opportunity in many managed care plans as gatekeepers scrutinized referrals to specialty providers and worked to reduce the volume of services through tough utilization review procedures. When the backlash against managed care erupted, fueled by the complaints of patients and medical providers alike, much of the furor concerned the difficulties being experienced by consumers seeking access to the mental health benefits offered in their plans, and the regulatory remedies adopted by many states specifically addressed mental health issues.[30]

Parity Reforms at the Federal Level

Ironically, the impact of managed care was to provide another argument on behalf of the feasibility of parity legislation. In response to complaints from insurers and employers that expanded coverage would lead to soaring costs, parity proponents, a group that included mental health advocates, professional providers, community mental health agencies, researchers, and the Clinton administration, could point to managed care as a proven mechanism for checking inappropriate utilization. In 1996, Congress passed the

Mental Health Parity Act. The law required equal coverage of mental health and physical health problems with respect to annual and lifetime benefit limits. However, it did not do the same for copayments or limitations on number of visits and days of care, it did not encompass substance abuse treatment, it did not apply to Medicare and Medicaid, it did not apply to companies with fifty employees or fewer, and it did not require coverage of mental health problems in company health plans.[31]

To move beyond this largely symbolic version of parity under federal law, states reentered the fray. By 2001, the majority of the states had enacted their own parity statutes. These were important political victories for the parity movement, and some new laws could be described as model legislation. Yet there was great inconsistency in the rules being put in place across the country regarding such things as the definition of eligible disorders and the details of benefit design. Federal prohibitions against state regulation of self-insuring companies continued to pose a barrier to enlarging the scope of mental health insurance protections via state action.

When parity advocates went back to Congress in the first decade of the twenty-first century seeking a more consistent approach applicable to a larger segment of the business community, they continued framing their issue as an antidiscrimination measure. In addition, they came armed with extensive empirical evidence from the past decade demonstrating the effective control of mental health spending by means of managed care techniques. The National Institute of Mental Health, an ally inside the federal government, helped both to sponsor such studies and to disseminate the findings. Clear evidence was in hand that "Managed care had fundamentally altered mental health care delivery by shifting from demand-side mechanisms (e.g., cost-sharing requirements, benefit limits) to supply-side mechanisms (e.g., utilization review) for controlling mental health spending."[32] This was essential information in moderating employers' objections to an expanded benefit. In addition, advocates presented information on the efficacy of new medications in treating problems like depression, and they stressed the value of timely mental health care in reducing other health care costs as well as productivity losses in the workplace. The parity proposal enjoyed the political advantage of bipartisan backing from a small phalanx of respected leaders in the House and Senate who had direct experience, either personally or through a family member, with mental health and substance abuse problems. The fact that another bill simultaneously was moving toward passage in Congress to reduce cost-sharing for outpatient mental health services in Medicare helped impart momentum to the parity cause. Also, in one of the stranger synergies of the legislative process, the parity statute ultimately became combined with the Troubled Asset Relief Program, a bailout of financial institutions to stabilize the economy during the subprime mortgage crisis. Through canny exploitation of the opportunities offered in each legislative body, a high-profile group shepherded the Mental Health Parity and Addiction Equity Act of 2008 into law. The outcome produced a great improvement over existing protections by including equal benefits for behavioral health and medical/surgical services, elimination of any special annual or lifetime expenditure limits for mental health as well as addiction treatment, and an end (through regulatory rule-making) to the practice of separate deductibles for mental health and substance abuse benefits.[33]

Three nagging issues remained under the 2008 parity law, however. First was the fact that employers still were not required to offer health plans that included behavioral health benefits. Second was the law's restricted application only to businesses having more than fifty employees. Third was lack of specificity concerning the types of services and settings of care to be encompassed by the law. While not a total corrective, the PPACA built on this parity statute in a number of important ways.

THE AFFORDABLE CARE ACT AND MENTAL HEALTH REFORM

Writing in *The New York Times* in July 2012, Professor of Psychiatry Richard A. Friedman commented, "Americans with mental illness had good reason to celebrate when the Supreme Court upheld President Obama's Affordable Care Act." Indeed, the impact of the law will be felt along multiple lines: expanded insurance coverage, greater comprehensiveness of benefits, and innovations in the system of care.

As of 2010, the uninsured population in the United States included an estimated 7.6 million people who were in need of mental health treatment.[34] According to the National Alliance for Mental Illness, in 2007, as many as one in five people with a serious mental disorder did not possess health insurance, and 15 percent of the uninsured had a serious mental disorder. The consequences include undertreatment and lack of treatment, with potentially devastating impacts on employment, family life, social participation, and other areas of functioning. The PPACA is projected to make it possible eventually for more than 90 percent of Americans to have health insurance. This will diminish substantially the incidence of coverage problems among individuals with mental illnesses.[35] PPACA provisions that promise to be most significant in their impact on this population group include new regulations prohibiting private insurers from denying coverage for preexisting conditions, an extension until age twenty-six for young adults to remain on their parents' health insurance, rules encouraging the expansion of employment-based coverage, the increased availability of affordable health benefit plans through new health insurance exchanges, and the expansion of Medicaid eligibility up to 133 percent of the federal poverty level.

At the same time that more Americans with mental health problems will be gaining access to insurance, the quality of that coverage for mental health conditions will be strengthened. This is because the PPACA requires all plans purchased through the new exchanges to include a minimum set of mental health and substance abuse services consistent with established parity standards.[36] Changes in the Medicare drug benefit will help those relying on expensive psychiatric medications. In addition, for states participating in Medicaid expansion, there is also the flexibility (and fiscal incentive over the next few years) to cover an extensive range of mental health services such as community-based care and supports, rehabilitation, and chronic care management and prevention.[37]

To be sure, these changes brighten the health insurance picture considerably for people with mental health problems. Just as interesting and potentially far-reaching, however, are those provisions in the Patient Protection and Affordable Care Act intended to transform how mental health care is organized, paid for, and delivered in our society. One thoughtful review of the opportunity for "reinventing" mental health and substance abuse care under PPACA identifies five key initiatives or pathways for change:

1. Provisions that encourage states and federal agencies to develop and assess financial and organizational tools reducing fragmentation of services

2. Use of new approaches like "health homes" that focus on enhancing services to individuals dealing with both serious mental illness and other chronic conditions

3. An effort at better coordination of social service and housing programs in Medicaid in addressing the problem of homelessness and mental illness

4. Greater attention to the interconnections between serious mental illness and substance abuse

5. A focus on documenting and disseminating effective mental health treatments based on measured clinical results and other relevant personal and systemic outcomes. Areas of special interest include integration of care for groups with multiple service needs, such as the Medicare and Medicaid dual-eligible population, and patients able to benefit from supported employment programs[38]

THE CONTEMPORARY SCENE IN PERSPECTIVE

According to information compiled in 2012 by the Substance Abuse and Mental Health Services Administration (SAMHSA), one in five adults, or more than sixty million

Americans, suffer from a diagnosable mental disorder in a given year. The frequency of disorder is greater among individuals who are younger, who are female, who are poor, and who are unemployed. Anxiety disorders are the most common category of mental illness, followed by impulse disorders, mood disorders, and substance disorders. Among specific disease entities, major depressive disorder affects a large number of individuals and is also one of the conditions most likely to be classified as meeting the standard for serious severity.

An estimated 6.5 percent of adults experience major depressive disorder over the course of a year. Children, too, are highly impacted by mental illness. Perhaps as many as one in eight had an emotional or behavioral disorder during the past year, with attention deficit hyperactivity disorder being the most common difficulty among the eight- to fifteen-year-olds. Of course, when the time perspective shifts from one-year to lifetime prevalence, these statistics rise considerably. Nearly one-half of all adults are believed to experience a mental disorder at some point during life.[39] While researchers continue to debate a variety of methodological issues concerning rival measuring instruments, the accuracy of distinguishing among diagnosable disorders, and estimating the severity of illness, there is no question that enormous strides have been made in the field of psychiatric epidemiology compared to the basic work in the early days of community mental health care.[40] When taken together with widespread media coverage of the mental health implications of such events as the 9/11 and Boston Marathon terrorist attacks, natural disasters like Hurricane Katrina, the psychological challenges faced by military service personnel in Iraq and Afghanistan, and various mass shootings here at home, the compilation of these statistics has done much to sensitize the public to both the scope of mental health problems and treatment possibilities.

Between 1955, the peak year of mental hospital populations, and 1994, patient care episodes in mental health organizations in the United States increased nearly sixfold.[41] Accompanying this growth was a shift between residential and nonresidential care, with the former modality dominant (by a ratio of 3:1) at the beginning of this time period and the latter modality dominant (by the same ratio) at the end. Both the mental health system's rapid growth and a striking reversal in the setting of care are emblematic of the progress of community mental health care in the postwar era.

Dynamic growth combined with a sharply circumscribed role for hospital care has continued to characterize use of mental health services into the current era. According to recent data, an estimated 13.3 percent of the adult population received some type of mental health treatment and/or counseling in 2009.[42] Less than 1 percent of these patients received inpatient mental health treatment. Far and away, prescription medication was the most common type of treatment received. Between 1996 and 2008, the number of prescription fills for mental health/substance abuse medications more than doubled.

As the provision of mental health care has expanded inside the specialty mental health and general medical sectors, the costs of treatment have climbed. A report published in the journal *Health Affairs* gives a careful accounting of this investment between 1986 and 2005.[43] In 2005, $113 billion was spent on mental health care in the United States, and another $22 billion was spent on substance abuse treatment. Since 1986, behavioral health spending grew more slowly than all health spending in the country, but the annual increases still were substantial (6.9 percent on average for mental health and 4.8 percent for substance abuse, compared with 7.9 percent for all health). Over this time period, spending on mental health and substance abuse kept up with the growth of the nation's gross national product and then some, going from 0.92 percent to 1.07 percent. In recent years, a major cost driver in this area has been the growing use and rising cost of prescriptions. However, the rate of inflation for drugs is now declining with widespread use of generics. Despite the spread of parity rules in connection with the 1996 federal statute and various state laws, only about 4 percent of all spending by private insurers

Among teens and young adults, suicide is the third leading cause of death, accounting for about 15 percent of the deaths in the age group between fifteen and twenty-four. The National Institute of Mental Health provides a wide variety of materials, including this poster, concerning suicide prevention as well as a hotline for individuals with suicidal thoughts.

SOURCE: U.S. Department of Defense.

Report on Posttraumatic Stress Disorder

The psychological problems of soldiers experiencing combat have not only posed a challenge to management of the U.S. military, but also shaped the evolution of psychiatry and public policy development for mental health care. The high number of "shell shock" cases in World War I (1914–1918) led to the establishment of a division of neurology and psychiatry in the Surgeon General's office, which worked hand in hand with the private National Committee for Mental Hygiene on diagnosing and treating these conditions. Neuropsychiatric problems during World War II (1939–1945) inspired new conceptions of the relationship between the environment and mental disorder that subsequently informed the community mental health movement. One of the bitterest controversies of the Vietnam War (1945–1975) concerned the adjustment difficulties faced by veterans with mental disorders who returned to a society rife with anti-war sentiment. Not until 1980 did the acronym PTSD, for posttraumatic stress disorder, enter the psychiatric lexicon when it was added to DSM-III in part due to the lobbying efforts of veterans groups. According to this standard reference source, the experience of war constitutes one kind of extreme stressor whose presence is pivotal in applying such a diagnosis.

In 2012, concerns surfaced that the army had been underdiagnosing cases of PTSD coming out of the conflicts in Iraq and Afghanistan. A preliminary Army investigation spurred by soldier complaints found that a high percentage of soldiers initially classified as suffering from PTSD later had this diagnosis reversed possibly due to the anticipated costs of medical benefits. Based on this information, Army officials charged a special Task Force on Behavioral Health with carrying out an independent nationwide review of its methods of diagnosing and treating mental health problems.

The task force report, titled *Corrective Action Plan*, was released in January 2013. Following examination of approximately 150,000 medical records of soldiers for the period of October 2001 to April 2012, the study group revalidated a high percentage of the original diagnoses of PTSD, and it concluded that no systematic bias had been revealed in the screening process. However, the task force also identified a need for numerous improvements in the military's handling of the behavioral health area. A total of forty-seven recommendations address such measures as better coordination of services among the Army organizations involved in the Integrated Disability Evaluation System along with better tracking of soldiers as they move through this process of disability determination; establishment of a system of Directors of Psychological Health at the state and regional levels to oversee the integration of psychiatry, psychology, and social work services in a multidisciplinary Department of Behavioral Health; and better dissemination of information to ensure that soldiers understand the care options available to them from different federal and state agencies. The report also highlighted the necessity of involving family members in the transition of soldiers with behavioral health conditions from active duty to discharge, calling for Soldier Family Assistance Centers "to connect Soldiers and Families with education, financial, job search assistance, and other transition support."

SOURCES: Albert Deutsch, *The Mentally Ill in America,* 2nd ed. (New York: Columbia University Press, 1949); Gerald N. Grob, *From Asylum to Community: Mental Health Policy in Modern America* (Princeton, NJ: Princeton University Press, 1991); Mathew J. Friedman, "Finalizing PTSD in DSM-5: Getting Here from There and Where to Go Next," *Journal of Trauma Stress* 26: 5 (2013): 548–546; Steve Vogel, "Army Orders Reforms for Mental Health Care Treatment," *Washington Post,* March 8, 2013.

went for mental health treatment in 2005. This figure compares to 10 percent of total Medicaid spending. The adoption of the 2008 federal parity statute, the passage of the PPACA in 2010, the related broadening of eligibility for Medicaid in most states, and the economic recession of the past five years all make the current era one of potentially important changes in behavioral health spending. The researchers who compiled these data stress their value as a benchmark for gauging future trends and outcomes of the new policies.

A dramatic sea change in philosophy, treatments, and financing that recast mental health care in the United States has occurred over the past half-century. Some of the most central goals of community care have now been achieved, to a great extent, with increased access to services, ongoing integration of mental health care and general medicine, development of effective model programs as alternatives to hospitalization, and new sources of payment. Yet even as some past issues have been addressed, others continue to call out for attention, and new concerns have come to the

fore. It is appropriate to end this survey of U.S. mental health care by mentioning a few areas of contemporary debate that promise to engage consumers, professionals, advocates, and policymakers for a good while to come.

Although use of services has risen sharply over the decades, it remains the case that not all people with mental health problems receive treatment. According to data from SAMHSA, only about 38 percent with any type of mental illness received mental health treatment in 2009. The treatment rate rises higher, to about 60 percent, if we focus on individuals with "serious mental illness," which is defined as "a diagnosable mental, behavioral, or emotional disorder . . . resulting in substantial impairment in carrying out major life activities." For both comparison groups, those with moderate problems and those with severe problems, definitive increases in treatment have taken place over time, but the numbers outside the treatment system are large.[44]

Difficulties arise when trying to go from statistics such as these to goal setting for service provision. While it may be tempting simply to say we should eliminate the gap between illness and treatment, this objective arguably would never be achievable in economic terms, and it may also be a poor way to define true clinical need and the potential to benefit from mental health care. In short, there is a danger of adopting a utopian notion of positive mental health, one that mental health professionals are poorly equipped to deliver and that could actually divert limited resources from the most devastating disorders.[45] Not all mental health problems require treatment because some are mild and they may be transitory or self-limiting.

ONGOING ISSUES AND NEEDS

The essential source for mental health diagnosis is the *Diagnostic and Statistical Manual* (DSM) published by the American Psychiatric Association. First released in 1952, the manual has now gone through seven editions (counting DSM-III-Revised, 1987, and DSM IV-Text Revision, 2000), with the latest, DSM-5, published in 2013. Although selected diagnostic categories have been removed from the manual over the course of time, by far the dominant tendency has been for expansion. In fact, the number of diagnoses listed in DSM has increased nearly threefold since the first edition.[46] There is controversy regarding the contents of DSM-5 due to the creation of various new disorder "subtypes."[47] Further, DSM-5 has been criticized for being insensitive to the "social determinants of mental disorders and their diagnosis."[48] No doubt, DSM has been an indispensable tool in improving the definition and detection of mental disorders over the decades. Yet credibility concerns are significant as the manual exercises its powerful sway over the conceptualization of, and insurance payments for, mental illness in our society.

Another issue in contemporary mental health care concerns the emergence of drugs as the dominant form of treatment across a whole host of diagnostic problems and patient groups. According to SAMHSA, by a factor of almost 2:1, prescription medication was the most common intervention for adults who received mental health treatment in 2009. The estimate is that 25.5 million Americans over eighteen years of age were given psychiatric drugs, the most common being different classes of antidepressants. Psychiatrists and general practitioners also write a large number of mental health prescriptions for children. Between 1987 and 1996, the overall use of psychotropic medications by children increased nearly 300 percent. Stimulants were the most common type, followed by antidepressants.[49] Parallel to this rise in medication has been psychotherapy's decline. One national study for the period between 1998 and 2007 found significant reductions in psychotherapy, whether given as a stand-alone treatment or in combination with medication.[50] This tendency toward medication alone as the standard method of mental health treatment conflicts with

research indicating the efficacy of psychotherapy for certain illnesses and patient groups, as well as the demonstrated clinical value of combining medication with therapy in many cases. It also raises questions about the formidable role of pharmaceutical companies in marketing their products to clinicians as well as to the public.

Deeply disturbing as it was, Newtown is only one of a series of memorably violent events perpetrated by someone previously suspected of having, or being treated for, mental health problems. The place names of such tragedies echo in the national consciousness—Aurora, Colorado; Tucson, Arizona; the Washington Navy Yard; and more. An instinctive response at these times on the part of many is to call for strict new measures protecting the public from people with mental illnesses. In a national survey conducted in January 2013, shortly after the Newtown shooting, 46 percent of respondents agreed that "people with serious mental illness are, by far, more dangerous than the general population."[51] This belief, however, is contradicted by research showing no direct link between mental illness and violence, although it is true that risk of violence rises for individuals with the most severe disorders who go untreated.[52] In his battle against proposed new gun control legislation, Wayne LaPierre, executive vice president of the National Rifle Association, has often tried to focus attention on dangerousness and mental illness and away from broader regulatory measures affecting the nation's gun owners. In one interview, he complained, "We have a completely cracked mentally ill system that's got these monsters walking the streets."[53] Such comments are not only deeply stigmatizing, they come close to a sweeping denunciation of the concept of community-based care.

Proposals to enforce existing background checks to keep guns out of the hands of individuals judged to pose the greatest threat to society, such as patients who have been involuntarily hospitalized, are reasonable and widely supported. However, more extreme approaches have also surfaced, including measures to compel mental health professionals to report persons "likely" to engage in harm to self or others.[54] The potentially deleterious effects of such a change in practice include large-scale overidentification of people who pose a risk of violence, discouragement against help-seeking for mental health problems, and invasion of patient privacy.[55]

In the end, the Obama administration opted for a more circumspect approach. With respect to mental health care, its 2013 "Now Is the Time" plan emphasized the elimination of barriers for reporting threats that are "direct and credible." Beyond this, the administration proposed greater access to mental health services and particularly the strengthening of innovative programs aimed at early identification of mental illness and appropriate treatment referrals. The plan also lays out steps to maximize coverage of mental health services under authority of the Patient Protection and Affordable Care Act and the 2008 federal parity statute. Subsequently, the president included $235 million for new mental health programs in his budget for Fiscal Year 2014.[56] When the U.S. Department of Health and Human Services at last issued final regulations for implementing the parity statute of 2008, it addressed long-standing questions concerning the meaning of comparable benefits in such areas as residential treatment and the "nonquantitative limits" embodied in definitions of medical necessity under managed care.[57] For the Obama administration, the expansion of mental health care via this rule-making also marked the fulfillment of all twenty-three executive actions promised by the president and vice president as their response to the Newtown massacre in the face of legislative intransigence.

U.S. mental health policy has always been undermined by a gap between ideals and capacity, as the administration's response to Newtown recognizes. A comprehensive system, one that includes a full spectrum of community and hospital services with appropriate utilization of different modalities by patients in need, remains a visionary goal rooted in our democratic commitment to health care access and human rights. A clearer understanding exists than ever before as to how this system might be organized, how further progress in treatment efficacy might be pursued, and what level of resources is involved in this undertaking. The essential challenge, then, is deciding where mental health care stands among the priorities that claim our nation's attention.

See also Chapter 22: Aging and Health Care Policy (1990s–Present); Chapter 23: Fifty Years of Progress in Disease and Injury Prevention (1950s–Present); Chapter 25: Nutrition, Physical Activity, and the Obesity Epidemic: Issues, Policies, and Solutions (1960s–Present); Chapter 26: Interest Groups, Think Tanks, and Health Care Policy (1960s–Present).

NOTES

1. Mary E. O'Leary, "Newtown Tragedy Spurs National Discussion on Mental Health Treatment," *West Hartford News,* December 18, 2012.

2. Liza Long, "I Am Adam Lanza's Mother," *The Blue Review,* December 15, 2012, http://thebluereview.org/i-am-adam-lanzas-mother.

3. "Republicans Pushing Mental Health Care over Gun Control Were Once against Mental Health Laws," *Huffington Post,* March 28, 2013.

4. Michael F. Hogan and Lloyd I. Sederer, "Mental Health Crises and Public Policy: Opportunities for Change?" *Health Affairs* 28: 3 (June 2009): 805–808.

5. Gerald N. Grob, *Mental Institutions in America: Social Policy to 1875* (New York: Free Press, 1973).

6. David J. Rothman, *The Discovery of the Asylum: Social Order and Disorder in the New Republic* (Boston: Little, Brown, 1971).

7. David A. Rochefort, *From Poorhouses to Homelessness: Policy Analysis and Mental Health Care,* 2nd ed. (Westport, CT: Auburn House, 1997).

8. Grob, *Mental Institutions in America,* 169.

9. Rochefort, *From Poorhouses to Homelessness.*

10. David J. Rothman, *Conscience and Convenience: The Asylum and Its Alternatives in Progressive America* (Boston: Little, Brown, 1980).

11. John W. Kingdon, *Agendas, Alternatives, and Public Policies* (Boston: Little, Brown, 1995).

12. Rochefort, *From Poorhouses to Homelessness.*

13. Leo Srole et al., *Mental Health in the Metropolis: The Midtown Manhattan Study* (New York: McGraw-Hill, 1962).

14. James M. Cameron, "A National Community Mental Health Program: Policy Initiation and Progress," in *Handbook on Mental Health Policy in the United States,* edited by David A. Rochefort, 121–142 (Westport, CT: Greenwood Press, 1989).

15. Ibid., 129.

16. Rochefort, *From Poorhouses to Homelessness.*

17. Henry A. Foley, *Community Mental Health Legislation: The Formative Process* (Lexington, MA: D.C. Heath, 1975).

18. Henry A. Foley and Steven S. Sharfstein, *Madness and Government: Who Cares for the Mentally Ill?* (Washington, DC: American Psychiatric Press, 1983).

19. David Mechanic and David A. Rochefort, "Deinstitutionalization: An Appraisal of Reform," *Annual Review of Sociology* 16 (1990): 301–327.

20. H. Richard Lamb and Robert W. Grant, "The Mentally Ill in an Urban County Jail," *Archives of General Psychiatry* 39: 1 (1982): 17–22; John R. Belcher, "Are Jails Replacing the Mental Health System for the Homeless Mentally Ill?" *Community Mental Health Journal* 24 (1988): 185–195; David Mechanic, "Correcting Misconceptions in Mental Health Policy: Strategies for Improved Care of the Seriously Mentally Ill," *Milbank Quarterly* 65: 2 (1987): 203–230.

21. Douglas Shenson, Nancy Dubler, and David Michaels, "Jails and Prisons: The New Asylums?" *American Journal of Public Health* 80: 6 (1990): 655–656, 655.

22. David Mechanic, Donna D. McAlpine, and David A. Rochefort, *Mental Health and Social Policy: Beyond Managed Care,* 6th ed. (Upper Saddle River, NJ: Pearson, 2014).

23. Irene Shifren Levine and Lorreta K. Haggard, "Homelessness as a Public Mental Health Problem," in *Handbook on Mental Health Policy in the United States,* edited by David A. Rochefort, 293–310 (Westport, CT: Greenwood Press, 1989).

24. Mechanic et al., *Mental Health and Social Policy.*

25. Charles A. Kiesler and Amy Sibulkin, *Mental Hospitalization: Myths and Facts about a National Crisis* (Newbury Park, CA: Sage, 1987).

26. Ibid.

27. Richard G. Frank, Howard H. Goldman, and Michael Hogan, "Medicaid and Mental Health: Be Careful What You Ask For," *Health Affairs* 22: 1 (January 2003): 101–113, 101.

28. Rochefort, *From Poorhouses to Homelessness,* 190–196.

29. Richard G. Frank, Chris Koyanagi, and Thomas G. McGuire, "The Politics and Economics of Mental Health Parity Laws," *Health Affairs* 16: 4 (July 1997): 108–119.

30. David A. Rochefort, "The Backlash against Managed Care," in *The New Politics of State Health Policy,* edited by Robert B. Hackey and David A. Rochefort, 113–141 (Lawrence: University Press of Kansas, 2001).

31. Rochefort, *From Poorhouses to Homelessness.*

32. Colleen Barry, Haiden A. Huskamp, and Howard H. Goldman, "A Political History of Federal Mental Health and Addiction Insurance Parity," *Milbank Quarterly* 88 (2010): 404–433, 412.

33. Ibid.

34. Isabelle T. Walker, "Mentally Ill and Uninsured in America," *American Journal of Nursing* 110: 3 (March 2010): 27–28.

35. Chris Koyanagi, *How Will Health Reform Help People with Mental Illnesses?* (Washington, DC: Bazelon Center for Mental Health Law, 2010).

36. Ibid.

37. Bazelon Center for Mental Health Law, *Taking Advantage of New Opportunities to Expand Medicaid under the Affordable Care Act* (Washington, DC: Bazelon Center for Mental Health Law, July 2102).

38. David Mechanic, "Seizing Opportunities under the Affordable Care Act for Transforming the Mental and Behavioral Health System," *Health Affairs* 31: 2 (2012): 376–382.

39. Ronald C. Kessler et al., "Lifetime Prevalence and Age-of-Onset Distributions of DSM-IV Disorders in the National Comorbidity Survey Replication," *Archives of General Psychiatry* 62: 6 (2005): 593–602.

40. Mechanic et al., *Mental Health and Social Policy.*

41. Michael J. Witkin et al., "Highlights of Organized Mental Health Services in 1994 and Major National and State Trends," in *Mental Health, United States, 1998,* edited by Ronald W. Manderscheid and Marilyn J. Henderson (Rockville, MD: U.S. Department of Health and Human Services, Substance Abuse and Mental Health Services Administration, 1998).

42. Substance Abuse and Mental Health Services Administration, *Mental Health, United States, 2010* (Rockville, MD: U.S. Department of Health and Human Services, 2012).

43. Tami L .Mark et al., "Changes in US Spending on Mental Health and Substance Abuse Treatment, 1986–2005," *Health Affairs* 30: 2 (February 2011): 284–292.

44. Ibid.

45. Mechanic et al., *Mental Health and Social Policy.*

46. Johnathan Fish, "Overcrowding on the Ship of Fools: Health Care Reform, Psychiatry, and the Uncertain Future of Normality," *Houston Journal of Health Law and Policy* 11 (2011): 1534–7907.

47. Robin S. Rosenberg, "Abnormal Is the New Normal," *Slate,* April 12, 2013, http://www.slate.com/articles/health_and_science/ medical_examiner/2013/04/diagnostic_and_statistical_manual_ fifth_edition_why_will_half_the_u_s_population.html.

48. Helena B. Hansen et al., "Independent Review of Social and Population Variation in Mental Health Could Improve Diagnosis in DSM Revisions," *Health Affairs* 32: 5 (May 2013): 984–993, 984.

49. Mark Olfson et al., "National Trends in the Use of Psychotropic Medications by Children," *Journal of the American Academy of Child and Adolescent Psychiatry* 415: 5 (2002): 514–521.

50. Ibid.

51. Colleen Barry et al., "After Newtown—Public Opinion on Gun Policy and Mental Illness," *New England Journal of Medicine* 368 (March 21, 2013): 1077–1081.

52. David Shern and Wayne Lindstrom, "After Newtown: Mental Illness and Violence," *Health Affairs* 32: 3 (March 2013): 447–450.

53. Lexington, "Why the NRA Keeps Talking about Mental Illness, Rather Than Guns," *The Economist,* March 13, 2013, http://www.economist.com/blogs/lexington/2013/03/guns-and-mentally-ill.

54. Benedict Carey and Anemona Hartocollis, "Warning Signs of Violent Acts Often Unclear," *New York Times,* January 15, 2013.

55. Jeffrey Swanson, "Mental Illness and New Gun Reform Laws: The Promise and Peril of Crisis-Driven Policy," *Journal of the American Medical Association* 309: 12 (2013): 1333–1234.

56. Sarah Kliff, "Obama's Proposed Budget to Seek $235 Million for New Mental Health Programs," *Washington Post,* April 9, 2013.

57. Jackie Calmes and Robert Pear, "Rules to Require Equal Coverage for Mental Ills," *New York Times,* November 8, 2013.

FURTHER READING

Frank, Richard G., and Sherry A. Glied. *Better but Not Well: Mental Health Policy in the United States since 1950.* Baltimore: Johns Hopkins University Press, 2006.

Grob, Gerald N. *The Mad among Us: A History of Care of America's Mentally Ill.* New York: Free Press, 1994.

Horwitz, Allan V. *Creating Mental Illness.* Chicago: University of Chicago, 2002.

Mechanic, David, Donna D. McAlpine, and David A. Rochefort. *Mental Health and Social Policy: Beyond Managed Care,* 6th ed. Upper Saddle River, NJ: Pearson, 2014.

Rochefort, David A. *From Poorhouses to Homelessness: Policy Analysis and Mental Health Care,* 2nd ed. Westport, CT: Auburn House, 1997.

Whitaker, Robert. *Mad in America: Bad Science, Bad Medicine, and the Enduring Mistreatment of the Mentally Ill.* Cambridge, MA: Perseus, 2001.

Nutrition, Physical Activity, and the Obesity Epidemic

Issues, Policies, and Solutions (1960s–Present)

Thomas D. Fahey and Michael W. Fahey

The United States is in the midst of an obesity epidemic, with more than two-thirds of the population either overweight or obese. Since 1960, the average American man's weight has increased from 166 to 191 pounds, and the average American woman's weight has increased from 140 to 164 pounds. The prevalence of obesity has increased from about 13 percent in 1960 to 35.7 percent in 2014. More than 68 percent of American adults are now overweight.[1] Obesity rates finally leveled off in 2014, after a consistent increase since 1980. Even with this promising statistic, obesity rates exceed 30 percent of the population in thirteen states and 25 percent of the population in forty-one states (see Figure 25.1).

Obesity rates also leveled off between 2007 and 2010 in school-aged children for the first time since the introduction of large-scale surveys on body mass index (see Figure 25.2). However, the prevalence of obesity was consistently higher among non-Hispanic black and Hispanic children and adolescents than among non-Hispanic white youth. Obesity is defined as a measure of body mass index (weight [kilograms] / height^2 [meters]) of 30 or more.

A NATIONAL CRISIS

The obesity epidemic has had severe consequences in the United States. Obesity increases the risk of premature death by 100 percent and can reduce life expectancy by ten to twenty years. Obesity and being overweight increase the risk of the metabolic syndrome, a group of symptoms that include insulin resistance, hypertension (high blood pressure), dyslipidemia (abnormal blood fats), abdominal fat deposition, and inflammation. Two-thirds of Americans suffer from the metabolic syndrome, which increases the risk of heart attack, stroke, and diabetes. Other health problems associated with obesity and overweight include impaired immune function, gallbladder and kidney diseases, skin problems, sleep and breathing disorders, erectile dysfunction, depression, pregnancy complications, back pain, arthritis, and other bone and joint disorders.[2] Obesity also impairs movement capacity, self-image, and emotional well-being.

Type 2 Diabetes and Obesity

Even mild to moderate overweight is associated with a substantial increase in the risk of type 2 diabetes. Obese people are more than three times as likely as non-obese people to develop type 2 diabetes, and the incidence of this disease among Americans has increased dramatically as the rate of obesity has climbed. About twenty-four million Americans (8 percent of the population) have one of two major forms of diabetes (see Figure 25.1). About 5 to 10 percent of people with diabetes have the more serious form, known as type 1 diabetes. In this type of diabetes, because the pancreas produces little or no insulin, daily doses of insulin are required. Type 1 diabetes usually strikes before age thirty.

The remaining 90 to 95 percent of Americans with diabetes have type 2 diabetes. This condition can develop slowly, and about 25 percent of affected people are unaware of their condition. In type 2 diabetes, the pancreas does not produce enough insulin, cells are resistant to insulin, or both. This condition is usually diagnosed in people over age forty, although there has been a tenfold increase in type 2 diabetes in children in the past two decades. About one-third of people with type 2 diabetes must take insulin; others may take medications that increase insulin production or stimulate cells to take up glucose (blood sugar).

The term *pre-diabetes* describes blood sugar levels that are higher than normal but not high enough for a diagnosis of full-blown diabetes. About fifty-seven million Americans have pre-diabetes, and most people with the condition will develop type 2 diabetes unless they adopt preventive lifestyle

FIGURE 25.1   **Changes in the Prevalence of Obesity and Diabetes between 1994 and 2010**

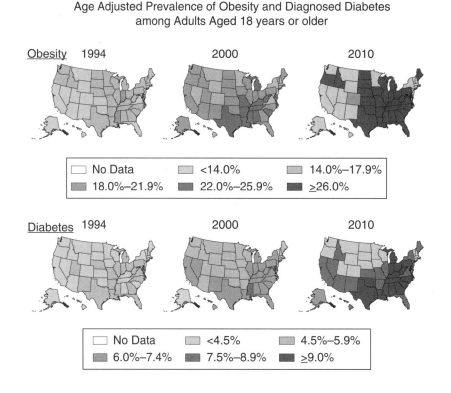

SOURCE: Centers for Disease Control, "Diabetes Data and Trends," http://apps.nccd.cdc.gov/DDTSTRS/default.aspx.

measures. The major factors involved in the development of diabetes are age, obesity, physical inactivity, a family history of diabetes, and lifestyle. Excess body fat reduces cell sensitivity to insulin, and insulin resistance is usually a precursor of type 2 diabetes. According to the Centers for Disease Control and Prevention (CDC), the rate of diagnosed diabetes cases is highest among Native Americans and Alaska Natives (16.5 percent), followed by African Americans (11.8 percent), Hispanics (10.4 percent), Asian Americans (7.5 percent), and white Americans (6.6 percent). Across all races, about 25 percent of Americans age sixty and older have diabetes.[3]

Ninety percent of cases of type 2 diabetes could be prevented if people led healthier lifestyles, including regular exercise, a healthy diet containing a variety of foods, and modest weight loss. For people with pre-diabetes, healthy lifestyle is more effective than prescription drugs for delaying or preventing the development of diabetes. Studies of people with pre-diabetes show that a 5 to 7 percent weight loss can lower diabetes onset by nearly 60 percent. Exercise (endurance and/or strength training) makes cells more sensitive to insulin and helps stabilize blood sugar levels; it also helps keep body fat at healthy levels. Obesity is also associated with an increased risk of death from many types of cancer.

The Obesity Epidemic

The annual cost of the obesity epidemic is $150 billion to $200 billion per year.[3] Obese people spend nearly twice as much on medical care as people with healthier weights. This is money that could be spent on education, defense, infrastructure, or reducing the tax rate. Obesity is a national emergency that is more dangerous to our country than terrorism or nuclear proliferation.

The causes of the obesity epidemic are complex and controversial, involving a combination of increased caloric intake and decreased physical activity. According to the National Health and Nutrition Examination Survey, energy intake increased from 1,955 kilocalories in 1971 to 2,269 kilocalories in 2003 and then decreased to 2,195 kilocalories in 2010. Caloric intake from fat decreased from 37 percent in 1971 to 33 percent in 2006.[4] During this time period, carbohydrate calories in the diet increased by 11 percent. In spite of these recent positive dietary changes, the rate of obesity has remained steady or increased. Excess caloric consumption remains a serious problem because of more meals eaten outside the home, greater consumption of fast food, increased portion sizes, increased consumption of soft drinks and convenience foods, and limited access to healthy foods.

FIGURE 25.2 **Prevalence of Obesity in U.S. Males and Females Aged Two through Nineteen Years between 1999 and 2010**

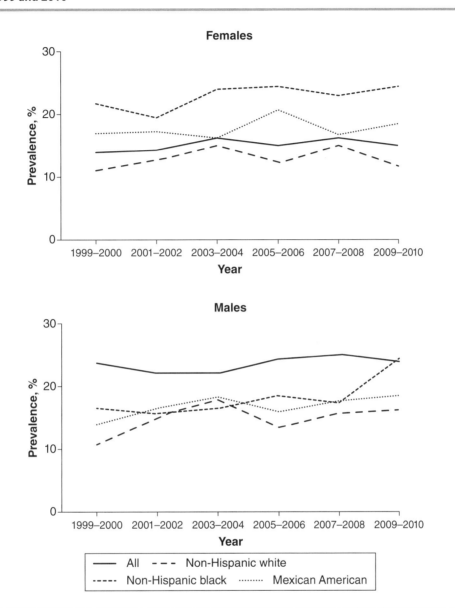

SOURCE: Cynthia L. Ogden, Margaret D. Carrol, Brian K. Kit, and Katherine M. Flegal, "Prevalence of Obesity and Trends in Body Mass Index among US Children and Adolescents, 1999–2010," *Journal American Medical Association*. 307: 5 (2012): 483–490.

People are less physically active than in past years. Possible explanations include more time spent in sedentary work and leisure activities, fewer short trips on foot and more by automobile, and fewer daily physical education classes for students. The National Health Interview Survey of 2012[5] reported that 50 percent of adults failed to meet the 2008 minimum physical activity recommendations by the U.S. Department of Health and Human Services (HHS)[6] of 150 minutes a week of moderate physical activity or 75 minutes per week of vigorous physical activity. Only 21 percent met the physical activity recommendations for both aerobic and muscle-strengthening activity (large muscle exercises,

two times per week). Table 25.1 shows that activity levels vary by age, race, gender, and educational level. Government programs should specifically target deficient groups.

Public policy since World War II (1939–1945) has inadvertently contributed to the obesity epidemic. Early policies sought to make inexpensive food available to the population through farm subsidies, improved infrastructure, suburbanization, and more efficient food processing. Nutritional recommendations based on little objective evidence shifted dietary patterns away from fat intake toward and increased consumption of carbohydrates. Educational policies that reduced recess time and physical education

TABLE 25.1 **Percentage of People Meeting Aerobic Physical Activity Guidelines in Select Groups**

Group	Inactive (%)	Insufficiently Active (%)	Met Guidelines (%)
Total	30.2	20.2	49.6
Gender			
Males	28.7	17.6	53.7
Females	31.6	22.6	45.8
Age			
18–44	24.5	19.3	56.1
45–64	31.8	21.4	46.9
65–74	35.7	19.7	44.6
75 and over	51.4	20.6	28.1
Race or ethnic group			
White	29.4	20.0	50.6
Black	38.5	19.9	41.6
Native American	28.4	23.2	48.4
Asian	28.0	22.6	49.4
Pacific Islander	11.7	18	70.3
Hispanic	37.8	17.9	44.4
Education			
Less than high school	51.8	18.1	30.1
High school or GED	41.2	21.2	37.6
Some college	29.1	21.0	49.9
Bachelor's degree or higher	15.8	20.7	63.5

SOURCE: National Center for Health Statistics, "Summary Health Statistics for U.S. Adults: National Health Interview Survey, 2012," *Vital and Health Statistics* 10: 260 (2014).

NOTE: The guideline is 150 minutes per week of moderate-intensity exercise or 75 minutes per week of vigorous-intensity exercise, or a combination of both.

combined with technological advances to decrease physical activity levels in school children.

Public policy can also reverse the trends of increased obesity rates and decreased physical activity. Accurate food labeling, taxing high-sugar soft drinks, subsidizing supermarkets in inner-city neighborhoods, developing activity-friendly parks and streets, and ensuring quality physical education and sports programs in the schools are only a few of the public policies that have been suggested to help fight obesity and promote active lifestyles.

PUBLIC POLICIES ON DIET, EXERCISE, AND OBESITY: 1960 TO 1980

Following World War II, the United States was the leading economic power in the world. Dietary policies were aimed at increasing the availability of food in the United States and war-torn Europe and Asia. Obesity was not considered a significant problem, but cardiovascular diseases were.

Longevity increased progressively during most of the twentieth century. In 1900, men lived an average of 46.3 years, while women lived 48.3 years.[7] That increased to 66.3 and 72.0 years in 1950 and 76.3 and 81.1 years in 2011. In 1900, heart disease was the fourth leading cause of death, behind infectious diseases such as influenza, pneumonia, tuberculosis, and gastrointestinal infections. By 1950, deaths from heart disease had increased from 137.4 to 355.5 deaths per 100,000 people. By 2010, the heart disease death rate had fallen to 192.9 deaths per 100,000 people.

In 1951, the Framingham Study,[8] a long-term epidemiological study of more than five thousand people living in Framingham, Massachusetts, identified high cholesterol, hypertension, and cigarette smoking as significant risk factors of cardiovascular disease. In 1947, Ancel Keys from the University of Minnesota led studies that established a link between elevated cholesterol and heart disease. The most significant investigation was the Seven Countries Study, a longitudinal study that investigated the relationship between diet and heart disease in the United States, Finland, the Netherlands, Italy, Yugoslavia, Greece, and Japan.[9] This study established the relationship between elevated cholesterol and coronary artery disease.

The Framingham and Seven Countries studies had significant effects on public policy. They established the concepts of risk factors of coronary artery disease, which were expanded from high cholesterol, hypertension, and smoking to include obesity, physical inactivity, stress, and diabetes. Initially, government efforts were aimed at funding research on risk factors of coronary artery disease and drugs to lower blood pressure and cholesterol. The establishment of the National High Blood Pressure Education Program in 1972 and the National Cholesterol Education Program in 1985 followed this.[10] However, even as late as 1976, national policies on nutrition focused more on nutritional inadequacies than on nutritional excesses.

Diet

National educational programs designed to alter diet included publications on diet and heart disease by the American Heart Association in 1952, 1965, 1968, and 1978; recommendations on preventing obesity from the National Institutes of Health in 1974 and 1977; the Surgeon General's Report on Health Promotion and Disease Prevention in 1979; and the *Dietary Guidelines for Americans* from the U.S. Department of Agriculture in 1980. Early public policies on diet were aimed at reducing the risk of heart disease. The integration of diet and exercise to prevent obesity, initiated in 1952, began in earnest in the 1980s.

The U.S. Senate Select Committee on Nutrition and Human Needs, headed by Senator George McGovern (in office 1963–1981) promoted a change in the national diet that recommended the consumption of more carbohydrates and less fat.[11] This was a hasty decision with little scientific support. A landmark study in 2014 led by Rajiv Chowdhury, which combined the results of more than seventy studies, showed that the fat content of the diet had no effects on the risk of coronary artery disease.[12] The overall composition of the diet is more important than individual foods.

POLITICS AND HEALTH CARE POLICY

The Long-Running Controversy about Dietary Fat

The most significant public policy activity on nutrition, physical activity, and obesity during the past fifty years was the diet recommendations of the McGovern Committee in 1977. They suggested an increase in carbohydrate consumption to 55 to 60 percent of the total caloric intake, reduction of overall fat consumption from 40 to 30 percent of daily calories, reduction of daily cholesterol consumption to three hundred milligrams, decreased consumption of meat and increased consumption of poultry and fish, decreased consumption of foods high in fat, substituting nonfat milk for whole milk, and decreased consumption of butterfat. Included in the report was a letter from the American Medical Association (April 18, 1977) to the Nutrition Committee that stated, "the value of dietary change remains controversial and that science cannot at this time insure that an altered diet will provide protection from certain killer diseases such as heart disease and cancer."

This policy, which was not supported by firm evidence, promoted reductions in fat intake and increases in carbohydrate intake. The dietary policy succeeded. An analysis of the U.S. diet between 1971 and 2006 using data from the National Health and Nutrition Examination Survey (1971–1975 and 2005–2006) showed that fat intake decreased in people who were normal weight, overweight, and obese, while carbohydrate intake increased substantially. However, the prevalence of obesity increased from 11.9 percent to 33.4 percent. In other words, Americans consumed less fat in 2006 than they did in the early 1970s, but they got substantially fatter. They also consumed more carbohydrates and calories. The percentage of carbohydrates in the diet was 44 percent in the 1970s and nearly 49 percent in 2006. Energy intake increased substantially in normal weight, overweight, and obese people.

In 2014, a large meta-analysis of published studies led by Rajiv Chowdhury from the University of Cambridge in the United Kingdom, supported by a large body of recent research, concluded that high consumption of saturated fats or polyunsaturated fats did not affect the risk of cardiovascular disease. High intake of trans fats increased the risk of heart disease by 16 percent. The researchers compared heart disease risk between people consuming the highest and lowest amounts of various kinds of fat. The results were based on an analysis of seventy-six studies involving nearly 700,000 people. The study refuted the dietary recommendations of the McGovern Committee that people reduce saturated fat intake and replace it with foods high in unsaturated fats such as nuts, fish, and vegetable oils. Factors such as obesity, physical activity, total calories, and intake of refined carbohydrates and salt also affect cardiovascular health and the development of obesity. Researchers concluded that overall dietary composition is more important for promoting health than single foods.

Some researchers have charged that a political decision made in 1977 might be partially responsible for the obesity epidemic. The combination of a political decision to push carbohydrates and the increased availability and affordability of corn-based sweeteners triggered significant changes in the U.S. diet that led to excessive caloric intake.

SOURCES: U.S. Senate, Select Committee on Nutrition and Human Needs, *Dietary Goals for the United States* (Washington, DC: U.S. Government Printing Office, 1977);, Gregory L. Austin, Lorraine G. Ogden, and James O. Hill, "Trends in Carbohydrate, Fat, and Protein Intakes and Association with Energy Intake in Normal-Weight, Overweight, and Obese Individuals: 1971–2006," *American Journal Clinical Nutrition* 93:4 (2011): 836–843. Rajiv Chowdhury et al., "Association of Dietary, Circulating, and Supplement Fatty Acids with Coronary Risk: A Systematic Review and Meta-analysis," *Annals of Internal Medicine* 160: 6 (2014): 398–406.

Exercise

Early exercise recommendations for Americans were based on the physical readiness of young men for the military. While the 1952 recommendations of the American Heart Association mentioned the importance of physical activity for weight control and heart disease prevention, physical education programs in schools were heavily centered on sports rather than metabolic fitness for preventing obesity or heart disease.

In 1954, a landmark study by Hans Kraus and Ruth Hirschland found that 57.9 percent of U.S. school children failed basic tests of strength and flexibility compared to only 8.7 percent of European children.[13] The study concluded that Europeans walked or rode bicycles and performed vigorous household chores such as chopping wood, while U.S. children rode in automobiles and school buses and performed typically minimal chores.

Jack Kelly, former Olympian and father of actress Grace Kelly (later Princess Grace of Monaco), brought the study to the attention of President Dwight D. Eisenhower (1953–1961). Alarmed, Eisenhower ordered the formation of a national study group composed of leading educators, physicians, sports figures, and government officials that met at the U.S. Naval Academy in June 1956. The meeting resulted in the formation of the President's Council on Physical Fitness and Sports, an organization charged with promoting exercise and sport in the United States.

The program was expanded during the John F. Kennedy (1961–1963) and Lyndon B. Johnson (1963–1969) administrations. Kennedy popularized fifty-mile hikes (a fitness requirement for Marine officers) and promoted improved physical education in schools. During the Johnson administration, the Council developed the Presidential Physical Fitness Award for exceptional physical fitness in school children. The Richard M. Nixon (1969–1974) and Gerald R. Ford (1974–1977) administrations placed more emphasis on adult fitness. These programs had little effect on physical fitness of U.S. school children. In 1975, a physical fitness survey showed that school children were less fit than were children in 1965.

In 1954, a group of physicians and scientists led by J.B. Wolf founded the Federation of Sports Medicine. This group would change its name to the American College of Sports Medicine (ACSM), which would become the leading proponent of physical activity for health. Its exercise recommendations and guidelines would become the basis for policies on physical activity from government agencies such as HHS. In 1975, the first edition of *ACSM's Guidelines for Graded Exercise Testing and Exercise Prescription* was published. Since then, these guidelines have served as a basis for public policies on exercise testing and prescription.

In the 1970s, the ACSM initiated certifications for program directors and exercise leaders. They began publishing the journals *Medicine and Science in Sports* (later called *Medicine and Science in Sports and Exercise*) and *Exercise and Sport Sciences Reviews*. These publications disseminated information on exercise and sports sciences and served as the early basis for establishing public policies on physical activity and sport.

Additionally, the Interstate Highway System had a major impact on exercise habits and food availability. President Eisenhower considered the system vital for national defense after observing the German Autobahn during World War II. The National Interstate and Defense Highways Act of 1956 initiated the extensive highway network we have today.[14] The interstate highway system improved national infrastructure by enhancing the quality and quantity of state, county, and city roads that allowed access to the new highways. Spending public funds on roads and highways rather than mass transit increased automobile usage and facilitated food deliveries.

More people moved to the suburbs, which made them dependent on automobiles for transportation. This resulted in decreased physical activity, because people drove cars instead of walking or cycling. Suburbanization often increased commute distances to work, but it also increased distances to parks, sports facilities, and recreational venues. Improved food delivery systems made food more affordable and readily available, which eventually promoted overeating and obesity.

PUBLIC POLICIES ON DIET, EXERCISE, AND OBESITY: 1981 TO PRESENT

World War II saw a large influx of women into the workforce, which changed family and social structures. Government-funded research made the performance of household chores easier and increased the availability of cheap, easy-to-prepare foods. Agricultural policies promoted the availability of cheap, high-calorie foods. Obesity rates soared, which in turn focused public policy on reducing obesity, improving the diet, and promoting physical activity.

Agricultural Policies and Nutrition

According to statistics from the U.S. Department of Agriculture, caloric intake was 400 kilocalories per day greater in 2007 than in 1985 and 600 kilocalories per day greater than in 1970.[15] At least part of this increased caloric intake was due to farm policy in the United States, which subsidized the production of corn, wheat, rice, milk, and soybeans. Farm policy after World War II was aimed at stabilizing supplies and preventing undernutrition at home and abroad. Farms became larger and more efficient, which led to overproduction.

The 1996 farm bill provided incentives for overproduction and subsidized farmers to protect them against low prices. Between 1985 and 2000, the inflation-adjusted price of high-sugar soft drinks decreased by 24 percent, while the prices of fresh fruit and vegetables increased 39 percent.[15] Agricultural subsidies support high-calorie foods but generally do not support healthier fruits and vegetables.

There is no easy solution. Agricultural subsidies support a strong national farm network that is vital to national security. Farm policy should be partially redirected to promote production of healthier fruits and vegetables without hurting farm economy.

Agricultural policy affects what crops farmers grow, but it also influences what people eat. These policies rarely consider their effects on public health. Policy must consider both sides of the spectrum. A policy that supports the production of cheap, high-calorie crops increases health care costs by promoting degenerative diseases linked to obesity, insulin resistance, and diabetes. Unfortunately, there is little direct evidence on the effects of farm policy on diet or obesity.[16]

Public Guidelines on Obesity

In the 1960s and 1970s, obesity rates remained stable at about 13 percent of the population. By 2000, obesity rates were 8.1 percent in infants and toddlers, 16.9 percent in children two to nineteen, and 34.9 percent in adults aged twenty years and older. In most groups, obesity rates remained stable between 2003 and 2012, except among women aged sixty years and older, which increased from 31.5 percent to 38.1 percent. While obesity rates have leveled off in recent years, they are still extremely high and account for a significant proportion of health care spending in the United States and other developed countries.[17]

Since 1980, the most significant public efforts to reduce obesity were led by the U.S. Department of Agriculture and U.S. Department of Health and Human Services. These departments published the *Dietary Guidelines for Americans* and generated national health goals outlined in Healthy People 2000, Healthy People 2010, and Healthy People 2020. Although obesity was not emphasized as a health priority in Healthy People 2000, it was prominently discussed in the 2010 and 2020 Healthy People reports. The U.S. Department of Health and Human Services and the U.S. Department of Agriculture have jointly produced the *Dietary Guidelines for Americans* every five years since 1980.

A progress update on Healthy People 2020 goals shows mixed results. While obesity rates accelerated between 1980 and 2000, they have remained high but stable since. Obesity is linked to hypertension, diabetes and insulin resistance, physical inactivity, and elevated cholesterol. Between 2005 and 2011, some health factors related to obesity have improved, while others have remained unchanged. Adults with hypertension whose blood pressure is under control improved from 43.7 percent of the

population in 2005 to 48.9 percent in 2011. Obesity was unchanged in adults (33.9 vs. 35.3 percent) and among children and adolescents (16.1 vs. 16.9 percent). Mean daily intake of total vegetables (cup equivalents per 1,000 kilocalories) remained constant at 0.8 serving. Hemoglobin A1c, a measure of blood sugar control and diabetes, was 17.9 percent in 2005 and 21 percent in 2012 among people diagnosed with diabetes. Adults meeting federal guidelines aerobic and physical activity and muscle-strengthening federal guidelines increased from 18.2 percent in 2008 to 20.6 percent in 2012.

Public Guidelines on Physical Activity

Before 1980, exercise recommendations emphasized vigorous exercise and participation in team sports in activities such as jogging and basketball. The first exercise recommendations from the American College of Sports Medicine were issued in 1975, which recommended exercise three to five days per week for fifteen to sixty minutes at 50 to 85 percent of heart rate reserve (maximum heart rate – resting heart rate). These guidelines were modified in 1978, 1990, 1998, and 2011 to reflect current knowledge on the effects of exercise on health and body composition.

During the 1980s and 1990s, research showed that moderate intensity exercise promoted health and longevity. This led to changes in exercise recommendations from the U.S. Surgeon General (issued in 1996), the Department of Health and Human Services (issued in 2005 and 2008), and the American College of Sports Medicine and American Heart Association (issued in 2007 and 2011).

In 2008 and 2010, the U.S. Surgeon General issued *The Surgeon General's Vision for a Healthy and Fit Nation,* and HHS made specific recommendations for promoting exercise and health. These reports stressed the importance of regular physical activity and emphasized that some physical activity is better than none. The reports also presented evidence that regular activity promotes health and prevents premature death and a variety of diseases.

Physical Activity Guidelines for Americans and the Surgeon General's recommendations included the following key guidelines for adults:

- For substantial health benefits, adults should do at least 150 minutes a week of moderate-intensity aerobic physical activity, or 75 minutes a week of vigorous-intensity aerobic physical activity, or an equivalent combination of moderate- and vigorous-intensity aerobic activity. Activity should preferably be spread throughout the week.
- For additional and more extensive health benefits, adults should increase their aerobic physical activity to 300 minutes a week of moderate-intensity activity, or 150 minutes a week of vigorous-intensity activity, or

an equivalent combination of moderate- and vigorous-intensity activity. Additional health benefits are gained by engaging in physical activity beyond this amount.

- Adults should also do muscle-strengthening activities that are moderate or high intensity and involve all major muscle groups on two or more days a week, as these activities provide additional health benefits.
- People should avoid inactivity. Adults, teenagers, and children should spend less time in front of a television or computer screen, because these activities contribute to a sedentary lifestyle and increase the risk of obesity.

The reports stated that physical activity benefits people of all ages and of all racial and ethnic groups, including people with disabilities. The reports emphasized that the benefits of activity outweigh the dangers. These levels of physical activity promote health and wellness by lowering the risk of high blood pressure, stroke, heart disease, type 2 diabetes, colon cancer, and osteoporosis. They also reduce feelings of mild to moderate depression and anxiety.

What is moderate physical activity? Activities such as brisk walking, dancing, swimming, cycling, and yard work can all count toward the daily total. A moderate amount of activity uses about 150 kilocalories of energy and causes a noticeable increase in heart rate, such as would occur with a brisk walk. You can burn the same number of calories by doing a lower intensity activity for a longer time or a higher intensity activity for a shorter time. In contrast to moderate-intensity activity, vigorous physical activity causes rapid breathing and a substantial increase in heart rate, as exemplified by jogging.

Public Policies to Prevent Obesity

Public health organizations such as the American College of Sports Medicine, American Heart Association, and Robert Wood Johnson Foundation as well as government agencies such as the Surgeon General's Office, U.S. Department of Health and Human Services, and U.S. Department of Agriculture promote strategies for preventing obesity by emphasizing healthy diet and increased physical activity. Figure 25.3 lists the CDC's suggested strategies for preventing obesity.

Healthy People 2020

This program, directed by the U.S. Department of Health and Human Services,[18] established national health goals, including those related to diet, exercise, and obesity. Specific goals of the program include consuming a variety of nutrient-dense foods within and across the food groups, especially whole grains, fruits, vegetables, low-fat or fat-free milk or milk products, and lean meats and other protein sources;

FIGURE 25.3 **CDC's Recommended Strategies for Obesity Prevention**

Communities should do the following:

1. Increase availability of healthier food and beverage choices in public service venues

2. Improve availability of affordable healthier food and beverage choices in public service venues

3. Improve geographic availability of supermarkets in underserved areas

4. Provide incentives to food retailers to locate in and/or offer healthier food and beverage choices in underserved areas

5. Improve availability of mechanisms for purchasing foods from farms

6. Provide incentives for the production, distribution, and procurement of foods from local farms

7. Restrict availability of less healthy foods and beverages in public service venues

8. Institute smaller portion size options in public service venues

9. Limit advertisements of less healthy foods and beverages

10. Discourage consumption of sugar-sweetened beverages

11. Increase support for breastfeeding

12. Require physical education in schools

13. Increase the amount of physical activity in physical education programs in schools

14. Increase opportunities for extracurricular physical activity

15. Reduce screen time in public service venues

16. Improve access to outdoor recreational facilities

17. Enhance infrastructure supporting bicycling

18. Enhance infrastructure supporting walking

19. Support locating schools within easy walking distance of residential areas

20. Improve access to public transportation

21. Zone for mixed-use development

22. Enhance personal safety in areas where persons are or could be physically active

23. Enhance traffic safety in areas where persons are or could be physically active

24. Participate in community coalitions or partnerships to address obesity

SOURCE: U.S. Department of Health and Human Services, *Recommended Community Strategies and Measurements to Prevent Obesity in the United States* (Washington, DC: Centers for Disease Control and Prevention, July 2009).

Physical Activity and Health: A Surgeon General's Report

The Framingham study identified cigarette smoking, hypertension, and high cholesterol as the most significant risk factors for developing coronary artery disease. In 1964, the Surgeon General's office issued a landmark report on smoking, which began to change the national consciousness against cigarettes. Secretary of Health and Human Services Donna Shalala (in office 1993–2001) commented on a landmark report that elevated physical inactivity to a major risk factor for heart disease:

> The United States has led the world in understanding and promoting the benefits of physical activity. In the 1950s, we launched the first national effort to encourage young Americans to be physically active, with a strong emphasis on participation in team sports. In the 1970s, we embarked on a national effort to educate Americans about the cardiovascular benefits of vigorous activity, such as running and playing basketball. And in the 1980s and 1990s, we made breakthrough findings about the health benefits of moderate-intensity activities, such as walking, gardening, and dancing.
>
> Now, with the publication of this first Surgeon General's report on physical activity and health, which I commissioned in 1994, we are poised to take another bold step forward. This landmark review of the research on physical activity and health—the most comprehensive ever—has the potential to catalyze a new physical activity and fitness movement in the United States. It is a work of real significance, on par with the Surgeon General's historic first report on smoking and health published in 1964.
>
> This report is a passport to good health for all Americans. Its key finding is that people of all ages can improve the quality of their lives through a lifelong practice of moderate physical activity. You don't have to be training for the Boston Marathon to derive real health benefits from physical activity. A regular, preferably daily regimen of at least 30–45 minutes of brisk walking, bicycling, or even working around the house or yard will reduce your risks of developing coronary heart disease, hypertension, colon cancer, and diabetes. And if you're already doing that, you should consider picking up the pace: this report says that people who are already physically active will benefit even more by increasing the intensity or duration of their activity.
>
> This watershed report comes not a moment too soon. We have found that 60 percent—well over half—of Americans are not regularly active. Worse yet, 25 percent of Americans are not active at all. For young people—the future of our country—physical activity declines dramatically during adolescence. These are dangerous trends. We need to turn them around quickly, for the health of our citizens and our country.
>
> We will do so only with a massive national commitment—beginning now, on the eve of the Centennial Olympic Games, with a true fitness Dream Team drawing on the many forms of leadership that make up our great democratic society. Families need to weave physical activity into the fabric of their daily lives. Health professionals, in addition to being role models for healthy behaviors, need to encourage their patients to get out of their chairs and start fitness programs tailored to their individual needs. Businesses need to learn from what has worked in the past and promote worksite fitness, an easy option for workers. Community leaders need to reexamine whether enough resources have been devoted to the maintenance of parks, playgrounds, community centers, and physical education. Schools and universities need to reintroduce daily, quality physical activity as a key component of a comprehensive education. And the media and entertainment industries need to use their vast creative abilities to show all Americans that physical activity is healthful and fun—in other words, that it is attractive, maybe even glamorous!
>
> We Americans always find the will to change when change is needed. I believe we can team up to create a new physical activity movement in this country. In doing so, we will save precious resources, precious futures, and precious lives. The time for action—and activity—is now.

SOURCE: U.S. Department of Health and Human Services, *Physical Activity and Health: A Report of the Surgeon General* (Atlanta, GA: U.S. Department of Health and Human Services, Centers for Disease Control and Prevention, National Center for Chronic Disease Prevention and Health Promotion, 1996).

limiting the intake of saturated and trans fats, cholesterol, added sugars, sodium, and alcohol; and limiting caloric intake to meet caloric needs. The program warns that all Americans should avoid unhealthy weight gain and that those whose weight is too high may also need to lose weight.

The program recognized that promoting healthy diets and preventing overeating must consider conditions at worksites, schools, restaurants, and homes. People must develop the knowledge and skills necessary to make healthy dietary choices. They must also have access to healthy, affordable foods. Improving the dietary habits of Americans includes increasing dietary knowledge and developing healthy attitudes and skills; changing societal and cultural norms about diet and obesity; examining government food, agricultural, and food assistance policies; and reassessing economic price systems.

Healthy People 2020 also addresses the physical activity compliance of Americans based on the *Physical Activity Guidelines for Americans*.[6] More than 80 percent of Americans do not meet physical activity guidelines for aerobic exercise and muscle strengthening activities. Also, 80 percent of children and adolescents do not get enough exercise.

First Lady Michelle Obama introduces My Plate, a graphic that illustrates the five food groups in a place setting. My Plate replaced the Food Pyramid, which had been used by the U.S. Department of Agriculture for nineteen years. Mrs. Obama stated, "Parents don't have the time to measure out exactly three ounces of chicken. . . . But we do have time to take a look at our kids' plates. . . . And as long as they're eating proper portions, as long as half of their meal is fruits and vegetables alongside their lean proteins, whole grains and low-fat dairy, then we're good. It's as simple as that."

SOURCE: Chris O'Meara/AP Photo.

Objectives of Healthy People 2020 include educating people about the importance of physical activity, increasing the proportion of Americans who meet the physical activity guidelines; improving community infrastructure by increasing the availability of sidewalks, bike lanes, trails, and parks; and promoting legislation that improves access to facilities that promote physical activity. For children, public policy should promote physical activity in childcare facilities, limiting television viewing and promoting physical education in schools, including recess time in class schedules. Children should have safe neighborhoods, access to recreational facilities, instruction in physical activity and sport, and access to public transportation. Facilities should be accessible to people with disabilities.

Government and Obesity

Obesity is a serious problem that affects 20 to 35 percent of the population in the United States, Mexico, Great Britain, Australia, New Zealand, and Greece.[19] However, obesity rates are only 3 to 10 percent in Japan, Switzerland, France, Denmark, Italy, and Sweden; even though they are highly industrialized like the United States, these countries have lower obesity rates. Although the United States spends more money per person ($8,915 in 2012) on health care than any other country, we are number one in obesity, thirtieth in life expectancy, and fifth in years living in ill health. The nation also has high rates of death from heart disease and cancer. Obviously, throwing money at the problem is not the answer.

Health organizations such as CDC, the Trust for America's Health, and the Robert Wood Johnson Foundation believe that government can help fight the obesity epidemic by increasing the availability and lowering the cost of healthy foods such as fruits and vegetables, providing incentives for healthy food distribution to poor urban areas, restricting the availability of unhealthy foods such as high-sugar soft drinks, increasing physical education in schools, broadening access to physical activity in towns and cities, and improving attitudes toward healthy lifestyles. As noted earlier, every ten years, the U.S. government sets health goals for the nation (i.e., Healthy People 2020, Healthy People 2010, etc.). Overall, the nation's health improved between 2000 and 2010: fewer people smoked, blood cholesterol decreased, and life expectancy increased. However, current trends in obesity and physical activity levels suggest that health care costs will continue to escalate and public health may deteriorate. Obesity rates increased from 23 percent of the population in 1988 to 35 percent in 2010. Fifty percent of people do not meet the minimum physical activity recommendations of 150 minutes per week of moderate-intensity exercise. Ominously, physical activity levels in children and young adults decreased for both aerobic and strength exercises. Although obesity rates recently leveled off, current trends indicate that teens and young adults are getting fatter, consuming more calories, and doing less exercise.

Obesity and the Patient Protection and Affordable Care Act of 2010

In June 2013, the AMA classified obesity as a disease. Obesity and being overweight are linked to metabolic diseases such as diabetes, insulin resistance, hypertension, and dyslipidemia (abnormal blood fats). This is significant because prior to the Patient Protection and Affordable Care Act (PPACA), many people were denied medical insurance coverage because of preexisting conditions. This legislation, informally known as Obamacare, mandated that people could not be denied coverage, charged more, or denied treatment based on health status.

The PPACA provides incentives for preventing chronic disease. For example, section 4108 provides $100 million for demonstration grants to help people lose weight, exercise, and control blood pressure and cholesterol. The act requires that HHS provide guidance to the states regarding the prevention and treatment of obesity and related diseases.[20]

Public education and awareness of the dangers of obesity and the role of diet and exercise in preventing it have probably influenced the leveling off of obesity rates in the last ten years. Insuring health care coverage to obese Americans should further these efforts and help reduce the problem. Obesity, poor diet, and physical inactivity remain significant health problems.

Personal Responsibility

Government programs might promote an atmosphere for healthy lifestyles, but people must take personal responsibility for their health if they want to lose fat and improve fitness. The major causes of obesity include lack of exercise and diets high in calories and refined sugars. Principles for reducing body fat include the following:

- Limit intake of trans fats. Do this by cutting down on processed foods and eating at fast food restaurants.
- Eat more meals at home. Eating at restaurants, particularly fast food restaurants, promotes overeating. When going to restaurants, avoid "super-sizing" meals.
- Cut out high-sugar soft drinks. Switch to water instead.
- Limit alcohol consumption to two drinks a day or less. Alcohol is high in calories and contributes to abdominal obesity when consumed with high-calorie foods.
- Exercise at a moderate intensity for 150 minutes per week or vigorous intensity for 75 minutes per week. Increase daily activity by walking up stairs, parking farther from the store, and performing active outdoor chores.
- Increase fiber intake.
- Watch less television. Abdominal fat deposition is greater in people who watch too much television. Substitute something more active.
- Lift weights. Combining weight training, aerobics, and sensible diet is the best way to lose whole body fat and decrease abdominal fat.

Consistency is the key. Long-term weight control depends on a caloric deficit of only 300 calories per day. That does not sound like much, but people have a hard time sustaining it. The easiest way to achieve this is by making small changes in lifestyle. For example, go for a walk or work out on an elliptical trainer for thirty minutes as soon as you get out of bed. You will burn at least 300 kilocalories. Make this workout a vital part of your day. Eat an apple after your morning workout. Apples are high in fiber and help curb appetite. A short walk and an apple are small steps toward effective weight control. These small changes will not cause substantial weight loss, but they will promote metabolic health and enhance weight management over time.

THE CONSEQUENCES OF PUBLIC POLICY ON DIET AND OBESITY

Public policy can promote physical activity levels by providing exercise-friendly environments, which include sidewalks, bike paths, parks, and trails, and by subsidizing healthier foods. Policies such as taxing high-calorie foods might disproportionally impact the poor and have no proven track record. Government can help by changing the social atmosphere to one that promotes and values physical activity as well as a healthy diet in children and adults. Obesity and poor metabolic health are insidious problems with no easy solutions. Failing to address these issues through effective public policies will increase health care costs and impact the health of Americans.

See also **Chapter 19: Children's Health and Health Care Policy (1960s–Present); Chapter 20: Women's Issues and American Health Care Policy (1960s–Present); Chapter 21: Minorities, Immigrants, and Health Care Policy: Disparities and Solutions (1960s–Present); Chapter 22: Aging and Health Care Policy (1990s–Present); Chapter 23: Fifty Years of Progress in Disease and Injury Prevention (1950s–Present); Chapter 24: Mental Health and Social Policy (1960s–Present).**

NOTES

1. Trust for America's Health, *F as in Fat: How Obesity Threatens America's Future* (Washington, DC: Trust for America's Health, 2013).
2. Thomas D. Fahey, Paul Insel, and Walton Roth, *Fit and Well: Core Concepts and Labs in Physical Fitness and Wellness,* 11th ed. (New York: McGraw-Hill, Forthcoming).
3. Centers for Disease Control and Prevention, "Diabetes Data and Trends," http://apps.nccd.cdc.gov/DDTSTRS/default .aspx.
4. Gregory L. Austin, Lorraine G. Ogden, and James O. Hill, "Trends in Carbohydrate, Fat, and Protein Intakes and Association with Energy Intake in Normal-Weight, Overweight, and Obese Individuals: 1971–2006," *American Journal of Clinical Nutrition* 93: 4 (2011): 836–843.

5. Centers for Disease Control and Prevention, "Leisure Time Physical Activity" (Sample adult core component of the 1997–June 2008 NHI Survey), http://www.cdc.gov/nchs/data/nhis/earlyrelease/200912_07.pdf.

6. Physical Activity Guidelines Advisory Committee, *Physical Activity Guidelines Advisory Committee Report* (Washington, DC: U.S. Department of Health and Human Services, 2008).

7. Pearson Education, "Life Expectancy by Age, 1850–2011," http://www.infoplease.com/ipa/A0005140.html.

8. Thomas R. Dawber, Gilson F. Meadors, and Felix E. Moore, "Epidemiological Approaches to Heart Disease: The Framingham Study," *American Journal of Public Health and the Nations Health* 41: 3 (1951): 279–286.

9. Ancel Keys, ed., *Seven Countries: A Multivariate Analysis of Death and Coronary Heart Disease* (Cambridge, MA: Harvard University Press, 1980).

10. Centers for Disease Control and Prevention, "Achievements in Public Health, 1900–1999: Decline in Deaths from Heart Disease and Stroke—United States, 1900–1999," *Morbidity and Mortality Weekly Report* 48: 30 (1999): 649–656.

11. U.S. Senate, Select Committee on Nutrition and Human Needs, *Dietary Goals for the United States* (Washington, DC: U.S. Government Printing Office, 1977).

12. Rajiv Chowdhury et al., "Association of Dietary, Circulating, and Supplement Fatty Acids with Coronary Risk: A Systematic Review and Meta-analysis," *Annals of Internal Medicine* 160: 6 (2014): 398–406.

13. Hans Kraus and Ruth P. Hirschland, "Minimum Muscular Fitness Tests in School Children," *Research Quarterly. American Association for Health, Physical Education and Recreation* 25: 2 (1954): 178–188.

14. U.S. Department of Transportation, "History of the Interstate Highway System," http://www.fhwa.dot.gov/interstate/history.htm.

15. David Wallinga, "Agricultural Policy and Childhood Obesity: A Food Systems and Public Health Commentary," *Health Affairs* 29: 3 (2010): 405–410.

16. Alan D. Dangour et al., "Can Nutrition Be Promoted through Agriculture-Led Food Price Policies? A Systematic Review," *BMJ Open* 3 (2013): e002937.

17. Cynthia L. Ogden et al., "Prevalence of Childhood and Adult Obesity in the United States, 2011–2012," *Journal of the American Medical Association* 311: 8 (2014): 806–814.

18. U.S. Department of Health and Human Services, "Healthy People 2020," http://www.healthypeople.gov/2020.

19. NationMaster, "Obesity: Countries Compared," http://www.nationmaster.com/country-info/stats/Health/Obesity.

20. Kathleen Sebelius, *Preventive and Obesity-Related Services Available to Medicaid Enrollees* (Washington, DC: U.S. Department of Health and Human Services, 2010).

FURTHER READING

Bray, George A., and Claude Bouchard, eds. *Handbook of Obesity,* Vol. 1, 3rd ed. Boca Raton, FL: CRC Press, 2014.

Fahey, Thomas, Paul Insel, and Walton Roth. *Fit and Well: Core Concepts and Labs in Physical Fitness and Wellness,* 11th ed. New York: McGraw-Hill, Forthcoming.

Physical Activity Guidelines Advisory Committee. *Physical Activity Guidelines Advisory Committee Report, 2008.* Washington, DC: U.S. Department of Health and Human Services, 2008. http://www.health.gov/paguidelines/report/pdf/committeereport.pdf.

Trust for America's Health. *F as in Fat: How Obesity Threatens America's Future.* Washington, DC: Trust for America's Health, 2013. http://www.rwjf.org/content/dam/farm/reports/reports/2013/rwjf407528.

U.S. Department of Health and Human Services. "HealthyPeople.gov." http://www.healthypeople.gov/2020.

Interest Groups, Think Tanks, and Health Care Policy (1960s–Present)

Susan Giaimo

I N U.S. POLITICS, INTEREST GROUPS AND RESEARCH institutes have served as important sources of policy proposals for members of Congress and the executive branch. The nation's porous political system's institutional fragmentation contains numerous "veto points" at which organized interests can modify and even block legislation they dislike. Interest groups can enter the fray during the multiple points of the legislative process. They can lobby the executive branch at federal and state levels to modify the rules governing the implementation of a law. They can challenge a law in the courts.

Time and again, interest groups have blocked the enactment of health policies. Repeated failed efforts by politicians to expand health care coverage to the American people in the twentieth century is a case in point, as associations representing health care providers, insurers, employers, and even senior citizens succeeded in blocking or repealing such laws. However formidable organized interests are in the policy process, they are neither impregnable nor static. On the contrary, their policy preferences and policy influence can and do change as conditions in the economy and in the health care sector change. Coalitions in favor of or opposed to the expansion of health insurance, and national health insurance in particular, have changed in both their composition and strength. Although interest groups successfully opposed Democratic and Republican presidents' efforts to introduce universal government health insurance, in some cases they have supported the creation of public insurance programs for particular segments of the population or the expansion of private insurance under the shadow of government sponsorship.

The health care arena has become a dynamic and increasingly crowded policy field with a bewildering array of stakeholders seeking to influence policymakers. Until the 1960s, the number of interest groups in health policy was small and concentrated, and their positions were fairly constant and predictable. Since then, new interest groups have entered the arena, many of them focused on fairly narrow concerns of their members. This teeming environment reflects broader changes in the interest group landscape, with the explosion in the number of interest groups associated with social movements of the 1960s and 1970s. It also highlights the mobilization of new health care stakeholders in reaction to the growing role of the federal and state governments in health care financing and provision following the enactment of Medicare and Medicaid in 1965.

The overarching lines of conflict in U.S. health policy have been over the balance between public and private, or government and market, forces in health care financing and provision. These battle lines were drawn in the early twentieth century with the first ill-fated attempt to introduce national health insurance and have continued ever since. Interest groups have been key players in public battles over such fundamental questions. Yet they also have worked behind the scenes to shape the details of health care legislation and its implementation to serve the interests of their members.

In exploring interest group activity in U.S. health policy since the 1960s, we concentrate here on three major efforts to expand health insurance coverage during this time period: the passage of Medicare and Medicaid, the failure to enact the Clinton Health Security plan, and the enactment of the Patient Protection and Affordable Care Act (PPACA). We do not, however, attempt to portray interest group activity on the range of health policy issues that do not involve high-level officials and partisan maneuvering or to describe interest group influence on state health policies.

EARLY OPPOSITION TO NATIONAL HEALTH CARE INSURANCE

The major forces opposed to a larger government role in national health insurance were a constellation of health care providers led by the American Medical Association (AMA) and its allies in business and the insurance industry who joined forces with members of Congress to block social policy initiatives of (mostly) Democratic presidents. From the 1930s until 1964, an anti-reform coalition composed of the AMA, private insurers, and employers was able to thwart national health insurance initiatives by teaming up with a conservative coalition of southern Democrats and northern Republicans in Congress. The passage of Medicare and Medicaid in 1965 under President Lyndon B. Johnson (1963–1969) was a rare defeat for this anti-reform coalition and reflected a new partisan reality in Congress following the watershed election of 1964. Yet both programs, by deliberate design, fell far short of universal coverage and targeted subgroups of the U.S. population. While extending health insurance to seniors, the poor, and the disabled, Medicare and Medicaid made concessions to the medical profession and private insurers in order to win their participation and support.[1]

The next major attempt at national health insurance occurred in 1993–1994 under President William J. Clinton (1993–2001). His effort to wed market competition with government regulation and compulsory national insurance was met by fierce and successful resistance among key stakeholders in the insurance industry and business community whose oppositional stance found common ground in a disciplined Republican Party and Democratic defectors in Congress. The executive branch's strategy of excluding health care stakeholders from meaningful negotiations on the terms of health care reform alienated opponents and contributed to the defeat of the initiative.[2]

President Barack Obama (2009–), however, succeeded where President Clinton had failed. Unlike Clinton, Obama at the outset pursued a strategy of inclusion with major health care stakeholders, making concessions to former foes of reform and thereby neutralizing health care providers and insurers and employers who had blocked previous reform efforts. Determined Democrats in Congress held together and withstood unified Republican opposition to enact a law that greatly expanded health insurance coverage while still falling short of universal national health insurance. In following this strategy of inclusion, Obama accepted limits to the scope of reform: the PPACA preserved the premier role of private insurance

and introduced only cautious provisions to alter the health care delivery system and the payment of providers.

RESEARCH INSTITUTES AND INTEREST GROUPS IN AMERICAN HEALTH POLICY

Research institutes (commonly known as think tanks) often serve as the wellspring of policy ideas, with interest groups acting as the vessels that carry such ideas along the stream of policymaking. The separation, however, is not always so neat; often, interest groups play a greater role than simply transmitting policy ideas. Indeed, groups seek to mold such ideas into legislative proposals that stand a chance of passage by Congress and approval by the president. To succeed in this endeavor, they must often forge alliances with each other and with partisan forces in Congress and the executive branch. Often, they will undertake public campaigns to influence public opinion in order to win policy battles.

Research institutes offer policy ideas that interest groups or political parties take up and translate into legislative initiatives. Research institutes also undertake policy analysis of legislative proposals or existing programs, and their reports can influence the process and content of legislative proposals. Some think tanks are independent entities; others promote policies that toe a clear ideological line and are closely identified with particular interest groups or political parties. Research institutes are patient players in the policy fray: unlike elected politicians, who must face the timetable of frequent elections, research institutes can wait; the policy ideas they promote often suffer several legislative defeats over the course of decades before becoming law.

Many major research institutes in the health policy arena are active in the political arena. Those that seek to analyze policy and disseminate information in a more dispassionate manner and using accepted social scientific research methods are the Kaiser Family Foundation and the Commonwealth Fund. Others produce respected analyses using scholarly and social scientific research methods, but have an identifiable leaning either for or against government intervention in health care. Among the former are the Brookings Institution, the Urban Institute, and the Robert Wood Johnson Foundation, while the American Enterprise Institute is among the latter. Increasingly, research institutes that adopt a clear ideological or partisan line have become active players in health policy debates. For example, the Cato Institute and the Heritage Foundation have advocated free market ideas and disparaged what they see as "big government" in health care. The chief think tank promoting an active government role in health care is the Public Policy Research Institute.

The relationships between research institutes and policymakers may be close. For example, the Heritage Foundation has been a champion of "premium support" as a way to reform Medicare and control the costs of the program. Premium support is a fixed-premium contribution from the federal government that seniors would use to purchase coverage from competing private insurers or from the traditional government Medicare plan. It is a controversial proposal, not least because it would transform Medicare from a defined benefit to defined contribution plan and would require seniors who chose a plan that was more expensive than the government's premium support to shoulder the additional cost. Although not the originator of premium support, the Heritage Foundation has promoted the idea in its publications and also has written favorably on Representative Paul Ryan's (R-WI; in office 1999–) versions of it in his budget proposals. The foundation also provided economic analysis of Ryan's budget proposals at his request.[3]

Interest Groups

Interest groups represent in the policy process those who share a common concern. They do not run candidates for political office themselves, but they may support particular candidates and parties. Interest groups transmit the demands of civil society to government policymakers. The theory of pluralism holds that interest groups compete with one another in an effort to influence policymakers, and the government is a neutral arbiter or referee among them. The policies enacted reflect the free play of ideas. In reality, however, some groups are more powerful than others. They may be better organized and have more money with which to fund their political activities than their rivals. Groups that represent the business interests tend to be more powerful in terms of money spent on political campaigns and lobbying than those representing labor unions, the environment, or consumers.

Interest groups seek to influence policymakers through a number of ways. Chief among them is money to finance election campaigns. Political action committees (PACs) are the entities created by interest groups to channel campaign contributions to candidates whom they believe will be sympathetic to their policy concerns. While larger interest groups had created their own PACs in the 1940s, these organizations became more prominent in the 1970s. In the wake of the Watergate scandal, Congress enacted reforms in the 1970s designed to weaken the say of party leaders in selecting candidates at national party conventions and to set out rules for channeling campaign contributions to PACs. Perversely, these laws displaced party bosses only to make interest groups the chief players in candidate selection and election campaign finance. By 2009, 4,618 PACs were registered with the Federal Election Commission (FEC), the government agency that oversees them.[4]

Money and Interest Groups

Beginning with the presidential election of 2000, the influence of money in politics became more pronounced through the rise of soft money and issue advocacy groups, known by their Internal Revenue Service designations, 527s and 501(c)(4)s. Unlike PACs, which must abide by FEC rules limiting the amount of contributions and specifying strict reporting requirements, 527s and 501(c)(4)s are largely unregulated and have become an avenue for interest groups to give unlimited amounts of money to election campaigns and issue advocacy efforts. Donors to such financing vehicles do not face any limits to their contribution amounts. Furthermore, the Supreme Court's ruling in *Citizens United v. Federal Election Commission* (2010) declared corporations to be persons possessing the right of free speech under the First Amendment, essentially freeing them from prior campaign and issue advocacy contribution restrictions.[5]

Interest groups also influence policymaking through lobbying members of Congress and the executive branch. Lobbyists meet with policymakers and seek to persuade them to adopt their group's position on a bill. Lobbyists provide key information to policymakers and may even help craft legislation or administrative rules. Groups may also mobilize their grassroots members to contact members of Congress or the president at critical moments in the legislative process. Finally, interest groups will also mount public campaigns and political advertising to try to shape public opinion and the position of policymakers. Lobbying activities are less subject to government regulation than campaign financing. Groups must report their lobbying expenditures to the federal government but, unlike contributions to PACs and election campaigns, face no limits on such spending.[6]

Hyperpluralism

The interest group landscape has become much more crowded since the late 1960s, so hyperpluralism is an apt description. Starting in the 1960s, the cozy world of a relatively small number of interest groups representing the economic interests of business and labor in closed-door meetings with congressional committee leaders and the cabinet was transformed by an explosion of new groups promoting particular causes, such as civil rights, feminism, peace, and environmentalism. In 2011, there were 12,220 registered lobbyists in the nation's capital.[7]

Not only do policymakers confront a far greater number of interest groups, but these associations are also narrower in scope than their economic predecessors.[8] Such hyperpluralism makes it difficult for interest groups and their contacts in Congress or the executive branch to forge durable alliances on policy initiatives, particularly those proposing sweeping health care reforms. Indeed, several different associations represent the business community and are often at odds with each other on health policy reform. Interest group power in this environment is better described as negative power: groups are too numerous and fragmented to take positive action, but they can block a policy initiative.[9] Their ability to veto a policy initiative is made easier by the porousness of the U.S. political system, in which separation of powers and federalism offer numerous points of entry to organized interests. Numerous points in the legislative process give groups access to block a policy initiative, from the subcommittee and committee stages to floor votes in the House of Representatives and the Senate, to watering down a law by lobbying executive agencies or state governments at the rule-making and implementation stages, and finally, mounting lawsuits through the courts.

The growth in the number of interest groups since the 1960s not only reflects the activities of social movements and citizen groups but also is the product of government health policies. President Johnson's domestic policy initiatives of the Great Society aimed to eliminate poverty in the nation. The Great Society, which constituted the biggest expansion of the federal government in social policy since the New Deal of the 1930s, created two important government health insurance programs, Medicare for senior citizens and Medicaid for the poor and disabled. These programs, like others associated with the Great Society, created new stakeholders and interest groups with a direct interest in the implementation of these programs.

Interest Groups and Their Allies

Interest group power also depends on alliances forged among different organized stakeholders (that is, with other groups) as well as the partisan allies in Congress and the executive branch. Democrats and Republicans are more sympathetic to some groups than others. While the rules are not hard and fast, Democrats are more inclined to listen to groups promoting organized labor, women, minorities, and patient advocates, while Republicans tend to identify with business interests more generally and with providers and insurers in the health care arena.

However, the power and influence of interest groups change over time. Seemingly impregnable alliances may unravel and new coalitions may take their place. Such alterations in interest group politics may occur for a number of reasons. New groups may enter the health policy arena to challenge existing coalitions. Coalitions may change in response to new challenges in the broader economy or within the health care system itself. In the face of such an altered environment, groups may redefine their interests, their policy preferences, and their partnerships. Changes in the partisan composition in Congress and the executive branch and in the ideological outlook in the Democratic and Republican parties themselves may provide organized interests and policymakers with opportunities to forge novel alliances around policy initiatives. All of these factors must be kept in mind when seeking to understand the form of a policy initiative and its fate in the policymaking process.

Major Interest Groups in Health Policy

The health policy universe has greatly expanded since President Johnson's enactment of Medicare and Medicaid in 1965. The major groups are those representing health care providers, insurers, employers, unions, and patients. In the battle over Medicare, the major interests were the AMA, representing doctors; the American Hospital Association (AHA); the American Federation of Labor and the Congress of Industrial Organizations (AFL-CIO), the peak association representing trade unions; and a handful of groups representing the business community and insurers.[10] The AMA spent $1.2 million (or $10 million in 2010 dollars) in 1965.[11] In 1993, when President Clinton attempted national health insurance, health care stakeholders numbered more than eleven hundred interest groups.[12] The power of the AMA and AFL-CIO was greatly diminished, and they were two voices among many, including employers, consumers, insurers, and providers. Employers were represented by a number of competing associations, including the Business Roundtable, the Chamber of Commerce, and the National Federation of Independent Business. Likewise, the insurance industry was represented by two different groups: the American Association of Health Plans (AAHP), representing large managed care plans, and the Health Insurance Association of America (HIAA), whose members included smaller insurers.

In 2009, when President Obama embarked on his health care reform effort, he encountered many of the same interest groups as well as those representing the pharmaceutical industry (Pharmaceutical Research and Manufacturers of America) and medical device manufactures, and new citizens' groups and political movements that coordinated the efforts of interest groups into broad pro- and anti-reform coalitions. Among the latter were Organizing for America and MoveOn in support of health care reform and the Tea Party groups in opposition to it. Groups on both sides of the divide spent $3.3 billion in lobbying in 2009.[13] The health care reform effort also led to the founding of new groups, such as the National Association of State Health Cooperatives.

THE PASSAGE OF MEDICARE AND MEDICAID IN 1965

In 1960, the health care system in the United States was largely a private affair. Voluntary employer-provided private insurance covered the majority of working-age Americans and their dependents. This state of affairs was the product of previous failures to enact universal national health insurance.[14] Yet for those outside the labor force, insurance was hard to come by. Private insurers shunned the aged, poor, and disabled as unprofitable risks. Because these groups were outside the labor market, they were not covered by the system of voluntary occupationally based insurance. It was precisely these categories of the "deserving" and "truly needy" who were deemed eligible for government intervention.

A diverse reform coalition brought together actors with different but reconcilable interests. Health care reformers in the Democratic Party viewed the provision of health insurance to senior citizens as a policy that could muster public support and expand their voting base among the elderly, while also appeasing interest groups that had opposed national health insurance initiatives in the past, such as commercial insurers and employers. The proposal also found favor with traditional Democratic allies such as organized labor, which wanted to shift responsibility for retiree health insurance from collective bargaining agreements to the government. President Johnson pursued a strategy of co-optation to neutralize potential opponents in the health care community.

The initial reform proposal was a contributory social insurance program modeled on Social Security pensions and financed from payroll taxes. Medicare would be a universal compulsory social insurance program for all seniors once they reached sixty-five years of age. As with Social Security, all seniors would be automatically enrolled in the program. The insurance would be a single-payer government program covering hospital care, which was far and away the most expensive portion of medical care at that time. The proposal carried a high degree of legitimacy and public support; after all, no one expected senior citizens to remain in the workforce. It was also difficult to justify medical bankruptcy or forgoing necessary health care due to old age.

The interest group universe in the battle over Medicare and Medicaid was sparsely populated by contemporary standards. The groups in favor of Medicare were peak associations representing organized labor, retirees, and those health care providers who provided care for seniors, such as the AFL-CIO, the American Association of Retired Workers, the American Geriatrics Society, and the National Coalition of Senior Citizens (itself a creation of the AFL-CIO). Except for the AFL-CIO, most of these groups lacked political muscle. This pro-reform coalition faced a much more powerful alliance of health care providers, insurers, and employers. These consisted of the American Medical Association, the American Hospital Association, the National Association of Blue Shield Plans (the health insurance for doctors' services run by state branches of the AMA), the Life Insurance Association of America, the National Association of Manufacturers, the Chamber of Commerce, the American Farm Bureau Federation (the mainstream group representing farmers in the political arena), and the American Legion.[15]

Interest Groups Gain Concessions

Given the forces arrayed against Medicare and Medicaid, how did these programs ever get enacted into law? The answer lies in a combination of factors. The new partisan political terrain in Washington following the 1964 election set the stage for enactment of the Great Society programs, the biggest expansion of the welfare state since the New Deal of the 1930s. In addition, President Johnson and congressional leaders forged a bipartisan agreement on a compromise proposal that created the new social insurance programs of Medicare and Medicaid but fell far short of national health insurance, which served to mute potential opposition to reform.[16]

The first factor was the emergence of a new interest group alliance supporting government health insurance for senior citizens and the poor. The new coalition drove a wedge between stakeholders that had long opposed national health insurance while bringing together groups that were normally at odds with each other: the AFL-CIO representing organized labor and the HIAA representing commercial insurers, and the nonprofit, provider-run Blue Cross-Blue Shield plans. The AFL-CIO supported social insurance for seniors because it would relieve it of the task of negotiating retiree health benefits, which ate into the benefits of current workers. Removing retirees from collective bargaining would allow unions to focus their efforts on winning higher wages and fringe benefits for current workers. Insurance companies were predisposed to government insurance for seniors because this demographic tended to have higher medical costs and was therefore not profitable to insure. Besides, most seniors could not afford to purchase individual health plans because of the practice of experience rating, whereby insurers set premiums to a person's medical condition. A government program for all seniors would allow commercial and nonprofit insurers to focus on working-age adults and their families who were profitable. Like they did with the elderly, commercial insurers also shunned the poor and disabled because of their unprofitability. Moreover, these groups were long considered the responsibility of state and local government welfare programs.

Concessions Concerning Medicare and Medicaid

The AMA, however, vociferously opposed Medicare and Medicaid and resorted to the same argument of "socialized medicine" that it had used so effectively to defeat national health insurance efforts in earlier decades. Yet this time, it could not count on the insurance industry as an ally. Thus isolated, the AMA lacked the muscle to halt the enactment of Medicare and Medicaid.

Even so, doctors, along with hospitals and insurers, won significant concessions in the final bill that secured their place in the new programs. Policymakers did so in a preemptive fashion; they wanted to be sure that doctors and hospitals would participate in the new public insurance programs, so they sweetened them to buy off the support of powerful health care stakeholders. Hence, providers in

Medicare and Medicaid would receive fee-for-service reimbursement. Of course, this form or reimbursement is inherently inflationary, because it encourages volume and expensive high-tech procedures, allowing providers to bill for each item of service and rewarding high-tech procedures. Hospitals won an additional concession of "cost plus 2 percent," which allowed them to bill an additional 2 percent on their fee-for-service itemizations. Not only did the AMA preserve fee-for-service, but doctors also evaded anything approaching nationally set prices. Instead, they would be reimbursed the "usual, customary, and reasonable" rates prevailing in their locality. Insurers also did quite well under Medicare and Medicaid. Responsibility for claims processing and provider reimbursement of these public insurance programs fell not to a government agency but instead to commercial and nonprofit insurers such as Blue Cross and Blue Shield.

The new political environment was the second factor that set the stage for the enactment of Medicare and Medicaid. The assassination of President John F. Kennedy (1961–1963) in November 1963 was a traumatic event for the country and directly and forcefully contributed to the outcome of the momentous 1964 presidential and congressional elections. Along with the election of Lyndon B. Johnson as president, Democrats swept both houses of Congress, securing majorities of sixty-eight seats in the Senate and 295 seats in the House of Representatives. The biggest change was the entry of liberal-minded Democrats from the urban north and the concomitant fading of the power of conservative southern Democrats in Congress who had stymied social reform by Democratic presidents since the 1930s and 1940s. President Johnson secured an electoral mandate and the congressional votes to enact his antipoverty programs.

This new political terrain fed directly into the bipartisan deal on Medicare and Medicaid. The Democratic chairman of the House Ways and Means Committee, Wilbur Mills (D-AR; in office 1939–1977), created a bill that combined three different reform approaches to forge an agreement between Democrats and Republicans in Congress. The "three-layer cake" proposal drew together an AFL-CIO proposal for hospital insurance, an AMA proposal for optional insurance to cover physician services, and the existing Kerr-Mills program enacted in 1960, which provided limited federal grants to states to care for their impoverished elderly. This three-layer cake became Medicare Part A, mandatory insurance for seniors to cover hospital and limited skilled nursing care expenses; Medicare Part B, optional insurance to cover physician services; and Medicaid, the joint federal-state insurance program covering the disabled and defined categories of the poor.[17]

Medicare and Medicaid represented a complex compromise that deliberately addressed the concerns of an array of stakeholders. President Johnson enhanced the chances of passage of these programs by pursuing a strategy of inclusion and co-optation of powerful potential opponents. Thus, Medicare Part A addressed concerns of the AFL-CIO and other groups representing the elderly who wanted hospital insurance for seniors. Part B's concessions to the AMA and private insurers muted their opposition. Medicaid brought needed federal assistance to state and local governments for the case of the poor and disabled. The bipartisan nature of the deal allowed both parties to claim credit for legislation that had broad public support.

Medicare and Medicaid constituted a mixed legacy in the history of social policy in the United States. The creation of new government insurance programs for the most vulnerable groups of the population was the biggest single expansion of the welfare state since the New Deal. Yet Medicare and Medicaid did not represent the stepping stone to imminent national health insurance as supporters of Medicare Part A had envisioned. Instead, grafting separate government insurance programs for seniors, the poor, and the disabled onto the system of voluntary employment-based insurance for able-bodied working-age Americans only served to dampen calls for comprehensive national health insurance in the United States for the time being.[18] Subsequent Republican and Democratic administrations considered national health insurance proposals, but these went nowhere. The next major push for national health insurance would come in the late 1980s and early 1990s, with interest groups far more splintered and seemingly incapable of forging a coalition for positive politics action.

HYPERPLURALISM AND THE DEATH OF HEALTH SECURITY IN 1994

The 1980s saw skyrocketing health care costs, which translated into a 90 percent hike in premiums for employment-based insurance between 1987 and 1993.[19] U.S. employers came to view this trend as an unsustainable assault on their profitability and survival. In the brave new world of globalization, manufacturing giants like General Motors faced stiffer competition from overseas competitors enjoying the advantage of much lower labor costs. Even on their home turf, firms offering health insurance had to shoulder higher labor costs, which put them at a competitive disadvantage to rivals who did not. In 1989 Chrysler took the unheard-of step of publicly calling on the government to enact national health insurance.[20] If all firms were forced to offer insurance to their workforce, it would level the competitive playing field. This new reality, in turn, drove a wedge in the coalition that had long opposed national health insurance, as employers began to resent the profits of health care providers and insurers at their expense. However, the hyperpluralistic interest group universe in U.S. politics made it difficult to assemble a successful coalition able to support a national health insurance plan. Instead, interest groups proved themselves far better at blocking reform rather than fostering or sustaining it.

President Clinton and Health Security

Yet the chances for the passage of national health insurance were encouraging at the start of Democrat Bill Clinton's presidency in 1993. Clinton had made health care reform, along with economic issues, a centerpiece of his presidential campaign, and for good reason. In 1991, Harris Wofford scored an upset victory in a special election for a Senate seat in Pennsylvania by running on a platform promising to enact universal health insurance. More Americans were losing health insurance as they lost their jobs in the recession or as their employers, facing unacceptable premium hikes, dropped coverage. Opinion polls showed that Americans were deeply worried about losing their workplace health insurance, with majorities agreeing that the health care system needed to be "totally rebuilt" and in favor of the federal government guaranteeing universal coverage.[21]

Clinton believed that national health insurance, based in the familiar setting of employment and provided by private insurers, would inoculate himself and his party against charges of socialized medicine and would appeal not only to the uninsured, but also to the middle class facing economic insecurity in the recession and to the business community complaining about rising costs. Representing the "New Democrat" wing of his party, Clinton sought to jettison the party's tax-and-spend, big-government image that had cost it the support of the middle and working classes that had defected to President Ronald Reagan (1981–1989). The New Democrat wing championed public-private initiatives and market solutions to public policy problems, in contrast to some of their older colleagues who had been active in the New Deal and Great Society battles. New Democrats also reckoned that their strategy would help forge a new electoral coalition among the middle class, the working class, and the poor and would overcome traditional wedge issues, such as social welfare, which divided voters on race and class lines.[22] This calculus was plausible, because Clinton enjoyed Democratic majorities in both houses of Congress, even though he was elected president on a plurality of 43 percent of the popular vote.[23]

Content of Health Security

Clinton's national health insurance plan, which he dubbed Health Security, reflected this effort to span this wide electoral and interest group divide. It would build on existing employment-based private insurance but would achieve universal coverage by mandating all employers to offer coverage to their workforce. Insurance would be financed primarily by payroll taxes but also excise taxes. Small businesses would receive federal tax credits to make such coverage affordable. Medicare and Medicaid would have survived as separate entities but would have been subjected to cuts in their budgets.

The Clinton plan contained several innovations intended to realize the twin goals of universal access and cost containment in health care. Foremost among these was managed competition, which involved government regulation of the insurance market to ensure universal access to care and competition and choice among health plans to encourage cost containment. The idea for managed competition came from Stanford health economist Alain Enthoven, who first proposed such a scheme in 1980 and refined it in subsequent journal articles.[24] Managed competition under Health Security would require all employers to offer their workers at least three plans that would differ in terms of cost-sharing, premiums, and choice of providers. The reformers expected that employees would choose the lower cost plans, thus bringing down health care costs. At the same time, managed competition set new restrictions on insurers to bar them from competing by cream-skimming. Instead of enrolling healthy people and excluding the sick from coverage through coverage denials and preexisting conditions exclusions, insurers would now be required to offer a comprehensive basic benefits package to all applicants, charge community-rated premiums that would effectively spread health risks by levying the same rate for all in a region rather than differentiating by a person's medical condition, and have plans with healthier members make risk-adjusted payments to plans with sicker members. Further, insurers would not be able to deny coverage to enrolled members when they became sick by means of invoking preexisting condition exclusions. Responsibility for administration of the health care system would be split between the federal and state governments. State governments would create and administer the individual and small-group insurance markets (or delegate this job to a nonprofit entity). Employers with at least five thousand employees could opt out of the state exchanges and instead assume their own financial risk for insuring their members, which many already did as self-insured plans. At the national level, Congress would set and update the basic benefits package. Finally, a National Insurance Board with members appointed by the president would have the authority to regulate alliances and health plans, and even to limit premium increases to the rate of inflation in the event that competition failed to deliver health care cost containment.

Clinton publicly launched his health care reform plan in a speech to Congress and the American people on September 22, 1993. Opinion polls shortly following the speech showed that most Americans were supportive of Health Security. Yet hopes for passage of Health Security were dashed in the ensuing year. The president's proposal never made it to a floor vote in Congress even though the

Democratic Party enjoyed majorities in both the House and Senate. By August 1994, health care reform was dead. In the congressional midterm elections, the Democrats lost control of both houses of Congress to the Republicans, a political event not seen since 1952.

Shutting Out Stakeholders

This spectacular turn of events was owed to the mobilization of an anti-reform coalition led chiefly by health insurers and employers allied with congressional Republicans. The strategy that President Clinton chose to undertake health care reform had to bear much of the blame for this outcome. It was as though he and his advisers had ignored the realities of U.S. politics, especially separation of powers, party indiscipline, and the extreme pluralism of the interest group universe. The president created a special task force in early 1993 to draw up health care reform, but the way he did so alienated potential allies. Clinton appointed his spouse, Hillary Rodham Clinton, and his close friend and political adviser Ira Magaziner to head the task force. Though Hillary Clinton possessed ample expertise and knowledge in health policy, neither she nor Magaziner were cabinet members subject to Senate confirmation. As a result, they lacked legitimacy that such a confirmation process might have provided. Far worse was that the task force and its affiliated committees of experts worked behind closed doors and shut out Democratic members of Congress with years of experience in health policy. Feeling snubbed by the president, Democratic and Republican members of Congress produced their own competing versions of health care reform so that as many as seven bills were being considered by Congress in 1994. The task force was equally insensitive to the need to win over important health care stakeholders, such as associations representing employers and insurers. While formally consulted in task force hearings, they were not official members of the task force and therefore were denied the opportunity to take part in real negotiations and the resultant give-and-take that would have accompanied such a process. With the growing opposition to Health Security, the Clinton administration also made matters worse by embarking on a public campaign to demonize the insurance industry, which only further riled up the opposition. In short, the exclusionary strategy the Clintons adopted proved to be a recipe for disaster. Notably, it was the polar opposite of President Johnson's strategy of co-optation of key interest groups and congressional leaders that culminated in the successful enactment of Medicare and Medicaid.

Interest Groups and Health Security

The interest group universe in 1994 was very different from 1965. It was a much more crowded field, with more than eleven hundred groups with a stake in the outcome of health care reform.[25] The sheer number of groups made it difficult to build a broad coalition in favor of health care reform. Nor were there a few peak associations that could speak authoritatively for their sector. Interest groups were far better at exerting negative power to block policy than to take positive action to enact it.[26]

Nowhere was this more apparent than with the business community, which lacked an overarching peak association to speak authoritatively on its behalf. Instead, businesses had several different organizations representing them, and they were badly divided on health care reform. The Business Roundtable and the U.S. Chamber of Commerce initially supported national health insurance but backed off in the face of revolts from their membership. The Chamber of Commerce also had to stanch the hemorrhaging of members who were defecting to the National Federation of Independent Business (NFIB), a rival association that was vocal in its opposition to the employer mandate.[27] Business associations thus proved far more adept at representing the interests of their own firm or sector, exerting negative power to block legislation they did not like.[28]

This disarray among large firms and other potential allies of Health Security left the field open to groups firmly set against reform and far better able to mobilize their grassroots members. The two most effective foes to enter the fray were the NFIB and the HIAA, which mobilized their base among smaller insurers who feared for their survival in the world of managed care, and they ran a highly effective series of television ads targeted to sway members of Congress in key districts. In contrast, the forces favoring national health insurance expressed at best lukewarm support for Health Security. Groups such as AARP and organized labor proved no match for the opponents in getting their members involved. Also notable was the phenomenon of "reverse lobbying" by Republican congressional leaders who pressured business associations such as the Chamber of Commerce to take a neutral stance on health care reform or else risk the loss of congressional action on other legislation that business held dear.[29] The AMA, however, was striking in its lack of influence over the reform debate. Like other interest groups, the president's task force had shut it out of negotiations on Health Security. Moreover, with the loss of members and the growth of rival physician organizations in the years since the passage of Medicare and Medicaid, the association could no longer plausibly claim to be the exclusive voice of the medical profession. Instead, the AMA was just another interest group in the battle over health care reform.[30]

Finally, Health Security contained some key elements that proved to be difficult to sell to the American public. Chief among these were the health alliances.

Although the president insisted that they were not government entities, the nonpartisan Congressional Budget Office thought otherwise and figured them into its cost estimates for Health Security. Congressional Republicans, meanwhile, seized on the complexity of Health Security and the unfamiliarity of many of its provisions, especially health maintenance organizations (HMOs), and won the battle for public opinion by portraying the legislation as a government leviathan that would stifle patients' choice of doctor and kill off small businesses. With Health Security's allies sitting on the sidelines and belatedly launching an anemic counteroffensive, the field was left to health care stakeholders and Republicans who waged a spectacular campaign of opposition through an onslaught of lobbying and political ads. Opinion polls reflected the effectiveness of this campaign: while 59 percent of poll respondents had expressed support for Health Security right after Clinton's September 1993 speech, that dropped to 46 percent by February 1994 and never recovered, hovering between 42 and 44 percent by summer 1994.[31]

AARP (formerly the American Association of Retired Persons) calls for citizens age fifty and older to make their views known about Medicare and Social Security. With more than thirty-seven million members, AARP is usually a powerful and outspoken lobbying group on issues of concern to older Americans.

SOURCE: Mario Tama/Getty Images.

Employers and Health Care Cost-Cutting Strategies

Following the government immobility on health care reform, employers followed a go-it-alone strategy to control their own health care outlays. In essence, they used competitive forces and managed care but with none of the rules to safeguard the sick that Health Security would have provided. Instead, employers herded their workers into managed care plans that controlled costs by means of preauthorizing (often denying) expensive high-tech procedures and referrals to specialists, putting physicians at financial risk for the health of their patients via capitated payments. Some of the goals and practices of managed care were laudatory, such as coordinating care through primary care doctors and moving away from the perverse more-is-better incentives of fee-for-service reimbursement. Other practices, however, were less benign and even harmful to patient care. These included financial bonuses to physician reviewers who met a targeted level of treatment denials, paying bonuses to groups of doctors for staying within a preset financial target, and basing medical treatment denials on the absence of agreed-upon clinical practice guidelines based in scientific research. Whereas fee-for-service reimbursement had encouraged physicians to perform

more procedures and more expensive ones, the managed care revolution contained equally perverse incentives but in the opposite direction, tempting insurers and providers to reduce access to care even if it was medically necessary. In the absence of good information on clinical effectiveness and of a legal framework to prohibit insurers from engaging in such practices or mandating coverage to all patients, competition became a sledgehammer to pulverize the weakest market players, especially small firms and sicker patients. At the same time, the utilization review processes adopted by insurers spawned a gargantuan private sector bureaucracy of medical reviewers and claims processors.

Managed care without adequate regulation allowed insurers and employers to trim health care costs for a few years in the mid-1990s, but at the expense of inciting a backlash. Managed care horror stories abounded.[32] Facing rising employee dissatisfaction with their health insurance, employers retreated and offered them health plans with more choices and less management of patients' treatments. With this accommodation, however, the upward trend in health insurance premiums resumed. Between 1999 and 2011, premiums for employer-based health insurance more than doubled. Coverage of an individual employee rose from $2,196 to $5,791 in those years, while premiums for family coverage jumped from $5,429 to $15,073.[33] Firms responded by shifting the rising cost of health insurance onto their employees by means of passing on the premium hikes. In addition, high-deductible health plans became more common, especially among smaller firms, as did

The Fight against Health Security

The battle over President William J. Clinton's Health Security proposal dramatically illustrated the negative influence of interest groups in the policy process. Along with more traditional techniques of lobbying legislators and mobilizing grassroots members, the episode also witnessed the deployment of novel lobbying techniques, such as politicians reversing the usual direction of influence and leaning heavily on interest groups for their particular stances on health care reform.

The myriad interest groups representing health care stakeholders also made the forging of a unified coalition in favor of reform extremely challenging. Groups representing a specific interest or sector often were at odds with one another. Nowhere was this more apparent than with employers, who lacked a single peak association to speak on their behalf or to coordinate their political strategies. Associations such as the Business Roundtable, which represented large corporations, tended to be supportive of Health Security. However, the small business association, the National Federation of Independent Business (NFIB), was virulently opposed to the Clinton plan and, in particular, its employer mandate. The Chamber of Commerce found itself in the crossfire. The association had endorsed universal coverage and some form of employer mandate to finance it. Yet it took flak for its stance from its own base, which in turn had been goaded to action by congressional Republicans. The Chamber of Commerce also saw defections to its rival, the NFIB. In the face of these pressures, the Chamber reversed its position and officially abandoned its support for universal coverage and an employer mandate.

Insurers were also badly split on health care reform. Larger commercial insurers, which already had HMO plans, anticipated the influx of millions of new customers under the Clinton plan. Small insurers viewed managed competition with trepidation, believing they might not survive. The Health Insurance Association of America (HIAA) was the trade group representing large and small insurers. Its internal divisions prompted larger insurers to exit the HIAA and form its own organization to lobby in favor of Health Security. The HIAA took up the cause of small insurers and launched a series of television ads deriding Health Security. The ads featured a fictional middle-class, middle-aged couple, Harry and Louise, poring over Health Security and opining that the Clinton plan would amount to government intrusion into the patient-doctor relationship, with the government making choices about one's personal health care. The ads were very effective in tapping into Americans' vague but deep-seated fears of big government. Moreover, the HIAA targeted the ads to run in key congressional districts in order to have maximum impact on the most vulnerable legislators.

The once-powerful American Medical Association (AMA) was just another interest group in this crowded health policy field. For one thing, it no longer had the majority of doctors as members and had to contend with rival medical associations. This reality undermined its claim as the sole and legitimate voice of the medical profession. In addition, the coalition of doctors, insurers, and employers that had led successful charges against national health insurance in previous decades by now had splintered, with cost-conscious employers challenging insurers and providers, and insurers, in turn, questioning doctors' unlimited professional freedom in treatment and income decisions. The AMA itself was deeply divided over health care reform and sent a mixed message publicly supporting some aspects of the Clinton plan (such as universal coverage) while stopping short of endorsing it outright. Many members feared the reforms would limit their incomes and clinical freedom. Coming under heavy fire from the NFIB and congressional Republicans, the AMA eventually backtracked on its timid support of health care reform.[34]

The overall effect of this tidal surge of interest groups arrayed against Health Security was telling: erstwhile allies turned into opponents of reform or just retreated to the sidelines. Public support for the Clinton plan tumbled. Congress, in turn, decided to take a pass and let the various reform proposals die in committee. Interest groups may not have been solely responsible for the death of health care reform, but they certainly were "accessories to the crime."

SOURCES: Susan Giaimo, *Markets and Medicine: The Politics of Health Care Reform in Britain, Germany, and the United States* (Ann Arbor: University of Michigan Press, 2002), 168–176; Cathi Jo Martin, *Stuck in Neutral: Business and the Politics of Human Capital Investment Policy* (Princeton, NJ: Princeton University Press, 2000), ch. 6; Theda Skocpol, *Boomerang: Clinton's Health Security Effort and the Turn against Government in U.S. Politics* (New York: W.W. Norton, 1996).

health plans with substantial coinsurance and copayments provisions that were shouldered by employees as out-of-pocket expenses. According to Milliman, the total cost of health insurance for a typical family of four, which included not only premium hikes but also the cost-sharing arrangements just described, jumped from $9,235 in 2002 to $19,393 in 2011.[35]

Nor did managed care or an expanding economy in the 1990s do much to stanch the rising tide of uninsured, which stood at 40.6 million, or 15.4 percent of the nonelderly population, in 1995 to 47 million, or 17 percent, in 2007, the year before the onset of the Great Recession.[36]

BRINGING STAKEHOLDERS BACK IN: THE PATIENT PROTECTION AND AFFORDABLE CARE ACT OF 2010

The Great Recession that hit in 2008 ushered in an era of economic insecurity not seen in the United States since the Great Depression of the 1930s. The root cause lay in the reckless lending and trading practices of investment banks in the real estate market. When the housing bubble burst, it brought the rest of the economy to the brink. Unemployment, which had stood at only 4.4 percent in 2007, rose quickly to peak at 10 percent in October 2009.[37] To avert a complete breakdown of the international financial system and a major economic depression, national governments in the United States and Europe had to intervene with massive taxpayer bailouts of the banks. In the United States, government bailouts also extended to the car industry, which faced steeply falling demand and the near bankruptcy of General Motors and Chrysler. Such government intervention in the economy had not been seen since the Great Depression and World War II (1939–1945).

Naturally, the turbulent economy had major repercussions in health care, because most working-age Americans and their dependents received health insurance from their workplace. Mass unemployment drove up the numbers of uninsured. Each 1 percent increase in unemployment translated into one million Americans losing their health insurance coverage. The U.S. Census Bureau estimated that 49.2 million people, or nearly 20 percent of Americans under age sixty-five, were uninsured at the peak of the recession in 2009.[38] Yet government programs like Medicaid and the Children's Health Insurance Program for the poor and near-poor were unable to cover all of these uninsured people.[39] The state and federal governments fund these programs jointly, but the states were facing huge budget gaps owing to the recession-induced fall in tax revenues plus greater demand for such health care programs and unemployment benefits. Furthermore, state governments did not have much maneuvering room; unlike the federal government, nearly all state constitutions require their governments to balance their budgets annually. This foreclosed the option of deficit spending. Other than in states such as California, most governors did not want to raise taxes to pay for additional state outlays. Lastly, the Medicaid and Children's Health Insurance Program coverage rules excluded certain people by design: they covered poor families with children but left out low-income childless adults. The health care safety net was stretched so tightly that it was fraying in many places.

Barack Obama and Health Care Reform

The political terrain had also shifted, with Democrats recapturing the White House after eight years of Republican rule. Democratic President Barack Obama soundly beat his Republican rival Senator John McCain in the November 2008 election, and Democrats also secured comfortable majorities in both houses of Congress. Obama had placed health care reform at the front and center of his campaign, and the election results indicated that he had a mandate for action. Even so, the economic crisis at first glance seemed an inauspicious environment in which to undertake any major health care reform. Paradoxically, however, the desperate economy provided an opening for a health care overhaul. The federal government had already intervened in the economy with its bailout of the banks and the car industry.

If the banks, which were responsible for the mess, could receive billions of dollars of government aid, should not the millions of ordinary Americans experiencing unemployment and loss of their health insurance obtain a helping hand from the government? With this argument, Obama and his advisers turned vice into virtue and transformed the economic crisis into a window of opportunity to move forward the plan for health care for all.

What sort of health care reform would Obama and the Democrats enact? How would it expand access to the growing millions of uninsured? Also, how could it avert potential opposition from key health care interest groups who had wrecked past efforts at reform? The left wing of the Democratic Party and labor union allies wanted a single-payer tax-financed government insurance plan, or "Medicare for all," along the lines of Canada's plan, but the fiscally conservative "Blue Dog" wing of the party could not countenance such an expansion of government outlays. Others seeking a third way between these two wings proposed a government health plan to compete alongside private employment-based insurance. This "public option," or "Medicare for some," would have stopped well short of a universal government plan and accordingly would have put less strain on the federal budget. Yet like the Medicare program, it would have enjoyed the economies of scale and the market power to negotiate lower reimbursement rates with providers and hopefully would force private insurers to do the same in order to stay competitive.[40] The public option naturally offended insurers, who foresaw smaller profits as a result, as well as providers like the AMA and AHA, who feared lower reimbursements. Liberal Democrats hoped that the public option would be the first step toward a single-payer insurance plan for all Americans, while conservatives feared the same fate. In the end, the plan did not have enough votes to pass the Senate, and President Obama declared his willingness to jettison the proposal in order to ensure passage of health care reform in that chamber.

The Need for Compromise

The compromise solution that Democrats finally agreed on retained employment-based private insurance for most Americans (since they already had it) while making it more affordable to them via income-based tax credits. In addition, Medicaid would be expanded to cover all individuals, even adults without children, but with incomes at or below 138 percent of the federal poverty limit. An online marketplace, or exchange, for health insurance for individuals and small businesses would operate in each state. The exchanges would put into practice the theory of managed competition: insurers in the exchanges would compete on price of premium and associated cost-sharing, but not on health risks. A transparent easy-to-compare format, much like the site Travelocity for airfares, would make it easy for consumers to shop for the plan that fit their needs. All insurers, whether inside or outside the exchanges, would no longer be able to exclude the sick from coverage through preexisting conditions clauses or experience-rated premiums. Instead, they would have to accept all applicants, would not be able to drop coverage based on health status, and would have to charge community-rated premiums that would vary only by sex, family size, region, and whether a person smoked. In addition, insurers in the exchanges that had a disproportionate share of sicker members would receive risk-adjusted payments from those that did not.

Many of the features of the Patient Protection and Affordable Care Act, then, looked very similar to President Clinton's Health Security plan of nearly two decades earlier. Instead of alliances there were now exchanges, competition coupled with consumer safeguards would control costs, and employment-based insurance would remain the norm for most Americans. There were also important differences. Unlike the Clinton plan, the PPACA went beyond reform of the insurance market to address, albeit tentatively, the inflationary features inherent in the organization and delivery of health care. Thus, the government encouraged but did not mandate experiments with bundled payments to providers (flat-rate payments per case or per episode of care) paired with financial rewards for improved patient health outcomes, encouraged new forms of medical practice such as accountable care organizations and patient-centered medical homes to coordinate the care of patients with chronic diseases, and provided funding for providers to adopt electronic medical records to make such coordinated care and measurement of health outcomes a reality.

The major departure from the Clinton plan concerned the question of financing health insurance. Instead of mandating all employers to offer insurance as the Clinton plan had proposed, the PPACA imposed the insurance mandate on individuals. However, it would come with tax credits up to 400 percent of the federal poverty limit so that insurance would be affordable for those in the lower and middle classes. The PPACA stopped short of an employer mandate, but it gave firms incentives to do so under a "play-or-pay" scheme: employers who refused to provide insurance would pay a financial penalty for each of their full-time workers. This fine would be used to pay for their employees seeking insurance in the individual market. However, small businesses would be exempt from play-or-pay.

Interestingly, the idea of an individual mandate had long been proposed by political conservatives. They had proposed the individual mandate as a way to decouple health insurance from employment. The individual mandate would place responsibility for health insurance on individuals but would also give them the freedom to shop around for a health plan that met their needs rather than have their employer choose one for them. In the 2008 presidential election campaign, the individual mandate was the centerpiece of John McCain's health care reform proposal. Candidate Obama himself was initially skeptical of the need for such a mandate and believed that subsidies for lower income people would be sufficient to convince them to sign up for insurance voluntarily. However, his advisers subsequently convinced him that the mandate was critical to the survival of insurance markets because it would allow for the pooling of the healthier with the sicker.

The PPACA not only based itself on the theoretical model of managed care laid out in the Clinton health plan, but it also drew on the real-world example of the Massachusetts Health Plan. Enacted by a Democratic-controlled legislature and Republican governor Mitt Romney (in office 2003–2007), who signed it into law in 2006,[41] the Massachusetts Health Plan introduced near-universal coverage of state residents through private employment-based insurers. It outlawed insurers' practices that discriminated against the sick. It created an online exchange where small businesses and individuals in the state could shop around for coverage from competing private insurers. Finally, an individual mandate and the play-or-pay provisions for employers were also features, as were tax credits for those on low incomes to make insurance affordable.

Cutting Deals with Health Care Stakeholders

If the PPACA borrowed much from the ill-fated Clinton plan, why did Congress enact it? Also, why did health care stakeholders not set out to destroy it as they had Health Security nearly two decades earlier? The answer lies in the very different strategy that President Obama and congressional Democrats pursued, which was quite the opposite of the one that the Clintons had followed. Obama and Democratic leaders in Congress took into account the dangers presented by powerful health care interest groups and the fragmented political system's capacity to destroy party unity and to provide numerous veto points to organized interests, and they plotted their strategy accordingly. That strategy entailed maintaining intraparty unity and bringing key interest groups early on into real negotiations in order to gain their support of reform. Obama showed a willingness to make strategic concessions with both congressional Democrats and health care interest groups in order to keep reform on track. At the same time, allies of the PPACA were far more effective in mobilizing grassroots support and maintaining unity than in 1994.

Democratic leaders decided to unify the different committee bills into a single piece of legislation for consideration in each chamber. Such action focused Democratic minds on one bill rather than on several competing versions of reform that had exerted such a centrifugal effect on party unity during 1993 and 1994. In a further departure from the Clinton strategy, Obama also decided to give Congress the lead in drafting health care reform legislation. This deference did much to forge a partisan bond able to traverse the institutional chasm created by separation of powers.

The most important concession that Obama made to ensure party unity was to drop the public option from the final version of health care reform. This was done as the politics of necessity, in large part to ensure Democratic Party unity across the different branches of government. House Democrats, who enjoyed a comfortable majority and whose Speaker was among the liberal wing of the party, had the votes (just barely, as it turned out) to include a watered-down version of the public option in their reform bill. The situation in the Senate was quite different. In that chamber, the moderate wing of the Democratic Party was stronger and the party's majority of seats was less assured under the filibuster, which allowed a minority of forty-one senators to block a floor vote on a bill. Were the public option included in the Senate reform bill, the defection of even a few moderate Democratic senators would have been enough to kill the legislation in a Republican-led filibuster. Aware of the numbers in the Senate, Obama announced his willingness to drop the public option from the final reform bill. Accordingly, the bill that made it out of the Senate did not have this feature, and House Democrats grumblingly reconciled themselves to this reality.

Aside from compromising and including congressional Democrats in the project of health care reform, the other striking difference was the approach of the Obama administration and traditional advocates of national health insurance toward groups normally opposed to reform. Instead of trying to freeze out health care stakeholders as the Clintons had done, the president brought key interest groups to the negotiating table early on. The hope was to forge a consensus on the content of reform that could withstand the onslaught from opponents of reform that was certain to follow during the long and tortuous legislative process. The strategy of stakeholder inclusion consisted of two parts. The first was bringing interest groups to the table as genuine negotiating partners. The second was the mobilization of a powerful and unified interest group coalition that brought together previous foes who were now determined to see reform through.

The effort to win over powerful interests that had blocked past efforts at national health insurance was not just the administration's purview. Rather, Obama relied on key politicians and interest group leaders as well. Senator Edward "Ted" Kennedy (D-MA; in office 1962–2009), a longtime advocate of universal health coverage who was suffering from terminal brain cancer, held closed-door talks with major health care stakeholders, many of whom had bitterly opposed the Clinton plan, to see if he could build a consensus on a new health care reform effort that would expand access to insurance and control costs. Health

insurers and providers were attracted to gaining new markets among the uninsured, while employers wanted a solution to their skyrocketing labor costs.[42] In May 2009, Obama announced the outlines of a breakthrough with major health care stakeholders. In a letter addressed to the president, the interest groups pledged to work together to slow the rate of health care inflation by 1.5 percent in the decade from 2010 through 2019. The list of participants at the announcement was a who's-who of the medical industrial complex: the AMA; the AHA; the Pharmaceutical Research and Manufacturers of America (PhRMA); the Advanced Medical Technology Association, which represented medical device manufacturers; America's Health Insurance Plans (AHIP) representing health insurance companies large and small; and the Service Employees' International Union (SEIU). Published in *The New York Times* on May 11, 2009, the letter noted, in part:

> We are committed to taking action in public-private partnership to create a more stable and sustainable health care system that will achieve billions in savings through:
>
> Implementing proposals in all sectors of the health care system, focusing on administrative simplification, standardization, and transparency that supports effective markets;
>
> Reducing over-use and under-use of health care by aligning quality and efficiency incentives among providers across the continuum of care so that physicians, hospitals, and other health care providers are encouraged and enabled to work together towards the highest standards of quality and efficiency;
>
> Encouraging coordinated care, both in the public and private sectors, and adherence to evidence-based best practices and therapies that reduce hospitalization, manage chronic disease more efficiently and effectively, and implement proven clinical prevention strategies; and,
>
> Reducing the cost of doing business by addressing cost drivers in each sector and through common sense improvements in care delivery models, health information technology, workforce deployment and development, and regulatory reforms.

None of the groups specified what exactly they would do to reach this ambitious goal but instead pledged to work with the president and each other to get there. All realized, however, that they would have to accept some responsibility for financing the expansion of coverage to the uninsured. It was in their self-interest to do so, as fewer uninsured translated into more certain incomes for providers and new markets for insurers.[43]

Interestingly, the person instrumental in bringing representatives of the health care industry to the agreement in May 2009 was not one of their own but Dennis Rivera, who led the health care reform campaign of the powerful SEIU and saw affordable employment-based insurance as vital to preserving union jobs. Thus, Rivera got employers (including Wal-Mart), health care providers, and insurers on board with health care reform. The SEIU's president, Andy Stern (himself a maverick reformist labor leader on the left wing of the labor movement, who had taken his union out of the AFL-CIO in 2005 over differences in organized labor's strategy), justified his union's strategy to forge an alliance on health care reform with traditional labor foes:

> If the business community, the pharmaceutical industry and Wal-Mart all opposed health care reform, this bill would be dead. . . . What keeps it alive is that conservatives are isolated from their traditional business base. The business community appreciates that our country needs to do something about health care.[44]

The Obama administration and its Democratic allies in Congress offered key concessions to providers, insurers, and employers in order to prevent a repetition of their obstruction that had been so damaging to the fate of Health Security in 1994. One by one, their associations cut deals with the administration. In some cases, the deals were sweet, in other cases, they were not. The pharmaceutical industry was the first to move. PhRMA agreed to close the gap in Medicare Part D drug coverage insurance (the so-called donut hole) by granting discounts of 50 percent for name-brand drugs and promising to spend $150 million in ads supportive of health care reform. In return, Obama agreed to keep many of the Medicare Part D provisions that would maintain the hefty profit margins of the industry. Under the PPACA, the Medicare program would not be able to negotiate drug prices with manufacturers or reimport cheaper prescription medicines from abroad.

Like the pharmaceutical industry, other provider groups made concessions in exchange for new revenues that an expansion of coverage to the millions of uninsured would bring them. The AMA publicly came out in favor of the House version of reform on the eve of that chamber's vote. The association was relieved at Obama's subsequent decision to drop the public option. Many of the AMA's members were well acquainted with the lower Medicare reimbursements compared with those of private insurers and feared that a public option would do the same for their treatment of working-age Americans. Hospitals, too, were satisfied with the elimination of the public option for similar reasons as physicians. To be sure, the AHA had to give some ground. Hospitals agreed to cuts in government reimbursements of $155 billion over ten years in order to finance the expansion of coverage to the uninsured. Fewer uninsured meant fewer cases of uncompensated charity care for the hospitals to bear. However, the AHA successfully negotiated a ten-year exemption from the introduction of such cuts.

Rejecting the Public Option

Obama's decision to jettison the public option was crucial to neutralizing the health insurance lobby, represented by AHIP, a merger of AAHP and HIAA. Private insurers feared and loathed the public option because it posed a real threat to their profit margins and perhaps their survival. Indeed, AHIP complained that the public option would enjoy unfair advantages in the marketplace and would essentially drive it out of business. Obama's decision to drop the public option, however, came with a price: insurers had to accept the prohibition of their medical underwriting practices that had allowed them to shun less healthy individuals and small businesses that employed them. At the same time, Obama and the insurance industry found common ground on the need for the individual mandate. Insurance reform entailed that insurance companies would have to accept all applicants and set modified community-rated premiums in place of those based on an applicant's health risk. Yet placing new requirements on insurance companies without also requiring everyone to buy insurance would likely lead to adverse selection, a problem long recognized by many health economists. That is, sicker individuals who had been denied coverage or priced out of the health insurance market would now rush to sign up for insurance. Without healthier people enrolling and offsetting these bad risks, the profits and even survival of insurers might be threatened. By requiring everybody to carry health insurance, the individual mandate would ensure the risk pooling necessary to the proper functioning of insurance markets. The provision for risk-adjusted payments among insurers was also expected to correct for any subtle forms of cream-skimming that insurance companies might try.

Despite these concessions, the insurance industry was unhappy with the direction of negotiations with congressional Democrats and the administration. AHIP argued that its members had already agreed to cuts in reimbursement for the private Medicare plans they offered to seniors. While AHIP recognized the new business that covering thirty million uninsured would bring in, it disagreed with the Democrats' estimates and maintained that it would impose hardship on insurers. However, it proved difficult for the insurance industry to plead hardship under the provisions of the PPACA. After all, the industry had enjoyed ample profits for a number of years. When AHIP tried to mount a campaign to sabotage the passage of the bill, its efforts seemed disingenuous and self-serving. An AHIP-commissioned analysis of the PPACA by the accounting firm PricewaterhouseCoopers found that the law would lead to much higher premiums than the government had indicated. However, the accounting firm later distanced itself from the report and news media exposed its flawed data. Nor did it help that Anthem announced a premium hike of 30 percent for the small-group market. The insurance industry's position was increasingly untenable.

Concessions to Employers

The Obama administration also made a number of key concessions to employers that muted their opposition to reform. Chief among these was the requirement that responsibility for insurance rest with individuals rather than employers. The decision to forgo an employer mandate assuaged the fears of many firms over their labor costs. So, too, did the exemption of small firms from the play-or-pay provisions of the law as well as the reward of tax credits to small businesses that opted to provide insurance anyway. These provisions satisfied most large employers. To be sure, the NIFB and U.S. Chamber of Commerce were vocal in their opposition to the PPACA and ran negative ads on the law. However, Obama's accommodations to employers' concerns made business opposition to reform less convincing, and, in fact, many large employers (and even some small ones) supported the PPACA.[45]

The second prong in the reform strategy was engaging grassroots supporters of reform in coordinated action. This was in effect a continuation of the mobilization of the electorate that had swept Obama into office in 2008; the leading groups in this issue-based campaign centering on health care reform were Health Care for America Now (HCAN), Organizing for America (OFA), and MoveOn. These groups coordinated their work and that of other groups favoring reform, such as groups representing segments of the medical profession as well as nurses and other allied health professions, labor unions, and consumer groups. HCAN and OFA organized rallies, circulated Internet petitions, and garnered online contributions to finance this issue campaign. These tactics sustained ordinary citizens' support for health care reform and targeted congressional Democrats in vulnerable districts whose votes for the PPACA were not assured. For example, in 2009, volunteers at a phone bank in Wisconsin called registered Democratic voters living in Ohio whose representative was wavering on reform and whose reelection was not assured. The phone bank volunteer would explain the PPACA to that member's constituents and urge them to vote for their incumbent representative in the upcoming election. This type of mobilization was designed to keep Democratic politicians honest and minimize their defections from the PPACA.

The mobilization of grassroots supporters succeeded on a number of levels. First, proponents of reform would not let differences of opinion destroy health care reform efforts as they had in the past. Though some groups such MoveOn and the AFL-CIO initially pushed hard for the public option, when President Obama made it clear that he would not sacrifice the entire reform project for the preservation of this one idea, they acquiesced. Moreover, they continued to rally their members to support reform and to pressure congressional Democrats to do the same. Their efforts paid off,

with Congress just barely enacting the Patient Protection and Affordable Care Act in March 2010.

Impact of the Tea Party Movement

The pro-reform coalition faced a formidable array of groups that mobilized to kill the bill, but not primarily from the insurance or provider groups. Instead, the main challenge came from the Tea Party movement. The Tea Party movement was not an organized interest group as such, nor was it a political party. Rather, it was a conservative backlash that developed among citizens and erstwhile Republicans in reaction to that party's fiscal profligacy and bank bailouts under President George W. Bush (2001–2009). It consisted largely of higher income white Americans. They generally abhorred big government and especially the Democrats' health care reform plans. While many Tea Party adherents formed spontaneously among grassroots citizens, the movement was also supported financially and otherwise by powerful conservative elites, such as former Republican representative Dick Armey's Freedom Works and the conservative industrialist Koch brothers.[46] Tea Partiers engaged in a number of actions to try to stop health care reform. In summer 2009, they disrupted town hall meetings, which Democrats had organized to explain and build public support for Obama's reform plans.

Tea Partiers were very effective in shouting down speakers and garnering widespread media coverage in the process. In addition to such direct action, the Tea Party movement sought to reorient the Republican Party by running conservative candidates in Republican primaries for Congress and the presidency. Rather than form a breakaway third party, the Tea Party movement intended to infiltrate the Republican Party in order to steer it back to its true small-government roots. Though failing to block the passage of the Patient Protection and Affordable Care Act, Tea Party candidates did well enough to help the Republicans regain control of the House of Representatives in the 2010 midterm elections; however, they fell short of their aim to retake the White House or the Senate in the 2012 elections.

Critics of the Administration's Strategy

Critics of the strategy of securing interest group buy-in charged that it was little more than Democrats selling out their principles and buying off their foes. Clearly, health care providers, insurers, and employers look set to do well under the new law. Defenders of this approach, however, argued that it was simply a matter of political necessity, that it was far better for the Democrats to transform traditional foes of health care reform into allies by means of inclusion and co-optation. However, such a strategy required compromise, by many pro-reform leaders and their supporters.

It also remains to be seen whether the deals struck with health care stakeholders during the enactment of the PPACA will hold. Having failed to gain Republican majorities that could repeal the law outright, the Tea Party's strategy has been to pressure congressional Republicans to block the health care reform law either by delaying its implementation or by defunding the law's key provisions. The Tea Party precipitated a partial federal government shutdown in October 2013 with its insistence on delaying implementation of the PPACA. Providers and insurers may seek to renegotiate or renege on earlier agreements they struck with the Obama administration. Medical device manufacturers pressured House Republicans to include a repeal of the tax on their equipment in their ultimatum on the shutdown in fall 2013, though the measure did not make it through the Democratic-controlled Senate. Wishing to preempt an electoral backlash in the 2014 congressional elections, the Obama administration decided to delay by one year the introduction of the play-or-pay provisions for large employers.

HEALTH CARE POLICY: GOING FORWARD

Health care policy in the United States amply illustrates the hyperpluralism of the interest group universe, which has become more crowded with the ascendancy of interest group campaign donations and lobbying in U.S. politics. It is also the result of the unplanned development of employment-based private insurance and the tacking on of public insurance programs for the poor and elderly later on. The result is a health policy arena full of narrow interests with a stake in preserving the status quo. A radical policy shift in this environment is extremely unlikely.[47] Instead, health care reformers have had to build on the existing edifice of private and public insurance, even if those twin pillars are showing the limits of their ability to uphold the system.

The sheer number of competing groups, even within a specific sector of the economy, poses enormous difficulty for policymakers seeking to forge a compromise agreement. Such agreements, while rare, do happen. They depend on

KEY DECISIONS: HEALTH CARE CRISES AND SOLUTIONS

The Repeal of the Medicare Catastrophic Coverage Act

In 1989, Congress enacted the Medicare Catastrophic Coverage Act (MCCA). The law would have extended Medicare coverage of hospital and doctor bills above a certain threshold. To pay for these new benefits, wealthier seniors would have faced higher premiums. AARP initially supported the bill but reversed its position after encountering a backlash from its own members. The ensuing opposition from both AARP and the National Committee to Preserve Social Security and Medicare led Congress to repeal the law the following year. Representative Donald L. Ritter (R-PA) introduced the bill to repeal the MCCA on January 3, 1989:

Mr. RITTER. Mr. Speaker, since its passage, I haven't heard one of the 72 Members who voted against the Medicare Catastrophic Coverage Act express regret over their vote, but I've heard complaints from many of those who are sorry they voted for it.

Lately, we've been reading more financial reports advising senior citizens on how to adjust their incomes in 1989 to reduce their tax liabilities. They are coming up with clever strategies to avoid paying the new surtax on their income tax that was imposed on them to pay for a Catastrophic Coverage Act they didn't want. But, this is one New Year's gift from Congress which taxpaying seniors find unwelcome.

In reducing tax liabilities to avoid the surtax, taxpaying seniors will withdraw moneys available for benefits. I'd like to ask my colleagues if they know that the Catastrophic Coverage Act contains a provision requiring that "The Secretary would increase the flat premium to replace revenue" in the case of a revenue shortfall. I fear this might result in not only higher Medicare part B payments, but also higher deductibles, lower levels of service and fewer people covered.

The funding mechanism is self-defeating. . . . At a time when society is craving greater savings and investment by seniors to cover retirement expenses, the Medicare Catastrophic Act is a mistake. It's a raw deal for seniors who have saved and invested wisely for their later years. Not only will they have to pay income taxes, but also new surcharges on those taxes for a bill that doesn't even encompass long-term care.

My constituents are writing and calling my office to protest the surtax and the sharp increases in Medicare part B. I understand that's happening in other congressional districts, too. The financing mechanisms in the bill are onerous for our tax-paying senior citizens, given the inevitable reduction of taxable income and assets, they sow the seeds of their own failure. For these reasons, I am introducing a bill to repeal the Medicare Catastrophic Act of 1988 and to establish a bipartisan advisory group to study and develop proposals to provide protection against excessive costs of catastrophic illness beyond the scope of current Medicare coverage.

SOURCE: "Introduction of the Bill to Repeal the Medicare Catastrophic Coverage Act of 1989—Hon. Don Ritter (Extension of Remarks—January 03, 1989)," *Congressional Record*, 101st Congress (1989–1990), http://thomas.loc.gov/cgi-bin/query/D?r101:101:./temp/~r101uZ6aBC::.

political and interest group leaders willing to engage in meaningful bargaining with each other and able to bring their base along. When reform does occur, it is invariably drawn out and ugly. Yet such is the pattern of interest group politics in the United States today.

See also **Chapter 6: The Centers for Medicare and Medicaid Services (1965–Present); Chapter 19: Children's Health and Health Care Policy (1960s–Present); Chapter 20: Women's Issues and American** **Health Care Policy (1960s–Present); Chapter 21: Minorities, Immigrants, and Health Care Policy: Disparities and Solutions (1960s–Present); Chapter 22: Aging and Health Care Policy (1990s–Present); Chapter 23: Fifty Years of Progress in Disease and Injury Prevention (1950s–Present); Chapter 24: Mental Health and Social Policy (1960s–Present); Chapter 25: Nutrition, Physical Activity, and the Obesity Epidemic: Issues, Policies, and Solutions (1960s–Present).**

NOTES

1. Theodore R. Marmor, *The Politics of Medicare,* 2nd ed. (New York: Aldine de Gruyter, 2000).
2. Theda Skocpol, *Boomerang: Clinton's Health Security Effort and the Turn against Government in U.S. Politics* (New York: W.W. Norton, 1996); Cathi Jo Martin, *Stuck in Neutral: Business and the Politics of Human Capital Investment Policy* (Princeton, NJ: Princeton University Press, 2000); Susan Giaimo, *Markets and Medicine: The Politics of Health Care Reform in Britain, Germany, and the United States* (Ann Arbor: University of Michigan Press, 2002).
3. Premium support for Medicare was first proposed by Henry J. Aaron and Robert D. Reischauer, "The Medicare Reform Debate: What Is the Next Step?" *Health Affairs* 14: 4 (1995): 8–30. For the Heritage Foundation's proposals, see Heritage Foundation, *Saving the American Dream: The Heritage Plan to Fix the Debt, Cut Spending, and Restore Prosperity* (Washington, DC: Heritage Foundation, 2011). The Heritage Foundation's economic analysis of Representative Ryan's budget proposals was done by the Center for Data Analysis, "Economic Analysis of the House Budget Resolution by the Center for Data Analysis at the Heritage Foundation," April 5, 2011. For Ryan's proposals on Medicare, see Paul Ryan, *Description of the Legislation: A Roadmap for America's Future,* January 27, 2010, 50–52. http://www.americanroadmap.org; Paul Ryan, *The Path to Prosperity,* House Budget Committee, March 2012, http://budget.house.gov/prosperity; Alice Rivlin and Paul Ryan, "A Long-Term Plan for Medicare and Medicaid," November 17, 2010, http://budget.house.gov/news/documentsingle.aspx?DocumentID=225826; and Ron Wyden and Paul Ryan, *Guaranteed Choices to Strengthen Medicare and Health Security for All,* December 15, 2011, http://budget.house.gov/uploaded files/wydenryan.pdf.
4. Allan J. Cigler and Burdett A. Loomis, *Interest Group Politics* (Washington DC: CQ Press, 2002); Leon D. Epstein, *Political Parties in the American Mold* (Madison: University of Wisconsin Press, 1986); William G. Weissert and Carol S. Weissert, *Governing Health: The Politics of Health Policy,* 4th ed. (Baltimore: Johns Hopkins University Press, 2012), 174.
5. Weissert and Weissert, *Governing Health,* 177–179.
6. Ibid., 160–161, 170–171.
7. Ibid., 135.
8. Kay Lehman Schlozman and John T. Tierney, *Organized Interests and American Democracy* (New York: Harper and Row, 1986).
9. Cigler and Loomis, *Interest Group Politics*; David Vogel, "Why Businessmen Distrust Their State: The Political Consciousness of American Corporate Executives," *British Journal of Political Science* 8 (January 1978): 45–78.
10. Marmor, *The Politics of Medicare,* 18.
11. Weissert and Weissert, *Governing Health,* 130.
12. Ibid., 132.
13. Ibid., 135.
14. Donald L. Madison, "From Bismarck to Medicare—A Brief History of Medical Care Payment in America," in *The Social Medicine Reader, Vol. III: Health Policy, Markets, and Medicine,* 2nd ed., edited by Jonathan Oberlander, 31-66 (Durham, NC: Duke University Press, 2005); Jacob S. Hacker, *The Divided Welfare State: The Battle over Public and Private Social Benefits in the United States* (Cambridge, UK: Cambridge University Press, 2002).
15. Marmor, *The Politics of Medicare,* 18; Jill Quadagno, *One Nation, Uninsured: Why the U.S. Has No National Health Insurance* (Oxford, UK: Oxford University Press, 2005), 64.
16. Marmor, *The Politics of Medicare,* chs. 1–5; Quadagno, *One Nation, Uninsured,* 55–76.
17. Quadagno, *One Nation, Uninsured,* 73–74; Marmor, *The Politics of Medicare,* 47–55.
18. Marmor, *The Politics of Medicare,* 56–61.
19. Philip F. Cooper and Barbara Steinberg Schone, "More Offers, Fewer Takers for Employment-Based Health Insurance: 1987 and 1996," *Health Affairs* 16: 6 (1997): 142.
20. Milt Freudenheim. "A Health Care Taboo Is Broken," *New York Times,* May 8, 1989.
21. Jacob S. Hacker, *The Road to Nowhere: The Genesis of President Clinton's Plan for Health Security* (Princeton, NJ: Princeton University Press, 1997), 17–20; Skocpol, *Boomerang,* 13, 21–23.
22. Hacker, *The Road to Nowhere,* 16–17.
23. In the 1992 presidential race, incumbent Republican President George H.W. Bush faced a challenge from Democrat Bill Clinton and independent candidate H. Ross Perot. Perot's candidacy drew away support from Bush, allowing Clinton to win with a 43 percent plurality of the popular vote.
24. Alain C. Enthoven, *Health Plan: The Only Practical Solution to the Soaring Cost of Medical Care* (Boston: Addison-Wesley, 1980); Alain C. Enthoven, "Managed Competition: An Agenda for Action," *Health Affairs* 7: 3 (1988): 25-47.
25. Weissert and Weissert, *Governing Health,* 132.
26. See Vogel, "Why Businessmen Distrust Their State," for his formulation on the negative power of business groups in U.S. policy.
27. Martin, *Stuck in Neutral*; Giaimo, *Markets and Medicine,* ch. 6.

28. Vogel, "Why Businessmen Distrust Their State."

29. Skocpol, *Boomerang*.

30. Mark A. Peterson, "From Trust to Political Power: Interest Groups, Public Choice, and Health Care," *Journal of Health Politics, Policy and Law* 26: 5 (2001): 1145–1163.

31. Skocpol, *Boomerang*, 75.

32. Robert J. Blendon et al., "Understanding the Managed Care Backlash," *Health Affairs* 17: 4 (1998): 80–94.

33. Kaiser Family Foundation and Health Research and Educational Trust, *Employer Health Benefits, 2011 Annual Survey*, http://kaiserfamilyfoundation.files.wordpress.com/2013/04/8225.pdf.

34. Giaimo, *Markets and Medicine*, 175; Skocpol, *Boomerang*, 161–162.

35. Milliman Medical Index, May 2011, http://www.milliman.com/mmi.

36. Robert L. Bennefield, "Health Insurance Coverage: 1995," *U.S. Census Bureau Current Population Reports, P60-195* September 1996, p. 1; Kaiser Family Foundation, *Key Facts about the Uninsured Population*, September 2013, http://kff.org/uninsured/fact-sheet/key-facts-about-the-uninsured-population.

37. Bureau of Labor Statistics, "Labor Force Statistics from the Current Population Survey," http://data.bls.gov/timeseries/LNS14000000.

38. Kaiser Family Foundation 2013, p. 3.

39. The Children's Health Insurance Program is the current name of the Medicaid expansion program for children of the working poor. It was originally enacted in 1997 as the State Children's Health Insurance Program.

40. Jacob S. Hacker, "Putting Politics First," *Health Affairs* 27: 3 (2008): 718–723; Jacob S. Hacker, The Case for Public Plan Choice in National Health Reform: Key to Cost Control and Quality Coverage (Berkeley: Center on Health, Economic and Family Security, University of California School of Law, and Institute for America's Future, 2008), https://www.law.berkeley.edu/files/Jacob_Hacker_Public_Plan_Choice.pdf.

41. On the Massachusetts Health plan, see Kaiser Family Foundation, *Massachusetts Health Care Reform: Six Years Later*, May 2012, http://kff.org/health-costs/issue-brief/massachusetts-health-care-reform-six-years-later.

42. Stuart Altman and David Shactman, *Power, Politics, and Universal Health Care: The Inside Story of a Century-long Battle* (Amherst, NY: Prometheus Books, 2011), ch. 12, esp. 254–255.

43. Steven Greenhouse, "Dennis Rivera Leads Labor Charge for Health Reform," *New York Times*, August 27, 2009; Robert Pear, "Industry Pledges to Control Health Care Costs," *New York Times*, May 11, 2009.

44. Greenhouse, 2009.

45. Altman and Shactman, *Power, Politics, and Universal Health Care*, ch. 12.

46. Edward Luce and Alexandra Ulmer, "Obama Foes Turn to '60s Radical for Tactical Tips," *Financial Times*, August 17, 2009, 2; Kate Zernike and Megan Thee-Brenan, "Poll Finds Tea Party Backers Wealthier and More Educated," *New York Times*, April 14, 2010.

47. Hacker, *The Divided Welfare State*.

FURTHER READING

Altman, Stuart, and David Shactman. *Power, Politics, and Universal Health Care: The Inside Story of a Century-long Battle*. Amherst, NY: Prometheus Books, 2011.

Jacobs, Lawrence R., and Theda Skocpol. *Health Care Reform and American Politics: What Everyone Needs to Know*. Rev. ed. Oxford, UK: Oxford University Press, 2012.

Marmor, Theodore R. *The Politics of Medicare*. 2nd ed. New York: Aldine de Gruyter, 2000.

Quadagno, Jill. *One Nation, Uninsured: Why the U.S. Has No National Health Insurance*. Oxford, UK: Oxford University Press, 2005.

Skocpol, Theda. *Boomerang: Clinton's Health Security Effort and the Turn against Government in U.S. Politics*. New York: W.W. Norton, 1996.

Weissert, William G., and Carol S. Weissert. *Governing Health: The Politics of Health Policy*. 4th ed. Baltimore: Johns Hopkins University Press, 2012.

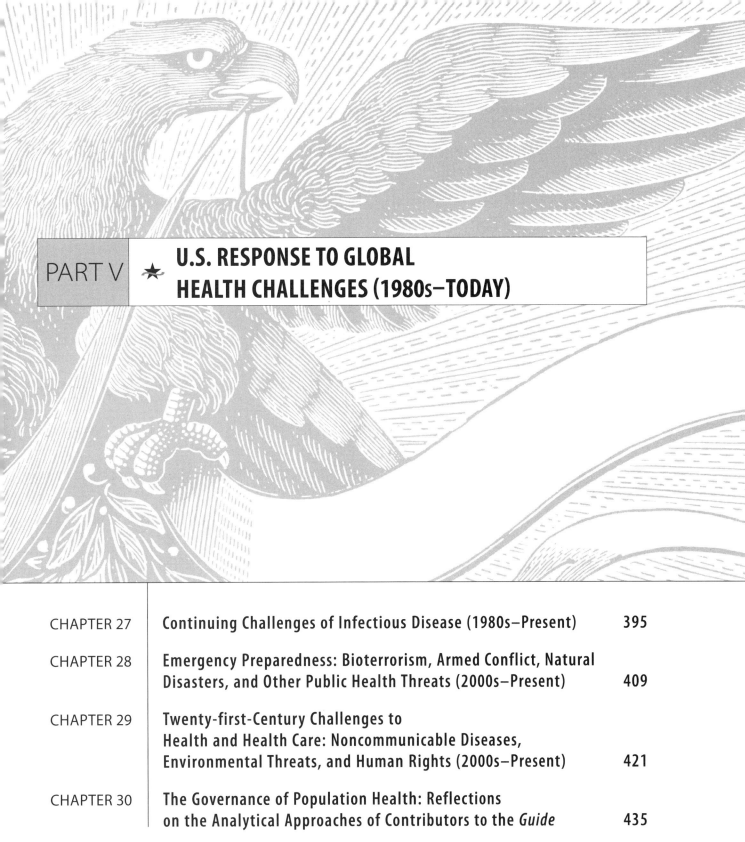

chapter 27

Continuing Challenges of Infectious Disease (1980s–Present)

Kenrad E. Nelson

N 1980, PUBLIC HEALTH PROFESSIONALS WERE optimistic that the major infectious diseases that had been responsible for serious morbidity and mortality in the Unites States had been controlled. The important contagious diseases of infants and young children, including diphtheria, pertussis, measles, and polio, had been controlled with effective vaccines. Many potentially serious bacterial infections that caused gastrointestinal infections, sepsis, or bacterial meningitis could be effectively treated with an array of antibiotics. Even though treatment sometimes failed because it was ineffective or the infecting bacteria were resistant to the drug, treatment was usually helpful.

EMERGENCE OF NEW INFECTIOUS DISEASES

The early successes in controlling infectious diseases had prompted the U.S. Surgeon General Dr. William Stewart (in office 1965–1969) to proclaim in 1968, "We can now close the book on infectious disease and concentrate our attention on chronic noninfectious diseases." However, despite the optimism concerning continued control and prevention of infectious disease in the United States, several new challenges have appeared since that time. There were outbreaks of hemorrhagic fevers, including the Ebola and Marburg viruses in the 1970s as well as Lassa fever earlier in Nigeria; large outbreaks of dengue and dengue hemorrhagic fever appeared in Asia. Although fatalities occurred

among laboratory workers who had handled materials containing these viruses in Europe and the United States, there were large outbreaks in developing countries.

Of greater concern were the outbreaks of Legionnaire's disease in 1976 in Philadelphia and the nationwide outbreaks of toxic shock syndrome from tampons contaminated with the toxin producing staphylococci. These outbreaks in particular alerted the public health medical community that previously unrecognized pathogens could emerge and cause serious and extensive outbreaks of new

A vivid HIV/AIDS poster reminds health care providers of the worldwide seriousness of this infectious disease. In 2013, to commemorate World AIDS Day, President Barack Obama addressed leaders of the Office of National AIDS Policy: "We created the first comprehensive National HIV/AIDS Strategy, rooted in a simple vision that every person should get access to life-extending care, regardless of age or gender, race or ethnicity, sexual orientation, gender identity or socio-economic status. . . . Here in the United States, we need to keep focusing on investments to communities that are still being hit hardest."

SOURCE: KTSImage/Thinkstock.

infectious diseases, even in the United States. Indeed, in the next thirty years, a large array of new infectious pathogens emerged in the United States and in other countries. The emergence of new infectious diseases provoked a new focus on research and coordinated efforts to identify and control newly emerging as well as reemerging infectious diseases.

Without question, the most important global emerging infection in the last thirty years has been HIV/AIDS. However, the international cooperative public health effort that was developed to control the global HIV/AIDS pandemic has strengthened the prevention efforts to control other global infectious diseases as well, such as influenza, tuberculosis, and malaria.

HIV/AIDS

It is not an exaggeration to say that the emergence of HIV/AIDS in the early 1980s completely changed the landscape of "infectious diseases" and redefined the characteristics of an emerging infectious disease throughout the world. Discovery of Pneumocystis pneumonia in five men who have sex with men was initially reported in the June 5, 1981, issue of *Morbidity and Mortality Reports*; this report was followed by descriptions of many other infectious diseases that were eventually linked to an HIV infection, after the virus was identified four years later. Prominent among many infections that are classified as opportunistic infections, which define AIDS in HIV-infected persons, are tuberculosis, many systemic fungal infections such as Cryptococcus neoformans, Histoplasma capsulatum, and Penicillium marneffei, as well other microorganisms. The opportunistic infections that predominate in an HIV-infected population depend in part on the risk behaviors leading to their HIV infection, their age and previous experience with currently inactive infections, and the geographic area of their residence. Since its original description in 1981, HIV/AIDS has spread to nearly every country in the world; it is truly a pandemic. It was estimated by the World Health Organization (WHO) that in 2010, 34 million people were living with HIV infections and an estimated 35 million had died from the disease. An estimated 2.7 million new HIV infections occurred in 2010. The highest prevalence and incidence of HIV infection is in the countries of sub-Saharan Africa, where the adult prevalence is above 5 percent in most countries.

Origins and Spread of HIV

The original transmission of HIV to humans is believed to have occurred in Central Africa, probably in the Democratic Republic of the Congo, from a reservoir in chimpanzees. There were likely sporadic human infections beginning in the 1890s from infected chimpanzees to hunters of "bush meat," who were exposed to infected blood and tissue of the animal during butchering.[1,2] The earliest documented human infection with HIV was from serum samples collected in Zaire (now the Democratic Republic of the Congo) in 1959.[3] Another human immunodeficiency virus, HIV-2, subsequently was discovered in the African Green Monkey in West Africa.[4] Humans can be infected with either HIV-1 or HIV-2, and infections with either virus can cause immunodeficiency and lead to AIDS with similar clinical features. However, the prevalence of HIV-2 infection is less than HIV-1 and the progression of AIDS is much slower. Without therapy, HIV-1 infections progress to AIDS in about ten to twelve years.[5] However, the time to AIDS varies by the age of the subject, the host's immune response, the presence of several co-infections, and other factors. In the absence of antiretroviral therapy, mortality occurs about one to one-and-a-half years after the appearance of AIDS, which is defined as the occurrence of one or more AIDS-defining opportunistic infections or a CD4 cell count of two hundred cells per million or less.

Risk Factors for HIV and the Global Distribution of Infection

HIV-1 and HIV-2 are not easily transmitted. Infections are acquired most frequently by sexual contact or perinatal exposure to infections from an infected person. High-risk behaviors for transmission include genital, rectal, or oral sex; injection drug use with shared equipment; needle stick exposure; transfusion of infected blood; and perinatal or breast milk transmission. The most important risk behaviors differ in various regions of the world.

Sub-Saharan Africa

Sub-Saharan Africa is the region with the highest proportion of persons living with HIV/AIDS. UNAIDS has estimated that 22.9 million persons in this region are infected with HIV. In 2012, it estimated that 1.9 million new infections and 1.2 million deaths occurred.[6] The region accounts for almost one-half of the total deaths from AIDS, while it contains only 12 percent of the global population. However, the number of new HIV infections decreased by 26 percent, from 2.6 million in 1997.[7] Most infections in the region were acquired by heterosexual sex. Mother-to-infant transmission remains a common means of transmission as well. However, successful prevention efforts have focused on the interruption of maternal to infant transmission in recent years. The latest UNAIDS report estimates that 59 percent of HIV- infected pregnant mothers in sub-Saharan Africa have been treated with antiretroviral drugs during and after their pregnancy to prevent transmission to their infant.[8]

The Caribbean Region

The Caribbean area is the second most infected region in the world. Among persons fifteen to forty-four years of age in this region, AIDS is the leading cause of death. The adult HIV prevalence has been estimated to be 0.9 percent and approximately 200,000 persons are living with HIV infections. Haiti was one of the first countries in the Western Hemisphere to be heavily affected by HIV/AIDS.[9] The infection was most likely introduced to Haiti from Africa. Early in the epidemic in the United States, HIV infections among men who have sex with men had been acquired in Haiti. The incidence of HIV in the Caribbean decreased by one-third between 2001 and 2012, but by only 12 percent in Haiti. Sexual transmission, both heterosexual and homosexual, and injection drug use are the important means of transmission among persons in the Caribbean.[10]

Asia

The prevalence of HIV is quite variable among countries in Asia. Several countries have generalized epidemics with HIV prevalence above 1 percent in the general population. These include Thailand, Cambodia, and Myanmar. More recently, expansion of the epidemic has occurred in Nepal, Vietnam, Malaysia, and China.[11] A rapidly expanding epidemic of heterosexual transmission among sex workers and their clients in Thailand was controlled by an extensive public health program that promoted condom use.[12,13] Epidemics of HIV among injection drug users have accounted for most infections in Vietnam and the southern provinces of China. A recent epidemic of HIV from transmission of a recombinant HIV virus imported from China in 2004 into the injection drug–using population of Taiwan has been controlled by implementation of an extensive harm reduction program.[14] Men who have sex with men are an important risk group for HIV infection for most countries in Asia.[15]

Eastern Europe and Central Asia

Eastern Europe and Central Asia are the only WHO regions where the estimated number of persons with HIV infection has continued to increase in recent years. An estimated 1.5 million persons are infected with HIV in Eastern Europe.[16] The most important risk populations in this region are injection drug users. The Russian Federation and Ukraine account for nearly 90 percent of the HIV infections in this region, an estimated 2.5 million to 3 million injection drug users.[17] Methadone replacement therapy and other harm reduction services are illegal in Russia and have only recently been introduced in Ukraine.

Latin America

An estimated 1.5 million people are living with HIV infection in Latin America. In 2010, an estimated 62,000 persons in the region died of AIDS.[18] Two countries in the region, Guatemala and Honduras, have high HIV prevalence in the general population. However, several other countries have faced epidemics. Brazil's population includes about one-third of the HIV-infected persons in the region. Early in the

epidemic, HIV infection in Brazil was primarily among men who have sex with men; recently, the epidemic has expanded among injection drug users and heterosexuals.

Oceania

An estimated 54,000 persons in Oceania are infected with HIV.[19] The main risk group among people living in the area is men who have sex with men. An extensive harm reduction program in Australia has been associated with low prevalence and incidence of HIV among injection drug users. Between 1997 and 2004, injection drug users accounted for 2.5 percent and heterosexual intercourse for 8.5 percent of HIV infections in Australia.

Middle East and North Africa

An estimated 330,000 persons in the Middle East and North Africa were infected with HIV in 2009.[20] The most severely affected country in the region is Sudan, which has been affected by a civil war and a humanitarian crisis. Injection drug use accounts for many infections in the region: this route of infection is especially significant in Libya, Algeria, Egypt, Iran, Bahrain, Kuwait, and Oman. Iran has established a harm reduction program including both methadone replacement therapy and needle/syringe exchanges in an attempt to prevent transmission among the large number of opiate users in the country.

Western and Central Europe

In 2010, UNAIDS estimated that 840,000 people were living with HIV infection in Western and Central Europe. An estimated 30,000 persons were newly infected with HIV in 2010, similar to the estimated number of new infections in 2001. The adult HIV prevalence is estimated at 0.2 percent. The number of new infections among men who have sex with men has increased in the last decade, while the incidents among injection drug users have decreased. Although the most important risk population in Europe is men who have sex with men, efforts to control HIV transmission in this population have not been successful in Europe or other regions.[21]

North America

Newly reported HIV infections in the United States increased until 1993 and then declined until 1997. Since then HIV incidents have leveled off at about 50,000 new infections each year. In 2008, the thirty-seven states with name and risk factor reporting determined there were 31,545 males and 10,662 females with newly diagnosed HIV infections. Among females, 84 percent had acquired their infection by heterosexual contact and 15 percent by injection drug use. Among males, 72 percent of new infections were acquired through male-to-male sexual contact, 15 percent were from heterosexual contact, and 9 percent were from injection drug use. Among males, 40 percent were African American, 37 percent were white, and 20 percent were Latino. Among females, 61 percent were African American, 19 percent were Latina, and 18 percent were white. New HIV infections in the United States are concentrated in the African American population of men who have sex with men.[22]

The epidemic in Mexico is less intense than in the United States. It has been estimated that more than 250,000 persons have been infected. Overall, approximately 40 percent of reported cases have been in homosexual or bisexual men, 7 percent in transfusion recipients, 20 percent in heterosexuals, 31 percent in injection drug users, and 1 percent in paid plasma donors, transmitted by contaminated equipment.

An estimated ninety thousand persons are living with HIV infection in Canada. The most significant risk group is young men who have sex with men. HIV infections among injection drug users constituted 33 percent of all new HIV infections in 1997, but the number of new infections in this group had subsequently declined to 15 percent by 2004 due to the implementation of a comprehensive harm reduction program to prevent transmission in the population.[23]

SUMMARY OF THE SPREAD OF HIV

In summary, HIV infections have spread to every region and nearly every country in the world since the emergence of the virus from Africa in the early 1980s. It is remarkable that a viral infection that can be transmitted only by sexual contact or parenteral inoculation, including injections and needle sticks, could spread so widely in thirty years.[24] The global spread of HIV/AIDS, together with the usual inexorable downward clinical course of the disease in the ten years or so after an untreated infection, has energized an unprecedented global research effort and public health response to implement strategies to prevent transmission of the virus and treat infected persons to control the progression of the disease. The research to develop strategies to prevent transmission of the virus and implement those that have proved to be effective globally will be reviewed in the next section of the chapter.

EVALUATION OF INTERVENTIONS TO PREVENT TRANSMISSION OF HIV

Although there has been global spread of the HIV epidemic, several effective interventions have been evaluated and implemented, including the use of male or female condoms and other barrier methods to prevent sexual transmission, adult male circumcision, screening of the blood supply and organs for transplantation, needle/syringe exchange, methadone replacement therapy and, probably most important, detection and treatment of HIV-infected

persons with antiviral drugs to decrease the viral load. Humans are the reservoir for the HIV virus.

The rate of transmission of HIV by uncomplicated heterosexual intercourse has been found to be about 0.3 percent per sexual act among a study of discordant couples in Uganda.[25] Transmission is considerably higher if one partner has an sexually transmitted disease (STD), especially a genital ulcer disease, during rectal or traumatic sex and if the infected partner has a high HIV viral load.[26] Interventions to prevent sexual transmission have included the following:

1. Barrier methods. Methods such as male or female condoms, have been shown to be at least 80 percent effective among "consistent condom users" compared to "inconsistent users."[27]

2. Male circumcision. This has been found to be about 60 percent protective in preventing transmission from infected women to uninfected men in three controlled clinical trials in Africa. It has also afforded significant protection to the insertive partner in rectal sex when the receptive partner is infected.[28,29,30]

3. Vaginal microbicides. Early research on the use of surfactants or acidifying agents proved them to be ineffective in preventing HIV transmission. However, the local use of vaginal gels containing antiretroviral drugs has shown promise of efficacy.[31] Vaginal microbicides are an attractive intervention because they are under the control of the female and could be used when the infection status of the partner is unknown, such as commonly occurs among female and male sex workers.

4. Sexual behavior change. Obviously, reducing or eliminating penetrative sexual contact with an HIV-infected partner would be an effective method of prevention of HIV transmission. However, large-scale changes in sexual behavior at the population level have not been easy to accomplish. Nevertheless, there has been some increase in non-genital, especially oral, sex in recent years, some of which may have occurred in an effort to prevent HIV. However, HIV transmission can still occur through oral sex, although likely at a much lower rate. The increase in oral sex has been suggested by the results of a study among college students that found an increase in the incidence of HIV-1 rather than HIV-2 as a cause of genital herpes from 31 percent in 1991 to 78 percent in 2008.[32]

5. Antiretroviral therapy to reduce viral load. Currently and in the foreseeable future, the most effective strategy to prevent HIV transmission will be the detection of HIV infections as early as possible by widespread testing and treating infected persons to prevent transmission as well as to preserve their immune function and prevent

AIDS-related illnesses. The remarkable efficiency of this approach was documented in the AIDS Clinical Trials Group study 052 in which the transmission of HIV was reduced by 96 percent among 1,763 couples who were enrolled in this double blinded clinical trial.[33] Implementing more widespread treatment successfully will depend on more extensive testing to detect infected persons before they are symptomatic. It will also require expanding the indications for HIV testing beyond the acknowledged risk groups (e.g., injection drug users, STD patients, men who have sex with men). Thus, it is currently recommended that an "opt-out" strategy be used to test everyone having a medical encounter. The opt-out strategy has been found effective in screening more than 85 percent of all pregnant women in a study where a group of women was tested for HIV unless they specifically refused testing (i.e., opted out).[34] With more widespread testing and therapy of all identified HIV-infected persons regardless of their CD4 cell count or HIV viral load, the "community viral load" could be reduced and the rise of transmission by sexual contact or parenteral exposure to blood from HIV-infected persons reduced, especially if the person has lower viral load because of treatment. The World Health Organization has attempted to follow the policy of more widespread testing and treating HIV-infected persons by recommending that all pregnant women be tested for HIV and, if positive, be treated permanently regardless of the CD4 cell count or viral load. As well as increasing the indication to treating all HIV infected persons from those with a CD4 cell count of below 200 cells/µl to those below 350 cells/µl.[35]

6. Injection drug use. The main strategy for preventing HIV transmission among injection drug users, aside from testing persons for HIV infections and treating those who are infected with antiretroviral drugs, is what is commonly known as "harm reduction." This includes access to and use of sterile injection equipment (i.e., needle exchange) and methadone or buprenorphine maintenance therapy to reduce the injection of opiates and avoid withdrawal symptoms after heroin injection is stopped or reduced. The implementation of widespread, easily accessible harm reduction services can be quite effective in preventing HIV transmission among opiate injectors, as shown in the experience in Australia and several European countries.[36] Harm reduction services, when effectively organized and deployed, can also reverse a rapidly emerging HIV epidemic among injection drug users, as seen recently in Taiwan. An additional strategy to prevent the transmission of HIV among injection drug users is pre-exposure or post-exposure prophylaxis, that is, treating HIV negative drug users previous to or after they share injection equipment or paraphernalia (e.g., cotton, water) with a drug user who is HIV positive or whose HIV status is unknown.[37,38]

7. Perinatal transmission. The prevention of HIV transmission to an infant by testing and identifying HIV-infected pregnant women by treating all those who are HIV-infected is an important strategy that has been introduced in the last few years. It is recommended that once antiretroviral therapy is begun, it should be continued. Also, it is critical that the viral load be monitored regularly to document that it has decreased to very low or undetectable levels to avoid transmission to the infant and to maintain the mother's health. Failure of therapy can occur among women who are non-adherent to therapy or those infected with a virus that is resistant to the drug being given. In the latter instance the therapy should be changed. However, if the virus found does not decrease adequately on antiretroviral therapy, the woman should not breastfeed her infant, because HIV can be transmitted through breast milk.[39]

8. Transfusion transmissions. The transmission of HIV by the transfusion of infected blood is very efficient. In the early 1980s, prior to the identification of HIV and the possibility of screening donors, an estimated 2,145 transmissions likely occurred in San Francisco prior to exclusion of high-risk donors, who commonly donated blood because their male sex partner was ill with AIDS. This risk is still a problem in some low-income countries in sub-Saharan Africa, where family members are recruited to locate blood to be administered to an AIDS patient. However, the risk of transfusion transmission of HIV has been markedly reduced with the development and availability of rapid tests to detect infected donors.[40] All blood donors in high-income and many middle-income countries are screened currently with tests to detect HIV RNA, to exclude donors who are in the seronegative window period during early infection, as well as sensitive HIV antibody tests. The rate of a false negative donor has declined from about 1 in 50,000 to 100,000 donors when screening donors only with the first-generation antibody tests to about 1 in 4,500,000 donors screened with currently available nucleic acid amplification tests plus antibody tests.[41] Another important public health procedure to exclude potential infected blood donors is risk factor screening and excluding any donors who have injected drugs or had high-risk sex and exposures, especially male-to-male sex. Screening and exclusion of high-risk donors is more difficult in Africa, since the epidemic is predominantly heterosexual and it is therefore more difficult to identify those at high risk of exposure on a questionnaire.[42]

RESPONSES TO THE HIV/AIDS PANDEMIC

While the global spread of HIV/AIDS during the past thirty years has been extensive and somewhat surprising, given the type of contact necessary for transmission, the international response to control this pandemic has been unprecedented in relation to any other disease. Soon after the disease was recognized among homosexual men, AIDS was reported among other populations, including persons with hemophilia, injection drug users, and transfusion recipients. Some of the public reacted negatively, believing that AIDS was "divine retribution" for sinful sexual behavior among homosexuals following an era of greater sexual freedom. However, other segments of the population were horrified at the evolution and spread of this new disease. Members of the devastated male homosexual community in the United States became involved in effective political activities. The public health community quickly recognized that this new disease was a threat to national stability that had to be confronted. In 1988, U.S. Surgeon General Dr. C. Everett Koop (in office 1982–1989) spearheaded an effort to educate the public about AIDS. Congress appropriated nearly $25 million authorizing legislation for the Centers for Disease Control and Prevention (CDC) to create a pamphlet on the newly recognized disease and then mail the brochure, *Understanding AIDS,* to every U.S. household. *Understanding AIDS* became an essential tool to combat the stigma and prejudice associated with AIDS among homosexual men, injection drug users, and other populations. It also signaled a new willingness to publicly discuss sexual behavior, which eventually led to the public's current familiarity with terms such as *safe sex* and *unprotected sex.*

The Ryan White Act

In 1990, another milestone dealing with the increasing numbers and diversity of AIDS patients in the United States occurred when President George H.W. Bush (1989–1993) signed the Ryan White Care Act, named after a young boy in Indiana with hemophilia who had contracted HIV infection through a blood transfusion. After White's Indiana school district excluded him from school because he was HIV-infected, he sued and won his court case against the district. The federal legislation provided funds to provide services to patients with HIV who have exhausted other sources of medical care.

United Nations General Assembly Special Session on AIDS

From June 25 to June 27, 2005, the UN General Assembly held its first special session devoted to coping with the effects of a single disease. At this session, governments from 189 countries committed themselves to a comprehensive program of international and national action to fight the HIV/AIDS pandemic by adopting the Declaration of Commitment on HIV/AIDS.[43] The declaration included a pledge on the part of the UN General Assembly that would devote at least one full day annually to reviewing the joint UN program on HIV/AIDS (UNAIDS). This meeting was followed by the establishment of the Global Fund to Combat HIV, Tuberculosis and Malaria, the three major lethal epidemic diseases affecting less developed countries. Developed countries pledged to support the activities of UNAIDS through contributions to the Global Fund, and developing countries experiencing significant problems with these three diseases could apply for funding to combat them.

Emerging Infections Secondary to HIV Infections

Because HIV infection targets critical cells of the human immune system, it impedes the normal protective response to many other pathogens. After an average duration of HIV infection of seven to ten years, an untreated patient develops AIDS, which is classified as a CD4 cell count of lower than two hundred cells per cubic millimeter or the occurrence of a clinical AIDS-defining condition. The CDC lists twenty-eight clinical characteristics that define the diagnosis of AIDS in addition to the low CD4 cell count, which in some patients may be accompanied only by nonspecific symptoms, such as fatigue, malaise, recurrent fever, and/or wasting.

POLITICS AND HEALTH CARE POLICY

The President's Emergency Plan for AIDS Relief

A major boost to the global effort to control the AIDS pandemic occurred in January 2003, when President George W. Bush (2001–2009) announced in his State of the Union Address the intention of the U.S. government to initiate the President's Emergency Plan for AIDS Relief (PEPFAR) with funding of $15 billion for the next five years. PEPFAR is administered through the Office of the Global AIDS Coordinator (OGAC). The head of OGAC has ambassador status, facilitating access to world leaders in all countries. Initially, the PEPFAR program focused on reducing the sexual transmission of HIV in fifteen of the worst affected countries. In May 2009, President Barack Obama (2009–) announced his administration's intention to provide $48 billion to support PEPFAR for the next six years.

The global effort to control the AIDS pandemic has truly been a groundbreaking effort. It has been estimated that PEPFAR and the Global Fund have averted 1.1 million deaths in developing countries and reduced the overall death rate by 10 percent in low-income countries heavily affected by AIDS. It has also given birth to the discipline of *global health.* Nearly every major educational institution in the developing world now has a focus on global health. Such a focus is critically needed in the closely connected global environment of the twenty-first century.

SOURCES: http://georgewbush-whitehouse.archives.gov/infocus/hivaids.

Various opportunistic infections occur commonly at different stages in the natural history of untreated HIV infection. Often, the first infection to appear is oral thrush. Also, genital or oral herpes is an early sign of immunocompromise from an HIV infection. Tuberculosis and esophageal candidiasis often occur at relatively higher CD4 cell counts, prior to a decline to a CD4 cell count below two hundred cells/µl. The global AIDS epidemic was one of the earliest events that promoted the emergence of several new human pathogens and the resurgence of many serious infections that were previously controlled, at least in economically advanced Western countries. The fact that populations in the United States and other high-income countries were heavily affected by the HIV/AIDS epidemic in the 1980s and 1990s was critical in provoking a coordinated global effort to control the pandemic.

Tuberculosis

Tuberculosis (TB) is the most important AIDS-related infection globally. Previous methods to control TB were compromised by the AIDS epidemic. Tuberculosis has become the most common AIDS-defining illness and the most common cause of AIDS mortality in sub-Saharan Africa. The risk of clinical tuberculosis after an acute TB infection is only about 5 to 10 percent in a person with an uncompromised immune system, and the lifetime risk of reactivation is only about 10 percent. However, among patients who are HIV-infected, an acute TB infection is often clinically progressive or disseminated. Among patients who control the initial TB infection, reactivation commonly occurs when the HIV infection progresses to further compromise the immune system. Also, the laboratory diagnosis of tuberculosis may be impeded in HIV-positive patients, since the inflammatory response less frequently results in cavitary lesions in the lungs with the production by the patient of sputum, which can be examined microscopically and cultured. In addition, the treatment of patients who are co-infected with tuberculosis and HIV is challenging. When patients are given effective antiretroviral drugs, the potential for a more effective immune response is restored. If the patient has latent tuberculosis on an inactive disseminated infection, treatment of HIV can lead to immune reconstitution inflammatory syndrome (IRIS). Because death from disseminated or extensive pulmonary tuberculosis can occur more quickly than with HIV/AIDS if untreated and a severe IRIS reaction can be fatal, clinicians questioned whether HIV/AIDS therapy should be delayed until the tuberculosis can be controlled. However, this strategy places the patients at risk of mortality from AIDS due to delayed antiretroviral therapy while the tuberculosis is being treated. The question of when to initiate therapy for HIV and TB was answered by a clinical trial in South Africa in which patients were randomized to early HIV treatment after

treatment of tuberculosis was under some control or delay of the antiretroviral therapy until the tuberculosis infection had been controlled.

Earlier treatment of an HIV infection (e.g., four to six weeks after instituting treatment of tuberculosis in co-infected patients) was associated with 56 percent lower mortality.[44] Thirty patients who developed IRIS reactions from early therapy were treated with steroids to control their reactions.

Pneumocystis carinii pneumonia

In the United States and Western Europe, the most common clinical presentation of AIDS in HIV-infected men who have sex with men was Pneumocystis carinii pneumonia (PCP). Before the AIDS epidemic, PCP was very rare and only reported in a few patients with congenital immune deficiency syndrome and immune compromises from cancers involving the immune system. When PCP occurred in an HIV-infected patient the CD4 cell count was nearly always below two hundred cells/µl. Because the organism is generally susceptible to antibiotics, especially trimethoprim sulfamethoxisole (bactrim), prophylaxis of HIV-infected persons with the drug is recommended. The organism has been studied by biologists and reclassified as a fungus. Although the organism has been renamed Pneumocystis jirovici, the clinical syndrome is still usually called PCP.

Cryptococcus neoformans

Disseminated infections, especially meningitis, from infection with the globally present fungal pathogen Cryptococcus neoformans are very common among patients with AIDS. In fact, substantial increases in patients presenting to health centers in Africa with Cryptococcus neoformans was seen early in the AIDS epidemic in the region.

Penicillium marneffei

One of the most dramatic examples of the emergence of infection from a regionally localized human pathogen affecting AIDS patients was the epidemic of Penicillium marneffei infections in Southeast Asia. P. marneffei infections in AIDS patients were especially common in northern Thailand, Vietnam, and southern China. After the HIV/AIDS epidemic spread in Thailand in the 1990s, disseminated P. marneffei emerged from a dozen or so cases reported in the world's literature from the original identification of the organism in a splenic abscess of a missionary in Vietnam in 1959 to hundreds of cases between 1990 and 1996 to become the most common AIDS-defining, opportunistic infections at Chiang Mai University hospital in Northern Thailand.[45,46] P. marneffei infections were much less common in central and southern Thailand. However, when the AIDS epidemic emerged later among injection drug users in Vietnam, disseminated P. marneffei infections became an extremely common AIDS-defining infection.

The environmental reservoir for P. marneffei, like several other human fungal pathogens, is likely soil. However, bamboo rats have been found to commonly have disseminated P. marneffei infections, probably because they burrow in the soil to create nests and feed. Similar to other dimorphic fungal pathogens, P. marneffei is acquired by humans from inhaling the aerosolized conidia from the infectious mold in the environment. The yeast that causes human infections is not transmittable from person to person. Although patients with HIV/AIDS are at increased risk of disseminated infections from several fungal pathogens, they are not a reservoir for transmission to other persons. In this way, they are a contrast to other AIDS-related infections, such as tuberculosis, herpes simplex virus (HSV-2, HSV-1) and several sexually transmitted pathogens, which increase the risk of exposure to other HIV-infected and non-infected persons.

Kaposi's Sarcoma

Another AIDS-defining illness that unexpectedly blossomed among patients with HIV infection early in the epidemic was Kaposi's sarcoma (KS). Prior to that time KS was endemic in a few southern Mediterranean and central and east African countries. It was believed to be a slowly growing tumor of peripheral vascular tissue that in some patients involved deeper structures and could lead to mortality. Why it occurred frequently among patients with HIV was a mystery. Then in 1994 Chang and Moore succeeding in identifying the genetic sequences of a previously undescribed herpes virus, HHV-8, from KS tissues. Subsequent studies have documented that all KS tissues contain the causative virus. The virus is carried in the upper respiratory tract and transmitted from person to person by inhalation of virus-infected respiratory secretions. However, there is a human genetic predisposition to develop KS after HHV-8 infection in addition to the increased risk associated with HIV immunosuppression. KS is also seen in patients with other immunocompromised conditions, such as after an organ or marrow transplant or with certain immunological malignances.

Mycobacterium avium Complex Infections

Patients with HIV/AIDS are at increased risk of infections with some non-tuberculosis mycobacteria, especially Mycobacterium avium Complex (MAC) organisms. These organisms are common in the environment, but persons with intact immunity are very rarely infected. However, HIV-infected patients commonly develop persistent MAC infections early after an HIV infection. Therefore, diagnosis of a MAC infection is an early sign that an HIV infection could be compromising the immune system.

Other AIDS-related Infections

Numerous other human pathogens have emerged as a result of immune compromise from AIDS infections. In fact, the natural history and severity of infections with most pathogens is worse in patients with HIV infection. Clearly, the chronic progressive course of HIV with the severe immune deterioration that usually occurs in an untreated patient with HIV/AIDS has revolutionized the medical and public health focus on infectious diseases and their treatment and prevention.

EMERGENCE OF INFECTIOUS DISEASES UNRELATED TO THE HIV/AIDS PANDEMIC

Although the HIV/AIDS pandemic has been directly responsible for the emergence of some new infectious diseases, several other serious infectious diseases have emerged due to other factors involving human activities and interactions with other humans, animals, and the environment.

Factors Promoting the Emergence of Infectious Diseases

Many factors are involved either individually or in combination in promoting the emergence of infectious diseases. These are the most important:

- Population growth and increased crowding
- Speed and ease of travel
- Increases in human contact with animals
- Genetic mutations of pathogens
- Changes in the food industry
- Antibiotic use and abuse
- Building of large dams
- Expansion of human populations into previously uninhabited forested and suburban areas
- Global climate change
- War and social disruption
- Changes in the susceptible population, including day care, nursing homes, and increase in the populations of immune-compromised patients, such as persons receiving treatment for cancer or after an organ or bone marrow transplant
- Bioterrorism

Severe Acute Respiratory Syndrome (SARS)

In November 2002, an outbreak of an unusually severe acute respiratory infectious disease occurred in rural Guangdong Province in southeastern China. Initially, public health officials at WHO and in China were concerned that a new highly lethal strain of influenza virus had emerged. In January 2003, cases with similar symptoms were reported in patients in Beijing, the capital city. However, the diagnosis of the infecting pathogen was unclear. On February 21, 2003, a sixty-five-year-old physician checked into a hotel in Hong Kong. He had been ill for six days with respiratory symptoms; the following day, his illness became worse and he was hospitalized. He had a severe cough with vomiting but had not shared a hotel room with anyone. In the next couple of weeks, cases of the mysterious illness were reported in many other countries that were visited by transient guests at the hotel on the same days as the index case. Several large outbreaks occurred in Hong Kong, including 330 cases among residents of a large apartment complex, the Amoy Gardens, caused by an aerosol traveling up the elevator shaft of a multistory building. Large outbreaks occurred in Beijing, Hanoi, Bangkok, Toronto, Taipei, and Hong Kong. Eventually, 8,450 cases of the disease occurred, resulting in 850 deaths. Massive public health efforts were initiated by some countries to control the spread of SARS, including quarantining 131,132 persons in Taiwan. The Chinese government rapidly constructed a new hospital in Beijing to isolate and care for SARS patients and quarantined 30,000 exposed persons in their homes. These traditional infection control measures of isolating infectious cases and quarantining exposed contacts were quite effective. Several epidemiological characteristics of SARS were critical in the success of the public health intervention:

- SARS had a fairly long incubation period of about twelve days.
- Most important, the SARS coronavirus spread only from symptomatic patients, not during the incubation period.
- There were very few, if any, asymptomatic infected subjects who could spread the infection.
- The general public was very compliant with the public health intervention.

No human cases of SARS have occurred in the last ten years, because the SARS epidemic has been controlled. In fact, researchers found bats in China to be infected with SARS. During the epidemic, SARS coronavirus infection was acquired by consuming Civet cats, a local delicacy in rural Guangdong Province, which also commonly carried the virus.

MERS CoV

Recently, another coronavirus was identified in persons in Saudi Arabia. One-hundred fifty-eight human cases of infection with Middle East respiratory virus coronavirus (MERS CoV) have been reported, with 30 percent mortality from Saudi Arabia and five other countries. MERS CoV was transmitted less efficiently than the SARS virus. Several small clusters of infection occurred, but transmission between humans eventually stopped. The Ro (the number of susceptible persons acquiring the infection from a case) has been estimated at 0.8, meaning less than one person on average has acquired the infection from an index case. This low Ro, if it is accurate, suggests that there will not be a

global epidemic from MERS CoV as there was from SARS. The Ro for SARS was 2.4, therefore a large epidemic ensued.

West Nile Virus

West Nile Virus (WNV) is a flavivirus that was first isolated in 1937 from the blood of a febrile patient in the West Nile district of northern Uganda. Outbreaks of WNV infection were reported in the 1960s in Egypt and France and in the 1970s in Israel, France, the Soviet Union, South Africa, and Romania. Studies during the outbreak found that birds were the reservoir and amplifying host and that infections in humans, horses, and birds were spread by mosquitoes.

In 1999, six patients with acute encephalitis were diagnosed in Queens, New York. Near the same time, deaths were reported in several bird species in the Bronx Zoo. The organism responsible for both the human cases and the bird deaths was identified as WNV, and these were the first such infections in the Western Hemisphere. During the next several years, outbreaks of WNV encephalitis or febrile illnesses spread from the original focus in New York to include persons in every state during the summer transmission season from June to October.

Between 1999 and 2001, WNV became the most frequent cause of reported neuroinvasive arboviral disease in the United States. Fatal WNV infections were most frequently reported among persons over fifty years old. However, only about 20 percent of WNV infections were symptomatic, and only about 2 percent caused the neurological disease. Although Culex species mosquitoes are the major vectors of WNV, the virus can be spread by a wide range of mosquitoes, a factor possibly important in the recurring seasonal outbreaks.

Genetic analysis of WNV from New York found the virus to be nearly identical to viruses from Israel. How the virus was transported from Israel to New York is unknown. It is very unlikely that the virus was brought by an infected person because the level of virus in humans is usually too low to infect mosquitoes. Could an infected bird or mosquito have transported WNV on a plane or a ship? We will never know. However, an important lesson from this outbreak is that human pathogens do not respect national borders. In addition, international travel is very efficient not only for people but also for animals and mosquitoes.

Dengue

Dengue is another very important mosquito-borne viral infection that has expanded in recent years. It has been estimated that more than one hundred million cases occur each year worldwide. The symptoms of dengue, dengue hemorrhagic fever, and dengue shock syndrome were first described in Southeast Asia in 1954, and clinically serious dengue infections have gradually spread worldwide. This more severe form of dengue is associated with a mortality rate of

5 to 15 percent. Dengue was first reported in the Western Hemisphere in 1981, when an outbreak of dengue 2 occurred in Cuba. Since then, very large outbreaks have occurred in several countries in South America and the Caribbean region. Recently, several cases occurred among residents of southern Florida. The dengue viruses are transmitted by Aedes aegypti mosquitoes, which are found worldwide in tropical and subtropical areas. However, Aedes albopictus mosquitoes are also a competent vector for the transmission of dengue and are found in the more temperate climates in the United States.

Influenza

Recurrent seasonal and year-round epidemics of influenza occur regularly in populations throughout the world. The reason for recurrent epidemics is related to the genetic instability of influenza viruses and the often weak immune responses to infection among humans.

However, occasionally influenza viruses can recombine their genome in animals by tracking gene segments to create a completely new virus to which humans are totally susceptible. When this occurs the new influenza virus can cause a pandemic, spreading worldwide and causing high morbidity and mortality in populations everywhere. The most severe pandemic occurred in 1918 with the emergence of the H1N1 swine influenza pandemic, which killed more than one hundred million persons worldwide. The H1N1 virus persisted until the late 1950s. It was replaced by the Asian H2N2 influenza virus in 1957, which caused another pandemic. In 1968, another new influenza virus emerged. The Hong Kong strain, which has acquired some gene segments from birds and swine, a "triple reassortant" virus, spread globally to cause a moderately severe pandemic.

In the last few years, persons having direct contact with infected poultry have developed severe influenza with high mortality from an H5N1 recombination virus. Another recombination H7N9 virus has been identified recently to cause very severe influenza among persons who have direct contact with animals such as swine or poultry. These viruses have infected more than 150 persons in small, self-limited outbreaks that have not spread further to other persons not having direct close contact with infected animals. The mortality rate among persons infected with these viral recombination influenza viruses is 15 percent for H5N1 and 30 percent for H7N9. Therefore, there is great concern among public health officials about the possibility that either of these viruses could acquire the capability of human-to-human transmission. This concern has resulted in more intense surveillance for influenza-like illnesses among persons having contact with poultry or swine and among their contacts.

The current working hypothesis developed by Robert G. Webster and his colleagues is that avian influenza strains are the source for all influenza viruses seen in birds and mammals. All of the fifteen Hemaglutiin types and nine Neuraminidase strains of influenza viruses have been isolated from avian sources. Only certain serotypes are found in humans and other mammals. Certain genetic characteristics of influenza viruses allow them to attack lung cells and invade, causing pneumonia. Other genetic properties are associated with transmission, causing epidemics.

Escherichia coli 0157:H7 and Escherichia coli 0104:H4

Escherichia coli (E. coli) are aerobic Gram negative organisms that are normal inhabitants of the colon. Most strains do not cause infection, but a few E. coli have acquired genetic characteristics that allow them to invade through the intestines and cause illness.

E. coli 0157:H7 organisms are carried in the intestinal tract of 1 to 10 percent of healthy cattle and sheep throughout the world. These organisms were first identified as the cause of severe infections in humans in 1982. Since then, they have caused both large epidemics and sporadic illness in humans. The organisms have acquired a plasmid coding for two pathogenic traits, a hemolysis and Shiga toxin. These two traits enhance the survival of the organism when ingested and allow invasion of the organism, causing bloody diarrhea. Some patients develop hemolysis and acute renal failure, the so-called hemolytic uremic syndrome (HUS), from infections with these organisms.

The organism can be acquired by food, raw milk, and water as well as by direct person-to-person spread of the organism from an infected person. Large outbreaks in the United States have been associated with consumption of inadequately cooked hamburger. In addition, some infections have been associated with other foods, such as apple juice. This product is often prepared from apples that have fallen on the ground and may have had contact with contaminated cow manure. As a result of these outbreaks, current public health recommendations include thorough cooking of hamburger and pasteurizing apple juice prior to consumption. A large epidemic from another related pathogen, E. coli 0104:H4, occurred in Germany in 2011. This outbreak included 3,222 cases, 810 of whom developed HUS. The source of this outbreak was eventually identified as bean sprouts from a single farm in Saxony.

Research has shown that a very small number of these organisms can survive passage through the acid environment of the stomach. Also, a review of forty outbreaks of E. coli 0157:H7 found 20 percent transmission from an infected person. The commonly infectious zoonotic reservoir in cattle, and other animals, and the high infectivity and virulence of the organisms for humans make prevention of outbreaks and sporadic cases quite challenging.

Food-Borne Outbreaks

Modern industrial methods of food preparation and distribution have virtually guaranteed that when a food is contaminated with an infectious dose of a human pathogen, a nationwide outbreak will occur. Recent large outbreaks caused by salmonella-contaminated peanuts and peppers are examples.

In addition, an increasing proportion of food consumed in the United States is imported. In 1997, an outbreak of 762 cases of cyclosporiasis, an intestinal parasite infection, occurred among persons in the United States and Canada who had consumed contaminated raspberries imported from Guatemala.

Epidemic of Systematic Fungal Infections from Steroid Injections

On September 18, 2012, a clinician in Tennessee reported meningitis due to Apergillus fumigatus in a patient who was receiving steroid injections to alleviate chronic low back pain. Subsequently, eight additional cases of fungal meningitis were identified in Tennessee and North Carolina. The organism involved in these cases was another fungus, Exserohilum rostatum. The steroid medications were all compounded by a pharmacy in Massachusetts. Three different lots of infected methyl-prednisolone were found to be contaminated with a variety of fungal pathogens. The pharmacy had been reported to have serious environment contamination problems and had been previously inspected by the Massachusetts authorities. This outbreak continued for another five months, and ultimately 733 patients and fifty-three deaths were reported in nineteen states. This pharmacy had compounded and sold 17,500 vials of methyl-prednisolone from the three lots that were proven to be contaminated, which had been distributed to seventy-five clinical facilities in twenty-three states.

This very large outbreak highlights the potential for serious infectious diseases related to medical care. There are an estimated 7,500 compounding pharmacies in the United States. Unlike pharmaceutical manufacturers, compounding pharmacies do not have to demonstrate the safety and efficacy of their products or adhere to manufacturing and labeling standards. They are not regulated by the Food and Drug Administration but rather by pharmacy boards and individual states.

Although the epidemic of fungal meningitis from contaminated steroid injections may be one of the most dramatic examples of emerging infections from medical care, it is certainly not the only example. Among the others are the emergence of Methicillin-resistant Staphylococcus aureus organisms as a very common cause of serious infections among hospitalized patients and those in the community. Also, Clostridium difficile infections of the gastrointestinal tract are very common following antibiotic use and may be difficult to cure. Recent studies have suggested that most C. difficile infections, which can cause chronic diarrhea, are acquired in the community, rather than in a hospital or clinic. Hepatitis C virus (HCV) infections have become epidemic following the Schistosomiasis eradication campaign in Egypt. Also, HCV infections can spread commonly in the community among injection drug users but also in medical facilities where injection equipment is not carefully sterilized. HCV infections are very common among the population of people born in the United States between 1945 and 1975, among injection drug users, and among persons who received a blood transfusion before 1992, when routine screening of blood donors was implemented. Persons with chronic HCV infections frequently are not aware they are infected because chronic HCV infections are asymptomatic until the infected person develops cirrhosis or liver cancer.

Bioterrorism

Bioterrorism, or the intentional distributions of a human pathogen, is a serious concern of public health experts and governments in the past few decades. Although the intentional use of pathogens during conflicts or for political purposes is not a new idea, the outbreak of twenty-two cases of inhalation anthrax with five deaths in September and November 2001, when thirteen envelopes containing anthrax spores were sent to various locations through the U.S. Postal Service, raised awareness about this possibility. Potential bioterrorism infectious agents have been classified according to their ability to be disseminated or transmitted, their mortality, their potential to cause panic, and the requirements for special public health preparedness to prevent disaster. Among those presenting the highest risk are plague, anthrax, tularemia, Ebola, and other viral pathogens and influenza viruses that cause high mortality, for example, H5N1 and H7N9.

GOING FORWARD: EVALUATION AND CONTROL OF NEW INFECTIOUS DISEASES

The several example of significant infectious diseases that have emerged in the United States since 1980 clearly demonstrate many of the conditions in modern life that support the emergence of new infectious disease. Many of the newly recognized human pathogens have been acquired from animals. They have been transmitted to humans in food or water; amplified by arthropods, which then transmitted them by biting; or delivered in medicines by injection or intentionally as an attack of bioterrorism. There are diverse reservoirs, vectors, and means of transmission of infection as well as many new potential human pathogens. Certainly, the emergence of new infectious diseases will continue in the future. Table 27.1 shows existing diseases and factors that have influenced their emergency.

Preventing Biological Weapons Proliferation and Bioterrorism

On December 9, 2009, Ellen Tauscher, the under secretary for arms control and international security, addressed the Annual Meeting of the States Parties to the Biological Weapons Convention in Geneva, Switzerland. There, she presented President Barack Obama's strategy to prevent the spread of biological weapons and bioterrorism.

The United States is confident that with your leadership [Chairman, Ambassador Marius Grinius of Canada], progress made this year on disease surveillance can translate into sustainable commitments. . . . The United States intends to implement this strategy through renewed cooperation and more thorough consultations with our international counterparts in order to prevent the misuse and abuse of science while working together to strengthen health security around the world.

When it comes to the proliferation of bio weapons and the risk of an attack, the world community faces a greater threat based on a new calculus. President Obama fully recognizes that a major biological weapons attack on one of the world's major cities could cause as much death and economic and psychological damage as a nuclear attack. . . . Our new strategy has a clear, overarching goal . . . to protect against the misuse of science to develop or use biological agents to cause harm. . . .

First, we will work with the international community to promote the peaceful and beneficial use of life sciences, in accordance with the BWC's [Biological Weapons Convention] Article Ten, to combat infectious diseases regardless of their cause. We will work to promote global health security by increasing the availability of and access to knowledge and products of the life sciences to help reduce the impact from outbreaks of infectious disease whether of natural, accidental or deliberate origin.

Second, we will work toward establishing and reinforcing norms against the misuse of the life sciences. We need to ensure a culture of responsibility, awareness, and vigilance among all who use and benefit from the life sciences to ensure that they are not diverted to harmful purpose.

Third, we will implement a coordinated approach to influence, identify, inhibit, and interdict those who seek to misuse scientific progress to harm innocent people. We will seek to obtain timely and accurate information on the full spectrum of threats and challenges. This information will allow us to take appropriate actions to manage the evolving risk.

Finally, and most relevant to this body, we want to reinvigorate the Biological Weapons Convention as the premier forum for global outreach and coordination. The Biological Weapons Convention embodies the international community's determination to prevent the misuse of biological materials as weapons. But it takes the active efforts of its States Parties—individually, and collectively—to uphold these commitments that continue to bolster the BWC as a key international norm."

SOURCE: U.S. Department of State, "Preventing Biological Weapons Proliferation and Bioterrorism," http://www.state.gov/t/us/133335.htm.

TABLE 27.1 **Factors in the Emergence of Infectious Diseases**

Disease	Factors Promoting Emergence	Disease	Factors Promoting Emergence
SARS	Human contact with exotic animals (civet cats); international travel	Hantavirus sin Nombre Virus (HPS)	Climate changes allowing expansion of the mice reservoir due to a larger supply of Pinon nuts (i.e., mouse food)
Monkey pox	Human contact with exotic animals, animal contact	Rift Valley Fever	Dams, irrigation, climate change
Anthrax	Bioterrorism	Filoviridae Species Ebola-Marburg virus	Increased contact between infected primates and humans; nosocomial spread; importation of animals
Arenaviruses	Changes in agriculture allowing closer contact with infected rodents		
Junin virus (Argentine hemorrhagic fever [HF])	Arena virus #1	Dengue	Increased global travel; urbanization; increased mosquito reservoir in urban areas
Machupo virus (Bolivian HF)	Arena virus #2	Influenza	Integrated pig-duck agriculture in Asia; increased global travel
Guanarito virus (Venezuelan HF)	Arena virus #3	HIV/(AIDS) HTLV	Changes in sexual behavior; urbanization, increased illicit drug use; global shipment of blood products

Disease	Factors Promoting Emergence
Raccoon rabies	Shipment of infected raccoons
Cyclospora cayetanensis	International shipment of raspberries from Guatemala
Cholera	El Niño climate change; international travel; shipment of foods
Borrelia burgdorferi (Lyme disease)	Increased deer population; increased human contact with ticks in nature from increase in suburban populations
Malaria	Growth and movement of human populations; declining use and effectiveness of insecticides; crowding
Escherichia coli (E. coli) 0157:H7	Growth of centralized agriculture promoting cross-contamination; global distribution of foods
Pfisteria pisticida	Changes in agricultural practices leading to pollution of rivers and estuaries; overgrowth of dinoflagellates

Disease	Factors Promoting Emergence
Campylobacter	Overuse and misuse of antibiotics in agriculture and in clinical settings
TB/Drug-resistant TB	Misuse of antibiotics; crowding in prisons, slums, hospitals, etc., allowing transmission
Cryptosporidium parvum	Contamination of municipal water supplies; increases in immunocompromised populations
Gram Negatives with NDMA (New Delhi Metallo-beta lactamase)	Antibiotic use/misuse; contaminated water in Asia
Hepatitis E	Contaminated drinking water; infected pork; deer
E. coli 0104:H4	Infected bean sprouts in Germany
Severe Fever Thrombocytopenia Syndrome (China)	Tick exposure in China
Heartland disease (USA)	Tick exposure in the United States

When new infectious diseases appear, the first step in their control is recognition that a new disease has appeared through the use of effective surveillance. Then a case definition needs to be developed so a case of the newly emerging infections can be evaluated. The evaluation initially must include the defining of two important characteristics:

- How is the disease acquired?
  - By contact
  - Airborne
  - By food or water ingestion
  - By a vector (e.g., mosquito, tick, snail)

- What is the reservoir?
  - Humans
  - Animals
  - Water (environment)
  - Soil (environment)

Then, efforts should be made to identify a pathogen, using culture, microscopy, or electron microscopy amplification of genetic material and other methods. Clearly, effective surveillance is the critical first step. When adequate surveillance is missing, control of mortality for infectious disease is unlikely to be possible. Governmental policies that provide insufficient resources for public health surveillance, investigation, and control of newly emerging infectious disease have been shown on numerous occasions to result in unexpected and needless increases in morbidity and mortality.

See also **Chapter 23: Fifty Years of Progress in Disease and Injury Prevention (1950s–Present); Chapter 28: Emergency Preparedness: Bioterrorism, Armed Conflict, Natural Disasters, and Other Public Health Threats (2000s–Present); Chapter 29: Twenty-first-Century Challenges to Health and Health Care: Noncommunicable Diseases, Environmental Threats, and Human Rights (2000s–Present); Chapter 30: The Governance of Population Health: Reflections on the Analytical Approaches of Contributors to the *Guide*.**

NOTES

1. Feng Gao et al., "Origin of HIV-1 in the Chimpanzee, Pan Troglodytes," *Nature* 197 (1999): 436–441.
2. Jacques Pepin, *The Origins of AIDS* (Cambridge, UK: Cambridge University Press, 2011).
3. A.J. Nahmias et al., "Evidence for Human Infection with an HTLV/LAV-like Virus in Central Africa in 1959," *Lancet* 327: 8492 (1986): 1279–1280.
4. V.M. Hirsch et al., "An African Primate Lentivirus (SIV(sm)) Closely Related to HIV-2," *Nature* 339 (1989): 389–392.

5. Richard Marlink et al., "Reduced Rate of Disease Development after HIV-2 Infection as Compared to HIV-1," *Science* 256 (1994): 1587–1590.

6. UNAIDS/World Health Organization, *AIDS Epidemic Update* (Geneva, Switzerland: UNAIDS/World Health Organization, December 2013).

7. Ibid.

8. Ibid.

9. Pepin, *The Origins of AIDS*; Victoria R. Harden, *AIDS at 30: A History* (Dulles, VA: Potomac Books, 2012).

10. UNAIDS/World Health Organization, *AIDS Epidemic Update.*

11. Ibid.

12. Kenrad E. Nelson et al., "Sex and Behavior and a Decline in HIV Infection among Young Men in Thailand," *New England Journal of Medicine* 335 (1996): 297–303.

13. Wiwat Rojanapithayakorn and Robert Hanenberg, "The 100% Condom Program in Thailand," *AIDS* 10 (1996): 1–7.

14. Yen-Fang Huang et al., "HIV Incidence among People Who Inject Drugs in Taiwan Following Introduction of a Harm Reduction Program: A Study of Two Cohorts," *PLoS Medicine* 11: 4 (2014): e1001625.

15. Harden, *AIDS at 30.*

16. UNAIDS/World Health Organization, *AIDS Epidemic Update.*

17. Yuriy V. Kruglov et al., "The Most Severe HIV Epidemic in Europe: Ukraine's National HIV Prevalence Estimates for 2007," *Sexually Transmitted Infections* 84 (2008): i37–i41.

18. UNAIDS/World Health Organization, *AIDS Epidemic Update.*

19. Ibid.

20. Ibid.

21. Ibid.

22. Ibid.

23. Ibid.

24. Harden, *AIDS at 30.*

25. Maria J. Wawer et al., "Rates of HIV-1 Transmission per Coital Act by Stage of HIV-1 Infection, in Rakai, Uganda," *Journal of Infectious Diseases* 189 (2004): 1785–1792.

26. Rachel A. Royce et al., "Sexual Transmission of HIV," *New England Journal of Medicine* 336 (1997): 1072–1078.

27. Susan C. Weller and Karen Davis, "Condom Effectiveness in Reducing Heterosexual HIV Transmission," *Cochrane Database of Systematic Reviews* 1 (2002): CD003215.

28. Ronald H. Gray et al., "Male Circumcision for HIV Prevention in Men in Rakai, Uganda: A Randomized Trial," *Lancet* 369 (2007): 657–666.

29. Robert C. Bailey et al., "Male Circumcision for HIV Prevention in Young Men in Kisumo, Kenya: A Randomized Controlled Trial," *Lancet* 369 (2007): 645–656.

30. Bertran Auvert et al., "Randomized Control Intervention Trial of Male Circumcision for Reduction of HIV Infection Risk: The ANRS 1265 Trial," *PLOS Medicine* 2 (2005): e298.

31. Gita Ramjee, Anatoli Kamali, and Sheena McCormack," "The Last Decade of Microbicide Clinical Trials in Africa: From Hypothesis to Facts," *AIDS* 24: Suppl 4 (2010): 590–594.

32. Heather Bradley et al., "Seroprevalence of Herpes Simplex Virus Types 1 and 2—United States, 1999–2010," *Journal of Infectious Diseases* 209 (2014): 325–333.

33. Myron S. Cohen et al., "Prevention of HIV-1 Infection with Early Antiretroviral Therapy," *New England Journal of Medicine* 365 (2011): 493–505.

34. John G. Bartlett et al., "Opt-Out Testing for Human Immunodeficiency Virus in the United States: Progress and Challenges," *Journal of the American Medical Association* 200 (2008): 945–951.

35. United Nations, "Declaration of Commitment on HIV/AIDS—Global Crisis, Global Action," http://www.un.org/gq/aids/coverage/finaldeclarationHIV/AIDS.html.

36. Erik J. C. Van Amerijden et al., "The Harm Reduction Approach and Risk Factors for Human Immunodeficiency Virus (HIV) Seroconversion in Injecting Drug Users, Amsterdam," *American Journal of Epidemiology* 136 (1991): 236–243.

37. Robert M. Grant et al., "Pre-exposure Chemoprophylaxis for HIV Prevention in Men Who Have Sex with Men," *New England Journal of Medicine* 364 (2010): 1370–1375.

38. Jared M. Baeton et al., "Antiretroviral Prophylaxis for HIV Prevention in Heterosexual Men and Women," *New England Journal of Medicine* 367 (2012): 399–410.

39. Stefan Z. Wiktor, Ehounou Ekpeni, and Ruth W. Nduati, "Prevention of Mother-to-Child Transmission of HIV-1 in Africa," *AIDS* 11: Suppl B (1997): S79–S87.

40. Michael P. Busch et al., "Factors Influencing Human Immunodeficiency Virus Type 1 Transmission by Blood Transfusion," *Journal of Infectious Diseases* 174 (1996): 26–33.

41. Roger Dodd, Edward P. Notari, and Susan L. Stramer, "Current Prevalence and Incidence of Infectious Disease Markers and Estimated Window-Period Risk in the American Red Cross Blood Donor Population," *Transfusion* 42 (2002): 975–979.

42. Ibid.

43. United Nations, "Declaration of Commitment on HIV/AIDS."

44. Salim S. Abdool Karim et al., "Integration of Antiretroviral Therapy with Tuberculosis Treatment," *New England Journal of Medicine* 365: 16 (2011): 1492–1501.

45. Khuanchai Supparatpinyo et al., "Disseminated Penicillium marneffei Infection in Southeast Asia," *Lancet* 344 (1994): 110–113.

46. Suwat Chariyalertsak et al., "Clinical Presentation and Risk Behaviors of Patients with Acquired Immunodeficiency Syndrome in Thailand, 1994–1998: Regional Variation and Temporal Trends," *Clinical Infectious Diseases* 32 (2001): 955–962.

FURTHER READING

Centers for Disease Control and Prevention. *Emerging Infectious Diseases.* (A public access journal published monthly)

Heymann, David. *Control of Communicable Diseases Manual.* Washington, DC: American Public Health Association, 2008.

Nelson, Kenrad E., and Carolyn Williams. *Infectious Disease Epidemiology*, 3rd ed. Burlington, MA: Bartlett Learning, 2013.

chapter 28

Emergency Preparedness

Bioterrorism, Armed Conflict, Natural Disasters, and Other Public Health Threats (2000s–Present)

Lance Gable

T HE EVENTS OF THE FIRST DOZEN YEARS OF the twenty-first century have reaffirmed the long-standing reality that emergencies and disasters can arise suddenly to threaten the health, well-being, and security of people in the United States and throughout the world. Sudden and extraordinary threats to life and health—whether arising from infectious diseases, natural disasters, bioterrorism, armed conflict, environmental contamination, or other circumstances—have repeatedly challenged our communities, institutions, and governments.

The significant public health emergencies of the past fifteen years have spurred a substantial expansion and reorganization of laws, policies, and institutions related to emergency preparedness at all levels of government and have prompted efforts to increase the preparation, emergency response capacity, and systemic resiliency across all sectors of society. These changes in turn have led to the development of new infrastructure supporting public health preparedness and homeland security, concepts largely unknown to the general population before 2001.

The impetus for these major changes in law and policy related to emergency preparedness came from two precipitating events of great political and social magnitude: the September 11, 2001, terrorist attacks on New York, Washington, D.C., and Somerset County, Pennsylvania, and Hurricane Katrina, which struck New Orleans and the Gulf Coast of the United States in August 2005. Each of these events provided a window into the vulnerabilities of the nation's emergency response systems and infrastructure and catalyzed efforts to reorient how to prepare for and respond to large-scale emergencies that have public health implications. These two events similarly triggered a wave of law and policy changes that continues to unfold up to the present day and whose impact on long-term emergency preparedness and public health remains unclear. Notably, both the

September 11, 2001, attacks and Hurricane Katrina serve as reminders that governance failures can undermine emergency preparedness and response and may even worsen the severity of the emergency and its health impact.

The sections that follow outline the substantial efforts that government, the health care system, and other institutions have taken to confront these challenges and prepare for public health emergencies. Over the past dozen years or so, these efforts have been at the forefront of discussions of law, public policy, and public health. Emergency preparedness efforts have prompted new laws, major changes to the design of health systems, and the establishment of major new federal and state government bureaucracy. Moreover, these systemic changes have altered the legal, policy, and institutional landscapes surrounding emergency preparedness and, in the process, generated a robust debate about the appropriate role of government and private sector institutions in avoiding, preparing for, and responding to public health emergencies. This debate over governance animates the current discourse about emergency preparedness nearly as much as discussions of logistical or practical considerations.

DEFINING EMERGENCY PREPAREDNESS IN A HISTORICAL CONTEXT

The terms *emergency, public health emergency, disaster, crisis,* and *catastrophe* are often used interchangeably. Indeed, these words contain considerable overlap in context and conception. Each of these terms denotes a situation in which circumstances have arisen that create a significant risk to the lives and health of the population. Particularly concerning are public health emergencies, significant threats to the health of the population that due to their "scale, timing, or unpredictability threaten to overwhelm routine capabilities."[1] The Model State Emergency Health

Powers Act defines public health emergencies according to their characteristics and causes:

> [A]n occurrence or imminent threat of an illness or health condition that: (1) is believed to be caused by any of the following: (i) bioterrorism; (ii) the appearance of a novel or previously controlled or eradicated infectious agent or biological toxin; (iii) a natural disaster; (iv) a chemical attack or accidental release; or (v) a nuclear attack or accident; and (2) poses a high probability of any of the following harms: (i) a large number of deaths in the affected population; (ii) a large number of serious or long-term disabilities in the affected population; or (iii) widespread exposure to an infectious or toxic agent that poses a significant risk of substantial future harm to a large number of people in the affected population.[2]

The nature and scope of public health emergencies set them apart from ordinary health care challenges and obligations. Public health emergencies occur when a discrete event or sequence of events creates a threat to population health that exceeds the typical health challenges endemic to the population. As a result, public health emergencies do not give rise to perpetual conditions of risk to health; rather, they occur for a limited duration and have predictable stages of preparedness, response, mitigation, and recovery. Public health emergencies arise without advance warning in many cases, and their scope and timing often cannot be accurately predicted. Nevertheless, the general categories of public health emergencies—infectious disease pandemics, natural disasters, bioterrorism, and so on—can be predicted and planned for in advance. The characteristics of indeterminate timing, severity, scale, and duration create challenges for emergency preparedness planners who must devise flexible, adaptable, and scalable systems that can be implemented in any location on short notice. Consequently, public health emergencies require specific planning, training, and resources to adequately address these issues.[3]

Public health emergency preparedness, then, "is the capability of the public health and health care systems, communities, and individuals, to prevent, protect against, quickly respond to, and recover from health emergencies, particularly those whose scale, timing, or unpredictability threatens to overwhelm routine capabilities."[4] At the national level, Presidential Policy Directive 8: National Preparedness (PPD-8) further conceives of five core capabilities integral to the National Preparedness Goal that span a continuum of preventing threats to life and health; protecting people and assets from the greatest threats and hazards; mitigating the impact of disasters; responding quickly to save lives and property; and recovering from emergencies to restore, strengthen, and revitalize all aspects of a community.[5]

Emergencies can occur in many areas of our society and often overlap boundaries of all sorts. Threats to health in particular are notably unrestrained by political or social borders. The influenza virus does not care about the nationality of the person it infects, and in our interconnected world an infectious disease from the other side of the globe is just a plane ride away. Likewise, the effects of health emergencies intersect with other important aspects of human activity, complicating efforts to prepare and respond. It is noteworthy that the emergency preparedness efforts under PPD-8 cover not only health but also other considerations, including security, environmental, and economic concerns. Threats to security and the environment often have significant health implications and vice versa. For instance, the extensive and devastating spread of HIV/AIDS in sub-Saharan Africa has created significant threats to social stability and national security in addition to its direct toll on human health.[6] Crises in the economic system can endanger health by limiting the resources available to protect health or to prevent and respond to public health emergencies. Relatedly, impacts on population health have consequences on the economy. Thus, recognizing the interconnectedness of threats to human well-being provides a vital insight in successfully combating these threats.

A History of Preparedness in the United States

Emergency preparedness has a long history dating back to colonial times in America. Early preparedness efforts arose from nascent efforts at public health necessitated by the constant threats posed by outbreaks of infectious diseases such as smallpox, cholera, yellow fever, plague, influenza, and typhoid. Outbreaks of these diseases caused significant morbidity and mortality among residents in the American colonies and later in the early decades of the United States. Early efforts to mitigate the harm incurred by the populace from these predictable but deadly outbreaks helped to solidify the authority of early local governments, particularly in major cities such as Philadelphia, New York, and Boston. Local public health departments played a key role in coordinating the response to major outbreaks throughout the nineteenth and twentieth centuries.[7]

Over time, the rise of state-level public health departments expanded the capacity, coordination, and in many cases the professionalism of response to disease outbreaks. Massachusetts formed the first state health department in the 1860s, and other states soon followed suit. State health departments had several advantages over local governance. First, state-level departments had legal authority beyond that exercised by local health departments, which allowed for a greater deployment of efforts to protect public health. Second, state health departments had a broader mandate to address health problems across the state and to coordinate efforts to stem the spread of diseases easily spread between local jurisdictions. Both the legal powers and ability to coordinate proved helpful in addressing disease outbreaks.

While infectious diseases remained the most significant menace to public health in the nineteenth century, threats to the life and health of the population came from other sources as well. The outbreak of the Civil War (1861–1865) led to thousands of deaths in combat and many more resulting from the spread of infectious disease facilitated by armed conflict. As was the case in every armed conflict before the discovery of antibiotics, effective blood transfusions, and advanced emergency field triage techniques, many more combatants and civilians perished from infectious diseases than from the fighting itself. The ballooning populations in large cities yielded numerous threats to public health: airborne and waterborne diseases spread easily in crowded tenements,[8] and dense urban centers provided fertile kindling for large municipal fires, with New York City and Chicago sustaining widespread damage from major conflagrations in 1835 and 1871, respectively.[9]

By the dawn of the twentieth century, the rise of the germ theory, vaccinations, and the sanitary innovations championed by the Progressive movement promised to usher in a new era of better health.[10] Nevertheless, attempts to reduce the health impacts of major public health emergencies were constrained by scientific, political, and infrastructural limitations. Once again, the confluence of armed conflict and infectious disease proved to be a formidable combination. Trench warfare and poison gas claimed millions of lives in Europe during World War I (1914–1918), but the global influenza pandemic that began during the war and continued through 1920 inflicted a massive toll worldwide, with up to fifty million dead. An estimated 675,000 people in the United States succumbed to this pandemic, most within a twenty-four-week period. As the outbreak unfolded, state and local governments, hospitals, and other organizations had little success in preventing the spread of the virulent influenza strain or mitigating the harm it caused.[11] Natural disasters also took their toll during this era. The Galveston Hurricane of 1900, the San Francisco earthquake of 1906, and the 1927 flood of the Mississippi River revealed the limitations of early twentieth century response and recovery capacity. This latter event, which affected millions of people in the southern United States, marked the first time the federal government took direct action to assist with emergency response and recovery, an approach that would expand greatly over subsequent years.[12]

The onset of the Great Depression and the New Deal government reforms that followed it would fundamentally shift the role of the federal government. The recognition of greater authority in the federal government would eventually give rise to the expansive emergency preparedness infrastructure that now exists. While World War II (1939–1945) brought another round of death and illness from armed conflict and the advent of the nuclear age brought new potential threats to life and health from

nuclear weaponry and environmental contamination, other trends such as the discovery of penicillin and the rise of the environmental and civil rights movements changed U.S. society. Life expectancy increased, as did the average prosperity of Americans and their access to health care, particularly following the establishment of the Medicare and Medicaid programs in 1965. Legal recognition of individual rights and the gradual dismantling of institutionalized discrimination also positively impacted health. Americans began to see the effects of the slow but persistent epidemiological transition that had been taking place for decades due to improvements in sanitation and advances in medical and scientific technology, as infectious diseases gave way to chronic conditions as the most significant factors causing human disease and death.

Federal infrastructure related to emergency preparedness grew sporadically along with the overall post–New Deal expansion of the federal government. The 1950 Federal Disaster Assistance Program authorized the president to respond to disasters of great magnitude. The Disaster Relief Act of 1970, which expanded the federal role in disaster relief with the introduction of increased funding and federal authority to engage in efforts to mitigate disasters, was followed closely by the Disaster Relief Act of 1974, which created the process for presidential disaster declarations.[13] The Robert T. Stafford Disaster Relief and Emergency Assistance Act—enacted in 1988 and still the primary legal authority for federal emergency preparedness and response efforts—authorizes federal assistance comprising funding, supplies, personnel, and expertise to be allocated for use by state and local governments during emergencies and major disasters.[14] However, the Stafford Act does not place emergency response under government control; rather, much of the authority to act remains with state and local government officials.

The establishment of the Federal Emergency Management Agency (FEMA) by President Jimmy Carter (1977–1981) in 1979 represented the first attempt to consolidate federal preparedness functions under a single agency. The creation of FEMA coincided almost exactly with the near-meltdown at the Three Mile Island nuclear power plant in Pennsylvania, an incident that galvanized the public's attention on the dangers of nuclear power generation. FEMA's focus initially was on responding to natural disasters such as floods, hurricanes, tornadoes, and earthquakes, and human-made disasters such as nuclear or environmental contamination and civil defense. FEMA's response capacity was tested throughout the 1980s. The passage of the Stafford Act in 1988 provided a more robust mechanism for the federal government to provide economic, logistical, and technical support during emergency response efforts, and FEMA became the lead agency responsible for implementing the Stafford Act. Nevertheless, the agency received substantial criticism for its insufficient response to Hurricane Andrew, a massive Category 5 storm that caused widespread damage in Florida in 1992. During the 1990s, FEMA Director James Lee Witt (in office 1993–2001) professionalized the agency and guided it through an expansion of its resources and mission. Reforms enacted in 1993, which reoriented the agency toward preparedness and mitigation, guided responses to major incidents such as the Northridge, California, earthquake in 1994 and the bombing of the Alfred P. Murrah Building in Oklahoma City in 1995.[15] By the end of the 1990s, FEMA had expanded its scope and expertise as a vital component of a greater federal role in emergency preparedness and response.

MODERN EMERGENCY PREPAREDNESS: SEPTEMBER 11, 2001, AND THE SECURITIZATION OF EMERGENCY PREPAREDNESS

On September 11, 2001, the United States witnessed the most devastating terrorist attack the country had ever experienced and the greatest single-day loss of life on its soil as a result of a hostile attack in history. The September 11, 2001, attacks involved the hijacking of four planes by terrorists who intentionally crashed them into the World Trade Center's twin towers in New York City, the Pentagon in Northern Virginia, and a field in Pennsylvania after passengers brought down the fourth plane in a struggle with the hijackers.[16]

While the country was recovering from this terrorist attack, an unknown person mailed several envelopes containing anthrax (*Bacillus anthracis*) to media and government offices in New York, Washington, D.C., and Florida. Eighteen people who handled or were in close proximity to the envelopes contracted anthrax, and five people died as a result of their exposure. An unprecedented 33,000 people received post-exposure prophylaxis as medical and public health officials scrambled to respond to, test, and treat those exposed to anthrax and to clean up contaminated facilities. While the perpetrator of this bioterrorist event remains uncertain, the anthrax releases revealed glaring weaknesses in biopreparedness and response capacity in the United States.[17]

The Federal Response

The combination of these two events so close together in time created a strong political incentive for quick and decisive action to increase emergency preparedness. Because both the September 11, 2001, attacks and the anthrax letters were attributable to intentional actions of terrorists, the law and policy reaction focused on health, security, and law enforcement initiatives. In the tense aftermath of the attacks, the federal government moved swiftly to pass several new laws that would allow for a greater level of preparedness for

future terrorist attacks and bioterrorism as well as an expansion of federal powers in addressing these types of potential threats. Changes to law and policy focused both on expanding the capacity to deal with the health effects of bioterrorism and mass casualty terrorist attacks and on the ability to prevent and/or prosecute those who would seek to cause harm to the public intentionally. The section that follows discusses three major legislative changes at the federal level: the passage of the PATRIOT Act, the creation of the Department of Homeland Security, and the passage of the Bioterrorism and All-Hazards Preparedness Act.

The PATRIOT Act

Within days of the September 11, 2001, terrorist attacks, Congress quickly moved to enact antiterrorism bills with expanded government powers. Bipartisan coalitions of legislators in both the Senate and the House of Representatives introduced multiple bills on this topic, some of which were soon consolidated to form the USA PATRIOT Act.[18] The bill was passed with substantial support in both houses of Congress and President George W. Bush (2001–2009) signed the law on October 26, 2001. Five years later, Congress passed the USA PATRIOT Improvement and Reauthorization Act of 2005,[19] again with strong bipartisan support.

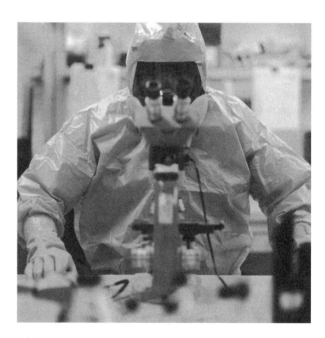

A bioterrorism specialist examines potentially contaminated spores through a microscope. Federal agencies, such as the Centers for Disease Control and Prevention, employ bioterrorism specialists to prepare for and react to emergency situations including biological agent attack, radiation and chemical emergencies, natural disasters such as hurricanes, and recent outbreaks such as the flu.

SOURCE: Ben Edwards/Stockbyte/Getty Images.

The PATRIOT Act sought to provide law enforcement and U.S. intelligence communities with enhanced tools to combat terrorism and crime both in and outside of the United States. The changes established by the PATRIOT Act can be divided into four general categories. First, the act expanded the use of electronic surveillance tools such as wiretaps that were available to investigators when investigating terrorism or potential terrorism. Second, the act facilitated cooperation and sharing of information between government agencies, alleviating barriers that had previously prevented this kind of information sharing and allowing for increased interagency cooperation. Third, the act updated U.S. law to reflect the reach of new technologies utilized in criminal activity by requiring only a single warrant to investigate suspected illegal activity, even if such activity crossed multiple jurisdictional borders. Finally, the act increased the penalties that could be imposed against those who were convicted of committing terrorism and certain crimes.[20]

The PATRIOT Act proved to be a divisive law despite its bipartisan political support. While streamlining the tools of investigation and information sharing seemed necessary to many supporters, opponents decried the law as an emblematic example of reactive government overreach and warned that these extensive government powers could be abused to circumvent legal rights.

The PATRIOT Act had two important effects on the governance of emergency preparedness. First, its surveillance tools could be used to thwart intentional attacks that posed a threat to the public's health or to facilitate rapid response and recovery through information sharing and interagency coordination. Second, the suspicion and anti-government sentiment that arose from the debate over the PATRIOT Act carried over into other legislative and policy debates about emergency preparedness. Fairly or not, subsequent efforts to expand government powers for public health emergency preparedness were deemed by some to be an extension of the PATRIOT Act, a perception that complicated the politics of these other pieces of legislation.

The Department of Homeland Security

Less than two weeks after the September 11, 2001, attacks, Pennsylvania Governor Tom Ridge (in office 1995–2001) was appointed the director of the Office of Homeland Security in the White House. The goal of the office was to oversee and coordinate a national strategy that would safeguard the United States against terrorism and properly respond to future attacks. The creation of this new office was the first step toward establishing the U.S. Department of Homeland Security (DHS). In November 2002, Congress passed the Homeland Security Act and on March 1, 2003, the department formally opened its doors as a stand-alone, cabinet-level department. The department incorporated twenty-two federal departments and agencies seeking a more effective and comprehensive homeland security effort.

The establishment of DHS heralded several major changes to the governance of public health emergencies. While preventing terrorism and enhancing national security make up the primary focus of DHS, the agency plays a key role in coordinating responses to natural disasters and other emergencies. Initially, FEMA was among the existing federal agencies placed under the umbrella of DHS. Situating FEMA within the large new federal bureaucracy of DHS was intended to achieve better efficiency and coordination across the federal government and to organize emergency preparedness and response efforts between different agencies, different levels of government, and disparate public and private actors. However, the consolidation of security and emergency preparedness agencies in a single department also generated criticism. Some longtime experts expressed concern about the increased focus on national security as a justification for emergency preparedness, noting that emergency response activities should be viewed as a component of public health rather than of national security. Some in the public health community voiced concern that this increased focus on national security would ultimately lead to a decimation of funding and support for public health programs that did not explicitly have a connection to security or emergency preparedness.[21] Other critics lamented FEMA's loss of independence. The Post-Katrina Emergency Management Reform Act of 2006 would later restore FEMA as an independent agency outside of DHS after Hurricane Katrina revealed concerns about the agency's effectiveness.

The Bioterrorism and All-Hazards Preparedness Act and Project BioShield

Congress also enacted several statutes designed specifically to prepare for and respond to bioterrorism incidents. The Public Health Security and Bioterrorism Preparedness and Response Act of 2002 (BPRA) created new federal infrastructure related to public health preparedness through the authorization of grants to states supporting capacity development for preparedness, the establishment of a high-level position in the U.S. Department of Health and Human Services (HHS) responsible for public health preparedness, the imposition of new requirements on laboratories in possession of dangerous agents, food and water security provisions, and bolstering the strategic national stockpile.[22] The Project BioShield Act of 2004 further developed federal public health emergency preparedness capacity, creating incentives for private entities to create tests and countermeasures for potentially harmful biological and chemical agents and toxins.[23] These incentives, however, did not result in a substantial increase in the private development of pharmaceutical countermeasures.[24] Nevertheless, these legislative efforts represented a shift toward much greater federal involvement in public health emergency preparedness.

The State and Local Response

State and local governments also strove to expand and enhance their emergency preparedness in the immediate aftermath of the September 11, 2001, attacks and anthrax mailings. Because state governments possess substantial police powers to address threats to public health and safety, many state legislatures reviewed and revised their legislative powers addressing disaster response and public-health emergencies. Similarly, states worked together through interstate compacts to assist each other and to share resources when needed to more effectively respond to public health emergencies and disasters.

Revisions to State Law: The Model State Emergency Health Powers Act

Even prior to September 2001, a number of ongoing efforts sought to evaluate and recalibrate public health law at the state level. Many state public health laws had become outdated and ill suited to addressing modern public health challenges. Often, these laws had evolved slowly and in a piecemeal way, resulting in a patchwork of public health powers that addressed different threats to health inconsistently and did not provide sufficient legal protections for members of the public.[25] Simultaneously, emergency preparedness experts warned of the possibility of bioterrorism using infectious agents or chemical compounds. Several planning exercises designed to test the systems that would respond to such attacks were held in the late 1990s. The "Dark Winter" exercise revealed that federal and state infrastructure and laws did not provide sufficient authority or capacity to sustain an adequate response to a large-scale bioterrorism attack.[26]

In late 2001, the Center for Law and the Public's Health, an academic center located at Georgetown and Johns Hopkins Universities, drafted a model state law designed to specify and enhance state public health emergency powers. The Model State Emergency Health Powers Act (Model Act) contained provisions that authorized state officials to plan for public health emergencies and to utilize extraordinary powers in response to emergencies under specified circumstances. Specifically, once a public health emergency had been declared, the Model Act allowed for rapid information sharing between state agencies, seizure and destruction of property that posed a continuing threat to public health, and the use of police powers to quarantine, isolate, test, or treat affected people, among other powers. The Model Act also built in procedural protections and checks and balances to ensure that state emergency powers were not employed inappropriately.[27] In addition to the Model Act provisions that addressed state powers to effectuate emergency preparedness and response, other provisions allowed the state to loosen licensing restrictions for professionals in short supply, honor reciprocity agreements with other states, and grant civil immunity to those professionals helping to respond to the emergency.

The Model Act proved to be both influential and controversial. In the first few years after it was drafted, provisions of the Model Act were adopted in dozens of states.[28] Consequently, its influence on state emergency preparedness law continues to be seen across the country. The Model Act was criticized for granting too much authority to state and local government officials and insufficiently protecting the civil liberties of individuals.[29] It also received criticism for not giving government officials enough discretion to rapidly react to public health emergencies, particularly those likely caused by the intentional actions of terrorists. Supporters of the Model Act defended its composition and the necessity of allowing additional state powers to respond to the extraordinary conditions that could occur during a public health emergency.[30]

The Emergency Management Assistance Compact

State governments possess yet another mechanism to respond to public health emergencies when they arise. All of the states have entered into the Emergency Management Assistance Compact (EMAC), an interstate compact that promises support between the states to assist with an emergency response.[31] Under EMAC, state officers or employees can travel to another state and these officers or employers will be able to assist in their professional capacities without concern about licensure or liability. EMAC provides for immunity from civil liability for EMAC volunteers and permits professional practice without an in-state license. Workers' compensation is also available to EMAC volunteers, ensuring that they have insurance coverage if they are injured during their service. The EMAC system essentially creates a network of state emergency response units that have worked out a legal framework to allow states to share resources during emergencies without complications.

In sum, the legislative and structural changes at both the federal and state levels after the September 11, 2001, attacks were substantial. Enactment of the PATRIOT Act and the BPRA and creation of the Department of Homeland Security represented an unprecedented securitization and centralization of emergency preparedness functions at the federal level, although state and local power to control emergency response activities remained a core component of the overall system. Likewise, state laws and institutions changed significantly as state and local governments moved to strengthen their ability to respond quickly to public health emergencies. The political and, perhaps even more important, economic support for emergency preparedness at the federal and state levels ballooned, and a large influx of resources flooded into

SARS and the Peril of Global Pandemics

In spring 2003, a mysterious new illness emerged from rural China. The disease caused flu-like symptoms of fever and chills, and more ominously, had a very high mortality rate. For several months, the outbreak of this disease—which would eventually be named severe acute respiratory syndrome (SARS)—was contained within China's borders and hidden from the rest of the world. Then, one infected individual traveled to Hong Kong and stayed overnight in an international hotel, in the process managing to infect dozens of others who were working and staying at that location. The detection of this new, dangerous disease that spread easily and rapidly put the entire world on high alert. Travelers who had stayed at the hotel in Hong Kong had dispersed to other places around the globe. Governments in these countries scrambled to identify people who could have been exposed and to take steps to separate them from others until their health status could be verified.

The SARS outbreak challenged the legal and medical frameworks for dealing with infectious diseases. Because SARS was a new virus in humans, no test or treatment was available and public health officials were forced to return to pre-therapeutic methods of disease control. In countries that had infected individuals, legal powers were employed to isolate those infected and quarantine those suspected of potentially being exposed to the virus. After a few cases emerged in Toronto, the Canadian government asked more than twenty thousand people to undergo a ten-day voluntary quarantine. In Hong Kong, Taiwan, and Singapore, the restrictions on individuals were even more severe, with mandatory mass quarantines being imposed on large segments of the population.

In the United States, emergency preparedness plans were implemented to screen incoming travelers from affected areas and public health officials remained on high alert to intervene should the outbreak proliferate. While the United States ultimately did not experience a significant outbreak, with fewer than one hundred SARS cases and no deaths, the threat of this new disease revealed major structural limitations in the capacity of the federal government to respond to infectious diseases. Federal quarantine powers apply to travelers entering the country and crossing state borders, but federal officials lack authority to quarantine or isolate individuals not moving between states. Since state and local officials have broader power to quarantine and isolate, federal officials would need to rely on them to take these steps if necessary. Similarly, federal law did not require SARS infections to be reported to the Centers for Disease Control and Prevention, since disease reporting is limited to specifically named diseases. President George W. Bush added SARS to the list of reportable conditions in April 2003.

Fortunately, the SARS outbreak was quickly contained thanks to aggressive surveillance, contact tracing, travel restrictions, and social separation of exposed individuals in affected countries and an unprecedented effort to identify the virus causing the disease. However, in a nine-month period, the virus infected more than eight thousand people and killed more than eight hundred. At the international level, the SARS outbreak motivated the World Health Organization to revise its International Health Regulations to build in more flexibility to respond to new diseases. In the United States, SARS served as test of the new federal public health preparedness infrastructure for responding to infectious disease that would be further challenged in the H1N1 influenza outbreak of 2009. Further, SARS affirmed the need for a strengthened emergency preparedness system and a reinforced public health infrastructure capable of handling emerging infectious diseases as well as extraordinary terrorist threats and natural disasters.

SOURCES: Mark Rothstein et al., *Quarantine and Isolation: Lessons Learned from SARS* (Atlanta, GA: Centers for Disease Control and Prevention, 2003); Lawrence O. Gostin et al., "Ethical and Legal Challenges Posed by Severe Acute Respiratory Syndrome: Implications for the Control of Severe Infectious Disease Threats," *Journal of the American Medical Association* 290: 24 (2003): 3229–3237; David P. Fidler, "SARS: Political Pathology of the First Post-Westphalian Pathogen," *Journal of Law, Medicine, and Ethics* 31: 4 (2003): 485–505.

preparedness programs across the country. This set the stage for further refinement of the emergency preparedness systems after Hurricane Katrina.

NATURAL DISASTER AND THE REIMAGINING OF EMERGENCY GOVERNANCE

With expansion of federal legal and physical infrastructure in place, by early 2005 the level of preparedness to deal with a major natural disaster should have been outstanding. Yet the arrival of Hurricane Katrina in late August 2005 revealed an emergency response system easily overwhelmed by a large natural disaster and called into question whether the numerous initiatives over the previous four years had improved emergency preparedness.

Hurricane Katrina and the Disintegration of Emergency Preparedness

In late August 2005, a large hurricane came ashore on the Gulf Coast of the United States. The affected areas—primarily the coastal regions of Louisiana, Mississippi, and Alabama—are areas well accustomed to hurricanes. Yet Hurricane Katrina was no ordinary storm; the destruction it caused was enormous and devastating. The levee system protecting large sections of New Orleans burst under the weight of the storm surge and whole city neighborhoods were flooded. Nearly 1,400 people were killed, and thousands more were stranded without food, water, or medical care. More than 700,000 people were displaced by the storm. The city and state governments had difficulty responding, as did federal response teams.[32]

Despite the intensive efforts to improve the capacity, functioning, and success of the emergency response system, the response to Hurricane Katrina failed. This failure stemmed from deficiencies in the design of the emergency preparedness system and in the execution of the preparedness plans. In short, neither the infrastructure nor the implementation were adequate.

Systemically, the division of authority across many levels of government and the presence of dual declarations of emergency and parallel lines of authority created challenges for execution of response efforts.[33] Likewise, the legal environment precluded willing volunteers, in most cases from nongovernmental entities, from taking a robust role in the response efforts.[34]

Similarly, the operational execution of the Hurricane Katrina response was lacking. The magnitude of the storm rendered many of the usual emergency response systems inoperable or weakened. In light of this, effective leadership and an adaptable system become especially important. Unfortunately, communication broke down and coordination between responders faltered. Federal, state, and local officials did not share information effectively, leading first to an underestimation of the magnitude of the disaster and later to a misallocation of responders and resources that were available. The key decision makers leading the emergency response, including elected officials, made poor decisions and worsened the situation.[35]

Legislative Changes after Hurricane Katrina

The shocking aftermath of Hurricane Katrina and the persistent contemporaneous concerns about the potential for a resurgent influenza pandemic spurred another round of federal legislation and policymaking to strengthen systems available to improve public health emergency preparedness.[36] The Pandemic and All-Hazards Preparedness Act of 2006 (PAHPA) reflected the continued evolution of legislative authority to facilitate national preparedness for public health emergencies, including chemical, biological, radiological, and nuclear attacks and infectious disease outbreaks. In addition to reauthorizing expiring preparedness and response programs from previous acts, PAHPA also established a new office in HHS to coordinate and oversee development of vaccines and biodefense mechanisms as part of the countermeasures program. PAHPA also created the Biomedical Advanced Research and Development Authority.[37]

Although the Pandemic and All-Hazards Preparedness Act Reauthorization Act of 2013 built on the foundation of the 2006 act, it made some alterations. Specifically, the 2013 act included provisions to ensure medical surge capacity and emphasized the importance of coordinated medical triage and regionalized systems of care with integrated policy coordination for federal response plans. It also further detailed the development of strategic countermeasures for biological, chemical, nuclear, and other agents. Further, the 2013 PAHPA implemented preparedness goals and budget planning. This reflects Congress's concern with the real-life functional implications of public health emergencies. The revised PAHPA contained additional provisions outlining cooperation between HHS and the Food and Drug Administration (FDA), including consultation and research, particularly to ensure competency of the countermeasure stockpiling and response protocol. This indicates that Congress recognized the key role the FDA plays in ensuring the availability and reliability of medical resources that are used to respond to emergencies and builds on the existing Strategic National Stockpile of emergency medical supplies. The emphasis on coordination suggests movement by the federal government to more clearly recognize that local, state, and private emergency response plans have become more common or comprehensive, signaling the need to coordinate for maximum efficiency.

The National Response Framework and the National Incident Management System

Congress passed the Post-Katrina Emergency Management Reform Act of 2006 to address the governance failures of the Hurricane Katrina response.[38] Among the significant changes effected by this law were the removal of FEMA from DHS and the development of the National Response Framework (NRF).[39] The restoration of FEMA as an independent agency reflected the prevailing sentiment that situating FEMA within DHS had hindered its flexibility and effectiveness during the Hurricane Katrina response.[40] While both DHS and HHS have retained important roles in emergency preparedness, this reorganization of federal infrastructure made FEMA both more independent and more accountable for its decision-making and response operations.

The development of the NRF, however, represents the most significant advance in federal emergency preparedness policy in the past decade. As one of the five National Planning Frameworks that make up the National Preparedness System, the NRF has become a more flexible and adaptable version of previous federal efforts to support and coordinate efforts to govern emergency preparedness and response. Unlike previous iterations of federal preparedness policy, the NRF is always in effect and may be implemented fully or partially at any time.[41] Its scope of application ranges from purely local incidents to those of national scale. It provides guidance on the key tasks related to the core capabilities that are to be completed by each component of the whole community. A guiding principle is that incident response efforts "should be handled at the lowest jurisdictional level capable of handling the mission."[42] With regard to timing, response activities occur in anticipation and during an incident, as well as in the short-term recovery period immediately following an incident.

KEY DECISIONS: HEALTH CARE CRISES AND SOLUTIONS

The Evolution of the National Preparedness System

The National Preparedness System (NPS) was established in Presidential Policy Directive 8: National Preparedness in response to the Post-Katrina Emergency Management Reform Act of 2006. It is the overarching policy structure that guides the nation's efforts toward achievement of the National Preparedness Goal (NPG), which was finalized in 2011. The NPG describes a "secure and resilient nation with the capabilities required across the whole community to prevent, protect against, mitigate, respond to, and recover from the threats and hazards that pose the greatest risk." The NPG outlines the structure that would become the NPS: five mission areas supported by capabilities implemented by a whole community of actors. The whole-community approach is a manifestation of the growing recognition that preparedness is not only the government's responsibility, but is the responsibility of individuals, businesses, and organizations at all levels.

The National Response Framework (NRF), a wide-reaching federal policy framework for emergency response, replaced both the 1992 Federal Response Plan (FRP) and the Department of Homeland Security's 2004 National Response Plan (NRP). While the FRP focused primarily on federal roles and responsibilities, the NRP was vastly integrative and innovative, expanding response planning to include all levels of government, private sector actors, and nongovernmental organizations. The NRP emerged from an emphasis on "common incident management and response principles," and it was an early step in a sequence of rapid changes. The NRP was superseded almost immediately by the first NRF in 2008, which included an even wider array of actors and "integrated lessons learned from Hurricane Katrina and other incidents." Following additional policy changes, the NRF was updated to its current version in May 2013 and is a major element of the NPS.

The NRF is one of the five National Planning Frameworks that was developed to support the NPS's mission areas: prevention, protection, mitigation, response, and recovery. Because it emerged from federal response guidance spanning twenty years, it is considered the most mature of the five frameworks. Its capabilities include those "necessary to save lives, protect property and the environment, and meet basic human needs after an incident has occurred." Specifically included are "planning, public information and warning, operational coordination, critical transportation, environmental response/health and safety, fatality management services, infrastructure systems, mass care services, mass search and rescue operations, on-scene security and protection, operational communications, public and private services and resources, public health and medical services, and situational assessment." These capabilities are not exclusive to the NRF, however; there is some overlap of capabilities across the five National Planning Frameworks.

SOURCES: P.L. 109-295, 120 Stat. 1355 (October 4, 2006); U.S. Department of Homeland Security, *National Preparedness Goal* (Washington, DC: U.S. Department of Homeland Security, September 2011), 1, http://www.fema.gov/pdf/prepared/npg.pdf; U.S. Department of Homeland Security, *National Response Framework* (Washington, DC: U.S. Department of Homeland Security, May 2013), 3, http://www.fema.gov/media-library-data/20130726-1914-250451246/final_national_response_framework_20130501.pdf.

The NRF is part of a comprehensive incident management infrastructure that evolved from lessons learned in recent major incidents. It contains principles that are integrated and coordinated with other incident management systems and includes the concepts of scalability, flexibility, and adaptability described in the National Incident Management System (NIMS).[43] In addition to describing the core response mission, it describes the coordinating structures necessary to support the response mission and their integration with the other four mission areas' coordinating structures. Finally, it describes the coordination of government-level operations and operational planning, which is an important contributor to effective and efficient operations such that responsible entities can mobilize swiftly when needed.

NIMS was established in 2004 as required by the Homeland Security Presidential Directive 5 (HSPD-5) to "provide a consistent nationwide approach for Federal, State, and local governments to work effectively and efficiently together to prepare for, respond to, and recover from domestic incidents, regardless of cause, size, or complexity."[44] HSPD-5 mandated use of NIMS by "all

Federal departments and agencies" for the management of domestic incidents and emergency governance.[45] Furthermore, it required adoption by states and local entities starting in 2005 as a prerequisite for federal preparedness assistance.

An update to NIMS in 2008 reflected the growing whole-community approach and clarified incident management roles for all levels of government, private sector actors, and nongovernmental organizations. NIMS works in tandem with the NRF, providing the "core set of doctrines, concepts, principles, terminology, and organizational processes that enables effective, efficient, and collaborative incident management."[46] The NIMS incident management practices are focused on five key integrated components: preparedness, communications and information management, resource management, command and management, and ongoing management and maintenance.[47] NIMS provides comprehensive guidance on the use of these components that is flexible enough to be adapted to small- to large-scale incidents, involving key stakeholders at all levels. Importantly, NIMS is intended to adapt along with additional research and development.

MODERN EMERGENCY PREPAREDNESS: INTO THE FUTURE

The numerous law and policy changes over the past dozen years have culminated in a system of emergency preparedness that differs in scope, organization, approach, and sophistication from what came before. The role of the federal government has expanded, particularly as a source of funding and coordination of emergency preparedness and response efforts. State and local governments have clarified, and in some cases expanded, their legal authority to engage in emergency response activities. Additionally, many state and local governments have utilized the federal resources designated for preparedness to enhance their own capacity for emergency response and public health initiatives.[48] This final section discusses several important developments in this area of law and policy: the rise of collaborative governance in emergency preparedness, the ongoing debates about the appropriate scope of government powers during emergencies, and the potential need for a crisis standard of care to address shortages during public health emergencies.

The Rise of Collaborative Governance

Creating a system that functions well under the difficult conditions created during a public health emergency poses a major challenge for governing public health emergencies. The community approach model adopted by the NRF, which takes into account the capacity and potential contributions of multiple responders across all sectors, provides a good template going forward. This approach recognizes that emergency preparedness and response cannot succeed if response efforts rely solely on formal institutions. Likewise, while concentration of legal powers and resources may make intuitive sense when responding to an urgent, large-scale emergency situation, often concentration and linear infrastructure and lines of authority prove to be insufficiently adaptable to address systemic failures. A governance structure that builds in pluralistic governance—using the strengths of all levels of government, nongovernmental organizations, and private sector entities—could allow for this additional flexibility provided that emergency preparedness planning incorporates coordination and harmonization of capabilities, resources, and effort.[49] This approach has been used with some success in the response efforts to recent major disasters, such as Superstorm Sandy in 2012, which reflected a more effective level of implementation and coordination across levels of government and between all institutions involved in emergency response efforts.

The Use of Coercive Powers

The use of coercive powers has generated another perennial debate surrounding emergency preparedness. Legal authority grants government officials the power to restrict individual liberty and property to protect the public's health. Powers to limit movement through quarantine, isolation, travel restrictions, mandatory evacuations, and other forms of social distancing may be appropriate to stem the spread of an infectious disease or to remove people from a dangerous area immediately after a disaster. However, coercive powers have been abused or applied discriminatorily in the past, which requires caution and oversight in their application. Likewise, powers that authorize restrictions on property use, including the commandeering or destruction of property to protect public health, can be necessary but should be used sparingly. Some commentators, while endorsing these powers, urge that the least restrictive alternative be used in applying coercive emergency powers.[50] Others have voiced opposition to coercive emergency powers on principle, out of a concern that their use cannot be easily constrained.[51]

Crisis Standards of Care and Scarce Resource Allocation

In severe public health emergencies, shortages of vital resources threaten to exacerbate already difficult circumstances. Emergency preparedness plans often include strategies to bolster medical supplies and personnel when shortages arise. Programs authorizing licensure reciprocity for health care professionals, such as the Emergency System for Advance Registration of Volunteer Health Professionals, and stockpiling commonly needed medical resources, such as the Strategic National Stockpile, recognize this concern. State governments and federal policymakers have begun to develop preparedness plans specifically to address legal and ethical issues related to scarce resource allocation during crisis standards of care, where normal medical and public health practices are limited by shortages.[52] Answering difficult questions about how to prioritize access to scarce medical resources and services while preserving effective medical outcomes, social functioning, and fairness remains a challenge for policymakers, public officials, and health care professionals developing preparedness policies.

The tumultuous years that began with the September 11, 2001, attacks ended with an emergency preparedness system in the United States that is quite different in scope and focus. The emergency preparedness infrastructure has expanded at the federal, state, and local levels, thanks to an influx of federal resources to build capacity and a focus on preparedness through the development of law, policy, and best practices unlike any previous period in U.S. history. While both the resources directed to emergency preparedness and the focus of policymakers on this issue have diminished in recent years, the results remain impressive; the nation is more prepared for emergencies than ever before. It is incontrovertible that the capacity, professionalism, and infrastructure available to respond to public health emergencies has never been greater in the United States. What remains to be determined is whether this improved capacity and organization can be maintained and whether it will result in better, more effective responses in the future.

See also Chapter 4: The Centers for Disease Control and Prevention: Anticipatory Action in the Face of Uncertainty (1946–Present); Chapter 27: Continuing Challenges of Infectious Disease (1980s–Present); Chapter 29: Twenty-first-Century Challenges to Health and Health Care: Noncommunicable Diseases, Environmental Threats, and Human Rights (2000s–Present); Chapter 30: The Governance of Population Health: Reflections on the Analytical Approach of Contributors to the *Guide*.

NOTES

1. Christopher Nelson et al., *Conceptualizing and Defining Public Health Emergency Preparedness* (Santa Monica, CA: RAND), http://www.rand.org/content/dam/rand/pubs/working_papers/2008/RAND_WR543.pdf.
2. Center for Law and the Public's Health at Georgetown and Johns Hopkins Universities, *Model State Emergency Health Powers Act* (December 21, 2001), Art. I, § 104(m), http://www.publichealthlaw.net/MSEHPA/MSEHPA2.pdf.
3. Lance Gable, "Evading Emergency: Strengthening Emergency Responses through Integrated Pluralistic Governance," *Oregon Law Review* 91 (2013): 375–454.
4. Nelson et al., *Conceptualizing and Defining Public Health.*
5. U.S. Department of Homeland Security, *National Preparedness Goal* (September 2011), http://www.fema.gov/media-library-data/20130726-1828-25045-9470/national_preparedness_goal_2011.pdf.
6. Laurie Garrett, "The Lessons of HIV/AIDS," *Foreign Affairs* 84: 4 (2005): 51–65.
7. George Rosen, *A History of Public Health* (Baltimore: Johns Hopkins University Press, 1993), 216–223.
8. Steven Johnson, *The Ghost Map: The Story of London's Most Terrifying Epidemic—and How It Changed Science, Cities, and the Modern World* (New York: Riverhead Books, 2006).
9. John J. Pauly, "The Great Chicago Fire as a National Event," *American Quarterly* 36: 5 (1984): 668–683.
10. Ronald Bayer, Amy Fairchild, and James Colgrove, *Searching Eyes: Privacy, the State, and Disease Surveillance in America* (Berkeley: University of California Press, 2007).
11. John Barry, *The Great Influenza: The Epic Story of the Deadliest Plague in History* (New York: Viking Penguin, 2004), 450.
12. Federal Emergency Management Agency, *The Federal Emergency Management Agency Publication 1* (November 2010), 4, http://www.fema.gov/media-library-data/20130726-1823-25045-8164/pub_1_final.pdf.
13. Ibid., 5–6.
14. 42 U.S. Code sec. 5121 et seq.
15. Federal Emergency Management Agency, *The Federal Emergency Management Agency,* 8–10.
16. National Commission on Terrorist Attacks upon the United States, *The 9/11 Commission Report* (New York: W.W. Norton, 2004).
17. David Heyman, *Lessons from the Anthrax Attacks: Implications for U.S. Bioterrorism Preparedness* (Washington, DC: Center for Strategic and International Studies, 2002).
18. P.L. 107-56 (2001).
19. P.L. 109-177 (2005).
20. P.L. 107-56 (2001).
21. Century Foundation, *Are Bioterrorism Dollars Making Us Safer?* (January 12, 2005), http://tcf.org.
22. P.L. 107-188 (2002).
23. P.L. 108-276 (2004).
24. Frank Gottron, *Project BioShield: Authorities, Appropriations, Acquisition, and Issues for Congress* (Washington, DC: Congressional Research Service, May 27, 2011).
25. Lawrence O. Gostin, "Public Health Law in an Age of Terrorism: Rethinking Individual Rights and Common Goods," *Health Affairs* 21 (2002): 86–91.
26. Tara O'Toole, Michael Mair, and Thomas V. Inglesby, "Shining Light on 'Dark Winter,'" *Clinical Infectious Diseases* 34 (2002): 979–982.
27. Center for Law and the Public's Health at Georgetown and Johns Hopkins Universities, *Model State Emergency Health Powers Act.*
28. Center for Law and the Public's Health at Georgetown and Johns Hopkins Universities, *Model State Emergency Health Powers Act: State Legislative Activity* (2006), http://www.publichealthlaw.net/MSEHPA/MSEHPA%20Leg%20Activity.pdf.
29. George J. Annas, "Blinded by Bioterrorism: Public Health and Liberty in the 21st Century," *Health Matrix* 13 (2003): 45–54.
30. Gostin, "Public Health Law in an Age of Terrorism."
31. P.L. 104-321 (1996).
32. U.S. Department of Homeland Security, Office of Inspector General, *A Performance Review of FEMA's Disaster Management Activities in Response to Hurricane Katrina* (OIG-06-32) (Washington, DC: U.S. Department of Homeland Security, March 2006).
33. Erin Ryan, "How the New Federalism Failed Katrina Victims," in *Law and Recovery from Disaster: Hurricane Katrina*, edited by Robin Paul Malloy (Surrey, UK: Ashgate, 2009), 173, 201–211.
34. James G. Hodge Jr., Lance Gable, and Stephanie Calves, "The Legal Framework for Meeting Surge Capacity through the Use of Volunteer Health Professionals during Public Health Emergencies and Other Disasters," *Journal of Contemporary Health Law & Policy* 22 (2005): 13–14.
35. Gable, "Evading Emergency."
36. Sarah Lister and Frank Grotten, "The Pandemic and All Hazards Preparedness Act (P.L. 109-417): Provisions and Changes to Preexisting Law" (Washington, DC: Congressional Research Service, January 25, 2007), http://www.ncdhhs.gov/dhsr/EMS/aspr/pdf/papareport.pdf.
37. P.L. 109-417 (2006).
38. P.L. 109-295, 120 Stat. 1355 (October 4, 2006).
39. Federal Emergency Management Agency, *The Federal Emergency Management Agency Publication 1.*
40. U.S. Department of Homeland Security, *A Performance Review of FEMA's Disaster Management Activities.*
41. U.S. Department of Homeland Security, *National Response Framework* (Washington, DC: U.S. Department of Homeland

Security, May 2013), 5, http://www.fema.gov/media-library-data/20130726-1914-25045-1246/final_national_response_framework_20130501.pdf.

42. Ibid., i.

43. Ibid., 1.

44. "Homeland Security Presidential Directive/HSPD-5— Management of Domestic Incidents" (February 28, 2003), 231, http://www.gpo.gov/fdsys/pkg/PPP-2003-book1/pdf/PPP-2003-book1-doc-pg229.pdf.

45. Ibid., 232.

46. U.S. Department of Homeland Security, *National Incident Management System* (Washington, DC: U.S. Department of Homeland Security, December 2008), 3, http://www.fema.gov/pdf/emergency/nims/NIMS_core.pdf.

47. Ibid., 7.

48. Trust for America's Health, *Ready or Not? Protecting the Public's Health from Diseases, Disasters, and Bioterrorism* (Washington, DC: Trust for America's Health, 2012), http://healthyamericans.org/reports/bioterror09/pdf/TFAHReadyorNot200906.pdf

49. Gable, "Evading Emergency."

50. Lawrence O. Gostin, "When Terrorism Threatens Health: How Far Are Limitations on Personal and Economic Liberties Justified?" *Florida Law Review* 55 (2003): 105.

51. Griffin Trotter, *The Ethics of Coercion in Mass Casualty Medicine* (Baltimore: Johns Hopkins University Press, 2007).

52. Institute of Medicine, *Crisis Standards of Care: A Systems Framework for Catastrophic Disaster Response* (Washington, DC: National Academies Press, 2012).

FURTHER READING

Birkland, Thomas A. *Lessons of Disaster: Policy Change after Catastrophic Events.* Washington, DC: Georgetown University Press, 2006.

Farber, Daniel A., Jim Chen, Robert V.M. Verchick, and Lisa Grow Sun. *Disaster Law and Policy.* 2nd ed. New York: Aspen, 2010.

Fidler, David P., and Lawrence O. Gostin. *Biosecurity in the Global Age: Biological Weapons, Public Health, and the Rule of Law.* Stanford, CA: Stanford University Press, 2007.

Institute of Medicine. *Crisis Standards of Care: A Systems Framework for Catastrophic Disaster Response.* Washington, DC: National Academies Press, 2012.

Rosner, David, and Gerald Markowitz. *Are We Ready? Public Health since 9/11.* Berkeley: University of California Press, 2006.

chapter 29

Twenty-first-Century Challenges to Health and Health Care

Noncommunicable Diseases, Environmental Threats, and Human Rights (2000s–Present)

Diana M. Bowman, Andrew S. Jessmore, and Scott L. Greer

PUBLIC HEALTH CHALLENGES DO NOT RESPECT national borders. As history illustrates, human influenza viruses cross countries and continents, as do, for examples, zoonoses.[1,2,3] The economic and social costs of such health challenges similarly affect many jurisdictions and often require multilateral and multisector responses. The eradication of small pox during the twentieth century,[4] and the more recent Multilateral Initiative on Malaria,[5,6] are testament of the need for well-funded transnational and collaborative multi-stakeholder partnerships.

While communicable diseases receive much of the attention, threats to human health are far more diversified. Noncommunicable diseases (NCDs), which include cancers, cardiovascular disease, and lifestyle diseases associated with obesity, such as diabetes, are increasingly challenging the economic and intellectual capacity of governments and the public health community more generally. Injuries and mental health disorders are similarly burdening the national and international health infrastructure. These largely preventable deaths and associated disabilities arguably present some of the most pressing and significant challenges to health and health care delivery at this time. Moreover, it would seem that without significant investment and a multilateral approach to addressing these challenges, their human and economic toll will continue to rise.[7]

The global community, including the United States, also must reduce exposure to environmental contaminants such as dioxins, air pollution, and waste—including nuclear waste.[8] Similarly, humanitarian crises, such as civil war, acts of aggression (including the use of biological and chemical weapons), and complex environmental conditions that range from famine to water scarcity, create additional layers of complexity and bureaucracy. These environmental and humanitarian threats add to the overall health burden that must be addressed by state and non-state actors in their attempts to promote public health. It is important to note the competing agendas, the multitude of actors and

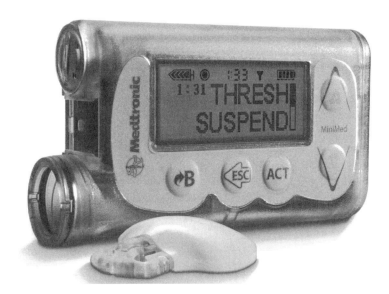

New technology helps monitor diabetes, a growing noncommunicable disease. Many new wearable devices wirelessly connect to smartphones (or other devices) and measure heart rate, exercise intensity and duration, blood pressure, and weight. The associated software connects to Web sites where the gathered information is stored in the "cloud" and can be accessed anywhere, making it easier to share information with health care providers and family.

SOURCE: Medtronic, Inc.

421

instruments that are at play in this global landscape. Only then can one have a real appreciation of the tensions between national and international goals, questions of sovereignty, resourcing, and accountability.

While it is important to be aware of these ongoing threats and challenges to human health, most fall outside the scope of this chapter. Our focus is on NCDs in their various forms and the way in which the most pressing NCDs are being addressed through the global architecture by relevant stakeholders.

THE CURRENT STATE OF PLAY

Public health practice and public health infrastructure have traditionally focused on communicable diseases (CDs). However, the increasing prevalence of NCDs, and the global burden created by these diseases, has forced governments and other stakeholders to shift priorities and spending.[9] What exactly do we mean by NCDs, and how significant is their global burden?

According to the World Health Organization (WHO),

> noncommunicable diseases (NCDs), mainly cardiovascular diseases, cancers, chronic respiratory diseases and diabetes represent a leading threat to human health and development. These four diseases are the world's biggest killers, causing an estimated 35 million deaths each year—60% of all deaths globally—with 80% in low- and middle-income countries. These diseases are preventable.[10]

They represent a "global crisis," affecting individuals "in almost all countries and in all income groups, men, women and children."[11] Figure 29.1 provides an illustration of the total deaths associated with NCDs by region, socioeconomic status, and sex.

The disproportionate impact of NCDs on low to middle incomes is highlighted by Figure 29.1, as to the role that injury—as discussed below—plays in preventable deaths for both males and females.[12] Yet despite this shocking reality, estimates suggest that if the status quo remains, the burden of NCDs will increase globally by 17 percent within the next decade (2013–2023); Africa will be the most adversely impacted continents, with estimates suggesting that the increase in this region will be 27 percent.[13] It is therefore not surprising that Abdullah Daar and his colleagues[14] have sought to go one step further, classifying NCDs as "chronic noncommunicable diseases." While this is an apt classification, for the purposes of this chapter, we shall continue to adopt the convention of NCDs.

The Global Economic Burden of NCDs

The economic burden of NCDs is, arguably, momentous. The World Economic Forum (WEF) and Harvard School of Public Health have suggested that the direct and indirect costs of the five leading NCDs and mental health conditions is likely to be $47 trillion over the next two decades (2011 to 2031), or 4 percent of annual global gross domestic product.[15] The WHO and WEF note that, "[o]n a per-person basis, the annual losses amount to an average of US $25 in low-income countries, US$ 50 in lower middle-income countries and US $139 in upper middle-income countries."[16]

Given their prevalence and ubiquity, NCDs represent a significant threat to economic development, while "also endangering industry competitiveness across borders."[17] It is well recognized that low- and middle-income countries are not adequately equipped with the necessary infrastructure, systems, or expertise to adequately address this growing epidemic and its associated economic challenges,[18] thus ensuring that a unified approach is required.[19]

Injuries as Part of the NCD Challenge

Global health care challenges extend beyond those posed by NCDs. Intentional and unintentional injuries, which include road traffic accidents, falls, firearm injuries, and suicides, similarly represent a significant global public health challenge, despite having been largely ignored by the global health community. The global burden of injury deaths has been estimated by the WHO at 5.8 million people, or 10 percent of global deaths, annually. Figure 29.2 places this information in context.

This equates to fifteen thousand people dying each and every day as a result of injuries.[20] The burden of these injuries is disproportionately felt in those countries and regions with more limited resources, specifically low- and middle-income countries[21] and former Communist countries.[22]

As illustrated by Figure 29.3, 23 percent of injury-related deaths occur on our roads; such deaths are the leading cause of death in those fifteen to twenty-nine years of age and are among the top three leading causes of death for those aged five to fourteen years and thirty to forty-four years.[23]

Injuries caused by violence, to oneself or to others, similarly represent a significant health care challenge in the twenty-first century. In 2004, suicides accounted for 15 percent of all injury-related deaths and were ranked as the sixteenth leading cause of death. Suicide was the fifth leading cause of death for those five to fourteen and fifteen to twenty-nine years of age.[24] Homicides accounted for 11 percent of these deaths, being the sixth leading cause of death for those three to forty-four years of age.

Impact of Injuries on International Infrastructure

The significance of injures on domestic and the international health infrastructure should not be underestimated, with the WHO acknowledging that the burden of injuries is increasing. According to its estimates, without effective intervention, road traffic crashes will have moved from being the ninth

FIGURE 29.1 **Total NCD Deaths by Region, Status, and Sex, 2008**

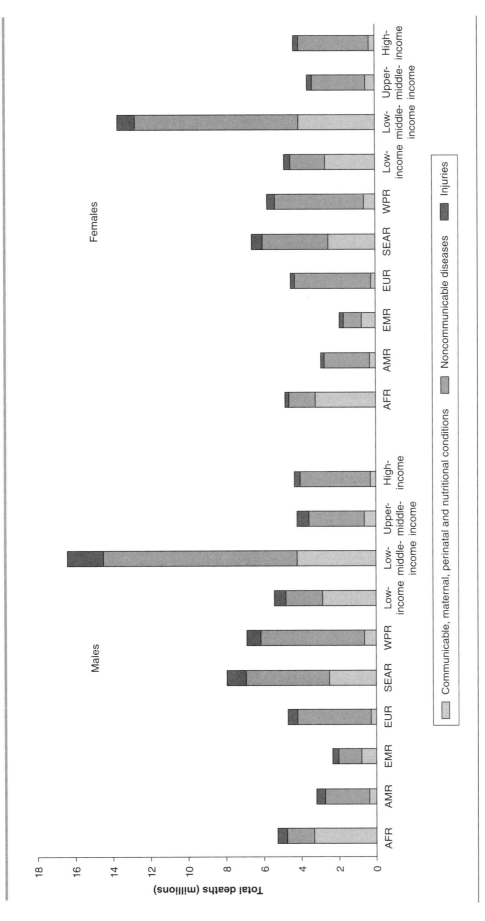

SOURCE: World Health Organization, *Global Status Report on Noncommunicable Diseases 2010* (Geneva, Switzerland: World Health Organization, 2011).

FIGURE 29.2 **The Scale of the Injury Problem**

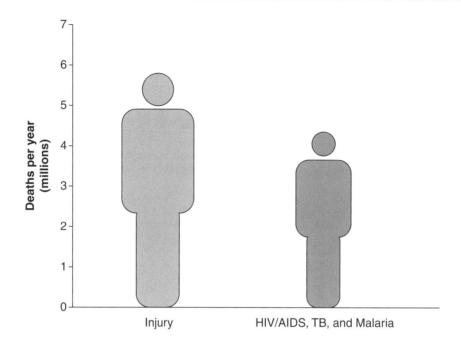

SOURCES: World Health Organization, *The Global Burden of Disease: 2004 Update* (Geneva, Switzerland: World Health Organization, 2004); World Health Organization, "Injuries and Violence: The Facts" (Geneva, Switzerland: World Health Organization, 2010), 2.

FIGURE 29.3 **How Injuries Claim Lives**

Causes of injury deaths, World, 2004.

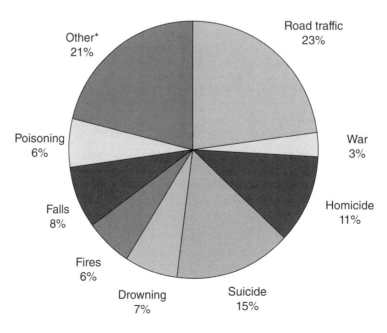

SOURCE: World Health Organization, "Injuries and Violence: The Facts" (Geneva, Switzerland: World Health Organization, 2010), with data from 2004.

leading cause of death in 2004 to the fifth by 2030, following only ischemic heart disease (first), cerebrovascular disease (second), chronic obstructive pulmonary disease (third), and lower respiratory infections (fourth).[25] Similarly, by 2030, it is anticipated that suicide will have increased from the sixteenth leading cause of death to the twelfth, ranking just behind HIV/AIDS (tenth) and nephritis and nephrosis (eleventh), with homicide moving up the list from twenty-second place in 2004 to sixteenth place by 2030.[26]

What of the hidden injury toll? The figures presented above represent only those who die as a result of injuries and violence. As noted by the WHO, these are "only a small fraction of those injured. Tens of millions of people suffer injuries that lead to hospitalization, emergency department or general practitioner treatment, or treatment that does not involve formal medical care."[27] With men more likely to die or be incapacitated as the result of an intentional or unintentional injury,[28] the economic burden of fatal and nonfatal injuries is felt beyond the individual and immediate family.

It is important to define NCDs as broadly as possible so as to encompass not only the types of diseases identified by the WHO but also intentional and unintentional injuries as well as mental health–related conditions. Only through adopting such a broad scope are we able to appropriately example the real burden being faced by all countries, including the United States, and the responses that have been initiated to address these challenges to date.

Liberty, Autonomy, and Self-Determination: Tensions with Today's Public Health Agenda

The global pandemics of NCDs, including obesity, cancer, and injury, may be largely attributed to behavioral risk factors, decisions associated with self-determination, and the broader socioeconomic context. As noted in the *Vienna Declaration on Nutrition and Noncommunicable Diseases in the Context of Health 2020,* two of the most notable—or significant—risk factors for NCDs are "unhealthy diet and physical inactivity."[29] This includes tobacco use, excessive or harmful use of alcohol, calorie-rich diets, and diets high in saturated and/or trans fats.[30,31] Individually, and combined, these behaviors increase the risk of high blood pressure, elevated cholesterol (high-density lipoproteins) levels, and obesity, and are risk factors for diabetes, cardiovascular disease, and other chronic diseases.[32,33] The U.S. population is not immune to the health crisis associated with NCDs.[34] Importantly, many of the most significant risk factors are modifiable. The injury burden may be similarly attributed to a range of behavioral risk factors and lifestyle choices; for example, decisions not to wear a seat belt or motorbike helmet are often made on the basis of personal freedom and/or autonomy.[35]

Government attempts to mitigate such behavioral risk factors through law have, and continue to be, met with resistance. Such attempts by government to limit or control, for example, the maximum size of sugary beverages, compulsory helmet wearing, and access to, and storage of, firearms continue to be challenged by those who see their liberties being increasingly encroached upon.[36] In examining the potential role for the U.S. government in relation to the obesity epidemic, Michelle Mello and her colleagues observed that "antiobesity laws encounter strong opposition from some quarters on the grounds that they constitute paternalistic intervention into lifestyle choices and enfeeble the notion of personal responsibility."[37]

Inherent within these tensions is the question of balance. Where is the appropriate balance between the individual rights and freedoms and that of the common good?[38,39] While such questions and balancing acts are not new, the perceived curtailing of individual rights by the state in relation to NCDs, in which harm is inflicted on the individual, appears to have exacerbated these tensions.[40] Bayer eloquently summarizes the tensions with the following question: "What is the legitimate role of the state in modifying, discouraging, burdening or even prohibiting behaviors that increase both morbidity and mortality?"[41]

Global Framework for Action

The ability for countries, including the United States, to respond to global health challenges relies to a large extent on the multilateral architecture and instruments created by states over the last seventy years. The world of global health governance is complex and fragmented,[42] but there are a few key arenas and agendas for global NCD policy.

The WHO

At the core of the framework sits the WHO, an organ of the United Nations (UN) established in 1948. As set out in Article 1 of the WHO's constitution, the overarching object of the agency is "the attainment by all peoples of the highest possible level of health." This is achieved through, for example, providing leadership, coordinating research, establishing evidence-based policies, and providing support to member countries on global health matters.[43] One hundred ninety-four nations—three fewer than are members of the UN—have ratified the Constitution of the World Health Assembly, granting them member-state status in the WHO. All UN member states are eligible for WHO membership (contingent on their ratification of the WHO constitution), and those nations who are not UN members may apply and be admitted through simple majority vote.[44] Other, nonstate entities have also gained associate or observer status through provisions in the WHO constitution.

Each member state elects delegates to represent their nation's interests at the World Health Assembly (WHA), the legislative body of the WHO and the preeminent forum on health. Delegates meet annually in Geneva, Switzerland, the location of WHO headquarters. The WHA addresses not only administrative concerns (such as approving the WHO work program and budget, and electing the director general), but also establishes the priorities, positions, and strategy of the WHO. The assembly also elects thirty-four members of the executive board, the nominees for which are experts in a variety of public health fields. These members determine the subjects and concerns demanding the WHO's attention, set the agenda for the WHA meetings, facilitate conversations, and give effect to the policies created by the WHA.

Through a network of regional and country-specific offices and affiliated collaborating centers, the WHO disseminates information and action plans as well as aid to member states, their health departments, and all types of health providers and practitioners. Six regional committees, formed in accordance with the WHO constitution "to meet the special needs of [each defined] area," represent geographically defined clusters of member states.[45] These

regional committees hold great sway over the policies, programming, and budgeting relevant to their region, and approve those delegates appointed to the WHA. Beyond the regional offices, each country typically will have an in-state headquarters as well as a network of smaller offices, as needed. A WHO representative leads these country-specific headquarters and works closely with the nation's health department, elected officials, and other relevant governmental and nongovernmental bodies to align national priorities, policies, and programming with those of the WHO.

The architecture of the WHO is notably open to pressures and preferences from the numerous poorer member states in the WHA, and in the 1970s, these states tried to enlist the WHO in their search for a more redistributive international order. From the 1980s onward, the response from wealthier states was a successful campaign to freeze the WHO permanent budget. This move reduced the power of low- and middle-income states and made the WHO

KEY DECISIONS: HEALTH CARE CRISES AND SOLUTIONS

Global Action Plans at the World Health Assembly, 2013

Addressing the sixty-sixth World Health Assembly gathered in Geneva, Switzerland, Dr. Margaret Chan, director-general of the World Health Organization (in office 2007–), welcomed the delegates and spoke on the importance of policymaking:

Ladies and gentlemen,

You will be considering three draft global action plans, for noncommunicable diseases, mental health, and the prevention of avoidable blindness and visual impairment.

All three plans call for a life-course approach, aim to achieve equity through universal health coverage, and stress the importance of prevention. All three give major emphasis to the benefits of integrated service delivery.

Global strategies and action plans make an important contribution to international coordination and promote a unified approach to shared problems.

But sound health policies at the national level matter most.

Public health has known for at least two decades that good health can be achieved at low cost, if the right policies are in place.

We know this from comparative studies of countries at the same level of economic development that reveal striking differences in health outcomes.

Last month, a study from the Rockefeller Foundation revisited this issue with new data from a number of countries. That study leads me to a positive conclusion.

Member States, we are doing a lot of things right, on the right track.

According to the study, factors that contribute to good health at low cost include a commitment to equity, effective governance systems, and context-specific programmes that address the wider social and environmental determinants of health. An ability to innovate is also important.

Specific policies that can make the greatest difference include a national medicines policy that makes maximum use of generic products, and a commitment to primary health care and the education and training of health care workers, which is fast becoming a top priority in many countries.

Above all, governments need to be committed and they need to have a vision set out in a plan.

This is also true for WHO.

SOURCE: Margaret Chan, "Director General Addresses the Sixty-sixth World Health Assembly," May 20, 2013, http://www.who.int/dg/speeches/2013/world_health_assembly_20130520/en.

much more dependent on its ability to work with wealthy donor states.[46] Wealthier states also sidelined the WHO by engaging in their own initiatives, such as creating the Global Fund to Fight AIDS, Tuberculosis and Malaria, or the impressive President's Emergency Plan for AIDS Relief program in the United States. Under Gro Harlem Brundtland (in office 1998–2003), the WHO adapted, focusing on public-private partnerships and work with the richer states, the international financial institutions that they dominate, notably the World Bank, and large foundations such as the Gates Foundation.[47]

Beyond the member-state nations and WHO offices worldwide, a number of international non-governmental organizations (NGOs), universities, research institutions, and relief organizations collaborate with the WHO to develop, refine, and implement policy and research worldwide. In fact, a number of these organizations sit as official or non-official observers to the WHA, lacking voting rights but serving as experts and partners.[48]

Mental, Neurological, and Substance Use Disorders

Mental, neurological, and substance use (MNS) disorders contribute to morbidity and premature mortality across every populated region of the world. The statistics associated with MNS disorders bring light to change that needs to be made. In the 2011 Mental Health Atlas, WHO states that worldwide more than 450 million people suffer from an MNS disorder. The 2011 Mental Health Atlas also explains that about 14 percent of the global burden of disease, when measured in disability-adjusted life years, can be explained by complications due to MNS disorders. The WHO recognizes the importance of mental health in its definition of health as "not merely the absence of disease or infirmity," but rather "a state of complete physical, mental, and social well-being."[49]

In 2013, the sixty-sixth World Health Assembly passed WHA66.8, the Comprehensive Mental Health Action Plan 2013–2020.[50] The resolution created a formal recognition of the status of mental health for WHO's 194 member states as well as their understanding of the importance of taking actions to improve mental health and to provide support in the achievement of a set of agreed global objectives:

1. Strengthen effective leadership and governance for mental health

2. Provide comprehensive, integrated, and responsive mental health and social care services in community-based settings

3. Implement strategies for promotion and prevention in mental health

4. Strengthen information systems, evidence and research for mental health

The resolution also offered a set of corresponding measurable global targets,[51] a first of their kind for mental health:

GT 1.1 80 percent of countries will introduce or update a national mental health plan in line with international and regional human rights instruments.

GT 1.2 50 percent of countries will have develop or update mental health legislation to protect human rights.

GT 2 Service coverage for severe mental disorders will increase by 20%.

GT 1.1 80 percent of countries will create two multisectoral programmes for the promotion of mental health and the prevention of disorders.

GT 1.2 The suicide rate will go down by 10 percent.

GT 4 80 percent of countries will routinely collect and report on a core set of mental health indicators.[52]

The action plan and associated objectives and targets come from a call for action supported by research from WHO and collaborating centers.[53,54,55,56] Drafting the act was a WHO-led consultation team that brought together member states, WHO collaborating centers, NGOs, academic institutions, and experts in the field.[57] To implement the action plan, WHO will aid countries in catering the action plan to their own needs, while the other partners provide their support in their areas of expertise.

The action plan shows WHO's growing shift in the perceived importance of NCDs and mental health.[58,59,60,61] While passing the resolution shows member state support, the implementation of the action plan could face challenges. Member states must reverse their investments into antiquated models of segregated treatment and invest in cost-effective and proven interventions and treatments.[62] The WHO and its partners must also work to urge health policy planners, local political leaders, and health professionals to advocate for and create the change outlines in the action plan. With effort from all stakeholders identified in the plan, the WHO can work to ensure that it better addresses health as "a state of complete physical, mental, and social well-being."[63,64,65]

Injury Prevention and Road Safety

In an effort to reduce the global carnage associated with road traffic accidents, the WHO has sought to use a different approach to addressing this NCD. The Decade of Action on Road Safety 2011–2020 is one such approach. Officially launched in May 2011 by the WHO, the Decade of Action represents the culmination of a number of high-profile reports and articles articulating the impact of road trauma on the global community[66,67,68] and increasing political pressure for global action. This includes, for example, two special resolutions on road safety by the UN General Assembly.[69,70]

The Framework Convention on Tobacco Control

The evolution of the WHO from an agency primarily focused on communicable diseases to one that is increasingly focused on the broader health agenda is evident in the period following 2000. The implementation of the Framework Convention on Tobacco Control (FCTC) in 2003, in an attempt by the agency to curb the growing global smoking epidemic—responsible for approximately six million deaths annually—is testament to this.

The bold vision to curb the tobacco epidemic was first articulated a decade prior to its entry into force. It was here, in 1993, that the idea to curb the epidemic through a binding international legal instrument was first formulated. To this group of scholars, the unexploited lawmaking power of the WHO was deemed to be the most advantageous approach. Given the global industry and economic powers at play, it is not surprising that conception to entry into force involved a long, and often hard-fought, battle.[71] As of today, eleven years after the fact, there are more than 170 signatories to the convention. The United States is one of these. However, the FCTC has not been ratified by the United States. Accordingly, while the Family Smoking Prevention and Tobacco Control Act of 2007 is in the "spirit" of the FCTC, the U.S. government is not bound by the obligations set out in the convention.

Pursuant to Article 3 of the FCTC, the overarching objective of the convention is to protect present and future generations from the devastating health, social, environmental, and economic consequences of tobacco consumption and exposure to tobacco smoke by providing a framework for tobacco control measures to be implemented by the parties at the national, regional, and international levels in order to reduce continually and substantially the prevalence of tobacco use and exposure to tobacco smoke. Accordingly, the FCTC goes to the very heart of addressing the challenges and burdens that have been created by one of the most pervasive, and expensive, NCDs of our time.

The manner in which this overarching objective, and other goals, is to be achieved is set within the body of the convention. Within these articles, the governance framework, guiding principles, and substantive provisions may be found. Importantly, these articles provide the legal foundation for domestic legislative and regulatory action in relation to tobacco control measures. In giving effect to their obligations under the FCTC, a country's legislative action must not, however, be in breach of their constitution and/or international public law.

The adoption of the FCTC by the member states of the WHO is testament to the fact that political will can be coordinated and marshaled around a global health challenge. Moreover, despite focus having been traditionally on communicable diseases, the growing health disaster caused by tobacco usage resulted in the WHO using its underutilized lawmaking power to address an NCD. This action was without precedent. The fact that the Framework Convention addresses a lifestyle disease, rather than a communicable disease such as HIV, and a disease that is extremely divisive in nature and politically charged, is arguably illustrative of the increasing importance of NCDs on the global health agenda.

There are two ways to think about, and evaluate, international initiatives such as the FCTC. One is to regard them as a way to influence member-state policymaking: do signatory states do what they agreed to do in the FCTC? The other way is more nuanced, and we will return to it: does the presence of the FCTC alter the dynamics of other areas of law, especially trade law, in order to defend public health policies against the demands of commercial rights and freedoms? The presence of the FCTC, which is evidence of a global commitment to tobacco control in general and specific policies toward that end, is a powerful argument against those who claim tobacco control measures infringe on free trade, investors' rights, or intellectual property rights (including trademark protection).

Looking forward, it may be argued that the passage of the FCTC provides the WHO and member states with a model for creating binding international agreements that address global public health challenges, including NCDs. While we are not so naïve to think that such agreements shall be created with ease, or in an expedient manner, the passage of the FCTC does provide hope for the creation of other such binding instruments. Others have expressed similar sentiment, with scholars calling for the creation of analogous conventions across various health fields, ranging from a Framework Convention on Global Health to instruments dealing with more narrowly defined topics, including alcohol consumption. The benefit of such a strategy would be to both "trade-proof" more areas of public health law and expand global debates and consensuses about public health questions.

SOURCES: Diana M. Bowman and Michael G. Bennett, "The Next Chapter of the Tobacco Wars: Unpacking and Unraveling the Latest Round of Constitutional Challenges," *American Journal of Public Health* 103: 8 (2013): e11–e13; Lawrence O. Gostin, "A Proposal for a Framework Convention on Global Health," *Journal of International Economic Law* 10: 4 (2007): 989–1008; Lawrence O. Gostin, "A Framework Convention on Global Health: Health for All, Justice for All," *Journal of the American Medical Association* 307: 19 (2012): 2087–2092: Holly Jarman, "Attack on Australia: Tobacco Industry Challenges to Plain Packaging," *Journal of Public Health Policy* 34: 3 (2013): 375–387; Holly Jarman, *The Politics of Trade and Tobacco Control* (Basingstoke, UK: Macmillan, 2014): Ruth Roemer et al., "Origins of the WHO Framework Convention on Tobacco Control," *American Journal of Public Health* 95: 6 (2005): 936–938; Ilona Kickbush and Martina Marianna Cassar Szabo, "A New Governance Space for Health," *Global Health Action* 7 (2014): 23507; Robin Room et al., "International Regulation of Alcohol," *BMJ* 337 (2008): 2364; Ruth Roemer, Allyn Taylor, and Jean Lariviere, "Origins of the WHO Framework Convention on Tobacco Control," *American Journal of Public Health* 95: 6 (2005): 936–938; World Health Organization, "10 Facts on the Global Tobacco Epidemic," http://www.who.int/features/factfiles/tobacco_epidemic/en/index.html; World Health Organization, *World Health Organization Framework Convention on Tobacco Control* (Geneva, Switzerland: World Health Organization, May 21, 2003), art. 3, http://whqlibdoc.who.int/publications/2003/9241591013.pdf.

While these resolutions sought to welcome, encourage, and urge the WHO, governments, and civil society to take action on road safety, they did not compel action at either the national or global level.[72] The catalyst, instead, occurred during the First Global Ministerial Conference on Road Safety in 2009, when road safety was, for the first time, "reframed as a humanitarian issue. It was also reframed as a developmental issue and an economic issue, both of which could no longer be ignored by the world at large."[73] The Moscow Declaration, the substantive output of the Ministerial Conference, is a four-page call to arms by "Ministers and heads of delegations as well as representatives of international, regional and sub-regional governmental and nongovernmental organizations and private bodies."[74]

Through the Declaration, these parties have: "[i]nvite[d] the United Nations General Assembly to declare the decade 2011–2020 as the 'Decade of Action for Road Safety' with a goal to stabilize and then reduce the forecast level of global road deaths by 2020."[75]

The Moscow Declaration sets out five areas for action which, when combined, span the road safety spectrum:

1. Strengthen road safety management capacity

2. Improve the safety of infrastructure (Safer Roads and Safer Transportation Systems)

3. Improve the safety of vehicles (Safer Vehicles)

4. Improve the safety behaviour of road users (Safer Road Users)

5. Improve post-crash care[76]

The WHO anticipates that by focusing on these five areas, and implementing evidence-based policies and best practices under each theme, as many as five million lives could be saved across the world from 2011 to 2020.

The call to arms, and the resulting work plan, were crystallized with the passage of UN Resolution A/64/255 on Improving Road Safety, an aspirational document designed to drive road safety measures. The document contains no firm commitments or specific targets; in this respect, the language and structure are analogous to that of the FCTC. Moreover, neither the Declaration nor Resolution A/64/255 provides resources for countries to obtain the aspirational goals set down (although donor assistance is noted in the text).

Coordination of the Decade of Action rests with the WHO after express invitation to be a leading agency in the events underpinning the actions and activities designed to drive the Decade. It is, however, supported in this role by a global coalition of partners, including the United States, which is a signatory to the Moscow Declaration. With the National Highway Traffic Safety Administration estimating that some 34,080 people died on U.S. roads in 2012 alone,[77] the interest of the U.S. government, and the Centers for Disease Control and Prevention in particular, in promoting road safety at home is clear. Yet with "[r]oad traffic crashes . . . [as] the leading cause of death for healthy U.S.

citizens traveling abroad,"[78] the United States has a vested interest in ensuring that best practice and evidence-based policies are implemented not only in the nation but also across all jurisdictions.

The WHO has been, and shall continue to be, at the forefront of addressing global health challenges. The power vested in the body by its constitution, when used, has the capacity to provide the agency with vast authority over member states—including the United States—in relation to CDs and NCDs. Limited resourcing of the WHO, and issues of state sovereignty, as illustrated by U.S. refusal to ratify the FCTC, have the capacity to reduce the role and overall effectiveness of the organization in addressing global health challenges. For this reason it is important to look beyond the walls of the WHO in order to examine how global health challenges are being addressed, including by the United States.

LOOKING BEYOND THE WHO TO ADDRESS NCDs

Global health and trade are inextricably linked. In 2007, Nick Drager and David Fidler framed this relationship as one of "global health diplomacy."[79] To them, the interdependence between global health and trade was not new. An analysis of the relationship enables "us to see how countries historically dealt with health in their trade and foreign policies, particularly with respect to ensuring that health measures did not unnecessarily restrict international commerce."[80] It is in these negotiations that the attainment of health goals has often been secondary to the economic goals associated with trade objectives. Drager and Fidler go on to suggest, however, that through mechanisms such as the WHO's Fifty-Ninth WHA resolution on international trade and health the balance between the two has begun to shift, with greater emphasis being placed on public health priorities, including those aspects directly associated with the trade agenda.

The World Trade Organization (WTO) therefore has played a critical role in global health diplomacy since its establishment in 1995, despite being a body focused on trade liberalization between member states.[81] Trade is promoted by the WTO through the formation of a multilateral system; the terms of engagement are established through a number of binding agreements, each of which works to create "the legal ground rules for international commerce."[82] These include, for example, The General Agreement on Tariffs and Trade, 1994 (GATT); the General Agreement on Trade in Services (GATS); the Agreement on Technical Barriers to Trade (TBT Agreement); the Agreement on the Application of Sanitary and Phytosanitary Measures (SPS Agreement); and the Agreement on Trade-Related Aspects of Intellectual Property Rights (TRIPS Agreement). The breadth of activities covered by such agreements is, in short, overwhelming and includes goods, services, and intangible property, ranging from agriculture, food, animal and plant safety, to intellectual property (such as patents, copyright, and geographical indications). The United States, as a member of the WTO and thereby a contracting party, is bound by the terms of engagement set out in these instruments.

Health and health-related issues are continual themes that appear in WTO negotiations and before the WTO Dispute Settlement Body in the form of trade-related disputes. For example, access to medicines is heavily regulated through the patent provisions set out in Section 5 of the TRIPS Agreement.[83] This includes key and highly contentious public health measures such as compulsory licensing provisions for essential medicines.[84,85] For scholars such as Philippe Cullett, the competing pressures of profit, patent protection, and access to medicines in developing countries highlights the potential human rights challenges, including access to life-saving drugs in a timely manner and at a fair price, which are brought to the fore in a trade-based system.[86] The 2001 Ministerial Declaration on the TRIPS Agreement and Public Health (the Doha Declaration) may be viewed as an acknowledgment of these tensions, and the need for some countries to have greater flexibility in the employment of the TRIPS Agreement in relation to public health activities, including access to medicine, primarily for communicable diseases. Pursuant to paragraph 4 of the Doha Declaration:

> We agree that the TRIPS Agreement does not and should not prevent Members from taking measures to protect public health. Accordingly, while reiterating our commitment to the TRIPS Agreement, we affirm that the Agreement can and should be interpreted and implemented in a manner supportive of WTO Members' right to protect public health and, in particular, to promote access to medicines for all.[87]

The impact of the Doha Declaration on public health was examined in 2011 by Carlos Correa and Duncan Matthews in a discussion paper prepared for the United Nations Development Progamme. As noted by the authors:

> The adoption of the Doha Declaration was a significant achievement for developing countries. It recognized the "gravity" of the public health problems afflicting many developing and least-developed countries (LDCs), especially those resulting from HIV, tuberculosis, malaria and other epidemics. However, the Declaration is not limited to those diseases and epidemics, but applies to *any* disease, including NCDs.[88]

As such, while the focus of the discussion leading up to the Doha meeting was on more traditional public health challenges, such as those presented by the HIV/AIDS epidemic, countries could theoretically invoke the greater flexibility provided by the declaration in relation to patents and access to medicines for NCDs associated with obesity, high cholesterol, and diabetes. However, for this to occur, any such country would first have to meet the criteria set out in the declaration.

This brings the United States back around to one of the underappreciated roles for the FCTC, the WHO, and possible future framework conventions on public health: trade-proofing. There is a global governance structure, and much of it is economic, with the WTO and a variety of other organizations and bilateral dispute mechanisms dedicated to promoting free trade and protecting intellectual property and investors' rights. These organizations, and the treaties underpinning them, are not designed to promote health, let alone regulations on business in the interests of health. On one hand, this means that health regulations must conform to their requirements, such as nondiscrimination by national origin.[89] Not all of these requirements pose a problem for evidence-based public health policymaking. On the other hand, there are also ways that public health policies are constrained by economic law in, for example, the challenge of proportionality analysis that tends to be biased against policy innovation.[90] International economic law, including intellectual property, trade, and investor protection law, tends to stack the deck in favor of business engaged in cross-border trade and investment. The response, seen in the FCTC above all, is to secure international agreement on the importance of public health, the legitimacy of policies designed to promote it, and thereby force tribunals to balance between economic rights and public health rather than following the law to focus on economic rights alone.

The idea that public health can legitimately outweigh commerce and restrain trade is well entrenched in the case of communicable diseases (even to the extent of major countries, such as Brazil and the United States, breaking or threatening to break patents in order to deal with major CDs). It is no accident that NCDs are a front line; they are often caused by the very same economic actors whose actions are enabled by international economic law. When we talk about the challenges of NCDs, we almost automatically talk about the activities, investments, and intellectual property of multinational tobacco companies, for example, and therefore find ourselves challenging aspects of the structure of the world economy.

LOOKING AHEAD

The relationship among NCDs, human rights, and global governance involves a wide range of issues, some of which we have discussed in depth (such as tobacco regulation) and some of which we have barely mentioned (such as the global human rights movement and its take on health and mental health issues, from incarceration of the ill to female genital mutilation). What they have in common, beyond complexity, is that they involve the tensions between free-dom (of consumers and businesses alike) and public health, between long and short terms and between national poli-cies and a global context.

The structure of global governance combines two kinds of governance challenges.[91] In some situations, there is too little governance as in, for example, the difficulty of securing international agreement on pollution, climate change, or mental health. There is no one actor or forum that can decide what the world is doing. In other situations, there is too much governance, as in, for example, the use of investor protection mechanisms in trade law to oppose tobacco control policies. In these cases, a single-purpose mechanism dedicated to promoting trade or intellectual property influences, even if unintentionally, the governance of other policy areas such as public health.

In the case of NCDs, the tensions among human rights, economics, and public health take a variety of forms, which are then spread across multiple levels of global governance. Intervening to reduce NCDs can take public health into areas that are vulnerable to backlash, as with road safety measures (speed cameras, compulsory helmet wearing laws, and random breath and drug testing) and gun control in many countries. For many, government intervention in these areas of life may be viewed as an unwarranted impingement on autonomy and self-determi-nation and accordingly may be met with various forms of societal resistance. Public backlash against state interven-tion can subsequently appeal to human rights arguments that frame such public health initiatives as being authori-tarian and paternalistic.

On the other side, arguing against commercial threats to health (such as those that tobacco and many food com-panies pose), and arguing against environmental injustice, involves rhetoric that is not to be found in the world of business and economics. This is the appeal of human rights for proponents of public health; a human right to a clean environment or healthy society, or more minimally a human right to use roads or suffer mental illness without punishment, is a powerful thing to invoke. Human rights are particularly influential in these areas because of the paucity of other politically powerful arguments against economic liberalism in this day and age.

The result is that human rights are invoked on both sides, both as a counterweight to "authoritarian" public health measures and as a counterweight to economic argu-ments that do not account for health externalities. There are commercial interests on both sides; pharmaceutical companies have reason to be interested in NCDs, because they are often amenable to treatments that involve a life-time of medication (although it is not to be assumed that these firms' interests really run toward prevention). Recognition of such factors, including the commercial interests of both sides, is fundamental to moving the debate forward.

In short, the nexus of NCDs, human rights, and global governance has a way of bringing to the fore all of the prob-lems involved in all three arenas. There are a variety of opportunistic alliances on all sides, such as those who would connect human rights and international organizations, those who would connect human rights and opposition to public health policies, and those who would connect NCD policies with a right to health. In each case, they show the still unformed, and therefore promising, nature of this pol-icy area. The politics of public health, lifestyle, and business might be old, but the economy, governance, and associated debates are new and challenging.

See also **Chapter 23: Fifty Years of Progress in Disease and Injury Prevention (1950s–Present); Chapter 27: Continuing Challenges of Infectious Disease (1980s–Present); Chapter 28: Emergency Preparedness: Bioterrorism, Armed Conflict, Natural Disasters, and Other Public Health Threats (2000s–Present).**

NOTES

1. Neil M. Ferguson et al., "Strategies for Mitigating an Influenza Pandemic," *Nature* 442: 7101 (2006): 448–452.
2. Kamran Khan et al., "Spread of a Novel Influenza A (H1N1) Virus via Global Airline Transportation," *New England Journal of Medicine* 361: 2 (2009): 212–214.
3. Nina Marano and Marguerite Pappaioanou, "Historical, New, and Reemerging Links between Human and Animal Health," *Emerging Infectious Disease* 10: 2065 (2004): 6.
4. Joel G. Breman and Isao Arita, "The Confirmation and Maintenance of Smallpox Eradication," *New England Journal of Medicine* 303: 22 (1980): 1263–1273.
5. Moses Bockarie et al., *Review of the Multilateral Initiative on Malaria* (Bethesda, MD: MIM Secretariat, 2002), http://www.mimalaria.org/eng/docs/pdfs/Review_MIM_2002.pdf.
6. Pedro L. Alonso et al., "A Research Agenda to Underpin Malaria Eradication," *PLoS Medicine* 8: 1 (2011): e1000406.
7. Liam Donaldson and Nicholas Banatvala, "Health Is Global: Proposals for a UK Government-wide Strategy," *Lancet* 369: 9564 (2007): 857–861.
8. Lorenzo Giusti, "A Review of Waste Management Practices and Their Impact on Human Health," *Waste Management* 29: 8 (2009): 2227–2239.
9. Derek Yach et al., "The Global Burden of Chronic Diseases: Overcoming Impediments to Prevention and Control,"

Journal of the American Medical Association 291: 21 (2004): 2616–2622.

10. World Health Organization, "2008–2013 Action Plan for the Global Strategy for the Prevention and Control of Noncommunicable Diseases" (Geneva: World Health Organization, 2009), http://whqlibdoc.who.int/publications/2009/9789241597418_eng.pdf.

11. Robert Beaglehole et al., "Priority Actions for the Noncommunicable Disease Crisis," *Lancet* 377: 9775 (2011): 1438–1447.

12. Ibid., 14.

13. NCD Alliance, "The Global Epidemic," http://ncdalliance.org/globalepidemic.

14. Abdallah S. Daar et al., "Grand Challenges in Chronic Noncommunicable Diseases," *Nature* 450: 7169 (2007): 494–496.

15. David E. Bloom et al., *The Global Economic Burden of Noncommunicable Diseases* (Geneva, Switzerland: World Economic Forum, 2011).

16. World Health Organization and World Economic Forum, *From Burden to "Best Buys"; Reducing the Economic Impact of Noncommunicable Diseases in Low- and Middle-Income Countries* (Geneva: World Economic Forum, 2011).

17. George Alleyne, David Stuckler, and Ala Alwan, "The Hope and the Promise of the UN Resolution on Noncommunicable Diseases," *Global Health* 6 (2010): 15.

18. U.S. Department of State, "Addressing the Challenges of Noncommunicable Diseases," http://www.state.gov/documents/organization/172760.pdf.

19. World Health Organization and World Economic Forum, *From Burden to "Best Buys."*

20. World Health Organization, "Injuries and Violence: The Facts" (Geneva, Switzerland: World Health Organization, 2010).

21. Christopher J.L. Murray and Alan D. Lopez, "Measuring the Global Burden of Disease," *New England Journal of Medicine* 369: 5 (2013): 448–457.

22. Marc Suhrcke et al., *Economic Consequences of Noncommunicable Diseases and Injuries in the Russian Federation* (Geneva, Switzerland: World Health Organization, 2007).

23. World Health Organization, "Injuries and Violence."

24. Ibid.

25. Ibid.

26. Ibid.

27. Ibid.

28. Ibid.

29. World Health Organization, "Vienna Declaration on Nutrition and Noncommunicable Diseases in the Context of Health 2020," July 5, 2013, http://www.euro.who.int/__data/assets/pdf_file/0009/193878/Vienna-Declaration.pdf.

30. Robert Beaglehole and Derek Yach, "Globalisation and the Prevention and Control of Noncommunicable Disease: The Neglected Chronic Diseases of Adults," *Lancet* 362: 9387 (2003): 903–908.

31. Beaglehole et al., "Priority Actions."

32. Aviva Must et al., "The Disease Burden Associated with Overweight and Obesity," *Journal of the American Medical Association* 282: 16 (1999): 1523–1529.

33. Ali H. Mokdad et al., "Prevalence of Obesity, Diabetes, and Obesity-related Health Risk Factors, 2001," *Journal of the American Medical Association* 289: 1 (2003): 76–79.

34. Goodarz Danaei et al., "The Preventable Causes of Death in the United States: Comparative Risk Assessment of Dietary, Lifestyle, and Metabolic Risk Factors," *PLoS Medicine* 6: 4 (2009): e1000058.

35. Ronald Bayer, "The Continuing Tensions between Individual Rights and Public Health," *EMBO Reports* 8: 12 (2007): 1099–1103.

36. Lawrence O. Gostin, "A Proposal for a Framework Convention on Global Health," *Journal of International Economic Law* 10: 4 (2007): 989–1008.

37. Michelle M. Mello, David M. Studdert, and Troyen A. Brennan, "Obesity—the New Frontier of Public Health Law," *New England Journal of Medicine* 354: 24 (2006): 2601–2610.

38. David R. Buchanan, "Autonomy, Paternalism, and Justice: Ethical Priorities in Public Health," *American Journal of Public Health* 98: 1 (2008): 15–21.

39. James Colgrove and Ronald Bayer, "Manifold Restraints: Liberty, Public Health, and the Legacy of *Jacobson v. Massachusetts,*" *American Journal of Public Health* 95: 4 (2005): 571–576.

40. Julio Frenk and Suerie Moon, "Governance Challenges in Global Health," *New England Journal of Medicine* 368 (2013): 936 942.

41. Bayer, "The Continuing Tensions."

42. Kent Buse, Wolfgang Hein, and Nick Drager, *Making Sense of Global Health Governance* (Basingstoke, UK: Palgrave Macmillan, 2009).

43. World Health Organization, "Working for Health: An Introduction to the World Health Organization" (Geneva, Switzerland: World Health Organization, 2007).

44. World Health Organization, *Constitution of the World Health Organization* (Geneva, Switzerland: World Health Organization, 1946).

45. World Health Organization, *Constitution of the World Health Organization*, 45th ed., supplement (Geneva, Switzerland: World Health Organization, 2006), http://apps.who.int/gb/bd/PDF/bd47/EN/constitution-en.pdf.

46. Nitsan Chorev, *The World Health Organization between North and South* (Cornell University Press, 2012).

47. Buse, Hein, and Drager, *Making Sense of Global Health Governance.*

48. World Health Organization, *Constitution of the World Health Organization* (1946).

49. World Health Organization, *Constitution of the World Health Organization*, 45th ed.

50. World Health Organization, *Comprehensive Mental Health Action Plan 2013–2020* (Geneva, Switzerland: World Health Organization, May 27, 2013).

51. Ibid.

52. Ibid.

53. Ibid.

54. Daniel Chisholm et al., "Scale Up Services for Mental Disorders: A Call for Action," *Lancet* 370: 9594 (2007): 1241–1252.

55. Pamela Y. Collins et al., "Grand Challenges in Global Mental Health," *Nature* 475: 7354 (2011): 27–30.

56. World Health Organization, "The Global Burden of Mental Disorders and the Need for a Comprehensive, Coordinated Response from Health and Social Sectors at the Country Level" (Geneva, Switzerland: World Health Organization, May 26, 2012).

57. Ibid.

58. Ibid., 56

59. United Nations, "64/265 Prevention and Control of Noncommunicable Disease" (New York: United Nations, May 20, 2010).

60. World Health Organization. "Global Status Report of Noncommunicable Diseases 2010" (Geneva, Switzerland: World Health Organization, 2011).

61. Victoria K. Ngo et al., "Grand Challenges: Integrating Mental Health Care into the Noncommunicable Disease Agenda," *PLoS Medicine* 10: 5 (2013): e1001443.

62. Ritsuko Kakuma et al., "Human Resources for Mental Health Care: Current Situation and Strategies for Action," *Lancet* 378: 9803 (2011): 1654–1663.

63. Ibid., 55.

64. Ibid., 56.

65. Ibid., 60.

66. Margie Peden et al., eds., *World Report on Road Traffic Injury Prevention* (Geneva, Switzerland: World Health Organization, 2004), http://apps.who.int/bookorders/anglais/detart1.jsp?cod lan=1&codcol=15&codcch=572.

67. World Health Organization, *World Health Organization Global Status Report on Road Safety: Time for Action* (Geneva, Switzerland: World Health Organization, 2009), 5–6, http://whqlibdoc.who.int/publications/2009/9789241563840_eng .pdf.

68. Kevin Watkins and Devi Sridhar, *Road Traffic Injuries: The Hidden Development Crisis* (London: Make Roads Safe, 2009), 7, 9.

69. G.A. Res 57/309, U.N. GAOR, 57th Sess., Doc. A/57/L.77 and Add. 1 (May 29, 2003).

70. G.A. Res 58/289, U.N. GAOR, 58th Sess., Doc. A/58/L.60/ Rev.1 and Add. 1 (May 11, 2004).

71. Ruth Roemer, Allyn Taylor, and Jean Lariviere, "Origins of the WHO Framework Convention on Tobacco Control," *American Journal of Public Health* 95: 6 (2005): 936–938.

72. Diana M. Bowman, Michael P. Fitzharris, and Ray Bingham, "Making a Positive Impact: Striking a Balance between Legislative Reach and Road Safety," *Annals of Health Law* 22 (2013): 281–306.

73. Ibid.

74. World Health Organization, "First Global Ministerial Conference on Road Safety: Time for Action, Moscow Declaration" (November 2009), http://www.who.int/road safety/ministerial_conference/declaration_en.pdf.

75. World Health Organization, *Global Plan for the Decade of Action for Road Safety 2011–2020* (Geneva, Switzerland: World Health Organization, 2011).

76. World Health Organization, "First Global Ministerial Conference."

77. National Highway Traffic and Safety Administration, "Early Estimate of Motor Vehicle Traffic Fatalities in 2012" (May 2013), http://www-nrd.nhtsa.dot.gov/Pubs/811741.pdf

78. Centers for Disease Control and Prevention, "Global Road Safety," http://www.cdc.gov/features/globalroadsafety.

79. Nick Drager and David P. Fidler, "Foreign Policy, Trade and Health: At the Cutting Edge of Global Health Diplomacy," *Bulletin of the World Health Organization* 85: 3 (2007): 162–162.

80. Ibid.

81. World Trade Organization, "Understanding the WTO: The Organization," http://www.wto.org/english/thewto_e/ whatis_e/tif_e/org6_e.htm.

82. World Trade Organization, *Annual Report 2013* (Geneva, Switzerland: World Trade Organization, 2013), http://www .wto.org/english/res_e/booksp_e/anrep_e/anrep13_e.pdf.

83. Frederick M. Abbott and Jerome H. Reichman, "The Doha Round's Public Health Legacy: Strategies for the Production and Diffusion of Patented Medicines under the Amended TRIPS Provisions," *Journal of International Economic Law* 10: 4 (2007): 921–987.

84. Frederic M. Scherer and Jayashree Watal. "Post-TRIPS Options for Access to Patented Medicines in Developing Nations," *Journal of International Economic Law* 5: 4 (2002): 913–939.

85. Duncan Matthews, "WTO Decision on Implementation of Paragraph 6 of the DOHA Declaration on the TRIPs Agreement and Public Health: A Solution to the Access to Essential Medicines Problem?" *Journal of International Economic Law* 7: 1 (2004): 73–107.

86. Jillian Claire Cohen-Kohler, "The Morally Uncomfortable Global Drug Gap," *Clinical Pharmacology & Therapeutics* 82: 5 (2007): 610–614.

87. World Trade Organization, "Understanding the WTO."

88. Duncan Matthews and Carlos Correa, *The Doha Declaration Ten Years on and Its Impact on Access to Medicines and the Right to Health* (New York: United Nations Development Programme, Bureau for Development Policy, 2011).

89. Holly Jarman, Judith Schmidt, and Daniel B. Rubin, "When Trade Law Meets Public Health Evidence: The World Trade Organization and Clove Cigarettes," *Tobacco Control* 21: 6 (2012): 596–598.

90. Holly Jarman, *The Politics of Trade and Tobacco Control* (Basingstoke, UK: Macmillan, 2014).

91. Scott L. Greer, "Global Health Policy: Governing Health Systems across Borders," In *Healthcare Management*, 2nd ed., edited by Kieran Walshe and Judith Smith, 120–143 (New York: McGraw-Hill, 2011).

FURTHER READING

Alleyne, George, David Stuckler, and Ala Alwan. "The Hope and the Promise of the UN Resolution on Noncommunicable Diseases." *Global Health* 6 (2010): 15.

Beaglehole, Robert, and Derek Yach. "Globalisation and the Prevention and Control of Noncommunicable Disease: The Neglected Chronic Diseases of Adults." *Lancet* 362: 9387 (2003): 903–908.

Buse, Kent, Wolfgang Hein, and Nick Drager. *Making Sense of Global Health Governance.* New York: Palgrave Macmillan, 2009.

Centers for Disease Control and Prevention. "Global Health— Noncommunicable Diseases." http://www.cdc.gov/global health/ncd.

Chorev, Nitsan. *The World Health Organization between North and South.* Ithaca, NY: Cornell University Press, 2012.

McQueen, David V. *Global Handbook on Noncommunicable Diseases and Health Promotion.* New York: Springer, 2013.

World Health Organization. "Global Action Plan for the Prevention and Control of NCDs 2013–2020." http://www .who.int/nmh/en.

World Health Organization. "WHO Framework Convention on Tobacco Control." http://www.who.int/fctc/en.

chapter 30

The Governance of Population Health

Reflections on the Analytical Approaches of Contributors to the *Guide*

Daniel M. Fox

I HOPE TO HELP READERS USE THIS BOOK BY SHARING how it contributes to understanding the governance of health affairs in the United States during the last century. I begin by defining governance and population health. Then I summarize different approaches to examining the governance and scope of American health policy among the contributors of the preceding chapters. I conclude by suggesting how readers can use and supplement what they read in this book.

I call one analytical approach used by authors "structural/functionalist," another "historical," and a third "cataloguing." Structural/functionalists examine data about politics and policies primarily to test theories and models about governance and their results. Authors who use a historical approach assess the strength and relevance of evidence mainly to explain political events and the policy that results from them. Cataloguers consider it sufficient to array statistics and descriptions of disease and other health problems, policies, and the agencies that formulate and implement them. Although I prefer the historical approach, in order to help readers examine, or perhaps formulate, their own preferences and therefore how they will use this book, I turn next to defining governance and population health.

GOVERNANCE AND POPULATION HEALTH: DEFINITIONS

Numerous definitions of governance are available in the literature of the disciplines and subdisciplines of the policy sciences, which include economics, history, international affairs, law, political science, political sociology, and public management. The definition I use is grounded in this literature, but I augment it with what I have learned during half a century of working in and writing about the politics of making and implementing policies as they occur in streets and homes, on dirt roads and highways, in offices,

corridors, conference rooms, and legislative chambers. In my experience, understanding governance requires knowing who does what, with, for, and to whom to achieve what purposes—and why they do it.[1]

People who have reliable answers to these questions, and who are sensitive to when and how changes in these answers occur in a jurisdiction or one of its sectors, are equipped to study, teach about, or participate in governance. Standard sources for answering the questions include experience as a student, teacher, practicing professional, friend, family member, and voter; critical reading of published and unpublished articles, books, and documents; and skeptical attention to print and electronic media.

A variety of assumptions have proven useful for describing and explaining the governance of any jurisdiction or sector. Two are particularly relevant to readers who want to make informed judgments about the evidence in this book and how authors selected and interpreted it. One is that those who tell sometimes do not know, while those who know often cannot tell. The other assumption is that it is helpful for participants and students of governance to establish categories for arraying the endless supply of evidence about it. I have found it useful to array evidence about the history of governance and its effects in four categories: ideas (which includes ideology as well as philosophical and scientific concepts), interests (usually involving commercial, professional, and issue-based advocacy groups), institutions (both formal organizations and customary behavior), and illness (the burden of disease and disability). These categories inform my inquiries, as a participant as well as a researcher, about any aspect of health policy.[2]

In contrast, most persons who have studied and participated in the governance of health affairs since early in the twentieth century have prioritized categories that relate more precisely to activities. They usually distinguish, for instance, between the governance of personal health services and of public health activities.

In recent decades, prominent participants in health policy research and governance have advocated categorizing activities within and outside the health sector on the basis of their effects on the health of populations. Their purpose in promoting a new category of population health is to focus attention on the multiple determinants of the health status of a population and on the role of governance in producing and responding to the effects of particular determinants. Prominent determinants include access (or lack of it) to health care and services related to it, the quality and safety of care (or lack of attention to these characteristics), and potential risks to the health status of populations and individuals as a result of characteristics of particular physical, political, economic, and social environments.

This population health perspective is acquiring significant national and international salience and is very much part of the thinking behind the organization and content of this book (hence, chapters on prevention, preparedness, global health, as well as population groups—minorities, women, children). It is currently informing the politics of health policy in many countries and their sub-jurisdictions. Leaders of numerous international organizations, with both public and private financing, routinely describe their work as measuring and intervening to improve population health, which they frequently describe as "global health."

Explicit attention to the multiple determinants of population health has recently become a prominent aspect of U.S. policy. Most visibly, officials of the federal Medicare program have, since 2010, promoted a "triple aim" of improving the quality of care, containing the growth of its costs, and improving population health. This policy currently defines populations as persons served by provider systems. In addition, regulations issued in 2013 by the Internal Revenue Service to implement a section of the Patient Protection and Affordable Care Act of 2010 require nonprofit health care facilities to document the health status of residents of the communities they serve in order to plan and then measure the benefits they provide to them.

APPROACHES TO THE GOVERNANCE OF POPULATION HEALTH IN THE *GUIDE TO U.S. HEALTH AND HEALTH CARE POLICY*

Readers who came to this chapter after studying or skimming all or some of those that precede it are likely to have noticed diversity among them. Authors chose to emphasize particular aspects of their assigned subjects. As a result, the titles of the book chapters are actually statements of intent. Issues discussed in chapters on the evolution of health policy overlap with many in chapters about government organizations. Most of the chapters that readers may initially assume are about current rather than past events—those on contemporary policy issues and responses to global health care challenges—are explicitly rooted in history.

Regardless of which approach the author or co-authors of each chapter employ to explain health politics and policy, most imply rather than articulate the approach they use and the assumptions that underlie it. Approximately one-third of the chapters use a structural/functionalist approach; most chapters use a variant of historical methodology.

What are the predominant features of each analytical approach? The structural/functionalists prioritize concepts, principles, and cross-cutting themes in U.S. government and political history. That is, they explain events in health politics and policy as evidence of, for example,

- Americans' deeply rooted commitment to individualism, or of predictable behavior by particular interest and advocacy groups;
- the problems of enforcing the separation of powers or of conducting federalism, or of the influence of market-oriented behavior;
- key factors in how agendas for policymaking are set;
- or, more generally, what some scholars call "American exceptionalism," the idea that life in the United States has always been different, and often better, than life in other countries that are now called industrial democracies.

The structural/functionalists foreground theory, often without acknowledging explicitly that they do. These authors seek evidence to test the applicability of theoretical constructs or models that are familiar to persons who identify themselves as practitioners of particular disciplines of the policy sciences, particularly economics, political science, political sociology, and public administration or management. The potential contribution of such analysis is to illustrate how a specific area of health policy follows a more general pattern in politics and governance of complex systems. The structural/functionalists, that is, demonstrate the validity of political economist Albert O. Hirschman's landmark insight that a "model is never defeated by facts, however damaging, but only by another model."[3]

Those chapters based predominantly on research using historical methods accord priority to telling credible stories rather than testing theories and models; the authors identify themselves with work in different disciplines of the policy sciences, especially with history, law, and their various subdisciplines. Some of these authors also identify with colleagues in political science or sociology who also are reluctant to theorize and test models. They prioritize, for example, describing:

- struggles for scarce power among the three branches of government rather than about the separation of powers;
- conflicts between federal and state officials, rather than about federalism; or

- the influence of critical events, individual or organizational decisions, and social context in the course of policy development.

In prioritizing empiricism over modeling, these authors tend to address a broader range of issues. They also accord greater attention to the influence on policy of, for example:

- the changing burden of disease on populations of various ages,
- the social history of religion and racism,
- the interaction of interest and advocacy groups with public officials, and
- the politics of organizing and running public agencies.

WHY APPROACHES TO THE POLITICS OF HEALTH POLICY DIFFER

Because it may help readers of this book to assess its chapters, I will try to explain the significant differences in their authors' approaches that I have described. I begin with personal experience and then summarize relevant contemporary literature.

I experience most painfully the difference between structural/functionalist and historical methods when political scientists accuse me of being wrong about generalizations that my colleagues in the politics of policymaking regard as self-evidently true. Throughout my career, political scientists have told me at conferences and in journals that something I said or wrote about politics was not in their literature and hence was wrong. When I reported such criticism to colleagues in government and politics, however, they often replied that anyone who rejects my point would not survive in our work.

I frequently tease friends who are political scientists about when and why so many of their colleagues decided they disliked politics so intensely that they preferred theorizing and modelling to observing, documenting, and even participating in it. A more diplomatic statement of this question would be why some colleagues who study politics have less interest in what people who do politics professionally say about their work than in testing theories and models.

I found some guidance to answering this question in recent literature about methodology in the policy sciences. In *Bureaucracy in a Democratic State: A Governance*

In order to positively impact the health of the U.S. population, President Lyndon B. Johnson (1963–1969) signs the Medicare bill into law on July 30, 1965. Looking on (from left to right) are First Lady Claudia "Lady Bird" Johnson, Vice President Hubert H. Humphrey (in office 1965–1969), former President Harry S. Truman (1945–1953), and former First Lady Bess Truman. As President Truman had supported nationwide health coverage while he was in the White House, the signing of Medicare brought Truman's plans to fruition.

SOURCE: © Bettmann/Corbis.

Perspective,[4] two scholars define as a struggle for "political control" what those of us in politics consider the normal resistance of subject-matter specialists in civil service positions to many of the goals of persons to whom they are accountable, people who have been elected to legislative office or govern countries and their subjurisdictions.

Another prevalent assumption among scholars of politics is that they already know from their literature what public servants could tell them. For example, the authors of a heralded study of "policy bureaucracy" in the United Kingdom decided they need not interview "senior civil servants, ministers, interest groups, parliamentarians…."[5]

Similarly, a distinguished political scientist, Daniel Carpenter, defined "bureaucratic autonomy" as the happy result of "bureaucrats' tak[ing] actions consistent with their own wishes … to which politicians and organized interests defer."[6] I have not yet encountered an elected official or the appointed head of an agency in the executive branch who would contemplate deference to bureaucrats.

In sharp contrast to the dominant views in the literature, another distinguished political scientist, Paul Pierson, wrote that theories and models are an aspect of "a rich tradition of historical research in the social sciences." He recommended that his colleagues devise "theoretical understandings of the different ways in which history matters in explaining social phenomenon."[7]

SUGGESTIONS FOR READING THE *GUIDE*

The preceding chapters describe and assess how health politics and policy in the United States have been and continue to be governed in response to and in the context of the multiple determinants of the health of U.S. populations. I proposed definitions of governance and of population health and then described and briefly assessed different methods used by the authors who contributed to this book.

My goal is to assist readers to understand and, as a result, decide how they might best use this book in their own activities, especially as students, teachers, and scholars. I suggest that readers judge how well each chapter addresses these key questions about governance and population health:

• Governance: Does the chapter describe precisely who did what, to, for, and with whom and why they did it in order to explain epidemiological trends or important outcomes in health care access, quality, or costs? Does the chapter describe and explain changes in the governance of the health sector and of the United States more generally that account for the events that are its subject? Does the methodology used to write the chapter, and findings based on applying it, lead to a persuasive explanation for particular events and policies and for the role of governance in shaping them?

• Population health: Does the chapter provide data about and a convincing explanation for each of the determinants of health that created, or at times constrained, demand for the policies it discusses? Does the chapter offer evidence about the effects of particular policies on each determinant of health associated with it and the factors that created demand to make and then to change or maintain particular policies? Does the methodology used in the chapter lead to persuasive generalizations about the effects of the policies it discusses on population health over time?

In reading the *Guide to U.S. Health and Health Care Policy,* I hope readers find these suggestions helpful.

NOTES

1. Daniel M. Fox, *The Convergence of Science and Governance: Research Health Policy and American States* (Berkeley: University of California Press, 2010).

2. Daniel M. Fox, *Power and Illness: The Failure and Future of American Health Policy* (Berkeley: University of California Press, 1993,1995).

3. Albert O. Hirschman, *Exit, Voice and Loyalty: Responses to Decline in Firms, Organizations, and States* (Cambridge, MA: Harvard University Press, 1970), 68.

4. Kenneth J. Meier, and Laurence J. O'Toole, Jr., *Bureaucracy in a Democratic State: A Governance Perspective* (Baltimore, MD: Johns Hopkins University Press, 2006).

5. Edward C. Page, and Bill Jenkins, *Policy Bureaucracy: Government with a Cast of Thousands* (Oxford, UK: Oxford University Press, 2005), xiv.

6. Daniel P. Carpenter, *The Forging of Bureaucratic Autonomy: Reputations, Networks, and Policy Innovation in Executive Agencies, 1862-1928* (Princeton, NJ: Princeton University Press, 2001), 21–44.

7. Paul Pierson, *Politics in Time: History, Institutions and Social Analysis* (Princeton, NJ: Princeton University Press, 2004), 4–6.

FURTHER READING

Fox, Daniel M. *The Convergence of Science and Governance: Research Health Policy and American States.* Berkeley: University of California Press, 2010.

Selected Federal Health and Health Care Agencies and Offices

The vast majority of health-related agencies and offices are located in the U.S. Department of Health and Human Services and the U.S. Department of Agriculture. In general, these two cabinet departments have the greatest impact on governmental health policy and on U.S. citizens' health. Nevertheless, many agencies of the federal government bear some public health or health care responsibilities. Among those agencies are the following:

U.S. Department of Health and Human Services

- Administration for Children and Families (ACF)
- Administration for Community Living (ACL)
- Agency for Healthcare Research and Quality (AHRQ)
- Centers for Disease Control and Prevention (CDC)
- Office of Infectious Diseases
- Office of Noncommunicable Diseases, Injury and Environmental Health
- Office of Public Health and Science
- Office of Population Affairs
- Office of Women's Health
- Vaccines for Children (VFC)
- Centers for Medicare and Medicaid Services (CMS)
- Children's Health Insurance Program (CHIP)
- Federal Coordinated Health Care Office
- Program for All-Inclusive Care for the Elderly (PACE)
- National Breast and Cervical Cancer Early Detection Program (NBCCEDP)
- Food and Drug Administration (FDA)
- Health Resources and Services Administration (HRSA)
- Indian Health Service (IHS)
- National Institutes of Health (NIH)
- National Institute of Mental Health (NIMH)
- Substance Abuse Mental Health Services Administration (SAMHSA)
- National Institute of Child Health and Human Development (NICD)
- National Institute on Drug Abuse
- Administration on Children, Youth and Families
- Office of Head Start
- Office of Child Care
- Office of Early Childhood Development
- Office of the Inspector General

U.S. Department of Agriculture

- Food and Nutrition Services (FNS)
- National School Lunch Program (NSLP)
- School Breakfast Program (SBP)
- Special Milk Program (SMP)
- Summer Food Service Program (SFSP)
- Center for Nutrition Policy and Promotion (CNPP)
- Supplemental Nutrition Assistance Program (SNAP)
- Child and Adult Care Food Program (CACFP)
- Commodity Supplemental Food Program (CSFP)
- Food Distribution Program on Indian Reservations (FDPIR)
- The Emergency Food Assistance Program (TEFAP)
- Special Supplemental Nutrition Program for Women, Infants, and Children (WIC)
- Food Safety and Inspection Service (FSIS)
- Fresh Fruit and Vegetable Program

U.S. Department of Labor

- Occupational Safety and Health Administration (OSHA)
- Mine Safety and Health Administration (MSHA)

U.S. Department of Defense

- Defense Environment Safety and Occupational Health Network and Information Exchange (DENIX)
- Military Health System
- Civilian Health and Medical Program of the Uniformed Services (CHAMPUS)
- Office of Medical Services

U.S. Department of Energy

- Office of Health, Safety, and Security

U.S. Department of State

- United States Agency for International Development (USAID)
- Office of the Global AIDS Coordinator

U.S. Department of Education

- Office of Safe and Healthy Students (OSHS)
- Office of Elementary and Secondary Education
- Office of Special Education and Rehabilitation Services
- Office of English Language Acquisition, Language Enhancement and Academic Achievement for Limited English Proficient Students

U.S. Department of Commerce

- International Trade Administration (ITA)

U.S. Department of Transportation

- National Highway and Traffic Safety Administration (NHTSA)

U.S. Department of Justice

- Drug Enforcement Agency (DEA)
- Bureau of Alcohol, Tobacco, Firearms and Explosives (ATF)
- Criminal Division, Fraud Section

U.S. Department of Homeland Security

- Federal Emergency Management Agency (FEMA)
- Office of Health Affairs

U.S. Department of Veterans Affairs

- Veterans Health Administration (VHA)
- Veterans Benefits Administration
- Office of Disability Assistance
- Defense Health Agency

Environmental Protection Agency

- Office of Air and Radiation (OAR)
- Office of Chemical Safety and Pollution Prevention (OCSPP)
- Office of Solid Waste and Emergency Response (OSWER)
- Office of Water
- Office of Children's Health Protection

Federal Trade Commission

- Bureau of Competition
- Bureau of Consumer Protection
- Bureau of Economics

Bibliography

PART I—EVOLUTION OF AMERICAN HEALTH CARE POLICY (BEGINNINGS TO TODAY)

Abramson, John. *Overdosed America: The Broken Promise of American Medicine.* New York: HarperCollins, 2004.

Altman, Stuart, and David Shactman. *Power, Politics and Universal Health Care: The Inside Story of a Century-Long Battle.* Amherst, NY: Prometheus Books, 2011.

Baer, John M. "Wofford Uses Soft Sell in His First TV Ads." *Philly .com.* http://articles.philly.com/1991-09-10/news/25801370_1_ democrat-harris-wofford-dick-thornburgh-tv-ads.

Ball, Robert. "What Medicare's Architects Had in Mind." *Health Affairs* 14: 4 (1995): 62–72.

Bernstein, Merton C., and Joan B. Bernstein. *Social Security: The System That Works.* New York: Basic Books, 1988.

Blumenthal, David, and James A. Morone. *The Heart of Power: Health and Politics in the Oval Office.* Berkeley: University of California Press, 2009.

Breslaw, Elaine G. *Lotions, Potions, Pills, and Magic: Health Care in Early America.* New York: New York University Press, 2012.

Broder, David, and Haynes Johnson. *The System: The American Way of Politics at a Breaking Point.* Boston: Little, Brown, 1996.

Brown, Lawrence, and Michael Sparer. "Poor Program's Progress: The Unanticipated Politics of Medicaid Policy." *Health Affairs* 22: 1 (2003): 31–44.

Brownlee, Shannon. *Overtreated: How Too Much Medicine Is Making Us Sicker and Poorer.* New York: Bloomsbury, 2007.

Buchmueller, Thomas C., and Alan C. Monheit. "Employer-Sponsored Health Insurance and the Promise of Health Insurance Reform" (NBER Working Paper Series). Cambridge, MA: National Bureau of Economic Research, 2009. http:// www.nber.org/papers/w14839.

Budrys, Grace. *Our Unsystematic Health Care System.* 3rd ed. Lanham, MD: Rowman & Littlefield, 2011.

Burton, John D. "'The Awful Judgments of God upon the Land': Smallpox in Colonial Cambridge." *New England Quarterly* 74: 3 (2001): 495–506.

Clemens-Cope, Lisa, Stephen Zuckerman, and Dean Resnick. "Limiting the Tax Exclusion of Employer-Sponsored Health Insurance Premiums: Revenue Potential and Distributional Consequences." Washington, DC: Urban Institute, 2013. http://www.rwjf.org/content/dam/farm/reports/issue_ briefs/2013/rwjf405948.

"Clinton's Health Plan: Transcript of President's Address to Congress on Health Care." *New York Times.* http://www .nytimes.com/1993/09/23/us/clinton-s-health-plan-tran script-president-s-address-congress-health-care .html?pagewanted=all&src=pm.

Cohn, Jonathan. "How They Did It." *The New Republic,* May 20, 2010.

———. *Sick: The Untold Story of America's Health Care Crisis—and the People Who Pay the Price.* New York: HarperCollins, 2008.

Coughlin, Teresa A., and Stephen Zuckerman. "State Responses to New Flexibility in Medicaid." *Milbank Quarterly* 86: 2 (2008): 209–240.

Dentzer, Susan. "America's Scandalous Health Care." *U.S. News and World Report* 108: 10 (1990): 24–28, 30.

Deutsch, Albert. "The Sick Poor in Colonial Times." *American Historical Review* 45: 3 (1941).

Dinan, John. "Shaping Health Reform: State Government Influence in the Patient Protection and Affordable Care Act." *Publius* 41: 3 (2011): 395–420.

Duffy, John. *The Sanitarians: The History of American Public Health.* Chicago: University of Illinois Press, 1990.

Ehrenreich, Barbara. "Our Health-Care Disgrace." *Time* 136: 25 (1990): 1–12.

Elhauge, Einer, ed. *The Fragmentation of U.S. Health Care: Causes and Solutions.* New York: Oxford University Press, 2010.

Feingold, Eugene. *Medicare: Policy and Politics: A Case Study and Policy Analysis.* San Francisco: Chandler, 1966.

Garrison, Fielding H. *An Introduction to the History of Medicine.* Philadelphia: Saunders, 1960.

Ginsberg, David L. "Health Care Policy in the Reagan Administration: Rhetoric and Reality." *Public Administration Quarterly* 11: 1 (1987): 59–70.

Goodman, Christopher J., and Stephen M. Mance. "Employment Loss and the 2007–2009 Recession: An Overview." *Monthly Labor Review* (April 2011): 3–12.

Gordon, Colin. *Dead on Arrival: The Politics of Health Care in Twentieth-Century America.* Princeton, NJ: Princeton University Press, 2003.

Hacker, Jacob S. *The Road to Nowhere: The Genesis of President Clinton's Plan for Health Security.* Princeton, NJ: Princeton University Press, 1997.

———. *The Divided Welfare State: The Battle over Public and Private Social Benefits in the United States.* New York: Cambridge University Press, 2002.

Hayes, Katherine. "Overview of Policy, Procedure, and Legislative History of the Affordable Care Act." *National Academy of Elder Law Attorneys* 7: 1 (2011): 1–9.

Hirshfield, Daniel. *The Lost Reform: The Campaign for Compulsory Health Insurance in the United States from 1932–1943.* Cambridge, MA: Harvard University Press, 1970.

Hoffman, Beatrix. *Health Care for Some: Rights and Rationing in the United States Since 1930.* Chicago: University of Chicago Press, 2012.

———. *The Wages of Sickness: The Politics of Health Insurance in Progressive America.* Chapel Hill: University of North Carolina Press, 2001.

Jacobs, Lawrence R., and Theda Skocpol. *Health Care Reform and American Politics: What Everyone Needs to Know.* New York: Oxford University Press, 2010.

Kenney, Genevieve, Jennifer Haley, and Alexandra Tabay. "Children's Insurance Coverage and Service Use Improve." In *Snapshots of American Families III.* Washington, DC: Urban Institute, July 2003.

Kleinke, J. D. *Oxymorons: The Myth of a U.S. Health Care System.* San Francisco: Jossey-Bass, 2001.

Kornick, Richard, and Todd Gilmer. "Explaining the Decline in Health Insurance Coverage, 1979–1995." *Health Affairs* 18: 2 (1999): 30–47.

Kulczyski, Andrzej. "Ethics, Ideology, and Reproductive Health Policy in the United States." *Studies in Family Planning* 38: 4 (2007): 333–351.

Levit, Katharine R., et al. "National Health Expenditures, 1993." *Health Care Financing Review* 16: 1 (1994): 247–294.

Lewis, Anthony. "A Sick System." *New York Times,* June 3 1991, A17.

Lynn, Joanne. *Sick to Death and not Going to Take It Anymore! Reforming Health Care for the Last Years of Life.* Berkeley: University of California Press, 2004.

Marmor, Theodore. *The Politics of Medicare.* New York: Aldine, 1973.

Mayes, Rick. *Universal Coverage: The Elusive Quest for National Health Insurance.* Ann Arbor: University of Michigan Press, 2001.

McCarthy, Michael. "Fragmented US Health-Care System Needs Major Reform." *Lancet* 357: 9258 (2001): 782.

McDonough, John E. *Inside National Health Reform.* Berkeley: University of California Press, 2009.

McFarlane, Deborah R. "Reproductive Health Policy in President Bush's Second Term: Old Battles and New Fronts in the United States and Internationally." *Journal of Public Health Policy* 27: 4 (2006): 405–426.

Means, James H. "Homo Medicus Americanus." *Daedalus* 92: 4 (1963): 701–723.

Mickey, Robert. "Dr. StrangeRove; or, How Conservatives Learned to Stop Worrying and Love Community Health Centers." In *The Health Care Safety Net in a Post-Reform World,* edited by Mark A. Hall, 21–66. New Brunswick, NJ: Rutgers University Press, 2012).

Morone, James A. "Enemies of the People: The Moral Dimension to Public Health." *Journal of Health, Politics, Policy and Law* 22: 4 (1997): 993–1020.

———. *Hellfire Nation.* New Haven, CT: Yale University Press, 2004.

Mushkin, Selina. "The Internal Revenue Code of 1954 and Health Programs." *Public Health Reports* 70: 8 (1955): 791–800.

Myers, Robert J. *Medicare.* Bryn Mawr, PA: McCahan Foundation, 1970.

Nixon, Richard. "Message to Congress." *Weekly Compilation of Presidential Documents.* Washington, DC: Office of the Federal Register, February 18, 1971.

———. "Special Message to the Congress Proposing a National Health Strategy." February 18, 1971. http://www.presidency.ucsb.edu/ws/?pid=3311.

Numbers, Ronald. *Almost Persuaded: American Physicians and Compulsory Health Insurance.* Baltimore: Johns Hopkins University Press, 1978.

Oberlander, Jonathan. "Learning from Failure in Health Care Reform." *New England Journal of Medicine* 357: 17 (2007): 1677–1679.

———. "Long Time Coming: Why Health Reform Finally Passed." *Health Affairs* 29: 6 (2010): 1112–1116.

———. *The Political Life of Medicare.* Chicago: University of Chicago Press, 2003.

Patel, Kant, and Mark Rushefsky. *Health Care Politics and Policy in America.* 5th ed. New York: M.E. Sharpe, 2014.

———. *The Politics of Public Health in the United States.* New York: M.E. Sharpe, 2005.

Poen, Monte M. *Harry S. Truman versus the Medical Lobby: The Genesis of Medicare.* Columbia: University of Missouri Press, 1979.

Quadagno, Jill. *One Nation Uninsured: Why the U.S. Has No National Health Insurance.* New York: Oxford University Press, 2005.

Quazi, Khalid J. "Health Care Reform in the United States: Fact, Fiction and Drama." *British Journal of Medical Practitioners* 2: 4 (2009): 5–7.

Reagan, Michael D. *The Accidental System: Health Care Policy in America.* Boulder, CO: Waterview Press, 1999.

Rosenberg, Charles E. *The Care of Strangers: The Rise of American Hospital System.* New York: Basic Books, 1987.

Rothman, David J. *Beginnings Count: The Technological Imperative in American Health Care.* New York: Oxford University Press, 1997.

Schneider, Anne L., and Helen M. Ingram. *Deserving and Entitled: Social Constructions and Public Policy.* Albany: State University of New York Press, 2004.

Shyrock, Richard H. "The Health of the American People: An Historical Survey." *Proceedings of the American Philosophical Society* 90: 4 (1946): 251–258.

Silva, Cristobal. "Miraculous Plagues: Epidemiology on New England's Colonial Landscape." *Early American Literature* 43: 2 (2008): 249–275.

Skocpol, Theda. *Boomerang: Health Care Reform and the Turn against Government.* New York: W.W. Norton, 1997.

Starbuck, David R. "Military Hospitals on the Frontier of Colonial America." *Expedition* 39: 1 (1997): 33–46.

Starr, Paul. *Remedy and Reaction: The Peculiar American Struggle over Health Care Reform.* New Haven, CT: Yale University Press, 2011.

———. *The Social Transformation of American Medicine.* New York: Basic Books, 1982.

———. "What Happened to Health Care Reform?" *American Prospect* 20 (Winter 1995): 20–31.

Stevens, Rosemary A. *American Medicine and the Public Interest.* Berkeley: University of California Press, 1998.

———. *In Sickness and in Wealth: American Hospitals in the Twentieth Century.* New York: Basic Books, 1989.

———. *The Public-Private Health Care State: Essays on the History of American Health Care Policy.* Piscataway, NJ: Transaction, 2007.

Stevens, Rosemary A., Charles E. Rosenberg., and Lawton R. Burns. *History and Health Policy in the Unites States.* New Brunswick, NJ: Rutgers University Press, 2006.

Taylor, Humphrey. "U.S. Health Care: Built for Waste." *New York Times,* April 17, 1990, A25.

Terris, Milton. "A Wasteful System That Doesn't Work." *Progressive* 54: 10 (1990): 14–16.

Thomasson, Melissa A. "The Importance of Group Coverage: How Tax Policy Shaped U.S. Health Insurance" (Working Paper

7543). Cambridge, MA: National Bureau of Economic Research, 2000. http://www.nber.org/papers/w7543.pdf.

Thompson, Frank J., and Courtney Burke. "Executive Federalism and Medicaid Demonstration Waivers: Implications for Policy and Democratic Process." *Journal of Health Politics, Policy and Law* 32: 6 (2007): 971–1004.

———. "Federalism by Waiver: Medicaid and the Transformation of Long-Term Care." *Publius* 39: 1 (2008): 22–48.

Truman, Harry. "Special Message to the Congress Recommending a Comprehensive Health Program." November 19, 1945. http://www.trumanlibrary.org/publicpapers/index.php?pid=483.

U.S. Health Resources Administration. *Health in America: 1776–1976.* Rockville, MD: U.S. Department of Health, Education and Welfare, 1976.

Von Drehle, David, Alex Altman, Michael Crowley, Michael Grunwald, and Michael Scherer. "Here's What We Know for Sure: Obama's Health Care Reform Is Constitutional, Congress May not Hold States Hostage to Its Every Whim." *Time* 180: 3 (2012): 30–41.

Warner, John H., and Janet A. Tighe. *Major Problems in the History of American Medicine and Public Health: Documents and Essays.* Boston: Houghton Mifflin, 2001.

Waxman, Henry A. "Politics and Science: Reproductive Health." *Health Matrix: Journal of Law-Medicine* 16: 1 (2006): 5–25.

Welch, Gilbert H., Lisa Swartz, and Steve Woloshin. *Overdiagnosed: Making People Sick in the Pursuit of Health.* Boston: Beacon Press, 2011.

PART II—GOVERNMENT ORGANIZATIONS THAT DEVELOP, FUND, AND ADMINISTER HEALTH POLICY (1789–TODAY)

Aaron, Henry J. "Budget Crisis, Entitlement Crisis, Health Care Financing Problem—Which Is It?" *Health Affairs* 26: 6 (2007): 1622–1633.

Altman, Drew E., Richard Greene, and Harvey M. Sapolsky. *Health Planning and Regulation: The Decision-making Process.* Washington, DC: AUPHA Press, 1981.

Antos, Joseph R. "Is There a Right Way to Promote Health Insurance through the Tax System?" *National Tax Journal* 54: 3 (2006): 477–490.

Armstrong, Drew. "Medicare Patch Habit Too Painful to Break." *CQ Weekly,* June 16, 2008, 1595–1596.

Bakke, Olav M., Michael Manocchia, Francisco de Abajo, Kenneth I. Kaitin, and Louis Lasagna. "Drug Safety Discontinuations in the U.K., the U.S. and Spain from 1974–1993: A Regulatory Perspective." *Clinical Pharmacology & Therapeutics* 58: 1 (1995): 108–117.

Belknap, Michal R. *The Supreme Court under Earl Warren, 1953–1969.* Columbia: University of South Carolina Press, 2005.

Bell, Jordan B., and Ella C. Nye. "Specific Symptoms Predict Suicidal Ideation in Vietnam Combat Veterans with Chronic Post-traumatic Stress Disorder." *Military Medicine* 172: 11 (2007): 1144–1147.

Blow, Frederic C., John E. Zebe, John F. McCarthy, Marcia Valenstein, Leah Gillon, and C. Raymond Bingham. "Ethnicity and Diagnostic Patterns in Veterans with Psychoses." *Social Psychiatry and Psychiatric Epidemiology* 39: 10 (2004): 841–851.

Bossarte, Robert M. *Veteran Suicide: A Public Health Imperative.* Washington, DC: American Public Health Association, 2013.

Bray, Robert M., and Laura L. Hourani. "Substance Use Trends among Active Duty Military Personnel: Findings from the United States Department of Defense Health Related Behavior Surveys, 1980–2005." *Addiction* 102: 7 (2007): 1092–1101.

Bushy, Angeline. "Health Issues of Women in Rural Environments: An Overview." *Journal of American Medical Women's Association* 53: 2 (1998): 53–56.

Carpenter, Daniel. *Reputation and Power: Organizational Image and Pharmaceutical Regulation at the FDA.* Princeton, NJ: Princeton University Press, 2010.

Center for Disease Control and Prevention. "Emergency Preparedness and Response." May 2, 2013. http://www.bt.cdc.gov/lrn.

Centers for Medicare and Medicaid Services. *Actuarial Report on the Financial Outlook for Medicaid.* 2012. http://medicaid.gov/Medicaid-CHIP-Program-Information/By-Topics/Financing-and-Reimbursement/Downloads/medicaid-actuarial-report-2012.pdf.

———. *Blueprint for Approval of Affordable State-Based and State Partnership Insurance Exchanges.* 2012. http://www.cms.gov/CCIIO/Resources/Files/Downloads/hie-blueprint-11162012.pdf.

Chandra, Amitabh, Jonathan Holmes, and Jonathan Skinner. *The 2013 Long-Term Budget Outlook.* Washington, DC: Congressional Budget Office, September 2013.

Congressional Budget Office. *Approaches to Reducing Federal Spending on Military Health Care.* Washington, DC: Congressional Budget Office, 2014.

———. *Quality Initiatives Undertaken by the Veterans Health Administration.* Washington, DC: Congressional Budget Office, 2009.

———. *The Sustainable Growth Rate Formula for Setting Medicare's Physician Payment Rates.* Washington, DC: Congressional Budget Office, September 6, 2006. http://www.cbo.gov/sites/default/files/cbofiles/ftpdocs/75xx/doc7542/09-07-sgr-brief.pdf.

———. *The Veterans Health Administration's Treatment of PTSD and Traumatic Brain Injury among Recent Combat Veterans.* Washington, DC: CreateSpace, 2012.

Conlan, Timothy J., and Paul L. Posner. "Inflection Point? Federalism and the Obama Administration." *Publius* 41: 3 (2011): 421–446.

Cutler, David M., Karen Davis, and Kristof Stremikis. "Why Health Reform Will Bend the Cost Curve." New York: Commonwealth Fund, December 2009.

Cutler, David M., and Judy Feder. *Financing Health Care Reform: A Plan to Ensure the Cost of Reform Is Budget-Neutral.* Washington, DC: Center for American Progress, 2009.

Defense Health Agency. *About DHA.* http://www.tricare.mil/tma/aboutDHA.aspx.

Derthick, Martha. "Going Federal: The Launch of Medicare Part D Compared to SSI." *Publius* 37: 3 (2007): 351–370.

DiMasi, Joseph A., Ronald W. Hansen, and Henry G. Grabowski. "The Price of Innovation: New Estimates of Drug Development Costs." *Journal of Health Economics* 22: 2 (2003): 151–185.

Doonan, Michael. *American Federalism in Practice: The Formulation and Implementation of Contemporary Health Policy.* Washington, DC: Brookings Institution, 2013.

Eibner, Christine. *Invisible Wounds of War: Quantifying the Societal Costs of Psychological and Cognitive Injuries.* Santa Monica, CA: RAND, 2008.

Ellis, Christopher, and James A. Stimson. *Ideology in America.* New York: Cambridge University Press, 2012.

Elster, Eric, Eric Schoomaker, and Charles Rice. "The Laboratory of War: How Military Trauma Care Advances Are Benefiting Soldiers and Civilians." *Health Affairs,* December 18, 2013. http://healthaffairs.org/blog/2013/12/18/the-laboratory-of-war-how-military-trauma-care-advances-are-benefiting-soldiers-and-civilians/

Emanuel, Ezekiel, et al. "A Systemic Approach to Containing Health Care Spending." *New England Journal of Medicine* 367 (2012): 949–954.

Etheridge, Elizabeth W. *Sentinel for Health: A History of the Centers for Disease Control.* Berkeley: University of California Press, 1992.

Evans, Robert G. "The TSX Gives a Short Course in Health Economics: It's the Prices, Stupid!" *Healthcare Policy* 6: 2 (2010): 13–23.

Families USA. "Implementing Exchanges." *Families USA: The Voice for Health Care Consumers.* October 2012.

FDA and Stakeholders Public Meeting. December 7, 2001. Executive Summary. http://www.fda.gov/cder/pdufa/default.htm.

Feder, Judith M. *The Politics of Federal Hospital Insurance.* Lexington, MA: Lexington Books, 1977.

Finley, Erin P. *Fields of Combat: Understanding PTSD among Veterans of Iraq and Afghanistan (The Culture and Politics of Health Care Work).* Ithiaca, NY: Cornell University Press, 2011.

Follette, Glenn, and Louise Sheiner. "The Sustainability of Health Spending Growth." *National Tax Journal* 58: 3 (2005): 391–408.

Fox, Daniel M. *Health Policies, Health Politics: The British and American Experience, 1911–1965.* Princeton, NJ: Princeton University Press, 1986.

Frederickson, David G., and H. George Frederickson. *Measuring the Performance of the Hollow State.* Washington, DC: Georgetown Press, 2006.

Freidson, Eliot. *Professionalism, the Third Logic: On the Practice of Knowledge.* Chicago: University of Chicago Press, 2001.

Gabel, Jon R. "Congress's Health Care Numbers Don't Add Up." *New York Times,* August 26, 2009.

Gais, Thomas, and James Fossett. "Federalism and the Executive Branch." In *The Executive Branch,* edited by Joel D. Aberbach and Mark A. Peterson, 486–524. New York: Oxford University Press, 2005.

Garrett, Laurie. *Betrayal of Trust: The Collapse of Global Public Health.* New York: Hyperion, 2000.

General Accounting Office. "Medicaid: States Use Illusory Approaches to Shift Program Costs to Federal Government." Washington, DC: General Accounting Office, August 1994.

Grabowski, Henry, Genia Long, and Richard Mortimer. "Implementation of the Biosimilar Pathway: Economic and Policy Issues," *Seton Hall Law Review* 41: 2 (2011): Article 2.

Grabowski, Henry, and John Vernon. "Longer Patents for Increased Generic Competition in the US." *PharmacoEconomics* 10: Suppl 2 (1996): 110–123.

Grabowski, Henry, John Vernon, and Lacy Glenn Thomas. "Estimating the Effects of Regulation on Innovation: An International Comparative Analysis of the Pharmaceutical Industry." *Journal of Law and Economics* 21 (1978): 133–163.

Gray, Bradford H., Michael K. Gusmano, and Sara R. Collins. "ACHPR and the Changing Politics of Health Services Research." *Health Affairs* (2003): W3-283–W3-307.

Greenwood, John T., and F. Clifton Berry Jr. *Medics at War: Military Medicine from Colonial Times to the 21st Century.* Annapolis, MD: Naval Institute Press, 2005.

Happell, Brenda, David Scott, Chris Platania-Phung, and Janette Nankivell. "Rural Physical Health Care Services for People with Serious Mental Illness: A Nursing Pperspective." *Australian Journal of Rural Health* 20: 5 (2012): 248–253.

Heymann, Phil, and Esther Scott. "Taking on Big Tobacco: David Kessler and the Food and Drug Administration, Kennedy School of Government Case Program." Cambridge, MA: Harvard University, Kennedy School of Government, 1997.

Ho, Alfred. "The Governance Challenges of the Government Performance and Results Act: A Case Study of the Substance Abuse and Mental Health Administration." *Public Performance and Management Review* 30 (March 2007): 369–397.

Holahan, John, Linda J. Blumberg, Stacy McMorrow, Stephen Zuckerman, Timothy Waidmann, and Karen Stockley. "Containing the Growth of Spending in the U.S. Health System." Washington, DC: Urban Institute, October 2011.

Holahan, John, Matthew Buettgens, and Stan Dorn. "The Cost of Not Expanding Medicaid." Washington, DC: Kaiser Commission on Medicaid and the Uninsured, July 2013.

Holohan, John, Alan Weil, and Joshua Wiener. *Federalism and Health Policy.* Washington, DC: Urban Institute Press, 2003.

Iglehart, John. "Doing More with Less: A Conversation with Kerry Weems." *Health Affairs* 28: 4 (2009): 688–696.

Institute of Medicine. *HHS in the 21st Century: Charting a New Course for a Healthier America.* Washington, DC: National Academies Press, 2009.

Institute of Medicine, Committee on the Assessment of the U.S. Drug Safety System. *The Future of Drug Safety: Promoting and Protecting the Health of the Public.* Washington, DC: National Academy Press, 2007.

Institute of Medicine, Committee on Health Planning Goals and Standards. *Health Planning in the United States: Selected Policy Issues.* 2 vols. Washington, DC: National Academy Press, 1981.

Jacobs, Lawrence R., and Theda Skocpol. *Health Care Reform and American Politics: What Everyone Needs to Know.* New York: Oxford University Press, 2010.

Jaycox, Lisa H., and Terri Tanielian. *Invisible Wounds of War: Psychological and Cognitive Injuries, Their Consequences, and Services to Assist Recovery.* Santa Monica, CA: RAND, 2008.

Jha, A.K., J.B. Perlin, K.W. Kizer, and R.A. Dudley. "Effect of the Transformation of the Veterans Affairs Health Care System on the Quality of Care." *New England Journal of Medicine* 348: 22 (2003): 2218–2227.

Joyce, Philip G. *The Congressional Budget Office: Honest Numbers, Power, and Policymaking.* Washington, DC: Georgetown University Press, 2011. Chs. 6 and 7.

———. *The Costs of Budget Uncertainty: Analyzing the Impact of Late Appropriations.* Washington, DC: IBM Center for the Business of Government, 2012.

Kaiser Family Foundation. *The Medicaid Program at a Glance.* March 2013. http://kff.org/medicaid/fact-sheet/the-medicaid-program-at-a-glance-update.

———. *State Decisions For Creating Health Insurance Marketplaces.* May 2013. http://kff.org/health-reform/state-indicator/health-insurance-exchanges.

Kaitin, Kenneth I., and Catherine Cairns. "The New Drug Approvals of 1999, 2000, and 2001: Drug Development Trends after the Passage of the Prescription Drug User Fee Act of 1992." *Drug Information Journal* 37 (2003): 357–371.

Kaitin, Kenneth, Nancy Mattison, Frances Northington, and Louis Lasagna. "The Drug Lag: An Update of New Drug Introductions in the United States and in the United Kingdom, 1977 through 1987." *Clinical Pharmacology & Therapeutics* 46: 2 (1989): 121–138.

Kane, Tim. *Who Bears the Burden? Demographic Characteristics of U.S. Military Recruits before and after 9/11.* Washington, DC: Heritage Center for Data Analysis, 2005.

Kazmier, Janice L. *Health Care Law.* Independence, KY: Cengage Learning, 2008.

Kenny, Genevieve M., Stephen Zuckerman, Lisa Dubay, Michael Huntress, Victoria Lynch, Jennifer Haley, and Nathaniel Anderson. "Opting in to the Medicaid Expansion under the ACA: Who Are the Uninsured Adults Who Could Gain Health Insurance Coverage?" Washington, DC: Urban Institute, 2012.

Kessler, David. *A Question of Intent: A Great American Battle with a Deadly Industry.* New York: Public Affairs, 2001.

King, Kathleen M., Sheila Burke, and Elizabeth Docteur, eds. *Final Report of the Study Panel on Medicare's Governance and Management.* Washington, DC: National Academy of Social Insurance, 2002.

Kirsch, Richard. *Fighting for Our Health.* Albany, NY: Rockefeller Institute Press, 2011.

Kizer, Kenneth W. *Prescription for Change: The Guiding Principles and Strategic Objectives Underlying the Transformation of the Veterans Health Administration.* Washington, DC: Department of Veterans Affairs, 1996.

———. *Vision for Change: A Plan to Restructure the Veterans Health Administration.* Washington, DC: Department of Veterans Affairs, 1995.

Kosterlitz, Julie. "Broad Coalition Prepares to Do Battle on Taxing Employee Fringe Benefits." *National Journal,* May 5, 1985, 956–960.

Kweder, Sandra. "Statement of Sandra Kweder, Deputy Director, Office of New Drugs, FDA." Hearings Before the Senate Finance Committee, U.S. Senate, FDA, Merck, and Vioxx: Putting Patient Safety First, November 18, 2004. http://finance.senate.gov/sitepages/hearing111804.htm.

Ladenheim, Kala. "Health Insurance in Transition: The Health Insurance Portability and Accountability Act of 1996." *Publius* 27: 2 (1997): 33–51.

Lapierre, Cody B., Andria F. Schwegler, and Bill J. Labauve. "Posttraumatic Stress and Depression Symptoms in Soldiers Returning from Combat Operations in Iraq and Afghanistan." *Journal of Traumatic Stress* 20: 6 (2007): 933–943.

Lefkowitz, Bonnie. With contributions by Eleanor D. Kinney and Cheryl Ulmer. *Health Planning: Lessons for the Future.* Rockville, MD: Aspen Systems, 1983.

Leuchtenburg, William E. *The Supreme Court Reborn: The Constitutional Revolution in the Age of Roosevelt.* New York: Oxford University Press, 1995.

Lipset, Seymour Martin. *American Exceptionalism: A Double-Edged Sword.* New York: W.W. Norton, 1996.

Longman, Phillip. *Best Care Anywhere: Why VA Health Care Would Work Better for Everyone.* 3rd ed. San Francisco: Berrett-Koehler, 2012.

Lurie, Philip M., Richard R. Bannick, and Elder Granger. *The Department of Defense's TRICARE Health Benefits Program as a Critical Plank in the Federal Platform for Health Care Reform.* Arlington, VA: Institute for Defense Analysis, 2009.

Mackenzie, Todd A., Amy E. Wallace, and William B. Weeks. "Impact of Rural Residence on Survival of Male Veterans Affairs Patients after Age 65." *Journal of Rural Health* 26: 4 (2010): 318–324.

Maltz, Earl M. *The Chief Justiceship of Warren Burger 1969–1986.* Columbia: University of South Carolina Press, 2000.

Marciarille, Ann Marie, and J. Bradford DeLong. "Bending the Health Cost Curve: The Promise and Peril of the Independent Payment Advisory Board." *Health Matrix* 22: 1 (2012): 75–121.

Marone, James. *The Democratic Wish: Popular Participation and the Limits of American Government.* New York: Basic Books, 1990.

Martinez, Barbara, and Scott Hensley. "Cardiologist Calls for Inquiry into FDA's Handling of Vioxx." *Wall Street Journal,* October 7, 2004, B8.

Mathews, Anna W. "FDA Study Estimates Vioxx Linked to 27,000 Heart Attacks." Dow Jones Newswires, October 6, 2004.

Mayes, Rick, and Thomas R. Oliver. "Chronic Disease and the Shifting Focus on Public Health: Is Prevention Still a Political Lightweight?" *Journal of Health Politics, Policy and Law* 37: 2 (2012): 181–200.

McCarthy, John F., Marcia Valenstein, and Frederic C. Blow. "Residential Mobility among Patients in the VA Health System: Associations with Psychiatric Morbidity, Geographic Accessibility, and Continuity of Care." *Administration and Policy in Mental Health and Mental Health Services Research* 34: 5 (2007): 448–455.

McDonough, John E. *Inside National Health Reform.* Berkeley: University of California Press, 2011.

Melhado, Evan M., Walter Feinberg, and Harold M. Swartz, eds. *Money, Power, and Health Care.* Ann Arbor, MI: Health Administration Press, 1988.

Meyers, Roy T. "The 'Ball of Confusion' in Federal Budgeting: A Shadow Agenda for Deliberative Budget Process Reform." *Public Administration Review* 69 (March/April 2009): 211–223.

———. "Late Appropriations and Government Shutdowns: Frequency, Causes, Consequences, and Remedies." *Public Budgeting and Finance* 17 (Fall 1997): 25–38.

Miles, Rufus E., Jr. *The Department of H.E.W.* New York: Praeger, 1974.

Milliken, Charles S., Jennifer L. Auchterlonie, and Charles W. Hoge. "Longitudinal Assessment of Mental Health Problems among Active and Reserve Component Soldiers Returning from the Iraq War." *Journal of the American Medical Association* 298: 18 (2007): 2141–2148.

Morone, Theodore R. *The Politics of Medicare.* 2nd ed. New York: Transaction, 2000.

National Academy of Social Insurance and National Academy of Public Administration. *Administrative Solutions in Health Reform.* Washington, DC: National Academy of Social Insurance, July 2009.

National Governors Association and the National Association of State Budget Officers. *The Fiscal Survey of States.* Washington, DC: National Association of State Budget Officers, 2013.

Neustadt, Richard E., and Harvey V. Fineberg, *The Swine Flu Affair: Decision-making on a Slippery Disease.* Washington, DC: U.S. Department of Health, Education, and Welfare, 1978.

Oberlander, Jonathan. *The Political Life of Medicare.* Chicago: University of Chicago Press, 2003.

Office of Management and Budget. "Analytical Perspectives, Budget of the United States Government, Fiscal Year 2014" 244–245. http://www.whitehouse.gov/omb/budget/Analytical_Perspectives.

———. *Fiscal Year 2013 Historical Tables: Budget of the U.S. Government.* 2013.

Office of the Inspector General. *FDA's Review Process for New Drug Applications: A Management Review* (OEI-01-01-00590).

Washington, DC: U.S. Department of Health and Human Services, March 2003.

Oliver, Thomas R., Philip R. Lee, and Helene L. Lipton. "A Political History of Medicare and Prescription Drug Coverage." *Milbank Quarterly* 82: 2 (2004): 283–354.

Olson, Mary K. "Are Novel Drugs More Risky for Patients than Less Novel Drugs?" *Journal Health Economics* 23: 6 (2004): 1135–1158.

———. "Explaining Regulatory Behavior in the FDA: Political Control vs. Agency Discretion." In *Advances in the Study of Entrepreneurship, Innovation, and Economic Growth,* Volume 7, edited by Gary Libecap, 71–108. Bingley, UK: Emerald, 1996.

———. "How Have User Fees Affected the FDA?" *Regulation* 25: 1 (2002): 20–25.

———. "Pharmaceutical Policy Change and the Safety of New Drugs." *Journal of Law and Economics* 45: 2 (2002): 615–642.

———. "Political Influence and Regulatory Policy: The 1984 Drug Legislation." *Economic Inquiry* 32: 3 (1994): 363–382.

———. "Regulation of Safety, Efficacy, and Quality." In *Elsevier Encyclopedia of Health Economics,* edited by Anthony Culyer. United Kingdom: Elsevier, 2014.

———. "Regulatory Agency Discretion among Competing Industries: Inside the FDA." *Journal of Law, Economics & Organization* 11: 2 (1995): 379–405.

———. "Regulatory Reform and Bureaucratic Responsiveness to Firms: the Impact of User Fees in the FDA." *Journal of Economics & Management Strategy* 9: 3 (2000): 363–395.

———. "The Risk We Bear: The Effects of Review Speed and Industry User Fees on Drug Safety." *Journal Health Economics* 27: 2 (2008): 175–200.

Osterholm, Michael. "Getting Prepared." *Foreign Affairs* 84: 4 (2005): 24–37.

Owens, Gina P., Catherine J. Herrera, and Allison A. Whitesell. "A Preliminary Investigation of Mental Health Needs and Barriers to Mental Health Care for Female Veterans of Iraq and Afghanistan." *Traumatology* 15: 2 (2009): 31–37.

Patient Protection and Affordable Care Act, Public Law 111-148 (March 23, 2010), as modified by the Health Care and Education Reconciliation Act of 2010, Public Law 111-152 (March 30, 2010), Title 1, Subtitle D, Section 1311.

Peltzman, Sam. "An Evaluation of Consumer Protection Legislation: The 1962 Drug Amendments." *Journal of Political Economy* 81 (1973): 1049–1091.

Pendergrast, Mark. *Inside the Outbreaks: The Elite Medical Detectives of the Epidemic Intelligence Service.* New York: Mariner Books, 2011.

Perlin, Jonathan B., Robert M. Kolodner, and Robert H. Roswell. "The Veterans Health Administration: Quality, Value, Accountability, and Information as Transforming Strategies for Patient-Centered Care." *American Journal of Managed Care* 10: 11, Pt 2 (2004): 828–836.

Peterson, Paul. *The Price of Federalism.* Washington, DC: Brookings Institution, 1995.

Posner, Paul, Steve Redburn, Phil Joyce, and Roy T. Meyers, "Strengthening the Federal Budget Process." Washington, DC: National Academy of Public Administration and American Society for Public Administration, July 12, 2012.

Powe, Lucas A., Jr. *The Supreme Court and the American Elite 1789–2008.* Cambridge, MA: Harvard University Press, 2009.

Quirk, Paul J. "The Food and Drug Administration." In *The Politics of Regulation,* edited by James Q. Wilson. New York: Basic Books, 1980, chap. 6.

Radin, Beryl A. *The Accountable Juggler: The Art of Leadership in a Federal Agency.* Washington, DC: CQ Press, 2002.

———. "Demeaning Professionals: Throwing Out the Baby with the Bathwater?" In *Challenging the Performance Movement: Accountability, Complexity and Democratic Values.* Washington, DC: Georgetown University Press, 2006.

———. *Managing in a Decentralized Department: The Case of the US Department of Health and Human Services.* Arlington, VA: PricewaterhouseCoopers Endowment for the Business of Government, October 1999.

———. "When Is a Health Department Not a Health Department: The Case of the US Department of Health and Human Services." *Social Policy & Administration* 44: 2 (2012): 142–154.

Radin, Beryl A., and Joshua M. Chanin, eds. *Federal Government Reorganization: A Policy and Management Perspective.* Boston, MA: Jones and Bartlett, 2009.

Ramchand, Rajeev, Joie Acosta, Rachel M. Burns, Lisa H. Jaycox, and Christopher G. Pernin. *The War Within: Preventing Suicide In the U.S. Military.* Santa Monica, CA: RAND, 2011.

Redhead, Stephen C. "Budget Control Act: Potential Impact of Sequestration on Health Reform Spending." Washington, DC: Congressional Research Service, May 1, 2013.

Reschovsky, James D., and Andrea B. Staiti. "Access and Quality: Does Rural America Lag Behind?" *Health Affairs* 24: 4 (2005): 1128–1139.

Robinson, Stephen L. *Hidden Toll of the War in Iraq: Mental Health and the Military.* Washington, DC: Center for American Progress, 2004.

Rogne, Leah, Carroll E. Estes, Brian R. Grossman, Brooke A. Hollister, and Erica Solway. *Social Insurance and Social Justice.* New York: Springer, 2009.

Rose, Shanna. *Financing Medicaid: Federalism and the Growth of America's Health Care Safety Net.* Ann Arbor: University of Michigan Press, 2013.

Rovner, Julie. "Congress, Administration Duel over State Medicaid Funds." *CQ Weekly,* October 26, 1991, 3130–3131.

Rural Assistance Center. "Returning Soldier and Veteran Health Frequently Asked Questions." http://www.raconline.org/topics/veterans/veteransfaq.php.

Sasich, Larry, Peter Lurie, and Sidney M. Wolfe. *The Drug Industry's Performance in Finishing Postmarketing Research (Phase IV) Studies,* 2005. http://www.citizen.org/hrg1520.

Schoenbaum, Michael. *Health Benefits for Medicare-Eligible Military Retirees: Rationalizing TRICARE for Life.* Santa Monica, CA: RAND, 2004.

Scully, Thomas A. "Policy High Points: Medicare and Medicaid in the New Millennium." *Health Affairs* (July 26, 2005): W5-339–W5-340. doi:10.1377/hlthaff.w5.339

Seal, Karen H., Daniel Bertenthal, Christian R. Miner, Saunek Sen, and Charles Marmar. "Bringing the War Back Home: Mental Health Disorders among 103,788 US Veterans Returning from Iraq and Afghanistan Seen at Department of Veterans Affairs Facilities." *Archives of Internal Medicine* 167: 5 (2007): 476–482.

Seal, Karen H., Shira Maguen, Beth Cohen, Kristian S. Gima, Thomas J. Metzler, Li Ren, Daniel Bertenthal, and Charles R. Marmar. "VA Mental Health Services Utilization in Iraq and Afghanistan Veterans in the First Year of Receiving New Mental Health Diagnoses." *Journal of Traumatic Stress* 23: 1 (2010): 5–16.

Shulman, Sheila R., and Jeffrey S. Brown. "The Food and Drug Administration's Early Access and Fast-Track Approval

Initiatives: How Have They Worked?" *Food & Drug Law Journal* 50 (1995): 503–531.

Skydell, Barbara. "Restructuring the VA Health Care System: Safety Net, Training, and Other Considerations." *National Health Policy Forum* 716 (1998): 14.

Smalley, K. Bryant, C. Thresa Yancey, Jacob C. Warren, Karen Naufel, Rebecca Ryan, and James L. Pugh. "Rural Mental Health and Psychological Treatment: A Review for Practitioners." *Journal of Clinical Psychology* 66: 5 (2010): 479–489.

Smith, David Barton. *Health Care Divided: Race and Healing a Nation.* Ann Arbor: University of Michigan Press, 1999.

Smith, David G. *Entitlement Politics.* New York: Aldine de Gruyter, 2002.

Sparrow, Malcolm K. *License to Steal: How Fraud Bleeds America's Health Care System.* Boulder, CO: Westview Press, 2000.

Starr, Paul. *Remedy and Reaction.* New Haven, CT: Yale University Press, 2011.

———. *The Social Transformation of American Medicine.* New York: Basic Books, 1982.

Steiner, John E., Jr. *Problems in Health Care Law: Challenges for the 21st Century.* Burlington, MA: Jones & Bartlett, 2013.

Stevens, Rosemary A. *In Sickness and In Wealth: American Hospitals in the Twentieth Century.* New York: Basic Books, 1989.

Taft, Casey T., Danny G. Kaloupek, Jeremiah A. Schumm, Amy D. Marshall, Jillian Panuzio, Daniel W. King, and Terence M. Keane. "Posttraumatic Stress Disorder Symptoms, Physiological Reactivity, Alcohol Problems, and Aggression among Military Veterans." *Journal of Abnormal Psychology* 116: 3 (2007): 498–507.

Temin, Peter. *Taking Your Medicine: Drug Regulation in the United States.* Cambridge, MA: Harvard University Press, 1980.

Thompson, Frank J. *Federalism, Policy Durability, and Health Reform.* Washington DC: Georgetown University Press, 2012.

———. *Medicaid Politics: Federalism, Policy Durability, and Health Reform.* Washington, DC: Georgetown University Press, 2012.

Tick, Edward. *War and the Soul: Healing Our Nation's Veterans from Post-tramatic Stress Disorder.* Wheaton, IL: Quest Books, 2012.

Topel, Eric J. "Failing the Public Health—Rofecoxib, Merck, and the FDA." *New England Journal of Medicine* 351: 17 (2004): 1707–1709.

Trask, Roger R. *The Department of Defense, 1947–1997: Organization and Leaders.* Washington, DC: U.S. Government Printing Office, 1997.

Tushnet, Mark V. *A Court Divided: The Rehnquist Court and the Future of Constitutional Law.* New York: W.W. Norton, 2005.

U.S. Congress, Office of Technology Assessment. *Pharmaceutical R&D: Costs, Risks and Rewards, OTA-H-522.* Washington, DC: U.S. Government Printing Office, February 1993.

U.S. Department of Defense. "About the Department of Defense." http://www.defense.gov/about.

———. "Military Health System History." http://www.health.mil/About_MHS/history.aspx.

———. *Strategic Management Plan: The Business of Defense FY2014—FY2015.* Arlington, VA: U.S. Department of Defense, 2013.

U.S. Department of Defense, Task Force on the Prevention of Suicide by Members of the Armed Forces. *The Challenge and the Promise: Strengthening the Force and Preventing Suicide and Saving Lives.* Arlington, VA: U.S. Department of Defense, 2010.

U.S. Department of Health and Human Services. http://www.hhs.gov.

U.S. Department of Justice. http://www.justice.gov.

U.S. Department of the Treasury. *Final Monthly Treasury Statement of Receipts and Outlays of the United States Government.* January 2014. https://www.fms.treas.gov/mts/mts0913.pdf.

U.S. Department of Veterans Affairs. "Annual Budget Submission." 2013. http://www.va.gov/budget/products.asp.

———. *The Assessment and Treatment of Individuals with History of Traumatic Brain Injury and Post-traumatic Stress Disorder: A Systematic Review of the Evidence.* Washington, DC: U.S. Department of Veterans Affairs, 2013.

———. "History—VA History." http://www.va.gov/about_va/vahistory.asp.

———. "Patient Aligned Care Team (PACT)." http://www.va.gov/primarycare/pcmh.

———. *VA History in Brief.* 2006. http://www.va.gov/opa/publications/archives/docs/history_in_brief.pdf.

U.S. Department of Veterans Affairs and U.S. Department of Health and Human Services. *Interagency Task Force on Military and Veterans Mental Health: 2013 Interim Report.* Washington, DC: U.S. Department of Veterans Affairs, 2013.

U.S. General Accounting Office. *Defense Health Care: Despite TRICARE Procurement Improvements, Problems Remain.* Washington, DC: U.S. General Accounting Office, 1995.

———. *Management of HHS: Using the Office of the Secretary to Enhance Departmental Effectiveness* (GAO HRD-90-51). Washington, DC: U.S. General Accounting Office, February 1990.

U.S. Government Accountability Office. *Defense Health Care: Implementation Issues for New TRICARE Contracts and Regional Structure.* Washington, DC: Ulan Press, 2011.

———. *Defense Health Care Reform: Additional Implementation Details Would Increase Transparency of DOD's Plans and Enhance Accountability* (GAO-14-49). Washington, DC: U.S. Government Accountability Office, November 2013.

———. *Electronic Health Records: Long History of Management Challenges Raises Concerns about VA's and DOD's New Approach to Sharing Health Information.* 2013.

———. *VA Mental Health: Number of Veterans Receiving Care, Barriers Faced, and Efforts to Increase Access.* 2011.

U.S. Government Printing Office. H.R. 3116 (103rd): Department of Defense Appropriations Act, 1994. 1993.

U.S. Senate Committee on the Budget, Republican Staff. "Informed Budgeteer: The ABC&D's of the Trigger." April 3, 2008.

U.S. Supreme Court. http://www.supremecourt.gov.

Veterans Crisis Line. "About the Veterans Crisis Line." http://veteranscrisisline.net/About/AboutVeteransCrisisLine.aspx.

Veterans Health Administration. "About VHA." http://www.va.gov/health/aboutVHA.asp.

Vladeck, Bruce. "Paralysis by Analysis." *Roll Call,* July 28, 2009.

Walker, David B. *The Rebirth of Federalism: Slouching Toward Washington.* 2nd ed. Chatham, NJ: Chatham House, 2000.

Wallace, Amy E., William B. Weeks, Stanley Wang, Austin F. Lee, and Lewis E. Kazis. "Rural and Urban Disparities in Health-related Quality of Life among Veterans with Psychiatric Disorders." *Psychiatric Services* 57: 6 (2006): 851–856.

Wardell, William M. "The Drug Lag Revisited: Comparison by Therapeutic Area of Patterns of Drugs Marketed in the United States and Great Britain from 1972 through 1976." *Clinical Pharmacology &Therapeutics* 24 (1978): 499–524.

Wardell, William M., Maureen S. May, and A. Gene Trimble. "New Drug Development by United States Pharmaceutical Firms." *Clinical Pharmacology and Therapeutics* 32 (1982): 407–417.

Waxman, Henry, and Thomas Davis. "Letter to Harvey V. Fineberg, President of the Institute of Medicine." June 20, 2007.

Wayne, Alex. "Getting in Front of Health Fraud." *CQ Weekly,* February 16, 2009, 344–50.

Weissert, Carol S. "Medicaid in the 1990s: Trends, Innovations and the Future." *Publius* 22: 3 (1992): 93–109.

Weissert, William, and Edward Miller. "Punishing the Pioneers: The Medicare Modernization Act and State Pharmacy Assistance Programs." *Publius* 35: 1 (2005): 115–141.

Weissert, William G., and Carol S. Weissert. *Governing Health: The Politics of Health Policy,* 5th ed. Baltimore: Johns Hopkins University Press, 2014.

Wennberg, John E. *Tracking Medicine: A Researcher's Quest to Understand Health Care.* New York: Oxford University Press, 2010.

White, Barry. "Examining Budgets for Chief Executives." In *Handbook of Government Budgeting,* edited by Roy T. Meyers, 462–484. San Francisco, CA: Jossey-Bass, 1999.

White, Joseph. "Cost Control after the ACA." *Public Administration Review* 73 (September 2013): S24–S33.

White, Joseph. *False Alarm: Why the Greatest Threat to Social Security and Medicare Is the Campaign to "Save" Them.* Baltimore: Johns Hopkins University Press, 2003.

Wilson, James Q. *Bureaucracy.* New York: Basic Books, 1989.

Wolf, Douglas, and Nancy Folbre. *Universal Coverage of Long-Term Care in the United States: Can We Get There from Here?* New York: Russell Sage Foundation, 2012.

Ziller, Erika C., Nathaniel J. Anderson, and Andrew F. Coburn. "Access to Rural Mental Health Services: Service Use and Out-of-Pocket Costs." *Journal of Rural Health* 26: 3 (2010): 214–224.

PART III—CONTEMPORARY HEALTH POLICY ISSUES: GOALS AND INITIATIVES (1920s–TODAY)

Abercrombie, Stoney, Todd Shaffer, Brian Crownover, Grant Hoekzema, Nathan Krug, Lisa Maxwell, Michael Mazzone, Karen Mitchel, Stephen Schultz, and Michael Tuggy. GME Reform. *Annals of Family Medicine* 11: 1 (2013): 90.

Abramson, John. *Overdo$ed America: The Broken Promise of American Medicine.* New York: HarperCollins, 2004.

Adeyi, Olusoji, Owen Smith, and Sylvia Robles. *Public Policy and the Challenge of Chronic Noncommunicable Diseases.* Washington, DC: World Bank, 2007.

Aiken, Linda H., Charles E. Lewis, John Craig, Robert C. Mendenhall, Robert J. Blendon, and David E. Rogers. "The Contribution of Specialists to the Delivery of Primary Care: A New Perspective." *New England Journal of Medicine* 300 (1979): 1363–1370.

Alcorn, Ted. "What Has the US Global Health Initiative Achieved?" *Lancet* 380: 9849 (2012): 1215–1216.

Altarum Institute. *Health Market Insights from the Bureau of Labor Statistics (BLS) December 2011 Employment Data.* Washington, DC: Altarum Institute, 2012.

Altman, Drew E., Richard Greene, and Harvey M. Sapolsky. *Health Planning and Regulation: The Decision-making Process.* Washington, DC: AUPHA Press, 1981.

Altman, Lawrence. "When a Novel Flu Is Involved, Health Officials Get Jumpy." *New York Times.* December 30, 1997. http://www .nytimes.com/1997/12/30/science/the-doctor-s-world-when-a-novel-flu-is-involved-health-officials-get-jumpy.html?n=To p%2fNews%2fHealth%2fColumns%2fThe%20 Doctor%27s%20World.

Altman, Stuart, and David Shactman. *Power, Politics, and Universal Health Care: The Inside Story of a Century-long Battle.* Amherst, NY: Prometheus Books, 2011.

Amadeo, Kimberly. "Why Reform Health Care." *About.com.* July 2013. http://useconomy.about.com/od/fiscalpolicy/a/health care_reform.htm.

American College of Obstetricians and Gynecologists. "New Recommendations for Down Syndrome Call for Offering Screening to All Pregnant Women." http://www.acog.org/ About_ACOG/News_Room/News_Releases/2006/New_ Recommendations_for_Down_Syndrome.

American Public Health Association. "Prevention and Public Health Fund." 2014. http://www.apha.org/advocacy/Health+ Reform/PH+Fund.

Ameringer, Carl F. *The Health Care Revolution: From Medical Monopoly to Market Competition.* California/Milbank Books on Health and the Public, Vol. 19. Berkeley: University of California Press, 2008.

Angell, Marcia. *The Truth about Drug Companies: How They Deceive Us and What to Do about It.* New York: Random House, 2004.

Association of American Medical Colleges. *AAMC Statement on the Physician Workforce.* Washington, DC: Association of American Medical Colleges, June 2006.

Avorn, Jerry. *Powerful Medicines: Benefits, Risks, and Costs of Prescription Drugs.* New York: Alfred Knopf, 2004.

Baird, Karen L. "The New NIH and FDA Medical Research Policies: Targeting Gender, Promoting Justice." *Journal of Health Politics, Policy and Law* 24: 3 (1999): 531–565.

Baldwin, Kathleen A., Rebecca J. Sisk, Parris Watts, Jan McCubbin, Beth Brockschmidt, and Lucy N. Marion. "Acceptance of Nurse Practitioners and Physician Assistants in Meeting the Perceived Needs of Rural Communities." *Public Health Nursing* 15: 6 (1998): 389–397.

Ball, Robert M. "What Medicare's Architects Had in Mind." *Health Affairs* 14: 4 (1995): 62–72.

Baxter, James Phinney. *Scientists against Time.* Boston: Little, Brown, 1968.

Begun, James W., and Ronald C. Lippencott. *Strategic Adaptation in the Health Professions.* San Francisco, CA: Jossey-Bass, 1993.

Bentkover, Judith, et al. "Medicare's Payment of Hospitals." In *Renewing the Promise: Medicare and Its Reform,* edited by David Blumenthal, Mark Schlesinger, and Pamela Brown Drumheller, 90–114. New York: Oxford University Press, 1988.

Berenson, Robert A., and Eugene C. Rich. "US Approaches to Physician Payment: The Deconstruction of Primary Care." *Journal of General Internal Medicine* 25: 6 (2010): 613–618. http://www.ncbi.nlm.nih.gov/pmc/articles/PMC2869428.

Bernstein, Jill, Deborah Chollet, and Stephanie Peterson. "Financial Incentives for Health Care Providers and Consumers" (Issue Brief No. 5). Oakland, CA: Mathematica Policy Research, 2010.

Bernstein, Robert. "A Seat at the Table: Trend or an Illusion?" *Health Affairs* 25: 3 (2006): 730–733.

Berwick, Donald. "A User's Manual for the IOM's 'Quality Chasm' Report." *Health Affairs* 21: 3 (2002): 80–90.

Bevan, Gwyn, and Christopher Hood. "Have Targets Improved Performance in the English NHS?" *BMJ* 332 (2006): 419.

Bielaszka-DuVernay, Christina. "Improving Quality and Safety" (Health Policy Brief). *Health Affairs,* April 15, 2011.

Blumenthal, David, and Charles M. Kilo. "A Report Card on Continuous Quality Improvement." *Milbank Quarterly* 76: 4 (2001): 625–648.

Braun, Susan. 2001. "The History of Breast Cancer Advocacy." *Breast Journal* 9: Suppl 2 (2003): S101–S103.

Brook, Robert H. "Practice Guidelines and Practicing Medicine: Are They Compatible?" *Journal of the American Medical Association* 262 (1989): 3027–3030.

Brook, Robert H., Mark R. Chassin, Arlene Fink, David H. Solomon, Jacqueline Kosecoff, and R.E. Park. "A Method for Detailed Assessment of the Appropriateness of Medical Technologies." *International Journal of Technology Assessment in Health Care* 2 (1986): 53–63.

Brook, Robert H., Kathleen N. Lohr, Mark Chassin, Jacqueline Kosecoff, Arlene Fink, and David Solomon. "Geographic Variations in the Use of Services: Do They Have Any Clinical Significance?" *Health Affairs* 3: 2 (1984): 64–73.

Brook, Robert H., Kathleen N. Williams, John E. Rolph, and Bryant M. Mori. "Controlling the Use and Cost of Medical Services: The New Mexico Experimental Medical Care Review Organization—A Four Year Case Study." *Medical Care* 16: 9, Suppl (1978): 1–76.

Brower, Vicki. "The Squeaky Wheel Gets the Grease," *EMBO Reports* 6: 11 (2005): 1014–1017.

Brown, Lawrence D. *Politics and Health Care Organizations: HMOs as Federal Policy.* Washington, DC: Brookings Institution, 1982.

Buerhaus, I. "Is a Nursing Shortage on the Way?" *Nursing Management* 30: 2 (1999): 54–55.

Bureau of Health Professions. *Physician Supply and Demand.* Rockville, MD: Health Resources and Services Administration, U.S. Department of Health and Human Services, October 2006.

Burke, Mary Anne, and Stephen A Matlin, eds. *Monitoring Financial Flows for Health Research 2008.* Geneva, Switzerland: Global Forum for Health Research, 2008.

Bush, Vannevar. *Science—The Endless Frontier.* Washington, DC: Office of Scientific Research and Development, 1945.

Callahan, Daniel. "Must We Ration Health Care for the Elderly?" *Journal of Law, Medicine & Ethics* 40: 1 (2012): 10–16.

———. *What Price Better Health? Hazards of the Research Imperative.* Berkeley: University of California Press, 2003.

Cannon, Michael. "Perspectives on an Individual Mandate." Cato Institute. October 17, 2008. http://www.cato.org/publications/commentary/perspectives-individual-mandate.

Caplinger, Dan. "Medicare Explained: Understanding the Basics from Part A to Part D." *Daily Finance,* May 14, 2013. http://www.dailyfinance.com/2013/05/14/medicare-explained-part-a-b-c-d/#!slide=976885.

Carpenter, Daniel. *Reputation and Power: Organizational Image and Pharmaceutical Regulation at the FDA.* Princeton, NJ: Princeton University Press, 2010.

Casamayou, Maureen Hogan. *The Politics of Breast Cancer.* Washington, DC: Georgetown University Press, 2001.

Center for Data Analysis. "Economic Analysis of the House Budget Resolution." Washington, DC: Heritage Foundation, April 5, 2011.

Center for Economic and Policy Research. "States Could Save $73 Billion by Negotiating Medicare Drug Prices." March 19, 2013. http://www.cepr.net/index.php/press-releases/press-releases/states-save-billions-negotiating-prescription-drug-prices.

Centers for Disease Control and Prevention. "CDC Timeline." http://www.cdc.gov/about/history/timeline.htm, 2014.

———. "Global Health." March 4, 2014. http://www.cdc.gov/globalhealth/what/default.htm.

———. "Global Health Funding." July 15, 2013. http://www.cdc.gov/globalhealth/globalhealthfunding.htm.

———. "Global HIV/AIDS at CDC—Overview." November 14, 2013. http://www.cdc.gov/globalaids/global-hiv-aids-at-cdc/default.html.

———. "Impact of Malaria." November 9, 2012. http://www.cdc.gov/malaria/malaria_worldwide/impact.html.

———. "Number (in Millions) of Civilian, Noninstitutionalized Adults with Diagnostic Diabetes, United States, 1980–2011." 2011. http://www.cdc.gov/diabetes/statistics/prev/national/figadults.htm.

———. "Preparedness 101: Zombie Apocalypse." May 16, 2011. http://blogs.cdc.gov/publichealthmatters/2011/05/preparedness-101-zombie-apocalypse.

———. "Smoking and Tobacco Use." February 14, 2014. http://www.cdc.gov/tobacco/data_statistics/fact_sheets/fast_facts.

Centers for Medicare and Medicaid Services. "CMS Improves Patient Safety for Medicare and Medicaid by Addressing Never Events." August 4, 2008. http://www.cms.gov/Newsroom/MediaReleaseDatabase/Fact-Sheets/2008-Fact-Sheets-Items/2008-08-042.html.

Chakma, Justin, Gordon H. Sun, Jeffrey D. Steinberg, Stephen M. Sammut, and Reshma Jagsi. "Asia's Ascent—Global Trends in Biomedical R&D Expenditures." *New England Journal of Medicine* 370: 3 (2014): 3–6.

Chassing, Mark R., Jacqueline Kosecoff, R.E., Park, Constance M. Winslow, Katherine L. Kahn, Nancy J. Merrick, Joan Keesey, Arlene Fink, David H. Solomon, and Robert H. Brook. "Does Inappropriate Use Explain Geographic Variations in the Use of Health Care Services? A Study of Three Procedures." *Journal of the American Medical Association* 258: 18 (1987): 2533–2537.

Chassing, Mark R., and Margaret E. O'Kane. "History of the Quality Improvement Movement." In *Toward Improving the Outcome of Pregnancy III,* edited by Scott D. Berns, 1–8. White Plains, NY: March of Dimes, 2010.

Cockburn, Ian, and Rebecca M. Henderson. "Absorptive Capacity, Coauthoring Behavior, and the Organization of Research in Drug Discovery." *Journal of Industrial Economics* 46 (1998): 157–182.

Cohen, Joshua T., Peter J. Neumann, and Milton C. Weinstein. "Does Preventative Care Save Money? Health Economics and the Presidential Candidates." *New England Journal of Medicine* 358 (2008): 661–663.

Cohen, Wesley M., and John P. Walsh. "Public Research, Patents and Implications for Industrial R&D in the Drug, Biotechnology, Semiconductor and Computer Industries." In *Capitalizing on New Needs and New Opportunities: Government-Industry Partnerships in Biotechnology and Information Technologies,* edited by Charles W. Wessner, 223–243. Washington, DC: National Academy Press, 2002.

Collins, Sara, Jennifer L. Kriss, Michelle M. Doty, and Sheila D. Rustgi. *Losing Ground: How the Loss of Adequate Health Insurance Is Burdening Working Families—Findings from the Commonwealth Fund Biennial Health Insurance Surveys, 2001–2007.* New York: Commonwealth Fund (August 2008). http://www.commonwealthfund.org/Publications/Fund-Reports/2008/Aug/Losing-Ground–How-the-Loss-of-Adequate-Health-Insurance-Is-Burdening-Working-Families–8212-Finding.aspx.

Committee on the Costs of Medical Care. "Health Care for the American People: The Report of the Committee on the Costs of Medical Care." *Western Journal of Medicine* (1933).

Cook-Deegan, Robert, and Michael McGeary. "The Jewel in the Federal Crown? History, Politics, and the National Institutes of Health." In *History & Health Policy in the United States: Putting the Past Back In,* edited by Rosemary A. Stevens, Charles E. Rosenberg, and Lawton R. Burns, 176–201. New Brunswick, NJ: Rutgers University Press, 2006.

Cooper, Richard A., and Thomas E. Getzen. "The Coming Physician Shortage." *Health Affairs* 21: 2 (2002): 296–299.

Cotter, Dennis. "The National Center for Health Technology: Lessons Learned." *Health Affairs,* January 22, 2009. http://healthaffairs.org/blog/2009/01/22/the-national-center-for-health-care-technology-lessons-learned.

Crabtree, Susan. "Health Care Law's Prevention Money Called Slush Fund." *Washington Times.* May 9, 2012. http://www.washingtontimes.com/news/2012/may/9/health-care-laws-prevention-money-called-slush-fun.

Crichton, Michael. *Jurassic Park.* New York: Ballantine Books, 2012.

Cutler, David M., and Judy Feder. "Financing Health Care Reform: A Plan to Ensure the Cost of Reform Is Budget-Neutral." Washington, DC: Center for American Progress, June 2009.

De Cock, Kevin M. "Trends in Global Health and CDC's International Role, 1961–2011." *Morbidity and Mortality Weekly Report* 60: 4 (2011): 104–111.

Deming, W. Edwards. *Out of the Crisis.* Cambridge, MA: Massachusetts Institute of Technology, Center for the Advanced Engineering Science, 2000.

Donabedian, Avedis. "Evaluating the Quality of Medical Care." *Milbank Quarterly* 44: 3, pt. 2 (1966): 166–203.

Earle, Jeff. "Domenici Slams Specter and NIH 'Pigs.'" *The Hill* (March 17, 2004). http://psychrights.org/education/Congress/NIHPigs.htm.

Edelstein, Burton. "The Dental Safety Net, Its Workforce, and Policy Recommendations for Its Enhancement." *Journal of Public Health Dentistry* 70: Suppl 1 (2010): S32–S39.

Ehrenfeld, Ellie. "From the CSR Director's Desk." *Peer Review Notes.* Bethesda, MD: Center for Scientific Review, National Institutes of Health, May 2000.

Eichner, Judith, and Bruce Vladeck. "Medicare as a Catalyst for Reducing Health Disparities." *Health Affairs* 24: 2 (2005): 365–375.

Elbel, Brian, and Mark Schlesinger. "Responsive Consumerism: Empowerment in Markets for Health Plans." *Milbank Quarterly* 87: 3 (2009): 633–682.

Elmore, Richard. "National Health Expenditures Top 17% of GDP." *Health Care Technology News.* February 10, 2010. http://news.avancehealth.com/2010/02/growth-in-health-care-expenditure.html.

Emanuel, Ezekiel. *Health Care Guaranteed: A Simple, Secure Solution for America.* New York: Public Affairs, 2008.

Epstein, Andrew J. "Do Cardiac Surgery Report Cards Reduce Mortality? Assessing the Evidence." *Medical Care Research and Review* 63 (2006): 403–426.

Erdey, Nancy Carol. "The Armor of Patience: The National Cancer Institute and the Development of Medical Research Policy in the United States, 1937–1971." Doctoral dissertation, Case Western University, 1995.

Etheridge, Elizabeth W. *Sentinel for Health: A History of the Centers for Disease Control.* Berkeley: University of California Press, 1992.

Fabrizio, Kira R. "Absorptive Capacity and Innovation: Evidence from Pharmaceutical and Biotechnology Firms." *Research Policy* 38 (2009): 255–267.

Faust, Halley S. "Prevention vs. Cure: Which Takes Precedence?" *Medscape Public Health & Prevention.* May 2005. http://www.medscape.com/viewarticle/504743.

Federal Emergency Management Agency. "Preparedness." February 20, 2013. http://www.fema.gov/preparedness.

Foote, Susan Bartlett. "Why Medicare Cannot Promulgate a National Coverage Rule: A Case of Regula Mortis." *Journal of Health Politics, Policy and Law* 2: 5 (2002): 707–730.

Foulks, Edward. "Advocating for Persons Who Are Mentally Ill: A History of Mutual Empowerment of Patients and Profession." *Administration and Policy in Mental Health* 27: 5 (2000): 353–367.

Fox, Daniel M. *Health Policies, Health Politics: The British and American Experience, 1911–1965.* Princeton, NJ: Princeton University Press, 1986.

———. "The Politics of the NIH Extramural Program, 1937–1950." *Journal of the History of Medicine and Allied Sciences* 42 (1987): 447–466.

Fraher, Erin P., Andy Knapton, George F. Sheldon, Anthony Meyer, and Thomas C. Ricketts. "Projecting Surgeon Supply Using a Dynamic Model." *Annals of Surgery* 257: 5 (2013): 867–872.

Frank Miele, "The Man Who Would Be Cloned." *Skeptic* (March 22, 1999). http://www.highbeam.com/doc/1G1-56222095.html.

Frieden, Thomas R. "Why Global Health Security Is Imperative." *The Atlantic.* February 13, 2014. http://www.theatlantic.com/health/archive/2014/02/why-global-health-security-is-imperative/283765.

Friedman, Thomas L. *The World Is Flat: A Brief History of the Twenty-first Century.* New York: Farrar, Straus and Giroux, 2005.

Fuchs, Victor. "Major Trends in the U.S. Health Economy since 1950." *New England Journal of Medicine* 366 (2012): 973–977.

Fukuyama, Francis. *Our Post Human Future.* New York: Farrar, Straus and Giroux, 2002.

Gabel, John R., Ryan Lore, Roland D. McDevitt, Jeremy D. Pickreign, Heidi Whitmore, Michael Slover, and Ethan Levy-Forsythe. "More than Half of Individual Health Plans Offer Coverage That Falls Short of What Can Be Sold through Exchanges as of 2014." *Health Affairs* 31: 6 (2012): 1–8.

Garrett, Laurie. *Betrayal of Trust: The Collapse of Global Public Health.* New York: Hyperion, 2000.

Gawande, Atul. "Testing, Testing." *The New Yorker.* December 4, 2009. http://www.newyorker.com/reporting/2009/12/14/091214fa_fact_gawande.

Gellad, Walid F., Sebastian Schneeweiss, Phyllis Brawarsky, Stuart Lipsitz, and Jennifer S. Haas. "What If the Federal Government Negotiated Pharmaceutical Prices for Seniors? An Estimate of National Savings." *Journal of Internal Medicine* 23: 9 (2008): 1435–1440.

Ginzberg, Eli, and Anna B. Dutka. *The Financing of Biomedical Research.* Baltimore: Johns Hopkins University Press, 1989.

Goldby, Stephen, Saul Krugman, M.H. Pappworth, and Geoffrey Edsall. "The Willowbrook Letters: Criticisms and Defense." *Lancet,* April 10, May 8, June 5, and July 10, 1971.

Goodman, David C., Elliott S. Fisher, Thomas A. Bubolz, Jack E. Mohr, James F. Poage, and John E. Wennberg. "Benchmarking the US Physician Workforce: An Alternative to Needs-based or Demand-based Planning." *Journal of the American Medical Association* 276: 22 (1996): 1811–1817.

Goozner, Merrill. *The $800 Million Pill: The Truth behind the Cost of New Drugs.* Berkeley: University of California Press, 2004.

Grabowski, Henry, John Vernon, and Lacy Glenn Thomas. "Estimating the Effects of Regulation on Innovation: An International Comparative Analysis of the Pharmaceutical Industry." *Journal of Law and Economics* 21 (1978): 133–163.

Graduate Medical Education National Advisory Committee. *Interim Report of the Graduate Medical Education National Advisory Committee to the Secretary, Department of Health Education and Welfare.* Washington, DC: U.S. Department of Health, Education and Welfare, Public Health Service, Health Resources Administration, 1979.

———. *Report of the Graduate Medical Education National Advisory Committee to the Secretary, Department of Health and Human Services. Volume 1.* Washington, DC: Office of Graduate Medical Education, 1980.

———. *Report to the Secretary, Department of Health and Human Services, Volume III Geographic Distribution Technical Panel.* Washington, DC: Office of Graduate Medical Education, Health Resources Administration, U.S. Department of Health and Human Services, 1981.

Gray, Bradford H. "The Legislative Battle Over Health Services Research." *Health Affairs,* Winter: 246.

———. *The Profit Motive and Patient Care: The Changing Accountability of Doctors and Hospitals.* Cambridge, MA: Harvard University Press, 1991.

Gray, Bradford, and Marilyn Fields, eds. *Controlling Costs and Changing Patient Care?: The Role of Utilization Management.* Washington, DC: National Academy Press, 1989.

Gray, Bradford H., Michael K. Gusmano, and Sara Collins. "AHCPR and the Politics of Health Services Research." *Health Affairs.* June 25, 2003. http://content.healthaffairs.org/content/early/2003/06/25/hlthaff.w3.283.citation.

Green, Linda V., Sergei Savin, and Yina Lu. "Primary Care Physician Shortages Could Be Eliminated through Use of Teams, Nonphysicians, and Electronic Communication." *Health Affairs* 32: 1 (2013): 11–19.

Greenberg, Daniel S. *Science, Money, and Politics: Political Triumph and Ethical Erosion.* Chicago: University of Chicago Press, 2001.

Grob, Rachel. "Behind the Jargon: The Heart of Patient-Centered Care." *Journal of Health Politics, Policy and Law* 38: 2 (2013): 457–465.

Grogan, Colleen M., and Michael K. Gusmano. *Healthy Voices/Unhealthy Silence: Advocacy and Health Policy for the Poor.* Washington, DC: Georgetown University Press. 2007.

Grover, Atul, and Lidia M. Niecko-Najjum. "Physician Workforce Planning in an Era of Health Care Reform." *Academic Medicine* 88: 12 (2013): 1822–1826.

Gusmano, Michael K. "Health Systems Performance and the Politics of Cancer Survival." *World Medical & Health Policy* 5: 1 (2013): 76–84.

Gusmano, Michael K., and Daniel Callahan. "Value for Money: Use with Care." *Annals of Internal Medicine* 154: 3 (2011): 207–208.

Gusmano, Michael K., Gerry Fairbrother, and Heidi Park. "Exploring the Limits of the Safety Net: Community Health Centers and Care for the Uninsured." *Health Affairs* 21: 6 (2002): 188–194.

Halpern, Sydney A. "Medical Authority and the Culture of Rights." *Journal of Health Politics, Policy and Law* 29: 4–5 (2004): 835–852.

Harris, Dean M. *Ethics in Health Services and Policy: A Global Approach.* San Francisco, CA: Jossey-Bass, 2011. Esp. chs. 7–9, 11–12.

Healy, Andrew, and Neil Malhotra. "Myopic Voters and Natural Disaster Policy." *American Political Science Review* 103: 3 (2009): 387–406.

Hibbard, Judith H., and Ellen Peters. "Supporting Informed Consumer Health Care Decisions: Data Presentation Approaches That Facilitate the Use of Information in Choice." *Annual Review of Public Health* 24 (2003): 413–433.

Himmelstein, David U., Elizabeth Warren, Deborah Thorne, and Steffie Woolhandler. "Illness and Injury as Contributors to Bankruptcy." *Health Affairs.* February 2005. http://content.healthaffairs.org/content/suppl/2005/01/28/hlthaff.w5.63.DC1.

Hoffman, Beatrix. "Health Care Reform and Social Movements in the United States." *American Journal of Public Health* 93 (2003): 75–85.

Hoffman, Beatrix, Nancy Tomes, Rachel Grob, and Mark Schlesinger, eds. *Patients as Policy Actors (Critical Issues in Health and Medicine).* New Brunswick, NJ: Rutgers University Press, 2011.

Howard, David H. "Quality and Consumer Choice in Healthcare: Evidence from Kidney Transplantation." *Topics in Economic Analysis and Policy* 5: 1 (2005): 1–20.

Hsiao, C. William, L. Daniel Dunn, and Diana K. Verrilli. "Assessing the Implementation of Physician-Payment Reform." *New England Journal of Medicine* 328: 13 (1993): 928–933.

Hurley, Robert E. "The Puzzling Popularity of the PPO." *Health Affairs* 23 (2004): 56–68.

Hutchins, Vince L. "Maternal and Child Health Bureau: Roots." *Pediatrics* 94: 5 (1994): 695–699.

Iglehart, John K. "Changing with the Times: The Views of Bruce C. Vladeck." *Health Affairs* 16: 3 (1997): 58–71.

———. "Financing Graduate Medical Education—Mounting Pressure for Reform." *New England Journal of Medicine* 366 (2012): 1562–1563.

———. "A New Day Dawns for Workforce Redesign." *Health Affairs* 32: 11 (2013): 1870.

———. "The Political Fight over Comparative Effectiveness Research." *Health Affairs* 29: 10 (2010): 1757–1760.

Institute of Medicine. *The Future of Drug Safety: Promoting and Protecting the Health of the Public.* Washington, DC: National Academy Press, 2007.

———. *The Future of Nursing.* Washington, DC: National Academies Press, 2010. http://www.iom.edu/Reports/2010/the-future-of-nursing-leading-change-advancing-health.aspx.

———. *HHS in the 21st Century: Charting a New Course for a Healthier America.* Washington, DC: National Academies Press, 2009.

———. *Responding to Health Needs and Scientific Opportunity: The Organizational Structure of the National Institutes of Health.* Washington, DC: National Academy Press, 1984.

Institute of Medicine, Board of Health Promotion and Disease Prevention, Committee on Assuring the Health of the Public in the Twenty-First Century. *The Future of the Public's Health in the Twenty-first Century.* Washington, DC: National Academy Press, 2003.

Institute of Medicine, Board on Population Health and Public Health Practice, Committee on Valuing Community-Based, Non-clinical Prevention Policies and Wellness Strategies. *An Integrated Framework for Assessing the Value of Community-based Prevention.* Washington, DC: National Academy Press, 2012.

Institute of Medicine, Committee on Health Planning Goals and Standards. *Health Planning in the United States: Selected Policy Issues.* 2 vols. Washington, DC: National Academy Press, 1981.

Jenks, Stephen F., and Gail R. Wilensky. "The Health Care Quality Improvement Initiative." *Journal of the American Medical Association* 268: 7 (1992): 900–903.

Johnson, Haynes, and David Broder. *The System: The American Way of Politics at the Breaking Point.* Boston: Little, Brown, 1996.

Jones, Kenneth Macdonald. "The Endless Frontier." *Prologue* 8 (1976): 35–46.

Juran, Joseph M. *A History of Managing for Quality.* Milwaukee, WI: ASQC Quality Press, 1995.

Kaiser Family Foundation. "Five Key Questions about Medicaid and Its Role in State/Federal Budgets and Health Reform." May 1, 2012. http://www.kff.org/medicaid/upload/8139-02.pdf.

——. "Medicare: A Primer." http://kaiserfamilyfoundation.files.wordpress.com/2013/01/7615-03.pdf.

——. "The Uninsured and the Difference Health Insurance Makes." September 1, 2012. http://www.kff.org/uninsured/upload/1420-14.pdf.

Kaiser Health News Daily Report. "CBO Finds Health Overhaul Will Cost $940 Billion over 10 Years but Trim Deficit." March 18, 2010. http://www.kaiserhealthnews.org/Daily-Reports/2010/March/18/New-CBO-Numbers.aspx.

Kant, Immanual. *The Groundwork of the Metaphysics of Morals* (Trans. by H. J. Paton). New York: Harper and Row, 1964.

Kass, Leon. *Human Cloning and Human Dignity: The Report of the President's Council on Bioethics.* New York: Public Affairs Press, 2002.

Kassirer, Jerome. *On the Take: How Big Business Is Corrupting American Medicine.* New York: Oxford University Press, 2004.

Kay, W.D. *Defining NASA: The Historical Debate over the Agency's Mission.* Albany: State University of New York Press.

Kellermann, Arthur L., John W. Saultz, Ateev Mehrotra, Spencer S. Jones, and Siddartha Dalal. "Primary Care Technicians: A Solution to the Primary Care Workforce Gap." *Health Affairs* 32: 11 (2013): 1893–1898.

Kerry, John, Kathleen Sebelius, and Lisa Monaco. "Why Global Health Security Is a National Priority." *CNN.* February 14, 2014. http://www.cnn.com/2014/02/12/opinion/kerry-sebelius-health-security/.

Kessler, Daniel P., William M. Sage, and David J. Becker. "Impact of Malpractice Reforms on the Supply of Physician Services." *Journal of the American Medical Association* 293: 21 (2005): 2618–2625.

Kingdon, John W. *Agendas, Alternatives and Public Policies.* 2nd ed. New York: HarperCollins, 1995.

Kirch, Darrell G., Mackenzie K. Henderson, and Michael J. Dill. "Physician Workforce Projections in an Era of Reform." *Annual Review of Medicine* 63 (2011): 435–445.

Kliff, Sarah. "The Incredible Shrinking Prevention Fund." *Washington Post.* April 19, 2013. http://www.washingtonpost.com/blogs/wonkblog/wp/2013/04/19/the-incredible-shrinking-prevention-fund.

Kocher, Robert, and Nikhil R. Sahn. "Rethinking Health Care Labor." *New England Journal of Medicine* 365 (2013): 1370–1372.

Koh, Howard K., and Kathleen G. Sebelius. "Promoting Prevention through the Affordable Care Act." *New England Journal of Medicine* 363 (2010): 1296–1299.

Kohler, Robert E. *Partners in Science: Foundations and Natural Scientists, 1900–1945.* Chicago: University of Chicago Press, 1991.

Kotch, Jonathan B., ed. *Maternal and Child Health: Programs, Problems and Policies in Public Health.* 3rd ed. Burlington, MA: Jones & Bartlett Learning, 2013.

Kuo, Yong-Fang, Figaro Loresto Jr., Linda Rounds, and James Goodwin. "States with the Least Restrictive Regulations Experienced the Largest Increase in Patients Seen by Nurse Practitioners." *Health Affairs* 32: 7 (2013): 1236–1243.

Lake, Tim, Chris Kvam, and Marsha Gold. "Literature Review: Using Quality Information for Health Care Decisions and Quality Improvement, Final Report." Oakland, CA: Mathematica Policy Research, May 2005.

Laurant, Miranda, Mirjam Harmsen, Hub Wollersheim, Richard Grol, Marjan Faber, and Bonnie Sibbald. "The Impact of Nonphysician Clinicians: Do They Improve the Quality and Cost-effectiveness of Health Care Services?" *Medical Care Research and Review* 66: 6, Suppl (2009): 36S–89S.

Lawton, S., and J. Glisson. "Congressional Deliberations: A Commentary." In *Deliberations and Compromise: The Health Professions Educational Assistance Act of 1976,* edited by Lauren LeRoy and Philip R. Lee, 1–19. Cambridge, MA: Ballinger, 1977.

Lefkowitz, Bonnie, with contributions by Eleanor D. Kinney and Cheryl Ulmer. *Health Planning: Lessons for the Future.* Rockville, MD: Aspen Systems, 1983.

LeRoy, Lauren, and Philip R. Lee, eds. *Deliberations and Compromise: the Health Professions Educational Assistance Act of 1976.* Cambridge, MA: Ballinger, 1977.

Litow, Mark E. "Medicare versus Private Health Insurance: The Cost of Administration" January 6, 2006. http://www.cahi.org/cahi_contents/resources/pdf/CAHIMedicareTechnicalPaper.pdf.

Locke, John. *Two Treatises of Government.* Cambridge, UK: Cambridge University Press, 1970.

Lohr, Kathleen, ed. *Medicare: A Strategy for Quality Assurance,* Volume I. Washington, DC: National Academy Press, 1990.

——. *Peer Review Organizations: Quality Assurance in Medicare.* Santa Monica, CA: RAND, 1985.

Luce, Bryan R., and Rebecca S. Cohen. "Health Technology Assessment in the United States." *International Journal of Technology Assessment in Health Care* 25: Suppl 1 (2009): 33–41.

Luft, Harold S. "How Do Health Maintenance Organizations Achieve Their Savings?" *New England Journal of Medicine* 298: 24 (1978): 1336–1343.

Mansfield, Caroline, Suellen Hopfer, and Theresa M. Marteau. "Termination Rates after Prenatal Diagnosis of Down Syndrome, Spina Bifida, Anencephaly, and Turner and Klinefelter Syndromes: A Systemic Literature Review." *Prenatal Diagnosis* 19 (1999): 808–812.

Marder, William D., Phillip R. Kletke, Anne B. Silberger, and Richa J. Willke. *Physician Supply and Utilization by Specialty: Trends and Projections.* Chicago: American Medical Association, 1988.

Marmor, Theodore. *The Politics of Medicare.* Chicago: Aldine, 1973.

Marmor, Theodore, and Jonathan Oberlander. "From HMOs to ACOs: The Quest for the Holy Grail in U.S. Health Policy." *Journal of General Internal Medicine* 27: 9 (2012): 1215–1218.

Mayes, Rick, and Robert Berenson. *Medicare Prospective Payment and the Shaping of U.S. Health Care.* Baltimore: Johns Hopkins University Press, 2008.

Mayes, Rick, and Thomas R. Oliver. "Chronic Disease and the Shifting Focus of Public Health: Is Prevention Still a Political Lightweight?" *Journal of Health Politics, Policy and Law* 37: 2 (2012): 181–200.

McCormick, Richard. "Experimentation on the Fetus: Policy Proposals." *Appendix to Report and Recommendations: Research on the Fetus.* Washington, DC: National Commission for the Protection of Human Subjects of Biomedical and Behavioral Research, 1976.

McKenna, Maryn. *Beating Back the Devil: On the Front Lines with the Disease Detectives of the Epidemic Intelligence Service.* New York: Free Press, 2004.

Medicare Payment Advisory Commission. *Report to the Congress: Improving Medicare's Payments for Inpatient Care and for Teaching Hospitals.* Washington, DC: Medicare Payment Advisory Commission, June 2000.

Melhado, Evan M., Walter Feinberg, and Harold M. Swartz, eds. *Money, Power, and Health Care.* Ann Arbor, MI: Health Administration Press, 1988.

Mello, Michelle M., and Allen Kachalia. *Evaluation of Options for Medical Malpractice System Reform.* Washington, DC: Medicare Payment Advisory Commission, January 29, 2010.

Miles, Rufus, Jr. *The Department of Health, Education, and Welfare.* New York: Praeger, 1974.

Mitchell, C. Ben, Edmund D. Pellegrino, Jean Bethke Elshtain, John F. Kilner, and Scott Rae. *Biotechnology and the Human Good.* Washington, DC: Georgetown University Press, 2007.

Moon, Marilyn. *Medicare Now and in the Future.* Washington, DC: Urban Institute Press, 1993.

More, Max, and Natasha Vita-More. *The Transhumanist Reader: Classical and Contemporary Essays on the Science, Technology, and Philosophy of the Human Future.* Chichester, UK: Wiley-Blackwell.

Morone, James A. *The Democratic Wish: Popular Participation and the Limits of American Government.* New York: Basic Books, 1990.

Moses, Hamilton, E. Ray Dorsey, David H. M. Matheson, and Samuel O. Thier. "Financial Anatomy of Biomedical Research." *Journal of the American Medical Association* 294 (2005): 1333–1342.

Mowery, David C., Richard R. Nelson, Bhaven N. Sampat, and Arvids A. Ziedonis. *Ivory Tower and Industrial Innovation: University-Industry Technology Transfer before and after the Bayh-Dole Act.* Stanford, CA: Stanford Business Books, 2004.

Mundinger, Mary O., Robert L. Kane, and Elizabeth R. Lenz, et al. "Primary Care Outcomes in Patients Treated by Nurse Practitioners or Physicians: A Randomized Trial." *Journal of the American Medical Association* 283: 1 (2000): 59–68.

National Academy of Social Insurance and the National Academy of Public Administration. *Administrative Solutions in Health Reform.* Washington, DC: National Academy of Social Insurance, July 2009.

National Commission for the Protection of Human Subjects of Biomedical and Behavioral Research. *The Belmont Report.* April 18, 1979. http://www.hhs.gov/ohrp/humansubjects/guidance/belmont.html.

National Research Council and Institute of Medicine. *Children's Health, the Nation's Wealth: Assessing and Improving Child Health.* Washington, DC: National Academies Press. 2004.

———. *Enhancing the Vitality of the National Institutes of Health: Organizational Change to Meet New Challenges.* Washington, DC: National Academies Press, 2003.

National Resources Committee. *Research—A National Resource.* 76th Congress, 1st session, House Document No. 122, 1939.

Neustadt, Richard E., and Harvey V. Fineberg. *The Swine Flu Affair: Decision-making on a Slippery Disease.* Washington, DC: U.S. Department of Health, Education and Welfare, 1978.

Nightingale, Florence. *Notes on Nursing: What It Is and What It Is Not.* New York: D. Appleton, 1912.

Northern Virginia Community College. "Community Health Services and Facilities Act—1961 and Beyond. Healthcare Professions Delivery Systems." http://www.nvcc.edu/home/bhays/dogwood/facilitiesact.htm.

Nussbaum, Martha. "Non-Relative Virtues: An Aristotelian Approach." *Midwest Studies in Philosophy* 13 (1988): 32–53.

Office of Technology Assessment. *Nurse Practitioners, Physician Assistants, and Certified Nurse Midwives: A Policy Analysis.* Washington, DC: Office of Technology Assessment, 1986.

O'Kane, Margaret. "Increasing Transparency on Health Care Costs, Coverage and Quality." Testimony before the Senate Commerce, Science & Transportation Committee. February 27 2013. http://www.ncqa.org/Portals/0/Newsroom/2013/NCQA%20POK%20Senate%20Commerce%20Testimony.pdf.

Oliver, Thomas R. "Analysis, Advice, and Congressional Leadership: The Physician Payment Review Commission and the Politics of Medicare." *Journal of Health Politics, Policy and Law* 18: 1 (1993): 113–174.

———. "Policy Entrepreneurship in the Social Transformation of American Medicine: The Rise of Managed Care and Managed Competition." *Journal of Health Politics, Policy and Law* 29. 4–5 (2004): 701–734.

Olson, Mary K. "Explaining Regulatory Behavior in the FDA: Political Control vs. Agency Discretion." In *Advances in the Study of Entrepreneurship, Innovation, and Economic Growth,* Volume 7, edited by Gary Libecap, 71–108. Greenwich, CT: JAI Press, 1996.

———. "Pharmaceutical Policy Change and the Safety of New Drugs." *Journal of Law and Economics* 45: 2, Part 2 (2002): 615–642.

———. "Regulatory Agency Discretion among Competing Industries: Inside the FDA." *Journal of Law, Economics & Organization* 11: 2 (1995): 379–405.

Osterholm, Michael. "Getting Prepared." *Foreign Affairs* 84: 4 (2005): 24–37.

Panel on Scientific Boundaries for Review. "Phase 1 Report." Bethesda, MD: Center for Scientific Review, National Institutes of Health, 2000. http://www.csr.nih.gov/archives/summary012000.htm.

Patel, Kavita. "Health Reform's Tortuous Route to the Patient-Centered Outcomes Research Institute." *Health Affairs* 29: 10 (2010): 1777–1782.

Patterson, James T. *The Dread Disease: Cancer and Modern American Culture.* Cambridge, MA: Harvard University Press, 1987.

Peltzman, Sam. "An Evaluation of Consumer Protection Legislation: The 1962 Drug Amendments." *Journal of Political Economy* 81 (1973): 1049–1091.

Pence, Gregory E. *Classic Cases in Medical Ethics: Accounts of the Cases That Shaped and Define Medical Ethics.* 5th ed. Boston: McGraw-Hill, 2008.

Pendergrast, Mark. *Inside the Outbreaks: The Elite Medical Detectives of the Epidemic Intelligence Service.* New York: Mariner Books, 2011.

Persad, G., A. Wertheimer, and E. Emanuel, "Principles for Allocation of Scarce Medical Interventions." *Lancet* 373: 9661 (2009): 423–431.

Peterson, M.A. "From Trust to Political Power: Interest Groups, Public Choice, and Health Care Markets." *Journal of Health Politics, Policy and Law* 26 (2001): 1145–1163.

Petterson, Lars E., Robert L. Phillips, James C. Puffer, Andrew Bazemore, and Stephen Petterson. "Most Family Physicians Work Routinely with Nurse Practitioners, Physician Assistants, or Certified Nurse Midwives." *Journal of the American Board of Family Medicine* 26: 3 (2013): 244–245.

Physicians for a National Health Program. "What Is Single Payer?" 2014. http://www.pnhp.org/facts/what-is-single-payer.

Pies, Ronald. "The Libertarian Mind," http://thehealthcareblog.com/blog/2010/12/03/the-libertarian-mind.

Pisacano, N.J. "History of the Specialty." https://www.theabfm.org/about/history.aspx.

Poon, Michael, et al. "Associations between Routine Coronary Computed Tomographic Angiography and Reduced Unnecessary Hospital Admissions, Length of Stay, Recidivism

Rates, and Invasive Coronary Angiography in the Emergency Department Triage of Chest Pain." *Journal of the American College of Cardiology* 62: 6 (2013): 543–552.

Pronovost, Peter, Brian Sexton, and David Thompson. "Five Years after to Err Is Human." *Journal of Critical Care* 20: 1 (2005): 76–78.

Quirk, Paul J. "The Food and Drug Administration." In *The Politics of Regulation,* edited by James Q. Wilson. New York: Basic Books, 1980.

Radin, Beryl A. *The Accountable Juggler: The Art of Leadership in a Federal Agency* Washington, DC: CQ Press, 2002.

———. "When Is a Health Department Not a Health Department: The Case of the US Department of Health and Human Services." *Social Policy & Administration* 44: 2 (2012): 142–154.

Rawls, John. *A Theory of Justice.* Cambridge, MA: Harvard University Press, 1971.

Redman, Eric. *The Dance of Legislation: An Insider's Account of the Workings of the United States Senate.* New York: Simon & Schuster, 1973.

Reinhardt, Uwe E. *Physician Productivity and the Demand for Health Manpower: An Economic Analysis.* Cambridge, MA: Ballinger, 1975.

———. "US Health Care Stands Adam Smith on His Head." *British Medical Journal* 335: 7628 (2007): 1020.

Rich, Eugene C., Mark Liebow, Malathi Srinivasan, David Parish, James O. Wolliscroft, Oliver Fein, and Robert Blaser. "Medicare Financing of Graduate Medical Education." *Journal of General Internal Medicine* 17: 4 (2002): 283–292.

Ricketts, Tom C. "Public Health Policy and the Policy Making Process." In *Principles of Public Health Practice,* 3rd ed., edited by F. Douglas Scutchfield and William Keck, 86–115. Stamford, CT: Cengage Learning, 2011.

Rigby, Elizabeth. "How the National Prevention Council Can Overcome Key Challenges and Improve Americans' Health." *Health Affairs* 30: 11 (2011): 2149–2156.

Riter, Bob. "A Very Brief History of the Breast Cancer Advocacy Movement." http://www.ibca.net/about_us/brief_history.php.

Robert Wood Johnson Foundation. "Can Medicare Be Preserved while Reducing the Deficit?" *Timely Analysis of Immediate Health Policy Issues.* Princeton, NJ: Robert Wood Johnson Foundation, 2013.

Rodwin, Marc A. "Patient Accountability and Quality of Care: Lessons from Medical Consumerism, Patients' Rights, Women's Health and Disability Rights Movements." *American Journal of Law & Medicine* 22: 1&2 (1994): 147–167.

Rothman, David, and David Blumenthal. *Medical Professionalism in the New Information Age.* New Brunswick, NJ: Rutgers University Press, 2010.

Rudolph, Linda, Julia Caplan, Karen Ben-Moshe, and Lianne Dillon. *Health in All Policies: A Guide for State and Local Governments.* Washington, DC: American Public Health Association, 2013. http://www.apha.org/NR/rdonlyres/882690FE-8ADD-49E0-8270-94C0ACD14F91/0/HealthinAllPoliciesGuide169pages.pdf.

Samanta, Ash, Michelle M. Mello, Charles Foster, John Tingle, and Jo Samanta. "The Role of Clinical Guidelines in Medical Negligence Litigation: A Shift from the Bolam Standard?" *Medical Law Review* 14: 3 (2006): 321–366.

Sapolsky, Harvey. *Science and the Navy: The History of the Office of Naval Research.* Princeton, NJ: Princeton University Press, 1990.

Sardell, Alice. *The U.S. Experiment in Social Medicine: The Community Health Center Program, 1965–1986.* Pittsburgh, PA: University of Pittsburgh Press, 1988.

Saward, Ernest W., ed. *The Regionalization of Personal Health Services.* Rev. ed. New York: Prodist, 1976.

Schlesinger, Mark, and Pamela Brown Drumheller. "Medicare and Innovative Insurance Plans." In *Renewing the Promise: Medicare and Its Reform,* edited by David Blumenthal, Mark Schlesinger, and Pamela Brown Drumheller, 133–59. New York: Oxford University Press, 1988.

Schlesinger, Mark J., and Leon Eisenberg, eds. *Children in a Changing Health System: Assessments and Proposals for Reform.* Baltimore: Johns Hopkins University Press, 1990.

Schlesinger, Mark, and David Mechanic. "Challenges for Managed Competition from Chronic Illness." *Health Affairs* Suppl (1993): 123–137.

Shannon, James. "The Background of Some Contemporary Problems." Paper presented at Conference No. 3 on the Biomedical Sciences, Macy Foundation, 1975.

Shewhart, Walter A. *Statistical Method from the Viewpoint of Quality Control.* Mineola, NY: Dover, 1986.

Siegel, Marc. "A Pandemic of Fear." *Washington Post.* March 26, 2006. http://www.washingtonpost.com/wp-dyn/content/article/2006/03/24/AR2006032401716.html.

Sklar, David P. "How Many Doctors Will We Need? A Special Issue on the Physician Workforce." *Academic Medicine* 88: 12 (2003): 1785–1787.

Skloot, Rebecca. *The Immortal Life of Henrietta Lacks.* New York: Crown, 2010.

Sloan, Frank A. "Access to Medical Care and the Local Supply of Physicians." *Medical Care* 15: 4 (1977): 338–346.

Smith, David G. *Paying for Medicare: The Politics of Reform.* New York: Aldine Transaction, 1993.

Smith, Jane S. *Patenting the Sun: Polio and the Salk Vaccine.* New York: William Morrow, 1990.

Snyder, Lynn Page. "Passage and Significance of the 1944 Public Health Service Act." *Public Health Reports* 109 (November-December 1994): 721–724.

Sommers, Anna, and Peter J. Cunningham. "Medical Bill Problems Steady for U.S. Families, 2007–2010." *Tracking Report* 28. http://www.hschange.com/CONTENT/1268/1268.pdf. 2011.

Sorenson, Corinna, Michael K. Gusmano, and Adam Oliver. "The Politics of Comparative Effectiveness Research: Lessons from Recent History." *Journal of Health Politics, Policy and Law* 39: 1 (2014): 139–170.

Squires, David A. "The US Health Care System in Perspective: A Comparison of 12 Industrialized Nations." *Issues in International Health Policy* (July, 2011). http://www.commonwealthfund.org/~/media/Files/Publications/Issue%20Brief/2011/Jul/1532_Squires_US_hlt_sys_comparison_12_nations_intl_brief_v2.pdf.

Staiger, Douglas O., David I. Auerbach, and Peter I. Buerhaus. "Comparison of Physician Workforce Estimates and Supply Projections." *Journal of the American Medical Association* 302: 15 (2009): 1674–1680.

Starfield, Barbara. "Public Health and Primary Care: A Framework for Proposed Linkages." *American Journal of Public Health* 86: 10 (1996): 1365–1369.

Starr, Paul. *Remedy and Reaction: The Peculiar American Struggle over Health Care Reform.* New Haven, CT: Yale University Press, 2013.

———. *The Social Transformation of American Medicine.* New York: Basic Books, 1982.

Steelman, John R. *The Nation's Medical Research,* Volume 5. Washington, DC: U.S. Government Printing Office, 1947.

Steinwachs, Donald M. "GMENAC's Projection of a Future Physician Surplus: Implications for HMOs." *Group Health Journal* 4: 1 (1983): 7–11.

Steinwachs, Donald M., Jonathan P. Weiner, Sam Shapiro, Paul Batalden, Kathy Coltin, and Fred Wasserman. "A Comparison of the Requirements for Primary Care Physicians in HMOs with Projections Made by the GMENAC." *New England Journal of Medicine* 314: 4 (1986): 217–222.

Stevens, Rosemary A. *In Sickness and In Wealth: American Hospitals in the Twentieth Century.* New York: Basic Books, 1989.

Stewart, Irvin. *Organizing Scientific Research for War: The Administrative History of the Office of Scientific Research and Development.* Boston: Little, Brown, 1948.

Stitzenberg, Karyn B., and George F. Sheldon. "Progressive Specialization within General Surgery: Adding to the Complexity of Workforce Planning." *Journal of the American College of Surgeons* 201: 6 (2005): 925–932.

Stobbe, Mike. "CDC's Zombie Apocalypse Advice an Internet Hit." *Huffington Post.* May 20, 2011. http://www.huffingtonpost.com/2011/05/21/zombie-apocalypse-advice-cdc_n_865078.html.

Stolberg, Sheryl Gay. "Shortage of Vaccine Poses Political Test for Obama." *New York Times.* October 28, 2009. http://www.nytimes.com/2009/10/29/us/politics/29shortage.html.

Stone, Deborah. "AIDS and the Moral Economy of Insurance." *The American Prospect,* December 4, 2000. http://prospect.org/article/aids-and-moral-economy-insurance.

Strickland, Stephen P. *Politics, Science, and Dread Disease: A Short History of United States Medical Research Policy.* Cambridge, MA: Harvard University Press, 1972.

Studdert, David M., Michelle Mello, Atul Gawande, et al. "Claims, Errors, and Compensation Payments in Medical Malpractice Litigation." *New England Journal of Medicine* 354: 19 (2006): 2024–2033.

Susser, Ida, ed. *The Castells Reader on Cities and Social Theory.* Hoboken, NJ: Wiley-Blackwell, 2002.

Tannenbaum, Sandra J. "Pay for Performance in Medicare: Evidentiary Irony and the Politics of Value." *Journal of Health Politics, Policy and Law* 34: 5 (2009): 717–746.

———. "Reducing Variation in Health Care: The Rhetorical Politics of a Policy Idea." *Journal of Health Politics, Policy and Law* 38: 1 (2013): 5–26.

Task Force on the Professional Doctorate. *A Report to the Board of Trustees from the Task Force on the Professional Doctorate.* Urbana, IL: Higher Learning Commission, North Central Association of Colleges and Schools, 2006.

Temin, Peter. *Taking Your Medicine: Drug Regulation in the United States.* Cambridge, MA: Harvard University Press, 1980.

Thacker, Stephen B., Andrew L. Dannenberg, and Douglas H. Hamilton. "Epidemic Intelligence Service of the Centers for Disease Control and Prevention: 50 Years of Training and Service in Applied Epidemiology." *U.S. National Library of Medicine* 154: 11 (2001): 985–992.

Thompson, Frank J. *Federalism, Policy Durability, and Health Reform.* Washington, DC: Georgetown University Press, 2012.

Tierney, Kathleen J., Michael K. Lindell, and Ronald W. Perry. *Facing the Unexpected: Disaster Preparedness and Response in the United States.* Washington, DC: Joseph Henry Press, 2001.

Tocqueville, Alexis de. *Democracy in America* (Translated by Harvey Mansfield and Delba Winthrop). Chicago: University of Chicago Press, 2000.

Trust for America's Health. "Trust for America's Health Statement on the Anniversary of the National Prevention Strategy." June 13, 2012. http://healthyamericans.org/newsroom/releases/?releaseid=265.

U.S. Bureau of the Census. "Number of Firms, Number of Establishments, Employment, and Annual Payroll by Enterprise Employment Size for the United States, All Industries: 2011." Washington, DC: U.S. Bureau of the Census, 2012.

U.S. Congress. *Subcommittee of the Committee on Interstate and Foreign Commerce on S. 191.* House of Representatives, 79th Congress, 2nd session. Hospital Survey and Construction Act/Hill–Burton Act of March, 1946.

U.S. Department of Health and Human Services. "Indian Health Service. Final Report to the Secretary of HHS, of the Negotiated Rulemaking Committee on the Designation of Medically Underserved Populations and Health Professional Shortage Areas." http://www.ihs.gov.

———. "National Prevention Strategy." June 16, 2011. http://www.surgeongeneral.gov/initiatives/prevention/strategy.

U.S. President's Emergency Plan for AIDS Relief. "PEPFAR's Role in the United States Global Health Initiative." 2014. http://www.pepfar.gov/documents/organization/149853.pdf.

Varmus, Harold. "Proliferation of the National Institutes of Health." *Science* 291 (March 9, 2001): 1903, 1905.

———. "Shattuck Lecture: Biomedical Research Enters the Steady State." *New England Journal of Medicine* 333 (September 21, 1995): 811–815.

Vladeck, Bruce C., Emily J. Goodwin, Lois P. Myers, and Madeline Sinisi. "Consumers and Hospital Use: The HCFA 'Death List.'" *Health Affairs* 7: 1 (1988): 122–125.

Vladeck, Bruce C., and Thomas Rice. "Market Failure and the Failure of Discourse: Facing up to the Power of Sellers." *Health Affairs* 28: 5 (2009): 1305–1315.

Wechsler, J. "FDA User Fee Renewal Addresses Drug Shortages, New Drug Development." *Formulary* 47 (2011): 125–126.

Weight-Control Information Network. "Overweight and Obesity Statistics." March 12, 2013. http://www.win.niddk.nih.gov/statistics/#ref2.

Weiner, Jonathan P., Donald M. Steinwachs, Sam Shapiro, Kathryn L. Coltin, Dan Ershoff, and J. Paul O'Connor. "Assessing a Methodology for Physician Requirement Forecasting: Replication of GMENAC's Need-based Model for the Pediatric Specialty." *Medical Care* 25: 5 (1987): 426–436.

Wennberg, John E. "Dealing with Medical Practice Variations: A Proposal for Action." *Health Affairs* 3: 2 (1984): 6–32.

———. "The More Things Change . . . : The Federal Government's Role in the Evaluative Sciences." *Health Affairs* Suppl (2003): W3-308–W3-310.

———. *Tracking Medicine: A Researcher's Quest to Understand Health Care.* New York: Oxford University Press, 2010.

Wennberg, John E., Benjamin A. Barnes, and Michael Zubkoff. "Professional Uncertainty and the Problem of Supplier-Induced Demand." *Social Science & Medicine* 16 (1982): 811–824.

Wennberg, John E., Jean L. Freeman, and William J. Culp. "Are Hospital Services Rationed in New Haven or Over-utilised in Boston?" *Lancet* 329: 8543 (1987): 1185–1189.

Wennberg, John E., and Alan Gittelsohn. "Small Area Variations in Health Care Delivery." *Science* 182 (1973): 1102–1108.

———. "Variations in Medical Care among Small Areas." *Scientific American* 246 (1982): 120–135.

White, Joseph. "Prices, Volume, and the Perverse Effects of the Variations Crusade." *Journal of Health Politics, Policy and Law* 36: 4 (2011): 775–790.

Willman, David. "National Institutes of Health: Public Servant or Private Marketeer?" *Los Angeles Times.* December 22, 2004, A1ff.

———. "Stealth Merger: Drug Companies and Government Medical Research." *Los Angeles Times.* December 7, 2003.

Wilper, Andrew P., Steffie Woolhandler, Karen E. Lasser, Danny McCormick, David H. Bor, and David U. Himmelstein. "Health Insurance and Mortality in US Adults." *American*

Journal of Public Health 99: 12 (2009): 1–7. http://www.ncpa .org/pdfs/2009_harvard_health_study.pdf.

Wilson, John Rowan. *Margin of Safety.* Garden City, NY: Doubleday, 1963.

Woolhandler, Steffie, Terry Campbell, and David U. Himmelstein, "Costs of Health Care Administration in the United States and Canada." *New England Journal of Medicine* 349 (2003): 768–775. http://www.pnhp.org/news/Admin%20Cost%20 study.pdf.

World Health Organization. "Fact File on Health Inequalities." 2014. http://www.who.int/sdhconference/background/news/ facts/en.

———. "Noncommunicable Diseases." March 2013. http://www .who.int/mediacentre/factsheets/fs355/en.

Yett, D. "The Nursing Shortage and the Nurse Training Act of 1964." *Industrial and Labor Relations Review* 19: 2 (1966): 190–200.

Zelman, Walter A., and Robert A. Berenson. *The Managed Care Blues and How to Cure Them.* Washington, DC: Georgetown University Press, 1998.

PART IV—CONTEMPORARY HEALTH POLICY ISSUES: PEOPLE AND POLICIES (1960s–TODAY)

Aaron, Henry J., and Robert D. Reischauer. "The Medicare Reform Debate: What Is the Next Step?" *Health Affairs* 14: 4 (1995): 8–30.

Agency for Health Care Research and Quality. *National Health Care Disparities Report 2011.* Rockville, MD: Agency for Health Care Research and Quality, 2012. http://www.ahrq .gov/research/findings/nhqrdr/nhdr11/nhdr11.pdf.

Alan Guttmacher Institute. "Facts on Publicly Funded Contraceptive Services in the United States." http://www.guttmacher.org/ pubs/fb_contraceptive_serv.html.

Alexander, Greg R., and Milton Kotelchuck. "Assessing the Role and Effectiveness of Prenatal Care: History, Challenges, and Directions for Future Research." *Public Health Reports* 116: 4 (2001): 306–316.

Almond, Douglas V., Kenneth Y. Chay, and Michael Greenstone. *The Civil Rights Act of 1964, Hospital Desegregation and Black Infant Mortality in Mississippi.* New York: Columbia University Press, 2008.

Altman, Stuart, and David Shactman. *Power, Politics, and Universal Health Care: The Inside Story of a Century-long Battle.* Amherst, NY: Prometheus Books, 2011.

American Bar Association Commission on Domestic and Sexual Violence. "Domestic Violence Statistics." http://www.american bar.org/groups/domestic_violence/resources/statistics.html.

Andersen, LeAnn D., Patrick Remington, Amy Trentham-Dietz, and Mathew Reeves. "Assessing a Decade of Progress in Cancer Control." *The Oncologist* 7 (2002): 200–204.

Appleby, Julie. "Physicians Wade into Efforts to Curb Unnecessary Treatments." *Kaiser Health News,* April 4, 2012. http://www .kaiserhealthnews.org/Stories/2012/April/04/physicians- unnecessary-treatments.aspx.

Atwell, Jessica E., Josh Van Otterloo, Jennifer Zipprich, Kathleen Winter, Kathleen Harriman, Daniel A. Salmon, Neal A. Halsey, and Saad B. Omer. "Nonmedical Vaccine Exemptions and Pertussis in California, 2010." *Pediatrics* 132: 4 (2013): 624–630.

Bailar, John C., III, and Elaine M. Smith. "Progress against Cancer?" *New England Journal of Medicine* 314 (1986): 1226–1232.

Beardsley, Edward H. "Goodbye to Jim Crow: The Desegregation of Southern Hospitals, 1945–70." *Bulletin of the History of Medicine* 60 (1986): 367–386.

Beckwith, J. Bruce. "Defining the Sudden Infant Death Syndrome." *Archives of Pediatric and Adolescent Medicine* 157 (2003): 286–290.

Belcher, John R. "Are Jails Replacing the Mental Health System for the Homeless Mentally Ill?" *Community Mental Health Journal* 24 (1988): 185–195.

Bennefield, Robert L. "Health Insurance Coverage: 1995" (Current Population Reports P60-195). Washington, DC: U.S. Census Bureau. September 1996.

Bergman, Abraham. *The "Discovery" of Sudden Infant Death Syndrome.* Seattle: University of Washington Press, 1988.

Blendon, Robert J., Mollyann Brodie, John M. Benson, Drew E. Altman, Larry Levitt, Tina Hoff, and Larry Hugick. "Understanding the Managed Care Backlash." *Health Affairs* 17: 4 (1998): 80–94.

Boushey, Carol J., Shirley A.A. Beresford, Gilbert S. Omenn, and Arno G. Motulsky. "A Quantitative Assessment of Plasma Homocysteine as a Risk Factor for Vascular Disease: Probable Benefits of Increasing Folic Acid Intakes." *Journal of the American Medical Association* 274 (1995): 1049–1057.

Branch, Taylor. *Parting the Waters: America in the King Years 1954–63.* New York: Simon & Schuster, 1988.

Bray, George A., and Claude Bouchard, eds. *Handbook of Obesity,* Volume 1, 3rd ed. Boca Raton, FL: CRC Press, 2014.

Brennan, Meghan B., Christine Kolehmainen, Joshua Barocas, Carol Isaac, Christopher J. Crnich, and James M. Sosman. "Barriers and Facilitators of Universal HIV Screening among Internal Medicine Residents." *Wisconsin Medical Journal* 112: 5 (2013): 199–205.

Brodie, Janet Farrell. *Contraception and Abortion in Nineteenth Century America.* Ithaca, NY: Cornell University Press, 1994.

Cameron, James M. "A National Community Mental Health Program: Policy Initiation and Progress." In *Handbook on Mental Health Policy in the United States.* Greenwood: Westport, CT: Greenwood, 1989.

Campbell, Andrea Louise. *How Policies Make Citizens: Senior Political Activism and the American Welfare State.* Princeton, NJ: Princeton University Press, 2003.

Campsmith, Michael L., Philip H. Rhodes, H. Irene Hall, and Timothy A. Green. "Undiagnosed HIV Prevalence among Adults and Adolescents in the United States at the End of 2006." *Journal of Acquired Immune Deficiency Syndrome* 53 (2010): 619–624.

Casamayou, Maureen Hogan. *The Politics of Breast Cancer.* Washington, DC: Georgetown University Press, 2001.

Centers for Disease Control and Prevention. "Ambulatory Health Care Data: National Ambulatory Medical Care Survey: 2010 Summary Tables."

———. "Cancer Screening—United States, 2010." *Morbidity and Mortality Weekly Report* 61: 3 (2012): 41–45.

———. "CDC Grand Rounds: Public Health Approaches to Reducing U.S. Infant Mortality." *Morbidity and Mortality Weekly Report* 62: 31 (1013): 625–628.

———. "CDC's Sudden Unexpected Infant Death Initiative." http:// www.cdc.gov/sids/SUIDAbout.htm.

———. "Estimates of New HIV Infections in the United States." CDC Fact Sheet (August 2008): 1–6.

———. "Hepatitis C FAQs for Health Professionals." http://www .cdc.gov/hepatitis/HCV/HCVfaq.htm#section1.

——. "Hepatitis C Testing for Anyone Born during 1945–1965: New CDC Recommendations." http://www.cdc.gov/features/hepatitisctesting/.

——. "Measles—United States, January 1—August 24, 2013." *Morbidity and Mortality Weekly Report* 62: 36 (2013): 741–743.

——. "Recommendations for the Use of Folic Acid to Reduce the Number of Cases of Spina Bifida and Other Neural Tube Defects." *Morbidity and Mortality Weekly Report* 41 (1991): RR-14.

——. "Revised Recommendations for HIV Testing of Adults, Adolescents, and Pregnant Women in Health-Care Settings." *Morbidity and Mortality Weekly Report* 55: RR14 (2006): 1–17.

——. "Spina Bifida and Anencephaly before and after Folic Acid Mandate—United States, 1995–1996 and 1999–2000." *Morbidity and Mortality Weekly Report* 53: 17 (2004): 362–365.

——. "Sudden Unexpected Infant Death (SUID)." http://www.cdc.gov/sids/.

——. "Timeline: Thimerosal in Vaccines (1999–2010)." http://www.cdc.gov/vaccinesafety/concerns/thimerosal/thimerosal_timeline.html.

——. "Ten Great Public Health Achievements—United States, 1900–1999." *Morbidity and Mortality Weekly Report* 48: 12 (1999): 241–243.

——. "Unintentional Drug Poisoning in the United States." July 2010. http://www.cdc.gov/homeandrecreationalsafety/pdf/poison-issue-brief.pdf.

Centers for Medicare and Medicaid Services. "Pregnant Women." http://www.medicaid.gov/Medicaid-CHIP-Program-Information/By-Population/Pregnant-Women/Pregnant-Women.html.

Cigler, Allan J., and Burdett A. Loomis. *Interest Group Politics.* Washington, DC: CQ Press, 2002.

Clark, Nina A., Paul A. Demers, Catherine J. Karr, Mieke Koehoorn, Cornel Lencar, Lilian Tamburic, and Michael Brauer. "Effect of Early Life Exposure to Air Pollution on Development of Childhood Asthma." *Environmental Health Perspectives* 118: 2 (2010): 284–290.

Colgrove, James, Sara Abiola, and Michelle M. Mello. "HPV Vaccination Mandates—Lawmaking amid Political and Scientific Controversy." *New England Journal of Medicine* 363: 8 (2010): 785–791.

Colgrove, James, and Ronald Bayer. "Manifold Restraints: Liberty, Public Health, and the Legacy of *Jacobson v. Massachusetts.*" *Government, Politics, and Law* 95: 4 (2005): 571–576.

Commission on Social Determinants of Health. *Closing the Gap in a Generation: Health Equity through Action on the Social Determinants of Health.* Geneva, Switzerland: World Health Organization. 2008.

Commonwealth Fund. "Why Not the Best? Results from the National Scorecard on U.S. Health System Performance, 2011." New York: Commonwealth Fund, October 2011.

Cooper, Philip F., and Barbara Steinberg Schone. "More Offers, Fewer Takers for Employment-based Health Insurance: 1987 and 1996." *Health Affairs* 16: 6 (1997): 142–149.

Coppy, Andrew J., and Nicholas D. Green. "Neural Tube Defects—Disorders of Neurulation and Related Embryonic Processes." *Wiley Interdisciplinary Reviews: Developmental Biology* 2: 2 (2013): 213–227.

Coppy, Andrew J., Philip Sanier, and Nicholas D. Green. "Neural Tube Defects: Recent Advances, Unsolved Questions, and Controversies." *Lancet Neurology* 12: 8 (2013): 799–810.

Corlin, Richard F. "The Secrets of Gun Violence in America: What We Don't Know Is Killing Us." *International Journal of Trauma Nursing* 8: 2 (2002): 42–47.

Czeizel, Andrew E., and Istvan Dudás. "Prevention of the First Occurrence of Neural-Tube Defects by Periconceptional Vitamin Supplementation." *New England Journal of Medicine* 327: 6 (1992): 1832–1835.

Dahlberg, Linda L., Robin M Ikeda, and Marcie-jo Kresno. "Guns in the Home and Risk of a Violent Death in the Home: Findings from a National Study." *American Journal of Epidemiology* 160: 10 (2004): 929–936.

D'Aiuto, Francesco, Marco Orlandi, and John C. Gunsolley. "Evidence that Periodontal Treatment Improves Biomarkers and CVD Outcomes." *Journal of Periodontology* 84: 4, Suppl (2013): S85–S105.

DeClerque, Julia L., Janice A. Freedman, Sarah Verbiest, and Stuart Bondurant. "North Carolina's Infant Mortality Problems Persist: Time for a Paradigm Shift." *North Carolina Medical Journal* 65: 3 (2004): 138–146.

Donabedian, Avedis. *Exploring Quality Assessment and Monitoring: The Definition of Quality and Approaches to Its Assessment.* Volume 1. Ann Arbor, MI: Health Administration Press, 1980.

Elbel, Brian, and Mark Schlesinger. "Responsive Consumerism: Empowerment in Markets for Health Plans." *Milbank Quarterly* 87: 3 (2009): 633–682.

Elizhauser, Anne, Bernard Friedman, and Elizabeth Stranges. *Septicemia in U.S. Hospitals, 2009* (HCUP Statistical Brief #122). Rockville. MD: Agency for Healthcare Research and Quality, October 2011. http://www.hcupus.ahrq.gov/reports/statbriefs/sb122.pdf.

Enthoven, Alain C. *Health Plan: The Only Practical Solution to the Soaring Cost of Medical Care.* Boston: Addison-Wesley, 1980.

——. "Managed Competition: An Agenda for Action." *Health Affairs* 7: 3 (1988): 25–47.

Epstein, Leon D. *Political Parties in the American Mold.* Madison: University of Wisconsin Press, 1986.

Fahey, Thomas, Paul Insel, and Walton Roth. *Fit and Well: Core Concepts and Labs in Physical Fitness and Wellness,* 11th ed. New York: McGraw-Hill, Forthcoming.

Faulk, Isidore S., Margaret Kem, and Nathan Sinai. *The Incidence of Illness and the Receipt and Costs of Medical Care among Representative Families: Committee on the Cost of Medical Care Report No. 27.* Chicago: University of Chicago Press, 1933.

Faulkner, W. *Requiem for a Nun.* New York: Random House, 1950.

Federal Highway Administration Safety Program. "Section 402 Highway Safety Funds." http://safety.fhwa.dot.gov/policy/section402.

Fell, James C., John H. Lacey, and Robert B. Voas. "Sobriety Checkpoints: Evidence of Effectiveness Is Strong, But Use Is Limited." *Traffic Injury Prevention* 5: 3 (2004): 220–227.

Finer, Lawrence B., and Mia R. Zolna. "Unintended Pregnancy in the United States: Incidence and Disparities, 2006." *Contraception* 84 (2011): 478–485.

Fish, Johnathan. "Overcrowding on the Ship of Fools: Health Care Reform, Psychiatry, and the Uncertain Future of Normality." *Houston Journal of Health Law and Policy* 11 (2011): 1534–7907.

Fix, Michael, and Margery A. Turner, eds. *A National Report Card on Discrimination in America: The Role of Testing.* Washington, DC: Urban Institute, 1998.

Fleegler, Eric W., Lois K. Lee, Michael C. Monuteaux, David Hemenway, and Rebekah Mannix. "Firearm Legislation and Firearm-related Fatalities in the United States." *Journal of the*

American Medical Association Internal Medicine 173: 9 (2013): 732–740.

Foley, Henry A. *Community Mental Health Legislation: The Formative Process.* Lexington, MA: D.C. Heath, 1975.

Foley, Henry A., and Steven S. Sharfstein. *Madness and Government: Who Cares for the Mentally Ill?* Washington, DC: American Psychiatric Press, 1983.

Forest, Patti. "The Role of North Carolina Medicaid in Women's Health and Wellness." *North Carolina Medical Journal* 70: 5 (2009): 441–442.

Frank, Richard G., and Sherry A. Glied. *Better but Not Well: Mental Health Policy in the United States since 1950.* Baltimore: Johns Hopkins University Press, 2006.

Frank, Richard G., Howard H. Goldman, and Michael Hogan. "Medicaid and Mental Health: Be Careful What You Ask For." *Health Affairs* 22: 1 (2003): 101–113.

Freudenheim, Milt. "A Health Care Taboo Is Broken." *New York Times.* May 8, 1989.

Friedman, Michael S., Kenneth E. Powell, Lori Hutwagner, LeRoy M. Graham, and W. Gerald Teague. "Impact of Changes in Transportation and Commuting Behaviors during the 1996 Summer Olympic Games in Atlanta on Air Quality and Childhood Asthma." *Journal of the American Medical Association* 285: 7 (2001): 897–905.

Friedman, Richard A. "Good News for Mental Illness in Health Law." *New York Times.* July 9, 2012.

Fryar, Cheryl D., Rosemarie Hirsch, Kathryn S. Porter, Benny Kottiri, Debra J. Brody, and Tatiana Louis. "Drug Use and Sexual Behaviors Reported by Adults: United States, 1999–2002." *Advance Data from Vital and Health Statistics* 384 (2007).

Galva, Jorge E., Christopher Atchison, and Samuel Levey. "Public Health Strategy and the Police Powers of the State." *Public Health Reports* 120: Suppl 1 (2005): 20–27.

Gao, F., G. Bailes, and D.L. Robertson, et al. "Origin of HIV-1 in the Chimpanzee, Pan Troglodytes." *Nature* 197 (1999): 436–437.

Garland, Suzanne M. "The Australian Experience with the Human Papillomavirus Vaccine." *Clinical Therapeutics* 36: 1 (2014): 17–23.

Gase, Lauren N., Radha Pennotti, and Kenneth D. Smith. "'Health in All Policies': Taking Stock of Emerging Practices to Incorporate Health in Decision Making in the United States." *Journal of Public Health Management and Practice* 19: 6 (2013): 529–540.

Giaimo, Susan. *Markets and Medicine: The Politics of Health Care Reform in Britain, Germany, and the United States.* Ann Arbor: University of Michigan Press, 2002.

Goodnough, Abby. "U.S. Infant Mortality Rate Fell Steadily from '05 to '11." *New York Times.* April 17, 2013. http://www.nytimes.com/2013/04/18/health/infant-mortality-rate-in-us-declines.html?_r=0.

Grabow, Maggie L., Scott N. Spak, Tracy Holloway, Brian Stone Jr., Adam C. Mednick, and Jonathan A. Patz. "Air Quality and Exercise-Related Health Benefits of Reduced Car Travel in the Midwestern United States." *Environmental Health Perspectives* 120: 1 (2012): 68–76.

Grant, Robert M., Javier R. Lama, Peter I. Anderson, et al. "Pre-exposure Chemoprophylaxis for HIV Prevention in Men Who Have Sex with Men." *New England Journal of Medicine* 364 (2010): 1370–1375.

Greenhouse, Steven. "Dennis Rivera Leads Labor Charge for Health Reform." *New York Times,* August 27, 2009.

Grob, Gerald N. *The Mad among Us: A History of Care of America's Mentally Ill.* New York: Free Press, 1994.

———. *Mental Illness and American Society, 1875–1940.* Princeton, NJ: Princeton University Press, 1983.

———. *Mental Institutions in America: Social Policy to 1875.* New York: Transaction Publishers, 2008.

Hacker, Jacob S. "The Case for Public Plan Choice in National Health Reform: Key to Cost Control and Quality Coverage." Berkeley: Center on Health, Economic and Family Security, University of California School of Law, and Institute for America's Future, 2008. https://www.law.berkeley.edu/files/Hacker_final_to_post.pdf.

———. *The Divided Welfare State: The Battle over Public and Private Social Benefits in the United States.* Cambridge, UK: Cambridge University Press, 2002.

———. "Putting Politics First." *Health Affairs* 27: 3 (2008): 718–723.

———. *The Road to Nowhere: The Genesis of President Clinton's Plan for Health Security.* Princeton, NJ: Princeton University Press, 1997.

Harden, Victoria R. *AIDS at 30: A History.* Dulles, VA: Potomac Books, 2012.

Heen, Mary L. "Ending Jim Crow Life Insurance Rates." *Northwestern Journal of Law & Social Policy* 4: 2 (2009): 360–399.

Hepburn, Lisa, and David Hemenway. "Firearm Availability and Homicide: A Review of the Literature." *Aggressive & Violent Behavior* 9 (2004): 417–440.

Heritage Foundation. *Saving the American Dream: The Heritage Plan to Fix the Debt, Cut Spending, and Restore Prosperity.* Washington, DC: Heritage Foundation, 2011.

Himmelfarb, Richard. *Catastrophic Politics: The Rise and Fall of the Medicare Catastrophic Coverage Act of 1988.* University Park: Pennsylvania State University Press, 1995.

Hoek, Gerard, Ranjini M. Krishnan, Rob Beelen, Annette Peters, Bart Ostro, Bert Brunekreef, and Joel D. Kaufman. "Long-Term Air Pollution Exposure and Cardio-respiratory Mortality: A Review." *Environmental Health* 12: 43 (2013): 1–15.

Hoffman, Beatrix. "Health Care Reform and Social Movements in the United States." *American Journal of Public Health* 93 (2003):75–85.

———. *Health Care for Some: Rights and Rationing in the United States since 1930.* Chicago: University of Chicago Press, 2012.

Hogan, Michael F., and Lloyd I. Sederer. "Mental Health Crises and Public Policy: Improved Care of the Seriously Mentally Ill." *Milbank Quarterly* 65: 2 (1987): 203–230.

Holman, Dawn M., Vicki Benard, Katherine B. Roland, Meg Watson, Nicole Liddon, and Shannon Stokley. "Barriers to Human Papillomavirus Vaccination among US Adolescents: A Systematic Review of the Literature." *Clinical Review and Education* 168: 1 (2014): 76–82.

Honein, Margaret A., Leonard J. Paulozzi, T.J. Mathews, J. Davidson Erickson, and Lee-Yang C. Wong. "Impact of Folic Acid Fortification of the US Food Supply on the Occurrence of Neural Tube Defects." *Journal of the American Medical Association* 285: 23 (2001): 2981–2986.

Horwitz, Allan V. *Creating Mental Illness.* Chicago: University of Chicago, 2002.

Institute of Medicine. *Toward Quality Measures for Population Health and the Leading Health Indicators.* Washington, DC: National Academies Press, 2012.

Jacobs, Lawrence R., and Theda Skocpol. *Health Care Reform and American Politics: What Everyone Needs to Know.* Rev. ed. Oxford, UK: Oxford University Press, 2012.

Jacobsen, Grant D., and Kathryn H. Jacobsen. "Health Awareness Campaigns and Diagnosis Rates: Evidence from National Breast Cancer Awareness Month." *Journal of Health Economics* 30: 1 (2011): 55–61.

Johnson, Lyndon B. *Public Papers of the Presidents of the United States: Lyndon Baines Johnson, 1965, Entry 546.* Washington, DC: U.S. Government Printing Office, 1966.

Johnson, Michael P., and Karl Hufbauer. "Sudden Infant Death Syndrome as a Medical Research Problem since 1945." *Social Problems* 30: 1 (1982): 65–81.

Jones, James H. *Bad Blood: The Tuskegee Syphilis Experiment.* New York: Free Press, 1981.

Kaiser Commision on Medicaid and the Uninsured. *Immigrants' Health Care Coverage and Access.* Washington DC: Kaiser Family Foundation, 2003.

Kaiser Family Foundation. "Infant Mortality Rate (Deaths per 1,000 Live Births), Linked Files, 2007–2009." http://kff.org/other/state-indicator/infant-death-rate.

———. "Key Facts about the Uninsured Population." September 2013. http://kff.org/uninsured/fact-sheet/key-facts-about-the-uninsured-population.

———. "Massachusetts Health Care Reform: Six Years Later." May 2012. http://kff.org/health-costs/issue-brief/massachusetts-health-care-reform-six-years-later.

———. "Medicaid: A Timeline of Key Developments." http://kff.org/medicaid/timeline/medicaid-a-timeline-of-key-developments.

———. "Where Are States Today? Medicaid and CHIP Eligibility Levels for Children and Non-Disabled Adults as of January 1, 2014." http://kff.org/medicaid/fact-sheet/where-are-states-today-medicaid-and-chip.

Kaiser Family Foundation and Health Research and Educational Trust. *Employer Health Benefits Survey, 2011.* Washington DC: Kaiser Family Foundation, September 27, 2011.

Kennedy, Bruce P., Ichiro Kawachi, Deborah Prothrow-Stith, Kimberly Lochner, and Vanita Gupta. "Social Capital, Income Inequality, and Firearm Violent Crime." *Social Science & Medicine* 47 (1998): 7–17.

Kennedy, John F. "Special Message to Congress on Civil Rights and Job Opportunities, June 19, 1963." In *Public Papers of the Prsidents of the United States: John F. Kennedy.* Washington, DC: U.S. Government Printing Office, 1964.

Kessler, Ronald C., Patricia Berglund, Olga Demler, Robert Jin, Kathleen R. Merikangas, and Ellen E. Walters. "Lifetime Prevalence and Age-of-Onset Distributions of DSM-IV Disorders in the National Comorbidity Survey Replication." *Archives of General Psychiatry* 62: 6 (2005): 593–602.

Kiesler, Charles A., and Amy Sibulkin. *Mental Hospitalization: Myths and Facts about a National Crisis.* Newbury Park: Sage, 1987.

Kingdon, John W. *Agendas, Alternatives, and Public Policies.* Boston: Little, Brown, 1995.

Kliff, Sarah. "Obama's Proposed Budget to Seek $235 Million for New Mental Health Programs." *Washington Post.* April 9, 2013.

Koh, Howard K. "A 2020 Vision for Healthy People." *New England Journal of Medicine* 362 (2010): 1653–1656.

Kolata, Gina. "Hopeful Glimmers in Long War on Cancer." *New York Times.* November 4, 2013. http://www.nytimes.com/2013/11/04/booming/hopeful-glimmers-in-long-war-on-cancer.html?ref=health.

Kotch, Jonathan B., ed. *Maternal and Child Health: Programs, Problems and Policies in Public Health,* 3rd ed. Burlington, MA: Jones & Bartlett Learning, 2013.

Krieger, Nancy, David H. Rehkopf, Jarvis T. Chen, Pamela D. Waterman, Enrico Marcelli, and Malinda Kennedy. "The Fall and Rise of US Inequalities in Premature Mortality 1960–2002." *PLoS Medicine* 5: 2 (2008): e46.

Lewis, Dale P., Don C. Van Dyke, Phyllis J. Stumbo, and Mary J. Berg. "Drug and Environmental Factors Associated with Adverse Pregnancy Outcomes Part III: Folic Acid: Pharmacology, Therapeutic Recommendations, and Economics." *Annals of Pharmacotherapy* 32 (1998): 1087–1095.

Lexington. "Rand Paul and Anti-Terror Laws: A Waste of a Tender Conscience." *The Economist.* March 8, 2013. http://www.economist.com/blogs/lexington/2013/03/guns-and-mentally-ill.

———. "Why the NRA Keeps Talking About Mental Illness, Rather than Guns." *The Economist.* March 13, 2013.

Li, Yi, Wen Wang, Jizhi Wang, Xiaoling Zhang, Weili Lin, and Yuanqin Yang. "Impact of Air Pollution Control Measures and Weather Conditions on Asthma During the 2008 Summer Olympic Games in Beijing." *International Journal of Biometeorology* 55 (2011): 547–554.

Littler, Eddy, and Bo Oberg. "Achievements and Challenges in Antiviral Drug Discovery." *Antiviral Chemistry & Chemotherapy* 16 (2005): 155–168.

Livingwood, William C., Carol Brady, Kimberly Pierce, Hani Atrash, Tao Hou, and Thomas Bryant. "Impact of Preconception Health Care: Evaluation of a Social Determinants Focused Intervention." *Maternal and Child Health Journal* 14: 3 (2010): 382–391.

Long, Liza. "I Am Adam Lanza's Mother." *The Blue Review.* December 15, 2012. http://thebluereview.org/i-am-adam-lanzas-mother.

Lu, Michael C., and Neal Halfon. "Racial and Ethnic Disparities in Birth Outcomes: A Life-course Perspective." *Maternal and Child Health Journal* 7: 1 (2003): 13–30.

Luce, Edward, and Alexandra Ulmer. "Obama Foes Turn to '60s Radical for Tactical Tips." *Financial Times.* August 17, 2009, p. 2.

Manchikanti, Laxmaiah, Burt Fellows, Hary Ailinani, and Vidyasagar Pampati. "Therapeutic Use, Abuse, and Nonmedical Use of Opioids: A Ten-Year Perspective." *Pain Physician* 13: 5 (2010).

Marinho, Rui T., and David P. Barreira. "Hepatitis C, Stigma and Cure." *World Journal of Gastroenterology* 19: 40 (2013): 6703–6709. http://www.wjgnet.com/1007-9327/full/v19/i40/6703.htm.

Marmor, Theodore. *The Politics of Medicare.* Hawthorne, NY: Aldine de Gruyter, 2000.

Marmot, Michael. *The Status Syndrome: How Social Standing Affects Our Health and Longevity.* New York: Holt Paperbacks, 2005.

Martin, Cathi Jo. *Stuck in Neutral: Business and the Politics of Human Capital Investment Policy.* Princeton, NJ: Princeton University Press, 2000.

Mason, Joel B., Aaron Dickstein, Paul F. Jacques, Paul Haggarty, Jacob Selhub, Gerard Dallal, and Irwin H. Rosenberg. "A Temporal Association between Folic Acid Fortification and an Increase in Colorectal Cancer Rates May Be Illuminating Important Biological Principles: A Hypothesis." *Cancer Epidemiology, Biomarkers & Prevention* 16: 7 (2007): 1325–1329.

Mayes, Rick, and Robert Berenson. *Medicare Prospective Payment and the Shaping of U.S. Health Care.* Baltimore: Johns Hopkins University Press, 2008.

McFarlane, Deborah R., and Kenneth J. Meier. *The Politics of Fertility Control: Family Planning and Abortion Policies in the American States.* Washington, DC: CQ Press, 2001.

McGlynn, Elizabeth A., Steven M. Asch, John Adams, Joan Keesey, Jennifer Hicks, Alison DeCristofaro, and Eve A. Kerr. "The Quality of Health Care Delivered to Adults in the United

States." *New England Journal of Medicine* 348: 26 (2003): 2635–2645.

McKenna, Matthew, and Janet Collins. "Current Issues and Challenges in Chronic Disease Control." In *Chronic Disease Epidemiology and Control*, 3rd ed., edited by Patrick L. Remington, Ross C. Brownson, and Mark V. Wegner. Washington, DC: American Public Health Association, 2010.

Mechanic, David. "Seizing Opportunities under the Affordable Care Act for Transforming the Mental and Behavioral Health System." *Health Affairs* 31: 2 (2012): 376–382.

Mechanic, David, Donna D. McAlpine, and David A. Rochefort. *Mental Health and Social Policy: Beyond Managed Care*. 6th ed. Upper Saddle River, NJ: Pearson, 2014.

Mechanic, David, and David A. Rochefort. "Deinstitutionalization: An Appraisal of Reform." *Annual Reviews* 16 (1990): 301–327. http://www.annualreviews.org/doi/abs/10.1146/annurev.so.16.080190.001505.

Miller, Anthony B., Claus Wall, Cornelia J. Baines, Ping Sun, Teresa To, and Steven A. Narod. "Twenty-five Year Follow-up for Breast Cancer Incidence and Mortality of the Canadian National Breast Screening Study: Randomized Screening Trial." *BMJ* 348 (2014): g366.

Miller, Matthew, Steven J. Lippmann, Deborah Azrael, and David Hemenway. "Household Firearm Ownership and Rates of Suicide across the 50 United States." *Journal of Trauma, Injury, Infection, and Critical Care* 62: 4 (2007): 1029–1035.

Milliman. "Milliman Medical Index." May 2011. http://www.milliman.com/mmi.

Moffit, Robert E., and Kathryn Nix. "Transforming Medicare into a Modern Premium Support System: What Americans Should Know." Washington, DC: Heritage Foundation, April 15, 2011.

Moon, Rachel Y., and Linda Fu. "Sudden Infant Death Syndrome: An Update." *Pediatrics in Review* 33 (2012): 314–319.

Morgen, Sandra. *Into Our Own Hands: The Women's Health Movement in the United States, 1969–1990*. New Brunswick, NJ: Rutgers University Press, 2002.

Morse, Tim F., Albert Deloreto, Thomas St. Luis, and John D. Meyer. "Are Employment Shifts into Non-manufacturing Industries Partially Responsible for the Decline in Occupational Injury Rates?" *American Journal of Industrial Medicine* 52 (2009): 735–741.

Murphy, S.L., J. Xu, and K.D. Kochanek. "Deaths: Final Data for 2010." *National Vital Statistic Reports* 61: 4 (2013).

National Alliance on Mental Illness. "The Uninsured." *NAMI Fact Sheet*. Arlington, VA: National Alliance on Mental Illness.

National Center for Health Statistics. "Health, United States, 2012: With Special Feature on Emergency Care." Hyattsville, MD: National Center for Health Statistics, 2013.

National Heart, Lung, and Blood Institute. "National High Blood Pressure Education Program." http://www.nhlbi.nih.gov/about/nhbpep/nhbp_pd.htm.

National Institute of General Medical Sciences. "Sepsis Fact Sheet." November 22, 2013. http://www.nigms.nih.gov/Education/factsheet_sepsis.html.

National Prevention Council. *National Prevention Strategy*. Washington, DC: U.S. Department of Health and Human Services, Office of the Surgeon General, 2011.

National Research Council and Institute of Medicine. *Children's Health, the Nation's Wealth: Assessing and Improving Child Health*. Washington, DC: National Academies Press, 2004.

Nichols, James L., and Katherine A. Ledingham. "NCHRP Report 601: The Impact of Legislation, Enforcement, and Sanctions on Safety Belt Use." Washington, DC: National Cooperative Highway Research Program, 2008.

"North Carolina Program Helps Keep More Babies Alive." *New York Times*. September 2, 1991. http://www.nytimes.com/1991/09/02/us/north-carolina-program-helps-keep-more-babies-alive.html.

O'Conner, Elizabeth, Bradley N. Gaynes, Brittany U. Burda, Clara Soh, and Evelyn P. Whitlock. "Screening for and Treatment of Suicide Risk Relevant to Primary Care: A Systematic Review for the U.S. Preventive Services Task Force." *Annals of Internal Medicine* 158 (2013): 741–754.

Obama, Barack. "Remarks by the President on World AIDS Day." December 2, 2013.

Običan, Sarah G., Richard H. Finnell, James L. Mills, Gary M. Shaw, and Anthony R. Scialli. "Folic Acid in Early Pregnancy: A Public Health Success Story." *FASEB Journal* 24 (2010): 4167–4174.

Occupational Health and Safety Administration. "Commonly Used Statistics." https://www.osha.gov/oshstats/commonstats.html.

Office of Equal Health Opportunity. "Roster of Speakers, Program Staff, Consultants and Compliance Officer Trainees, Training Sessions April 4 & 5, 1966 and April 6 & 7, 1966." Atlanta, Georgia.

Office of National Drug Control Policy. "National Drug Control Strategy." http://www.whitehouse.gov/sites/default/files/ondcp/policy-and research/ndcs2010.pdf.

Olfson, Mark, Steven C. Marcus, Myrna M. Weissman, and Peter S. Jensen. "National Trends in the Use of Psychotropic Medications by Children." *Journal of the American Academy of Child and Adolescent Psychiatry* 415: 5 (2002): 514–521.

Organisation for Economic Co-operation and Development. "OECD Family Database, CO1.1." http://www.oecd.org/social/family/database.

Pallon, A., and E. Arias. Paradox Lost: Explaining the Adult Hispanic Mortality Advantage. *Demography* 41: 3 (2004): 385–415.

Parker, Theodore. "Of Justice and Conscience." In *Ten Sermons on Religion*. Boston: Crosby, Nichols, 1853.

Patel, Kant, and Mark Rushefsky. *Health Care Politics and Policy in America*, 3rd ed.. Armonk, NY: M.E. Sharpe, 2006.

Pear, Robert. "Industry Pledges to Control Health Care Costs." *New York Times*. May 11, 2009.

Pepin, Jacques. *The Origins of AIDS*. Cambridge, UK: Cambridge University Press, 2011.

Peterson, Mark A. "From Trust to Political Power: Interest Groups, Public Choice, and Health Care." *Journal of Health Politics, Policy and Law* 26: 5 (2001): 1145–1163.

Physical Activity Guidelines Advisory Committee. *Physical Activity Guidelines Advisory Committee Report, 2008*. Washington, DC: U.S. Department of Health and Human Services, 2008. http://www.health.gov/paguidelines/report/pdf/committeereport.pdf.

Pringle, Beverly, Lisa J. Colpe, Robert K. Heinssen, Michael Schoenbaum, Joel T. Sherrill, Cynthia A. Claassen, and Jane L. Pearson. "A Strategic Approach for Prioritizing Research and Action to Prevent Suicide." *Psychiatric Services* 64: 1 (2013): 71–75.

Pronovost, Peter, Brian Sexton, and David Thompson. "Five Years after to Err Is Human." *Journal of Critical Care* 20: 1 (2005), 76–78.

Quadagno, Jill. *One Nation, Uninsured: Why the U.S. Has No National Health Insurance*. Oxford, UK: Oxford University Press, 2005.

Rabinoff, Michael. *Ending the Tobacco Holocaust: How Big Tobacco Affects Our Health, Pocketbook and Political Freedom—And What We Can Do about It*. Santa Rosa, CA: Elite Books, 2010.

Remington, Patrick L., and Ross C. Brownson. "Fifty Years of Progress in Chronic Disease Epidemiology and Control." *Morbidity and Mortality Weekly Report* 60: Suppl (2011): 70–77.

Richardson, Erin G., and David Hemenway. "Homicide, Suicide, and Unintentional Firearm Fatality: Comparing the United States with Other High-Income Countries, 2003." *Journal of Trauma: Injury, Infection, & Critical Care* 70: 1 (2011): 238–243.

Rochefort, David A. "The Backlash against Managed Care." In *The New Politics of State Health Policy*, edited by Robert B. Hackey and David A. Rochefort. Lawrence: University Press of Kansas, 2001.

———. *From Poorhouses to Homelessness: Policy Analysis and Mental Health Care*. 2nd ed. Westport, CT: Auburn House, 1997.

———. *Handbook on Mental Health Policy in the United States*. Westport, CT: Greenwood Press, 1989.

Rosenberg, Robin. "Abnormal Is the New Normal." *Slate*. April 12, 2013. http://www.slate.com/articles/health_and_science/medical_examiner/2013/04/diagnostic_and_statistical_manual_fifth_edition_why_will_half_the_u_s_population.html.

Ruiz, John M., Patrick Steffen, and Timothy B. Smith. "Hispanic Mortality Paradox: A Systematic Review and Meta-analysis of the Longitudinal Literature." *American Jounal of Public Health* 103: 3 (2012): e52–e60.

Russell, Anne, Robert B. Voas, William Dejong, and Marla Chaloupka. "MADD Rates the States: A Media Advocacy Event to Advance the Agenda Against Alcohol-Impaired Driving." *Public Health Reports* 110: 3 (1995): 240–245.

Russell, Kelly F., Ben Vandermeer, and Lisa Hartling. "Graduated Driver Licensing for Reducing Motor Vehicle Crashes among Young Drivers." *Cochrane Database of Systematic Reviews* (2011).

Russell, Louise B. *Educated Guesses: Making Policy about Medical Screening Tests*. Berkeley: University of California Press, 1994.

Ruther, Martin, and Allen Dobson. "Equal Treatment and Unequal Benefits: A Re-examination of the Use of Medicare Services by Race: 1967–1976." *Health Care Financing Review* 2: 3 (1981): 55–83.

Ryan, Paul. *The Path to Prosperity*. House Budget Committee. March 2012. http://budget.house.gov/prosperity.

———. *A Roadmap for America's Future*. http://roadmap.republicans.budget.house.gov.

Schlesinger, Mark J., and Leon Eisenburg, eds. *Children in a Changing Health System: Assessments and Proposals for Reform*. Baltimore: Johns Hopkins University Press, 1990.

Schlozman, Kay Lehman, and John T. Tierney. *Organized Interests and American Democracy*. New York: Harper & Row, 1986.

Schneider, Anne, and Helen Ingram. "Social Construction of Target Populations: Implications for Politics and Policy." *American Political Science Review* 87: 2 (1993): 334–347.

Schulman, Kevin, Jesse A. Berlin, and William Harless, et al. "The Effect of Race and Sex on Physicians' Recommendations for Cardiac Catheterization." *New England Journal of Medicine* 340 (1999): 618–626.

Schulz, James H., and Robert H. Binstock. *Aging Nation: The Economics and Politics of Growing Older in America*. Baltimore: Johns Hopkins University Press, 2006.

Schuster, Mark A., Elizabeth A. McGlynn, and Robert H. Brook. "How Good Is the Quality of Health Care in the United States?" *Millbank Quarterly* 76 (1998): 517–563.

Sen, Amartya. "Why Health Equity?" *Health Economics* 11 (2002): 659–666.

Shenson, Douglas, Nancy Dubler, and David Michaels. "Jails and Prisons: The New Asylums?" *American Journal of Public Health* 80: 6 (1990): 655–656.

Shern, David, and Wayne Lindstrom. "After Newtown: Mental Illness and Violence." *Health Affairs* 32: 3 (2013): 447–450.

Shilts, Randy. *And the Band Played On: Politics, People, and the AIDS Epidemic*. New York: St Martin's, 1987.

Skocpol, Theda. *Boomerang: Clinton's Health Security Effort and the Turn against Government in U.S. Politics*. New York: W.W. Norton, 1996.

Sleet, David A., Shawna L. Mercer, Krista H. Cole, Ruth A. Shults, Randy W. Elder, and James L. Nichols. "Scientific Evidence and Policy Change: Lowering the Legal Blood Alcohol Limit for Drivers to 0.08% in the USA." *Global Health Promotion* 18: 1 (2011): 23–26.

Smedley, Brian, Adrienne Y. Stiths, and Alan R. Nelson, eds. *Unequal Treatment: Confronting Racial and Ethnic Disparities in Health Care*. Washington, DC: National Academies Press, 2002.

Smith, David B. "Desegregating the Hospitals in Jackson, Mississippi." *Milbank Quarterly* 83: 5 (2005): 247–269.

———. *Health Care Divided: Race and Healing a Nation*. Ann Arbor: University of Michigan Press, 1999.

———. *Reinventing Care: Assisted Living in New York City*. Nashville, TN: Vanderbilt University Press, 2003.

Starfield, Barbara. "Refocusing the System." *New England Journal of Medicine* 359 (2008): 2087–2091.

Starr, Paul. *Remedy and Reaction: The Peculiar American Struggle over Health Care Reform*. New Haven, CT: Yale University Press, 2011.

———. *Social Transformation of American Medicine*. New York: Basic Books, 1982.

Steenkamp, Malinda, et al. "The National Violent Death Reporting System: An Exciting New Tool for Public Health Surveillance." *Injury Prevention* 12: Suppl II (2006): ii3–ii5.

Stone, Deborah. *Policy Paradox: The Art of Political Decision Making*. 3rd ed. New York: W.W. Norton, 2012.

Strickland, David L. "Statement to the U.S. House, House Committee on Transportation and Infrastructure, Subcommittee on Highways and Transit: How Autonomous Vehicles Will Shape the Future of Surface Transportation." Hearing, 19 November 2013.

Substance Abuse and Mental Health Services Administration. *Mental Health, United States, 2010*. Rockville, MD: U.S. Department of Health and Human Services, 2012.

Tannenbaum, Sandra J. "Pay for Performance in Medicare: Evidentiary Irony and the Politics of Value." *Journal of Health Politics, Policy and Law* 34: 5 (2009): 717–746.

Tavernise, Sabrina. "F.D.A. Ruling Would All but Eliminate Trans Fats." *New York Times*. November 7, 2013. http://www.nytimes.com/2013/11/08/health/fda-trans-fats.html.

Tracy, Erin E., Susan Haas, and Michelle R. Laurina. "Newborn Care and Safety: The Black Box of Obstetric Practices and Residency Training." *Obstetrics and Gynecology* 120: 3 (2012): 643–464.

Trust for America's Health. *F as in Fat: How Obesity Threatens America's Future*. Washington, DC: Trust for America's Health, 2013. http://www.rwjf.org/content/dam/farm/reports/reports/2013/rwjf407528.

UN AIDS and World Health Organization. "AIDS Epidemic Update." December 2013. Geneva, Switzerland: World Health Organization.

University of Chicago Medicine. "From a No-Name Virus to a Cure: Treatment Options Blossom for Hepatitis C." January 2013. http://www.uchospitals.edu/news/features/hepatitisc-cure.html.

U.S. Bureau of the Census. *American Community Survey, 2010.* Washington, DC: U.S. Bureau of the Census, 2010.

———. *Dicennial Census.* Washington, DC: U.S. Bureau of the Census, 1960.

U.S. Bureau of Labor Statistics. *The Health Consequences of Smoking: A Report of the Surgeon General.* Atlanta, GA: U.S. Department of Health and Human Services, Centers for Disease Control and Prevention, National Center for Chronic Disease Prevention and Health Promotion, Office on Smoking and Health, 2004.

———. "Labor Force Statistics from the Current Population Survey." http://data.bls.gov/timeseries/LNS14000000.

U.S. Department of Health and Human Services. *Healthy People 2010 Final Review.* Washington, DC: U.S. Government Printing Office, 2011.

———. "Healthy People 2020." http://www.healthypeople.gov/2020/default.aspx.

U.S. Department of Housing and Urban Development. "Racial and Ethnic Minorities Face More Subtle Housing Discrimination" (Press Release). June 11, 2013. http://portal.hud.gov/hudportal/HUD?src=/press/press_releases_media_advisories/2013/HUDNo.13-091.

U.S. Department of Transportation, National Highway Traffic Safety Administration. "Strategies to Increase Seat Belt Use: An Analysis of Levels of Fines and the Type of Law." Washington, DC: U.S. Department of Transportation, 2010.

U.S. Food and Drug Administration. "Food Standards: Amendments of Standards of Identity for Enriched Grain Products to Require Addition of Folic Acid." *Federal Register* 61 (1996): 8781–8797.

U.S. Preventive Services Task Force. *Screening for HIV: Final Recommendation Statement* (AHRQ Publication No. 12-05173-EF-3). http://www.uspreventiveservicestaskforce.org/uspstf13/hiv/hivfinalrs.htm.

van Panhuis, William G., John Grefenstette, and Su Yon Jung, et al. "Contagious Diseases in the United States from 1888 to the Present." *New England Journal of Medicine* 369: 22 (2013): 2152–2158.

VanWormer, Jeffrey J., Amit Acharya, Robert T. Greenlee, and Francisco J. Nieto. "Oral Hygiene and Cardiometabolic Disease Risk in the Survey of the Health of Wisconsin." *Community Dentistry and Oral Epidemiology* 41 (2013): 374–384.

Vogel, David. "Why Businessmen Distrust Their State: The Political Consciousness of American Corporate Executives." *British Journal of Political Science* 8 (January 1978): 45–78.

Walker, Isabelle T. "Mentally Ill and Uninsured in America." *American Journal of Nursing* 110: 3 (2010): 27–28.

Weech-Maldanado, Robert, Adam Carle, Beverly Weidmer, Margarita Hurtado, Quyen Ngo-Metzger, and Ron D. Hays. "The Consumer Assessment of Healthcare Providers and Systems (CAHPS) Cultural Competence (CC) Item Set." *Medical Care* 50: 5 (2012): S22–S31.

Weisman, Carol S. *Women's Health Care.* Baltimore: Johns Hopkins University Press, 1998.

Weissert, William G., and Carol S. Weissert. *Governing Health: The Politics of Health Policy.* 4th ed. Baltimore: Johns Hopkins University Press, 2012.

Whitaker, Robert. *Mad in America: Bad Science, Bad Medicine, and the Enduring Mistreatment of the Mentally Ill.* Cambridge, MA: Perseus, 2001.

White House. *Now Is the Time: The President's Plan to Protect Our Children and Times.* July 9, 2012. http://www.whitehouse.gov/sites/default/files/docs/wh_now_is_the_time_full.pdf.

Whitehead, Margaret. "The Concepts and Principles of Equity and Health." Copenhagen, Denmark: World Health Organization, Regional Office for Europe. 1990.

Wilkerson, Isabel. *The Warmth of Other Suns: The Epic Story of America's Great Migration.* New York: Random House, 2010.

Witkin, Michael J., Joanne E. Atay, Ronald W. Manderscheid, Jason DeLozier, Alisa Male, and Robert Gillespe. "Highlights of Organized Mental Health Services in 1994 and Major National and State Trends." In *Mental Health, United States, 1998,* edited by Ronald W. Manderscheid and Marilyn J. Henderson. Rockville, MD: U.S. Department of Health and Human Services, Substance Abuse and Mental Health Services Administration, 1998.

Wolff, Megan J. "The Myth of the Actuary: Life Insurance and Frederick L. Hoffman's Race Traits and Tendencies of the American Negro." *Public Health Reports* 121 (January-February 2006): 84–91.

World Health Organization. "Tobacco Free Initiative." http://www.who.int/tobacco/mpower/en.

Wyden, Ron, and Paul Ryan. *Guaranteed Choices to Strengthen Medicare and Health Security for All.* December 15, 2011. http://budget.house.gov/uploadedfiles/wydenryan.pdf.

Zernike, Kate, and Megan Thee-Brenan. "Poll Finds Tea Party Backers Wealthier and More Educated." *New York Times.* April 14, 2010.

Zimring, Franklin E. "Firearms, Violence, and the Potential Impact of Firearms Control." *Journal of Law, Medicine & Ethics* 32 (2004): 34–37.

zur Hausen, Harald. "Viruses in Human Cancers." *Science* 254: 5035 (1991): 1167–1173.

PART V—U.S RESPONSE TO GLOBAL HEALTH CHALLENGES (1980s–TODAY)

Abbott, Frederick M., and Jerome H. Reichman. "The Doha Round's Public Health Legacy: Strategies for the Production and Diffusion of Patented Medicines Under the Amended TRIPS Provisions." *Journal of International Economic Law* 10: 4 (2007): 921–987.

Alleyne, George, David Stuckler, and Ala Alwan. "The Hope and the Promise of the UN Resolution on Noncommunicable Diseases." *Global Health* 6 (2010): 15.

Annas, George J. "Blinded by Bioterrorism: Public Health and Liberty in the 21st Century." *Health Matrix* 13 (2003): 45–54.

Barry, John. *The Great Influenza: The Epic Story of the Deadliest Plague in History.* New York: Viking, 2004.

Bayer, Ronald. "The Continuing Tensions Between Individual Rights and Public Health." *EMBO Reports* 8: 12 (2007): 1099–1103.

Bayer, Ronald, Amy Fairchild, and James Colgrove. *Searching Eyes: Privacy, the State, and Disease Surveillance in America.* Berkley: University of California Press, 2007.

Beaglehole, Robert, Ruth Bonita, Richard Horton, Cary Adams, George Alleyne, Perviz Asaria, Vanessa Baugh, et al. "Priority Actions for the Non-communicable Disease Crisis." *Lancet* 377: 9775 (2011): 1438–1447.

Beaglehole, Robert, and Derek Yach. "Globalisation and the Prevention and Control of Noncommunicable Disease: The Neglected Chronic Diseases of Adults." *Lancet* 362: 9387 (2003): 903–908.

Bertazzi, Pier Alberto, Dario Consonni, Silvia Bachetti, Maurizia Rubagotti, Andrea Baccarelli, Carlo Zocchetti, and Angela C. Pesatori. "Health Effects of Dioxin Exposure: A 20-Year Mortality Study." *American Journal of Epidemiology* 153: 11 (2001): 1031–1004.

Birkland, Thomas A. *Lessons of Disaster: Policy Change after Catastrophic Events.* Washington, DC: Georgetown University Press, 2006.

Bloom, David E., Elizabeth Cafiero, Eva Jané-Llopis, Shafika Abrahams-Gessel, Lakshmi Reddy Bloom, Sana Fathima, Andrea B. Feigl, et al. *The Global Economic Burden of Noncommunicable Diseases.* Geneva, Switzerland: World Economic Forum, 2012.

Bowman, Diana M., and Michael G. Bennett. "The Next Chapter of the Tobacco Wars: Unpacking the Latest Round of Constitutional Challenges." *American Journal of Public Health* 103: 8 (2013): e11–e13.

Bowman, Diana M., Michael Fitzharris, and Ray Bingham. "Making a Positive Impact: Striking a Balance between Legislative Reach and Road Safety." *Annals of Health Law* 22 (2013): 281–306.

Buchanan, David R. "Autonomy, Paternalism, and Justice: Ethical Priorities in Public Health." *American Journal of Public Health* 98: 1 (2008): 15–21.

Buse, Kent, Wolfgang Hein, and Nick Drager. *Making Sense of Global Health Governance.* New York: Palgrave Macmillan, 2009.

Center for Law and the Public's Health at Georgetown and Johns Hopkins Universities. *Model State Emergency Health Powers Act.* Art. I, § 104(m), December 21, 2001. http://www.publichealthlaw.net/MSEHPA/MSEHPA%20Leg%20Activity.pdf.

Centers for Disease Control and Prevention. *Emerging Infectious Diseases* (A public access journal published monthly).

———. "Global Health—Noncommunicable Diseases." http://www.cdc.gov/globalhealth/ncd.

Century Foundation. *Are Bioterrorism Dollars Making Us Safer?* January 12, 2005. http://tcf.org /media-center/2005/pr44.

Chan, Margaret. "Director General Addresses the Sixty-sixth World Health Assembly." May 20, 2013. http://www.who.int/dg/speeches/2013/world_health_assembly_20130520/en.

Chisholm, Daniel, Alan J. Flisher, Crick Lund, Vikram Patel, Shekhar Saxena, Graham Thornicroft, and Mark Tomlinson. "Scale Up Services for Mental Disorders: A Call for Action." *Lancet* 370: 9594 (2007): 1241–1252.

Chorev, Nitsan. *The World Health Organization between North and South.* Ithaca, NY: Cornell University Press, 2012.

Colgrove, James, and Ronald Bayer. "Manifold Restraints: Liberty, Public Health, and the Legacy of *Jacobson v Massachusetts.*" *Government, Politics, and Law* 95:.4 (2005): 571–576.

Collins, Pamela Y., Vikram Patel, Sarah S. Joestl, Dana March, Thomas R. Insel, Abdallah S. Daar, Isabel A. Bordin, et al. "Grand Challenges in Global Mental Health." *Nature* 475: 7354 (2011): 27–30.

Cullet, Philippe. "Patents and Medicines: The Relationship between TRIPS and the Human Right to Health." *International Affairs* 79: 1 (2003): 139–160.

Daar, Abdallah S., Peter A. Singer, Deepa Leah Persad, Stig K. Pramming, David R. Matthews, Robert Beaglehole, Alan Bernstein, et al. "Grand Challenges in Chronic Non-communicable Diseases." *Nature* 450: 7169 (2007): 494–496.

Danaei, Goodarz, Eric L. Ding, Dariush Mozaffarian, Ben Taylor, Jürgen Rehm, Christopher J.L. Murray, and Majid Ezzati. "The Preventable Causes of Death in the United States: Comparative Risk Assessment of Dietary, Lifestyle, and Metabolic Risk Factors." *PLoS Medicine* 6: 4 (2009): e1000058.

Drager, Nick, and David P. Fidler. "Foreign Policy, Trade and Health: At the Cutting Edge of Global Health Diplomacy." *Bulletin of the World Health Organization* 85: 3 (2007): 162–162.

Evans, Robert, Morris Bayer, and Theodore Marmor, eds. *Why Are Some People Healthy and Others Not? The Determinants of Health of Populations.* New York: Aldine de Gruyter, 2004.

Farber, Daniel A., Jim Chen, Robert V.M. Verchick, and Lisa Grow Sun. *Disaster Law and Policy.* 2nd ed. New York: Aspen, 2010.

Fidler, David P., and Lawrence O. Gostin. *Biosecurity in the Global Age: Biological Weapons, Public Health, and the Rule of Law.* Stanford, CA: Stanford University Press, 2007.

Gable, Lance. "Evading Emergency: Strengthening Emergency Responses through Integrated Pluralistic Governance." *Oregon Law Review* 91 (2013): 375–454.

Giusti, L. "A Review of Waste Management Practices and Their Impact on Human Health." *Waste Management* 29: 8 (2009): 2227–2239.

Gostin, Lawrence. "Health for All, Justice for All: A Framework Convention on Global Health." *Journal of the American Medical Association* 307: 19 (2012): 2087–2092.

———. "Public Health Law in an Age of Terrorism: Rethinking Individual Rights and Common Goods." *Health Affairs* 21 (2002): 86–91.

———. *Public Health Law: Power, Duty, Restraint.* Volume 3. Berkeley: University of California Press, 2000.

———. "When Terrorism Threatens Health: How Far Are Limitations on Personal and Economic Liberties Justified?" *Florida Law Review* 55 (2003): 1105–1170.

Greer, Scott L. "Global Health Policy: Governing Health Systems across Borders." In *Healthcare Management,* edited by Kieran Walshe and Judith Smith. New York: McGraw-Hill International, 2011.

Heymann, David. *Control of Communicable Diseases Manual.* Washington, DC: American Public Health Association, 2008.

———. *Lessons from the Anthrax Attacks: Implications for U.S. Bioterrorism Preparedness.* Washington, DC: Center for Strategic and International Studies, 2002.

Hodge, James G., Jr., Lance Gable, and Stephanie Calves. "The Legal Framework for Meeting Surge Capacity through the Use of Volunteer Health Professionals during Public Health Emergencies and Other Disasters." *Journal of Contemporary Health Law & Policy* 22 (2005): 13–14.

Homeland Security Presidential Directive. *Management of Domestic Incidents.* February 28, 2003. http://www.gpo.gov/fdsys/pkg/PPP-2003-book1/pdf/PPP-2003-book1-doc-pg229.pdf.

Institute of Medicine. *Crisis Standards of Care: A Systems Framework for Catastrophic Disaster Response.* Washington, DC: National Academies Press, 2012.

Jarman, Holly. "Attack on Australia: Tobacco Industry Challenges to Plain Packaging." *Journal of Public Health Policy* 34: 3 (2013): 375–387.

———. *The Politics of Trade and Tobacco Control.* Basingstoke, UK: Palgrave Macmillan, 2014.

Jarman, Holly, Judith Schmidt, and Daniel B. Rubin. "When Trade Law Meets Public Health Evidence: The World Trade Organization and Clove Cigarettes." *Tobacco Control* 21: 6 (2012): 596–598.

Johnson, Steven. *The Ghost Map: The Story of London's Most Terrifying Epidemic—and How It Changed Science, Cities, and the Modern World.* New York: Riverhead Books, 2006.

Kakuma, Ritsuko, Harry Minas, Nadja van Ginneken, Mario R. Dal Poz, Keshav Desiraju, Jodi E. Morris, Shekhar Saxena, and Richard M. Scheffler. "Human Resources for Mental Health Care: Current Situation and Strategies for Action." *Lancet* 378: 9803 (2011): 1654–1663.

Kampa, Marilena, and Elias Castanas. "Human Health Effects of Air Pollution." *Environmental Pollution* 151: 2 (2008): 362–367.

Kindig, David. "Understanding Population Health Terminology." *Milbank Quarterly* 85: 1 (2007): 139–161.

Lister, Sarah, and Frank Grotten. "The Pandemic and All Hazards Preparedness Act (P.L. 109-417): Provisions and Changes to Preexisting Law." Washington, DC: Congressional Research Service, January 25, 2007. http://www.ncdhhs.gov/dhsr/EMS/aspr/pdf/papareport.pdf.

Marmot, Michael, and Richard Wilkinson, eds. *Social Determinants of Health*, 2nd ed. Oxford, UK: Oxford University Press, 2006.

Matthews, Duncan. "WTO Decision on Implementation of Paragraph 6 of the DOHA Declaration on the TRIPs Agreement and Public Health: A Solution to the Access to Essential Medicines Problem?" *Journal of International Economic Law* 7: 1 (2004): 73–107.

McQueen, David V. *Global Handbook on Noncommunicable Diseases and Health Promotion*. New York: Springer, 2013.

Mello, Michelle M., David M. Studdert, and Troyen A. Brennan. "Obesity—The New Frontier of Public Health Law." *New England Journal of Medicine* 354: 24 (2006): 2601–2610.

Mokdad, Ali H., Earl S. Ford, Barbara A. Bowman, William H. Dietz, Frank Vinicor, Virginia S. Bales, and James S. Marks. "Prevalence of Obesity, Diabetes, and Obesity-related Health Risk Factors, 2001." *Journal of the American Medical Association* 289: 1 (2003): 76–79.

Murray, Christopher J.L., and Alan D. Lopez. "Measuring the Global Burden of Disease." *New England Journal of Medicine* 369: 5 (2013): 448–457.

Must, Aviva, Jennifer Spadano, Eugenie H. Coakley, Alison E. Field, Graham Colditz, and William H. Dietz. "The Disease Burden Associated with Overweight and Obesity." *Journal of the American Medical Association* 282: 16 (1999): 1523–1529.

National Commission on Terrorist Attacks upon the United States. *The 9/11 Commission Report*. New York: W.W. Norton, 2004.

National Highway Traffic Safety Administration. *Early Estimate of Motor Vehicle Traffic Fatalities in 2012*. http://www-nrd.nhtsa.dot.gov/Pubs/811741.pdf.

NCD Alliance. "The Global Epidemic." http://ncdalliance.org/globalepidemic.

Nelson, Christopher, Nicole Lurie, Jeffrey Wasserman, Sarah Zakowski, and Kristin J. Leuschner. *Conceptualizing and Defining Public Health Emergency Preparedness*. Santa Monica, CA: RAND, May 2008. http://www.rand.org/content/dam/rand/pubs/working_papers/2008/RAND_WR543.pdf.

Nelson, Kenrad E., and Carolyn Williams. *Infectious Disease Epidemiology*. 3rd ed. Burlington, MA: Bartlett Learning, 2013.

Ngo, Victoria K., Adolfo Rubinstein, Vijay Ganju, Pamela Kanellis, Nasser Loza, Cristina Rabadan-Diehl, and Abdallah S. Daar. "Grand Challenges: Integrating Mental Health Care into the Non-communicable Disease Agenda." *PLoS Medicine* 10: 5 (2013): e1001443.

O'Toole, Tara, Michael Mair, and Thomas V. Inglesby. "Shining Light on 'Dark Winter.'" *Clinical Infectious Diseases* 34 (2002): 979–982.

Pauly, John J. "The Great Chicago Fire as a National Event." *American Quarterly* 36: 5 (1984): 668–683.

Peden, Margie, et al., eds. *World Report on Road Traffic Injury Prevention*. Geneva, Switzerland: World Health Organization, 2004. http://apps.who.int/bookorders/anglais/detart1.jsp?codlan=1&codcol=15&codcch=572.

Roemer, Ruth, Allyn Taylor, and Jean Lariviere. "Origins of the WHO Framework Convention on Tobacco Control." *American Journal of Public Health* 95: 6 (2005): 936–938.

Room, Robin, Laura Schmidt, Jurgen Rehm, and Pia Makela. "International Regulation of Alcohol." *BMJ* 337: 2364 (2008): a2364.

Rosen, George. *A History of Public Health*. Baltimore: Johns Hopkins University Press, 1993.

Rosner, David, and Gerald Markowitz. *Are We Ready? Public Health since 9/11*. Berkeley: University of California Press, 2006.

Ryan, Erin. "How the New Federalism Failed Katrina Victims." In *Law and Recovery from Disaster: Hurricane Katrina*, edited by Robin Paul Malloy, 174–211. Farnham, UK: Ashgate, 2009.

Scherer, Frederic M., and Jayashree Watal. "Post-TRIPS Options for Access to Patented Medicines in Developing Nations." *Journal of International Economic Law* 5: 4 (2002): 913–939.

Suhrcke, Marc, Lorenzo Rocco, Martin McKee, Stefano Mazzuco, Dieter Urban, and Alfred Steinherr. *Economic Consequences of Noncommunicable Diseases and Injuries in the Russian Federation*. Geneva, Switzerland: World Health Organization, 2007.

Trotter, Griffin. *The Ethics of Coercion in Mass Casualty Medicine*. Baltimore: Johns Hopkins University Press, 2007.

United Nations. *Prevention and Control of Non-communicable Disease*. New York: United Nations, May 20, 2010.

U.S. Department of Homeland Security, Federal Emergency Management Agency. *The Federal Emergency Management Agency Publication 1*. Washington, DC: U.S. Department of Homeland Security, November 2010. http://www.fema.gov/media-library-data/20130726-1823-25045-8164/pub_1_final.pdf.

———. *National Incident Management System*. December 2008. http://www.fema.gov/pdf/emergency/nims/NIMS_core.pdf.

———. *National Preparedness Goal*. September 2011. http://www.fema.gov/media-library-data/20130726-1828-25045-9470/national_preparedness_goal_2011.pdf.

———. *National Response Framework*. May 2013. http://www.fema.gov/media-library-data/20130726-1914-25045.

———. *A Performance Review of FEMA's Disaster Management Activities in Response to Hurricane Katrina* (OIG-06-32). Washington, DC: U.S. Department of Homeland Security, March 2006. http://www.oig.dhs.gov/assets/Mgmt/OIG_06-32_Mar06.pdf

U.S. Department of State. *Addressing the Challenges of Noncommunicable Diseases*. http://www.state.gov/documents/organization/172760.pdf.

U.S. Department of Transportation. "Early Estimate of Motor Vehicle Traffic Fatalities in 2012." Washington, DC: U.S. Department of Transportation, 2013. http://www-nrd.nhtsa.dot.gov/Pubs/811741.pdf.

Watkins, Kevin, and Devi Sridhar. *Road Traffic Injuries: The Hidden Development Crisis*. London: Make Roads Safe, 2009.

World Health Organization. "Annual Report 2013." Geneva: WTO, 2013. http://www.wto.org/english/res_e/booksp_e/anrep_e/anrep13_e.pdf.

———. *Constitution of the World Health Organization*. 45th ed. Geneva, Switzerland: World Health Organization, 2006. http://apps.who.int/gb/bd/PDF/bd47/EN/constitution-en.pdf.

———. "Draft Comprehensive Mental Health Action Plan, 2013–2020." Geneva, Switzerland: World Health Organization, May 27, 2013.

———. "First Global Ministerial Conference on Road Safety: Time for Action, Moscow Declaration." http://www.who.int/road-safety/ministerial_conference/declaration_en.pdf.

———. "Global Action Plan for the Prevention and Control of NCDs 2013–2020." http://www.who.int/nmh/en.

———. "The Global Burden of Disease: 2004 Update." Geneva, Switzerland: World Health Organization, 2008. http://www.who.int/features/factfiles/tobacco_epidemic/en/index.html.

———. "The Global Burden of Mental Disorders and the Need for a Comprehensive, Coordinated Response from Health and Social Sectors at the Country Level." Geneva, Switzerland: World Health Organization, May 26, 2012.

———. "Global Status Report of Noncommunicable Diseases 2010." Geneva, Switzerland: World Health Organization, 2011.

———. "Injuries and Violence: The Facts." Geneva, Switzerland: World Health Organization, 2010.

———. "Mental Health Atlas 2011." Geneva, Switzerland: World Health Organization, 2011.

———. "Mental Health Gap Action Programme: Scaling Up Care for Mental, Neurological and Substance Use Disorders." Geneva, Switzerland: World Health Organization, 2008.

———. "Parties to the WHO Framework Convention on Tobacco Control." Geneva, Switzerland: World Health Organization, 2012.

———. "Ten Facts on the Global Tobacco Epidemic." Geneva, Switzerland: World Health Organization, 2012.

———. "United National Road Safety Collaboration." http://www.who.int/roadsafety/en.

———. "Working for Health: An Introduction to the World Health Organization," Geneva, Switzerland: World Health Organization, 2007.

———. "World Health Organization European Ministerial Conference on Nutrition and Noncommunicable Diseases in the Context of Health 2020." Geneva, Switzerland: World Health Organization. http://www.euro.who.int/__data/assets/pdf_file/0009/193878/Vienna-Declaration.pdf.

———. "WHO Framework Convention on Tobacco Control." http://www.who.int/fctc/en.

World Health Organization and World Economic Forum. "From Burden to 'Best Buys': Reducing the Economic Impact of Non-communicable Diseases in Low- and Middle-Income Countries." Geneva, Switzerland: World Health Organization, 2011.

Index

Note: References to figures, illustrations, maps, photos, and tables are labeled (fig.), (illus.), (map), (photo), (table).